AA007908

26th Conference on Computational Natural Language Learning (CoNLL 2022)

Abu Dhabi, United Arab Emirates and Online
7-8 December 2022

ISBN: 978-1-7138-6762-3

Printed from e-media with permission by:

Curran Associates, Inc.
57 Morehouse Lane
Red Hook, NY 12571

Some format issues inherent in the e-media version may also appear in this print version.

Printed with permission by Curran Associates, Inc. (2023)

Association for Computational Linguistics
209 N. Eighth Street
Stroudsburg, Pennsylvania 18360

Phone: 1-570-476-8006
Fax: 1-570-476-0860

acl@aclweb.org

Additional copies of this publication are available from:

Curran Associates, Inc.
57 Morehouse Lane
Red Hook, NY 12571 USA
Phone: 845-758-0400
Fax: 845-758-2633
Email: curran@proceedings.com
Web: www.proceedings.com

CoNLL 2022

The 26th Conference on Computational Natural Language Learning

Proceedings of the Conference

December 7-8, 2022

Introduction

Welcome to the 26th edition of the Conference on Computational Natural Language Learning (CoNLL). For the fifth time in a row, CoNLL is collocated and co-organized with EMNLP. The COVID-19 pandemic is still not behind us, but possibilities of traveling and meeting in person are increasing again. As such, this year's edition is hybrid with both in-person and online talks and poster presentations.

CoNLL 2022 follows CoNLL 2020 and CoNLL 2021 in making this the third edition that specifically "focuses on theoretically, cognitively and scientifically motivated approaches to computational linguistics." Just like in the previous two editions, this new focus was specified in the call for papers, in the instructions to reviewers and area chairs and is emphasized in publicity around the conference. Following EMNLP, we had a hybrid call accepting both direct and ARR submissions.

We received 102 direct submissions and 5 ARR submissions. From the direct submissions, 94 were sent out to reviewers (the other 8 being either retracted or desk rejected). The 5 ARR submissions were directly sent to our area chairs with their ARR reviews. We accepted 28 papers, 26 being direct submissions and 2 ARR submissions. In addition, CoNLL will feature two keynote talks by Noah Goodman and Allyson Ettinger. We thank both of them for accepting our invitation and are looking forward to their talks. We furthermore would like to thank all members of our program committee, listed on page iv, and our Area Chairs for many of whom the schedule overlapped with their Summer Break, in alphabetical order: Andrew Caines, Tanmoy Chakraborty, Kai-wei Chang, Ryan Cotterell, Dan Goldwasser, Micha Elsner, Rob van der Goot, Jena Hwang, Nora Hollenstein, Dieuwke Hupkes, Joseph Le Roux, Dipendra Misra, Preslav Nakov, Nanyun Peng, Maja Popovic, Emily Prud'hommeaux, Roi Reichart, Nathan Schneider, Kevin Small, Rui Wang, Adina Williams, Mark Yatskar.

Special thanks go to our publication chair R. Thomas McCoy, our publicity chair Jack Hessel and Webmaster Jens Lemmens. Without them, these proceedings could not have been completed or authors and other interested community members would have missed important information.

We received many useful tips and pieces of information from last year's organizers, Arianna Bisazza and Omri Abend as well as from SiGNLL President Julia Hockemaier and SiGNLL Chair Afra Alishahi. Thank you for your support!

We hope you enjoy these proceedings.

Antske Fokkens and Vivek Srikumar
CoNLL 2022 conference co-chairs

Organizing Committee

Conference Chairs

Antske Fokkens, Vrije Universiteit Amsterdam and Eindhoven University of Technology, The Netherlands
Vivek Srikumar, University of Utah, USA

Publicity Chair

Jack Hessel, Allen Institute for AI, USA

Publication Chair

R. Thomas McCoy, Princeton University, USA

Area Chairs

Andrew Caines, University of Cambridge, UK
Tanmoy Chakraborty, IIT Delhi, India
Kai-wei Chang, University of California Los Angeles, USA
Ryan Cotterell, ETH Zürich, Switzerland
Dan Goldwasser, Purdue University, USA
Micha Elsner, The Ohio State University, USA
Rob van der Goot, University of Copenhagen, Denmark
Jena Hwang, Allen Institute for AI, USA
Nora Hollenstein, University of Copenhagen, Denmark
Dieuwke Hupkes, Facebook AI Research, France
Joseph Le Roux, Universite Sorbonne Paris Nord-CNRS UMR 70301, France
Dipendra Misra, Microsoft Research, USA
Preslav Nakov, Mohamed Bin Zayed University of Artificial Intelligence, UAE
Nanyun Peng, University of California Los Angeles, USA
Maja Popovic, Dublin City University, Ireland
Emily Prud'hommeaux, Boston College, USA
Roi Reichart, Technion - Israel Institute of Technology, Israel
Nathan Schneider, Georgetown University, USA
Kevin Small, Amazon, USA
Rui Wang, Shanghai Jiao Tong University, China
Adina Williams, FAIR, USA
Mark Yatskar, University of Pennsylvania, USA

Invited Speakers

Noah Goodman, Stanford University, USA
Allyson Ettinger, University of Chicago, USA

Program Committee

Reviewers

Omri Abend, Rodrigo Agerri, Željko Agić, Chris Alberti, Afra Alishahi, Aida Amini, Mark Anderson, Reut Apel, Jun Araki, Christoph Aurnhammer

Miguel Ballesteros, Leslie Barret, Barend Beekhuizen, Robert Berwick, Yevgeni Berzak, Shohini Bhattasali, Eduardo Blanco, Bernd Bohnet, Gosse Bouma

José G. C. de Souza, Spencer Caplan, Giovanni Cassani, Rahma Chaabouni, Hanjie Chen, Xinchi Chen, Emmanuele Chersoni, Christos Christodoulopoulos, Alexander Clark, Ailís Cournane, Francisco M Couto

Forrest Davis, Angel Daza, Aniello De Santo, Steven Derby, Lucia Donatelli, Li Dong, Zi-Yi Dou, Rotem Dror, Andrew Drozdov, Li Du, Jonathan Dunn, Maria Pia di Buono

Akiko Espinosa Anke

Amir Feder, Andrea Fischer, Abdellah Fourtassi, Daniel Freudenthal, Yoshinari Fujinuma

Kim Gerdes, Kripabandhu Ghosh, Dan Goldwasser, Zebulon Goriely, Kartik Goyal, Onur Gungor, Ashim Gupta

Michael Hahn, Sadid A. Hasan, Daniel Hershcovich, Cong Duy Vu Hoang, Cuong Hoang, Mark Hopkins, Jennifer Hu, Kuan-Hao Huang

Ganesh Jawahar, Zhanming Jie, Lifeng Jin, Kristen Johnson, Jaap Jumelet

Diptesh Kanojia, Alina Karakanta, Casey Kennington, Tracy Holloway King, Amrith Krishna

John P. Lalor, Ni Lao, Alberto Lavelli, Phong Le, Jiaxuan Li, Tao Li, Marina Litvak, Nelson F. Liu, Zhengzhong Liu, Zoey Liu

Sean MacAvaney, Andreas Maletti, Stella Markantonatou, Bruno Martins, David Martins de Matos, Yevgen Matusevych, Kate McCurdy, Stephen McGregor, Maitrey Mehta, Stephan Meylan, Petar Milin, Kanishka Misra, Daichi Mochihashi, Manuel Montes

Massimo Nicosia, Tong Niu

Tim O'Gorman, Fredrik Olsson, Yohei Oseki

Ankur Padia, Aishwarya Padmakumar, Alexandros Papangelis, Chan Young Park, Tiago Pimentel, Christopher Potts

Ella Rabinovich, Daniele Radicioni, Sagnik Ray Choudhury, Anthony Rios, Aiala Rosá

Elizabeth Salesky, Vicente Ivan Sanchez Carmona, Sashank Santhanam, Nikunj Saunshi, Thomas Schatz, William Schuler, Abu Awal Md Shoeb, Miikka Silfverberg, Efstathios Stamatatos, Mark Steedman, Karl Stratos, Yoshi Suhara, Alane Suhr

Anaïs Tack, Ran Tian, Amalia Toneva

Clara Vania, Shikhar Vashishth, Prashanth Vijayaraghavan, David Vilar, Esau Villatoro-Tello

Miaosen Wang, Rui Wang, Yizhong Wang, Taro Watanabe

Eduardo Xamena, Yang Xu

Fan Yin, Michael Yoder

Omnia Zayed, Rowan Zellers, Mike Zhang, Mozhi Zhang, Tianlin Zhang, Zhisong Zhang, Kai Zhao, Yichu Zhou, Vilém Zouhar

Table of Contents

A Multilingual Bag-of-Entities Model for Zero-Shot Cross-Lingual Text Classification
Sosuke Nishikawa, Ikuya Yamada, Yoshimasa Tsuruoka and Isao Echizen 1

Collateral facilitation in humans and language models
James Michaelov and Benjamin Bergen 13

How Hate Speech Varies by Target Identity: A Computational Analysis
Michael Yoder, Lynnette Ng, David West Brown and Kathleen Carley 27

Continual Learning for Natural Language Generations with Transformer Calibration
Peng Yang, Dingcheng Li and Ping Li 40

That's so cute!: The CARE Dataset for Affective Response Detection
Jane Yu and Alon Halevy 50

A Fine-grained Interpretability Evaluation Benchmark for Neural NLP
Lijie Wang, Yaozong Shen, Shuyuan Peng, Shuai Zhang, Xinyan Xiao, Hao Liu, Hongxuan Tang, Ying Chen, Hua Wu and Haifeng Wang 70

Towards More Natural Artificial Languages
Mark Hopkins 85

Causal Analysis of Syntactic Agreement Neurons in Multilingual Language Models
Aaron Mueller, Yu Xia and Tal Linzen 95

Combining Noisy Semantic Signals with Orthographic Cues: Cognate Induction for the Indic Dialect Continuum
Niyati Bafna, Josef van Genabith, Cristina España-Bonet and Zdeněk Žabokrtský 110

Detecting Unintended Social Bias in Toxic Language Datasets
Nihar Sahoo, Himanshu Gupta and Pushpak Bhattacharyya 132

Incremental Processing of Principle B: Mismatches Between Neural Models and Humans
Forrest Davis 144

Parsing as Deduction Revisited: Using an Automatic Theorem Prover to Solve an SMT Model of a Minimalist Parser
Sagar Indurkhya 157

Entailment Semantics Can Be Extracted from an Ideal Language Model
William Merrill, Alex Warstadt and Tal Linzen 176

On Neurons Invariant to Sentence Structural Changes in Neural Machine Translation
Gal Patel, Leshem Choshen and Omri Abend 194

Shared knowledge in natural conversations: can entropy metrics shed light on information transfers?
Eliot Maës, Philippe Blache and Leonor Becerra 213

Leveraging a New Spanish Corpus for Multilingual and Cross-lingual Metaphor Detection
Elisa Sanchez-Bayona and Rodrigo Agerri 228

Cognitive Simplification Operations Improve Text Simplification
Eytan Chamovitz and Omri Abend 241

On Language Spaces, Scales and Cross-Lingual Transfer of UD Parsers
Tanja Samardžić, Ximena Gutierrez-Vasques, Rob van der Goot, Max Müller-Eberstein, Olga Pelloni and Barbara Plank 266

Visual Semantic Parsing: From Images to Abstract Meaning Representation
Mohamed Ashraf Abdelsalam, Zhan Shi, Federico Fancellu, Kalliopi Basioti, Dhaivat Bhatt, Vladimir Pavlovic and Afsaneh Fazly 282

Syntactic Surprisal From Neural Models Predicts, But Underestimates, Human Processing Difficulty From Syntactic Ambiguities
Suhas Arehalli, Brian Dillon and Tal Linzen 301

OpenStance: Real-world Zero-shot Stance Detection
Hanzi Xu, Slobodan Vucetic and Wenpeng Yin 314

Optimizing text representations to capture (dis)similarity between political parties
Tanise Ceron, Nico Blokker and Sebastian Padó 325

Computational cognitive modeling of predictive sentence processing in a second language
Umesh Patil and Sol Lago 339

PIE-QG: Paraphrased Information Extraction for Unsupervised Question Generation from Small Corpora
Dinesh Nagumothu, Bahadorreza Ofoghi, Guangyan Huang and Peter Eklund 350

Probing for targeted syntactic knowledge through grammatical error detection
Christopher Davis, Christopher Bryant, Andrew Caines, Marek Rei and Paula Buttery 360

An Alignment-based Approach to Text Segmentation Similarity Scoring
Gerardo Ocampo Diaz and Jessica Ouyang 374

Enhancing the Transformer Decoder with Transition-based Syntax
Leshem Choshen and Omri Abend 384

Characterizing Verbatim Short-Term Memory in Neural Language Models
Kristijan Armeni, Christopher Honey and Tal Linzen 405

Program

Wednesday, December 7, 2022

09:00 - 09:10 *Opening Remarks*

09:10 - 10:30 *Keynote 1: Noah Goodman*

10:30 - 11:00 *Coffee Break*

11:00 - 12:30 *Oral Session 1: Machine Learning for NLP, Model Interpretation*

Continual Learning for Natural Language Generations with Transformer Calibration
Peng Yang, Dingcheng Li and Ping Li

Towards More Natural Artificial Languages
Mark Hopkins

Probing for targeted syntactic knowledge through grammatical error detection
Christopher Davis, Christopher Bryant, Andrew Caines, Marek Rei and Paula Buttery

Enhancing the Transformer Decoder with Transition-based Syntax
Leshem Choshen and Omri Abend

12:30 - 14:00 *Lunch Break*

14:00 - 15:30 *Oral Session 2: Multilingual Work and Translation*

A Multilingual Bag-of-Entities Model for Zero-Shot Cross-Lingual Text Classification
Sosuke Nishikawa, Ikuya Yamada, Yoshimasa Tsuruoka and Isao Echizen

Combining Noisy Semantic Signals with Orthographic Cues: Cognate Induction for the Indic Dialect Continuum
Niyati Bafna, Josef van Genabith, Cristina España-Bonet and Zdeněk Žabokrtský

On Neurons Invariant to Sentence Structural Changes in Neural Machine Translation
Gal Patel, Leshem Choshen and Omri Abend

On Language Spaces, Scales and Cross-Lingual Transfer of UD Parsers
Tanja Samardžić, Ximena Gutierrez-Vasques, Rob van der Goot, Max Müller-Eberstein, Olga Pelloni and Barbara Plank

15:30 - 16:00 *Coffee Break*

16:00 - 17:30 *Poster Session 1: Virtual*

How Hate Speech Varies by Target Identity: A Computational Analysis
Michael Yoder, Lynnette Ng, David West Brown and Kathleen Carley

OpenStance: Real-world Zero-shot Stance Detection
Hanzi Xu, Slobodan Vucetic and Wenpeng Yin

Characterizing Verbatim Short-Term Memory in Neural Language Models
Kristijan Armeni, Christopher Honey and Tal Linzen

Parsing as Deduction Revisited: Using an Automatic Theorem Prover to Solve an SMT Model of a Minimalist Parser
Sagar Indurkhya

An Alignment-based Approach to Text Segmentation Similarity Scoring
Gerardo Ocampo Diaz and Jessica Ouyang

A Fine-grained Interpretability Evaluation Benchmark for Neural NLP
Lijie Wang, Yaozong Shen, Shuyuan Peng, Shuai Zhang, Xinyan Xiao, Hao Liu, Hongxuan Tang, Ying Chen, Hua Wu and Haifeng Wang

Thursday, December 8, 2022

09:10 - 10:30 *Keynote 2: Allyson Ettinger*

10:30 - 11:00 *Coffee Break*

11:00 - 12:30 *Poster session 2: In-person*

That's so cute!: The CARE Dataset for Affective Response Detection
Jane Yu and Alon Halevy

Causal Analysis of Syntactic Agreement Neurons in Multilingual Language Models
Aaron Mueller, Yu Xia and Tal Linzen

Detecting Unintended Social Bias in Toxic Language Datasets
Nihar Sahoo, Himanshu Gupta and Pushpak Bhattacharyya

Leveraging a New Spanish Corpus for Multilingual and Cross-lingual Metaphor Detection
Elisa Sanchez-Bayona and Rodrigo Agerri

Cognitive Simplification Operations Improve Text Simplification
Eytan Chamovitz and Omri Abend

Optimizing text representations to capture (dis)similarity between political parties
Tanise Ceron, Nico Blokker and Sebastian Padó

PIE-QG: Paraphrased Information Extraction for Unsupervised Question Generation from Small Corpora
Dinesh Nagumothu, Bahadorreza Ofoghi, Guangyan Huang and Peter Eklund

12:30 - 14:00 *Lunch Break*

14:00 - 15:30 *Oral Session 3: Psycholinguistics and Language Models*

Collateral facilitation in humans and language models
James Michaelov and Benjamin Bergen

Thursday, December 8, 2022 (continued)

Incremental Processing of Principle B: Mismatches Between Neural Models and Humans
Forrest Davis

Syntactic Surprisal From Neural Models Predicts, But Underestimates, Human Processing Difficulty From Syntactic Ambiguities
Suhas Arehalli, Brian Dillon and Tal Linzen

Computational cognitive modeling of predictive sentence processing in a second language
Umesh Patil and Sol Lago

15:30 - 16:00 *Coffee Break*

16:00 - 17:00 *Oral Session 4: Semantics and Grounding*

Entailment Semantics Can Be Extracted from an Ideal Language Model
William Merrill, Alex Warstadt and Tal Linzen

Shared knowledge in natural conversations: can entropy metrics shed light on information transfers?
Eliot Maës, Philippe Blache and Leonor Becerra

Visual Semantic Parsing: From Images to Abstract Meaning Representation
Mohamed Ashraf Abdelsalam, Zhan Shi, Federico Fancellu, Kalliopi Basioti, Dhaivat Bhatt, Vladimir Pavlovic and Afsaneh Fazly

17:00 - 17:15 *Best Paper Awards and Closing*

A Multilingual Bag-of-Entities Model for Zero-Shot Cross-Lingual Text Classification

Sosuke Nishikawa[1,2*]
sosuke-nishikawa@alumni.u-tokyo.ac.jp

Ikuya Yamada[2,4]
ikuya@ousia.jp

Yoshimasa Tsuruoka[1]
tsuruoka@logos.t.u-tokyo.ac.jp

Isao Echizen[1,3]
iechizen@nii.ac.jp

[1]The University of Tokyo [2]Studio Ousia
[3]National Institute of Informatics [4]RIKEN AIP

Abstract

We present a multilingual bag-of-entities model that effectively boosts the performance of zero-shot cross-lingual text classification by extending a multilingual pre-trained language model (e.g., M-BERT). It leverages the multilingual nature of Wikidata: entities in multiple languages representing the same concept are defined with a unique identifier. This enables entities described in multiple languages to be represented using shared embeddings. A model trained on entity features in a resource-rich language can thus be directly applied to other languages. Our experimental results on cross-lingual topic classification (using the MLDoc and TED-CLDC datasets) and entity typing (using the SHINRA2020-ML dataset) show that the proposed model consistently outperforms state-of-the-art models.

1 Introduction

In the zero-shot approach to cross-lingual transfer learning, models are trained on annotated data in a resource-rich language (the source language) and then applied to another language (the target language) without any training. Substantial progress in cross-lingual transfer learning has been made using multilingual pre-trained language models (PLMs), such as multilingual BERT (M-BERT), jointly trained on massive corpora in multiple languages (Devlin et al., 2019; Conneau and Lample, 2019; Conneau et al., 2020a). However, recent empirical studies have found that cross-lingual transfer learning with PLMs does not work well for languages with insufficient pre-training data or between distant languages (Conneau et al., 2020b; Lauscher et al., 2020), which suggests the difficulty of cross-lingual transfer based solely on textual information.

We propose a multilingual bag-of-entities (M-BoE) model that boosts the performance of zero-shot cross-lingual text classification by automatically generating links to a language-agnostic knowledge base (KB) and injecting features of these entities into PLMs. KB entities, unlike words, can capture unambiguous semantics in documents and be effectively used to address text classification tasks (Gabrilovich and Markovitch, 2006; Chang et al., 2008; Negi and Rosner, 2013; Song et al., 2016; Yamada and Shindo, 2019). In particular, our model extends PLMs by using Wikidata entities as input features (see Figure 1). A key idea behind our model is to leverage the multilingual nature of Wikidata: entities in multiple languages representing the same concept (e.g., *Apple Inc.*, *애플*, *アップル*) are assigned a unique identifier across languages (e.g., Q312). Given a document to be classified, our model extracts Wikipedia entities from the document, converts them into the corresponding Wikidata entities, and computes the entity-based document representation as the weighted average of the embeddings of the extracted entities. Inspired by previous work (Yamada and Shindo, 2019; Peters et al., 2019), we compute the weights using an attention mechanism that selects the entities relevant to the given document. We then compute the sum of the entity-based document representation and the text-based document representation computed using the PLM and feed it into a linear classifier. Since the entity vocabulary and entity embedding are shared across languages, a model trained on entity features in the source language can be directly transferred to multiple target languages.

We evaluate the performance of the M-BoE model on three cross-lingual text classification tasks: topic classification on the MLDoc (Schwenk and Li, 2018) and TED-CLDC (Hermann and Blunsom, 2014) datasets and entity typing on the SHINRA2020-ML (Sekine et al., 2020) dataset. We train the model using training data in the source language (English) and then evaluate it on the target languages. It outperforms our base PLMs (i.e.,

* Work done as an intern at Studio Ousia.

Proceedings of the 26th Conference on Computational Natural Language Learning (CoNLL), pages 1 - 12
December 7-8, 2022 ©2022 Association for Computational Linguistics

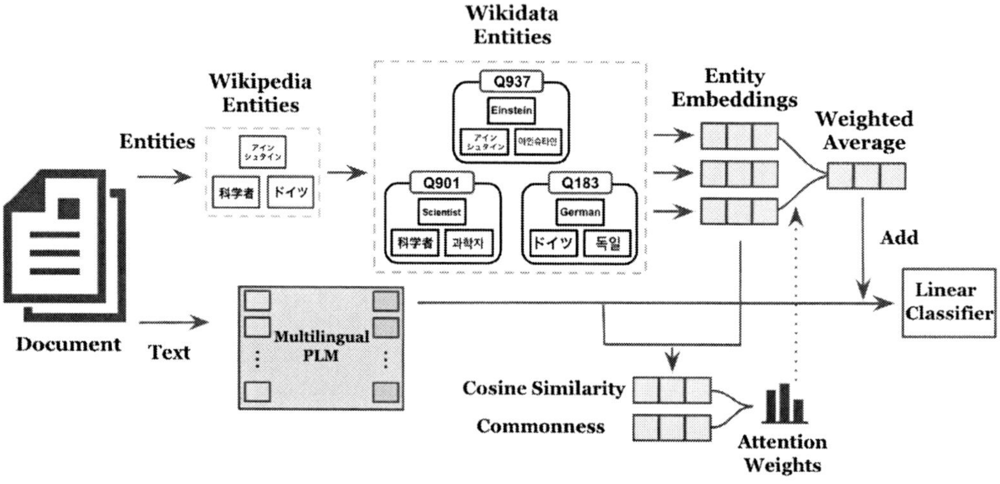

Figure 1: Architecture of M-BoE. Given a document, the model extracts Wikipedia entities, converts them into corresponding Wikidata entities, and calculates the entity-based document representation by using the weighted average of the embeddings of the entities selected by an attention mechanism. The sum of the entity-based representation and the representation computed using a multilingual PLM is used to perform linear classification for the task.

M-BERT (Devlin et al., 2019) and the XLM-R model (Conneau et al., 2020a)) for all target languages on all three tasks, thereby demonstrating the effectiveness of the entity-based representation. Furthermore, our model performs better than state-of-the-art models on the MLDoc dataset.

Our contributions are as follows:

- We present a method for boosting the performance of cross-lingual text classification by extending multilingual PLMs to leverage the multilingual nature of Wikidata entities. Our method successfully improves the performance on multiple target languages simultaneously without expensive pre-training or additional text data in the target languages.
- Inspired by previous work (Yamada and Shindo, 2019; Peters et al., 2019), we introduce an attention mechanism that enables entity-based representations to be effectively transferred from the source language to the target languages. The mechanism selects entities that are relevant to address the task.
- We present experimental results for three cross-lingual text classification tasks demonstrating that our method outperforms our base PLMs (i.e., M-BERT and XLM-R) for all languages on the three tasks and outperforms state-of-the-art methods on the MLDoc dataset.

2 Related Work

Cross-lingual PLMs Zero-shot cross-lingual transfer learning approaches have relied on parallel corpora (Xu and Wan, 2017) or multilingual word representation (Duong et al., 2017). Considerable progress has been made on PLMs for various cross-lingual transfer tasks. The representative models are M-BERT (Devlin et al., 2019) and XLM-R (Conneau et al., 2020a), which are multilingual extensions of BERT (Devlin et al., 2019) and RoBERTa (Liu et al., 2019), respectively. Both models are pre-trained on massive corpora of approximately 100 languages. LASER (Artetxe and Schwenk, 2019) is a PLM trained on a parallel corpus of 93 languages by using a sequence-to-sequence architecture.

Improving cross-lingual transfer learning Several studies have attempted to improve cross-lingual transfer learning by using additional text data in the target language. Lai et al. (2019) proposed using an unlabeled corpus in the target language to bridge the gap between the language and the domain. Dong et al. (2020) and Keung et al. (2019) incorporated adversarial training using unlabeled target language examples. Dong and de Melo (2019) and Eisenschlos et al. (2019) presented methods for data augmentation in which pseudo-labels are assigned to an unlabeled corpus in the target language. Conneau and Lample (2019) additionally pre-trained BERT-based models using a parallel corpus. However, these methods require extra training on additional text data for each target language, and their resulting models work well only on a single target language. Unlike these methods, our method does not require extra training and improves performance simultaneously for all target languages with only a single PLM. Furthermore, our method can be easily applied to these models since it is a simple extension of a PLM and does not modify its internal architecture.

Enhancing monolingual PLMs using entities Several methods have been proposed for improving the performance of PLMs through pre-training using entities. ERNIE (Zhang et al., 2019) and KnowBert (Peters et al., 2019) enrich PLMs by using pre-trained entity embeddings. LUKE (Yamada et al., 2020b) and EaE (Févry et al., 2020) train entity embeddings from scratch during pre-training. However, all of these methods are aimed at improving the performance of monolingual tasks and require pre-training with a large corpus, which is computationally expensive. Our method dynamically injects entity information into PLMs during fine-tuning without expensive pre-training.

Several studies have attempted to incorporate entity information into PLMs after pre-training to enhance the performance of monolingual tasks. Ostendorff et al. (2019) concatenated contextualized representations with knowledge graph embeddings to represent author entities and used them as features for the book classification task. E-BERT (Poerner et al., 2020) inserts KB entities next to the entity names in the input sequence to improve BERT's performance for entity-centric tasks. Verlinden et al. (2021) introduced a mechanism for combining span representations and KB entity representations within a BiLSTM-based end-to-end information extraction model. Unlike these methods, our method aims to improve the cross-lingual text classification by combining PLMs with language-agnostic entity embeddings.

Text classification models using entities Several methods have been commonly used to address text classification using entities. Explicit semantic analysis (ESA) is a representative example; it represents a document as a bag of entities, which is a sparse vector in which each dimension is a score reflecting the relevance of the text to each entity (Gabrilovich and Markovitch, 2006; Chang et al., 2008; Negi and Rosner, 2013). More recently, Song et al. (2016) proposed cross-lingual explicit semantic analysis (CLESA), an extension of ESA, to address cross-lingual text classification. CLESA computes sparse vectors from the intersection of Wikipedia entities in the source and target languages using Wikipedia language links. Unlike CLESA's approach, we address cross-lingual text classification by extending state-of-the-art PLMs with a language-agnostic entity-based document representation based on Wikidata.

The most relevant to our proposed approach is the neural attentive bag-of-entities (NABoE) model proposed by Yamada and Shindo (2019). It addresses monolingual text classification using entities as inputs and uses an attention mechanism to detect relevant entities in the input document. Our model can be regarded as an extension of NABoE by (1) representing documents using a shared entity embedding across languages and (2) combining an entity-based representation and attention mechanism with state-of-the-art PLMs.

3 Proposed Method

Figure 1 shows the architecture of our model. The model extracts Wikipedia entities, converts them into Wikidata entities, and computes the entity-based document representation using an attention mechanism. The sum of the entity-based document representation and the text-based document representation computed using the PLM is fed into a linear classifier to perform classification tasks.

3.1 Entity detection

To detect entities in the input document, we use two dictionaries that can be easily constructed from the KB: (1) a mention-entity dictionary, which binds an entity name (e.g., "Apple") to possible referent KB entities (e.g., *Apple Inc.* and *Apple (food)*) by using the internal anchor links in Wikipedia (Guo et al., 2013), and (2) an inter-language entity dictionary, which links multilingual Wikipedia entities (e.g., *Tokyo, 도쿄, 東京*) to a corresponding identifier (e.g., Q7473516) of Wikidata.

All words and phrases are extracted from the given document in accordance with the mention-entity dictionary[1], and all possible referent entities

[1]Following past work (Yamada and Shindo, 2019), name overlap bounds are resolved by detecting only the earliest and

Dataset	Language	Train	Dev.	Test
MLDoc	8	1,000	1,000	4,000
TED-CLDC	12	936	105	51–106
SHINRA	30	417,387	21,967	30k–920k

Table 1: Number of examples in MLDoc, TED-CLDC, and SHINRA2020-ML datasets.

are detected if they are included as entity names in the dictionary. Note that all possible referent entities are detected for each entity name rather than a single resolved entity. For example, we detect both *Apple Inc.* and *Apple (food)* for entity name "Apple". Next, the detected entities are converted into Wikidata entities if they are included in the inter-language entity dictionary.

3.2 Model

Each Wikidata entity is assigned a representation $\boldsymbol{v}_{e_i} \in \mathbb{R}^d$. Since our method extracts all possible referent entities rather than a single resolved entity, it often extracts entities that are not related to the document. Therefore, we introduce an attention mechanism inspired by previous work (Yamada and Shindo, 2019; Peters et al., 2019) to prioritize entities related to the document. Given a document with K detected entities, our method computes the entity-based document representation $\boldsymbol{z} \in \mathbb{R}^d$ as the weighted average of the entity embeddings:

$$\boldsymbol{z} = \sum_{i=1}^{K} a_{e_i} \boldsymbol{v}_{e_i}, \qquad (1)$$

where $a_{e_i} \in \mathbb{R}$ is the attention weight corresponding to entity e_i and calculated using

$$\boldsymbol{a} = \text{softmax}(\boldsymbol{W}_a^\top \boldsymbol{\phi}), \qquad (2)$$

$$\phi(e_i, d) = \begin{bmatrix} \text{cosine}(\boldsymbol{h}, \boldsymbol{v}_{e_i}) \\ p_{e_i} \end{bmatrix} \qquad (3)$$

where $\boldsymbol{a} = [a_{e_1}, a_{e_2}, \cdots, a_{e_K}]$ are the attention weights; $\boldsymbol{W}_a \in \mathbb{R}^2$ is a weight vector; $\boldsymbol{\phi} = [\phi(e_1, d), \phi(e_2, d), \cdots, \phi(e_K, d)] \in \mathbb{R}^{2 \times K}$ represents the degree to which each entity e_i is related to document d; and $\phi(e_i, d)$ is calculated by concatenating commonness[2] p_{e_i} with the cosine similarity between the document representation computed using the PLM, $\boldsymbol{h} \in \mathbb{R}^d$ (e.g., the final hidden state of the [CLS] token), and entity embedding, $\boldsymbol{v}_{e_i}$.

The sum of this entity-based document representation $\boldsymbol{z}$ and text-based document representation $\boldsymbol{h}$ is fed into a linear classifier[3] to predict the probability of label c:

$$p(c \mid \boldsymbol{h}, \boldsymbol{z}) = Classifier(\boldsymbol{h} + \boldsymbol{z}). \qquad (4)$$

4 Experimental Setup

In this section, we describe the experimental setup we used for the three cross-lingual text classification tasks.

4.1 Entity preprocessing

We constructed a mention-entity dictionary from the January 2019 version of Wikipedia dump[4] and an inter-language entity dictionary from the March 2020 version in the Wikidata dump,[5] which contains 45,412,720 Wikidata entities (e.g., Q312). We computed the commonness values from the same versions of Wikipedia dumps in the corresponding language, following the work of Yamada and Shindo (2019).

We initialized Wikidata entity embeddings using pre-trained English entity embeddings trained on the KB. To train these embeddings, we used the open-source Wikipedia2Vec tool (Yamada et al., 2020a). We used the January 2019 English Wikipedia dump mentioned above and set the dimension to 768 and the other parameters to the default values. We initialized an entity embedding using a random vector if the entity did not exist in the Wikipedia2Vec embeddings. Note that we used only English Wikipedia to train the entity embeddings.

4.2 Data

We evaluated our model using three datasets: MLDoc (Schwenk and Li, 2018), TED-CLDC (Hermann and Blunsom, 2014), and SHINRA2020-ML (Sekine et al., 2020).

MLDoc is a dataset for multi-class text classification, i.e., classifying news articles into four

longest ones.

[2]Commonness (Mihalcea and Csomai, 2007) is the probability that an entity name refers to an entity in Wikipedia.

[3]In preliminary experiments, we also tested concatenation, but observed worse overall results than with summation.

[4]`https://dumps.wikimedia.org/`

[5]`https://dumps.wikimedia.org/wikidatawiki/entities/`

Model	en	fr	de	ja	zh	it	ru	es	target avg.
MultiCCA (Schwenk and Li, 2018)	92.2	72.4	81.2	67.6	74.7	69.4	60.8	72.5	71.2
LASER (Artetxe and Schwenk, 2019)	89.9	78.0	84.8	60.3	71.9	69.4	67.8	77.3	72.8
M-BERT	94.0	79.4	75.1	69.3	68.0	67.1	65.3	75.2	71.4 ± 1.4
+M-BoE	94.1	84.0	76.9	71.1	72.2	70.0	68.9	75.5	74.1 ± 0.7
XLM-R	94.4	84.9	86.7	78.5	85.2	73.4	71.3	81.5	80.2 ± 0.5
+M-BoE	**94.6**	**86.4**	**88.9**	**80.0**	**87.4**	**75.6**	**73.7**	**83.2**	**82.2 ± 0.6**

Table 2: Classification accuracy for topic classification on MLDoc dataset; "target avg." indicates average scores for target languages.

Model	en	fr	de	it	ru	es	ar	tr	nl	pt	pl	ro	target avg.
M-BERT	51.6	47.7	43.9	50.6	47.9	53.1	41.3	44.2	49.4	46.2	45.1	45.4	47.1 ± 1.4
+M-BoE	**52.9**	49.5	46.2	**53.3**	49.2	**54.7**	44.7	49.1	51.0	47.6	47.7	48.2	49.6 ± 1.1
XLM-R	51.5	49.5	49.7	48.7	48.3	51.2	45.6	51.3	48.8	46.3	48.3	48.4	49.1 ± 1.8
+M-BoE	51.7	**50.0**	**53.8**	51.3	**52.3**	52.9	**50.5**	**53.1**	**52.0**	**49.3**	**50.5**	**49.6**	**51.8 ± 0.9**

Table 3: F1 score for topic classification on TED-CLDC dataset.

categories in eight languages. We used the english.train.1000 and english.dev datasets, which contain 1000 documents for training and validation data. As in the previous work (Schwenk and Li, 2018; Keung et al., 2020), we used accuracy as the metric.

TED-CLDC is a multi-label classification dataset covering 15 topics in 12 languages based on the transcripts of TED talks. This topic classification dataset is exactly like the MLDoc dataset except that the classification task is more difficult because of its colloquial nature and because the amount of training data is small. Following the previous work (Hermann and Blunsom, 2014), we used micro-average F1 as the metric.

SHINRA2020-ML is an entity typing dataset that assigns fine-grained entity labels (e.g., Person, Country, Government) to a Wikipedia page. We used this dataset for multi-label classification tasks; we used all datasets in 30 languages except English for the test data. Note that our model does not use information in the test data during training because we only use the English Wikipedia to train our entity embeddings. Following the original work (Sekine et al., 2020), we used micro-average F1 as the metric.

We created a validation set by randomly selecting 5% of the training data in TED-CLDC and 5% of the training data in SHINRA2020-ML. In all experiments, we trained our model on English training data, optimized hyper-parameters using English development data, and evaluated it on the remaining languages. A summary of the datasets is shown in Table 1.

4.3 Models

We used M-BERT (Devlin et al., 2019) and XLM-R_{base} (Conneau et al., 2020a) as the baseline multilingual PLMs to evaluate the proposed method. We added a single fully-connected layer on top of the PLMs and used the final hidden state $\boldsymbol{h}$ of the first [CLS] token as the text-based document representation. For the MLDoc dataset, we trained the model by minimizing the cross-entropy loss with softmax activation. For the TED-CLDC and SHINRA2020-ML datasets, we trained the model by minimizing the binary cross-entropy loss with sigmoid activation. For these two tasks, we regarded each label as positive if its corresponding predicted probability was greater than 0.5 during inference.

For topic classification using MLDoc, we compared the performance of the proposed model with those of two state-of-the-art cross-lingual models: LASER (Artetxe and Schwenk, 2019) (see Section 2), and MultiCCA (Schwenk and Li, 2018), which is based on a convolutional neural network with multilingual word embeddings. To ensure a fair comparison, we did not include models that use additional unlabeled text data or a parallel corpus to train models for each target language.

For entity typing, we tested a model that uses oracle entity annotations (i.e., hyperlinks) contained in the Wikipedia page to be classified instead of entities detected using the entity detection method described in Section 3.1. Note that this model also uses attention mechanisms and pre-trained entity embeddings.

	fr	de	ja	zh	it	ru	es	ar	tr	nl	pt	pl	ro	hi	no
M-BERT	68.5	84.2	81.3	80.7	85.2	81.4	85.6	57.4	50.7	55.6	80.4	77.7	76.9	81.8	83.6
+M-BoE	69.3	**85.1**	**82.5**	**82.2**	**86.4**	**83.2**	**86.6**	61.9	54.0	59.0	**81.7**	79.4	**80.5**	82.9	**84.8**
+Oracle M-BOE	75.4	85.2	81.9	81.8	86.5	83.0	86.5	61.9	53.7	61.7	81.8	79.7	79.9	83.0	84.8
XLM-R	73.0	82.6	77.4	75.1	84.2	81.0	85.3	58.9	69.1	63.7	79.8	80.0	76.9	83.3	82.4
+M-BoE	**77.4**	84.5	79.0	77.0	85.6	**83.2**	85.8	**63.3**	**72.3**	**65.5**	80.7	**81.8**	77.8	**84.8**	84.0
+Oracle M-BOE	76.5	84.8	79.6	77.2	85.5	83.4	86.2	63.0	71.8	67.6	80.4	81.5	78.8	84.8	83.2
	th	ca	da	fa	id	sv	vi	bg	cs	fi	he	hu	ko	uk	target avg.
M-BERT	84.0	81.5	80.1	80.2	72.4	79.4	79.3	74.0	74.6	75.7	74.0	77.1	81.3	78.0	76.6 ± 0.7
+M-BoE	**85.1**	**83.2**	81.4	82.1	75.4	**82.4**	81.2	76.1	76.8	**77.6**	**78.1**	**79.2**	82.9	**80.0**	78.7 ± 0.5
+Oracle M-BOE	85.3	83.2	82.3	82.4	75.5	82.0	81.6	76.6	77.4	77.4	77.8	78.7	83.3	79.9	79.0 ± 0.5
XLM-R	81.4	79.0	81.0	82.4	75.5	75.5	80.7	76.0	77.9	74.7	70.5	73.1	82.6	74.3	77.1 ± 1.2
+M-BoE	82.1	80.9	**83.3**	**84.1**	**78.2**	78.7	**81.9**	**79.1**	**79.6**	76.9	71.9	75.5	**84.0**	77.0	**79.2 ± 0.9**
+Oracle M-BOE	81.8	81.2	82.9	83.9	78.3	78.2	82.5	79.1	79.9	77.1	71.8	75.8	83.92	76.9	79.2 ± 0.9

Table 4: F1 score for entity typing on SHINRA2020-ML dataset.

4.4 Detailed settings

We tuned the hyper-parameters on the basis of the English validation set. The details on the hyperparameters of the models can be found in Appendix A. We trained the models using the AdamW optimizer with a gradient clipping of 1.0.

In all experiments, we trained the models until the performance on the English validation set converged. We conducted all experiments ten times with different random seeds, and recorded the average scores and 95% confidence intervals.

5 Results

Tables 2, 3, and 4 show the results of our experiments. Overall, the M-BoE models outperformed their baselines (i.e., M-BERT and XLM-R) for all target languages on all three datasets. Furthermore, there was a significant difference in the mean scores for the target languages for those models in a paired t-test ($p < 0.05$). In particular, the performance of our model clearly exceeded that of the M-BERT baseline by 2.7% in accuracy, 2.5% in F1, and 2.1% in F1, on the MLDoc, TED-CLDC, and SHINRA2020-ML datasets, respectively.

For entity typing, using the entities detected with our simple dictionary-based approach achieved comparable performance to using gold entity annotations (Table 4: Oracle M-BoE) on the SHINRA2020-ML dataset, which clearly demonstrates the effectiveness of our attention-based entity detection method.

6 Analysis

We conducted a series of experiments to analyze the performance of our model on the MLDoc dataset (Table 5). We first analyzed the impact on the performance of each component in the M-BoE model, including the attention mechanism, pre-trained entity embeddings, and entity detection methods. We then evaluated the sensitivity of the model's performance to differences in the number of detected entities for each language. Finally, we conducted qualitative analysis by visualizing important entities.

Setting	M-BoE (M-BERT) target avg.	M-BoE (XLM-R) target avg.
Full model	**74.1**	**82.2**
Attention mechanism:		
without attention	70.5	81.1
commonness only	72.4	81.8
cosine only	72.8	81.8
Entity embeddings:		
random vectors	73.0	80.9
KG embedding	73.2	81.4
Entity detection method:		
entity linking	71.7	80.5
entity linking + att	73.0	81.9
Baseline	71.4	80.2

Table 5: Results of analysis of our model on MLDoc.

6.1 Attention mechanism

We examined the effect of the attention mechanism on performance. When the attention mechanism was removed (Table 5: **Attention mechanism**), the performance was substantially lower than with the proposed model. This indicates that the attention mechanism selects the entities that are effective in solving the classification task. Next, we examined the effectiveness of the two features (i.e., cosine and commonness) in the attention mechanism by excluding them one at a time from the M-BoE model. Table 5 shows that there was a slight drop in performance when either of them was not used, indicating that both features are effective.

Model	en (train)	fr	de	ja	zh	it	ru	es	avg.
External entity linking	20.0	19.2	14.6	8.15	5.2	11.7	12.7	13.8	13.2
Dictionary-based method (ours)	105.8	97.8	78.9	47.9	34.5	53.2	64.6	72.3	64.2

Table 6: Comparison of the number of detected entities on MLDoc dataset. Numbers indicate average number of entities detected for each example.

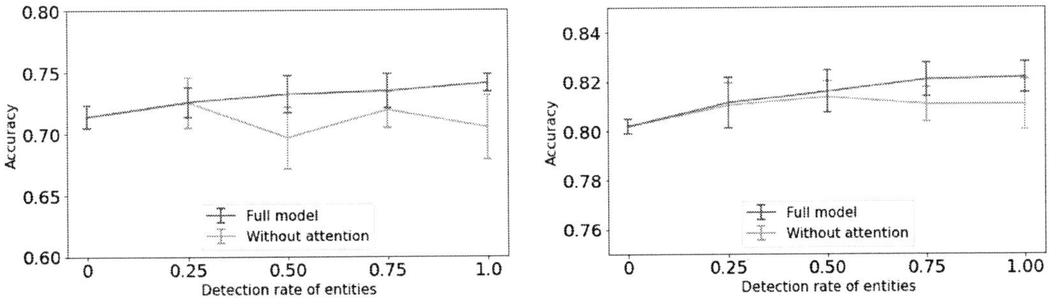

(a) M-BoE (M-BERT) (b) M-BoE (XLM-R)

Figure 2: Classification accuracy for each entity detection rate using MLDoc dataset.

6.2 Entity embeddings

To investigate the effect of entity embedding initialization, we replaced Wikipedia2Vec with (1) random vectors and (2) knowledge graph (KG) embeddings (Table 5: **Entity embeddings**). For KG embedding, we used ComplEx (Trouillon et al., 2016), a state-of-the-art KG embedding method. We trained the ComplEx embeddings on the wikidata5m dataset (Wang et al., 2021) using the kge tool.[6] We set the dimension to 768 and used the default hyper-parameters for everything else in the `wikidata5m-complex configuration` in the tool. The results show that using Wikipedia2Vec was the most effective although using KG embeddings was better than using random vectors.

6.3 Entity detection method

To verify the effectiveness of our dictionary-based entity detection method, we simply replaced it with a commercial multilingual entity linking system, Google Cloud Natural Language API[7] (Table 5: **Entity detection method**). All entities were detected with the API and converted into Wikidata entities, as explained in Section 3.1. Note that unlike our dictionary-based method, the entity linking system detects a single disambiguated entity for each entity name.

The results show that our entity detection method outperformed the API. We attribute this to the number of entities detected with our dictionary-based detection method. As shown in Table 6, the number of entities detected with the entity linking system was substantially lower than with our entity detection method because, unlike our method, the system detects only disambiguated entities and does not detect non-named entities. Therefore, we attribute the better performance of our method compared with that of the API to (1) non-named entities also being important features and (2) the inability to use the correct entity if the disambiguation error is caused by entity linking.

Furthermore, as described in Section 5, our entity detection method performed competitively with the human-labeled entity annotations on the SHINRA2020-ML dataset.

Next, we examined the performance impact of the number of detected Wikidata entities. For the full model and no attention model, we observed a change in performance when some percentage of the entities were randomly removed during training and inference. Figure 2 shows that, the higher the entity detection rate, the better the performance of the full model. When the attention mechanism was removed, however, there was no consistent trend. The performance remained the same or even dropped. These results suggest that the more enti-

[6] `https://github.com/uma-pi1/kge`
[7] `https://cloud.google.com/natural-language`

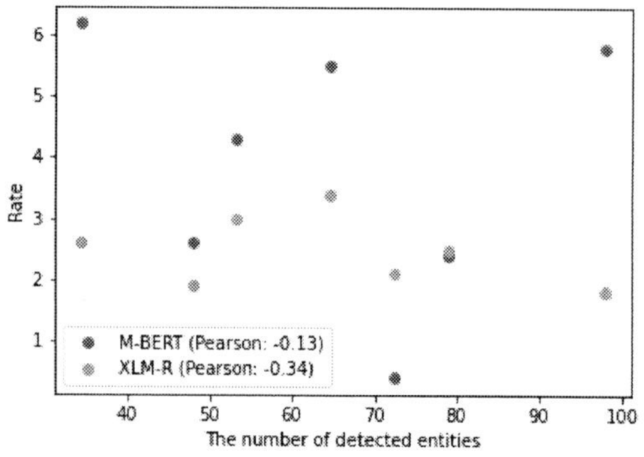

(a) MLDoc

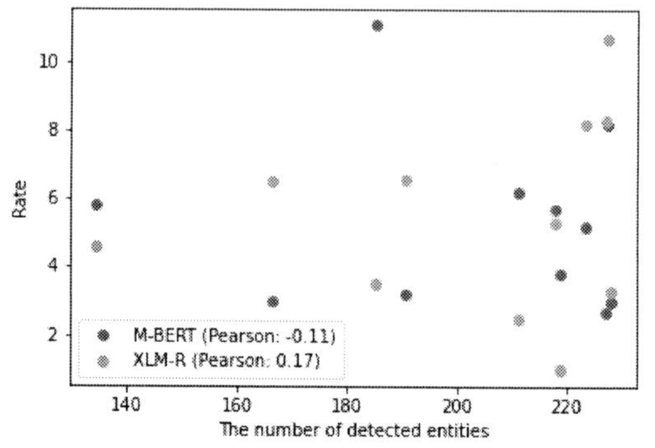

(b) TED-CLDC

Figure 3: Pearson correlation coefficient and scatter plot of average number of detected entities and rate of improvement in performance (Rate) for each target language.

Language	Document	Label	Probability distribution (M-BERT, M-BoE)	Top three entities
Ja	[台北 2日 ロイター] 引け前の台湾株式市場で、加権指数が3.28%急落した。フローカーらによると、工業株に売りが集中したため、という。大引け前10分(0350gmt)現在、加権指数は278. 07ポイント(3. 28%)急落し、8207. 59。売買代金は、1090億台湾ドル。	**MCAT** (Markets)	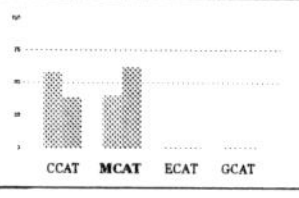	**"Stock certificate"** **"Share price"** **"Taiwan Capitalization Weighted Stock Index"**
Zh	〔路透社東京19日電〕日本大藏省一顧問小組週四促請大藏省取消目前只允許被授權外匯銀行進行外匯交易的管制,完全開放外匯市場交易資格的限制. 這項限制的取消將使投資人進出外匯市場更為容易;此外,銀行業也可藉此增進競爭力,並促進市場的流動性及活絡匯市的交易.(完)	**ECAT** (Economics)	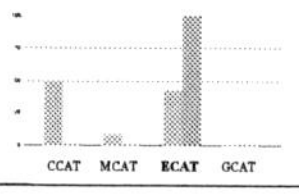	**"Ministry of the Treasury"** **"Financial transaction"** **"Competition (economics)"**
Ru	москва, 17 мар (рейтер) - президент рф борис ельцин подписал федеральные законы о внесении изменении и дополнении в статьи 100 и 110 закона рф "о государственных пенсиях в рф", сообщила пресс-служба президента рф. статья 100 закона излагается в следующеи редакции: "в заработок для исчисления пенсии включаются все виды выплат (дохода), полученных в связи с выполнением работы, предусмотреннои статьеи 89 закона, на которые начисляются страховые взносы в пенсионный фонд рф". пресс-служба президента рф сообщила, что виды выплат, на которые не начисляются страховые взносы в пенсионный фонд рф, определяются правительством рф.	**GCAT** (Government Social)	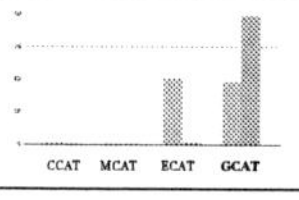	**"Federal law"** **"Pension Fund of the Russian Federation"** **"Kremlin Press Secretary"**

Figure 4: Example results for MLDoc. "Top three entities" indicates the three most influential entities selected by attention mechanism.

ties detected, the better the performance, and that the attention mechanism is important for this consistent improvement.

6.4 Performance sensitivity to language differences

In our method, the number of detected Wikidata entities during inference differs depending on the target languages. We investigated how this affects performance. For each of the datasets, we computed the Pearson's correlation coefficient between the number of detected entities and the rate of improvement over the baseline performance for each language (Figure 3). As a result, there was no clear trend in the correlation coefficients, which ranged from -0.3 to 0.2. These results indicate that the performance was consistently improved for languages with a small number of detected entities. We attribute this to the ability of our method to detect a sufficient number of entities, even for languages with a relatively small number of entity detections.

6.5 Qualitative analysis

To further investigate how the M-BoE model improved performance, we took the MLDoc documents that our model classified correctly while M-BERT did not and examined the influential entities that were assigned the largest attention weights by the M-BoE model. Figure 4 shows three examples in which the M-BoE model effectively improved performance. Overall, it identified the entities that were highly relevant to the document. For example, the first document is a Japanese document about the Taiwanese stock market, and the M-BoE model correctly identified the relevant entities, including ***Stock certificate***, ***Share price***, and ***Taiwan Capitalization Weighted Stock Index***.

7 Conclusions

Our proposed M-BoE model is a simple extension of multilingual PLMs: language-independent Wikidata entities are used as input features for zero-shot cross-lingual text classification. Since the Wikidata entity embeddings are shared across languages, and the entities associated with a document are further selected by the attention mechanism, a model trained on these features in one language can efficiently be applied to multiple target languages. We achieved state-of-the-art results on three cross-lingual text classification tasks, which clearly shows the effectiveness of our method.

As future work, we plan to evaluate our model on low-resource languages and a variety of natural language processing tasks, such as cross-lingual document retrieval. We would also like to investigate whether our method can be combined with other methods, such as using additional textual data in the target language.

Acknowledgements

This work was partially supported by JSPS KAKENHI Grants JP16H06302, JP18H04120, JP20K23355, JP21H04907, and JP21K18023, and by JST CREST Grants JPMJCR18A6 and JPMJCR20D3, Japan.

References

Mikel Artetxe and Holger Schwenk. 2019. Massively multilingual sentence embeddings for zero-shot cross-lingual transfer and beyond. *Transactions of the Association for Computational Linguistics*, 7:597–610.

Ming-Wei Chang, Lev Ratinov, Dan Roth, and Vivek Srikumar. 2008. Importance of semantic representation: Dataless classification. In *Proceedings of the 23rd National Conference on Artificial Intelligence - Volume 2*, AAAI'08, page 830–835.

Alexis Conneau, Kartikay Khandelwal, Naman Goyal, Vishrav Chaudhary, Guillaume Wenzek, Francisco Guzmán, Edouard Grave, Myle Ott, Luke Zettlemoyer, and Veselin Stoyanov. 2020a. Unsupervised cross-lingual representation learning at scale. In *Proceedings of the 58th Annual Meeting of the Association for Computational Linguistics*, pages 8440–8451.

Alexis Conneau and Guillaume Lample. 2019. Cross-lingual language model pretraining. In *Advances in Neural Information Processing Systems*, volume 32, pages 7059–7069.

Alexis Conneau, Shijie Wu, Haoran Li, Luke Zettlemoyer, and Veselin Stoyanov. 2020b. Emerging cross-lingual structure in pretrained language models. In *Proceedings of the 58th Annual Meeting of the Association for Computational Linguistics*, pages 6022–6034.

Jacob Devlin, Ming-Wei Chang, Kenton Lee, and Kristina Toutanova. 2019. BERT: Pre-training of deep bidirectional transformers for language understanding. In *Proceedings of the 2019 Conference of the North American Chapter of the Association for Computational Linguistics: Human Language Technologies, Volume 1 (Long and Short Papers)*, pages 4171–4186.

Xin Dong and Gerard de Melo. 2019. A robust self-learning framework for cross-lingual text classification. In *Proceedings of the 2019 Conference on Empirical Methods in Natural Language Processing and the 9th International Joint Conference on Natural Language Processing*, pages 6306–6310.

Xin Dong, Yaxin Zhu, Yupeng Zhang, Zuohui Fu, Dongkuan Xu, Sen Yang, and Gerard de Melo. 2020. Leveraging adversarial training in self-learning for cross-lingual text classification. In *Proceedings of the 43rd International ACM SIGIR Conference on Research and Development in Information Retrieval*, SIGIR '20, page 1541–1544.

Long Duong, Hiroshi Kanayama, Tengfei Ma, Steven Bird, and Trevor Cohn. 2017. Multilingual training of crosslingual word embeddings. In *Proceedings of the 15th Conference of the European Chapter of the Association for Computational Linguistics: Volume 1, Long Papers*, pages 894–904.

Julian Eisenschlos, Sebastian Ruder, Piotr Czapla, Marcin Kadras, Sylvain Gugger, and Jeremy Howard. 2019. MultiFiT: Efficient multi-lingual language model fine-tuning. In *Proceedings of the 2019 Conference on Empirical Methods in Natural Language Processing and the 9th International Joint Conference on Natural Language Processing*, pages 5702–5707.

Thibault Févry, Livio Baldini Soares, Nicholas FitzGerald, Eunsol Choi, and Tom Kwiatkowski. 2020. Entities as experts: Sparse memory access with entity supervision. In *Proceedings of the 2020 Conference on Empirical Methods in Natural Language Processing*, pages 4937–4951.

Evgeniy Gabrilovich and Shaul Markovitch. 2006. Overcoming the brittleness bottleneck using wikipedia: Enhancing text categorization with encyclopedic knowledge. In *Proceedings of the 21st National Conference on Artificial Intelligence - Volume 2*, AAAI'06, page 1301–1306.

Stephen Guo, Ming-Wei Chang, and Emre Kiciman. 2013. To link or not to link? a study on end-to-end tweet entity linking. In *Proceedings of the 2013 Conference of the North American Chapter of the*

Association for Computational Linguistics: Human Language Technologies, pages 1020–1030.

Karl Moritz Hermann and Phil Blunsom. 2014. Multilingual models for compositional distributed semantics. In *Proceedings of the 52nd Annual Meeting of the Association for Computational Linguistics (Volume 1: Long Papers)*, pages 58–68.

Phillip Keung, Yichao Lu, and Vikas Bhardwaj. 2019. Adversarial learning with contextual embeddings for zero-resource cross-lingual classification and NER. In *Proceedings of the 2019 Conference on Empirical Methods in Natural Language Processing and the 9th International Joint Conference on Natural Language Processing*, pages 1355–1360.

Phillip Keung, Yichao Lu, Julian Salazar, and Vikas Bhardwaj. 2020. Don't use English dev: On the zero-shot cross-lingual evaluation of contextual embeddings. In *Proceedings of the 2020 Conference on Empirical Methods in Natural Language Processing (EMNLP)*, pages 549–554.

Guokun Lai, Barlas Oguz, Yiming Yang, and Veselin Stoyanov. 2019. Bridging the domain gap in cross-lingual document classification. *arXiv preprint arXiv:1909.07009*.

Anne Lauscher, Vinit Ravishankar, Ivan Vulić, and Goran Glavaš. 2020. From zero to hero: On the limitations of zero-shot language transfer with multilingual Transformers. In *Proceedings of the 2020 Conference on Empirical Methods in Natural Language Processing*, pages 4483–4499.

Yinhan Liu, Myle Ott, Naman Goyal, Jingfei Du, Mandar Joshi, Danqi Chen, Omer Levy, Mike Lewis, Luke Zettlemoyer, and Veselin Stoyanov. 2019. Roberta: A robustly optimized BERT pretraining approach. *arXiv preprint arXiv:1907.11692*.

Rada Mihalcea and Andras Csomai. 2007. Wikify!: Linking documents to encyclopedic knowledge. In *Proceedings of the Sixteenth ACM Conference on Conference on Information and Knowledge Management*, CIKM '07, pages 233–242.

Sapna Negi and Michael Rosner. 2013. UoM: Using explicit semantic analysis for classifying sentiments. In *Second Joint Conference on Lexical and Computational Semantics (*SEM), Volume 2: Proceedings of the Seventh International Workshop on Semantic Evaluation (SemEval 2013)*, pages 535–538.

Malte Ostendorff, Peter Bourgonje, Maria Berger, Julian Moreno-Schneider, and Georg Rehm. 2019. Enriching BERT with Knowledge Graph Embedding for Document Classification. In *Proceedings of the GermEval 2019 Workshop*, Erlangen, Germany.

Matthew E. Peters, Mark Neumann, Robert Logan, Roy Schwartz, Vidur Joshi, Sameer Singh, and Noah A. Smith. 2019. Knowledge enhanced contextual word representations. In *Proceedings of the 2019 Conference on Empirical Methods in Natural Language Processing and the 9th International Joint Conference on Natural Language Processing*, pages 43–54.

Nina Poerner, Ulli Waltinger, and Hinrich Schütze. 2020. E-BERT: Efficient-yet-effective entity embeddings for BERT. In *Findings of the Association for Computational Linguistics: EMNLP 2020*, pages 803–818.

Holger Schwenk and Xian Li. 2018. A corpus for multilingual document classification in eight languages. In *Proceedings of the Eleventh International Conference on Language Resources and Evaluation.*

Satoshi Sekine, Masako Nomoto, Kouta Nakayama, Asuka Sumida, Koji Matsuda, and Maya Ando. 2020. Overview of shinra2020-ml task. In *Proceedings of the NTCIR-15 Conference.*

Yangqiu Song, Shyam Upadhyay, Haoruo Peng, and Dan Roth. 2016. Cross-lingual dataless classification for many languages. In *Proceedings of the Twenty-Fifth International Joint Conference on Artificial Intelligence*, IJCAI'16, page 2901–2907.

Théo Trouillon, Johannes Welbl, Sebastian Riedel, Eric Gaussier, and Guillaume Bouchard. 2016. Complex embeddings for simple link prediction. In *Proceedings of The 33rd International Conference on Machine Learning*, volume 48 of *Proceedings of Machine Learning Research*, pages 2071–2080. PMLR.

Severine Verlinden, Klim Zaporojets, Johannes Deleu, Thomas Demeester, and Chris Develder. 2021. Injecting knowledge base information into end-to-end joint entity and relation extraction and coreference resolution. In *Findings of the Association for Computational Linguistics: ACL-IJCNLP 2021*, pages 1952–1957.

Xiaozhi Wang, Tianyu Gao, Zhaocheng Zhu, Zhengyan Zhang, Zhiyuan Liu, Juanzi Li, and Jian Tang. 2021. KEPLER: A Unified Model for Knowledge Embedding and Pre-trained Language Representation. *Transactions of the Association for Computational Linguistics*, 9:176–194.

Kui Xu and Xiaojun Wan. 2017. Towards a universal sentiment classifier in multiple languages. In *Proceedings of the 2017 Conference on Empirical Methods in Natural Language Processing*, pages 511–520.

Ikuya Yamada, Akari Asai, Jin Sakuma, Hiroyuki Shindo, Hideaki Takeda, Yoshiyasu Takefuji, and Yuji Matsumoto. 2020a. Wikipedia2Vec: An efficient toolkit for learning and visualizing the embeddings of words and entities from Wikipedia. In *Proceedings of the 2020 Conference on Empirical Methods in Natural Language Processing: System Demonstrations*, pages 23–30.

Ikuya Yamada, Akari Asai, Hiroyuki Shindo, Hideaki Takeda, and Yuji Matsumoto. 2020b. LUKE: Deep contextualized entity representations with entity-aware self-attention. In *Proceedings of the 2020 Conference on Empirical Methods in Natural Language Processing*, pages 6442–6454.

Ikuya Yamada and Hiroyuki Shindo. 2019. Neural attentive bag-of-entities model for text classification. In *Proceedings of the 23rd Conference on Computational Natural Language Learning*, pages 563–573.

Zhengyan Zhang, Xu Han, Zhiyuan Liu, Xin Jiang, Maosong Sun, and Qun Liu. 2019. ERNIE: Enhanced language representation with informative entities. In *Proceedings of the 57th Annual Meeting of the Association for Computational Linguistics*, pages 1441–1451.

Appendix for "A Multilingual Bag-of-Entities Model for Zero-Shot Cross-Lingual Text Classification"

A Hyper-parameter Details

We conduct a grid-search for batch size $\in \{16, 32, 64, 128\}$ and learning rate $\in \{1e-05, 2e-05, 5e-05\}$. The chosen hyperparameters for each model are shown in Table 7.

Model	MLDoc	TED-CLDC	SHINRA2020-ML
M-BERT	32 / 2e-05	16 / 2e-05	128 / 5e-05
XLM-R	32 / 2e-05	16 / 5e-05	64 / 2e-05
M-BoE (M-BERT)	32 / 2e-05	16 / 2e-05	128 / 5e-05
M-BoE (XLM-R)	32 / 2e-05	16 / 5e-05	64 / 2e-05

Table 7: Hyper-parameters used for experiments. In each cell, the left value indicates batch size, and the right value indicates learning rate.

Collateral facilitation in humans and language models

James A. Michaelov
Department of Cognitive Science
University of California, San Diego
j1michae@ucsd.edu

Benjamin K. Bergen
Department of Cognitive Science
University of California, San Diego
bkbergen@ucsd.edu

Abstract

Are the predictions of humans and language models affected by similar things? Research suggests that while comprehending language, humans make predictions about upcoming words, with more predictable words being processed more easily. However, evidence also shows that humans display a similar processing advantage for highly anomalous words when these words are semantically related to the preceding context or to the most probable continuation. Using stimuli from 3 psycholinguistic experiments, we find that this is also almost always also the case for 8 contemporary transformer language models (BERT, ALBERT, RoBERTa, XLM-R, GPT-2, GPT-Neo, GPT-J, and XGLM). We then discuss the implications of this phenomenon for our understanding of both human language comprehension and the predictions made by language models.

1 Introduction

Humans process words more easily when they more contextually predictable, whether predictability is determined by humans (Fischler and Bloom, 1979; Brothers and Kuperberg, 2021) or language models (McDonald and Shillcock, 2003; Levy, 2008; Smith and Levy, 2013). Work on the N400, a neural signal of processing difficulty, has provided evidence that the neurocognitive system underlying human language comprehension preactivates words based on the extent to which they are predictable from the preceding context—thus, predictable words are easier to process because they or their features have already been activated before they are encountered (Kutas and Hillyard, 1984; Van Petten and Luka, 2012). This has led many to argue that we should consider the human language comprehension system to be engaging in prediction (DeLong et al., 2005; Kutas et al., 2011; Van Petten and Luka, 2012; Bornkessel-Schlesewsky and Schlesewsky, 2019; Kuperberg et al., 2020; DeLong and Kutas, 2020; Brothers and Kuperberg, 2021).

However, words that are either semantically related to the elements of the preceding context or to the most likely next word are also processed more easily, even if they are semantically implausible and ostensibly unpredictable. These are known as *related anomaly* effects. For an example of the former, consider the sentences in (1) that were used as experimental stimuli by Metusalem et al. (2012).

(1) My friend Mike went mountain biking recently. He lost control for a moment and ran right into a tree. It's a good thing he was wearing his ______.

(a) *helmet*
(b) *dirt*
(c) *table*

Helmet is the most predictable continuation of the sentence, as determined based on cloze probability (Taylor, 1953, 1957)—the proportion of people to fill in a gap in a sentence with a specific word. Thus, unsurprisingly, *helmet* elicited the smallest N400 response, indicating that it is most easily processed. *Dirt* and *table* are both implausible continuations, and equally improbable based on human responses (both have a cloze probability of zero). Yet Metusalem et al. (2012) found that *dirt*, which is semantically related to the preceding context of *mountain biking*, elicits a smaller N400 response than *table*, which is not. This suggests that something about *dirt*'s relation to the *mountain biking* event causes it to be preactivated more than *table*, despite their seemingly equal implausibility and unpredictability.

The sentences in (2), used as experimental stimuli by Ito et al. (2016), provide an example of the other previously-discussed form of related anomaly—where a word semantically related to the most probable continuation (in this case, that

Proceedings of the 26th Conference on Computational Natural Language Learning (CoNLL), pages 13 - 26
December 7-8, 2022 ©2022 Association for Computational Linguistics

with the highest cloze) is easier to process than one that is not. Even though *tail* and *tyre* are both implausible continuations with a cloze probability of zero, Ito et al. (2016) find that *tail*, which is semantically-related to the highest-cloze continuation *dog*, elicits a smaller N400 response than *tyre*, which is not.

(2) Meg will go to the park to walk her ______ tomorrow.

(a) *dog*

(b) *tail*

(c) *tyre*

In sum, words related to elements of the preceding context or to the most probable continuation of a sequence appear to be more preactivated in the brain than words that are not, even when both are highly anomalous. This effect has been replicated many times (Kutas and Hillyard, 1984; Kutas et al., 1984; Kutas, 1993; Federmeier and Kutas, 1999; Metusalem et al., 2012; Rommers et al., 2013; Ito et al., 2016; DeLong et al., 2019; for review see DeLong et al., 2019).

The key question, therefore, is whether the same neurocognitive system underlying the predictability effects on the N400 also underlie related anomaly effects. Under one account (DeLong et al., 2019; DeLong and Kutas, 2020), the predictive system that underlies predictability effects also leads to these related anomalous words being 'collaterally facilitated' (DeLong and Kutas, 2020, p. 1045) due to their shared semantic features. Under this account, therefore, related anomaly effects can all be explained as by-products of our predictive system and the semantic organization of information in the brain. However, there is no direct evidence that this is the case—in fact, given the metabolic costs of preactivation (Brothers and Kuperberg, 2021), it may intuitively seem unlikely that an efficient predictive system would lead to implausible and otherwise anomalous words being preactivated. In fact, many researchers have argued that one or more associative mechanisms are required to explain related anomaly and other similar effects (Lau et al., 2013; Ito et al., 2016; Frank and Willems, 2017; Federmeier, 2021).

As systems designed specifically to predict the probability of a word given its context, language models offer a means to test the viability of the former hypothesis. If language models calculate that related but anomalous words are more predictable than unrelated anomalous words, this would demonstrate that related anomaly effects can be produced by a system engaged in prediction alone. This would show that it is possible that related anomalies can be 'collaterally facilitated' (DeLong and Kutas, 2020, p. 1045) by a predictive mechanism in human language comprehension. Thus, it would remove the need to posit additional associative mechanisms on the basis of related anomaly effects, which could greatly simplify our understanding of human language comprehension.

This is what we test in the present study. We run the stimuli from 3 psycholinguistic experiments carried out in English (Ito et al., 2016; DeLong et al., 2019; Metusalem et al., 2012) through 8 contemporary transformer language models (Devlin et al., 2019; Radford et al., 2019; Liu et al., 2019; Lan et al., 2020; Conneau et al., 2020; Black et al., 2021; Wang and Komatsuzaki, 2021; Lin et al., 2021), calculating the surprisal (negative log-probability) of each word for which the N400 was measured. We then compare whether, in line with the N400 response, anomalous words that are semantically related to the context have significantly lower surprisals than unrelated words.

2 Related work

There have been a wide range of attempts to computationally model the N400 (Parviz et al., 2011; Laszlo and Plaut, 2012; Laszlo and Armstrong, 2014; Rabovsky and McRae, 2014; Frank et al., 2015; Ettinger et al., 2016; Cheyette and Plaut, 2017; Brouwer et al., 2017; Rabovsky et al., 2018; Venhuizen et al., 2019; Fitz and Chang, 2019; Aurnhammer and Frank, 2019; Michaelov and Bergen, 2020; Merkx and Frank, 2021; Uchida et al., 2021; Szewczyk and Federmeier, 2022; Michaelov et al., 2022). One of the most successful and influential approaches has been to model the N400 using the surprisal calculated from neural language models—surprisal has been found to be a significant predictor of single-trial N400 data (Frank et al., 2015; Aurnhammer and Frank, 2019; Merkx and Frank, 2021; Michaelov et al., 2021; Szewczyk and Federmeier, 2022; Michaelov et al., 2022), and has been found to be similar to the N400 response in how it is affected by a range of experimental manipulations (Michaelov and Bergen, 2020; Michaelov et al., 2021). A key finding is that better-performing and more sophisticated language models perform better at predicting the N400 (Frank et al., 2015; Aurnhammer and Frank, 2019; Michaelov and Bergen, 2020; Merkx and Frank, 2021; Michaelov et al., 2021, 2022). For this reason, we use contemporary transformer language models in the present study.

We use experimental stimuli from 3 experiments. Stimuli from one of these experiments (Ito et al., 2016) have been previously used in computational analyses of the N400. This is one of several sets that Michaelov and Bergen (2020) attempt to model using recurrent neural network (RNN) language models, finding that they can indeed calculate that words related to the highest-cloze continuation are more predictable than unrelated words. In the present study, we test whether this result can be replicated on a larger number of language models, and specifically, transformer language models.

There has also been work looking at how language models deal with semantic relatedness to the highest-cloze continuation based on stimuli from other N400 experiments. Michaelov and Bergen (2020), for example, find that in cases where the related and unrelated words are both plausible, the related continuations are more strongly predicted by RNNs (Gulordava et al., 2018; Jozefowicz et al., 2016), in line with the original N400 results (Kutas, 1993). Michaelov et al. (2021) conceptually replicate this finding on a different dataset (Bardolph et al., 2018) using one of the same RNNs (Jozefowicz et al., 2016) and GPT-2 (Radford et al., 2019). However, these prior efforts differ from the present study in that they investigate N400s and surprisal to words that are all plausible continuations of the sentence, and where they both have a low but generally non-zero cloze probability. In the stimuli analyzed in the present study, by contrast, both the related and unrelated words are anomalous—they have a cloze probability of zero, and are implausible continuations. Thus, their preactivation does, at least intuitively, appear to be more clearly 'collateral'.

We are only aware of one previous study that directly compares the predictions of transformers and the human N400 response on related anomaly stimuli. Ettinger (2020) evaluates BERT in terms of its similarity to cloze—because the predictions of a language model, being incremental, may show similar effects to those found in the N400 (see also Michaelov and Bergen, 2020 for discussion). For this reason, Ettinger (2020) tests how good BERT is at predicting the highest-cloze (most probable) continuations in the stimuli over anomalous but semantically related continuations, but does not directly look at the related anomaly effect—whether the related anomalous continuations are more strongly predicted than the unrelated anomalous continuations. Thus, to the best of our knowledge, the present study is the first to investigate whether the predictions of transformer language models display related anomaly effects like humans do.

Finally, there has been some work investigating whether language models display priming effects (e.g. Prasad et al., 2019; Misra et al., 2020; Kassner and Schütze, 2020; Lin et al., 2021; Lindborg and Rabovsky, 2021). The effect found by Metusalem et al. (2012)—that words related to the events described in the context are preactivated more strongly than words that are not—is a form of semantic priming, as it results in the increased preactivation of a word based on the semantic content stimulus that has been recently encountered (i.e. the event described in the preceding linguistic context). Thus, our investigation of the patterns in the prediction of the the stimuli from Metusalem et al. (2012) is intended to further our knowledge of priming in language models—specifically, whether there are systematic ways in which context shapes the extent to which anomalous words are predicted.

3 General Method

In this study, we took the stimuli from a range of experiments (Ito et al., 2016; DeLong et al., 2019; Metusalem et al., 2012) and ran them through a number of transformer language models. We used the *transformers* (Wolf et al., 2020) implementations of the (largest and most up-to-date versions of each of the) following models: BERT (Devlin et al., 2019), RoBERTa (Liu et al., 2019), ALBERT (Lan et al., 2020), XLM-R (Conneau et al., 2020), GPT-2 (Radford et al., 2019), GPT-Neo (Black et al., 2021), GPT-J (Wang and Komatsuzaki, 2021), and XGLM (Lin et al., 2021). We chose these models to cover a number of both autoregressive (GPT-2, GPT-Neo, GPT-J, XGLM) and masked (BERT, RoBERTa, ALBERT, XLM-RoBERTa) language model architectures. Given the recent increase in popularity of multilingual language models, we also made sure to include one autoregressive (XGLM) and one masked (XLM-RoBERTa) multilingual language model, in case there is a difference based on the number of languages that a model is trained on.

All experimental stimuli used in the present study have been made available by the original authors of their respective papers as appendices or supplementary materials. In our analysis, we truncated all stimuli to be the preceding context of the critical word (the word for which the N400 was measured). We then used the language models to calculate the probability of the next word, and negative log-transformed (using a logarithm of base 2, following Futrell et al., 2019) these probabilities to calculate the surprisal of each word. For words not present in the vocabulary of each model, we tokenized the word, and then progressively calculated the surprisal of each sub-word token given the preceding context; with the sum of all the surprisals (equivalent to the the negative log-probability of the product of all the probabilities) being used as the total surprisal for the word. In this way, we calculated the surprisal of each critical word given its preceding context only.

All graphs and statistical analyses were created and run in *R* (R Core Team, 2020) using *Rstudio* (RStudio Team, 2020) and the *tidyverse* (Wickham et al., 2019), *lme4* (Bates et al., 2015), and *lmerTest* (Kuznetsova et al., 2017) packages. All reported p-values are corrected for multiple comparisons based on false discovery rate across all statistical tests carried out (Benjamini and Hochberg, 1995). Because of this correction procedure, if any models display related anomaly effects, this is evidence that prediction alone can account for them.

All of the code for running the experiments and carrying out the statistical analyses is provided at `https://github.com/jmichaelov/collateral-facilitation`.

4 Experiment 1: Ito et al. (2016)

4.1 Introduction

We begin with Ito et al. (2016), who investigated whether relatedness to the highest-cloze continuation of a given sentence impacts the amplitude of the N400 response. They presented human participants with experimental stimuli that included a word that was either the highest-cloze continuation of a sentence, semantically related to that highest-cloze continuation, similar to the highest-cloze continuation in terms of their form (e.g. *hook* and *book*), or unrelated. For the purposes of the present study, we are interested in semantic relatedness and thus do not consider the formal relatedness condition. Thus, we look at the stimuli from the three experimental conditions exemplified in (3)—an example of Predictable, Related, and Unrelated continuations for one sentence frame.

(3) Lydia cannot eat anymore as she is so ______ now.

- *full* (Predictable)
- *half* (Related)
- *mild* (Unrelated)

Ito et al. (2016) find that related continuations elicit a smaller N400 response than unrelated continuations. As stated, this finding was successfully modeled using the surprisal of two RNN language models by Michaelov and Bergen (2020).

In the present study, we aim to investigate whether this can be replicated with contemporary transformer language models. Thus far, only one study (Merkx and Frank, 2021) has directly compared the N400 prediction capabilities of RNNs and transformers while matching number of parameters, training data, and language modeling performance, finding that transformers are better predictors of N400 amplitude overall. We might therefore expect that the transformers used in the present study should model the related anomaly effect found by Ito et al. (2016) at least as well as the RNNs used by Michaelov and Bergen (2020). However, a key feature of Merkx and Frank's (2021) study is that it uses naturalistic stimuli. This makes the experiment more ecologically valid, but as has been pointed out (Michaelov and Bergen, 2020; Brothers and Kuperberg, 2021), this means that we cannot tell whether the higher correlation between surprisal and N400 amplitude is due to any factors that we are interested in investigating—Merkx and Frank (2021) do not consider how relatedness to a previously-mentioned event or to most predictable continuation impacts surprisal and the N400. For this reason, it is in fact far from clear that we should expect this specific related anomaly effect to be modeled as well by transformers as by RNNs. However, if it is, this would demonstrate the effect in two different language model architectures, further strengthening the idea that a predictive system alone can explain related anomaly effects.

Thus, in the present study, we investigate whether the results of Michaelov and Bergen (2020) replicate beyond the two RNNs tested, and crucially, whether the results replicate with transformer language models. Specifically, we test whether the surprisal elicited by implausible stimuli related to the highest-cloze continuation is lower

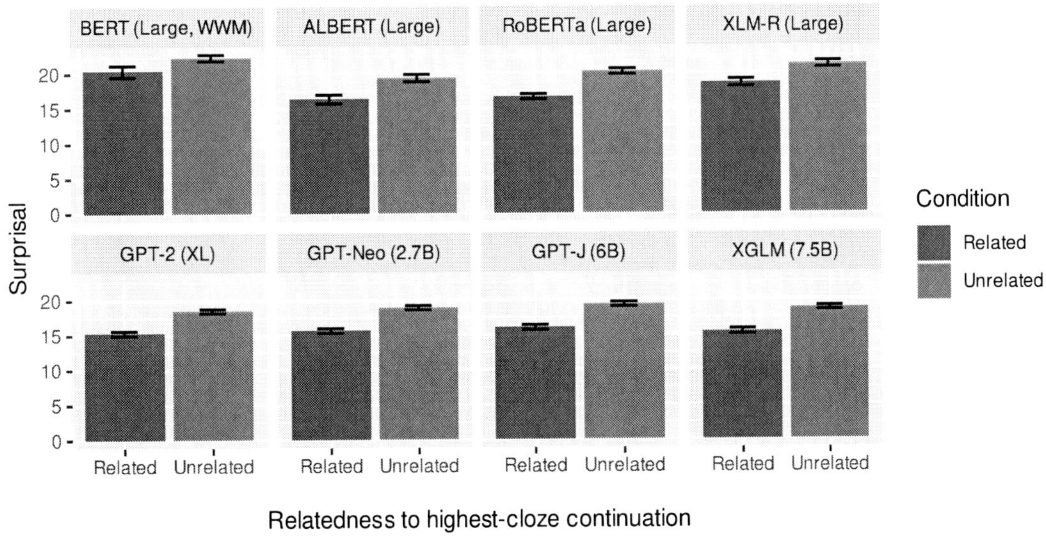

Figure 1: Mean surprisal elicited by each language model for the Ito et al. (2016) stimuli related and unrelated to the most probable (highest-cloze) continuation of each sentence. Error bars indicate standard error.

Model	Test Statistic	Corrected *p*
BERT	$F(1, 120) = 7.15$	0.0093
ALBERT	$F(1, 92) = 20.6$	< 0.0001
RoBERTa	$F(1, 159) = 60.8$	< 0.0001
XLM-R	$F(1, 126) = 21.2$	< 0.0001
GPT-2	$F(1, 157) = 64.0$	< 0.0001
GPT-Neo	$F(1, 152) = 64.1$	< 0.0001
GPT-J	$F(1, 149) = 62.5$	< 0.0001
XGLM	$F(1, 146) = 72.6$	< 0.0001

Table 1: The results of a Type III ANOVA (using Satterthwaite's method for estimating degrees of freedom; Kuznetsova et al., 2017) on the Ito et al. (2016) stimuli, testing for which language models experimental condition (related or unrelated) is a significant predictor of their surprisal. This is the case for all language models.

than the surprisal elicited by implausible stimuli unrelated to the highest-cloze continuation.

4.2 Results

The results of the experiment are shown in Figure 1. As can be seen, numerically, related words elicit lower surprisals than unrelated words, indicating that they were more highly predicted by the language models. This in turn suggests that these models do in fact collaterally predict the related continuations.

In order to test this more directly, we ran statistical analyses of the surprisals elicited by the language models. This was done by constructing linear mixed-effects regressions for each language model surprisal with experimental condition as a main effect, and the maximal random effects structure that would successfully converge for all models (see Barr et al., 2013). For all regressions except for that predicting RoBERTa surprisal, this random effects structure was a random intercept of sentence frame and of critical word. For the RoBERTa surprisal regression, the latter random intercept was removed due to it causing a singular fit. As creating null models with only the random effects structure resulted in singular fits for multiple regressions, we were unable to run likelihood ratio tests to test whether experimental condition—that is, whether the word was semantically related or unrelated to the highest-cloze continuation—was a significant predictor of surprisal. For this reason, we instead tested whether experimental condition was a significant predictor of surprisal by running a Type III ANOVA using Satterthwaite's method for estimating degrees of freedom (Kuznetsova et al., 2017) on the aforementioned linear mixed-effects models that included experimental condition as a fixed effect.

The results of the tests are shown in Table 1. As can be seen, condition is a significant predictor of the surprisal from every language model, confirm-

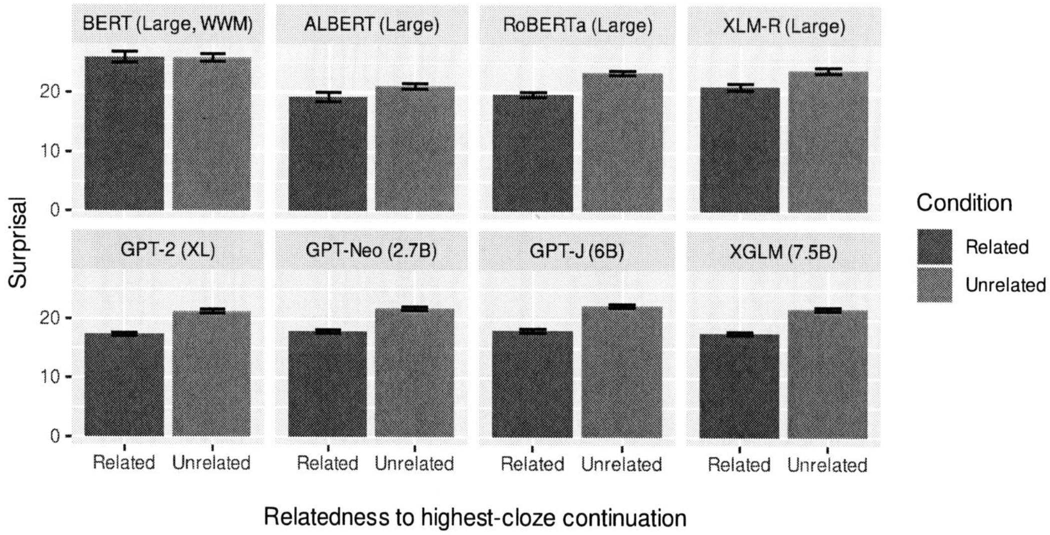

Figure 2: Mean surprisal elicited by each language model for the DeLong et al. (2019) stimuli related and unrelated to the most probable (highest-cloze) continuation of each sentence. Error bars indicate standard error.

ing that language models predict related stimuli to be more likely than unrelated stimuli.

The results of this experiment demonstrate that all the language models tested—BERT, ALBERT, RoBERTa, XLM-R, GPT-2, GPT-Neo, GPT-J, and XGLM—display the related anomaly effect in response to the Ito et al. (2016) stimuli. All eight models predict implausible continuations that are related to the most probable continuations to be more likely those that are unrelated.

5 Experiment 2: DeLong et al. (2019)

5.1 Introduction

DeLong et al. (2019) also investigated the difference between the N400 amplitude elicited by implausible words that are related or unrelated to the most predictable (highest-cloze) continuation. As in Ito et al. (2016), these stimuli were chosen such that both related and unrelated words were highly implausbile—in this case, 'unpredictable words were strategically chosen not to make sense in their given contexts' (DeLong et al., 2019, p. 4). These stimuli are exemplified by the set shown in (4).

(4) The commuter drove to work in her ______ after breakfast.

- *car* (Predictable)
- *brakes* (Related)
- *poetry* (Unrelated)

Model	Test Statistic	Corrected p
BERT	$F(1,159) =< 0.1$	0.9322
ALBERT	$F(1,112) = 6.3$	0.0138
RoBERTa	$F(1,159) = 50.7$	< 0.0001
XLM-R	$F(1,132) = 18.2$	0.0001
GPT-2 XL	$F(1,134) = 120.7$	< 0.0001
GPT-Neo	$F(1,142) = 111.7$	< 0.0001
GPT-J	$F(1,141) = 132.6$	< 0.0001
XGLM	$F(1,159) = 122.4$	< 0.0001

Table 2: The results of a Type III ANOVA (using Satterthwaite's method for estimating degrees of freedom; Kuznetsova et al., 2017) on the DeLong et al. (2019) stimuli, testing for which language models experimental condition (related or unrelated) is a significant predictor of their surprisal. This is the case for all language models except BERT.

Like Ito et al. (2016), DeLong et al. (2019) find that overall, related continuations elicit a smaller N400 response than unrelated continuations.

5.2 Results

As in Experiment 1, we ran the stimuli from the original experiment through the 8 language models and calculated the surprisal of each critical word. The results of the experiment are shown in Figure 2.

In all models except BERT, related stimuli all elicit numerically lower surprisals than unrelated stimuli, indicating that they were more highly-predicted by the language models.

We again ran the same statistical test as in Experiment 1, testing whether experimental condition (related or unrelated to the highest-cloze continuation) is a significant predictor of the surprisal elicited by the stimuli in each language model. The ALBERT, XLM-R, GPT-2, GPT-Neo, and GPT-J regressions had random intercepts of sentence frame and critical word, while the BERT, RoBERTa, and XGLM regressions had only random intercepts for sentence frame. The results of the Type III ANOVA are shown in Table 2. Condition is a significant predictor of the surprisal of every model except BERT—in these models, related stimuli are predicted to be more likely continuations of the sentence than unrelated stimuli. Thus, with the exception of BERT, we replicate the findings of Experiment 1.

6 Experiment 3: Metusalem et al. (2012)

6.1 Introduction

Metusalem et al. (2012) investigated the extent to which relatedness to the event described in the preceding context impacts the amplitude of the N400 response. Metusalem et al. (2012) presented human participants with experimental stimuli that included either the most probable (highest-cloze) continuation of a sentence, an implausible continuation that was related to the event described, or an implausible continuation that was unrelated to the event described. All of the implausible stimuli also had a cloze probability of zero. The stimuli are exemplified by the set for a single sentence frame shown in (5).

(5) We're lucky to live in a town with such a great art museum. Last week I went to see a special exhibit. I finally got in after waiting in a long ______.

- *line* (Predictable)
- *painting* (Related)
- *toothbrush* (Unrelated)

Metusalem et al. (2012) found that despite their implausibility and improbability (based on cloze), critical words related to the event described in the context preceding them elicited smaller N400 responses than words that were unrelated to the event, a clear example of a related anomaly effect.

6.2 Results

As in Experiments 1 and 2, we ran the stimuli from the original experiment through the 8 language models and calculated the surprisal of each critical word. The results of the experiment are shown in Figure 3. As in Experiment 1, numerically, in all models related stimuli elicit lower surprisals than unrelated surprisals, indicating that they were more highly predicted by the language models.

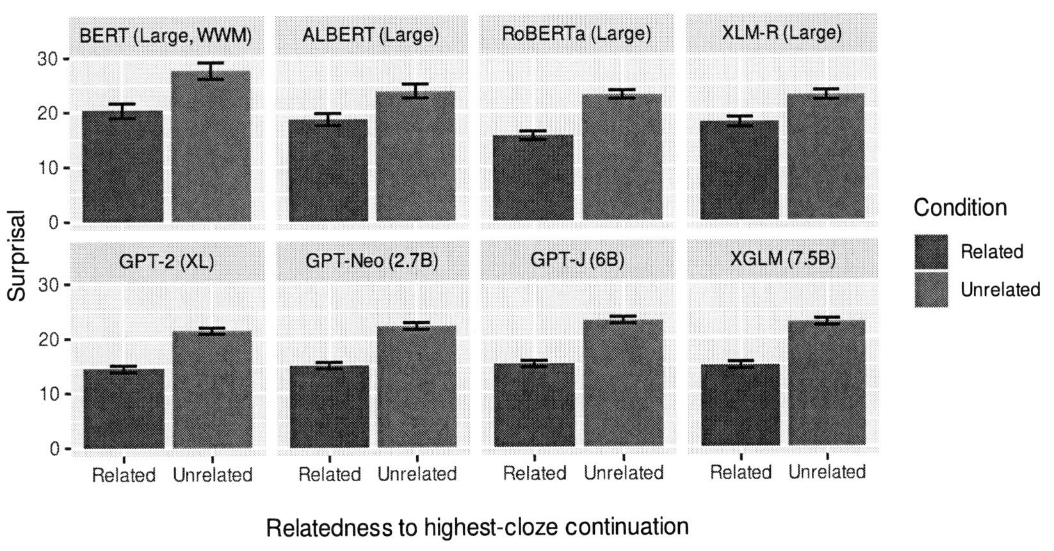

Figure 3: Mean surprisal elicited by each language model for the Metusalem et al. (2012) stimuli related and unrelated to the most probable (highest-cloze) continuation of each sentence. Error bars indicate standard error.

Model	Test Statistic	Corrected p
BERT	$F(1,29) = 77.1$	< 0.0001
ALBERT	$F(1,29) = 78.7$	< 0.0001
RoBERTa	$F(1,28) = 188.1$	< 0.0001
XLM-R	$F(1,34) = 83.4$	< 0.0001
GPT-2 XL	$F(1,35) = 211.5$	< 0.0001
GPT-Neo	$F(1,42) = 200.1$	< 0.0001
GPT-J	$F(1,35) = 265.5$	< 0.0001
XGLM	$F(1,33) = 222.5$	< 0.0001

Table 3: The results of a Type III ANOVA (using Satterthwaite's method for estimating degrees of freedom; Kuznetsova et al., 2017) on the Metusalem et al. (2012) stimuli, testing for which language models experimental condition (related or unrelated) is a significant predictor of their surprisal. This is the case for all language models.

We again ran the same statistical analyses as in Experiments 1 and 2, constructing linear mixed-effects regression models, all of which had random intercepts of sentence frame and critical word. Using a Type III ANOVA, we tested whether experimental condition (related or unrelated to the event described in the preceding context) is a significant predictor of N400 amplitude. The results are shown in Table 3. As can be seen, experimental condition was a significant predictor of the surprisal of all models.

7 General Discussion

7.1 Summary of Results

In all but one specific case—BERT in Experiment 2—experimental condition significantly predicted language model surprisal in the same direction as human N400 responses. The results of Experiments 1 and 2, therefore demonstrate convincingly that, like humans, language models do tend to predict that anomalous words related to the most probable continuation are more probable than anomalous words that are not. The results of Experiments 3, analogously, demonstrate that like humans, language models tend to predict that anomalous words related to a relevant event described in the preceding context are more probable than anomalous words that are not. Thus, like the human language comprehension system, language models exhibit related anomaly effects.

7.2 Psycholinguistic implications

These results have clear implications for psycholinguistic research on the effects of related anomalies on human language processing. First, a predictive system can display the effects—in fact, there is only one set of stimuli for which not all models do. This demonstrates the sufficiency of a predictive system for preactivating related anomalous stimuli to a greater degree than unrelated anomalous stimuli. In other words, based on a parsimony criterion, there is no need to posit that related anomaly effects on human language processing require something beyond a predictive system such as an associative system, either instead of or in addition to a predictive one.

Second, both kinds of related anomaly effect explored—the reduction in N400 amplitude correlated with relatedness to the most probable continuation and that correlated with relatedness to the event in the preceding context—are explainable by a single mechanism. This may seem counterintuitive, given how intuitively different the effects may seem. Yet this finding is consistent with the idea in the literature that the two effects can be considered different variants of the same phenomenon (DeLong et al., 2019; DeLong and Kutas, 2020).

Given that this study is based on computational modeling, we should note that the results do not constitute direct proof of a neurocognitive predictive system or of the lack of the involvement of an additional associative mechanism. However, they are consistent with such accounts, and open the door for future research, both computational and experimental. For example, it may be the case that other phenomena that have been argued to constitute evidence for a separate associative mechanism (see Federmeier, 2021, for review) may also be explainable on the basis of prediction. On the other hand, the approach we use here can also be used to design stimuli that do not differ in probability in order to further test whether prediction can explain all related anomaly effects.

7.3 Implications for NLP

The results of the present study demonstrate that related anomaly effects occur in contemporary transformer language models. Based on the present study, this does not appear to be impacted by whether the model is an autoregressive or masked language model; or by whether the model is monolingual or multilingual. In fact, the only model that does not show the effect every time is BERT, the least powerful model tested (all other models are either larger, trained on more data, or both). Thus, in line with previous research showing that higher-quality language models better predict human processing metrics (Merkx and Frank, 2021), the present results suggest that better language models are also more likely to display human-like patterns of prediction.

The results of this study also have several implications for understanding how the predictions of humans and language models relate. As has been previously discussed, some researchers have argued that we should evaluate the predictions of language models based on cloze probability (Ettinger, 2020). In fact, some have suggested training models on cloze probabilities (Eisape et al., 2020). However, the results of this study, along with others (Frank et al., 2015; Aurnhammer and Frank, 2019; Michaelov and Bergen, 2020; Aurnhammer and Frank, 2019; Merkx and Frank, 2021; Szewczyk and Federmeier, 2022; Michaelov et al., 2022), suggest that the predictions of language models are highly correlated with N400 amplitude; and recent work has argued that that the activation states of transformers are highly correlated with activation in the brain during language comprehension more generally (Schrimpf et al., 2020). Thus, while it may be useful for certain tasks to have cloze-like predictions, it may be the case that we are generally more likely to get N400-like predictions from language models.

If so, this is a cause for both optimism and pessimism. Given that humans are the gold-standard in natural language tasks generally, if a language model can make predictions that closely match those that humans make as part of language comprehension, this may also suggest that the representations learned are at least in some ways functionally similar to those that humans use to generate the same predictions. On the other hand, by the same token, it may suggest a limit to the possibilities of language modeling alone—there is much more to language comprehension than the kinds of prediction that underlie the N400 response (see, e.g., Ferreira and Yang, 2019; DeLong and Kutas, 2020; Kuperberg et al., 2020).

8 Conclusion

In order to better understand related anomaly effects in humans, we investigated whether contemporary transformer language models display them. We found that in all but one case, they do, suggesting that related anomaly effects in both humans and language models may be driven by prediction alone.

Acknowledgements

We would like to thank the authors of the original N400 experiment papers—Wen-Hsuan Chan, Martin Corley, Katherine A. DeLong, Jeffrey L. Elman, Mary Hare, Aine Ito, Marta Kutas, Andrea E. Martin, Ken McRae, Ross Metusalem, Mante S. Nieuwland, Martin J. Pickering, and Thomas P. Urbach—for making their stimuli available. We would also like to thank the anonymous reviewers for their helpful comments, the other members of the Language and Cognition Lab at UCSD for their valuable discussion, and the San Diego Social Sciences Computing Facility Team for their technical assistance. This work was partially supported by a 2021-2022 Center for Academic Research and Training in Anthropogeny Annette Merle-Smith Fellowship awarded to James A. Michaelov, and the RTX A5000 used for this research was donated by the NVIDIA Corporation.

References

Adam Amram, Anat Ben David, and Reut Tsarfaty. 2018. Representations and Architectures in Neural Sentiment Analysis for Morphologically Rich Languages: A Case Study from Modern Hebrew. In *Proceedings of the 27th International Conference on Computational Linguistics*, pages 2242–2252, Santa Fe, New Mexico, USA. Association for Computational Linguistics.

Christoph Aurnhammer and Stefan L. Frank. 2019. Evaluating information-theoretic measures of word prediction in naturalistic sentence reading. *Neuropsychologia*, 134:107198.

Megan Bardolph, Cyma Van Petten, and Seana Coulson. 2018. Single Trial EEG Data Reveals Sensitivity to Conceptual Expectations (N400) and Integrative Demands (LPC). In *Twelfth Annual Meeting of the Society for the Neurobiology of Language*, Quebec City, Canada.

Dale J. Barr, Roger Levy, Christoph Scheepers, and Harry J. Tily. 2013. Random effects structure for confirmatory hypothesis testing: Keep it maximal. *Journal of Memory and Language*, 68(3):255–278.

Douglas Bates, Martin Mächler, Ben Bolker, and Steve Walker. 2015. Fitting linear mixed-effects models using lme4. *Journal of Statistical Software*, 67(1):1–48.

Emily Bender. 2019. The #BenderRule: On naming the languages we study and why it matters. *The Gradient*.

Emily M. Bender. 2009. Linguistically Naïve != Language Independent: Why NLP Needs Linguistic Typology. In *Proceedings of the EACL 2009 Workshop on the Interaction between Linguistics and Computational Linguistics: Virtuous, Vicious or Vacuous?*, pages 26–32, Athens, Greece. Association for Computational Linguistics.

Emily M. Bender. 2011. On Achieving and Evaluating Language-Independence in NLP. *Linguistic Issues in Language Technology*, 6.

Yoav Benjamini and Yosef Hochberg. 1995. Controlling the False Discovery Rate: A Practical and Powerful Approach to Multiple Testing. *Journal of the Royal Statistical Society. Series B (Methodological)*, 57(1):289–300.

Sid Black, Leo Gao, Phil Wang, Connor Leahy, and Stella Biderman. 2021. GPT-Neo: Large scale autoregressive language modeling with mesh-tensorflow. Zenodo.

Ina Bornkessel-Schlesewsky and Matthias Schlesewsky. 2019. Toward a Neurobiologically Plausible Model of Language-Related, Negative Event-Related Potentials. *Frontiers in Psychology*, 10.

Trevor Brothers and Gina R. Kuperberg. 2021. Word predictability effects are linear, not logarithmic: Implications for probabilistic models of sentence comprehension. *Journal of Memory and Language*, 116:104174.

Harm Brouwer, Matthew W. Crocker, Noortje J. Venhuizen, and John C. J. Hoeks. 2017. A Neurocomputational Model of the N400 and the P600 in Language Processing. *Cognitive Science*, 41(S6):1318–1352.

Tom Brown, Benjamin Mann, Nick Ryder, Melanie Subbiah, Jared D Kaplan, Prafulla Dhariwal, Arvind Neelakantan, Pranav Shyam, Girish Sastry, Amanda Askell, Sandhini Agarwal, Ariel Herbert-Voss, Gretchen Krueger, Tom Henighan, Rewon Child, Aditya Ramesh, Daniel Ziegler, Jeffrey Wu, Clemens Winter, Chris Hesse, Mark Chen, Eric Sigler, Mateusz Litwin, Scott Gray, Benjamin Chess, Jack Clark, Christopher Berner, Sam McCandlish, Alec Radford, Ilya Sutskever, and Dario Amodei. 2020. Language Models are Few-Shot Learners. In *Advances in Neural Information Processing Systems*, volume 33, pages 1877–1901. Curran Associates, Inc.

Samuel J. Cheyette and David C. Plaut. 2017. Modeling the N400 ERP component as transient semantic overactivation within a neural network model of word comprehension. *Cognition*, 162:153–166.

Aakanksha Chowdhery, Sharan Narang, Jacob Devlin, Maarten Bosma, Gaurav Mishra, Adam Roberts, Paul Barham, Hyung Won Chung, Charles Sutton, Sebastian Gehrmann, Parker Schuh, Kensen Shi, Sasha Tsvyashchenko, Joshua Maynez, Abhishek Rao, Parker Barnes, Yi Tay, Noam Shazeer, Vinodkumar Prabhakaran, Emily Reif, Nan Du, Ben Hutchinson, Reiner Pope, James Bradbury, Jacob Austin, Michael Isard, Guy Gur-Ari, Pengcheng Yin, Toju Duke, Anselm Levskaya, Sanjay Ghemawat, Sunipa Dev, Henryk Michalewski, Xavier Garcia, Vedant Misra, Kevin Robinson, Liam Fedus, Denny Zhou, Daphne Ippolito, David Luan, Hyeontaek Lim, Barret Zoph, Alexander Spiridonov, Ryan Sepassi, David Dohan, Shivani Agrawal, Mark Omernick, Andrew M. Dai, Thanumalayan Sankaranarayana Pillai, Marie Pellat, Aitor Lewkowycz, Erica Moreira, Rewon Child, Oleksandr Polozov, Katherine Lee, Zongwei Zhou, Xuezhi Wang, Brennan Saeta, Mark Diaz, Orhan Firat, Michele Catasta, Jason Wei, Kathy Meier-Hellstern, Douglas Eck, Jeff Dean, Slav Petrov, and Noah Fiedel. 2022. PaLM: Scaling Language Modeling with Pathways.

Jonathan H. Clark, Dan Garrette, Iulia Turc, and John Wieting. 2022. Canine: Pre-training an Efficient Tokenization-Free Encoder for Language Representation. *Transactions of the Association for Computational Linguistics*, 10:73–91.

Alexis Conneau, Kartikay Khandelwal, Naman Goyal, Vishrav Chaudhary, Guillaume Wenzek, Francisco Guzmán, Edouard Grave, Myle Ott, Luke Zettlemoyer, and Veselin Stoyanov. 2020. Unsupervised Cross-lingual Representation Learning at Scale. In *Proceedings of the 58th Annual Meeting of the Association for Computational Linguistics*, pages 8440–8451, Online. Association for Computational Linguistics.

Katherine A. DeLong, Wen-hsuan Chan, and Marta Kutas. 2019. Similar time courses for word form and meaning preactivation during sentence comprehension. *Psychophysiology*, 56(4):e13312.

Katherine A. DeLong and Marta Kutas. 2020. Comprehending surprising sentences: Sensitivity of post-N400 positivities to contextual congruity and semantic relatedness. *Language, Cognition and Neuroscience*, 35(0):1044–1063.

Katherine A DeLong, Thomas P Urbach, and Marta Kutas. 2005. Probabilistic word pre-activation during language comprehension inferred from electrical brain activity. *Nature Neuroscience*, 8(8):1117–1121.

Jacob Devlin, Ming-Wei Chang, Kenton Lee, and Kristina Toutanova. 2019. BERT: Pre-training of Deep Bidirectional Transformers for Language Understanding. In *Proceedings of the 2019 Conference of the North American Chapter of the Association for Computational Linguistics: Human Language Technologies, Volume 1 (Long and Short Papers)*, pages

4171–4186, Minneapolis, Minnesota. Association for Computational Linguistics.

Tiwalayo Eisape, Noga Zaslavsky, and Roger Levy. 2020. Cloze Distillation: Improving Neural Language Models with Human Next-Word Prediction. In *Proceedings of the 24th Conference on Computational Natural Language Learning*, pages 609–619, Online. Association for Computational Linguistics.

Allyson Ettinger. 2020. What BERT Is Not: Lessons from a New Suite of Psycholinguistic Diagnostics for Language Models. *Transactions of the Association for Computational Linguistics*, 8:34–48.

Allyson Ettinger, Naomi Feldman, Philip Resnik, and Colin Phillips. 2016. Modeling N400 amplitude using vector space models of word representation. In *Proceedings of the 38th Annual Conference of the Cognitive Science Society*, Philadelphia, USA.

Kara D. Federmeier. 2021. Connecting and considering: Electrophysiology provides insights into comprehension. *Psychophysiology*, n/a(n/a):e13940.

Kara D. Federmeier and Marta Kutas. 1999. A Rose by Any Other Name: Long-Term Memory Structure and Sentence Processing. *Journal of Memory and Language*, 41(4):469–495.

Fernanda Ferreira and Zoe Yang. 2019. The Problem of Comprehension in Psycholinguistics. *Discourse Processes*, 56(7):485–495.

Ira Fischler and Paul A. Bloom. 1979. Automatic and attentional processes in the effects of sentence contexts on word recognition. *Journal of Verbal Learning and Verbal Behavior*, 18(1):1–20.

Hartmut Fitz and Franklin Chang. 2019. Language ERPs reflect learning through prediction error propagation. *Cognitive Psychology*, 111:15–52.

Stefan L. Frank, Leun J. Otten, Giulia Galli, and Gabriella Vigliocco. 2015. The ERP response to the amount of information conveyed by words in sentences. *Brain and Language*, 140:1–11.

Stefan L. Frank and Roel M. Willems. 2017. Word predictability and semantic similarity show distinct patterns of brain activity during language comprehension. *Language, Cognition and Neuroscience*, 32(9):1192–1203.

Richard Futrell, Ethan Wilcox, Takashi Morita, Peng Qian, Miguel Ballesteros, and Roger Levy. 2019. Neural language models as psycholinguistic subjects: Representations of syntactic state. In *Proceedings of the 2019 Conference of the North American Chapter of the Association for Computational Linguistics: Human Language Technologies, Volume 1 (Long and Short Papers)*, pages 32–42, Minneapolis, Minnesota. Association for Computational Linguistics.

Kristina Gulordava, Piotr Bojanowski, Edouard Grave, Tal Linzen, and Marco Baroni. 2018. Colorless Green Recurrent Networks Dream Hierarchically. In *Proceedings of the 2018 Conference of the North American Chapter of the Association for Computational Linguistics: Human Language Technologies, Volume 1 (Long Papers)*, pages 1195–1205, New Orleans, Louisiana. Association for Computational Linguistics.

Aine Ito, Martin Corley, Martin J. Pickering, Andrea E. Martin, and Mante S. Nieuwland. 2016. Predicting form and meaning: Evidence from brain potentials. *Journal of Memory and Language*, 86:157–171.

Rafal Jozefowicz, Oriol Vinyals, Mike Schuster, Noam Shazeer, and Yonghui Wu. 2016. Exploring the Limits of Language Modeling. *arXiv:1602.02410 [cs]*.

Nora Kassner and Hinrich Schütze. 2020. Negated and Misprimed Probes for Pretrained Language Models: Birds Can Talk, But Cannot Fly. In *Proceedings of the 58th Annual Meeting of the Association for Computational Linguistics*, pages 7811–7818, Online. Association for Computational Linguistics.

Yoon Kim, Yacine Jernite, David Sontag, and Alexander M. Rush. 2016. Character-Aware Neural Language Models. In *Thirtieth AAAI Conference on Artificial Intelligence*.

Gina R. Kuperberg, Trevor Brothers, and Edward W. Wlotko. 2020. A Tale of Two Positivities and the N400: Distinct Neural Signatures Are Evoked by Confirmed and Violated Predictions at Different Levels of Representation. *Journal of Cognitive Neuroscience*, 32(1):12–35.

Marta Kutas. 1993. In the company of other words: Electrophysiological evidence for single-word and sentence context effects. *Language and Cognitive Processes*, 8(4):533–572.

Marta Kutas, Katherine A. DeLong, and Nathaniel J. Smith. 2011. A look around at what lies ahead: Prediction and predictability in language processing. In Moshe Bar, editor, *Predictions in the Brain: Using Our Past to Generate a Future*, pages 190–207. Oxford University Press, New York, NY, US.

Marta Kutas and Steven A. Hillyard. 1984. Brain potentials during reading reflect word expectancy and semantic association. *Nature*, 307(5947):161–163.

Marta Kutas, Timothy E Lindamood, and Steven A Hillyard. 1984. Word expectancy and event-related brain potentials during sentence processing. In S. Kornblum and J. Requin, editors, *Preparatory States and Processes*, pages 217–237. Lawrence Erlbaum, Hillsdale, NJ.

Alexandra Kuznetsova, Per B. Brockhoff, and Rune H. B. Christensen. 2017. lmerTest Package: Tests in Linear Mixed Effects Models. *Journal of Statistical Software*, 82:1–26.

Zhenzhong Lan, Mingda Chen, Sebastian Goodman, Kevin Gimpel, Piyush Sharma, and Radu Soricut. 2020. ALBERT: A Lite BERT for Self-supervised Learning of Language Representations. In *International Conference on Learning Representations*.

Sarah Laszlo and Blair C. Armstrong. 2014. PSPs and ERPs: Applying the dynamics of post-synaptic potentials to individual units in simulation of temporally extended Event-Related Potential reading data. *Brain and Language*, 132:22–27.

Sarah Laszlo and David C. Plaut. 2012. A neurally plausible Parallel Distributed Processing model of Event-Related Potential word reading data. *Brain and Language*, 120(3):271–281.

Ellen F. Lau, Phillip J. Holcomb, and Gina R. Kuperberg. 2013. Dissociating N400 Effects of Prediction from Association in Single-word Contexts. *Journal of Cognitive Neuroscience*, 25(3):484–502.

Roger Levy. 2008. Expectation-based syntactic comprehension. *Cognition*, 106(3):1126–1177.

Xi Victoria Lin, Todor Mihaylov, Mikel Artetxe, Tianlu Wang, Shuohui Chen, Daniel Simig, Myle Ott, Naman Goyal, Shruti Bhosale, Jingfei Du, Ramakanth Pasunuru, Sam Shleifer, Punit Singh Koura, Vishrav Chaudhary, Brian O'Horo, Jeff Wang, Luke Zettlemoyer, Zornitsa Kozareva, Mona Diab, Veselin Stoyanov, and Xian Li. 2021. Few-shot Learning with Multilingual Language Models. *arXiv:2112.10668 [cs]*.

Alma Lindborg and Milena Rabovsky. 2021. Meaning in brains and machines: Internal activation update in large-scale language model partially reflects the N400 brain potential. *Proceedings of the Annual Meeting of the Cognitive Science Society*, 43(43).

Yinhan Liu, Myle Ott, Naman Goyal, Jingfei Du, Mandar Joshi, Danqi Chen, Omer Levy, Mike Lewis, Luke Zettlemoyer, and Veselin Stoyanov. 2019. RoBERTa: A Robustly Optimized BERT Pretraining Approach. *arXiv:1907.11692 [cs]*.

Scott A. McDonald and Richard C. Shillcock. 2003. Eye Movements Reveal the On-Line Computation of Lexical Probabilities During Reading. *Psychological Science*, 14(6):648–652.

Danny Merkx and Stefan L. Frank. 2021. Human Sentence Processing: Recurrence or Attention? In *Proceedings of the Workshop on Cognitive Modeling and Computational Linguistics*, pages 12–22, Online. Association for Computational Linguistics.

Ross Metusalem, Marta Kutas, Thomas P. Urbach, Mary Hare, Ken McRae, and Jeffrey L. Elman. 2012. Generalized event knowledge activation during online sentence comprehension. *Journal of Memory and Language*, 66(4):545–567.

James A. Michaelov, Megan D. Bardolph, Seana Coulson, and Benjamin K. Bergen. 2021. Different kinds of cognitive plausibility: Why are transformers better than RNNs at predicting N400 amplitude? In *Proceedings of the 43rd Annual Meeting of the Cognitive Science Society*, pages 300–306, University of Vienna, Vienna, Austria (Hybrid).

James A. Michaelov and Benjamin K. Bergen. 2020. How well does surprisal explain N400 amplitude under different experimental conditions? In *Proceedings of the 24th Conference on Computational Natural Language Learning*, pages 652–663, Online. Association for Computational Linguistics.

James A. Michaelov, Seana Coulson, and Benjamin K. Bergen. 2022. So Cloze yet so Far: N400 Amplitude is Better Predicted by Distributional Information than Human Predictability Judgements. *IEEE Transactions on Cognitive and Developmental Systems*.

Sabrina J. Mielke. 2016. Language diversity in ACL 2004 - 2016.

Kanishka Misra, Allyson Ettinger, and Julia Rayz. 2020. Exploring BERT's Sensitivity to Lexical Cues using Tests from Semantic Priming. In *Findings of the Association for Computational Linguistics: EMNLP 2020*, pages 4625–4635, Online. Association for Computational Linguistics.

Robert Munro. 2015. Languages at ACL this year.

Mehdi Parviz, Mark Johnson, Blake Johnson, and Jon Brock. 2011. Using Language Models and Latent Semantic Analysis to Characterise the N400m Neural Response. In *Proceedings of the Australasian Language Technology Association Workshop 2011*, pages 38–46, Canberra, Australia.

Grusha Prasad, Marten van Schijndel, and Tal Linzen. 2019. Using Priming to Uncover the Organization of Syntactic Representations in Neural Language Models. In *Proceedings of the 23rd Conference on Computational Natural Language Learning (CoNLL)*, pages 66–76, Hong Kong, China. Association for Computational Linguistics.

R Core Team. 2020. *R: A Language and Environment for Statistical Computing*. R Foundation for Statistical Computing, Vienna, Austria.

Milena Rabovsky, Steven S. Hansen, and James L. McClelland. 2018. Modelling the N400 brain potential as change in a probabilistic representation of meaning. *Nature Human Behaviour*, 2(9):693–705.

Milena Rabovsky and Ken McRae. 2014. Simulating the N400 ERP component as semantic network error: Insights from a feature-based connectionist attractor model of word meaning. *Cognition*, 132(1):68–89.

Alec Radford, Jeffrey Wu, Rewon Child, David Luan, Dario Amodei, and Ilya Sutskever. 2019. Language Models are Unsupervised Multitask Learners. page 24.

Joost Rommers, Antje S. Meyer, Peter Praamstra, and Falk Huettig. 2013. The contents of predictions in sentence comprehension: Activation of the shape of objects before they are referred to. *Neuropsychologia*, 51(3):437–447.

RStudio Team. 2020. *RStudio: Integrated Development Environment for r*. RStudio, PBC., Boston, MA.

Martin Schrimpf, Idan Blank, Greta Tuckute, Carina Kauf, Eghbal A. Hosseini, Nancy Kanwisher, Joshua Tenenbaum, and Evelina Fedorenko. 2020. The neural architecture of language: Integrative reverse-engineering converges on a model for predictive processing. *bioRxiv*, page 2020.06.26.174482.

Nathaniel J. Smith and Roger Levy. 2013. The effect of word predictability on reading time is logarithmic. *Cognition*, 128(3):302–319.

Jakub M. Szewczyk and Kara D. Federmeier. 2022. Context-based facilitation of semantic access follows both logarithmic and linear functions of stimulus probability. *Journal of Memory and Language*, 123:104311.

Wilson L. Taylor. 1953. "Cloze Procedure": A New Tool for Measuring Readability. *Journalism Quarterly*, 30(4):415–433.

Wilson L. Taylor. 1957. "Cloze" readability scores as indices of individual differences in comprehension and aptitude. *Journal of Applied Psychology*, 41(1):19–26.

Romal Thoppilan, Daniel De Freitas, Jamie Hall, Noam Shazeer, Apoorv Kulshreshtha, Heng-Tze Cheng, Alicia Jin, Taylor Bos, Leslie Baker, Yu Du, YaGuang Li, Hongrae Lee, Huaixiu Steven Zheng, Amin Ghafouri, Marcelo Menegali, Yanping Huang, Maxim Krikun, Dmitry Lepikhin, James Qin, Dehao Chen, Yuanzhong Xu, Zhifeng Chen, Adam Roberts, Maarten Bosma, Vincent Zhao, Yanqi Zhou, Chung-Ching Chang, Igor Krivokon, Will Rusch, Marc Pickett, Pranesh Srinivasan, Laichee Man, Kathleen Meier-Hellstern, Meredith Ringel Morris, Tulsee Doshi, Renelito Delos Santos, Toju Duke, Johnny Soraker, Ben Zevenbergen, Vinodkumar Prabhakaran, Mark Diaz, Ben Hutchinson, Kristen Olson, Alejandra Molina, Erin Hoffman-John, Josh Lee, Lora Aroyo, Ravi Rajakumar, Alena Butryna, Matthew Lamm, Viktoriya Kuzmina, Joe Fenton, Aaron Cohen, Rachel Bernstein, Ray Kurzweil, Blaise Aguera-Arcas, Claire Cui, Marian Croak, Ed Chi, and Quoc Le. 2022. LaMDA: Language Models for Dialog Applications.

Reut Tsarfaty, Djamé Seddah, Sandra Kübler, and Joakim Nivre. 2013. Parsing Morphologically Rich Languages: Introduction to the Special Issue. *Computational Linguistics*, 39(1):15–22.

Takahisa Uchida, Nicolas Lair, Hiroshi Ishiguro, and Peter Ford Dominey. 2021. A Model of Online Temporal-Spatial Integration for Immediacy and Overrule in Discourse Comprehension. *Neurobiology of Language*, 2(1):83–105.

Cyma Van Petten and Barbara J. Luka. 2012. Prediction during language comprehension: Benefits, costs, and ERP components. *International Journal of Psychophysiology*, 83(2):176–190.

Noortje J. Venhuizen, Matthew W. Crocker, and Harm Brouwer. 2019. Expectation-based Comprehension: Modeling the Interaction of World Knowledge and Linguistic Experience. *Discourse Processes*, 56(3):229–255.

Ben Wang and Aran Komatsuzaki. 2021. GPT-J-6B: A 6 billion parameter autoregressive language model.

Hadley Wickham, Mara Averick, Jennifer Bryan, Winston Chang, Lucy D'Agostino McGowan, Romain François, Garrett Grolemund, Alex Hayes, Lionel Henry, Jim Hester, Max Kuhn, Thomas Lin Pedersen, Evan Miller, Stephan Milton Bache, Kirill Müller, Jeroen Ooms, David Robinson, Dana Paige Seidel, Vitalie Spinu, Kohske Takahashi, Davis Vaughan, Claus Wilke, Kara Woo, and Hiroaki Yutani. 2019. Welcome to the tidyverse. *Journal of Open Source Software*, 4(43):1686.

Thomas Wolf, Lysandre Debut, Victor Sanh, Julien Chaumond, Clement Delangue, Anthony Moi, Pierric Cistac, Tim Rault, Remi Louf, Morgan Funtowicz, Joe Davison, Sam Shleifer, Patrick von Platen, Clara Ma, Yacine Jernite, Julien Plu, Canwen Xu, Teven Le Scao, Sylvain Gugger, Mariama Drame, Quentin Lhoest, and Alexander Rush. 2020. Transformers: State-of-the-Art Natural Language Processing. In *Proceedings of the 2020 Conference on Empirical Methods in Natural Language Processing: System Demonstrations*, pages 38–45, Online. Association for Computational Linguistics.

Susan Zhang, Stephen Roller, Naman Goyal, Mikel Artetxe, Moya Chen, Shuohui Chen, Christopher Dewan, Mona Diab, Xian Li, Xi Victoria Lin, Todor Mihaylov, Myle Ott, Sam Shleifer, Kurt Shuster, Daniel Simig, Punit Singh Koura, Anjali Sridhar, Tianlu Wang, and Luke Zettlemoyer. 2022. OPT: Open Pre-trained Transformer Language Models.

A Limitations

As mentioned the discussion section, one limitation of the present study is that while it demonstrates that it is possible for related anomaly effects to emerge from a system engaged in prediction alone, it does not directly demonstrate that this is what is occurring in humans.

A further limitation is that we model the results of three related anomaly experiments out of the larger total number that have been carried out (for review, see DeLong et al., 2019). However, given how consistent related anomaly effects appear to be (DeLong et al., 2019), and how consistent our results are (after statistical correction for multiple comparisons, all three related anomaly effects are modeled by all but one transformer, which only fails to model one effect), we do not believe this presents a problem for our analysis.

Finally, the three experiments modeled were all carried out in English. Related anomaly effects have been reported in other languages (DeLong et al., 2019) such as Dutch (Rommers et al., 2013); and these are not modeled in our study. Thus, it is an open question whether our results generalize to related anomaly effects in languages other than English. However, we also note the evidence that higher-quality models are better at predicting N400 amplitude (Merkx and Frank, 2021). For this reason, given the overwhelming focus on English in computational linguistics (Bender, 2009, 2011; Tsarfaty et al., 2013; Munro, 2015; Mielke, 2016; Kim et al., 2016; Amram et al., 2018; Bender, 2019; Clark et al., 2022), current language model architectures are likely to be best suited to predicting English—indeed, current state-of-the-art models such as GPT-3 (Brown et al., 2020), OPT (Zhang et al., 2022), PaLM (Chowdhery et al., 2022), and LaMDA (Thoppilan et al., 2022) are trained mostly or only on English data. Thus, while the focus on modeling English may be an issue for the field as a whole, in this case, focusing on experiments carried out in English may in fact give us the best possible chance to evaluate what the human predictive system *could* predict.

B Models used

The details of the models used in this study are provided in Table 4.

Model Name	Full Name on the Hugging Face Model Hub	Reference
BERT	`bert-large-cased-whole-word-masking`	Devlin et al. (2019)
ALBERT	`albert-xxlarge-v2`	Lan et al. (2020)
RoBERTa	`roberta-large`	Liu et al. (2019)
XLM-R	`xlm-roberta-large`	Conneau et al. (2020)
GPT-2 XL	`gpt2-xl`	Radford et al. (2019)
GPT-Neo	`EleutherAI/gpt-neo-2.7B`	Black et al. (2021)
GPT-J	`EleutherAI/gpt-j-6B`	Wang and Komatsuzaki (2021)
XGLM	`facebook/xglm-7.5B`	Lin et al. (2021)

Table 4: Transformer langauge models used in the present study. All were accessed using the transformers (Wolf et al., 2020) package.

How Hate Speech Varies by Target Identity: A Computational Analysis

Michael Miller Yoder[1] **Lynnette Hui Xian Ng**[1] **David West Brown**[2] **Kathleen M. Carley**[1]
[1]School of Computer Science [2]Department of English
Carnegie Mellon University
Pittsburgh, Pennsylvania, USA
{mamille3,huixiann,dwb2,carley}@andrew.cmu.edu

Abstract

This paper investigates how hate speech varies in systematic ways according to the identities it targets. Across multiple hate speech datasets annotated for targeted identities, we find that classifiers trained on hate speech targeting specific identity groups struggle to generalize to other targeted identities. This provides empirical evidence for differences in hate speech by target identity; we then investigate which patterns structure this variation. We find that the targeted demographic category (e.g. gender/sexuality or race/ethnicity) appears to have a greater effect on the language of hate speech than does the relative social power of the targeted identity group. We also find that words associated with hate speech targeting specific identities often relate to stereotypes, histories of oppression, current social movements, and other social contexts specific to identities. These experiments suggest the importance of considering targeted identity, as well as the social contexts associated with these identities, in automated hate speech classification.

Warning: *This paper contains offensive and hateful terms and concepts. We have chosen to reproduce these terms for clarity in aiding efforts against hate speech.*

1 Introduction

Researchers working in natural language processing (NLP) often treat hate speech as a binary, unified, concept that can be detected from language alone. However, as a linguistic concept that relies heavily on social context, hate speech contains a variety of related phenomena (Brown, 2017). Hate speech is characterized by variation in linguistic features (e.g. implicit vs. explicit), context (e.g. platforms, prior conversations), and communities (social histories and hierarchies). This paper focuses on a crucial aspect of this variation: how hate speech varies by the identity groups it targets.

To study this variation, we analyze hate speech datasets that include annotations for which identity group is targeted. Drawing from multiple of these datasets, we sample new corpora that target the same identity group. These identity groups vary according to several dimensions, including relevant demographic category (e.g. gender, religion) and relative social power (e.g. socially marginalized or dominant). We empirically test which dimensions most clearly separate different forms of hate speech by evaluating how well classifiers trained on one set of identities generalize to hate speech directed at different sets of identities.

We find that hate speech varies most prominently by the targeted demographic category and less so by the social power of the targeted identity group. Theorists working in philosophy and sociolinguistics have drawn attention to how hate speech directed at marginalized groups differs from hate directed toward socially dominant groups (Butler, 1997; Lakoff, 2000). However, we do not find that hate speech toward dominant groups is sufficiently different to consistently increase classification performance when removed from existing datasets.

Analyzing the most representative terms in hate speech directed toward different identities, we find that many words reflect identity-specific context such as histories of oppression or stereotypes. These results have implications for NLP researchers building generalizable hate speech classifiers, as well as for a more general understanding of variation in hate speech.

Contributions

1. An empirical analysis of variation in hate speech by target identity. Specifically, how well classifiers trained on hate speech directed toward specific identities generalize to hate speech directed at other identities.

2. An analysis of which dimensions of social difference (demographic category, power) among targeted identities reflect the most variation in hate speech.

Proceedings of the 26th Conference on Computational Natural Language Learning (CoNLL), pages 27 - 39
December 7-8, 2022 ©2022 Association for Computational Linguistics

3. A qualitative analysis of the hate speech terms most strongly associated with specific target identities.

2 Hate Speech

Hate speech is an example of a "thick concept" with a set of related, but difficult to define meanings and understandings (Pohjonen and Udupa, 2017). Legal theorist Alexander Brown (2017) argues for a set of attributes that make an expression more or less likely to be considered hate speech, similar to Wittgenstein's "family resemblances" concept. Key attributes include an incitement of emotion and violence, and a direction of that incitement toward a targeted identity group (Sanguinetti et al., 2018; Poletto et al., 2021). Though others have studied the linguistic properties of this incitement (Marsters, 2019; Wiegand et al., 2021), we focus on how variation in the identity group targeted by hate speech affects the linguistic characteristics of hate speech.

2.1 Variation by identity

Identities are central to hate speech. Classifiers often learn to associate the presence of identity terms, especially derogatory ones, with hate speech and abusive language (Dixon et al., 2017; Uyheng and Carley, 2021). Computational studies of the targets of online hate speech have included measurement studies of its prevalence toward different targets. Silva et al. (2016) and Mondal et al. (2017) searched for templates such as "I hate ___" to measure hate toward different identity groups. We analyze datasets manually annotated with the targets of hate speech. This captures a broader range of hate speech, including indirect hate speech and stereotypes. ElSherief et al. (2018a,b) investigated differences between hate toward groups versus individual targets. In contrast, we compare differences among identity targets. Rieger et al. (2021) measured multiple types of variation, including by identity target, in hate speech from fringe platforms such as 4chan and 8chan. We test if such differences affect the generalization of hate speech classifiers.

Many identities are involved in the production and recognition of hate speech, including the identities of those who produce hate speech and those who annotate hate speech datasets. The post history and inferred gender of social media users have been found to be useful in predicting hate speech (Waseem and Hovy, 2016; Unsvåg and Gambäck, 2018; Qian et al., 2018). Waseem (2016) find differences in hate speech annotations between crowdworkers and experts, while Sap et al. (2022) find differences by the political ideology of annotators. We focus on identities presented in the hate speech itself.

2.2 Generalizability

In this paper, we evaluate the ability of hate speech classifiers to generalize across targeted identities. Gröndahl et al. (2018) find that hate speech models generally perform poorly on data that differs from their training data; we look at how shifts in the distribution of identity targets affects generalization. Swamy et al. (2019) look at generalizability across subtasks of abusive language detection and find that a larger proportion of hateful instances aids generalization. Pamungkas et al. (2020) and Fortuna et al. (2020) find that hate speech models using variants of BERT (Devlin et al., 2019) generalize better than other models. We thus use a variant of BERT in our generalization experiments. See Yin and Zubiaga (2021) for a more thorough survey on generalizability in hate speech detection.

3 Data

From surveys of hate speech datasets (Vidgen and Derczynski, 2020; Poletto et al., 2021) and the Hate Speech Dataset Catalogue[1], we selected datasets with annotations for targeted identities. We only selected datasets that do not restrict target identities in order to minimize differences in other properties (e.g, domain, year) when comparing across targeted identities. This excludes hate speech datasets and shared tasks that focus on particular targeted identity groups, such as women or immigrants (Kwok and Wang, 2013; Basile et al., 2019).

We also did not consider hate speech datasets that label targeted demographic category, such as race or gender (Waseem, 2016), but do not specify the identity group targeted. Demographic category is just one of the dimensions of similarities and differences among identity groups that we wish to compare for their affect on hate speech. We included datasets from all domains, except those with synthetic data.

Since we only found one non-English dataset that contained unrestricted annotations for targeted identities (Ousidhoum et al., 2019), we focus on hate speech in English in this work.

[1]https://hatespeechdata.com/

For generalization analyses, we sampled corpora specific to identity groups across datasets large enough to contain a minimum number of instances of hate speech against enough groups (described in Section 4.1). These are the first 4 datasets noted in Table 1. All datasets are used in the analysis of removing dominant groups (Section 6.2).

Datasets are resampled to a 30/70 ratio of hate to non-hate to eliminate a source of variance among hate speech datasets known to affect generalization (Swamy et al., 2019). Non-hate instances are upsampled or downsampled to meet this ratio, which was chosen as typical of hate speech datasets (Vidgen and Derczynski, 2020). If they do not already contain a binary hate speech label, dataset labels are binarized as described in Appendix A.

3.1 Target identity label normalization

Annotations for targeted identities vary considerably across datasets. Some of these differences are variations in naming conventions for identity groups with significant similarity ('Caucasian' and 'white people', for example). Other identities are subsets of broader identities, such as 'trans men' as a specific group within 'LGBTQ+ people'.

To construct identity-based corpora across datasets, we normalized and grouped identities annotated in each dataset. One of the authors, who has taken graduate-level courses on language and identity, manually normalized the most common identity labels in each dataset and assigned these normalized identity labels into broader identity groups (such as 'LGBTQ+ people'). Intersectional identities, such as 'Chinese women', were assigned to multiple groups (in this case 'Asian people' and 'women'). Hate speech was often directed at conflated, problematic groupings such as 'Muslims and Arabs'. Though we do not condone these groupings, we use them as the most accurate descriptors of identities targeted.

4 Cross-Identity Generalization

We examine variation among hate speech targeting different identities in a bottom-up, empirical fashion. In order to do this, we construct corpora of hate speech directed at the most commonly annotated target identities, grouped and normalized as described in Section 3.1. We then trained hate speech classifiers on each target identity corpus and evaluated on corpora targeting other identities.

Along with practical implications for hate speech classification generalization, this analysis suggests which similarities and differences among identities are most relevant for differentiating hate speech.

4.1 Data sampling

In order to have enough data targeting many identities and to generalize beyond the particularities of specific datasets, we assembled identity-specific corpora from multiple source datasets. To mitigate dataset-specific effects, we uniformly sampled hate speech instances directed toward target identities from the first 4 datasets listed in Table 1. We select these datasets since they contain enough data to train classifiers targeting a sufficient variety of identities. The corpus for each target identity contains an equal amount of hate speech drawn from each of these datasets, though the total number of instances may differ among corpora. Negative instances were also uniformly sampled across datasets, and were restricted to those which had no target identity annotation or an annotation that matched the target identity of the hate speech.

We selected target identities that contained a minimum of 900 instances labeled as hate across these four datasets after grouping and normalization. We selected this threshold as a balance between including a sufficient number of identities and having enough examples of hate speech toward each identity to train classifiers. In order to include a variety of identities in the analysis while maintaining uniform samples for each dataset, we upsample identity-specific hate speech from individual datasets up to 2 times if needed. Corpora are split into a 60/40 train/test split. Selected target identities and the size of each corpus can be found in Table 2. These identity-specific corpora, which are samples of existing publicly available datasets, are available at `https://osf.io/53tfs/`.

4.2 Cross-identity hate speech classification

Due to the high performance of BERT-based models on hate speech classification (Mozafari et al., 2019; Samghabadi et al., 2020), we trained and evaluated a DistilBERT model (Sanh et al., 2019), which has been shown to perform very similarly to BERT on hate speech detection with fewer parameters (Vidgen et al., 2021). Models were trained with early stopping after no improvement for 5 epochs on a development set of 10% of the training set. An Adam optimizer was used with an initial learning rate of 10^{-6}. Input data was lowercased

Dataset	Domain	Original size
Civil Comments (Borkan et al., 2019)	News comments	1999516
Social Bias Inference Corpus (Sap et al., 2020)	Reddit, Twitter, Gab, Stormfront	44781
Kennedy et al. (2020)	YouTube, Twitter, Reddit	39565
HateXplain (Mathew et al., 2021)	Twitter, Gab	20148
Contextual Abuse Dataset (Vidgen et al., 2021)	Reddit	27494
ElSherief et al. (2021)	Twitter	19650
Salminen et al. (2018)	YouTube, Facebook	3222

Table 1: Overview of datasets used in this study. Original size is the number of instances before resampling for experiments. The last 3 datasets are only used in the experiment removing hate toward dominant social groups (section 6.2).

Corpus	Train size	Test size
Women	27960	18624
Black people	17664	11776
Muslims, Arabs	13712	9136
LGBTQ+ people	10544	7000
Asian people	7968	5312
Latinx people	7016	4688
Jews	5080	3400
White people	2328	1560
Men	1832	1232
Christians	1816	1224
Race/ethnicity	71024	47240
Gender/sexuality	63032	42056
Religion	32144	21376
Marginalized	168904	112792
Dominant	7952	5368

Table 2: Number of instances in corpora used in generalization experiments. These corpora are sampled by target identity uniformly from the first 4 datasets listed in Table 1.

Train \ Test	Asian	Black	Christians	Jews	Latinx	LGBTQ+	Men	Muslims, Arabs	White	Women
Asian	71.5	40.2	30.6	39.4	49.9	24.4	26.6	35.9	42.2	24.9
Black	39.5	78.2	29.7	32.7	48.4	23.9	30.3	28.4	49.3	28.6
Christians	23.7	27.1	52.1	40.5	27.1	25.4	22.2	33.5	25.6	21.5
Jews	20.6	21.2	35.0	79.9	18.3	17.7	14.8	25.5	21.7	14.3
Latinx	44.5	39.4	33.4	35.5	68.2	24.1	23.2	30.1	48.0	23.2
LGBTQ+	15.7	22.2	27.8	20.3	15.2	72.4	32.4	15.2	14.8	29.1
Men	24.0	39.3	33.0	26.5	27.3	45.5	47.2	28.2	31.0	39.9
Muslims, Arabs	40.8	38.6	51.5	57.3	40.8	28.0	30.8	77.0	34.1	30.1
White	29.1	36.9	27.6	25.7	35.7	15.8	24.9	19.8	70.6	19.3
Women	35.2	48.5	47.7	45.0	36.2	57.3	58.6	42.4	40.7	70.1

Table 3: Hate speech classification performance (F1 score) across identity-specific corpora

and an uncased base DistilBERT model was fine-tuned using the Hugging Face Transformers package, Keras, and Tensorflow. We removed URLs, hashtags and @mentions of users, but kept emoji in preprocessing. To mitigate random variation, we trained separate DistilBERT models 5 times and report the average performances.

As a baseline, we also evaluated a logistic regression classifier with TF-IDF unigram features over the entire vocabulary. This classifier used L2 regularization with a constant $C = 1$.

Results from only the DistilBERT models are reported as they consistently outperformed the logistic regression model by 0.1 F1 or more. Generalization performance trends across identities were similar for DistilBERT and logistic regression. Code for these analyses are available at `https://github.com/michaelmilleryoder/hate_speech_identities`.

4.3 Results

Table 3 shows generalization performance, measured by F1-score on the positive class of hate speech, across identity splits. We choose F1 on the 'hate' class since that focuses on performance in detecting hate speech across different target identities, rather than the non-hate instances which may or may not target identities. Generalization across target identities is poor, often dropping from over 70 F1-score when training and test sets match by targeted identity to less than 40 when they do not.

Following Uyheng and Carley (2021), we perform a PCA dimensionality reduction of this generalization performance to 2 factors in order to visualize which target identities exhibit similarities (Figure 1).

Evident from this PCA is a clustering of iden-

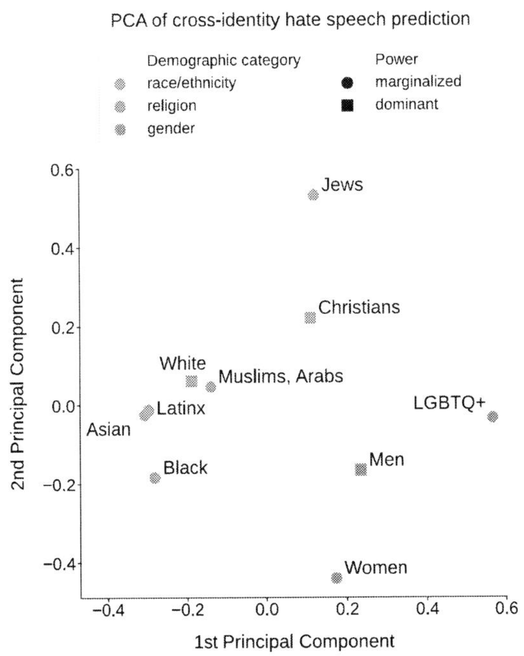

Figure 1: PCA of cross-identity hate speech classification performance. Hate speech classifiers trained on data targeting identities in the same demographic categories perform most similarly.

tity targets by demographic category. In particular, three clusters are evident: identities that reference religion are in a similar space, while identities that reference race and ethnicity are in a different space, as are terms that reference gender and sexuality. We look specifically at the effect of these distinctions on hate speech in Section 5.

Three identities included have relative social power in the European and North American English-speaking contexts from which our datasets were drawn: white people, Christians, and men. These identities do not form a clear cluster in Figure 1, though they contain factor loadings relatively close to 0 for both factors. In Section 6, we investigate how hate speech varies according to the relative social power of the identities targeted.

5 Variation by Demographic Category

Poor generalization results across identity targets (Table 3) suggest that hate speech varies significantly by the identities it targets. Our results also suggest that this variation patterns largely by demographic categories such as race/ethnicity, gender/sexuality, and religion (Figure 1). We hypothesize that if demographic categories are particularly discriminative, hate speech classification performance will drop sharply when attempting to generalize across categories.

Train \ Test	Race/ethnicity	Religion	Gender/sexuality
Race/ ethnicity	76.6	73.7	41.8
Religion	56.3	78.5	30.2
Gender/ sexuality	48.1	48.4	70.9

Table 4: Hate speech generalization performance (F1 on hate) by demographic category.

To test this, we manually assigned normalized and grouped identities to the categories referenced by the identity. For example, the identity of 'Asian' references race/ethnicity, while 'Asian women' references both race/ethnicity and gender/sexuality. In cases where target groups fit multiple categories (which is not common), we include instances in all corpora they reference. Though targeted identities sometimes reference categories such as politics, interests, and age, the only categories that met a threshold of 900 hate speech instances uniformly sampled across datasets were race/ethnicity, religion, and gender/sexuality. Details on corpora constructed by category can be found in Table 2.

We then train DistilBERT hate speech classification models on each corpus and test on all others to measure generalization performance in the same way as for identity generalization. Results can be found in Table 4.

Performance drops across identity categories, sometimes falling by almost half of the F1-score. This suggests that for purposes of automatic classification, hate speech varies significantly by demographic category. Classifiers generalize particularly poorly from race/ethnicity and religion to gender/sexuality, and less poorly between race/ethnicity and religion. This may be because of the blurred lines in hate speech targets between racial and religious categories, for example, by conflating Muslims and Arabs or targeting Jews by both religious and racial characteristics.

6 Variation by Power

Another significant dimension of variation among targeted identities is relative social power in the societies from which hate speech data has been drawn. Work on hate speech detection in NLP is often motivated as an effort to fight sexism, racism, homophobia, and other oppressions of marginalized groups, and improve participation of these groups online (Mathew et al., 2021; Jurgens et al., 2019). However, this work often frames hate speech as a property of language without considering social context. Abstracting away from the particulars of targeted identities, datasets often include hate speech directed at any identity group, regardless of the social context of power or marginalization. Such datasets thus include hate speech directed toward groups with relative social power, such as white people or men in English-speaking European and American contexts.

Calls are growing to consider the role of power and historical oppression in NLP work (Blodgett et al., 2020; Field et al., 2021). Moreover, some theorists of social meaning in language argue that hate speech is fundamentally different when directed at social groups with power (Butler, 1997; Lakoff, 2000). They note that such speech does not reference the same historical threat of possible violence and recurring oppression as does hate directed toward marginalized groups. From a lens of social dominance theory (Sidanius and Pratto, 1999), hate speech serves either to perpetuate or challenge group hierarchies depending on its target. Activists have called for social media platforms to incorporate this social context by treating hate speech toward marginalized groups as more serious than hate directed toward groups with relative social power (Nurik, 2019; Dwoskin et al., 2020).

For these theoretical and practical reasons, we consider empirical differences in hate speech based on the social power of targeted identity groups. Similar to previous experiments, we test the generalization of classifiers across identities with different levels of social power. We also test for effects on classification performance when removing hate directed toward socially dominant identity groups from hate speech datasets. If this type of hate is sufficiently different, including it could "muddy" the concept we are after and reduce the effectiveness of classifiers in identifying hate speech. Removing it would more closely match commonly stated motivations of NLP work on hate speech.

6.1 Generalization

Just as with demographic categories, we construct separate corpora of hate speech directed at identities with relative social power and identities with relative social marginalization.

We manually label normalized, grouped identity terms with a coarse-grained label as either *dominant*, *marginalized*, or *other*. This labeling was done by one of the authors familiar with the North American and European English-speaking contexts from which hate speech datasets were drawn. Identity groups certainly have different social power depending on the setting. For example, though LGBTQ+ people are generally marginalized, gay men in LGBTQ+ spaces can have higher social power relative to people with more marginalized genders and sexualities (Stulberg, 2018). Our goal in annotation was to label identity groups for which there would be broad agreement of enduring dominance or marginalization in North American and European English-speaking societies. All other cases were marked *other*. This included political identities such as 'Republican' or 'liberal', since political power is generally transient in these societies. Some targeted identities were intersectional, that is, contained multiple identity groups, such as "white women" or "transgender men". These cases were taken case-by-case, considering the marginalization of each identity component and marking *other* for many tough cases. A full list of identities labeled as dominant and marginalized is available in Table 7 in Appendix A. Any identities not in these lists were marked *other* by default.

Some datasets all annotators to mark multiple targeted identities. We marked these instances as directed to *marginalized* groups if there was only *marginalized* or *other* identities targeted. Instances with both *marginalized* and *dominant* identities targeted were marked as *other*. Details on corpora constructed by power are in Table 2.

As with identities and demographic categories, we evaluated the ability of DistilBERT hate speech classification models to generalize across marginalized and dominant identity targets (Table 5).

Generalization does not suffer as much across target identities with differences in social power, particularly when trained on the corpus of hate directed at marginalized identities. This suggests that which target identities have power does not structure variation in hate speech as much as differences in demographic category.

Train \ Test	Dominant	Marginalized
Dominant	57.9	42.1
Marginalized	61.3	72.8

Table 5: Hate speech generalization performance (F1 on hate) by relative social power.

6.2 Removing hate speech toward socially dominant groups

We further evaluate the effect of removing hate speech toward socially dominant groups on classification performance. We hypothesize that if it is sufficiently different, as some theorists argue, then it may act as noise. For this experiment, we resample all 7 hate speech datasets listed in Table 1 separately instead of combining across datasets as in generalization experiments. This allows us to see trends across even more datasets than we could examine if uniformly sampling from just those with enough to reach a certain threshold.

We resample each dataset to exclude or include hate toward dominant social groups. All instances are the same between these samples except for instances of hate speech toward dominant social groups and those instances replaced by them. This allows a comparison across samples of equal size and hate speech ratio.

Removing hate speech toward any set of target identities could improve performance since the remaining instances are more likely to be similar to each other. For this reason we compare removing hate speech toward dominant groups with removing hate speech toward a set of non-dominant identities. We select these "control" identities to be similar in frequency across datasets to identities labeled as dominant. Specifically, we match each identity labeled as dominant with the non-dominant identity that has the closest log frequency distribution across datasets (by Euclidean distance).

We perform 5x2-fold cross-validation with a DistilBERT model to estimate performance with and without dominant or control identities. Parameters are the same as were used with the models built to test generalization, and 10% of training sets are used as development sets for early stopping.

Two out of the 7 datasets, ElSherief et al. (2021) and HateXplain, show significant improvement after removing hate speech toward dominant social identities. However, when removing the control identities, 2 out of the 7 datasets, Civil Comments and HateXplain, also show significant improvements, while the Social Bias Inference Corpus shows a significant decrease in performance. This does not show convincing evidence that hate speech toward dominant groups is sufficiently different to act as noise for hate speech classification.

7 Lexical Variation Across Target Identities

To explore how hate speech varies by target identity, we examine the words most strongly associated with each target identity and grouping of identities. We use the Sparse Additive Generative Model (SAGE; Eisenstein et al., 2011) to find words that are most representative of each hate speech corpus. SAGE finds representative words by learning a generative model that contrasts terms in documents in a section of a corpus with a background frequency distribution over the whole corpus. We run SAGE over 3 separate corpora: one where each section is an identity-specific split, another with category splits, and another with splits by relative social power. We run SAGE with a vocabulary size of the most frequent 3000 words and a smoothing rate of 50. Larger vocabulary sizes and lower smoothing included less informative, specialty words that did not occur frequently in the corpus. The 10 most representative terms for each of these splits are shown in Table 6.

Identity terms, many of them derogatory, form the bulk of these representative words. This provides more evidence for the centrality of identities to hate speech (Uyheng and Carley, 2021). Some representative words relate to identity-specific histories of oppression. For example, 'oven' and 'gas' are representative terms of antisemitic hate speech. Identity-specific stereotypes are also visible: 'terrorist' and 'bomb' are top terms in hate speech against Muslims and Arabs. Current culture wars issues are also relevant. For example, transphobic attitudes around bathrooms are reflected in the top terms in hate speech targeting LGBTQ+ people. 'BLM', for the Black Lives Matter movement, is a top term associated with anti-Black hate speech.

The difficulty in a binary distinction of dominance and marginalization can be seen through the

Identity	Top terms
Asian	chinese, china, asian, ching, chong, asians, japanese, chinaman, ch*nk, japan
Black	n*ggas, black, n*gga, n*gger, africa, blm, negro, ethiopian, blacks, african
Christians	priest, catholic, jesus, priests, bible, christians, christianity, christian, church
Jews	jewish, jews, holocaust, jew, israel, hitler, gas, oven, zionist, k*ke
Latinx	latinos, latino, mexico, mexican, mexicans, beaner, sp*c, latin, hispanic, beaners
LGBTQ+	transgender, transgendered, transgenders, bisexual, queers, bathroom, f*g, gay
Men	divorce, dudes, men, male, negative, movies, man, priests, soy, dad
Muslims, Arabs	islam, muslim, islamic, muslims, isis, terrorist, terrorists, iran, bomb, radical
White	redneck, white, supremacist, supremacy, mudshark, trash, fascist, shootings
Women	hoes, sexist, woman, hoe, feminist, women, feminists, feminism, slut, bitches
Category	
Gender/sexuality	hoes, dyke, transgender, f*ggot, f*g, sexist, sexual, lesbian, hoe, dykes
Race/ethnicity	chinese, black, blacks, asian, asians, mexicans, whites, africa, supremacist
Religion	catholic, priest, christians, christian, christianity, religion, church, jesus, koran
Power	
Dominant	priest, catholic, priests, jesus, catholics, virgin, church, devil, dress
Marginalized	muslim, muslims, she, islam, her, woman, n*gger, black, jews, women

Table 6: Most representative terms (lowercased) in corpora divided by different target identity sets from SAGE.

most representative words in hate directed toward groups with high relative social power. As a marker of Christianity, 'Catholic', for example, could be seen as dominant in European and American contexts where Christianity has historically been a religion with relative social and cultural prominence. However, some white nationalist groups such as the Ku Klux Klan have targeted Catholics as outside idealized Christian Protestantism (Burris et al., 2000; Berlet and Vysotsky, 2006). 'Redneck' and 'trash' are top terms in hate targeting white people, and 'virgin', a top term in hate targeting dominant groups, is used in jokes stereotyping incest. Such terms target poor white people based mainly on class. Also in the top terms against white people is 'mudshark', a derogatory term targeting white women who have relationships with Black men. These terms target groups that are marginalized within broadly dominant groups: white women, poor white people, and Catholics. Such examples show how social power is relative, complex, and intersectional. They also evidence a tendency for hate speech to target marginalized groups, even within groups that have higher relative social power.

8 Discussion

Our results demonstrate that hate speech varies considerably according to which identities are targeted. We show evidence that classifiers trained on hate toward one target identity generalize poorly to other target identities, especially across demographic categories such as race/ethnicity, religion and gender/sexuality.

These results suggest that the designers of hate speech classifiers pay attention to the distribution of targeted identities in training data. Many commonly used hate speech datasets do not specify this information. If the distribution skews toward a particular identity group (such as anti-Black racism), then using such a classifier on data that has a different distribution (e.g., mostly antisemitic) would likely give poor performance. More generally, these results suggest a value in treating hate speech as a social and linguistic category with lots of internal variance. This variance depends in part on the social context around targeted identities.

Classifiers trained on hate speech toward dominant or marginalized groups suffered somewhat when tested on the opposite group. However, we did not find evidence that removing hate speech toward dominant groups clarifies the hate speech signal enough to consistently increase performance beyond what might be expected by removing a random set of targeted identities. This suggests that differences based on the social context of power do not affect the language of hate speech enough to be easily detectable by machine learning classifiers. Differences in severity between hate speech targeting socially marginalized or powerful groups is more likely a matter of interpretation by those with social knowledge of power in a particular society.

9 Conclusion

We present a meta-analysis of hate speech datasets annotated for identity group targets. This analysis shows that hate speech differs significantly by target identity, as classifiers trained on hate speech toward one identity do not generalize well to other identities. We then examine what factors of social context structure this variation by target identity. We find evidence for hate speech varying substantially by demographic category, and less so by the relative social power of targeted identities.

These results reinforce the importance of variation by social context within hate speech and suggest that researchers pay attention to variation by target identity. Future work may address improving generalization across target identities by strategically sampling training data or incorporating multiple identity-specific classifiers. Similar analyses may also be conducted on multilingual hate speech datasets in future work.

10 Limitations and Ethics

As a meta-analysis of existing datasets, this study is limited by the availability of hate speech data labeled with target identity. Performance estimates with and without hate speech toward dominant groups would be more reliable with more labeled hate speech toward socially dominant groups. The scarcity of hate speech against socially dominant groups is not coincidental: this speech is less prototypically considered hate speech than that against marginalized groups. This can be seen in the dataset from Kennedy et al. (2020), for example, where annotators rate the average severity of hate against dominant groups as less than the average severity of hate against marginalized groups.

Another limitation is that datasets each have their own definitions of hate speech and associated annotation criteria, which may vary considerably. We attempted to mitigate the effects of any one dataset's definition with uniform sampling (see Section 4.1). Since we take these annotations as representative of hate speech, it is necessary to be mindful that we are not capturing any true sense of "hate speech", but simply what annotators have identified as hate speech. However, we wished to investigate the role of target identity in existing hate speech classification approaches, for which existing datasets and their associated definitions are most relevant.

These datasets are only in English and largely reflect European and American societies. Our findings are specific to this context. Experiments on multilingual datasets may reveal other trends and reflect different social associations around identity terms, which are culturally specific.

When sampling identity-based corpora from datasets, we attempted to control for the idiosyncrasies of any particular dataset. However, the sizes of the resulting identity-specific corpora vary depending on how much hate speech directed toward them occurs across datasets. This could influence our generalization experiments. Classifiers trained on identities with small corpora still perform well on test sets of identities with the same demographic category, the general trend we report. As seen in Figure 1, identities with lots of data sometimes exhibit behavior similar to identities with not as much data. These factors lead us to doubt that corpus size has a large impact on generalization results.

Care must always be taken to specify that differences based on identity, in this case hate speech directed toward identities, are due to social, not biological, factors (Hanna et al., 2020; Lu et al., 2022). We attempt to be clear that these differences are the result of social context.

Acknowledgements

This work was supported in part by the Collaboratory Against Hate: Research and Action Center at Carnegie Mellon University and the University of Pittsburgh. The Center for Informed Democracy and Social Cybersecurity at Carnegie Mellon University also provided support. We thank the researchers who made their annotated hate speech data publicly available, which enabled this meta-analysis.

References

Valerio Basile, Cristina Bosco, Elisabetta Fersini, Debora Nozza, Viviana Patti, Francisco Rangel, Paolo Rosso, and Manuela Sanguinetti. 2019. SemEval-2019 Task 5: Multilingual Detection of Hate Speech Against Immigrants and Women in Twitter. In *Proceedings of the 13th International Workshop on Semantic Evaluation (SemEval-2019)*, pages 54–63.

Chip Berlet and Stanislav Vysotsky. 2006. Overview of

U.S. white supremacist groups. *Journal of Political and Military Sociology*, 34:11–48.

Su Lin Blodgett, Solon Barocas, Hal Daumé III, and Hanna Wallach. 2020. Language (technology) is power: A critical survey of "bias" in NLP. In *Proceedings of the 58th Annual Meeting of the Association for Computational Linguistics*, pages 5454–5476, Online. Association for Computational Linguistics.

Daniel Borkan, Lucas Dixon, Jeffrey Sorensen, Nithum Thain, and Lucy Vasserman. 2019. Nuanced metrics for measuring unintended bias with real data for text classification. In *Companion Proceedings of the 2019 World Wide Web Conference*, pages 491–500. Association for Computing Machinery.

Alexander Brown. 2017. What is hate speech? part 2: Family resemblances. *Law and Philosophy*, 36:561–613.

Val Burris, Emery Smith, and Ann Strahm. 2000. White supremacist networks on the Internet. *Source: Sociological Focus*, 33:215–235.

Judith Butler. 1997. *Excitable Speech*, 1st edition. Routledge.

Jacob Devlin, Ming-Wei Chang, Kenton Lee, and Kristina Toutanova. 2019. BERT: Pre-training of deep bidirectional transformers for language understanding. In *Proceedings of the 2019 Conference of the North American Chapter of the Association for Computational Linguistics: Human Language Technologies, Volume 1 (Long and Short Papers)*, pages 4171–4186, Minneapolis, Minnesota. Association for Computational Linguistics.

Lucas Dixon, John Li, Jeffrey Sorensen, Nithum Thain, and Lucy Vasserman. 2017. Measuring and mitigating unintended bias in text classification. In *AAAI/ACM Conference on Artificial Intelligence, Ethics, and Society (AIES)*.

Elizabeth Dwoskin, Nitasha Tiku, and Heather Kelly. 2020. Facebook to start policing anti-black hate speech more aggressively than anti-white comments, documents show. *The Washington Post*.

Jacob Eisenstein, Amr Ahmed, and Eric P. Xing. 2011. Sparse additive generative models of text. In *Proceedings of the 28th International Conference on Machine Learning*, pages 1041–1048.

Mai ElSherief, Vivek Kulkarni, Dana Nguyen, William Yang Wang, and Elizabeth Belding. 2018a. Hate lingo: A target-based linguistic analysis of hate speech in social media. In *Proceedings of the International AAAI Conference on Web and Social Media*, volume 12.

Mai ElSherief, Shirin Nilizadeh, Dana Nguyen, Giovanni Vigna, and Elizabeth Belding. 2018b. Peer to peer hate: Hate speech instigators and their targets. In *Proceedings of the Twelfth International AAAI Conference on Web and Social Media (ICWSM 2018)*, pages 52–61.

Mai ElSherief, Caleb Ziems, David Muchlinski, Vaishnavi Anupindi, Jordyn Seybolt, Munmun De Choudhury, and Diyi Yang. 2021. Latent hatred: A benchmark for understanding implicit hate speech. In *Proceedings of the 2021 Conference on Empirical Methods in Natural Language Processing*, pages 345–363.

Anjalie Field, Su Lin Blodgett, Zeerak Waseem, and Yulia Tsvetkov. 2021. A survey of race, racism, and anti-racism in NLP. In *Proceedings of the 59th Annual Meeting of the Association for Computational Linguistics and the 11th International Joint Conference on Natural Language Processing (Volume 1: Long Papers)*, pages 1905–1925, Online. Association for Computational Linguistics.

Paula Fortuna, Juan Soler, and Leo Wanner. 2020. Toxic, hateful, offensive or abusive? what are we really classifying? an empirical analysis of hate speech datasets. In *Proceedings of the 12th Language Resources and Evaluation Conference*, pages 6786–6794, Marseille, France. European Language Resources Association.

Tommi Gröndahl, Luca Pajola, Mika Juuti, Mauro Conti, and N. Asokan. 2018. All you need is "love": Evading hate speech detection. In *Proceedings of the 11th ACM Workshop on Artificial Intelligence and Security (AISec '18)*, pages 2–12. Association for Computing Machinery.

Alex Hanna, Emily Denton, Andrew Smart, and Jamila Smith-Loud. 2020. Towards a critical race methodology in algorithmic fairness. In *FAT* 2020 - Proceedings of the 2020 Conference on Fairness, Accountability, and Transparency*, pages 501–512.

David Jurgens, Eshwar Chandrasekharan, and Libby Hemphill. 2019. A just and comprehensive strategy for using NLP to address online abuse. In *Proceedings of the 57th Annual Meeting of the Association for Computational Linguistics*, pages 3658–3666. Association for Computational Lingustics.

Chris J. Kennedy, Geoff Bacon, Alexander Sahn, and Claudia von Vacano. 2020. Constructing interval variables via faceted Rasch measurement and multitask deep learning: a hate speech application.

Irene Kwok and Yuzhou Wang. 2013. Locate the hate: Detecting tweets against blacks. In *Twenty-Seventh AAAI Conference on Artificial Intelligence*, pages 1621–1622.

Robin Tolmach Lakoff. 2000. *The Language War*. University of California Press.

Christina Lu, Jackie Kay, and Kevin R. McKee. 2022. Subverting machines, fluctuating identities: Relearning human categorization. In *FAccT '22: 2022 ACM Conference on Fairness, Accountability, and Transparency*, pages 1005–1014.

Alexandria Marsters. 2019. *When hate speech leads to hateful actions: A corpus and discourse analytic approach to linguistic threat assessment of hate speech.* Ph.D. thesis, Georgetown University.

Binny Mathew, Punyajoy Saha, Seid Muhie Yimam, Chris Biemann, Pawan Goyal, and Animesh Mukherjee. 2021. Hatexplain: A benchmark dataset for explainable hate speech detection. In *Proceedings of the AAAI Conference on Artificial Intelligence*, volume 35, pages 14867–14875.

Mainack Mondal, Leandro Araújo Silva, and Fabrício Benevenuto. 2017. A measurement study of hate speech in social media. In *HT 2017 - Proceedings of the 28th ACM Conference on Hypertext and Social Media*, pages 85–94. Association for Computing Machinery.

Marzieh Mozafari, Reza Farahbakhsh, and Noël Crespi. 2019. A BERT-Based Transfer Learning Approach for Hate Speech Detection in Online Social Media. In *International Conference on Complex Networks and Their Applications.*, pages 928–940.

Chloé Nurik. 2019. "Men Are Scum": Self-Regulation, Hate Speech, and Gender-Based Censorship on Facebook. *International Journal of Communication*, 13:2878–2898.

Nedjma Ousidhoum, Zizheng Lin, Hongming Zhang, Yangqiu Song, and Dit-Yan Yeung. 2019. Multilingual and Multi-Aspect Hate Speech Analysis. In *Proceedings of the 2019 Conference on Empirical Methods in Natural Language Processing and the 9th International Joint Conference on Natural Language Processing*, pages 4675–4684.

Endang Wahyu Pamungkas, Valerio Basile, and Viviana Patti. 2020. Misogyny detection in twitter: a multilingual and cross-domain study. *Information Processing and Management*, 57.

Matti Pohjonen and Sahana Udupa. 2017. Extreme speech online: An anthropological critique of hate speech debates. *International Journal of Communication*, 11:1173–1191.

Fabio Poletto, Valerio Basile, Manuela Sanguinetti, Cristina Bosco, and Viviana Patti. 2021. Resources and benchmark corpora for hate speech detection: a systematic review. In *Language Resources and Evaluation*, volume 55, pages 477–523. Springer Science and Business Media B.V.

Jing Qian, Mai Elsherief, Elizabeth M Belding, and William Yang Wang. 2018. Leveraging Intra-User and Inter-User Representation Learning for Automated Hate Speech Detection. In *Proceedings of NAACL-HLT 2018*, pages 118–123.

Diana Rieger, Anna Sophie Kümpel, Maximilian Wich, Toni Kiening, and Georg Groh. 2021. Assessing the Extent and Types of Hate Speech in Fringe Communities: A Case Study of Alt-Right Communities on 8chan, 4chan, and Reddit. *Social Media and Society*, 7(4).

Joni Salminen, Hind Almerekhi, Milica Milenković, Soon-gyo Jung, Jisun An, Haewoon Kwak, and Bernard J Jansen. 2018. Anatomy of online hate: developing a taxonomy and machine learning models for identifying and classifying hate in online news media. In *Twelfth International AAAI Conference on Web and Social Media*, pages 330–339.

Niloofar Safi Samghabadi, Parth Patwa, Srinivas Pykl, Prerana Mukherjee, Amitava Das, and Thamar Solorio. 2020. Aggression and misogyny detection using bert: A multi-task approach. In *Proceedings of the Second Workshop on Trolling, Aggression and Cyberbullying*, pages 11–16.

Manuela Sanguinetti, Fabio Poletto, Cristina Bosco, Viviana Patti, and Marco Stranisci. 2018. An Italian Twitter Corpus of Hate Speech against Immigrants. In *Proceedings of the Eleventh International Conference on Language Resources and Evaluation (LREC'18)*, pages 2798–2895.

Victor Sanh, Lysandre Debut, Julien Chaumond, and Thomas Wolf. 2019. DistilBERT, a distilled version of BERT: smaller, faster, cheaper and lighter. In *5th Workshop on Energy Efficient Machine Learning and Cognitive Computing*.

Maarten Sap, Saadia Gabriel, Lianhui Qin, Dan Jurafsky, Noah A. Smith, and Yejin Choi. 2020. Social bias frames: Reasoning about social and power implications of language. In *Proceedings of the 58th Annual Meeting of the Association for Computational Linguistics*, pages 5477–5490.

Maarten Sap, Swabha Swayamdipta, Laura Vianna, Xuhui Zhou, Yejin Choi, and Noah A Smith. 2022. Annotators with attitudes: How annotator beliefs and identities bias toxic language detection. In *Proceedings of the 2022 Conference of the North American Chapter of the Association for Computational Linguistics: Human Language Technologies*.

Jim Sidanius and Felicia Pratto. 1999. *Social Dominance*. Cambridge University Press.

Leandro Silva, Mainack Mondal, Denzil Correa, Fabricio Benevenuto, and Ingmar Weber. 2016. Analyzing the targets of hate in online social media. In *Proceedings of the Tenth International AAAI Conference on Web and Social Media (ICWSM 2016)*, pages 687–690.

Lisa M Stulberg. 2018. *LGBTQ social movements*. John Wiley & Sons.

Steve Durairaj Swamy, Anupam Jamatia, and Björn Gambäck. 2019. Studying generalisability across abusive language detection datasets. In *Proceedings of the 23rd Conference on Computational Natural Language Learning*, pages 940–950. Association for Computational Linguistics.

Elise Fehn Unsvåg and Björn Gambäck. 2018. The Effects of User Features on Twitter Hate Speech Detection. In *Proceedings of the Second Workshop on Abusive Language Online (ALW2)*, pages 75–85.

Joshua Uyheng and Kathleen M. Carley. 2021. An identity-based framework for generalizable hate speech detection. In *International Conference on Social Computing, Behavioral-Cultural Modeling and Prediction and Behavior Representation in Modeling and Simulation*, pages 121–130.

Bertie Vidgen and Leon Derczynski. 2020. Directions in abusive language training data, a systematic review: Garbage in, garbage out. *PLoS ONE*, 15.

Bertie Vidgen, Dong Nguyen, Helen Margetts, Patricia Rossini, and Rebekah Tromble. 2021. Introducing CAD: the contextual abuse dataset. In *Proceedings of the 2021 Conference of the North American Chapter of the Association for Computational Linguistics: Human Language Technologies*, pages 2289–2303, Online. Association for Computational Linguistics.

Zeerak Waseem. 2016. Are You a Racist or Am I Seeing Things? Annotator Influence on Hate Speech Detection on Twitter. In *Proceedings of the First Workshop on NLP and Computational Social Science*, pages 138–142.

Zeerak Waseem and Dirk Hovy. 2016. Hateful Symbols or Hateful People? Predictive Features for Hate Speech Detection on Twitter. In *Proceedings of the NAACL-HLT 2016*, pages 88–93.

Michael Wiegand, Josef Ruppenhofer, and Elisabeth Eder. 2021. Implicitly abusive language – what does it actually look like and why are we not getting there? In *Proceedings of the 2021 Conference of the North American Chapter of the Association for Computational Linguistics: Human Language Technologies*, pages 576–587, Online. Association for Computational Linguistics.

Wenjie Yin and Arkaitz Zubiaga. 2021. Towards generalisable hate speech detection: a review on obstacles and solutions. *PeerJ Computer Science*, 7:1–38.

A Appendix

We applied the following transformations to datasets for binary hate speech labels:

- Civil Comments (Borkan et al., 2019): toxicity value >= 0.5 was labeled hate
- Social Bias Inference Corpus (Sap et al., 2020): offensive value > 0.5 was labeled hate, following the original paper's binarization
- Kennedy et al. (2020): hate speech value > 1 was labeled hate
- HateXplain (Mathew et al., 2021): labeled hate if any annotator labeled the instance as hate
- Contextual Abuse Dataset (Vidgen et al., 2021): labeled hate if any of the following labels was present: `AffiliationDirectedAbuse`, `Slur`, `IdentityDirectedAbuse`
- ElSherief et al. (2021): we paired implicit hate (which was annotated with identity targets) with non-hate from stage 1 annotations
- Salminen et al. (2018): labeled hate if the class was labeled `hateful`

Marginalized	women, people with mental disabilities, black people, gay men, transgender people, muslims, jewish people, gay people, sexual and gender minorities, feminists, chinese women, people with autism, lgbtqa community, people from china, illegal immigrants, people from pakistan, working class people, elderly people, non-white people, people from mexico, people from india, people with aspergers, people with mental health issues, people with disabilities, romani people, ethnic minorities, immigrants, minorities, jews, blacks, black folks, illegals, people of color, non-whites, islamic people, gays, mexicans, illegal aliens, arabs, africans, refugees, indians, hispanics, black men, arabians, hindus, black lives matter, iranians, mexican, latino folks, asian folks, foreigners, jewish folks, muslim folks, latino/latina folks, physically disabled folks, mentally disabled folks, lesbian women, folks with mental illness/disorder, holocaust victims, native american/first nation folks, trans women, arabic folks, folks with physical illness/disorder, overweight/fat folks, trans men, rape victims, bisexual women, children, poor folks, african folks, ethiopians, bisexual men, sexual assault victims, harassment victims, africa, old folks, orphans, mexican folks, indian folks, child rape victims, ethiopian folks, child sexual assault victims, young children, ethiopian, genocide victims, pregnant folks, ethiopia, pedophilia victims, kids, japanese, chinese folks, holocaust survivors, asian, black, latinx, middle eastern, native american, pacific islander, hindu, jewish, muslim, immigrant, migrant worker, undocumented, non_binary, transgender_men, transgender_unspecified, transgender_women, bisexual, gay, lesbian, seniors, disability_physical, disability_cognitive, disability_neurological, disability_visually_impaired, disability_hearing_impaired, disability_unspecific, disability_other, disability, xenophobia, islam, jews/judaism, special_needs, african_descent, indian/hindu, asians, asian people, muslims and arabic/middle eastern people, lgbtq+ people, victims of violence, non-binary people, older people, bisexual people, chinese people, arabic/middle eastern people, african people, indian people, ethiopian people, japanese people, mexican people, transgender men, undocumented immigrants, latinx people, native american people, people with physical disabilities, transgender women, buddhists, indigenous people, gay or lesbian people, gay and lesbian people
Dominant	involuntary celibates, white people, police officers, people from america, men, christians, rich people, white men, whites, white folks, conservative males, white conservatives, white liberals, americans, white nationalists, male conservatives, cops, police, white, conservative men, christian folks, christian, straight, middle_aged, law enforcement, wealthy people, corporations, military, armed forces, straight people, middle-aged people
Other	left-wing people, moderators, liberals, communists, left-wing people (social justice), non-gender dysphoric transgender people, right-wing people, democrats, activists (anti-fascist), donald trump supporters, republicans, conservatives, gamers, activists (animal rights), people with drug problems, fans of anthropomorphic animals ("furries"), catholics, progressives, leftists, white women, antifa, germans, journalists, islamists, southerners, media, religious people, assault victims, mass shooting victims, terrorism victims, ugly folks, atheist, buddhist, mormon, specific country, teenagers, young_adults, terrorism, humanity, left_wing_people, terrorists, mormons, atheists, young adults, nonreligious people

Table 7: Labels of relative social power assigned to lowercased identity terms from hate speech datasets. Any identities not in these lists were marked *other* by default.

Continual Learning for Natural Language Generations with Transformer Calibration

Pang Yang, Dingcheng Li, Ping Li
Cognitive Computing Lab
Baidu Research
10900 NE 8th St. Bellevue, WA 98004, USA
{pengyang5612, dingchengl, pingli98}@gmail.com

Abstract

Conventional natural language process (NLP) generation models are trained offline with a given dataset for a particular task, which is referred to as isolated learning. Research on sequence-to-sequence language generation aims to study continual learning model to constantly learning from sequentially encountered tasks. However, continual learning studies often suffer from catastrophic forgetting, a persistent challenge for lifelong learning. In this paper, we present a novel NLP transformer model that attempts to mitigate catastrophic forgetting in online continual learning from a new perspective, i.e., attention calibration. We model the attention in the transformer as a calibrated unit in a general formulation, where the attention calibration could give benefits to balance the stability and plasticity of continual learning algorithms through influencing both their forward inference path and backward optimization path. Our empirical experiments, paraphrase generation and dialog response generation, demonstrate that this work outperforms state-of-the-art models by a considerable margin and effectively mitigate the forgetting.

1 Introduction

Sequence-to-sequence (Seq2Seq) generation has been widely applied in artificial learning (AI) system to deal with various challenging tasks, e.g., paraphrase, dialogue system (Bordes et al., 2016), machine translation, etc. In addition, powerful representation learning (e.g., Transformer) have been used in Seq2Seq models, which have taken the state-of-the-art of generation models to a new level. Generally, nature language generation (NLG) models leverage an encoder to create a vector representation for source inputs, and then pass this representation into a decoder so as to output a target sequence word by word. For example, Bart (Lewis et al., 2019) is such a transformer-based NLG architecture that is equipped with the BERT-type network structure (Devlin et al., 2019) as its encoder and with the GPT-type structure as the decoder.

Despite the remarkable ability on sequence generation, the conventional paradigm aims to learn a Seq2Seq model on the whole available dataset, which limits its ability in accumulating knowledge in continual learning scenario. When switching to a new task from some previously learned ones, the fine-tuned model on the new task sometimes faces a significant performance drop on previous learned data, where such a phenomenon is also referred to as *catastrophic forgetting* (Parisi et al., 2019; Mai et al., 2021; Yin et al., 2021; Li et al., 2022a,b). In contrast, humans and animals exhibit remarkable ability to deal with new tasks by effectively adapting their acquired knowledge without forgetting the previously learned skills. If one desires to build a human-like NLG model, continual learning ability is a necessary skill for achieving this goal.

The existing replay-based continual learning approaches have taken into account of different perspectives of the model training process to remedy the *catastrophic forgetting* dilemma, such as regularizing the parameter change during training (Chaudhry et al., 2018; Parisi et al., 2019), selective memory storage or replay (Aljundi et al., 2019), Bayesian and variational Bayesian training (Kirkpatrick et al., 2017; Nguyen et al., 2018), and task-specific parameterization of the model (Pham et al., 2021; Singh et al., 2020). In this paper,we tackle the problem from a novel angle that is distinct to all the aforementioned attempts, i.e., seeking a better balance between stability and plasticity with neuron calibration. Specifically, we refer to neuron calibration as a process of mathematically adjusting the transformation functions in various layers of transformer-based architecture. In this way, the neuron calibration is able to prioritize both model parameter and feature map that are suitable to new tasks. In detail, our proposed neuron calibration approach regularizes the param-

Proceedings of the 26th Conference on Computational Natural Language Learning (CoNLL), pages 40 - 49
December 7-8, 2022 ©2022 Association for Computational Linguistics

eter update against catastrophic forgetting via posing a trainable soft mask on the attention and feature maps, which then influences both the model inference process and the model training process through the forward inference path and the backward optimization path.

The contributions of our work are three-fold: (i) we introduce a general and light-weight feature calibration approach to tackle task-incremental continual learning problems where the models are formulated as feed-forward transformer-based function approximations; (ii) we formulate a novel task-incremental learning paradigm to train the calibrated model with an interleaved optimization scheme to mitigate the forgetting issue; (iii) we indicate through extensive empirical experiments that the proposed method could outperform the recent continual learning algorithms on Seq2Seq language generation applications.

2 Related Work

Continual Learning. Existing continual learning methods can be classified into three categories. The *regularization approaches* (Li and Hoiem, 2017; Zenke et al., 2017; Schwarz et al., 2018) impose a regularization constraint to the objective function to mitigate the catastrophic forgetting. The *rehearsal approaches* (Rolnick et al., 2019; Aljundi et al., 2019; Buzzega et al., 2020; Wang et al., 2022) allocate a small memory buffer to store and replay the exemplar from the previous task to consolidate the historical knowledge. The *architectural* approaches (Rusu et al., 2016; Serra et al., 2018; Singh et al., 2020; von Oswald et al., 2020) avoid catastrophic forgetting through approximating the training of the task-specific network and allowing the expansion of the parameters during continual learning. Nonetheless, all these methods are confined to supervised classification problem, which limits their application in real-life problems. Lifelong GAN (Zhai et al., 2019) tackles the generation problem of continual learning and learn task-specific representation on shared parameters. Their method is restricted to image generation tasks and not directly applicable to NLP benchmark datasets.

Continual Language Generation. Few work has been done in continual learning for Seq2seq language generation. The most relevant work is from Mi et al. (2020), which propose a continual learning framework that builds a human-like dialogue system in an incremental learning manner. Specifically, this method combines the memory replay with the regularization technique to address the catastrophic forgetting, and empirically achieves a promising result on the MultiWoZ-2.0 dataset. Nonetheless, their system is specifically designed for the dialogue task and lacks generalization to Seq2Seq tasks. Our method differs from Mi et al. (2020) in terms of the following three points: (i) our method is built upon a neuron calibration approach, where such contribution is orthogonal to that from all the previous works; (ii) our proposed method does not engage any task-specific part; (iii) we do not store the historical exemplar from the episodic memories during training. In addition, our proposed method could be adapted to various seq2seq language generation applications, such as summarization, translation, paraphrases, dialog response generation.

3 Method

3.1 Preliminary

We introduce the setting of online continual learning. Formally, we denote the sequence of training tasks in continual learning as $\{\mathcal{T}_1, \cdots, \mathcal{T}_T\}$. The tasks come and go in an online fashion, and the training data for each task is available only at that time slot. When the new task arrives, the previous task's data is deleted and cannot be used any more. For the t-th task, we denote its training dataset as $\mathcal{D}_t$. The objective of the task is to learn a transformer-based generation model. Our work tackles the natural language generation (NLG)-based continual learning problems and thus the model is typically modeled as a feed-forward transformer with L-blocks (i.e, $\{l_i\}_{i=1}^L$), with its corresponding parameters denoted as $\{\theta_i\}_{i=1}^L$.

3.2 Transformer Calibration

We introduce a general calibration mechanism to tackle the continue learning problems on Seq2Seq generation, where the models are parameterized by the transformer-based NLG models. By applying neuron calibration, we aim to adapt the transformation function in the deep transformer layers. Our proposed learning paradigm with neuron calibration could perform both model selection and feature selection to effectively avoid catastrophic change on the model parameters while accomplishing a stable consolidation of knowledge among tasks. In this framework, the calibration module is independent from the pre-trained base model in order to

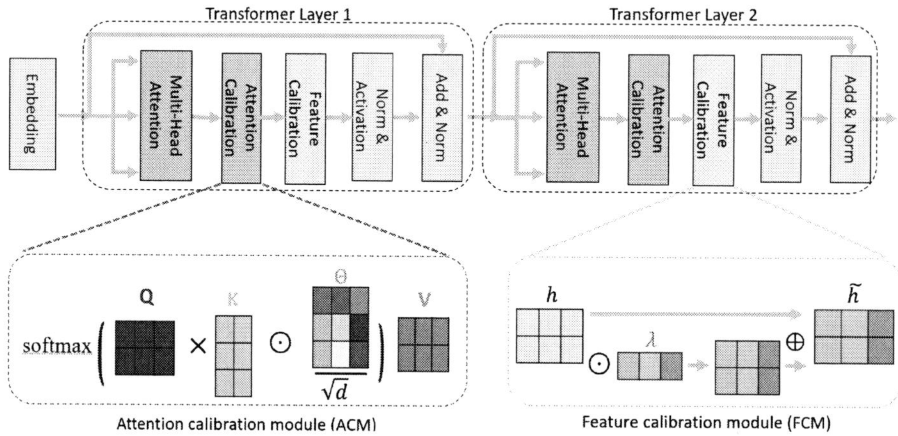

Figure 1: Overview of our proposed transformer calibration for continual learning framework. This method consists of two types of calibration modules: attention calibration module (ACM) and feature calibration module (FCM), which are sequentially applied to the layers in the multi-head attention model (as shown in the figure) to calibrate the attention signals and feature maps, respectively.

preserve the learned knowledge and avoid catastrophic forgetting. Figure 1 provides an illustration of our neuron calibration process.

Formally, we introduce two types of general calibration modules to be applied on the transformer-based NLG models: (i) attention calibration module (ACM) and (ii) feature calibration module (FCM). The attention calibration module learns to scale the attentions of the *transformer function* whereas the feature calibration module learns to scale the *feature map* output from the transformer block. When calibrating the i-th layer of the transformer block, we use A_i to denote its scaled attention function after applying attention calibration (ACM). Meanwhile, we use $\mathbf{h}_i$ and $\widetilde{\mathbf{h}}_i$ to denote the output feature maps before and after applying feature calibration (FCM), respectively.

We first introduce the formulation for ACM. To calibrate the attention, we first define a learnable matrix $\Phi_i \in \mathbb{R}^{N \times N}$, which presents the importance of each pair of words, where N is the maximal number of words in the sentence and a subset of parameters is used according to sentence length. The scale dot-product attention is formulated as:

$$\text{Atten} = \text{Softmax}\left(Q_i K_i^\top \odot \left(\frac{\Phi_i}{\sqrt{d}}\right)\right) V_i \quad (1)$$

where $\odot$ is the element-wise product. As Φ_i is learned across the sequential tasks, the task-aware attention can serve as a task representation instead of traditional task embedding. The overall calibrated attention can be decoupled into two parts: the $QK^\top$ term presents the content-based attention, and $\Phi_i/\sqrt{d}$ term acts as the soft mask for attention calibration. This united design offers more task adaptation by suppressing the unrelated attention values and highlighting the important ones. With the ACM, the calibrator module plays a crucial role during the model training process: at the forward inference path, it scales the value of the attention in the attention block to make prediction; at the backward learning path, it serves as a prioritized weight to regularize the update on parameters.

By applying attention calibration on transformer blocks, the attention function at the i-th layer $\text{Atten}(Q_i, K_i, V_i, \Phi_i)$ is parameterized by Φ_i and produces the output as follows,

$$h_i = \mathcal{F}_{A_i}(h_{i-1}), \text{s.t. } A_i = \text{Atten}(Q_i, K_i, V_i, \Phi_i) \quad (2)$$

The output h_i of the attention function is then processed by a feature calibration module (FCM) to generate the calibrated feature map for that layer. We use $\Omega_{\lambda_i}(\cdot)$ to denote the feature transformation function at the i-th layer, parameterized by λ_i. With FCM, the calibration parameters also interact with the feature map h_i with a multiplicative operation. Specifically, the calibrated feature is computed as:

$$\Omega_{\lambda_i}(h_i) = \text{tile}(\lambda_i) \odot h_i, \;\; \lambda_i \in \mathbb{R}^d, h_i \in \mathbb{R}^{N \times d} \quad (3)$$

given the dimension of feature map d.

In the end, the outputs from (2) and (3) get added up in an element-wise manner by a residual connection. This is followed by normalization and activation operations to produce a final output for that layer. In summary, the overall calibration process for the i-th layer could be formulated as follows,

$$\tilde{h}_i = \sigma\left(\mathcal{LN}\left(\Omega_{\lambda_i}\left(\mathcal{F}_{A_i}\left(h_{i-1}\right)\right) \oplus \mathcal{F}_{A_i}\left(h_{i-1}\right)\right)\right), \tag{4}$$

where $\mathcal{LN}(\cdot)$ denotes the layer normalization, $\oplus$ denotes an element-wise addition operator, and $\sigma(\cdot)$ is an activation function. Then $\tilde{h}_i$ is sent as input to the $i+1$-th layer in the feed-forward network. All the aforementioned calibrator parameters are initialized with a value of 1 at the start of training. We illustrate an example case of applying the calibration on a transformer-based model in Figure 1.

3.3 Learning Calibration Parameters

We propose an interleaved learning paradigm to train the calibrated transformer model. In the training procedure, we aim to exploit the training of the calibrator parameters to mitigate the catastrophic forgetting on the continual learning. Since the 'forgetting' in the training is often attributed to dramatic changes in parameter values, we design the learning objective for the calibrator learning as to regularize the parameter change after accessing the new knowledge not to be biased too much from the model values learned from previous ones.

To formulate the objective function for the calibrated model training, we inherit the *elastic weight consolidation* (EWC) approach proposed in Kirkpatrick et al. (2017) . Specifically, EWC approximates the true posterior distribution for the continual learning parameters by a Gaussian distribution given by the mean from the previous tasks and a diagonal precision from the Fisher information matrix. In this work, we formulate a weight calibration process to prevent the catastrophic change on model parameters. Then we train the calibrator parameters with the following loss function,

$$\mathcal{L}_c = \underbrace{\text{vec}\left(\theta-\theta^t\right)^\top \Lambda_t \text{vec}\left(\theta-\theta^t\right)}_{\text{term (a)}} + \underbrace{\beta\mathcal{L}_t(\Psi,\lambda,\theta)}_{\text{term (b)}} \tag{5}$$

where β is a trade-off parameter, and the operator *vec* $(\cdot)$ stacks the tensor into a vector.

The matrix Λ_t in term (a) are the Fisher information matrix, which is obtained from the data training loss for previous observed tasks, while the $\mathcal{L}_t(\Psi,\lambda,\theta)$ in term (b) is the loss for the current task. The two terms perform the consolidation process to retain the essential parameters towards past knowledge when the base model parameters are trained to absorb new tasks. To consolidate the knowledge on the calibrated model, the Fisher information matrix is computed upon the gradients on calibrated parameters.

3.4 Optimization

We formulate the optimization process to train the calibrated model under an iterative optimization schema, with the parameters from the base model and those from the calibration module being optimized by the loss function (5). During the interleaved optimization process, we first fix θ_t and take gradient steps with regard to $\{\Psi,\lambda\}$ as follows:

$$\Psi_{t+1} \leftarrow \Psi_t - \alpha \nabla_\Psi \mathcal{L}_c\left((\Psi,\lambda),\theta_t,\mathcal{D}_t\right), \tag{6}$$

$$\lambda_{t+1} \leftarrow \lambda_t - \alpha \nabla_\lambda \mathcal{L}_c\left((\Psi,\lambda),\theta_t,\mathcal{D}_t\right), \tag{7}$$

Then, we go on to optimize the base model parameter when the inference takes place with the updated base model,

$$\theta_{t+1} \leftarrow \theta_t - \alpha \nabla_\theta \mathcal{L}_c\left(\theta,(\psi_{t+1},\lambda_{t+1}),\mathcal{D}_t\right) \tag{8}$$

where α is the learning rate. By employing the calibrated parameterization of the transformer-based network, and optimizing it with the iterative learning scheme, our method achieves the trade-off between new data adaptation and past knowledge consolidation. We present the details in Algorithm 1.

Algorithm 1: Transformer Calibration for Continual Learning Algorithm (TCCL)

Input: Base model θ, calibrator (Φ,λ) learning rate α, trade-off parameter β, training data $\{\mathcal{D}_1^{tr},...,\mathcal{D}_T^{tr}\}$, test data $\{\mathcal{D}_1^{te},...,\mathcal{D}_T^{te}\}$

Output: Base model $\mathcal{F}_\theta$, calibrator $\mathcal{F}_{(\Phi,\lambda)}$.

function *train_and_eval*

Randomly initialize θ, Ψ and λ.

for $t \leftarrow 1\, to\, T$ **do**

for $b \leftarrow 1\, to\, n_{batch}$ **do**

Observe a batch of data $\mathcal{B}^t = \{x_i, y_i\}_{i=1}^{bs}$ from $\mathcal{D}_t^{tr}$.

$\Phi' \leftarrow \Phi - \alpha\nabla_\Phi\mathcal{L}_c(\mathcal{B}^t;\theta,\Phi,\lambda)$

$\lambda' \leftarrow \lambda - \alpha\nabla_\psi\mathcal{L}_c(\mathcal{B}^t;\theta,\Phi,\lambda)$

$\theta' \leftarrow \theta - \alpha\nabla_\theta\mathcal{L}_c(\mathcal{B}^t;\theta,\Phi',\lambda')$

Compute Λ_t according to $\nabla_\theta\mathcal{L}_c$

for $te \leftarrow 1\, to\, t$ **do**

Evaluate testing accuracy for the current model on $\mathcal{D}_{1,...,t}^{te}$:

$\hat{y}_{1,...,t} \leftarrow \mathcal{F}(\mathcal{D}_{1,...,t}^{te};\theta_t,\Phi_t,\lambda_t)$

4 Empirical Experiments

We evaluated the proposed algorithm on seq2seq generation tasks. We applied the algorithms on two datasets for seq2seq generation tasks in the continual learning. We also conducted the ablation study with respect to attention calibration and feature calibration to evaluate the robustness and effectiveness of the proposed calibration techniques.

4.1 Application: Paraphrase Generation

Dataset. For paraphrase generation, we train the model over three existing paraphrase datasets, Quora[1], Twitter[2] and Wiki_data (linked-wiki-text2)[3], in a sequential manner, where the model observes the three sequential tasks (i.e., datasets) one by one. See Table 1 for Statistics of the datasets.

	train	valid	test
Quora	111,947	8,000	37,316
Twitter	85,970	1,000	3,000
Wiki_data	78,392	8,154	9,324
total	276,309	17,154	49,640

Table 1: Statistics of Dataset on Paraphrase Generation

Experimental Setting. We exploit the SOTA generation model, BART, as the generation model backbone in the continual learning framework. We compare our approach with the following baselines:

- Finetune: for each new task, the model is initialized with the parameters learned from previous observed tasks, and then fine-tuned with data of the current new task.
- Full: the model is trained with all the available instances from three datasets together, which regarded as the up-bounded performance for the continual learning techniques.
- EWC: the EWC (Kirkpatrick et al., 2017) is introduced in the objective function to train the model over the sequential tasks.

For evaluation metrics, we use Bleu4, RougeL and Meteor for the Seq2Seq generation tasks. To measure the forgetting rates of different methods, we basically exploit the model learned on t-th task to evaluate its performance on previous tasks, i.e., $1, \cdots, t-1$ task. We tune the learning rate α from $\{10^{-3}, 10^{-2}, ..., 10^{0}\}$ for both model parameter and calibrator parameter, and trade-off parameter β from $\{0.1, 0.5, 1, 5, 10\}$. Meanwhile, the batch size is set to be $\{128, 256, 512\}$ on all datasets. All training and evaluation experiments are performed using Tesla V100S GPUs. The whole learning process takes around 0.5 GPU day.

4.1.1 Experimental Results

Accuracy Measurement: Table 2 presents the accuracy results in the continual learning setting, where the model is evaluated after the model has been trained on sequential tasks one after another. In the table, the first three models are *independent* baselines trained on either one of three datasets. As expected, model trained on new dataset may suffer the significant performance drop on previous instances, due to the data distribution gap between old and new datasets. For example, twitter includes the short casual text while Wiki_data contains formal academic text.

For the fine-tune, the model is trained in a Quora-Tweeter-Wiki (QTW) order, in which the model is initialized with the model parameters learned on the previous task and then fine tuned over the following task. We observe that finetune results on Quora and Wiki_data are comparable with those when building the model from scratch. In addition, EWC can achieve a better performance than Finetune and independent training over any evaluation metrics on Quora and most metrics on Twitter and Wiki, demonstrating the effectiveness of EWC in continual learning. Nonetheless, our calibration model consistently achieves the best performance across all sequential tasks, demonstrating that the calibration model yields a promising domain adaptation in continual learning.

Forgetting Measurement. Table 3 presents the results when the current models are evaluated on testing data from the previous tasks. The purpose of this experimental setting is to measure the forgetting rate of the models in the sequential training. In the order of QTW, the results are evaluated on Quora after the model is trained on Twitter, as well as on Quora and Twitter after the model is trained on Wiki. Our method is compared with independent baseline, finetune and EWC. Table 3 indicates that our method obtains a less performance drop than Finetune and EWC, with a low forgetting rate. Moreover, after the model is trained on

[1]https://huggingface.co/datasets/quora

[2]https://metatext.io/datasets/paraphrase-and-semantic-similarity-in-twitter-(pit)

[3]https://paperswithcode.com/dataset/wikitext-2

	Quora Test			Twitter Test			Wiki Test		
Models	bleu4*	rougeL	meteor	bleu4*	rougeL	meteor	bleu4*	rougeL	meteor
Quora-trained	30.11	55.85	57.17	2.12	6.13	5.49	4.51	11.21	12.13
Twitter-trained	3.18	11.46	9.01	35.47	57.49	54.57	4.60	9.76	7.50
Wiki_data-trained	22.38	43.44	46.23	9.32	17.93	21.03	42.12	73.86	73.10
Finetune	30.11	55.85	57.17	35.79	56.32	54.93	42.12	73.86	73.10
EWC	30.25	56.16	57.98	33.52	54.41	54.21	42.15	73.53	73.59
Ours	**32.14**	**58.12**	**59.13**	**36.81**	**58.46**	**55.32**	**44.47**	**74.49**	**73.66**
Full	33.99	59.56	61.67	38.56	58.76	56.01	46.86	76.59	75.91

Table 2: Results of model evaluations on QTW setting
(bleu4* denotes a more strict scoring version for the baseline evaluation)

Train: Twitter → Test: Quora

Models	bleu4*	rougeL	meteor
Quora-trained	30.11	55.85	57.17
Finetune	15.80	46.59	**47.31**
EWC	15.63	41.53	46.03
Ours	**15.93**	**46.65**	45.81

Train: Wiki_data → Test: Quora

Models	bleu4*	rougeL	meteor
Quora-trained	30.11	55.85	57.17
Finetune	19.07	51.76	55.95
EWC	19.63	49.35	53.02
Ours	**21.39**	**53.62**	**56.44**

Train: Wiki_data → Test: Twitter

Models	bleu4*	rougeL	meteor
Twitter-based	35.79	56.32	54.93
Finetune	14.09	37.97	45.89
EWC	14.84	38.65	46.33
Ours	**16.62**	**40.25**	**48.44**

Table 3: Results of all the methods when testing new models on previous domains (from 2nd row to the last).

Wiki, the performance on Quora is even improved from the one after trained on Twitter. Moreover, this work outperforms EWC on all the evaluation domains with a noticeable margin, which demonstrates that our calibration module is effective to boost the performance for continual learning via properly regularizing the parameter update against catastrophic forgetting. Overall, the empirical result demonstrates that the calibration mechanism can mitigate the forgetting issue greatly.

Ablation Study. We conduct the ablation study where several simplified versions of the calibration framework are evaluated in order to understand the effects of different components. Specifically, we evaluate the model variants without attention calibration module (i.e., w/o ACM), or feature calibration module (i.e., w/o FCM), or EWC regularization term (i.e., w/o R), and present the comparison result in Table 4. From the table, we can observe that (i) equipped with ACM or FCM, the performance is apparently better than the original backbone since dropping the calibration module ("w/o ACM" and "w/o FCM") would degrade the performance; (ii) EWC regularization is also effective, indicated by the better result than the one without EWC regularization term ("w/o R"). Overall, the results demonstrate that calibrating on latent feature and attention value is a promising direction.

	Quora Test		Wiki_data Test	
Models	bleu4*	meteor	bleu4*	meteor
Finetune	30.11	57.17	42.12	73.10
w/o FCM	33.32	59.32	43.33	73.10
w/o ACM	32.25	58.91	42.15	72.59
w/o R	33.77	59.57	43.51	72.93
Ours	**35.44**	**61.45**	**44.47**	**73.66**

Table 4: Ablation studies on the proposed calibration components and regularizion terms.

Next we aim to investigate the effect of the attention calibration that is performed on three different attentions in the transformer model. Specifically, we equipped the calibration component on either one of the self-attention of encoder, the self-attention of decoder and the encoder-decoder (ED) attention. The comparison results in Table 5 indicate that (i) the self-attention calibration on encoder is more effective to boost the performance; (ii) the calibration on encoder-decoder attention yields

	Quora Test		
Model Variants	bleu4*	rougeL	meteor
Self-Attention (E)	33.31	59.94	59.56
Self-Attention (D)	32.65	58.76	58.34
ED-Attention (D)	34.81	60.55	60.33
Ours (All)	**35.44**	**61.37**	**61.45**

Table 5: Ablation studies of the calibration different attention blocks in language model.

SOURCE	BART	Ours	TARGET
What is the best home workout to reduce waist fat?	How can I reduce my waist fat through a diet?	What is best home remedy for reducing belly fats?	What is best home remedy for reducing belly fats?
What's it like to be in a relationship with a married man?	What is it like for a married man to be in a relationship?	What's it like to be in a relationship with a married man?	What's it like to be in a relationship with a married man?
which provides a conventional sonic underscore to the onscreen action	which provides a sonic underscore to the onscreen action	which provides a conventional sonic underscoring to the onscreen action	which provides a conventional underscore to the onscreen action
Example gymnasium scene's first encounter with Angela	Example gymnasium scene, Angela 's first encounter with Angela	For example, the gymnasium scene, Pfaster 's first encounter with Angela	One example is the gymnasium scene, Lester 's first encounter with Angela.

Table 6: Examples of the generated paraphrases by BART and Ours on QTW data setting.

much better results than other two self-attentions. Overall, the results demonstrate that the attention calibration plays an important role for boosting the performance of the transformer-based generation model.

Case Study. In Table 6, we perform the case studies on paraphrase generation tasks. All examples are results generated by the final model, e.g., the model trained on Wiki_data is used to generate samples on Quora, Twitter, Wiki_data. Among the four examples, the first two is from Quora, and the others from Wiki_data. We compare our generated sentence with ones from BART backbone. From the table, we observe that our method has a better generation on all four cases. In those generation samples, the colored parts are key words. Yet, BART model either fails to generate those key words or creates the examples of false causality. In contrast, our method is able to generate key words in all cases with correct word relations.

4.2 Application: Dialog Response Generation

Dataset. The proposed model is evaluated on the dialog response generation task using the MultiWoZ-2.0 dataset (Budzianowski et al., 2018), which contains 6 domains (Attraction, Hotel, Restaurant, Booking, Taxi and Train) and 7 DA intents ("Inform, Request, Select, Recommend, Book, Offer-Booked, No-Offer"). We follow the setting (Mi et al., 2020) to generate the train/validation/test splits of MultiWoz. The details of the dataset is present in Table 7.

Experimental Setting. To evaluate the method performance, we exploit the slot error rate (SER) and BLEU4 score as the evaluation metrics. The lower value of SER indicates a better performance. To estimate the forgetting rate, the above met-

Domain and Intents of MultiWoZ-2.0 Data			
Domains	#. Total	Intents	#. Total
Attraction	8,823	Inform	28,700
Hotel	10,918	Request	7,621
Restaurant	10,997	Select	865
Booking	8,154	Book	4,525
Taxi	3,535	Recommend	3,678
Train	13,326	Offer-Booked	2,099
		No-Offer	1,703

Table 7: Statistics on the Dialog Response dataset

rics are reported in two continual learning settings (Kemker et al., 2018): $\Omega_{all} = \frac{1}{T}\sum_{i=1}^{T}\Omega_{all,i}$ and $\Omega_{first} = \frac{1}{T}\sum_{i=1}^{T}\Omega_{first,i}$, where T is total number of tasks in the sequential order. $\Omega_{all,i}$ is the test performance on all the tasks evaluated by the model learned with the i-th task, while $\Omega_{first,i}$ is the test result on the first task after the i-th task has been learned.

Our work exploits the well-known seq2seq generation model, conditional variational encoder (CVAE) as the backbone model, and the proposed model is compared with the following baselines:

a) **Finetune**: the model trained from previous observed tasks is used to be fine-tuned with data of the current new task.
b) **Full**: this model is trained with the data from current tasks and all historical tasks together.
c) **ARPER** (Mi et al., 2020): the model introduces memory replay and adaptive regularization together to mitigate the catastrophic forgetting issue.
d) **ER**: the model with the chosen exemplars that best approximate the mean DA vector (Rebuffi et al., 2017).

For CVAE, we equipped the feature calibration module on the backbone, due to no attention on the CVAE. In the following experiment, we follow the setting (Mi et al., 2020) and utilize the selected exemplars to compute the Fisher information as in the function (5).

4.2.1 Comparison Result

We conduct comparison experiments with baselines with various number of exemplars. The first one is that all methods do not use any exemplars. The reason for this comparison is that our proposed method is memory-free, i.e., no memory buffer required to store and replay the exemplar for data rehearsal. In such setting, ARPER reduces to the general regularization technique. Table 8 gives the evidence that without any exemplars, our method achieves a better performance than ARPER in both Ω_{all} and Ω_{first}, with a noticeable margin. We observe that the ARPER severely relies on the exemplars. Without the exemplars, the ARPER suffer a significant performance drop in terms of the accuracy, even poorer than Finetune.

With the increased number of exemplars, our method can obtain a better performance since the fisher matrix in our objective can cumulative the informative data throughout the training process. In addition, ER and APRE are memory-based techniques and are obviously beneficial from the exemplars. Nonetheless, our method can consistently outperform APRER and ER in both settings of 250 exemplars and 500 exemplars. That indicates that our memory-free calibration technique can effectively exploit the exemplar knowledge without the need of data storage for the exemplars.

Zero exemplars in total				
	Ω_{all}		Ω_{first}	
Models	SER	BLEU4	SER	BLEU4
Finetune	64.46	0.361	107.27	0.253
ER	67.23	0.360	105.33	0.181
ARPER	63.54	0.360	102.87	0.192
Ours	**56.90**	**0.395**	**68.60**	**0.258**
ALL	4.26	0.599	3.60	0.616
250 exemplars in total				
	Ω_{all}		Ω_{first}	
Models	SER	BLEU4	SER	BLEU4
Finetune	64.46	0.361	107.27	0.253
ER	16.89	0.535	9.89	0.532
ARPER	5.22	0.590	2.99	0.624
Ours	**4.41**	**0.603**	**2.33**	**0.635**
ALL	4.26	0.599	3.60	0.616
500 exemplars in total				
	Ω_{all}		Ω_{first}	
Models	SER	BLEU4	SER	BLEU4
Finetune	64.46	0.361	107.27	0.253
ER	12.25	0.555	4.53	0.568
ARPER	5.12	0.598	2.81	0.627
Ours	**4.33**	**0.606**	**2.21**	**0.638**
ALL	4.26	0.599	3.60	0.616

Table 8: Average Results of all the methods when learning six domains using 0/250/500 exemplars. (BLEU4 follows the setting in Mi et al. (2020))

4.2.2 Dynamic Results in Continual Learning

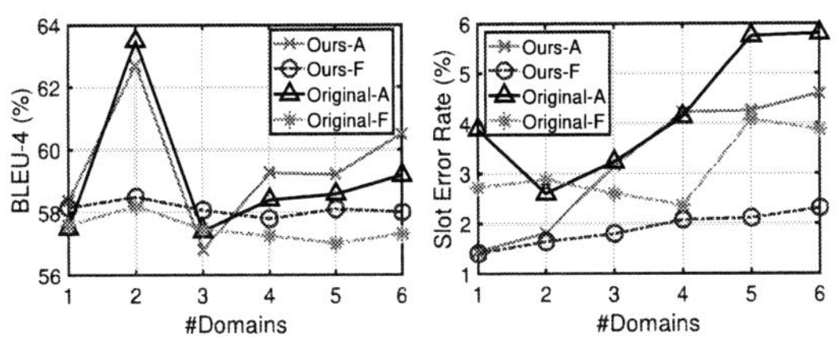

Figure 2: BLEU-4 and SER on all observed domains (solid) and on the first domain (dashed) over the six continually observed domains using 250 exemplars.

Figure 2 presents the comparison results along the six continually observed domains of dialog response. We compare the performance of the calibrated model with the original CVAE backbone. With more tasks continually learned, our method gradually performs better performance than the original backbone. On the first task (dashed lines), the calibrated model outperforms the original one on both metrics. These results illustrate the advantage of our calibration components throughout the entire continual learning process.

5 Conclusions

We propose an efficient seq2seq generation model with the calibration on the transformer, where a fixed architecture network after calibration can dynamically adjust the function with respect to each individual task. To optimize our method, we further propose a reproductive learning equipped with an iterative optimization objective that trade-off between plasticity and stability. Moreover, our calibration module is very light-weight without introducing any task-specific parameters. Extensive empirical experiments indicate that our approach outperforms the baselines and achieves a promising result. We also indicate that the calibration module and interleaved optimization play a vital role to boost the performance. Finally, extending the calibration module to multi-lingual pre-trained model is a promising future research direction.

References

Rahaf Aljundi, Eugene Belilovsky, Tinne Tuytelaars, Laurent Charlin, Massimo Caccia, Min Lin, and Lucas Page-Caccia. 2019. Online continual learning with maximal interfered retrieval. In *Advances in Neural Information Processing Systems (NeurIPS)*, pages 11849–11860, Vancouver, Canada.

Antoine Bordes, Y-Lan Boureau, and Jason Weston. 2016. Learning end-to-end goal-oriented dialog. *arXiv preprint arXiv:1605.07683*.

Pawel Budzianowski, Tsung-Hsien Wen, Bo-Hsiang Tseng, Iñigo Casanueva, Stefan Ultes, Osman Ramadan, and Milica Gasic. 2018. Multiwoz - A large-scale multi-domain wizard-of-oz dataset for task-oriented dialogue modelling. pages 5016–5026.

Pietro Buzzega, Matteo Boschini, Angelo Porrello, Davide Abati, and Simone Calderara. 2020. Dark experience for general continual learning: a strong, simple baseline. In *Advances in Neural Information Processing Systems (NeurIPS)*, virtual.

Arslan Chaudhry, Puneet Kumar Dokania, Thalaiyasingam Ajanthan, and Philip H. S. Torr. 2018. Riemannian walk for incremental learning: Understanding forgetting and intransigence. In *Proceedings of the 15th European Conference on Computer Vision (ECCV), Part XI*, pages 556–572, Munich, Germany.

Jacob Devlin, Ming-Wei Chang, Kenton Lee, and Kristina Toutanova. 2019. BERT: pre-training of deep bidirectional transformers for language understanding. In *Proceedings of the 2019 Conference of the North American Chapter of the Association for Computational Linguistics: Human Language Technologies (NAACL-HLT)*, pages 4171–4186, Minneapolis, MN.

Ronald Kemker, Marc McClure, Angelina Abitino, Tyler L. Hayes, and Christopher Kanan. 2018. Measuring catastrophic forgetting in neural networks. In *Proceedings of the Thirty-Second AAAI Conference on Artificial Intelligence (AAAI)*, pages 3390–3398, New Orleans, LN.

James Kirkpatrick, Razvan Pascanu, Neil Rabinowitz, Joel Veness, Guillaume Desjardins, Andrei A Rusu, Kieran Milan, John Quan, Tiago Ramalho, and Agnieszka Grabska-Barwinska. 2017. Overcoming catastrophic forgetting in neural networks. *Proceedings of the national academy of sciences*, 114(13):3521–3526.

Mike Lewis, Yinhan Liu, Naman Goyal, Marjan Ghazvininejad, Abdelrahman Mohamed, Omer Levy, Ves Stoyanov, and Luke Zettlemoyer. 2019. Bart: Denoising sequence-to-sequence pre-training for natural language generation, translation, and comprehension. *arXiv preprint arXiv:1910.13461*.

Dingcheng Li, Zheng Chen, Eunah Cho, Jie Hao, Xiaohu Liu, Fan Xing, Chenlei Guo, and Yang Liu. 2022a. Overcoming catastrophic forgetting during domain adaptation of seq2seq language generation. In *Proceedings of the 2022 Conference of the North American Chapter of the Association for Computational Linguistics: Human Language Technologies*, pages 5441–5454.

Dingcheng Li, Peng Yang, Zhuoyi Wang, and Ping Li. 2022b. Power norm based lifelong learning for paraphrase generations. *preprint*.

Zhizhong Li and Derek Hoiem. 2017. Learning without forgetting. *IEEE transactions on pattern analysis and machine intelligence*, 40(12):2935–2947.

Zheda Mai, Ruiwen Li, Jihwan Jeong, David Quispe, Hyunwoo Kim, and Scott Sanner. 2021. Online continual learning in image classification: An empirical survey. *arXiv preprint arXiv:2101.10423*.

Fei Mi, Liangwei Chen, Mengjie Zhao, Minlie Huang, and Boi Faltings. 2020. Continual learning for natural language generation in task-oriented dialog systems. In *Findings of the Association for Computational Linguistics (EMNLP Findings)*, volume EMNLP 2020, pages 3461–3474, Online Event.

Cuong V. Nguyen, Yingzhen Li, Thang D. Bui, and Richard E. Turner. 2018. Variational continual learning. In *Proceedings of the 6th International Conference on Learning Representations (ICLR)*, Vancouver, Canada.

German Ignacio Parisi, Ronald Kemker, Jose L. Part, Christopher Kanan, and Stefan Wermter. 2019. Continual lifelong learning with neural networks: A review. *Neural Networks*, 113:54–71.

Quang Pham, Chenghao Liu, Doyen Sahoo, and Steven C. H. Hoi. 2021. Contextual transformation networks for online continual learning. In *Proceedings of the 9th International Conference on Learning Representations (ICLR)*, Virtual Event.

Sylvestre-Alvise Rebuffi, Alexander Kolesnikov, Georg Sperl, and Christoph H. Lampert. 2017. iCaRL: Incremental classifier and representation learning. In *Proceedings of the 2017 IEEE Conference on Computer Vision and Pattern Recognition (CVPR)*, pages 5533–5542, Honolulu, HI.

David Rolnick, Arun Ahuja, Jonathan Schwarz, Timothy P. Lillicrap, and Gregory Wayne. 2019. Experience replay for continual learning. In *Advances in Neural Information Processing Systems (NeurIPS)*, pages 348–358, Vancouver, Canada.

Andrei A Rusu, Neil C Rabinowitz, Guillaume Desjardins, Hubert Soyer, James Kirkpatrick, Koray Kavukcuoglu, Razvan Pascanu, and Raia Hadsell. 2016. Progressive neural networks. *arXiv preprint arXiv:1606.04671*.

Jonathan Schwarz, Wojciech Czarnecki, Jelena Luketina, Agnieszka Grabska-Barwinska, Yee Whye Teh, Razvan Pascanu, and Raia Hadsell. 2018.

Progress & compress: A scalable framework for continual learning. In *Proceedings of the 35th International Conference on Machine Learning (ICML)*, pages 4535–4544, Stockholm, Sweden.

Joan Serra, Didac Suris, Marius Miron, and Alexandros Karatzoglou. 2018. Overcoming catastrophic forgetting with hard attention to the task. In *International Conference on Machine Learning*, pages 4548–4557. PMLR.

Pravendra Singh, Vinay Kumar Verma, Pratik Mazumder, Lawrence Carin, and Piyush Rai. 2020. Calibrating cnns for lifelong learning. In *Advances in Neural Information Processing Systems (NeurIPS)*, virtual.

Johannes von Oswald, Christian Henning, João Sacramento, and Benjamin F. Grewe. 2020. Continual learning with hypernetworks. In *Proceedings of the 8th International Conference on Learning Representations (ICLR)*, Addis Ababa, Ethiopia.

Zhuoyi Wang, Dingcheng Li, and Ping Li. 2022. Latent coreset sampling based data-free continual learning. In *Proceedings of the 31st ACM International Conference on Information and Knowledge Management (CIKM)*, Atlanta, GA.

Haiyan Yin, Peng Yang, and Ping Li. 2021. Mitigating forgetting in online continual learning with neuron calibration. In *Advances in Neural Information Processing Systems (NeurIPS)*, pages 10260–10272, virtual.

Friedemann Zenke, Ben Poole, and Surya Ganguli. 2017. Continual learning through synaptic intelligence. In *Proceedings of the 34th International Conference on Machine Learning (ICML)*, pages 3987–3995, Sydney, Australia.

Mengyao Zhai, Lei Chen, Frederick Tung, Jiawei He, Megha Nawhal, and Greg Mori. 2019. Lifelong GAN: continual learning for conditional image generation. In *Proceedings of the 2019 IEEE/CVF International Conference on Computer Vision (ICCV)*, pages 2759–2768, Seoul, Korea.

"That's so cute!": The CARE Dataset for Affective Response Detection

Jane Dwivedi-Yu
Meta AI
janeyu@meta.com

Alon Y. Halevy
Meta AI
ayh@meta.com

Abstract

Social media plays an increasing role in our communication with friends and family, and in our consumption of entertainment and information. Hence, to design effective ranking functions for posts on social media, it would be useful to predict the affective responses of a post (e.g., whether it is likely to elicit feelings of entertainment, inspiration, or anger). Similar to work on emotion detection (which focuses on the affect of the publisher of the post), the traditional approach to recognizing affective response would involve an expensive investment in human annotation of training data.

We create and publicly release CARE_{db}, a dataset of 230k social media post annotations according to seven affective responses using the Common Affective Response Expression (CARE) method. The CARE method is a means of leveraging the signal that is present in comments that are posted in response to a post, providing high-precision evidence about the affective response to the post without human annotation. Unlike human annotation, the annotation process we describe here can be iterated upon to expand the coverage of the method, particularly for new affective responses. We present experiments that demonstrate that the CARE annotations compare favorably with crowdsourced annotations. Finally, we use CARE_{db} to train competitive BERT-based models for predicting affective response as well as emotion detection, demonstrating the utility of the dataset for related tasks.

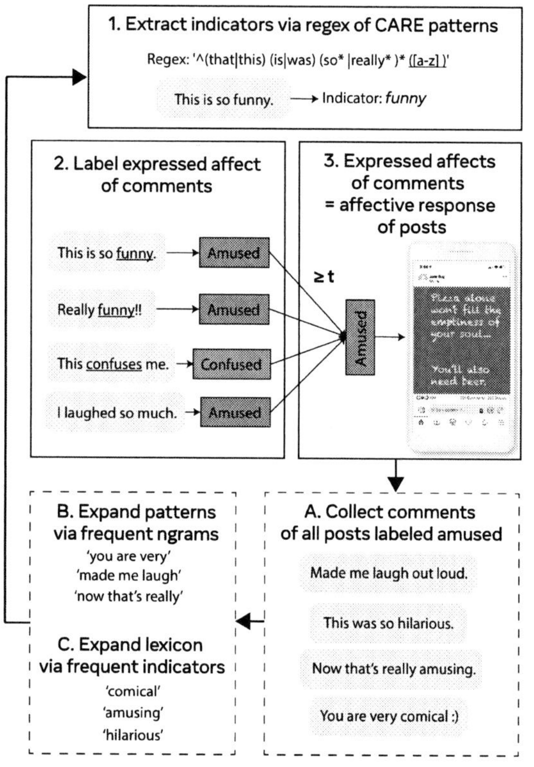

Figure 1: Overview of the CARE Method (pseudo-code in Appendix, Algorithm 1). The top half of the figure (steps 1–3) shows how the affective response to a post is computed by aggregating the expressed affects in comments from users viewing the post. The bottom half of the figure (steps A–C) shows how we expand the collection of CARE patterns and the lexicon based on labels that have been obtained from prior iterations.

1 Introduction

Social media and other online media platforms have become a common means of not only interacting and connecting with others, but also finding interesting, informing, and entertaining content. Users of those platforms depend on the ranking systems of the recommendation systems to show them information they will be most interested in and to safeguard them against unfavorable experiences.

Towards this end, a key technical problem is to predict the *affective response* that a user may have when they see a post. Some affective responses can be described by emotions (e.g., angry, joyful), and others may be described more as experiences (e.g., entertained, inspired). Predicting affective response differs from emotion detection in that the latter focuses on the emotions expressed by the publisher of the post (referred to as the *publisher*

Proceedings of the 26th Conference on Computational Natural Language Learning (CoNLL), pages 50 - 69
December 7-8, 2022 ©2022 Association for Computational Linguistics

affect in Chen et al. (2014)) and not on the viewer of the content. While the publisher's emotion may be relevant to the affective response, it only provides a partial signal (Dwivedi-Yu et al., 2022), and the two are not always equivalent (see Figure 2 for an illustrative example). Affective response for recommender systems has shown to be critical in several applications such as music, emotional health monitoring systems, product and travel recommendations (Rosa et al., 2015, 2018; Akram et al., 2020; Artemenko et al., 2020; Dwivedi-Yu et al., 2022).

Figure 2: An example case of differing publisher affect and affective response. This work focuses on affective response through signals such as comments and reactions. Post image sourced from Shutterstock (Tapia).

Current approaches to predicting affective response require obtaining training data from human annotators who try to classify content into classes of a given taxonomy. However, obtaining enough training data can be expensive, and moreover, due to the subjective nature of the problem, achieving consensus among annotators can be challenging. Some methods explore inferring responses from physiological data or facial expressions from users, but this is a highly invasive process and can be difficult to scale to multiple users. (Tkalčič et al., 2017, 2019; Angelastro et al., 2019).

This paper introduces the Common Affective Response Expression method (CARE for short), a means of obtaining labels for affective response in an unsupervised way from the comments written in response to online posts. CARE uses patterns and a keyword-affect mapping to identify expressions in comments that provide high-precision evidence about the affective response of the readers to the post. For example, the expression "What a hilarious story" may indicate that a post is humorous and "This is so cute" may indicate that a post is adorable. We seed the system with a small number of high-precision patterns and mappings. We then iteratively expand on the initial set by considering frequent patterns and keywords in unlabeled comments on posts labeled by the previous iteration.

Using CARE, we create the largest dataset to date for affective response, CARE_{db}, which contains 230k posts annotated according to 7 affective responses. We validate the effectiveness of CARE by comparing the CARE annotations with crowdsourced annotations. Our experiments show that there is a high degree of agreement between the annotators and the labels proposed by CARE (e.g., in 90% of the cases, at least two out of three annotators agree with all the CARE labels). Furthermore, we show that the CARE patterns/lexicon have greater accuracy than applying SOTA emotion recognition techniques to the comments. Using CARE_{db}, we train CARE-BERT[1], a BERT-based model that can predict affective response *without* relying on comments. CARE-BERT provides strong baseline performance for the task of predicting affective response, on par with the SOTA models for emotion recognition. Furthermore, we show that CARE-BERT can be used for transfer learning to a different emotion-recognition task, achieving similar performance to Demszky et al. (2020), which relied on manually-labeled training data.

In summary, our contributions are as follows:

- CARE, a novel method for leveraging the signal present in comments in order to label the affective response of a post, without the need for human annotation.
- CARE_{db}, a dataset of 230k annotated posts according to 7 affective responses using CARE.
- Error analysis using human annotations for a sampled set of posts from CARE_{db}.
- Quantitative results that demonstrate CARE performs better than a method leveraging a state-of-the-art publisher-affect classifier.

[1]The CARE patterns, lexicon, CARE_{db}, and CARE-BERT are made available at `https://github.com/facebookresearch/care`.

- CARE-BERT: A model for labeling affective response from the post text, without the need for comments.
- Transfer learning experiments that demonstrate transferability to different emotion-recognition tasks under low-resource settings.

2 Related work

We first situate our work with respect to previous research on related tasks.

2.1 Emotion detection in text

Approaches to emotion detection can be broadly categorized into three groups: lexicon-based, machine learning, and combinations of the first two. The lexicon-based approach typically leverages lexical resources such as lexicons and encoded rules to guide emotion prediction (Tao, 2004; Ma et al., 2005; Asghar et al., 2017). Though these methods can be fast and interpretable, they are often not as robust and flexible because of the constraints of the lexicon (Alswaidan and Menai, 2020; Acheampong et al., 2020). Additionally, the scope of emotions predicted by these works is usually fairly small, ranging from two to five, and most datasets utilized are usually smaller than 10k, making it unclear if they extrapolate well. Among the ML approaches, many SOTA works employ deep learning methods (Demszky et al., 2020; Felbo et al., 2017; Barbieri et al., 2018; Huang et al., 2019a; Baziotis et al., 2017; Huang et al., 2019b), but while these show significant improvement over prior techniques, they are highly uninterpretable and often require prohibitively large human-labeled datasets to train. In both the lexicon-based approach and the ML-approach, the classes of emotions predicted in these works are usually non-extendable or require additional labeled data.

While there are some commonalities between works in emotion detection and affective response detection, the problems are distinct enough that we cannot simply apply emotion recognition techniques to our setting. Emotion recognition focuses on the publisher affect (the affect of the person writing the text). The publisher affect may provide a signal about the affective response of the reader, but there is no simple mapping from one to the other. For example, being 'angered' is an affective response that does not only result from reading an angry post—it can result from a multitude of different publisher affects (e.g. excited, angry, sympathetic, embarrassed, or arrogant). For some affective responses, such as feeling 'grateful' or 'connected' to a community, the corresponding publisher affect is highly unclear.

2.2 Affective response detection

There have been some works that address affective response through natural language in limited settings, such as understanding reader responses to online news (Katz et al., 2007; Strapparava and Mihalcea, 2007; Lin et al., 2008; Lei et al., 2014). In contrast, our goal is to address the breadth of content on social media. There are works which use Facebook reactions as a proxy for affective response, but these are constrained by the pre-defined set of reactions (Clos et al., 2017; Raad et al., 2018; Pool and Nissim, 2016; Graziani et al., 2019; Krebs et al., 2017). The work described in Rao et al. (2014) and Bao et al. (2012) attempts to associate emotions with *topics*, but a single topic can have a large variety of affective responses when seen on social media, and therefore their model does not apply to our case. Some works in the computer vision community study affective response to images (Chen et al., 2014; Jou et al., 2014); as they note, most of the work in the vision community also focuses on publisher affect.

2.3 Methods for unsupervised labeling

A major bottleneck in developing models for emotion and affective response detection is the need for large amounts of training data. As an alternative to manually-labeled data, many works utilize metadata such as hashtags, emoticons, and Facebook reactions as pseudo-labels (Wang et al., 2012; Suttles and Ide, 2013; Hasan et al., 2014; Mohammad and Kiritchenko, 2015). However, these can be highly noisy and limited in scope. For example, there exist only seven Facebook reactions, and they do not necessarily correspond to distinct affective responses. Additionally, for abstract concepts like emotions, hashtagged content may only capture a superficial interpretation of the concept. For example, searching #inspiring on Instagram will return many photos featuring selfies or obviously inspirational quotes, which do not sufficiently represent inspiration. The work we present here extracts labels from free-form text in comments rather than metadata. The work done in Sintsova and Pu (2016) is similar to our work in that it pseudo-labels tweets and extends its lexicon, but the classifier itself is a keyword, rule-based approach and is heavily reliant on the capacity of these lexicons. In contrast, our work leverages the high precision of CARE and uses these results to train a model, which is not constrained by the lexicon size in its predictions. Our method also employs bootstrapping to expand the set of patterns and lexicon, similar to Agichtein and Gravano (2000) and Jones et al. (1999) but focuses on extracting affect rather than relation tuples.

3 The CARE Method

In this section, we provide a formal description of CARE for annotating the affective response of posts. Before we proceed, we note two aspects of affective responses. First, there is no formal definition for what qualifies as an affective response. In practice, we use affective responses to understand the experience that the user has when seeing a piece of content, and these responses may be both emotional and cognitive. Second, the response a user may have to a particular piece of content is clearly a very personal one. Our goal here is to predict whether a piece of content is generally likely to elicit a particular affective response. In practice, if the recommendation system has models of user interests and behavior, these would need to be combined with the affect predictions for personalized predictions.

3.1 CARE patterns and the CARE lexicon

CARE is composed of two major components: CARE patterns, regular expressions used to extract information from the comments of a post, and the CARE lexicon, a keyword-affect dictionary used to map the comment to an affect.

CARE patterns are not class or affect-specific and leverage common structure present in comments for affective response extraction. There is an unlimited number of possible CARE patterns, but we seeded the system with six CARE patterns and an additional 17 more were automatically discovered using the expansion method. In the same spirit as Hearst Patterns (Hearst, 1992), CARE patterns are tailored to extract specific relationships and rely on two sets of sub-patterns:

- Exaggerators $\{E\}$: words that intensify or exaggerate a statement, e.g., *so*, *very*, or *really*.
- Indicators $\{I\}$: words (up to 3) that exist in the CARE lexicon, which maps the indicator to a particular class. For example, 'funny' in "This is so funny" would map to *amused*.

We present the six CARE patterns below that were used to seed the system: (The symbol * (resp. $^+$) indicates that zero (resp. one) or more matches are required.) Example: *This is so amazing!*

- Demonstrative Pronouns:
  $\{\text{this}|\text{that}|\text{those}|\text{these}\}\{\text{is}|\text{are}\}^*\{E\}^*\{I\}^+$
  Example: *This is so amazing!*
- Subjective Self Pronouns:
  $\{\text{i}|\text{we}\}\{\text{am}|\text{is}|\text{are}|\text{have}|\text{has}\}^*\{E\}^*\{I\}^+$
  Example: *I am really inspired by this recipe.*
- Subjective Non-self Pronouns:
  $\{\text{he}|\text{she}|\text{they}\}\{\text{is}|\text{are}|\text{have}|\text{has}\}^*\{E\}^*\{I\}^+$
  Example: *They really make me mad.*
- Collective Nouns:
  $\{\text{some people}|\text{humans}|\text{society}\}\{E\}^+\{I\}^+$
  Example: *Some people are so dumb.*
- Leading Exaggerators: $\{E\}^+\{I\}^+$
  Example: *So sad to see this still happens.*
- Exclamatory Interrogatives:
  $\{\text{what a}|\text{how}\}\{E\}^+\{I\}^+$
  Example: *What a beautiful baby!*

Given the indicators extracted by the CARE patterns, the CARE lexicon is responsible for mapping the comment to particular affective responses. The lexicon contains 163 indicators for the 7 classes we consider (123 of which were automatically identified in the expansion process described in the next section). We also considered using other lexicons (Strapparava and Valitutti, 2004; Poria et al., 2014; Staiano and Guerini, 2014; Esuli and Sebastiani, 2006; Mohammad et al., 2013), but we found that they were lacking enough application context to be useful in our setting. Table 1 shows the affects in the CARE lexicon and corresponding definitions and example comments that would fall under each affect (or class). The classes *excited*, *angered*, *saddened*, and *scared* were chosen since they are often proposed as the four basic emotions (Wang et al., 2011; Jack et al., 2014; Gu et al., 2016; Zheng et al., 2016). The classes *adoring*, *amused*, and *approving* were established because they are particularly important in the context of social media for identifying positive content that users enjoy. Overall, a qualitative inspection indicated that these seven have minimal conceptual overlap and sufficiently broad coverage. We note, however, that one of the benefits of the method we describe is that it is relatively easy to build a model for a new class of interest compared to the process of human annotation.

3.2 Labeling posts

Here we describe how to combine and use the two major components (CARE patterns and lexicon) at the comment-level in order to annotate the post-level affective response. The pipeline for labeling posts is shown in steps 1–3 of Figure 1 and described in detail in Appendix, Algorithm 1. We begin with reg-ex matching of CARE patterns and individual sentences of the comments. We truncate the front half of a sentence if it contains words like 'but' or 'however' because the latter half usually indicates their predominant sentiment. We also reject indicators that contain negation words such as 'never', 'not', or 'cannot' (although one could theoretically map this to the opposite affective response using Plutchik's Wheel of Emotions (Plutchik, 1980)). Note that contrary to traditional rule-based or machine-learning methods, we do not strip stop words (e.g., 'this' and 'very') because it is often crucial to the regular expression matching, and this specificity has a direct impact on the precision of the pipeline.

Given the reg-ex matches, we use the lexicon to map the indicators to the publisher affect of the comment (e.g., *excited*). It is important to note that the expressed affects of the comments should intuitively equate to the affective responses of a post. Consequently, we obtain post-level affective response labels by aggregating the comment-level labels and filtering out labels that have a support smaller than t. Specifically, a post would be labeled with the affective response a if at least t of the comments were labeled with a. In our experiments, we used a value of $t = 5$, after qualitative inspection of CARE$_{db}$, discussed in Section 4. We note, however, that it is possible for a comment to be labeled according to multiple classes if it has multiple indicators. In reality, the program should be permissive of multiple labels for a single comment, because emotions are in many cases not mutually exclusive—an individual, for example, could be experiencing both sadness and anger simultaneously.

3.3 Expanding CARE patterns/lexicon

We seeded our patterns and lexicon with a small intuitive set. We then expanded these by looking at common n-grams that appear across posts with the same label (steps A–C of Figure 1). At a high level, for a given affect a, consider the set, $comm(a)$, of all the comments on posts that were labeled a, but did not match any CARE pattern. From these comments, we extract new keywords (e.g. 'dope' for *approving* as in 'This is so dope.') for the CARE lexicon by taking the most frequent n-grams in $comm(a)$ but infrequent in $comm(b)$, where b includes all classes except a. On the other hand, the most common n-grams co-occuring with multiple classes were converted to regular expressions and then added as new CARE patterns (see Table B1 for a few examples). We added CARE patterns according to their frequency and stopped when we had sufficient data to train our models. After two expansion rounds, the set of patterns and indicators increased from 6 to 23 and 40 to 163, respectively. Counting the possible combinations of patterns and indicators, there are roughly 3500 distinct expressions. *When considering the possible 23 CARE patterns, 163 CARE lexicon indicators, and 37 exaggerators, there are a total of 130k possible instantiations of a matching comment.*

4 Evaluating CARE$_{db}$

In this section we apply our method to social media posts and validate these annotations using human evaluation (Section 4.1). Section 4.2 discusses class-wise error analysis, and in Section 4.3, we explore the alternative possibility of creating CARE$_{db}$ using a SOTA publisher-affect classifier (Demszky et al., 2020) to label the comments instead of using the CARE patterns/lexicon.

CARE$_{db}$: Our experiments use a dataset that is created from Reddit posts and comments in the pushshift.io database that were created between 2011 and 2019. We create our dataset, CARE$_{db}$, as follows. We used CARE patterns and the CARE lexicon to annotate 34 million comments from 24 million distinct posts. After filtering with a threshold of $t = 5$, we obtained annotations for 400k posts (the total number of posts that have at least 5 comments was 150 million). The low recall is expected given the specificity of CARE patterns/lexicon. We also filtered out posts that have less than 10 characters, resulting in a total of 230k posts in CARE$_{db}$. Table 1 shows the breakdown of cardinality per affective response. 195k of the posts were assigned a single label, whereas 26k (resp. 8k) were assigned two (resp. three) labels. Note that the distribution of examples per class in

AR	Definition	Example comment	Size
Adoring	Finding someone or something cute, adorable, or attractive.	*He is the cutest* thing ever.	36
Amused	Finding something funny, entertaining, or interesting.	*That was soooo funny.*	30
Approving	Expressing support, praise, admiration, or pride.	*This is really fantastic!*	102
Excited	Expressing joy, zeal, eagerness, or looking forward to something.	*Really looking forward to* this!	41
Angered	Expressing anger, revulsion, or annoyance.	*I'm so frustrated* to see this.	26
Saddened	Expressing sadness, sympathy, or disappointment.	*So sad from reading this.*	34
Scared	Expressing worry, concern, stress, anxiety, or fear.	*Extremely worried* about finals.	2

Table 1: Definition of affective responses (AR), examples of comments which would map to each affective response, and the number of posts (in thousands) per class in CARE$_{db}$. The portion of each example which would match a CARE pattern in a reg-ex search is italicized.

CARE$_{db}$ is not reflective of the distribution in the original data, because different classes have different recall rates. The CARE$_{db}$ dataset features the pushshift.io ID and text of the post as well as the annotations using CARE.

4.1 Human evaluation

In our next experiment, we evaluate the labels predicted by CARE with the help of human annotators using Amazon Mechanical Turk (AMT), restricting to those who qualify as AMT Masters and have a lifetime approval rating greater than 80%. The dataset for annotation was created as follows. We sub-sampled a set of 6000 posts from CARE$_{db}$, ensuring that we have at least 500 samples from each class and asked annotators to label the affective response of each post. Annotators were encouraged to select as many as appropriate and also permitted to choose 'None of the above' as shown in Figure C1. In addition to the post, we also showed annotators up to 10 sampled comments from the post in order to provide more context. This was also done in an effort to make the comparison to CARE more fair, since CARE relies upon having access to the comments of the post. Every post was shown to three of the 91 distinct annotators. For quality control, we also verified that there no individual annotator provided answers that disagreed with the CARE labels more than 50% of the time on more than 100 posts.

We observed an average Fleiss' kappa score of 0.59, which is considered moderate agreement, the breakdown of which is shown in Table C1. Table 2 shows that the rate of agreement between the annotators and the labels proposed by the CARE method is high. For example, 94% of posts had at least one label proposed by CARE that was confirmed by 2 or more annotators, and 90% had *all* the labels confirmed. The last column measures the agreement among annotators on labels that were not suggested by CARE, which was 53% when confirmed by 2 or more annotators. We expected this value for 'other' to be reasonably large because the CARE patterns/lexicon were designed to generate a highly precise set of labels, rather than highly comprehensive ones. However, the value is still much smaller relative to the agreement rate for the CARE labels (53% versus 94%). On average, each annotation answer contained around 1.8 labels per post (with a standard deviation of 0.9). We note that 'None of the above' was chosen less than 0.2% of the time. Table C2 and Figure C2 present annotator agreement statistics and label prevalence, respectively, broken down by class.

# Agree	Any CARE	All CARE	Other
≥ 1	98	96	82
≥ 2	94	90	53
$= 3$	80	76	24

Table 2: The rate of agreement between the annotators and the labels proposed by CARE. The first column specifies the number of annotators to be used for consensus. The rest of the columns shows, for all posts, the average rate of intersection of the human labels with at least one CARE label, all CARE labels, and any label that is not a CARE label.

4.2 Error Analysis

Evaluating CARE reveals that the accuracy of CARE varies by class (Figure C2), and in particular, is lower for *amused* and *excited*. As can be seen from the interclass Spearman correlations (Figure G4) and a two-dimensional projection of the embeddings of the labeled comments (Figure G3), there appears to be non-trivial overlap amongst the classes *amused*, *excited*, and *approving*. To better understand if certain pattern or indicator matches are at fault here, we investigate the precision and recall at the pattern and lexicon level.

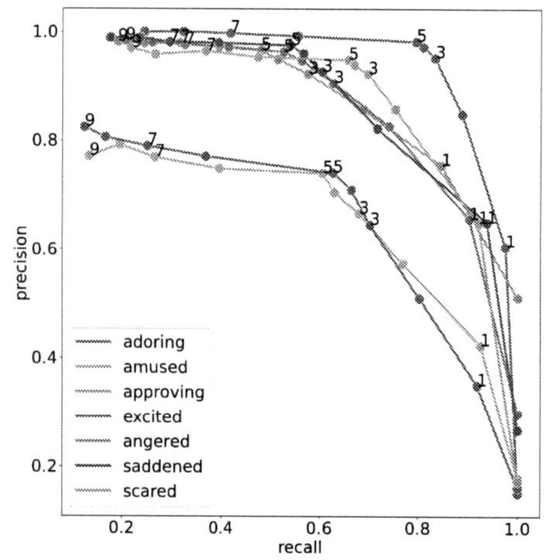

Figure 3: Precision versus recall of each class using varying thresholds (t = 0 to 9). Ground truth labels utilized are those which have at least 2 out of 3 annotator agreement. For clarity, only odd values of t are labeled.

Recall that instantiating a match for a comment involves choosing a (pattern, keyword) combination. Separating the lexicon from the patterns enables us to encode a large number of instantiated patterns parsimoniously, but some pair combinations provide a much weaker signal than others, particularly for the class *amused* (see Figure H6 for examples). Hence, for future iterations of CARE, we intend to implement a mechanism to exclude certain pattern and keyword combinations and a means for using different thresholds for each class.

Alternatively, another mechanism for accommodating these class-wise discrepancies in performance is by tuning for each class an optimal threshold t (i.e., the number of matched comments we need to see in order to reliably predict a label). Figure 3 shows how the precision and recall of each class varies according to different threshold values. To achieve precision and recall greater than 0.7, a threshold of 1 actually seems viable for most classes, while for *amused* and *excited* a threshold of at least 3 is needed. In fact, for most of the classes, using thresholds larger than 3 has negligible impact on the precision score, but does reduce the recall.

4.3 Can we leverage emotion classification?

Recall, steps 1 and 2 of Figure 1 uses the CARE patterns and lexicon to label the publisher affect of the comments. Conceivably, this could have been done instead by using a SOTA emotion classifier such as the GoEmotions classifier (Demszky et al., 2020), which is trained specifically to predict the publisher affect of Reddit comments. Here, we show that our method for labeling the publisher affect of comments performs comparatively better. Let us define the method CARE^G, a modified version of the CARE method where steps 1 and 2 are replaced with labels using the GoEmotions classifer. We apply CARE^G to our human annotated dataset (Section 4.1) by first applying the GoEmotions classifier to all comments of the posts. These GoEmotion labels are then mapped to our taxonomy in Table 1 using the mapping defined in Table 3, which is based on the grouping of emotions at the Ekman level used in Demszky et al. (2020). We then, as usual, aggregate and filter post labels according to a threshold t.

CARE^G (Table F4) shows a relative decrease of 12.9% and 18.0% in the rate of annotator agreement with any and all labels, respectively, compared to that of CARE. These decreases hold even when partitioning on each individual class. The comparatively lower performance of CARE^G is most likely due to the low F1-scores (<0.4) of the GoEmotions classifer for nearly half of the 28 classes, as reported in the original work Demszky et al. (2020, Table 4). It is also important to note that in addition to demonstrating higher precision, CARE patterns and lexicon are valuable because they do not require human annotated data, unlike GoEmotions. It may, however, be useful to leverage multiple emotion detection approaches. Section F discusses a potential ensembling strategy for this.

To validate the mapping in Table 3, we applied steps 1 and 2 of CARE to the GoEmotions dataset (see Section E), and computed the rate of agreement among the labels in our defined mapping. We find this rate of agreement to be high (87.3% overall). Note, we perform this equivalence at the publisher affect level, because as discussed before, the affective response and publisher affect are not always equivalent. In addition to prior work (Dwivedi-Yu et al., 2022), Section D presents experiments that indicate that affective response and publisher affect labels intersect only 44% of the time.

5 Predicting affective response for posts without comments

In this section we describe CARE-BERT, a multi-label affective response classifier that is trained only on the post-level text and annotations in CARE$_{db}$. Such a model is important in order to

AR	GoEmotion label	% agree
Amused	Amusement	79.8
Approving	Admiration, Approval	89.3
Excited	Joy	81.3
Angered	Anger, Annoyance, Disgust	93.3
Saddened	Disappointment, Sadness	90.9
Scared	Fear, Nervousness	84.9

Table 3: CARE to GoEmotions mapping. The last column summarizes the rate at which the mapping holds. The average across all datapoints was 87.3%.

make predictions early in the life of the post and in cases where the comments may not exist or may not match any CARE patterns or keywords. Note that *the model is not given the comments* text and is therefore not restricted to the CARE pattern/lexicon semantics. In section 5.2, we describe how CARE-BERT can be further fine-tuned for related tasks like emotion detection.

5.1 Creating and evaluating CARE-BERT

We train CARE-BERT with the CARE labels in $CARE_{db}$, using the pre-trained model bert-base-uncased from the Huggingface library (Wolf et al., 2020). We use a max length of 512 and we add a dropout layer with a rate of 0.3 and a dense layer to allow for multi-label classification. We used an Adam optimizer with a learning rate of 5e-5, a batch size of 16, and 5 epochs. We used a train/validation/test split of 80/10/10%. See Section I for other settings we explored.

The evaluation on the human-annotated set (held out from training) is shown in Table 4. We use labels with support from all annotators as ground truth. The classes of lowest prevalence, such as *scared*, had the poorest results, while the more frequent classes (*adoring*, *approving*, *saddened*) had the highest results. To put these results in perspective, we use the mapping in Table 3 and compare with the numbers from Demszky et al. (2020). Note, the comparison is *not* for the same dataset—our results pertain to predicting on the post, whereas GoEmotions predicts the comments. Still, CARE-BERT demonstrates a 35% improvement in the overall micro-averaged F1-score.

CARE vs. CARE-BERT: Compared to the human annotators and CARE, CARE-BERT is disadvantaged by not having access to the comments. We use human annotated set of $CARE_{db}$ and find that 0.89 of the CARE labels are also proposed by human annotators, while this value is 0.72 for CARE-BERT (Table J6). In Table J7 we display select examples that may illustrate reasons for this discrepancy. Firstly, one of the challenges that CARE-BERT faces is that there may not be sufficient context in the post alone. In the example "Who is this LIRIK guy, and why does he have 50K subscribers" it is challenging to predict that some people find the subject adorable without additional context. Relatedly, the conversation that the post initiates can be challenging to foresee. The last example reads "AskReddit: Imagine the last thing you ate has been made illegal. What would that be?" In some cases, commenters just ate something they didn't like and are therefore content with the premise. In other cases, commenters just ate something they very much enjoy and are saddened by the hypothetical. Our results show that this is not particular to 'AskReddit' posts, and given these challenges, it is reasonable that the CARE method provides more reliable labels.

Affect	P	R	F1	GoEmotions F1
Adoring	0.73	0.66	0.70	-
Amused	0.63	0.54	0.60	**0.80**
Approving	0.73	0.72	**0.75**	0.53
Excited	0.58	0.52	**0.58**	0.51
Angered	0.70	0.61	**0.69**	0.40
Saddened	0.78	0.62	**0.73**	0.39
Scared	0.68	0.3	0.47	**0.54**
micro-avg	0.70	0.68	**0.69**	0.51
macro-avg	0.69	0.62	**0.65**	0.53
stdev	0.06	0.12	0.09	0.14

Table 4: Precision (P), recall (R), and F1 of CARE-BERT using $CARE_{db}$ on the post text of the human-annotated set and F1-scores of the GoEmotions classifier from Demszky et al. (2020) on comments.

5.2 Transfer learning to emotion detection

We now demonstrate that CARE-BERT is also useful for pre-training of another related task in a setting with limited annotated data. We consider transfer learning to the ISEAR Dataset (Scherer and Wallbott, 1994), which is a collection of 7666 statements from a diverse set of 3000 individuals labeled according to six categories (anger, disgust, fear, guilt, joy, sadness, and shame). The labels pertain to the *publisher affect* and not affective response, as considered in this work. Our experiment explores transfer learning to predict the labels in the ISEAR dataset using an additional drop-out layer of 0.3 and a dense layer.

Our experiments follow closely to that of Demszky et al. (2020) and uses different training set sizes (500, 1000, 2000, 4000, and 6000) for 10 different train-test splits. We plot the average and standard deviation in the F1-scores across these 10 splits in Figure 4. We compare four different fine-tuning setups: the first two are trained using CARE-BERT and then fine-tuned on the benchmark dataset, one with no parameter freezing (no_freeze), and one with all layers but the last two frozen (freeze). The third setup is similar to CARE-BERT (no_freeze) but is trained on GoEmotions rather than CARE$_{db}$. The last setup is the bert-base-uncased model trained only on ISEAR, where all setups use the same architecture and hyperparameters as discussed in Section 5.

Our values differ slightly from that cited in Demszky et al. (2020) due to the small differences in architecture and hyperparameters. However, the overall results corroborate that of Demszky et al. (2020) in that models with additional pre-training perform better than the baseline (no additional pre-training) for limited sample sizes. From Figure 4, it is apparent that CARE-BERT and the model built from GoEmotions perform essentially on par in these transfer learning experiments, in spite of the fact that CARE-BERT does not utilize human annotations. It is also worth noting that GoEmotions and the ISEAR dataset address the same task (emotion detection) while CARE-BERT predicts affective response. The comparable performance of CARE-BERT with the GoEmotions models demonstrates the utility of CARE-BERT for other tasks with limited data and the promise of CARE as a means of reliable unsupervised labeling.

6 Conclusion

We described a method for extracting training data for models that predict the affective responses of a post on social media. CARE is an efficient, accurate, and scalable way of collecting unsupervised labels and can be extended to new classes. Using CARE, we created CARE$_{db}$, a large dataset which can be used for affective response detection and other related tasks, as demonstrated by the competitive performance of CARE-BERT to similar BERT-based models in emotion detection. We release the annotations and models in the hopes that this will unlock future research.

In particular, there are two main cases in which CARE can be improved upon: (1) when there does not exist a set of common phrases that are indicative of an affect, and (2) when an indicator maps to multiple affects. In the latter case, there is still partial information that can be gleaned from the labels. In addition to developing methods for the above cases, future work also includes incorporating emojis, negations, and punctuation, extending to new classes, or possibly using embedding similarity rather than exact match for the CARE patterns. Finally, we also plan to investigate the use of CARE for predicting the affective response to images as well as multi-modal content such as memes.

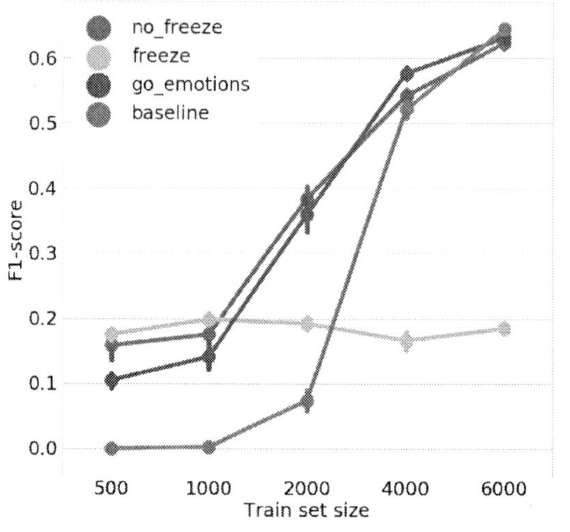

Figure 4: The F1-score of each model using varying training set sizes of the ISEAR dataset. The light blue line refers to using CARE-BERT, but with freezing all parameters except in the last layer. The dark blue is the same but without freezing. Lastly, the purple line refers to the same architecture as CARE-BERT (no freezing) but trained on GoEmotions instead of CARE$_{db}$, and the red line is trained only on the ISEAR dataset using a bert-base-uncased model with the same hyperparameters.

References

Francisca Adoma Acheampong, Chen Wenyu, and Henry Nunoo-Mensah. 2020. Text-based emotion detection: Advances, challenges, and opportunities. *Engineering Reports*, page e12189.

Eugene Agichtein and Luis Gravano. 2000. Snowball: Extracting relations from large plain-text collections. In *Proceedings of the fifth ACM conference on Digital libraries*, pages 85–94.

Sheeraz Akram, Shariq Hussain, Ibrahima Kalil Toure, Shunkun Yang, and Humza Jalal. 2020. Choseamobile: A web-based recommendation system for mobile phone products. *Journal of Internet Technology*, 21(4):1003–1011.

Nourah Alswaidan and Mohamed Menai. 2020. A survey of state-of-the-art approaches for emotion recognition in text. *Knowledge and Information Systems*, 62.

Sergio Angelastro, B Carolis, and Stefano Ferilli. 2019. Predicting user preference in pairwise comparisons based on emotions and gaze. In *International Conference on Industrial, Engineering and Other Applications of Applied Intelligent Systems*, pages 253–261. Springer.

Olga Artemenko, Volodymyr Pasichnyk, Nataliia Kunanets, and Khrystyna Shunevych. 2020. Using sentiment text analysis of user reviews in social media for e-tourism mobile recommender systems. In *COLINS*, pages 259–271.

Dr. Muhammad Asghar, Aurangzeb Khan, Afsana Bibi, Fazal Kundi, and Hussain Ahmad. 2017. Sentence-level emotion detection framework using rule-based classification. *Cognitive Computation*, 9:1–27.

Shenghua Bao, Shengliang Xu, Li Zhang, Rong Yan, Zhong Su, Dingyi Han, and Yong Yu. 2012. Mining social emotions from affective text. *IEEE Transactions on Knowledge and Data Engineering*, 24(9):1658–1670.

Francesco Barbieri, Jose Camacho-Collados, Francesco Ronzano, Luis Espinosa-Anke, Miguel Ballesteros, Valerio Basile, Viviana Patti, and Horacio Saggion. 2018. SemEval 2018 task 2: Multilingual emoji prediction. In *Proceedings of The 12th International Workshop on Semantic Evaluation*, pages 24–33, New Orleans, Louisiana. Association for Computational Linguistics.

Christos Baziotis, Nikos Pelekis, and Christos Doulkeridis. 2017. DataStories at SemEval-2017 task 4: Deep LSTM with attention for message-level and topic-based sentiment analysis. In *Proceedings of the 11th International Workshop on Semantic Evaluation (SemEval-2017)*, pages 747–754, Vancouver, Canada. Association for Computational Linguistics.

Yan-Ying Chen, Tao Chen, Winston H Hsu, Hong-Yuan Mark Liao, and Shih-Fu Chang. 2014. Predicting viewer affective comments based on image content in social media. In *proceedings of international conference on multimedia retrieval*, pages 233–240.

Jérémie Clos, Anil Bandhakavi, Nirmalie Wiratunga, and Guillaume Cabanac. 2017. Predicting emotional reaction in social networks. In *European Conference on Information Retrieval*, pages 527–533. Springer.

Michael AA Cox and Trevor F Cox. 2008. Multidimensional scaling. In *Handbook of data visualization*, pages 315–347. Springer.

Dorottya Demszky, Dana Movshovitz-Attias, Jeongwoo Ko, Alan Cowen, Gaurav Nemade, and Sujith Ravi. 2020. GoEmotions: A dataset of fine-grained emotions. In *Proceedings of the 58th Annual Meeting of the Association for Computational Linguistics*, pages 4040–4054, Online. Association for Computational Linguistics.

Jane Dwivedi-Yu, Yi-Chia Wang, Lijing Qin, Cristian Canton-Ferrer, and Alon Y Halevy. 2022. Affective signals in a social media recommender system. In *Proceedings of the 28th ACM SIGKDD Conference on Knowledge Discovery and Data Mining*, pages 2831–2841.

Andrea Esuli and Fabrizio Sebastiani. 2006. SENTIWORDNET: A publicly available lexical resource for opinion mining. In *Proceedings of the Fifth International Conference on Language Resources and Evaluation (LREC'06)*, Genoa, Italy. European Language Resources Association (ELRA).

Bjarke Felbo, Alan Mislove, Anders Søgaard, Iyad Rahwan, and Sune Lehmann. 2017. Using millions of emoji occurrences to learn any-domain representations for detecting sentiment, emotion and sarcasm. In *Proceedings of the 2017 Conference on Empirical Methods in Natural Language Processing*, pages 1615–1625, Copenhagen, Denmark. Association for Computational Linguistics.

Karën Fort, Gilles Adda, and Kevin Bretonnel Cohen. 2011. Amazon mechanical turk: Gold mine or coal mine? *Computational Linguistics*, pages 413–420.

Lisa Graziani, Stefano Melacci, and Marco Gori. 2019. Jointly learning to detect emotions and predict facebook reactions. In *International Conference on Artificial Neural Networks*, pages 185–197. Springer.

Simeng Gu, Wei Wang, Fushun Wang, and Jason H Huang. 2016. Neuromodulator and emotion biomarker for stress induced mental disorders. *Neural plasticity*, 2016.

Maryam Hasan, Emmanuel Agu, and Elke Rundensteiner. 2014. Using hashtags as labels for supervised learning of emotions in twitter messages. In *ACM SIGKDD workshop on health informatics, New York, USA*.

Marti A. Hearst. 1992. Automatic acquisition of hyponyms from large text corpora. In *COLING 1992 Volume 2: The 15th International Conference on Computational Linguistics*.

Chenyang Huang, Amine Trabelsi, and Osmar Zaïane. 2019a. ANA at SemEval-2019 task 3: Contextual emotion detection in conversations through hierarchical LSTMs and BERT. In *Proceedings of the 13th International Workshop on Semantic Evaluation*, pages 49–53, Minneapolis, Minnesota, USA. Association for Computational Linguistics.

Yen-Hao Huang, Ssu-Rui Lee, Mau-Yun Ma, Yi-Hsin Chen, Ya-Wen Yu, and Yi-Shin Chen. 2019b. Emotionx-idea: Emotion bert–an affectional model for conversation. *arXiv preprint arXiv:1908.06264*.

Rachael E Jack, Oliver GB Garrod, and Philippe G Schyns. 2014. Dynamic facial expressions of emotion transmit an evolving hierarchy of signals over time. *Current biology*, 24(2):187–192.

Rosie Jones, Andrew McCallum, Kamal Nigam, and Ellen Riloff. 1999. Bootstrapping for text learning tasks. In *IJCAI-99 Workshop on Text Mining: Foundations, Techniques and Applications*, volume 1. Citeseer.

Brendan Jou, Subhabrata Bhattacharya, and Shih-Fu Chang. 2014. Predicting viewer perceived emotions in animated gifs. In *Proceedings of the 22nd ACM international conference on Multimedia*, pages 213–216.

Phil Katz, Matt Singleton, and Richard Wicentowski. 2007. SWAT-MP:the SemEval-2007 systems for task 5 and task 14. In *Proceedings of the Fourth International Workshop on Semantic Evaluations (SemEval-2007)*, pages 308–313, Prague, Czech Republic. Association for Computational Linguistics.

Florian Krebs, Bruno Lubascher, Tobias Moers, Pieter Schaap, and Gerasimos Spanakis. 2017. Social emotion mining techniques for facebook posts reaction prediction. *arXiv preprint arXiv:1712.03249*.

Jingsheng Lei, Yanghui Rao, Qing Li, Xiaojun Quan, and Liu Wenyin. 2014. Towards building a social emotion detection system for online news. *Future Generation Computer Systems*, 37:438 – 448. Special Section: Innovative Methods and Algorithms for Advanced Data-Intensive Computing Special Section: Semantics, Intelligent processing and services for big data Special Section: Advances in Data-Intensive Modelling and Simulation Special Section: Hybrid Intelligence for Growing Internet and its Applications.

Kevin Hsin-Yih Lin, Changhua Yang, and Hsin-Hsi Chen. 2008. Emotion classification of online news articles from the reader's perspective. In *2008 IEEE/WIC/ACM International Conference on Web Intelligence and Intelligent Agent Technology*, volume 1, pages 220–226. IEEE.

Chunling Ma, Helmut Prendinger, and Mitsuru Ishizuka. 2005. Emotion estimation and reasoning based on affective textual interaction. In *Proceedings of the First International Conference on Affective Computing and Intelligent Interaction*, ACII'05, page 622–628, Berlin, Heidelberg. Springer-Verlag.

Saif M Mohammad and Svetlana Kiritchenko. 2015. Using hashtags to capture fine emotion categories from tweets. *Computational Intelligence*, 31(2):301–326.

Saif M Mohammad, Svetlana Kiritchenko, and Xiaodan Zhu. 2013. Nrc-canada: Building the state-of-the-art in sentiment analysis of tweets. *arXiv preprint arXiv:1308.6242*.

Gabriele Paolacci and Jesse Chandler. 2014. Inside the turk: Understanding mechanical turk as a participant pool. *Current directions in psychological science*, 23(3):184–188.

Robert Plutchik. 1980. Chapter 1 - a general psychoevolutionary theory of emotion. In Robert Plutchik and Henry Kellerman, editors, *Theories of Emotion*, pages 3 – 33. Academic Press.

Chris Pool and Malvina Nissim. 2016. Distant supervision for emotion detection using Facebook reactions. In *Proceedings of the Workshop on Computational Modeling of People's Opinions, Personality, and Emotions in Social Media (PEOPLES)*, pages 30–39, Osaka, Japan. The COLING 2016 Organizing Committee.

Soujanya Poria, Alexander Gelbukh, Erik Cambria, Amir Hussain, and Guang-Bin Huang. 2014. Emosenticspace: A novel framework for affective common-sense reasoning. *Knowledge-Based Systems*, 69:108 – 123.

Bin Tareaf Raad, Berger Philipp, Hennig Patrick, and Meinel Christoph. 2018. Aseds: Towards automatic social emotion detection system using facebook reactions. In *2018 IEEE 20th International Conference on High Performance Computing and Communications; IEEE 16th International Conference on Smart City; IEEE 4th International Conference on Data Science and Systems (HPCC/SmartCity/DSS)*, pages 860–866. IEEE.

Yanghui Rao, Qing Li, Liu Wenyin, Qingyuan Wu, and Xiaojun Quan. 2014. Affective topic model for social emotion detection. *Neural Networks*, 58:29 – 37. Special Issue on "Affective Neural Networks and Cognitive Learning Systems for Big Data Analysis".

Nils Reimers and Iryna Gurevych. 2019. Sentence-bert: Sentence embeddings using siamese bert-networks. In *Proceedings of the 2019 Conference on Empirical Methods in Natural Language Processing*. Association for Computational Linguistics.

Renata L Rosa, Demsteneso Z Rodriguez, and Graça Bressan. 2015. Music recommendation system based on user's sentiments extracted from social networks. *IEEE Transactions on Consumer Electronics*, 61(3):359–367.

Renata Lopes Rosa, Gisele Maria Schwartz, Wilson Vicente Ruggiero, and Demóstenes Zegarra Rodríguez. 2018. A knowledge-based recommendation system that includes sentiment analysis and deep learning. *IEEE Transactions on Industrial Informatics*, 15(4):2124–2135.

Klaus R. Scherer and Harald Wallbott. 1994. Evidence for universality and cultural variation of differential emotion response patterning. *Journal of personality and social psychology*, 66(2):310.

Valentina Sintsova and Pearl Pu. 2016. Dystemo: Distant supervision method for multi-category emotion recognition in tweets. *ACM Trans. Intell. Syst. Technol.*, 8(1).

Jacopo Staiano and Marco Guerini. 2014. Depeche mood: a lexicon for emotion analysis from crowd annotated news. In *Proceedings of the 52nd Annual Meeting of the Association for Computational Linguistics (Volume 2: Short Papers)*, pages 427–433, Baltimore, Maryland. Association for Computational Linguistics.

Luke Stark and Jesse Hoey. 2021. The ethics of emotion in artificial intelligence systems. In *Proceedings of the 2021 ACM Conference on Fairness, Accountability, and Transparency*, pages 782–793.

Carlo Strapparava and Rada Mihalcea. 2007. Semeval-2007 task 14: Affective text. *Association for Computational Linguistics*, pages 308–313.

Carlo Strapparava and Alessandro Valitutti. 2004. WordNet affect: an affective extension of WordNet. In *Proceedings of the Fourth International Conference on Language Resources and Evaluation (LREC'04)*, Lisbon, Portugal. European Language Resources Association (ELRA).

Jared Suttles and Nancy Ide. 2013. Distant supervision for emotion classification with discrete binary values. In *International Conference on Intelligent Text Processing and Computational Linguistics*, pages 121–136. Springer.

Jianhua Tao. 2004. Context based emotion detection from text input. In *Eighth International Conference on Spoken Language Processing*.

Luis Tapia. *Clown on black background*. Shutterstock.

Marko Tkalčič, Nima Maleki, Matevž Pesek, Mehdi Elahi, Francesco Ricci, and Matija Marolt. 2017. A research tool for user preferences elicitation with facial expressions. In *Proceedings of the eleventh acm conference on recommender systems*, pages 353–354.

Marko Tkalčič, Nima Maleki, Matevž Pesek, Mehdi Elahi, Francesco Ricci, and Matija Marolt. 2019. Prediction of music pairwise preferences from facial expressions. In *Proceedings of the 24th International Conference on Intelligent User Interfaces*, pages 150–159.

Kaiyu Wang, Yanmeng Guo, Fei Wang, and Zuoren Wang. 2011. Drosophila trpa channel painless inhibits male–male courtship behavior through modulating olfactory sensation. *PLoS One*, 6(11):e25890.

Wenbo Wang, Lu Chen, Krishnaprasad Thirunarayan, and Amit P Sheth. 2012. Harnessing twitter "big data" for automatic emotion identification. In *2012 International Conference on Privacy, Security, Risk and Trust and 2012 International Confernece on Social Computing*, pages 587–592. IEEE.

Thomas Wolf, Lysandre Debut, Victor Sanh, Julien Chaumond, Clement Delangue, Anthony Moi, Pierric Cistac, Tim Rault, Remi Louf, Morgan Funtowicz, Joe Davison, Sam Shleifer, Patrick von Platen, Clara Ma, Yacine Jernite, Julien Plu, Canwen Xu, Teven Le Scao, Sylvain Gugger, Mariama Drame, Quentin Lhoest, and Alexander Rush. 2020. Transformers: State-of-the-art natural language processing. In *Proceedings of the 2020 Conference on Empirical Methods in Natural Language Processing: System Demonstrations*, pages 38–45, Online. Association for Computational Linguistics.

Zheng Zheng, Simeng Gu, Yu Lei, Shanshan Lu, Wei Wang, Yang Li, and Fushun Wang. 2016. Safety needs mediate stressful events induced mental disorders. *Neural plasticity*, 2016.

A Broader Impact

Any work that touches upon emotion recognition or recognizing affective response needs to ensure that it is sensitive to the various ways of expressing affect in different cultures and individuals. Clearly, applying the ideas described in this paper in a production setting would have to first test for cultural biases. To make "broad assumptions about emotional universalism [would be] not just unwise, but actively deleterious" to the general community (Stark and Hoey, 2021). We also note that emotion recognition methods belong to a taxonomy of conceptual models for emotion (such as that of Stark and Hoey (2021) and these "paradigms for human emotions [...] should [not] be taken naively ground truth."

Before being put in production, the method would also need to be re-evaluated when applied to a new domain to ensure reliable performance in order to prevent unintended consequences. Additionally, our work in detecting affective response is intended for understanding content, not the emotional state of individuals. This work is intended to identify or recommend content, which aligns with the user's preferences. This work should not be used for ill-intended purposes such as purposefully recommending particular content to manipulate a user's perception or preferences.

B Details on expanding CARE

n-gram	frequency	class
adorable	9000	Adoring
gorgeous	8422	Adoring
fantastic	7796	Approving
interesting	5742	Amused
sorry for your	5202	Saddened
brilliant	4205	Approving
fake	2568	Angered
sorry to hear	2323	Saddened
why i hate	1125	Angered
i feel like	293	pattern
you are a	207	pattern
this is the	173	pattern
this made me	110	pattern
he is so	102	pattern

Table B1: Examples of n-grams resulting from `GetNgrams` in Algorithm 1 and steps B1 and B2 of Figure 1. The n-grams above the middle line are added to the lexicon under the specific class listed, while the n-grams below are used for further expansion of CARE patterns after translating to reg-ex format manually.

Algorithm 1 on page 18 presents pseudo-code for the process of labeling posts and expanding CARE patterns and the CARE lexicon. Table B1 presents example results from the expansion process.

C Annotation details

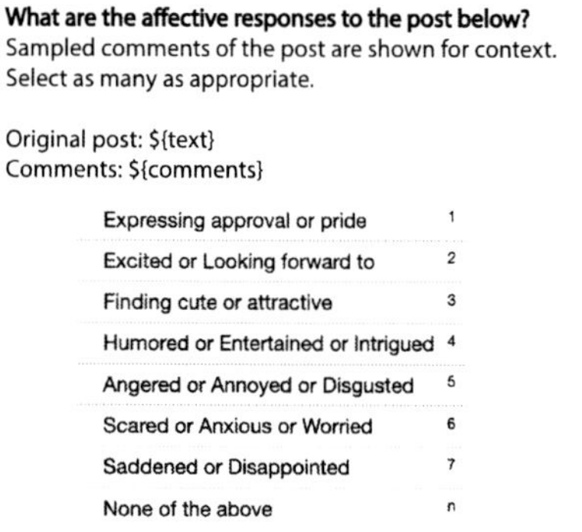

Figure C1: Interface for crowdsourcing process using Amazon Mechanical Turk. Three distinct annotators were used to annotate each post. Annotators were told an affective response is an emotion or cognitive response to the post and the definitions and examples in Table 1 were shown to them.

AR	% w/ support	Avg support	Fleiss' kappa
Adoring	99.2	2.8	0.78
Amused	93.2	2.1	0.43
Approving	98.8	2.8	0.51
Excited	83.6	2.1	0.58
Angered	99.4	2.8	0.59
Saddened	99.6	2.9	0.61
Scared	98.8	2.6	0.64
Average	**96.1**	**2.6**	**0.59**

Table C2: The percent of CARE-labeled examples (maximum of 100) with agreement from at least one labeler by class and of those examples, the average number of annotator agreement (maximum of 3). The third column shows the Fleiss' kappa, which was computed for class a based on the presence and absence of label a by each annotator for a given post. The bottom row is the average over all classes.

The annotators were paid a competitive wage in order to temper the effects of the ethical and sampling limitations and concerns as described in Fort et al. (2011) and Paolacci and Chandler (2014). Figure C1 shows the interface used for crowdsourcing human annotations for evaluating CARE patterns. To better understand annotation results for each class, we present Table C2, which shows annotator agreement statistics broken down by class.

We also computed Fleiss' kappa for each class, where a value between 0.41-0.60 is generally considered moderate agreement and a value between 0.61-0.80 is substantial agreement. As can be seen, classes such as *adoring* have high average annotator support and Fleiss' kappa while others like *amused* have low average annotator support and Fleiss' kappa, an observation that aligns with the findings in Section 4.2.

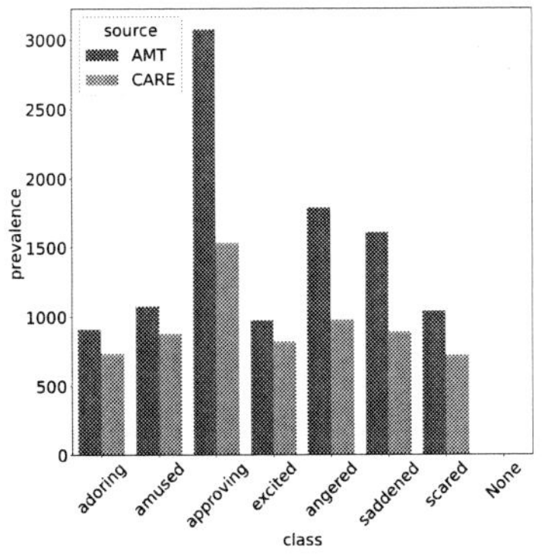

Figure C2: Prevalence of class labels according to annotations from AMT on which at least two annotators agree upon (blue) and according to CARE (orange). The prevalence of *approving* was much higher from AMT, likely due to a large perceived overlap in the definitions of *approving* and other classes such *excited.*

D Are affective response and publisher affect the same?

The GoEmotions dataset and classifier target the publisher affect (of comments), whereas CARE-BERT and CARE target the affective response (of posts). In an effort to study the correlation between affective response and publisher affect, we compare the following sets of labels: 1) human annotations of GoEmotion and the predicted affective responses using CARE-BERT applied to GoEmotions and 2) CARE labels for posts in CARE$_{db}$ and the predicted publisher affects using the GoEmotions classifier applied to CARE$_{db}$. Specifically, for every annotated label (i.e., not from a classifier) we count the percentage of the time where there is intersection with the set of predicted labels (i.e., from a classifier).

The results of these experiments are shown in Table D3, broken down according to the class of the annotated label. Overall, the percentage of affective response and publisher affect label agreement (44%) is moderate but seems to indicate that the affective response detection and emotion detection are not necessarily the same problem, in particular for *scared* and *approving*. The classes *approving*, *excited*, and *angered* have a large variance between the two datasets, where the first (Table D3, second column) uses comments and the second (Table D3, third column) uses posts. This could be due to the classification errors (either by GoEmotions or by CARE-BERT) or due to the type of the text (comment or post). More research and data collection is needed to understand the relationship between affective response and publisher affect.

AR	GoEmotions	CARE$_{db}$	Average
Amused	63	54	59
Approving	8	47	28
Excited	52	24	38
Angered	4	74	39
Saddened	60	62	61
Scared	44	34	39
Average	**39**	**49**	**44**

Table D3: Rate of intersection between affective response and publisher affect labels. The first column denotes the class. The second column denotes the percent of the time an annotated label in GoEmotions exists in the set of predicted labels by CARE-BERT when applied to the GoEmotions dataset. The third column denotes the percent of the time an annotated label in CARE-BERT exists in the set of predicted labels by the GoEmotions classifier when applied to CARE$_{db}$. The last column is the row-wise average.

E Using CARE patterns/lexicon to predict publisher affect in GoEmotions

The GoEmotions dataset (Demszky et al., 2020) is a collection of 58k Reddit comments labeled according to the publisher affect from a taxonomy of 28 emotions. There exists a natural mapping from 6 of our classes to those of GoEmotions (the exception being *adoring*) based on the definitions alone. Hence, applying CARE patterns/lexicon to the GoEmotions dataset presents another way of validating the quality of steps 1 and 2 of CARE. The number of examples in GoEmotions with labels belonging to these 6 classes was 21.0k and the number of comments that were labeled by CARE patterns/lexicon was 1259. Table 3 compares the human annotations in the GoEmotions dataset with the labels that CARE patterns/lexicon assigned to the comments and shows that they have a high degree of agreement.

While the low recall is certainly a limitation of CARE patterns and lexicon when applied to a specific small dataset, we emphasize that the primary intention of CARE patterns is to generate a labeled dataset in an unsupervised manner, so one can start training classifiers for that affective response. Given the abundance of freely available unlabeled data (e.g., on Reddit, Twitter), recall is not a problem in practice. In the next section and in Section 4.3, however, we discuss how existing emotion classifiers, such as the GoEmotions classifier (Demszky et al., 2020) can also be leveraged in the CARE method.

F CARE and CARE^G evaluation details

CARE^G refers to the CARE method, where steps 1 and 2 of Figure 1 use the GoEmotions classifier instead of CARE patterns. To evaluate how CARE and CARE^G compares, we use the same human-labeled dataset described in Section 4.1 and applied the GoEmotions classifier to all the comments belonging to these posts (72k comments). We then mapped the predicted GoEmotion labels to CARE pattern labels using the mapping in Table 3. GoEmotion and CARE labels not in the mapping are excluded from this analysis.

Threshold	Any CARE^G	All CARE^G	Other
$t = 1$	95	34	25
$t = 2$	91	61	42
$t = 3$	87	71	51
$t = 4$	81	73	57
$t = 5$	73	67	62
$t = 6$	58	56	70
$t = 7$	47	45	76
$t = 8$	38	37	81
$t = 9$	30	29	84
$t = 10$	24	23	88
max	89	89	60
CARE	93	89	54
ensemble	94	83	49

Table F4: The rate of intersection between labels agreed upon by at least two annotators and the labels proposed by CARE^G. The first column indicates the threshold t used in CARE^G. Using annotations agreed upon by at least two annotators, the rest of the columns show the rate of agreement with at least one predicted label, all predicted labels, and any human-annotated label that was not predicted. The row labeled 'max' refers to choosing the comment-level label with the highest frequency for each post. For context, the results for CARE using $t = 5$ are shown in the penultimate row. The last row presents results from combining the CARE pattern labels and the GoEmotion labels using $t = 4$.

The same metrics for ≥ 2 annotator agreement in Table 2 are shown in Table F4 for multiple thresholds and for all classes, excluding *adoring*. CARE labels consistently demonstrate higher agreement with human annotations than those of CARE^G. The last row of Table F4 shows results for an ensembling approach where steps 1 and 2 use labels from both CARE patterns in addition to the labels from the GoEmotions classifier, where the former uses $t = 5$ and the latter uses $t = 4$ in step 3 (optimal values for each approach, respectively). This ensembling approach does reasonably well and can be used to include classes in the GoEmotions taxonomy that do not exist in the taxonomy of Table 1. Given other emotion classifiers, one could potentially include those as well.

G Multi-dimensional scaling pairwise plots

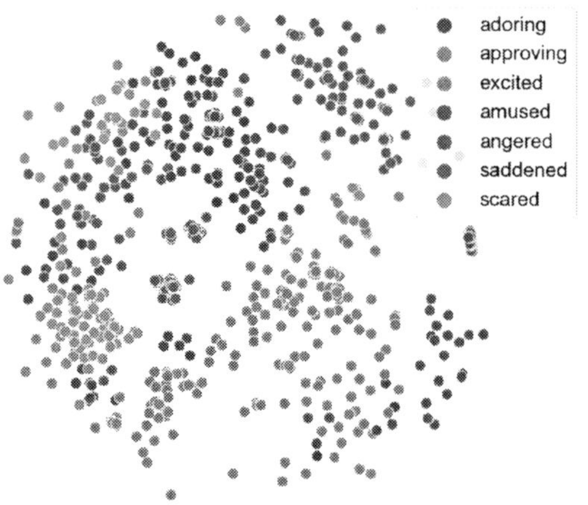

Figure G3: The two-dimensional projection (using MDS) of sentence embeddings of comments suggests that the CARE-based predictions correspond to similarity in the embedding space. Colors correspond to the labels given by CARE labeling, which were not given to the embedding model or the MDS.

We visualize the degree of overlap between the sentence embeddings (using Sentence-Bert (Reimers and Gurevych, 2019)) of 100 comments in CARE$_{db}$ for each class. We then use multi-dimensional scaling or MDS (Cox and Cox, 2008) to map the embeddings to the same two-dimensional space using euclidean distance as the similarity metric, as shown in Figure G3 and Figure G5. Note that the MDS process does not use the class labels. As can be seen, there is substantial overlap between *amused* and other classes, as well as between *excited* and *approving*. Figure G4 shows the Spearman correlation between each class and a hierarchical clustering using the AMT-annotated dataset, and corroborates that *approving* and *excited* indeed do have the highest degree of correlation. Given that the average number of human annotations per post was 1.8 (Section 4.1), it is likely that a portion of this overlap can be attributed to the multi-label nature of the problem as well as the moderate correlation between certain classes such as *excited* and *approving* (Figure G4). See Figure G5 for plots of multi-dimensional scaling for every pair of classes, as referenced in Section 4.2.

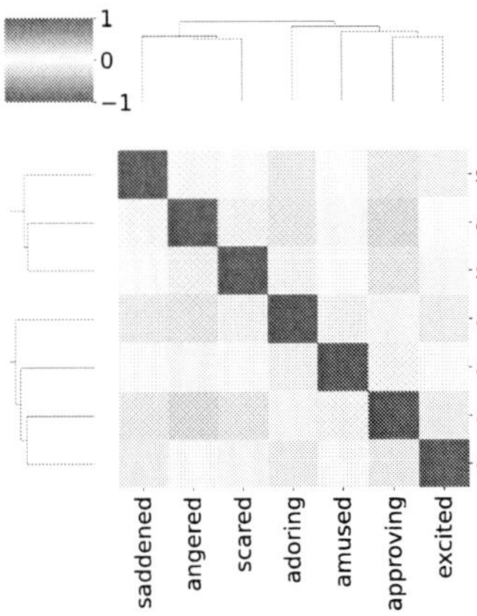

Figure G4: Pairwise Spearman correlation between each pair of classes, computed using the degree of annotator support for each class given a post. The dendrogram represents a hierarchical clustering of the data, correctly capturing the distinction between positive and negative classes.

H Pattern match analysis

To investigate why higher thresholds would be needed for certain classes, we analyze the CARE patterns and lexicon at the class level.

Let us define a match as a tuple containing the pattern name and the word or phrase which maps the comment to an affect according to the CARE lexicon. We could also consider exaggerators in our analysis, but here we assume a negligible effect on differentiating reliability. We previously assumed that each instantiated match should have the same weight of 1, but this may not be appropriate, considering that some patterns or words may be more reliable.

As can be seen in Figure H6, there are some cases in which the keyword in general seems to have a high false positive rate (e.g., happy) and in other cases it appears the erroneous combination of a particular pattern and keyword can lead to high false positive rates. For example, while the match '(so very, funny)' has a low false positive rate of 0.2, '(I, funny)' has a much higher false positive rate of 0.57, which intuitively makes since 'I'm funny' does not indicate being amused. We also investigated whether individual patterns are prone to higher false positive rates, which does not seem to be the case. For future iterations of CARE, one could also use the true positive rate as the weight of a match to obtain a weighted sum when aggregating over comments to label a post.

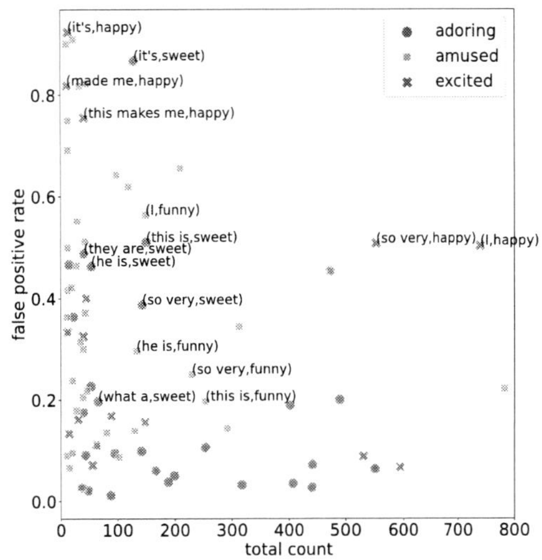

Figure H6: Scatter plot of the total frequency of a match versus its false positive rate. Ground truth labels used here are those from AMT and agreed upon by at least 2 annotators. For clarity, a match is shown only if its total count was 10 or more and if it belongs to one of the three classes (*adoring*, *amused*, and *excited*). Only those which contain the keywords 'sweet' (*adoring*), 'funny' (*amused*), and 'happy' (*excited*) are labeled.

I Modeling details

AR	Precision	Recall	F1
Positive	0.95	0.95	0.94
Negative	0.77	0.77	0.78
micro-avg	**0.89**	**0.91**	**0.90**
macro-avg	**0.86**	**0.86**	**0.86**
stdev	**0.10**	**0.13**	**0.11**

Table I5: Accuracy of CARE-BERT for the two-class case: POSITIVE versus NEGATIVE. Note that amused, excited, adoring, and approving were mapped to positive and angered, saddened, and scared were mapped to negative.

We began with the hyper-parameter settings in Demszky et al. (2020) and explored other hyper-parameter settings (batch sizes [16, 32, 64], max length [64, 256, 512], drop out rate [0.3, 0.5, 0.7], epochs [2-10]) but found minimal improvements in the F1-score, as computed by the `scikit-learn` package in python. Running this on two Tesla P100-SXM2-16GB GPUs took roughly 19 hours. We also experimented with higher thresholds for the parameter t (see Section 3.2) but saw marginal improvements, if any.

We developed two versions of CARE-BERT: one using the classes in Table 1, and a simpler one using only the classes POSITIVE, and NEGATIVE. The first four rows in Table 1 are considered positive while the last three are negative, the results of which are featured in Table I5. Naturally, the two-class model that blurs the differences between classes with the same valence has higher results.

J Modeling Analysis

	Human	CARE	CARE-BERT
Human	1.0	0.55	0.51
CARE	0.89	1.0	0.72
CARE-BERT	0.72	0.62	1.0

Table J6: Percentage of agreement between annotation schemes. Each entry corresponds to the percentage of all labels the annotation scheme along the row agrees with the annotation scheme along the column.

Algorithm 1: Algorithm for producing candidates for new CARE patterns and indicators in the CARE lexicon. The algorithm uses three hyperparameters t (the minimum number of comments to label a post), $f\_lexicon$ (the minimum frequency of a n-gram to be added to the lexicon), and $f\_pattern$ (the minimum frequency of an n-gram to be a candidate pattern) which was set to 5, 1000, and 100, respectively. The resulting list of candidate patterns needs to be manually converted into a regular expression matching the structure outlined in Section 3.1.

```
Data: C: set of comments, P: set of corresponding posts, L: dictionary of keywords to class
      (CARE lexicon), D: list of non-class-specific regular expressions (CARE patterns)
lexicon_candidates ← [], pattern_candidates ← []
labeled_posts ← LabelPosts (C, P, L, D), ngrams ← GetNgrams (labeled_posts, C)
for a in all classes do
    // Add an ngram as a lexicon candidate if it is exclusively in high frequency with class a
    for ngram in ngrams[a] do
        if frequency of ngram in ngrams[a] ≥ f_lexicon then
            for b in all classes where b ≠ a do
                if ngram in ngrams[b] and frequency of ngram in ngrams[b] ≥ f_lexicon then
                    Break and continue to new n-gram
            Append ngram to lexicon_candidates, if not added already
    // Add an ngram as a pattern candidate if in high enough frequency and present in another class
    for ngram in ngrams[a] do
        if total freq. of ngram in ngrams ≥ f_pattern and ngram in ngrams[b] for b ≠ a then
            Append ngram to pattern_candidates, if not added already
Result: lexicon_candidates, pattern_candidates

Function LabelPosts (C, P, L, D):
    labeled_comments ← {}, labeled_posts ← {}
    // For each comment, apply reg-ex and map indicator to affect using the lexicon
    for c in C do
        if indicator is non-empty after reg-ex matching and in lexicon then
            Append c to labeled_comments[L[indicator]]
    // For each post, aggregate comment labels to label post
    for p in P do
        for a in all classes do
            if number of comments belonging to post p and labeled as class a ≥ t then
                Append p to labeled_posts[a]
    return labeled_posts

Function GetNgrams (labeled_posts, C):
    ngrams ← {}
    for a in all classes do
        // Get the n-grams of all comments belonging to a post labeled as a
        for p in labeled_posts[a] do
            for c in C belonging to post p do
                Add 1-grams, 2-grams, and 3-grams of comment c to ngrams[a]
    return ngrams
```

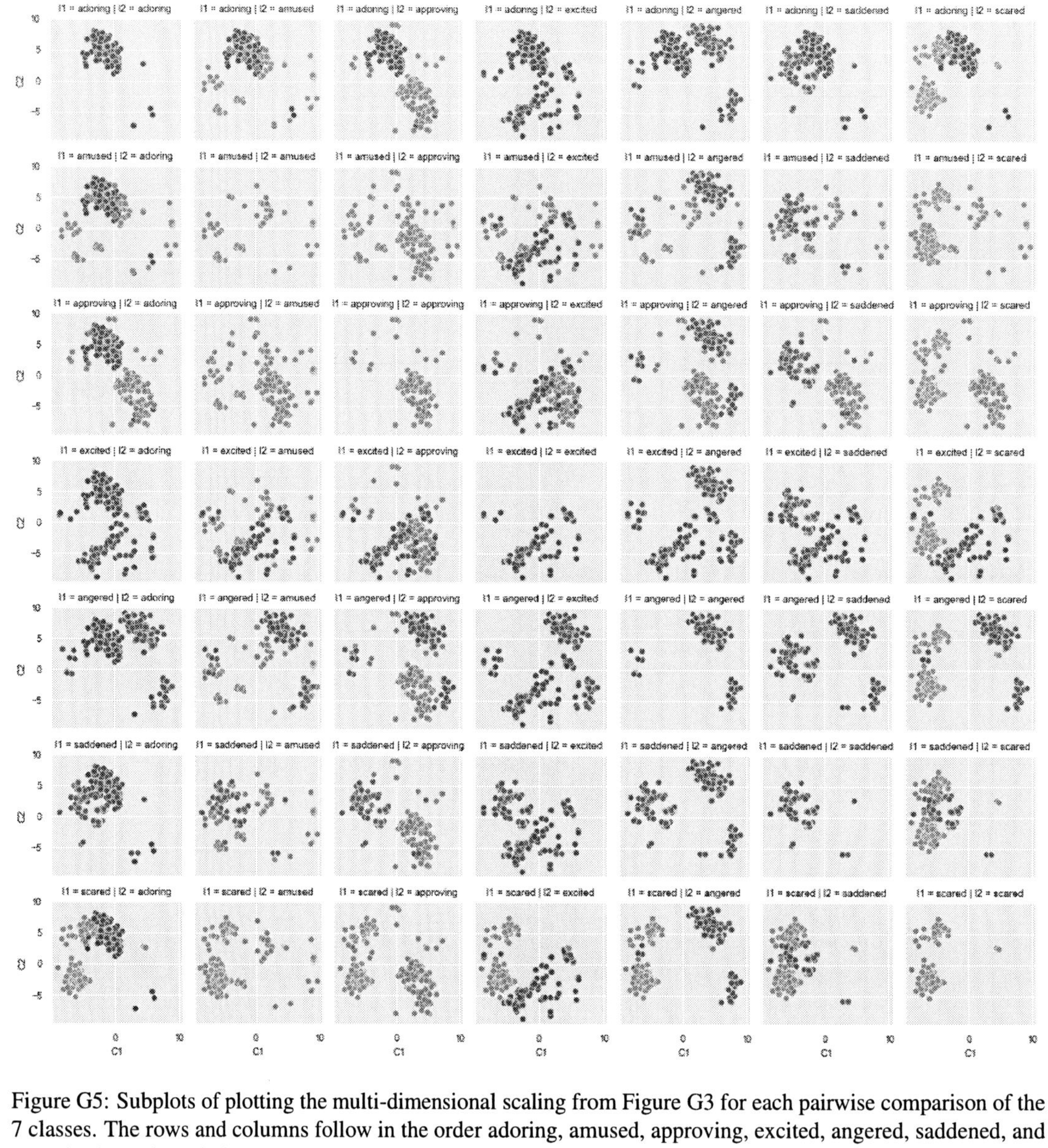

Figure G5: Subplots of plotting the multi-dimensional scaling from Figure G3 for each pairwise comparison of the 7 classes. The rows and columns follow in the order adoring, amused, approving, excited, angered, saddened, and scared. The entire grid is symmetric for ease of exploration.

Table J7: Examples of posts labeled according to human annotators, CARE, and CARE-BERT. The first three show examples where all three labeling schemes agree, the second three demonstrates examples where external knowledge may be needed, and the last three shows examples where the trajectory of the discussion may be more unpredictable. **Note:** CARE-BERT **does not get access to the comments.**

Post	**Comments**	**Human**	**CARE**	CARE-BERT
Anxiety: I just want to say that I'm trying...I may not be successful, but I'm trying.	Dude, very proud of you my friend. Don't give up.; Good for you. I'm proud of you for trying. Keep at it.; Happy for you.	approving	approving	approving
AskReddit: What's something you've been wanting to get off your chest but are too scared to?	I'm scared to end up alone and unloved.; I'm so scared to graduate college.; I just got engaged, but I'm not actually happy about it.	saddened; scared	saddened; scared	saddened; scared
AskReddit: What movie really emotionally impacted you?	A Walk to Remember. So sad.; It's a Wonderful Life. Makes me so teary-eyed.; Dead Ringer. Made me so depressed.	saddened; approving	saddened; approving	saddened; approving
Hockey: The Vancouver Canucks have landed a spot in the playoffs!	This is excellent news!; Holy shit, this is exciting!; Hell yeah, fuck the kings!	angered; excited; approving	excited	excited
Panthers: Divisional Playoffs - Panthers vs. 49ers - Discussion Thread Let's do this!	I'M SO MAD; I'm freakin' scared, man.; Screw the whiners! They're going to regret the day they stepped on our turf!	angered; approving	angered	angered; excited
InfertilityBabies: Going to be a line jumper! The doctor says my BP isn't stellar so I am in L and amp;D until Monday morning (37 weeks) induction!	Good luck! So exciting!; Congrats! You're about to be a mom! I'm very excited for you!!!; Super exciting!	excited	excited	approving
AskReddit: What is your favorite TV series ever?	Arrow. It's amazing!; Walking Dead. So excited for the new season!; Teen Titans. It's the best show ever.	approving; excited	approving	approving; amused
Hearthstone: Who is this LIRIK guy, and why does he have 50K subscribers?	This is hilarious; What an idiot. Do more research before posting; He's an adorable guy.	amused; angered; adoring	amused	excited
AskReddit: Imagine that the last thing you ate has been made illegal. What would that be?	Pizza, and now I'm super sad.; Frozen lasagna. Good riddance.; French onion dip. I love that stuff.	approving; saddened	saddened	approving

A Fine-grained Interpretability Evaluation Benchmark for Neural NLP

Lijie Wang, Yaozong Shen, Shuyuan Peng, Shuai Zhang, Xinyan Xiao,
Hao Liu, Hongxuan Tang, Ying Chen, Hua Wu, Haifeng Wang
Baidu Inc, Beijing, China
{wanglijie,shenyaozong@baidu.com}

Abstract

While there is increasing concern about the interpretability of neural models, the evaluation of interpretability remains an open problem, due to the lack of proper evaluation datasets and metrics. In this paper, we present a novel benchmark to evaluate the interpretability of both neural models and saliency methods. This benchmark covers three representative NLP tasks: sentiment analysis, textual similarity and reading comprehension, each provided with both English and Chinese annotated data. In order to precisely evaluate the interpretability, we provide token-level rationales that are carefully annotated to be sufficient, compact and comprehensive. We also design a new metric, i.e., the consistency between the rationales before and after perturbations, to uniformly evaluate the interpretability on different types of tasks. Based on this benchmark, we conduct experiments on three typical models with three saliency methods, and unveil their strengths and weakness in terms of interpretability. We will release this benchmark[1] and hope it can facilitate the research in building trustworthy systems.

1 Introduction

In the last decade, deep learning (DL) has been rapidly developed and has greatly improved various artificial intelligence tasks in terms of accuracy (Deng and Yu, 2014; Litjens et al., 2017; Pouyanfar et al., 2018). However, as DL models are black-box systems, their inner decision processes are opaque to users. This lack of transparency makes them untrustworthy and hard to be applied in decision-making applications in fields such as health, commerce and law (Fort and Couillault, 2016). Consequently, there is a growing interest in explaining the predictions of DL models (Simonyan et al., 2014; Ribeiro et al., 2016; Alzantot et al., 2018; Bastings et al., 2019; Jiang et al., 2021). Accordingly, many

Sentiment Analysis (SA)
Instance^{o}: although it bangs a very cliched drum at times, this crowd-pleaser's fresh dialogue, energetic music, and good-natured spunk are often infectious. **Sentiment label**: positive
Instance^{p}: although it bangs a very cliched drum at times, this crowd-pleaser's novel dialogue, vigorous music, and good-natured spunk are often infectious. **Sentiment label**: positive
Semantic Textual Similarity (STS)
Instance1^{o}: Is there a reason why we should travel alone? **Instance2^{o}**: What are some reasons to travel alone? **Similarity**: same
Instance1^{p}: Is there any reason why we travel alone? **Instance2^{p}**: List some reasons to travel alone? **Similarity**: same
Machine Reading Comprehensive (MRC)
Question: What part of France were the Normans located? **Article^{o}**: ...and customs to synthesize a unique "Norman" culture in the north of France. ... **Answer**: north
Question: Where in France were the Normans located? **Article^{p}**: ...and customs to synthesize a unique "Norman" culture in the north of France. ... **Answer**: north

Table 1: Examples from our benchmark. In each instance, colored tokens are rationales, and tokens in the same color constitute an independent rationale set. Each perturbed example (^{p}) is created on an original example (^{o}), where underlined tokens in the original example have been altered. The consistency of rationales under perturbations is used to evaluate interpretability.

evaluation datasets are constructed and the corresponding metrics are designed to evaluate related works (DeYoung et al., 2020; Jacovi and Goldberg, 2020).

In order to accurately evaluate model interpretability[2] with human-annotated rationales[3] (i.e., evidence that supports the model prediction), many researchers successively propose the properties that a rationale should satisfy, e.g., sufficiency, compact-

[1]https://www.luge.ai/#/luge/task/taskDetail?taskId=15

[2]Despite fine-grained distinctions between "interpretability" and "explainability", we use them interchangeably.

[3]In this paper, we focus on highlight-based rationales, which consist of input elements, such as words and sentences, that play a decisive role in the model prediction.

Proceedings of the 26th Conference on Computational Natural Language Learning (CoNLL), pages 70 - 84
December 7-8, 2022 ©2022 Association for Computational Linguistics

ness and comprehensiveness (see Section 3.3 for their specific definitions) (Kass et al., 1988; Fischer et al., 1990; Lei et al., 2016; Yu et al., 2019). However, the existing datasets are designed for different research aims with different metrics, and their rationales do not satisfy all properties needed, as shown in Table 2, which makes it difficult to track and facilitate the research progress of interpretability. In addition, all existing datasets are in English.

Meanwhile, many studies focus on designing guidelines and metrics for interpretability evaluation, where plausibility and faithfulness are proposed to measure interpretability from different perspectives (Herman, 2017; Alvarez Melis and Jaakkola, 2018; Yang et al., 2019; Wiegreffe and Pinter, 2019; Jacovi and Goldberg, 2020). Plausibility measures how well the rationales provided by models align with human-annotated rationales. With different annotation granularities, token-level and span-level F1-scores are proposed to measure plausibility (DeYoung et al., 2020; Mathew et al., 2021). Faithfulness measures to what extent the provided rationales influence the corresponding predictions. Some studies (Yu et al., 2019; DeYoung et al., 2020) propose to compare the model's prediction on the full input to its prediction on input masked according to the rationale and its complement (i.e., non-rationale). However, it is difficult to apply this evaluation method to non-classification tasks, such as machine reading comprehension. Furthermore, the model prediction on the non-rationale has gone beyond the standard output scope, e.g., the prediction label on the non-rationale should be neither positive nor negative in the sentiment classification task. Thus the metric provided by this method can not generally and may not precisely evaluate the interpretability.

In order to address the above problems, we release a new interpretability evaluation benchmark which provides fine-grained rationales for three tasks and a new evaluation metric for interpretability. Our contributions include:

- Our benchmark contains three representative tasks in both English and Chinese, i.e., sentiment analysis, semantic textual similarity and machine reading comprehension. Importantly, all annotated rationales meet the requirements of sufficiency, compactness and comprehensiveness by being organized in the set form.
- To precisely and uniformly evaluate the interpretability of all tasks, we propose a new evaluation metric, i.e., the consistency between the rationales provided on examples before and after perturbation. The perturbations are crafted in a way that will not change the model decision mechanism. This metric measures model fidelity under perturbations and could help to find the relationship between interpretability and other metrics, such as robustness.
- We give an in-depth analysis based on three typical models with three popular saliency methods, as well as a comparison between our proposed metrics and the existing metrics. The results show that our benchmark can be used to evaluate the interpretability of DL models and saliency methods. Meanwhile, the results strongly indicate that the research on interpretability of NLP models has much further to go, and we hope our benchmark will do its bit along the way.

2 Related Work

As our work provides a new interpretability evaluation benchmark with human-annotated rationales, in this section, we mainly introduce saliency methods for the rationale extraction, interpretability evaluation datasets and metrics.

Saliency Methods In the post-hoc interpretation research field, saliency methods are widely used to interpret model decisions by assigning a distribution of importance scores over the input tokens to represent their impacts on model predictions (Simonyan et al., 2014; Ribeiro et al., 2016; Murdoch et al., 2018). They are mainly divided into four categories: gradient-based, attention-based, erasure-based and linear-based. In gradient-based methods, the magnitudes of the gradients serve as token importance scores (Simonyan et al., 2014; Smilkov et al., 2017; Sundararajan et al., 2017). Attention-based methods use attention weights as token importance scores (Jain and Wallace, 2019; Wiegreffe and Pinter, 2019). In erasure-based methods, the token importance score is measured by the change of output when the token is removed (Li et al., 2016; Feng et al., 2018). Linear-based methods use a simple and explainable linear model to approximate the evaluated model behavior locally and use the learned token weights as importance scores (Ribeiro et al., 2016; Alvarez-Melis and Jaakkola, 2017). These methods have their own advantages and limitations from aspects of computational efficiency, interpretability performance and so on (Nie

Datasets	Granularity	Properties		
		Sufficiency	Compactness	Comprehensiveness
e-SNLI* (Camburu et al., 2018)	word	✗	✓	✗
HUMMINGBIRD (Hayati et al., 2021)	word	✓−	✗	–
HateXplain (Mathew et al., 2021)	word	✓−	–	✓
Movie Reviews* (Zaidan and Eisner, 2008)	snippet	✓	✗	✗
CoS-E* (Rajani et al., 2019)	snippet	✓−	✗	✓
Evidence Inference* (Lehman et al., 2019)	snippet	✓	✗	✗
BoolQ* (DeYoung et al., 2020)	snippet	✓	✗	✓
WikiQA (Yang et al., 2015)	sentence	✓	✗	–
MultiRC* (Khashabi et al., 2018)	sentence	✓	✗	✓
HotpotQA (Yang et al., 2018)	sentence	✓	✗	✓
FEVER* (Thorne et al., 2018)	sentence	✓	✗	–
SciFact (Wadden et al., 2020)	sentence	✓	✗	–
Ours	word	✓	✓	✓

Table 2: Statistics of existing datasets with highlight-based rationales. The datasets marked with * are collected and modified by ERASER (DeYoung et al., 2020). ERASER manually reviews and constructs snippet-level rationales to make them satisfy sufficiency and comprehensiveness. ✓− represents the rationale contains key words, but does not contain enough information for the prediction. The value '-' represents the property is not mentioned in the paper.

et al., 2018; Jain and Wallace, 2019; De Cao et al., 2020; Sixt et al., 2020).

Interpretability Datasets Many datasets with human-annotated rationales have been published for interpretability evaluation, e.g., highlight-based rationales (DeYoung et al., 2020; Mathew et al., 2021), free-text rationales (Camburu et al., 2018; Rajani et al., 2019) and structured rationales (Ye et al., 2020; Geva et al., 2021). To create high-quality highlight-based rationales, many studies give their views on the properties that a rationale should satisfy. Kass et al. (1988) propose that a rationale should be understood by humans. Lei et al. (2016) point that a rationale should be compact and sufficient, i.e., it is short and contains enough information for a prediction. Yu et al. (2019) introduce comprehensiveness as a criterion, requiring all rationales to be selected, not just a sufficient set. Although the above criteria have been proposed for highlight rationales, the existing datasets in Table 2 are built with part of them, as they are conducted on different tasks with individual aims.

Interpretability Metrics For highlight-based rationales, plausibility and faithfulness are often used to measure interpretability from the aspects of human cognition and model fidelity (Arras et al., 2017; Mohseni et al., 2018; Weerts et al., 2019). DeYoung et al. (2020) propose to use IOU (Intersection-Over-Union) F1-score and AUPRC (Area Under the Precision-Recall curve) score to measure plausibility of snippet-level rationales. Mathew et al. (2021) use token F1-score to evaluate plausibility of token-level rationales. Jacovi and Goldberg (2020) provide concrete guidelines for the definition and evaluation of faithfulness. DeYoung et al. (2020) propose to evaluate faithfulness from the perspectives of sufficiency and comprehensiveness of rationales (Equation 4). However, this evaluation manner is only applicable to classification tasks and brings uncontrollable factors to interpretability evaluation. Thus Yin et al. (2022) propose sensitivity and stability as complementary metrics for faithfulness. Ding and Koehn (2021) evaluate faithfulness of saliency methods on natural language models by measuring how consistent the rationales are regarding perturbations.

In this work, we provide a new interpretability evaluation benchmark, containing fine-grained annotated rationales, a new evaluation metric and the corresponding perturbed examples.

3 Evaluation Data Construction

As illustrated in Figure 1, the construction of our datasets mainly consists of three steps: 1) data collection for each task; 2) perturbed data construction; 3) iterative rationale annotation and checking. We first introduce the annotation process, including the annotation criteria for perturbations and rationales. Then we describe our data statistics. In addition, we show other annotation details in Appendix A.

3.1 Data Collection

In order to provide a general and unified interpretability evaluation benchmark, we construct

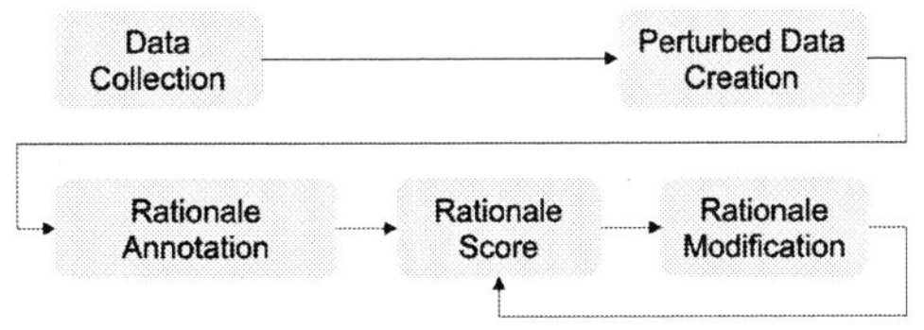

Figure 1: The construction workflow of our datasets.

evaluation datasets for three representative tasks, i.e., sentiment analysis, semantic textual similarity, and machine reading comprehension. Meanwhile, we create both English and Chinese evaluation datasets for each task.

Sentiment Analysis (SA), a single-sentence classification task, aims to predict a sentiment label for the given instance. For English, we randomly select 1,500 instances from Stanford Sentiment Treebank (SST) (Socher et al., 2013) dev/test sets, and 400 instances from Movie Reviews (Zaidan and Eisner, 2008) test set. For Chinese, we randomly sample 60,000 instances from the logs of an open SA API[4] with the permission of users. The annotators select instances for annotation (see Appendix A for details) and label a sentiment polarity for each unlabeled instance. Then 2,000 labeled instances are chosen for building evaluation set.

Semantic Textual Similarity (STS), a sentence-pair similarity task, is to predict the similarity between two instances. We randomly select 2,000 pairs from Quora Question Pairs (QQP) (Wang et al., 2018) and LCQMC (Liu et al., 2018) to build English and Chinese evaluation data respectively.

Machine Reading Comprehension (MRC), a long-text comprehension task, aims to extract an answer based on the question and the corresponding passage. We randomly select 1,500 triples with answers and 500 triples without answers from SQUAD2.0 (Rajpurkar et al., 2018) and DuReader (He et al., 2018) for building English and Chinese evaluation set respectively.

3.2 Perturbed Data Creation

Recent studies (Jacovi and Goldberg, 2020; Ding and Koehn, 2021) claim that a saliency method is faithful if it provides similar rationales for similar inputs and outputs. Inspired by them, we propose to evaluate the model faithfulness via measuring how consistent its rationales are regarding perturbations that are supposed to preserve the same model decision mechanism. In other words, under perturbations, a model is considered to be faithful if the change of its rationales is consistent with the change of its prediction. Consequently, we construct perturbed examples for each original input.

Perturbation Criteria Perturbations should not change the model internal decision mechanism. We create perturbed examples from two aspects: 1) perturbations do not influence model rationales and predictions; 2) perturbations cause the alterations of rationales and may change predictions. Please note that the influence of perturbations comes from human's basic intuition on model's decision-making mechanism. Based on the literature (Jia and Liang, 2017; McCoy et al., 2019; Ribeiro et al., 2020), we define three perturbation types.

- **Alteration of dispensable words**. Insert, delete and replace words that should have no effect on model predictions and rationales, e.g., the sentence "*what are* some reasons to travel alone" is changed to "*list* some reasons to travel alone".
- **Alteration of important words**. Replace important words which have an impact on model predictions with their synonyms or related words, such as "i dislike you" instead of "i hate you". In this situation, the model prediction and rationale should change with perturbations.
- **Syntax transformation**. Transform the syntax structure of an instance without changing its semantics, e.g., "the customer commented the hotel" is transformed into "the hotel is commented by the customer". In this case, the model prediction and rationale should not be affected.

For each original input, the annotator first selects a perturbation type, then creates a perturbed example according to the definition of this perturbation type. Please note that the annotators can select more than one perturbation type for an original input. We ask the annotator to create at least one perturbed example for each original input. And they need to create at least 100 perturbed examples for each perturbation type. For each task, we have two annotators to create perturbed examples and label golden results for these examples, i.e., sentiment label for SA, similarity label for STS and answer for MRC. According to the perturbation criteria, most of the perturbed examples have the same results as their original ones. Then we ask the other

[4] `https://ai.baidu.com/tech/nlp_apply/sentiment_classify`. Due to the diversity of these logs, we choose instances from these logs for annotation.

two annotators to review and modify the created examples and their corresponding results. Since the annotation task in this step is relatively easy, the accuracy of created examples after checking is more than 95%.

3.3 Iterative Rationale Annotation Process

Given an input and the corresponding golden result, the annotators highlight important input tokens that support the prediction of golden result as the rationale. Then we introduce the rationale criteria and the annotation process used in our work.

Rationale Criteria As discussed in recent studies (Lei et al., 2016; Yu et al., 2019), a rationale should satisfy the following properties.

- **Sufficiency**. A rationale is sufficient if it contains enough information for people to make the correct prediction. In other words, people can make the correct prediction only based on tokens in the rationale.
- **Compactness**. A rationale is compact if all of its tokens are indeed required in making a correct prediction. That is to say, when any token is removed from the rationale, the prediction will change or become difficult to make.
- **Comprehensiveness**. A rationale is comprehensive if its complements in the input can not imply the prediction, that is, all evidence that supports the output should be labeled as rationales.

Annotation Process To ensure the data quality, we adopt an iterative annotation workflow, consisting of three steps, as described in Figure 1.

Step 1: rationale annotation. Based on human's intuitions on the model decision mechanism, given the input and the corresponding golden result, the ordinary annotators who are college students majoring in languages label all critical tokens to guarantee the rationale's comprehensiveness. Then they organize these tokens into several sets, each of which should be sufficient and compact. That is to say, each set can support the prediction independently. As described in Table 1, the first example contains three rationale sets, and tokens in the same color belong to the same set. Based on this set form, the rationale satisfies the above three criteria.

Step 2: rationale scoring. Our senior annotators[5] double-check the annotations by scoring the given rationales according to the annotation criteria. For each rationale set, the annotators rate their confidences for sufficiency and compactness. The confidences for **sufficiency** consist of three classes: *can not support result (1)*, *not sure (2)* and *can support result (3)*. And the confidences for **compactness** compose of four classes: *include redundant tokens (1)*, *include disturbances (2)*, *not sure (3)* and *conciseness (4)*. Then based on all rationale sets for each input, the annotators rate their confidences for **comprehensiveness** on a 3-point scale including *not be comprehensive (1)*, *not sure (2)*, *be comprehensive (3)*.

A rationale is considered to be of high-quality if its average score on sufficiency, compactness and comprehensiveness is equal to or greater than 3.0, 3.6, 2.6. That is to say, at least two-thirds of the annotators give the highest confidence, and less than one-third of the annotators give the confidence of "*not sure*". Then all unqualified data whose average score on a property is lower than the corresponding threshold goes to the next step.

Step 3: rationale modification. Low-quality rationales are shown to the ordinary annotators again. The annotators correct the rationales to meet the properties with scores below the threshold.

Then the corrected rationales are scored by senior annotators again. The unqualified data after three loops is discarded. This iterative annotation-scoring process can ensure the data quality.

Other annotation details, such as annotator information, annotation training and data usage instructions, are described in Appendix A.

[5]They are full-time employees, and have lots of experience in annotating data for NLP tasks.

Tasks	English			Chinese		
	Size	RLR	RSN	Size	RLR	RSN
SA	1,999	20.1%	2.1	2,160	27.6%	1.4
STS	2,248	50.4%	1.0	2,146	66.6%	1.0
MRC	1,969	10.4%	1.0	2,315	9.8%	1.0

Table 3: Overview of our datasets. "Size" shows the number of original/perturbed pairs. "RLR" represents the ratio of rationale length to its input length. "RSN" represents the number of rationale sets in an input. We report the average RLR and RSN over all data.

3.4 Data Statistics

We give a comparison between our benchmark and other existing datasets, as shown in Table 2. Compared with existing datasets, our benchmark contains three NLP tasks with both English and Chinese annotated data. Compared with ERASER which collects seven existing English datasets in

Models	SA		STS		MRC	
	Acc^f	Acc^r	Acc^f	Acc^r	F1^f	F1^r
English						
LSTM	78.2	**86.2**	74.6	69.8	54.4	53.4
RoBERTa-base	93.8	92.4	92.7	89.3	71.7	**80.8**
RoBERTa-large	95.4	91.5	93.2	88.8	76.0	**76.7**
Chinese						
LSTM	60.0	**70.4**	75.2	**80.7**	66.4	**82.2**
RoBERTa-base	59.8	**77.0**	85.5	**88.1**	65.8	**89.3**
RoBERTa-large	62.6	**80.6**	86.0	**87.4**	67.8	**83.3**

Table 4: Model performance on the original full input (Acc^f) and human-annotated rationale (Acc^r).

its benchmark and provides snippet-level rationales to satisfy sufficiency and comprehensiveness, our benchmark provides token-level rationales and satisfies all three primary properties of rationales.

Table 3 shows the detailed statistics of our benchmark. We can see that the length ratio and the number of rationales vary with datasets and tasks, where the length ratio affects the interpretability performance on plausibility, as shown in Table 6.

Meanwhile, we evaluate the sufficiency of human-annotated rationales by evaluating model performance on rationales, as shown in Table 4. Despite the input construction based on rationales has destroyed the distribution of original inputs, model performance on human-annotated rationales is competitive with that on full inputs, especially on MRC task and Chinese datasets. We can conclude that human-annotated rationales are sufficient. Meanwhile, we give more data analysis in Table 7, such as model performance on non-rationales, sufficiency and comprehensiveness scores.

4 Metrics

Following existing studies (DeYoung et al., 2020; Ding and Koehn, 2021; Mathew et al., 2021), we evaluate interpretability from the perspectives of plausibility and faithfulness. Plausibility measures how well the rationales provided by the model agree with human-annotated ones. And faithfulness measures the degree to which the provided rationales influence the corresponding predictions.

Different from existing work, we adopt **token-F1** score for plausibility and propose a new metric **MAP** for faithfulness.

Token F1-score is defined in Equation 1, which is computed by overlapped rationale tokens. Since an instance may contain multiple golden rationale sets, for the sake of fairness, we take the set that has the largest F1-score with the predicted rationale as the ground truth for the current prediction.

$$\begin{aligned} \texttt{Token-F1} &= \frac{1}{N}\sum_{i=1}^{N}(2 \times \frac{P_i \times R_i}{P_i + R_i}) \\ \text{where} \quad P_i &= \frac{|S_i^p \cap S_i^g|}{|S_i^p|} \text{ and } R_i = \frac{|S_i^p \cap S_i^g|}{|S_i^g|} \end{aligned} \tag{1}$$

where S_i^p and S_i^g represent the rationale set of i-th instance provided by models and human respectively; N is the number of instances.

MAP (Mean Average Precision) measures the consistency of rationales under perturbations and is used to evaluate faithfulness. According to the original/perturbed input pair, MAP aims to calculate the consistency of two token lists sorted by token importance score, as defined in Equation 2. The high MAP indicates the high consistency.

$$\texttt{MAP} = \frac{\sum_{i=1}^{|X^p|}(\sum_{j=1}^{i} G(x_j^p, X_{1:i}^o))/i}{|X^p|} \tag{2}$$

where X^o and X^p represent the sorted rationale token list of the original and perturbed inputs, according to the token important scores assigned by a specific saliency method. $|X^p|$ represents the number of tokens in X^p. $X_{1:i}^o$ consists of top-i important tokens of X^o. The function $G(x, Y)$ is to determine whether the token x belongs to the list Y, where $G(x, Y) = 1 \, \texttt{iff} \, x \in Y$.

Meanwhile, we also report results of metrics proposed in DeYoung et al. (2020), i.e., IOU F1-score for plausibility, and the joint of sufficiency and comprehensiveness for faithfulness.

IOU F1-score is proposed on span-level rationales, which is the size of token overlap in two sets divided by the size of their union, as shown by S_i in Equation 3. A rationale is considered as a match if its S_i is equal to or greater than 0.5, as illustrated by the $Greater$ function.

$$\begin{aligned} \texttt{IOU-F1} &= \frac{1}{N}\sum_{i=1}^{N} Greater(S_i, 0.5) \\ \text{where} \quad S_i &= \frac{|S_i^p \cap S_i^g|}{|S_i^p \cup S_i^g|} \end{aligned} \tag{3}$$

The joint of **sufficiency** (Score-Suf) and **comprehensiveness** (Score-Com) is shown in Equation 4. A lower sufficiency score implies the rationale is more sufficient and a higher comprehensiveness score means the rationale is more influential in the prediction. A faithful rationale should have a low sufficiency score and a high comprehensiveness

Models	SA (Acc)		STS (Acc)		MRC (F1)	
	Ori	Ours	Ori	Ours	Ori	Ours
English						
LSTM	78.6	78.2	78.6	74.6	58.6	54.4
RoBERTa-base	92.1	93.8	91.5	92.7	78.4	71.7
RoBERTa-large	91.3	95.4	91.4	93.2	83.8	76.0
Chinese						
LSTM	86.7	60.0	77.4	75.2	75.0	66.4
RoBERTa-base	95.1	59.8	88.1	85.5	74.4	65.8
RoBERTa-large	95.0	62.6	88.1	86.0	77.8	67.8

Table 5: Conventional performance of base models on three tasks, where "Acc" is short for accuracy. The "Ori" dev/test set comes from the same dataset as training set. "Ours" represents our evaluation datasets.

score.

$$\begin{aligned} \texttt{Score-Suf} &= \frac{1}{N}\sum_{i=1}^{N}(F(x_i)_j - F(r_i)_j) \\ \texttt{Score-Com} &= \frac{1}{N}\sum_{i=1}^{N}(F(x_i)_j - F(x_i \setminus r_i)_j) \end{aligned} \tag{4}$$

where $F(x_i)_j$ represents the prediction probability provided by the model F for class j on the input x_i; r_i represents the rationale of x_i, and $x_i \setminus r_i$ represents its non-rationale.

5 Experiments

5.1 Experiment Settings

We implement three widely-used models and three saliency methods. We give brief descriptions of them and leave the implementation details to Appendix B. The source code will be released with our evaluation datasets.

Saliency Methods We adopt integrated gradient (**IG**) method (Sundararajan et al., 2017), attention-based (**ATT**) method (Jain and Wallace, 2019) and linear-based (**LIME**) (Ribeiro et al., 2016) method in our experiments. IG assigns importance score for each token by integrating the gradient along the path from a defined input baseline to the original input. ATT uses attention weights as importance scores, and the acquisition of attention weights depends on the specific model architecture. LIME uses the token weights learned by the linear model as importance scores.

For each saliency method, we take the top-k^d important tokens to compose the rationale for an input, where k^d is the product of the current input length and the average rationale length ratio of a dataset d, as shown by *RLR* in Table 3.

Comparison Models For each task, we re-implement three typical models with different network architectures and parameter sizes, namely LSTM (Hochreiter and Schmidhuber, 1997), RoBERTa-base and RoBERTa-large (Liu et al., 2019). Based on these backbone models, we then fine-tune them with commonly-used datasets of three specific tasks. For SA, we select training sets of SST and ChnSentiCorp[6] to train models for English and Chinese respectively. For STS, training sets of QQP and LCQMC are used to train English and Chinese models. For MRC, SQUAD2.0 and DuReader are used as training sets for English and Chinese respectively. For each task, we select the best model on the original dev set.

In order to confirm the correctness of our implementation, Table 5 shows model performances on both original dev/test and our evaluation datasets. We can see that our re-implemented models output close results reported in related works (Liu et al., 2018; WANG and JIANG; Liu et al., 2019). Meanwhile, the results of Chinese SA and MRC tasks decrease significantly on our evaluation sets. This may be caused by the poor generalization and robustness of the model, as our evaluation datasets contain perturbed examples and Chinese data for SA is not from the ChnSentiCorp dataset.

5.2 Evaluation Results

Table 6 shows the evaluation results of interpretability from the plausibility and faithfulness perspectives. Within the scope of baseline models and saliency methods used in our experiments, there are three main findings. First, based on all models and saliency methods used in our experiments, our metrics for interpretability evaluation, namely token-F1 score and MAP, are more fine and generic, especially MAP, which applies to all three tasks. Second, IG method performs better on plausibility and ATT method performs better on faithfulness. Meanwhile, ATT method achieves best performance in sentence-pair tasks. Third, with all three saliency methods, in these three tasks, LSTM model is comparable with transformer model (i.e., RoBERTa based model in our experiments) on interpretability, though LSTM performs worse than transformer in term of accuracy. We think that the generalization ability of LSTM model is weak, leading to low accuracy, even with relatively reasonable rationales.

In the following paragraphs, we first give a comparison between our proposed metrics and those

[6] https://github.com/pengming617/bert_classification

Models + Methods	SA					STS					MRC		
	Plausibility		Faithfulness			Plausibility		Faithfulness			Plausibility		Faithfulness
	Token-F1↑	IOU-F1↑	MAP↑	Suf↓	Com↑	Token-F1	IOU-F1	MAP	Suf	Com	Token-F1	IOU-F1	MAP
LSTM + IG	36.9	12.1	67.2	-0.025	0.708	54.1	17.3	69.0	0.048	0.441	40.7	11.0	72.3
RoBERTa-base + IG	37.4	10.4	64.1	0.059	0.392	52.9	24.2	65.3	0.153	0.478	42.1	11.0	66.9
RoBERTa-large + IG	35.0	7.9	40.6	0.130	0.260	52.7	35.9	49.7	0.224	0.400	18.0	0.1	18.0
LSTM + ATT	36.6	12.4	67.8	0.123	0.298	49.6	11.8	76.0	0.221	0.313	19.9	0.4	88.3
RoBERTa-base + ATT	33.2	9.4	69.2	0.267	0.128	66.5	54.2	73.6	0.185	0.337	22.6	2.6	55.0
RoBERTa-large + ATT	23.3	3.1	75.9	0.301	0.095	56.8	35.9	75.4	0.136	0.399	26.6	1.3	76.0
LSTM + LIME	36.6	11.3	63.2	-0.040	0.762	54.5	19.2	60.0	0.134	0.311	-	-	-
RoBERTa-base + LIME	41.5	13.8	61.0	0.032	0.568	58.7	34.9	70.5	0.064	0.509	-	-	-
RoBERTa-large + LIME	41.4	14.3	62.9	0.053	0.505	61.2	42.3	71.8	0.019	0.524	-	-	-

Table 6: Interpretability evaluation results on English datasets of three tasks. The metric with ↑ means the higher the score, the better the performance. Conversely, ↓ means a low score represents a good performance. As LIME is specially designed for classification tasks, we have not applied it to MRC. Meanwhile, the sufficiency score (Suf) and the comprehensiveness score (Com) are also only suitable for classification tasks, as shown in Equation 4. Thus we do not report these two scores on MRC.

used in related studies. Then we give a detailed analysis about the interpretability results of three saliency methods and three evaluated models.

Comparison between Evaluation Metrics We report results of token-F1 and IOU-F1 scores for plausibility. The higher the scores, the more plausible the rationales. It can be seen that the two metrics have the similar trends in all three tasks with all three saliency methods. But token-F1 is much precise than IOU-F1, as the IOU-F1 score of a rationale is 1 only if its overlap with ground truth is no less than 0.5 (Equation 3). However, in all three tasks, overlaps of most instances are less than 0.5, especially in the task with a low *RLR*. Thus IOU-F1 is too coarse to evaluate token-level rationales. Instead, token-F1 focuses on evaluating token impact on model predictions, so as to be more suitable for evaluating compact rationales.

For faithfulness evaluation, we report results of MAP, sufficiency and comprehensiveness scores. We can see that our proposed MAP is an efficient metric for faithfulness evaluation. Specifically, it applies to most tasks, especially non-classification tasks. Moreover, in the two classification tasks (i.e., SA and STS), with IG and LIME methods, MAP has the same trend as the other two metrics over all three models, which further indicates that MAP can well evaluate the faithfulness of rationales. With ATT method, there is no consistent relationship between these three metrics. We think this is because the calculations of sufficiency and comprehensiveness scores with ATT method are not accurate and consistent enough. For example, in the SA task, from the comparison of three saliency methods with LSTM model, we can see that the rationales extracted by these methods have similar plausibility scores, but the sufficiency score with ATT method is much higher than that with the other two methods. Please note that a low sufficiency score means a sufficient rationale. Similarly, in the STS task with RoBERTa-base model, the rationales extracted by ATT method have a higher plausibility score, as well as a higher sufficiency score. Finally, we believe that other metrics can be proposed based on our benchmark.

Evaluation of Saliency Methods LIME, which uses a linear model to approximate a DL classification model, is model-agnostic and task-agnostic. It obtains the highest performance on token-F1 and sufficiency scores in SA and STS tasks, as the rationales extracted by it more accurately approximate the decision process of DL models. But how to better apply LIME to more NLP tasks is very challenging and as the future work.

When comparing IG and ATT, we find ATT performs better on faithfulness and sentence-pair tasks. In SA and MRC, IG performs better on plausibility and ATT method achieves better results on faithfulness, which is consistent with prior works (Jain and Wallace, 2019; DeYoung et al., 2020). In STS, ATT method achieves higher results both on plausibility and faithfulness than IG method. We think this is because the cross-sentence interaction attentions are more important for sentence-pair tasks. Interestingly, on all three tasks, there is a positive correlation between MAP (faithfulness) and token-F1 (plausibility) with IG method.

Evaluation of Models While analyzing interpretability of model architectures, we mainly focus on IG and ATT methods, as LIME is model-agnostic. We find that interpretability of model architectures vary with saliency methods and tasks.

Compared with transformer models, based on IG method, LSTM is competitive on plausibility and performs better on faithfulness in all three tasks. On the contrary, based on ATT method, transformer models outperform LSTM on plausibility and are competitive on faithfulness in STS and MRC tasks. As discussed above, the interaction between inputs is more important in these two tasks.

From the comparison between two transformer models with different parameter sizes, i.e., RoBERTa-base and RoBERTa-large, we find that RoBERTa-base outperforms RoBERTa-large on plausibility with these two saliency methods. Interestingly, for faithfulness evaluation, RoBERTa-base performs better than RoBERTa-large with IG method, and RoBERTa-large performs better than RoBERTa-base with ATT method.

We believe these findings are helpful to the future work on interpretability.

6 Limitation Discussion

We provide a new interpretability evaluation benchmark which contains three tasks with both English and Chinese annotated data. There are three limitations in our work.

- How to evaluate the quality of human-annotated rationales is still open. We have several annotators to perform quality control based on human intuitions and experiences. Meanwhile, we compare model behaviors on full inputs and human-annotated rationales to evaluate the sufficiency and comprehensiveness of rationales, as shown in Table 4 and Table 7. However, this manner has damaged the original input distribution and brings uncontrollable factors on model behaviors. Therefore, how to automatically and effectively evaluate the quality of human-annotated rationales should be studied in the future.
- We find that the interpretability of model architectures and saliency methods vary with tasks, especially with the input form of the task. Thus our benchmark should contain more datasets of each task type (e.g., single-sentence task, sentence-pair similarity task and sentence-pair inference task) to further verify these findings. And we will build evaluation datasets for more tasks in the future.
- Due to space limitation, there is no analysis of the relationships between metrics, e.g., the relationship between plausibility and accuracy, and the relationship between faithfulness and robustness. We will take these analyses in our future work.

Finally, we hope more evaluation metrics and analyses are proposed based on our benchmark. And we hope our benchmark can facilitate the research progress of interpertability.

7 Conclusion

We propose a new fine-grained interpretability evaluation benchmark, containing token-level rationales, a new evaluation metric and corresponding perturbed examples for three typical NLP tasks, i.e., sentiment analysis, textual similarity and machine reading comprehension. The rationales in this benchmark meet primary properties that a rationale should satisfy, i.e., sufficiency, compactness and comprehensiveness. The experimental results on three models and three saliency methods prove that our benchmark can be used to evaluate interpretability of both models and saliency methods. We will release this benchmark and hope it can facilitate progress on several directions, such as better interpretability evaluation metrics and causal analysis of NLP models.

Acknowledgements

We are very grateful to our anonymous reviewers for their helpful feedback on this work. This work is supported by the National Key Research and Development Project of China (No.2018AAA0101900).

References

David Alvarez-Melis and Tommi Jaakkola. 2017. A causal framework for explaining the predictions of black-box sequence-to-sequence models. In Proceedings of the 2017 Conference on Empirical Methods in Natural Language Processing, pages 412–421, Copenhagen, Denmark. Association for Computational Linguistics.

David Alvarez Melis and Tommi Jaakkola. 2018. Towards robust interpretability with self-explaining neural networks. Advances in neural information processing systems, 31.

Moustafa Alzantot, Yash Sharma, Ahmed Elgohary, Bo-Jhang Ho, Mani Srivastava, and Kai-Wei Chang. 2018. Generating natural language adversarial examples. In Proceedings of the 2018 Conference on Empirical Methods in Natural Language Processing, pages 2890–2896, Brussels, Belgium. Association for Computational Linguistics.

Leila Arras, Franziska Horn, Grégoire Montavon, Klaus-Robert Müller, and Wojciech Samek. 2017. " what is relevant in a text document?": An interpretable machine learning approach. PloS one, 12(8):e0181142.

Jasmijn Bastings, Wilker Aziz, and Ivan Titov. 2019. Interpretable neural predictions with differentiable binary variables. In Proceedings of the 57th Annual Meeting of the Association for Computational Linguistics, pages 2963–2977, Florence, Italy. Association for Computational Linguistics.

Oana-Maria Camburu, Tim Rocktäschel, Thomas Lukasiewicz, and Phil Blunsom. 2018. e-snli: Natural language inference with natural language explanations. Advances in Neural Information Processing Systems, 31.

Nicola De Cao, Michael Sejr Schlichtkrull, Wilker Aziz, and Ivan Titov. 2020. How do decisions emerge across layers in neural models? interpretation with differentiable masking. In Proceedings of the 2020 Conference on Empirical Methods in Natural Language Processing (EMNLP), pages 3243–3255, Online. Association for Computational Linguistics.

Li Deng and Dong Yu. 2014. Deep learning: methods and applications. Foundations and trends in signal processing, 7(3–4):197–387.

Jay DeYoung, Sarthak Jain, Nazneen Fatema Rajani, Eric Lehman, Caiming Xiong, Richard Socher, and Byron C. Wallace. 2020. ERASER: A benchmark to evaluate rationalized NLP models. In Proceedings of the 58th Annual Meeting of the Association for Computational Linguistics, pages 4443–4458, Online. Association for Computational Linguistics.

Shuoyang Ding and Philipp Koehn. 2021. Evaluating saliency methods for neural language models. In Proceedings of the 2021 Conference of the North American Chapter of the Association for Computational Linguistics: Human Language Technologies, pages 5034–5052, Online. Association for Computational Linguistics.

Shi Feng, Eric Wallace, Alvin Grissom II, Mohit Iyyer, Pedro Rodriguez, and Jordan Boyd-Graber. 2018. Pathologies of neural models make interpretations difficult. In Proceedings of the 2018 Conference on Empirical Methods in Natural Language Processing, pages 3719–3728, Brussels, Belgium. Association for Computational Linguistics.

Gerhard Fischer, Thomas Mastaglio, Brent Reeves, and John Rieman. 1990. Minimalist explanations in knowledge-based systems. In Twenty-Third Annual Hawaii International Conference on System Sciences, volume 3, pages 309–317. IEEE.

Karën Fort and Alain Couillault. 2016. Yes, we care! results of the ethics and natural language processing surveys. In Proceedings of the Tenth International Conference on Language Resources and Evaluation (LREC'16), pages 1593–1600, Portorož, Slovenia. European Language Resources Association (ELRA).

Mor Geva, Daniel Khashabi, Elad Segal, Tushar Khot, Dan Roth, and Jonathan Berant. 2021. Did aristotle use a laptop? a question answering benchmark with implicit reasoning strategies. Transactions of the Association for Computational Linguistics, 9:346–361.

Shirley Anugrah Hayati, Dongyeop Kang, and Lyle Ungar. 2021. Does BERT learn as humans perceive? understanding linguistic styles through lexica. In Proceedings of the 2021 Conference on Empirical Methods in Natural Language Processing, pages 6323–6331, Online and Punta Cana, Dominican Republic. Association for Computational Linguistics.

Wei He, Kai Liu, Jing Liu, Yajuan Lyu, Shiqi Zhao, Xinyan Xiao, Yuan Liu, Yizhong Wang, Hua Wu, Qiaoqiao She, Xuan Liu, Tian Wu, and Haifeng Wang. 2018. DuReader: a Chinese machine reading comprehension dataset from real-world applications. In Proceedings of the Workshop on Machine Reading for Question Answering, pages 37–46, Melbourne, Australia. Association for Computational Linguistics.

Bernease Herman. 2017. The promise and peril of human evaluation for model interpretability. NIPS 2017 Symposium on Interpretable Machine Learning.

Sepp Hochreiter and Jürgen Schmidhuber. 1997. Long short-term memory. Neural computation, 9(8):1735–1780.

Alon Jacovi and Yoav Goldberg. 2020. Towards faithfully interpretable NLP systems: How should we define and evaluate faithfulness? In Proceedings of the 58th Annual Meeting of the Association for Computational Linguistics, pages 4198–4205, Online. Association for Computational Linguistics.

Sarthak Jain and Byron C. Wallace. 2019. Attention is not Explanation. In Proceedings of the 2019 Conference of the North American Chapter of the Association for Computational Linguistics: Human Language Technologies, Volume 1 (Long and Short Papers), pages 3543–3556, Minneapolis, Minnesota. Association for Computational Linguistics.

Robin Jia and Percy Liang. 2017. Adversarial examples for evaluating reading comprehension systems. In Proceedings of the 2017 Conference on Empirical Methods in Natural Language Processing, pages 2021–2031, Copenhagen, Denmark. Association for Computational Linguistics.

Zhongtao Jiang, Yuanzhe Zhang, Zhao Yang, Jun Zhao, and Kang Liu. 2021. Alignment rationale for natural language inference. In Proceedings of the 59th Annual Meeting of the Association for Computational Linguistics and the 11th International Joint Conference on Natural Language Processing (Volume 1: Long Papers), pages 5372–5387, Online. Association for Computational Linguistics.

Robert Kass, Tim Finin, et al. 1988. The need for user models in generating expert system explanations. International Journal of Expert Systems, 1(4).

Daniel Khashabi, Snigdha Chaturvedi, Michael Roth, Shyam Upadhyay, and Dan Roth. 2018. Looking beyond the surface: A challenge set for reading comprehension over multiple sentences. In Proceedings of the 2018 Conference of the North American Chapter of the Association for Computational Linguistics: Human Language Technologies, Volume 1 (Long Papers), pages 252–262, New Orleans, Louisiana. Association for Computational Linguistics.

Eric Lehman, Jay DeYoung, Regina Barzilay, and Byron C. Wallace. 2019. Inferring which medical treatments work from reports of clinical trials. In Proceedings of the 2019 Conference of the North American Chapter of the Association for Computational Linguistics: Human Language Technologies, Volume 1 (Long and Short Papers), pages 3705–3717, Minneapolis, Minnesota. Association for Computational Linguistics.

Tao Lei, Regina Barzilay, and Tommi Jaakkola. 2016. Rationalizing neural predictions. In Proceedings of the 2016 Conference on Empirical Methods in Natural Language Processing, pages 107–117, Austin, Texas. Association for Computational Linguistics.

Jiwei Li, Will Monroe, and Dan Jurafsky. 2016. Understanding neural networks through representation erasure. arXiv preprint arXiv:1612.08220.

Geert Litjens, Thijs Kooi, Babak Ehteshami Bejnordi, Arnaud Arindra Adiyoso Setio, Francesco Ciompi, Mohsen Ghafoorian, Jeroen Awm Van Der Laak, Bram Van Ginneken, and Clara I Sánchez. 2017. A survey on deep learning in medical image analysis. Medical image analysis, 42:60–88.

Xin Liu, Qingcai Chen, Chong Deng, Huajun Zeng, Jing Chen, Dongfang Li, and Buzhou Tang. 2018. LCQMC:a large-scale Chinese question matching corpus. In Proceedings of the 27th International Conference on Computational Linguistics, pages 1952–1962, Santa Fe, New Mexico, USA. Association for Computational Linguistics.

Yinhan Liu, Myle Ott, Naman Goyal, Jingfei Du, Mandar Joshi, Danqi Chen, Omer Levy, Mike Lewis, Luke Zettlemoyer, and Veselin Stoyanov. 2019. Roberta: A robustly optimized bert pretraining approach. arXiv preprint arXiv:1907.11692.

Binny Mathew, Punyajoy Saha, Seid Muhie Yimam, Chris Biemann, Pawan Goyal, and Animesh Mukherjee. 2021. Hatexplain: A benchmark dataset for explainable hate speech detection. In AAAI.

Tom McCoy, Ellie Pavlick, and Tal Linzen. 2019. Right for the wrong reasons: Diagnosing syntactic heuristics in natural language inference. In Proceedings of the 57th Annual Meeting of the Association for Computational Linguistics, pages 3428–3448, Florence, Italy. Association for Computational Linguistics.

Sina Mohseni, Jeremy E Block, and Eric D Ragan. 2018. A human-grounded evaluation benchmark for local explanations of machine learning. arXiv preprint arXiv:1801.05075.

W James Murdoch, Peter J Liu, and Bin Yu. 2018. Beyond word importance: Contextual decomposition to extract interactions from lstms. In International Conference on Learning Representations.

Weili Nie, Yang Zhang, and Ankit Patel. 2018. A theoretical explanation for perplexing behaviors of backpropagation-based visualizations. In International Conference on Machine Learning, pages 3809–3818. PMLR.

Samira Pouyanfar, Saad Sadiq, Yilin Yan, Haiman Tian, Yudong Tao, Maria Presa Reyes, Mei-Ling Shyu, Shu-Ching Chen, and Sundaraja S Iyengar. 2018. A survey on deep learning: Algorithms, techniques, and applications. ACM Computing Surveys (CSUR), 51(5):1–36.

Nazneen Fatema Rajani, Bryan McCann, Caiming Xiong, and Richard Socher. 2019. Explain yourself! leveraging language models for commonsense reasoning. In Proceedings of the 57th Annual Meeting of the Association for Computational Linguistics, pages 4932–4942, Florence, Italy. Association for Computational Linguistics.

Pranav Rajpurkar, Robin Jia, and Percy Liang. 2018. Know what you don't know: Unanswerable questions for SQuAD. In Proceedings of the 56th Annual Meeting of the Association for Computational Linguistics (Volume 2: Short Papers), pages 784–789, Melbourne, Australia. Association for Computational Linguistics.

Marco Tulio Ribeiro, Sameer Singh, and Carlos Guestrin. 2016. " why should i trust you?" explaining the predictions of any classifier. In Proceedings of the 22nd ACM SIGKDD international conference on knowledge discovery and data mining, pages 1135–1144.

Marco Tulio Ribeiro, Tongshuang Wu, Carlos Guestrin, and Sameer Singh. 2020. Beyond accuracy: Behavioral testing of NLP models with CheckList. In Proceedings of the 58th Annual Meeting of the Association for Computational Linguistics, pages 4902–4912, Online. Association for Computational Linguistics.

Karen Simonyan, Andrea Vedaldi, and Andrew Zisserman. 2014. Deep inside convolutional networks: Visualising image classification models and saliency maps.

Leon Sixt, Maximilian Granz, and Tim Landgraf. 2020. When explanations lie: Why many modified bp attributions fail. In International Conference on Machine Learning, pages 9046–9057. PMLR.

Daniel Smilkov, Nikhil Thorat, Been Kim, Fernanda Viégas, and Martin Wattenberg. 2017. Smoothgrad: removing noise by adding noise. arXiv preprint arXiv:1706.03825.

Richard Socher, Alex Perelygin, Jean Wu, Jason Chuang, Christopher D. Manning, Andrew Ng, and Christopher Potts. 2013. Recursive deep models for semantic compositionality over a sentiment treebank. In Proceedings of the 2013 Conference on Empirical Methods in Natural Language Processing, pages 1631–1642, Seattle, Washington, USA. Association for Computational Linguistics.

Mukund Sundararajan, Ankur Taly, and Qiqi Yan. 2017. Axiomatic attribution for deep networks. In Proceedings of the 34th International Conference on Machine Learning-Volume 70, pages 3319–3328.

James Thorne, Andreas Vlachos, Christos Christodoulopoulos, and Arpit Mittal. 2018. FEVER: a large-scale dataset for fact extraction and VERification. In Proceedings of the 2018 Conference of the North American Chapter of the Association for Computational Linguistics: Human Language Technologies, Volume 1 (Long Papers), pages 809–819, New Orleans, Louisiana. Association for Computational Linguistics.

David Wadden, Shanchuan Lin, Kyle Lo, Lucy Lu Wang, Madeleine van Zuylen, Arman Cohan, and Hannaneh Hajishirzi. 2020. Fact or fiction: Verifying scientific claims. In Proceedings of the 2020 Conference on Empirical Methods in Natural Language Processing (EMNLP), pages 7534–7550, Online. Association for Computational Linguistics.

Alex Wang, Amanpreet Singh, Julian Michael, Felix Hill, Omer Levy, and Samuel Bowman. 2018. GLUE: A multi-task benchmark and analysis platform for natural language understanding. In Proceedings of the 2018 EMNLP Workshop BlackboxNLP: Analyzing and Interpreting Neural Networks for NLP, pages 353–355, Brussels, Belgium. Association for Computational Linguistics.

Shuohang WANG and Jing JIANG. Machine comprehension using match-lstm and answer pointer.(2017). In ICLR 2017: International Conference on Learning Representations, Toulon, France, April 24-26: Proceedings, pages 1–15.

Hilde JP Weerts, Werner van Ipenburg, and Mykola Pechenizkiy. 2019. A human-grounded evaluation of shap for alert processing. Proceedings of KDD workshop on Explainable AI 2019 (KDD-XAI).

Sarah Wiegreffe and Yuval Pinter. 2019. Attention is not not explanation. In Proceedings of the 2019 Conference on Empirical Methods in Natural Language Processing and the 9th International Joint Conference on Natural Language Processing (EMNLP-IJCNLP), pages 11–20, Hong Kong, China. Association for Computational Linguistics.

Thomas Wolf, Lysandre Debut, Victor Sanh, Julien Chaumond, Clement Delangue, Anthony Moi, Pierric Cistac, Tim Rault, Rémi Louf, Morgan Funtowicz, et al. 2019. Huggingface's transformers: State-of-the-art natural language processing. arXiv preprint arXiv:1910.03771.

Fan Yang, Mengnan Du, and Xia Hu. 2019. Evaluating explanation without ground truth in interpretable machine learning. arXiv preprint arXiv:1907.06831.

Yi Yang, Wen-tau Yih, and Christopher Meek. 2015. WikiQA: A challenge dataset for open-domain question answering. In Proceedings of the 2015 Conference on Empirical Methods in Natural Language Processing, pages 2013–2018, Lisbon, Portugal. Association for Computational Linguistics.

Zhilin Yang, Peng Qi, Saizheng Zhang, Yoshua Bengio, William Cohen, Ruslan Salakhutdinov, and Christopher D. Manning. 2018. HotpotQA: A dataset for diverse, explainable multi-hop question answering. In Proceedings of the 2018 Conference on Empirical Methods in Natural Language Processing, pages 2369–2380, Brussels, Belgium. Association for Computational Linguistics.

Qinyuan Ye, Xiao Huang, Elizabeth Boschee, and Xiang Ren. 2020. Teaching machine comprehension with compositional explanations. In Findings of the Association for Computational Linguistics: EMNLP 2020, pages 1599–1615, Online. Association for Computational Linguistics.

Fan Yin, Zhouxing Shi, Cho-Jui Hsieh, and Kai-Wei Chang. 2022. On the sensitivity and stability of model interpretations in NLP. In Proceedings of the 60th Annual Meeting of the Association for Computational Linguistics (Volume 1: Long Papers), pages 2631–2647, Dublin, Ireland. Association for Computational Linguistics.

Mo Yu, Shiyu Chang, Yang Zhang, and Tommi Jaakkola. 2019. Rethinking cooperative rationalization: Introspective extraction and complement control. In Proceedings of the 2019 Conference on Empirical Methods in Natural Language Processing and the 9th International Joint Conference on Natural Language Processing (EMNLP-IJCNLP), pages 4094–4103, Hong Kong, China. Association for Computational Linguistics.

Omar Zaidan and Jason Eisner. 2008. Modeling annotators: A generative approach to learning from annotator rationales. In Proceedings of the 2008 Conference on Empirical Methods in Natural Language Processing, pages 31–40, Honolulu, Hawaii. Association for Computational Linguistics.

A Other Details of Our Datasets

Other Annotation Details We give more details about data collection, annotator information, annotation training and payment, and instructions for data usage.

Data collection. Except for Chinese data of SA, the annotated instances for other datasets are collected from the existing datasets, as described in Section 3.1. In the process of collection, we ask annotators to discard instances that contain: 1) offensive content, 2) information that names or uniquely identifies individual people, 3) discussions about politics, guns, drug abuse, violence or pornography.

Annotator information. We have two ordinary annotators for each task, and three senior annotators for all tasks. The ordinary annotators annotate the rationales and modify the rationales according to the scores from the senior annotators. They are college students majoring in languages. Our senior annotators are full-time employees, and perform quality control. Before this work, they have lots of experience in annotating data for NLP tasks.

Annotation training and payment. Before real annotation, we train all annotators for several times so that they understand the specific task, rationale criteria, etc. During real annotation, we have also held several meetings to discuss common mistakes and settle disputes. Our annotation project for each task lasts for about 1.5 month. And we cost about 15.5 RMB for the annotation of each instance.

Instructions of data annotation and usage. Before annotation, we provide a full instruction to all annotators, including the responsibility for leaking data, disclaimers of any risks, and screenshots of annotation discussions. Meanwhile, our datasets are only used for interpretability evaluation. And we will release a license with the release of our benchmark.

Data Analysis We report sufficiency and comprehensiveness scores of human-annotated rationales, as shown in Table 7. The sufficiency scores of human-annotated rationales are lower than those of rationales provided by transformer models or extracted by IG and ATT methods. We can conclude that our human-annotated rationales are sufficient. However, with IG and LIME methods, the comprehensiveness scores of human-annotated rationales are lower than those of rationales provided by models. As discussed before, the model performance on non-rationales is not accurate enough, as shown by Acc^{nr}, which achieves about 50% on non-rationales. How to effectively evaluate the quality of human-annotated rationales should be studied in the future.

B Implementations Details

B.1 Implementations of Evaluated Models

We utilize HuggingFace's Transformer (Wolf et al., 2019) to implement RoBERTa based models for three tasks. Please refer to their source codes[7] for more details. The LSTM model architectures for three tasks are shown in Figure 2.

B.2 Implementations of Saliency Methods

We first describe experimental setups for three saliency methods. Then we introduce implementation details of attention-based method. Finally, we illustrate the limitations of LIME in STS and MRC tasks.

Experimental setup. In IG-based method, token importance is determined by integrating the gradient along the path from a defined baseline x_0 to the original input. In the experiments, a sequence of all zero embeddings is used as the baseline x_0. And the step size is set to 300.

LIME uses the token weight learned by the linear model as the token's importance score. For each original input, N perturbed samples which contains K tokens of it are created. Then the weighted square loss is used to optimize the selection of tokens that are useful for the model prediction. In the experiments, we set N to $5,000$ and K to 10. In the STS task, an input is a pair of two instances. Each perturbed sample for an input consists of a perturbed example for one instance and the original input for the other instance.

ATT method on LSTM models. Figure 2 shows the architectures of LSTM models in three tasks. In the SA task, given the input instance Q, an LSTM encoder is used to get the representation for each token, denoted as h_i^Q. And a full connected layer (FC) is used to get the instance representation based on the last hidden representation. We use h^{fc} to represent the representation after the FC layer. Then the instance representation h^{fc} is fed into the softmax layer to get the predicted label. The attention weight for token i in Q is calculated by $\frac{h^{fc} \cdot h_i^Q}{\sum_{j=1}^{|Q|} h^{fc} \cdot h_j^Q}$, where $|Q|$ represents the number of tokens in Q. Then the attention weight of the

[7] https://huggingface.co/transformers/

Models	SA					STS					MRC	
	Acc^f	Acc^r	Acc^{nr}	Suf	Com	Acc^f	Acc^r	Acc^{nr}	Suf	Com	$F1^f$	$F1^r$
English												
LSTM	78.2	**86.2**	60.7	0.151	0.217	74.6	69.8	61.3	0.152	0.291	54.4	53.4
RoBERTa-base	93.8	92.4	70.6	0.084	0.251	92.7	89.3	54.8	0.075	0.418	71.7	**80.8**
RoBERTa-large	95.4	91.5	74.4	0.086	0.234	93.2	88.8	53.9	0.085	0.420	76.0	**76.7**
Chinese												
LSTM	60.0	**70.4**	48.7	0.172	0.135	75.2	**80.7**	51.2	0.083	0.339	66.4	**82.2**
RoBERTa-base	59.8	**77.0**	50.2	0.252	0.207	85.5	**88.1**	48.8	0.048	0.399	65.8	**89.3**
RoBERTa-large	62.6	**80.6**	47.6	0.212	0.147	86.0	**87.4**	48.9	0.051	0.433	67.8	**83.3**

Table 7: Model performance on the original full input (Acc^f), human-annotated rationale (Acc^r), and non-rationale (Acc^{nr}) by removing human-annotated rationale from the original full input. Suf and Com represent the sufficiency score and comprehensiveness score of the human-annotated rationales, as shown in Equation 4. We do not report $F1^{nr}$ on the MRC task, as the golden answer is not from the non-rationale.

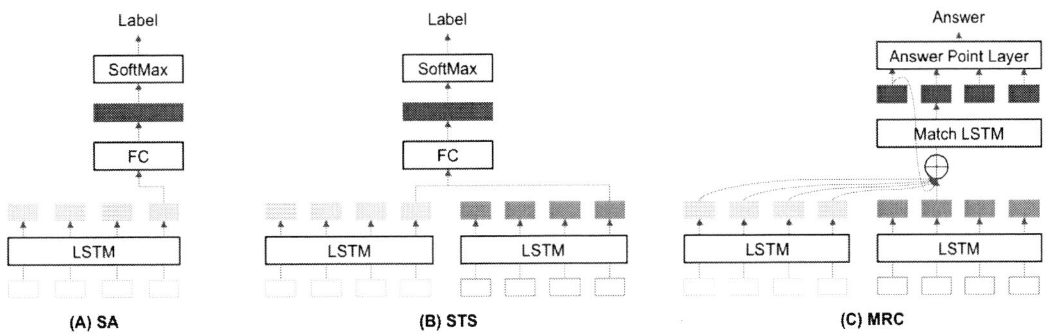

Figure 2: LSTM model architectures for three tasks.

token is used as its importance score for the model prediction.

Similarly, in the STS task, the model architecture is mostly the same as that of SA. The main difference is that the input of STS consists of two instances, denoted as Q and P, and the concatenation of their last hidden representations is fed into an FC layer. Then, referring to the attention weight calculation of Q, the attention weight for the token in P is calculated by $\frac{h^{fc} \cdot h_i^P}{\sum_{j=1}^{|P|} h^{fc} \cdot h_j^P}$, where $|P|$ represents the number of tokens in P. For each instance in a pair, we select top-k^d important tokens as the rationale.

In the MRC task, the input also consists of two sequences: the question Q and the passage P. We adopt the match-LSTM model (WANG and JIANG) as our baseline model. The match-LSTM model uses two LSTMs to encode the question and passage respectively. Then it uses the standard word-by-word attention mechanism to obtain the attention weight for each token in the passage. And the final representation of each token in the passage is obtained by combining a weighted version of the question. We use $\bar{h}_i^P$ to represent the representation of i-th token in the passage. Then the importance score of j-th token is calculated by Equation 5.

$$a_j = \frac{\sum_{i=1}^{|Q|} e_{ij}}{|Q|} \qquad e_{ij} = \frac{h_i^Q \cdot \bar{h}_j^P}{\sum_{k=1}^{|Q|} h_i^Q \cdot \bar{h}_k^P} \tag{5}$$

where a_j is used as the importance score of token j.

ATT method on pre-trained models. Following related studies (Jain and Wallace, 2019; DeYoung et al., 2020), on transformer-based pre-trained models, attention scores are taken as the self-attention weights induced from the [CLS] token index to all other indices in the last layer. As the pre-trained model uses wordpiece tokenization, we sum the self-attention weights assigned to its constituent pieces to compute a token's score. Meanwhile, as the pre-trained model has multi-heads, we average scores over heads to derive a final score. In the MRC task, for each token in the passage, importance score is taken as the average self-attention weights induced from this token index to all indices of the question in the last layer.

Limitations of LIME. Given an input, LIME constructs a token vocabulary for it and aims to assign an important score for each token in this vocabulary. That is to say, for the token that appears multiple times, LIME neglects its position

Models + Methods	SA					STS					MRC		
	Plausibility		Faithfulness			Plausibility		Faithfulness			Plausibility		Faithfulness
	Token-F1↑	IOU-F1↑	MAP↑	Suf↓	Com↑	Token-F1	IOU-F1	MAP	Suf	Com	Token-F1	IOU-F1	MAP
LSTM + IG	38.2	9.8	60.6	-0.131	0.707	68.2	61.5	58.6	0.336	0.419	19.9	0.6	87.1
RoBERTa-base + IG	35.2	12.5	51.5	0.118	0.489	71.9	71.4	62.1	0.139	0.470	34.0	9.1	67.9
RoBERTa-large + IG	37.9	12.9	43.6	0.123	0.381	71.8	72.0	58.1	0.251	0.547	25.2	1.7	61.9
LSTM + ATT	24.0	9.8	72.6	0.171	0.225	72.7	72.1	77.3	0.110	0.359	2.7	0.0	79.6
RoBERTa-base + ATT	25.7	6.0	69.5	0.191	0.320	67.2	55.4	71.3	0.201	0.399	28.5	5.3	61.4
RoBERTa-large + ATT	30.7	8.2	67.9	0.173	0.248	68.0	59.8	67.0	0.251	0.547	28.5	5.5	48.8
LSTM + LIME	38.6	10.1	59.4	-0.130	0.701	74.8	79.0	65.9	-0.015	0.411	-	-	-
RoBERTa-base + LIME	37.3	14.3	56.6	0.051	0.660	77.3	83.2	74.8	-0.041	0.494	-	-	-
RoBERTa-large + LIME	39.0	14.5	53.0	-0.013	0.653	76.8	82.9	74.3	-0.024	0.562	-	-	-

Table 8: Interpretability evaluation results on Chinese datasets of three tasks.

information and only assigns one score for it. However, in STS and MRC, the position of a token is very important. Therefore, It can not guarantee the effectiveness of evaluation on these two tasks with LIME. In addition, as LIME is designed for classification models, it is difficult to apply it to the MRC task.

C Interpretability Evaluation on Chinese Datasets

We report interpretability results of three baseline models with three saliency methods on Chinese evaluation datasets in Table 8. It can be seen that interpretability results on Chinese datasets have the similar trends as those on English datasets. Different from the conclusions on English datasets, on all three tasks, IG-based method outperforms ATT-based method on plausibility. And ATT method performs better than IG on faithfulness in SA and STS tasks.

Towards More Natural Artificial Languages

Mark Hopkins
Department of Computer Science
Williams College
mh24@williams.edu

Abstract

A number of papers have recently argued in favor of using artificially generated languages to investigate the inductive biases of linguistic models, or to develop models for low-resource languages with underrepresented typologies. But the promise of artificial languages comes with a caveat: if these artificial languages are not sufficiently reflective of natural language, then using them as a proxy may lead to inaccurate conclusions. In this paper, we take a step towards increasing the realism of artificial language by introducing a variant of indexed grammars that draw their weights from hierarchical Pitman-Yor processes. We show that this framework generates languages that emulate the statistics of natural language corpora better than the current approach of directly formulating weighted context-free grammars.

1 Introduction

In the World Atlas of Linguistic Structures, Dryer (2013) reports that the plurality of world languages follow a subject-object-verb (SOV) word order. However, relatively few SOV languages (Japanese, Turkish, Persian) have a significant Internet footprint. Today, the Internet is dominated by subject-verb-object (SVO) languages like English, Spanish, and Chinese. The resulting paucity of non-SVO data makes it difficult to study whether linguistic models have an inductive bias towards particular word orders, or to develop models that perform well on low-resource languages from underrepresented linguistic families. In recent work, Wang and Eisner (2016), Ravfogel et al. (2019) and White and Cotterell (2021) argue that artificial languages could be an effective tool for addressing challenges like these, enabling researchers to create large cor pora that manifest targeted linguistic phenomena.

An obvious objection presents itself: what if the models aren't realistic enough? If not, then conclusions drawn from artificial languages may not transfer to natural languages. One response to this objection would be to abandon the entire enterprise, and with it the potential advantages of simulated data. An alternative is to follow the tradition of other disciplines who model natural systems (e.g. physics, geology, meteorology) and iterate on these models until they are sufficiently good predictors of observed phenomena.

In this spirit, this paper builds upon the framework of White and Cotterell (2021), who used weighted context-free grammars to construct artificial languages for studying the inductive biases of neural language models towards particular word orders. Observing that their framework did not account for selectional preference (the linguistic phenomenon that head words and their syntactic dependents are not probabilistically independent), we generalize weighted context-free grammars by introducing the *weighted random-access indexed grammar*, which facilitates the development of artificial languages that manifest selectional preference. We also present a methodology for building grammars that emulate statistical relationships observed in natural language corpora. Inspired by Teh (2006), we use hierarchical Pitman-Yor processes (Pitman and Yor, 1997) as the token-generating distributions for open-class categories (like noun, verb, and adjective). We set the hyperparameters by matching the statistics of the produced artificial languages with natural language corpora. As a pilot experiment for our framework, we partially replicate an experiment performed by White and Cotterell (2021) that studied the inductive bias of transformer and LSTM-based language models towards languages featuring various syntactic parameter configurations (Chomsky, 1981; Baker, 2008).

Finally, we accompany this paper with a Python package called `testperanto`[1], to allow researchers to use and refine our framework for further linguis-

[1] `https://github.com/Mark-Hopkins-at-Williams/testperanto` (Apache 2.0 license)

Proceedings of the 26th Conference on Computational Natural Language Learning (CoNLL), pages 85 - 94
December 7-8, 2022 ©2022 Association for Computational Linguistics

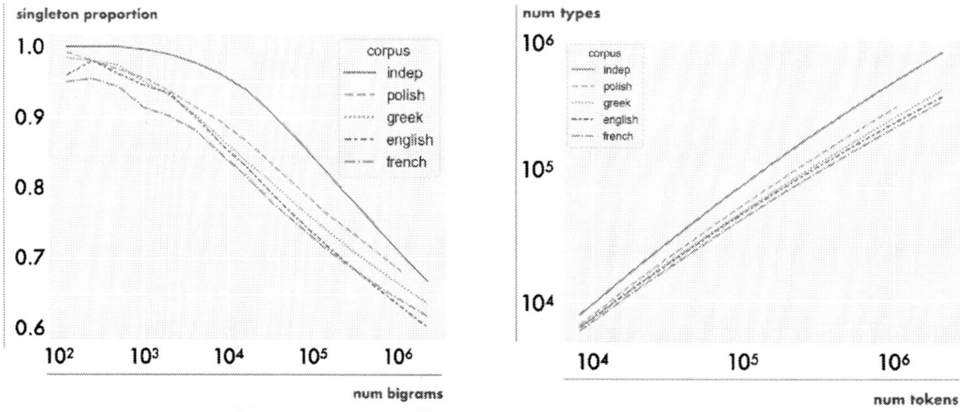

Figure 1: A comparison of the singleton proportion curves of adjective-noun bigrams in the Europarl corpus with bigrams generated using independent adjective and noun distributions.

tic studies.

2 Related Work

Both Wang and Eisner (2016) and Ravfogel et al. (2019) constructed artificial languages by manipulating sentences from existing natural language corpora. Both approaches made use of a dependency parser (or a gold parsed corpus) to inform these manipulations, altering syntactic constituent order (Wang and Eisner, 2016; Ravfogel et al., 2019) or token morphology (Ravfogel et al., 2019).

White and Cotterell (2021) argued that manipulated natural language corpora have downsides. Based on a series of negative results (Cotterell et al., 2018; Mielke et al., 2019), they suggested that it may not be possible to remove confounding linguistic features from an existing corpus, making it difficult to isolate typological features for study. To maximize the ability to run a controlled experiment, they generated fully artificial languages from hand-built weighted context-free grammars. However, although their grammars modeled certain syntactic dependencies (e.g. conjugating a verb with its subject), they did not model semantic dependencies. We assert that it is prohibitively difficult to directly formulate weighted context-free grammars that model semantic dependencies (e.g. selectional preference), motivating our extension – the weighted random-access indexed grammar.

3 Motivation

White and Cotterell (2021) generated artificial language using a *weighted context-free grammar* (WCFG). A WCFG augments a context-free grammar (CFG) with a function q that assigns a non-negative weight $q(r)$ to each grammar rule r. This induces a weight for each derivation: the product of the weights of the rules used in the derivation. More formal details can be found in Collins (2013).

WCFGs produce terminal symbols (words) according to probability distributions that depend exclusively on the grammar nonterminals. Consider the following CFG:

$$\begin{array}{rcl} \mathsf{S} & \rightarrow & \mathsf{NN\ VP} \\ \mathsf{VP} & \rightarrow & \mathsf{VB\ NN} \\ \mathsf{VB} & \rightarrow & \texttt{drank} \mid \texttt{ate} \\ \mathsf{NN} & \rightarrow & \texttt{you} \mid \texttt{it} \mid \texttt{water} \mid \texttt{food} \end{array}$$

By using plain nonterminals like VB and NN, the respective probabilities of sentences `it drank water` and `it drank food` depend only on the probability of the rules VB $\rightarrow$ `water` and VB $\rightarrow$ `food`. Crucially, the verb choice does not differentiate the sentence probabilities. This is unrealistic – it is more common to drink water than to drink food, whereas it is more common to eat food than to eat water. This phenomenon (that linguistic arguments are not independent of their predicates) is known as *selectional preference*.

One way to detect selectional preference (Teh, 2006) is to collect dependency relationships from a parsed natural language corpus (e.g. `amod`, `nsubj`, `dodj`) and extract the dependency bigrams (e.g. for `amod`, the first three dependency bigrams in Europarl are `internal market`, `European citizens`, and `cultural exception`). Then, as we stream through the dependency bigrams, we plot either the number of observed bigram types

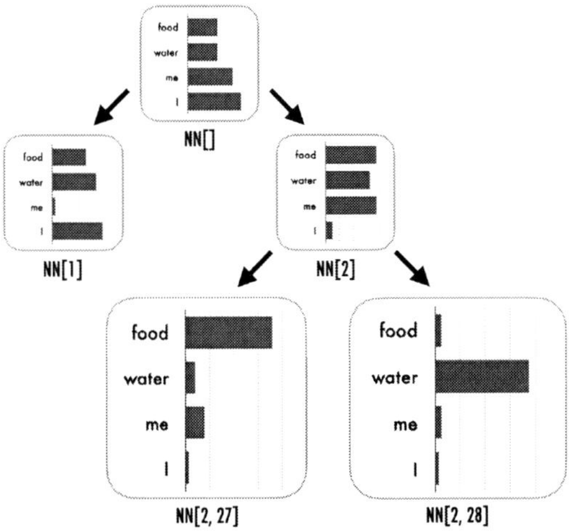

Figure 2: An example hierarchical Pitman-Yor process. NN[] is the global noun distribution. NN[1] and NN[2] respectively represent the likelihood that a noun is the subject or object of a verb. NN[2, 27] and NN[2, 28] respectively represent the likelihood that a noun is the object of verb 27 (eat) or verb 28 (drink) of the vocab.

(a type-token curve) or the proportion of bigrams whose type has been observed exactly once (a singleton proportion curve). In Figure 1, we contrast the curves generated[2] using four Europarl corpora (Koehn, 2005) with a bigram corpus constructed by sampling one adjective and one noun from independent distributions respectively derived from adjective and noun frequency in the English Europarl corpus. The curves generated using the independent bigram corpus are outliers. For instance, when the number of observed bigrams is plotted on a log scale, the natural corpora have roughly linear singleton proportion curves, whereas the independent corpus has a considerable bow in the curve.

We would like to generate artificial languages such that the dependencies have similar statistics to naturally observed dependencies. Rather than independently generating open-class words, Teh (2006) suggests using a hierarchical Pitman-Yor process (Pitman and Yor, 1997) – a tree-structured set of distributions over the same domain, in which child distributions are resamplings of their parents. Figure 2 shows an example. A hierarchical Pitman-Yor process allows us to model context-specific word distributions (e.g. `food` is more likely to appear as the object of the verb `eat` than `water`, `I`, or `me`) that are jointly influenced by global word frequency priors. A Pitman-Yor process $\mathsf{PY}(d, \theta, P_{\mathsf{base}})$ is characterized by a *discount* parameter $d \in [0, 1)$, a *strength* parameter $\theta \in (-d, \infty)$, and a *base distribution* P_{base} over integers $\{1, \ldots, V\}$. We follow (Teh, 2006) in describing a Pitman-Yor process as a stochastic process that generates samples $\langle x_1, x_2, ...\rangle$ from i.i.d. samples $\langle y_1, y_2, ...\rangle$ drawn from base distribution P_{base}. Intuitively, it is a "rich-get-richer" process, in which the jth sample x_j is set to either the value y_i assigned to a previous x-sample (with probability proportional to the number of previous x-samples that were assigned the value y_i), or the next y-sample in the sequence that hasn't yet been used. Formally, let $b_1 = 1$ and draw subsequent binary values b_{n+1} from a Bernoulli (coin-flip) distribution where:

$$P(b_{n+1} = 1) = \frac{\theta + d \sum_{1 \leq i \leq n} b_i}{\theta + n}$$

Variable b_{n+1} determines whether the $(n+1)$th sample is set to the value of a previous assignment ($b_{n+1} = 0$) or the next unused y_i sample ($b_{n+1} = 1$). Now define $t_1 = 1$ and consider $j, n \in \mathbb{Z}^+$. If $b_{n+1} = 0$, then let $t_{n+1} = j$ with probability:

$$\frac{1}{n} \sum_{1 \leq i \leq n} \mathbb{1}(t_i = j)$$

Otherwise, if $b_{n+1} = 1$:

$$t_{n+1} = 1 + \sum_{1 \leq i \leq n} b_i$$

The nth sample drawn from the Pitman-Yor process is $x_n = y_{t_n}$. A Pitman-Yor process, for all practical purposes, can generate an "open-class" of words by using a uniform base distribution P_{unif} with a sufficiently large vocabulary size V (for our experiments, we use the space of all 32-bit integers).

A hierarchical Pitman-Yor process is simply a Pitman-Yor process that uses another Pitman-Yor process as its base distribution. For instance, we could define a global adjective distribution $P_{\mathsf{adj}} = \mathsf{PY}(0.4, 500, P_{\mathsf{unif}})$, and then for noun y_1 of our vocabulary, we could define a noun-dependent adjective distribution $P_{\mathsf{adj}, \mathsf{y}_1} = \mathsf{PY}(d, \theta, P_{\mathsf{adj}})$.

4 Approach

The main challenge: how do we construct a WCFG that derives its weights from the linked distributions of a hierarchical Pitman-Yor process? Concerned with the induction of better n-gram language

[2] To generate Figure 1, we shuffled the Europarl sentences and extracted the adjective-noun dependencies using `spaCy`. The shuffling smooths irregularities caused by topic shift.

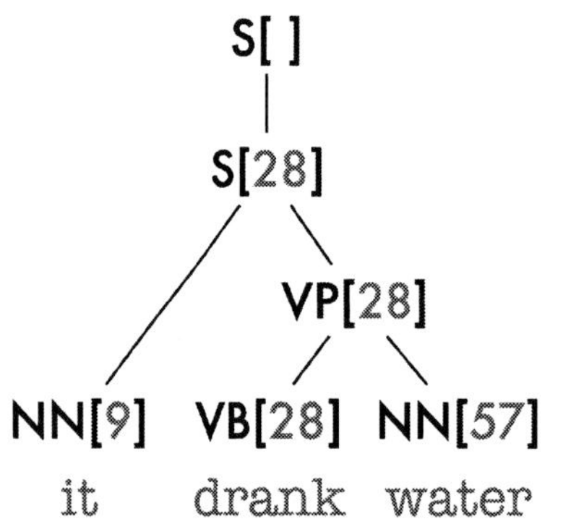

Figure 3: An example derivation, using the indexed grammar from Figure 4.

			ζ
S[]	$\rightarrow$	S[z_1]	$z_1 \mapsto$ VB[]
S[y_1]	$\rightarrow$	NN[z_1] VP[y_1]	$z_1 \mapsto$ NN[1, y_1]
VP[y_1]	$\rightarrow$	VB[y_1] NN[z_1]	$z_1 \mapsto$ NN[2, y_1]
VB[27]	$\rightarrow$	ate	
VB[28]	$\rightarrow$	drank	
NN[9]	$\rightarrow$	it	
NN[56]	$\rightarrow$	food	
NN[57]	$\rightarrow$	water	

Figure 4: An example indexed grammar. The base weight $w_0(\rho)$ of each indexed rule ρ is 1.

models, previous work (Teh, 2006; Blunsom and Cohn, 2011) mainly focused on how to incorporate hierarchical Pitman-Yor processes into sequential models like Hidden Markov Models. Here, our concern is how to incorporate these distributions into a generative syntactic model convenient for engineering artificial languages with specific linguistic typologies. There exist many syntactic models to choose from, including dependency grammars (Eisner, 1996), tree-adjoining grammars (Joshi, 1987), lexical functional grammars (Kaplan, 1985), CCGs (Steedman and Baldridge, 2011), HPSGs (Pollard and Sag, 1994) and GPSGs (Gazdar et al., 1985). In this work, we choose to extend context-free grammars, partly because of their popularity and partly to facilitate comparison with (White and Cotterell, 2021), who used WCFGs – however, our approach can be adapted to other syntactic formalisms.

4.1 Intuition

Our approach is a variation on indexed grammars (Aho, 1968; Hopcroft et al., 2001), which augment CFG nonterminals with a sequence of symbols called *indices*. Before going through the formalism, we briefly preview how it works, using a derivation (Figure 3) for an example indexed grammar (Figure 4). At the top level, it applies CFG rule S[] $\rightarrow$ S[28], which involves two choices:

1. the choice of "indexed rule": S[] $\rightarrow$ S[z_1]
2. the choice of indices to assign to its z-variables: $\{z_1 \mapsto 28\}$

Next, the derivation expands S[28] by applying the CFG rule S[28] $\rightarrow$ NN[9] VP[28]. Again, this involves two choices:

1. the choice of indexed rule: S[y_1] $\rightarrow$ NN[z_1] VP[y_1]
2. the choice of indices to assign to its z-variables: $\{z_1 \mapsto 9\}$

Note the role of the variables: y-variables match LHS indices and copy them to the RHS, whereas z-variables introduce new indices on the RHS. Each z-variable z_i of an indexed rule is associated with a key $\zeta(z_i)$ (Figure 4, right column) that references a distribution in a "distribution table" τ. The weight associated with a derivation rule (e.g. S[28] $\rightarrow$ NN[9] VP[28]) is the product of the base weight w_0 of the indexed rule (e.g. w_0(S[y_1] $\rightarrow$ NN[z_1] VP[y_1]), and the probabilities of the z-assignments (e.g. τ(NN[1, 28])(9)). As with CFGs, the weight of a derivation is the product of the derivation rules.

4.2 Random-access Indexed Grammars

Let $Y = \{y_1, y_2, ...\}$ and $Z = \{z_1, z_2, ...\}$ be reserved symbols called y- and z-variables. A *random-access indexed grammar (RIG)*[3] is a 5-tuple (N, T, F, S, R) where:

- N is a set of *nonterminal* symbols
- T is a set of *terminal* symbols
- F is a set of *index* symbols, or *indices*[4]
- $S \in N$ is the *start symbol*

[3]The standard definition of indexed grammars (Hopcroft et al., 2001) treats the indices as a stack, rather than as a random-access array. Our departure from the standard definition (introducing y- and z-variables to allow random-access matching) prioritizes the ease of grammar engineering over definitional conciseness and representational power. Moreover, since our use case is generation, we are not concerned with indexed grammar variants that prioritize efficiency of parsing or induction (e.g. (Gazdar, 1987)).

[4]In this paper, we will use the set of nonnegative 32-bit integers as our set F of indices.

- R is a finite set of *indexed rules* (to be defined shortly)

In contrast to standard CFG rules, indexed rules use *indexed nonterminals*, symbols of the form $\mathsf{A}[\phi]$, where $\mathsf{A} \in N$ and $\phi \in (F \cup Y \cup Z)^*$. A *grounded indexed nonterminal* is an indexed nonterminal $\mathsf{A}[\phi]$ such that $\phi \in F^*$. An *indexed rule* has the form:

$$\mathsf{A}[\phi] \rightarrow \mathsf{rhs}$$

where $\mathsf{A}[\phi]$ is an indexed nonterminal without z-variables, and rhs is a sequence of terminals and indexed nonterminals whose y-variables all appear in ϕ.

To define the semantics of a RIG, let a *substitution* be a function $\sigma : D \rightarrow F$ with domain $D \subseteq Y \cup Z$. We apply a substitution σ to a indexed nonterminal $\mathsf{A}[\phi_1, \ldots, \phi_n]$ as follows:

$$\sigma(\mathsf{A}[\phi_1, \ldots, \phi_n]) = \mathsf{A}[\bar{\sigma}(\phi_1), \cdots, \bar{\sigma}(\phi_n)]$$

where:

$$\bar{\sigma}(x) = \begin{cases} \sigma(x) & \text{if } x \in D \\ x & \text{if } x \notin D \end{cases}$$

for $x \in F \cup Y \cup Z$. We apply a substitution σ to an indexed rule ρ by applying σ to every indexed nonterminal in ρ. For example, if:

$$\begin{aligned} \sigma &= \{\mathsf{y}_1 \mapsto 52, \mathsf{z}_1 \mapsto 14\} \\ \rho &= \mathsf{S}[\mathsf{y}_1] \rightarrow \mathsf{NN}[\mathsf{z}_1]\ \mathsf{VP}[\mathsf{y}_1] \end{aligned}$$

then:

$$\sigma(\rho) = \mathsf{S}[52] \rightarrow \mathsf{NN}[14]\ \mathsf{VP}[52]$$

Each indexed rule ρ implicitly represents the set of CFG rules that can be obtained by applying a substitution to the variables of the indexed rule:

$$\mathcal{R}(\rho) = \{\sigma(\rho) \mid \sigma : V(\rho) \rightarrow F\}$$

Here, $V(\rho) \subseteq Y \cup Z$ is the set of variables that appear in indexed rule ρ. The RIG encodes a CFG consisting of the union $\bigcup_{\rho \in R} \mathcal{R}(\rho)$ of these rules.

4.3 Weighted RIGs

Next, we introduce weights from a hierarchical Pitman-Yor process. We reference the process distributions via a *distribution table* – a function τ that maps grounded indexed nonterminals to distributions (e.g. the distributions of a hierarchical Pitman-Yor process). For instance, in the distribution table τ implied by Figure 2, $\tau(\mathsf{NN}[2, 28])$ corresponds to the lower right distribution.

A weighted random-access indexed grammar (WRIG) is a tuple (G, τ, w_0, ζ) where:

- $G = (N, T, F, S, R)$ is a RIG
- τ is a distribution table
- w_0 assigns a nonnegative weight (called the *base weight*) to each indexed rule $\rho \in R$
- ζ assigns a z-*weighting* to each indexed rule $\rho \in R$. The z-weighting $\zeta(\rho)$, abbreviated ζ_ρ for clarity, is a function that assigns an indexed nonterminal (that may contain y- but not z-variables) to each z-variable of the rule.

Every WRIG encodes a WCFG. Each CFG rule $r = \sigma(\rho)$ encoded by indexed rule ρ (where $\sigma : V(\rho) \rightarrow F$ is a substitution) has weight:

$$q(r) = w_0(\rho) \cdot \prod_{\mathsf{z} \in Z(\rho)} w_{\mathsf{z}}(\sigma(\mathsf{z}))$$

where $Z(\rho) \subseteq Z$ is the set of z-variables that appear in indexed rule ρ, and $w_{\mathsf{z}} = \tau(\sigma(\zeta_\rho(\mathsf{z})))$ is the distribution associated with grounded indexed nonterminal $\sigma(\zeta_\rho(\mathsf{z}))$ in the distribution table τ.

Example: The second rule of the RIG in Figure 4 encodes (among others) the CFG rule:

$$\mathsf{S}[28] \rightarrow \mathsf{NN}[9]\ \mathsf{VP}[28]$$

The weight of this CFG rule is:

$$\begin{aligned} & w_0(\mathsf{S}[\mathsf{y}_1] \rightarrow \mathsf{NN}[\mathsf{z}_1]\ \mathsf{VP}[\mathsf{y}_1]) \\ \cdot\ & \tau(\mathsf{NN}[1, 28])(9) \end{aligned}$$

In other words, it is the base weight of the indexed rule, multiplied by the probability of word 9 (`it`) being the subject of verb 28 (`drink`).

4.4 Voiceboxes

Using a WRIG, syntax can be specified with relative ease, i.e. without the need to manually formulate an arduous number of rules. However, terminal rules (i.e. rules that generate the lexemes) are a different story. We need an auxiliary mechanism to automatically invent lexemes from grounded indexed preterminals, i.e. a mechanism that will translate a preterminal (see Figure 4) like `VB[27]` – the 27th verb of the vocabulary – into a lexeme (e.g., `ate`). To do so, we pair the WRIG with a *voicebox*,

			ζ
$\mathsf{S}[]$	$\rightarrow$	$\mathsf{S}[z_1, z_2]$	$z_1 \mapsto \mathsf{VB}[], z_2 \mapsto \mathsf{COUNT}[]$
$\mathsf{S}[y_1, y_2]$	$\rightarrow$	$\mathsf{IC}[y_1, y_2]$, $\mathsf{DC}[z_1, z_2]$	$z_1 \mapsto \mathsf{VB}[], z_2 \mapsto \mathsf{COUNT}[]$
$\mathsf{IC}[y_1, y_2]$	$\rightarrow$	$\mathsf{NP}[z_1, y_2, 1]$ $\mathsf{VP}[y_1, y_2]$	$z_1 \mapsto \mathsf{NN}[1, y_1]$
$\mathsf{DC}[y_1, y_2]$	$\rightarrow$	`weil` $\mathsf{NP}[z_1, y_2, 1]$ $\mathsf{VPD}[y_1, y_2]$	$z_1 \mapsto \mathsf{NN}[1, y_1]$
$\mathsf{VP}[y_1, y_2]$	$\rightarrow$	$\mathsf{VB}[y_1, y_2]$ $\mathsf{NP}[z_1, z_2, 2]$	$z_1 \mapsto \mathsf{NN}[2, y_1], z_2 \mapsto \mathsf{COUNT}[]$
$\mathsf{VPD}[y_1, y_2]$	$\rightarrow$	$\mathsf{NP}[z_1, z_2, 2]$ $\mathsf{VB}[y_1, y_2]$	$z_1 \mapsto \mathsf{NN}[2, y_1], z_2 \mapsto \mathsf{COUNT}[]$
$\mathsf{NP}[y_1, y_2, y_3]$	$\rightarrow$	$\mathsf{DT}[y_2, y_3]$ $\mathsf{NN}[y_1, y_2, y_3]$	

Figure 5: A WRIG capturing simple German syntax and morphology. Each indexed rule has base weight 1.

x	$\tau(x)$	description
$\mathsf{VB}[]$	$\mathsf{PY}(0.4, 1, P_{\mathsf{unif}})$	global verb distribution
$\mathsf{NN}[]$	$\mathsf{PY}(0.4, 500, P_{\mathsf{unif}})$	global noun distribution
$\mathsf{NN}[1]$	$\mathsf{PY}(0.4, 500, \tau(\mathsf{NN}[]))$	global subject distribution
$\mathsf{NN}[1, y_1]$	$\mathsf{PY}(0.4, 10, \tau(\mathsf{NN}[1]))$	subject distribution for head verb y_1
$\mathsf{NN}[2]$	$\mathsf{PY}(0.4, 500, \tau(\mathsf{NN}[]))$	global object distribution
$\mathsf{NN}[2, y_1]$	$\mathsf{PY}(0.4, 0.1, \tau(\mathsf{NN}[2]))$	object distribution for head verb y_1
$\mathsf{COUNT}[]$	$\mathsf{Unif}(\{1, 2\})$	global count distribution (1=singular, 2=plural)

Figure 6: Distribution table for the WRIG in Figure 5. P_{unif} is a uniform distribution over all 32-bit integers.

a function that maps grounded indexed nonterminals (specifically, preterminals) to lexemes. The voicebox is then used to generate terminal rules on-the-fly. Note that the voicebox can also support morphology. For example, if the preterminal `VB[27, 3, 1]` encodes the third-person singular conjugation of verb 27, then the voicebox might produce $\beta(\texttt{VB}[27, 3, 1]) = \texttt{eats}$.

5 Demo: Simple German Syntax with Selectional Preference

To demonstrate how linguistic phenomena can be modeled by a WRIG, we present a small example in Figure 5, whose distribution table is given by Figure 6. It models various aspects of German syntax: word order (independent clauses are SVO, whereas dependent clauses are SOV), verb conjugation (present singular and present plural), and case roles (nominative and accusative). Figure 7 shows the first five sentences of a corpus generated by the WRIG. To interpret the indexed nonterminals, note that subject count (1=singular, 2=plural) and case (1=nominative, 2=accusative) are encoded as integer indices:

- $\mathsf{S}[y_1, y_2], \mathsf{IC}[y_1, y_2], \mathsf{DC}[y_1, y_2]$: respectively produce a sentence, independent clause, and dependent clause with subject count y_2, whose head is the $y_1{}^{\mathsf{th}}$ verb of the vocabulary
- $\mathsf{NP}[y_1, y_2, y_3]$: produces a noun phrase with count y_2 and case y_3, whose head is the $y_1{}^{\mathsf{th}}$ noun of the vocabulary
- $\mathsf{VP(D)}[y_1, y_2]$: produces a (dependent clause) verb phrase with subject count y_2, whose head is the $y_1{}^{\mathsf{th}}$ verb of the vocabulary
- $\mathsf{NN}[y_1, y_2, y_3]$: produces the $y_1{}^{\mathsf{th}}$ noun of the vocabulary, declined for count y_2 and case y_3
- $\mathsf{VB}[y_1, y_2]$: produces the $y_1{}^{\mathsf{th}}$ verb of the vocabulary, conjugated for subject count y_2
- $\mathsf{DT}[y_1, y_2]$: produces a determiner for a noun with count y_1 and case y_2

Terminal rules for open-class nonterminals $\mathsf{NN}[y_1, y_2, y_3]$ and $\mathsf{VB}[y_1, y_2]$ are generated by a voicebox that randomly concatenates German syllables to create new words, and adds German morphological endings based on count and case. For the closed-class $\mathsf{DT}[y_1, y_2]$, the voicebox generates the German definite determiner for the specified count and case. For instance (see Figure 7), the noun hunghub[5] appears as `den` hunghub when it is accusative singular and `die` hunghuben when it is accusative plural.

[5]In this grammar, all nouns are masculine. See the `testperanto` tutorials for an example of how to model noun gender.

der zerheimherrun konzumschlage den lagfrischhan , weil der terterfin die wirnachparen kennjahre
der dungtun milchsichkeite die hunghuben **, weil die vorsamrichen den tagwohn jahrkolen**
der derver milchsichkeite den hunghub **, weil der tiktikflach** die hunghuben milchsichkeite
die kenngunhungen milchsichkeiten **den milchmanmilch , weil der tiklang den frauhung telmonhane**
der niedlang milchsichkeite **den dichgeh , weil die frauhungrungen die langterleren samkenntelen**

Figure 7: Example sentences generated by the simple German WRIG. Observe that the verb `milchsichkeiten` strongly tends to take the noun hunghub as its object – the hyperparameters of this particular WRIG have been set to encourage atypically strong selectional preference between verbs and their objects.

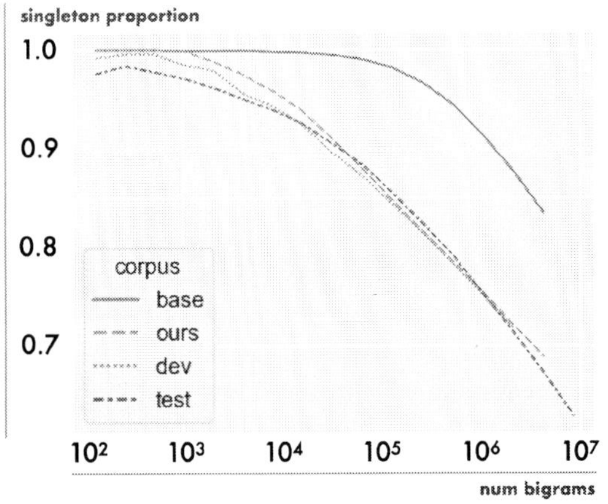

Figure 8: Singleton proportion of verb-object dependency bigrams as corpus size increases.

		singleton proportion		type-token ratio	
		`dev`	`test`	`dev`	`test`
amod	base	0.099	0.094	0.23	0.23
	ours	**0.0074**	**0.013**	**0.016**	**0.018**
nsubj	base	0.045	0.057	0.083	0.12
	ours	**0.0044**	**0.010**	**0.014**	**0.041**
dobj	base	0.081	0.088	0.18	0.22
	ours	**0.0081**	**0.014**	**0.036**	**0.054**

Figure 9: Absolute difference of singleton proportion and type-token ratio between artificial corpora (ours and base) and natural corpora (dev and test), averaged over power-of-two corpora sizes from 2^7 to 2^{22}.

By associating the noun distributions with the distributions of a hierarchical Pitman-Yor process, we also model selectional preference. By assigning a Pitman-Yor process of very low strength (0.1) to the verb-dependent object distributions, we enforce unusually strong selectional preference between verbs and objects, allowing us to see its manifestation of in just a small sample of generated sentences (Figure 7). In particular, the invented verb `milchsichkeiten` frequently takes the noun hunghub as its object.

6 Experiment: Word Order Bias

As a pilot study of our framework, we re-created an experiment performed by White and Cotterell (2021), who used WCFGs to investigate the inductive biases of neural language models for various word orders exhibited by natural language. We created a WRIG based on their WCFG description, which produces simple declarative sentences with relative clauses, prepositional phrases, and clausal complements. We used a voicebox that assigned concatenations of random syllables to each generic noun, verb, and adjective. It used English prepositions, determiners, and morphology (e.g. verbs with a singular subject were suffixed with the letter "s"). We set the parameters of our Pitman-Yor processes by specifying discount and strength parameters so that our produced sentences closely matched the type-token ratio and singleton proportion curves of the English side of the WMT 2014 German-English parallel corpus (Bojar et al., 2014; Luong et al., 2015) for the following dependency bigrams: adjective-noun (amod), verb-subject (nsubj), verb-object (dobj). Figure 8 compares the singleton proportion curves of verb-object dependencies for our generated corpus, versus the development corpus (WMT 2014 Ger-Eng) and a held-out test corpus: the English side of the JParaCrawl 3.0 Jpn-Eng corpus (Morishita et al., 2022). We also compare our corpus statistics to a baseline that attempts to replicate (White and Cotterell, 2021), using independent adjective, noun, and verb distributions rather than tied hierarchical Pitman-Yor distributions. Visual inspection shows that the independent baseline is an outlier, unrepresentative of the statistics manifested by natural corpora. We can distill these curves into a single numeric indicator by averaging the absolute difference between an artificial corpus curve (`ours` or `base`) and a natural corpus curve

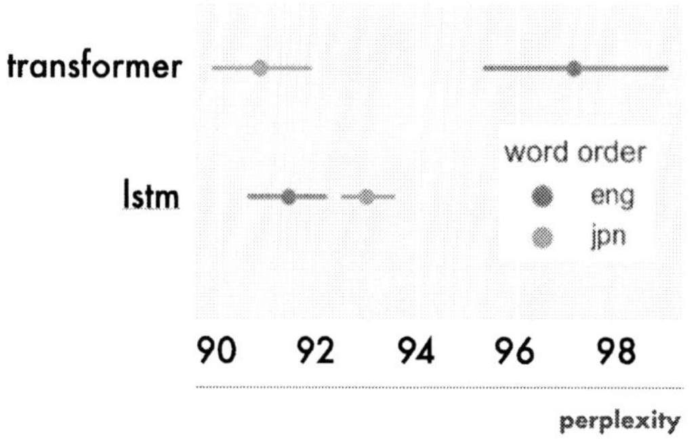

Figure 10: Visualization of experimental results using a point plot. The transformer produces lower-perplexity language models for the artificial languages that follow a Japanese word order, while the LSTM produces lower-perplexity language models for the artificial languages that follow an English word order.

(dev or test) for each power of two on the x-axis. Figure 9 presents these numbers for singleton proportion and the type-token ratio: the statistics for our generated corpus are an order-of-magnitude closer to natural corpora than the baseline.

We created two variants of the WRIG, corresponding to the standard word orders of English and Japanese. For instance, as a head-final language, the Japanese WRIG included the rule[6]:

$$\mathsf{VP}[y_1, y_2] \rightarrow \mathsf{NP}[z_1, z_2]\ \mathsf{VB}[y_1, y_2]$$

and as a head-initial language, the English WRIG included the rule:

$$\mathsf{VP}[y_1, y_2] \rightarrow \mathsf{VB}[y_1, y_2]\ \mathsf{NP}[z_1, z_2]$$

Following (White and Cotterell, 2021), the WRIGs also differed in:

- the position of the complementizer in complements, relative to the sentential component
- the position of the adposition in adpositional phrases, relative to the adpositional object
- the position of a relative clause, relative to the noun it modifies

We generated 1,000,000 sentences for each WRIG variant, and divided these into ten evenly sized corpora. Each corpus of 100,000 sentences was further divided into an 80k-10k-10k train-dev-test partition. On each train set, we trained[7] a transformer-based and an LSTM-based language model, resulting in 10 trained language models (LMs) per choice of neural architecture and WRIG. Finally, we evaluated these LMs on the respective test sets.

For each architecture (transformer and LSTM) and word order (English and Japanese), Figure 10 visualizes the test perplexity over the ten trials using a point plot[8]. For transformer LMs, we obtained lower perplexity on the languages that followed a Japanese word order. For LSTM LMs, we observed the opposite: a (statistically significant) lower perplexity on the languages that followed an English word order. While these results generally support the findings of White and Cotterell (2021), White and Cotterell (2021) did not find significant differences between the LSTM LMs. We find it encouraging that our results do not differ wildly from White and Cotterell (2021) (it would be troubling for the prospects of artificial languages if each iterative improvement dramatically reversed the conclusions of the previous iteration). At the same time, we also find it encouraging that the differences between their results and ours offer a possible reconciliation between White and Cotterell (2021) and Ravfogel et al. (2019), who reported, based on experiments with naturally-derived corpora, that LSTM LMs performed better on SVO (versus SOV) languages.

7 Conclusion

With this work, our goal is to enable researchers to more easily develop models for typologically diverse languages, and to investigate under what conditions such models perform effectively. By demonstrating that RIGs (weighted by hierarchical Pitman-Yor processes) can model realistic syntactic and semantic dependencies, we hope to provide some confidence that the framework can prove a useful proxy for real-world data, when such data is not readily available. To facilitate adoption of our framework, we are also releasing an open-source Python package called `testperanto` for building WRIGs, providing fellow researchers with a means to generate artificial languages that emulate the typology of the natural languages they seek to study.

[6]A brief guide to the referenced indexed nonterminals of the WRIG: $\mathsf{VP}[y_1.y_2]$ produces a verb phrase with subject count y_2, whose head is the $y_1{}^{th}$ verb of the vocabulary. $\mathsf{NP}[y_1, y_2]$ produces a noun phrase with count y_2, whose head is the $y_1{}^{th}$ noun of the vocabulary. $\mathsf{VB}[y_1, y_2]$ produces the $y_1{}^{th}$ verb of the vocabulary, conjugated for subject count y_2.

[7]Like White and Cotterell (2021), we used the `fairseq` implementation (Ott et al., 2019) of these language models.

[8]We used `seaborn` to generate the plot. A point plot shows the mean of the ten trials (the dot) and the 95% confidence interval (the line).

References

Alfred V Aho. 1968. Indexed grammars—an extension of context-free grammars. *Journal of the ACM (JACM)*, 15(4):647–671.

Mark C Baker. 2008. *The atoms of language: The mind's hidden rules of grammar*. Basic books.

Phil Blunsom and Trevor Cohn. 2011. A hierarchical Pitman-Yor process HMM for unsupervised part of speech induction. In *Proceedings of the 49th Annual Meeting of the Association for Computational Linguistics: Human Language Technologies*, pages 865–874, Portland, Oregon, USA. Association for Computational Linguistics.

Ondřej Bojar, Christian Buck, Christian Federmann, Barry Haddow, Philipp Koehn, Johannes Leveling, Christof Monz, Pavel Pecina, Matt Post, Herve Saint-Amand, Radu Soricut, Lucia Specia, and Aleš Tamchyna. 2014. Findings of the 2014 workshop on statistical machine translation. In *Proceedings of the Ninth Workshop on Statistical Machine Translation*, pages 12–58, Baltimore, Maryland, USA. Association for Computational Linguistics.

Noam Chomsky. 1981. Principles and parameters in syntactic theory. *Explanation in linguistics*, pages 32–75.

Michael Collins. 2013. Lexicalized probabilistic context-free grammars. *Lecture Notes*.

Ryan Cotterell, Sabrina J. Mielke, Jason Eisner, and Brian Roark. 2018. Are all languages equally hard to language-model? In *Proceedings of the 2018 Conference of the North American Chapter of the Association for Computational Linguistics: Human Language Technologies, Volume 2 (Short Papers)*, pages 536–541, New Orleans, Louisiana. Association for Computational Linguistics.

Matthew S. Dryer. 2013. Order of subject, object and verb. In Matthew S. Dryer and Martin Haspelmath, editors, *WALS Online*. Max Planck Institute for Evolutionary Anthropology, Leipzig.

Jason M. Eisner. 1996. Three new probabilistic models for dependency parsing: An exploration. In *COLING 1996 Volume 1: The 16th International Conference on Computational Linguistics*.

Gerald Gazdar. 1987. COMIT ==> PATR II. In *Theoretical Issues in Natural Language Processing 3*.

Gerald Gazdar, Ewan Klein, Geoffrey K Pullum, and Ivan A Sag. 1985. *Generalized phrase structure grammar*. Harvard University Press.

John E Hopcroft, Rajeev Motwani, and Jeffrey D Ullman. 2001. Introduction to automata theory, languages, and computation. *Acm Sigact News*, 32(1):60–65.

Aravind K Joshi. 1987. An introduction to tree adjoining grammars. *Mathematics of language*, 1:87–115.

Ronald M. Kaplan. 1985. Structural correspondences and Lexical-Functional Grammar. In *Proceedings of the first Conference on Theoretical and Methodological Issues in Machine Translation of Natural Languages*, Hamilton, NY.

Philipp Koehn. 2005. Europarl: A parallel corpus for statistical machine translation. In *Proceedings of Machine Translation Summit X: Papers*, pages 79–86, Phuket, Thailand.

Thang Luong, Hieu Pham, and Christopher D. Manning. 2015. Effective approaches to attention-based neural machine translation. In *Proceedings of the 2015 Conference on Empirical Methods in Natural Language Processing*, pages 1412–1421, Lisbon, Portugal. Association for Computational Linguistics.

Sabrina J. Mielke, Ryan Cotterell, Kyle Gorman, Brian Roark, and Jason Eisner. 2019. What kind of language is hard to language-model? In *Proceedings of the 57th Annual Meeting of the Association for Computational Linguistics*, pages 4975–4989, Florence, Italy. Association for Computational Linguistics.

Makoto Morishita, Katsuki Chousa, Jun Suzuki, and Masaaki Nagata. 2022. Jparacrawl v3. 0: A large-scale english-japanese parallel corpus. *arXiv preprint arXiv:2202.12607*.

Myle Ott, Sergey Edunov, Alexei Baevski, Angela Fan, Sam Gross, Nathan Ng, David Grangier, and Michael Auli. 2019. fairseq: A fast, extensible toolkit for sequence modeling. In *Proceedings of the 2019 Conference of the North American Chapter of the Association for Computational Linguistics (Demonstrations)*, pages 48–53, Minneapolis, Minnesota. Association for Computational Linguistics.

Jim Pitman and Marc Yor. 1997. The two-parameter poisson-dirichlet distribution derived from a stable subordinator. *The Annals of Probability*, pages 855–900.

Carl Pollard and Ivan A Sag. 1994. *Head-driven phrase structure grammar*. University of Chicago Press.

Shauli Ravfogel, Yoav Goldberg, and Tal Linzen. 2019. Studying the inductive biases of RNNs with synthetic variations of natural languages. In *Proceedings of the 2019 Conference of the North American Chapter of the Association for Computational Linguistics: Human Language Technologies, Volume 1 (Long and Short Papers)*, pages 3532–3542, Minneapolis, Minnesota. Association for Computational Linguistics.

Mark Steedman and Jason Baldridge. 2011. Combinatory categorial grammar. *Non-Transformational Syntax: Formal and Explicit Models of Grammar. Wiley-Blackwell*, pages 181–224.

Yee Whye Teh. 2006. A hierarchical Bayesian language model based on Pitman-Yor processes. In *Proceedings of the 21st International Conference on Computational Linguistics and 44th Annual Meeting of the Association for Computational Linguistics*, pages 985–992, Sydney, Australia. Association for Computational Linguistics.

Dingquan Wang and Jason Eisner. 2016. The galactic dependencies treebanks: Getting more data by synthesizing new languages. *Transactions of the Association for Computational Linguistics*, 4:491–505.

Jennifer C. White and Ryan Cotterell. 2021. Examining the inductive bias of neural language models with artificial languages. In *Proceedings of the 59th Annual Meeting of the Association for Computational Linguistics and the 11th International Joint Conference on Natural Language Processing (Volume 1: Long Papers)*, pages 454–463, Online. Association for Computational Linguistics.

Causal Analysis of Syntactic Agreement Neurons in Multilingual Language Models

Aaron Mueller[ʃ], **Yu Xia**[ɕ], **Tal Linzen**[ɕ]
[ʃ]Johns Hopkins University [ɕ]New York University
amueller@jhu.edu, yx1675@nyu.edu, linzen@nyu.edu

Abstract

Structural probing work has found evidence for latent syntactic information in pre-trained language models. However, much of this analysis has focused on monolingual models, and analyses of multilingual models have employed correlational methods that are confounded by the choice of probing tasks. In this study, we causally probe multilingual language models (XGLM and multilingual BERT) as well as monolingual BERT-based models across various languages; we do this by performing counterfactual perturbations on neuron activations and observing the effect on models' subject-verb agreement probabilities. We observe where in the model and to what extent syntactic agreement is encoded in each language. We find significant neuron overlap across languages in autoregressive multilingual language models, but not masked language models. We also find two distinct layer-wise effect patterns and two distinct sets of neurons used for syntactic agreement, depending on whether the subject and verb are separated by other tokens. Finally, we find that behavioral analyses of language models are likely underestimating how sensitive masked language models are to syntactic information.

1 Introduction

Syntactic information is necessary for robust generalization in natural language processing tasks (for a case study using the natural language inference task, see McCoy et al. 2019). The success of pre-trained language models (LMs) such as RoBERTa (Liu et al., 2019) and GPT-3 (Brown et al., 2020) in many NLP tasks has prompted hypotheses that they accomplish their performance through structural representations induced during pre-training, rather than only lexical or positional representations (Manning et al., 2020); behavioral evidence for LMs' syntactic abilities has been found in masked LMs (MLMs; Warstadt et al., 2020; Warstadt and Bowman, 2020; Goldberg, 2019) and autoregressive LMs (ALMs; Hu et al., 2020). Evidence for structural representations has been reported for multilingual pre-trained LMs (Goldberg, 2019; Mueller et al., 2020) and in sequence-to-sequence models (Mueller et al., 2022).

Despite efforts to understand the structural information encoded by pre-trained LMs (Hewitt and Manning, 2019; Chi et al., 2020; Elazar et al., 2021; Ravfogel et al., 2021; Finlayson et al., 2021; *inter alia*), it remains unclear how and where multilingual models encode this information. Most multilingual probing studies are *correlational* and use dependency parsing or labeling as a proxy task indicative of syntactic information (Chi et al., 2020; Stańczak et al., 2022). This is problematic: Models do not need structural or word order information to achieve high performance on dependency labeling (Sinha et al., 2021), and training a parametric probing classifier introduces many confounds (Hewitt and Liang, 2019; Antverg and Belinkov, 2022).

Causal probing, however, enables non-parametric analyses of models through counterfactual interventions on inputs or model representations. Causal probing studies have argued for the existence of specific syntactic agreement neurons and units in neural language models (Finlayson et al., 2021; Lakretz et al., 2019; De Cao et al., 2021), but these studies have focused on monolingual models—usually (though not always) in English. Causal methods allow us to make stronger arguments about where and how syntactic agreement is performed in pre-trained LMs, and we can apply them to answer questions about the language specificity and construction specificity of syntactic agreement neurons.

In this study, we extend causal mediation analysis (Pearl, 2001; Robins, 2003; Vig et al., 2020) to multilingual language models, including an autoregressive LM and a masked LM. We also analyze a series of monolingual MLMs across languages. We employ the syntactic interventions approach

Proceedings of the 26th Conference on Computational Natural Language Learning (CoNLL), pages 95 - 109
December 7-8, 2022 ©2022 Association for Computational Linguistics

of Finlayson et al. (2021) on stimuli in languages typologically related to English, such that we can observe whether there exist syntax neurons that are shared across a set of languages that are all relatively high-resource and grammatically similar. Our contributions include the following:

1. We causally probe for syntactic agreement neurons in an autoregressive language model, XGLM (Lin et al., 2021); a masked language model, multilingual BERT (Devlin et al., 2019); and a series of monolingual BERT-based models. We find two distinct layer-wise effect patterns, depending on whether the subject and verb are separated by other tokens.
2. We quantify the degree of neuron overlap across languages and syntactic structures, finding that many neurons are shared across structures and fewer are shared across languages.
3. We analyze the sparsity of syntactic agreement representations for individual structures and languages, and find that syntax neurons are more sparse in MLMs than ALMs, but also that the degree of sparsity is similar across models and structures.

Our data and code are publicly available.[1]

2 Related Work

Multilingual language modeling. Multilingual language models enable increased parameter efficiency per language, as well as cross-lingual transfer to lower-resource language varieties (Wu and Dredze, 2019). This makes both training and deployment more efficient when support for many languages is required. A common approach for training multilingual LMs is to concatenate training corpora for many languages into one corpus, often without language IDs (Conneau et al., 2020; Devlin et al., 2019).

These models present interesting opportunities for syntactic analysis: Do multilingual models maintain similar syntactic abilities despite a decreased number of parameters that can be dedicated to each language? Current evidence suggests slight interference effects, but also that identical models maintain much of their monolingual performance when trained on multilingual corpora (Mueller et al., 2020). Is syntactic agreement, in particular, encoded independently per language or shared across languages? Some studies suggest that syntax is encoded in similar ways across languages (Chi et al., 2020; Stańczak et al., 2022), though these rely on correlational methods based on dependency parsing, which introduce confounds and may not rely on syntactic information *per se*.

Syntactic probing. Various behavioral probing studies have analyzed the syntactic behavior of monolingual and multilingual LMs (Linzen et al., 2016; Marvin and Linzen, 2018; Ravfogel et al., 2019; Mueller et al., 2020; Hu et al., 2020). Results from behavioral analyses are generally easier to interpret and present clearer evidence for *what* models' preferences are given various contexts. However, these methods do not tell us *where* or *how* syntax is encoded.

A parallel line of work employs parametric probes. Here, a linear classifier or multi-layer perceptron probe is trained to map from a model's hidden representations to dependency attachments and/or labels (Hewitt and Manning, 2019) to locate syntax-sensitive regions of a model. This approach has been applied in multilingual models (Chi et al., 2020), and produced evidence for parallel dependency encodings across languages. However, if such probes are powerful, they may learn the target task themselves rather than tap into an ability of the underlying model (Hewitt and Liang, 2019), leading to uninterpretable results. When controlling for this, even highly selective probes may not need access to syntactic information to achieve high structural probing performance (Sinha et al., 2021). There are further confounds when analyzing individual neurons using correlational methods; for example, probes may locate encoded information that is not actually used by the model (Antverg and Belinkov, 2022).

Causal probing has recently become more common for interpreting various phenomena in neural models of language. Lakretz et al. (2019) and Lakretz et al. (2021) search for syntax-sensitive units in English and Italian monolingual LSTMs by intervening directly on activations and evaluating syntactic agreement performance. Vig et al. (2020) propose causal mediation analysis for locating neurons and attention heads implicated in gender bias in pre-trained language models; this method involves intervening directly on the inputs or on individual neurons. Finlayson et al. (2021) extend this approach to implicate neurons in syntactic agreement. This study extends their data and

[1] https://github.com/aaronmueller/multilingual-lm-intervention

method to multilingual stimuli and models.

Other causal probing work uses interventions on model representations, rather than inputs. This includes amnesic probing (Elazar et al., 2021), where part-of-speech and dependency information is deleted from a model using iterative nullspace projection (INLP; Ravfogel et al., 2020). Ravfogel et al. (2021) employ INLP to understand how relative clause boundaries are encoded in BERT.

3 Methods

3.1 Causal Metrics

We first define terms to represent the quantities we measure before and after the intervention. We are interested in the impact of an intervention $\mathbf{x}$ on a model's preference $y_{\mathbf{x}}$ for grammatical inflections over ungrammatical ones. We start with the original input, on which we apply the `null` intervention: This represents performing no change to the original input. Given prompt u and verb v, we first calculate the following ratio:

$$y_{\texttt{null}}(u, v) = \frac{p(v_{pl} \mid u_{sg})}{p(v_{sg} \mid u_{sg})} \quad (1)$$

Here, u_{sg} represents a prompt that would require a singular verb inflection v_{sg} at the [MASK] for the sentence to be grammatical; for example, "The doctor near the cars [MASK] it". v_{sg} is the third-person singular present inflection of verb v, and v_{pl} is the plural present inflection; for example, v_{sg} ="observes" and v_{pl} ="observe". Note that this ratio has the incorrect inflection as the numerator; this entails that if the model computes agreement correctly, we will have $y < 1$.

We now define the `swap-number` intervention, where the grammatical number of u is flipped (resulting in "The doctors near the cars [MASK] it" for the previous example). This results in the following expression for y:

$$y_{\texttt{swap-number}}(u, v) = \frac{p(v_{pl} \mid u_{pl})}{p(v_{sg} \mid u_{pl})} \quad (2)$$

Now, the numerator is the correct inflection, so we expect $y > 1$.

As we are interested in the contribution of individual model components to the model's overall preference for correct inflections, we focus on *indirect effects*, where we perform interventions on individual model components and observe the change in y. In particular, we measure the **natural indirect effect** (NIE), as follows.

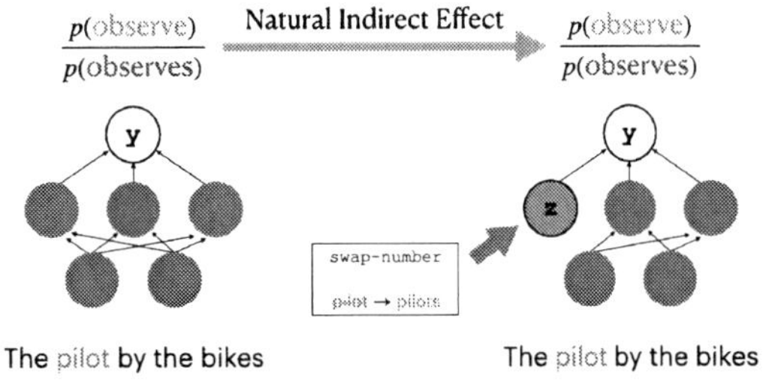

Figure 1: Example of computing the natural indirect effect (NIE). We change a neuron's activation to what it would have been if we had intervened on the prompt, then measure the relative change in y.

We intervene on an individual neuron $\mathbf{z}$. We change $\mathbf{z}$'s original activation given u and v (denoted $\mathbf{z}_{\texttt{null}}(u, v)$) to the activation it *would have* taken if we had performed the intervention on u (denoted $\mathbf{z}_{\texttt{swap-number}}(u, v)$). The rest of the neurons retain their original activations. "Natural" here refers to the fact that our intervention changes the activation $\mathbf{z}$ to the value it would have in another natural setting u', rather than setting it to some predefined constant (such as 0) that it may or may not obtain given natural inputs. We measure the relative change in y after applying the intervention (see Figure 1 for a visual example):

$$\overline{\text{NIE}}(\texttt{swap-number, null}; y, \mathbf{z}) = \mathbb{E}_{u,v}\left[\frac{y_{\texttt{null},\mathbf{z}_{\texttt{swap-number}}(u,v)}(u, v) - y_{\texttt{null}}(u, v)}{y_{\texttt{null}}(u, v)}\right] = \mathbb{E}_{u,v}\left[\frac{y_{\texttt{null},\mathbf{z}_{\texttt{swap-number}}(u,v)}(u, v)}{y_{\texttt{null}}(u, v)} - 1\right] \quad (3)$$

If a neuron encodes useful information for syntactic agreement, we expect y to *increase* after the intervention, making the numerator positive. Positive NIEs indicate that a neuron encodes preferences for correct verb inflections, and negative NIEs indicate that the neuron prefers incorrect inflections. The closer the NIE is to 0, the less of a contribution a neuron makes to syntactic agreement in either direction.

3.2 Models

Finlayson et al. (2021) analyzed a series of monolingual autoregressive language models (ALMs): GPT-2 (Radford et al., 2019), TransformerXL (Dai

Model	Layers	Neurons	Parameters
BERT	12	9126	110M
mBERT	12	9126	110M
GPT-2	24	25600	345M
XGLM	24	25600	564M

Table 1: The size of each model used in this study. Each monolingual BERT variant (including the RoBERTa-based CamemBERT) has the same number of layers, neurons, and parameters as BERT.

et al., 2019), and XLNet (Yang et al., 2019). Here, we apply their analysis approach to multilingual models. Multilingual ALMs are rare in the literature; to our knowledge, the only ALM designed to be multilingual is XGLM (Lin et al., 2021),[2] which we employ in this study.

Multilingual MLMs are much more common. We focus on multilingual BERT (Devlin et al., 2019). We were unable to analyze XLM-R (Conneau et al., 2020), a more recent multilingual MLM that performs better than mBERT on certain benchmarks, since its tokenizer splits a large proportion of our nouns and verbs into multiple tokens, which greatly constrained the stimuli we could use. In future work, we intend to address this issue by developing methods that enable multi-token interventions, as well as calibrated comparisons across variable-length sequences.

We also analyze a series of monolingual MLMs—one for each language included in our sample. Four of these models were based on BERT: BERT (English), GermanBERT,[3] BERTje (Dutch; de Vries et al., 2019), and FinnishBERT (Virtanen et al., 2019). Our French MLM, CamemBERT (Martin et al., 2020), is based on RoBERTa (Liu et al., 2019), which is very similar to BERT.

3.3 Materials

We translate the stimuli from Finlayson et al. (2021) (Figure 2) to French, German, Dutch, and Finnish. Since the subjects and verbs on which we intervene must be one token each,[4] we are restricted

Simple Agreement:
The athlete investigates/*investigate...

Across Prepositional Phrase:
The manager behind the bikes observes/*observe...

Across Object Relative Clause:
The farmers that the parent loves *confuses/confuse...

Figure 2: Constructions used in this study, grouped by whether the subject and verb are adjacent. We use a subset of constructions from Finlayson et al. (2021), directly translating the stimuli to French, German, Dutch, and Finnish. See Appendix A for examples of each structure in each language.

to very frequent words in the pre-training corpus which do not get split into subwords by a model's tokenizer. This limits us to high-resource language varieties—and as most of the top languages in mBERT and XGLM's pre-training corpora are Indo-European, this also limits the typological range of this method. A virtue of our sample of languages, however, is that is allows us to study whether neurons are shared across typologically similar languages, where shared neurons and similar layer-wise effect patterns are most likely to occur: If syntactic agreement neurons are not shared across similar languages, they are unlikely to be shared across *any* languages.

For each structure, we sample up to 200 sentences. If there are fewer than 200 sentences where the subjects and verbs are single tokens, we take the entire set of valid stimuli. When we use the original stimuli from Finlayson et al. (2021), we often have very few sentences where the subjects and verbs are single tokens. Thus, we also create short-word versions of the stimuli, where we use shorter and more common words (e.g., instead of "managers" or "observe", we can use "cats" or "see"). Our results are consistent when using the original and short nouns and verbs; see Appendix B.

The original stimuli were generated from a grammar given a list of manually selected terminals. By generating artificial stimuli and *not* sampling sentences from a corpus, we partially control for memorized sequences or token collocations in the pre-training corpus.

[2]GPT-3 (Brown et al., 2020) is technically multilingual, as its training corpus contains data from other languages. However, it was not designed with multilinguality in mind, and the vast majority of its training data is English.

[3]`https://www.deepset.ai/german-bert`

[4]It is not clear how to compare the probability of variable-length sequences in masked language models, and autoregressive language models tend to prefer sequences containing fewer tokens. There have been attempts to compare variable-length sequence probabilities using iterative approaches (e.g., Schick and Schütze, 2021), though this generally requires fine-tuning to work properly.

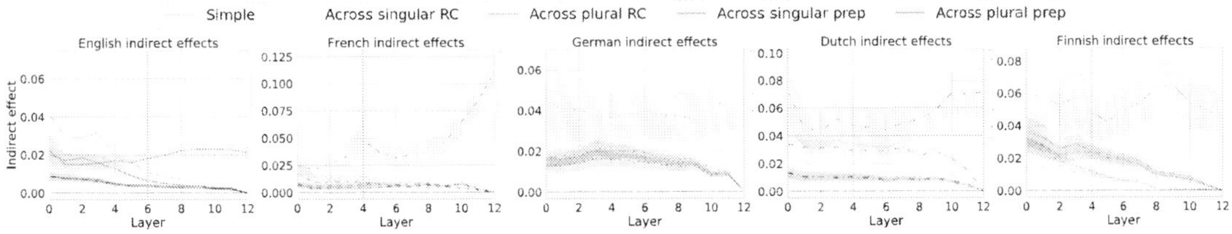

(a) BERT (b) CamemBERT (c) GermanBERT (d) BERTje (e) FinnishBERT

Figure 3: Natural indirect effects for the top 5% of neurons in each layer for monolingual masked language models. There are two distinct layer-wise NIE contours in each language, depending on whether the subject and verb are separated by other tokens (as in 'across a relative clause' and 'across a prepositional phrase' structures) or not (as in 'simple agreement').

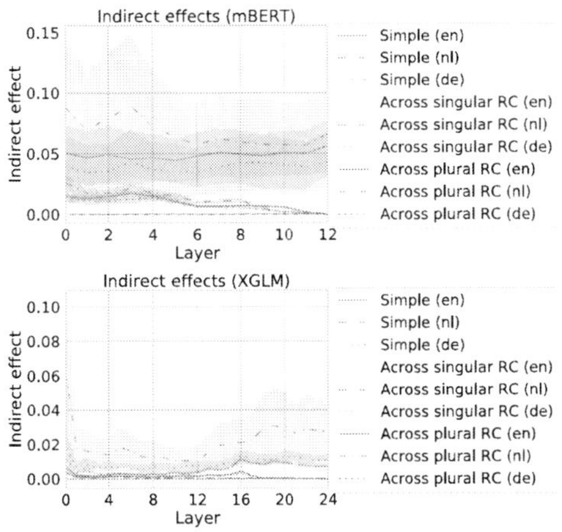

Figure 4: Natural indirect effects for mBERT (top) and XGLM (bottom) for Germanic languages. There are two distinct layer-wise NIE patterns in each language. NIE patterns for the same structure look very similar across languages.

Finlayson et al. (2021) found two distinct layer-wise NIE patterns for syntactic agreement: one when the subject and verb are adjacent (the *short-range* effect), and another when they are separated by any number of tokens (the *long-range* effect). To understand whether the short-range effect is due to preferences for frequent bigrams (rather than specifically grammatical subject-verb bigrams), we also design a bigram swap intervention. We use high-mutual-information adjective-noun English bigrams as the original inputs and intervene by randomly swapping the first or second words in the bigram with words from a different bigram. For example, given the bigrams coaxial cable and police officer, we can define $y_{\texttt{null}} = \frac{p(\text{officer}|\text{coaxial})}{p(\text{cable}|\text{coaxial})}$ and $y_{\texttt{swap-bigram}} = \frac{p(\text{officer}|\text{police})}{p(\text{cable}|\text{police})}$. Then we can compute the NIE as in Equation 3.

Finally, to test whether separate neurons are used for short- and long-range token collocations in general, we also define short- and long-range *semantic plausibility* baselines, where nouns are associated with stereotypical adjectives (e.g., square T.V. and red apple). The short-range semantic plausibility intervention is the same as for the bigram intervention: We compute the probability ratio of the first and second noun in a pair of bigrams before and after swapping the adjective. For long-range semantic plausibility, the prompt u is "The T.V./apple is", and v is the probability ratio of the *adjectives* before and after swapping the nouns.

4 Results

4.1 Layer-wise NIE contours are similar across languages

We present indirect effects for monolingual masked language models (Figure 3), as well as mBERT and XGLM (Figure 4). Here, we select the top 5% of neurons per layer by NIE. In each language, whether in a monolingual or multilingual MLM or ALM, **there are two distinct layer-wise NIE effect patterns for number agreement**: one for short-range dependencies and one for long-range dependencies. This agrees with the findings of Finlayson et al. (2021) on autoregressive English LMs. However, these effects look more distinct across monolingual models, whereas **multilingual models exhibit more similar layer-wise NIE patterns across languages.** In other words, monoligual models accomplish syntactic agreement in different layers and neurons depending on the language (even though these languages are typologically similar), but in multilingual models agreement computations implicate the same layers across languages. This does not necessarily mean that the same individual neuron are being used cross-linguistically in multilingual models (we explore this question in more detail in §4.2.1); rather, the model may simply be learning similar layer-wise strategies for each language.

While prior work finds that syntactic agreement is easier to learn in languages that have more explicit morphological cues to hierarchical structure (Ravfogel et al., 2019; Mueller et al., 2020),[5] this does not necessarily imply that different agreement mechanisms are learned in such languages. We find similar layer-wise NIEs in mBERT across each language we consider, including Finnish, a non-Indo-European (specifically, Uralic) language.

4.2 Syntax neurons are shared across structures, but not with semantic baselines

Here, we analyze to what extent the same neurons are implicated across syntactic structures and languages in mBERT. For each structure, we take the top 30 neurons by indirect effect (from any layer); we then compute the proportion of such high-NIE neurons that are shared across structures.

First, we investigate to what extent the neurons that have high NIE for the syntactic structures are selective to syntax. We do so by computing the overlaps in English between neurons with high NIE for syntactic structures and the neurons with high NIE for our bigram and semantic plausibility baselines. We find that the top syntactic agreement neurons for any structure are *not* shared with the neurons implicated in semantic plausibility or bigram collocation (Figure 5). In other words, **the neurons used for syntactic agreement are *specific to agreement*** and do not track common bigrams more generally.

Figure 5 also shows that **neurons are shared across syntactic structures**, providing evidence for an abstract notion of syntactic agreement encoded in mBERT that is separate from the individual structures that the model is presented with. However, the varying extents of overlap indicate that there are also neurons specialized to particular structures. To further contextualize these overlap proportions, we also compute overlaps for simple agreement in a randomly initialized mBERT, as a baseline. This experiment yields near-zero overlaps, indicating that the overlaps across structures we obtain for mBERT and XGLM are unlikely to be due to random chance.[6]

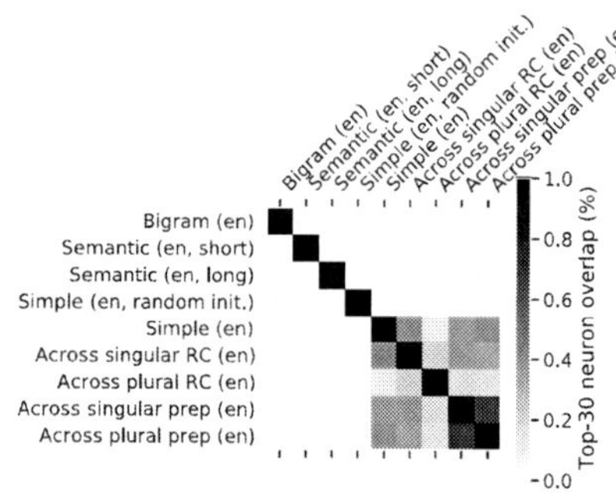

(a) mBERT

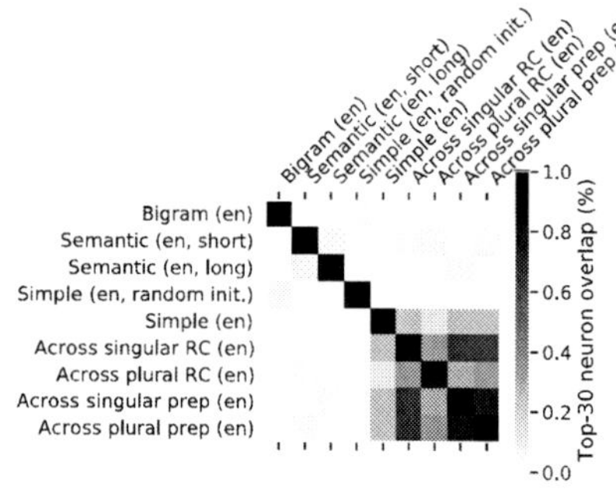

(b) XGLM

Figure 5: Neuron overlap across structures (including baselines) in English for (a) mBERT and (b) XGLM. There is zero or near-zero overlap between the baselines and all syntactic agreement structures, whereas overlap is relatively high (and statistically significant) for all other structures.

4.2.1 Neurons are shared across languages in autoregressive language models

The overlap in neurons across languages (Figure 6) is significant for all structures in XGLM. For mBERT, overlap is significant between "across a PP" structures and other long-distance agreement structures, but not for any other structure pairs. Note that in XGLM, the diagonal is no darker than most other squares; in other words, there is *not* more cross-lingual neuron overlap for the same syntactic structure relative to other structures. **These may be generic cross-lingual syntax neurons which are not specialized to any particular structure or language.** We found in §4.2 that there is almost no overlap between syntactic agreement neurons and bigram collocation/semantic plausibility neurons in English, which is further evidence

[5] Explicit case marking correlates well with performance on syntactic evaluations (Ravfogel et al., 2019), so we would expect German and Finnish to exhibit different results if these cues give rise to different agreement computations.

[6] For reference, the probability of at least one neuron being shared between two random samples of 30 neurons in (m)BERT-base is $1 - \frac{\binom{9984-30}{30}}{\binom{9984}{30}} \approx .086$.

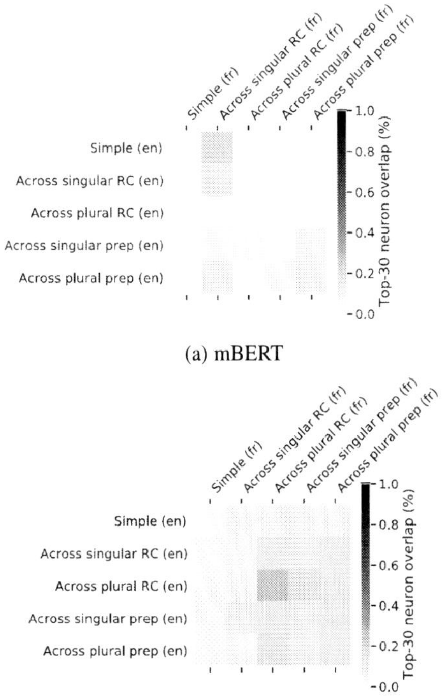

(a) mBERT

(b) XGLM

Figure 6: Cross-lingual neuron overlaps for the top 30 neurons by NIE in (a) mBERT and (b) XGLM. We present English-French overlaps; overlaps between other language pairs look similar (see Appendix C). The overlap percentages in (b) are significantly higher than random chance. Overlaps for most structure pairs in (a) are not significant, except for overlaps between 'Across a preposition' structures and other long-range agreement structures.

that these may be more general syntactic agreement neurons. Nonetheless, overlap is very low across languages compared to across structures within a given language. Thus, **in autoregressive language models, syntactic agreement neurons can be language-specific or cross-lingual, but most are language-specific. For masked language models, syntactic agreement neurons are rarely shared across languages.**

4.3 Neuron sparsity differs across structures, but not across languages

What proportion of LMs' neurons encode subject-verb agreement? The sparsity of syntax neurons in pre-trained models may vary depending on which language and structure we observe. Lakretz et al. (2019) and Lakretz et al. (2021) found that agreement neurons are sparse in LSTMs, but it is not clear whether this would hold for MLMs or large

Language	Model	% Neurons for TE	% Neurons for Max. NIE
en	BERT	1.0%	5.8%
	mBERT	1.0%	8.7%
	GPT-2	17.5%	25.0%
	XGLM	4.5%	16.5%
fr	CamemBERT	6.7%	10.6%
	mBERT	3.8%	29.8%
	XGLM	3.5%	24.0%
de	GermanBERT	1.0%	8.7%
	mBERT	1.0%	6.7%
	XGLM	1.5%	18.0%
nl	BERTje	1.0%	5.8%
	mBERT	1.0%	2.9%
	XGLM	0.5%	37.5%
fi	FinnishBERT	1.0%	4.8%

Table 2: Neuron sparsities for the "simple agreement" structure across languages and models. Multilingual models do not necessarily encode syntax more sparsely than monolingual models. Sparsities are generally consistent across languages for the same model.

Transformer-based ALMs. Given our consistent results across languages, we hypothesize that the neuron sparsity of subject-verb agreement will be similar across monolingual models. Given the consistent distinction thus far in how neurons encode short- and long-range agreement, we also hypothesize that neuron sparsity will differ between agreement distances. Due to lower parameterization per language in multilingual models, however, we hypothesize that multilingual models encode agreement more sparsely than monolingual models.

We measure sparsity by iteratively selecting the top k neurons by NIE, intervening on them simultaneously, and computing the natural indirect effect after performing the `swap-number` intervention. We continue sampling k more neurons and computing NIEs until we have selected all neurons; the NIE after intervening on all neurons is equivalent to the *total effect* (TE).[7] Computing effects for each neuron and each structure is computationally expensive, so we use $k = 128$ for XGLM and GPT-2 (0.5% of neurons selected at a time) and $k = 96$ for (m)BERT ($\approx$1.0% of neurons selected at a time).

We report two metrics: (1) the percentage of neurons at which we see the maximum NIE, and (2) the minimum percentage of neurons required for the NIE to reach the TE of the model. These correspond to the peak NIE and the point at which the NIEs cross the dashed line in Figure 7.

For 'simple agreement' (Table 2), the proportion of neurons to reach the TE is generally small, espe-

[7] Intuitively, the TE can be thought of as the preference of the model as a whole for correct verbs over incorrect verbs.

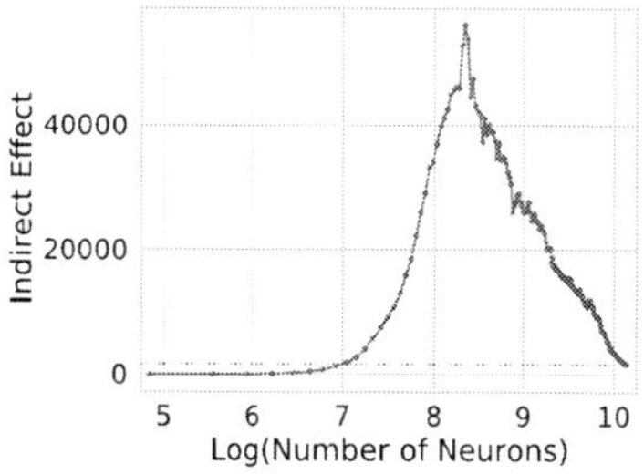

(a) Simple agreement

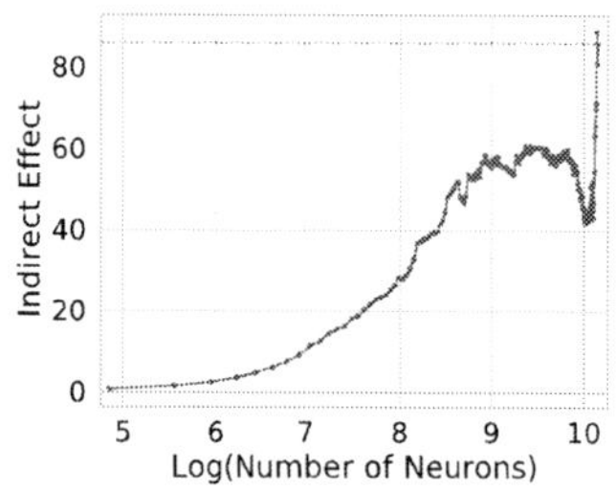

(b) Across a singular RC

Figure 7: Indirect effects when intervening on increasing numbers of neurons in XGLM. The dashed line represents the total effect. For 'simple agreement', there exists a set of neurons that strongly prefers grammatical completions; however, there are many more neurons that have weak preferences against them, and this results in the model as a whole having weak preferences for correct verb inflections. For 'across a singular RC', however, almost every set of neurons seems to have preferences for grammatical inflections.

cially for MLMs. However, the TE itself is often a couple orders of magnitude smaller for MLMs than for ALMs; thus, these percentages are not comparable across model architectures.

The proportion of neurons required to achieve the maximum NIE is typically lower for MLMs than ALMs. In other words, **syntax neurons are more sparse in masked language models than autoregressive language models.**[8]

The percentage of neurons to reach the maximum NIE does not significantly differ across monolingual and multilingual models, however. This means that **multilingual models do not consistently encode syntactic agreement in a more sparse way than monolingual models**. This and our neuron overlap results suggest that multilingual models encode syntactic information in a similar way to monolingual models (including the proportion of neurons sensitive to syntax), though most syntax-sensitive neurons tend to be language-specific rather than shared across languages.

Sparsity also differs across syntactic structures. For 'simple agreement', NIEs peak at around 5–20% of neurons. For 'across a singular RC', the addition of every k neurons almost always increases the NIEs. **Long-range syntactic information seems to be distributed throughout the majority of neurons in XGLM, but short-range syntactic information is more sparsely encoded.**

These numbers hide more interesting trends, however. The TEs for mBERT are often close to 0 across structures, while the maximum NIEs are in the hundreds for those same structures.[9] This has interesting implications for interpreting behavioral analyses: studies such as Hu et al. (2020) and Mueller et al. (2020) suggest that mBERT does not have strong syntax-sensitive preferences compared to autoregressive language models, and the low TEs we observe support this. However, this obscures that **there are actually many neurons in mBERT which are highly sensitive to syntactic agreement**, as indicated by the high maximum NIEs: we observe weak agreement preferences in the model as a whole because there are many more neurons which have weak preferences *against* syntactic agreement (i.e., small negative NIEs), perhaps because those neurons are specializing in other phenomena (e.g., token collocations or semantic agreement). Thus, behavioral analyses of model behavior may be underestimating the sensitivity of models to syntactic phenomena, for there is negative interference from neurons that prefer non-syntax-sensitive completions.

5 Discussion

We observe two distinct layer-wise NIE patterns for syntactic agreement, depending on whether the subject and verb are adjacent or separated by other tokens. This extends the findings of Finlayson et al. (2021) to multilingual MLMs and ALMs, as well as monolingual MLMs in various languages. Going beyond their findings, we ruled out the possibility that these neurons do not simply track semantic plausibility or bigram collocations more generally. While this is not conclusive evidence that these neurons are specialized to syntax, evidence from other behavioral and probing studies also supports

[8]French is an exception: there are more syntax-sensitive neurons in both monolingual and multilingual models.

[9]The effect contours for mBERT have a similar contour to those in Figure 7, though the TE ($\approx$0) and maximum NIE ($\approx$340) for 'simple agreement' are far smaller.

the existence of neurons focused on syntax (Hewitt and Manning, 2019; Elazar et al., 2021; Goldberg, 2019). De Cao et al. (2021) found neurons focused *purely* on syntax, while Tucker et al. (2022) found redundantly encoded syntactic information across neurons. It is not clear how much of the neuron overlap we observe is due to redundantly encoded information, but future work could investigate this.

A consistent trend across our experiments is that ALMs encode syntactic agreement in a distinct way from MLMs. In ALMs, there is more cross-lingual and cross-structure neuron overlap than in MLMs; more similar layer-wise effect patterns across structures and languages (though they are still distinct); and a greater proportion of neurons which are sensitive to agreement. This could be partially explained by ALMs' left-to-right processing of natural language input, which more closely resembles incremental inputs to human learners. MLMs are able to perform syntactic agreement (Hu et al., 2020; Goldberg, 2019), but their fill-in-the-blank pre-training objectives may induce distinct representations of sentence structure as compared to models that process or predict inputs incrementally.

Why do we observe different indirect effect contours for short- and long-range agreement? Perhaps syntactic agreement is encoded using a single mechanism, but the way that syntactic information is used for predicting output tokens depends on the structure of the input or prior output tokens. Alternatively, there could be two completely distinct agreement mechanisms that function in different ways entirely. While our findings do not disambiguate between these possibilities (or some other separate type or amount of mechanisms), future work could employ methods like those in Meng et al. (2022) to observe this distinction more explicitly. The findings of Meng et al. (2022) suggest that the model regions that are implicated in *saying* something are distinct from those implicated in *knowing* something—that is, knowledge retrieval and predicting particular tokens are separate mechanisms in pre-trained language models. Perhaps their method could be extended to study syntactic agreement, such that we can better understand what, exactly, these distinct indirect effect trends represent.

6 Conclusions

We have used causal mediation analysis to observe which neurons track syntactic agreement in multilingual pre-trained language models, and in which layers they are concentrated. We found two distinct layer-wise contours for syntactic agreement regardless of the language, multilinguality, or architecture of the model (§4.1); that syntax-sensitive neurons are shared across languages in autoregressive language models (§4.2.1); and that the neuron sparsity of syntactic agreement is similar in monolingual and multilingual models (§4.3). We also found that behavioral analyses of masked language models obscure the extent to which their neurons are sensitive to syntactic agreement (§4.3).

Acknowledgments

We thank the members of NYU's Computation and Psycholinguistics Lab for valuable feedback on earlier versions of this work.

This material is based upon work supported by the National Science Foundation (NSF) under Grant No. BCS-2114505. Aaron Mueller was supported by a National Science Foundation Graduate Research Fellowship (Grant #1746891). This work was also supported by supported in part through the NYU IT High Performance Computing resources, services, and staff expertise.

References

Omer Antverg and Yonatan Belinkov. 2022. On the pitfalls of analyzing individual neurons in language models.

Tom Brown, Benjamin Mann, Nick Ryder, Melanie Subbiah, Jared D Kaplan, Prafulla Dhariwal, Arvind Neelakantan, Pranav Shyam, Girish Sastry, Amanda Askell, Sandhini Agarwal, Ariel Herbert-Voss, Gretchen Krueger, Tom Henighan, Rewon Child, Aditya Ramesh, Daniel Ziegler, Jeffrey Wu, Clemens Winter, Chris Hesse, Mark Chen, Eric Sigler, Mateusz Litwin, Scott Gray, Benjamin Chess, Jack Clark, Christopher Berner, Sam McCandlish, Alec Radford, Ilya Sutskever, and Dario Amodei. 2020. Language models are few-shot learners. In *Advances in Neural Information Processing Systems*, volume 33, pages 1877–1901. Curran Associates, Inc.

Ethan A. Chi, John Hewitt, and Christopher D. Manning. 2020. Finding universal grammatical relations in multilingual BERT. In *Proceedings of the 58th Annual Meeting of the Association for Computational Linguistics*, pages 5564–5577, Online. Association for Computational Linguistics.

Alexis Conneau, Kartikay Khandelwal, Naman Goyal, Vishrav Chaudhary, Guillaume Wenzek, Francisco Guzmán, Edouard Grave, Myle Ott, Luke Zettlemoyer, and Veselin Stoyanov. 2020. Unsupervised cross-lingual representation learning at scale. In *Proceedings of the 58th Annual Meeting of the Association for Computational Linguistics*, pages 8440–8451, Online. Association for Computational Linguistics.

Zihang Dai, Zhilin Yang, Yiming Yang, Jaime Carbonell, Quoc Le, and Ruslan Salakhutdinov. 2019. Transformer-XL: Attentive language models beyond a fixed-length context. In *Proceedings of the 57th Annual Meeting of the Association for Computational Linguistics*, pages 2978–2988, Florence, Italy. Association for Computational Linguistics.

Nicola De Cao, Leon Schmid, Dieuwke Hupkes, and Ivan Titov. 2021. Sparse interventions in language models with differentiable masking. *CoRR*, arXiv:2112.06837.

Wietse de Vries, Andreas van Cranenburgh, Arianna Bisazza, Tommaso Caselli, Gertjan van Noord, and Malvina Nissim. 2019. BERTje: A Dutch BERT model. *CoRR*, arXiv:1912.09582.

Jacob Devlin, Ming-Wei Chang, Kenton Lee, and Kristina Toutanova. 2019. BERT: Pre-training of deep bidirectional transformers for language understanding. In *Proceedings of the 2019 Conference of the North American Chapter of the Association for Computational Linguistics: Human Language Technologies, Volume 1 (Long and Short Papers)*, pages 4171–4186, Minneapolis, Minnesota. Association for Computational Linguistics.

Yanai Elazar, Shauli Ravfogel, Alon Jacovi, and Yoav Goldberg. 2021. Amnesic Probing: Behavioral Explanation with Amnesic Counterfactuals. *Transactions of the Association for Computational Linguistics*, 9:160–175.

Matthew Finlayson, Aaron Mueller, Sebastian Gehrmann, Stuart Shieber, Tal Linzen, and Yonatan Belinkov. 2021. Causal analysis of syntactic agreement mechanisms in neural language models. In *Proceedings of the 59th Annual Meeting of the Association for Computational Linguistics and the 11th International Joint Conference on Natural Language Processing (Volume 1: Long Papers)*, pages 1828–1843, Online. Association for Computational Linguistics.

Yoav Goldberg. 2019. Assessing BERT's syntactic abilities. arXiv preprint 1901.05287.

John Hewitt and Percy Liang. 2019. Designing and interpreting probes with control tasks. In *Proceedings of the 2019 Conference on Empirical Methods in Natural Language Processing and the 9th International Joint Conference on Natural Language Processing (EMNLP-IJCNLP)*, pages 2733–2743, Hong Kong, China. Association for Computational Linguistics.

John Hewitt and Christopher D. Manning. 2019. A structural probe for finding syntax in word representations. In *Proceedings of the 2019 Conference of the North American Chapter of the Association for Computational Linguistics: Human Language Technologies, Volume 1 (Long and Short Papers)*, pages 4129–4138.

Jennifer Hu, Jon Gauthier, Peng Qian, Ethan Wilcox, and Roger Levy. 2020. A systematic assessment of syntactic generalization in neural language models. In *Proceedings of the 58th Annual Meeting of the Association for Computational Linguistics*, pages 1725–1744, Online. Association for Computational Linguistics.

Yair Lakretz, Dieuwke Hupkes, Alessandra Vergallito, Marco Marelli, Marco Baroni, and Stanislas Dehaene. 2021. Mechanisms for handling nested dependencies in neural-network language models and humans. *Cognition*, page 104699.

Yair Lakretz, German Kruszewski, Theo Desbordes, Dieuwke Hupkes, Stanislas Dehaene, and Marco Baroni. 2019. The emergence of number and syntax units in LSTM language models. In *Proceedings of the 2019 Conference of the North American Chapter of the Association for Computational Linguistics: Human Language Technologies, Volume 1 (Long and Short Papers)*, pages 11–20, Minneapolis, Minnesota. Association for Computational Linguistics.

Xi Victoria Lin, Todor Mihaylov, Mikel Artetxe, Tianlu Wang, Shuohui Chen, Daniel Simig, Myle Ott, Naman Goyal, Shruti Bhosale, Jingfei Du, Ramakanth Pasunuru, Sam Shleifer, Punit Singh Koura, Vishrav Chaudhary, Brian O'Horo, Jeff Wang, Luke Zettlemoyer, Zornitsa Kozareva, Mona T. Diab, Veselin Stoyanov, and Xian Li. 2021. Few-shot learning with multilingual language models. *CoRR*, arXiv:2112.10668.

Tal Linzen, Emmanuel Dupoux, and Yoav Goldberg. 2016. Assessing the ability of LSTMs to learn syntax-sensitive dependencies. *Transactions of the Association for Computational Linguistics)*, 4:521–535.

Yinhan Liu, Myle Ott, Naman Goyal, Jingfei Du, Mandar Joshi, Danqi Chen, Omer Levy, Mike Lewis, Luke Zettlemoyer, and Veselin Stoyanov. 2019. RoBERTa: A robustly optimized BERT pretraining approach. *CoRR*, arXiv:1907.11692.

Christopher D Manning, Kevin Clark, John Hewitt, Urvashi Khandelwal, and Omer Levy. 2020. Emergent linguistic structure in artificial neural networks trained by self-supervision. *Proceedings of the National Academy of Sciences*, 117(48):30046–30054.

Louis Martin, Benjamin Muller, Pedro Javier Ortiz Suárez, Yoann Dupont, Laurent Romary, Éric de la Clergerie, Djamé Seddah, and Benoît Sagot. 2020. CamemBERT: a tasty French language model. In *Proceedings of the 58th Annual Meeting of the Association for Computational Linguistics*, pages 7203–7219, Online. Association for Computational Linguistics.

Rebecca Marvin and Tal Linzen. 2018. Targeted syntactic evaluation of language models. In *Proceedings of the 2018 Conference on Empirical Methods in Natural Language Processing*, pages 1192–1202, Brussels, Belgium. Association for Computational Linguistics.

Tom McCoy, Ellie Pavlick, and Tal Linzen. 2019. Right for the wrong reasons: Diagnosing syntactic heuristics in natural language inference. In *Proceedings of the 57th Annual Meeting of the Association for Computational Linguistics*, pages 3428–3448, Florence, Italy. Association for Computational Linguistics.

Kevin Meng, David Bau, Alex Andonian, and Yonatan Belinkov. 2022. Locating and editing factual knowledge in gpt.

Aaron Mueller, Robert Frank, Tal Linzen, Luheng Wang, and Sebastian Schuster. 2022. Coloring the blank slate: Pre-training imparts a hierarchical inductive bias to sequence-to-sequence models. *CoRR*, arXiv:2203.09397.

Aaron Mueller, Garrett Nicolai, Panayiota Petrou-Zeniou, Natalia Talmina, and Tal Linzen. 2020. Cross-linguistic syntactic evaluation of word prediction models. In *Proceedings of the 58th Annual Meeting of the Association for Computational Linguistics*, pages 5523–5539, Online. Association for Computational Linguistics.

Judea Pearl. 2001. Direct and indirect effects. In *Proceedings of the Seventeenth Conference on Uncertainty in Artificial Intelligence*, pages 411–420.

Alec Radford, Jeff Wu, Rewon Child, David Luan, Dario Amodei, and Ilya Sutskever. 2019. Language models are unsupervised multitask learners. *OpenAI Blog*.

Shauli Ravfogel, Yanai Elazar, Hila Gonen, Michael Twiton, and Yoav Goldberg. 2020. Null it out: Guarding protected attributes by iterative nullspace projection. In *Proceedings of the 58th Annual Meeting of the Association for Computational Linguistics*, pages 7237–7256, Online. Association for Computational Linguistics.

Shauli Ravfogel, Yoav Goldberg, and Tal Linzen. 2019. Studying the inductive biases of RNNs with synthetic variations of natural languages. In *Proceedings of the 2019 Conference of the North American Chapter of the Association for Computational Linguistics: Human Language Technologies, Volume 1 (Long and Short Papers)*, pages 3532–3542, Minneapolis, Minnesota. Association for Computational Linguistics.

Shauli Ravfogel, Grusha Prasad, Tal Linzen, and Yoav Goldberg. 2021. Counterfactual interventions reveal the causal effect of relative clause representations on agreement prediction. In *Proceedings of the 25th Conference on Computational Natural Language Learning*, pages 194–209, Online. Association for Computational Linguistics.

James M. Robins. 2003. Semantics of causal DAG models and the identification of direct and indirect effects. *Oxford Statistical Science Series*, pages 70–82.

Timo Schick and Hinrich Schütze. 2021. Exploiting cloze-questions for few-shot text classification and natural language inference. In *Proceedings of the 16th Conference of the European Chapter of the Association for Computational Linguistics: Main Volume*, pages 255–269, Online. Association for Computational Linguistics.

Koustuv Sinha, Robin Jia, Dieuwke Hupkes, Joelle Pineau, Adina Williams, and Douwe Kiela. 2021. Masked language modeling and the distributional hypothesis: Order word matters pre-training for little. In *Proceedings of the 2021 Conference on Empirical Methods in Natural Language Processing*, pages 2888–2913, Online and Punta Cana, Dominican Republic. Association for Computational Linguistics.

Karolina Stańczak, Edoardo Ponti, Lucas Torroba Hennigen, Ryan Cotterell, and Isabelle Augenstein. 2022. Same neurons, different languages: Probing morphosyntax in multilingual pre-trained models.

Mycal Tucker, Tiwalayo Eisape, Peng Qian, Roger Levy, and Julie Shah. 2022. When does syntax mediate neural language model performance? evidence from dropout probes.

Jesse Vig, Sebastian Gehrmann, Yonatan Belinkov, Sharon Qian, Daniel Nevo, Yaron Singer, and Stuart Shieber. 2020. Investigating gender bias in language models using causal mediation analysis. In *Advances in Neural Information Processing Systems*, volume 33, pages 12388–12401. Curran Associates, Inc.

Antti Virtanen, Jenna Kanerva, Rami Ilo, Jouni Luoma, Juhani Luotolahti, Tapio Salakoski, Filip Ginter, and Sampo Pyysalo. 2019. Multilingual is not enough: BERT for Finnish.

Alex Warstadt and Samuel R. Bowman. 2020. Can neural networks acquire a structural bias from raw linguistic data? In *Proceedings of the 42nd Annual Meeting of the Cognitive Science Society*, Online. Cognitive Science Society.

Alex Warstadt, Yian Zhang, Xiaocheng Li, Haokun Liu, and Samuel R. Bowman. 2020. Learning which features matter: RoBERTa acquires a preference for linguistic generalizations (eventually). In *Proceedings of the 2020 Conference on Empirical Methods in Natural Language Processing (EMNLP)*, pages 217–235, Online. Association for Computational Linguistics.

Shijie Wu and Mark Dredze. 2019. Beto, Bentz, Becas: The surprising cross-lingual effectiveness of BERT. In *Proceedings of the 2019 Conference on Empirical Methods in Natural Language Processing and the 9th International Joint Conference on Natural Language*

Processing (EMNLP-IJCNLP), pages 833–844, Hong Kong, China. Association for Computational Linguistics.

Zhilin Yang, Zihang Dai, Yiming Yang, Jaime Carbonell, Russ R Salakhutdinov, and Quoc V Le. 2019. XLNet: Generalized autoregressive pretraining for language understanding. In *Advances in Neural Information Processing Systems*, volume 32. Curran Associates, Inc.

A Example Sentences

Here, we present examples of each syntactic structure we observe in each language.

(1) *Simple agreement (English)*:

The woman observes/*observe.

(2) *Simple agreement (French)*:

L' homme approuve/*approuvent.
The man approves/*approve.

(3) *Simple agreement (German)*:

Der Arzt weiß/*wissen.
The physician knows/*know.

(4) *Simple agreement (Dutch)*:

De schrijver begrijpt/*begrijpen.
The writer understands/*understand.

(5) *Simple agreement (Finnish)*:

Täti ymmärtää/*ymmärtävät.
Aunt understands/*understand.
"The aunt understands/*understand."

For each of the following syntactic structures containing a grammatical number attractor, we separate structures by whether the attractor is singular or plural. For concision, we simply present examples of each structure without separating out examples by the number of the attractor. Note that Finnish mainly uses *postpositions* rather than prepositions; the attractor still intervenes between the main subject and its verb, but the order of the preposition and noun phrase is different compared to the Indo-European languages we consider.

(6) *Across a relative clause (English)*:

The woman that the guards like observes/*observe.

(7) *Across a relative clause (French)*:

L' homme que le chef suit approuve/*approuvent.
The man that the boss follows approves/*approve.

(8) *Across a relative clause (German)*:

Der Arzt den die Tiere vergeben weiß/*wissen.
The physician that the animals forgive knows/*know.

(9) *Across a relative clause (Dutch)*:

De schrijver die de ouder roept begrijpt/*begrijpen.
The writer that the parent calls understands/*understand.

(10) *Across a relative clause (Finnish)*:

Täti jota luistelijat kehuvat ymmärtää/*ymmärtävät.
Aunt that skaters praise understands/*understand.

"The aunt that the skaters praise understands/*understand."

(11) *Across a prepositional phrase (English)*:

The woman behind the cars observes/*observe.

(12) *Across a prepositional phrase (French)*:

L' homme devant le chat approuve/*approuvent.
The man in-front-of the cat follows approves/*approve.

(13) *Across a prepositional phrase (German)*:

Der Arzt nahe den Äpfeln weiß/*wissen.
The physician near the apples knows/*know.

(14) *Across a prepositional phrase (Dutch)*:

De schrijver achter de fiets begrijpt/*begrijpen.
The writer behind the bike understands/*understand.

(15) *Across a* ***post**positional phrase (Finnish)*:

Täti puiden lähellä ymmärtää/*ymmärtävät.
Aunt trees near understands/*understand.

"The aunt near the trees understands/*understand."

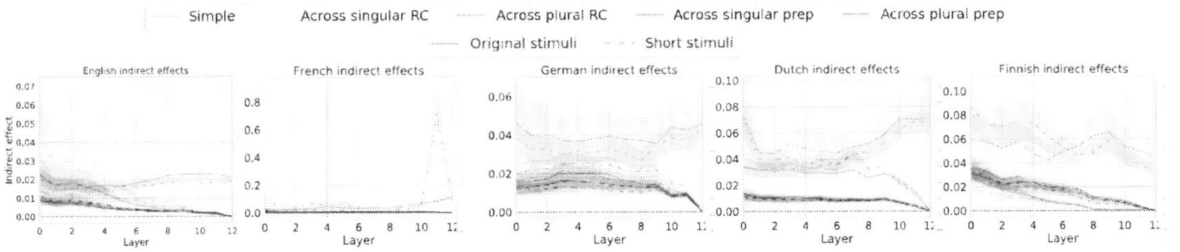

(a) BERT (b) CamemBERT (c) GermanBERT (d) BERTje (e) FinnishBERT

Figure 8: Natural indirect effects for the top 5% of neurons in each layer for monolingual masked language models. The indirect effect contours we observe do not vary significantly when replacing the nouns and verbs with shorter, more frequent words—except in layer 11 of CamemBERT.

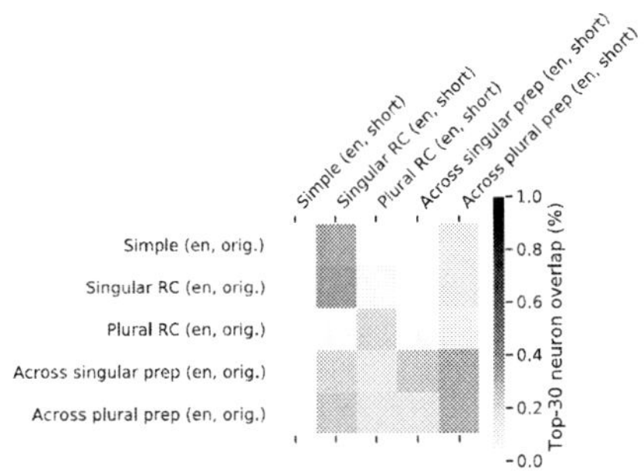

(a) mBERT

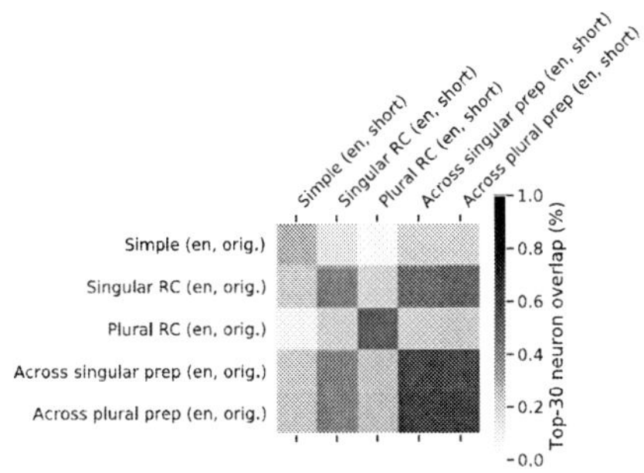

(b) XGLM

Figure 9: Neuron overlap across structures (including baselines) in English for (a) mBERT and (b) XGLM. There is significant overlap between the original stimuli and short-word stimuli, though this is more the case for XGLM than mBERT.

B Invariance to Short- and Long-Word Stimuli

When using the stimuli from Finlayson et al. (2021), most of the subjects and verbs are split into multiple tokens. These are generally long and relatively infrequent nouns and verbs like "managers" and "observe". We could use more stimuli if we replace each word with words that are shorter and more frequent in pre-training corpora, such as "cats" and "see".

Will these lexical replacements change the trends we observe? We observe the layer-wise natural indirect effect of the top neurons in each layer for the original stimuli and the short-word stimuli to see if lexical replacements have an effect on the way neurons encode syntactic agreement in monolingual BERT models. Our results (Figure 8) are nearly identical for the original stimuli and the short stimuli. A notable exception is layer 11 of CamemBERT, where indirect effects are so large that the rest of the effects are dwarfed by comparison. However, when excluding this result, indirect effect contours look similar between original and short stimuli.

We also compare the extent of neuron overlap between original and short stimuli for multilingual BERT and XGLM. Our results (Figure 9) show a relatively high degree of overlap, especially for XGLM. However, overlap is somewhat lower than when we use only one stimulus type (Figure 5). Ideally, overlap should be nearly 100% along the diagonal of both matrices if these neurons account only for syntactic agreement rather than specific lexical items, so these results suggest that lexical (and not syntactic) features may account for a notable proportion of the neuron overlap we observe in our previous experiments. Alternatively, it could mean that these neurons attend both syntactic *and* lexical information. Nonetheless, overlaps are still significant and indirect effects still look similar when swapping our nouns and verbs, so it is likely that models are picking up on some abstraction for syntactic agreement that generalizes across specific token sequences.

These results suggest that the neuron-level effects we observe are not simply spurious lexical correlations. More significantly, this is further evidence that **the neuron-level effects we observe are**

not word-level effects, but some more abstract structural feature(s) that the model has learned.

C Neuron Overlap Across Languages: Full Results

Here, we present neuron overlaps across languages for mBERT and XGLM (Figure 10). As in §4.2.1, we present overlaps for the top 30 neurons (in *any* layer of the model) per structure per language. As before, we find that neuron overlap is generally greater in autoregressive LMs than masked LMs.

Neuron overlaps are most prominent between English and French; while not typologically the most closely related language pair, English and French share a great deal of vocabulary and have similar SVO word orders when pronominal objects are not present. German, meanwhile, uses SOV with V2 in main clauses.

D Limitations

Perhaps the greatest limitation of our method—and many other causal probing methods (Vig et al., 2020; Finlayson et al., 2021; Ravfogel et al., 2021)—is that we are limited to stimuli where the subjects on which we intervene and the competing verb forms are one token each. This greatly limits the range of subjects and verbs (and languages) we can consider in this study, especially for more multilingual models where a greater proportion of words are split into subwords by the tokenizer. Models may use a different mechanism altogether to calculate the probability of two competing verbs given the presence or lack of a morpheme like {-s} which expresses number information, and our method would not allow us to understand where and how models are performing this kind of agreement. While one can, in theory, compare the probability of variable-length token sequences in autoregressive language models, there is no principled way to do this in masked language models. And in practice, autoregressive language models tend to prefer shorter sequences. Future work could consider probing methods which allow for variable-length span predictions.

There are also more general issues with probing individual neurons. Complex phenomena like syntactic agreement are likely to be encoded in *sets of* neurons, rather than individual neurons; indeed, we find evidence for this in §4.3. This means that analyzing individual neurons can result in oversimplified understandings of where and how certain phenomena are encoded and used. Future causal probing work could focus on non-parametric methods which allow one to probe multiple neurons simultaneously, such that we may causally implicate model *regions* rather than just individual components like neurons or attention heads.

(a) mBERT:

(b) XGLM:

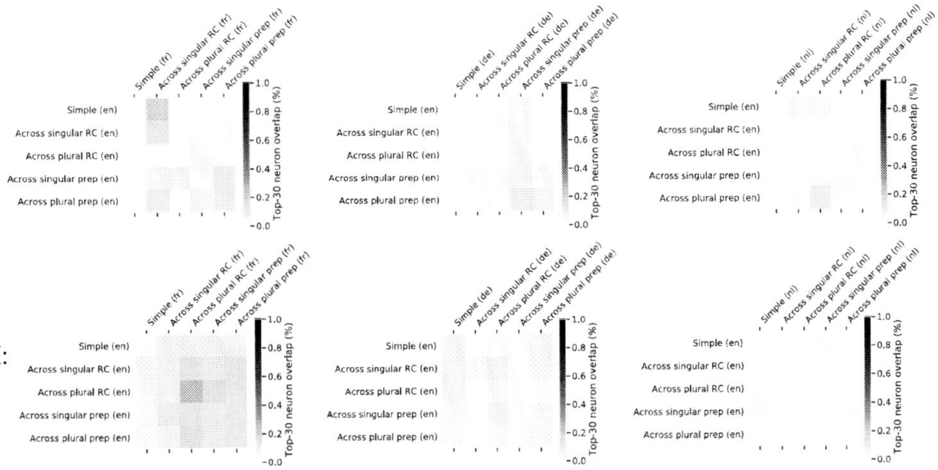

Figure 10: Neuron overlap for the top 30 neurons in mBERT (top row) and XGLM (bottom row). We show overlaps between English and French (left), German (center), and Dutch (right).

Combining Noisy Semantic Signals with Orthographic Cues: Cognate Induction for the Indic Dialect Continuum

Niyati Bafna[1,3,4*], **Josef van Genabith**[1,2], **Cristina España-Bonet**[2], **Zdeněk Žabokrtský**[3]
[1]Saarland Informatics Campus, Saarland University, Germany
[2]DFKI GmbH, Germany
[3]Institute of Formal and Applied Linguistics, Charles University, Prague
[4]Inria, Paris, France
niyatibafna13@gmail.com, {josef.van_genabith, cristinae}@dfki.de,
zabokrtsky@ufal.mff.cuni.cz

Abstract

We present a novel method for unsupervised cognate/borrowing identification from monolingual corpora designed for low and extremely low resource scenarios, based on combining noisy semantic signals from joint bilingual spaces with orthographic cues modelling sound change. We apply our method to the North Indian dialect continuum, containing several dozens of dialects and languages spoken by more than 100 million people. Many of these languages are zero-resource and therefore natural language processing for them is nonexistent. We first collect monolingual data for 26 Indic languages, 16 of which were previously zero-resource, and perform exploratory character, lexical and subword cross-lingual alignment experiments for the first time at this scale on this dialect continuum. We create bilingual evaluation lexicons against Hindi for 20 of the languages. We then apply our cognate identification method on the data, and show that our method outperforms both traditional orthography baselines as well as EM-style learnt edit distance matrices. To the best of our knowledge, this is the first work to combine traditional orthographic cues with noisy bilingual embeddings to tackle unsupervised cognate detection in a (truly) low-resource setup, showing that even noisy bilingual embeddings can act as good guides for this task. We release our multilingual dialect corpus, called HinDialect, as well as our scripts for evaluation data collection and cognate induction.[2]

1 Introduction

Hindi is listed as one of the 22 official languages of India, with the latest census showing 43.63% of Indians as having Hindi as their mother tongue.[3] However, this figure counts speakers of the languages of the whole Indic/Indo-Aryan (IA) dialect continuum, the "Hindi Belt", that stretches from Rajasthan in the West to Bihar and Jharkhand in the East, and of which modern standard Hindi is only a part.[4] This continuum, spread out over North and Central India, contains a wide variety of languages/dialects that may even be mutually incomprehensible, and form subfamilies of their own, e.g. the Rajasthani, Bihari, or Pahari subfamilies.[5]

Natural language processing (NLP) resources for these languages are sorely lacking; most of these languages, despite having millions of speakers, have little or no monolingual data, no linguistic resources such as lexicons, grammars, taggers, let alone more elaborate resources such as parallel data or pretrained embeddings.

We focus on 26 languages of the Hindi Belt written in the Devanagari script and make the following contributions: *(i)* we collect the first monolingual resources for many of these languages, and *(ii)* we develop a novel strategy for cognate lexicon induction in asymmetric truly low-resource scenarios, tackling this problem for the first time with the under-researched Indic dialect continuum. Cognate induction is an important first step towards obtaining bilingual lexicons, one of the most basic and all-purpose bilingual resources a language can have. Bilingual lexicons are especially useful in low-resource scenarios, e.g. for word-by-word translation, bilingual transfer, and as seeds for a variety of tasks; they also have applications in historical linguistics. Finally, in the case of severely under-supported languages, they are crucial for building dictionaries for speakers and language learners. In this work, we perform cognate induction for each language against Hindi, since Hindi

*This work was done at Charles University and Saarland University as a Masters' Thesis.

[2]See http://hdl.handle.net/11234/1-4839 and https://github.com/niyatibafna/north-indian-dialect-modelling, respectively.

[3]https://en.wikipedia.org/wiki/2011_Census_of_India

[4]We also see a shallower north-south dimension to the continuum, i.e. from Haryana to northern Maharashtra.

[5]See https://glottolog.org/resource/languoid/id/indo1321 for the full language tree.

Proceedings of the 26th Conference on Computational Natural Language Learning (CoNLL), pages 110 - 131
December 7-8, 2022 ©2022 Association for Computational Linguistics

is the most well-studied and resource-rich of this set, and therefore the most logical language from which bilingual transfer may be attempted.

We crawl monolingual data for the continuum, forming the largest collection (in number of languages) of a dialect continuum as far as we know. This also introduces the first monolingual data for 16 zero-resource IA languages to the NLP community. Such a corpus has wide applications for work in transfer, historical linguistics, dialect continua, and building language support for these communities. We probe the resulting multilingual collection at a character, subword and lexical level, finding a general link between relatedness and genealogically and geographically proximal languages.

Secondly, we use the corpus for cognate/borrowing induction (CI) for each target language with Hindi:[6] identifying cognates from monolingual corpora containing fully inflected word forms in a completely unsupervised manner.[7] We work in an asymmetric data scarcity situation: we have abundant monolingual resources for Hindi, but only a few thousands/ten thousands of monolingual tokens for target languages. These constraints set this task apart from most of the previous literature on cognate identification (List, 2014; Fourrier et al., 2021; List, 2019; Artetxe et al., 2018); however, this setting is realistic when attempting to build resources for truly low-resource languages. We present two simple but novel strategies for cognate identification, evaluating on synthetically created test sets. We experiment with iteratively learning substitution probabilities within an edit distance paradigm, as well as combining noisy semantic signals from a subword embedding space with orthographic distance measures, reporting qualitative improvements over the baseline.

2 Related Work

Data and Resources. Languages in the continuum differ in the amount of resources available. For the highest resourced languages (this corresponds to Band 1 in Section 5) one can find raw and annotated corpora, pretrained embeddings, and evaluation resources (Kunchukuttan et al., 2020; Bojar et al., 2014; Nivre et al., 2016). For medium-resourced languages (Band 2), we have some collection efforts,[8] mostly monolingual (Ojha, 2019; Ojha et al., 2020; Goldhahn et al., 2012) but including some parallel data. Zampieri et al. (2018) presented a shared task for language identification for Awadhi, Braj, Bhojpuri, Magahi, and Hindi providing 15k sentences for each language. Mundotiya et al. (2021) collect monolingual corpora for Bhojpuri, Magahi, and Maithili, as well as POS-tagged annotated corpora and WordNets[9] aligned with the larger IndoWordNet effort (Sinha et al., 2006) Mundotiya et al. (2022) presents NER-annotated corpora and trained NER models for the same 3 languages. The least resourced languages (Band 3) lack any kind of systematic resource and are the main focus of our work.

Bi/Multilingual Lexicon Induction Much previous work has been based on *non-neural methods*. Batsuren et al. (2019) use semantic relationships from the Universal Knowledge Core (Giunchiglia et al., 2018) which is built from existing WordNets,[10] gold annotations as well as geographical-orthographic similarity measures for cognate identification. Çöltekin (2019) compares linear and neural models to predict the next edit-distance based action to perform crosslingual morphological inflection. In earlier works, Scherrer and Sagot (2014), inspired by Koehn and Knight (2002), induced cognate sets in a completely unsupervised manner using a character-based alignment algorithm, as well as co-occurrence-based context vectors. List (2012) induce cognate sets over aligned word lists of languages in a language family by iteratively learning phonological rules; this is implemented in the software LingPy (List, 2014). Hall and Klein (2010) work with unaligned word lists for languages in the same family, modelling transfer within a tree-based framework and learning edit-distance based transformation matrices for each vertical edge. Although the idea of learning edit distance matrices is quite old (Bilenko and Mooney, 2003), it has not been used in combination with modern embeddings-based methods for cognate identification as far as we know.

Recently, *neural and embeddings-based methods* have been gaining importance. Conneau et al. (2018) is one of the earliest works to link bilingual

[6]Henceforth, we use the term "cognate" as including borrowings.

[7]While we do have lexical resources for Band 1 and 2 languages including WordNets for *some* Band 1 languages (see Table 1 for bands), we simulate low-resource scenarios consistent with the truly low-resource Band 3 languages

[8]See www.ldcil.org/resourcesTextCorp.aspx

[9]Not publicly available yet

[10]CogNet contains only Band 1 Indic languages

lexicon induction (BLI) with bilingual embedding spaces, or the alignment of monolingual embeddings. This idea has been explored by other works that seek to adapt it to low-resource settings or relax its strong isometry assumption (Dou et al., 2018; Patra et al., 2019), sometimes using a bootstrapping strategy for embedding alignment and bilingual lexicon induction (Artetxe et al., 2018; Cao and Zhao, 2021). Fourrier et al. (2021) frame cognate induction as a machine translation problem, finding that SMT beats NMT over smaller datasets; Kanojia et al. (2019) identify cognate sets for (Band 1) Indian languages using the IndoWordNet combined with lexical similarity measures, training neural models over the resulting data.

3 Orthographic Distance for Cognate Induction

3.1 Baseline Approach

A straightforward approach for CI involves using orthographic distance as a stand-in for phonological distance, motivated by the fact that Devanagari is orthographically shallow, that is, spellings closely represent associated pronunciations. We consider source words from Hindi; the best cognate candidate in the other language is chosen by minimizing orthographic distance. We use two distances: normalized edit distance (**NED**), that is, the edit distance normalized by the maximum of the 2 word lengths, thus scaling to 0-1; and Jaro-Winkler (**JW**) distance (Winkler, 1990), which weights differences higher in the beginnings of strings.

For all approaches, we use a minimum source frequency of 5, maximum lexicon size of 5000, and we collect 5 best candidates per source word; this ensures identical recall over all approaches given a fixed source language corpus and test lexicon.

3.2 Expectation-Maximisation Approach

A limiting theoretical deficiency in the baseline approach is that it treats substitutions of any two characters equally (similarly for insertions and deletions). By contrast, the expectation-maximisation (EM) approach optimises substitution probabilities iteratively while simultaneously learning cognate pairs, given two lexicons, in an expectation-maximization style algorithm. We call it **EMT**, EM for "Transform probabilities".

Setup. Given two word lists (that may overlap) WL_s and WL_t, let the set of all characters of the source and target side be χ_s and χ_t respectively. We use a scoring function $S(c_i, c_j)$, that contains a "score" for replacing any character $c_i \in \chi_s$ with $c_j \in \chi_t$;[11] for a given character in a source word, S is modelled as a transformation probability distribution over χ_t. S is initialized by giving high probability (in practice, 0.5) to self-transforms and distributing the remaining probability mass equally over other characters.

Given that $C(a, b)$ is the number of times we have seen $a \to b$, and $T(a)$ is the total number of times we have seen a on the source side, our score is the conditional probability:

$$S(c_i, c_j) = \frac{C(c_i, c_j)}{T(c_i)} \qquad (1)$$

We maintain a list of cognates found over all EM loops, so that we only update model parameters once per cognate pair. Note that a word may appear in many different cognate pairs in this setup.

The EMT Algorithm is composed of two steps. *1) Expectation step.* Given a candidate source and target pair (s, t), we can find $Ops(s, t)$, which is the *minimal list* of the operations we need to perform to get from s to t. Each member in Ops is of the type (c_i, c_j). In addition to "insert"/ "delete"/"replace" operations, we also use a "retain" operation, for characters that remain the same; we also want to estimate $S(a, a)\ \forall\ a$.

The score for the pair (s, t) is computed as

$$\zeta(s,t) = - \sum_{(a,b) \in Ops} log_{10}(S(a, b)), \qquad (2)$$

where the lower the ζ the more probable a pair is a cognate. For a given s, we can then always find the word that is the most probable cognate as $t = min_{t_i \neq s}(\zeta(s, t_i))$.

Note that in the training phase, we disallow $s = t$, to mitigate exploding self-transform probabilities. Finally, we choose the best K of all cognate pairs i.e. those with the highest confidence, equivalent to the lowest ζ values.

2) Maximisation step. We update the model parameters based on the newly identified cognates in the previous step. This is done by increasing the counts of all observed edit distance operations:

$$C(a, b) := C(a, b) + 1 \quad \forall (a, b) \in Ops(s, t)$$

[11]We model insertion and deletion as special cases of replacement, by introducing a null character.

$$T(a) := T(a) + 1 \qquad \forall (a, b) \in Ops(s, t)$$

Inference is performed by choosing the K best target candidates that minimise $\zeta(s, t)$ as described above, now allowing self-matches.

4 Semantic Similarity for Cognate Induction

Orthographic matching, even with tailored and learnt substitution matrices for a given pair of languages, may be inherently inadequate, as it pays no heed to the shared semantics of cognates. We use bilingual subword embeddings (BE) to address this problem in the following way: we use the semantic space to narrow down possible candidates, and then apply orthographic matching in order to select the top K candidates. This is a two-stage approach that relies mainly on two separate metrics: first, the quality of semantic similarity judgments provided by a semantic embedding space, and second, orthographic similarity judgments provided by the distance/similarity metric we choose to use.

SEM_JW: BE+JW In this approach, we retrieve K nearest neighbours of each source word. These candidates are scored by an interpolation of semantic similarity and orthographic distance, with equal weighting. We use cosine similarity for the former, and JW for the latter. All words that are not within the K nearest neighbours (50 in our experiments) are discarded from consideration. The idea is to mitigate the effect of chance orthographic similarities.

For candidates, if $E(s)$ is the embedding vector for string s, we minimize:

$$D(a, b) = 1 - scos(E(a), E(b)) \cdot J(a, b), \quad (3)$$

where $scos(v_1, v_2)$ captures the cosine similarity (scaled to [0, 1]) between vectors v_1 and v_2, and $J(a, b)$ is the **JW** similarity.

SEM_EMT: BE+EMT We seek to combine the benefits of iteratively learning transformation probabilities with those of semantic spaces. This approach is almost identical to that in Section 3.2, except for the fact that only $K = 50$ nearest neighbours of a source word in the semantic space are used as its potential cognate candidates, both during training and inference.

5 Data Collection

We apply the methods described above to the Indic dialect continuum. Since these languages cover a range of resource situations, we divide them into three categories, Band 1, 2 and 3, based on amount of resources, with Band 1 containing the best resourced languages, and Band 3 containing (previously) zero-resource languages. See Table 1 for a description of the languages under consideration.

5.1 Monolingual Corpora Crawl

Digital presence of Band 3 languages is low to non-existent; automatic crawling for content faces the primary problems of scarcity, script handling, and automatic language identification between closely related variants.

Kavita Kosh,[12] translating roughly to "poetry collection", is an online collection of folksongs and poems in 31 languages from the IA continuum. Content is manually curated by the organization; the poetry consists of works by early contemporary writers, mostly from the late twentieth century. All content is in Devanagari (transliterated in case of e.g. Bengali content). The website categorizes pieces by type, language, author/theme, and possibly additional labels such as anthology. We collect data for a total of 31 languages, of which we have folksong data for 26 languages, and poetry data for 18 languages.[13,14] We leave out 5 languages for cognate induction: Bangla, Gujarati, Punjabi (written primarily in a different script), Sanskrit and Pali (extinct languages). The data is cleaned at a character-level, we filter out words with any character not within a specified UTF-8 code-point range and tokenization is performed by white-space splitting. See total counts in tokens in Table 1. Poem and token counts are reported in Appendix A.[15]

5.2 Evaluation Data for Cognate Induction

Band 3 languages lack standardized gold bilingual lexicons that may be used for supervision. After a survey of possible digital resources for this purpose (see Appendix B for a listing), we choose to use Languages Home, an online language learning website,[16] containing translations of 80–90 artificially simple English sentences (e.g. "He ate an apple",

[12] `http://kavitakosh.org/kk/`

[13] We also include Korku as an outlier datapoint; it is *not* an Indic language and therefore lacks the genealogical similarities of the others.

[14] We preserve the distinction made by the website between Khadi Boli and Hindi; the former is the closest to what we consider modern Hindi.

[15] We have been authorized by the organization to make the folksongs data available but not the poetry. However, our crawler is publicly available to use.

[16] `https://www.languageshome.com`

Language	Primary Regions	Language (Sub-)Family	Data (Tok.)	Collected (Tok.)	# native speakers
BAND 1					
Hindi	Uttar Pradesh*, Bihar*, Rajasthan*, 13 others	IA Central, Western Hindi	1.86B[1]	7127997	250M†
Marathi	Maharastra*, Goa*	IA Southern, Marathic	551M[1]	3327	73M
Nepali	Nepal*, West Bengal*	IA Northern, Eastern Pahari	14M[2]	692657	16M
Sindhi	Sindh*, Pakistan, Rajasthan, Gujarat	IA Northwestern, Sindhi-Lahnda	61M[5]	51458	25M
BAND 2					
Bhojpuri	Bihar, Jharkhand*	IA, Bihari	259K[3]	197639	40M
Awadhi	Bihar	IA, Bihari	123K[3]	500079	38M
Magahi	Bihar, Jharkand*	IA, Bihari	234K[3]	84754	40M
Maithili	Bihar*, Jharkhand*	IA, Bihari	300K[4]	218339	14M
Brajbhasha	Uttar Pradesh	IA Central, Western Hindi	249K[3]	160039	1M
BAND 3					
Rajasthani	Rajasthan	IA Central, Gujarati-Rajasthani	-	187724	50M
Hariyanvi	Haryana, Rajasthan	IA Central, Western Hindi	-	233003	13M
Bhili	Rajasthan, Gujarati, Madhya Pradesh	IA Central, Bhil	-	27326	3M
Korku	Madhya Pradesh, Maharashtra	Austro-Asiatic, North Munda	-	15509	0.7M
Baiga	Chattisgarh	IA Central, Chattisgarhi	-	13848	UNK
Nimaadi	Rajasthan, Madhya Pradesh	IA Central, Bhil	-	14056	2M
Malwi	Rajasthan, Madhya Pradesh	IA Central, Bhil	-	9626	5M
Bhadavari	Jammu Kashmir	IA Northern, Western Pahari	-	990	0.1M
Himachali	Himachal Pradesh	IA Northern, Himachali	-	466	2M
Garwali	Uttarakhand	IA Northern, Central Pahari	-	92668	6M
Kumaoni	Uttarakhand	IA Northern, Central Pahari	-	1028	2M
Kannauji	Uttar Pradesh	IA Central, Western Hindi	-	327	9.5M
Bundeli	Madhya Pradesh, Uttar Pradesh	IA Central, Western Hindi	-	26928	5.6M
Chattisgarhi	Chattisgarh*	IA Central, Eastern Hindi	-	83226	18M
Bajjika	Bihar	IA, Bihari	-	7414	12M
Angika	Bihar, Jharkhand*	IA, Bihari	-	1265146	15M
Khadi Boli	Delhi	IA Central, Western Hindi	-	4507	UNK

Table 1: Language bands. Note that Band 1 languages may have much more data available from other sources such as Wikipedia; for Band 2 languages, we may have other sources with the same order of magnitude of data. "Primary Regions" only mentions places in the Indian subcontinent; * indicates official status. Corpora from which data counts are taken: [1](Kakwani et al., 2020), [2](Yadava et al., 2008), [3](Zampieri et al., 2018), [4](Goldhahn et al., 2012) [5](Conneau et al., 2020). Speaker counts taken from (latest) 2011 census if available. †: probably inflated

"He will come") into 76 Indian languages (including some Dravidian languages and IA languages for which we do not have data). This resource has the best coverage as well as consistency over Band 3 languages. Of these, 20 languages are of our interest, including 12 Band 3 languages. This data is considerably noisy, with problems including the fact that it is written in "casual" Roman transliteration, inconsistent parenthetic explanations, and code-switching.

We develop a pipeline to extract the aligned lexicons. The pipeline consists of cleaning, transliteration of the Indic side into Devanagari with indic-trans (Bhat et al., 2015), parallelizing with Hindi instead of English,[17] and finally extracting word-alignments over the given Hindi-parallel data with FAST-ALIGN (Dyer et al., 2013).

The resulting lexicons have an average size of 153.6 elements, a minimum size of 118, and a maximum of 177. We manually evaluate the Hindi-Marathi lexicon, finding that 73.5% of 130 source words contain at least one correct target.[18] Despite clear problems of noise, and acknowledging that these lexicons should be post-edited by native speakers, this is the best possible evaluation data that we can use, given its coverage and uniform format; however, we consider it as a relative rather than absolute indicator of performance.

6 Experiments and Results

6.1 Probing the Monolingual Corpora

We seek to capture a high-level picture of the data on the character, subword, and lexical level, comparing observations with language-specific characteristics from prior knowledge as well as with expected cross-lingual relationships. For this, we perform 3 types of experiments.

Character-level. We inspect the symmetric KL-Divergence[19] over characters as well as char-gram distributions of the languages. For the latter, the final metric is simply the average over divergence values for each char-gram length. Since IA languages are orthographically shallow, inspecting such distributions of a language may give us a fairly good idea of the general usage of consonants and vowels in the language.

Lexical Overlap. If L_i and L_j are the filtered lexicons of two languages i and j, we calculate

$$O_{ij} = \frac{|L_i \cap L_j|}{min(|L_i|, |L_j|)} \tag{4}$$

for all pairs. We apply a corpus-dependent frequency threshold to the data: we discard all words in a corpus with size N_L that occur with a frequency less than $T(N_L) = log_{100}(N_L) - 1$. The exponent 100 and the constant -1 were chosen such that the threshold does not grow too quickly, and that datasets with less than 1000 tokens are fully retained.

Subword-level. We calculate pairwise subword-level overlap measures, captured by character grams of length 2–4,[20] thinking of subwords as approximating morphemic units of the language. Let's define L_{ic} as the inventory/lexicon of c-length char-grams for language i, then the c-char-gram overlap O_{ijc} for languages i and j is calculated identically to lexical overlap in Eqn 4.

We would like to weight O_{ijc} according to c, capturing the idea that it is more of a similarity signal for two languages to share c-char-grams for a higher c. For this purpose, we calculate the "universe of possibilities" for each c; i.e. the total number U_c of unique c-char-grams that occur in the entire corpus. Since we want normalizing weights that are inversely related to the probability of an accidentally shared c-char-gram, we calculate subword similarity as follows:

$$O_{ij} = \sum_c \left(O_{ijc} \cdot \frac{U_c}{\sum_c U_c} \right) \tag{5}$$

Finally, we also calculate pairwise symmetric KL-Divergence over subword distributions.

Results. Figure 1 is generally representative of our results across character, subword and lexical results, both overlap-based and information-theoretic (see Appendix A for related heatmaps). The following general observations emerge from all the above experiments. The Purvanchal and eastern languages from Kannuaji to Angika (represented in the bottom right), show the highest similarity/overlap within themselves over all calculated measures. This is expected and confirms that the

[17]Word alignment of Indic languages with Hindi sentences as compared to English sentences is likelier to be accurate.

[18]Note that a word equivalent used here may not be a cognate even if a cognate does exist in the language.

[19]Specifically, for probability distributions P and Q, we calculate the symmetric quantity $D_{KL}(P||Q) + D_{KL}(Q||P)$

[20]Different ranges yield the same trend.

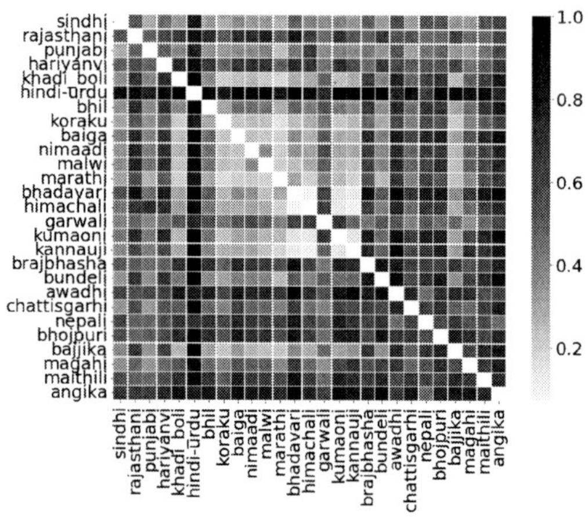

Figure 1: Overlap-based similarity over i-char-grams.

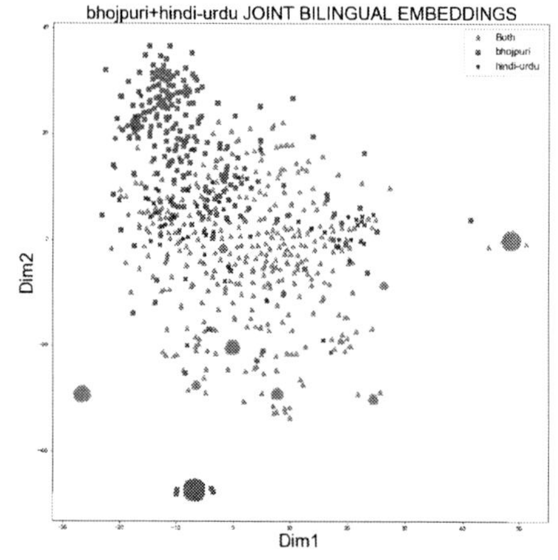

Figure 2: t-SNE visualization (Van der Maaten and Hinton, 2008). Bhojpuri words cluster together.

corpus represents the close genealogical and cultural ties between these languages.

We see that Hindi has high lexical/subword-level similarities with almost every language. This could be the result of the widespread use of Hindi, or its large dataset, including noise even after filtering. We also notice that some languages have consistently low lexical similarities with others. In the case of Korku, this is expected, given that Korku is a genealogical outlier. In other cases, such as with Malwi and Himachali, this is probably because the collected dataset is too small to be representative of the vocabulary of these languages. In general, and as expected, the eastern cluster as well as the western cluster of languages show close relationships with each other.

6.2 Bilingual Embeddings

We use FASTTEXT (Bojanowski et al., 2017) for training bilingual embeddings in a simple **joint** manner, with minimum corpus frequency according to the corpus-dependent threshold $T(N_L)$, described in Section 6.1; we hope to leverage its usage of subword information, given that that we are dealing with data-scarce morphologically rich languages.

Visualizations reveal that low-resource target language words often cluster around each other, whereas Hindi words and words belonging to both languages are more meaningfully distributed. (See Figure 2, Appendix C for other language plots.) A possible diagnosis is an effect pointed out by Gong et al. (2018) who show that low-frequency words tend to cluster together regardless of their semantics. This, along with the fact that we are unfairly applying the same minimum frequency threshold (better suited for the high-resource anchor) for both languages by mixing the data, may explain the poor quality of the target language embeddings. In order to mitigate the problem, we **upsample** the target language data to bring it to the same order of magnitude as the Hindi data.

Results We use the Nepali WordNet to extract a Hindi–Nepali bilingual lexicon, and we calculated Recall@50 (given 50 nearest neighbours). We also use basic visualizations and a crosslingual integration metric *cl_integ*, which measures the fraction of nearest neighbours per word that belong to the other language, to compare the two sets of embeddings, on average. That is, if $\nu_E(w, K)$ is the set of K nearest neighbours of w in the embedding space E and $\psi_n(L)$ is a sample of n words from a language with lexicon L, then

$$cl\_integ_{12} = \frac{1}{n \cdot K} \left(\sum_{\substack{w \in \\ \psi_n(L_1)}} \sum_{\substack{w' \in \\ \nu_E(w,K)}} I(w' \in L_2) \right)$$

We report scores as a percentage, with $n = 500$ and $K = 10$.

The UPSAMPLE Nepali model has better Recall@50 for the Hindi–Nepali gold lexicon (33% vs. 29%).[21] Representing *cl_integ* scores as a pair of integration values in either direction, i.e. (target-Hindi, Hindi-target), we find that the UPSAMPLE

[21]We also evaluated differently sized subsets of Nepali data for over the WordNet lexicon, which yielded consistent results; see Appendix C for details and more visualizations.

	NED	JW	EMT	SEM_JW	SEM_EMT	Gold
1	कहा	कहा	कहा	कहा	कहा	कहलाह
2	कहना	कहना	कहना	कहात	क	कहल
3	कहाँ	कहाँ	कहाँ	कहाई	कहीं	-
4	एकहा	कहमा	एकहा	कहनाम	लजाते	-
5	कहमा	कहां	-	कह	पूछा	-

Figure 3: Hindi source word: /kəha:/ (said). SEM_JW approach performs the best, resulting in Bhojpuri equivalents (except the third prediction) and inflections. SEM_EMT also results in semantically correct outputs (for all but the fourth prediction). The NED/JW approaches produce orthographically close words that are semantically unrelated, e.g. /kəhã:/ (where).

models show scores of (43%, 27%), and the JOINT models show (91%, 14%), averaged over all languages. We see that the UPSAMPLE models show less skew by direction, and higher scores for the latter direction (which is what we use).

Finally, visualizations for different languages (see Appendix C.1 for an example) show the target language words to be better distributed in the UPSAMPLE approach, with more meaningful collocations. All of these are good indications that upsampling did indeed improve the quality of the bilingual embedding space. We use these for the subsequent approaches.

6.3 Cognate Induction

Our main results are presented in Table 2. There is no clear quantitative winner; SEM_JW performs slightly better than the other approaches on average. Cognate identification methods usually work at a much higher accuracy (Beinborn et al., 2013; Fourrier et al., 2021), 70–90%. The low accuracies that we record are due to a number of factors: a much lower resource range, lack of aligned word lists, lemmatizers, or supervision and evaluation, as well as noise in the evaluation data. While most literature assumes lemmatized word lists as input for this task, we do not have lemmatizers for these languages and work with fully inflected word forms; this is a further challenge for our CI strategies.

Qualitatively, we observe significant differences across models. See Figure 3 for example outputs.

NED/JW: The NED/JW approaches are often able to capture the correct answer for longer words, because the closest candidate in edit distance is likely to be in the ballpark for closely related languages. However, we also often get outputs (especially the second or third prediction) that are entirely off, as is expected from this naive idea.

EMT: Taking a look into the substitution distributions learnt by EMT, we see that it learns some expected relationships e.g. the relationship between /i/ and /i:/, shifts between other vowels, or the fact that some rarely used characters are likely to be deleted. However, the approach is not able to produce good final outputs. We attribute this to a bad seed; this approach basically depends on the seed obtained from simple NED to get started, and if it meanders down a mistaken path, that error tends to magnify itself due to the iterative nature of the algorithm, sometimes resulting in even worse final outputs than simple NED/JW.

SEM_*: The SEM_* approaches are intended to address the fundamental inadequacy in the above approaches: the fact that they do not exploit the shared semantics of cognates. SEM_JW is accordingly better at producing outputs that are semantically related, besides the required cognates. Top predictions tend to be similar to those of NED/JW, but SEM_JW produces a better collection of outputs, from the perspective of bilingual lexicons, especially since it is less biased against a higher number of substitutions. However, for many words, the method produces rather Hindi-like outputs, probably as a result of the persisting problem of language-wise clustering in the spaces.[22] SEM_EMT still suffers from the same problems as before; we see therefore that a stronger orthographic distance metric such as JW is better able to spot the cognate from semantically related words.

7 Discussion and Conclusion

We analyse the performance of the approaches with respect to the different facets of cognacy.

Variant inflectional endings: Learning the correspondences between inflections in a dialect pair is a crucial task when it comes to cognate identification for fully inflected word forms. In terms of producing the right answer, we see an intuitive split between common and rare words when it comes to other approaches. For common words, SEM_JW

[22]This problem may be mitigated with a higher target frequency threshold.

	Total	Found	NED	JWM	EMT	SEM_JW	SEM_EMT
Kumaoni	138.0	118.0	**5.1**	4.2	**5.1**	**5.1**	4.2
Marathi	138.0	116.0	**7.8**	5.2	4.3	1.7	3.4
Bajjika	149.0	123.0	13.8	**15.4**	13.8	14.6	11.4
Malwi	153.0	125.0	**24.8**	22.4	20.0	20.0	15.2
Koraku	140.0	116.0	**1.7**	0.9	**1.7**	**1.7**	0.9
Bundeli	139.0	117.0	26.5	25.6	25.6	**30.8**	26.5
Bhil	156.0	128.0	19.5	**21.1**	17.2	18.8	18.0
Sindhi	134.0	114.0	10.5	**13.2**	7.9	10.5	9.6
Magahi	159.0	129.0	17.8	**20.9**	18.6	**20.9**	17.1
Chattisgarhi	136.0	115.0	25.2	26.1	24.3	**28.7**	26.1
Garwali	143.0	120.0	**15.8**	**15.8**	15.0	**15.8**	14.2
Brajbhasha	155.0	127.0	33.9	**34.6**	32.3	33.9	32.3
Rajasthani	144.0	120.0	30.8	29.2	27.5	**31.7**	30.0
Bhojpuri	139.0	115.0	31.3	28.7	**32.2**	30.4	29.6
Maithili	140.0	117.0	17.9	17.1	16.2	18.8	**20.5**
Hariyanvi	153.0	126.0	38.1	41.3	37.3	**43.7**	42.9
Awadhi	148.0	123.0	**28.5**	26.8	22.0	26.0	25.2
Nepali	105.0	95.0	**12.6**	**12.6**	9.5	9.5	7.4
Angika	141.0	116.0	21.6	20.7	21.6	**22.4**	21.6
Average	142.6	118.9	20.1	20.2	18.5	**20.3**	18.7

Table 2: Results for CI, precision (%) over bilingual lexicons presented in Section 5.2. A precision point is calculated per source word such that any predicted target exists in the evaluation target set.

is likely to perform better than the other approaches because the word is well embedded and the correct word form is likely to be nearby in the semantic space, and subsequently selected by JW. In these cases, especially for short words, NED/JW are likely to be derailed by irrelevant words.

Correct semantics: We would like to have semantically sensible outputs even if the predicted words are not cognates. Naturally, this is performed best by the SEM_* approaches, although the NED/JW approaches do better than expected.

Sound changes: Sound change is one of the fundamental phenomena of cognacy, and can be understood in the case of borrowing in the sense of changed pronunciations. Unfortunately, we do not have the theoretical data of attested sound changes across these dialects in order to be best able to check which approach performs best in this respect.

The SEM_JW produces overall the most respectable outputs, although this is more true for common words. The main inadequacy of all these approaches is their inability to capture language-pair specific correspondences. An extension of this work could focus on refining something akin to the SEM_EMT, which has the most theoretical potential in this direction. Improvements could include searching the hyperparameter space for better priors. An investigation into better bi/multilingual spaces is crucial to generalize good performance over rare words; future work can look into using orthographic similarities explicitly while training the space itself, as well as the utility of zero-shot multilingual contextual embeddings for this task.

We have presented a new approach to unsupervised cognate identification from monolingual corpora under conditions of asymmetric data scarcity. We collected monolingual data for 26 Indian languages of the Indic dialect continuum, 16 of which previously zero-resource, as well as synthetic evaluation data. Our experiments show the benefits of combining weak semantic signals from static bilingual embeddings with orthographic cues.

8 Acknowledgements

This work has been using data, tools and services provided by the LINDAT/CLARIAH-CZ Research Infrastructure (`https://lindat.cz`), supported by the Ministry of Education, Youth and Sports of the Czech Republic (Project No. LM2018101). The first author was supported by the Erasmus+ Programme, European Masters Program in Language and Communication Technologies, EU grant no. 2019-1508. The second and third author were supported by the German Federal Ministry of Education and Research (BMBF) under funding code 01IW20010 (CORA4NLP) and the German Research Foundation (Deutsche Forschungsgemeinschaft) under grant SFB 1102: Information Density and Linguistic Encoding.

References

Mikel Artetxe, Gorka Labaka, and Eneko Agirre. 2018. A Robust Self-Learning Method for Fully Unsupervised Cross-lingual Mappings of Word Embeddings. In *Proceedings of the 56th Annual Meeting of the Association for Computational Linguistics (Volume 1: Long Papers)*, pages 789–798, Melbourne, Australia. Association for Computational Linguistics.

Khuyagbaatar Batsuren, Gábor Bella, and Fausto Giunchiglia. 2019. CogNet: A Large-Scale Cognate Database. In *Proceedings of the 57th annual meeting of the association for computational linguistics*, pages 3136–3145.

Lisa Beinborn, Torsten Zesch, and Iryna Gurevych. 2013. Cognate Production using Character-Based Machine Translation. In *Proceedings of the sixth international joint conference on natural language processing*, pages 883–891.

Irshad Ahmad Bhat, Vandan Mujadia, Aniruddha Tammewar, Riyaz Ahmad Bhat, and Manish Shrivastava. 2015. IIIT-H System Submission for FIRE2014 Shared Task on Transliterated Search. In *Proceedings of the Forum for Information Retrieval Evaluation*, FIRE '14, pages 48–53, New York, NY, USA. ACM.

Mikhail Bilenko and Raymond J Mooney. 2003. Employing Trainable String Similarity Metrics for Information Integration. In *IIWeb*, pages 67–72.

Piotr Bojanowski, Edouard Grave, Armand Joulin, and Tomas Mikolov. 2017. Enriching Word Vectors with Subword Information. *Transactions of the association for computational linguistics*, 5:135–146.

Ondřej Bojar, Vojtěch Diatka, Pavel Rychlý, Pavel Straňák, Vít Suchomel, Aleš Tamchyna, and Daniel Zeman. 2014. HindMonoCorp 0.5. LINDAT/CLARIAH-CZ digital library at the Institute of Formal and Applied Linguistics (ÚFAL), Faculty of Mathematics and Physics, Charles University.

Hailong Cao and Tiejun Zhao. 2021. Word Embedding Transformation for Robust Unsupervised Bilingual Lexicon Induction. *arXiv preprint arXiv:2105.12297*.

Çağrı Çöltekin. 2019. Cross-lingual Morphological Inflection with Explicit Alignment. In *Proceedings of the 16th Workshop on Computational Research in Phonetics, Phonology, and Morphology*, pages 71–79.

Alexis Conneau, Kartikay Khandelwal, Naman Goyal, Vishrav Chaudhary, Guillaume Wenzek, Francisco Guzmán, Édouard Grave, Myle Ott, Luke Zettlemoyer, and Veselin Stoyanov. 2020. Unsupervised Cross-lingual Representation Learning at Scale. In *Proceedings of the 58th Annual Meeting of the Association for Computational Linguistics*, pages 8440–8451.

Alexis Conneau, Guillaume Lample, Marc'Aurelio Ranzato, Ludovic Denoyer, and Hervé Jégou. 2018. Word Translation without Parallel Data. In *Proceedings of the 6th International Conference on Learning Representations*.

Chakrabarti Debasri, Narayan Dipak Kumar, Pandey Prabhakar, and Bhattacharyya Pushpak. 2002. Experiences in building the Indo-Wordnet: A Wordnet for Hindi. In *Proceedings of the First Global WordNet Conference*.

Zi-Yi Dou, Zhi-Hao Zhou, and Shujian Huang. 2018. Unsupervised Bilingual Lexicon Induction via Latent Variable Models. In *Proceedings of the 2018 Conference on Empirical Methods in Natural Language Processing*, pages 621–626, Brussels, Belgium. Association for Computational Linguistics.

Pankaj Dwivedi and Somdev Kar. 2016. Sociolinguistics and Phonology of Kanauji. In *International Conference on Hindi Studies*.

Chris Dyer, Victor Chahuneau, and Noah A Smith. 2013. A Simple, Fast, and Effective Reparameterization of IBM model 2. In *Proceedings of the 2013 Conference of the North American Chapter of the Association for Computational Linguistics: Human Language Technologies*, pages 644–648.

Clémentine Fourrier, Rachel Bawden, and Benoît Sagot. 2021. Can Cognate Prediction Be Modelled as a Low-Resource Machine Translation Task? In *Findings of the Association for Computational Linguistics: ACL-IJCNLP 2021*, Bangkok, Thailand.

Fausto Giunchiglia, Khuyagbaatar Batsuren, and Abed Alhakim Freihat. 2018. One World–Seven Thousand Languages. In *Proceedings 19th international conference on computational linguistics and intelligent text processing, CiCling2018*, pages 18–24.

Dirk Goldhahn, Thomas Eckart, and Uwe Quasthoff. 2012. Building Large Monolingual Dictionaries at the Leipzig Corpora Collection: From 100 to 200 languages. In *Proceedings of the Eighth International Conference on Language Resources and Evaluation (LREC'12)*, pages 759–765.

Chengyue Gong, Di He, Xu Tan, Tao Qin, Liwei Wang, and Tie-Yan Liu. 2018. FRAGE: Frequency-agnostic Word Representation. *Advances in neural information processing systems*, 31.

David Hall and Dan Klein. 2010. Finding Cognate Groups using Phylogenies. In *Proceedings of the 48th Annual Meeting of the Association for Computational Linguistics*, pages 1030–1039. Citeseer.

Divyanshu Kakwani, Anoop Kunchukuttan, Satish Golla, Gokul N.C., Avik Bhattacharyya, Mitesh M. Khapra, and Pratyush Kumar. 2020. IndicNLPSuite: Monolingual corpora, evaluation benchmarks and pre-trained multilingual language models for Indian languages. In *Findings of the Association for Computational Linguistics: EMNLP 2020*, pages 4948–4961, Online. Association for Computational Linguistics.

Diptesh Kanojia, Kevin Patel, Malhar Kulkarni, Pushpak Bhattacharyya, and Gholemreza Haffari. 2019. Utilizing Wordnets for Cognate Detection among Indian Languages. In *Proceedings of the 10th Global Wordnet Conference*, pages 404–412.

Philipp Koehn and Kevin Knight. 2002. Learning a Translation Lexicon from Monolingual Corpora. In *Proceedings of the ACL-02 workshop on Unsupervised lexical acquisition*, pages 9–16.

Anoop Kunchukuttan, Divyanshu Kakwani, Satish Golla, Avik Bhattacharyya, Mitesh M Khapra, Pratyush Kumar, et al. 2020. AI4Bharat-IndicNLP Corpus: Monolingual corpora and Word Embeddings for Indic languages. *arXiv preprint arXiv:2005.00085*.

Johann-Mattis List. 2012. LexStat: Automatic Detection of Cognates in Multilingual Wordlists. In *Proceedings of the EACL 2012 Joint Workshop of LINGVIS & UNCLH*, pages 117–125.

Johann-Mattis List. 2019. Automatic Inference of Sound Correspondence Patterns across Multiple Languages. *Computational Linguistics*, 45(1):137–161.

Mattis List. 2014. Sequence Comparison in Historical Linguistics. In *Sequence Comparison in Historical Linguistics*. Düsseldorf university press.

Rajesh Kumar Mundotiya, Shantanu Kumar, Ajeet Kumar, Umesh Chandra Chaudhary, Supriya Chauhan, Swasti Mishra, Praveen Gatla, and Anil Kumar Singh. 2022. Development of a Dataset and a Deep Learning Baseline Named Entity Recognizer for Three Low Resource Languages: Bhojpuri, Maithili and Magahi. *ACM Trans. Asian Low-Resour. Lang. Inf. Process.*

Rajesh Kumar Mundotiya, Manish Kumar Singh, Rahul Kapur, Swasti Mishra, and Anil Kumar Singh. 2021. Linguistic Resources for Bhojpuri, Magahi, and Maithili: Statistics about Them, Their Similarity Estimates, and Baselines for Three Applications. *Transactions on Asian and Low-Resource Language Information Processing*, 20(6):1–37.

Joakim Nivre, Marie-Catherine De Marneffe, Filip Ginter, Yoav Goldberg, Jan Hajic, Christopher D Manning, Ryan McDonald, Slav Petrov, Sampo Pyysalo, Natalia Silveira, et al. 2016. Universal dependencies v1: A multilingual treebank collection. In *Proceedings of the Tenth International Conference on Language Resources and Evaluation (LREC'16)*, pages 1659–1666.

Atul Kr Ojha. 2019. English-Bhojpuri SMT System: Insights from the Karaka Model. *arXiv preprint arXiv:1905.02239*.

Atul Kr. Ojha, Valentin Malykh, Alina Karakanta, and Chao-Hong Liu. 2020. Findings of the LoResMT 2020 Shared Task on Zero-Shot for Low-Resource languages. In *Proceedings of the 3rd Workshop on Technologies for MT of Low Resource Languages*, pages 33–37, Suzhou, China. Association for Computational Linguistics.

Barun Patra, Joel Ruben Antony Moniz, Sarthak Garg, Matthew R Gormley, and Graham Neubig. 2019. Bilingual Lexicon Induction with Semi-supervision in Non-Isometric Embedding Spaces. In *Proceedings of the 57th Annual Meeting of the Association for Computational Linguistics*, pages 184–193.

Yves Scherrer and Benoît Sagot. 2014. A Language-independent and Fully Unsupervised Approach to Lexicon Induction and Part-of-Speech Tagging for Closely Related Languages. In *Language Resources and Evaluation Conference*.

Manish Sinha, Mahesh Reddy, and Pushpak Bhattacharyya. 2006. An Approach Towards Construction and Application of Multilingual Indo-Wordnet. In *3rd Global Wordnet Conference (GWC 06), Jeju Island, Korea*. Citeseer.

Laurens Van der Maaten and Geoffrey Hinton. 2008. Visualizing data using t-sne. *Journal of machine learning research*, 9(11).

William E Winkler. 1990. String Comparator Metrics and Enhanced Decision Rules in the Fellegi-Sunter Model of Record Linkage. *Proceedings of the Section on Survey Research Methods (American Statistical Association)*.

Yogendra P Yadava, Andrew Hardie, Ram Raj Lohani, Bhim N Regmi, Srishtee Gurung, Amar Gurung, Tony McEnery, Jens Allwood, and Pat Hall. 2008. Construction and Annotation of a Corpus of Contemporary Nepali. *Corpora*, 3(2):213–225.

Marcos Zampieri, Shervin Malmasi, Preslav Nakov, Ahmed Ali, Suwon Shon, James Glass, Yves Scherrer, Tanja Samardzic, Nikola Ljubešić, Jörg Tiedemann, et al. 2018. Language identification and Morphosyntactic Tagging: The second VarDial evaluation campaign. In *Proceedings of the Fifth Workshop on NLP for Similar Languages, Varieties and Dialects (VarDial 2018)*, pages 1–17.

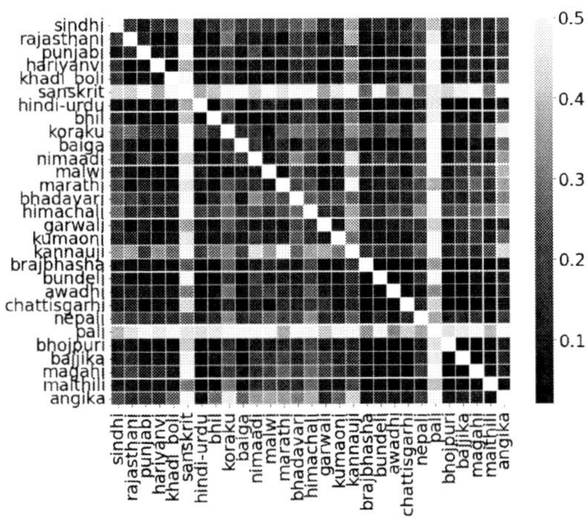

Figure 4: Character-level symmetric KL-Divergence for all languages

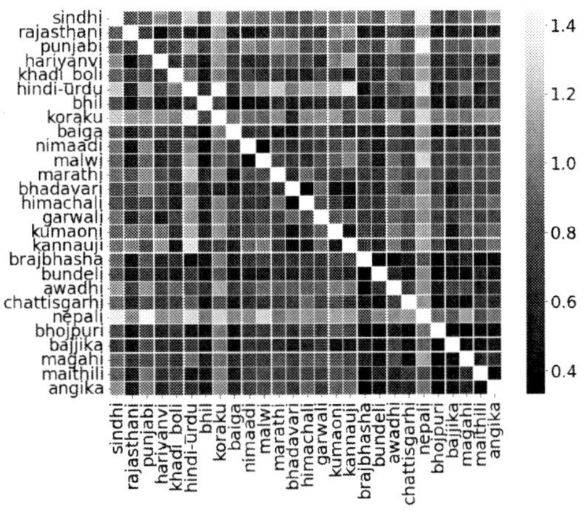

Figure 5: Pairwise KL-Divergence over distributions of i-char-grams. Lower is better.

A Data Collection and Probing

We record counts of tokens from the folksongs and poetry in Table 3.

A.1 Character-level probes

We inspect a table of character distributions over the language data after it has been cleaned. As expected, the commonest and most widely used consonants and vowels in the IA family form the bulk of the distributions of most languages, e.g. /t/, /ð/, /a/, /e/. We see some conspicuously low numbers, e.g. /ʃ/, /v/, and /ɳ/, fairly common consonants in the rest of the languages, seem to be very little used (in this corpus) from Kannauji. This is in part corroborated by Dwivedi and Kar (2016), who say that the first two are not native to Kannuaji but borrowed from Hindi.

We also see spikes in more endemic consonants as expected, for example /ɭ/ only shows reasonable percentages in Marathi and Nimaadi. Finally, the "avagraha" symbol /s/, used in Sanskrit to denote the deletion of the inherent vowel of the previous consonant, has only been inherited into the scripts of certain languages like Nepali and Magahi; in Hindi, it is sometimes used to denote the elongation of the previous vowel especially in lyrical texts. See Figure 4 for a heatmap over pairwise symmetric KL-divergence for character distributions.

A.2 Lexical measures

See Figure 6 for a depiction of pairwise lexical overlap. We also take a "close-up" look at sections of the pairwise results for language clusters that we expect to have closer relationships within the cluster. See Figures 7a,7b,7c. There are 3 such geographically motivated bands that we are interested in.

Firstly, we observe the "north" band, including Sindhi, Haryanvi, Punjabi, and the Pahari languages. Then we have the "north-central" band, which follows the heartland of the Gangetic plains, from Rajasthan (Rajasthani) across Delhi (Khadi Boli), Uttar Pradesh (Awadhi, Kannauji), Chattisgarh (Chattisgarhi), and Bihar (Bhojpuri, Magahi, Angika). Finally, we have the "central" band across southern Rajasthan (Bhili), Madhya Pradesh (Nimaadi, Malwi) and Maharashtra (Marathi).

We see that the "north-central" band indeed has the highest inter-similarities with some pairs (even excluding Hindi) showing similarities at around 70% (Bundeli-Angika, Kannauji-Awadhi). The "north" band follows; we see that Haryanvi and Nepali generally have high overlap with surrounding languages. Finally, the "central" band shows Rajasthani as having high lexical similarity with languages spoken in nearby regions, e.g. Bhili and Nimaadi; this makes sense, since Rajasthani is a catch-all for many related languages with high influence over nearby languages. Baiga shows generally low similarities except with Chattisgarhi, of which it is supposed to be a variant.[23]

Also see a dendrogram induced from lexical similarity measures in Figure 8. We see that some languages expected to be similar are grouped in the same subtrees e.g. Haryanvi and Rajasthani, {Awadhi, Angika, Bhojpuri}, as well as {Nimaadi,

[23] `https://glottolog.org/resource/languoid/id/baig1238`

Language	Band	Folksongs	Poetry	Folksongs tokens	Poetry tokens	Total Pieces	Total tokens
Rajasthani	3	67	1790	7404	180320	1857	187724
Gujarati	1	14	624	1795	73363	638	75158
Himachali	3	3	0	466	0	3	466
Hindi-Urdu	1	1	54408	100	7127897	54409	7127997
Magahi	2	340	376	37587	47167	716	84754
Awadhi	2	47	1333	4942	495137	1380	500079
Punjabi	1	754	0	69595	0	754	69595
Koraku	3	177	0	15509	0	177	15509
Baiga	3	35	0	13848	0	35	13848
Nimaadi	3	157	0	14056	0	157	14056
Khadi Boli	3	42	0	4507	0	42	4507
Bhojpuri	2	131	1275	20350	177289	1406	197639
Garwali	3	128	449	33380	59288	577	92668
Chattisgarhi	3	92	378	33504	49722	470	83226
Brajbhasha	2	83	1441	8883	151156	1524	160039
Bhil	3	155	0	27326	0	155	27326
Sanskrit	3	2	248	184	95450	250	95634
Angika	3	96	6773	21419	1243727	6869	1265146
Hariyanvi	3	554	930	49122	183881	1484	233003
Kannauji	3	6	0	327	0	6	327
Bundeli	3	326	0	26928	0	326	26928
Bangla	1	12	0	838	0	12	838
Malwi	3	129	0	9626	0	129	9626
Marathi	1	5	30	1412	1915	35	3327
Kumaoni	3	9	0	1028	0	9	1028
Bhadavari	3	8	0	990	0	8	990
Nepali	1	0	4753	0	692657	4753	692657
Maithili	2	0	1552	0	218339	1552	218339
Pali	3	0	27	0	5859	27	5859
Bajjika	3	0	71	0	7414	71	7414
Sindhi	1	0	500	0	51458	500	51458

Table 3: Showing crawled corpus counts for all collected languages.

Malwi, Bhili, and Baiga}. More distantly related languages like Gujarati, Pali, Bangla and Sanskrit are placed on the outer parts of the tree. However, we would have also expected to see Khadi Boli closer to Haryanvi, and Bajjika closer to Angika and Bhojpuri.

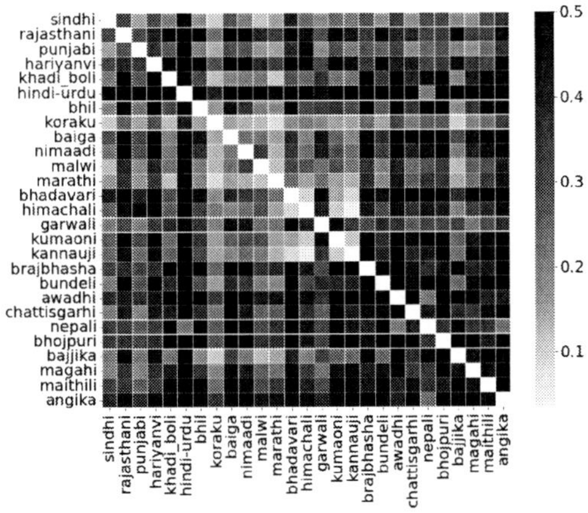

Figure 6: Lexical Overlap, all languages

A.3 Subword-level

See Figure 5 for a heatmap capturing pairwise symmetric KL-Divergence over subword distributions. Trends are similar to those seen in overlap-based measures; however, we see that the similarities against Hindi are lower, suggesting lower influence of corpus size on the measure.

B Evaluation Data

B.1 Existing resources

For some Band 1 languages (specifically, Hindi, Nepali, and Marathi), we have WordNets from the IndoWordNet project (Sinha et al., 2006; Debasri et al., 2002), from which we can extract equivalents across languages. We are not concerned, therefore, with searching for multilingual lexical resources for Band 1 languages. For some Band 2 languages (Bhojpuri, Magahi, and Maithili), WordNets are under way (Mundotiya et al., 2021) but as yet unavailable.

For Band 3, as discussed, we do not have any pre-existing bilingual or multilingual lexical resources in a convenient format. We therefore look for bilingual lexicons in the "wild"; that is, blogs, websites, scanned dictionaries, etc. We list all such raw material that we found that could be potentially useful for this purpose in Table 4. The names of these resources are listed separately in Table 5.

We exclude a few other resources we found due to too small a length ($<$ 30 word pairs), or too unstructured a format; these are unlikely to be of much help to the NLP community.

B.2 Overview of existing resources

The listed resources cover 4 Band 2 languages and 7 Band 3 languages: this is counting "Bihari" as the same as Bhojpuri, and Rajasthani the same as Marwari. Note that these resources may cover more languages; we have only listed the ones relevant to this project in the "Languages" column. These resources have widely different domains, content types, and formats.

Four of the listed websites disable copying and webpage inspection, discouraging crawling or re-using their data; this means that 3 Band 3 languages are once more resource-less.

Content-wise, we see that many resources have explanations on the target side (Hindi or English), rather than equivalents. For this project, that means that the resource is not really ready-to-use as a bilingual lexicon, but will require further work in terms of extracting equivalents from the explanations for the target side, or recasting it as a lexicon of similar words on the target side, etc. $R11$ for Rajasthani also requires transliteration for the source side before it is useful. Finally, we note that even the resources listed as containing equivalents in Table 4 usually contain a mixture of equivalents, explanations, and examples. That is, each resource would require considerable processing, possibly manual, to yield a relatively noiseless bilingual lexicon.

As we discussed, for the purposes of this project, we would like to have not only bilingual lexicons per language with an anchor (preferably Hindi), but also considerable intersections between the lexicons to allow the potential of testing multilingual interactions beyond Hindi-*lang* tasks. This too, unfortunately, is likely to be a problem when gathering resources from different sources with rather small lists, although we can hope to find some common words.

Given the above problems, including potential extensive manual efforts to the above individual resources usable, probable multilingual mismatch, and low coverage of Band 3 languages despite it all, we decided not to attempt garnering lexicons from these different resources for individual languages with the intention of putting them together.

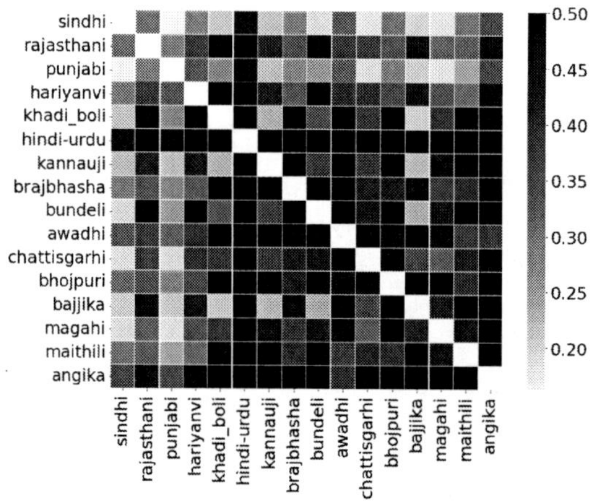

(a) Lexical Overlap, "North central" cluster of languages

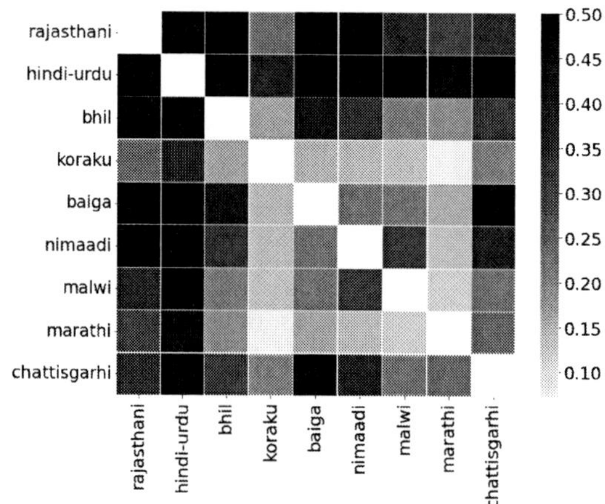

(b) Lexical Overlap, "Central" cluster of languages

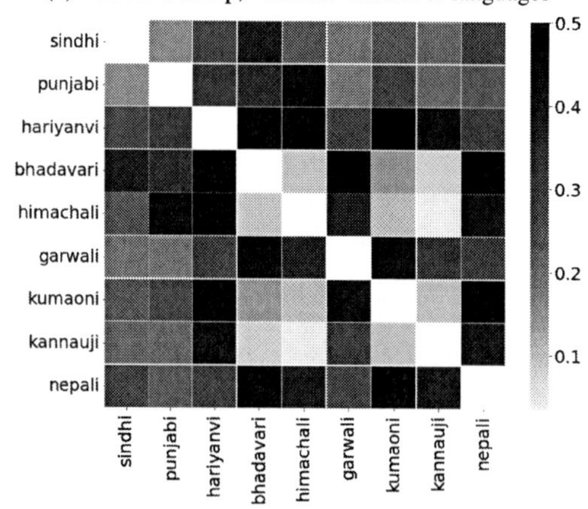

(c) Lexical Overlap, "Northern" cluster of languages

Figure 7: Pairwise lexical overlap for different subsets of languages

Resource	Languages	Anchor language	Content notes	Format	Approx. length
R1	Rajasthani^r	Eng.^{r}	Explanations in English	Simple list	>500
R2	Rajasthani^d	Hin^d, Eng^r	Hindi equivalents, English explanation	Webpages by initial letter	> 500
R3	Angika^d	Hin^d, Eng^r	Explanations	Each word on diff. page, disabled copying	102
R4	Bundeli^d	Hin^d	Equivalents	Simple listing, disabled copying	Few 100s
R5	Haryanvi^d	Hin^d	Equivalents	Simple list	< 100
R6	Chattisgarhi^d	Hin^d	Explanations	Webpage per word, disabled copying	< 100
R7	Chattisgarhi^d	Hin^d	Equivalents	List, disabled copying	Few 100s
R8	Kumaoni$^{d\ r}$	Hin^d, Eng^r	Equivalents, categorized by themes	Simple list	< 100
R9	Brajbhasha^d	Hin^d	Equivalents/ explanations	Mixture of paragraphs and lists, rather disorganized	Few 100s
R10	Bhojpuri^d	Hin^d	Mostly equivalents, also Hindi synonyms	Simple list	400
R11	Hindi^r, Marathi^i, Nepali^i, "Bihari"^{i}, Magahi^{d,i}, Marwari^i	-	Cognates	Swadesh list	207
R12	{Bhojpuri, Garwali, Hindi, Marathi, Nepali, Magahi, Maithili, Sindhi}^{d,i}	Eng^r	Short phrase translations	Simple list	45 phrases (on avg.)

Table 4: Raw resources found for different languages. The superscripts ^{d}, ^{r} and ^{i} indicate that the script used for the language is Devanagari, Roman or IPA respectively. The lexicon length given is an approximation because some of these formats make it difficult to get the exact number of entries.

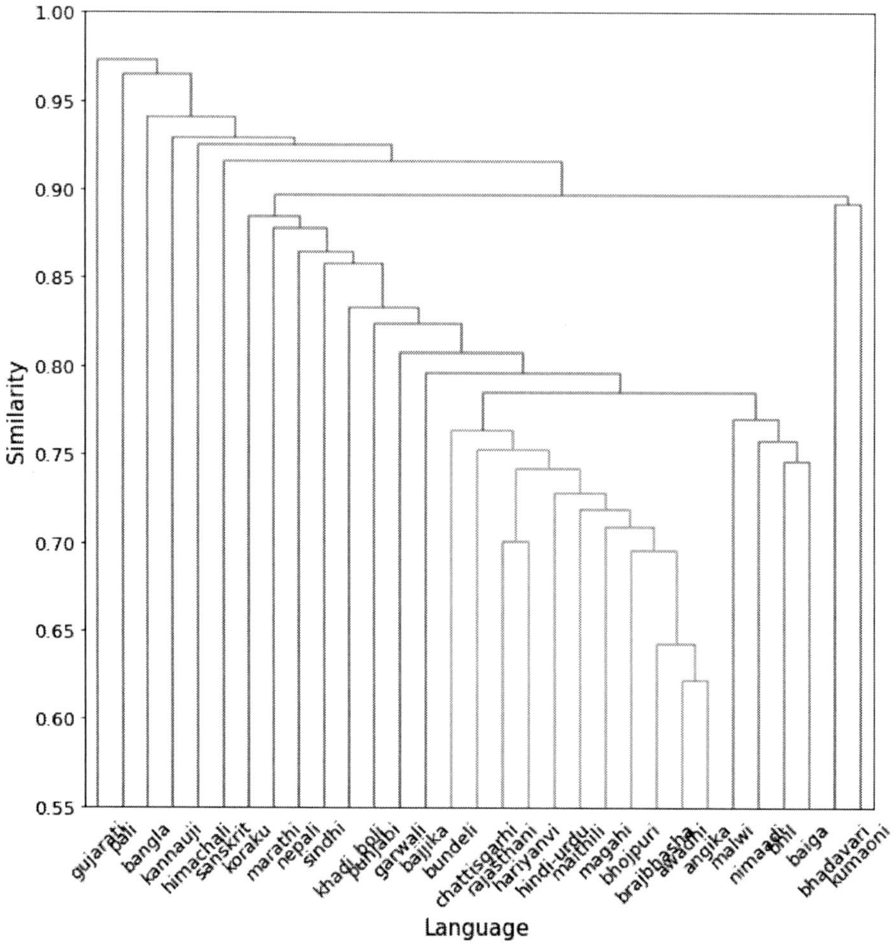

Figure 8: Dendrogram based on lexical overlap.

R11 is naturally exactly what we would have liked to find, although, again, it may require transliteration from IPA from most languages to be useful (and for Hindi, from a "casual" Roman script). The main problem, however, is that it deals with 3 Band 1 languages (for which we already have lexicons), 2 Band 2 languages, and only 1 Band 3 language, making it a low-coverage resource for our situation.

R12 is another interesting multilingual resource, highly similar to the resource that we finally decided to use, discussed in Section 5.2.

Note that a couple of these resources are valuable on their own, e.g. *R10* for Bhojpuri is extensive, simply formatted, and relatively neat and consistent; it will not require too much manual work to convert it into a usable resource for linguists. Similarly, *R1* and *R2* in Rajasthani provide the raw material for good bilingual lexicons, although they will first require a good quality transliteration into Devanagari for the Rajasthani side.

B.3 Collected data

Example of parallel sentence from "Languages Home":

```
English: Will you give me your pen?
Hindi: Kya tum mujhe apna pen doge?
```

We see that the word "pen" is code-switched in Hindi, rather than using the Hindi word "kalam". However, in other languages such as Bagheli, we see the word "kalam" used instead.[24] Therefore, although the word "kalam" exists in both languages, this relationship is not obscured because the trans-

[24]By itself, this difference is not a bad thing given that the purpose of this website is language learning. In Hindi, the given parallel sentence is absolutely natural-sounding - people do often code-switch the word "pen". Code-switching with English may be less common in less urban languages such as Bagheli; thus accounting for the use of the native word "kalam".

Resource	Name
R1	Rajasthani Language Dictionary I Rangrasiya
R2	Glossary of Rajasthani Language - Jatland Wiki
R3	Angika Shabdkosh
R4	Bundeli Shabdkosh
R5	(Blog post) Learn Harayanvi Language Through Hindi Language
R6	Chattisgarhi-Hindi online dictionary
R7	(Post) HS MiXX Entertainment
R8	Kumaoni Boli
R9	(Blog post) Learn Brajbhasha Vocabulary
R10	(Blog post) Bhojpuri dictionary
R11	(Blog post) Swadesh Word List of Indo-European languages
R12	Omniglot

Table 5: Resource websites: indexed according to Table 4

lator chose to use a different equivalent instead (in this case, code-switched, but not necessarily so in other sentences).

We report per-language statistics of the Hindi-parallel transliterated data in Table 6.

C CI: Using semantic similarity

C.1 Training embeddings: Visualizations

We use t-SNE (Van der Maaten and Hinton, 2008) to obtain the following visualizations; we performed these for *joint* models of Bhojpuri, Rajasthani, Hariyanvi, Magahi, and Korku (with Hindi-Urdu). See Figure 10 for Bhojpuri (the others are similar).

The main observations we can make for this type of model, common to all the languages, is that the low-resource target language words seem to be clustered around each other, whereas Hindi words and words belonging to both languages are better situated according to their semantics.

For the UPSAMPLE models, we visualize the same words for these languages; we present a representative (Bhojpuri) plot in Figure 10 (lower figure). While it is not clear from the visualization that the JOINT_UPSAMPLED models are less language-wise clustered than the JOINT, the target language words seem at least much better distributed, and we see more meaningful collocations (both monolingual in the target language, and cross-lingual) that we did not see before, such as "we", "our" (cross-lingual) in the Bhojpuri. However, it is difficult to say from such visualizations which space is better

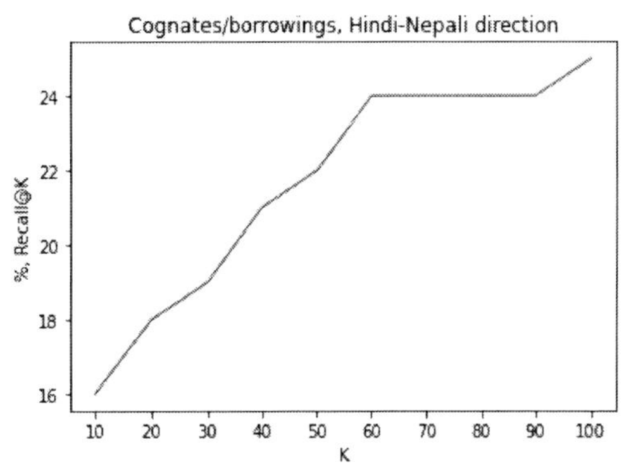

Figure 9: Recall@K for the bilingual FASTTEXT Nepali embeddings.

embedded.

C.2 Evaluating embeddings

C.2.1 Measuring Integration: *cl_integ*

See Table 7 for the evaluation for JOINT as well as UPSAMPLE embeddings for all languages over the *cl_integ* metric.

C.2.2 Evaluating embeddings: Nepali WordNet

As mentioned before, we do in fact have WordNets from the IndoWordNet project (Kakwani et al., 2020) for Nepali and Marathi, from which bilingual lexicons can easily be extracted. While the Marathi dataset in our current collection is not very representative as previously discussed, we evaluate the Nepali-Hindi bilingual space using the

Language	Total in corpus	Unique in corpus	Total in test	Unique in test	Common in corpus and test	Frac. covered in corpus[1]	Frac. covered in test[2]
Brajbhasha	156986	30194	299	161	93	0.12	0.65
Angika	1253545	91757	310	165	102	0.09	0.60
Maithili	218491	41434	273	147	81	0.09	0.54
Magahi	79405	16942	326	172	81	0.11	0.64
Hindi-Urdu	7100394	197355	336	171	165	0.25	0.98
Awadhi	490877	53103	281	145	109	0.05	0.82
Rajasthani	187708	34360	312	161	124	0.11	0.84
Hariyanvi	232526	27431	298	156	123	0.13	0.86
Bhil	27246	5557	319	177	68	0.12	0.48
Chattisgarhi	83073	14463	267	134	95	0.16	0.76
Nepali	688865	104687	203	118	65	0.04	0.62
Bajjika	7412	2788	317	149	55	0.13	0.53
Koraku	15508	2278	262	132	17	0.04	0.23
Malwi	9626	2883	325	163	51	0.12	0.46
Sindhi	52659	11850	250	141	55	0.09	0.51
Bhojpuri	196513	34051	303	146	110	0.16	0.83
Garwali	90234	22655	275	161	86	0.07	0.64
Marathi	3109	1685	230	130	29	0.05	0.37
Kumaoni	1013	441	250	171	16	0.10	0.16
Bundeli	26902	7991	272	147	82	0.12	0.63

Table 6: Evaluation token data statistics post-transliteration, after aligning with Hindi. [1] This reports the fraction of the corpus (token-wise) that is contained in the test, vice-versa for [2].

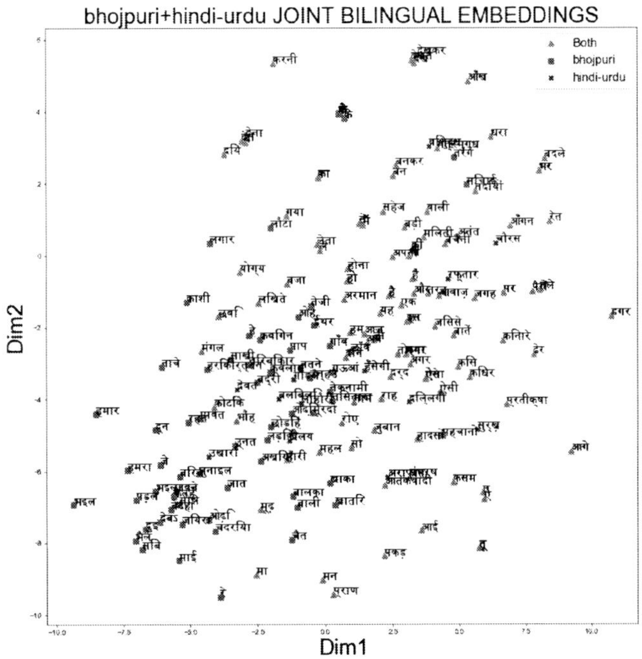

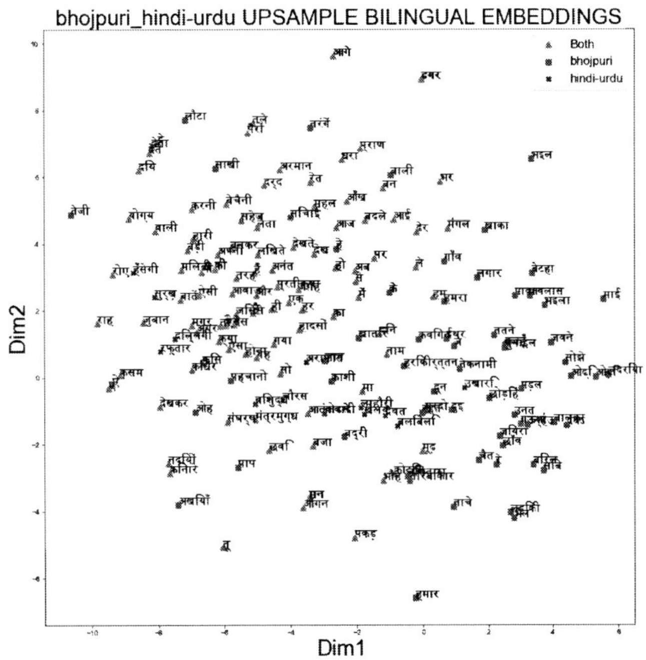

Figure 10: t-SNE (Van der Maaten and Hinton, 2008) Visualization of Bhojpuri-Hindi bilingual space, JOINT (up) and UPSAMPLE (down)

	J_12	J_21	U_12	U_21
Sindhi	0.53	0.23	0.31	0.33
Rajasthani	0.78	0.33	0.62	0.40
Punjabi	0.58	0.19	0.40	0.27
Hariyanvi	0.75	0.30	0.66	0.36
Khadi Boli	0.99	0.18	0.76	0.13
Sanskrit	0.33	0.28	0.12	0.26
Bhil	0.92	0.24	0.53	0.34
Koraku	0.59	0.13	0.34	0.10
Baiga	0.97	0.21	0.73	0.31
Nimaadi	0.87	0.16	0.47	0.21
Malwi	0.88	0.14	0.45	0.13
Marathi	0.95	0.20	0.32	0.15
Bhadavari	1.00	0.12	0.81	0.30
Himachali	1.00	0.07	0.48	0.07
Garwali	0.64	0.25	0.25	0.39
Kumaoni	0.97	0.09	0.74	0.05
Kannauji	1.00	0.04	0.66	0.14
Brajbhasha	1.00	0.32	0.74	0.38
Bundeli	0.99	0.21	0.58	0.36
Awadhi	0.69	0.34	0.45	0.43
Chattisgarhi	0.86	0.29	0.51	0.36
Nepali	0.37	0.39	0.31	0.48
Pali	0.57	0.11	0.07	0.10
Bhojpuri	0.91	0.32	0.74	0.41
Bajjika	1.00	0.20	0.74	0.30
Magahi	0.84	0.21	0.44	0.42
Maithili	0.85	0.38	0.57	0.49
Angika	0.63	0.44	0.50	0.40

Table 7: *cl_integ* values reported as 0-1 measure for both sets of embedding spaces, in both directions. 12 indicates that we consider the non-Hindi language as source, and look for the fraction of nearby Hindi words, 21 is vice versa.

# tokens	integ_12	integ_21	bl_12	bl_21
JOINT				
5000	0.43	0.37	0.30	0.21
50000	0.33	0.38	0.29	0.21
100000	0.29	0.37	0.29	0.20
500000	0.33	0.44	0.29	0.20
UPSAMPLE				
500000	0.29	0.42	0.33	0.15

Table 8: Recall@50 for Nepali data splits of different sizes against Hindi-Nepali lexicon obtained from IndoWordNet. 12: Nepali as source, 21: Hindi as source. We also show results for *cl_integ* and bilingual lexicon tests for UPSAMPLE Nepali model

Nepali WordNet. We used the WordNet to extract a Hindi/Urdu-Nepali bilingual lexicon, and we calculated Recall@K, in the following way: for each Hindi-Urdu word, we extract its K nearest neighbours. If any of those are the gold target, we count a full point for that word. Finally, we report the total such points as a percentage of the length of the gold bilingual lexicon.

See the results for the *joint* Nepali model in Figure 9.

Nepali is in the highest range of availability in our current dataset, so we do not expect these results to be representative for other languages with less data. We therefore also look at these results over artificially smaller cuts of the Nepali dataset. See Table 8. We also report these numbers for the UPSAMPLE Nepali model (all data included) in the same table.

C.2.3 Discussion

There are a couple of interesting things to note about the above results. We see that cl_integ shows high values from the LRL to Hindi direction, but not vice versa. Nepali happens to be an outlier in this case, which is perhaps unfortunate since it is unlikely to be representative of the other languages, and it is the only language we can evaluate with more detail.

We notice in Table 8 that the results for the WordNet bilingual lexicon test seem to be stable across different data splits. This is rather suspicious; however, a possible explanation is that the positives accrue from frequent words anyway, possible also present in the Hindi-Urdu data; therefore, reducing the number of Nepali tokens does not seem to affect this number. Note that this is not at all an indication that the resulting embeddings are of the same quality, simply that this metric is not able to capture possible underlying damage.

Detecting Unintended Social Bias in Toxic Language Datasets

Nihar Sahoo*, **Himanshu Gupta***, **Pushpak Bhattacharyya**
CFILT, Indian Institute of Technology Bombay, India
{nihar, himanshug, pb @cse.iitb.ac.in}

Abstract

Warning: This paper has contents which may be offensive, or upsetting however this cannot be avoided owing to the nature of the work.

With the rise of online hate speech, automatic detection of Hate Speech, Offensive texts as a natural language processing task is getting popular. However, very little research has been done to detect unintended social bias from these toxic language datasets. This paper introduces a new dataset *ToxicBias* curated from the existing dataset of Kaggle competition named "Jigsaw Unintended Bias in Toxicity Classification". We aim to detect social biases, their categories, and targeted groups. The dataset contains instances annotated for five different bias categories, viz., *gender, race/ethnicity, religion, political, and LGBTQ*. We train transformer-based models using our curated datasets and report baseline performance for bias identification, target generation, and bias implications. Model biases and their mitigation are also discussed in detail. Our study motivates a systematic extraction of social bias data from toxic language datasets. All the codes and dataset used for experiments in this work are publicly available[1].

Figure 1: An illustrative example of *ToxicBias*. During the annotation process, hate speech/offensive text is provided without context. Annotators are asked to mark it as biased/neutral and to provide category, target, and implication if it has biases.

1 Introduction

In the age of social media and communications, it is simpler than ever to openly express one's opinions on a wide range of issues. This openness results in a flood of useful information that can assist people in being more productive and making better decisions. According to statista [2], the global number of active social media users has just surpassed four billion, accounting for more than half of the world's population. The user base is expected to grow steadily over the next five years. Various studies (Plaisime et al., 2020) say that children and teenagers, who are susceptible, make up a big share of social media users. Unfortunately, this increasing number of social media users also leads to an increase in toxicity (Matamoros-Fernández and Farkas, 2021). Sometimes this toxicity gives birth to violence and hate crimes. It does not just harm an individual; most of the time, the entire community suffers as due to its intensity.

We have different perspectives based on race, gender, religion, sexual orientation, and many other factors. These perspectives sometimes lead to biases that influence how we see the world, even if we are unaware of them. Biases like this can lead us to make decisions that are neither intelligent nor just. Furthermore, when these biases are expressed as hate speech and offensive texts, it becomes painful for specific communities. While some of these biases are implied, most explicit biases can be found in the form of hate speech and offensive texts.

The use of hate speech incites violence and sometimes leads to societal and political instability.

*These authors contributed equally to this work

[1] https://github.com/sahoonihar/ToxicBias_CoNLL_2022

[2] https://www.statista.com/statistics/278414/number-of-worldwide-social-network-users/

Proceedings of the 26th Conference on Computational Natural Language Learning (CoNLL), pages 132 - 143
December 7-8, 2022 ©2022 Association for Computational Linguistics

BLM (Black Lives Matter) movement is the consequence of one such bias in America. So, to address these biases, we must first identify them. While the concepts of Social Bias and Hate Speech may appear to be the same, there are subtle differences.

This paper expands on the above ideas and proposes a new dataset ***ToxicBias*** for detecting social bias from toxic language datasets. The main contributions can be summarized as follows:

- To the best of our knowledge, this is the first study to extract social biases from toxic language datasets in English.
- We release a curated dataset of 5409 instances for detection of social bias, its categories, targets and bias reasoning.
- We present methods to reduce lexical overfitting using counter-narrative data augmentation.

In the following section we discuss various established works which are aligned with our work. Section 3 provides information about our dataset, terminology, annotation procedure, and challenges. In section 3, we describe our tests and results, followed by a discussion of lexical overfitting reduction via data augmentation in section 5. Section 6 discusses the conclusion and future works.

2 Related Work

Offensive Text: Unfortunately, offensive content poses some unique challenges to researchers and practitioners. First and foremost, determining what constitutes abuse/offensive behaviour is difficult. Unlike other types of malicious activity, e.g., spam or malware, the accounts carrying out this type of behavior are usually controlled by humans, not bots (Founta et al., 2018).The term "offensive language" refers to a broad range of content, including hate speech, vulgarity, threats, cyberbully, and other ethnic and racial insults (Kaur et al., 2021). There is no single definition of abuse, and phrases like "harassment," "abusive language," and "damaging speech" are frequently used interchangeably.

Hate Speech: Hate Speech is defined as speech that targets disadvantaged social groups in a way that may be damaging to them. (Davidson et al., 2017). Fortuna and Nunes (2018) defines Hate speech as follows: "Hate speech is a language that attacks or diminishes, that incites violence or hate against groups, based on specific characteristics such as physical appearance, religion, national or ethnic origin, sexual orientation, gender identity or other, and it can occur with different linguistic styles, even in subtle forms or when humor is used".

Bias in Embedding: The initial works to explore bias in language representations aimed at detecting gender, race, religion biases in word representations (Bolukbasi et al., 2016; Caliskan et al., 2017; Manzini et al., 2019). Some of recent works have focused on bias detection from sentence representations (May et al., 2019; Kurita et al., 2019) using BERT embedding.

In addition, there have been a lot of notable efforts towards detection of data bias in hate speech and offensive languages (Waseem and Hovy, 2016; Davidson et al., 2019; Sap et al., 2019; Mozafari et al., 2020). Borkan et al. (2019) has discussed the presence of unintended bias in hate speech detection models for identity terms like islam, lesbian, bisexual, etc. The biased association of different marginalized groups is still a major challenge in the models trained for toxic language detection (Kim et al., 2020; Xia et al., 2020). This is mainly due to the bias in annotated data which creates the wrong associations of many lexical features with specific labels (Dixon et al., 2018). Lack of social context of the post creator also affect the annotation process leading to bias against certain communities in the dataset (Sap et al., 2019).

Social bias datasets: More recently, many datasets (Nadeem et al., 2021; Nangia et al., 2020) have been created to measure and detect social biases like gender, race, profession, religion, age, etc. However, Blodgett et al. (2021) has reported that many of these datasets lack clear definitions and have ambiguities and inconsistencies in annotations. A similar study have been done in (Sap et al., 2020), where dataset has both categorical and free-text annotation and generation framework as core model.

There have been few studies on data augmentation (Nozza et al., 2019; Bartl et al., 2020) to decrease the incorrect association of lexical characteristics in these datasets. Hartvigsen et al. (2022) proposed a prompt based framework to generate large dataset of toxic and neutral statements to reduce the spurious correlation for Hate Speech detection.

However, no study has been done for detecting social biases from toxic languages, which is a challenging task due to the conceptual overlap between hate speech and social bias. Using a thorough guideline, we attempt to uncover harmful biases in toxic language datasets. The curated dataset is discussed in length in the next section, as are the definitions of each category label and the annotation procedure.

3 ToxicBias Dataset

We develop the manually annotated *ToxicBias* dataset to enable the algorithm to correctly identify social biases from a publicly available toxicity dataset. Below, we define social bias and the categories taken into account in our dataset. The comprehensive annotation process that we use for dataset acquisition is then covered.

3.1 Social Bias

People typically have preconceptions, stereotypes, and discrimination against other who do not belong to their social group. Positive and negative social bias refers to a preference for or against persons or groups based on their social identities (e.g., race, gender, etc.). Only the negative biases, however, have the capacity to harm target groups (Crawford, 2017). As a result, in our study, we *focus on identifying negative biases* in order to prevent harmful repercussions on targeted groups. Members of specific social groups (e.g., Women, Muslims, and Transgender individuals) are more likely to face prejudice as a result of living in a culture that does not sufficiently support fairness. In this work, we have considered five prevalent social biases:

- **Gender:** Favoritism towards one gender over other. It can be of the following types: Alpha, Beta or Sexism (Park et al., 2018).
- **Religion:** Bias against individuals on the basis of religion or religious belief. e.g. Christianity, Islam, Scientology etc (Muralidhar, 2021).
- **Race:** Favouritism for a group of people having common visible physical traits, common origins, language etc. It is related to dialect, color, appearance, regional or societal perception (Sap et al., 2019).
- **LGBTQ:** Prejudice towards LGBTQ community people. It can be due to societal perception or physical appearance.
- **Political:** Prejudice against/towards individuals on the basis of their political beliefs. For example: liberals, conservatives, etc.

Categories	Targets
Political	liberal, conservative, feminist, etc.
Religion	christian, jew, hindu, atheist, etc.
Gender	men, women
LGBTQ	gay, lesbian, homosexual, etc.
Race	black, white, asian, canadians, etc.

Table 1: Bias categories and corresponding targets.

For all of these categories, target terms are the communities towards which bias is targeted.

3.2 Social Bias *Vs* Hate Speech

While Social Bias and Hate Speech may appear the same at first look, they are not. The differences between them are quite subtle. While hate speech is always associated with negative sentiment, social bias can also have positive sentiments. Social bias is preconceived belief toward or against specific social identities, whereas hate speech is an explicit comment expressing hatred against an individual or a group. Not all hate speech is biased, and not all biased speech is hate speech. We will use the following examples to demonstrate the differences:

- Some comments are merely toxic without containing any social biases in them, e.g.
  *IM FREEEEE!!!! WORST EXPERIENCE OF MY F**K-ING LIFE*
- Toxic comments can be hate speech but not necessarily biased, e.g.
  you gotta be kidding. trump a Christian, nope, he is the devil, he hates blacks, Hispanics, muslims, gays, Asians, etc.
- Some comments are just biased with negating sentiment without containing any toxicity or hate speech in them, e.g.
  All Asian people are bad drivers.

3.3 Annotation Process

The dataset we used for annotation is collected from a Kaggle competition named "Jigsaw Unintended Bias in Toxicity Classification (jig, 2019; Research Data, 2018)". It has around two million Wikipedia comments annotated for toxicity. The data also has several other toxicity subtype attributes such as *severe toxicity, obscene, threat, insult, identity_attack, and sexual_explicit.*

We discovered that, with the exception of the *identity_attack* column, all of the columns in this dataset are redundant for the social bias detection

comment_text	label	category	target	implication
I wish gay men would just leave children alone.	bias	lgbtq	gays	gays are pedophiles
Islam, unfortunately, is a violent cult.	bias	religion	muslims	muslims are violent
Why does Netflix hate gay people?	neutral	-	-	-
Liberal women are so #k̊ing ugly!	bias	political, gender	liberals, women	prejudice against liberal women
Why are black thugs coming out here murdering locals? What is the real story? Please someone..hire an investigative journalist.	bias	race	blacks	prejudice against blacks

Table 2: Annotation of Bias along with its category, targeted groups and implication

task. *Identity_attack* shows denigration of the comment towards a identity. This identity could be related to race, religion, political affiliation, gender, or sexual orientation. So, we filtered out only those comments for which *identity_attack* values are greater than or equal to 0.5. We annotated this filtered dataset for the presence of social bias. We have considered only *five bias categories* for our annotation and *possible targets* listed in Table 1. We did not include other categories due to their low presence in the original dataset. The targets describe any social or demographic groups that is targeted in the comment. Bias implications are annotated in addition to bias categories and relevant targets. Table 2 shows a sample annotation of this filtered dataset. The bias implications are simple *free-text* reasons showing the stereotype towards the target group.

The final dataset contains 5409 cases with multiple label annotations. There are 120 distinct terms for target annotation divided into five categories. To check the consistency of our framework and to categorize biases, two different annotators annotated the data independently. Considering the complexity of the task, we provided a detailed guideline to each of the annotators. Following the thorough guidelines by Singh et al. (2022), we developed a series of questionnaires for each categories to assist the annotators. Inter-annotator agreement was assessed for the first 2500 occurrences, and a Cohen's Kappa value of 64.3 was found, indicating good agreement between annotators. The figure 2 depicts the distribution of data among multiple categories. All the disagreements between annotators were resolved by adjudication with the help of an expert. For details about the annotators, please refer A.2.

Out of 5409, our dataset has **4325** bias instances (80% of dataset) and **1084** neutral (not biased towards any identity). The number of instances for each category across train, dev., test are shown in Table 3.

Categories	train	dev	test	total
bias	3460	346	519	4325
neutral	867	86	131	1084
race	1769	181	252	2202
religion	1257	120	196	1573
gender	293	24	41	358
lgbtq	453	41	82	576
political	172	20	26	218

Table 3: Distribution of different categories across three splits of Train, Dev. and Test.

3.4 Annotation Challenges

Several issues were encountered while annotating harmful datasets, which must be handled to annotate and build a consistent dataset.

- Quoting someone else statements considered biased? Example:
  Trump said "Mexicans are rapists and drug dealers".

  One may argue that such statements are not biased as they are merely quoting someone else's opinions that are not theirs. However, we label them biased because quoting someone else's statement is just as detrimental and harmful.

- We believe that asking questions about an issue may not lead to bias. Example:
  Black idiot or white idiot. What is the difference?

  One would believe that this phrase is about idiots in general, without regard to race. As a result, there will be no prejudice. On the other hand, some may interpret that both blacks and whites are referred to as fools here.

- We also encountered statements lacking context. Example:
  Is that the white kind? I mean since you hate whites so much?

  Now here, we do not know whether the statement is talking about white colour or white race. We label these kinds of sentences as neutral

- Some statements were purely made as a personal attack. These instances were labeled appropriately as biased or neutral. Example: *Trump pig latin. Oink, oink, oink, grab em by the poo say*

  We label this statement as biased because Trump here represents a certain political party (community), unlike the below example: *settlers is a demeaning racist term. You Johnny are a white hating racist.*

  Here Johnny is not a big political leader (name). So we mark this as neutral.

- We have encountered many sarcastic instances in the dataset and label them appropriately. Example:
  Ah yes, re-education! That's what us nasty white folks need.

  We label this statement as neutral because it's a self-criticism sarcastically.

  Yeah - - because up until now, Islamic State really loved the US! And the West in general! They love us so much sometimes they cut off peoples heads to keep as a souvenir!

  The above statement was labeled as biased as it is sarcastically showing prejudice against Islam.

- Some statements are speaker dependent. Example:
  Shit still happenin and no one is hearin about it, but niggas livin it everyday.

  This statement will not be biased if said by an African-American; however, it becomes highly offensive and biased if stated by someone else.

4 Experimental Setup

In this section we will discuss about different models trained for detection of social biases and their categories. For all our experiment, we split the data into train, development, and test (80:8:12) set. Since the dataset was imbalanced with respect to bias column, we split it in stratified manner.

4.1 Metrices

We report accuracy, macro F1-score, and AUC-based scores in accordance with best practice.

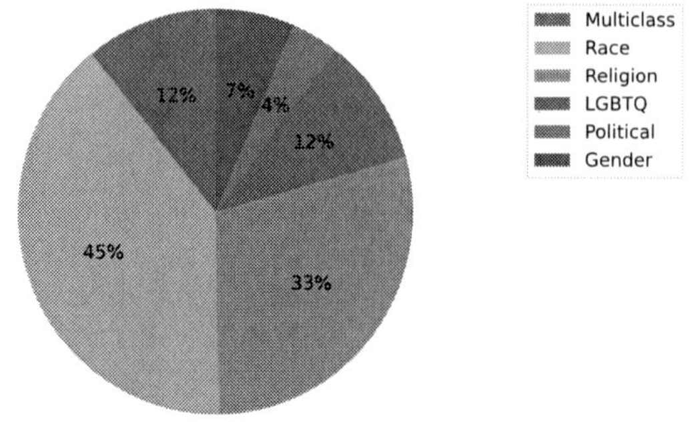

Figure 2: Distribution of bias categories in ToxicBias. It is observed that some instances qualified for multiple bias categories(12.22%)

These metrics would be used to assess the classifier's ability to distinguish between the bias and neutral texts along with bias categories. AUC stands for *Area under the ROC curve.* ROC curve depicts the tradeoff between true positive rate (TPR) and false positive rate (FPR). The AUC value is high when the TPR is high and the FPR is low.

Borkan et al. (2019) proposed AUC-based metrics to quantify the unintended model bias. These metrics compare the output distributions of instances that include the specific community word (subgroup distribution) with the rest (background distribution). The three AUC-based bias scores are as follows:

1. **Subgroup AUC (AUC_{sub}):** It calculates AUC exclusively on a subset of the data for a specified community word. A low score indicates that the model struggles to differentiate between bias and neutral comments related to the community word.
2. **Background Positive and Subgroup Negative AUC (AUC_{bpsn}):** AUC_{bpsn} uses the biased background instances and the neutral subgroup examples to determine AUC. A low score indicates that the model has high false positive rate. The model misinterprets neutral comments mentioning the community with biased comments missing it.
3. **Background Negative and Subgroup Positive AUC (AUC_{bnsp}):** It uses the neutral background instances and the biased subgroup examples to determine AUC. A low score suggests that the model has a high rate of false negatives. The model misunderstands biased comments that mention the community with neutral ones that do not.

	Model	P	R	F1	Acc
Baselines	Logistic Regression	0.67	0.50	0.46	0.84
	SVM	0.42	0.50	0.46	0.84
	Bi-LSTM + Glove	0.59	0.58	0.58	0.78
Transformers w/o Aug	BERT (Hierarchical)	0.62	0.66	**0.64**	**0.86**
	BERT (Multi-task)	0.90	0.52	0.49	0.81
	GPT2	0.62	0.66	0.62	0.71
Transformers /w Aug	BERT (Hierarchical)	0.86	0.86	**0.86**	**0.88**
	BERT (Multi-task)	0.86	0.86	**0.86**	0.87
	GPT2	0.81	0.86	0.84	0.81

Table 4: Performance of various models on bias detection task. We report results for baselines, and Transformer based training. For Transformer based training, we compare performances without data augmentation and with data augmentation. Best scores are shown in bold.

Model	Hierarchical				Multi-task			
	Acc	P	R	F1	Acc	P	R	F1
political	0.96	0.48	0.50	0.49	0.96	0.77	0.57	**0.61**
gender	0.95	0.47	0.50	0.49	0.95	0.84	0.71	**0.76**
race	0.84	0.81	0.83	0.82	0.86	0.86	0.88	**0.86**
religion	0.82	0.82	0.82	0.82	0.93	0.91	0.94	**0.92**
lgbtq	0.93	0.81	0.81	0.81	0.94	0.86	0.87	**0.86**

Table 5: Bias Category Detection Results. P, R, F1 and Acc are Precision, Recall, F1-score and Accuracy respectively. Best scores are shown in bold.

4.2 Baseline Models

We discuss several model architectures for detection of biases and their categories. For bias detection, which is a binary class classification task, we consider Logistic Regression (LR) with TF-IDF as our baseline model. Our baseline model gives 84% accuracy with 0.46 F1 score. The low F1 score clearly indicates that model has very high false positive rate and false negative rate. We also tried Support Vector Machine (linear kernel) with TF-IDF and LSTM (Huang et al., 2015) with Glove 300d word representation (Pennington et al., 2014). The best model is observed to be BERT (Devlin et al., 2019) with 0.64 F1 score. Two different model settings were used to detect biases and their categories. We will discuss each of them in detail in the following sections.

4.3 Hierarchical Model

In the hierarchical model, bias detection and category classification was done in two steps. Bias detection, a binary class classification task, is performed first. If the post has some biases, then its categories are detected next. Since a post may contain several biases, the bias category detection task was framed as multi-label classification. Bias detection results of several models in hierarchical model architecture is shown in Table 4. Bias category detection results in the hierarchical setting are shown in Table 5.

4.4 Multi-task Learning

In the context of classification, multi-Task Learning tries to improve the performance of numerous classification problems by learning them together. So instead of predicting bias and its category in two steps, we can train a model to predict them simultaneously in one step. Since there can be multiple biases in a post, we cannot use logistic regression or SVM in a multi-label classification task. Hence in this model architecture, we try LSTM and BERT models only. We use LSTM with a single output layer. The last dense layer of the LSTM comprises six neurons, one to detect bias and the other five to identify bias categories.

Precision (P), recall (R), F1 (macro values for all), and accuracy (Acc) for bias detection experiments in Multi-task architecture is shown in Table 4. Table 5 shows the comparison between hierarchical and multi-task model for category detection task.

4.5 Generation Framework

Considering the efficacy of GPT (Radford and Narasimhan, 2018) based model for classification, conditional generation tasks (Sap et al., 2020), we frame the prediction of categorical variables and implications as generation task. The input is a sequence of tokens as in Equation1, where w_i are the tokens corresponding to comment text and [BOS], [SEP], [EOS] are start token, separator token and end token respectively. Two task specific tokens ([BON], [BOFF]) were added to the token

comment_text	Ground truth label	Predicted label	Ground truth category	Predicted category
Quran is a holy book.	neutral	bias	-	religion
So then I was all like "I'd rather get the black plague and lock myself in an iron maiden than go out with you.	neutral	bias	-	race
Do they come in men's sizes?	neutral	bias	-	gender
What I've just shown is that this happens in every black hole.	neutral	bias	-	race

Table 6: Error analysis showing model biases from predictions of Multi-task BERT model without augmentation.

Variables	BLEU-2	RougeL
Categories	61.60±0.96	88.23±1.23
Target subgroup	52.95±2.84	77.58±4.21
Implications	33.4±1.55	39.5±1.20

Table 7: Evaluation of various generation tasks. The standard deviations for three runs are also reported.

vocabulary which were used as $w_{[\text{bias}]}$ in the input. Here, [BON], [BOFF] correspond to bias and neutral instances respectively. As we have many inputs with multiple bias categories and targets, we combine them using a comma separator in the raw text. While encoding the input we use $w_{[\text{C}]_i}, w_{[\text{T}]_i}$ as the token corresponding to them respectively. Similarly, $w_{[\text{R}]_i}$ is used for representing the tokens corresponding to implications.

$$\begin{aligned} \mathbf{x} = \{&[\text{BOS}], w_i, [\text{SEP}]\ w_{[\text{bias}]}, [\text{SEP}] \\ &w_{[\text{C}]_i}, [\text{SEP}] w_{[\text{T}]_i}, [\text{SEP}] w_{[\text{R}]_i}, [\text{EOS}]\} \end{aligned} \quad (1)$$

For this experiment, we finetune the GPT-2 (Radford et al., 2018) model with commonly used hyperparameters. For training we use cross-entropy loss as cost function. During inference, we first calculate the normalized probability of $w_{[\text{bias}]}$ conditioned on the initial part of input and then append the highest probable token to the input and generate rest of the tokens till [EOS].

We use BLEU-2 (Papineni et al., 2002) and RougeL (Fmeasure) (Lin, 2004) as the metrics to calculate the performance of the model for category, target and implication of the comment text(Table 7) and macro F1 as metric for bias evaluation(Table 4). Performance for category generation is better than other two variable as it has less ambiguity whereas the low performance for implications show the variability in the annotation for implications.

We report all the hyperparameters and training setup in appendix A.3.

4.6 Results and Discussion

From the above tables, we can infer that the BERT-based hierarchical model outperforms Multi-task and GPT-2 models for the bias detection task. In addition, category identification is performed more effectively by multi-task model. This is quite apparent from the fact that in multi-task learning each model aid each others due to shared parameters. We also see that F1 scores for political and gender categories are less when compared to other categories in the category detection task. One plausible explanation might be the low frequency of such biases in our dataset. The BLEU scores of category and target subgroup generation are higher than those of bias implication generation, as shown in Table 7. The fundamental reason for this is that the bias category and target have less distinct bigrams/tri-grams than the implications. We show an error analysis for categorical prediction tasks after training the models. We discovered that the model predicts incorrectly for some simple sentences. A few examples are also listed in the Table 6. This most likely occurred due to lexical overfitting/ model bias of the trained model towards some of the identity specific terminologies. In the next section, we discuss an approach to reduce this unwanted behavior of the model using counter-narrative augmentation.

5 Mitigation of Model Bias

When we look at the incorrectly classified comments in Table 6, we observe that they contain community words such as 'blacks,' 'Quran,' and so on. Sometimes, due to the presence of these community terms, our model predicts that these comments would be biased. In essence, our initial model is latching onto some community related terms and hence suffers from model bias. According to (Zueva et al., 2020), most existing models provide predictions with certain bias. Even if the statement itself is not toxic, the model commonly classifies it as toxic if it includes specific frequently

comment_text	Ground truth category	Prediction (**without** augmentation)	Prediction (**with** augmentation)
Quran is a holy book.	none	religion	none
Islam is a peaceful religion.	none	religion	none
Muslims are invaders.	religion	religion	religion
Do they come in men's sizes?	none	gender	none
What I've just shown is that this happens in every black hole.	none	race	none
I'm sick of niggers, it's a bad neighborhood. I don't like being around them, they're animals.	race	race	race

Table 8: Error analysis showing the effectiveness of counter-narrative augmentation. After training with augmented data, the resulting model does not latch on to the community related terms.

Subgroup	Count	% Bias
all comments	5409	79.92
black	1291	79.55
jewish	269	74.34
lgbt	778	77.24
muslim	1263	87.01
female	586	76.45

Table 9: Percentage of bias comments by identity terms such as black, jewish, lgbt, muslim, female in the *ToxicBias* dataset.

targeted identities (such as women, blacks, or Jews). Similarly, our model incorrectly labels comments referencing particular identities, such as Blacks, Muslims, and Whites, as social bias. Model biases emerge when identity words like Blacks, Whites, and Muslims appear more frequently in biased comments than in neutral comments. If the training data for a machine learning model is skewed towards certain terms, the final model is likely to acquire this bias. Table 9 shows the bias percentage in ***ToxicBias*** for several identities/subgroups, indicating the imbalance for bias labels among those identities and emphasising the importance of AUC-based metrics resilient to these data skews.

Counter-narratives: Despite enormous attempts to build suitable legal and regulatory responses to hate content on social media platforms, dealing with hatred online remains challenging. If hate speech is addressed with standard content deletion or user suspension methods, censorship may be accused. Actively addressing hate material through counter-narratives (i.e., informed textual responses) is one potential technique that has received little attention in the academic community thus far. A counter-narrative (also known as a counter-comment or counter-speech) is a reply that provides non-negative feedback through fact-based arguments and is often recognized as the most effective way to deal with hate speech.

subgroup	$AUC_{sub} \uparrow$	$AUC_{bpsn} \uparrow$	$AUC_{bnsp} \uparrow$
black	0.48	0.50	0.49
jewish	0.47	0.50	0.49
lgbt	0.81	0.83	0.82
muslim	0.82	0.82	0.82
female	0.81	0.81	0.81

Table 10: AUC based scores for subgroups on bias detection model trained without data augmentation. Higher AUC values for each target subgroup indicate reduced lexical overfitting/model bias for those targets.

subgroup	$AUC_{sub} \uparrow$	$AUC_{bpsn} \uparrow$	$AUC_{bnsp} \uparrow$
black	0.86	0.78	0.97
jewish	0.91	0.93	0.91
lgbt	0.89	0.91	0.93
muslim	0.96	0.97	0.86
female	0.93	0.94	0.93

Table 11: AUC based scores on bias detection model trained after data augmentation. Higher AUC values for each target subgroup indicate reduced lexical overfitting/model bias for those targets.

We use two counter-narrative datasets to reduce the model biases: CONAN (Chung et al., 2019) and Multi-target CONAN (Fanton, Margherita and Bonaldi, Helena and Tekiroğlu, Serra Sinem and Guerini, Marco, 2021). These datasets provide counter-narratives to hate speech or stereotypes directed towards social groups such as Muslims, Blacks, Women, Jews, and LGBT people. So they do not contain any negative social biases towards those groups. Combining these counter narratives ensures that the resulting dataset will have more neutral/positive instances mentioning those identity terms. Adding these counter narratives to our dataset significantly decreased model biases. We used total of 7219 counter-narratives related to jews (593), muslim (4996), black (352), homosexual_gay_or_lesbian (617), and female (661). As illustrated in table 10, black and jewish identities suffer from both high false positives and high false negatives. However, after counter-narrative augmentation, the resulting model appears to be capable of dealing with the problem of model bias. Table 11 shows the reduction in model bias using AUC-based metrics. Table 8 includes an error analysis to show how CONAN has helped reduce model bias.

6 Conclusion and Future Work

We have demonstrated that identity attacks or hate speech often incorporate social biases or stereotypes. However, not all hate speech can be labeled as social bias. Some of them are merely personal insults. Filtering out such biases from hate speech is not a trivial task. Furthermore, we have frequently observed that detecting bias without context for the comment or demographic information of the comment holder makes the annotation much more challenging. However, detecting these social biases from toxic datasets, which are available in relatively large amounts, will be a useful starting point for social bias research in other forms of text.

The issue of model bias is also observed during inference. The imbalanced existence of particular community terms (muslims, whites, etc.) might lead to a model labeling a comment as biased. To attenuate model biases, we used counter-narratives and showed that they help significantly to reduce model biases. From our study, we also observe that biases can have directions too. So basically, biases can occur against specific communities and in favour of a community. We intend to detect such biases in future work.

7 Acknowledgements

We would like to the the anonymous reviewers as well as the CoNLL action editors. Their insightful comments helped us in improving the current version of the paper. Additionally, we would like to thank Sandeep Singamsetty, Prapti Roy, Sandhya Singh for their contributions in data annotation and useful comments. This research work was supported by Accenture Labs, India.

8 Limitations

The most notable limitation of our work is the lack of external context and small-sized dataset. In our present models, we have not considered any external context that can be useful for the categorization task, such as the profile bio, user gender, post history, etc. Our work currently considers only five types of social biases, not all other possible dimensions of bias. We also concentrated on using only the English language in our work, and the dataset is oriented toward western culture. The bias annotations in the dataset may not be very relevant to people of non-western culture. Furthermore, Multilingual bias is not taken into account.

References

2019. Jigsaw unintended bias in toxicity classification.

Marion Bartl, Malvina Nissim, and Albert Gatt. 2020. Unmasking contextual stereotypes: Measuring and mitigating BERT's gender bias. In *Proceedings of the Second Workshop on Gender Bias in Natural Language Processing*, pages 1–16, Barcelona, Spain (Online). Association for Computational Linguistics.

Su Lin Blodgett, Gilsinia Lopez, Alexandra Olteanu, Robert Sim, and Hanna Wallach. 2021. Stereotyping norwegian salmon: an inventory of pitfalls in fairness benchmark datasets. In *Proceedings of the 59th Annual Meeting of the Association for Computational Linguistics and the 11th International Joint Conference on Natural Language Processing (Volume 1: Long Papers)*, pages 1004–1015.

Tolga Bolukbasi, Kai-Wei Chang, James Zou, Venkatesh Saligrama, and Adam Kalai. 2016. Man is to computer programmer as woman is to homemaker? debiasing word embeddings.

Daniel Borkan, Lucas Dixon, Jeffrey Sorensen, Nithum Thain, and Lucy Vasserman. 2019. Nuanced metrics for measuring unintended bias with real data for text classification.

Aylin Caliskan, Joanna J. Bryson, and Arvind Narayanan. 2017. Semantics derived automatically from language corpora contain human-like biases. *Science*, 356(6334):183–186.

Yi-Ling Chung, Elizaveta Kuzmenko, Serra Sinem Tekiroglu, and Marco Guerini. 2019. CONAN - COunter NArratives through nichesourcing: a multilingual dataset of responses to fight online hate speech. In *Proceedings of the 57th Annual Meeting of the Association for Computational Linguistics*, pages 2819–2829, Florence, Italy. Association for Computational Linguistics.

Kate Crawford. 2017. The trouble with bias.

Thomas Davidson, Debasmita Bhattacharya, and Ingmar Weber. 2019. Racial bias in hate speech and abusive language detection datasets. *CoRR*, abs/1905.12516.

Thomas Davidson, Dana Warmsley, Michael Macy, and Ingmar Weber. 2017. Automated hate speech detection and the problem of offensive language.

Jacob Devlin, Ming-Wei Chang, Kenton Lee, and Kristina Toutanova. 2019. BERT: Pre-training of deep bidirectional transformers for language understanding. In *Proceedings of the 2019 Conference of the North American Chapter of the Association for Computational Linguistics: Human Language Technologies, Volume 1 (Long and Short Papers)*, pages 4171–4186, Minneapolis, Minnesota. Association for Computational Linguistics.

Lucas Dixon, John Li, Jeffrey Sorensen, Nithum Thain, and Lucy Vasserman. 2018. Measuring and mitigating unintended bias in text classification. In *Proceedings of the 2018 AAAI/ACM Conference on AI, Ethics, and Society*, AIES '18, page 67–73, New York, NY, USA. Association for Computing Machinery.

Fanton, Margherita and Bonaldi, Helena and Tekiroğlu, Serra Sinem and Guerini, Marco. 2021. Human-in-the-Loop for Data Collection: a Multi-Target Counter Narrative Dataset to Fight Online Hate Speech. In *Proceedings of the 59th Annual Meeting of the Association for Computational Linguistics*. Association for Computational Linguistics.

Paula Fortuna and Sérgio Nunes. 2018. A survey on automatic detection of hate speech in text. *ACM Computing Surveys*, 51:1–30.

Antigoni-Maria Founta, Constantinos Djouvas, Despoina Chatzakou, Ilias Leontiadis, Jeremy Blackburn, Gianluca Stringhini, Athena Vakali, Michael Sirivianos, and Nicolas Kourtellis. 2018. Large scale crowdsourcing and characterization of twitter abusive behavior.

Thomas Hartvigsen, Saadia Gabriel, Hamid Palangi, Maarten Sap, Dipankar Ray, and Ece Kamar. 2022. Toxigen: A large-scale machine-generated dataset for adversarial and implicit hate speech detection.

Zhiheng Huang, Wei Xu, and Kai Yu. 2015. Bidirectional lstm-crf models for sequence tagging.

Simrat Kaur, Sarbjeet Singh, and Sakshi Kaushal. 2021. Abusive content detection in online user-generated data: A survey. *Procedia Computer Science*, 189:274–281. AI in Computational Linguistics.

Jae Yeon Kim, Carlos Ortiz, Sarah Nam, Sarah Santiago, and Vivek Datta. 2020. Intersectional bias in hate speech and abusive language datasets.

Keita Kurita, Nidhi Vyas, Ayush Pareek, Alan W Black, and Yulia Tsvetkov. 2019. Measuring bias in contextualized word representations.

Chin-Yew Lin. 2004. ROUGE: A package for automatic evaluation of summaries. In *Text Summarization Branches Out*, pages 74–81, Barcelona, Spain. Association for Computational Linguistics.

Ilya Loshchilov and Frank Hutter. 2019. Decoupled weight decay regularization.

Thomas Manzini, Lim Yao Chong, Alan W Black, and Yulia Tsvetkov. 2019. Black is to criminal as caucasian is to police: Detecting and removing multiclass bias in word embeddings. In *Proceedings of the 2019 Conference of the North American Chapter of the Association for Computational Linguistics: Human Language Technologies, Volume 1 (Long and Short Papers)*, pages 615–621, Minneapolis, Minnesota. Association for Computational Linguistics.

Ariadna Matamoros-Fernández and Johan Farkas. 2021. Racism, hate speech, and social media: A systematic review and critique. *Television & New Media*, 22(2):205–224.

Chandler May, Alex Wang, Shikha Bordia, Samuel R. Bowman, and Rachel Rudinger. 2019. On measuring social biases in sentence encoders. In *Proceedings of the 2019 Conference of the North American Chapter of the Association for Computational Linguistics: Human Language Technologies, Volume 1 (Long and Short Papers)*, pages 622–628, Minneapolis, Minnesota. Association for Computational Linguistics.

Marzieh Mozafari, Reza Farahbakhsh, and Noël Crespi. 2020. Hate speech detection and racial bias mitigation in social media based on BERT model. *CoRR*, abs/2008.06460.

Deepa Muralidhar. 2021. *Examining Religion Bias in AI Text Generators*, page 273–274. Association for Computing Machinery, New York, NY, USA.

Moin Nadeem, Anna Bethke, and Siva Reddy. 2021. StereoSet: Measuring stereotypical bias in pretrained language models. In *Proceedings of the 59th Annual Meeting of the Association for Computational Linguistics and the 11th International Joint Conference on Natural Language Processing (Volume 1: Long Papers)*, pages 5356–5371, Online. Association for Computational Linguistics.

Nikita Nangia, Clara Vania, Rasika Bhalerao, and Samuel R Bowman. 2020. Crows-pairs: A challenge dataset for measuring social biases in masked language models. *arXiv preprint arXiv:2010.00133*.

Debora Nozza, Claudia Volpetti, and Elisabetta Fersini. 2019. Unintended bias in misogyny detection. In *IEEE/WIC/ACM International Conference on Web Intelligence*, WI '19, page 149–155, New York, NY, USA. Association for Computing Machinery.

Kishore Papineni, Salim Roukos, Todd Ward, and Wei-Jing Zhu. 2002. Bleu: a method for automatic evaluation of machine translation. In *Proceedings of the 40th Annual Meeting of the Association for Computational Linguistics*, pages 311–318, Philadelphia, Pennsylvania, USA. Association for Computational Linguistics.

Ji Ho Park, Jamin Shin, and Pascale Fung. 2018. Reducing gender bias in abusive language detection. In *Proceedings of the 2018 Conference on Empirical Methods in Natural Language Processing*, pages 2799–2804, Brussels, Belgium. Association for Computational Linguistics.

Jeffrey Pennington, Richard Socher, and Christopher Manning. 2014. GloVe: Global vectors for word representation. In *Proceedings of the 2014 Conference on Empirical Methods in Natural Language Processing (EMNLP)*, pages 1532–1543, Doha, Qatar. Association for Computational Linguistics.

Marie Plaisime, Candace Robertson-James, Lidyvez Mejia, Ana Núñez, Judith Wolf, and Serita Reels. 2020. Social media and teens: A needs assessment exploring the potential role of social media in promoting health. *Social Media + Society*, 6(1):2056305119886025.

Alec Radford and Karthik Narasimhan. 2018. Improving language understanding by generative pre-training.

Alec Radford, Jeffrey Wu, Rewon Child, David Luan, Dario Amodei, and Ilya Sutskever. 2018. Language models are unsupervised multitask learners.

Civil Research Data. 2018. Civil comments.

Maarten Sap, Dallas Card, Saadia Gabriel, Yejin Choi, and Noah A. Smith. 2019. The risk of racial bias in hate speech detection. In *Proceedings of the 57th Annual Meeting of the Association for Computational Linguistics*, pages 1668–1678, Florence, Italy. Association for Computational Linguistics.

Maarten Sap, Saadia Gabriel, Lianhui Qin, Dan Jurafsky, Noah A Smith, and Yejin Choi. 2020. Social bias frames: Reasoning about social and power implications of language. *ACL*.

Sandhya Singh, Prapti Roy, Nihar Sahoo, Niteesh Mallela, Himanshu Gupta, Pushpak Bhattacharyya, Milind Savagaonkar, Nidhi Sultan, Roshni Ramnani, Anutosh Maitra, and Shubhashis Sengupta. 2022. Hollywood identity bias dataset: A context oriented bias analysis of movie dialogues. In *Proceedings of the Thirteenth Language Resources and Evaluation Conference*, pages 5274–5285, Marseille, France. European Language Resources Association.

Stefanie Ullmann and Marcus Tomalin. 2020. Quarantining online hate speech: technical and ethical perspectives. *Ethics and Information Technology*, 22(1):69–80.

Zeerak Waseem and Dirk Hovy. 2016. Hateful symbols or hateful people? predictive features for hate speech detection on twitter. In *Proceedings of the NAACL Student Research Workshop*, pages 88–93, San Diego, California. Association for Computational Linguistics.

Thomas Wolf, Lysandre Debut, Victor Sanh, Julien Chaumond, Clement Delangue, Anthony Moi, Pierric Cistac, Tim Rault, Rémi Louf, Morgan Funtowicz, Joe Davison, Sam Shleifer, Patrick von Platen, Clara Ma, Yacine Jernite, Julien Plu, Canwen Xu, Teven Le Scao, Sylvain Gugger, Mariama Drame, Quentin Lhoest, and Alexander M. Rush. 2020. Huggingface's transformers: State-of-the-art natural language processing.

Mengzhou Xia, Anjalie Field, and Yulia Tsvetkov. 2020. Demoting racial bias in hate speech detection. In *Proceedings of the Eighth International Workshop on Natural Language Processing for Social Media*, pages 7–14, Online. Association for Computational Linguistics.

Nadezhda Zueva, Madina Kabirova, and Pavel Kalaidin. 2020. Reducing unintended identity bias in Russian hate speech detection. In *Proceedings of the Fourth Workshop on Online Abuse and Harms*, pages 65–69, Online. Association for Computational Linguistics.

A Appendix

A.1 Ethical Considerations

Our work aims at capturing various social biases in toxic social media posts and demonstrates the annotation quality on biases in one of existing dataset. We also discuss the challenges we faced while doing the annotation of the dataset, specifically due to the absence of context for each instance in the dataset. Also, study of social biases come with ethical concerns of risks in deployment (Ullmann and Tomalin, 2020). As these toxic posts can create potentially harm to any user or community, it is required to conduct this kind of research to detect them. If done with precautions, such research can be quite helpful in automatic flagging of toxic and harmful online contents.

Researchers working the problem of social bias detection on any form of text would benefit from the dataset we have collated and from the inferences we got from multiple training strategies.

A.2 Annotator Demographics and Treatment

Both the annotators were trained and selected through extensive one-on-one discussions, and were working voluntarily. Both of them went through few days of initial training where they would annotate many examples which would then be validated by an expert and were communicated properly about any wrong annotations during training. As there are potential negative side effects of annotating such toxic comments, we used to have regular discussion sessions with them to make sure they are not excessively exposed to the harmful contents. Both the annotators were Asian male and were of age between 23 to 26. The expert was an Asian female with post-graduation degree in sociology.

A.3 Training Details

A.3.1 BERT Training

We finetune 12 layer BERT base uncased with batch size of 32 for two epochs. Max token length of 128 is used. We experiment with learning rates of $2e-5, 3e-5, 4e-5, 5e-5$ with AdamW(Loshchilov and Hutter, 2019) optimizer and epochs of $5, 10, 20$. We also use a dropout layer in our model. AdamW optimizer with learning rate = $5e-05$, epsilon = $1e-08$, decay = 0.01, clipnorm = 1.0 were used.

A.3.2 GPT-2 Training

We finetune GPT-2 with a training batch size of 1, gradient accumulation step as 4, and 200 warm up steps. Experiments were run with a single GeForce RTX 2080 Ti GPU. Finetuning one GPT-2 model took around 40 minutes for 5 epochs.

We have kept all the parameters of BERT and GPT-2 trainable. All of our implementations uses Huggingface's transformer library (Wolf et al., 2020).

Incremental Processing of Principle B: Mismatches Between Neural Models and Humans

Forrest Davis
Department of Linguistics and Philosophy
Massachusetts Institute of Technology
forrestd@mit.edu

Abstract

Despite neural language models qualitatively capturing many human linguistic behaviors, recent work has demonstrated that they underestimate the true processing costs of ungrammatical structures. We extend these more fine-grained comparisons between humans and models by investigating the interaction between Principle B and coreference processing. While humans use Principle B to block certain structural positions from affecting their incremental processing, we find that GPT-based language models are influenced by ungrammatical positions. We conclude by relating the mismatch between neural models and humans to properties of training data and suggest that certain aspects of human processing behavior do not directly follow from linguistic data.

1 Introduction

Neural models trained on text data alone have been shown to qualitatively capture aspects of a large variety of human linguistic behaviors (e.g., Gulordava et al., 2018; Wilcox et al., 2019; Warstadt et al., 2020; Hu et al., 2020; Jumelet et al., 2021). Investigations have evaluated a range of levels of linguistic knowledge, including: i) syntax (Marvin and Linzen, 2018; Warstadt et al., 2019; Wilcox et al., 2019, 2021a), ii) semantics (Pannitto and Herbelot, 2020; Misra et al., 2020), and iii) discourse structure and pragmatics (Schuster et al., 2020; Davis and van Schijndel, 2020).

Recent work has placed increased attention on finer-grained comparisons between neural models and humans (e.g., van Schijndel and Linzen, 2021; Wilcox et al., 2021b; Paape and Vasishth, 2022). The growing consensus is that neural models underestimate the processing costs seen with humans, while nonetheless capturing the broad patterns (see Wilcox et al., 2021b). The present study adds to this literature by comparing the incremental processing of coreference in humans and neural models.

While coreference, more generally, is modulated by discourse, pragmatics, and information structure (e.g., Arnold, 1998, 2001; Rohde et al., 2006; Hartshorne, 2014; Rohde and Kehler, 2014), there are sentential restrictions on coreference that have immediate effects on human incremental processing (e.g., Nicol, 1988; Clifton et al., 1997; Sturt, 2003; Chow et al., 2014). This study finds that, contrary to humans, autoregressive neural models do not similarly restrict their behavior in coreference processing.

In particular, the present study investigated the interaction between the Binding Principles, articulated in Chomsky (1981), and incremental processing. Binding Principles account for the constrained distribution of pronouns (and anaphora) and their possible linguistic antecedents:

(1) **Binding Principles**

PRINCIPLE A An anaphor is bound in its governing category

PRINCIPLE B A pronominal is free in its governing category

PRINCIPLE C An R-expression is free

Roughly, Principle A excludes examples like *John thinks that Mike hates himself* from meaning that "John thinks that Mike hates John". Conversely, Principle B excludes examples like *John thinks that Mike hates him* from meaning that "John thinks that Mike hates Mike". Finally, Principle C excludes *He hates John* from meaning "John hates John". These principles are mediated by a structural relation, c-command, rather than linear order. While the specific binding conditions have been refined within syntactic theory (e.g., Reinhart and Reuland, 1993), we focused here on the empirical results concerning Principle B and incremental processing, putting aside explicit theoretical commitments.

(2) Bill told Clark that Robert had deceived him.

Proceedings of the 26th Conference on Computational Natural Language Learning (CoNLL), pages 144 - 156
December 7-8, 2022 ©2022 Association for Computational Linguistics

In (2), despite *him* agreeing in gender with *Bill*, *Clark*, and *Robert*, only two of these are possible antecedents of *him*: *Bill* and *Clark*. Principle B blocks the structural location occupied by *Robert* from serving as an antecedent of *him*. In human incremental processing, this restriction has immediate effects, preventing the gender of this embedded subject from influencing the processing of the pronoun (see Chow et al., 2014). Moreover, Principle B can restrict the prediction of nouns following certain cataphoric pronouns – pronouns that occur before their coreferring noun phrase (Kush and Dillon, 2021). For example, in (3), *him* can only corefer with *Mark* and not *Michael*. In human incremental processing, the cataphoric pronoun *him* has no effect on the processing of the subject (e.g., *Michael*).

(3) Before offering him a fancy pastry, Michael politely asked Mark for help.

In what follows, we evaluate whether GPT-like autoregressive neural models use Principle B to restrict their incremental processing like humans. Specifically, we investigated two broad effects of Principle B: i) its interaction with "vanilla" pronouns (as in (2)), and ii) its interaction with cataphora (as in (3)).

While models appear to learn aspects of Principle B (treating apparent violations in unique ways), we find that neural models, in contrast to humans, do not categorically ignore structural positions blocked by Principle B. Ultimately, the present study suggests that, beyond underestimating the processing costs seen in humans, models fail, at least in some cases, to learn qualitatively similar patterns to humans. This suggests, in turn, that certain aspects of human parsing behavior are not directly evidenced in linguistic data.

2 Background

In human coreference processing, a major question is whether antecedent retrieval, triggered by the presence of a pronoun, is restricted first by agreement features (e.g., gender, number), returning possibly ungrammatical antecedents, or by structural constraints, like Principle B, which serve as an initial filter. As an illustration consider the following set of stimuli discussed in Chow et al. (2014):

(4) a. John thought that Bill liked him.
    b. John thought that Mary liked him.
    c. Jane thought that Bill liked him.
    d. Jane thought that Mary liked him.

If Principle B immediately restricts the set of possible antecedents of *him*, then we would expect the reading times at *him* to be the same for (4-a) and (4-b), as in both cases the structurally licit antecedent agrees in gender. If instead structurally ungrammatical antecedents can influence the immediate processing of *him*, then we would expect that (4-a)–(4-c) would pattern together, to the exclusion of (4-d), where no antecedent is given in the linguistic context. Put another way, whether the structurally ungrammatical antecedent influences reading times at *him* is indicative of the status of Principle B in human linguistic processing.

The bulk of work investigating these, and similar constructions, has found that structural constraints like Principle B do immediately influence human incremental processing (e.g., Clifton et al., 1997; Sturt, 2003; Chow et al., 2014; Kush and Phillips, 2014; Kush and Dillon, 2021). That is, finding that (4-a) and (4-b) pattern together and (4-c) and (4-d) pattern together.[1]

Within work in natural language processing, existing models have been claimed to capture aspects of Principle A (e.g., Warstadt et al., 2020; Hu et al., 2020). Principle C has received less attention, though see Mitchell et al. (2019) which found that LSTM language models failed to obey Principle C. Coreference, more broadly, has also been explored, with results suggesting that models encode features of coreference resolution (e.g., Sorodoc et al., 2020) and the interaction of implicit causality and pronouns (verb biases that influence preferred antecedents for pronouns; Upadhye et al., 2020; Davis and van Schijndel, 2021; Kementchedjhieva et al., 2021).

The present study straightforwardly extends existing studies of neural models to Principle B. While we cannot assess whether neural models truly "interpret" the pronoun as coreferring with certain antecedents (and thus fully verify whether they have learned Principle B, or even Principle A), we can compare the difference in model behavior conditioned on minimally contrastive stimuli. In fact, human online sentence comprehension stud-

[1]However, some other work has suggested that grammatically illicit antecedents can in fact have measurable effects (e.g., Badecker and Straub, 2002; Kennison, 2003). Such effects may be capturing later stages of processing (see Sturt, 2003). Nevertheless, the plurality of the evidence suggests that Principle B has immediate effects on human processing.

ies are similarly limited. Since we cannot directly measure the content retrieved in reading a pronoun, online reading times are taken as a proxy for the consideration of certain antecedents.

3 Neural Models and Measures

We analyzed four autoregressive models with GPT-like architectures: GPT-2 XL (1.5B parameters; Radford et al., 2019), GPT-Neo (2.7B parameters; Black et al., 2021), GPT-J (6B parameters; Wang and Komatsuzaki, 2021), and GPT-3 (175B parameters; Brown et al., 2020). GPT-2 XL, GPT-Neo, and GPT-J were accessed via HuggingFace (Wolf et al., 2020), and GPT-3 by using OpenAI's API.[2]

In evaluating model performance, we used *surprisal* (Hale, 2001; Levy, 2008):

$$-\log \text{Prob}(\text{word}|\text{context}) \quad (1)$$

Surprisal has a linear relationship with human reading times (Smith and Levy, 2013). We follow a growing body of work in utilizing this relationship to compare the behavior of neural models and humans (e.g., van Schijndel and Linzen, 2021; Wilcox et al., 2021b).[3]

To aid the interpretation of the results, we calculated by-item gender mismatch effects (GMMEs). GMMEs are used in human experiments to index the increased cost in processing incurred when encountering a pronoun (or a postcedent, in the case of cataphoric pronoun processing) that was not expected (e.g., van Gompel and Liversedge, 2003; Reali et al., 2015; Kush and Dillon, 2021). Thus, GMMEs are a means of measuring human predictions by providing evidence for mismatches between expectations and reality. We calculated two classes of GMMEs for neural models targeting gender prediction for, i) "vanilla" pronouns, and ii) subjects after reading cataphoric pronouns.

For predictions about upcoming pronouns, consider:

(5) a. Fred thought Kathy hated him
    b. Mike thought Kevin hated him

To calculate the GMME for (5), we took the difference between the surprisal for *him* in (5-a) and the surprisal for *him* in (5-b). More generally, we calculated a GMME by taking the difference in the surprisal of the target (either a pronoun or the subject noun) between minimal pairs. A positive GMME would suggest that the model was more surprised when the embedded subject mismatched in gender with the pronoun; in other words, the gender of the embedded subject influenced the surprisal of the pronoun. In this case, comparing the GMME for *him* and *his* is informative about the status of Principle B in neural models. Humans have been shown to exhibit no GMME dependent on the embedded subject with *him*, because Principle B blocks co-indexation between these positions. For *his*, however, co-indexation is possible, and a GMME is obtained (see Chow et al., 2014).[4]

For predictions about upcoming antecedents after cataphoric pronouns, consider:

(6) a. While he was at work, Fred ate food.
    b. While he was at work, Keisha ate food.

For (6) we calculated a GMME by taking the difference in surprisal of *Keisha* in (6-b) and the surprisal of *Fred* in (6-a). A positive GMME would indicate that the neural model was more surprised when the subject mismatched with the gender of the cataphoric subject pronoun.[5]

4 Principle B and Pronouns

Recall, humans restrict their incremental processing of coreference to just those antecedents which are grammatically licensed (e.g., Chow et al., 2014). That is, in sentences like *Fred thought Amy hated him*, *him* cannot be co-indexed with the structural position that *Amy* occupies, and thus, the gender of *Amy* does not hinder the processing of *him*. In this section, we evaluated the ability of GPT-like autoregressive neural models to replicate this qualitative effect across four experimental conditions.

4.1 Stimuli

In this section, we consider four experiments:

(7) **Experiments**

[2]We used the version of GPT-3 called text-davinci-002. All the stimuli, results, and scripts for recreating the statistics and figures can be found at `https://github.com/forrestdavis/PrincipleB`.

[3]For a more explicit comparison between human self-paced reading times and neural models see Section 6.1.

[4]Because the feminine pronoun *her* is ambiguous between a possessive and an object pronoun when processing left to right (e.g., *Sue loves her* and *Sue loves her friend*) only masculine pronouns were evaluated in pronoun prediction.

[5]All subject nouns investigated were encoded by the neural models as single tokens rather than being split into multiple tokens as in Randolf mapping to 'Rand' + 'olf' in GPT-J.

a. SIMPLE SUBJECT: Single clause with simple subject
b. COMPLEX SUBJECT: Single clause with complex subject containing a prepositional phrase
c. 2NP: Clause with embedding and simple subjects
d. 3NP: Clause with embedding and simple subjects and an object

Examples of each are included below:

(8) **Stimuli Examples**
a. SIMPLE SUBJECT: The boy meets him.
b. COMPLEX SUBJECT: The story about Eric hurt him.
c. 2NP: Jason hadn't expected that Adam was investigating him.
d. 3NP: Liam advised the nephew that Patrick can praise him.

We used the data generation scripts and vocabulary provided with the BLiMP dataset to create our stimuli (Warstadt et al., 2020). The sentences are all grammatical and generally semantically felicitous (despite certain interpretations being blocked by Principle B). The stimuli for COMPLEX SUBJECT always had a subject comprised of "the X about...", where X ranged over inanimate nouns like *book* or *story*.[6]

There were 1000 base sentences for each experiment, with each sentence having exponents that varied gender in all relevant positions (e.g., (8-c) has four forms varying whether the matrix subject is *Jason* or *Amanda* and whether the embedded subject is *Adam* or *Victoria*).[7] The applicability of Principle B varied by experiment. For SIMPLE SUBJECT, Principle B blocks co-indexation between the subject and the object pronoun. For COMPLEX SUBJECT, Principle B does not block co-indexation between the lower noun (e.g., *Eric* in (8-b)) and the pronoun. Principle B, however, does block the higher nouns (e.g., *the story* in (8-b)) from co-indexing with the pronoun *him*.[8] For 2NP and 3NP, Principle B blocks co-indexation between the embedded subject (e.g., *Adam* in (8-c) and *Patrick* in (8-d)) and the pronoun, but not the matrix subject (e.g., *Jason* in (8-c) and *Liam* in (8-d)) or matrix object for 3NP (e.g., *the nephew* in (8-d)). If neural models patterned like humans, then we should find no GMME when Principle B blocks co-indexation, and positive GMMEs elsewhere.

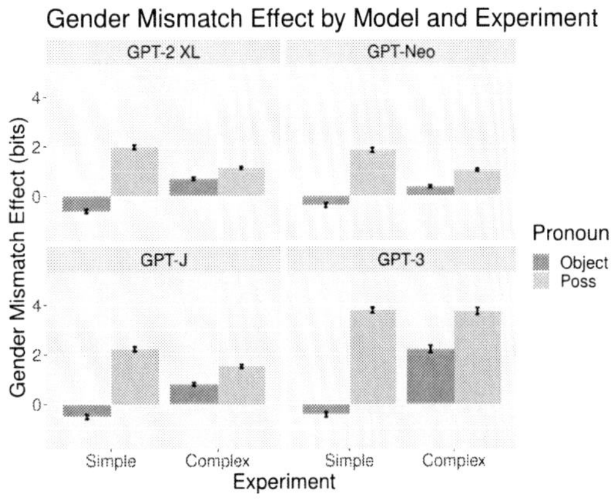

Figure 1: GMME for object pronoun (*him*) and possessive pronoun (*his*) for each neural model by two conditions: i) SIMPLE SUBJECT, and ii) COMPLEX SUBJECT (e.g., (*Bill|The book about Bill*) *worried him*). Error bars are 95% confidence intervals.

4.2 Simple Sentences and Pronoun Prediction

First, we investigated the influence on pronoun prediction that subjects had in single clause constructions (the SIMPLE SUBJECT and COMPLEX SUBJECT experiments; see (8-a) and (8-b) above for the relevant contrasts).

Results grouped by model, condition, and pronoun are given in Figure 1. Statistical analyses were conducted via linear-mixed effects models.[9]

Starting with the results for possessive pronouns, we found that all models showed a positive GMME. That is, models expected possessive pronouns to agree in gender with the subject, both in simple sentences (e.g., *Fred worried his...*) and sentences with complex subjects (e.g., *The book about Fred worried his...*).

For object pronouns, GMME differed by subject type. For complex subjects, where co-indexation between the object pronoun and the lower noun (e.g., *Fred* in *The book about Fred*) is possible,

[6]The full set contained *book, pamphlet, brochure, play, movie, newspaper article, story, essay, report, documentary, commentary,* and *show*.

[7]No noun was repeated in a single sentence. That is, there were no sentences like *The man advised the nephew that the man can praise him.*

[8]Additionally, all higher nouns were inanimate, again blocking the applicability of *him*.

[9]We used lmer (version 1.1.30; Bates et al., 2015) and lmerTest (version 3.1.3; Kuznetsova et al., 2017) in R. Models were fit to predict the surprisal of the pronoun *him* or *his* with a main effect of condition (i.e. whether the noun matched the gender of the pronoun) with by-item random intercepts.

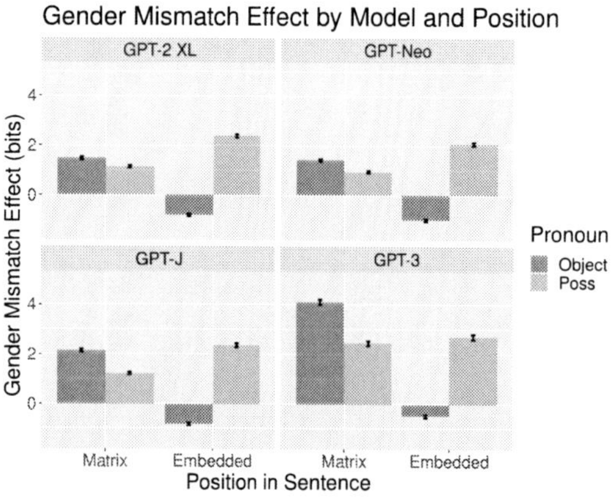

Figure 2: GMME for object pronoun (*him*) and possessive pronoun (*his*) for each neural model by whether i) the matrix subject, or ii) the embedded subject agrees in gender (e.g., *(Bill|Hannah) thinks that (Mark|Sue) hates him*). Error bars are 95% confidence intervals.

models again exhibited a positive GMME, suggesting that agreement between the object pronoun and the lower noun was expected. For simple subjects, where co-indexation between the subject and the pronoun is **not** possible (e.g., *him* cannot refer to *Fred* in *Fred worried him*), a negative GMME was obtained. That is, despite the subject not being a possible coreferent for the object pronoun, the gender of the subject (negatively) influenced the surprisal of the object pronoun.

4.3 Multiple NPs

We found evidence that, in cases where co-indexation is blocked by Principle B, models expected pronouns to mismatch with the gender of the antecedent. While suggesting that models consider antecedents that humans do not, it nonetheless suggests models capture aspects of the ungrammaticality of violations of Principle B. In this section, we evaluated models on more complex sentences containing two or three noun phrase antecedents (the 2NP and 3NP experiments; see examples (8-c) and (8-d) in Section 4.1 for the relevant contrasts).

Results for the 2NP case are given in Figure 2 (with results for the 3NP case given in Figure 7 in Appendix A). Statistical analyses were conducted via linear-mixed effects models.[10] Starting with the results for possessive pronouns, in both conditions, all models exhibited a positive GMME in all positions (e.g., matrix subject, embedded subject). That is, models predicted that possessive pronouns would agree with the antecedent nouns.

For object pronouns, we again found a mismatch in the direction of the GMME conditioned on the structural position of the relevant antecedent. When co-indexation is grammatically licensed (e.g., *him* can refer to *Bill* in *Bill knows that Mary loves him*), a positive GMME was obtained for all models. In cases where Principle B blocks co-indexation, all models exhibited a negative GMME instead. As in Section 4, this suggests that grammatically unavailable antecedents influenced the surprisal of object pronouns contrary to the results obtained in human incremental processing.

4.4 Interim Discussion

Broadly, the above experiments demonstrated that neural models exhibited GMMEs when pronouns mismatched in gender with preceding nouns. For the possessive pronoun *his*, this amounted to positive GMMEs across-the-board. That is, mismatches in gender between *his* and any antecedent increased the surprisal of *his*. For the object pronoun *him*, the GMME interacted with Principle B. Positive GMMEs were obtained when grammatically licit antecedents mismatched in gender, suggesting models predicted *him* to agree with these antecedents. However, when Principle B blocked the structural position from permitting co-indexation between the antecedent and the object pronoun, a negative GMME was obtained. That is, models expected *him* to mismatch in gender with grammatically unavailable antecedents.

As evidenced by the COMPLEX SUBJECT experiment, this negative GMME is not merely a dispreference for local agreement with object pronouns. For sentences like *The book about Fred surprised him*, the more recent noun in linear order agrees in gender with *him*, but we found a positive GMME. Rather, neural models appear to have learned, at least some, aspects of Principle B (in so far as certain structural positions are marked). However, the negative GMME was unexpected given the findings in the literature surrounding incremental processing of such constructions in English. Ultimately, neural models appear to use information in prediction that the human parser does not.

[10]Models were fit to predict the surprisal of the pronoun *him* or *his* with an interaction between the matrix subject gender (i.e. whether it matched with the pronoun) and the embedded subject gender, in the two noun phrase case, or the matrix subject gender, the matrix object gender, and the embedded subject gender (e.g., *Fred|Mary told Mark|Karen that Frank|Sue hated him*), in the three noun phrase case, and with by-item random intercepts.

5 Principle B and Cataphora

The above section explored the role Principle B plays in pronoun prediction for GPT-like neural models, finding a qualitative mismatch between the incremental processing of neural models and humans. Recent work in psycholinguistics has also demonstrated that Principle B can restrict the prediction of subjects following cataphoric object pronouns (Kush and Dillon, 2021).

(9) a. While baking him some cookies, Nicholas chatted with Mark.
b. While an employee baked him some cookies, Nicholas happily chatted with Mark.

In (9), *him* is a cataphoric pronoun – the noun phrase it corefers with comes later in the sentence. While *him* can be co-indexed with *Nicholas* in (9-b) (meaning Nicholas had some cookies baked for him), *him* cannot be co-indexed with *Nicholas* in (9-a).[11] Principle B excludes this latter co-indexation.[12] Kush and Dillon (2021) found that humans exhibited a GMME at the subject (e.g., *Nicholas*) only in cases where co-indexation between the catphoric *him* and the subject was possible (e.g., (9-b)). As with "vanilla" pronouns, it seems, then, that Principle B immediately restricts the human parser, such that grammatically unavailable structural positions are ignored.

In the following section, we evaluated whether neural models patterned like humans in this respect. That is, whether models exhibited a GMME only in cases where Principle B did not block co-indexation. First, we also verified that the neural models could use cataphoric pronouns to restrict the prediction of subjects more generally.

5.1 Stimuli

In this section, we consider two experiments:

(10) **Experiments**
a. SUBJECT CATAPHORA: Sentences with a cataphoric subject pronoun
b. OBJECT CATAPHORA: Sentences with a cataphoric object pronoun

[11]A natural interpretation of (9-a) is that Nicholas was baking cookies for Mark while chatting with Mark

[12]Obligatory control of the PRO in the adjunct is also implicated by this construction. We abstract from the relevant syntactic analysis here, and instead focus on the empirical findings from human experiments (for full discussion see Kush and Dillon, 2021, and references therein).

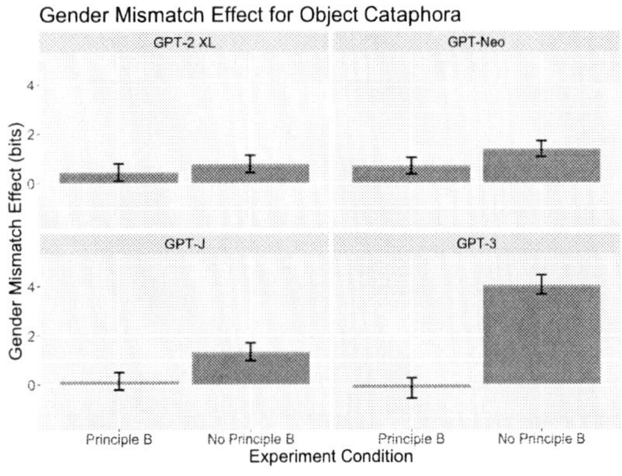

Figure 3: GMME for subject following a cataphoric object pronoun (*him*) for each neural model by whether Principle B applies (e.g., (*While driving him|While someone drove him*), (*Bill|Sue*)). Stimuli adapted from Kush and Dillon (2021). Error bars are 95% confidence intervals.

Examples of each are included below.

(11) **Stimuli Examples**
a. SUBJECT CATAPHORA: When **he** was off work, Richard...
b. OBJECT CATAPHORA: While driving **him** to school on Friday, Thomas...

For SUBJECT CATAPHORA, we used the 32 stimuli from Experiment 1 in van Gompel and Liversedge (2003). The gender of the cataphoric pronoun and the matrix subject (e.g., *he* and *Richard* in (11-a)) were manipulated resulting in male and female versions of each. Moreover, for each stimulus in van Gompel and Liversedge (2003), we evaluated models on ten unique subjects per gender.

For OBJECT CATAPHORA, we drew on the 24 stimuli from Experiment 2 in Kush and Dillon (2021), which were already balanced for gender (i.e. 12 with *him*). As with SUBJECT CATAPHORA, the experiment manipulated the gender match between the cataphoric pronoun and the subject noun. Additionally, Kush and Dillon (2021) manipulated whether Principle B applied to the construction. For instance, Principle B applies in (11-b), blocking *him* from co-indexing with *Thomas*. However, a minimal different string, *While a parent drove him to School on Friday, Thomas...*, does not implicate Principle B. We again evaluated models on ten unique subject nouns per sentence.

In this section, Principle B was only relevant for *Object Cataphora*, with *Subject Cataphora* serving as a baseline to ensure that models can, in fact, use cataphoric pronouns to predict the gender of upcoming subjects.

5.2 Simple Subject Cataphora

We turn first to the ability of neural models to modulate their predictions of upcoming subjects by the presence of cataphoric subject pronouns (see (11-a) for a relevant example). Results are given in Figure 8 of Appendix A, and statistical analyses were conducted via linear-mixed effects models.[13] All models exhibited a positive GMME, suggesting that models use cataphoric pronouns to constrain upcoming predictions about the gender of nouns.

5.3 Cataphora and Principle B

Given that neural models can use cataphoric pronouns in prediction, we evaluated whether models capture the interaction of cataphoric processing and Principle B (see Section 5.1 for discussion of the relevant contrast). Results are given by model and experimental condition in Figure 3. Statistical significance was determined via linear-mixed effects models.[14]

Recall, that humans exhibit a GMME only in the case that Principle B does not block coreference between the cataphoric pronoun and the subject (e.g., *him* cannot be co-indexed with *Fred* in *While driving him to the store, Fred...*). If neural models capture this aspect of human incremental processing, a GMME should be obtained only in cases where Principle B is not active. We found, however, that not all models captured this distinction.

GPT-3 and GPT-J demonstrated no significant GMME in cases where Principle B blocked coreference, in line with humans. GPT-2 XL and GPT-Neo, on the other hand, had a positive GMME suggesting that models used the gender of the cataphoric pronoun to predict the gender of the subject. That is, the models predicted that the gender of the subject would agree with the cataphoric pronoun, despite co-indexation being ungrammatical for humans. When Principle B was not implicated, all models showed a positive GMME suggesting that,

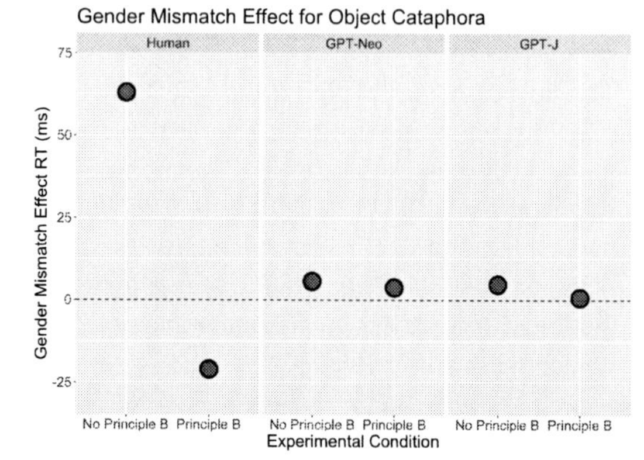

Figure 4: Mean GMME for subject following a cataphoric object pronoun (*him*) for humans (reported in Experiment 2 of Kush and Dillon (2021)), GPT-Neo, and GPT-J. Predicted reading times (in milliseconds) for the neural models were obtained by fitting the self-paced reading times for the fillers following the methodology outlined in van Schijndel and Linzen (2021).

as with subject cataphora, object cataphora can restrict the prediction of subjects.

6 General Discussion

This study investigated whether autoregressive neural models displayed similar incremental coreference processing to humans. Specifically, we examined the interaction between Principle B and coreference processing with two broad case studies: i) "vanilla" pronouns (where the antecedent precedes the pronoun), and ii) cataphoric pronouns (where the pronoun precedes its coreferring noun phrase). For the first case study, we found that the pronoun predictions of all models were influenced by structural positions deemed ungrammatical by Principle B, inconsistent with the incremental processing behavior of humans. For the second case study, we found that two of the four models (GPT-J and GPT-3), displayed human-like processing behavior in predicting subjects after cataphoric object pronouns (e.g., *him*), specifically with Principle B blocking the influence of the pronoun on the prediction of the later subject.

Three questions remain concerning the behavior of neural models: 1) how closely do models predict the observed processing cost in human studies, 2) why do GPT-J and GPT-3, and not the other models, pattern like humans in cataphoric processing, and 3) why do models consider ungrammatical antecedents in their incremental processing of pronouns.

[13]Models were fit to predict the surprisal of the subject noun with a main effect of contrast (whether the cataphoric pronoun agreed with the subject) and by-item and by-gender (*he* or *she*) random intercepts.

[14]Models were fit to predict the surprisal of the subject noun with an interaction of the gender agreement of the cataphoric pronoun (i.e. whether the pronoun and subject agreed in gender) and the presence of Principle B (i.e. whether co-indexation was possible between the cataphoric pronoun and the subject) with by-item random intercepts.

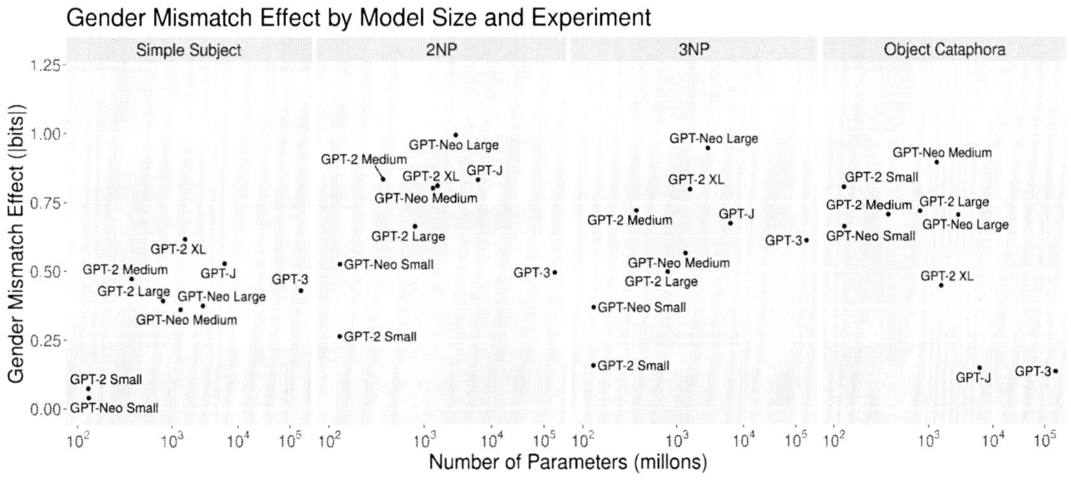

Figure 5: Absolute value of the GMME by model size (in millions of paramters) across four experiments: i) SIMPLE SUBJECTS (Section 4.2), ii) 2NP, iii) 3NP (Section 4.3), and iv) OBJECT CATAPHORA (Section 5.3).

6.1 Finer Comparison Between Model and Human Behavior

Following the methodology outlined in van Schijndel and Linzen (2021), we can directly compare the GMME observed in humans and in neural models. In what follows, we report on comparisons between the GMME observed for humans in Experiment 2 of Kush and Dillon (2021) and the predicted GMME in milliseconds from GPT-Neo (which was demonstrated to have non-human like behavior) and GPT-J (which did have qualitatively similar behavior to humans). To foreshadow the results, we found that both models greatly underestimate the processing cost observed in humans, even in cases of qualitative overlap.

We fit a linear-mixed effects model with reading times from the filler items in Kush and Dillon (2021) as the dependent variable, and, as fixed effects, the surprisal of the current word, the surprisal of each of the preceding three words, word length (of the current word and preceding three words), and frequency (of the current word and the preceding three words). Additional, we included fixed effects for the interaction between word length and frequency and by-participant random intercepts.[15] The predicted reading times (in milliseconds) at the subject (i.e. where we expect a GMME) were determined for GPT-Neo and GPT-J by applying the significant coefficients for the surprisal terms of their statistical model (as in van Schijndel and Linzen (2021)). For both models, the surprisal of the current word and the preceding two words were significant.[16]

Figure 4 gives the GMME for humans and the predicted GMME for the two neural models. As is visually apparent, neural models greatly underestimate the processing cost. For example, the GMME reported for humans in the condition without an interaction with Principle B was 63 milliseconds, while GPT-Neo predicted an average of around 5.7 milliseconds and GPT-J an average of around 4.7 milliseconds. Similar results have been obtained in prior work for non-pronominal constructions, suggesting a broader inability for surprisal measures from neural models to capture the processing cost of grammatical violations (van Schijndel and Linzen, 2021; Wilcox et al., 2021b; Paape and Vasishth, 2022).

6.2 Model Behavior and Scale

With regards to the second remaining question, GPT-J and GPT-3 differ from the other models in one obvious way: they are the two largest models we investigated. Scaling laws suggest that larger models will outperform smaller models (e.g., Kaplan et al., 2020; Wei et al., 2022). Figure 5 plots the absolute value of the GMMEs for four of the experiments investigated in this paper, including additional results from smaller versions of GPT-2

[15]That is, we fit the model (excluding the entropy and entropy reduction terms) given in Equation 1 of van Schijndel and Linzen (2021).

[16]In particular, for GPT-Neo, the coefficients were 1.857 ms/bit for the current word, 1.802 ms/bit for the preceding word, and 1.987 ms/bit for the word two time steps in the past. Similarly, for GPT-J, the coefficients were 1.929 ms/bit, 2.037 ms/bit, and 1.980 ms/bit.

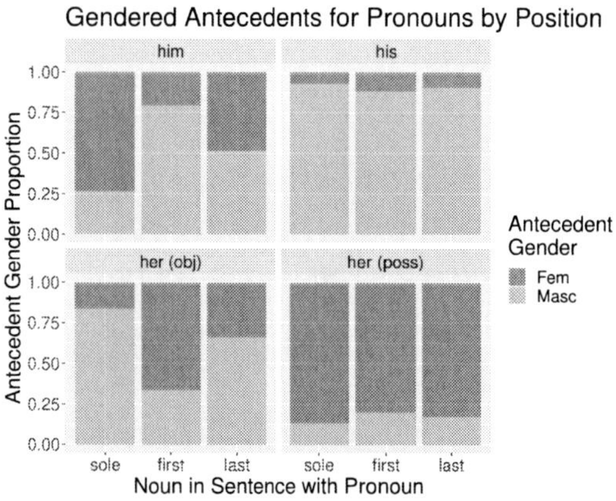

Figure 6: Proportion of each gender preceding pronouns in three positions: i) when there is exactly one antecedent, and when there is at leat two antecedents, ii) the first antecedent, and iii) the last antecedent. Data from the Pile (Gao et al., 2020) which is the training data for GPT-J and GPT-Neo.

and GPT-Neo for a larger range of model sizes. Generally, the GMME increases with model size (though GPT-3 is at times an outlier). However, for the experiment with cataphoric processing, we see that the GMME decreases with scale, suggesting that larger models learn to ignore ungrammatical positions in cataphoric pronouns, while simultaneously considering ungrammatical positions more strongly with "vanilla" pronouns.

6.3 Model Behavior and Training Data

Turning to the final remaining question (why models consider ungrammatical antecedents), the SIMPLE SUBJECT experiments are an instructive case study. Sentences like *Bill adores him* are not ungrammatical, only the interpretation that "Bill adores Bill" is blocked. Suppose the world is such the following two schema are produced at equal rates:

(12) a. Bill adores [MALE NOUN]
b. Bill adores [FEMALE NOUN]

(12-a) has two possible pronominal exponents, *Bill adores him* and *Bill adores himself*, while (12-b) has just one, *Bill adores her*. Suppose further, that the first exponent of (12-a) is twice as likely as the second. The resultant set of productions will be 50% *Bill adores her*, 33% *Bill adores him*, and 17% *Bill adores himself.*[17] Models trained on data of this sort would presumably come to favor pronouns that mismatch with the subject.

In fact, the training data for GPT-J and GPT-Neo (which is publicly available) bears resemblance to this. We took the Pile (Gao et al., 2020) and extracted all sentences with pronouns. These sentences were then parsed and chunked into noun phrases using Spacy and gender was assigned by checking for their inclusion in the male and female nouns in the BLiMP vocabulary.[18] The results are compiled in Figure 6. As is visually apparent, the data is highly indicative of a gender mismatch in the case just discussed, and skewed, to a lesser degree, towards a gender mismatch in more complex cases implicated by Principle B (e.g., 3NP stimuli).

The Binding Principles, in other words, distort the surface distribution of pronouns such that the models ultimately favor mismatches in gender in just those positions where co-indexation is impossible. Moreover, we see in the scaling figure discussed above (Figure 5), that smaller models show no, or weaker, GMMEs. Given the findings that large models have a higher capacity to memorize training data (e.g., Carlini et al., 2022; McCoy et al., 2021), we may take the GMME in the SIMPLE SUBJECT experiment to be a case of models overfiting their training data.

6.4 Conclusion

The present study argues that autoregressive models do not (uniformly) process pronouns like humans. We showed that models fail to capture the qualitative patterns of human incremental coreference processing, in addition to underestimating processing costs in constructions already noted in the literature (see van Schijndel and Linzen, 2021; Wilcox et al., 2021b). Models appear to learn only aspects of Principle B that have predictable reflexes in training data.[19] Therefore, models can mimic humans without a full human-like system. Ultimately, this work provides evidence suggesting that certain aspects of human parsing behavior do not directly follow from linguistic data. We leave bridging the gap to future work.

[17] That is, we are, for expository purposes, assuming the world consists of only structures drawn from the set {*Bill adores him, Bill adores her, Bill adores himself*} with *Bill adores herself* excluded. This is to highlight how Principle B restricts the possible strings in such a way that mismatch is more common.

[18] We used the small pretrained English model from Spacy.

[19] For a fuller discussion of mismatches between neural models and humans, as well as what these results may mean for a linguistic theory, see Davis (2022).

Acknowledgments

We would like to Dorit Abusch, Miloje Despić, Joseph Rhyne, Marten van Schijndel, Rachel Vogel, John Whitman and members of the C.Psyd lab and Cornell NLP Group, who gave feedback on earlier forms of this work. We would also like to thank the anonymous reviewers for their helpful suggestions and comments.

References

Jennifer E Arnold. 1998. *Reference Form and Discourse Patterns*. Ph.D. thesis, Stanford University.

Jennifer E Arnold. 2001. The effect of thematic roles on pronoun use and frequency of reference continuation. *Discourse Processes*, 31(2):137–162.

William Badecker and Kathleen Straub. 2002. The processing role of structural constraints on interpretation of pronouns and anaphors. *Journal of Experimental Psychology: Learning, Memory, and Cognition*, 28(4):748–769.

Douglas Bates, Martin Mächler, Ben Bolker, and Steve Walker. 2015. Fitting Linear Mixed-Effects Models Using lme4. *Journal of Statistical Software*, 67(1):1–48.

Emily M. Bender. 2009. Linguistically Naïve != Language Independent: Why NLP Needs Linguistic Typology. In *Proceedings of the EACL 2009 Workshop on the Interaction between Linguistics and Computational Linguistics: Virtuous, Vicious or Vacuous?*, pages 26–32, Athens, Greece. Association for Computational Linguistics.

Emily M. Bender and Alexander Koller. 2020. Climbing towards NLU: On Meaning, Form, and Understanding in the Age of Data. In *Proceedings of the 58th Annual Meeting of the Association for Computational Linguistics*, pages 5185–5198, Online. Association for Computational Linguistics.

Sid Black, Gao Leo, Phil Wang, Connor Leahy, and Stella Biderman. 2021. GPT-Neo: Large Scale Autoregressive Language Modeling with Mesh-Tensorflow.

Tom Brown, Benjamin Mann, Nick Ryder, Melanie Subbiah, Jared D Kaplan, Prafulla Dhariwal, Arvind Neelakantan, Pranav Shyam, Girish Sastry, Amanda Askell, Sandhini Agarwal, Ariel Herbert-Voss, Gretchen Krueger, Tom Henighan, Rewon Child, Aditya Ramesh, Daniel Ziegler, Jeffrey Wu, Clemens Winter, Chris Hesse, Mark Chen, Eric Sigler, Mateusz Litwin, Scott Gray, Benjamin Chess, Jack Clark, Christopher Berner, Sam McCandlish, Alec Radford, Ilya Sutskever, and Dario Amodei. 2020. Language models are few-shot learners. In *Advances in Neural Information Processing Systems*, volume 33, pages 1877–1901. Curran Associates, Inc.

Nicholas Carlini, Daphne Ippolito, Matthew Jagielski, Katherine Lee, Florian Tramer, and Chiyuan Zhang. 2022. Quantifying memorization across neural language models. arXiv.

Noam Chomsky. 1981. *Lectures on Government and Binding: The Pisa Lectures*. De Gruyter Mouton.

Wing-Yee Chow, Shevaun Lewis, and Colin Phillips. 2014. Immediate sensitivity to structural constraints in pronoun resolution. *Frontiers in Psychology*, 5:630.

Charles Clifton, Shelia M. Kennison, and Jason E. Albrecht. 1997. Reading the Words *Her, His, Him:* Implications for Parsing Principles Based on Frequency and on Structure. *Journal of Memory and Language*, 36(2):276–292.

Forrest Davis. 2022. *On the Limitations of Data: Mismatches between Neural Models of Language and Humans*. Ph.D. thesis, Cornell University.

Forrest Davis and Marten van Schijndel. 2020. Discourse structure interacts with reference but not syntax in neural language models. In *Proceedings of the 24th Conference on Computational Natural Language Learning*, pages 396–407, Online. Association for Computational Linguistics.

Forrest Davis and Marten van Schijndel. 2021. Uncovering constraint-based behavior in neural models via targeted fine-tuning. In *Proceedings of the 59th Annual Meeting of the Association for Computational Linguistics and the 11th International Joint Conference on Natural Language Processing (Volume 1: Long Papers)*, pages 1159–1171, Online. Association for Computational Linguistics.

Allyson Ettinger, Ahmed Elgohary, and Philip Resnik. 2016. Probing for semantic evidence of composition by means of simple classification tasks. In *Proceedings of the 1st Workshop on Evaluating Vector-Space Representations for NLP*, pages 134–139, Berlin, Germany. Association for Computational Linguistics.

Leo Gao, Stella Biderman, Sid Black, Laurence Golding, Travis Hoppe, Charles Foster, Jason Phang, Horace He, Anish Thite, Noa Nabeshima, et al. 2020. The Pile: An 800GB Dataset of Diverse Text for Language Modeling. *arXiv*.

Kristina Gulordava, Piotr Bojanowski, Edouard Grave, Tal Linzen, and Marco Baroni. 2018. Colorless Green Recurrent Networks Dream Hierarchically. In *Proceedings of the 2018 Conference of the North American Chapter of the Association for Computational Linguistics: Human Language Technologies, Volume 1 (Long Papers)*, pages 1195–1205, New Orleans, Louisiana. Association for Computational Linguistics.

John Hale. 2001. A Probabilistic Earley Parser as a Psycholinguistic Model. In *Second Meeting of the North American Chapter of the Association for Computational Linguistics*.

Joshua K. Hartshorne. 2014. What Is Implicit Causality? *Language, Cognition and Neuroscience*, 29(7):804–824.

Jennifer Hu, Sherry Yong Chen, and Roger Levy. 2020. A Closer Look at the Performance of Neural Language Models on Reflexive Anaphor Licensing . In *Proceedings of the Society for Computation in Linguistics 2020*, pages 323–333, New York, New York. Association for Computational Linguistics.

Jaap Jumelet, Milica Denic, Jakub Szymanik, Dieuwke Hupkes, and Shane Steinert-Threlkeld. 2021. Language Models Use Monotonicity to Assess NPI Licensing. In *Findings of the Association for Computational Linguistics: ACL-IJCNLP 2021*, pages 4958–4969, Online. Association for Computational Linguistics.

Jared Kaplan, Sam McCandlish, Tom Henighan, Tom B. Brown, Benjamin Chess, Rewon Child, Scott Gray, Alec Radford, Jeffrey Wu, and Dario Amodei. 2020. Scaling Laws for Neural Language Models. *arXiv*.

Yova Kementchedjhieva, Mark Anderson, and Anders Søgaard. 2021. John praised Mary because _he_? Implicit Causality Bias and Its Interaction with Explicit Cues in LMs. In *Findings of the Association for Computational Linguistics: ACL-IJCNLP 2021*, pages 4859–4871, Online. Association for Computational Linguistics.

S Kennison. 2003. Comprehending the pronouns her, him, and his: Implications for theories of referential processing. *Journal of Memory and Language*, 49(3):335–352.

Dave Kush and Brian Dillon. 2021. Principle B constrains the processing of cataphora: Evidence for syntactic and discourse predictions. *Journal of Memory and Language*, 120:104254.

Dave Kush and Colin Phillips. 2014. Local anaphor licensing in an SOV language: Implications for retrieval strategies. *Frontiers in Psychology*, 5:1252.

Alexandra Kuznetsova, Per B. Brockhoff, and Rune H.B. Christensen. 2017. lmerTest Package: Tests in Linear Mixed Effects Models. *Journal of Statistical Software*, 82(13):1–26.

Roger Levy. 2008. Expectation-based syntactic comprehension. *Cognition*, 106(3):1126–1177.

Tal Linzen, Emmanuel Dupoux, and Yoav Goldberg. 2016. Assessing the Ability of LSTMs to Learn Syntax-Sensitive Dependencies. *Transactions of the Association for Computational Linguistics*, 4(0):521–535.

Rebecca Marvin and Tal Linzen. 2018. Targeted Syntactic Evaluation of Language Models. In *Proceedings of the 2018 Conference on Empirical Methods in Natural Language Processing*, pages 1192–1202, Brussels, Belgium. Association for Computational Linguistics.

R. Thomas McCoy, Paul Smolensky, Tal Linzen, Jianfeng Gao, and Asli Celikyilmaz. 2021. How much do language models copy from their training data? evaluating linguistic novelty in text generation using raven.

Kanishka Misra, Allyson Ettinger, and Julia Rayz. 2020. Exploring BERT's Sensitivity to Lexical Cues using Tests from Semantic Priming. In *Findings of the Association for Computational Linguistics: EMNLP 2020*, pages 4625–4635, Online. Association for Computational Linguistics.

Jeffrey J Mitchell, Nina Kazanina, Conor J Houghton, and Jeffrey S Bowers. 2019. Do LSTMs know about Principle C? In *Proceedings of the 2019 Conference on Cognitive Computational Neuroscience*.

Janet Lee Nicol. 1988. *Coreference Processing during Sentence Comprehension*. Thesis, Massachusetts Institute of Technology.

Dario Paape and Shravan Vasishth. 2022. Estimating the true cost of garden-pathing: A computational model of latent cognitive processes. Preprint, PsyArXiv.

Ludovica Pannitto and Aurélie Herbelot. 2020. Recurrent babbling: Evaluating the acquisition of grammar from limited input data. In *Proceedings of the 24th Conference on Computational Natural Language Learning*, pages 165–176, Online. Association for Computational Linguistics.

Alec Radford, Jeffrey Wu, Rewon Child, David Luan, Dario Amodei, and Ilya Sutskever. 2019. Language Models are Unsupervised Multitask Learners.

Chiara Reali, Yulia Esaulova, Anton Öttl, and Lisa von Stockhausen. 2015. Role descriptions induce gender mismatch effects in eye movements during reading. *Frontiers in Psychology*, 6.

Tanya Reinhart and Eric Reuland. 1993. Reflexivity. *Linguistic Inquiry*, 24(4):657–720.

Hannah Rohde and Andrew Kehler. 2014. Grammatical and information-structural influences on pronoun production. *Language, Cognition and Neuroscience*, 29(8):912–927.

Hannah Rohde, Andrew Kehler, and Jeffrey L Elman. 2006. Event Structure and Discourse Coherence Biases in Pronoun Interpretation. In *28th Annual Conference of the Cognitive Science Society*, page 6.

Sebastian Schuster, Yuxing Chen, and Judith Degen. 2020. Harnessing the linguistic signal to predict scalar inferences. In *Proceedings of the 58th Annual Meeting of the Association for Computational Linguistics*, pages 5387–5403, Online. Association for Computational Linguistics.

Nathaniel J. Smith and Roger Levy. 2013. The effect of word predictability on reading time is logarithmic. *Cognition*, 128(3):302–319.

Ionut-Teodor Sorodoc, Kristina Gulordava, and Gemma Boleda. 2020. Probing for Referential Information in Language Models. In *Proceedings of the 58th Annual Meeting of the Association for Computational Linguistics*, pages 4177–4189, Online. Association for Computational Linguistics.

Patrick Sturt. 2003. The time-course of the application of binding constraints in reference resolution. *Journal of Memory and Language*, 48(3):542–562.

Shiva Upadhye, Leon Bergen, and Andrew Kehler. 2020. Predicting Reference: What do Language Models Learn about Discourse Models? In *Proceedings of the 2020 Conference on Empirical Methods in Natural Language Processing (EMNLP)*, pages 977–982, Online. Association for Computational Linguistics.

Roger P.G. van Gompel and Simon P. Liversedge. 2003. The Influence of Morphological Information on Cataphoric Pronoun Assignment. *Journal of Experimental Psychology. Learning, Memory & Cognition*, 29(1):128–139.

Marten van Schijndel and Tal Linzen. 2021. Single-Stage Prediction Models Do Not Explain the Magnitude of Syntactic Disambiguation Difficulty . *Cognitive Science*, 45(6).

Elena Voita and Ivan Titov. 2020. Information-Theoretic Probing with Minimum Description Length. In *Proceedings of the 2020 Conference on Empirical Methods in Natural Language Processing*, pages 183–196, Online. Association for Computational Linguistics.

Ben Wang and Aran Komatsuzaki. 2021. GPT-J-6B: A 6 Billion Parameter Autoregressive Language Model.

Alex Warstadt, Yu Cao, Ioana Grosu, Wei Peng, Hagen Blix, Yining Nie, Anna Alsop, Shikha Bordia, Haokun Liu, Alicia Parrish, Sheng-Fu Wang, Jason Phang, Anhad Mohananey, Phu Mon Htut, Paloma Jeretic, and Samuel R. Bowman. 2019. Investigating BERT's Knowledge of Language: Five Analysis Methods with NPIs. In *Proceedings of the 2019 Conference on Empirical Methods in Natural Language Processing and the 9th International Joint Conference on Natural Language Processing (EMNLP-IJCNLP)*, pages 2877–2887, Hong Kong, China. Association for Computational Linguistics.

Alex Warstadt, Alicia Parrish, Haokun Liu, Anhad Mohananey, Wei Peng, Sheng-Fu Wang, and Samuel R. Bowman. 2020. BLiMP: The Benchmark of Linguistic Minimal Pairs for English. *Transactions of the Association for Computational Linguistics*, 8:377–392.

Jason Wei, Yi Tay, Rishi Bommasani, Colin Raffel, Barret Zoph, Sebastian Borgeaud, Dani Yogatama, Maarten Bosma, Denny Zhou, Donald Metzler, Ed H. Chi, Tatsunori Hashimoto, Oriol Vinyals, Percy Liang, Jeff Dean, and William Fedus. 2022. Emergent Abilities of Large Language Models. *arXiv*.

Ethan Wilcox, Richard Futrell, and Roger Levy. 2021a. Using Computational Models to Test Syntactic Learnability. *LingBuzz*.

Ethan Wilcox, Roger Levy, and Richard Futrell. 2019. Hierarchical Representation in Neural Language Models: Suppression and Recovery of Expectations. In *Proceedings of the 2019 ACL Workshop BlackboxNLP: Analyzing and Interpreting Neural Networks for NLP*, pages 181–190, Florence, Italy. Association for Computational Linguistics.

Ethan Wilcox, Pranali Vani, and Roger Levy. 2021b. A Targeted Assessment of Incremental Processing in Neural Language Models and Humans. In *Proceedings of the 59th Annual Meeting of the Association for Computational Linguistics and the 11th International Joint Conference on Natural Language Processing (Volume 1: Long Papers)*, pages 939–952, Online. Association for Computational Linguistics.

Thomas Wolf, Lysandre Debut, Victor Sanh, Julien Chaumond, Clement Delangue, Anthony Moi, Pierric Cistac, Tim Rault, Remi Louf, Morgan Funtowicz, Joe Davison, Sam Shleifer, Patrick von Platen, Clara Ma, Yacine Jernite, Julien Plu, Canwen Xu, Teven Le Scao, Sylvain Gugger, Mariama Drame, Quentin Lhoest, and Alexander Rush. 2020. Transformers: State-of-the-Art Natural Language Processing. In *Proceedings of the 2020 Conference on Empirical Methods in Natural Language Processing: System Demonstrations*, pages 38–45, Online. Association for Computational Linguistics.

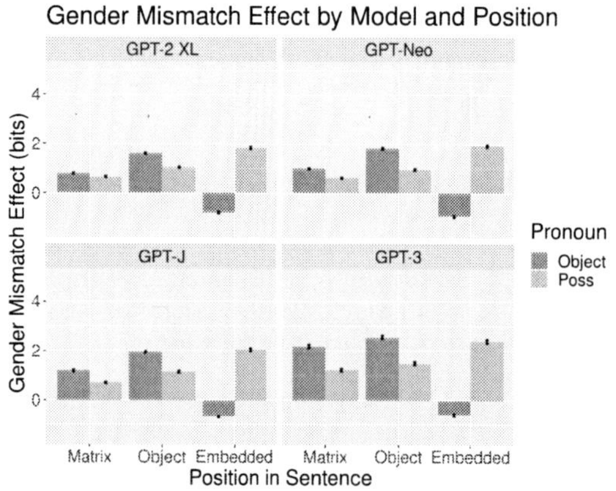

Figure 7: GMME for object pronoun (*him*) and possessive pronoun (*his*) for each neural model by whether i) the matrix subject, ii) the matrix object, or iii) the embedded subject agrees in gender (e.g., (*Bill|Hannah*) *told* (*Aaron|Amy*) that (*Mark|Sue*) *hates him*). Error bars are 95% confidence intervals.

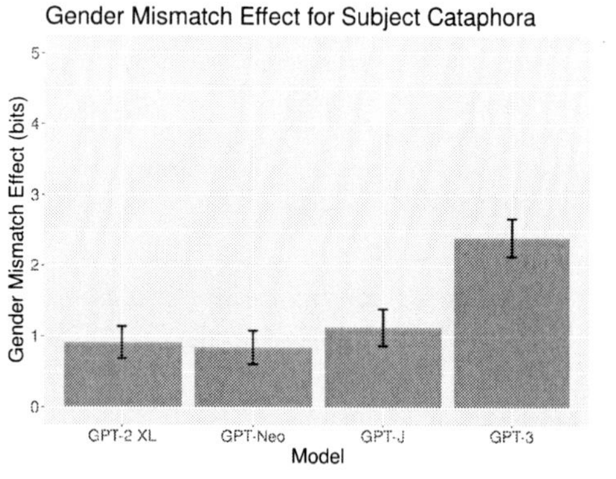

Figure 8: GMME for subject following a cataphoric subject pronoun, (e.g., *he*), for each neural model (e.g., *While he was working, (Bill|Sue)...*). Stimuli adapted from van Gompel and Liversedge (2003). Error bars are 95% confidence intervals.

A Appendix

Additional Figures

Results for the 3NP case are given in Figure 7. For the possessive pronoun *his*, we found a positive GMME for all positions, suggesting that models expected *his* to match the gender of any of the preceding antecedents. For the object pronoun *him*, a positive GMME was obtained when grammatically available antecedents (i.e. those not blocked by Principle B) mismatched in gender. A negative GMME was found for the grammatically unavailable antecedent (i.e. the embedded subject), suggesting models expected *him* to mismatch with antecedents in that structural position.

Results for subject cataphora are given in Figure 8. All models exhibited a positive GMME when the subject mismatched in gender with the cataphoric subject pronoun, suggesting that models use cataphoric subject prnouns to constrain their predictions of upcoming subjects.

Limitations

There are three main limitations: 1) whether models truly "interpret" the correct coreference relations, 2) our reliance on stereotypical gender, 3) we only investigated English.

The first was noted in Section 2. It applies to any investigation of coreference in neural models, including existing investigations of Principle A (e.g., Warstadt et al., 2020). While probing has been used to investigate model representations (e.g., Ettinger et al., 2016; Voita and Titov, 2020), which may be suggestive of something like co-indexation, we do not take models to be interpreting language, that is comprehending the meaning of sentences in a human-like fashion (see the discussion in Bender and Koller, 2020). At present, techniques are limited, and thus, we set aside the issue of whether models interpret pronouns in a human-like fashion, and instead, focus on comparing model behavior to humans, which has proved fruitful in other domains (e.g., Linzen et al., 2016). Future work might consider analyses of the attention mechanisms to dig deeper into what information models are using.

The second limitation has been noted in related literature (e.g., Warstadt et al., 2020). We rely on stereotypical associations between nouns and pronouns, which does not cleanly map on to the real world (e.g., for example, we do not consider singular *they*). In using the vocabulary items already actively manipulated in the literature, we can, nonetheless, make meaningful comparisons to existing work.

The final limitations is driven, primarily, by the existing resources in the field. There exist many pre-trained models for English, and less so for other languages (for discussion of the broader English bias in NLP, see Bender, 2009). Additional, the bulk of psycholinguistic work is focused on English, making comparisons between neural models and humans beyond English, challenging. Thus, the generalizability of the present study is limited to just those pronominal systems that are English-like.

Parsing as Deduction Revisited: Using an Automatic Theorem Prover to Solve an SMT Model of a Minimalist Parser

Sagar Indurkhya
Massachusetts Institute of Technology
32 Vassar St.
Cambridge, MA 02139
indurks@mit.edu

Abstract

We introduce a constraint-based parser for Minimalist Grammars (MG), implemented as a working computer program, that falls within the long established "Parsing as Deduction" framework. The parser takes as input an MG lexicon and a (partially specified) pairing of sound with meaning – i.e. a word sequence paired with a semantic representation – and, using an axiomatized logic, declaratively deduces syntactic derivations (i.e. parse trees) that comport with the specified interface conditions. The parser is built on the first axiomatization of MGs to use Satisfiability Modulo Theories (SMT), encoding in a constraint-based way the principles of minimalist syntax. The parser operates via a novel solution method: it assembles an SMT model of an MG derivation, translates the inputs into SMT formulae that constrain the model, and then solves the model using the Z3 SMT-solver, a high-performance automatic theorem prover; as the SMT-model has finite size (being bounded by the inputs), it is decidable and thus solvable in finite time. The output derivation is then recovered from the model solution. To demonstrate this, we run the parser on several representative inputs and examine how the output derivations differ when the inputs are partially vs. fully specified. We conclude by discussing the parser's extensibility and how a linguist can use it to automatically identify: (i) dependencies between input interface conditions and principles of syntax, and (ii) contradictions or redundancies between the model axioms encoding principles of syntax.

1 Introduction

Minimalist theories of syntax consider the *Human Language Faculty* (HLF) as a computational system capable of deriving from a finite lexicon and a single combinatorial operation, an unbounded set of hierarchical syntactic structures, pairing sounds (typically word sequences) with meaning representations (Chomsky, 1995). (In more technical language, the HLF pairs *Phonological Forms* [PF], where a PF is an encoding of information relevant to how a brain-internal structured expression gets pronounced, signed, etc, with *Logical Forms* [LF], where an LF is a structured semantic representation, e.g. predicate-argument structure.) This study introduces a novel computational model for the HLF, implemented as a working computer program,[1] that takes the form of a constraint-based parser for Minimalist Grammars (MG), grounded in the (first) axiomatization of minimalist syntax using Satisfiability Modulo Theories (SMT).[2] Working within the *"Parsing as Deduction"* framework (Pereira and Warren, 1983), the parser is a logic program that uses an automatic theorem prover to answer the question: *can a given lexicon yield a syntactic structure that encodes a given LF and/or PF?*

More specifically, the parser takes as input an MG lexicon and a (partial) specification of LF and PF interface conditions (i.e. constraints over the LF and PF encoded in a syntactic structure), and it outputs the set of MG derivations (i.e. syntactic structures) that the (input) lexicon can generate and that satisfy the (input) interface conditions. The parser operates by first constructing an SMT model of a lexicon and an SMT model of derivation, with the two models linked by shared free variables to form an SMT model of a minimalist parser. Next, the parser converts the inputs into constraints, expressed as SMT-formulae, that augment the SMT model and serve to constrain the space of model solutions. Finally, the parser obtains its output by using the Z3 SMT-solver,[3] a (modern) high-performance automatic theorem

[1]The program's source code is available at https://github.com/indurks/mgsmt.

[2]SMT is a propositional logic that may be extended with background theories – e.g. the theories of uninterpreted functions, bit-vectors and arithmetic (Dutertre and de Moura, 2006; Ranise and Tinelli, 2006; Nieuwenhuis and Oliveras, 2006; Nieuwenhuis et al., 2006; Moura and Bjørner, 2009).

[3]See (Moura and Bjørner, 2008; Bjørner, 2011).

Proceedings of the 26th Conference on Computational Natural Language Learning (CoNLL), pages 157 - 175
December 7-8, 2022 ©2022 Association for Computational Linguistics

prover, to check whether the SMT model is satisfiable – if it is, the SMT-solver enumerates valid model-interpretations from which the parser recovers the (output) set of minimalist derivations.

Notably, this model of HLF is declarative, and so encompasses both semantic parsing and natural language generation. E.g. one can use the parser to generate language by: (i) inputting a lexicon and LF constraints; (ii) ordering the parser to "solve for syntax" and recover a derivation from the model-solution; and (iii) obtaining the (output) generated PF from the recovered derivation. (Here the inputs are known quantities and the derivation is an unknown quantity being solved for.) Moreover, our model for HLF can be used to run experiments in which the input interface conditions are *partially* specified and the SMT-solver is instructed to identify dependencies between the principles of syntax (encoded in the parser) and the features in the input lexicon – in this way, one can determine whether (and how) the syntactic principles and the lexicon do not adequately constrain a derivation to compensate for the absent (LF or PF) interface conditions.

The remainder of this study is organized as follows. First, §2 reviews key principles of minimalist syntax and how they are modeled using MGs. Next, §3 reviews related prior work within the *Parsing as Deduction* framework, which this study seeks to extend, and that motivates our approach. Then, §4, §5 and §6 present the three key contributions of this study: §4 details the deductive parsing procedure, showing how the Z3 SMT-solver can be used to identify satisfiable interpretations of an SMT model of a minimalist parser; §5 details the SMT model of the minimalist parser, its underlying axiomatization of minimalist syntax, and how the model is constrained by user specified inputs; §6 details application of the parser to a representative set of example inputs and analyzes the output derivations, showing how the parser functions even when the input interface conditions are only partially specified. Finally, §7 discusses how: (i) the SMT model of the parser may be extended, and (ii) the parser can help linguists identify dependencies and contradictions between the model axioms encoding principles of syntax and the logical constraints derived from the input interface conditions.

2 Background: Minimalist Grammars

We opted to model minimalist syntax using the Minimalist Grammar (MG) formalism (Stabler, 1996) because MGs have been extensively characterized formally and appear to be sufficiently expressive for modeling the syntactic structures prescribed by contemporary theories of minimalist syntax.[4] The MG formalism (and minimalist syntax more generally) centers on: (i) a lexicon consisting of a finite set of lexical items (i.e. syntactic atoms), each pairing a word with a finite sequence of syntactic features, and (ii) *Merge*, a recursive, binary structure-building operation. Syntactic structures are derived from a multi-set of lexical items via repeated application of *Merge*, which has two (logically-disjoint) sub-cases, *external merge* (EM) and *internal merge* (IM),[5] that serve to model two basic facts of natural language, *combination* and *displacement* (respectively).[6]

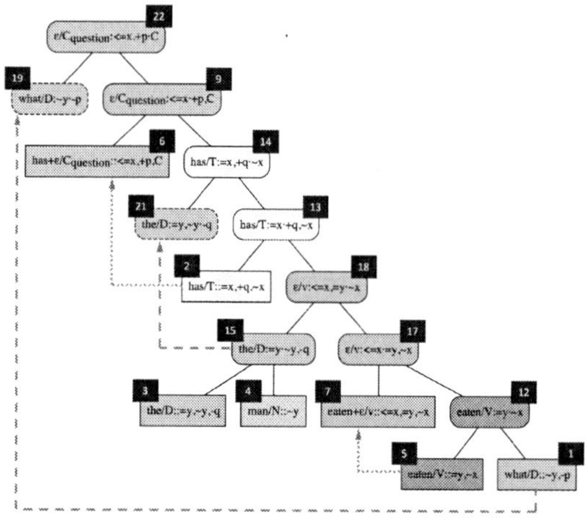

Figure 1: The parser outputs an MG derivation of *"What has the man eaten?"* that satisfies the LF & PF interface conditions in I_1 (of Table 2). The derivation was recovered from the model interpretation in Table 3, and each node is labeled with the index of a row in Table 3. The depicted structure is a multi-dominance tree, with nodes $\{1, 5, 12, 7, 17, 3, 4, 15, 18, 2, 13, 14, 6, 9, 22\}$ making up the derivation tree from which this multi-dominance tree was derived. Lexical and derived nodes are denoted by regular and rounded rectangles respectively. Constituents with the same head have the same color. Dashed and dotted arrows indicate phrasal and head movement respectively; a dashed border indicates that a node is the target of phrasal-movement, with the (raised) lower structure being copied to the target position.

[4]See (Michaelis, 1998; Michaelis et al., 2000; Michaelis, 2001; Graf, 2011, 2013; Kobele, 2011).

[5]*EM* merges two disjoint structures, whereas *IM* merges a structure with one of its sub-structures.

[6]Combination forms syntactic structures by (recursively) pairing separate structures; it is used to associate predicates with their arguments (i.e. the assignment of thematic roles like "Agent" and "Patient," also known as θ-roles). Displace-

To illustrate the MG formalism, let us see how the MG derivation (i.e. syntactic structure) for the sentence *"What has the man eaten?"*, shown in Fig. 1, is built bottom-up using the lexical items listed in Table 1. First, the lexical items for the determiner *"the"* and the nominal *"man"* are combined, via the application of external merge, to form the determiner phrase *"the man"*; note that this instance of *constituent selection* is allowed because the term *"the"* has a *selector* feature, $=y$, that matches the *selectee* feature, $\sim y$, on the term *"man"*.[7] Then, the lexical items for the (lexical) verb *"eaten"* is first (externally) merged with its complement, the (internal) argument *"what"* to form a VP, which is then (externally) merged with a covert light-verb, ϵ/v, with the resulting vP then merged with the external argument, *"the man"*, to form a (double) VP-shell structure in accordance with the Hale-Keyser model of predicate-argument structure (Hale and Keyser, 1993, 2002). Next, the VP-shell structure is merged with a tense marker, the auxiliary verb *"has"*, to form a TP. After this, per the *VP Internal Subject Hypothesis* (Radford, 2009), the internal argument, *"the man"* is moved, via application of *internal merge*, from its initial location (within the VP-shell) to the subject-position of the TP; note that this instance of movement is licensed by the *licensor* feature, $+q$, on *"has"* matching the *licensee* feature, $-q$, on *"the man"*. The TP is then (externally) merged with a (covert) complementizer, ϵ/C, to form a CP.[8] Finally, the internal argument *"what"* is raised (via internal merge) from the VP-shell to the specifier position of the CP, at which point the derivation is complete.[9]

In summary, to parse a sentence, a multi-set of lexical items is selected from the lexicon and (recursively) *merged* together to yield a derivation in which the terminal expression has only the special feature C remaining (because all of the selectional and licensing features have been consumed); if the ordering of the phonological forms in the resulting structure aligns with the order of the words in the sentence being parsed,[10] then the structure is considered to be a valid parse of the sentence.[11]

3 Related Work: Parsing as Deduction

We have developed an MG parser within the *Parsing as Deduction* framework, which was first described by Pereira and Warren (1983), who showed how an axiomatization of a context-free grammar could be combined with a logical deduction engine to formulate a chart parser as a logic program. As Pereira notes, key advantages of this framework include: (i) a connection between the deductions that yield a syntactic structure and the inferences needed to extract a semantic interpretation from said structure; (ii) the ability to handle filler-gap dependencies without altering the basic design of a chart parser. The *Parsing as Deduction* framework has since been employed to construct parsers for a variety of grammatical formalisms, including lexicalized context-free grammars, tree adjoining grammars, combinatory categorical grammars, and dependency grammars.[12] Notably, this framework has been used to develop parsers that model Government and Binding (GB) theory (a predecessor of minimalist syntax) by encoding principles of syntax within a system of axioms that mirrors the modular structure of GB theory (Chomsky, 1981; Johnson, 1989; Fong, 1991).

Normally, these parsers employ Prolog, the defacto language for Constraint Logic Programming (CLP).[13] However, we leverage recent advances in the performance of automated theorem provers for SMT, which enhances CLP by enabling us to focus entirely on formulating (declarative) model axioms while the computer is free to decide how best to deduce a model solution (De Moura and Bjørner,

ment, driven by syntactic movement, enables a phrase to be interpreted at both its (final) surfaced position as well as other positions within a syntactic structure – e.g., given the expression *"You, I love."*, *"You"* is the object of *"love"* and normally appears in *Object* position, but here it is displaced to the front of the sentence (where it is pronounced).

[7] Selector, selectee, licensor and licensee features are designated by a prefixed $=$, $\sim$, $+$, and $-$ respectively.

[8] The *extended projection*, $C{-}T{-}v{-}V$, forms the spine of each clause (Grimshaw, 2005; Adger and Svenonius, 2011).

[9] N.b. *head-movement* – i.e. the incorporation of a lower (lexical) head into the head it merges with – is applied when the completed derivation is sent to the PF-interface for externalization. Head-movement occurs twice in this derivation: (i) the V-to-v head-movement utilized in the Hale-Keyser model of predicate-argument structure; (ii) the T-to-C head-movement utilized in raising the auxiliary verb (as when forming a polar-interrogative from a declarative).

[10] E.g. using Specifier-Head-Complement linearization to model *Subject-Verb-Object* (SVO) ordering (Kayne, 1994).

[11] See Appendix-B for further commentary on MGs, including a presentation of an algebraic formulation of MGs based on (Stabler and Keenan, 2003).

[12] See (Shieber et al., 1995; Duchier, 1999; Tang and Mooney, 2001; Debusmann et al., 2004; Estratat and Henocque, 2004; Duchier et al., 2010; Lierler and Schüller, 2012; Schüller, 2013). See (Schabes and Waters, 1993; Joshi and Schabes, 1997; Steedman and Baldridge, 2011) for details of these grammatical formalisms.

[13] See (Jaffar and Lassez, 1987; Apt, 1990; Jaffar and Maher, 1994; Koller and Niehren, 2002).

1. $\epsilon/C_{Ques.} :: <=x, +p, C$	19. $he :: \sim y, -q$
2. $has :: =x, +q, \sim x$	20. $resigned :: \sim x$
3. $the :: =y, \sim y, -q$	21. $known :: =y, \sim x$
4. $man :: \sim y$	22. $everyone :: \sim y, -q, -p$
5. $\epsilon/v :: <=x, =y, \sim x$	23. $who :: =x, +p, \sim y$
6. $eaten :: =y, \sim x$	24. $loved :: =y, \sim x$
7. $what :: \sim y, -p$	25. $\epsilon/C_{Decl.} :: =x, C$
8. $\epsilon/v :: <=x, \sim x$	26. $knows :: =y, \sim x$
9. $\epsilon/C_{Ques.} :: <=x, C$	27. $john :: \sim y, -q$
10. $was :: =x, +q, \sim x$	28. $given :: =y, \sim x$
11. $she :: \sim y, -q$	29. $\epsilon/T :: =x, +q, \sim x$
12. $given :: =y, =y, \sim x$	30. $money :: \sim y, -q, -p$
13. $money :: \sim y$	31. $that :: =x, +p, \sim y$
14. $will :: =x, +q, \sim x$	32. $stolen :: =y, \sim x$
15. $who :: \sim y, -q, -p$	33. $fears :: =y, \sim x$
16. $her :: \sim y$	34. $money :: \sim y, -q$
17. $tell :: =y, =y, \sim x$	35. $\epsilon/C_{Ques.} :: =x, +p, C$
18. $that :: =x, \sim y$	36. $a :: =y, \sim y, -q$

Table 1: An MG lexicon that the parser may take as input. Each lexical item consists of: (i) a phonological form that is either overt or covert (ϵ); (ii) (optional) a categorical feature (e.g. entries 1 & 5); (iii) a sequence of syntactic features. The lexicon includes entries for auxiliary verbs (e.g. 2, 10 & 14), determiners (e.g. 3), nominals (e.g. 4, 11, 22, 27 & 30), tense markers (e.g. 2, 14, & 29), complementizers (e.g. 1, 9, 18 & 25), relative pronouns (e.g. 23), Wh-words (e.g. 7 & 15), intransitive verbs (e.g. 20), transitive verbs (e.g. 6, 26 & 32), and ditransitive verbs (e.g. 12 & 17).

2011). Hence, we extend prior work within the *Parsing as Deduction* framework by: (i) developing a (declarative) constraint-based *minimalist* parser, thereby advancing (linguistically) beyond earlier *GB*-based parsers; (ii) formulating an MG parser as a finite (and thus decidable) SMT-model that is solved using an SMT-solver (instead of Prolog).[14]

4 The Parsing Procedure

This section details the parsing procedure and illustrates it with a worked out example.

INPUT. The procedure takes as input: (i) an MG lexicon, $\mathcal{L}$; (ii) a pairing of LF and PF interface conditions, I, to be parsed; (iii) parameters, p, bounding the size of the SMT model (to be built).

INITIALIZATION. The procedure initializes the SMT-solver with an empty stack of constraints, $\mathcal{S}$.

CONSTRUCTING THE SMT MODEL. The SMT model of the parser is constructed as follows. First, the procedure instantiates the SMT model of the lexicon (detailed in §5) and constrains it with the input lexicon – this is carried out by:

(a) initializing an SMT model of a lexicon, $m_{\mathcal{L}}$, with size bound by p, and pushing $m_{\mathcal{L}}$ onto $\mathcal{S}$;

(b) constructing an SMT-formula, c_l, that restricts interpretations (i.e. model solutions) of $m_{\mathcal{L}}$ to align with $\mathcal{L}$, and then pushing c_l onto $\mathcal{S}$;

Next, the procedure instantiates an SMT model of a derivation (detailed in §5) and then constrains it with the (input) interface conditions – this involves:

(a) initializing an SMT model of a derivation, m_d, with size bound by p, and pushing m_d onto $\mathcal{S}$;

(b) translating I into an SMT-formula, c_I, that constrains m_d (detailed in §5) such that any derivation recovered from an interpretation of m_d must respect I, and pushing c_I onto $\mathcal{S}$.

Finally, the procedure "connects" the SMT model of the derivation to the SMT model of the lexicon – this is achieved by first creating an SMT-formula, m_b, that connects m_d with m_l by constraining interpretations of the free variables that appear in both m_d and m_l, and then pushing m_b onto the $\mathcal{S}$.

CHECKING THE SMT MODEL. The procedure uses the SMT-solver's model-checking routine (i.e. decision procedure) to determine whether there exists a satisfiable interpretation of the model (i.e. the conjunction of the SMT-formulae in $\mathcal{S}$) – if one exists, the procedure recovers it from the solver, and then (automatically) reconstructs an MG derivation from the (recovered) model interpretation. The procedure then pushes onto $\mathcal{S}$ a constraint (i.e. an SMT-formula) that prohibits the interpretation of m_d from being equivalent to any previously recovered (satisfiable) model interpretations;[15] this model-checking process is then run again to try and recover a (new) alternative MG derivation – this process is repeated until the solver cannot identify a (new) satisfiable model interpretation (because all model-solutions have already been identified).

OUTPUT. The procedure outputs the set of MG derivations that were reconstructed from the recovered (satisfiable) model interpretations – each (output) derivation accords with the (input) interface conditions, I, and can be generated from the (input) lexicon, $\mathcal{L}$.

Finally, we illustrate the parsing procedure with a worked out example. Consider the procedure taking as input the lexicon in Table 1 and the interface conditions (for the sentence *"What has the man eaten?"*) listed in entry I_1 of Table 2: after constructing the SMT model and constraining it with the input lexicon and interface conditions (detailed

[14]See (Harkema, 2001; Niyogi and Berwick, 2005; Stanojević, 2016; Torr et al., 2019) for earlier MG (chart) parsers.

[15]This further constrains the SMT model so that the solver cannot yield a model interpretation that encodes an MG derivation that the parser has already identified.

in §5), the procedure invokes the SMT-solver's model-checking (i.e. decision) routine to obtain the satisfiable model-interpretation presented in Table 3 (see also Appendix-Table 4); the procedure then recovers the output derivation shown in Fig. 1, which accords with I_1, from the satisfiable model-interpretation.

5 Specification of the SMT Model

This section details the SMT models of the MG derivation and MG lexicon - these models make up the heart of the parser introduced in this study.[16] These models consist of: (i) uninterpreted (i.e. free) finite sorts that represent model-objects such as words, syntactic features, categories, nodes in a derivation tree, etc; (ii) uninterpreted (free) functions that establish relationships between model-objects by mapping members of one or more sorts to another sort; (iii) model axioms – i.e. SMT-formulae – that constrain the valuation an SMT-solver may assign to each uninterpreted function.[17] (See Fig. 2 for a summary of the sorts and functions that make up the model.) Crucially, since the model of the parser has finite size (being bounded by the input parameter, p), we can explicitly quantify all of the SMT formulae in the model, *thereby yielding a decidable model that is solvable in finite time.*

We turn first to the **SMT model of the lexicon**. When constructing this model, the parsing procedure scans the input lexicon and instantiates several finite sorts: Σ, that models the set of PFs; $\mathbb{F}$, that models the set of feature-labels (e.g. $\{x, y, p, q\}$); and the *lexicon node sort*, Ω, that models the syntactic features appearing in the input lexicon.[18] The lexicon node sort is organized into disjoint subsets referred to as ***lexicon node sequences***, with each subset corresponding to one of the distinct lexical feature sequences appearing in the input lexicon.[19] Among the uninterpreted functions in the lexicon model, one plays an especially critical role: the successor function, ψ, which maps $a \in \Omega$ to $b \in \Omega$, where a corresponds to a node within a lexicon node sequence, and b corresponds to the subsequent node in that same lexicon node sequence;[20] the valuation of ψ is hard-coded by the parsing algorithm after Ω has been divided into lexicon node sequences.[21] The binary (uninterpreted) predicate, Δ_Ω, associates each lexical feature sequence with one or more (overt or covert) PFs, and these associations are hard-coded by the parsing procedure.[22] (E.g. Fig. 3 shows a lexicon node sequence and the lexical feature sequence it models.)

Next we turn to the **SMT model of the derivation**, which is composed of a finite sort, $\mathbb{N}$, that models the nodes in the derivation. The derivation takes the form of a *multi-dominance tree*[23] that is formed by augmenting the derivation tree with additional edges corresponding to the movement of phrases via internal merge (see Fig. 1). Members of $\mathbb{N}$ are sub-divided into ***derivation node sequences***, with each sequence corresponding to the projection of a lexical head within the derivation;[24] an important exception to this is a single member of $\mathbb{N}$, $\bot$, that serves as a *null-value* target for uninterpreted functions. The model's uninterpretable functions include:

(a) A unary function, p, that maps each node in a derivation node sequence to its successor node (in that sequence).
(b) A unary function, h, that maps each $x \in \mathbb{N}$ to the head (i.e. beginning) of the derivation node sequence to which x belongs; a derivation node $x \in \mathbb{N}$ is a head if and only if $h(h(x)) = h(x)$.
(c) A binary function, $\mathcal{M}$, that models *Merge*: given $x, y \in \mathbb{N}$, $\mathcal{M}(x, y)$ is the product of

[16]A complete, formal definition of these SMT models, including all model axioms, may be found in Ch. 2 of (Indurkhya, 2021a); see Appendix A for notes on reproducibility.

[17]All model axioms are written using propositional logic extended with (quantifier-free) theories of: (i) uninterpreted functions, (ii) Pseudo-Boolean constraints, and (iii) arithmetic.

[18]N.b. the sorts modeling the (fixed) sets of syntactic categories (e.g. N or V) and feature-types (e.g. $+$ or $=$) are pre-defined and do not depend on the input lexicon.

[19]E.g. the input lexicon in Table 1 has 29 distinct PFs, 4 distinct feature-labels, and 18 distinct lexical feature sequence, with each sequence having at most 3 features; therefore, the cardinality of the instantiated sorts Σ, $\mathbb{F}$ and Ω is 29, 4 and $18 \times 3 = 54$ (respectively).

[20]If a lexicon node $x \in \Omega$ corresponds to the terminal node in a lexicon node sequence, then $\psi(x) = x$.

[21]E.g. if, as in Fig. 3, $L_9, L_{14}, L_0, L_5 \in \Omega$ forms a lexicon node sequence that models the lexical feature sequence for entry 3 in Table 1, $[the :: =y, \sim y, -q]$, then the following constraint would be added to the SMT model of the lexicon: $(\psi(L_9){=}L_{14}) \wedge (\psi(L_{14}){=}L_0) \wedge (\psi(L_0){=}L_5)$.

[22]Encoding the SMT model of the lexicon with a representation that factors apart PFs and lexical feature sequences reduces the size of the model because lexical feature sequences are not duplicated, which in turn improves the performance of the SMT-solver. (E.g. in Table 1, the PFs for entries 24 and 28 will both map to the same lexicon node sequence.)

[23]Multi-dominance and derived trees are closely related (Kobele et al., 2007; Morawietz, 2008; Graf, 2013). Appendix-C details, and Appendix-Fig. 6 shows, how the *derivation node sequences* are organized so as to form a multi-dominance tree.

[24]*Derivation node sequences* are inspired by the closely related notion of "slices" (of a derivation tree) employed in Graf (2013). See Appendix-Fig. 6 for an illustration of how $\mathbb{N}$ is organized into derivation node sequences.

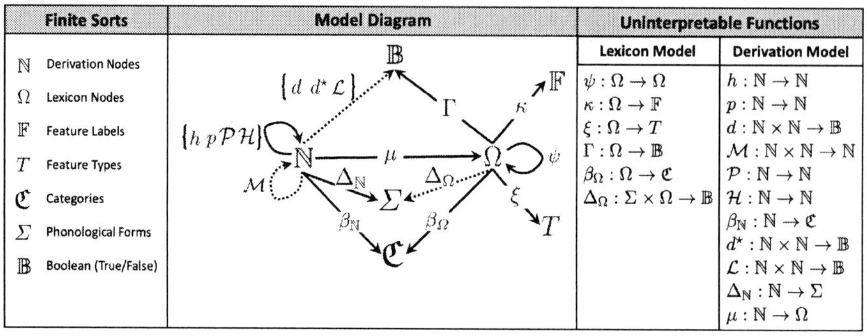

Figure 2: Arrangement of the uninterpreted functions and (finite) sorts that make up, and connect together, the SMT model of a derivation and the SMT model of a lexicon.

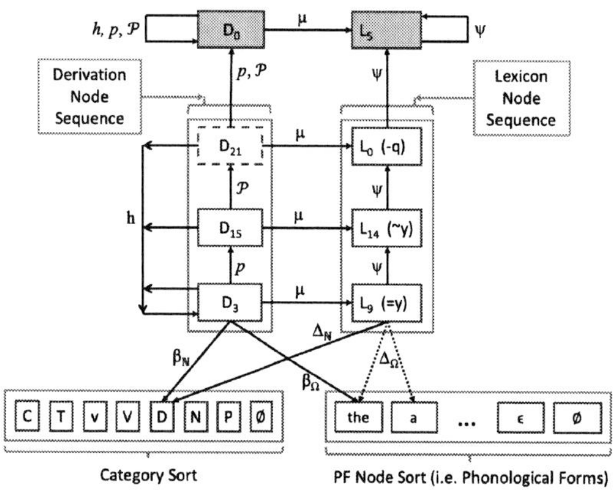

Figure 3: Model diagram showing how uninterpreted functions form commutative diagrams that connect the SMT model of the derivation to the SMT model of the lexicon – here they connect one of the *derivation node sequences* (from Fig. 1) to one of the *lexicon node sequences* (for entries 3 & 36 in Table 1). N.b. the lexicon node sequence maps to two PFs, and the derivation node sequence corresponds to one of those two PFs.

merging x with y.[25]

(d) A unary function, $\mathcal{P}$, that models the movement of phrases by mapping a node in the derivation tree to the location it is raised to.

(e) A unary function, $\mathcal{H}$, that models head-movement by mapping a lexical head to the lexical head that it incorporates with.

(f) Two binary predicates, d and $d^\star$, that encode the dominance relations making up the derivation (a multi-dominance tree), with d encoding dominance as imposed by p, and $d^\star$ encoding the dominance relations in the *derived tree* – i.e. the tree produced after all syntactic movement is completed (see Appendix-C for details).

[25]If x and y are not externally merged, then $\mathcal{M}(x, y) = \bot$; this illustrates one of the ways in which $\bot$ is utilized.

(g) A unary function, $\beta_{\mathbb{N}}$, that associates each term in the derivation with a category (in $\mathfrak{C}$).

(h) A binary function, $\mathcal{L}$, encoding (linear) precedence (in accordance with the *derived tree*).

We restrict (satisfiable) interpretations of the SMT model by constraining it with additional axioms that encode various principles of minimalist syntax,[26] including axioms requiring:

(a) $\forall x, y \in \mathbb{N}, \mathcal{M}(x, y) = \mathcal{M}(y, x)$ (symmetry).

(b) no self-merging: $\forall x \in \mathbb{N}, \mathcal{M}(x, x) = \bot$.

(c) no term is the target of multiple merges: $\forall x, y, z \in \mathbb{N}, z \neq y \rightarrow \mathcal{M}(x, y) \neq \mathcal{M}(x, z)$.

(d) every non-lexical (i.e. non-leaf) node in the derivation tree is in the range of $\mathcal{M}$.

(e) $\forall x \in \mathbb{N}, h(\mathcal{P}(x)) = h(x)$.

(f) $\forall x, y \in \mathbb{N}$, if x and y are lexical heads related by head-movement (i.e. $(h(x) = x) \wedge (h(y) = y) \wedge (\mathcal{H}(x) = y)$), then the maximal projection of x is merged with y (via EM) - i.e. $\exists z \in \mathbb{N}$ s.t. $(h(z) = x) \wedge d(z, x) \wedge (h(\mathcal{M}(\mathcal{H}(x), z)) = y)$.

(g) the root node of the derivation tree is a (maximal) projection of a *complementizer* head (C), and the functional heads in a clause are organized as an *extended projection* of the form $C \leftarrow T \leftarrow v \leftarrow V$ (Adger and Svenonius, 2011).

(h) if a phrase, $x \in \mathbb{N}$, undergoes IM with a (lower) phrase, $y \in \mathbb{N}$, so that $\mathcal{P}(y)$ is the sister of x (i.e. $\mathcal{M}(\mathcal{P}(x), y) \neq \bot$), then $\mathcal{M}(x, \mathcal{P}(y)) = p(x)$ and $h(\mathcal{M}(x, \mathcal{P}(y))) = h(x) \neq h(y)$.

Notably, the expressive power of SMT, particularly the composition of uninterpretable functions, allows the model to consist of a few dozen axioms, which we found to be manageable to reason about.

[26]E.g. the *Theory of Bare-Phrase Structure* (Chomsky, 1995), the *Inclusivess Principle* (Chomsky, 2001), the *No Tampering Condition* (Chomsky, 2005, 2013), the *Projection Principle* (Chomsky, 1986) and the *Principle of Economy of Derivation* (Collins, 2001).

Next the parsing procedure translates each of the (input) interface conditions (ICs) into SMT-formulae that constrain the SMT model of the derivation. LF ICs stipulating (subject-predicate) agreement and the assignment of θ-roles (i.e. semantic roles) to arguments are translated into model constraints (i.e. SMT-formulae) that require specific *local hierarchical relations* be established by *Merge*,[27] and the sentence type (i.e. declarative vs. interrogative) is translated into model constraints that dictate which type of complementizer, $C_{ques.}$ or $C_{decl.}$, heads the sentence. PF ICs are translated into constraints that require the *Subject-Verb-Object* (SVO) ordering of the derived tree, in which all phrasal-movement and head-movement has taken place, match the linear order of words in the input sentence.[28] Notably, the SMT-formulae encoding LF constraints are entirely separate from the SMT-formulae encoding PF constraints.

Finally, the SMT models of the lexicon and the derivation are connected by an uninterpreted function, μ, that maps each derivation node sequence to a lexicon node sequence, subject to the constraints: (i) $\mu \circ p = \psi \circ \mu$, which lines up each projection in the derivation with a lexical feature sequences (for a lexical entry) in the lexicon; (ii) $\beta_\Omega \circ \mu = \beta_\mathrm{N}$, which ensures that each lexical head in a derivation has the same category as the lexical entry it originates from. (Fig. 3 depicts these constraints and others as commutative diagrams.) There are also model-axioms that further restrict μ by requiring that pairs of nodes merged via EM or IM map to selectional or licensing features (respectively).

6 Parsing with Partially Specified Inputs

We validated the parsing procedure, and in particular the SMT-models it constructs, by using it to parse each pair of interface conditions in Table 2 using the lexicon in Table 1. Notably, this lexicon was designed so that, for each (LF, PF) pairing of interface conditions in Table 2, the lexicon can yield a derivation that satisfies the (input) interface conditions (ICs) and that matches the derivation prescribed by contemporary theories of minimalist syntax[29] – among these are derivations (in both active and passive voice) for declaratives, polar-interrogatives, *wh*-questions, relative clauses, and embedded sentences. Moreover, the (prescribed) derivations involve covert complementizers (C), tense-markers (T), and light-verbs (v), as well as various forms of movement including: *wh*-raising, subject-raising, T-to-C head-movement, and V-to-v head-movement (in *VP*-shells). The validation process succeeded, demonstrating that the parser, using the lexicon in Table 1, can yield (and internally model) the prescribed derivation for each entry in Table 2. E.g. see Fig. 7 & 8 for derivations, output by the parser, with an embedded sentence (for I_5) and a relative clause (for I_7), respectively.

We also measured, for each IC in Table 2, the

I_i		Interface Conditions
I_1	PF:	what has the man/N eaten/V?
	LF:	$\theta_{\text{eaten}}[s\colon$ the man, $o\colon$ what], $\mathcal{A}_{\text{has}}[s\colon$ the man]
I_2	PF:	was she/N given/V money/N?
	LF:	$\theta_{\text{given}}[o\colon$ money, $i\colon$ she], $\mathcal{A}_{\text{was}}[s\colon$ she]
I_3	PF:	who will tell/V her/N that he/N has resigned/V?
	LF:	$\theta_{\text{tell}}[s\colon$ who, $o\colon$ that he has resigned, $i\colon$ her], $\mathcal{A}_{\text{will}}[s\colon$ who], $\theta_{\text{resigned}}[s\colon$ he], $\mathcal{A}_{\text{has}}[s\colon$ he]
I_4	PF:	she/N has known/V everyone/N who was loved/V.
	LF:	$\theta_{\text{known}}[s\colon$ she, $o\colon$ everyone who was loved], $\mathcal{A}_{\text{has}}[s\colon$ she], $\theta_{\text{loved}}[o\colon$ everyone], $\mathcal{A}_{\text{was}}[s\colon$ everyone]
I_5	PF:	she/N knows/V that john/N has given/V money/N.
	LF:	$\theta_{\text{knows}}[s\colon$ she, $o\colon$ that john has given money], $\theta_{\text{given}}[s\colon$ john, $o\colon$ money], $\mathcal{A}_{\text{has}}[s\colon$ john]
I_6	PF:	john/N has given/V money/N that was stolen/V.
	LF:	$\theta_{\text{given}}[s\colon$ john, $o\colon$ money that was stolen], $\mathcal{A}_{\text{has}}[s\colon$ john], $\theta_{\text{stolen}}[o\colon$ money], $\mathcal{A}_{\text{was}}[s\colon$ money]
I_7	PF:	john/N fears/V everyone/N who knows/V her/N.
	LF:	$\theta_{\text{fears}}[s\colon$ john, $o\colon$ everyone who knows her], $\theta_{\text{knows}}[s\colon$ everyone, $o\colon$ her]
I_8	PF:	john/N fears/V that money/N was stolen/V.
	LF:	$\theta_{\text{fears}}[s\colon$ john, $o\colon$ that money was stolen], $\theta_{\text{stolen}}[o\colon$ money], $\mathcal{A}_{\text{was}}[s\colon$ money]

Table 2: Corpus of Paired (LF and PF) Interface Conditions (ICs). PF ICs provide surface order data, and some words are associated with a specified category (denoted by a slash followed by the category). LF ICs include relations for agreement ($\mathcal{A}$), predicate-argument structure (θ), and sentence-type (either declarative or interrogative as denoted by end-punctuation). N.b. LF ICs only encode hierarchical/structural relations – i.e. the values filling the slots consist of *sets* of tokens, not sequences of tokens. A predicate associates with one or more arguments: "s:" denotes an external argument, and "o:" and "i:" denote an internal argument serving as a direct or indirect object (respectively). Entries with an embedded clause – e.g. I_3 & I_8 – can have (separate) LF ICs stipulated for each clause.

[27] Specifically, per the *Uniformity of θ-Assignment Hypothesis* (Baker, 1988; Adger, 2003), internal (object or oblique) arguments are assigned a θ-role by establishing a local relationship (via EM) with the projection of a lexical verb, while external arguments are assigned a θ-role (e.g. AGENT) by establishing a local relationship with the light-verb within a VP-shell structure. Likewise, *subject-predicate agreement* requires a local relationship (established via IM) between a raised subject and the tense marker it agrees with.

[28] Following (Kayne, 1994), SVO ordering of the *derived tree* is obtained by requiring that *specifiers* precede their *head*, and that *heads* precede their *complement*.

[29] See (Adger, 2003; Hornstein et al., 2005; Hornstein and Pietroski, 2009; Collins and Stabler, 2016; Radford, 2016).

Node	$\beta_{\mathbb{N}}$	h	p	$\mathcal{P}$	$\mathcal{H}$	μ	$(\psi \circ \mu)$	$\Delta_{\mathbb{N}}$
D_0		D_0	D_0	D_0	D_0	L_5	L_5	
D_1	D	D_1	D_{12}	D_{19}	D_0	L_{37}	L_3	what
D_2	T	D_2	D_{14}	D_0	D_6	L_{32}	L_{36}	has
D_3	D	D_3	D_{15}	D_0	D_0	L_9	L_{14}	the
D_4	N	D_4	D_{15}	D_0	D_0	L_8	L_5	man
D_5	V	D_5	D_{12}	D_0	D_7	L_6	L_{33}	eaten
D_6	$C_{ques.}$	D_6	D_9	D_0	D_0	L_{23}	L_7	ϵ
D_7	v	D_7	D_{17}	D_0	D_0	L_{17}	L_4	ϵ
D_8		D_0	D_0	D_0	D_0	L_5	L_5	
D_9	C_{ques}	D_6	D_{22}	D_0	D_0	L_7	L_{27}	
D_{10}		D_0	D_0	D_0	D_0	L_5	L_5	
D_{11}		D_0	D_0	D_0	D_0	L_5	L_5	
D_{12}	V	D_5	D_{17}	D_0	D_0	L_{33}	L_5	
D_{13}	T	D_2	D_9	D_0	D_0	L_{24}	L_5	
D_{14}	T	D_2	D_{13}	D_0	D_0	L_{36}	L_{24}	
D_{15}	D	D_3	D_{18}	D_{21}	D_0	L_{14}	L_0	
D_{16}		D_0	D_0	D_0	D_0	L_5	L_5	
D_{17}	v	D_7	D_{18}	D_0	D_0	L_4	L_{35}	
D_{18}	v	D_7	D_{14}	D_0	D_0	L_{35}	L_5	
D_{19}	D	D_1	D_{22}	D_0	D_0	L_3	L_5	
D_{20}		D_0	D_0	D_0	D_0	L_5	L_5	
D_{21}	D	D_3	D_{13}	D_0	D_0	L_0	L_5	
D_{22}	$C_{ques.}$	D_6	D_0	D_0	D_0	L_{27}	L_5	

Table 3: Model interpretation for the derivation in Fig. 1. Each D_i is a member of the *derivation node sort*, $\mathbb{N}$. Valuations, recovered from the model interpretation, are listed for several of the uninterpreted functions (e.g. $h(D_{15})=D_3$ and $p(D_9)=D_{22}$) that make up: (i) the derivation model – i.e. h (head), p (parent), $\mathcal{P}$ (phrasal movement), $\mathcal{H}$ (head movement), $\Delta_{\mathbb{N}}$, and $\beta_{\mathbb{N}}$; (ii) the lexicon model – i.e. ψ (successor) and μ (bus). Not all members of $\mathbb{N}$ are used in the derivation (e.g. D_{11}); the bottom nodes, $D_0 \in \mathbb{N}$ and $L_0 \in \Omega$, serve as target nodes reserved for uninterpreted functions to map unused D_i to – e.g. $h(D_{11})=p(D_{11})=D_0$, and $\mu(D_{11})=L_0$.

runtime of the parser - i.e. the time the Z3 SMT-solver takes to check (i.e. solve) the constructed SMT model.[30] We found that I_1 and I_2 each took less than 12 seconds to parse, I_3-I_6 each took between 3 and 6 minutes to parse, and I_7 and I_8 took 31 and 41 minutes to parse (respectively). These differences in runtime are not unexpected when we observe that: (i) I_1 and I_2 have fewer tokens and no embedding structure (as compared to I_3-I_8); (ii) I_7 and I_8 require more instances of head-movement, empty categories and phrasal movement, so that the checked model is (substantively) larger than those of I_1-I_6. Moreover, we found in practice that there is a tradeoff between: (i) writing succinct, comprehensible model-axioms that make extensive use of compositions of uninterpretable functions, and (ii) the runtime of the Z3 SMT-solver. We believe navigating this tradeoff is an important avenue of future work for this parser, and that it is worth exploring the use of other higher-order theories supported by Z3, such as the theory of algebraic datatypes (Bjørner and Nachmanson, 2020), for modeling minimalist derivations and lexicons.

We next applied the parser to inputs in which either the LF or PF interface conditions are specified (but not both). We did this for each entry in Table 2, and present the analysis for I_1 below.

If the input is limited to the PF ICs in I_1, the parser can output a derivation (see Fig. 4) in which *"the man"* is the internal argument (as it merges with *"eaten"*) and *"what"* is the external argument (as it merges with the light-verb, v). This *alternative* derivation is possible because the external and internal arguments are selected using the same feature, $=y$, and swapping where the two arguments merge into the VP-shell structure compels the axiom encoding the *Uniformity of θ-Assignment Hypothesis* to assign semantic roles (to the arguments) that yield an incorrect reading of *"What has the man eaten?"* One solution is to refine the (selection) labels of nominal phrases (NP) to encode θ-roles; however, the model must be updated to propagate NP-labels to determiners (and complementizers and relative pronouns), or else the lexicon will grow untenably by multiplying out the determiners for each distinct selection label.

Conversely, if the input is instead limited to the LF ICs in I_1, then the parser can output a derivation (see Fig. 5) where the auxiliary verb *"has"* is not raised because T-to-C head-movement is compelled by PF ICs (and not by LF ICs); consequently, the surfaced form, *"What the man has eaten?"*, is ungrammatical. One solution is to add axioms that model Economy Conditions (Collins, 2001), so that T-to-C head-movement may be omitted if doing so leaves the surfaced form unchanged.

7 Conclusion

We have introduced an MG parser that is a computational model of HLF and is grounded in an SMT-model encoding a novel axiomatization of minimalist syntax. The parser uses the Z3 SMT-solver, an automatic theorem prover, to answer the question: *can the input lexicon yield a derivation that satisfies the input LF and PF interface conditions?* In this way, parsing is translated into an (SMT) decision problem, with model solutions corresponding to the derivations output by the parser.

We demonstrated that the parser, implemented within the *Parsing as Deduction* framework, can operate on partially specified interface conditions.[31]

[30] See Table 5 in the appendix for detailed results.

[31] More generally, we note that the flexibility of the parser's

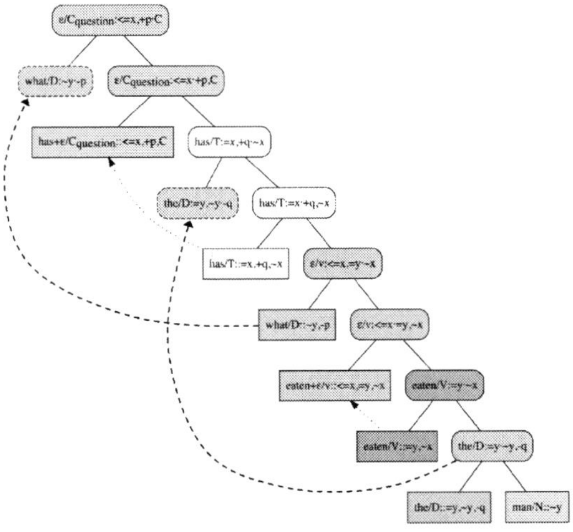

Figure 4: A derivation yielded by the parser, using the lexicon in Table 1, when only the PF interface conditions in entry I_1 (in Table 2) were input to the parser. In contrast with the (prescribed) derivation shown in Fig. 1, this derivation has the originating locations of the two arguments of the (lexical) verb *"eaten"* swapped; hence, although this derivation will be (correctly) externalized as *"What has the man eaten?"*, the derivation encodes an (incorrect) semantic interpretation in which the predicate *"eaten"* takes *"the man"* as its internal (object) argument, and *"what"* as its external (subject) argument (akin to the expression *"What has eaten the man?"*).

Figure 5: A derivation yielded by the parser, using the lexicon in Table 1, when only the LF interface conditions in entry I_1 (in Table 2) were input to the parser. In contrast with the (prescribed) derivation shown in Fig. 1, this derivation does not raise the auxiliary verb, *"has"*, via *T-to-C* head-movement; consequently, although this derivation accords with the LF interface conditions stipulated in I_1 (as it uses entry 36 in Table 1, which codes for an interrogative), it is externalized (i.e. surfaced) as the (un-grammatical) expression *"What the man has eaten?"*

This flexibility of the parser can be leveraged to observe when: (i) output derivations do not accord with the prescriptions of modern theories of minimalist syntax – inspecting these derivations can yield clues about how interface conditions and linguistic constraints cooperate to rule out derivations prohibited by the theory; (ii) the parser fails to output any derivation despite the theory prescribing a licit derivation – then the SMT-solver can identify the minimal subset of model-axioms that are mutually incompatible (Lynce and Silva, 2004; Guthmann et al., 2016), thus identifying conflicts between the axioms of minimalist syntax and the constraints derived from the interface conditions.

Finally, a key advantage of this parser is that it enables a division of labor: the SMT-solver is tasked with carrying out the logical deductions needed to find a model solution, leaving the linguist free to: (i) extend the parser, with the modular design of the SMT-model enabling related sets of axioms to be modified without impacting the remainder of the model;[32] (ii) investigate how principles of syntax cooperate to constrain the space of derivations, and identify redundant principles that may be dropped to yield a simpler theory of syntax.

design enables it to operate on partially specified inputs, with the SMT-solver in effect solving for the unspecified inputs (in addition to the derivation itself). E.g. if we specify the LF and PF interface conditions, but not the lexicon, then the parser will constrain the SMT model of the derivation using the interface conditions, but will not constrain the SMT model of the lexicon since no input lexicon was specified – then when the SMT-solver obtains a satisfiable interpretation of the SMT model of the parser, we can (automatically) recover from the interpretation of the lexicon model an MG lexicon that yields a derivation that satisfies the specified interface conditions. Moreover, if we augment the parser by connecting multiple SMT models of derivations, each constrained by a different pairing of interface conditions, to a single SMT model of a lexicon, then the composite SMT model can be used to infer an MG that can, for each pair of interface conditions, yield a derivation that satisfies that pairing – notably, this approach aligns with earlier work that used logic grammars to infer a lexicon (Rayner et al., 1988). See (Indurkhya, 2020) and (Indurkhya, 2022) for detailed discussions of how augmenting the parser in this manner can yield instantaneous and incremental (respectively) computational models of language acquisition.

Acknowledgements

I would like to thank three anonymous reviewers, as well as Robert C. Berwick, Sandiway Fong and Sanjoy Mitter for their comments and feedback.

[32]E.g. to support *head-final* languages (e.g. French or Japanese), the model-axioms encoding *SOV* ordering can be replaced (with axioms for *SOV* ordering) without altering model-axioms unrelated to the PF-interface (see Appendix D).

References

David Adger. 2003. *Core syntax: A minimalist approach*, volume 33. Oxford University Press Oxford.

David Adger and Peter Svenonius. 2011. Features in minimalist syntax. *The Oxford handbook of linguistic minimalism*, pages 27–51.

Krzysztof R Apt. 1990. Logic programming. *Handbook of Theoretical Computer Science, Volume B: Formal Models and Sematics (B)*, 1990:493–574.

Mark C Baker. 1988. *Incorporation: A theory of grammatical function changing*. University of Chicago Press.

Nikolaj Bjørner. 2011. Engineering theories with z3. In *Asian Symposium on Programming Languages and Systems*, pages 4–16. Springer.

Nikolaj Bjørner and Lev Nachmanson. 2020. Navigating the universe of z3 theory solvers. In *Brazilian Symposium on Formal Methods*, pages 8–24. Springer.

Noam Chomsky. 1981. *Lectures on Government and Binding*. Studies in generative grammar. Foris.

Noam Chomsky. 1986. *Knowledge of language: Its nature, origin, and use*. Greenwood Publishing Group.

Noam Chomsky. 1995. *The Minimalist Program*. Volume 28 of Current studies in linguistics series. MIT Press.

Noam Chomsky. 2001. Derivation by phase. In Michael Kenstowicz, editor, *Ken Hale: A life in language*, pages 1–52. MIT Press.

Noam Chomsky. 2005. Three factors in language design. *Linguistic Inquiry*, 36(1):1–22.

Noam Chomsky. 2013. Problems of projection. *Lingua*, 130:33–49.

Chris Collins. 2001. Economy conditions in syntax. *The Handbook of Contemporary Syntactic Theory*, pages 45–61.

Chris Collins and Edward Stabler. 2016. A formalization of minimalist syntax. *Syntax*, 19(1):43–78.

Leonardo De Moura and Nikolaj Bjørner. 2011. Satisfiability modulo theories: introduction and applications. *Communications of the ACM*, 54(9):69–77.

Ralph Debusmann, Denys Duchier, Marco Kuhlmann, and Stefan Thater. 2004. Tag parsing as model enumeration. In *Proceedings of the 7th International Workshop on Tree Adjoining Grammar and Related Formalisms*, pages 148–154.

Denys Duchier. 1999. Axiomatizing dependency parsing using set constraints. In *Sixth Meeting on the Mathematics of Language*, page 115–126.

Denys Duchier, Thi-Bich-Hanh Dao, Yannick Parmentier, and Willy Lesaint. 2010. Property grammar parsing seen as a constraint optimization problem. In *Formal Grammar*, pages 82–96. Springer.

Bruno Dutertre and Leonardo de Moura. 2006. A fast linear-arithmetic solver for DPLL(T). In *Computer Aided Verification*, pages 81–94, Berlin, Heidelberg. Springer Berlin Heidelberg.

Mathieu Estratat and Laurent Henocque. 2004. Parsing languages with a configurator. In *European Conference on Artificial Intelligence*, volume 16, page 591.

Sandiway Fong. 1991. *Computational properties of principle-based grammatical theories*. Ph.D. thesis, Massachusetts Institute of Technology.

Thomas Graf. 2011. Closure properties of minimalist derivation tree languages. In *International Conference on Logical Aspects of Computational Linguistics*, pages 96–111. Springer.

Thomas Graf. 2013. *Local and transderivational constraints in syntax and semantics*. Ph.D. thesis, University of California at Los Angeles.

Jane B Grimshaw. 2005. *Words and structure*. CSLI Publications.

Ofer Guthmann, Ofer Strichman, and Anna Trostanetski. 2016. Minimal unsatisfiable core extraction for smt. In *2016 Formal Methods in Computer-Aided Design (FMCAD)*, pages 57–64.

Kenneth Hale and Samuel J. Keyser. 1993. On argument structure and the lexical expression of syntactic relations. In Kenneth Hale and Samuel J. Keyser, editors, *The view from Building 20: Essays in linguistics in honor of Sylvain Bromberger*, pages 53–109. MIT Press.

Kenneth Hale and Samuel Jay Keyser. 2002. *Prolegomenon to a theory of argument structure*, volume 39 of *Linguistic Inquiry Monographs*. MIT Press.

Hendrik Harkema. 2001. *Parsing Minimalist Languages*. Ph.D. thesis, University of California Los Angeles.

Norbert Hornstein, Jairo Nunes, and Kleanthes K Grohmann. 2005. *Understanding minimalism*. Cambridge University Press.

Norbert Hornstein and Paul Pietroski. 2009. Basic operations: Minimal syntax-semantics. *Catalan Journal of Linguistics*, 8(1):113–139.

Sagar Indurkhya. 2020. Inferring Minimalist Grammars with an SMT-solver. In *Proceedings of the Society for Computation in Linguistics 2020*, pages 457–460, New York, New York. Association for Computational Linguistics.

Sagar Indurkhya. 2021a. *Solving for syntax*. Ph.D. thesis, Massachusetts Institute of Technology.

Sagar Indurkhya. 2021b. Using collaborative filtering to model argument selection. In *Proceedings of the International Conference on Recent Advances in Natural Language Processing (RANLP 2021)*, pages 629–639, Held Online. INCOMA Ltd.

Sagar Indurkhya. 2022. Incremental acquisition of a Minimalist Grammar using an SMT-solver. In *Proceedings of the Society for Computation in Linguistics 2022*, pages 212–216, online. Association for Computational Linguistics.

Sagar Indurkhya and Robert C. Berwick. 2021. Evaluating the cognitively-related productivity of a universal dependency parser. In *2021 IEEE 20th International Conference on Cognitive Informatics & Cognitive Computing (ICCI*CC)*, pages 7–15.

Joxan Jaffar and J-L Lassez. 1987. Constraint logic programming. In *Proceedings of the 14th ACM SIGACT-SIGPLAN symposium on Principles of programming languages*, pages 111–119.

Joxan Jaffar and Michael J Maher. 1994. Constraint logic programming: A survey. *The Journal of Logic Programming*, 19:503–581.

Mark Johnson. 1989. Parsing as deduction: The use of knowledge of language. *Journal of Psycholinguistic Research*, 18(1):105–128.

Aravind K Joshi and Yves Schabes. 1997. Tree-adjoining grammars. In *Handbook of formal languages*, pages 69–123. Springer.

Richard S Kayne. 1994. *The antisymmetry of syntax*. 25. MIT Press.

Gregory M Kobele. 2011. Minimalist tree languages are closed under intersection with recognizable tree languages. In *International Conference on Logical Aspects of Computational Linguistics*, pages 129–144. Springer.

Gregory M Kobele, Christian Retoré, and Sylvain Salvati. 2007. An automata-theoretic approach to minimalism. *Model Theoretic Syntax at 10*, pages 71–80.

Alexander Koller and Joachim Niehren. 2002. Constraint Programming in Computational Linguistics. In Dave Barker-Plummer, David I. Beaver, Johan van Benthem, and Patrick Scotto di Luzio, editors, *Words, Proofs, and Dialog*, volume 141, pages 95–122. CSLI Press.

Yuliya Lierler and Peter Schüller. 2012. Parsing combinatory categorial grammar via planning in answer set programming. In *Correct Reasoning*, pages 436–453. Springer.

Inês Lynce and João Silva. 2004. On computing minimum unsatisfiable cores. In *International Conference on Theory and Applications of Satisfiability Testing (SAT)*, pages 305–310.

Jens Michaelis. 1998. Derivational minimalism is mildly context-sensitive. In *International Conference on Logical Aspects of Computational Linguistics*, volume 98, pages 179–198. Springer.

Jens Michaelis. 2001. Transforming linear context-free rewriting systems into minimalist grammars. *Logical Aspects of Computational Linguistics*, pages 228–244.

Jens Michaelis, Uwe Mönnich, and Frank Morawietz. 2000. Algebraic description of derivational minimalism. *Algebraic Methods in Language Processing*, 16.

Frank Morawietz. 2008. *Two-Step Approaches to Natural Language Formalism*, volume 64. Walter de Gruyter.

Leonardo de Moura and Nikolaj Bjørner. 2008. Z3: An efficient smt solver. In *International conference on Tools and Algorithms for the Construction and Analysis of Systems*, pages 337–340. Springer.

Leonardo de Moura and Nikolaj Bjørner. 2009. Satisfiability modulo theories: An appetizer. In *Brazilian Symposium on Formal Methods*, pages 23–36. Springer.

Robert Nieuwenhuis and Albert Oliveras. 2006. On sat modulo theories and optimization problems. In *International conference on theory and applications of satisfiability testing*, pages 156–169. Springer.

Robert Nieuwenhuis, Albert Oliveras, and Cesare Tinelli. 2006. Solving sat and sat modulo theories: From an abstract Davis–Putnam–Logemann–Loveland procedure to DPLL(T). *Journal of the ACM (JACM)*, 53(6):937–977.

Sourabh Niyogi and Robert C Berwick. 2005. A minimalist implementation of Hale-Keyser incorporation theory. In *UG and External Systems: Language, Brain and Computation*, pages 269–288. John Benjamins Publishing.

Fernando C. N. Pereira and David H. D. Warren. 1983. Parsing as deduction. In *Proceedings of the 21st Annual Meeting on Association for Computational Linguistics*, ACL '83, pages 137–144. Association for Computational Linguistics.

David Pesetsky and Esther Torrego. 2001. T-to-c movement: Causes and consequences. *Current Studies in Linguistics Series*, 36:355–426.

Andrew Radford. 2009. *An introduction to English sentence structure*. Cambridge University Press.

Andrew Radford. 2016. *Analysing English sentences: A minimalist approach (Second Edition)*. Cambridge University Press.

Silvio Ranise and Cesare Tinelli. 2006. Satisfiability modulo theories. *Trends and Controversies-IEEE Intelligent Systems Magazine*, 21(6):71–81.

Manny Rayner, Asa Hugosson, and Goran Hagert. 1988. Using a logic grammar to learn a lexicon. In *Coling Budapest 1988 Volume 2: International Conference on Computational Linguistics*.

James Rogers and Rachel Nordlinger. 1998. *A descriptive approach to language-theoretic complexity*. MIT press.

Yves Schabes and Richard C Waters. 1993. Lexicalized context-fee grammars. In *31st Annual Meeting of the Association for Computational Linguistics*, pages 121–129.

Peter Schüller. 2013. Flexible combinatory categorial grammar parsing using the cyk algorithm and answer set programming. In *International Conference on Logic Programming and Nonmonotonic Reasoning*, pages 499–511. Springer.

Stuart M Shieber, Yves Schabes, and Fernando CN Pereira. 1995. Principles and implementation of deductive parsing. *The Journal of Logic Programming*, 24(1-2):3–36.

Edward Stabler. 1996. Derivational minimalism. In *International Conference on Logical Aspects of Computational Linguistics*, pages 68–95. Springer.

Edward P Stabler. 2013. Two models of minimalist, incremental syntactic analysis. *Topics in Cognitive Science*, 5(3):611–633.

Edward P. Stabler and Edward L Keenan. 2003. Structural similarity within and among languages. *Theoretical Computer Science*, 293(2):345–363.

Miloš Stanojević. 2016. Minimalist grammar transition-based parsing. In *International Conference on Logical Aspects of Computational Linguistics*, pages 273–290. Springer.

Mark Steedman and Jason Baldridge. 2011. Combinatory categorial grammar. *Non-Transformational Syntax: Formal and Explicit Models of Grammar. Wiley-Blackwell*, pages 181–224.

Lappoon R Tang and Raymond J Mooney. 2001. Using multiple clause constructors in inductive logic programming for semantic parsing. In *European Conference on Machine Learning*, pages 466–477. Springer.

John Torr, Milos Stanojevic, Mark Steedman, and Shay B Cohen. 2019. Wide-coverage neural a* parsing for minimalist grammars. In *Proceedings of the 57th annual meeting of the Association for Computational Linguistics*, pages 2486–2505.

A Reproducibility

We ran the computer programs detailed in this study on a MacBook Pro (Retina, 15-inch, Late 2013) with a 2.3 GHz Intel Core i7 processor, and 16GB of 1600MHz DDR3 RAM. We used Python v3.7.9 and v4.8.6 of the Z3 SMT-solver. The complete program source code for the parser, including the (python) source code for the SMT models, is available at `https://github.com/indurks/mgsmt`.

B Minimalist Grammar

This section provides additional details about the Minimalist Grammar formalism used in the present study. Notably, MGs are mildly-context sensitive (Michaelis, 1998) and are sufficiently expressive for modeling natural language in so far as they can model the syntactic constraints that appear in contemporary syntax (e.g. they can produce structures encoding cross-serial dependencies) – specifically, the syntactic constraints underlying HLF can be modeled by Monadic Second Order (MSO) logic (Rogers and Nordlinger, 1998), and MSO-expressible constraints over an MG derivation tree can be encoded within an MG lexicon (Graf, 2013).[33]

We now turn to reviewing the algebraic formulation of MGs presented in Stabler and Keenan (2003) – we encourage the reader to consult Fig. 1 and Table 1 to ground this formal presentation. A minimalist grammar, G, is defined by a tuple, $(\Sigma, Sel, Lic, Lex, \mathbb{M})$, and we will now define each member of this tuple in turn. First, Σ is a finite, non-empty set of phonological forms – a phonological form is either *overt* (i.e. a pronounced word) or *covert* (i.e. unpronounced), and we let ϵ denote a covert phonological form. Next, Sel and Lic are defined as non-empty (disjoint) finite sets of feature labels for *selection* and *licensing* respectively.[34] We then define F, the set of syntactic features, as the union of:

(i) the singleton set containing the special feature C, which marks the end of the derivation process;

(ii) the set of selectional features, formed by prefixing members of Sel with $=$ or $\sim$ to indicate if the feature is a *selector* or a *selectee* (respectively); furthermore, a $<$ or $>$ prefixed before a selector prefix – i.e. "<=" or ">=" – indicates that the selector triggers left or right head-movement respectively.[35]

(iii) the set of licensing features, formed by prefixing members of Lic with $+$ or $-$ to indicate if the feature is a *licensor* or a *licensee* (respectively).

Turning to the lexicon, Lex, we first define the set of *chains* as $H = \Sigma^* \times Types \times F^*$, where the set $Types = \{::, :\}$ designates whether a chain is *lexical* or *derived* (from *lexical* chains) respectively.[36] We can then define Lex as a non-empty finite set of lexical chains. Finally, the set of expressions, $E = H^+$, may be recursively combined together via the binary structure building operation *Merge*, denoted by $\mathbb{M}$, to produce another expression. *Merge* has two disjoint subcases:

(i) *external merge* (EM), which models combination, requires that both arguments of merge are disjoint from one another;

(ii) *internal merge* (IM), which models displacement, requires that one of the arguments is a constituent of the other.

Both sub-cases of *Merge* are driven by feature-checking, with M determining whether two expressions may be paired together based on their features; note that the syntactic features are uninterpretable, and *Merge* deletes the pairs of features that check one another.

Let us now formally detail the subcases of M.

[33]Notably, MGs are sufficiently expressive for modeling syntactic derivations that are systematically related by structural transformations. E.g. a declarative is (structurally) related to its corresponding polar-interrogative by way of the rule for *aux-raising* (i.e. T-to-C movement as modeled in contemporary minimalist syntax) in which the top most (i.e. root) complementizer triggers head-movement of the (hierarchically) closest tense-marker – we would thus expect that the syntactic structure assigned (by an MG parser) to a declarative could be transformed into a polar-interrogative by replacing lexical item 25 with lexical item 9 (in Table 1), and would also expect that running an MG parser on the polar-interrogative would yield the same derivation as obtained by applying *aux-raising* to the derivation of the declarative. This capability of MGs and their parsers stands in contrast with state-of-the-art UD parsers that have difficulty acquiring and encoding knowledge of the *aux-raising* rule (Indurkhya and Berwick, 2021).

[34]The feature system used here is based on checking theory as detailed in Chomsky (1995).

[35]Instances of head-movement include: (i) the V-to-v head-movement utilized in the Hale-Keyser model of predicate-argument structure (Hale and Keyser, 1993, 2002); (ii) T-to-C head-movement (Pesetsky and Torrego, 2001) that is utilized in fronting an auxiliary verb (e.g. when forming a polar-interrogative from a declarative).

[36]*Lexical chains* serve to track the sequence of movement operations that the (maximal) projection (of a lexical head) may undergo in the course of a derivation; in particular, they track terms in the derivation that have not yet finished moving (and thus need to be accessible to the Internal Merge operation.

Let $s, t \in \Sigma^*$, $f \in Sel$, $g \in Lic$, $\gamma \in F^*$ and $\delta \in F^+$. Furthermore, let $\alpha_1, ..., \alpha_k \in H$ for $0 \leq k$, and let $\iota_1, ..., \iota_l \in H$ for $0 \leq l$. We then define EM as the union of the following three (disjoint) functions, $\{EM_1, EM_2, EM_3\}$, that involve feature *selection*:

$$\frac{[\mathrm{s} :: {=}f, \gamma] \qquad [\mathrm{t} \cdot {\sim}f], \iota_1...\iota_l}{[\mathrm{st} : \gamma], \iota_1...\iota_l} \ \mathrm{EM}_1$$

$$\frac{[\mathrm{s} : {=}f, \gamma], \alpha_1...\alpha_k \qquad [\mathrm{t} \cdot {\sim}f], \iota_1...\iota_l}{[\mathrm{ts} : \gamma], \alpha_1...\alpha_k, \iota_1...\iota_l} \ \mathrm{EM}_2$$

$$\frac{[\mathrm{s} \cdot {=}f, \gamma], \alpha_1...\alpha_k \qquad [\mathrm{t} \cdot {\sim}f, \delta], \iota_1...\iota_l}{[\mathrm{s} : \gamma], \alpha_1...\alpha_k, [\mathrm{t} : \delta], \iota_1...\iota_l} \ \mathrm{EM}_3$$

The separation of the phonological form and the syntactic features by the symbol $\cdot$ designates that the chain could either be *lexical* or *derived*. IM is defined as the union of the two disjoint functions, $\{IM_1, IM_2\}$, that employ feature licensing:

$$\frac{[\mathrm{s} : {+}g, \gamma], \alpha_1...\alpha_{i-1}, [\mathrm{t} : {-}g], \alpha_{i+1}...\alpha_k}{[\mathrm{ts} : \gamma], \alpha_1...\alpha_{i-1}, \alpha_{i+1}...\alpha_k} \ \mathrm{IM}_1$$

$$\frac{[\mathrm{s} : {+}g, \gamma], \alpha_1...\alpha_{i-1}, [\mathrm{t} : {-}g, \delta], \alpha_{i+1}...\alpha_k}{[\mathrm{s} : \gamma], \alpha_1...\alpha_{i-1}, [\mathrm{t} : \delta], \alpha_{i+1}...\alpha_k} \ \mathrm{IM}_2$$

Furthermore, IM_1 and IM_2 are restricted by the *Shortest Move Constraint* (SMC): if a licensor, α, binds to a licensee, β, it must be the case that β is the only licensee to which α can bind. The SMC ensures that the licensor will always select the (hierarchically) nearest licensee, as at every step in the derivation, there can only be one possible licensee that can be licensed; this has the consequence of making IM deterministic (with respect to which licensee a licensor will license), so that a derivation can be determined entirely from knowledge of the order in which the various lexical heads (and projections thereof) are *externally* merged with one another.

Finally, we define a *derivation* as a sequence of expressions produced by recursively applying $\mathbb{M}$ to a group of chains; a derivation is deemed to be *complete* if there remains a single expression that has no chains and that has one feature, C (which serves to indicate the termination point of the derivation).[37]

	D_0	D_1	D_2	D_3	D_4	D_5	D_6	D_7	D_8	D_9	D_{10}	D_{11}	D_{12}	D_{13}	D_{14}	D_{15}	D_{16}	D_{17}	D_{18}	D_{19}	D_{20}	D_{21}	D_{22}
D_8	·	·	·	·	·	·	·	·	·	·	·	·	·	·	·	·	·	·	·	·	·	·	·
D_9	·	○	⊕	⊕	⊕	⊕	⊕	⊕	·	·	·	·	⊕	⊕	⊕	⊕	·	⊕	⊕	·	·	⊕	·
D_{10}	·	·	·	·	·	·	·	·	·	·	·	·	·	·	·	·	·	·	·	·	·	·	·
D_{11}	·	·	·	·	·	·	·	·	·	·	·	·	·	·	·	·	·	·	·	·	·	·	·
D_{12}	·	○	·	·	·	⊕	·	·	·	·	·	·	·	·	·	·	·	·	·	·	·	·	·
D_{13}	·	○	⊕	⊕	⊕	⊕	·	⊕	·	·	·	·	⊕	·	⊕	⊕	·	⊕	⊕	·	·	⊕	·
D_{14}	·	○	⊕	○	○	⊕	·	⊕	·	·	·	·	⊕	·	·	○	·	⊕	⊕	·	·	·	·
D_{15}	·	·	·	⊕	⊕	·	·	·	·	·	·	·	·	·	·	·	·	·	·	·	·	·	·
D_{16}	·	·	·	·	·	·	·	·	·	·	·	·	·	·	·	·	·	·	·	·	·	·	·
D_{17}	·	○	·	·	·	⊕	·	⊕	·	·	·	·	⊕	·	·	·	·	·	·	·	·	·	·
D_{18}	·	○	·	○	○	⊕	·	⊕	·	·	·	·	⊕	·	·	○	·	⊕	·	·	·	·	·
D_{19}	·	+	·	·	·	·	·	·	·	·	·	·	·	·	·	·	·	·	·	·	·	·	·
D_{20}	·	·	·	·	·	·	·	·	·	·	·	·	·	·	·	·	·	·	·	·	·	·	·
D_{21}	·	·	·	+	+	·	·	·	·	·	·	·	·	·	·	+	·	·	·	·	·	·	·
D_{22}	·	⊕	⊕	⊕	⊕	⊕	⊕	⊕	·	⊕	·	·	⊕	⊕	⊕	⊕	·	⊕	⊕	⊕	·	⊕	·

Table 4: Model interpretation of two binary uninterpreted functions, d and $d^\star$, for the derivation in Fig. 1. Given an entry at row D_i and column D_j: + indicates that the node D_i dominates the node D_j with respect to the derived tree but not the derivation tree; ○ indicates that D_i dominates D_j with respect to the derivation tree but not the derived tree; ⊕ indicates that D_i dominates D_j with respect to both the derivation tree and the derived tree; and · indicates that D_i does not dominate D_j (with respect to either the derivation tree or the derived tree). E.g. D_{18} dominates D_{15} with respect to the derivation tree but not the derived tree: notice in Table 3 that while $p(D_{15}) = D_{18}$, there is no $k \in [0, 22]$ such that $\mathcal{P}(D_k) = D_{18}$. Conversely, D_{21} dominates D_{15} with respect to the derived tree but not the derivation tree: notice in Table 3 that $\mathcal{P}(D_{15}) = D_{21}$, but there is no $k \in [0, 22]$ such that $p(D_k) = D_{21}$. The derivation's root node, D_{22}, dominates each of the other nodes in the derivation with respect to both the derivation tree and the derived tree. Finally, $D_1, D_2, \ldots, D_7$, which are leaf nodes (i.e. lexical heads) in the derivation, do not dominate any other nodes in the derivation, and for that reason rows $D_1 \ldots D_7$ are not shown as they would be entirely filled by · .

Assuming a *Subject-Verb-Object* word-ordering, the surface form associated with a complete derivation may be read out by recursively applying (top-down) a Specifier-Head-Complement linearization of each projection.[38]

C Multi-dominance and Derived Trees

This section details how a *minimalist derivation* takes the form of a *multi-dominance tree* – i.e. the *(bare) phrase structures* that linguists are familiar

[37] As defined here, an MG either can or cannot generate a given derivation. However, we can compute a relative likelihood for a given derivation to be generated by an MG by determining for each of the merge operations involving (constituent) selection (i.e. the *c-selection* that drives external merge), the degree to which the heads of the two merged projections tend to associate with one another – this pairwise associativity between phonological forms (corresponding to the two heads) can be computed by various methods, e.g. using a similarity metric to compute distance between the word embedding vectors for the two phonological forms, or using model-based collaborative filtering may be used to compute the associativity between predicates and arguments (Indurkhya, 2021b).

[38] In a projection of a lexical head, the complement is the first term the lexical head merges with, and the specifier is the subsequent term that the projection (of the head) merges with – e.g. in XBar-theoretic terms, given the two rules: $XP \rightarrow Spec, X'$, and $X' \rightarrow X, Comp$, the projection of the lexical head X will be linearized so that the surface ordering is $Spec, X, Comp$.

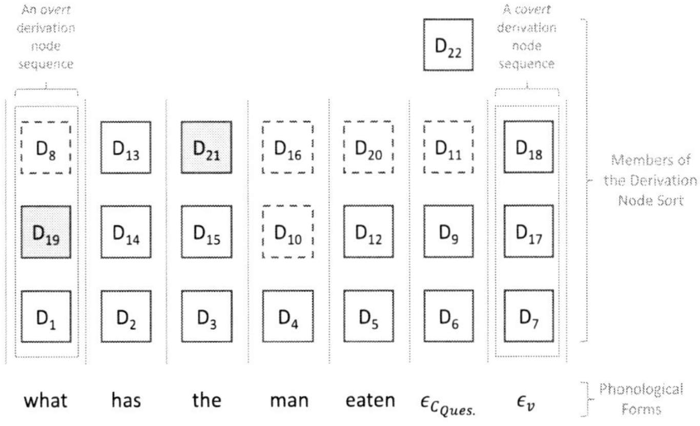

Figure 6: An illustration of how the members of the derivation node sort, $\mathbb{N}$, are arranged into *derivation node sequences*, with each sequence being associated with either an overt or covert phonological form. Each derivation node sequence is depicted as a column, with the first node in the sequence at the bottom and the last node in the sequence at the top. Note that the derivation node sequences shown here may be arranged so as to form the derivation (tree) shown in Fig. 1. Nodes that actively play a role in the derivation are depicted as white boxes, and active nodes that are in the same column have the same (lexical) head - e.g. the root node is D_{22}, and since D_{22} has the same head as D_9 and D_6, it is displayed here above the covert node-sequence associated with the (covert) phonological form $\epsilon_{C_{ques.}}$. (Note that the root node is not a member of any derivation node sequence, and is treated as a special case in the axioms.) Boxes with dashed boundaries correspond to inactive members of $\mathbb{N}$ that do not participate in the derivation (i.e. they do not appear in the derivation in Fig. 1). Boxes with solid boundaries are projections, whereas greyed out boxes are part of a lexical chain (i.e. the sequence of movement operations that a maximal projection may participate in). Importantly, the derivation node sequences together form an index over $\mathbb{N}$, and this index enables us to write model axioms that can explicitly reference the members of a *derivation node sequence* – i.e. the axioms that constrain uninterpreted functions operating over $\mathbb{N}$ can explicitly reference each individual step in the projection (and potential subsequent chain) of the lexical head associated with a given phonological form.

with.[39]

A multi-dominance tree is a super-position of the *derivation tree* – i.e. the tree made up of the external and internal merge operations that work together to combine a multi-set of lexical items drawn from the lexicon – and the *derived tree*, which is the tree that remains after a minimalist derivation has been generated and all movement operations have been applied. Each MG derivation tree is associated with a *multi-dominance tree*, which can be generated from the derivation tree by appending, for each occurrence of IM in the derivation tree, a node at the destination of the movement operation, and then establishing a dominance relation (via $d^{\star}$) between the destination node and the node at the source of movement.[40]

We observe that, for both the derivation and multi-dominance trees, each node is associated with a (lexical) *head*; then, since two nodes that are merged together cannot have the same head, we can identify which of two merged constituents projects by examining the head of the node that corresponds to the product of merge.[41]

- The *derivation tree* can be recovered from the multi-dominance tree by deleting each occurrence of movement (i.e. deleting the node at the raised location).
- The *derived tree* may be recovered from the multi-dominance tree by removing, for each node x in the multi-dominance tree that serves as a source of movement, the dominance relation (with respect to the derived tree) between

[39]Relatedly, see Pgs. 12-24 of Graf (2013) for a discussion of *"augmented derivation trees."*

[40]This is closely related to the two-step approach that involves first lifting information *implicitly* encoded within a derivation tree (i.e. the information encoded in the structure of the multi-dominance tree) so as to make the information explicit, and then reconstructing the (derived) phrase structure tree that linguists are more familiar with. See Pgs. 35-50 of Graf (2013) for a discussion of the two-step approach of (i) lifting an MG derivation to its associated the multi-dominance tree and then (ii) reconstructing the "derived tree"; see also (Kobele et al., 2007). See Morawietz (2008) (Pgs. 131-182) for a review of the two-step approach as applied to multiple context-free grammars (MCFGs), and note that MGs may be translated into MCFGs (Michaelis et al., 2000).

[41]N.b. the derivation and multi-dominance trees do not explicitly encode (linear) precedence relations between the lexical heads entering into the derivation.

x and its parent – i.e.:

$$d^\star(p(x), x) = \text{False}$$

Importantly, the multi-dominance tree can be viewed as a super-position of the derivation tree and the derived tree, and it is the multi-dominance tree associated with an MG derivation that serves as the domain of discourse in the SMT model of the derivation. Hence, whenever the present study refers to a derivation tree or a derived tree, the reader should understand that they are components of a multi-dominance tree.

Each *lexical item* that appears in a derivation has a (bottom-up) trajectory through the associated multi-dominance tree:

(i) the lexical item, starting as a lexical head, is first projected zero or more times – this process is driven by either external merge via (c-)selection or internal merge via licensing;

(ii) the (maximal) projection of the lexical item is then either the terminal point of the derivation (marked by the presence of the special symbol C) or is selected by some other lexical head (this is driven by the presence of a selectee feature);

(iii) finally, the lexical item is raised, via internal merge, zero or more times to form a movement-chain, with each movement operation forming a link in the chain.

Importantly, there are two key points to take away from this observation:

(a) Each node in the multi-dominance tree associates with a lexical item in the derivation (i.e. the lexical item that is the head of that node) and the nodes associated with a lexical head may be arranged as a sequence in the order in which they appear in the multi-dominance tree (starting from the bottom); ***for this reason, we refer to such a sequence as a "derivation node sequence" and observe that the multi-dominance tree associated with an MG derivation is a structural arrangement of derivation node sequences*** (Stabler, 2013).

(b) Given the multi-dominance tree that is associated with an MG derivation, we can recover the multiset of lexical items from which the multi-domimance tree is derived (except for the labels of the syntactic features); this can be seen by observing that each node in a derivation node sequence is associated with exactly one type of syntactic feature – i.e. selector, selectee, licensor, licensee, or the special symbol C – and noting that the feature-type of a node can be determined by the position of that node within the multi-domimance tree, so that given a derivation node sequence associated with a lexical entry, the corresponding sequence of syntactic feature-types (present in that lexical entry) can be obtained the path that the derivation node sequence takes through the multi-dominance tree.

(See Fig. 6 for an illustration of the derivation node sequences that are assembled to form the derivation presented in Fig. 1.) ***Consequently, an SMT model of a minimalist derivation can be constructed by: (i) modeling the derivation node sequences that form the associated multi-dominance tree, and (ii) constraining the topology of the multi-domimance tree by using the model axioms to restrict how the derivation node sequences may be assembled together.***

IC	Trial 1	Trial 2	Trial 3	Median
I_1	11.7	10.5	13.9	11.7
I_2	3.2	3.3	4.0	3.3
I_3	323.8	208.9	346.0	323.8
I_4	267.1	296.2	281.1	281.1
I_5	222.6	225.5	178.5	222.6
I_6	261.8	312.0	261.4	261.8
I_7	1213.3	2065.6	1857.2	1857.2
I_8	2445.1	1851.7	3275.9	2445.1

Table 5: Runtime performance, measured in seconds, of the parser (i.e. the time Z3 takes to check the constructed SMT-model of the parser).

D Limitations

This section briefly comments on two limitations of the parser introduced in this study.

One limitation of the parser is that it has only been tested on (Modern Standard) English, which has Subject-Verb-Object (SVO) ordering; however, we believe that the parser can be readily adapted to languages with Subject-Object-Verb (SOV) ordering (e.g. French or Japanese) by replacing a small number of the constraints (derived from PF interface conditions) that encode SVO-ordering by applying *Specifier-Head-Complement* linearization to the derived tree: namely, these constraints for SVO-ordering could be replaced with constraints that enforce SOV-ordering based on applying *Specifier-*

Complement-Head linearization (see the relevant footnote in §7). Moreover, it would be interesting to investigate whether the SMT model of the parser could be augmented with a (boolean) variable that serves as a switch, controlling whether the constraints for SVO or SOV are used; notably, such a switch could either be hard-coded by the user (to enforce which ordering the parser should use), or left un-valued, in which case the parser could use either (SVO or SOV) ordering, so long as the surfaced word-sequence (yielded by the output derivation) aligns with the input word-sequence (so that the input PF interface conditions are satisfied).

Another limitation of the parser is that it is primarily focused on modeling syntax, and does not explicitly model morphological inflection. We believe that, in future work, this limitation could be overcome (in part) by: (i) augmenting the SMT model of the lexicon to store the *root* of each (overt) phonological form and encoding morphological attributes within the labels of the syntactic features; (ii) updating the constraints (i.e. SMT-formulae) derived from the PF interface conditions to inflect each root form when comparing it against the relevant surface form (i.e. the inflected word listed in the input PF interface conditions) - this inflection would be realized by the constraints inspecting the morphological attributes encoded in the feature label associated with that root form.

We believe that both of these (current) limitations point to productive avenues for further research involving extending the parser presented in this study.

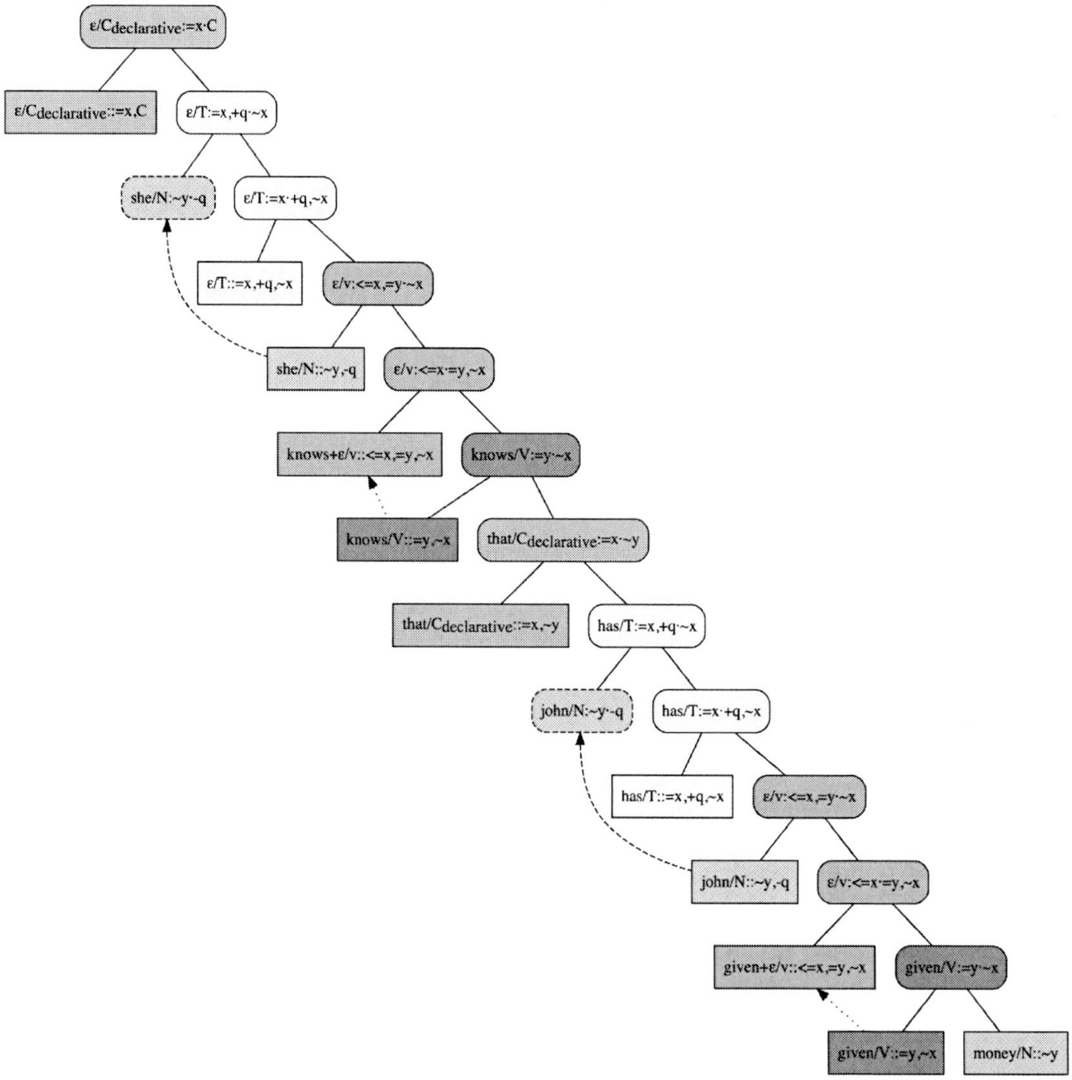

Figure 7: A derivation for the sentence: *"She knows that John has given money."* This derivation was output by the parser when it was applied to entry I_5 in Table 2, using the lexicon in Table 1, and matches the derivation prescribed by contemporary theories of minimalist syntax. This demonstrates the parser's capacity to model an input with an embedded sentence – i.e. *"John has given money"*.

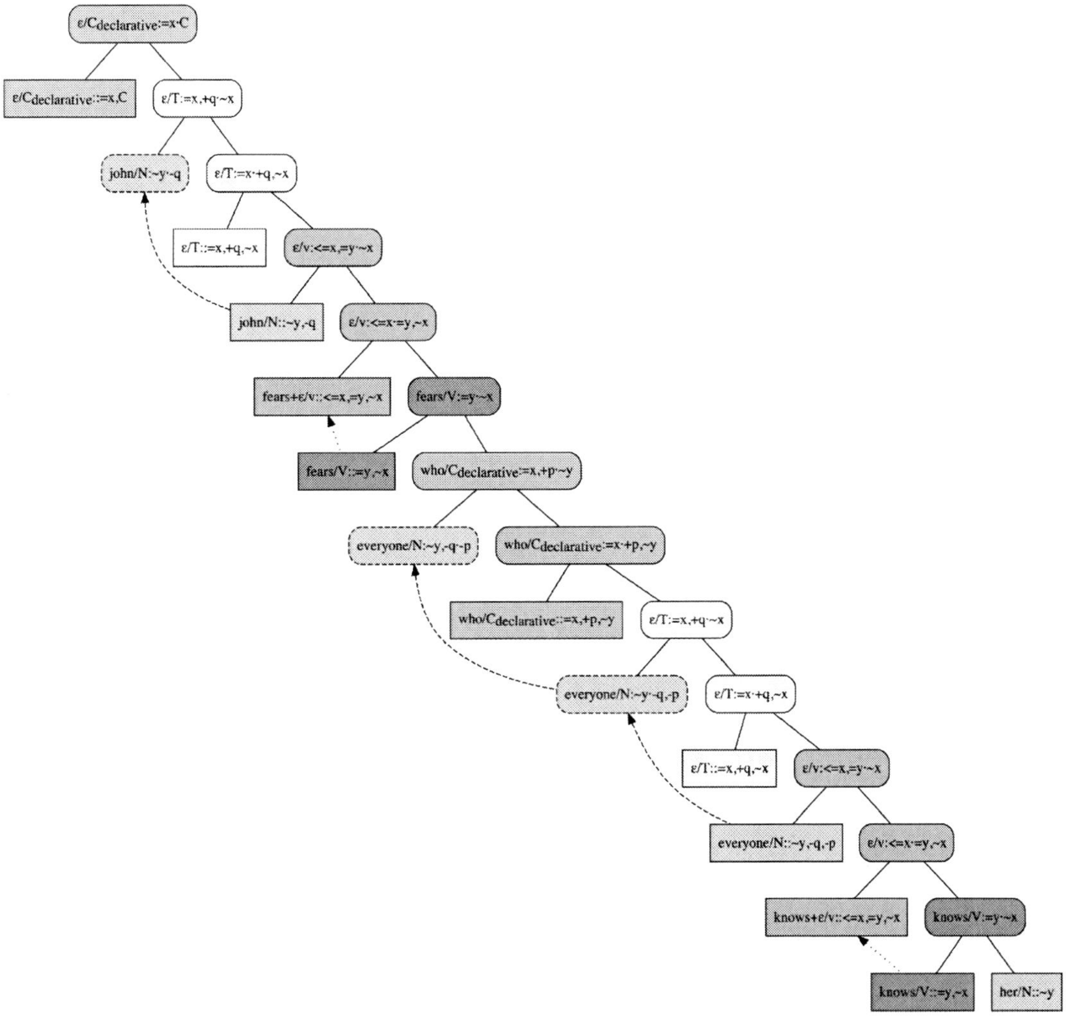

Figure 8: A derivation for the sentence: *"John fears everyone who knows her."* This derivation was output by the parser when it was applied to entry I_7 in Table 2, using the lexicon in Table 1, and matches the derivation prescribed by contemporary theories of minimalist syntax. This demonstrates the parser's capacity to model an input with a relative clause – i.e. *"everyone who knows her"*.

Entailment Semantics Can Be Extracted from an Ideal Language Model

William Merrill
New York University

Alex Warstadt
ETH Zürich

Tal Linzen
New York University

{willm,linzen}@nyu.edu alexanderscott.warstadt@inf.ethz.ch

Abstract

Language models are often trained on text alone, without additional grounding. There is debate as to how much of natural language semantics can be inferred from such a procedure. We prove that entailment judgments between sentences can be extracted from an ideal language model that has perfectly learned its target distribution, assuming the training sentences are generated by Gricean agents, i.e., agents who follow fundamental principles of communication from the linguistic theory of pragmatics. We also show entailment judgments can be decoded from the predictions of a language model trained on such Gricean data. Our results reveal a pathway for understanding the semantic information encoded in unlabeled linguistic data and a potential framework for extracting semantics from language models.

1 Introduction

Recent advances in building computational models of language have been powered by *distributional semantics*: the idea that a text span's surrounding context encodes its meaning (Firth, 1957). In particular, large pretrained language models (LMs; Peters et al., 2018; Devlin et al., 2019; Brown et al., 2020) have become an integral part of NLP systems: the representations that emerge from training to predict missing words in a text are empirically useful for natural language understanding tasks.

Despite this empirical progress, Bender and Koller (2020) argue LMs cannot learn to understand the semantics of sentences. This is because of a mismatch between the LM training objective—predicting missing words in text ("form")—and Bender and Koller's conception of meaning as the relation of a sentence to the external world. Thus Bender and Koller claim "that the language modeling task, because it only uses form as training data, cannot in principle lead to learning of meaning."

In this paper, we argue meaning *can* be learned from form because the communicative goals of human authors encode semantic information in unlabeled text. We show how this semantic information can be extracted to resolve semantic relations between sentences (e.g., whether one sentence entails another): in this inferentialist sense, ideal LMs encode the meaning of sentences. This argument has been raised speculatively by others (Michael, 2020; Potts, 2020; Bommasani et al., 2021), but we will rigorously justify it here with formal results.

To give the simplest (and least general) illustration of our argument, we first assume training data is generated by overly idealized *uniformly truthful* speakers: agents who decide what to say by picking sentences they consider true uniformly at random.[1] This very coarsely captures human authors' goal of being informative (rather than misleading) to their listeners (Grice, 1975). In Theorem 1, we prove a sentence x entails sentence y if and only if, after uttering x, a uniformly truthful speaker is just as likely to say y as to repeat x. Thus, entailment semantics can be extracted from probabilistic languages generated by uniformly truthful speakers.

Uniformly truthful speakers are not a realistic model of humans: while humans favor true sentences to false ones (Grice, 1975), not all true sentences are equally likely to be produced. It is a common principle in linguistic theories of pragmatics that human speakers choose their utterances in order to balance two competing objectives: (a) conveying information to their listener and (b) brevity (Levinson et al., 1983; Grice, 1975). We define a class of *Gricean* speakers who optimize for these objectives, and prove in Theorem 2 that x entails y if and only if a simple equation holds in terms of text probabilities produced by such speakers. Thus, entailment semantics can be decoded from probabilistic languages generated by Gricean speakers.

[1] Studying the ability of LMs to understand programming language semantics, Merrill et al. (2021) make a similar assumption that programmers are more likely to write true assertion statements than false ones.

Proceedings of the 26th Conference on Computational Natural Language Learning (CoNLL), pages 176 - 193
December 7-8, 2022 ©2022 Association for Computational Linguistics

The previous results assume access to a language's ideal likelihood function, but, in practice, one only ever receives a corpus *sampled* from the language. Moving to the corpus setting, we analyze how much data allows approximately computing our derived entailment test using probabilities estimated from sentence frequencies in a corpus. We find that the corpus size needed to guarantee the entailment test holds approximately is inversely related to the likelihood of the sentences. We estimate that approximating the entailment test between 4-word sentences using corpus frequencies is possible with $\sim 10^{10}$ sentences, about the size of the GPT-3 training data (Brown et al., 2020). On the other hand, approximating the entailment test for 10-word sentences should be possible with $\sim 10^{17}$ sentences, or $\sim 10^{7}$ GPT-3 corpora. Thus, extracting entailment judgments using corpus frequencies requires an infeasible amount of data—even by modern NLP standards.

To overcome this limitation, one might hope to use probabilities estimated by LMs to extract entailment judgments between longer sentences that are rare even in a large corpus. With synthetic data generated by Gricean speakers, we find that entailment can be decoded from n-gram LM predictions to some extent. However, we speculate that current neural LMs may not score the probability of rare text well enough to enable decoding entailment judgments between natural language sentences.

In summary, our main contribution is to show a correspondence between the semantics of text and its likelihood, assuming the likelihood function matches models of human text production from linguistic theory. Determining whether a sentence in a probabilistic language entails another sentence can be reduced to modeling the probabilities of strings in the language. In practice, entailment judgments between very short sentences can be extracted from corpus frequencies, but this becomes infeasible for slightly longer sentences. LMs can in principle be used to extrapolate the likelihood of longer strings, but we hypothesize current LMs are not well-suited for doing so well enough to enable extracting entailment from natural language. Our theory demonstrates a formal sense in which unlabeled text data encodes linguistic meaning and makes quantitative predictions for (a) how to extract semantics from text corpora and (b) how much data this requires.

2 Definitions

2.1 Sentences and Worlds

Let $\mathcal{X}$ be a finite set of sentences, and $\mathcal{W}$ a countable[2] set of possible world states. A sentence x is a string whose denotation $[\![x]\!]$ is a *proposition*, i.e., a set of world states ($\subseteq \mathcal{W}$) where x is true. Following standard conventions in formal semantics (cf. Heim and Kratzer, 1998), the set $[\![x]\!]$ can be equivalently viewed as a function mapping a world state w to $\{0, 1\}$ that indicates whether x is true in w, which we will write as $[\![x]\!](w)$. We imagine w to encode a partial description of the world, much like the concept of a *situation* in formal semantics (Kratzer, 2021). For simplicity, we assume an individual's subjective belief state can be modeled as the unique, maximal w that fully describes the facts which they believe to be true.

Example $x =$ `John has at least two cats`. Let $\mathcal{W} = \{w_0, w_1, w_2, w_3\}$ be the set of possible worlds, where w_n denotes the state in which John has n cats. Then $[\![x]\!] = \{w_2, w_3\}$, because John has at least two cats in these worlds. Furthermore, it holds that $[\![x]\!](w_2) = 1$, but $[\![x]\!](w_1) = 0$.

2.2 Speakers and Texts

We refer to a sequence of sentences $z \in \mathcal{X}^*$ as a *text*.[3] The meaning of a text is the set of worlds consistent with all its sentences, i.e.,

$$[\![z]\!] = \bigcap_{t=1}^{|z|} [\![z_t]\!].$$

We will imagine that a text $z \in \mathcal{X}^*$ is produced by iteratively sampling $z_t \in \mathcal{X} \cup \{\$\}$ from a *speaker model* $p(z_t \mid z_{<t}, w)$. $p(z_t \mid z_{<t}, w)$ represents the probability of saying sentence z_t with belief state w after having said $z_1 \cdots z_{t-1}$. Let $\$ \notin \mathcal{X}$ be a special *end of sequence* token satisfying $[\![\$]\!] = \mathcal{W}$. We refer to any text ending with \$ as *complete*. Given a world w, an incomplete text $z \in \mathcal{X}^*$ or complete text $z \in \mathcal{X}^*\$$ has *conditional probability*

$$p(z \mid w) = \prod_{t=1}^{|z|} p(z_t \mid z_{<t}, w).$$

The conditional probability of an incomplete text represents the probability of observing z as the

[2]Our results extend to uncountable sets of world states if entailment is relaxed to hold almost surely (cf. §B). Alternatively, our results apply as-is if we assume a countable set of equivalence classes over uncountably many worlds.

[3]Where $\mathcal{X}^*$ denotes the Kleene star closure of $\mathcal{X}$.

prefix of a text written by a human with beliefs w. In contrast, the probability of a complete text represents the probability that a speaker produces z and no further text. The conditional distribution $p(z \mid w)$ cannot be observed directly by a LM, since w is a latent variable missing from the training data. Rather, a LM has access to texts that have been generated by speakers across many possible belief states. Mathematically, this can be expressed by saying a LM's target distribution is a *marginal* distribution over $z \in \mathcal{X}^* \cup \mathcal{X}^*\$$ according to some *prior* distribution over worlds $p(w)$:

$$\begin{aligned} p(z) &= \mathop{\mathbb{E}}_{w \sim p(w)} [p(z \mid w)] \\ &= \mathop{\mathbb{E}}_{w \sim p(w)} \left[\prod_{t=1}^{\infty} p(z_t \mid z_{<t}, w) \right]. \end{aligned}$$

The prior $p(w)$ represents the probability that a speaker contributing to the corpus will have belief state w—we make no assumptions about its form besides that $p(w) > 0$ for all $w \in \mathcal{W}$, and, for every sentence, there is some world state that makes that sentence true. In contrast to $p(z)$, which corresponds to the expected corpus frequency of z, we denote by $p(\llbracket z \rrbracket)$ the probability that z is true.[4]

Example Let z be the 2-sentence text:[5]

$$z_1 = \texttt{We swung our swords.}$$
$$z_2 = \texttt{That was ever so long ago.}$$

Let p be the distribution of all possible English web texts. The marginal probability $p(z)$ can be decomposed across many possible worlds. One such world w_1 might be the world where the speaker is the semi-legendary Viking hero Ragnar Loðbrók (in modern English translation); another world w_2 might be the perspective of a Reddit user reviewing a coffee maker. Each of these worlds corresponds to one term in a sum over all worlds. We expect $p(z \mid w_1)$ to be higher than $p(z \mid w_2)$ since it is more likely for a medieval literary character to utter z than a modern product reviewer. Finally, $p(z \mid w_1)$ can be factored as

$$p(z_1 \mid w_1) p(z_2 \mid z_1, w_1).$$

In contrast to $p(z)$, which counts all contexts where z is the beginning of a longer text, $p(z\$)$ measures the frequency of $z_1 z_2$ followed by nothing else.

[4]The notation explicitly represents the probability mass assigned to the set of worlds where z is true.

[5]Text taken from the Wikipedia page for the skaldic poem *Krákumál*, written in Ragnar's voice.

2.3 Distributional and Semantic Relations

Distributional Relations A *distributional relation* d is a relation over sentences x and y defined in terms of likelihood of different texts under some distribution p. Let $d_p(x, y)$ be the value of the distributional relation d between sentences x, y according to distribution p. If we train an LM on texts sampled from a target distribution p, the LM estimates a predictive distribution $\hat{p}$. Thus, any LM parameterizes $d_{\hat{p}}$: an instantiation of the distributional relation d with respect to the probabilities learned by the LM. If the LM perfectly approximates $p(x)$ for all x, then $d_{\hat{p}} = d_p$ by construction.

Example Define the distributional relation d (with respect to some distribution p) such that $d^>_p(x, y) \iff p(x) > p(y)$. $d^>_p(x, y)$ says x is more likely than y according to p. If $\hat{p}$ represents LM predictions trained on the target distribution p, than $d^>_{\hat{p}}(x, y)$ says whether the LM predicts a sentence x is more likely than another sentence y.

Semantic Relations In contrast, a semantic relation between x and y is a relation defined in terms of their denotations $\llbracket x \rrbracket$ and $\llbracket y \rrbracket$. We will focus on the key semantic relation of entailment:

Definition 1 For two sentences $x, y \in \mathcal{X}$, x entails y if and only if $\llbracket x \rrbracket \subseteq \llbracket y \rrbracket$.

It is not clear *prima facie* if LMs can represent entailment relations. However, it could be that a semantic relation s can somehow equivalently be written as a distributional relation d_p. If so, a LM that perfectly approximates p could be understood to encode s, since s can be extracted from $\hat{p}$ via $d_{\hat{p}}$.

Formally, we can ask if a semantic relation can be alternatively expressed as a distributional relation by analyzing if there exists an isomorphism between a semantic relation $s(\llbracket x \rrbracket, \llbracket y \rrbracket)$ and some distributional relation $d_p(x, y)$:

Definition 2 (Isomorphism) A semantic relation s is isomorphic to a distributional relation d under speaker p if and only if, for all $x, y \in \mathcal{X}$,

$$s(\llbracket x \rrbracket, \llbracket y \rrbracket) \iff d_p(x, y).$$

If Definition 2 holds under a speaker model p, then predicting whether s holds between two sentences is reducible to perfectly modeling the probabilities of texts generated by p. Our goal going forward will be to derive distributional relations isomorphic to entailment assuming p models the goals of humans when they produce text.

3 Uniformly Truthful Speakers

We start by illustrating our research question and technical approach assuming an overly simple model of humans as *uniformly truthful* speakers. A uniformly truthful speaker chooses a sentence to produce by selecting one of the true sentences that holds in their belief state uniformly at random. This very coarsely captures the property of natural language pragmatics that subjectively true sentences tend to be more likely than false ones, although it does not account for many other factors that influence human speech patterns in complex ways (Grice, 1975).[6] Let $n(w)$ be the number of *sentences* true in world w. We can formally define a uniformly truthful speaker as follows:

Definition 3 A speaker p is *uniformly truthful* if, for all sentences $x \in \mathcal{X} \cup \{\$\}$,

$$p(x \mid w) = \frac{[\![x]\!](w)}{\sum_{x'} [\![x']\!](w)} = \frac{[\![x]\!](w)}{n(w)}.$$

In other words, p uniformly spreads probability mass across all sentences that are true in world w. We will show that, if the corpus consists of text written by uniformly truthful speakers, entailment can be decided by a distributional relation. The following lemma will be a core technical tool in our analysis. Informally, it is useful because it establishes a correspondence between relations over sets of worlds and probabilities.

Lemma 1 *Let $\mathbb{1}_{\mathcal{S}}$ be the indicator function for set $\mathcal{S}$. For sets $\mathcal{A}, \mathcal{B}$ such that $\mathcal{A} \subseteq \mathcal{B} \subseteq \mathcal{W}$, and $c : \mathcal{W} \to \mathbb{R}_+$, $\mathcal{A} = \mathcal{B}$ if and only if*

$$\sum_{w \in \mathcal{W}} \mathbb{1}_{\mathcal{A}}(w) c(w) = \sum_{w \in \mathcal{W}} \mathbb{1}_{\mathcal{B}}(w) c(w).$$

Proof. We will prove that $\mathcal{B} \subseteq \mathcal{A}$ by contradiction. Assume there exists $w \in \mathcal{B}$ such that $w \notin \mathcal{A}$. Then the right sum contains the positive term $c(w)$, while the left sum does not. Because all terms in the right sum are positive, the left sum must contain at least one term $c(w')$ that the right sum does not. Thus, $w' \in \mathcal{A}$ but $w' \notin \mathcal{B}$. But this has violated our assumption that $\mathcal{A} \subseteq \mathcal{B}$. □

We now use Lemma 1 to derive a simple distributional relation that is isomorphic to entailment.

[6]LMs sometimes generate objectively false statements (Lin et al., 2022), presumably due to the occurrence of such facts in their training data. This is actually consistent with a uniform truthfulness assumption, which only requires that speakers only produce sentences they believe are true, not sentences that are actually true in some objective sense.

Theorem 1 *If p is a uniformly truthful speaker, then entailment is isomorphic to a distributional relation. Specifically, for all sentences $x, y \in \mathcal{X}$,*

$$[\![x]\!] \subseteq [\![y]\!] \iff p(xy) = p(xx).$$

Proof. $d_p(x, y)$ holds if and only if

$$\begin{aligned} p(xy) &= p(xx) \\ \mathop{\mathbb{E}}_{w} \left[\frac{[\![x]\!](w)[\![y]\!](w)}{n(w)^2} \right] &= \mathop{\mathbb{E}}_{w} \left[\frac{[\![x]\!](w)[\![x]\!](w)}{n(w)^2} \right] \\ \mathop{\mathbb{E}}_{w} \left[\frac{[\![x]\!](w)[\![y]\!](w)}{n(w)^2} \right] &= \mathop{\mathbb{E}}_{w} \left[\frac{[\![x]\!](w)}{n(w)^2} \right]. \end{aligned}$$

An expectation in a countable space is a sum weighted by probability masses. So, by Lemma 1, this holds iff $[\![x]\!] = [\![xy]\!] = [\![x]\!] \cap [\![y]\!]$. We conclude $p(xy) = p(xx)$ if and only if $[\![x]\!] \subseteq [\![y]\!]$. □

A similar proof suffices to show that the following isomorphism also holds:

Corollary 1.1 *If p is a uniformly truthful speaker, the following isomorphism holds for all $x, y \in \mathcal{X}$:*

$$[\![x]\!] \subseteq [\![y]\!] \iff p(xy) = p(x\$).$$

3.1 Discussion

Uniformly truthful speakers resemble humans in that they mimic the *tendency* of humans to tell the truth about what they believe. However, they are clearly too simple to account for human speech patterns. Most crucially, humans generally aim to produce informative speech, rather than sampling true sentences at random. More fundamentally, natural language has a countably infinite number of possible sentences, so a uniform distribution over all true sentences is not even mathematically well-defined. These limitations motivate our more involved analysis of Gricean speakers, which will adapt the technical tools used in this section.

4 Gricean Speakers

In this section, we will define a new class of speakers who pick sentences in order to be informative to their listener, while also trying to be concise. To do this, we will draw on information theory to formalize what it means for a speaker to be informative. We will then derive a distributional relation that is isomorphic to entailment for Gricean speakers, which is a generalization of the relation for uniformly truthful speakers from §3.

4.1 Definition

Information The first step towards formalizing Gricean speakers is to define a notion of the semantic information contained in a sentence. We formalize a listener $\ell(w \mid z)$ as the inverse of a speaker: Given a text $z \in \mathcal{X}^*$, a listener produces a distribution over possible world states. Then, in a given world w we can define the information that a text conveys to the listener as the reduction in the number of bits needed to transmit w to ℓ after they have read z compared to before they have read z.

Definition 4 The information content of a text $z \in \mathcal{X}^* \cup \mathcal{X}^*\$$ to a listener $\ell(w \mid z)$ is[7]

$$I_\ell(z; w) = \log \ell(w \mid z) - \log \ell(w).$$

In other words, the information content of a text is the reduction in ℓ's code length for the world after having read the text compared to beforehand. We can naturally extend Definition 4 to measure the *conditional information* conveyed by sentence y given that x has already been produced:

Definition 5 The information content of $y \in \mathcal{X}^* \cup \mathcal{X}^*\$$ given $x \in \mathcal{X}^*$ to a listener $\ell(w \mid z)$ is

$$\begin{aligned} I_\ell(y \mid x; w) &= I_\ell(xy; w) - I_\ell(x; w) \\ &= \log \ell(w \mid xy) - \log \ell(w \mid x). \end{aligned}$$

Informative Speaker We now define a Gricean speaker in terms of I_ℓ. Our definition generalizes the rational speech acts model (Goodman and Frank, 2016), but makes weaker assumptions about the listener and allows a dynamic semantics where later sentences can condition on previous ones (Lewis, 1979; Kamp, 1981; Heim, 1982). We define an utterance's utility as a convex combination of its information content and its cost to produce, operationalizing the Gricean idea that speakers pick utterances by weighing their informativeness against their cost. The cost function $c : \mathcal{X}^* \cup \mathcal{X}^*\$ \to \mathbb{R}$ can be any measure of sentence complexity (e.g., length) satisfying $c(xy) = c(x) + c(y)$ for $x, y \in \mathcal{X}^* \cup \mathcal{X}^*\$$.[8]

Definition 6 A speaker p is *Gricean* if there exists a listener $\ell(w \mid z)$, some $\alpha > 0$, and a cost function c such that, for all $z \in \mathcal{X}^* \cup \mathcal{X}^*\$$:

$$p(z \mid w) \propto \exp\left(\alpha I_\ell(z; w) - c(z)\right).$$

[7]For convenience, we let $\log 0 = -\infty$ and $\infty - \infty = 0$.

[8]This is satisfied when $c(x)$ is the length of x, but also for other options like the corpus frequency of x (Goodman and Frank, 2016) or the depth of the syntactic tree of x.

Further, ℓ must satisfy the following for all $x \in \mathcal{X}^*$, $y \in \mathcal{X} \cup \{\$\}$, and $w \in \mathcal{W}$,

$$I_\ell(y \mid x; w) = 0 \iff [\![x]\!](w) \to [\![y]\!](w).$$

In other words, the speaker must be trying to convey information about the state of the world to some listener who fully absorbs the semantic information in all sentences they have already heard: clarifying already established information will not benefit the listener. We can formalize this by deriving $p(y \mid x, w)$ for $x \in \mathcal{X}^*$ and $y \in \mathcal{X} \cup \{\$\}$:

$$\begin{aligned} p(y \mid x, w) &= \frac{p(xy \mid w)}{p(x \mid w)} \\ &\propto \exp\left(\alpha I_\ell(y \mid x; w) - c(y)\right). \end{aligned}$$

Notably, the probability of y given x depends on the *conditional information* of y given x, which means only information conveyed by y that is nonredundant with x will make y more likely.[9]

4.2 Results

Proofs are in §C. Under a Gricean speaker, the cost of an utterance can be expressed:

Lemma 2 *For any Gricean speaker p and $x \in \mathcal{X}$,*

$$\frac{p(x\$)}{p(xx)} = \frac{\exp(c(x))}{\exp(c(\$))}.$$

Corollary 2.1 *Under a Gricean speaker, for all $x \in \mathcal{X}$, $c(x) = \log p(x\$) - \log p(xx) + c(\$)$.*

Corollary 2.1 says that a sentence is costly to the extent that it is unlikely to be repeated twice, giving an intuitive characterization of this quantity in terms of text probabilities. Now, we will use this characterization of cost to derive a distributional relation that is isomorphic to entailment.

Theorem 2 *Under any Gricean speaker p, entailment is isomorphic to a distributional relation. Specifically, for all sentences $x, y \in \mathcal{X}$,*

$$[\![x]\!] \subseteq [\![y]\!] \iff \frac{p(xy)}{p(x\$)} = \frac{p(yy)}{p(y\$)}.$$

If we allow our decision rule to depend on the cost function c in addition to probabilities, we can simplify Theorem 2 as follows:

[9]From a technical perspective, the exp in Definition 6 is justified by the fact that probabilities decompose multiplicatively, i.e., $p(xy \mid w) = p(x \mid w)p(y \mid x, w)$, but the information content and cost of text should decompose additively across different sentences. Applying basic exponent rules shows that Definition 6 satisfies this desideratum.

Corollary 2.1 *Under any Gricean speaker p, for all sentences $x, y \in \mathcal{X}$, $[\![x]\!] \subseteq [\![y]\!]$ if and only if*

$$\log p(x\$) - \log p(xy) = c(y) - c(\$).$$

If we imagine $c(y) - c(\$) = 0$ for a uniformly truthful speaker, we see the equation in Theorem 2 is a generalization of the equation in Theorem 1.

4.3 Discussion

Gricean speakers are a general enough model of humans speakers to capture the basic pragmatic principles influencing speech production. Thus, it is notable that Theorem 2 establishes a closed-form distributional relation isomorphic to entailment.

One conceptual limitation of Gricean speakers is that their simulated listener must fully consume information, such that redundantly conveying the same information twice will not lead to any information gain the second time. This contrasts with real speech, where potential interpretation errors by the listener incentivize the speaker to be somewhat redundant (Degen et al., 2019). Mathematically, this would violate the axiom of Definition 6 that

$$I_\ell(y \mid x; w) = 0 \iff [\![x]\!](w) \to [\![y]\!](w).$$

Extending Theorem 2 to speakers who use redundancy to account for noise and interpretation errors is an interesting direction for future work.

Another interesting extension would be formalizing speakers who aim to be informative regarding some question under discussion, rather than being generally informative about w (cf. Goodman and Lassiter, 2015). This could encompass both "what" questions that aim to clarify some aspect of the world, and "why" questions that aim to convey explanations for established facts.

5 Decoding Entailment from Empirical Text Frequencies

We have so far shown that entailment judgments can be extracted from the sentence probabilities in the ideal distribution $p(z)$. What happens if, more practically, we estimate the probability of a sentence by its frequency in a large corpus sampled from $p(z)$? We prove this method enables feasible extraction of entailment judgments between very short sentences, but the corpus size may become intractably large for longer sentences.

Imagine we have a finite corpus of *iid* sentences $\{Z_i\}_{i=1}^n$, each sampled from $p(z)$. Let $\hat{p}(z)$ be the empirical frequency of a text z in the corpus, i.e., if $\pi(z, z')$ returns whether text z is a prefix of text z',

$$\hat{p}(z) = \frac{1}{n} \sum_{i=1}^{n} \pi(z, Z_i).$$

Since $p(z)$ encodes entailment via our extraction rules, $\hat{p}(z)$ will encode entailment between sentences if $\hat{p}(z)$ is close to $p(z)$. A naive notion of closeness is to guarantee, for all ϵ, there exists some number of texts n such that, with high probability, $|p(z) - \hat{p}(z)| < \epsilon$. But this notion is not strict enough: if $p(z)$ is small, this difference will also be small, even if $\hat{p}(z)$ is not a good approximation of $p(z)$ on a relative scale. Instead, we want to guarantee that $\hat{p}(z)/p(z)$ converges to 1, or, equivalently, that their difference as log probabilities converges to 0. This ensures that convergence will still be meaningful for low-probability sentences, which most sentences are in natural language.

Under this standard, rarer sentences take more samples to approximate. Define the sentence complexity $\mathfrak{K}_p(z) = \frac{1}{p(z)}$. We bound the approximation error in terms of $\mathfrak{K}_p(z)$.[10]

Lemma 3 *For $z \in \mathcal{X}^* \cup \mathcal{X}^*\$$ and $\delta > 0$, it holds with probability at least $1 - \delta - (1 - p(z))^n$ that*

$$|\log p(z) - \log \hat{p}(z)| \leq \sqrt{\frac{\mathfrak{K}_p(z)}{\delta n}}.$$

To make this bound non-vacuous, n must be large enough to counteract $\mathfrak{K}_p(z)$ and bring $(1 - p(z))^n$ close to 0. Thus, good approximation requires fewer samples for more common sentences. To get a more concrete view of the number of samples required to extract entailment judgments from an LM, we analyze $\mathfrak{K}_p(z)$ for Gricean speakers.[11]

Recall that we write $c(z)$ for the cost that a Gricean speaker assigns to producing a sentence z. For Gricean speakers, $\mathfrak{K}_p(z)$ is related to $c(z)$ as well as the probability z is true.

Theorem 3 *Assume that $p(z \mid w)$ is a Gricean speaker with respect to listener ℓ and $[\![z]\!](w) = 1 \iff I_\ell(z; w) \geq 0$. Let $g_p(x, y) = \log \frac{p(xy)}{p(x\$)} - \log \frac{p(yy)}{p(y\$)}$. Let $q = 1 - \min\{p(xy), p(yy)\}$. Then, for all $x, y \in \mathcal{X}$ such that $[\![xy]\!](p) > 0$, for all $\delta > 0$, it holds with probability at least $1 - \delta - 4q^n$ that $|g_p(x, y) - g_{\hat{p}}(x, y)|$ is at most*

$$8\sqrt{\frac{\exp(\max\{c(xy), c(yy)\})}{p([\![xy]\!])} \cdot \frac{1}{\delta n}}.$$

[10] Omitted proofs from §5 are in §D.

[11] §D also analyzes uniformly truthful speakers.

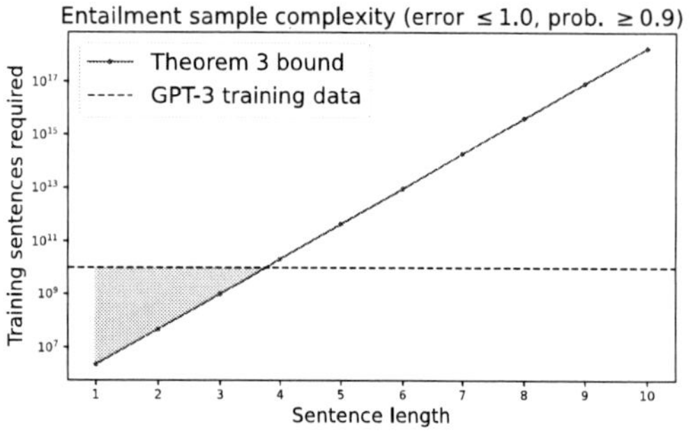

Figure 1: Estimated number of training sentences for guaranteeing $g_{\hat{p}}$ closely approximates g_p, where $\hat{p}$ is estimated using empirical text frequencies.

Theorem 3 says we can use text frequencies to decode entailment between sentences x, y from a Gricean corpus, but the number of training sentences to guarantee this grows exponentially with the cost of x and y. Thus, we probably cannot expect to extract entailment judgments from text frequencies except between *very short* sentences.

We make this more quantitative in Figure 1, where we estimate the number of training sentences needed to ensure g_p and $g_{\hat{p}}$ are close on sentences of length $\leq k$ as a function of k. The main assumption behind this calculation is that a sentence's probability vanishes exponentially in its length, where the exponential base is the perplexity of the language. §E documents the underlying assumptions in more detail. Figure 1 predicts g_p and $g_{\hat{p}}$ can be made close for length-4 sentences using $\sim 10^{10}$ training sentences: about as much data as GPT-3 was trained on. In contrast, handling (still short) sentences of length 10 can be done with $\sim 10^{17}$ training sentences, or $\sim 10^7$ GPT-3 corpora. Thus, relying solely on corpus frequencies is likely not a feasible way to extract entailment relations from text generated by Gricean speakers.

6 Decoding Entailment from LMs

We have just analyzed how many samples are necessary to decode entailment relations from the text frequencies in a finite corpus. As shown by Theorem 3, this approach will require intractably many samples for sentences of nontrivial length because longer strings will appear infrequently (if at all) in the corpus. In order to estimate the probability of rare, longer, strings what if we use an LM to estimate $\hat{p}(z)$ instead of text frequencies? Perhaps a smoothed LM should allow us to extrapolate $\hat{p}(z)$ well enough for long sentences to extract entailment judgments between them. In this section, we briefly discuss some limitations of this approach.

It is tempting to take low LM perplexity as evidence that an LM estimates sentence probabilities well enough to approximately satisfy the isomorphism in Theorem 2. After all, low test perplexity implies that $\hat{p}(z)$ is, on average, a good approximation of $p(z)$: if the perplexity is bounded below ϵ, then the KL divergence $\mathrm{KL}(p, \hat{p})$ is bounded below $\log \epsilon$. ϵ decreases with the amount of training data n at a rate between $\Omega(1/\sqrt{n})$ and $\Omega(1/n)$ (Wang et al., 2013; Li and Liu, 2021). Thus, with enough data, $\hat{p}(z)$ will closely approximate $p(z)$ for an average sentence z in the training distribution.

But low error on an average z does not establish entailment can be decoded from $\hat{p}$ because $d_{\hat{p}}$, as derived in Theorem 2, depends on the text $z = yy$, which is very unlikely in natural language.[12] Poorly estimating $p(yy)$ has little impact on $\mathrm{KL}(p, \hat{p})$, so LMs trained to minimize $\mathrm{KL}(p, \hat{p})$ have no reason to estimate $p(yy)$ well unless they are imbued with strong inductive biases. Thus, we expect that LMs trained with a standard cross-entropy loss may not produce reliable entailment judgments because they poorly estimate the probability of key valid (but unlikely) texts.[13] However, we find in the next section that they do succeed in the easier setting of small artificial languages and fully Gricean speakers.

7 Experiments: Extracting Semantics from Simulated Gricean Corpora

We test empirically whether we can extract entailment judgments from LMs trained on unlabelled text.[14] Natural language corpora are unlikely to adhere exactly to our idealized assumptions about the speakers generating texts, so we generate the training corpora from a simulated Gricean speaker (see §4). To make learning semantics more tractable with limited computation, we set $|\mathcal{W}| = 3$ and restrict the vocabulary $\mathcal{X}$ to 7 utterances, each denoting one of the 7 non-empty subsets of $\mathcal{W}$. Each sentence in the training corpus is generated by sampling utterances from a Gricean speaker, conditioned on a uniformly sampled world state and the

[12] yy is unlikely to be produced by a Gricean speaker because the second y conveys no information.

[13] Future work should more carefully analyze how much data is required to extract complex entailment relations from LM predictions (rather than corpus frequencies). This is beyond the scope of the current project. .

[14] `https://github.com/viking-sudo-rm/formal-language-understanding`

previously generated utterance, until the tautological utterance is generated. The semantic value of a sentence is taken to be the conjunction over all of its utterances. We set the rationality parameter α and the cost function heuristically (details in §G).

We generate training sets varying in size from 2 texts to 10M texts, and train two types of models on each: a simple empirical text frequency as described in Section 5, and a trigram model implemented using NLTK (Bird, 2006). Then for all sentence pairs (x, y), where x and y have 6 utterances or fewer and each denotes a non-empty proposition, we compute $g_{\hat{p}}(x, y)$ from §5. Theorem 2 shows that, under the true distribution p, $g_{\hat{p}}(x, y) = 0$ if and only if x entails y.

The results are plotted in Figure 2. We arrive at the following conclusions:

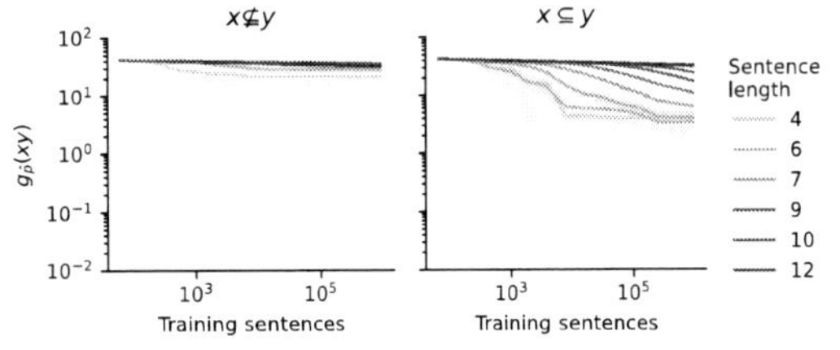

(a) $\hat{p}(x)$ given by text frequency model.

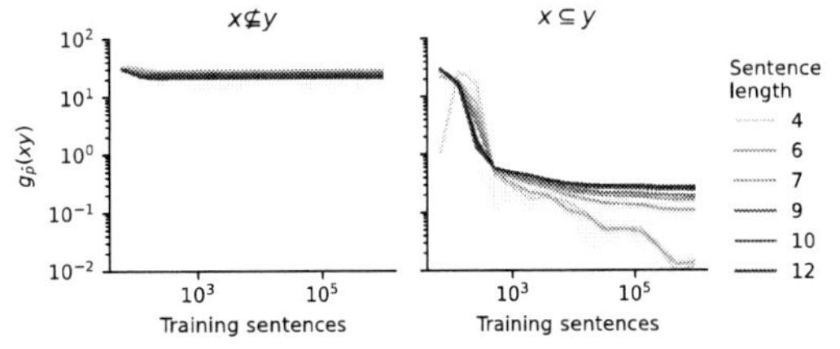

(b) $\hat{p}(x)$ given by trigram model.

Figure 2: Plot of $g_{\hat{p}}(x, y) = \log \frac{\hat{p}(xy)}{\hat{p}(x\$)} - \log \frac{\hat{p}(yy)}{\hat{p}(y\$)}$ as a function of the number of sentences in the training corpus and the length $|xy|$. Given the true distribution p, $g_p(x, y) = 0$ iff x entails y. We exclude pairs x, y where both xy and yy are absent from the training data.

Entailment relations can be extracted with greater-than-chance performance from LM predictions. The value of $g_{\hat{p}}(x, y)$ is much closer to 0 on average for entailed pairs than for non-entailed pairs. This is predicted by Theorem 2.

The size of the corpus needed to extract entailment grows predictably with sentence length. For entailed pairs, the average value of $g_{\hat{p}}(x, y)$ for shorter sentences approaches 0 more quickly with a large training corpus. This is in line with the predictions of Theorem 4.

Model inductive bias impacts the ease of extracting entailment. Entailed and non-entailed pairs are better distinguished by the trigram model than the text frequency model. Specifically, $g_{\hat{p}}(x, y)$ is closer to 0 for the trigram model for a given amount of data, and the trigram model's predictions are less sensitive to sentence length.

8 Generality of Extracting Semantics

Our main result that entailment judgments can be extracted from an ideal LM assumes the corpus was produced by Gricean speakers. While pragmatic theory supports this assumption, real human speakers are undoubtedly more complex. What if we relax the assumption that speakers are Gricean? In Theorem 6 in §F, we show that any semantic relation is isomorphic to some distributional relation as long as, for any pair of possible semantics, there is some text whose probability distinguishes between the two candidate semantics.

We take it to be uncontroversial that semantics influences speech production, so we interpret Theorem 6 to say all semantic relations are fully encoded in ideal LMs. In contrast to Theorem 2, however, this result is nonconstructive, so we do not know which algorithm to use to decide entailment between two sentences, even though one exists. Further, without further assumptions about the speaker, we cannot guarantee the extraction relation is efficiently computable or even computable at all.

9 Conclusion

Given a general, linguistically motivated model of human text production, we proved that entailment judgments can be decoded from the likelihood function for texts because of semantic artifacts created by human authors. We also showed empirically that entailment could be extracted n-gram LMs trained on simple formal languages. Thus, we have given one explanation for why distributional information encodes semantic information (Firth, 1957) and how semantic relations are, in principle, extractable from LMs. It is an open question whether entailment judgments might be extractable from current large LMs, but we hypothesize that the complexity of natural language makes this substantially more challenging than with our synthetic experiments, and that the loss function and inductive biases of current neural LMs are not well suited for doing so without an infeasible amount of data.

A natural next step for future work is to test this hypothesis empirically by measuring whether entailment judgments can be extracted from large LMs using our theory. Similarly, it would be interesting to think about how LMs could be modified so that they can better pick up on the semantic information encoded in their training distribution.

10 Acknowledgments

This project benefited from informal discussions with Chris Barker, Sam Bowman, Lucius Bynum, Kyunghun Cho, Tiwa Eisape, Yanai Elazar, Najoung Kim, Alexander Koller, Vishakh Padmakumar, Chris Potts, Naomi Saphra, Sebastian Schuster, and Noah A. Smith. We also thank the members of the CAP Lab and Semantics Group at NYU for their feedback. This work was supported in part through the NYU IT High Performance Computing resources, services, and staff expertise. It was funded by NSF award 1922658, and WM was supported by an NSF graduate research fellowship.

References

Emily M. Bender and Alexander Koller. 2020. Climbing towards NLU: On meaning, form, and understanding in the age of data. In *Proceedings of the 58th Annual Meeting of the Association for Computational Linguistics*, pages 5185–5198, Online. Association for Computational Linguistics.

Steven Bird. 2006. NLTK: The Natural Language Toolkit. In *Proceedings of the COLING/ACL 2006 Interactive Presentation Sessions*, pages 69–72, Sydney, Australia. Association for Computational Linguistics.

Rishi Bommasani, Drew A. Hudson, Ehsan Adeli, Russ Altman, Simran Arora, Sydney von Arx, Michael S. Bernstein, Jeannette Bohg, Antoine Bosselut, Emma Brunskill, Erik Brynjolfsson, Shyamal Buch, Dallas Card, Rodrigo Castellon, Niladri Chatterji, Annie Chen, Kathleen Creel, Jared Quincy Davis, Dora Demszky, Chris Donahue, Moussa Doumbouya, Esin Durmus, Stefano Ermon, John Etchemendy, Kawin Ethayarajh, Li Fei-Fei, Chelsea Finn, Trevor Gale, Lauren Gillespie, Karan Goel, Noah Goodman, Shelby Grossman, Neel Guha, Tatsunori Hashimoto, Peter Henderson, John Hewitt, Daniel E. Ho, Jenny Hong, Kyle Hsu, Jing Huang, Thomas Icard, Saahil Jain, Dan Jurafsky, Pratyusha Kalluri, Siddharth Karamcheti, Geoff Keeling, Fereshte Khani, Omar Khattab, Pang Wei Koh, Mark Krass, Ranjay Krishna, Rohith Kuditipudi, Ananya Kumar, Faisal Ladhak, Mina Lee, Tony Lee, Jure Leskovec, Isabelle Levent, Xiang Lisa Li, Xuechen Li, Tengyu Ma, Ali Malik, Christopher D. Manning, Suvir Mirchandani, Eric Mitchell, Zanele Munyikwa, Suraj Nair, Avanika Narayan, Deepak Narayanan, Ben Newman, Allen Nie, Juan Carlos Niebles, Hamed Nilforoshan, Julian Nyarko, Giray Ogut, Laurel Orr, Isabel Papadimitriou, Joon Sung Park, Chris Piech, Eva Portelance, Christopher Potts, Aditi Raghunathan, Rob Reich, Hongyu Ren, Frieda Rong, Yusuf Roohani, Camilo Ruiz, Jack Ryan, Christopher Ré, Dorsa Sadigh, Shiori Sagawa, Keshav Santhanam, Andy Shih, Krishnan Srinivasan, Alex Tamkin, Rohan Taori, Armin W. Thomas, Florian Tramèr, Rose E. Wang, William Wang, Bohan Wu, Jiajun Wu, Yuhuai Wu, Sang Michael Xie, Michihiro Yasunaga, Jiaxuan You, Matei Zaharia, Michael Zhang, Tianyi Zhang, Xikun Zhang, Yuhui Zhang, Lucia Zheng, Kaitlyn Zhou, and Percy Liang. 2021. On the opportunities and risks of foundation models.

Tom Brown, Benjamin Mann, Nick Ryder, Melanie Subbiah, Jared D Kaplan, Prafulla Dhariwal, Arvind Neelakantan, Pranav Shyam, Girish Sastry, Amanda Askell, Sandhini Agarwal, Ariel Herbert-Voss, Gretchen Krueger, Tom Henighan, Rewon Child, Aditya Ramesh, Daniel Ziegler, Jeffrey Wu, Clemens Winter, Chris Hesse, Mark Chen, Eric Sigler, Mateusz Litwin, Scott Gray, Benjamin Chess, Jack Clark, Christopher Berner, Sam McCandlish, Alec Radford, Ilya Sutskever, and Dario Amodei. 2020. Language models are few-shot learners. In *Advances in Neural Information Processing Systems*, volume 33, pages 1877–1901. Curran Associates, Inc.

Judith Degen, Robert XD Hawkins, Caroline Graf, Elisa Kreiss, and Noah D Goodman. 2019. When redundancy is rational: A Bayesian approach to "overinformative" referring expressions. *arXiv preprint arXiv:1903.08237.*

Jacob Devlin, Ming-Wei Chang, Kenton Lee, and Kristina Toutanova. 2019. BERT: Pre-training of deep bidirectional transformers for language understanding. In *Proceedings of the 2019 Conference of the North American Chapter of the Association for Computational Linguistics: Human Language Technologies, Volume 1 (Long and Short Papers)*, pages 4171–4186, Minneapolis, Minnesota. Association for Computational Linguistics.

John R Firth. 1957. A synopsis of linguistic theory, 1930-1955. *Studies in linguistic analysis.*

Noah D Goodman and Michael C Frank. 2016. Pragmatic language interpretation as probabilistic inference. *Trends in cognitive sciences*, 20(11):818–829.

Noah D Goodman and Daniel Lassiter. 2015. Probabilistic semantics and pragmatics: Uncertainty in language and thought. *The handbook of contemporary semantic theory, 2nd edition. Wiley-Blackwell.*

Herbert P Grice. 1975. Logic and conversation. In *Speech acts*, pages 41–58. Brill.

Irene Heim and Angelika Kratzer. 1998. *Semantics in Generative Grammar.* Blackwell.

Irene Roswitha Heim. 1982. *The semantics of definite and indefinite noun phrases*. University of Massachusetts Amherst.

Hans A Kamp. 1981. A theory of truth and semantic representation formal methods in the study of language, part 1, ed. by jeroen groenendijk, theo janssen and martin and stokhof. *Amsterdam: Mathematisch Centrum*.

Angelika Kratzer. 2021. Situations in Natural Language Semantics. In Edward N. Zalta, editor, *The Stanford Encyclopedia of Philosophy*, Winter 2021 edition. Metaphysics Research Lab, Stanford University.

Stephen C Levinson, Stephen C Levinson, and S Levinson. 1983. *Pragmatics*. Cambridge university press.

David Lewis. 1979. Scorekeeping in a language game. In *Semantics from different points of view*, pages 172–187. Springer.

Shaojie Li and Yong Liu. 2021. Towards sharper generalization bounds for structured prediction. *Advances in Neural Information Processing Systems*, 34.

Stephanie Lin, Jacob Hilton, and Owain Evans. 2022. TruthfulQA: Measuring how models mimic human falsehoods. In *Proceedings of the 60th Annual Meeting of the Association for Computational Linguistics (Volume 1: Long Papers)*, pages 3214–3252, Dublin, Ireland. Association for Computational Linguistics.

William Merrill, Yoav Goldberg, Roy Schwartz, and Noah A. Smith. 2021. Provable Limitations of Acquiring Meaning from Ungrounded Form: What Will Future Language Models Understand? *Transactions of the Association for Computational Linguistics*, 9:1047–1060.

Julian Michael. 2020. To dissect an octopus: Making sense of the form/meaning debate.

Matthew E. Peters, Mark Neumann, Mohit Iyyer, Matt Gardner, Christopher Clark, Kenton Lee, and Luke Zettlemoyer. 2018. Deep contextualized word representations. In *Proceedings of the 2018 Conference of the North American Chapter of the Association for Computational Linguistics: Human Language Technologies, Volume 1 (Long Papers)*, pages 2227–2237, New Orleans, Louisiana. Association for Computational Linguistics.

Christopher Potts. 2020. Is it possible for language models to achieve understanding?

Shaojun Wang, Russell Greiner, and Shaomin Wang. 2013. Consistency and generalization bounds for maximum entropy density estimation. *Entropy*, 15(12):5439–5463.

A Limitations

We derived a recipe for computing entailment in terms of text probabilities, hinting that entailment judgments may be decodable from LM predictions. Yet two key concerns qualify this conclusion.

Learnability We reduce entailment classification to computing probabilities in the *target distribution* of an LM, not probabilities predicted by an LM. In §6, we argue that the loss function of current LMs is not well suited to producing models from which entailment can be extracted.

Speaker Assumptions Gricean speakers capture important factors influencing speech production in pragmatic theory, but human speakers are undoubtedly more complex. Based on §8, we expect a similar isomorphism to hold under any reasonable speaker model, but the mathematical form may change and it may become harder to compute.

B Uncountable World Spaces

In this section, we assume $\mathcal{W}$ is an uncountably infinite set with a a probability density function $p(w)$. We then define "almost sure" entailment as follows:

Definition 7 For $x, y \in \mathcal{X}$, we say x almost surely entails y (i.e., $[\![x]\!] \sqsubseteq [\![y]\!]$) if and only if

$$p([\![x]\!] \setminus [\![y]\!]) = 0.$$

Note that if $\mathcal{W}$ is countable, then $\mathcal{A} \sqsubseteq \mathcal{B}$ reduces to $\mathcal{A} \subseteq \mathcal{B}$. We can generalize Lemma 1 as follows, which shows that all our results go through for almost sure entailment when $\mathcal{W}$ is uncountable.

Lemma 4 *Let $\mathbb{1}_{\mathcal{S}}$ be the indicator function for set $\mathcal{S}$. Let $f : \mathcal{W} \to \mathbb{R}$ be some function such that $\inf_{w \in \mathcal{W}} f(w) > 0$. For any sets $\mathcal{A}, \mathcal{B}$ such that $\mathcal{A} \subseteq \mathcal{B} \subseteq \mathcal{W}$, then $p(\mathcal{B} \setminus \mathcal{A}) = 0$ if and only if*

$$\mathop{\mathbb{E}}_{w \sim p(w)} [\mathbb{1}_{\mathcal{A}}(w) f(w)] = \mathop{\mathbb{E}}_{w \sim p(w)} [\mathbb{1}_{\mathcal{B}}(w) f(w)] .$$

Proof. If $p(\mathcal{B} \setminus \mathcal{A}) = 0$, then the condition follows by construction. We thus only need to show that the condition follows from $p(\mathcal{B} \setminus \mathcal{A}) = 0$. Let $q = p(\mathcal{B} \setminus \mathcal{A})$. By linearity of expectation, we rewrite the premise condition as

$$\begin{aligned}
0 &= \mathop{\mathbb{E}}_{w \sim p(w)} [(\mathbb{1}_{\mathcal{A}}(w) - \mathbb{1}_{\mathcal{B}}(w)) f(w)] \\
&= \mathop{\mathbb{E}}_{w \sim p(w)} [(\mathbb{1}_{\mathcal{A}}(w) - \mathbb{1}_{\mathcal{B}}(w)) f(w) \mid w \in \mathcal{B} \setminus \mathcal{A}] \, q \\
&+ \mathop{\mathbb{E}}_{w \sim p(w)} [(\mathbb{1}_{\mathcal{A}}(w) - \mathbb{1}_{\mathcal{B}}(w)) f(w) \mid w \notin \mathcal{B} \setminus \mathcal{A}] \, (1 - q) \\
&\geq \mathop{\mathbb{E}}_{w \sim p(w)} [f(w) \mid w \in \mathcal{B} \setminus \mathcal{A}] \, q.
\end{aligned}$$

Letting $f^* = \inf_{w \in \mathcal{W}} f(w) > 0$, we get $0 \geq f^* q$. Since $f^* > 0$ and $q \geq 0$, $q = p(\mathcal{B} \setminus \mathcal{A}) = 0$. □

C Gricean Speaker Proofs

Lemma 2 *For any Gricean speaker p and $x \in \mathcal{X}$,*

$$\frac{p(x\$)}{p(xx)} = \frac{\exp(c(x))}{\exp(c(\$))}.$$

Proof. Starting with the definition of an Gricean speaker, for any $x \in \mathcal{X}^*$ and $y \in \mathcal{X} \cup \{\$\}$,

$$p(xy) = \mathop{\mathbb{E}}_{w} [p(x \mid w) p(y \mid x, w)] .$$

Now, letting $g(x, w) \triangleq p(x \mid w) / \left(\sum_{y'} \exp\left(\alpha I_\ell(y' \mid x; w) - c(y')\right)\right)$,

$$p(xy) = \exp(-c(y)) \mathop{\mathbb{E}}_{w} [\exp(\alpha I_\ell(y \mid x; w)) g(x, w)] .$$

We apply this identity to both sides of the fraction in the lemma statement:

$$\frac{p(x\$)}{p(xx)} = \frac{\exp(-c(\$))\,\mathbb{E}_w\left[\exp(\alpha I_\ell(\$ \mid x; w))g(x, w)\right]}{\exp(-c(x))\,\mathbb{E}_w\left[\exp(\alpha I_\ell(x \mid x; w))g(x, w)\right]}$$
$$= \frac{\exp(c(x))}{\exp(c(\$))} \cdot \frac{\mathbb{E}_w\left[\exp(\alpha I_\ell(\$ \mid x; w))g(x, w)\right]}{\mathbb{E}_w\left[\exp(\alpha I_\ell(x \mid x; w))g(x, w)\right]}.$$

Since $[\![x]\!] \subseteq [\![\$]\!]$ and $[\![x]\!] \subseteq [\![x]\!]$, we know that the conditional information of both $\$$ and x given x is 0, and, thus,

$$\frac{p(x\$)}{p(xx)} = \frac{\exp(c(x))}{\exp(c(\$))} \cdot \frac{\mathbb{E}_w\left[\exp(0)g(x, w)\right]}{\mathbb{E}_w\left[\exp(0)g(x, w)\right]} = \frac{\exp(c(x))}{\exp(c(\$))}.$$

□

Theorem 2 *Under any Gricean speaker p, entailment is isomorphic to a distributional relation. Specifically, for all sentences $x, y \in \mathcal{X}$,*

$$[\![x]\!] \subseteq [\![y]\!] \iff \frac{p(xy)}{p(x\$)} = \frac{p(yy)}{p(y\$)}.$$

Proof. Recall from the proof of Lemma 2 that there exists a function $g(x, w)$ such that, for all $x \in \mathcal{X}^*$ and $y \in \mathcal{X} \cup \{\$\}$,

$$p(xy) \propto \exp(-c(y)) \mathop{\mathbb{E}}_{w}\left[\exp(\alpha I_\ell(y \mid x; w))g(x, w)\right].$$

Thus, by Lemma 2, the proposed distributional relation can be expanded as

$$\begin{aligned}
d_p(x, y) &\iff \frac{p(xy)}{p(x\$)} = \frac{p(yy)}{p(y\$)} \\
&\iff p(xy) \cdot \frac{p(y\$)}{p(yy)} = p(x\$) \cdot \frac{p(xx)}{p(xx)} \\
&\iff p(xy)\frac{\exp(c(y))}{\exp(c(\$))} = p(xx)\frac{\exp(c(x))}{\exp(c(\$))} \\
&\iff p(xy)\exp(c(y)) = p(xx)\exp(c(x)) \\
&\iff \mathop{\mathbb{E}}_{w}\left[\exp(\alpha I_\ell(y \mid x; w))g(x, w)\right] = \mathop{\mathbb{E}}_{w}\left[\exp(\alpha I_\ell(x \mid x; w))g(x, w)\right].
\end{aligned}$$

By Lemma 1, this holds if and only if, for all w,

$$\begin{aligned}
\exp(\alpha I_\ell(y \mid x; w)) &= \exp(\alpha I_\ell(x \mid x; w)) \\
I_\ell(y \mid x; w) &= I_\ell(x \mid x; w) \\
I_\ell(y \mid x; w) &= 0 \\
[\![x]\!](w) \rightarrow [\![y]\!](w) &= 1.
\end{aligned}$$

We conclude the distributional relation holds if and only if $[\![x]\!] \subseteq [\![y]\!]$. □

D Proofs for Learning Bounds

Lemma 3 *For $z \in \mathcal{X}^* \cup \mathcal{X}^*\$$ and $\delta > 0$, it holds with probability at least $1 - \delta - (1 - p(z))^n$ that*

$$|\log p(z) - \log \hat{p}(z)| \leq \sqrt{\frac{\mathfrak{K}_p(z)}{\delta n}}.$$

Proof. Without loss of generality, assume $p(z) > 0$. With probabiliy $1 - (1 - p(z))^n$ over the draw of our sample, the random variable $\log \hat{p}(z)$ has finite variance defined by

$$\mathrm{Var}\left[\log \hat{p}\right] = \frac{1}{n} \cdot \frac{1 - p(z)}{p(z)} \leq \frac{\mathfrak{K}_p(z)}{n}.$$

With finite variance, we can apply Chebyshev's inequality to conclude that

$$\Pr\left[|\log p(z) - \log \hat{p}(z)| \geq \epsilon\right] \leq \frac{\operatorname{Var}\left[\log \hat{p}\right]}{\epsilon^2} \leq \frac{\mathfrak{K}_p(z)}{n\epsilon^2}.$$

Solving for $\delta \leq \Pr\left[|\log p(z) - \log \hat{p}(z)|\right]$, we get

$$\begin{aligned}\delta &\leq \frac{\mathfrak{K}_p(z)}{n\epsilon^2} \\ \therefore \epsilon &\leq \sqrt{\frac{\mathfrak{K}_p(z)}{\delta n}}.\end{aligned}$$

We conclude that that with probability $1 - \delta - (1 - p(z))^n$,

$$|\log p(z) - \log \hat{p}(z)| \leq \sqrt{\frac{\mathfrak{K}_p(z)}{\delta n}}.$$

□

We now characterize the complexity factor $\mathfrak{K}_p(z)$ for uniformly truthful speakers.

Lemma 5 *For all $z \in \mathcal{X}^* \cup \mathcal{X}^*\$$ such that $[\![z]\!](p) > 0$, it holds that*

$$\mathfrak{K}_p(z) \leq \frac{|\mathcal{X}|}{p([\![z]\!])}.$$

Proof. We start by deriving a lower bound on $p(z)$.

$$\begin{aligned}p(z) &= \sum_w \frac{[\![z]\!](w)}{\sum_{z'} [\![z']\!](w)} p(w) \\ &\geq \sum_w \frac{[\![z]\!](w)}{|\mathcal{X}|} p(w) \\ &= \frac{[\![z]\!](p)}{|\mathcal{X}|}.\end{aligned}$$

Applying this inequality to the definition of $\mathfrak{K}_p(z)$, we conclude that

$$\mathfrak{K}_p(z) \leq \frac{|\mathcal{X}|}{[\![z]\!](p)}.$$

□

Lemma 5 lets us to derive the following guarantee for estimating entailment scores using a corpus produced by uniformly truthful speakers:

Theorem 4 *For a uniformly truthful speaker p, let $u_p(x, y) = \log p(x\$) - \log p(xy)$. For $x, y \in \mathcal{X}$ such that $[\![xy]\!](p) > 0$ and $\delta > 0$, it holds with probability at least $1 - \delta - 2(1 - p(xy))^n$ that*

$$|u_p(x, y) - u_{\hat{p}}(x, y)| \leq 2\sqrt{\frac{|\mathcal{X}|}{p([\![xy]\!])} \cdot \frac{2}{\delta n}}.$$

Proof. We expand the difference in scores as follows:

$$|u_p(x, y) - u_{\hat{p}}(x, y)| \leq |\log p(x) - \log \hat{p}(x\$)| + |\log p(xy) - \log \hat{p}(xy)|.$$

We then apply Lemma 3 with $\frac{\delta}{2}$. Since $p(x\$) \geq p(xy)$, this implies that with probability $1 - \delta - 2(1 - p(xy))^n$,

$$|u_p(x,y) - u_{\hat{p}}(x,y)| \leq \sqrt{\frac{2\mathfrak{K}_p(x\$)}{\delta n}} + \sqrt{\frac{2\mathfrak{K}_p(xy)}{\delta n}}$$
$$\leq 2\sqrt{\frac{2\max\{\mathfrak{K}_p(x\$), \mathfrak{K}_p(xy)\}}{\delta n}}.$$

Finally, we apply Lemma 5 to conclude that

$$|u_p(x,y) - u_{\hat{p}}(x,y)| \leq 2\sqrt{\frac{|\mathcal{X}|}{\min\{[\![x\$]\!](p), [\![xy]\!](p)\}} \cdot \frac{2}{\delta n}}$$
$$= 2\sqrt{\frac{|\mathcal{X}|}{[\![xy]\!](p)} \cdot \frac{2}{\delta n}}.$$

□

We now characterize the complexity factor for Gricean speakers.

Lemma 6 *Assume that $p(z \mid w)$ is a Gricean speaker with respect to listener ℓ and $[\![z]\!](w) = 1 \iff I_\ell(z; w) \geq 0$. Then, for all $z \in \mathcal{X}^* \cup \mathcal{X}^*\$$,*

$$\mathfrak{K}_p(z) \leq \frac{\exp(c(z))}{p([\![z]\!])}.$$

Proof. We start by writing out the form of $p(z)$:

$$p(z) = \frac{\sum_w \exp(\alpha I_\ell(z; w))p(w)}{\exp(c(z))}.$$

Because $z \in \mathcal{X}^* \cup \mathcal{X}^*\$$, all terms where $[\![z]\!](w) = 1$ contribute at least 0 information; other terms contribute negative information. Thus, we bound the information content of the "true" terms above 0, and ignore the other terms to get the lower bound

$$p(z) \geq \frac{\sum_w [\![z]\!](w) \exp(0)p(w)}{\exp(c(z))}$$
$$= \frac{\sum_w [\![z]\!](w)p(w)}{\exp(c(z))}$$
$$= \frac{[\![z]\!](p)}{\exp(c(z))}.$$

Plugging this into $\mathfrak{K}_p(z)$, we conclude that

$$\mathfrak{K}_p(z) \leq \frac{\exp(c(z))}{[\![z]\!](p)}.$$

□

Theorem 3 *Assume that $p(z \mid w)$ is a Gricean speaker with respect to listener ℓ and $[\![z]\!](w) = 1 \iff I_\ell(z; w) \geq 0$. Let $g_p(x,y) = \log \frac{p(xy)}{p(x\$)} - \log \frac{p(yy)}{p(y\$)}$. Let $q = 1 - \min\{p(xy), p(yy)\}$. Then, for all $x, y \in \mathcal{X}$ such that $[\![xy]\!](p) > 0$, for all $\delta > 0$, it holds with probability at least $1 - \delta - 4q^n$ that $|g_p(x,y) - g_{\hat{p}}(x,y)|$ is at most*

$$8\sqrt{\frac{\exp(\max\{c(xy), c(yy)\})}{p([\![xy]\!])} \cdot \frac{1}{\delta n}}.$$

Proof. We start by expanding $g_p(x,y)$:

$$\begin{aligned} g_p(x,y) &= \log \frac{p(xy)}{p(x\$)} - \log \frac{p(yy)}{p(y\$)} \\ &= \log p(xy) - \log p(x\$) - \log p(yy) + \log p(y\$). \end{aligned}$$

Thus, following Theorem 4, we can bound

$$\begin{aligned} |g_p(x,y) - g_{\hat{p}}(x,y)| \leq\ & |\log p(xy) - \log \hat{p}(xy)| + |\log p(x\$) - \log \hat{p}(x\$)| \\ & + |\log p(yy) - \log \hat{p}(yy)| + |\log p(y\$) - \log \hat{p}(y\$)|. \end{aligned}$$

We apply Lemma 3 to each term with $\frac{\delta}{4}$. Since $p(yy) \leq p(y\$)$ and $p(xy) \leq p(x\$)$, we get that with probability at least $1 - \delta - 4q^n$,

$$\begin{aligned} |g_p(x,y) - g_{\hat{p}}(x,y)| &\leq 4\sqrt{\frac{4\max\{\mathfrak{K}_p(xy), \mathfrak{K}_p(x\$), \mathfrak{K}_p(yy), \mathfrak{K}_p(y\$)\}}{\delta n}} \\ &= 8\sqrt{\frac{\max\{\mathfrak{K}_p(xy), \mathfrak{K}_p(x\$), \mathfrak{K}_p(yy), \mathfrak{K}_p(y\$)\}}{\delta n}}. \end{aligned}$$

Finally, we apply Lemma 6 to conclude that, with probability at least $1 - \delta - 4q^n$,

$$\begin{aligned} |g_p(x,y) - g_{\hat{p}}(x,y)| &\leq 8\sqrt{\max\left\{\frac{\exp(c(xy))}{[\![xy]\!](p)}, \frac{\exp(c(x\$))}{[\![x\$]\!](p)}, \frac{\exp(c(yy))}{[\![yy]\!](p)}, \frac{\exp(c(y\$))}{[\![y\$]\!](p)}\right\} \cdot \frac{1}{\delta n}} \\ &\leq 8\sqrt{\frac{\exp(\max\{c(xy), c(yy)\})}{[\![xy]\!](p)} \cdot \frac{1}{\delta n}}. \end{aligned}$$

□

We can use Corollary 2.1 to derive a tighter version of Theorem 3 by removing the dependence on the uncommon string yy:

Theorem 5 *Let* $s_p(x,y) = \log \frac{p(x\$)}{p(xy)} - c(y) + c(\$)$ *. Then, for all* $x, y \in \mathcal{X}$ *such that* $[\![xy]\!](p) > 0$*, for all* $\delta > 0$*, the following holds with probability* $1 - \delta - 2(1 - p(xy))^n$,

$$|s_p(x,y) - s_{\hat{p}}(x,y)| \leq 2\sqrt{\frac{\exp(c(xy))}{p([\![xy]\!])} \cdot \frac{2}{\delta n}}.$$

The proof follows analogously to Theorem 3. The main improvement of Theorem 5 compared to Theorem 3 is that the probability the bound holds no longer depends on the unlikely probability $p(yy)$. We also get the benefit that the cost complexity factor has been reduced to only depend on $c(xy)$ and obtain better constants ($2\sqrt{2}$ instead of 8), although these changes are likely less important than removing the dependence on $p(yy)$. Of course, the drawback is that we are assuming access to the cost function $c(y)$. If we have such access, though, the improvements in the bound suggest we may be able to extract entailment from a finite corpus of Gricean text with better sample complexity than if we did not.

E Sample Complexity Estimation Details

Assuming the approximation error in Theorem 3 is $\leq \epsilon$, we aim to solve the following inequality for n:

$$\epsilon \leq 8\sqrt{\frac{\exp(\max\{c(xy), c(yy)\})}{p([\![xy]\!])} \cdot \frac{1}{\delta n}}.$$

Sentence Length We make the simplifying assumption that $\max\{c(xy), c(yy)\} = 2w(\ell + 1)$, where ℓ is a variable representing sentence length.[15] Let Σ be the word-level vocabulary of English. We estimate the value w by assuming $q(z) = \exp(-w(|z| + 1))$ is a valid prior over Σ^* and solving for the unique value of w to satisfy this condition:

$$\sum_{z \in \Sigma^*} \exp(-w(|z| + 1)) = 1$$

$$\sum_{\ell=0}^{\infty} \frac{|\Sigma|^\ell}{\exp(w(\ell + 1))} = 1$$

$$\exp(-w) \sum_{\ell=0}^{\infty} \left(\frac{|\Sigma|}{\exp(w)} \right)^\ell = 1$$

$$\therefore w = \log(|\Sigma| + 1).$$

This reveals that w should be set ≥ 1, but the question remains how to set $|\Sigma|$. In practice, we assume the speaker prior is defined over the support of all syntactically valid or likely strings in English, not over all possible strings as derived above. Letting S be the word-level perplexity of English, we set w according to

$$w \approx \log(S + 1).$$

We set S to the value estimated by GPT-3: ~ 20 nats/word (Brown et al., 2020). Simplifying the numerator in the bound yields

$$\exp(\log(21)(\ell + 1)) = 21^{\ell+1}.$$

Making the prior less strong, i.e., increasing $|\Sigma|$ to be greater than this perplexity estimate, would only increase the number of samples needed to extract entailment judgments.

Truth Probability We conservatively assume $p([\![xy]\!]) = \frac{1}{2}$, although in practice it may be smaller for more informative sentences. Reducing it would lead to higher sample complexity estimates.

Final Form Putting together our estimates for sentence length and truth probability yields

$$\epsilon \leq 8\sqrt{\frac{2 \cdot 21^{\ell+1}}{\delta n}}$$

$$\therefore n \leq \frac{128 \cdot 21^{\ell+1}}{\delta \epsilon^2}.$$

The final form captures the intuition that the likelihood of a string vanishes exponentially with its length, and that the base of this decay is roughly inversely proportional to the perplexity of the language. In practice, we set $\delta = 0.1$ and $\epsilon = 1.0$. Changing the value of ϵ (the desired approximation accuracy) would shift the curve.

F General Relations and Speakers

So far, we have characterized concrete distributional relations that are isomorphic to entailment for different classes of speaker models. In this section, we analyze the conditions under which a distribution relation isomorphic to a semantic relation exists, given no assumptions about the speaker. Informally, we prove in Theorem 6 that a distributional isomorphism exists if and only if the speaker model depends on semantics "at all". This is a very weak condition, and should be satisfied by any reasonable model of natural speakers. Thus, we take this as evidence that any speaker model—not just the ones we have considered, admits a distributional relation isomorphic to entailment.

[15] We write $\ell + 1$ instead of ℓ here for technical reasons: we want to guarantee that $q(z)$ can be a valid probability distribution.

We now turn to the formal presentation of this result. Let M be the function that takes a set of worlds $\mathcal{W}$ and returns all semantic evaluation functions $\mu : \mathcal{X} \mapsto 2^{\mathcal{W}}$ over $\mathcal{W}$. For a semantic evaluation function $\mu = \lambda x.[\![x]\!]$, let p_μ be a speaker model parameterized by semantics μ.

Say two semantic evaluation functions μ, μ' are isomorphic with respect to s if and only if, for all x, y,

$$S(\mu(x), \mu(y)) \iff S(\mu'(x), \mu'(y)).$$

Theorem 6 *The following are equivalent for any speaker p and semantic relation s:*

1. *There exists a distribution relation d such that, for all $\mathcal{W}$, for all $\mu \in M(\mathcal{W})$, s is isomorphic to d_{p_μ}.*
2. *For all $\mathcal{W}, \mathcal{W}'$, for all $\mu \in M(\mathcal{W})$ and $\mu' \in M(\mathcal{W}')$ such that μ, μ' are not isomorphic w.r.t. s, there exists $z \in \mathcal{X}^*$ such that $p_\mu(z) \neq p_{\mu'}(z)$.*

Proof. We will show that equivalence holds in both directions.

Forward Direction: We assume the second statement does not hold by way of modus tollens. Thus, there exists $\mathcal{W}, \mathcal{W}'$ with $\mu \in M(\mathcal{W})$ and $\mu' \in M(\mathcal{W}')$ with μ, μ' not isomorphic such that, for all $z \in \mathcal{X}^*$, $p_\mu(z) = p_{\mu'}(z)$. Thus, for all d and sentences x, y,

$$d_{p_\mu}(x, y) \iff d_{p_{\mu'}}(x, y).$$

But μ and μ' are not isomorphic, so there exist x, y such that $S(\mu(x), \mu(y)) \not\Leftrightarrow S(\mu'(x), \mu'(y))$. Thus, we can conclude that one of the following must hold:

$$d_{p_\mu}(x, y) \not\Leftrightarrow S(\mu(x), \mu(y))$$
$$d_{p_{\mu'}}(x, y) \not\Leftrightarrow S(\mu'(x), \mu'(y)).$$

We conclude by modus tollens that the first statement implies the second.

Backward Direction: Assume the second statement holds. The function $f(\mu) = p_\mu$ is invertible up to isomorphism to s. In other words, there exists $g(p_\mu) = \mu^*$ such that, for all x, y,

$$S(\mu^*(x), \mu^*(y)) \iff S(\mu(x), \mu(y)).$$

Then we define d according to

$$\begin{aligned} d_{p_\mu}(x, y) &\iff S(g(p_\mu)(x), g(p_\mu)(y)) \\ &\iff S(\mu^*(x), \mu^*(y)) \\ &\iff S(\mu(x), \mu(y)). \end{aligned}$$

Thus, the second statement implies the first. □

G Experimental Details

G.1 Language Description

We set the vocabulary $\mathcal{X} = \{\texttt{100}, \texttt{010}, \texttt{001}, \texttt{110}, \texttt{011}, \texttt{111}\}$ and define $\mathcal{W} = \{1, 2, 3\}$. We refer to each three-digit binary string as an *utterance*, and define the evaluation function for an utterance x as $[\![x]\!](w) = 1 \iff x_w = 1$. Thus, `100` is true only in world 1, while `111` is true in all worlds (i.e., is tautological). We identify `111` with the end of sequence \$.

In line with our formal definitions, we define a *text* z as a concatenation of utterances $z_1 \cdots z_n$ ending with \$. Recall that we define the evaluation function over a text as the intersection of the evaluation functions of the utterances it contains. For our language, this reduces to $[\![z]\!](w) = 1 \iff \forall i\,(z_i = 1)$. Thus, `011 101 111` is true only in w_3, and `011 101 110 111` is true in no worlds (i.e., contradictory).

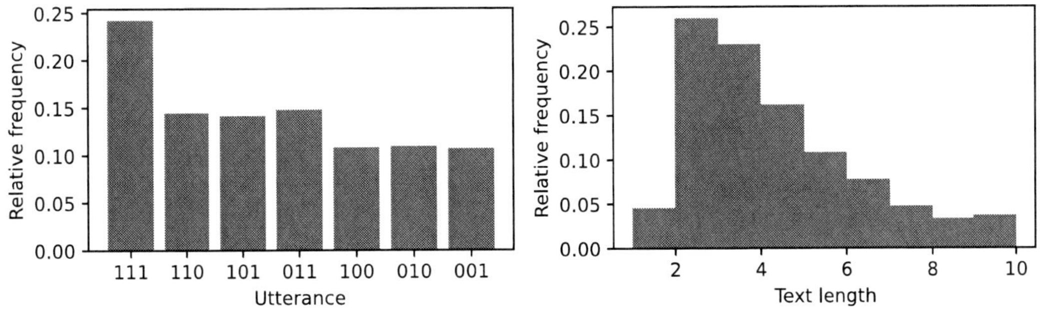

Figure 3: Properties of the data generated by the speaker in our experiments, with $\alpha = 5$ and $c(x) = 0.1 \cdot |x|$.

G.2 Speaker Model Parameters

We model the listener of the informative speaker as a literal listener (Goodman and Frank, 2016), which means our informative speaker is a rational speaker of depth 1 in the language of rational speech acts.

We set $c(x) = 0.1 \cdot |x|$, where $|x|$ is the length of the string x. We set the rationality parameter $\alpha = 5$. These choices were made heuristically, by inspecting the the properties of the speaker's output, as summarized in Figure 3. These parameters led to a relatively uniform distribution over utterances (except for the stop token `111` which is present in all texts), and a variety of text lengths without excessive redundancy. We found that larger values of α or of the coefficient for the cost function produced short texts, biasing maximally informative utterances (i.e., `100`, `010`, or `001`); while smaller values produced long, repetitive utterances or sometimes empty utterances.

G.3 Training and Evaluation

We sample a dataset from a speaker by independently sampling n texts from the speaker model. We generate datasets of varying size from each speaker, with the number of texts n decreasing by factors of 2 from 10^7 texts down to just 2 texts.

We train models of two kinds: a text frequency model, and a trigram model. The text frequency model simply assigns a probability to a text proportional to its frequency in the training data, assigning a small $\epsilon = 10^{-20}$ probability to an unknown sequence. The trigram model is trained using NLTK's (Bird, 2006) MLE implementation, i.e., the probabilities are unsmoothed. We do not need to use smoothing due to the small number of possible trigrams in the language.

For evaluation data, we generate pairs of texts labeled for entailments. We include all pairs where each text is 6 utterances or shorter, except for utterances that are contradictory or consist only of the end of sequence token. The total number of test pairs is about 1.1M.

On Neurons Invariant to Sentence Structural Changes in Neural Machine Translation

Gal Patel **Leshem Choshen** **Omri Abend**
School of Computer Science and Engineering
The Hebrew University of Jerusalem
`first.last@mail.huji.ac.il`

Abstract

We present a methodology that explores how sentence structure is reflected in neural representations of machine translation systems. We demonstrate our model-agnostic approach with the Transformer English-German translation model. We analyze neuron-level correlation of activations between paraphrases while discussing the methodology challenges and the need for confound analysis to isolate the effects of shallow cues. We find that similarity between activation patterns can be mostly accounted for by similarity in word choice and sentence length. Following that, we manipulate neuron activations to control the syntactic form of the output. We show this intervention to be somewhat successful, indicating that deep models capture sentence-structure distinctions, despite finding no such indication at the neuron level. To conduct our experiments, we develop a semi-automatic method to generate meaning-preserving minimal pair paraphrases (active-passive voice and adverbial clause-noun phrase) and compile a corpus of such pairs.[1]

1 Introduction

Understanding the roles neurons play is important for the interpretability of neural machine translation (NMT) models. Finding neurons that are either invariant or sensitive to particular structural distinctions may explain how such structures are encoded, and validates the robustness of translation systems, which is a challenging but important problem (He et al., 2020; Freitag et al., 2020). Furthermore, understating how these encodings are used by the network may potentially enable controlling the output by direct manipulation of neurons.

Previous work analyzing what aspects of sentence structure are encoded in network representations mostly took a probing approach or focused on syntactic agreements. Works that compared activations did so either across models with identical input (Dalvi et al., 2019; Bau et al., 2019; Wu et al., 2020) or by representation words, not sentences (Antverg and Belinkov, 2021). Our novelty lies in using the same model with paraphrased input pairs, to analyze sentence structure encoding, without probing (c.f. §7). We derive inspiration from Computer Vision works that analyze model behavior under non-semantic changes to the input (Lenc and Vedaldi, 2015; Goodfellow et al., 2009).

For our proposed approach, we provide a dataset of minimal paraphrases (along with a code to extend it). We take two phenomena as test cases: active to passive voice and an adverbial clause to a noun phrase (see Table 1 and section §2).

To compare the activation patterns of sentences that may be comprised of a different number of tokens, we aggregate tokens representations. We then measure the correlation of neuron activations between paraphrases and provide a confound analysis. We find that the main contributors to strong correlation are similar positional encodings and bag-of-words overlap, suggesting strong correlation is derived from similar input encoding and not high-level abstractions learned by the model. The identification of these confounds may be beneficial to future work on network analysis (see §4).

Our findings suggest that these paraphrase distinctions are nonetheless encoded and used, as evident by our experiments of manipulating neurons (§5). We control the structure of the translation output (e.g., active/passive) by translating neuron activations in a fixed direction. We show that this manipulation generates outputs that are more similar to the desired form with an in-depth evaluation, using BLEU, dependency parsing, and manual analysis. We provide ablation studies that show that the results are not simply random artifacts of manipulation, with a non-local effect. Lastly, we compare different methods for selecting subsets of neurons

[1]The dataset is provided with paraphrase generation code: `https://github.com/galpatel/minimal-paraphrases`

Proceedings of the 26th Conference on Computational Natural Language Learning (CoNLL), pages 194 - 212
December 7-8, 2022 ©2022 Association for Computational Linguistics

	Source	Paraphrased
Active Voice→ Passive Voice	*She **took** the book*	*The book **was taken** by her*
Adverbial Clause→ Noun Phrase	*The party died down before **she arrived***	*The party died down before **her arrival***

Table 1: Examples produced by our paraphrasing engine

to be manipulated (§6) with counter-intuitive results, attributed to neurons of general importance and multiple roles per neuron.

Overall, the similarity between neuron activation over paraphrases is mostly explained by shallow input features: the positional and token embeddings. Therefore, some neurons represent input features, but sentence-level information is not localized, even in higher layers. Moreover, we show that sentence phrasing can be naïvely controlled, with a manipulation of a large number of neurons. This suggests that the distinction between different sentence structures is encoded in the model, probably in a distributed manner. Lastly, the neurons most effective for such manipulations are the ones most correlated across paraphrases, not necessarily those that vary the most.

2 Dataset: Minimal Paraphrase Pairs

We curate datasets that isolate specific sentence structure distinctions. To achieve that, we require sentence pairs with the following attributes:

- **Similar Meaning**, to have invariant semantics.
- **Minimal Change**, to facilitate the experimental setup and the interpretation of the results.
- **Controlled Change**, where paraphrasing is consistent and well-defined. As opposed to lexical paraphrases that tend to be idiosyncratic, the same distinction is applied to all instances.
- **Reference Translation**, since we examine translation models.

Existing paraphrasing tools and datasets fail to satisfy these criteria (see §7). Therefore, we develop our own paraphrasing method, with which we compile two parallel sets: active voice to passive voice and an adverbial clause to a noun phrase. Sentence examples can be found in Table 1.

The proposed process is automatic, following predefined syntactic rules while utilizing several NLP models. First, we identify sentences that match some source patterns (active voice, adverbial clause) according to a Dependency Parsing and POS tags model (Honnibal et al., 2020) and a Semantic Role Labeling model (Gardner et al., 2018). Then, we rephrase the sentence to the desired structure. We complement missing prepositions by choosing the one with the highest probability as predicted by BERT (Devlin et al., 2019). For example, the adverbial clause sentence *"She felt accomplished when she met the investor"* requires the preposition "*with*" in the noun phrase form *"She felt accomplished during her meeting* with *the investor"*, and the temporal preposition *when* is replaced with *during*. In ambiguous instances, we choose whether or not to insert a preposition by opting for the sentence with the higher probability according to GPT2 Language Model (Radford et al., 2019). When replacing a verb with a noun (e.g., *arrival* is replaced with *arrive*), we look for the most suitable conversion in existing lexicons, including Nomlex (Macleod et al., 1998), AMR's and Verb Forms. See Appendix A for details and examples.[2]

	Paraphrased	Valid
Adverbial Clause to Noun Phrase	376	114
Active Voice to Passive Voice	3107	1169

Table 2: Minimal Paraphrase pairs count, as derived from WMT19 English-German dev set, before (left) and after (right) filtering.

We apply our paraphrasing engine to the WMT19 English-German development set (Barrault et al., 2019). Some results are disfluent. For example, the sentence *"He took his time"* is converted to *"His time was taken by him"*, which is syntactically well-formed, but anomalous. Therefore, we manually filter the data. For more details and other failed filtering approaches, see Appendix A.3. The number of pairs is given in Table 2.

3 Technical Setup

Model. We demonstrate our model-agnostic methodology with the Transformer model for Machine Translation (Vaswani et al., 2017). We use the fairseq implementation (Ott et al., 2019), which

[2]The dataset is provided with paraphrase generation code: `https://github.com/galpatel/minimal-paraphrases`

was trained on the WMT19 English-German train set (Barrault et al., 2019). The embedding dimension is 1024 with sinusoidal positional encoding.

Dataset. Minimal paraphrases (see §2). Due to space considerations, we present results on the active/passive set in the main paper. Clause/noun phrase results are in appendices §B.3 and §C.

Notations. We refer to trained models with a different random seed as m_1, m_2. We denote the set of source sentences $S = \{s_1, ..., s_n\}$, and its corresponding paraphrased set with $P = \{p_1, ..., p_n\}$ (e.g., s_i is an active voice sentence and p_i is its passive counterpart). We follow Liu et al. (2019); Wu et al. (2020) and take into account only the last sub-word token for each word (results with all sub-word tokens were similar). We consider as neurons the 1024 activation values in the output embedding of the 6 encoder layer blocks (following Wu et al., 2020)[3]. This leads to the following definition: the activation of some neuron l in model m, on sentence s_i is $x_S^{m,l}[i]$, while $x_S^{m,l}$ is a vector of size n (with n being the number of sentences in set S, i.e. one activation value per sentence, see §4.1).

4 Detecting Correlation Patterns

To detect activation patterns under experimental conditions, we measure Pearson correlation[4] between neural activations. While correlation analysis has been previously used to analyze neuron-level behavior (Bau et al., 2019; Dalvi et al., 2019; Wu et al., 2020; Meftah et al., 2021), our novelty lies with the independent variable being a property of the input (i.e., paraphrases) and not the model (e.g., architecture, initialization).

4.1 Sample Alignment Challenge

For every neuron, we measure its activation values while feeding a model with either the set of source sentences as input (e.g., active voice) or the paraphrased set (e.g., passive voice). Since the number of words may differ between paired sentences, so will the total number of tokens in these sentence sets. Consequently, the neural activation sample size will vary, which poses a challenge for testing correlation. Previous works did not face this difficulty, as they compared activation values given the same input corpus.

[3]Experiments on activations internal to each layer block have similar but weaker effects (Appendix B.2).

[4]Results with Spearman correlation were similar.

We overcome this with intra-sentence aggregation. Instead of having an activation value per word in the input corpus, we consider a single value per sentence, by pooling activations of words within a sentence. Ideally, this will allow for a sentence-level analysis of semantics and structure. Mean pooling was previously considered in several instances. Ethayarajh (2019) compared sentences by averaging their word vectors and Antverg and Belinkov (2021) aggregated words with specified attributes by averaging their representation, element-wise. The main results of this paper use mean pooling. In Appendix B.1 we also report results with min/max pooling, that show similar trends.

It is possible to consider other straightforward approaches, which we find less suitable. One option is a position-wise alignment of words (discarding the last words of the longer sentence). The difficulty here is that words of different semantics and syntactic roles are compared. For example, the third words of the active/passive sentence in Table 1 would be *the* and *was*, the former is a determiner of a direct object while the latter is an auxiliary of the root verb. Another option is functional correspondence alignment, where we measure correlation only between the functional tokens that indicate the structure change (e.g. *took* vs. *taken* and *arrived* vs. *arrival* from the examples in Table 1). That would result in an analysis based on similar single words with the same context words but in different syntactic forms. This could be problematic as it would capture a local syntactic change but not necessarily a sentence-level phrasing.

4.2 Baseline Experiments

We capture correlation across paraphrases, denoted with *ParaCorr*. Given the same model, we look at activations over a set of sentences and their correlation to the activations over the paraphrased set:

$$ParaCorr(l, l') = \rho(x_S^{m_1,l}, x_P^{m_1,l'}) \quad (1)$$

ParaCorr should examine how neural networks represent differences in sentence structure (or similarities in semantics). We follow by comparing it to *ModelCorr* - the correlation between any pair of neurons across models, when given the same input:

$$ModelCorr(l, l') = \rho(x_S^{m_1,l}, x_S^{m_2,l'}) \quad (2)$$

ModelCorr is based on Bau et al. (2019) who detected generally important neurons in this way.

Figures 1a and 1b show ParaCorr and ModelCorr

correlation maps.[5] Some of ParaCorr's observed effect also appears in ModelCorr, suggesting the observed correlations might be unrelated to the examined variable, i.e. paraphrases. Moreover, ModelCorr indicates a strong correlation between neurons of the same location in different models, but we had expected a different pattern as highly correlated neurons should be distributed differently for randomly initialized models.

4.3 Controlling for Confounds

In this section, we show that strong activation correlations between paraphrases are a product of low-level cues. Namely, we inspect how the propagation of token identity and positional information greatly influences the correlation. This is a relevant confound to note for previous work adapting correlation analysis on neurons (Bau et al., 2019; Wu et al., 2020; Meftah et al., 2021). The positional encoding in our setting is sinusoidal, therefore the same positions are encoded exactly the same across models. Paraphrases present a minor change in sentence length: 2.0 ± 0.4 or 0.8 ± 0.8 token difference when paraphrasing active to passive or clause to noun phrase, respectively. The positional encodings are therefore similar. As for tokens, paraphrases have a large unigram overlap.

We define *PosCorr* as activation correlation between sentences with identical positional encoding but different token embeddings. Formally:

$$PosCorr(l, l') = \rho(x_S^{m_1,l}, x_{\hat{S}}^{m_1,l'}) \quad (3)$$

Where $\hat{S}$ is a set of random token sequences, uniformly sampled from the dictionary, with the same sequence lengths as S. PosCorr isolates the strong correlation effect observed both in ModelCorr and ParaCorr (Figure 1c). Repetition through the layers is probably due to the residual connections, which propagate the positional encoding. Indeed, when we looked at correlations of neurons inside the layer block – before the first residual connection – the effect seen in PosCorr was missing (see Appendix B.2). The implication is that input representation, and not higher-level learned representation, is likely the cause of strong correlations.

TokenCorr accounts for token embeddings. We strip an input set S from its positional encoding, denoted by $\tilde{S}$, and measure correlation:

$$TokenCorr(l, l') = \rho(x_S^{m_1,l}, x_{\tilde{S}}^{m_1,l'}) \quad (4)$$

TokenCorr (Figure 1d) captures the diagonals phenomenon of ParaCorr, explained by paraphrases having a large bag-of-words overlap (the effect is not present in ModelCorr since token embeddings are different across models). This implies that individual token identities, and not necessarily sentence-level semantics, contribute to strong correlations. This distinction is made apparent when we consider how word order may affect meaning. For example, *"Rose likes Josh"* has a different meaning than *"Josh likes Rose"*, although the sentences have the same bag of words. Even if word meaning is sufficient for a lot of cases, grammatical cues are still essential (Mahowald et al., 2022).

We further dissect the observed correlation for possible confounds. First, we compare activations of sentence pairs that share only the relevant syntactic structure (e.g., two random active voice sentences). No strong correlation is observed (between -0.17 to 0.20). This suggests that the effect observed in the TokenCorr experiment, where the same tokens are fed to the model (Figure 1d, Eq. 4) is not explained by a similar structure cue (i.e., active voice). In another experiment, we combine both PosCorr and TokenCorr: we strip the original sentence from its positional embedding and replace the tokens with random ones – i.e., nothing is shared between the compared conditions. As little correlation is detected (between -0.27 to 0.31), we rule out the possibility of neurons with constant values.

Overall, our confound analysis implies the following: (1) strong activation correlation is greatly due to low-level components and not high-level learned knowledge, (2) strong correlation detected across paraphrases may not be exclusive to sentences with similar meaning but different structures, and (3) sentence structure is not localized to a specific set of neurons in our analysis.

5 Manipulation of Neurons

Manipulation of neurons allows us to control the output translation (without additional training) and adds a causative explanation to the role neurons play. We look into changing the activation values to force the output to have a desired syntactic structural feature (e.g., active or passive voice). Although we did not observe individual neurons that have a strong positive/negative correlation across paraphrases in §4, these sentence-structure distinc-

[5]We feature only the first layer due to resolution constraints. Any effect shown is present in all layer block pairs but weakens when moving away from the main diagonal (i.e. correlation across layers) or when the layers are higher.

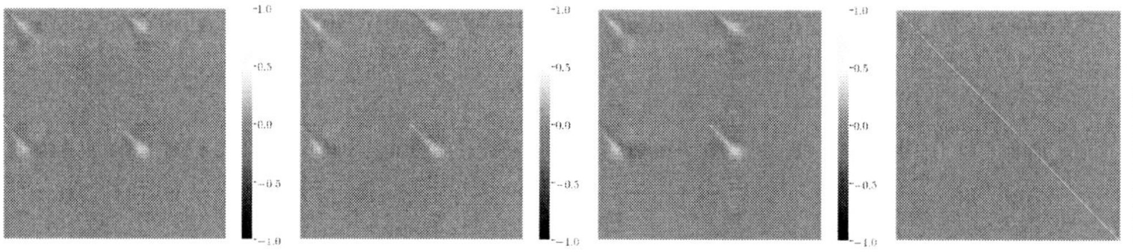

(a) ParaCorr (b) ModelCorr (c) PosCorr (d) TokenCorr

Figure 1: Activation correlation of neurons in the encoder, using the active-passive dataset.

tions could still be encoded in a decentralized manner in the model, and therefore susceptible to manipulation. We address three main questions:

1. Can we effectively control the output structural properties by changing neuron values?
2. Does the exact activation value matter or only the identity of the modified neurons?
3. How to choose a set of neurons to manipulate?

5.1 Setup

We denote with $\bar{x_c}[i]$ the average activation of neuron i given a set of input sentences with property c, e.g., the property of passive voice. For a model with a total of n neurons (in the encoder), we have a vector of average behavior $\bar{x_c} \in R^n$. An intervention on neuron i with a current value of $x[i]$ from property c_1 towards property c_2 is a linear translation between their averages:

$$\hat{x}[i] = x[i] - \beta(\bar{x_{c_1}} - \bar{x_{c_2}})[i] \quad (5)$$

So far, the formulation is based on previous work (Bau et al., 2019). Our preliminary experiments showed it is essential that the scaling factor β includes a normalization term because comparing the effects of different manipulations (i.e. different target properties c_2) can be confounded by activation magnitude. Therefore, $\beta = \frac{\alpha}{\|\bar{x_{c_1}} - \bar{x_{c_2}}\|}$. This leaves us with various parameters to experiment with: the properties c_1, c_2 we wish to manipulate, the subset of neurons we intervene with, and the scaling factor α. We explore the former two in §5.2 and the latter in Appendix C.5, having $\alpha = 1$ as default.

We evaluate whether manipulation increases the similarity of the output to a reference with the target form (c_2), relative to the similarity with the source form (c_1). We measure BLEU scores between our model's translation and Google translations, which (in the absence of manual references) we consider as references to both the source and target forms. This is a reasonable assumption given the performance gap between the models we use and Google Translate. Later we discuss evaluation by additional methods to complement BLEU (see §5.3).

5.2 Experiments

We present experiments on manipulating passive voice inputs toward active voice translations. The reverse manipulation (active input to passive translation) and the results on the clause/noun-phrase set can be found in Appendix C.

Baseline Manipulation. We modify an increasing amount of neurons, first selecting the neurons most correlated across paraphrases (i.e., we rank by $ParaCorr(l, l)$ with the higher values first). The motivation to use the correlation as a rank is based on Bau et al. (2019), who used it as an indicator of important neurons. We manipulate passive voice inputs toward active voice translations. Outputs become more similar to active voice than passive voice (Figure 2a), suggesting that sentence structure is indeed encoded in the model, even if we did not detect the distinction at the neuron-level in §4. Moreover, the information is *used* by the model when generating translations and it can be controlled.

Direction of Manipulation. We explore the importance of the manipulation direction, i.e. the value we shift towards. A random manipulation, with a random vector $y_r \in \mathbb{R}^n$, is defined by:

$$\hat{x}[i] = x[i] - \beta(\bar{x_{c_1}} - y_r)[i] \quad (6)$$

Repeating 100 different random vectors (Figure 2b), we find it to be substantially worse. This implies that success is tied to the specific values we manipulate, not an artifact of any modification.

Selection of Manipulation. We test whether there is a preferable subset of neurons to manipu-

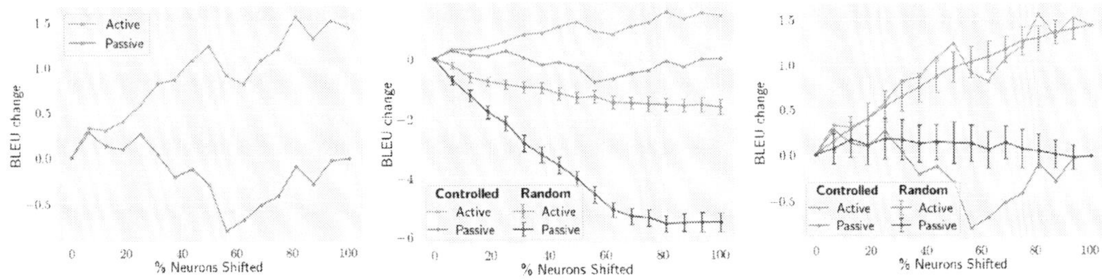

(a) Controlled baseline

(b) Random direction comparison

(c) Random selection comparison

Figure 2: Manipulating the outputted translation to be of active voice when feeding passive voice input. Lines present BLEU change with active and passive references, as a function of the amount of neurons manipulated (x-axis). For random experiments (b) and (c) we report the average of the measured BLEU and its standard deviation.

late by randomly selecting a subset of neurons.[6] Results (Figure 2c) do not indicate that a controlled selection of neurons (according to ParaCorr ranking) is better than random. Overall, it seems that a large subset of neurons has to be modified to obtain the desired outcome, which agrees with our correlation results, where the active-passive feature was not localized. Notwithstanding, we study subset choice even further in §6.

5.3 Beyond BLEU

BLEU score captures translation quality on the surface and not necessarily how good (or bad) it is at capturing form (active vs. passive). Therefore, we employ additional evaluation measures.

Passive Score. Specifically for the active-passive dataset, we use a dependency parser and a POS tagger to detect passive form[7]. The scorer is not intended to be perfect in capturing all passive instances[8], but it could serve as a complementary measure to indicate trends. We observe a decrease of detected passive voice when we manipulate the passive input towards active translation (see Figure 3b), solidifying the BLEU results.

Qualitative Analysis. A native German speaker examined a sample of output translations and found successful manipulations (see Appendix D). She discussed failed outputs – where the translation changed (i.e. unequal strings) but did not result in the desired form. They did not degrade the translation. In some cases, sentences changed between stative passive and dynamic passive, rather than between passive and active (the distinction between these passive types is more evident in German). In other cases, the manipulation was not applicable. For instance, some verbs could not be in an adverbial form in German, which demands them either to appear as a noun phrase or to be replaced with a synonym verb (an example is in Appendix D). These suggest that the manipulation has successfully modified the desired attributes in the sentence, even when not automatically detected as such. Moreover, it may be limited by the nature of the target language and the model's capabilities to generalize to synonyms while controlling the sentence structure.

Held-out Test Set. We repeated the manipulation experiment on a held-out test set: 552 active voice sentences from the WMT19 test set. This allows us to examine if the successful manipulation effect extends to a setting where the manipulated sentences do not contribute to the measure of average activation of the source form. As can be seen in C.2, the manipulation still results in the desired change in passive form detection.

Linearity Caveat. As Ravfogel et al. (2021) noted, positive results can indicate a causal effect, while negative results should be interpreted carefully since we have a linear manipulation in a non-linear setting. We leave the exploration of non-linear techniques for future work.

6 Specific Neuron Set Selection

Although finding a subset of neurons that carries a specific functionality is a difficult problem (Sajjad

[6]We also experimented with choosing random neurons under the constraint they have the same distribution among the 6 encoder layers as the controlled case, with similar results.

[7]Using Spacy (Honnibal et al., 2020), we consider a sentence to be in passive voice if the root lemmatization is *"werden"* and it has a child of dependency *"oc"* (i.e., clausal object) with a tag indicating a participle form.

[8]Limited recall: baseline translation of passive sentences (without manipulation) gets a score of 37.38%

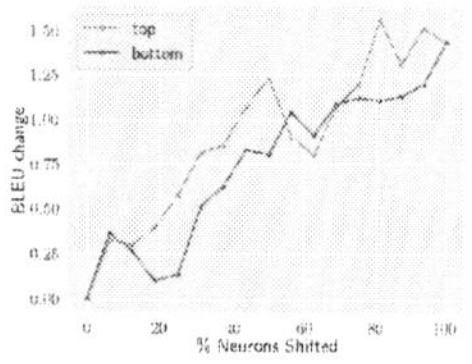

(a) BLEU

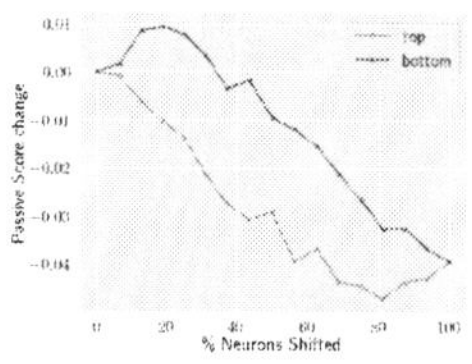

(b) Passive Score

Figure 3: Top ParaCorr neurons are better for manipulation. Manipulating the output translation to be in active voice when feeding passive voice as input. Comparing the choice of neurons to manipulate when starting from the top or bottom according to the rank given by ParaCorr. (1) Measuring by BLEU against active voice references and (2) measuring passive score that automatically detects passive voice.

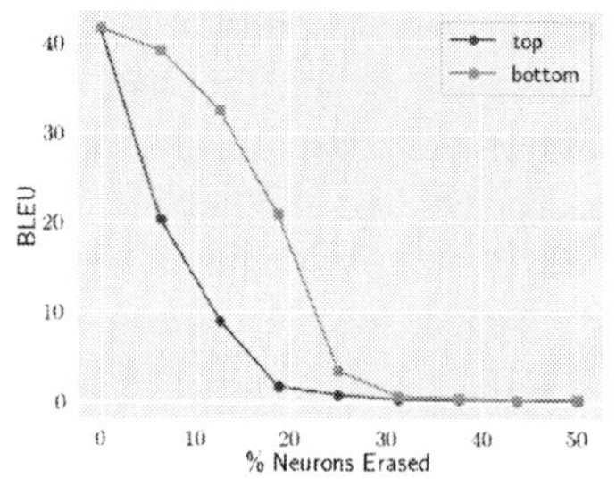

Figure 4: Top ranked neurons have a stronger impact on the translation quality of a test set, measured in BLEU. Erasure of neurons from the top or bottom of the rank given by the value of correlation between paraphrases.

et al., 2021), we look for subsets that are *relatively* better for manipulation. In our baseline (§5.2) we chose which neurons to manipulate according to the rank given by ParaCorr (i.e., sorting neurons by $ParaCorr(l, l)$, high to low). Under an intuitive interpretation, neurons that positively correlate when a systematic change is made to the input are those invariant to that change. Neurons with a negative correlation are specific to the change in sentence structure. Following these, we expect bottom-ranked neurons to be better for manipulation than top-ranked neurons. Contrarily, we observe the opposite phenomenon (Figure 3). The following tests may explain it.

Model Performance. Top-ranked neurons are important for overall performance. We follow Bau et al. (2019) who identified important neurons by deleting them (i.e., setting activations to zero) and examining the impact on the model performance. We delete an increasing amount of neurons, according to ParaCorr rank. We measure BLEU on a held-out set of 552 active voice sentences, and their references, extracted from the WMT19 test set. Results (Figure 4) show that top-ranked neurons have a stronger impact on the translation quality than bottom-ranked do, suggesting that ParaCorr partially ranks neurons by their general importance.

Role Overlap. Some of the top ParaCorr neurons account for lexical identity and positional information. This fact explains why they have the most impact when manipulating sentence structure. Word order is essential for active-passive paraphrasing, where the subject and direct object exchange places. Notably, when we tested non-paired active-passive sentences the phenomena did not repeat itself, see Appendix C.6. Word tokens are the building blocks for the semantic meaning of a sentence (which is the same across paraphrases), even when a bag-of-word is not exclusive to a single meaning. The first evidence to support this claim is seen in §4, where most of the strong correlations in ParaCorr are explained by similarity in the tokens and the positional embeddings between the inputs (i.e., TokenCorr and PosCorr, respectively). In an additional test, we check how many of the top ParaCorr neurons are also in the top PosCorr and TokenCorr neurons. Figure 5 shows that for any count x, the set of top x ParaCorr neurons have an intersection with the sets of top x PosCorr or TokenCorr neurons.

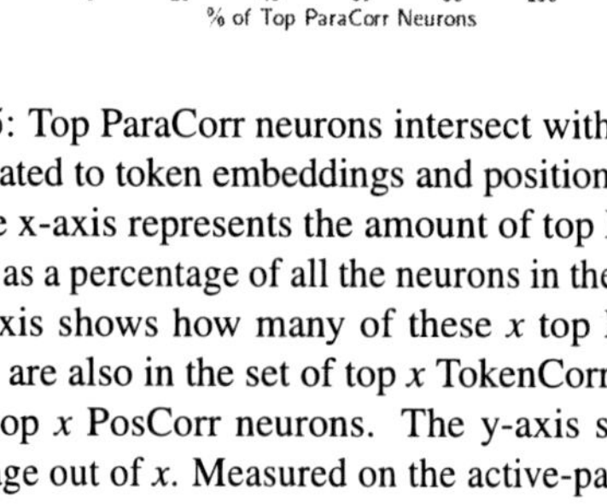

Figure 5: Top ParaCorr neurons intersect with neurons most related to token embeddings and positional encoding. The x-axis represents the amount of top ParaCorr neurons as a percentage of all the neurons in the encoder. The y-axis shows how many of these x top ParaCorr neurons are also in the set of top x TokenCorr neurons and/or top x PosCorr neurons. The y-axis scale is a percentage out of x. Measured on the active-passive set.

7 Related Work

Understanding NLP Neural Networks. Various approaches were previously proposed (Belinkov and Glass, 2019), each with a methodology that differs from ours. Probing tasks investigate whether linguistic properties of the input text can be effectively predicted from model representations (Jawahar et al., 2019; Tenney et al., 2019; Slobodkin et al., 2021). They shed light on what information is kept within a model, but not necessarily what is used, or how (Antverg and Belinkov, 2021). Others employ mediation analysis theory: Vig et al. (2020); Finlayson et al. (2021) study semantic behavior and syntactic agreement, respectively. Some works analyze attention heads (Voita et al., 2019) or follow attention flow (Abnar and Zuidema, 2020). Visualization tools interpret activations, but with some exceptions (e.g., Lenc and Vedaldi, 2015), they are mostly limited to qualitative examples. Durrani et al. (2020) interpreted individual neurons with probing-like methods for fine-grained analysis. Challenge sets (Choshen and Abend, 2019; Warstadt et al., 2020) and adversarial examples (Alzantot et al., 2018), expose challenging cases by analyzing the NMT system's behavior, rather than representation. Elazar et al. (2021) analyzes semantically equivalent inputs by clustering their embeddings. They improve prediction by continual training, while we manipulate translation post-training.

Interpretation in other domains. Some Computer Vision work inspired our approach. Lenc and Vedaldi (2015) study the interaction between input transformation and its representation through the layers, while Goodfellow et al. (2009) examine invariant neurons, those that are selective to high-level features but robust given semantically identical transformations. Their methodologies do not fit the NLP domain since they rely on a mathematically well-defined input transformation (e.g., rotation). We propose an alternative with our paraphrases in §2. Linguistic encoding in the human brain has been studied in neuroscience works. Friederici (2011) analyzed the correlation of neuroimaging where subjects are presented with sentences with subtle syntactic variations or violations, and found that well-correlated regions are considered to process syntax. Fedorenko et al. (2016) presented human subjects with various inputs, which are analogous to our correlation experiments: word lists (TokenCorr), meaningless grammatical sentences (PosCorr), non-words lists (combination of TokenCorr and PosCorr), and regular sentences (ParaCorr).

Individual neurons analysis with correlation. Bau et al. (2019) detected neurons that correlate across LSTM models while showing these are the most important for performance. They manipulated individual neurons to control single words in the output (e.g., gender, tense), with their linguistic role identified by probing with a GMM classifier. The technique to identify neurons that behave similarly in different models was previously suggested by Dalvi et al. (2019), who found neurons in LSTM models to have role polysemy, aligning with our discussion in §6. Later, Wu et al. (2020) employed correlation to examine similarities of different Transformer architectures. Meftah et al. (2021) adapted correlations to quantify the impact of fine-tuning by measuring activations of neurons before and after domain adaptation.

Controlling active-passive voice in translation. Yamagishi et al. (2016) controlled voice (active/passive) in RNN-based machine translation, from Japanese to English, when an indicator was given as input. Their method required additional model training, unlike ours.

Paraphrases. Existing paraphrasing tools vary by how localized their edits are. Some alter the lexical level (Ribeiro et al., 2018), other alter whole phrases (Ganitkevitch, 2013; Bhagat et al., 2009), some are sentence-level paraphrases (Dolan et al., 2004), while some split source sentences into subsentences (e.g., Dornescu et al., 2014; Lee and Don, 2017). Other than paraphrasing tools, existing datasets include the PPDB database (Pavlick et al., 2015) that contains sentence paraphrases that are lexical, phrasal, or syntactic. Zhang et al. (2019); Dolan and Brockett (2005) include paraphrase and non-paraphrase pairs, the former with high lexical overlap, while (Hu et al., 2019) contains multiple paraphrases of lexical diversity. None of these match our criteria for paraphrases (§2).

8 Conclusion

With our curated dataset, we introduced a model-agnostic methodology to detect activation patterns across paraphrases. By a meticulous confound analysis, we found that activation similarity is likely due to shallow features of sequence length or word identity, which are not exclusive to meaning-preserving variations. We emphasize how these confounds must be taken into account when attempting to detect local correlation under any experimental setup. We controlled syntactic structures of generated output, which provides evidence of the ability of models to capture them. While we found the modification technique to be important for manipulation success, the selection of a subset of neurons was more challenging. Future work should test additional architectures and language pairs or examine the representation significance of our paraphrase pairs in other NLP tasks.

Limitations

Our work has some limitations. First, we compile the minimal paraphrases dataset to analyze representations of an isolated difference. Even so, human language is complex and any input transformation could not be mathematically well-defined. Our paraphrases may have other differences than the ones we indicate, which may introduce noise to our analysis. For example, we don't know the effect specific verbs (e.g., more common/rare ones) have when they appear in noun form, or what possible bias 'by' introduces when we add it for passive voice.

Secondly, we demonstrate our model-agnostic methodology in a specific setting with a transformer model for en-de translation. Our insights of what is captured (or isn't) may change when experimenting on other architectures or language pairs.

We aggregate token representations to sentence representation, discussing our choice and other possible approaches in §4.1. We do this to overcome potential differences in the number of tokens the paraphrases contain. However, the aggregation may lose encoded information along the way. We find some evidence of that when examining other pooling techniques (min/max) in Appendix B.1.

Our manipulation shows that many neurons have to be modified for a successful outcome (at least 50%). Still, when manipulating more and more neurons, the effect is not always monotone in every setting (see Figure 9, Figure 12 and Figure 13). We conducted our qualitative analysis on the output with all of the encoder neurons modified and see positive results, with a discussion of how to choose neurons relatively better (§6).

In the following Appendix sections we also address: the filtering required for the automatically generated paraphrases (§A.3), analysis on neurons internal to the layer block (§B.2), possible alternative explanation for the observed results for top vs. bottom ranked neurons (§C.6), unsuccessful manipulation cases (§C.4) and manipulation magnitude (§C.5).

Acknowledgements

This work was supported by the Israel Science Foundation (grant no. 2424/21). We thank Yonatan Belinkov for helpful comments and discussion. We thank Nicole Gruber for her work on paraphrase annotation and qualitative analysis of German translations.

References

Samira Abnar and Willem Zuidema. 2020. Quantifying attention flow in transformers. In *Proceedings of the 58th Annual Meeting of the Association for Computational Linguistics*, pages 4190–4197, Online. Association for Computational Linguistics.

Moustafa Alzantot, Yash Sharma, Ahmed Elgohary, Bo-Jhang Ho, Mani Srivastava, and Kai-Wei Chang. 2018. Generating natural language adversarial examples. In *Proceedings of the 2018 Conference on Empirical Methods in Natural Language Processing*, pages 2890–2896, Brussels, Belgium. Association for Computational Linguistics.

Omer Antverg and Yonatan Belinkov. 2021. On the pitfalls of analyzing individual neurons in language models. *CoRR*, abs/2110.07483.

Loïc Barrault, Ondřej Bojar, Marta R Costa-Jussa, Christian Federmann, Mark Fishel, Yvette Graham, Barry Haddow, Matthias Huck, Philipp Koehn, Shervin Malmasi, et al. 2019. Findings of the 2019 conference on machine translation (wmt19). In *Proceedings of the Fourth Conference on Machine Translation (Volume 2: Shared Task Papers, Day 1)*, pages 1–61.

Anthony Bau, Yonatan Belinkov, Hassan Sajjad, Nadir Durrani, Fahim Dalvi, and James Glass. 2019. Identifying and controlling important neurons in neural machine translation. In *International Conference on Learning Representations*.

Yonatan Belinkov and James Glass. 2019. Analysis methods in neural language processing: A survey. *Transactions of the Association for Computational Linguistics*, 7:49–72.

Rahul Bhagat, Eduard Hovy, and Siddharth Patwardhan. 2009. Acquiring paraphrases from text corpora. In *Proceedings of the Fifth International Conference on Knowledge Capture*, K-CAP '09, page 161–168, New York, NY, USA. Association for Computing Machinery.

Leshem Choshen and Omri Abend. 2019. Automatically extracting challenge sets for non-local phenomena in neural machine translation. In *Proceedings of the 23rd Conference on Computational Natural Language Learning (CoNLL)*, pages 291–303, Hong Kong, China. Association for Computational Linguistics.

Fahim Dalvi, Nadir Durrani, Hassan Sajjad, Yonatan Belinkov, Anthony Bau, and James Glass. 2019. What is one grain of sand in the desert? analyzing individual neurons in deep nlp models. In *Proceedings of the AAAI Conference on Artificial Intelligence*, volume 33, pages 6309–6317.

Jacob Devlin, Ming-Wei Chang, Kenton Lee, and Kristina Toutanova. 2019. BERT: Pre-training of deep bidirectional transformers for language understanding. In *Proceedings of the 2019 Conference of the North American Chapter of the Association for Computational Linguistics: Human Language Technologies, Volume 1 (Long and Short Papers)*, pages 4171–4186, Minneapolis, Minnesota. Association for Computational Linguistics.

Bill Dolan, Chris Quirk, and Chris Brockett. 2004. Unsupervised construction of large paraphrase corpora: Exploiting massively parallel news sources. In *Proceedings of the 20th international conference on Computational Linguistics*, page 350. Association for Computational Linguistics.

William B. Dolan and Chris Brockett. 2005. Automatically constructing a corpus of sentential paraphrases. In *Proceedings of the Third International Workshop on Paraphrasing (IWP2005)*.

Iustin Dornescu, Richard Evans, and Constantin Orăsan. 2014. Relative clause extraction for syntactic simplification. In *Proceedings of the Workshop on Automatic Text Simplification - Methods and Applications in the Multilingual Society (ATS-MA 2014)*, pages 1–10, Dublin, Ireland. Association for Computational Linguistics and Dublin City University.

Nadir Durrani, Hassan Sajjad, Fahim Dalvi, and Yonatan Belinkov. 2020. Analyzing individual neurons in pre-trained language models. In *Proceedings of the 2020 Conference on Empirical Methods in Natural Language Processing (EMNLP)*, pages 4865–4880, Online. Association for Computational Linguistics.

Yanai Elazar, Nora Kassner, Shauli Ravfogel, Abhilasha Ravichander, Eduard H. Hovy, Hinrich Schütze, and Yoav Goldberg. 2021. Measuring and improving consistency in pretrained language models. *CoRR*, abs/2102.01017.

Kawin Ethayarajh. 2019. How contextual are contextualized word representations? Comparing the geometry of BERT, ELMo, and GPT-2 embeddings. In *Proceedings of the 2019 Conference on Empirical Methods in Natural Language Processing and the 9th International Joint Conference on Natural Language Processing (EMNLP-IJCNLP)*, pages 55–65, Hong Kong, China. Association for Computational Linguistics.

Evelina Fedorenko, Terri L. Scott, Peter Brunner, William G. Coon, Brianna Pritchett, Gerwin Schalk, and Nancy Kanwisher. 2016. Neural correlate of the construction of sentence meaning. *Proceedings of the National Academy of Sciences*, 113(41):E6256–E6262.

Matthew Finlayson, Aaron Mueller, Sebastian Gehrmann, Stuart Shieber, Tal Linzen, and Yonatan Belinkov. 2021. Causal analysis of syntactic agreement mechanisms in neural language models. In *Proceedings of the 59th Annual Meeting of the Association for Computational Linguistics and the 11th International Joint Conference on Natural Language Processing (Volume 1: Long Papers)*, pages 1828–1843, Online. Association for Computational Linguistics.

Markus Freitag, George Foster, David Grangier, and Colin Cherry. 2020. Human-paraphrased references improve neural machine translation. In *Proceedings of the Fifth Conference on Machine Translation*, pages 1183–1192, Online. Association for Computational Linguistics.

A. Friederici. 2011. The brain basis of language processing: from structure to function. *Physiological reviews*, 91 4:1357–92.

Juri Ganitkevitch. 2013. Large-scale paraphrasing for natural language understanding. In *Proceedings of the 2013 NAACL HLT Student Research Workshop*, pages 62–68, Atlanta, Georgia. Association for Computational Linguistics.

Matt Gardner, Joel Grus, Mark Neumann, Oyvind Tafjord, Pradeep Dasigi, Nelson F. Liu, Matthew Peters, Michael Schmitz, and Luke Zettlemoyer. 2018. AllenNLP: A deep semantic natural language processing platform. In *Proceedings of Workshop for NLP Open Source Software (NLP-OSS)*, pages 1–6, Melbourne, Australia. Association for Computational Linguistics.

Ian Goodfellow, Honglak Lee, Quoc Le, Andrew Saxe, and Andrew Ng. 2009. Measuring invariances in deep networks. In *Advances in Neural Information Processing Systems*, volume 22, pages 646–654. Curran Associates, Inc.

Yvette Graham, Timothy Baldwin, Alistair Moffat, and Justin Zobel. 2017. Can machine translation systems be evaluated by the crowd alone. *Natural Language Engineering*, 23(1):3–30.

Pinjia He, Clara Meister, and Zhendong Su. 2020. Structure-invariant testing for machine translation. In *Proceedings of the ACM/IEEE 42nd International Conference on Software Engineering*, ICSE '20, page 961 973, New York, NY, USA. Association for Computing Machinery.

Matthew Honnibal, Ines Montani, Sofie Van Landeghem, and Adriane Boyd. 2020. spacy: Industrial-strength natural language processing in python.

J. Edward Hu, Rachel Rudinger, Matt Post, and Benjamin Van Durme. 2019. Parabank: Monolingual bitext generation and sentential paraphrasing via lexically-constrained neural machine translation. *Proceedings of the AAAI Conference on Artificial Intelligence*, 33(01):6521–6528.

Ganesh Jawahar, Benoît Sagot, and Djamé Seddah. 2019. What does BERT learn about the structure of language? In *Proceedings of the 57th Annual Meeting of the Association for Computational Linguistics*, pages 3651–3657, Florence, Italy. Association for Computational Linguistics.

Katharina Kann, Sascha Rothe, and Katja Filippova. 2018. Sentence-level fluency evaluation: References help, but can be spared! In *Proceedings of the 22nd Conference on Computational Natural Language Learning*, pages 313–323, Brussels, Belgium. Association for Computational Linguistics.

John Lee and J. Buddhika K. Pathirage Don. 2017. Splitting complex English sentences. In *Proceedings of the 15th International Conference on Parsing Technologies*, pages 50–55, Pisa, Italy. Association for Computational Linguistics.

K. Lenc and A. Vedaldi. 2015. Understandinspacyg image representations by measuring their equivariance and equivalence. In *2015 IEEE Conference on Computer Vision and Pattern Recognition (CVPR)*, pages 991–999.

Nelson F. Liu, Matt Gardner, Yonatan Belinkov, Matthew E. Peters, and Noah A. Smith. 2019. Linguistic knowledge and transferability of contextual representations. In *Proceedings of the 2019 Conference of the North American Chapter of the Association for Computational Linguistics: Human Language Technologies, Volume 1 (Long and Short Papers)*, pages 1073–1094, Minneapolis, Minnesota. Association for Computational Linguistics.

Catherine Macleod, Ralph Grishman, Adam Meyers, Leslie Barrett, and Ruth Reeves. 1998. Nomlex: A lexicon of nominalizations. In *In Proceedings of Euralex98*, pages 187–193.

Kyle Mahowald, Evgeniia Diachek, Edward Gibson, Evelina Fedorenko, and Richard Futrell. 2022. Grammatical cues are largely, but not completely, redundant with word meanings in natural language. *CoRR*, abs/2201.12911.

Sara Meftah, N. Semmar, Y. Tamaazousti, H. Essafi, and F. Sadat. 2021. Neural supervised domain adaptation by augmenting pre-trained models with random units. *ArXiv*, abs/2106.04935.

Myle Ott, Sergey Edunov, Alexei Baevski, Angela Fan, Sam Gross, Nathan Ng, David Grangier, and Michael Auli. 2019. fairseq: A fast, extensible toolkit for sequence modeling. In *Proceedings of NAACL-HLT 2019: Demonstrations*.

Ellie Pavlick, Pushpendre Rastogi, Juri Ganitkevitch, Benjamin Van Durme, and Chris Callison-Burch. 2015. PPDB 2.0: Better paraphrase ranking, fine-grained entailment relations, word embeddings, and style classification. In *Proceedings of the 53rd Annual Meeting of the Association for Computational Linguistics and the 7th International Joint Conference on Natural Language Processing (Volume 2: Short Papers)*, pages 425–430, Beijing, China. Association for Computational Linguistics.

Alec Radford, Jeffrey Wu, Rewon Child, David Luan, Dario Amodei, and Ilya Sutskever. 2019. Language models are unsupervised multitask learners. *OpenAI blog*, 1(8):9.

Shauli Ravfogel, Grusha Prasad, Tal Linzen, and Yoav Goldberg. 2021. Counterfactual interventions reveal the causal effect of relative clause representations on agreement prediction. In *Proceedings of the 25th Conference on Computational Natural Language Learning*, pages 194–209, Online. Association for Computational Linguistics.

Marco Tulio Ribeiro, Sameer Singh, and Carlos Guestrin. 2018. Semantically equivalent adversarial rules for debugging NLP models. In *Proceedings of the 56th Annual Meeting of the Association for Computational Linguistics (Volume 1: Long Papers)*, pages 856–865, Melbourne, Australia. Association for Computational Linguistics.

Hassan Sajjad, Nadir Durrani, and Fahim Dalvi. 2021. Neuron-level interpretation of deep nlp models: A survey. *ArXiv*, abs/2108.13138.

Aviv Slobodkin, Leshem Choshen, and Omri Abend. 2021. Mediators in determining what processing bert performs first. *arXiv preprint arXiv:2104.06400*.

Ian Tenney, Dipanjan Das, and Ellie Pavlick. 2019. BERT rediscovers the classical NLP pipeline. In *Proceedings of the 57th Annual Meeting of the Association for Computational Linguistics*, pages 4593–4601, Florence, Italy. Association for Computational Linguistics.

Ashish Vaswani, Noam Shazeer, Niki Parmar, Jakob Uszkoreit, Llion Jones, Aidan N Gomez, Ł ukasz Kaiser, and Illia Polosukhin. 2017. Attention is all you need. In *Advances in Neural Information Processing Systems*, volume 30. Curran Associates, Inc.

Jesse Vig, Sebastian Gehrmann, Yonatan Belinkov, Sharon Qian, Daniel Nevo, Yaron Singer, and Stuart M. Shieber. 2020. Causal mediation analysis for interpreting neural NLP: the case of gender bias. *CoRR*, abs/2004.12265.

Elena Voita, David Talbot, Fedor Moiseev, Rico Sennrich, and Ivan Titov. 2019. Analyzing multi-head self-attention: Specialized heads do the heavy lifting, the rest can be pruned. In *Proceedings of the 57th Annual Meeting of the Association for Computational Linguistics*, pages 5797–5808, Florence, Italy. Association for Computational Linguistics.

Alex Warstadt, Alicia Parrish, Haokun Liu, Anhad Mohananey, Wei Peng, Sheng-Fu Wang, and Samuel R. Bowman. 2020. BLiMP: The Benchmark of Linguistic Minimal Pairs for English. *Transactions of the Association for Computational Linguistics*, 8:377–392.

Thomas Wolf, Lysandre Debut, Victor Sanh, Julien Chaumond, Clement Delangue, Anthony Moi, Pierric Cistac, Tim Rault, Remi Louf, Morgan Funtowicz, Joe Davison, Sam Shleifer, Patrick von Platen, Clara Ma, Yacine Jernite, Julien Plu, Canwen Xu, Teven Le Scao, Sylvain Gugger, Mariama Drame, Quentin Lhoest, and Alexander Rush. 2020. Transformers: State-of-the-art natural language processing. In *Proceedings of the 2020 Conference on Empirical Methods in Natural Language Processing: System Demonstrations*, pages 38–45, Online. Association for Computational Linguistics.

John Wu, Yonatan Belinkov, Hassan Sajjad, Nadir Durrani, Fahim Dalvi, and James Glass. 2020. Similarity analysis of contextual word representation models. In *Proceedings of the 58th Annual Meeting of the Association for Computational Linguistics*, pages 4638–4655, Online. Association for Computational Linguistics.

Hayahide Yamagishi, Shin Kanouchi, Takayuki Sato, and Mamoru Komachi. 2016. Controlling the voice of a sentence in japanese-to-english neural machine translation. In *WAT@COLING*.

Yuan Zhang, Jason Baldridge, and Luheng He. 2019. PAWS: paraphrase adversaries from word scrambling. *CoRR*, abs/1904.01130.

A Compilation of Minimal Paraphrase Pairs

A.1 Tools and Techniques

We explain, in greater detail, the main tools we use when we paraphrase, as briefly discussed in section §2.

Pattern Detection. Making sure we change form but not semantics, we rely on syntax-based patterns, not word-based. We use dependency parsing (including Part of Speech tagging) and Semantic Role Labeling combined (by Honnibal et al. (2020) and Gardner et al. (2018), respectively) to detect active form and adverbial clauses by type (see Table 3).

Sentence Probability Used for choosing between two sentence options (with or without a certain preposition). We use gpt2 model Radford et al. (2019) by huggingface Wolf et al. (2020) to get sentence probability for each option and opt for the higher.

Word Insertion.

Input: a sentence $X = x_1, x_2, ..., x_n$, a position *i*, and a set of possible words $W = \{w_1, ..., w_m\}$

1: Define $X' = x_1, \ldots, x_{i-1}, [MASK], x_i, \ldots, x_n$

2: Send X' into a trained BERT masked language model Devlin et al. (2019) by Wolf et al. (2020) and get $y \in \mathbb{R}^d$, a probability vector for each word in the vocabulary (*d* is the size of the vocabulary of the BERT model)

3: Define $w_k \in W$ s.t. $w_k = \max_{i=1,...m} y[w_i]$ to be a new word at position *i* of sentence X (the word with the highest probability, according to BERT, out of the given set W).

Output: a sentence $(x_1, x_2, \ldots, x_{i-1}, w_k, x_i, \ldots, x_n)$

We can make this an **Optional Word Insertion** by returning either the input or output sentence, using Sentence Probability.

Noun Derivation.

Input: a verb (lemma form)
We prioritize choosing the noun form from AMR morph verbalization [9]. If we don't find it there, we choose between Nomlex form (Macleod et al., 1998) and present participle form according to Verb Form Dictionaries[10] (if exists), deciding according to Word Insertion.
Output: either a noun or None

Preposition Sets. Using Word Insertion requires a set of options as input. In our paraphrasing process, we use the following predefined sets to insert prepositions. **Temporal prepositions:** 'as', 'aboard','along', 'around', 'at', 'during', 'upon', 'with', 'without'. **General prepositions:** 'as', 'aboard', 'about', 'above', 'across', 'after', 'against', 'along', 'around', 'at', 'before', 'behind', 'below', 'beneath', 'beside', 'between', 'beyond', 'but', 'by', 'down', 'during', 'except', 'following', 'for', 'from', 'in', 'inside', 'into', 'like', 'minus', 'minus', 'near', 'next', 'of', 'off', 'on', 'onto', 'onto', 'opposite', 'out', 'outside', 'over', 'past', 'plus', 'round', 'since', 'since', 'than', 'through', 'to', 'toward', 'under', 'underneath', 'unlike', 'until', 'up', 'upon', 'with', 'without'.

[9] `https://amr.isi.edu/download.html`

[10] `https://github.com/monolithpl/verb.forms.dictionary`

A.2 Active Voice to Passive Voice

The active-to-passive paraphrasing process is done on sentences that include a nominal subject and a direct object. We discard any sentence of question and coordination, possible passive form (root verb is in past participle), and those where the root verb has a *"to"* auxiliary.

1: If the subject is a proper noun, convert it to object form
2: If the direct object is a proper noun, convert it to subject form
3: Switch the subtree spans of subject and object
4: Add "by" just before the span of the new object
5: If an auxiliary verb is one of "can", "may", "shall", convert it to "could", "might", "should" respectively.
6: If root verb is a gerund or present participle, replace it with "being". Otherwise, remove it altogether.
7: Add suitable auxiliary according to the new subject form of singular/plural, and the tense.
8: If the sentence includes a negation word, remove it and add "not" before the auxiliary.
9: Replace the root verb to its past participle form (using the Verb Forms Dictionary[11]).
10: If the sentence includes a particle, move it after the root verb.
11: If the sentence includes a dative, try to replace it using Optional Word Insertion.

We'll go over an example:

Active to Passive: example

Input: He can't take the book.

1: "*He*" ← "*Him*"
2: NA
3: Switch *"him"* with *"The book"*
4: "*him*" ← "*by him*"
5: "*can*" ← "*could*"
6: NA
7: Add *"be"*
8: "*'t*" ← "*not*"
9: "*take*" ← "*taken*"
10: NA
11: NA

Output: The book could not be taken by him.

The complete process of paraphrasing a sentence with an adverbial clause to one with a noun phrase substituting it is detailed in Table 3. We'll demonstrate a few examples. [12]

Purpose clause

Input: She sat under the sun to enjoy the warmth.

1: Extract *"to enjoy the warmth"*
2: Found matching participle *"to"*
3: NA
4: "*enjoy*" ← "*enjoyment*"
5: NA
6: "*to*" ← "*for*"
7: "*thewarmth*" ← "*ofthewarmth*"

Output: She sat under the sun for enjoyment of the warmth.

Cause/Reason clause, possessive form

Input: She was at the library for a long time because she had an unresolved problem.

1: Extract *"because she had an unresolved problem"*
2: Found matching root *"had"* and a marker *"because"*
3: Remove *"had"*
4: Remove *"an"*
5: "*she*" ← "*her*"
6: "*because*" ← "*because of*"
7: NA

Output: She was at the library for a long time because of her unresolved problem.

Cause/Reason clause, non-possessive form

Input: This robot is very advanced because it flies itself.

1: Extract *"because it flies itself"*
2: Found matching root *"flies"* and a marker *"because"*
3: NA
4: "*flies*" ← "*flight*"
5: "*it*" ← "*its*"
6: "*because*" ← "*because of*"
7: "*flight*" ← "*self flight*"

Output: This robot is very advanced because of its self flight.

A.3 Filtering Results

As mentioned in §2, some sentences generated by our paraphrasing process are disfluent. Therefore,

[11] `https://github.com/monolithpl/verb.forms.dictionary`

[12] The flow of purpose clause conversion could arguably lack optional determiner addition before the new noun phrase. It could be easily added to the generation code for any future use.

<table>
<tr><td>1. Extract</td><td colspan="4">Extract Adverbial Clause
detect type by Semantic Role Labeling (Gardner et al., 2018)</td></tr>
<tr><td></td><td colspan="2">Cause/Reason</td><td rowspan="2">Temporal</td><td rowspan="2">Purpose</td></tr>
<tr><td></td><td>Possessive</td><td>Non-Possessive</td></tr>
<tr><td>2. Match pattern</td><td>root "have" and marker "because"</td><td>root isn't: "have"/ "be"/"do"/"can"</td><td>marker "as"/"before"/ "after"/"until"/"while" or adverbial modifier "when"</td><td>participle "to"</td></tr>
<tr><td>3. aux</td><td colspan="4">remove root's auxiliaries</td></tr>
<tr><td>4. det/Noun</td><td>remove direct object's determinants</td><td colspan="3">Noun Derivation A.1</td></tr>
<tr><td>5. Possession</td><td colspan="4">Nominal subject to possessive form</td></tr>
<tr><td>6. Preposition</td><td colspan="2">replace "because" with "because of"</td><td>If "as"/"while"/ "when", replace by Word Insertion A.1[a]</td><td>Replace "to" with "for"</td></tr>
<tr><td>7. Additions</td><td>If negation, add "lack of"</td><td colspan="3">If there is a direct object[b]
Optional Word Insertion A.1[c]</td></tr>
</table>

[a] Using temporal prepositions set.
[b] If there is a direct object of the form "<xxx>self" in the non-possessive cause/reason case, we instead add "self" before the derived noun and remove this object.
[c] Using general prepositions set.

Table 3: The paraphrasing process from an adverbial clause sentence to a noun phrase.

we manually filtered the data. Two in-house annotators made binary predictions as to whether the generated paraphrases are fluent, with 75% observed agreement and 0.6 Cohen's kappa. We also tried using Direct Assessment (Graham et al., 2017) and eliciting fluency scores through crowdsourcing, as well as attempting to threshold the probability given by GPT2 or SLOR (Kann et al., 2018). Neither of these approaches worked in a satisfactory manner.

B Detecting Correlation Patterns

B.1 Pooling Techniques

In section 4 we measure the correlation of activations over paraphrases. Since paraphrases vary in their sequence length, the subsequent random variables representing the activations for each sentence structure (i.e. activations over active voice versus activations over passive voice), vary as well. While previous works (Bau et al., 2019; Dalvi et al., 2019; Wu et al., 2020; Meftah et al., 2021) compared activations over all input words, our settings necessitate pooling. In §4 we presented the results where we used mean activation per sentence. In Figure 6 we compare the heatmaps of different poolings. As is evident, the major confounds (diagonals and concentrated neuron groups of strong correlation) are present across the techniques.

B.2 Inside the Layer Block

In section 4 we measure the correlation of activations only at the output of the encoder layer block, following previous work (Wu et al., 2020). We also take a look at intermediate activations, see Figure 7. This strengthens our hypothesis that the strong correlation seen in PosCorr (Figure 1c) is due to the sinusoidal positional encodings, as they are propagated through the network with residual connections. The PosCorr effect appears only after the first residual connection, weakens through the fully-connected layers, and strengthens again after additional residual connection.

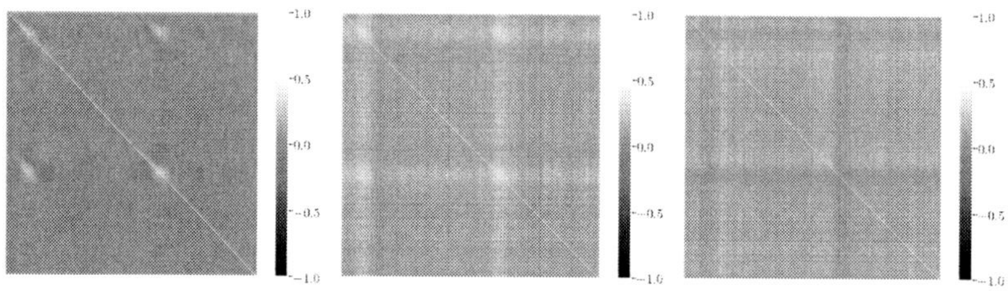

(a) Mean (b) Min (c) Max

Figure 6: Activation correlation between paraphrases (ParaCorr), using the active-passive dataset. The correlation is done sentence-wise, while the pooling technique of token activation varies. The major confounds are present across all techniques.

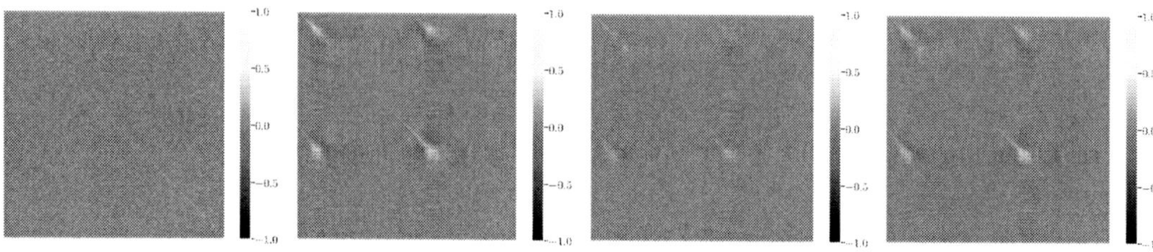

(a) Post Attention (b) Residual + Norm (c) Linear Layers (d) Residual + Norm

Figure 7: Activation correlation between paraphrases (ParaCorr), using the active-passive dataset. A view inside the first encoder layer block, step-by-step: (a) attention heads, (b) adding residual connections and applying normalization, (c) fully connected layer, followed by ReLU and another fully connected layer, (d) adding residual connections and applying normalization - the output of the layer block.

B.3 Adverbial Clause versus Noun Phrase

Here we present the same correlation methods detailed in section 4 but measured on the adverbial clause versus noun phrase sets. See Figure 8.

C Manipulation of Neurons

C.1 Active to Passive

To complete all variations of the manipulation experiment, we first showcase the shift from active voice input to passive voice translation (the opposite direction of what we showed in the main paper). We see that the translation is more similar to the target form (passive voice) than the input form (active voice). The positive change in BLEU is more subtle in this manipulation, and again getting maximal change requires many neurons to be modified (at least 50%), see Figure 9a. With the random experiments of direction (Figure 9b) and neurons selection (Figure 9c), we get similar results - our controlled direction is better while choosing an optimal subset of neurons is not easy.

C.2 Manipulation on a Test Set

We repeat the manipulation on a held-out test set: 552 sentences that we automatically detect as active voice sentences from the WMT19 test set. While our experiments on the dev set are valid, as we manipulate from one set (e.g. passive voice) by measuring another (e.g. active voice), one might argue that we can't know the effect of the shared semantic meaning (on the set level) has on the success rate. To cover all bases, we manipulate the test set according to average activations measured on the dev set. Here we do not have a passive voice counterpart, so we manipulate active voice inputs to passive voice translations. The passive voice detection score (see §5.3) shows a monotonous increase (up to 0.6% more) as we modify more neurons (see Figure 10). The trend matches our expectations. Moreover, we see again that manipulating top-ranked neurons (rank given by ParaCorr) has a greater effect than bottom-ranked ones. This is again consistent with what we saw with the development set and BLEU score in section 6.

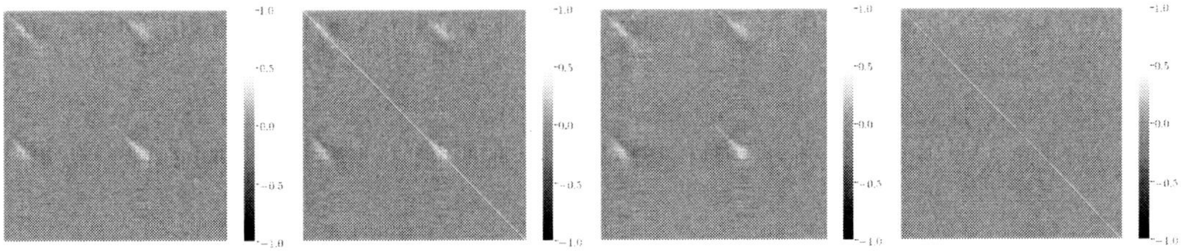

(a) ModelCorr (b) ParaCorr (c) PosCorr (d) TokenCorr

Figure 8: Activation correlation of first layer neurons in the Transformer encoder, using the clause/noun-phrase dataset.

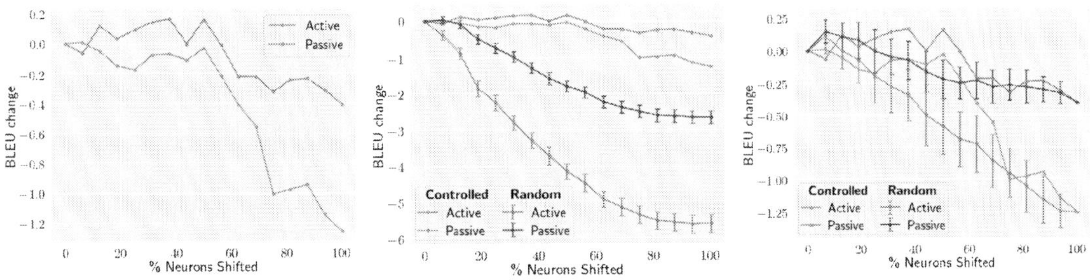

(a) Baseline (b) Random direction comparison (c) Random selection comparison

Figure 9: Manipulating output translation to be in passive voice when feeding active voice as input. Lines present BLEU change with active and passive references according to the amount of neurons manipulated (x).

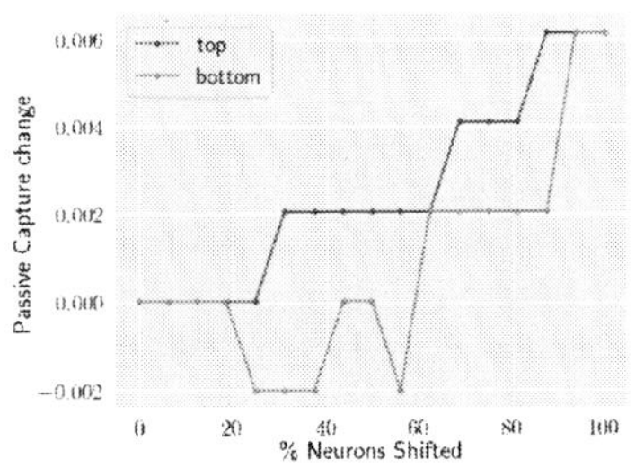

Figure 10: Manipulating neurons to get passive voice translation given an active voice input from the test set. Comparing the effect of manipulating first top versus bottom neurons, according to ParaCorr. We measure passive form detection

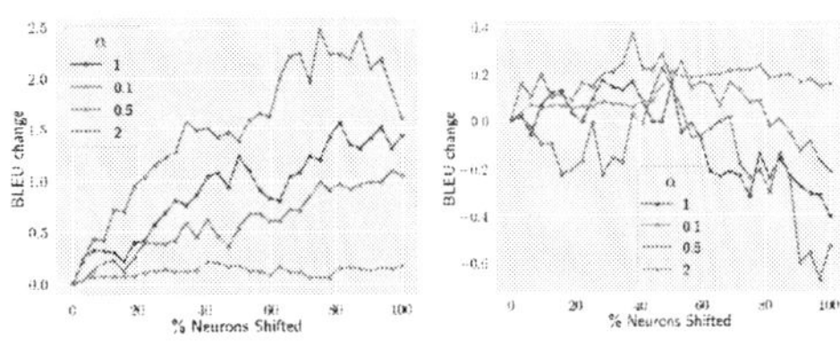

(a) Passive to Active (b) Active to Passive

Figure 11: Comparing various magnitudes α for manipulation step $\frac{\alpha}{\|\bar{x_{c_1}} - \bar{x_{c_2}}\|}(\bar{x_{c_1}} - \bar{x_{c_2}})$. BLEU score measured against reference of target form, when manipulating increasingly more neurons according to top rank of ParaCorr.

C.3 Noun Phrase to Adverbial Clause

Manipulating from a noun phrase to an adverbial clause is consistent with the results we saw for passive to active manipulation, see Figure 12 We repeat the same succession of experiments on the adverbial clause versus noun phrase dataset.

C.4 Adverbial Clause to Noun Phrase

Manipulating neurons to convert input with an adverbial clause to output translation with a noun phrase is not outright successful (see Figure 13). In the controlled case (where we employ direction by our records of average activation of each paraphrase form and select an increasing set of neurons to manipulate according to the top or bottom ParaCorr rank), we are still closer to the clause form than the noun phrase. We propose several possible explanations:

1. The clause versus noun phrase dataset is substantially smaller than the active versus passive one (114 examples compared to 1,169 instances). A small dataset may include more noise or simply make the target syntactic form

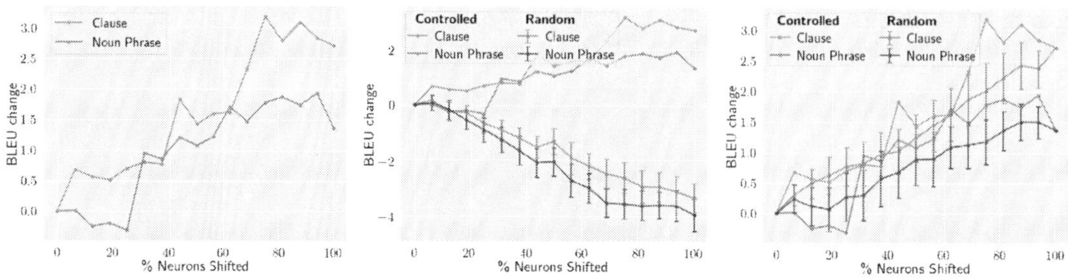

(a) Baseline (b) Random direction comparison (c) Random selection comparison

Figure 12: Manipulating output translation to be with an adverbial clause when feeding a sentence with a noun phrase as input. Lines present BLEU change with active and passive references according to the amount of neurons manipulated (x).

harder to capture.

2. Adverbial clause form may be more common in the train set so the model regularizes to the statistically more acceptable option. We see hints for that when we compare the manipulation towards active form as more successful than passive form (§5 and Figure 9).

3. Noun phrase form may not be distinctive enough to be encoded in the model.

4. The target form may not be natural in the target language. As we discuss in our qualitative analysis in section 5.3, fail cases revealed instances where the target form was either not possible for a native German speaker, or required a replacement of the verb to a synonym. This replacement demands another level of manipulation from the model, one that it may not even know to generalize.

C.5 Manipulation Magnitude

As defined in section 5, manipulation from sentence feature c_1 to c_2 is a subtraction of the term $\frac{\alpha}{\|\bar{x_{c_1}}-\bar{x_{c_2}}\|}(\bar{x_{c_1}} - \bar{x_{c_2}})$ (applied to chosen neurons). We experimented with a small grid search for possible values for the scaling factor α, without an apparent option being better than the baseline ($\alpha = 1$). See Figure 11 for results[13]. There is no definitive conclusion of what magnitude would be consistently better in every manipulation. Similar trends were found in the clause dataset: $\alpha = 2$ was best when manipulating from paraphrased form noun phrase back to the original form of the adverbial clause, and worse the other way around. This could be tied to the general effect we discuss in §C.4 where one direction of manipulation is more effective: changing from paraphrased form to original form. This should be further investigated in future work.

C.6 Unparalleled Sentences Manipulation

As seen in §6, top ParaCorr neurons were better for manipulation than those from the bottom of the rank. One possible explanation we introduced was the fact that many of those top ParaCorr neurons are also top PosCorr and TokenCorr neurons. Therefore, the effectiveness might be derived from the role polysemy of these neurons, especially when the paraphrasing calls for a change of word order (e.g. active-passive requires subject and object swap) or token identity (e.g. clause to noun phrase requires a transformation between verb and noun). This is true for cases where the paraphrases are parallel pairs, therefore they share those shallow features (tokens and word order).

Here we present an experiment of manipulation where there are no parallel pairs of paraphrases. We randomly split the sentence pairs into two sets. From one we take only the active sentences, and from the other we take only the passive sentences, resulting in an active set and passive set of unrelated sentences. We repeat the manipulation experiment as detailed in §5.2 but use those unparalleled sets for measuring the averaging activation of neurons under the active voice feature and under the passive voice feature (i.e., for measuring $\bar{x_{c_1}}$ and $\bar{x_{c_2}}$). We do so for 100 different splits of the data. Measuring the mean and standard deviation of the

[13]We experimented with even greater values ($\alpha \in \{5, 10, 100, 1000\}$), each with a more drastic BLEU drop, therefore we discard their inclusion in the figure to allow the y-axis range to capture the subtle trends of the variables presented.

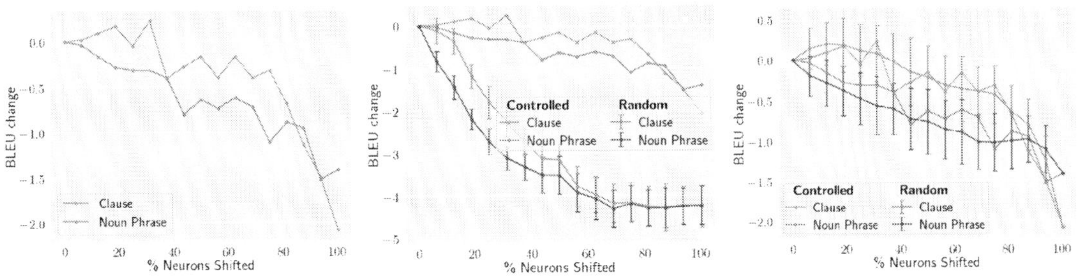

(a) Baseline (b) Random direction comparison (c) Random selection comparison

Figure 13: Manipulating output translation to be with a noun phrase when feeding a sentence with an adverbial clause as input. Lines present BLEU change with active and passive references according to the amount of neurons manipulated (x).

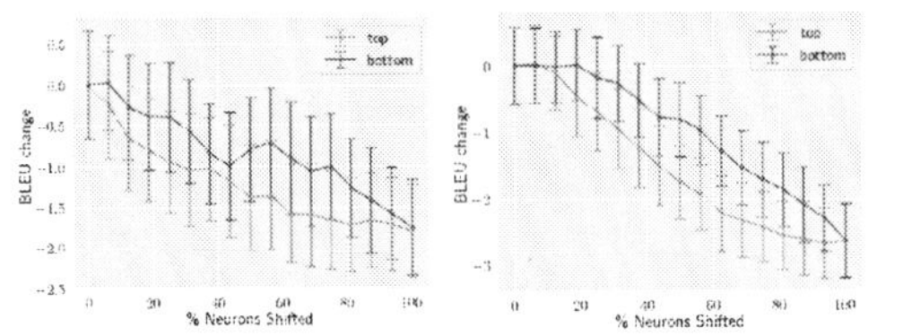

(a) Passive to Active (b) Active to Passive

Figure 14: Comparing the impact of manipulating top ParaCorr neurons versus bottom ones, where the modification value of neurons is determined by average activation under unparalleled sets of sentences, i.e. $\bar{x_{c_1}}$ and $\bar{x_{c_2}}$ are measured by active and passive non-pairs. The lines represent the mean and standard deviation over 100 different unparalleled sets.

BLEU against the objective reference, the results are presented in Figure 14. Notably, the standard deviation of the experiment is reported, not the standard error of the mean. The results may match the intuition where the least correlated neurons between paraphrases are those most sensitive to the active-passive feature, but since nothing is shared across those sentences, the expected noise level is high, and any measure is hard to explain.

When we measured the correlation of such unparalleled sentences, we got an average correlation (per neuron over 100 different splits of the dataset into unparalleled sets) ranging from -0.04 to 0.04, with a standard deviation between 0.03 to 0.06.

D Qualitative Analysis of Manipulation

Sentence examples of successful manipulation from passive voice input to active voice translation, as examined by a native German speaker, can be found in Table 4.

As we discuss in §5.3, sometimes a manipulation is not applicable in the target language. For example, the adverbial clause sentence from our dataset *"In Lyman's case, she reported the alleged rape to military police less than an hour after it occurred."*, is translated into a noun phrase sentence regardless of input form (i.e. if we insert either this as input or its noun phrase paraphrase) or manipulation (i.e. with or without manipulation). "it occurred" is immediately translated into the German parallel of "its occurrence" when translating the clause version, and it is translated into a wrong noun phrase when translating the noun phrase version (the German parallel of "appearance" rather than "occurrence" in this context, i.e. "Auftreten" and "Vorfall", respectively). A native German speaker suggested we opt to replace "occurred" with "happened", otherwise it could not be translated into a clause form. Even the human reference (of WMT) is with the "its occurrence" noun phrase. See Table 5.

Table 4: Example of successfully manipulated sentences, from passive voice input to active voice translation. Manipulation is done by shifting the values of all the neurons in the encoder toward their average activation on active voice sentences. Correctness of sentence voice and fluency was verified by a native German speaker.

Input sentence: passive voice	Baseline translation: passive voice	Manipulated translation: active voice
The scene was described by police as very gruesome.	Der Tatort wurde von der Polizei als sehr grauenvoll beschrieben.	Die Polizei beschrieb den Tatort als sehr grauenvoll.
During the excavations, the remains of a total of five creatures were collected by them.	Bei den Ausgrabungen wurden von ihnen die Überreste von insgesamt fünf Lebewesen gefunden.	Bei den Ausgrabungen fanden sie die Überreste von insgesamt fünf Lebewesen.
From "dream" to "megalomania": the Bit Galerie is discussed by TV readers	Vom "Traum" zum "Größenwahn": Die Bit-Galerie wird von TV-Lesern diskutiert	Vom "Traum" zum "Größenwahn": TV-Leser diskutieren über die Bit-Galerie

Table 5: Example of an adverbial clause and a noun phrase translations, showcasing the limitations of BLEU comparison to Google Translate references and the challenge of translating an output in adverbial clause form. Either manipulation here did not have any effect (e.g. manipulation from clausal input resulted in translation identical to the one without manipulation)

	Adverbial Clause	**Noun Phrase**
English	In Lyman's case, she reported the alleged rape to military police less than an hour after it occurred.	In Lyman's case, she reported the alleged rape to military police less than an hour after its occurrence.
Human Reference	In Lymans Fall meldete sie die mutmassliche Vergewaltigung der Militärpolizei weniger als eine Stunde nach dem überfall.	
Google Translate	In Lymans Fall meldete sie die mutmassliche Vergewaltigung weniger als eine Stunde nach ihrem Auftreten der Militärpolizei.	In Lymans Fall wurde die mutmassliche Vergewaltigung von ihr weniger als eine Stunde nach ihrem Auftreten der Militärpolizei gemeldet.
Our Translation	In Lymans Fall meldete sie die angebliche Vergewaltigung weniger als eine Stunde nach dem Vorfall der Militärpolizei.	In Lymans Fall meldete sie die angebliche Vergewaltigung weniger als eine Stunde nach ihrem Auftreten der Militärpolizei.

Shared knowledge in natural conversations: can entropy metrics shed light on information transfers?

Eliot Maës[1,3] **Philippe Blache**[2,3] **Leonor Becerra-Bonache**[1,3]
[1]Aix Marseille Univ, Université de Toulon, CNRS, LIS, Marseille, France
[2]LPL, CNRS & Aix-Marseille University
[3]ILCB (Institute of Language, Communication and the Brain)
{eliot.maes, leonor.becerra}@lis-lab.fr,
blache@ilcb.fr

Abstract

The mechanisms underlying human communication have been under investigation for decades, but the answer to how understanding between locutors emerges remains incomplete. Interaction theories suggest the development of a structural alignment between the speakers, allowing for the construction of a shared knowledge base (*common ground*). In this paper, we propose to apply metrics derived from information theory to quantify the amount of information exchanged between participants, the dynamics of information exchanges, to provide an objective way to measure the common ground instantiation. We focus on a corpus of free conversations augmented with prosodic segmentation and an expert annotation of thematic episodes. We show that during free conversations, the amount of information remains globally constant at the scale of the conversation, but varies depending on the thematic structuring, underlining the role of the speaker introducing the theme. We propose an original methodology applied to uncontrolled material.

1 Introduction

Theories of interaction explain how participants elaborate their discourse in the perspective of exchanging information, executing a task, establishing a joint action, etc. These theories stipulate in particular that such activity is correlated with the building of a shared knowledge between participant, also called *common ground* (Pickering and Garrod, 2004, 2021). In these frameworks, the quality of an interaction depends on the capacity of building such mutual knowledge, which to its turn depends on the alignment of linguistic representations between participants. These mechanisms are based on different levels of convergence between the participants, that can occur at any level: lexical, syntactic, prosodic, as well as gestures, behaviors, etc. One hypothesis is that this phenomenon is also visible at the semantic level, showing a coordination between participants in terms of information exchange that can be uncovered by studying the amount of such information and its dynamics during a conversation.

The goal of this work is therefore to evaluate these questions by means of information-theoretical measures (Shannon, 1948): sharing information relies on the use of simple symbols which can be combined, concatenated to transfer increasingly complex knowledge. Moreover, it is possible to analyze the dynamics of this process, whether the amount of transfer vary during a conversation, at what position, and whether an alignment between participants can also be observed at this level. An estimation of the quantity of information exchanged between participants and its dynamics could therefore constitute an objective way to measure the common ground instantiation.

Several works have been done in this direction, based on lexical information measured by entropy, and showing a convergence between participants. Inspired by Xu and Reitter (2016), we study the dynamics of information transfer at three levels: first globally, at the scale of an entire conversation, by taking into account productions from both speakers into a same system. Doing that, we propose to identify whether some specific phenomena (e.g. peaks) appear in the amount of exchanged information and that could be related with discourse-level structures (e.g. topic shift). Second, we will study the global evolution of entropy for each speaker, trying to exhibit some convergence patterns (e.g. phase synchronization). Third, we propose to apply the same type of analysis at the scale of a topic, by studying the dynamics of information exchange within a topic (e.g. decrease of entropy) as well as the complementary patterns between speakers. Last, but not least, this is the first work in this domain applied to unrestricted natural conversations.

This paper presents several contributions, corresponding to important differences with the litera-

Proceedings of the 26th Conference on Computational Natural Language Learning (CoNLL), pages 213 - 227
December 7-8, 2022 ©2022 Association for Computational Linguistics

ture. First, we propose to explore this question applied to free conversations instead of task-oriented or controlled ones. Second, in difference with existing works, we evaluate the dynamics of the exchange based on well-defined inter-pausal units instead of sentences (a not adequate notion for spoken languages). Finally, we base our analysis on thematic annotation made by an expert (human linguist) instead of an automatic topic segmentation.

The paper is organised as follows. In Section 2, we review the different approaches to these questions in the litterature. In Section 3, we describe our conversational dataset and the methodology we apply. Our experiments and a discussion of the results are presented in Section 4.

2 Related Works

Several studies have proposed to use information-theoretic measures to study language processing. The general idea is to approach an evaluation of the cognitive load through quantitative estimation. In a seminal work, Hale (2001) introduced the notion of *surprisal*, defined as the negative log-probability of a word given the preceding context, to measure processing difficulty. This approach has been picked up by many studies in psycholinguistic, showing in particular a correlation between reading times and surprisal (Monsalve et al., 2012; Frank et al., 2015). In the same vein, based on grammatical probability distributions, entropy reduction has been proposed to evaluate the informational contributions of each word as a complexity processing measure (Hale, 2016). At the lexical level, without any additional syntactic information than what is understood by the linguistic model, entropy has been proposed to estimate sentence information content in discourse. We offer in this section an overview of the main works done in this direction by first presenting the main approaches to measure information content and second the methods for studying variations of such measures at the discourse level.

2.1 Measuring Information Content

In discourse, each lexical choice can be described as a random variable X_i that is constrained by a number of influences, both short range (sentence structure, local topic) and long range (global context). As the relevant context builds up, the next word prediction is assumed to become easier and easier as more contextual cues are available to the discussion. The information density of this random variable is estimated as the entropy $H(X_i)$ defined by Shannon (1948). We especially follow Xu and Reitter 2018; Giulianelli et al. 2021 in modeling the information content.

The influence of the local context on the word choice is typically modelled at utterance or sentence level with conditional probabilities; sentence entropy is taken as the average entropy of the words comprising that sentence. Therefore, for a given sentence S comprising of a sequence of n words $w_1, w_2, ...w_n$

$$H(w_1...w_n) = -\frac{1}{n} \sum_{w_i \in S} logP(w_i|w_1...w_{i-1}) \tag{1}$$

Keller (2004) and Genzel and Charniak (2003) exposing a correlation between sentence length and entropy values, we also compute a *normalized* version of our entropy metric to remove dependence to sentence length, by dividing the previously computed metric by the average obtained on all sentences of the same length:

$$H'(S) = \frac{H(S)}{\frac{\sum_{W \in L(n)} H(W)}{\#\{L(n)\}}} \tag{2}$$

where $L(n)$ is the set of sentences of length n, ie sentences of the same length as our sentence S.

The initial studies use n-gram language models to estimate word probabilities, which fail to take more long range dependencies into account. The natural reaction is to question the effect of context, which is the approach taken by Giulianelli et al. (2021). They introduce the distinction between *decontextualised* entropy, that only uses the local sentence S as context, and *contextualised* entropy, which utilises the global context C, i.e. all previously mentioned sentences up to the current word, as context. The contextualised entropy of a word is therefore computed as the conditional entropy of a word depending on both the local and global context.

The difference between the amounts of information at the local and global contexts if carried by the mutual information term $MI(S|C)$:

$$H(S|C) = H(S) - MI(S|C) \tag{3}$$

2.2 Entropy variations in language processing

Genzel and Charniak (2002) proposed the *entropy rate constancy* principle stipulating that the rate of transmitted information remains approximately constant. Initially enunciated for written texts, this principle has been applied to natural conversation, albeit with some adaptations.

Following the entropy rate constancy principle, the conditional entropy remains constant through the dialogue. As a consequence, local entropy and mutual information have to vary in the same proportions. At the scale of a dialogue, it has been shown that the two arguments of this equation regularly increase in the same way (Genzel and Charniak, 2002). But at the same time, even though the entropy should remain constant throughout the dialogue, local variations are possible. This aspect has been explored by studying the entropy at specific positions, taking into account the role of the participants in the conversation (Xu and Reitter, 2016, 2018; Giulianelli and Fernández, 2021). These studies are based on a segmentation of the discourse in a sequence of separate topics, with the idea that this succession of thematic episodes could be associated with a variation in the entropy. In this perspective, Qian and Jaeger (2011) has shown a correlation between entropy decrease and potential topic shift in written text: topic shift corresponds to the drop of the mutual information term. More recently, Xu and Reitter (2016) exhibited a symmetry in the entropy fluctuations within a topic depending on the speakers' roles. A new topic corresponds to introducing new information into the context, which means high entropy at the beginning of a topic for the speaker who introduces it (topic *initiator*). Reciprocally, their partner (called in these studies *responders*) progressively update the context, which means that for them, entropy starts low and progressively increases until the next topic. As a consequence, these fluctuations show a convergence pattern between interlocutors within a topic.

3 Datasets and Models

3.1 Datasets

Previous work on information density focusing mostly on task-related conversational datasets such as MapTask (Anderson et al., 1991), we explore whether conclusions drawn on such specific data further generalise to natural conversation by applying the same methods on the Paco-Cheese corpus (Priego-Valverde et al., 2020; Amoyal et al., 2020). Indeed, since vocabulary is not as controlled in natural conversations as it is in tasks, the conversation might drift onto less predictable topics that rely more on common knowledge.

Paco-Cheese (PC) (Priego-Valverde et al., 2020) is a multimodal corpus containing audio and video recordings of 26 interactions between dyads of participants. Conversations are in French and lasting 15 to 20 minutes. Participants were given a short prompt to read to elicit conversation but were otherwise free to talk about the topics of their choice. About half (16) of the conversations happened between participants that were not acquainted. Manual transcription was obtained, then automatically aligned to the audio signal and segmented using SPPAS (Bigi, 2012). Consequently, the speech segments we consider here are inter-pausal units (IPUs) - segments boundaries are defined by pauses longer than 200ms of silence - which commonly are shorter than sentences. The corpus is also enriched with annotations for noise, laugh, pauses, feedbacks, head nods and smiles (Amoyal, 2018; Amoyal and Priego-Valverde, 2019). Expert thematic annotation has been added to 16 of the dialogues. Excerpts from the corpus can be found in Appendix A.

Relying on these annotations, we compute information content values for the dialogues and consider its evolution at two levels: *global evolution* throughout the conversation, and *local evolution* in a given conversational theme.

3.2 Language Models

We estimate information content throughout the dialogue by computing per-word entropy for each sentence, using language models trained on different corpora and finetuned on the dataset of interest.

Previous works relied both on n-gram models (Xu and Reitter, 2018) and Transformer models (Giulianelli et al., 2021). Models were then not straightly compared however the latter method provides with two advantages: first, Transformers allow for the possibility to take larger amounts of contextual information into account; second, default Tokenizers in the pipeline are trained using a Byte-Pair Encoding, which allows them to properly deal with out-of-vocabulary (OOV) tokens. Those rarer words would be especially important in predicting surprise and information content in the conversation.

After experimenting with n-gram models, RNNs and the GPT-2 language model (Radford et al., 2019) - we disregard more recent models using masking-based learning in order to focus on more

Table 1: Perplexity for the models used compared to that of GPT-2 pretrained models

model	lang.	pretraining	finetuning	perplexity	OOV
SRILM	FR	decoda	x	132,32	0.5%
RNN	FR	wikipedia	x	83,16	-
GPT-2	FR	wikipedia		125,39	-
GPT-2	FR	wikipedia	x	32,51	-

cognitive-plausible models - we chose to focus on the latter as GPT-2 demonstrates both lower perplexity and has been shown to better correlate with human surprisal in language understanding (Michaelov et al., 2021). We rely on HuggingFace's implementation of the model[1], using default tokenizers and parameters (Wolf et al., 2020). Finetuning is required to adapt the language model from written input to the specificities of natural conversation. We therefore finetune the models on a 70% split of each target corpus. As shown in Table 1, finetuning yields a substantial reduction in the model's perplexity.

The information content of an utterance is computed sequentially, using log-probabilities predicted by the model for each token in the sentence. Several lengths of context are considered (current utterance only $H(S)$; several utterances; every preceding utterance $H(S|C)$) and Mutual Information is computed from the difference between $H(S)$ and $H(S|C)$.

More information on models parameters and finetuning can be found in Appendix B.

3.3 Statistical Models

With our experiments, we study the dynamics of information transfers at two levels: i) globally, at the level of the entire conversation; ii) locally, at the level of topic episodes. We fit linear models on information content estimated by the language models on those two conditions. In those models, the logarithm of the information content is the response variable (*H(S|C)* or *H(S)*) and the logarithm of turn position (whether global, `logp`, or relative to the local theme, `logt`) is the fixed effect. Dialogues are considered a random effect in this analysis.

We also include in our analysis a comparison between utterance lengths to validate that using IPUs does not affect the conclusions we draw from the data.

[1]`https://huggingface.co/gpt2`, using weights from `dbddv01/gpt2-french-small` for the french model

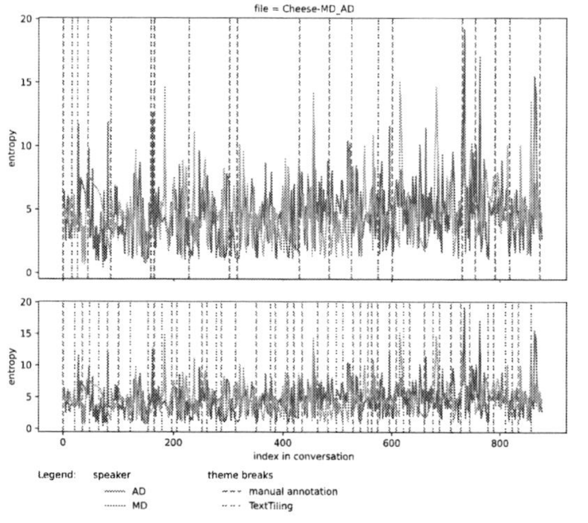

Figure 1: Evolution of normalised contextualised entropy on one example dialogue. The two speakers are plotted in different colors. Dashed lines indicate the start of new themes in the manual annotation (top) and automated annotation (bottom).

3.4 Peak identification and correlation to thematic annotation

Topic Segmentation Information content evolution is typically studied at the dialogue level (global context), but also locally, at the level of *topic episodes*. Annotations for this partitioning can be derived automatically using tools such as TextTiling (Hearst, 1997). This algorithm relies on lexical co-occurrences patterns to compute a similarity score between sentences and segment a text into subtopic shifts.

To complement the manual annotation of themes in Paco-Cheese, we obtain automatic extraction of theme changes using NLTK's implementation[2] of the TextTiling algorithm. This step furthermore allows to compare human sensitivity to topic change to lexical changes (see Figure 1), an analysis which has not been done on the corpus yet.

Entropy Peak Detection and Analysis Investigating the location of information exchanges, we consider peaks of entropy as potential locations for the introduction of new data to the conversation. Assimilating those values to outliers, two unsupervised methods are used to detect those values. Entropy series are detrended and scaled before

[2]`https://www.nltk.org/api/nltk.tokenize.html#module-nltk.tokenize.texttiling`

Table 2: Estimates and significance for the effect of position on information content for the linear mixed-effect models on Paco-Cheese

		interaction		theme	
global	log position	0.027	***		
	log position			-0.032	***
initiator	log position			-0.021	**
follower	log position			-0.015	

further computations. The first method of outlier detection involves local detection of unusual values; we rely on `scikit-learn` (Pedregosa et al., 2011) implementation of Local Outlier Factor for this. The second method (hereafter NormOutlier) involves globally comparing the values and selecting the highest two percent. For both methods, parameters were chosen as optimal values on a subset of the data based on accuracy, precision and recall metrics. We finally compare the performances of those methods in predicting thematic episodes boundaries, to basic classifiers from the `scikit-learn` dummy module.

We also leverage Part-of-Speech tagging and Feedback annotations from the dataset to explore which words are most unexpected for the model.

4 Experiments

In this section we present the results of our experiments with the Paco-Cheese dataset. Taking the values of $H(S)$ (i.e., the information content of a sentence) and $H(S|C)$ (i.e., the contextualised entropy) estimated by the language model, we also compute the difference between contextualised and decontextualised entropy (MI). We extend results obtained by previous works with this new corpora containing free conversations. We then explore those results using qualitative and quantitative analysis of locations with high information content.

4.1 Speakers behavior in natural conversation

Global evolution We find a positive effect of turn position on information content when taking the entire Paco-Cheese dialogues as the context unit (see Table 2). This effect can however be entirely attributed to the structure of the corpus as conversation usually start with a few sentences of explanation of the experiment and two one sided readings of the jokes. Indeed when focusing only on the free conversation, we find that this positive effect disappears (see Figure 2 for the difference of entropy evolution between the two conditions).

Local evolution: themes We do however observe an effect of turn position on information content at the level of themes (β = -0.032, $p < 0.001$) (see Figure 3), which seems to be entirely driven by the behavior of the topic initiator (β = -0.021, $p < 0.001$). We observe no effect of turn position on information content for the other locutor responding to the topic initiation.

We attribute the lack of overall effect of position to the structure of the conversation, as in a natural paradigm speakers will naturally shift from one topic to the next, without necessarily relying on previously mentioned context to move the conversation forward. Themes, however, make up smaller, coherent units of a conversation. The negative effect of turn position on information content in themes would seem to be going against the principle of Uniform Information Density (Jaeger and Levy, 2006) and its applications to dialogue which indicate that information content should be increasing; it is however in line with Xu and Reitter (2018)'s findings that the information content will be either constant or slightly decreasing the more the topic progresses. We postulate that the reason why we do not observe an effect of position is because the responder is active in helping constructing the theme and does not simply fall back into a passive role at the introduction of a new topic.

The full results of the statistical analysis and accuracy of theme change detection can be found in Appendix C.[3]

4.2 Units of sense in a conversation: IPUs vs. sentences?

Unlike other works that compute entropy at the level of a "sentence" (which is not valid when studying spoken language), the input to our models are inter-pausal units (speech separated by 200ms pauses). IPUs being shorter than sentences or turns and potentially made of fewer words, they offer the possibility of a finer granularity, more in line with linguistic characteristics of dialogues.

One might expect this change of scale to affect the patterns displayed in information content, as longer interventions would bring in more information at once. Differences between topic initiator and responder might appear more strongly with a more frequent use of short utterances and feedback.

[3]Codes and statistical analysis are available at `https://github.com/ejmaes/multimodal-itmodels`

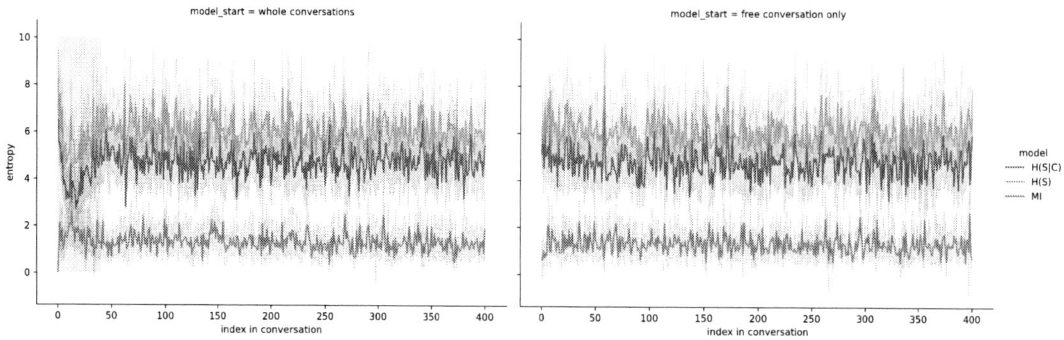

Figure 2: Average evolution of the entropy throughout the conversation for the Paco-Cheese corpus. Left: starting at file start; Right: removing introductions and prompt reading to start analysis at the beginning of the free conversation. In red, the approximate duration of conversation starters (varies between dialogues)

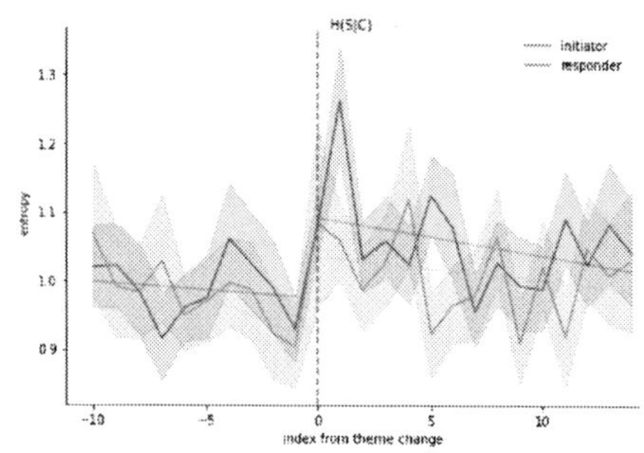

Figure 3: Average information content in the utterances surrounding the start of a new theme, for both speakers.

To test this hypothesis, we aggregated IPUs by a given speaker that were separated by silences shorter than 1 second and were not interupted by the other speaker. The obtained utterances are akin to sentences in terms of length and semantic content. For the comparison to be more accurate, we remove the IPUs of the first part of the dialogs, which correspond to the reading of jokes and not to actual conversation. We then fed this new data into the language model. Results (see Table 3) mostly appear robust to the aggregation, with a main effect of position on entropy at the level of themes and for the speaker initiating the theme.

Table 3: Comparison between IPUs and sentences - Estimates and significance for the effect of position on information content

		IPUs		sentence - 1s	
global	both speakers	0.015		-0.22	**
theme	both speakers	**-0.030**	***	**-0.029**	***
	initiator	**-0.024**	**	**-0.033**	**
	follower	-0.014		-0.017	

4.3 Distribution of entropy peaks against themes

The distribution of information in the conversation, despite being stable on a global level, is not smooth on a local scale, as the even flow of entropy is sometimes intersected with peaks of local uncertainty. We ponder whether those peaks only correlate to endemic features of the conversation, such as the introduction of new information to the discussion, or whether they inform on model shortcomings that need to be addressed to better understand the characteristics of information transmission and common ground instantiation in conversation.

4.3.1 Theme change in conversation: smooth or abrupt behavior?

Inspired by the behavior observed in entropy values around theme breaks (see Figure 3) and the decrease in entropy for the initiator throughout the theme they introduced, we wonder whether it is possible to predict theme breaks from entropy values and more specifically entropy peaks.

We first start by exploring how similar automatic and manual annotations actually are. A first quantitative approach reveals that TextTiling systematically overestimates the number of themes by conversation in our dataset (Figure 4), predicting 565 thematic episodes whereas the dataset only has 268 (see Table 4). This might be an indicator of the existence of subtopics in the conversations; however, locations indicated by TextTiling as the start of new themes only weakly correlate with expertly annotated locations. A first hypothesis as to explain those results involves the existence of *transitions* phases in-between two thematic episodes. Transitions are frequently annotated in the corpus, with

Table 4: Average number of themes per dialogue in each dataset, as annotated vs estimated by TextTiling

	Annotations	TextTiling
PACO-CHEESE	16.4 ($\pm$ 2.8)	34.5 ($\pm$ 7.0)

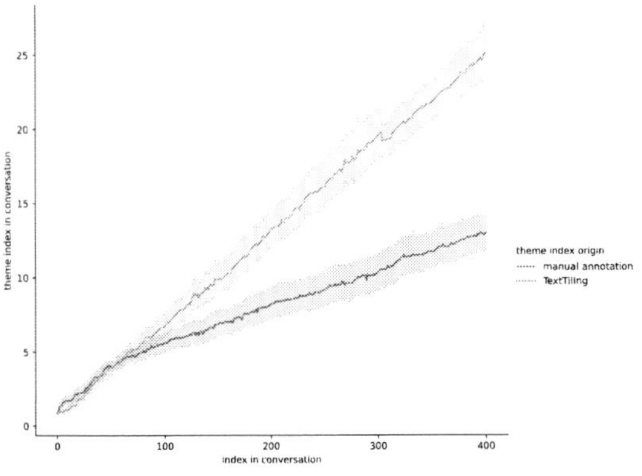

Figure 4: Average number of themes discussed in the conversation as a function of IPU index, according to manual annotation (blue) and automatic annotation (orange). Some conversations are shorter than others, which might cause the average number of themes to drop around some indexes.

13.6 ± 3.3 transitions per conversation, slightly less than the number of themes per dialogue. Indeed, if transitions are annotated, then boundaries between themes must be considered to be flexible enough. We then consider that a prediction falling within a small window of a boundary will be an accurate one; this yields better results, despite prediction accuracy remaining quite low (80 common locations out of 288 annotated theme changes, see Table 5).

Manual and automatic annotation therefore appear to consider different features and rules to establish thematic boundaries. But if automatic annotation is more sensitive to new vocabulary introduced in the conversation to label thematic changes, we hypothesize might also correlate more with entropy values. For this reason we compare the location of information content peaks to the distribution of topics both manually and automatically predicted.

Peak location does not accurately predict theme changes or TextTiling results, though correlating peaks to TextTiling yields slightly better results than manual annotation. For manual annotation, Local Outlier detection allows for the detection of the largest number the theme changes ($precision$ = 0.172 / $recall$ = 0.65 within a 5 IPUs window), predicting a larger number of locations of interest than annotated. Peak detection further correlates with automated annotation of theme changes, which further support the hypothesis of entropy peaks appearing around locations where new content is introduced. This method for predicting thematic boundaries however does not fare better than a baseline classifier trained directly on entropy values and sentence length to detect topic boundaries.

4.3.2 Language models and natural conversation

To further analyze model and participants behavior throughout the conversation, we shift our focus to per-word entropy. We focus on two aspects: words with high entropy on the one hand, and the way the model deals with conversational feedback on the other.

From peak locations, a set of vocabulary with the highest entropy values is extracted. We cross this list with part-of-speech tagging and feedback annotation available in the corpus before going further. We note that most of those words are nouns, with the stronger occurrences being proper nouns, which is expected since those words wouldn't be known to the model - or, in the case of locations, logical in the conversation - prior to encountering them. Some of those unexpected words would however not be evaluated by the speakers as this significant, since they are already part as their shared knowledge (nearby locations, daily life abbreviations, names of known individuals...). Thus most of these words may simply be unexpected in this context or too unusual for the model, and do not provide any new information to the topic at hand. However, a small percentage of words do; and in the case of words reappearing later in the conversation, a slight decrease in entropy is observed. A list of unusual words with high entropy causing the appearance of peaks is provided in Appendix D.1.

We finally turn our attention to backchannels, a discourse-specific occurrence through which a listener can interact with the speaker and notify them on their thought process without requiring taking the floor. Backchannels typically include movements (head nods, smiles or facial expressions), small words (*yes, okay, no, sure...*) or short utterances that do not disrupt the conversation flow. A qualitative analysis of peak locations had revealed the presence of feedbacks among the utterances of interest; further inspection actually reveals this is not an issue in modeling. Indeed, most feedbacks generate lower than average entropy. But

Table 5: Comparison of manually annotated theme changes locations to peak locations and theme breaks according to automated annotation. A baseline classifier (DumStrat) trained to predict theme breaks is added for reference.

	features	target	best result	True Positive	precision	recall
TextTiling	text	manual annotation	window=5	80	0.136	0.299
LocalOutlier	entropy		window=5	173	0.172	0.646
NormOutlier	entropy		window=5	23	0.174	0.086
DumStrat	entropy + text features		-	261	0.268	0.113
LocalOutlier	entropy	TextTiling	window=5	381	0.278	0.674

sometimes longer feedbacks conveying meaning a bit more specific generate uncertainty, same as other utterances in the dialogue, with the difference than those productions from the listener are more concise than utterances from the speaker. It is especially the fact for unexpected, negative input, but makes perfect sense on a cognitive standpoint.

A more detailed view into feedbacks types, frequencies and related entropy is available in Appendix D.2.

5 Conclusion

The results presented in this paper represent a new contribution for the study of information exchange during conversation. First, this work only relies on free natural conversations, without adding more controlled corpora. In particular, in difference with other works in the literature, we do not add any task-oriented dialogue (such as MapTask) nor telephone conversation (such as Switchboard), that have known specific impacts on turn taking and topic shift. In terms of methodology, we decided to use a prosodic segmentation of the input (pauses longer than 200ms) generating identify inter-pausal units usually used in studies on spoken language. IPUs are discourse segments with a certain coherence only identified on the basis of the acoustic signal. These segments offer a finer-grained view of the input in comparison with the segmentation into sentences that are usually used in the literature. This notion of sentence is not only problematic when applied to spoken language (the existing works do not precisely explain to what they correspond), but may also introduce a bias when studying topic shift, these two segments being possibly the same. Finally, we are using with this analysis a thematic segmentation that was done manually by experts, rather than relying on automatic segmentation as previous works might have done. TextTiling identifies topics based on semantic similarity; here annotations are based on higher-level information, bringing together all different linguistic and non-verbal information, providing a much more reliable segmentation.

Our results first confirm that at the scale of a conversation, entropy remains stable, as it has been observed in other works. At a local level, when segmenting the discourse in themes, we also observe a specific behavior, showing a decrease in the entropy of the speaker introducing the theme, which is expected. However, no significant pattern can be observed for the responder, for who the entropy remains approximately stable. To be more precise, we did not observe any increase in the entropy. As a consequence, we cannot say that a convergence in the entropy rate between the different speakers can be observed at the scale of a theme. This result is important in the study of conversational interactions. It means that convergence between speakers, which is necessary during a conversation, is a complex phenomenon that cannot be observed only on the basis of quantity measures. At the same time, the analysis of entropy constitutes a robust cue for evaluating how much and when information is transferred between speakers in a natural setup; however it must be complemented with data from other sources to assist the model in isolating truly important sections of the dialogue, from noise (rarer words that are logical in the context).

This work opens the door to further study. For starters, as previously mentioned, enriching the models with information, coming from other modalities would most likely refine the analysis. Among the modalities of interest are audio (speech rate is known to be modulated according to the difficulty of the information), video (gaze), and cerebral activity. Indeed, we think that the dynamics of the entropy is correlated with information exchange and more generally with the building of the common ground. It becomes therefore possible to start studying the brain basis of mutual understanding by looking specifically at the brain signal associated with entropy peaks. Our hypothesis is that this entropy-based indicator could offer the possibility to analyze the brain signal in a time-locked event paradigm (evoked-related potentials) as well as the time-frequency level (frequency bands).

Acknowledgements

This work, carried out within the Institut Convergence ILCB (ANR-16-CONV-0002), has benefited from support from the French government, managed by the French National Agency for Research (ANR).

References

Mary Amoyal. 2018. Analyse du sourire lors des transitions thématiques dans la conversation.

Mary Amoyal and Béatrice Priego-Valverde. 2019. Smiling for negotiating topic transitions in french conversation. In *GESPIN-Gesture and Speech in Interaction*.

Mary Amoyal, Béatrice Priego-Valverde, and Stéphane Rauzy. 2020. PACO : A corpus to analyze the impact of common ground in spontaneous face-to-face interaction. In *LREC procs*.

Anne H. Anderson, Miles Bader, Ellen Gurman Bard, Elizabeth Boyle, Gwyneth Doherty, Simon Garrod, Stephen Isard, Jacqueline Kowtko, Jan McAllister, and Jim Miller. 1991. The hcrc map task corpus. *Language and Speech*, 34(4):351–366.

Frederic Bechet, Benjamin Maza, Nicolas Bigouroux, Thierry Bazillon, Marc El-Beze, Renato De Mori, and Eric Arbillot. 2012. Decoda: a call-centre human-human spoken conversation corpus. In *Proceedings of the Eighth International Conference on Language Resources and Evaluation (LREC'12)*, pages 1343–1347.

Brigitte Bigi. 2012. Sppas: un outil« user-friendly» pour l'alignement texte/son (sppas: a tool to perform text/speech alignement)[in french]. In *JEP-TALN-RECITAL 2012, Workshop DEGELS 2012: Défi GEste Langue des Signes (DEGELS 2012: Gestures and Sign Language Challenge)*, pages 85–92.

Stefan L Frank, Leun J Otten, Giulia Galli, and Gabriella Vigliocco. 2015. The erp response to the amount of information conveyed by words in sentences. *Brain and language*, 140:1–11.

Dmitriy Genzel and Eugene Charniak. 2002. Entropy rate constancy in text. In *Proceedings of the 40th annual meeting of the Association for Computational Linguistics*, pages 199–206.

Dmitriy Genzel and Eugene Charniak. 2003. Variation of entropy and parse trees of sentences as a function of the sentence number. In *Proceedings of the 2003 conference on empirical methods in natural language processing*, pages 65–72.

Mario Giulianelli and Raquel Fernández. 2021. Analysing Human Strategies of Information Transmission as a Function of Discourse Context. In *Proceedings of the 25th Conference on Computational Natural Language Learning*, pages 647–660, Online. Association for Computational Linguistics.

Mario Giulianelli, Arabella Sinclair, and Raquel Fernández. 2021. Is Information Density Uniform in Task-Oriented Dialogues? In *Proceedings of the 2021 Conference on Empirical Methods in Natural Language Processing*, pages 8271–8283, Online and Punta Cana, Dominican Republic. Association for Computational Linguistics.

John Hale. 2001. A probabilistic earley parser as a psycholinguistic model. In *Proceeding of 2nd Conference of the North American Chapter of the Association for Computational Linguistics*, Pittsburgh, PA.

John Hale. 2016. Information-theoretical complexity metrics. *Language and Linguistics Compass*, 10(9):397–412.

Marti A Hearst. 1997. Text tiling: Segmenting text into multi-paragraph subtopic passages. *Computational linguistics*, 23(1):33–64.

T Jaeger and Roger Levy. 2006. Speakers optimize information density through syntactic reduction. volume 19.

Frank Keller. 2004. The entropy rate principle as a predictor of processing effort: An evaluation against eye-tracking data. In *Proceedings of the 2004 conference on empirical methods in natural language processing*, pages 317–324.

James A Michaelov, Megan D Bardolph, Seana Coulson, and Benjamin K Bergen. 2021. Different kinds of cognitive plausibility: why are transformers better than rnns at predicting n400 amplitude? *arXiv preprint arXiv:2107.09648*.

Irene Fernandez Monsalve, Stefan L. Frank, and Gabriella Vigliocco. 2012. Lexical surprisal as a general predictor of reading time. In *Proceedings of the 13th Conference of the European Chapter of the Association for Computational Linguistics*, EACL '12, pages 398–408. Association for Computational Linguistics.

F. Pedregosa, G. Varoquaux, A. Gramfort, V. Michel, B. Thirion, O. Grisel, M. Blondel, P. Prettenhofer, R. Weiss, V. Dubourg, J. Vanderplas, A. Passos, D. Cournapeau, M. Brucher, M. Perrot, and E. Duchesnay. 2011. Scikit-learn: Machine learning in Python. *Journal of Machine Learning Research*, 12:2825–2830.

Martin Pickering and Simon Garrod. 2021. *Understanding Dialogue*. Cambridge University Press.

Martin J. Pickering and Simon Garrod. 2004. Toward a mechanistic psychology of dialogue. *Behavioral and Brain Sciences*, 27(2):169–190.

Béatrice Priego-Valverde, Brigitte Bigi, and Mary Amoyal. 2020. "cheese!": a corpus of face-to-face french interactions. a case study for analyzing smiling and conversational humor. In *LREC*, pages 467–475.

Ting Qian and T Florian Jaeger. 2011. Topic shift in efficient discourse production. In *Proceedings of the Annual Meeting of the Cognitive Science Society*, volume 33.

Alec Radford, Jeffrey Wu, Rewon Child, David Luan, Dario Amodei, Ilya Sutskever, et al. 2019. Language models are unsupervised multitask learners. *OpenAI blog*, 1(8):9.

Claude Elwood Shannon. 1948. A mathematical theory of communication. *The Bell system technical journal*, 27(3):379–423.

Ashish Vaswani, Noam Shazeer, Niki Parmar, Jakob Uszkoreit, Llion Jones, Aidan N Gomez, Łukasz Kaiser, and Illia Polosukhin. 2017. Attention is all you need. *Advances in neural information processing systems*, 30.

Thomas Wolf, Lysandre Debut, Victor Sanh, Julien Chaumond, Clement Delangue, Anthony Moi, Tim Cistac, Pierand Rault, Rémi Louf, Joe towicz, Morgan Funand Davison, Sam Shleifer, Patrick Platen, Clara Ma, Yacine Jernite, Julien Plu, Teven Le Xu, Canand Scao, Sylvain Gugger, Mariama Drame, Quentin Lhoest, and Alexander M. Rush. 2020. Transformers: State-of-the-art natural language processing. In *Proceedings of the 2020 Conference on Empirical Methods in Natural Language Processing: System Demonstrations*, pages 38–45,. Online. Association for Computational Linguistics.

Yang Xu and David Reitter. 2016. Entropy Converges Between Dialogue Participants: Explanations from an Information-Theoretic Perspective. In *Proceedings of the 54th Annual Meeting of the Association for Computational Linguistics (Volume 1: Long Papers)*, pages 537–546, Berlin, Germany. Association for Computational Linguistics.

Yang Xu and David Reitter. 2017. Spectral Analysis of Information Density in Dialogue Predicts Collaborative Task Performance. In *Proceedings of the 55th Annual Meeting of the Association for Computational Linguistics (Volume 1: Long Papers)*, pages 623–633, Vancouver, Canada. Association for Computational Linguistics.

Yang Xu and David Reitter. 2018. Information density converges in dialogue: Towards an information-theoretic model. *Cognition*, 170:147–163.

A Corpus Excerpt

Table 6 shows an excerpt of a Paco-Cheese dialogue, annotated with utterance position in the dialogue, current discussion theme, speaker identifiers and information content estimates (contextualised, decontextualised, and difference between the two).

B Language Models Training and comparison

B.1 Transformers

We experiment with GPT-2 (Radford et al., 2019), an autoregressive Transformer-based (Vaswani et al., 2017) language model, relying on HuggingFace's implementation, pretrained models[4] and default tokenizers.

Considering the corpora peculiarity (dialogue) which differs from most of the training data, we finetune the models on 70% of the target corpora. The finetuned models yield significantly lower perplexity on the portion of the dataset reserved for testing. One epoch with a training loss of 5e-05 (default) and batches of size 8 leads to significant improvement on the English corpus. The French model is finetuned for 20 epochs with a learning rate of 1e-05 and batches of size 16.

For inference, the model's maximum sequence length is used (1024) so as to maximize the model's ability to extract context from the discourse.

To match the SRILM execution output as well as to give context to the prediction of the first sentence token, we include a sentence beginning token at the start of the sentence for the prediction, but this token's information content is not computed.

B.2 Other language models

RNN models Data in input of the RNN models is parsed using the same Tokenizers as GPT in order to facilitate comparison between models; the models are trained on the same fraction of the corpus. After a first pass on a set of wikipedia data, the model are finetuned for 2 epochs on the target dataset. The model's architecture is as follows: one embeddings layer, one GRU layer (`hidden_size=128`). The RNN cell output is then fed to a Linear layer through a Dropout layer.

SRILM Language Models Unlike neural network models which training relied on tokenizers which virtually removed the problem of out of vocabulary (OOV) tokens, SRILM Language Models can only rely on the vocabulary encountered during training for inference of probabilities. Choosing the model therefore involves balancing perplexity and number of OOV tokens matched during inference. The fraction of OOV in the held-out data

[4]Pretrained model used for English corpora was the default `gpt2` weights; for French corpora, weights from `dbddv01/gpt2-french-small` were used.

Table 6: 20 lines from the Paco-Cheese corpora, excerpt of the conversation between AA and OR.

index	theme	speaker	text	H(S|C)	H(S)	MI
120	exams	OR	ça venait de la psycho de l'anthropo enfin de plein de euh domaines	1.18	1.30	0.13
121	exams	AA	ouais ouais	0.31	0.43	0.12
122	exams	OR	je pense c'était juste simplement euh ça	1.04	1.01	-0.04
123	exams	AA	ben ouais mais moi le truc c'est que genre la veille ben du coup je l'avais revu et tout	0.76	0.77	0.01
124	exams	OR	et	0.40	0.62	0.21
125	exams	AA	genre les j'ai vu mes deux résumés je les ai regardés j'ai fait euh	0.95	0.91	-0.03
126	exams	AA	pouah c'est bon ça tombera non non j'ai fait non c'est bon ça tombera pas sur ça	0.76	0.74	-0.01
127	exams	OR	la flemme	1.38	1.03	-0.35
128	exams	OR	ouais	0.37	0.65	0.28
129	exams	AA	genre du coup je les ai lu vite fait en diagonale	1.51	1.55	0.04
130	exams	AA	et	0.51	0.62	0.11
131	exams	AA	après j'ai eu la première question du partiel j'ai fait	0.80	0.85	0.06
132	exams	AA	ah	0.74	0.79	0.05
133	exams	OR	ouais voilà	0.65	0.65	-0.00
134	exams	AA	ah bon	1.41	1.12	-0.29
135	exams	OR	et moi je m'étais même pas rendue compte que c'était là-dedans c'est après cristèle elle m'a dit mais tu vois que c'est tu as exactement ton résumé genre	0.80	0.88	0.08
136	exams	AA	j'aurais dû	0.78	0.75	-0.03
137	exams	OR	alors qu'en plus le résumé quand elle a corrigé il m'a dit très bon résumé	1.11	1.16	0.06
138	exams	AA	ouais moi aussi	0.72	0.76	0.04
139	exams	AA	du coup j'étais un petit peu deg quoi	1.77	1.57	-0.20

was between 1 and 5% with non-finetuned models, lower with finetuned models. Following Xu and Reitter (2017) who train their language model on a different corpus, we compare different data sources for the language model. We find that pretraining the model on a larger dialogue corpus (we use DECODA, (Bechet et al., 2012)) then finetuning it on a fraction of the target corpus yields the best balance in terms of perplexity and number of OOV tokens. Indeed perplexity will be lower with large corpus that are closer in structure to the target data; thus training on dialogue data will be better than training on written corpus such as wikipedia, especially considering that the larger the original corpus, the smaller the effect of finetuning.

B.3 Building up contextual information

One interrogation that came with using models with context was how context buildup allowed for better expectations of the upcoming words. The mind is capable of selecting relevant information from an utterance and reusing it long distance, albeit with limits, as the memory span is not infinite. How much pull would long distance information have in the predictions? The biggest information input happens with the addition of the previous sentence to the context (see Figure 5); further additions to the context have a more limited impact. Thus computed values of entropy for each sentence can

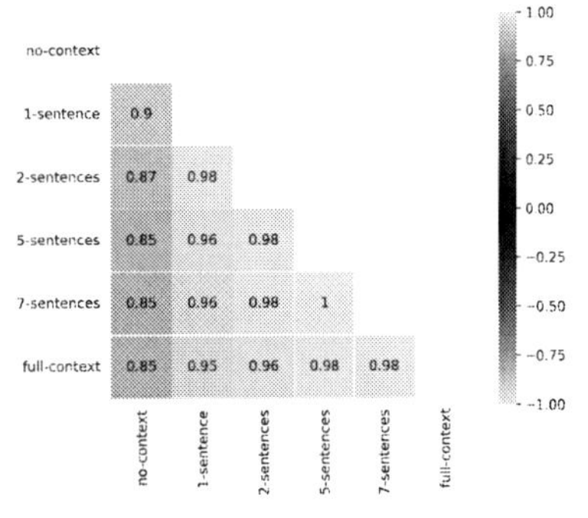

Figure 5: Correlation between entropy values given by the model, depending on the length of the contextual information, in IPUs

mostly be explained by language understanding and local structure of the sentence, with previous utterances and long distance information selection refining the predictions.

C Experimental Results

C.1 Linear Models results

Table 7 summarise the results of our statistical analysis. The same four linear models are fitted on information content estimated on different sets of the data: the utterance column refers to the length of the context, the IPU being the main condition, and `concat 1s` referring to paradigms where IPUs from one speaker are aggregated as long as they

Table 7: Results of linear mixed-effect models on the Paco-Cheese dataset

model	utterance	test_label	var	whole dialogues estimate	p	sig	free conversation only estimate	p	sig
H(S|C)	IPU	Position in INTERACTION	(Intercept)	-0.269	0.000	***	-0.009	0.863	
			logp	0.027	0.000	***	-0.015	0.111	
		Position in THEME	(Intercept)	-0.023	0.174		-0.010	0.577	
			logt	-0.032	0.000	***	-0.030	0.000	***
		Position in THEME - initiator	(Intercept)	-0.056	0.017	*	-0.010	0.668	
			logt	-0.021	0.002	**	-0.024	0.001	***
		Position in THEME - responder	(Intercept)	-0.082	0.032	*	-0.087	0.023	*
			logt	-0.015	0.114		-0.014	0.153	
	concat 1s	Position in INTERACTION	(Intercept)	-0.004	0.924				
			logp	-0.022	0.005	**			
		Position in THEME	(Intercept)	-0.016	0.570				
			logt	-0.029	0.000	***			
		Position in THEME - initiator	(Intercept)	0.003	0.891				
			logt	-0.033	0.002	**			
		Position in THEME - responder	(Intercept)	-0.082	0.059	.			
			logt	-0.017	0.123				
H(S)	IPU	Position in INTERACTION	(Intercept)	-0.112	0.000	***			
			logp	0.010	0.004	**			
		Position in THEME	(Intercept)	-0.011	0.344				
			logt	-0.015	0.000	***			
		Position in THEME - initiator	(Intercept)	-0.018	0.213				
			logt	-0.012	0.015	*			
		Position in THEME - responder	(Intercept)	-0.053	0.028	*			
			logt	-0.004	0.534				

are not interrupted by pauses longer than 1 second and are not interrupted by the other speaker. *Whole dialogue* and *free conversation only* refer to whether the dialogue data is considered as a whole or whether the start of the dialogue (introductions, reading of jokes to kickstart conversation) is removed only to keep the free flowing conversation. In those models, the logarithm of the information content is the response variable (H(S|C) or H(S)) and the logarithm of turn position (whether global, `logp`, or relative to the local theme, `logt`) is the fixed effect. Dialogues are considered a random effect in this analysis.

All models yield similar results in terms of estimates and p-value for the 4 conditions, with the exception of the effect of position in interaction that disappears in the free conversations only condition.

C.2 Peaks and Theme Change Locations

Manual annotation is compared to automated annotation based on lexical similarity using the TextTiling algorithm (Hearst, 1997). Figure 6 shows the distribution of annotated themes throughout two example conversations, with dashed lines indicated the start of new themes as annotated manually and automatically. TextTiling shows a higher sensitivity than human annotation to lexical changes in the conversation, resulting in a number of annotated themes twice as large on average.

Peak detection is run using two methods. The first method (LocalOutlier in the table) relies on the implementation of Local Outlier Factor by `scikit-learn` (Pedregosa et al., 2011), which allows for comparison of a value to its neighbors (n=5) to detect locally unusual values. The second method (NormOutlier) relies on a global, where only the top 2% values are considered outliers (see Figure 7). Both methods are applied to series of contextualised entropy H(S|C) as well as mutual information (MI) as both would be expected to be sensitive to the introduction of new information to the conversation. Neighbors number and percentage threshold value were chosen as optimal values based on accuracy, precision and recall, on a subset of the data.

Table 8 summarises how peak location and TextTiling theme break prediction fare in predicting the location of manually annotated theme changes. There is a total of 268 of theme changes in the dataset (excluding moments annotated as transitions between two themes). We consider that the location of a theme change might not be an accurate consideration since it depends on the annotator sensitivity and consider the prediction might match a location within a small window of IPUs centered around it. Windows of size 2 and 5 were consid-

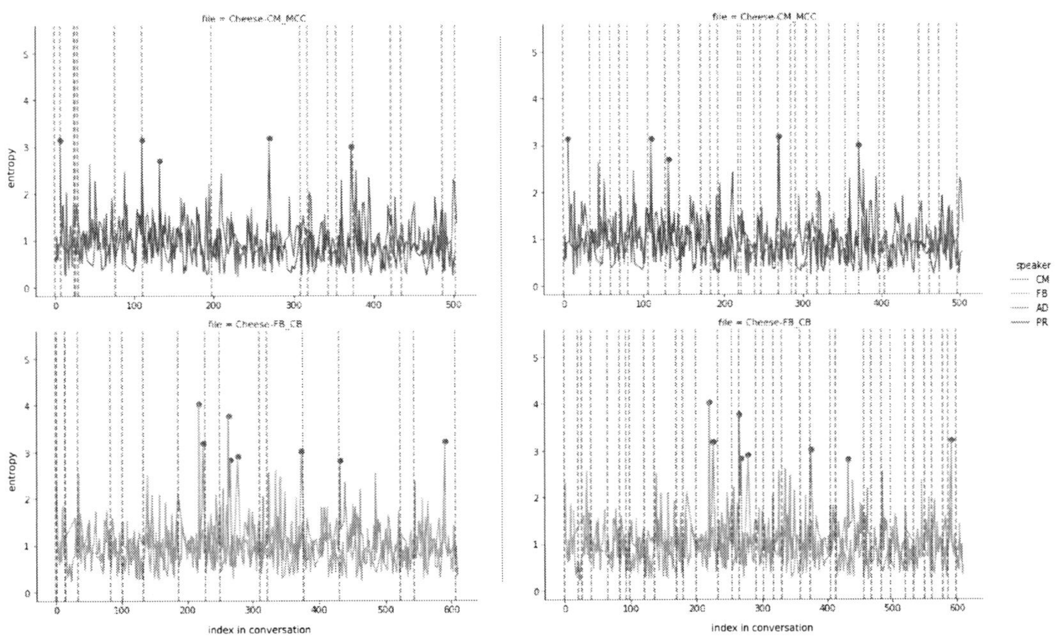

Figure 6: Evolution of normalised contextualised entropy on two dialogues. The two speakers are plotted in different colors. Bold points indicate outliers detected by the NormOutlier method. Dashed lines indicate the start of new themes - left: manual annotation; right: predicted by TextTiling

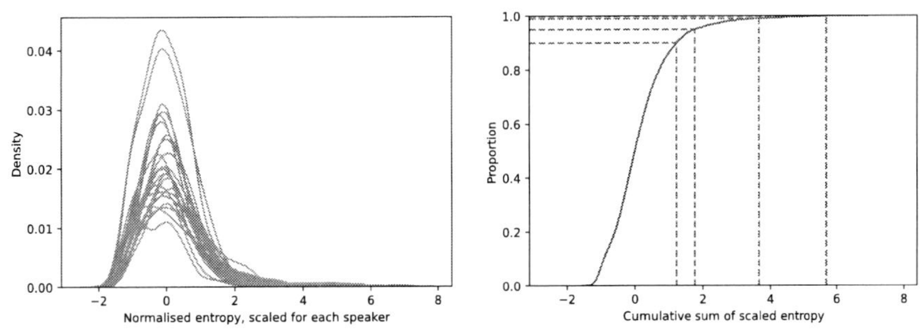

Figure 7: Probability distribution function of entropy (normalised and scaled) observed individually for the various speakers in the corpora (left) and cumulative (right), with ticks at 90, 95 and 99% density.

ered (larger windows were discarded as themes can change frequently). Table 9 compares the location of peaks and that of lexical changes as annotated by the TextTiling algorithm. In both tables, precision and recall refer to commonly used metrics counting the number of exact prediction (True Positives) compared to the number of peaks that weren't located at theme breaks (False Positives) and theme breaks which did not result in entropy peaks (False Negatives).

LocalOutlier systematically yields a larger number of locations identified as peaks whereas NormOutlier is more sparse - which was expected by design of NormOutlier. Focusing LocalOutlier on outliers that increase entropy does not improve prediction. Both algorithms detect a smaller number of locations of interest when only taking into account evolution of the contextualised entropy ($H(S|C)$) over the dialogue rather than mutual information. TextTiling is not more accurate than peak detection to detect manually annotated theme change locations, but a larger number of peaks matched theme change predicted by TextTiling. However none of those methods perform better than a baseline classifier (stratified Dummy Classifier from the `scikit-learn` library) trained to predict boundaries of thematic episodes based on values for $H(S|C)$, MI and utterance length.

Increasing the window size reliably increases the number of theme breaks matched, substantiating the hypothesis that theme changes involves adding new information to the conversation, which is detectable using entropy metrics.

D In-depth per-word entropy analysis

D.1 Choice of words and peaks of entropy in a discussion

We select the sentences which have been labelled as peaks of entropy and analyse entropy word by word, how each word contributes to the sentence, and what category those words fall into. Examples of these words are given in Table 10. What we find is that most words with high entropy are simply rare enough that they are deemed improbable; most of them are either nouns (48%), adjectives (20%) or verbs. Some peaks however are caused by words falling into one of the following categories (disregarding words from the transcription that still contain typos): Proper Nouns (*Arthur, Jas, Danemark, Luminy...*), contractions or abreviations (*FLE, QCM*), technical words that might be taken from other languages (*slides, rift...*) which would be highly unusual for the model, but part of the shared knowledge for the two interlocutors.

The more an unexpected word is linked to a theme, the more we would expect it to reappear, and if it had caused a peak of entropy at first, we would expect that surprise being smoothed over time. Indeed, on a conversational level, the more a word occurs in conversation, it becomes part of the shared knowledge and is expected to be reused by any locutor. As a consequence, reused references are subject to compression throughout a dialogue (Giulianelli and Fernández, 2021) as they are expected to be understood without much cognitive load the more they appear. Context (previous words mentioned in the conversation) being available to our models they should equally be able to not be surprised by the reappearance. In our case, most words causing peaks are not reoccurring (68%), but those that do indeed become slightly more predictable (generating slightly less entropy, $p < 0.1$)

D.2 The role of backchannels

Backchannels are words or movements (nods, smiles) that a listener will spontaneously produce to signal the speaker of their attention, encourage them to continue with their story or on the contrary signal their lack of understanding or disagreement. Several kinds of feedbacks are annotated in Paco-Cheese, based on speech production, nods, smiles and context: generic (*hm, yes, ok, sure...*) and specific (context-dependant productions, whether positive or negative).

Considering that some feedback productions seemed to appear in the list of peaks, we analyzed in more details how well the models - which were initially designed for written language, devoid of backchannels - adjust to such phenomena after fine-tuning. A supposition was that feedbacks might appear as "disruptive" in the written flow of conversation, since productions are often partial or context-dependent.

We expected generic feedbacks to be well adapted to; specific feedbacks however would be contextual and generate slightly more entropy. Indeed, productions labelled as generic feedback are associated with per-sentence entropy values that are lower ($p < 0.01$) that those of productions that do not contain feedbacks. Specific feedbacks are associated with higher entropy values than generic feedbacks, but in the majority of cases (negative-unexpected feedbacks excepted) associated with lower entropy values than the productions not containing any feedback ($p < 0.05$) (see Table 11).

Table 8: Comparing TextTiling theme change locations and information content peaks to manually annotated theme changes. Baseline classifier (DumStrat) is added for consideration. TP indicates the number of elements, that either directly match a manual annotation or fall within a small window of that point.

			exact prediction			window=2			window=5		
			TP	precision	recall	TP	precision	recall	TP	precision	recall
input data	algorithm	nb elements									
text	TextTiling	565	28	0.050	0.104	28	0.060	0.108	80	0.136	0.299
MI	LocalOutlier	2137	71	0.033	0.265	118	0.066	0.440	193	0.154	0.720
	NormOutlier	70	3	0.043	0.011	3	0.086	0.011	8	0.129	0.030
H(S|C)	LocalOutlier	1602	59	0.037	0.220	101	0.072	0.377	173	0.172	0.646
	NormOutlier	138	6	0.043	0.022	9	0.101	0.034	23	0.174	0.086
	DumStrat	261	15	0.057	0.027	28	0.115	0.050	64	0.268	0.113

Table 9: Comparing information content peaks to the locations of TextTiling theme changes. TP indicates the number of elements, that either directly match a manual annotation or fall within a small window of that point.

			exact prediction			window=2			window=5		
input		number of	TP	precision	recall	TP	precision	recall	TP	precision	recall
data	algorithm	elements									
H(S|C)	LocalOutlier	1602	112	0.070	0.198	162	0.125	0.287	318	0.280	0.563
	NormOutlier	138	15	0.109	0.027	14	0.159	0.025	31	0.225	0.055
MI	LocalOutlier	2137	122	0.057	0.216	203	0.117	0.359	381	0.278	0.674
	NormOutlier	70	1	0.014	0.002	2	0.071	0.004	14	0.200	0.025

Table 10: Words with the highest entropy that appear in utterances labelled as peaks

'arthur', 'improbable', 'rift', 'interagir', 'mesuré', 'aram', 'anthropologie', 'jugé', 'jas', 'autes', 'deg', 'opposés', 'ent', 'moinl', 'laide', 'pas', 'identifie', 'quarantaine', 'danemark', 'audience', 'ets', 'saint', 'conte', 'sû', 'comparent', 'qcm', 'coup', 'implicite', 'anonyme', 'explicite', 'dis', 'calédonie', 'didons', 'tain', 'maléfique', 'géologie', 'dirigés', 'exemp', 'londres', 'craintes', 'médhia', 'incompréhension', 'montrer', 'décennie', 'ydis', 'dit', 'tien', 'règles', 'temps', 'cont', 'pt', 'dénonce', 'allée', 'devoirs', 'discours', 'là', 'fle', 'vêtement', 'cing', 'lie', 'occupé', 'anova', 'emmener', 'énorme', 'suppose', 'bianca', 'trois', 'humoristique', 'obliger', 'professeur', 'particuliers', 'sociale', 'oculus', 'totallement', 'alcooliques', 'la', 'bas', 'intro', 'teint', 'techniquement', 'régression', 'suisse', 'interêt', 'luminy', 'clés', 'quantité', 'perspective', 'morphologie', 'vive', 'istres', 'smaines', 'cognitive', 'contraignant', 'stricto sensu', 'afrique', 'occupe', 'pénal', 'voyage', 'apprécies', 'psychologue'

Table 11: Number of feedbacks of each category in the corpus and length compared to that of productions that don't contain feedbacks

Production type	# occurrences	average length	average entropy	comparison (t.test) of entropy: pvalue	
				less than 'no-feedback'	more than 'generic'
no-feedback		8.2	1.084 ± 0.51		<0.001
generic	799	2.0	0.651 ± 0.41	<0.001	
négative-expected	339	4.4	0.920 ± 0.54	<0.001	<0.001
négative-unexpected	303	4.2	1.055 ± 0.55	0.32	<0.001
positive-expected	110	4.7	1.010 ± 0.60	0.01	<0.001
positive-unexpected	75	3.7	0.983 ± 0.55	<0.001	<0.001

Leveraging a New Spanish Corpus for Multilingual and Crosslingual Metaphor Detection

Elisa Sanchez-Bayona and **Rodrigo Agerri**
HiTZ Center - Ixa, University of the Basque Country UPV/EHU
elisa.sanchez@ehu.eus, rodrigo.agerri@ehu.eus

Abstract

The lack of wide coverage datasets annotated with everyday metaphorical expressions for languages other than English is striking. This means that most research on supervised metaphor detection has been published only for that language. In order to address this issue, this work presents the first corpus annotated with naturally occurring metaphors in Spanish large enough to develop systems to perform metaphor detection. The presented dataset, CoMeta, includes texts from various domains, namely, news, political discourse, Wikipedia and reviews. In order to label CoMeta, we apply the MIPVU method, the guidelines most commonly used to systematically annotate metaphor on real data. We use our newly created dataset to provide competitive baselines by fine-tuning several multilingual and monolingual state-of-the-art large language models. Furthermore, by leveraging the existing VUAM English data in addition to CoMeta, we present the, to the best of our knowledge, first cross-lingual experiments on supervised metaphor detection. Finally, we perform a detailed error analysis that explores the seemingly high transfer of everyday metaphor across these two languages and datasets.

1 Introduction

Metaphor can broadly be defined as the interpretation of a concept belonging to one domain in terms of another concept from a different domain (Lakoff and Johnson, 1980). Metaphorical expressions are recurrent in natural language as a mechanism to convey abstract ideas through specific experiences related to the real, physical world or to send a stronger message in a discourse. There is a large body of work from various fields such as linguistics, psychology or philosophy that tried to provide a theoretical characterization of metaphor. Some approaches are based on the semantic similarity shared between the domains involved (Gentner, 1983; Kirby, 1997), while others explain metaphorical uses of language in terms of violation of *selectional preferences* (Wilks, 1975, 1978). Other perspectives focus on the communicative impact of using a metaphorical expression in contrast to its literal counterpart (Searle, 1979; Black, 1962). Following previous work on metaphor detection in Natural Language Processing (NLP) (Steen et al., 2010; Leong et al., 2018), our approach is based on the Conceptual Metaphor Theory of Lakoff and Johnson (1980). They do not conceive metaphors just as a cognitive-linguistic phenomenon commonly used in our everyday utterances. Instead, metaphors are understood as a conceptual mapping that typically reshapes an entire abstract domain of experience (target) in terms of a different concrete domain (source).

The high frequency of metaphors in everyday language has increased the popularity of research for this type of figurative language in the NLP field. One of the reasons behind is the fact that the automatic processing of metaphors is essential to achieve a successful interaction between humans and machines. In this sense, it is considered that other NLP tasks performance could benefit from metaphor processing, such as Machine Translation (Mao et al., 2018), Sentiment Analysis (Zhang, 2010; Rentoumi et al., 2009), Textual Entailment (Agerri, 2008; Liu et al., 2022) or Hate Speech Detection (van Aken et al., 2018; Lemmens et al., 2021), among others.

However, the large majority of research on metaphor detection has been done for English, for which the public release of the VUAM dataset within the FigLang shared tasks from 2018 and 2020 marked a major milestone (Leong et al., 2018, 2020). In this paper we would like to contribute to research in multilingual and cross-lingual metaphor detection by presenting a new wide coverage dataset in Spanish with annotations for everyday metaphorical expressions.

Proceedings of the 26th Conference on Computational Natural Language Learning (CoNLL), pages 228 - 240
December 7-8, 2022 ©2022 Association for Computational Linguistics

In this context, the contributions of this work are the following: (i) A new publicly available dataset for metaphor detection in Spanish from a variety of domains, CoMeta; (ii) an in-depth discussion of problematic cases and of adapting the MIPVU method to annotate metaphor in Spanish; (iii) a quantitative and qualitative analysis of the resulting CoMeta corpus; (iv) competitive baselines using 18 large monolingual and multilingual language models in monolingual and cross-lingual evaluation settings, showing that modern language models such as DeBERTa (He et al., 2021) perform similarly to models specifically trained for metaphor processing like MelBERT (Choi et al., 2021); (v) error analysis shows that, for these languages and datasets, cross-lingual metaphor transfer is very high, mostly due to the presence of metaphorical usage of commonly used verbs; (vi) the CoMeta dataset, code and fine-tuned models are publicly available [1] to encourage research in multilingual and cross-lingual metaphor detection and to facilitate reproducibility of results.

2 Previous Work

Metaphorical expressions can be conveyed through multiple linguistic structures and can be classified according to different criteria (Rai and Chakraverty, 2020). A common distinction is that of **conventional** metaphors (as in Example (1)), highly extended among speakers and lexicalized, and **novel** metaphors (Example (2)), which are less frequent in everyday utterances (examples taken from Rai and Chakraverty (2020)).

(1) *Sweet* love.

(2) Snow *debuts* on Twitter.

Lakoff and Johnson (1980) argue that metaphors express a mapping across a source and targe domain which constitute a **conceptual metaphor**. Conceptual metaphors can be expressed through language resulting in **linguistic metaphors**. These in turn can be classified as **lexical metaphors** (as in (1), (2) and (3)) **multi-word metaphors** (5), and **extended metaphors**, which cover longer fragments of speech. With respect to the grammatical category to which they belong, we can find **verbal** (2), **adjectival** (1), **nominal** (3) or **adverbial** metaphors (4).

(3) My lawyer is an old *shark*

(4) Ram speaks *fluidly*.

(5) If you use that strategy, he'll *wipe* you *out*. (Lakoff and Johnson, 1980)

Automatic processing of metaphor is generally divided into three different tasks: **detection** of metaphorical expressions, their **interpretation**, namely, the identification of the literal meaning expressed by the linguistic metaphor, and the **generation** of new metaphorical expressions. From here on, we will center our attention on metaphor detection.

Most work on metaphor detection has focused on English texts. The VU Amsterdam Metaphor Corpus (VUAMC or VUAM) (Steen et al., 2010) is the most extensive dataset with annotations for the characterization of linguistic metaphor. It consists of English texts labeled with several typologies of metaphor following the the VU Metaphor Identification Procedure (MIPVU), discussed in Section 3.2.1. It was subsequently adapted to other languages (Nacey et al., 2019). However, Spanish was not included and, for the languages that were, this adaptation did not include the development of annotated corpora.

First attempts to tackle metaphor detection in English were corpus-based (Charteris-Black, 2004; Skorczynska and Deignan, 2006; Semino, 2017). Most recent approaches address the task as sequence labeling usually based on deep learning, neural networks and word embeddings (Wu et al., 2018; Bizzoni and Ghanimifard, 2018). In addition, syntactic and semantic features (WordNet, FrameNet, VerbNet, dependency analysis, morphology, etc.) are exploited in order to boost the performance of such models. The celebration of the 2018 and 2020 shared tasks (Leong et al., 2018, 2020) around the detection of metaphors using the VUAM dataset contributed to a huge jump in development and performance, although top results were achieved by classifying mostly conventional metaphors (Tong et al., 2021; Neidlein et al., 2020).

Others combine metaphor theories as features in addition to annotated data to feed pre-trained models based on the Transformers architecture (Devlin et al., 2019). For instance, the state-of-the-art system MelBERT (Choi et al., 2021) uses the Metaphor Identification Procedure (MIP) (Pragglejaz, 2007) and *selectional preferences* (Wilks, 1975, 1978; Percy, 1958). These theories argue that terms with matching semantic features tend to appear in

[1] https://ixa-ehu.github.io/cometa/

the same context, and metaphors usually do not comply with this hypothesis. Furthermore, the recently published model of MIss RoBERTa WiLDe (Babieno et al., 2022) benefits from dictionary definitions as an additional feature to train their model based on the architecture of MelBERT.

Due to the lack of labeled data to train supervised models, previous work addressing Spanish metaphor processing has mainly been based on unsupervised approaches. However, as it is often the case for many other NLP tasks, unsupervised approaches obtain far lower results than supervised methods (Tsvetkov et al., 2014; Shutova et al., 2017). Other issues are that most work in Spanish has focused either on a very specific type of conceptual metaphor (Williams Camus et al., 2016), or on the characterization of metaphor in very domain-specific data (Martínez Santiago et al., 2014). The development of CoMeta aims to compensate this lack of resources for the Spanish language. To the best of our knowledge, it constitutes the largest dataset of general domain texts with metaphorical annotations in Spanish that, despite not reaching the size of the VUAMC corpus, can be used as a starting point, suitable to be extended and improved in the future, to further advance multilingual and cross-lingual methods for metaphor detection.

3 Dataset Development

In the following subsections we detail the creation process of our dataset CoMeta, including the data collection and annotation.

3.1 Data Collection

In order to compile a general domain dataset with natural language utterances and everyday language metaphors, we gathered samples from existing datasets of Spanish texts with linguistic annotations. As a result, CoMeta consists of 3633 sentences with metaphor annotations at token level from texts of multiple genres, such as blog, Wikipedia, news, fiction, reviews and political discourse, extracted from the following two sources.

Universal Dependencies (UD): We used the two largest Spanish treebanks annotated within the UD framework, which include linguistic information, such as Part Of Speech (POS), lemmas or dependencies: **AnCora**[2] and **GSD**[3]. UD Spanish AnCora is a UD formatted version of the original Ancora Corpus (Taulé et al., 2008). It contains 17680 sentences from the news domain, from which we randomly extracted 2000 sentences. The GSD treebank is an automatic compilation of texts from miscellaneous domains, such as Wikipedia, blogs and reviews. We selected also randomly a subset of 1000 sentences out of 16013. After preprocessing and filtering to remove duplicates, a total number of 2862 instances were finally included in CoMeta (1925 from Ancora, 937 from GSD and 771 from PD).

Political Discourse (PD): In addition to UD texts, we manually collected political discourse transcripts from the Spanish [4] and the Basque Government (Escribano et al., 2022), five from each source. We chose this domain due to the higher frequency of appearance of metaphorical expressions, which are often used in order to convey a more powerful message (Prabhakaran et al., 2021; Díaz-Peralta, 2018). From this source, we collected 771 sentences with automatic linguistic information added with UDPipe (Straka and Straková, 2016).

3.2 Annotation Process

The labelling of CoMeta was mostly carried out by a single annotator, a Spanish native speaker and expert linguist over 3 months as part-time job. All annotations were revised up to a total of 6 times. Initial rounds consisted in annotating all kind of metaphorical expressions. Subsequent four rounds were dedicated to identify metaphorical expressions of each POS. Last two rounds were employed to revise annotations and resolve borderline cases. In order to evaluate the consistency of the annotations and inter-annotator agreement, 6 more Spanish linguists were also involved in the annotation of a subsample of the corpus. This procedure will be further described in next Subsection 3.2.4. We decided to use binary labels following the approach of the VUAM versions used in the shared tasks recently mentioned.

3.2.1 Annotation Guidelines

The task of metaphor annotation is inherently subjective, since it is sometimes based on personal experience and cultural knowledge. The Metaphor Identification Procedure (MIP) (Pragglejaz, 2007) constituted an attempt to provide a systematic

[2]https://universaldependencies.org/treebanks/es_ancora/index.html

[3]https://universaldependencies.org/treebanks/es_gsd/index.html

[4]https://www.lamoncloa.gob.es/consejodeministros/ruedas/Paginas/index.aspx

guideline that facilitates the process. It was later extended to MIPVU (Steen et al., 2010), to cover ambiguous cases and address more thoroughly complex issues such as Multiword Expressions (MWE) or polysemy. The development of MIPVU resulted in the VUAM corpus (Steen et al., 2010). This procedure was subsequently adapted to other languages in (Nacey et al., 2019), although no wide coverage annotated corpus resulted from that adaptation. We followed the MIPVU guidelines to label CoMeta. In broad terms, it consists of the following steps:

1. Read the entire text–discourse to establish a general understanding of the meaning.
2. Determine the lexical units in the text–discourse.
3. (a) For each lexical unit in the text, establish its meaning in context, that is, how it applies to an entity, relation, or attribute in the situation evoked by the text (contextual meaning). Take into account what comes before and after the lexical unit.
   (b) For each lexical unit, determine if it has a more basic contemporary meaning in other contexts than the one in the given context. For our purposes, basic meanings tend to be:
      - More concrete; what they evoke is easier to imagine, see, hear, feel, smell, and taste.
      - Related to bodily action.
      - More precise (as opposed to vague).
      - Historically older. Basic meanings are not necessarily the most frequent meanings of the lexical unit.
   (c) If the lexical unit has a more basic current–contemporary meaning in other contexts than the given context, decide whether the contextual meaning contrasts with the basic meaning but can be understood in comparison with it.
4. If yes, mark the lexical unit as metaphorical.

3.2.2 Scope of Annotations

The definition of "word" provokes continuous and unsolved debates in the linguistics field. In MIPVU they use the more general term "lexical unit", understood as the basic piece that bears meaning, either a segment with its own POS or MWE. We followed this criterion as well in CoMeta. With regard to the POS, we decided to label only semantically significant classes: nouns, verbs, adjectives and adverbs, since most metaphors belong to one of these types. Details about the resulting dataset are reported in Table 1.

In this work, we focus on metaphorical expressions constrained to lexical units in the context of sentences. Thus, extended metaphors, where the figurative meanings are recurrent along larger pieces of texts, are not taken into account.

3.2.3 Borderline Features

Other Forms of Figurative Language: The boundaries between metaphor and other types of figurative language are not always clearly discernible. Specially in the case of metonymic expressions.

In this work, we do not annotate metonymy, since we regard them as two different and distinguishable cognitive phenomena. In the case of metonymy, a concept is substituted by another from the same domain through a relationship of contiguity, e.g. *beber una botella de ginebra (lit. "to drink a bottle of gin")*. In this example, the container is used to refer to the beverage but both terms belong to the domain of drink consumption. On the other hand, metaphorical expressions associate two different concepts from two distinct domains. With respect to similes, we treat them as a form of metaphor with a linguistic cue that makes the association of concepts explicit, e.g. "like". Thus, similes are annotated in the same way as metaphors, marking the lexical units with figurative meaning.
Polysemy: MIPVU's guidelines establish a comparison between the contextual meaning of a lexical unit and a more basic one in order to spot metaphors. However, some cases are ambiguous, due to polysemy, and can lead to confusion in the annotation process. For instance, in the example (7) from CoMeta, the adjective *claro* (lit. "clear") presents various basic meanings in Diccionario de la Real Academia Española (DRAE) (RAE): "Que tiene abundante luz" (lit. "Having abundant light") and "Dicho de un color o de un tono: Que tiende al blanco, o se le acerca más que otro de su misma clase." (lit. "Said about a colour or tone: with a tendency to white or closer to it than any other of the same class"). These basic meanings are straightforward and match this contextual sense.

(6) Los otros nombres de modelos tenían un sig-

	CoMeta		UD		PD	
	Met	**No_met**	**Met**	**No_met**	**Met**	**No_met**
VERB	873	9803	570	7560	303	2243
NOUN + PROPN	847 + 1	20118 + 8418	507+0	15790+7010	340+1	4328+1408
ADJ	396	6922	313	5413	83	1509
ADV	28	3836	15	2779	13	1057
Total	2145	49097	1405	38552	740	10545

Table 1: Number of metaphorical and non-metaphorical tokens by POS in overall CoMeta and in the separate domains from Universal Dependencies (UD) and Political Discourse (PD).

nificado *claro* (lit. "The names of other models had a clear meaning").

(7) La reina Sofía vestía un abrigo verde claro (lit. "Queen Sofía was wearing a light green coat").

However, in (6) it is harder to distinguish which is the contextual meaning according to the nuanced definitions provided in DRAE (RAE): "Inteligible, fácil de comprender" (lit. "Intelligible, easy to understand"), "Que se percibe o distingue bien" (lit. "Properly perceivable or distinguishable"), "Expresado sin reservas, francamente" (lit. "Expressed without reservations"). Regardless the ambiguity of the contextual meaning, all these senses are opposed to the basic sense and belong to different domains: *claro* in (6) alludes to LANGUAGE or COMMUNICATION, while the basic meaning is from the LIGHT or COLOR domain. Thus, we labeled the adjective as a metaphor in despite of not being able to determine exactly the contextual meaning.

Pronominal Verbs: Some verbs in Spanish present a pronominal form, which consists of a verb and a pronoun, either prepended and graphically separated from the verb form or as a clitic: *se arrepienten* (lit. "they repent") or as a clitic: *no pueden arrepentirse* (lit. "they cannot repent"). This pronoun can have multiple functions depending on its context of appearance, namely, reflexive, reciprocal... Thus, it is important for annotators to be able to discern each use case. In our dataset pronouns are not within the scope of annotations but verbs are. This kind of lexical units is represented in CoMeta by three different tokens: a) verb and clitic pronoun: verb+se, e.g. *olvidarse* (lit. "to forget"); b) the verb form, e.g. *olvidar* ; c) the pronoun. In order to capture verbal metaphors and its semantic information, we tagged options a) and b) in case of metaphorical expressions materialized through this structure. For instance, in example (8), the presence of the clitic implies a difference in meaning. The pronominal variant of *enganchar* (lit. "to hook") in this context is used metaphorically, where the football player returns back to the league, so we tagged tokens *engancharse* and *enganchar*.

(8) Garrido tendrá hoy un partido especial, sobre todo por si puede *engancharse* a la Europa League (lit. "Garrido will have a special match today, mainly if he is able to rejoin the European League").

Multiword Expressions: Multiword expressions, generally speaking, can be understood as the result of two or more words that co-occur with high frequency and act as a single lexical unit. MIPVU (Steen et al., 2010) prompts to annotate the contextual meaning of a MWE as a whole. However, in the actual annotation process, doubts arise as to whether some expressions can be considered a MWE or not.

MIPVU used a list from the British National Corpus with MWEs as aid for their identification. In Spanish, there is no such resource, so we utilised the DRAE (RAE). If an expression is registered in the dictionary with an individual entry, we treated it as a single lexical unit.

MWEs included in dictionaries are often idiomatic, with non-compositional nor transparent meaning. Since the overall meaning of an idiomatic expression rarely has anything to do with the sum of its constituents, they behave as a black box. In practice, *corriente* in example (9) is part of the idiom collected in DRAE *estar al corriente*, which means "to be aware or know about something". Therefore it is not considered a lexical unit but a piece of a larger MWE which, in this case, is not metaphorical. On the contrary, *corriente* (lit. "current") in (10) can be treated as a single lexical unit with a contextual meaning of "trend" or a group of people that share similar principles that opposes to its most basic sense that alludes to the movement of some fluids, *corriente de aire* (lit. "airflow"), it is annotated as a metaphor.

(9) Estaba al corriente de sus secretos. (lit. "They were aware of their secrets").

(10) Una *corriente* cristiana que se originó en el siglo I. (lit. "A christian current that was originated in the I century").

3.2.4 Annotation Evaluation

To analyse quantitatively the consistency of CoMeta annotations, we randomly selected the 10% of sentences to be labeled by other annotators over the whole corpus. In other words, these sentences could belong either to train or test partitions. From this subset, 80% of the sentences contained at least one metaphorical expression labeled as such by the main annotator of CoMeta. The purpose is to examine the consensus in the metaphorical annotations.

A total of 6 annotators participated in the evaluation and all of them were also Spanish native speakers with linguistic background knowledge. Each one reviewed 60 sentences randomly distributed and non-overlapping. As an aid for the task, we presented them the MIPVU guidelines and illustrative examples in advance. For each sentence, we extracted randomly 4 lexical units. We added a check-box next to each of these potential metaphorical expressions. Annotators must check those they deemed were holding metaphorical meaning in the context of that sentence. We included two additional options: one check-box to be marked in case there were no metaphorical expressions; and another one for annotators to write spotted metaphors that were not among the 4 candidates presented. We computed inter-annotator agreement by means of Cohen's Kappa and obtained an average score of 0.631, which gives an account of the hardship and subjectivity of the task but also indicates a substantial consistency in the annotations.

3.3 Data Analysis

The most frequent metaphors arise from verbs, followed by nouns, adjectives and adverbs. Nevertheless, in political discourse texts, noun metaphors are more numerous than verbs, as shown in Table 1. Verbal metaphors usually involve verbs denoting motion or change of state, e.g. *abrir/cerrar* (lit. "to open/close"), *salir/entrar* (lit. "to go in/out"), *ascender/descender* (lit. "to ascend/descend"), *frenar/acelerar* (lit. "to accelerate/brake"), *partir/llegar* (lit. "to leave/arrive"), and many others. Personifications are frequent as well (11), through verbs that denote actions typically executed by an animate agent attributed to an inanimate entity (examples from CoMeta).

(11) Les *atrapó* la miseria humana. (lit. "Human misery caught them").

Adjectival metaphors arise in many cases through synesthesia and adjectives denoting physical dimensions applied to abstract or uncountable concepts (12, 13).

(12) *Tozudo* oleaje. (lit. "Stubborn waves").

(13) Foto *rancia*. (lit. "Rancid photograph").

Regarding the domains of the conceptual mappings, we have observed several instances of metaphorical expressions that depict politics in terms of the construction field (14, 15), and a virus or a disease as war (16, 17).

(14) Es imposible *construir* un proyecto de Estado. (lit. "It is impossible to build a State project").

(15) La candidatura de Osaka es muy *sólida* (lit. "Osaka's candidacy is very solid").

(16) Unidos conseguiremos de nuevo *vencer* al virus (lit. "Together we will defeat the virus again").

(17) El único *arma* terapéutica que tenemos en este momento para *luchar* contra el coronavirus (lit. "The only therapeutic weapon available at this time to fight against coronavirus").

4 Evaluation

In this section we present the experiments on metaphor detection in Spanish and English. Furthermore, we also report the results of the first supervised cross-lingual experiments for metaphor detection. The main objective of the cross-lingual evaluation setting was to examine which kind of metaphors carried more often across languages.

	VUAM			CoMeta	
	Train	Dev	Test	Train	Test
Metaphor	8668	2372	3982	1713	432
No_Metaphor	135896	34297	54347	91628	23342
Total	144564	36669	58329	93341	23774

Table 2: Number of metaphorical and non-metaphorical tokens in VUA and CoMeta datasets.

Dataset	Model	Prec	Rec	F1
CoMeta	ixabertes_v1	71.99	59.49	65.15
	mdeberta-v3-base	**78.70**	59.03	**67.46**
	xlm-roberta-large	75.57	**60.88**	67.44
VUAM	deberta-large	**79.95**	68.50	**73.79**
	deberta-base	73.06	**73.07**	73.07
	xlm-roberta-large	77.99	68.00	72.65
VUAM SOTA	MelBERT	76.4	68.6	72.3

Table 3: Monolingual results for Spanish and English.

4.1 Datasets

The two datasets used for experimentation are the VUAM dataset (Steen et al., 2010) in English, and CoMeta in Spanish. With respect to the VUAM dataset (Steen et al., 2010), we employed the original train and test splits provided in the shared task (Leong et al., 2020). We also extracted a development set by splitting the training set (0.8-0.2). Using the original train and test partitions will allow us to compare with previous results. In the case of CoMeta, and due to its smaller size, we did not create a development split. Table 2 provides the stats for each corpus. It should be noted that both datasets are imbalanced. In the case of CoMeta we decided not to alter this distribution since it represents the frequency of metaphor in natural language texts.

4.2 Experimental Setup

We perform experiments in two evaluation settings: monolingual and cross-lingual. For the monolingual setting, we evaluate on the English and Spanish datasets using the most commonly used large language models for each of the languages. In the cross-lingual setting we evaluate the best performing multilingual language model for each language in a zero-shot scenario, namely, fine-tuning in a source language and making the predictions in another language, not seen during fine-tuning.

Monolingual Experiments: The experiments performed in this setting aimed to establish a baseline with respect to the state-of-the-art in metaphor detection for English using the VUAM corpus, currently represented by MelBERT (Choi et al., 2021). This baseline will also help us to judge the performance on the CoMeta dataset. We picked the 9 most commonly used large language models for each language, both in their *base* and *large* versions (DeBERTa also includes mDeBERTa, a multilingual base model pre-trained for 100 languages). For English we experimented with BERT (Devlin et al., 2019), RoBERTa (Liu et al., 2019), DeBERTa (He et al., 2021) and XLM-RoBERTa (Conneau et al., 2020).

With respect to Spanish, we used BETO (Cañete et al., 2020), ixabertes_v1 and ixabertes_v2[5], ixambert (Otegi et al., 2020), RoBERTa-BNE models (Gutiérrez-Fandiño et al., 2022) and the multilingual models mDeBERTa and XLM-RoBERTa (base and large). Every model was fine-tuned via the Huggingface Transformers library (Wolf et al., 2020).

We performed hyperparameter tuning for batch size (8, 16, 36), linear decay (0.1, 0.01), learning rate (in the [1e-5-5e-5] interval) and epochs from 4 to 10. We keep a fixed seed of 42 for experimental reproducibility and a sequence length of 128. A warm-up of 6% is specified. The results of the hyperparameter tuning showed that after 4 epochs development loss started to increase, so every result reported here is obtained by performing 4 epochs only. Furthermore, the results of the best models are chosen according to their performance on the

[5]Avalaible in `http://www.deeptext.eus/es/node/2`

Train Dataset	Test Dataset	Model	Prec	Rec	F1
CoMeta	VUAM	mdeberta-v3-base	76.28	58.8	66.41
VUAM	CoMeta	xlm-roberta-large	73.95	70.36	72.11

Table 4: Results from cross-lingual experiments after 4 epochs.

development for each language. Finally, due to presentation reasons, we decided to include only the best three models: the best *base* and *large* models for each language, the best Spanish monolingual and the best multilingual for English. These are the results included in Table 3. Results of all models are gathered in Appendix A, Table 6.

Cross-lingual Experiments: The aim of this experiments is to explore: a) whether a model trained with metaphorical annotations from one language can achieve good results when evaluating metaphors in another language and, b) to what extent metaphors are shared between these languages. Thus, in this setting we picked the best performing multilingual model for each of the two monolingual evaluations and apply them in a zero-shot cross-lingual manner, namely, by fine-tuning the language model on the English dataset and evaluating it with the Spanish one, and viceversa, using the best hyperparameter configuration obtained in the monolingual setting.

4.3 Results

The first interesting result of our experiments is that the general purpose DeBERTa-large language model performs slightly better than the metaphor-specific MelBERT, with the base version not far behind. With respect to Spanish, the results are not as high in general as those obtained for English. In particular, the performance of XLM-RoBERTa-large for Spanish is substantially lower than for English. Apart from many other factors that may be involved, we attribute these lower results to the smaller size of the Spanish training set. It is also interesting to note that a base multilingual model, mDeBERTa, is the best performing model for Spanish, obtaining very similar results to XLM-RoBERTa-large. Still, the low results of the state-of-the-art models show that this remains a highly difficult task.

For the cross-lingual results, we picked the best multilingual model for each of the monolingual settings, mDeBERTa for Spanish and XLM-RoBERTa-large for English. The results reported in Table 4 show that the zero-shot performance is remarkably high, which is quite surprising, especially if we consider the performance of XLM-RoBERTa-large for Spanish. In fact, these results show that XLM-RoBERTa obtains better results for Spanish when fine-tuned in English. Next section will provide some analysis to attempt to explain this phenomenon. In any case, the results obtained for Spanish are promising and encourage us to continue improving the annotated resources for this language.

4.4 Error Analysis

In Table 5 we enumerated the most frequent predictions which are potentially interesting for error analysis. These predictions correspond to the model with best performance, DeBERTa-large in the case of VUAM and mDeBERTa for CoMeta. False positives (FP) represent lexical units that were labeled wrongly as metaphorical. False negatives (FN) include metaphorical expressions that were not detected as such by the model, whereas true positives (TP) gather which metaphorical expressions were accurately identified.

The FP and FN from the monolingual setup of VUAM show mostly verbs that tend to form collocations, like *go* or *get*, or highly lexicalised terms, such as *little, away, subject* or *back.* The high occurrence of these lexical units both with metaphorical and literal meaning and the high degree of polysemy difficult the possibility to learn patterns. In the case of CoMeta, FP and FN comprise terms that scarcely appear in our dataset with metaphorical meaning or in similar proportions with metaphorical and literal tags.

With respect to TP, in VUAM predictions, we can find again terms that occur in the dataset very frequently conforming collocations and phrasal verbs, which are commonly tagged as metaphors. Right predictions in CoMeta present lexical units that only appear with metaphorical meaning, such as *ola* (lit. "wave") in relation to the virus domain, which does not occur in CoMeta with a literal sense.

Results from cross-lingual experiments show an outcome which resembles that of the monolingual

		Monolingual	Cross-lingual			Monolingual	Cross-lingual
VUAMC	FP	get 33	get 21	CoMeta	FP	crecimiento 3	contempla 4
		got 22	got 20			paso 3	crecimiento 3
		little 16	go 14			espacio 3	espacio 3
		go 16	bloody 12			repaso 2	repaso 2
	FN	got 13	back 14		FN	estabilidad 6	estabilidad 6
		away 12	got 12			gran 4	ocupa 4
		back 12	plant 12			ocupa 4	dimensión 4
		subject 10	get 11			dimensión 4	seguimiento 3
	TP	make 50	make 48		TP	marco 8	marco 8
		take 33	take 34			ola 6	ola 6
		way 32	way 33			abrir 4	abrir 4
		got 26	got 27			escenario 4	escenario 4

Table 5: Top-4 terms of false positive (FP), true positive (TP) and false negative (FN) predictions from experiments performed with VUAM and CoMeta in monolingual and cross-lingual scenarios.

setup. This similarity between both setups was noticeable from the scores of the evaluation metrics in Tables 3 and 4. This suggests that, due to its current size, training on CoMeta obtains worse results than training in English. We hypothesize that, in addition to the size, the high frequency of commonly used verbal lexical units that are labelled as metaphors in both datasets help to obtain such good results in the cross-lingual setting.

5 Conclusions and Future Work

In this work we have created CoMeta, which to the best of our knowledge is the largest dataset with metaphor annotations in Spanish composed of texts from various domains to be publicly available. We also discussed in detail the main issues that emerged during the annotation process for Spanish. In order to evaluate the quality of CoMeta's annotations we carried out a series of experiments in both monolingual and cross-lingual environments, using the largest dataset with metaphor annotations in English, the VUAM corpus, as reference point.. Moreover, we set a new state of the art on the task of metaphor detection in English and set a strong baseline for the task in Spanish, which hopefully will encourage researchers to continue with this line of work.

The aim of this work is to lay the foundations for future development on metaphor detection in Spanish and cross-lingually. Regarding the dataset, a future line of work would introduce more fine-grained tags that represent the different kinds of metaphorical expressions. This task should be performed by multiple annotators, in order to explore agreement over the whole dataset, as well as to observe if doubtful cases share any feature that could be leveraged for their identification. The presence of more fine-grained tags would also enable a deeper statistical analysis of CoMeta that could be exploited to study how metaphor manifests in Spanish and whether there are similarities with the usage of metaphor in other languages.

Results obtained from our experiments encourage future research to continue with cross-lingual approaches. We hypothesize that these results may be due to the difference in size of the training data in both languages or the application of MIPVU guidelines to Spanish, which is not the language it was originally designed for. Future experimental work is needed to test these interpretations, which could benefit from the extension of the annotations in CoMeta we just mentioned.

Acknowledgements

This work has been supported by the HiTZ center and the Basque Government (Research group funding IT-1805-22). Elisa Sanchez-Bayona is funded by a UPV/EHU grant "Formación de Personal Investigador". Rodrigo Agerri acknowledges the support from the RYC-2017–23647 fellowship (MCIN/AEI /10.13039/501100011033 y por El FSE invierte en tu futuro), and from the projects DeepKnowledge (PID2021-127777OB-C21) by MCIN/AEI/10.13039/501100011033 and FEDER Una manera de hacer Europa, and Disargue (TED2021-130810B-C21) by MCIN/AEI /10.13039/501100011033 and European Union NextGenerationEU/PRTR .

Limitations

The presented dataset is limited in size compared to its English counterpart, the VUAM corpus. Therefore, a second version of CoMeta augmented with more texts of domains where metaphors are more abundant should be a priority of future work. This would be important both for monolingual and cross-lingual results, especially to analyze the cross-lingual transfer behaviour of the multilingual models. Furthermore, the process of metaphor labelling is inherently subjective and annotator-dependent, since personal experience and socio-cultural features may influence the identification of metaphors, as well as the domain of collected texts. Thus, the incorporation of a variety of annotators would alleviate this issue. In any case, we believe that CoMeta represents a worthy first contribution towards multilingual and cross-lingual metaphor detection and that the results obtained in this paper can be improved by further developing CoMeta to be a dataset of size similar to VUAM. Finally, even if we reported state-of-the-art results, the overall low performance means that further work on this task is required.

References

Rodrigo Agerri. 2008. Metaphor in Textual Entailment. In *COLING*, pages 3–6.

Mateusz Babieno, Masashi Takeshita, Dusan Radisavljevic, Rafal Rzepka, and Kenji Araki. 2022. MIss RoBERTa WiLDe: Metaphor Identification Using Masked Language Model with Wiktionary Lexical Definitions. *Applied Sciences*, 12(4).

Yuri Bizzoni and Mehdi Ghanimifard. 2018. Bigrams and BiLSTMs Two neural networks for sequential metaphor detection. In *Proceedings of the Workshop on Figurative Language Processing*, pages 91–101.

M. Black. 1962. *Models and Metaphors: Studies in Language and Philosophy*. Studies in language and philosophy. Cornell University Press.

José Cañete, Gabriel Chaperon, Rodrigo Fuentes, Jou-Hui Ho, Hojin Kang, and Jorge Pérez. 2020. Spanish pre-trained bert model and evaluation data. In *PML4DC at ICLR 2020*.

Jonathan Charteris-Black. 2004. *Corpus Approaches to Critical Metaphor Analysis*. Springer.

Minjin Choi, Sunkyung Lee, Eunseong Choi, Heesoo Park, Junhyuk Lee, Dongwon Lee, and Jongwuk Lee. 2021. MelBERT: Metaphor Detection via Contextualized Late Interaction using Metaphorical Identification Theories. In *Proceedings of the 2021 Conference of the North American Chapter of the Association for Computational Linguistics: Human Language Technologies, NAACL-HLT*, pages 1763–1773. Association for Computational Linguistics.

Alexis Conneau, Kartikay Khandelwal, Naman Goyal, Vishrav Chaudhary, Guillaume Wenzek, Francisco Guzmán, Edouard Grave, Myle Ott, Luke Zettlemoyer, and Veselin Stoyanov. 2020. Unsupervised Cross-lingual Representation Learning at Scale.

Jacob Devlin, Ming-Wei Chang, Kenton Lee, and Kristina Toutanova. 2019. BERT: Pre-training of deep bidirectional transformers for language understanding. In *Proceedings of the 2019 Conference of the North American Chapter of the Association for Computational Linguistics: Human Language Technologies, Volume 1 (Long and Short Papers)*, pages 4171–4186, Minneapolis, Minnesota. Association for Computational Linguistics.

Marina Díaz-Peralta. 2018. Metaphor and ideology: Conceptual structure and conceptual content in spanish political discourse. *Discourse & Communication*, 12(2):128–148.

Nayla Escribano, Jon Ander Gonzalez, Julen Orbegozo-Terradillos, Ainara Larrondo-Ureta, Simón Peña-Fernández, Olatz Perez-de Viñaspre, and Rodrigo Agerri. 2022. Basqueparl: A bilingual corpus of basque parliamentary transcriptions. In *Proceedings of the Language Resources and Evaluation Conference*, pages 3382–3390, Marseille, France. European Language Resources Association.

Dedre Gentner. 1983. Structure-Mapping: A Theoretical Framework for Analogy. *Cognitive science*, 7(2):155–170.

Asier Gutiérrez-Fandiño, Jordi Armengol-Estapé, Marc Pàmies, Joan Llop-Palao, Joaquin Silveira-Ocampo, Casimiro Pio Carrino, Carme Armentano-Oller, Carlos Rodriguez-Penagos, Aitor Gonzalez-Agirre, and Marta Villegas. 2022. Maria: Spanish language models. *Procesamiento del Lenguaje Natural*, 68(0):39–60.

Pengcheng He, Jianfeng Gao, and Weizhu Chen. 2021. Debertav3: Improving deberta using electra-style pretraining with gradient-disentangled embedding sharing. *ArXiv*, abs/2111.09543.

John T Kirby. 1997. Aristotle on Metaphor. *American Journal of Philology*, 118(4):517–554.

George Lakoff and Mark Johnson. 1980. Metaphors We Live By.

Jens Lemmens, Ilia Markov, and Walter Daelemans. 2021. Improving hate speech type and target detection with hateful metaphor features. In *Proceedings of the Fourth Workshop on NLP for Internet Freedom: Censorship, Disinformation, and Propaganda*, pages 7–16, Online. Association for Computational Linguistics.

Chee Wee (Ben) Leong, Beata Beigman Klebanov, Chris Hamill, Egon Stemle, Rutuja Ubale, and Xianyang Chen. 2020. A report on the 2020 VUA and TOEFL metaphor detection shared task. In *Proceedings of the Second Workshop on Figurative Language Processing*, pages 18–29, Online. Association for Computational Linguistics.

Chee Wee (Ben) Leong, Beata Beigman Klebanov, and Ekaterina Shutova. 2018. A Report on the 2018 VUA Metaphor Detection Shared Task. In *Proceedings of the Workshop on Figurative Language Processing*, pages 56–66, New Orleans, Louisiana. Association for Computational Linguistics.

Emmy Liu, Chen Cui, Kenneth Zheng, and Graham Neubig. 2022. Testing the Ability of Language Models to Interpret Figurative Language. arXiv.

Yinhan Liu, Myle Ott, Naman Goyal, Jingfei Du, Mandar Joshi, Danqi Chen, Omer Levy, Mike Lewis, Luke Zettlemoyer, and Veselin Stoyanov. 2019. RoBERTa: A Robustly Optimized BERT Pretraining Approach.

Rui Mao, Chenghua Lin, and Frank Guerin. 2018. Word embedding and WordNet based metaphor identification and interpretation. In *Proceedings of the 56th Annual Meeting of the Association for Computational Linguistics (Volume 1: Long Papers)*, pages 1222–1231, Melbourne, Australia. Association for Computational Linguistics.

Fernando Martínez Santiago, Miguel Angel García Cumbreras, Manuel Carlos Díaz Galiano, and Arturo Montejo Ráez. 2014. Etiquetado de metáforas lingüísticas en un conjunto de documentos en español.

Susan Nacey, Aletta G Dorst, Tina Krennmayr, and W Gudrun Reijnierse. 2019. *Metaphor Identification in Multiple Languages: MIPVU around the world* , volume 22. John Benjamins Publishing Company.

Arthur Neidlein, Philip Wiesenbach, and Katja Markert. 2020. An analysis of language models for metaphor recognition. In *Proceedings of the 28th International Conference on Computational Linguistics*, pages 3722–3736, Barcelona, Spain (Online). International Committee on Computational Linguistics.

Arantxa Otegi, Aitor Agirre, Jon Ander Campos, Aitor Soroa, and Eneko Agirre. 2020. Conversational question answering in low resource scenarios: A dataset and case study for basque. In *Proceedings of The 12th Language Resources and Evaluation Conference*, pages 436–442.

Walker Percy. 1958. Metaphor as Mistake. *The Sewanee Review*, 66(1):79–99.

Vinodkumar Prabhakaran, Marek Rei, and Ekaterina Shutova. 2021. How metaphors impact political discourse: A large-scale topic-agnostic study using neural metaphor detection. arXiv.

Group Pragglejaz. 2007. MIP: A method for identifying metaphorically used words in discourse. *Metaphor and symbol*, 22(1):1–39.

Real Academia Española RAE. *Diccionario de la lengua española, 23.ª ed., [versión 23.4 en línea].*

Sunny Rai and Shampa Chakraverty. 2020. A Survey on Computational Metaphor Processing. *ACM Comput. Surv.*, 53(2).

Vassiliki Rentoumi, George Giannakopoulos, Vangelis Karkaletsis, and George A. Vouros. 2009. Sentiment analysis of figurative language using a word sense disambiguation approach. In *Proceedings of the International Conference RANLP-2009*, pages 370–375, Borovets, Bulgaria. Association for Computational Linguistics.

John R Searle. 1979. *Expression and meaning: Studies in the theory of speech acts*. Cambridge University Press.

Elena Semino. 2017. Corpus linguistics and metaphor. *The Cambridge Handbook of Cognitive Linguistics*, pages 463–476.

Ekaterina Shutova, Lin Sun, Elkin Darío Gutiérrez, Patricia Lichtenstein, and Srini Narayanan. 2017. Multilingual metaphor processing: Experiments with semi-supervised and unsupervised learning. *Computational Linguistics*, 43(1):71–123.

Hanna Skorczynska and Alice Deignan. 2006. Readership and Purpose in the Choice of Economics Metaphors. *Metaphor and Symbol*, 21(2):87–104.

G.J. Steen, A.G. Dorst, J.B. Herrmann, A.A. Kaal, T. Krennmayr, and T. Pasma. 2010. *A method for linguistic metaphor identification. From MIP to MIPVU.*

Milan Straka and Jana Straková. 2016. UDPipe. LINDAT/CLARIAH-CZ digital library at the Institute of Formal and Applied Linguistics (ÚFAL), Faculty of Mathematics and Physics, Charles University.

Mariona Taulé, M. Antònia Martí, and Marta Recasens. 2008. AnCora: Multilevel annotated corpora for Catalan and Spanish. In *Proceedings of the Sixth International Conference on Language Resources and Evaluation (LREC'08)*, Marrakech, Morocco. European Language Resources Association (ELRA).

Xiaoyu Tong, Ekaterina Shutova, and Martha Lewis. 2021. Recent advances in neural metaphor processing: A linguistic, cognitive and social perspective. In *Proceedings of the 2021 Conference of the North American Chapter of the Association for Computational Linguistics: Human Language Technologies*, pages 4673–4686, Online. Association for Computational Linguistics.

Yulia Tsvetkov, Leonid Boytsov, Anatole Gershman, Eric Nyberg, and Chris Dyer. 2014. Metaphor Detection with Cross-Lingual Model Transfer. In *Proceedings of the 52nd Annual Meeting of the Association for Computational Linguistics (Volume 1: Long Papers)*, pages 248–258.

Betty van Aken, Julian Risch, Ralf Krestel, and Alexander Löser. 2018. Challenges for Toxic Comment Classification: An In-Depth Error Analysis. In *Proceedings of the 2nd Workshop on Abusive Language Online (ALW2)*, pages 33–42, Brussels, Belgium. Association for Computational Linguistics.

Yorick Wilks. 1975. A preferential, pattern-seeking, Semantics for natural language inference. *Artificial Intelligence*, 6(1):53–74.

Yorick Wilks. 1978. Making preferences more active. *Artificial Intelligence*, 11(3):197–223.

Julia Teresa Williams Camus et al. 2016. "get the metaphor right! Cancer treatment metaphors in the English and Spanish press". Universidad de Córdoba.

Thomas Wolf, Lysandre Debut, Victor Sanh, Julien Chaumond, Clement Delangue, Anthony Moi, Pierric Cistac, Tim Rault, Remi Louf, Morgan Funtowicz, Joe Davison, Sam Shleifer, Patrick von Platen, Clara Ma, Yacine Jernite, Julien Plu, Canwen Xu, Teven Le Scao, Sylvain Gugger, Mariama Drame, Quentin Lhoest, and Alexander Rush. 2020. Transformers: State-of-the-art natural language processing. In *Proceedings of the 2020 Conference on Empirical Methods in Natural Language Processing: System Demonstrations*, pages 38–45, Online. Association for Computational Linguistics.

Chuhan Wu, Fangzhao Wu, Yubo Chen, Sixing Wu, Zhigang Yuan, and Yongfeng Huang. 2018. Neural Metaphor Detecting with CNN-LSTM Model. In *Proceedings of the Workshop on Figurative Language Processing, New Orleans, LA*.

Li Zhang. 2010. Metaphor interpretation and context-based affect detection. In *COLING*.

A Appendix

In Table 6 we gather the performance of all models used in monolingual experiments over the test set. For each model, we only included the version that achieved the highest F1 score with the specified parameters after 4 epochs. Bold results correspond to the model that obtained top performance, while underscored results correspond to the second best score.

Dataset	Model	Batch Size	Weight Decay	Learning Rate	F1
CoMeta	*Monolingual*				
	bertin	8	0.01	0.00003	61.56
	beto	8	0.01	0.00005	64.28
	electricidad	8	0.1	0.00005	61.18
	ixabertes_v1	8	0.01	0.00005	65.15
	ixabertes_v2	8	0.01	0.00005	64.79
	ixambert	8	0.1	0.00005	62.04
	roberta-large-bne	16	0.1	0.00001	62.02
	roberta-base-bne	8	0.1	0.00005	63.07
	Multilingual				
	mbert	8	0.01	0.00005	61.78
	mdeberta-v3-base	8	0.01	0.00005	**67.46**
	xlm-roberta-base	8	0.1	0.00005	63.82
	xlm-roberta-large	8	0.01	0.00002	67.44
VUAM	*Monolingual*				
	bert-base	16	0.01	0.00005	69.99
	bert-large	32	0.01	0.00005	71.67
	deberta-base	32	0.1	0.00005	73.07
	deberta-large	8	0.01	0.00002	**73.79**
	roberta-base	8	0.01	0.00005	70.11
	roberta-large	32	0.1	0.00005	72.69
	Multilingual				
	mdeberta-v3-base	16	0.01	0.00005	70.40
	xlm-roberta-base	8	0.1	0.00002	66.59
	xlm-roberta-large	32	0.1	0.00003	72.11

Table 6: Results from monolingual experiments with all models, trained over 4 epochs, for English and Spanish.

Cognitive Simplification Operations Improve Text Simplification

Eytan Chamovitz
Department of Computer Science
Tel Aviv University
eytanc@gmail.com

Omri Abend
Department of Computer Science
Hebrew University of Jerusalem
omri.abend@mail.huji.ac.il

Abstract

Text Simplification (TS) is the task of converting a text into a form that is easier to read while maintaining the meaning of the original text. A sub-task of TS is Cognitive Simplification (CS), converting text to a form that is readily understood by people with cognitive disabilities without rendering it childish or simplistic. This sub-task has yet to be explored with neural methods in NLP, and resources for it are scarcely available. In this paper, we present a method for incorporating knowledge from the cognitive accessibility domain into a TS model, by introducing an inductive bias regarding what simplification operations to use. We show that by adding this inductive bias to a TS-trained model, it is able to adapt better to CS without ever seeing CS data, and outperform a baseline model on a traditional TS benchmark. In addition, we provide a novel test dataset for CS, and analyze the differences between CS corpora and existing TS corpora, in terms of how simplification operations are applied.

1 Introduction

Text Simplification (TS) is the task of converting text into a form that is easier to understand by modifying its syntax and/or the words used in it, while maintaining the original text's meaning (Alva-Manchego et al., 2020b).

TS is a very diverse task that can include simplifications aimed at different target audiences. TS is often operationalized in NLP using a number of particular corpora to train and evaluate neural models (see §3), whose target audiences are mostly second language learners, primary school students or adults with learning disabilities. For brevity, this paper will refer by TS to this concrete formulation of the simplification task, rather than the abstract, general notion of the task of simplifying text.

Cognitive Simplification (CS) is the task of converting text to a form that is clear, simple, and readily understood by people with cognitive disabilities (Yalon-Chamovitz, 2009; Yalon-Chamovitz et al., 2016; Yalon-Chamovitz and Avidan-Ziv, 2016).[1] The procedure includes structural and lexical modifications that reduce the text's complexity, while preserving *as much* of the meaning and information content as possible, and without rendering it childish or simplistic. See Figure 1.

The following example illustrates the differences and similarities between CS and TS. The sentence "*Some indigenous groups living in palm-rich areas use palms to make many of their necessary items and food.*" from the ASSET (Alva-Manchego et al., 2020a) validation set was simplified by one of the annotators as "*Groups who live in palm-rich areas use palms to make basic items and food.*". A CS, in this case, could be "*People who live in areas with a lot of palm trees use the trees for many things. People can eat the dates that grow on palm trees. People can make many things from palm trees, for example, baskets and plates.*".[2] This is an example of the common need in CS to explicitly state assumed prior knowledge, and the need to make the text "closer" to the reader ("people" vs. "groups"). See §5.1.

CS and TS appear to be similar tasks, as similar modifications can be applied in both. CS could even be considered a sub-task of TS, with a target audience of people with cognitive disabilities. However, there are two main differences between the two, that we believe motivate further investigation into CS as an independent task. First, CS is a well-defined procedure with manuals in multiple languages (PLAIN, 2011a; Uziel-Karl et al., 2011), while TS has general guidelines and, to the best of our knowledge, no common standards. Second, the goal of CS is to simplify texts to provide *cognitive accessibility* (Yalon-Chamovitz et al., 2016).

[1] People with developmental disabilities, head trauma patients, people with dementia or Alzheimer's Disease, etc. Not including people with learning disabilities such as dyslexia.

[2] Simplified by the authors with guidance from a professional cognitive simplifier.

Proceedings of the 26th Conference on Computational Natural Language Learning (CoNLL), pages 241 - 265
December 7-8, 2022

Original Source:	**Now, normally** during Disability Pride Month, we're **showcasing our disability pride** through *various* parades and events **throughout the country**.
Original Target:	**Most years**, during Disability Pride Month we have parades and events **all over the United States** to **show how proud we are**.
Operations:	<REPHRASE> <DEL> <REORDER>
Modified Source T5:	<mask_1> Now, normally during Disability Pride Month, we're showcasing our disability pride through various parades and events throughout the country.
Modified Target T5:	<mask_1> <REPHRASE> <DEL> <REORDER> <mask_2> Most years, during Disability Pride Month we have parades and events all over the United States to show how proud we are.
Modified Source BART:	<mask> Now, normally during Disability Pride Month, we're showcasing our disability pride through various parades and events throughout the country.
Modified Target BART:	<REPHRASE> <DEL> <REORDER> Most years, during Disability Pride Month we have parades and events all over the United States to show how proud we are.

Figure 1: Illustration of our approach on an example sentence from the CS dataset FestAbility Transcripts. The modified sources and targets for each model architecture include special operation tokens (see §5.2) added in the method appropriate for the model. For demonstration purposes in the original source and target, we **boldface** and color match areas that <REPHRASE> was applied to, we *italicize* areas that <DEL> was applied to, and underline areas that <REORDER> was applied to.

This goal of CS can also be at odds with TS's more general goal of improving comprehension, such as when simplifying an article for school students vs. for adults with cognitive disabilities at a similar language proficiency.

As a first step, we explore CS and TS in English, and leave exploration of other languages and intra-language comparisons for future work.

There are very few NLP works that tackle CS. As such, scarce data is available for training potential CS models. We propose a methodology to address this gap, by introducing an inductive bias to a model trained on TS, in the form of simplification operations. We propose a set of simplification operations based on CS manuals, and show that adding inductive bias regarding their use improves performance on the ASSET test set, compared to a strong baseline model.

In addition, we present an English parallel corpus aimed at CS, which we use as a test set.[3] We show that when fine-tuning models on TS data, our method improves the models' SARI score on the CS dataset, allowing better task adaptation from TS to CS. Finally, we compare how the operations are used in the new CS dataset and existing TS corpora, and show that CS differs from TS not only in goal, but also in data statistics.

2 Cognitive Simplification

The field of cognitive accessibility (Yalon-Chamovitz, 2009) is derived from defining accessibility to include the ability to use services, receive information, and participate in activities, in addition to the more commonly accepted physical ability to reach, navigate, and move in a place. This definition codified the accessibility measure of simplifying textual information to address the need of people with cognitive disabilities to understand textual information, i.e., Cognitive Simplification. Subsequent operationalizations of this notion were carried out by Uziel-Karl et al. (2011) and Yalon-Chamovitz et al. (2016). In particular, they emphasize the need to preserve as much of the meaning of the original text as possible, without rendering it childish or simplistic, while using the same written language as the original text. Although cognitively simplified texts can be easier to read for people with learning disabilities (such as dyslexia), people with learning disabilities are not the main target audience for them.

NLP research into TS for people with cognitive disabilities is relatively scarce. Most works focus on measuring the effect of cognitively simplified text on the comprehension of people with cognitive disabilities (Chen et al., 2017; Rochford, 2021) and without them (Djamasbi et al., 2016b,a). A different line of work explored how people with different cognition react to texts at different simplification levels (Yaneva et al., 2016).

Several works (Feng, 2009; Yaneva et al., 2016) detail parallel corpora of regular and EasyRead documents, documents that are created via the process of CS. Although these works provide details regarding linguistic phenomena in their corpora, we were not able to find any of the corpora detailed

[3]This dataset, together with all our code, is publicly available under CC BY-NC-SA 4.0 on GitHub and huggingface datasets.

therein to run evaluations on. In addition, we were not able to find any recent works that report results on these corpora, using neural techniques for TS.

Although some preliminary works reference the use of contemporary NLP methods for CS to generate simplification examples (e.g., Rochford, 2021), to the best of our knowledge none provide details regarding the model used, model hyperparameter choices, and evaluation methodology. As such, we consider our work to be one of the first to tackle CS as a rigorous, distinct NLP task.[4]

Two other tasks that are related to CS, and use contemporary NLP methods, are text2picto (Sevens et al., 2017; Vandeghinste et al., 2017) and picto2text (Sevens et al., 2015). These are the tasks of converting text to the Sclera[5] and Beta[6] pictogram languages, designed for people with IDD (intellectual or developmental disabilities), and vise versa. While the output of both tasks can improve access to information for people with cognitive disabilities, we believe this task to be distinct from CS and especially TS, that focus on written and spoken language.

3 Other Related Work

We would like to highlight key points from Alva-Manchego et al. (2020b) relevant to our work that relate to training and evaluation datasets and evaluation metrics.

The main datasets used to train and evaluate TS models are WikiLarge (Zhang and Lapata, 2017) and Newsela (Xu et al., 2015). Both corpora contain matching complex-simple document pairs, whose sentences are automatically or manually aligned to create the datasets. In WikiLarge, the matching document pairs are taken from English Wikipedia[7] and Simple English Wikipedia,[8] that aims to be more accessible to people with lower English skills, mainly language learners. In Newsela,[9] the matching document pairs are articles written professionally at four different reading levels, and are originally intended to be used to teach language skills at different school grade levels.

The latest training datasets, and the current de facto standard for TS training, are WikiAuto and NewselaAuto, created by Jiang et al. (2020) by using a neural CRF sentence alignment model. Both are split into training and validation sets. To train their neural CRF aligner, Jiang et al. (2020) also compiled two manually aligned datasets, WikiManual and NewselaManual, split into development, train, and test sets.

The two main datasets used for validation and evaluation of TS models are Turkcorpus (Xu et al., 2016) and ASSET (Alva-Manchego et al., 2020a). Both contain multiple references for each source sentence (8 and 10 respectively). They are crowd-sourced and validated professionally.

The main metric used for evaluating TS models is SARI (Xu et al., 2016), which is computed based on three token-level operations: ADD, KEEP, and DELETE. For the full calculation, see Appendix D.

Many previous works in TS also report BLEU (Papineni et al., 2002). However, several works (Sulem et al., 2018; Xu et al., 2016), have shown that BLEU scores are not suitable for the evaluation of TS models. Nevertheless, BLEU is still reported, and so we also report it for completeness.

A contemporaneous work (Alva-Manchego et al., 2021) argued for the value of manual evaluation in TS rather than automatic metrics. We defer this exploration for CS for future work.

Recent works have proposed methods to control TS outputs by prepending special tokens to the input of a TS model, in a similar manner to the one explored in this work. Such control allows adjusting the model's outputs to different target audiences, and to control what aspects of the simplification process are applied. ACCESS (Martin et al., 2020a), and MUSS (Martin et al., 2020b) both use four structural features of the input-output pairs to define what tokens to prepend during training, and at inference they predefine which tokens to use for all inputs. Sheang and Saggion (2021) add a fifth token to this methodology. Scarton and Specia (2018) use a combination of tokens to specify the type of simplification to perform and the grade level to which to simplify to. Similarly to these works, we also define special tokens to add to the input at training, while at inference we take a different approach (see §6).

Other recent work on TS focuses on particular simplification operations (Zhong et al., 2020; Srikanth and Li, 2021), or on combining different operation modules in a joint model (Maddela et al., 2021). Srikanth and Li (2021) define Elaborative

[4]Contemporaneous work by Rennes (2022) also addresses TS for people with cognitive disabilities in Swedish.

[5]http://www.sclera.be/

[6]https://www.betasymbols.com/

[7]https://en.wikipedia.org/

[8]https://simple.wikipedia.org/

[9]https://newsela.com/data/

Simplification as simplification by adding information to the source text, rather than just removing redundant information. This aligns with some of our proposed simplification operations (Adding Information and Explicitation, see §5.1). Similarly, Zhong et al. (2020) focus on whole sentence deletion, which aligns with some operations from our proposed list (Deleting information, and Operations on Sentences). Maddela et al. (2021) combine a module for sentence deletion and splitting with a paraphrasing module to generate final simplifications. We discuss all three operations in §5.1.

4 Our Approach

To learn how to simplify a text, a model needs to learn *what* types of modifications to apply to the input and *how* to apply each one. These modifications can be categorized into *operations*. Moreover, since TS has multiple large-scale datasets commonly used for training, while there are hardly any such datasets for CS, incorporation of some form of CS-focused inductive bias into a TS-trained model would be useful to allow it to adapt to the CS task. The inductive bias could also be useful for improving TS on its own, given the similarities between the two tasks (see §7 and §8).

As such, our hypothesis is that a TS-trained model that was trained to be aware of the use of CS simplification operations, will perform better at TS and adapt better to CS than a model that was trained end-to-end. We will now turn to testing this hypothesis empirically.

5 Simplification Operations

We adapt existing CS manuals (PLAIN, 2011a,b; U.S. OPM, 2011a,b; U.S. Dep. HHS, 2020; Uziel-Karl et al., 2011) into a list of eight main types of simplification operations. Seven of these apply to the simplification instance (SI) level, and the final main type applies to a whole document. An SI is a set of one or more sentences in regular language (source) aligned to one or more sentences in simplified language (target).[10] Each main type of operation has multiple sub-operations. For full details, see Appendix A.

Previous work define different lists of simplification operations (Caseli et al., 2009; Bott and Saggion, 2011) or focus on word-level operations (KEEP, ADD, DELETE and sometimes also MOVE (Dong et al., 2019)). Our list is based on independent sources (the CS manuals) and focus on intra- and inter-sentence operations applied mainly to a SI. §5.1 provides theoretical definitions for each operation. §5.2 describes how we integrate operations into a TS model.

5.1 Definitions

Below is the list of definitions for the main types of simplification operations.

1. **Proximation**: Reduces ambiguity in the source by making references in the text "closer" to the reader, such as converting a 3rd person point of view to 1st person's.
2. **Rephrasing**: Modifying the words used in the source such that simpler words and phrases are used in the target instead of complex, ambiguous, and hard to understand ones.
3. **Deleting Information**: Removing words and information from the source via summarization or deletion, to reduce the overall information load on the reader.
4. **Adding Information**: Adding information to the target of a SI, that did not appear implicitly or explicitly in the source, mainly through generating relevant examples.
5. **Explicitation**: Explicitly stating or explaining implied knowledge and information from the source[11], and explicitly resolving pronouns and co-references in the target.
6. **Intra-Sentence Rearrangement**: Reorder the information content and words of a sentence into a logical and easily followed order.
7. **Operations on Sentences**: Operations that apply to a whole sentence, including Sentence Splitting and Sentence Reordering.
8. **Document-Level Operations**: Operations that are applied to a document level, including paragraph reordering, and whole paragraph addition/deletion.

In this paper we focus on the first seven operations.

All the operations described above make texts easier to understand for any reader (PLAIN, 2011a; Uziel-Karl et al., 2011). They are especially important for people with cognitive disabilities, as each in their own way reduces the "mental load" required from a reader to understand a given text. For example, "Adding Information" by providing examples makes general or abstract concepts more concrete to a reader; "Explicitation" by clearly stating im-

[10]See Alva-Manchego et al. (2020b), section 2.1.1.

[11]Explicitation is different from Adding Information since the information that appears "new" in the target is actually implied to be understood by all readers in the source.

Task	Train	Model	SARI	ADD	KEEP	DELETE	BLEU	% Ident.
TS		GEM T5Base	30.35	3.11	62.24	25.7	0.898	40.66%
		GEM BART-Base	32.16	3.11	62.17	31.21	0.888	38.16%
	Auto	T5Large	32.92	2.92	61.70	34.12	0.901	39.28%
		T5Large+Classifier$^{♠,♠}$	36.90	**4.73**	61.10	44.87	0.855	23.68%
		T5Base*	32.01	3.04	61.96	31.05	0.903	35.93%
		T5Base+Classifier$^{♠,♠}$	38.13	4.55	61.20	48.65	0.860	23.68%
		BART-Large$^{♠}$	36.05	4.61	61.82	41.71	0.857	19.22%
		BART-Large+Classifier$^{\dagger,♠}$	**38.76**	**4.73**	60.78	**50.78**	0.845	11.70%
		BART-Base	32.43	3.24	61.91	32.13	0.885	33.70%
		BART-Base+Classifier$^{♠,♠}$	37.22	3.87	61.93	45.86	0.874	25.91%
CS		GEM T5Base	19.09	1.45	41.64	14.18	0.234	70.71%
		GEM BART-Base	21.77	2.43	42.63	20.24	0.238	64.17%
	Auto	T5Large	20.02	1.67	41.38	17.01	0.231	68.54%
		T5Large+Classifier*,*	21.71	2.74	41.81	20.58	0.229	57.94%
		T5Base	20.66	2.04	41.86	18.07	0.237	68.22%
		T5Base+Classifier$^{♠,♠}$	26.40	**3.02**	42.19	34.01	0.222	46.11%
		BART-Large$^{♠}$	25.12	2.97	42.91	29.46	0.231	48.91%
		BART-Large+Classifier$^{,♠}$	**27.13**	2.45	42.88	**36.05**	0.221	44.55%
		BART-Base*	23.19	2.69	42.81	24.06	0.237	58.26%
		BART-Base+Classifier,†	24.54	2.13	42.92	28.58	0.226	55.14%

Table 1: Results for all models trained on WikiAuto (Jiang et al., 2020) and the GEM baseline models (Gehrmann et al., 2021). Metrics include SARI and the percentage of identical generations (% Ident.). We also report BLEU for completeness (see text). The highest SARI scores for each fine-tuning setting are **boldfaced**. We tested significance for the overall SARI scores using Wilcoxon Signed-Rank tests (Wilcoxon, 1945) in two settings. First, for each model type and size, we compared the vanilla model and the matching +Classifier model. Second, compared each GEM baseline model with other models of matching types (T5 and BART). We did so for both TS and CS. Scores with $\rho < 0.00001$, $\rho < 0.001$, and $\rho < 0.01$ are marked with ♠, †, and * respectively. We mark each +Classifier model with two symbols, respectively for each significance test setting. E.g., in CS, BART-Base+Classifier is not significantly better than BART-Base, but has $\rho < 0.001$ when testing against GEM BART-Base.

plied prior knowledge eliminates the need to query that knowledge from memory; and "Proximation" by changing passive voice to active voice makes a sentence easier to follow, since "*Active voice makes it clear who is supposed to do what.*".[12]

5.2 Special Tokens for Operations

This section describes a method for introducing inductive bias regarding the use of operations to a TS model. For each operation, we create a special token that is added to an SI such that the model would learn to predict the token at inference. See Figure 1 for an example. For each operation, we formulate simple rules that can be applied automatically to determine whether it took place in a given SI. These rules depend on the source and target together, and cannot be discerned deterministically based on the source. To prevent overlap between operations that share similar indicators, such as Adding Information and Explicitation (when stating implied prior knowledge), we map the first seven operations into 9 unique tokens: Proximation to <PROX>; Rephrasing to <REPHRASE>; Deleting Information to <DEL>; Adding Information to <ADD> and <EXAMPLE>; Explicitation to <ADD>, <EXPLAIN>, and <EXPLICIT>; Intra-sentence Rearrangement to <REORDER>; and Operations on Sentences to <REORDER> and <SPLIT>. For a full description on the rules used to identify each token, see Appendix B.

While the use of simple rules to assign operation tokens to SIs is noisy, we see its quality as sufficient for testing our main hypothesis, namely about the value of the inductive bias implied by the operations. We do not stipulate that our operation classification is optimal, and leave the exploration of more sophisticated methods for future work.

To validate our automatic operation token assignment, we asked an in-house human annotator to manually assign operation tokens to 50 random SIs from the WikiAuto training set according to their definition in §5.1. Using these labels as ground truth, our automatic identification rules achieve a micro precision, recall, and F1 scores of 60.3%, 90.1%, and 72.2% respectively. The main fall in F-score is the accuracy of the <ADD> operation,

[12]Federal Plain Language Guide, Section III.a.1., (PLAIN, 2011b)

which is assigned by an admittedly over-simplistic rule. The two other most frequent operations have F-scores of around 90%. For further details, see Appendix F.

We further validated the reliability of the annotation by assigning a co-author of this paper to independently complete the same manual annotation task. This resulted in a remarkably high inter-annotator agreement. Indeed, measured by Cohen's κ, we get an agreement of $\kappa = 0.84$ for the <REPHRASE> operation, and perfect agreement for other operations. Taken together, these scores indicate the reliability of the automatic token assignment we employ, at least at the aggregate level.

6 Simplification Experiments

We use the huggingface[13] API to fine-tune pretrained language models. We select T5 (Raffel et al., 2020) and BART (Lewis et al., 2020) model architectures of two sizes each, Base and Large, to align with the recently published GEM benchmark's (Gehrmann et al., 2021) official baseline for TS that uses these two model architectures. In addition, we wanted to test if results are consistent across model architectures.

6.1 Training Setting

The main dataset we use for fine-tuning is WikiAuto (Jiang et al., 2020), the automatic alignment of WikiLarge (Zhang and Lapata, 2017). This dataset contains 483802/20000 SIs for training/validation respectively, and is the standard dataset used in recent works for TS training. This is also the training set used in the GEM benchmark.

We also experiment with a non-standard training setting, using the manually aligned datasets WikiManual and NewselaManual from Jiang et al. (2020), who used these datasets to train their respective automatic alignment models for the WikiLarge and Newsela corpora. We experiment with this setting since both datasets as well as our new CS dataset are manually aligned, and manual alignments can potentially capture more complex simplification phenomena. This dataset has 11728/1418 SIs in training/validation sets.

Models. For each model architecture and size, and each dataset, we fine-tune the model on two different settings: baseline and +Classifier. In the baseline setting, the model receives as input the source text, and the target output is the correct simplified sentence. This is the standard methodology used to train TS models. In the +Classifier setting, our goal is to force the model to predict simplification operations while simplifying the source sentence. For each model architecture this is achieved differently. For T5, since you can bind particular masking tokens to particular spans of the input, we format the input and target for the model such that a mask is bound to the operation tokens and the target remains the simplification. For BART, since masks cannot be bound to particular spans, we prepend a masking token to the source and prepend the simplification operations to the target. We illustrate both methods in Figure 1.

All models are fine-tuned on a single 24GB RAM GPU for 3 epochs, using a constant learning rate of 10^{-4} and the Adafactor optimizer (Shazeer and Stern, 2018). At inference, we use beam search with 4 beams and early stopping. We do not perform hyperparameter tuning. Due to computational limitations, we train one model of each (architecture, size, type, training data) combination.

We also compare each model architecture against the respective GEM baseline using a notebook provided by the original authors.

6.2 Evaluation Datasets

All models are evaluated on the ASSET (Alva-Manchego et al., 2020a) test set, which contains 359 SIs. This is the standard dataset for evaluating TS models, since it provides multiple reference simplifications for each source sentence. The way we decided whether a particular operation is applied to a source sentence in ASSET is by majority of the ten references, meaning, we consider an operation taking place only if more than 50% of annotators in ASSET used it in their simplifications of that source. In Appendix H we provide more details on the counts of actions in each dataset.

In addition, we evaluate each model on a new Cognitive Simplification test set, called FestAbility Transcripts. This dataset contains aligned transcripts of the virtual accessibility conference FestAbility[14] held in 2020 during the COVID-19 pandemic. The conference was simplified live according to the Yalon Method[15], and the transcripts were manually aligned by the authors to create 321 SIs. We use this dataset to test each model's perfor-

[13]https://huggingface.co/

[14]https://www.festability.org/

[15]https://www.yalonmethod.com/

mance in adapting from a TS setting to a CS one. Table 2 provides some details into the content of this dataset.

Metric	Value
Unique Tokens – source	1452
Unique Tokens – target	996
Shared Tokens	798
TER	0.92
Token Length Ratio	0.95
Nbchars Ratio	1.14
Levinstein Similarity	46.29
Wordrank Ratio	0.83
Deptree Depth Ratio	1.11

Table 2: Details for the new FestAbility Dataset. Using a SentencePiece tokenizer, we report the number of unique tokens in the source sentences and the target simplifications, and the number of shared tokens between them. We also report the four metrics from Martin et al. (2020a,b) for future comparisons between FestAbility and other datasets.

We report SARI[16] (Xu et al., 2016) for each model on each test set, and we also report separately the scores for each token-level operation (ADD, KEEP, DELETE) that are averaged together to compute SARI. For completeness, we report BLEU scores for each model as well. However, we should note that according to Sulem et al. (2018) and Alva-Manchego et al. (2021), BLEU is not a suitable metric for evaluating text simplification models. We also report what percentage of test outputs are identical to the source for each model.

7 Results

Our main results are presented in Table 1. Results on TS show that when trained on the standard WikiAuto dataset, the +Classifier variant of a model outperforms the baseline's SARI score in all cases, with 3.98 points for T5Large, 6.12 points for T5Base, 2.71 points for BART-Large, and 4.79 points for BART-Base. These are substantial improvements, considerably larger than differences in SARI scores between model sizes of the same variant, except for the BART baseline models. The difference between the T5 baseline models is 0.91 points, T5+Classifier models is 1.23, the BART baseline is 3.62 points, and the BART+Classifier models is 1.54 points.

[16]Using the EASSE (Alva-Manchego et al., 2019) implementation of the metric.

Focusing on CS performance, we find that the +Classifier variants achieved superior results for all model architectures and sizes. The improvement differs by architecture and size, with the largest difference being of 5.74 SARI point for the T5Base models trained on WikiAuto. The best performance is again obtained by the BART-Large+Classifier model, and is at least 2.01 SARI points higher than the score obtained by any baseline variant.

With respect to the Manual dataset training setting, we see similar trends. In particular, the +Classifier models outperform baseline models, and the best performing model is still BART-Large+Classifier. Due to space limitations, we discuss the results on this dataset in Appendix C.

Taken together, our results demonstrate the effectiveness of incorporating inductive bias using simplification operations for both TS and CS.

In order to ensure that the experimental setup we use is comparable in performance with the standard practice in the field of TS, we experiment with the original GEM baseline code-base, and our hyperparameter settings were chosen according to it. The results of models trained according to this code-base are indeed comparable to models of matching sizes of the baseline variants.

We further validated our results with significance tests, following the guidelines of Dror et al. (2018). We used the Wilcoxon Signed-Ranked (Wilcoxon, 1945) test as our main significance test. We compared each vanilla and +Classifier model pair, and also each model of a particular type (T5 and BART) to their respective GEM baselines. The results are shown in Table 1. Almost all tests, with only six exceptions, are significant with at least $\rho < 0.01$ and most with $\rho < 0.00001$. These results further support the validity of our analysis.

We attribute the improved performance of all +Classifier models to improvements in the token-level operations scores for ADD and DELETE. In the standard training setting on WikiAuto, all +Classifier models achieve substantially higher ADD and DELETE scores than their same-sized baseline counterparts, while all models achieve similar KEEP scores. Interestingly, for the BART models, the difference in ADD scores is less substantial than for the T5 models.

8 Simplification Dataset Comparison

We compare simplification datasets with respect to how the simplification operations are used in each.

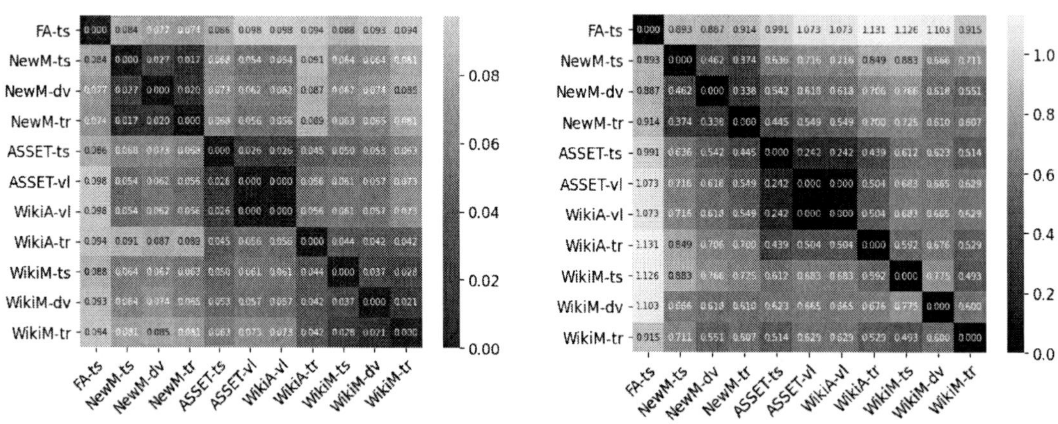

(a) $\overline{JSD}$ distances between distributions

(b) ℓ_2 distances between correlation matrices

Figure 2: Heatmaps of the distances between dataset sub-sets. We shorten dataset names as follows: FA=FestAbility, NewM=NewselaManual, WikiM/A=WikiManual/Auto. The final two letters signify ts=test, vl=valid, dv=dev, and tr=train sets. For each sub-set pair, we report the numerical distance in the matching cell.

We show that simplification operations can also be used to better characterize such datasets.

We analyze all available sub-sets (development, train, validation, and test) of all datasets, to provide a fine-grained analysis. We consider test sub-sets of datasets, to better understand the results of §7. This analysis was done after-the-fact, and did not influence the development of the models.[17]

The results presented in this section show that CS is different from TS in how the operations are applied. They also surface the known relationships between the datasets, validating our analysis. We believe that this type of aggregate analysis can be confidently performed given the validation at the end of §5.2, but acknowledge that the token assignment is noisy.

To understand how each simplification operation is applied individually, we compute the frequency with which each operation is applied in a given sub-set. These frequencies can be viewed as defining random variables X_o^S, stating the probability that each simplification operation o is used in a particular SI in sub-set S. As such, to understand the distance between sub-sets with respect to the individual application of each operation, we can compute the mean Jensen-Shannon distance (Lin, 1991; Fuglede and Topsoe, 2004) (which we mark $\overline{JSD}$) between matching random variables in different sub-sets. For further details on the action distributions for each dataset, see Appendix H.

As can be seen in Figure 2a, all sub-sets have $\overline{JSD} < 0.1$ from one another, which is not a large distance. However, we are still able to see distinct clusters for each dataset, with subsets having $\overline{JSD} < 0.04$ within clusters and $\overline{JSD} > 0.04$ to other sub-sets.[18] Interestingly, WikiAuto-test is closer to the WikiManual cluster than it is to WikiAuto-valid, which could be explained by the fact that WikiAuto was created based on the matching of complex-simple sentences presented in WikiManual. In addition, WikiAuto-valid and ASSET-valid appear to be identical, which could be explained by the fact that the source for ASSET-valid was taken from WikiAuto-valid. Regarding the CS dataset FestAbility, it is $\overline{JSD} > 0.07$ from all other sub-sets, and is the farthest sub-set from WikiAuto, ASSET, and WikiManual clusters, and the second or third farthest from sub-sets in the NewselaManual cluster.

To understand how simplification operation are applied together, we computed the Pearson correlations of the co-occurrence of each operation pair in a given subset S, to create a correlation matrix M^S. We then computed the pair-wise ℓ_2-distance between matrices. Results are in Figure 2b.

As can be seen in Figure 2b, the clusters of closest sub-sets are maintained for NewselaManual, and for ASSET and WikiAuto-val , while the sub-sets of WikiManual are no longer closest to one another. Also, WikiAuto-train is similarly distant from both WikiAuto-val and the WikiManual sub-sets, unlike when comparing with $\overline{JSD}$. In this

[17]We analyze the test sets also because the CS dataset only contains a test set at this point, due to their small size.

[18]For reference, if $p = (0.557, 0.443)$ and $q = (0.5, 0.5)$, then $JSD(p, q) = 0.0403$.

setting, the FestAbility dataset is the most distant sub-set from all other sub-sets, with $d_{\ell_2} > 0.88$ from all of them. All other sub-sets are $d_{\ell_2} < 0.75$ from one another, except NewselaManual-test from WikiAuto-train and WikiManual-test with $d_{\ell_2} = 0.85$ and $d_{\ell_2} = 0.88$ respectively.

Taken together, these results show that while each individual operation is applied with similar probability in every dataset, the operations are applied together differently. In CS in particular, they are applied in a more distinct fashion than in TS.

The difference in operation application could be attributed to the different domains from which each dataset pulls its sentences. In our CS dataset, all sentences are transcripts of human speech, taken from a formal conference. Thus, they may contain more informal language than a Wikipedia article. Given our datasets, we therefore cannot differentiate between domain difference and task difference. However, we are currently compiling a larger dataset for CS that contains more formal language, that will enable such analysis.

The analysis here can provide additional insight as to the performance patterns of the different models (§7). Since each operation is applied individually under a similar distribution in TS and CS, the +Classifier models could have potentially learned indicators of when to apply each action individually when training on TS. This could have been useful when adapting to CS, especially given that the operations co-occur differently in TS and CS.

9 Conclusion and Future Work

We formulated the task of Cognitive Simplification as an NLP task, and discussed its similarities and dissimilarities from the well-researched task of TS. The two tasks are similar in the types of simplification operations that are applied in each, and different in the distribution in which the operations are applied. They also differ in their target audience, at least when using standard datasets. We further release with this paper a readily available dataset directed at CS, providing a test set to evaluate CS models on.

Attempting to overcome the absence of training data for CS, we showed that by introducing to a TS-trained model inductive bias as to the simplification operations that need to be performed on the input, the model is able to better adapt to CS. We also showed that TS-trained models that are trained to predict simplification operations perform better than their baseline counterparts on TS.

We believe that comparing how simplification operations are applied in different languages can provide valuable insights into understanding the task of Text Simplification better. Future work will further explore the relation between the distribution of operations and the ability of the model to generalize to different domains and task formulations. Such an inquiry may reveal that simplification operations provide not only inductive bias, but also an analytical tool for comparing datasets and variants of TS. There are TS datasets in many languages, including Swedish (Rennes and Jönsson, 2015), Spanish (Saggion et al., 2015), German (Säuberli et al., 2020; Battisti et al., 2020), Danish (Klerke and Søgaard, 2012), Portuguese (Leal et al., 2018), and Russian (Dmitrieva and Tiedemann, 2021). We plan to compare these datasets in terms of their distribution of operations, so as to empirically characterize whether the notion of text simplification implicit in these datasets is similar or not.

We hope that our findings will spark interest in CS, as there is much more to solve in creating automatic simplification systems for people with cognitive disabilities. As stated above, we are currently working on compiling a larger and more robust CS dataset, that will enable improvements in CS technology, and allow to tease apart domain effects in the differences between TS and CS from more fundamental differences between the tasks.

Ethical Considerations

Use of existing datasets. The WikiAuto, WikiManual (Jiang et al., 2020), and ASSET (Alva-Manchego et al., 2020a) datasets are publicly available. We took the WikiAuto and ASSET from the huggingface dataset hub,[19] and WikiManual from the authors' GitHub.[20] We used and received access to Newsela with accordance to Newsela's terms of service.

The released FestAbility dataset. The FestAbility conference is available for viewing online, and we received approval to redistribute the simplifications and transcripts from the organization that simplified the conference.[21] The text in these transcripts deals with the following subjects: rights of people with cognitive disabilities, arts and performing arts in particular, accessibility, and personal

[19] https://huggingface.co/docs/datasets/

[20] https://github.com/chaojiang06/wiki-auto

[21] https://www.yalonmethod.com/

stories. None of the text is offensive or discriminatory in any way. Free public access to this dataset is available for future research under CC BY-NC-SA 4.0 on GitHub at `https:/github.com/eytan-c/CognitiveSimplification` and as a huggingface dataset at `https://huggingface.co/datasets/eytanc/FestAbilityTranscripts`.

Ethical risks. We do not see any immediate adverse effects that our methodology and dataset can lead to. On the contrary, further research into CS from an NLP context can only provide benefits to people with cognitive disabilities.

Other Considerations Gooding (2022) recently presented multiple different ethical considerations for text simplification research. These include stating explicitly the target audience for TS, using appropriate datasets, and evaluating using appropriate measures, among others. While contemporaneous, our paper aligns with the claims that Gooding (2022) present with how we define the task of CS. Furthermore, the methodology presented in §8 can be used to empirically measure some of the risks presented in Section 3 of Gooding (2022).

Limitations

Computational limitations. Each model trained in §6 requires a long time to train on the largest GPU available to the authors, with the largest models taking several days to complete the training. See Appendix E for details. These resources therefore prohibit experimentation with larger models.

Comparison to other TS systems. The TS literature contains many TS systems, using many different techniques (such as Martin et al. (2020a,b); Sheang and Saggion (2021); Scarton and Specia (2018); Zhong et al. (2020); Maddela et al. (2021); Zhao et al. (2018); Zhang and Lapata (2017)). Any one of these systems could be used as well for CS, and such a comparison is warranted. The goal of this paper however is to highlight the need and possibilities of further research into CS, and provide initial benchmarks and tools to do so. We do not presume that our methodology of adding simplification operations is the best methodology for CS. We leave investigating the answer to this question for future research. The authors are currently working on answering this question, in particular in conjunction with releasing additional CS data.

Using additional datasets. Although we did get permission to use NewselaAuto as a training dataset, we did not train models with that dataset to report results on. The reasoning behind this decision that we wanted the main results of this paper to be easily reproducible, and while WikiAuto is readily available for use by all, access to Newsela is provided under a restrictive license.

Adding simplification operations. The methodology proposed in the paper to add simplification operations to SI uses simplistic rules to do so. Some of the operations can be quite difficult to identify, even for humans. We believe that there probably is a better methodology for identifying the simplification operations, and leave identifying such a methodology for future research.

Acknowledgements

This work was partially supported by the Israel Science Foundation (grant No. 929/17). We would like to thank Prof. Shira Yalon-Chamovitz for helpful discussions and for providing us with the cognitive simplification guidelines and data. We would like to thank the authors of the GEM baseline for simplification, for providing the source code used to train their baseline models. We would also like to acknowledge the Adi Lautman Interdisciplinary Program, for providing the fertile ground in which the initial idea for this project grew.

References

Fernando Alva-Manchego, Louis Martin, Antoine Bordes, Carolina Scarton, Benoît Sagot, and Lucia Specia. 2020a. ASSET: A dataset for tuning and evaluation of sentence simplification models with multiple rewriting transformations. In *Proceedings of the 58th Annual Meeting of the Association for Computational Linguistics*, pages 4668–4679, Online. Association for Computational Linguistics.

Fernando Alva-Manchego, Louis Martin, Carolina Scarton, and Lucia Specia. 2019. EASSE: Easier automatic sentence simplification evaluation. In *Proceedings of the 2019 Conference on Empirical Methods in Natural Language Processing and the 9th International Joint Conference on Natural Language Processing (EMNLP-IJCNLP): System Demonstrations*, pages 49–54, Hong Kong, China. Association for Computational Linguistics.

Fernando Alva-Manchego, Carolina Scarton, and Lucia Specia. 2020b. Data-driven sentence simplification: Survey and benchmark. *Computational Linguistics*, 46(1):135–187.

Fernando Alva-Manchego, Carolina Scarton, and Lucia Specia. 2021. The (un)suitability of automatic evaluation metrics for text simplification. *Computational Linguistics*, 47(4):861–889.

Alessia Battisti, Dominik Pfütze, Andreas Säuberli, Marek Kostrzewa, and Sarah Ebling. 2020. A corpus for automatic readability assessment and text simplification of German. In *Proceedings of the 12th Language Resources and Evaluation Conference*, pages 3302–3311, Marseille, France. European Language Resources Association.

Stefan Bott and Horacio Saggion. 2011. An unsupervised alignment algorithm for text simplification corpus construction. In *Proceedings of the Workshop on Monolingual Text-To-Text Generation*, pages 20–26, Portland, Oregon. Association for Computational Linguistics.

Helena M Caseli, Tiago F Pereira, Lucia Specia, Thiago A S Pardo, Caroline Gasperin, and Sandra M Aluisio. 2009. Building a Brazilian Portuguese Parallel Corpus of Original and Simplified Texts. In *10th Conference on Intelligent Text Processing and Computational Linguistics (CICLing-2009)*, pages 59–70.

Ping Chen, John Rochford, David Kennedy, Soussan Djamasbi, Peter Fay, and Will Scott. 2017. Automatic Text Simplification for People with Intellectual Disabilities. In *2016 International Conference on Artificial Intelligence Science and Technology*, pages 725–731. World Scientific Publishing Co Pte Ltd.

Soussan Djamasbi, John Rochford, Abigail DaBoll-Lavoie, Tyler Greff, Jennifer Lally, and Kayla McAvoy. 2016a. Text Simplification and User Experience. In *International Conference on Augmented Cognition*, pages 285–295. Springer International Publishing.

Soussan Djamasbi, Mina Shojaeizadeh, Ping Chen, and John Rochford. 2016b. Text Simplification and Generation Y: An Eye Tracking Study. In *SIGHCI 2016 Proceedings*, 12. Association for Information Systems.

Anna Dmitrieva and Jörg Tiedemann. 2021. Creating an aligned Russian text simplification dataset from language learner data. In *Proceedings of the 8th Workshop on Balto-Slavic Natural Language Processing*, pages 73–79, Kiyv, Ukraine. Association for Computational Linguistics.

Yue Dong, Zichao Li, Mehdi Rezagholizadeh, and Jackie Chi Kit Cheung. 2019. EditNTS: An neural programmer-interpreter model for sentence simplification through explicit editing. In *Proceedings of the 57th Annual Meeting of the Association for Computational Linguistics*, pages 3393–3402, Florence, Italy. Association for Computational Linguistics.

Rotem Dror, Gili Baumer, Segev Shlomov, and Roi Reichart. 2018. The hitchhiker's guide to testing statistical significance in natural language processing. In *Proceedings of the 56th Annual Meeting of the Association for Computational Linguistics (Volume 1: Long Papers)*, pages 1383–1392, Melbourne, Australia. Association for Computational Linguistics.

Lijun Feng. 2009. Automatic readability assessment for people with intellectual disabilities. *SIGACCESS Access. Comput.*, (93):84–91.

Bent Fuglede and Flemming Topsoe. 2004. Jensen-shannon divergence and hilbert space embedding. In *International Symposium on Information Theory, 2004. ISIT 2004. Proceedings.*, pages 31–36. Institute of Electrical and Electronics Engineers.

Sebastian Gehrmann, Tosin Adewumi, Karmanya Aggarwal, Pawan Sasanka Ammanamanchi, Anuoluwapo Aremu, Antoine Bosselut, Khyathi Raghavi Chandu, Miruna-Adriana Clinciu, Dipanjan Das, Kaustubh Dhole, Wanyu Du, Esin Durmus, Ondřej Dušek, Chris Chinenye Emezue, Varun Gangal, Cristina Garbacea, Tatsunori Hashimoto, Yufang Hou, Yacine Jernite, Harsh Jhamtani, Yangfeng Ji, Shailza Jolly, Mihir Kale, Dhruv Kumar, Faisal Ladhak, Aman Madaan, Mounica Maddela, Khyati Mahajan, Saad Mahamood, Bodhisattwa Prasad Majumder, Pedro Henrique Martins, Angelina McMillan-Major, Simon Mille, Emiel van Miltenburg, Moin Nadeem, Shashi Narayan, Vitaly Nikolaev, Andre Niyongabo Rubungo, Salomey Osei, Ankur Parikh, Laura Perez-Beltrachini, Niranjan Ramesh Rao, Vikas Raunak, Juan Diego Rodriguez, Sashank Santhanam, João Sedoc, Thibault Sellam, Samira Shaikh, Anastasia Shimorina, Marco Antonio Sobrevilla Cabezudo, Hendrik Strobelt, Nishant Subramani, Wei Xu, Diyi Yang, Akhila Yerukola, and Jiawei Zhou. 2021. The GEM benchmark: Natural language generation, its evaluation and metrics. In *Proceedings of the 1st Workshop on Natural Language Generation, Evaluation, and Metrics (GEM 2021)*, pages 96–120, Online. Association for Computational Linguistics.

Sian Gooding. 2022. On the ethical considerations of text simplification. In *Ninth Workshop on Speech and Language Processing for Assistive Technologies (SLPAT-2022)*, pages 50–57, Dublin, Ireland. Association for Computational Linguistics.

Chao Jiang, Mounica Maddela, Wuwei Lan, Yang Zhong, and Wei Xu. 2020. Neural CRF model for sentence alignment in text simplification. In *Proceedings of the 58th Annual Meeting of the Association for Computational Linguistics*, pages 7943–7960, Online. Association for Computational Linguistics.

Sigrid Klerke and Anders Søgaard. 2012. DSim, a Danish parallel corpus for text simplification. In *Proceedings of the Eighth International Conference on Language Resources and Evaluation (LREC'12)*, pages 4015–4018, Istanbul, Turkey. European Language Resources Association (ELRA).

Sidney Evaldo Leal, Magali Sanches Duran, and Sandra Maria Aluísio. 2018. A nontrivial sentence corpus for the task of sentence readability assessment in

Portuguese. In *Proceedings of the 27th International Conference on Computational Linguistics*, pages 401–413, Santa Fe, New Mexico, USA. Association for Computational Linguistics.

Mike Lewis, Yinhan Liu, Naman Goyal, Marjan Ghazvininejad, Abdelrahman Mohamed, Omer Levy, Veselin Stoyanov, and Luke Zettlemoyer. 2020. BART: Denoising sequence-to-sequence pre-training for natural language generation, translation, and comprehension. In *Proceedings of the 58th Annual Meeting of the Association for Computational Linguistics*, pages 7871–7880, Online. Association for Computational Linguistics.

Jianhua Lin. 1991. Divergence measures based on the shannon entropy. *IEEE Transactions on Information Theory*, 37(1):145–151.

Mounica Maddela, Fernando Alva-Manchego, and Wei Xu. 2021. Controllable text simplification with explicit paraphrasing. In *Proceedings of the 2021 Conference of the North American Chapter of the Association for Computational Linguistics: Human Language Technologies*, pages 3536–3553, Online. Association for Computational Linguistics.

Louis Martin, Éric de la Clergerie, Benoît Sagot, and Antoine Bordes. 2020a. Controllable sentence simplification. In *Proceedings of the 12th Language Resources and Evaluation Conference*, pages 4689–4698, Marseille, France. European Language Resources Association.

Louis Martin, Angela Fan, Éric De La Clergerie, Antoine Bordes, and Benoît Sagot. 2020b. Multilingual unsupervised sentence simplification. *Computing Research Repository*, arXiv:2005.00352. Version 2.

Kishore Papineni, Salim Roukos, Todd Ward, and Wei-Jing Zhu. 2002. BLEU: a Method for Automatic Evaluation of Machine Translation. In *Proceedings of the 40th Annual Meeting of the Association for Computational Linguistics (ACL)*, July, pages 311–318, Philadelphia.

Ellie Pavlick and Chris Callison-Burch. 2016. Simple PPDB: A paraphrase database for simplification. In *Proceedings of the 54th Annual Meeting of the Association for Computational Linguistics (Volume 2: Short Papers)*, pages 143–148, Berlin, Germany. Association for Computational Linguistics.

PLAIN. 2011a. Federal Plain Language Guidelines. `https://www.plainlanguage.gov/guidelines/`. Accessed: 2021-06-07. Plain Language Action and Information Network.

PLAIN. 2011b. *Federal Plain Language Guidelines*, 1 edition. Plain Language Action and Information Network.

Colin Raffel, Noam Shazeer, Adam Roberts, Katherine Lee, Sharan Narang, Michael Matena, Yanqi Zhou, Wei Li, and Peter J. Liu. 2020. Exploring the limits of transfer learning with a unified text-to-text transformer. *Journal of Machine Learning Research*, 21(140):1–67.

Evelina Rennes. 2022. *Automatic Adaptation of Swedish Text for Increased Inclusion*. Ph.D. thesis, Linköping UniversityLinköping University, Human-Centered systems, Faculty of Science & Engineering.

Evelina Rennes and Arne Jönsson. 2015. A tool for automatic simplification of Swedish texts. In *Proceedings of the 20th Nordic Conference of Computational Linguistics (NODALIDA 2015)*, pages 317–320, Vilnius, Lithuania. Linköping University Electronic Press, Sweden.

John Rochford. 2021. Developing Simple Web Text for People with Intellectual Disabilities and to Train Artificial Intelligence. In *Actes des Ateliers d'INFORSID - Dessinons ensemble le futur des systèmes d'information*, pages 88–95. Conference and Labs of the Evaluation Forum.

Horacio Saggion, Sanja Štajner, Stefan Bott, Simon Mille, Luz Rello, and Biljana Drndarevic. 2015. Making it Simplext: Implementation and evaluation of a text simplification system for spanish. *ACM Trans. Access. Comput.*, 6(4).

Andreas Säuberli, Sarah Ebling, and Martin Volk. 2020. Benchmarking data-driven automatic text simplification for German. In *Proceedings of the 1st Workshop on Tools and Resources to Empower People with REAding DIfficulties (READI)*, pages 41–48, Marseille, France. European Language Resources Association.

Carolina Scarton and Lucia Specia. 2018. Learning simplifications for specific target audiences. In *Proceedings of the 56th Annual Meeting of the Association for Computational Linguistics (Volume 2: Short Papers)*, pages 712–718, Melbourne, Australia. Association for Computational Linguistics.

Leen Sevens, Vincent Vandeghinste, Ineke Schuurman, and Frank Van Eynde. 2015. Natural language generation from pictographs. In *Proceedings of the 15th European Workshop on Natural Language Generation (ENLG)*, pages 71–75, Brighton, UK. Association for Computational Linguistics.

Leen Sevens, Vincent Vandeghinste, Ineke Schuurman, and Frank Van Eynde. 2017. Simplified text-to-pictograph translation for people with intellectual disabilities. In *Natural Language Processing and Information Systems*, pages 185–196, Cham. Springer International Publishing.

Noam Shazeer and Mitchell Stern. 2018. Adafactor: Adaptive learning rates with sublinear memory cost. In *Proceedings of the 35th International Conference on Machine Learning*, volume 80 of *Proceedings of Machine Learning Research*, pages 4596–4604. PMLR.

Kim Cheng Sheang and Horacio Saggion. 2021. Controllable sentence simplification with a unified text-to-text transfer transformer. In *Proceedings of the 14th International Conference on Natural Language Generation*, pages 341–352, Aberdeen, Scotland, UK. Association for Computational Linguistics.

Neha Srikanth and Junyi Jessy Li. 2021. Elaborative simplification: Content addition and explanation generation in text simplification. In *Findings of the Association for Computational Linguistics: ACL-IJCNLP 2021*, pages 5123–5137, Online. Association for Computational Linguistics.

Elior Sulem, Omri Abend, and Ari Rappoport. 2018. BLEU is not suitable for the evaluation of text simplification. In *Proceedings of the 2018 Conference on Empirical Methods in Natural Language Processing*, pages 738–744, Brussels, Belgium. Association for Computational Linguistics.

U.S. Dep. HHS. 2020. Plain writing and clear communications. `https://www.hhs.gov/open/plain-writing/index.html`. Accessed: 2021-06-07. U.S. Department of Health and Human Services.

U.S. OPM. 2011a. Information Management Plain Language. `https://www.opm.gov/information-management/plain-language/#tips`. Accessed: 2021-06-07. U.S. Office of Personnel Management.

U.S. OPM. 2011b. *OPM Plain Writing Plan*. U.S. Office of Personnel Management.

Sigal Uziel-Karl, Michal Tenne Rinde, and Shira Yalon-Chamovitz. 2011. *Language Accessibility for people with Cognitive Disabilities: Instructions Booklet*. Ono Academic College and Israel Ministry of Labor, Social Affairs and Social Services.

Vincent Vandeghinste, Ineke Schuurman, Leen Sevens, and Frank Van Eynde. 2017. Translating text into pictographs. *Natural Language Engineering*, 23(2):217–244.

Frank Wilcoxon. 1945. Individual comparisons by ranking methods. *Biometrics Bulletin*, 1(6):80–83.

Wei Xu, Chris Callison-Burch, and Courtney Napoles. 2015. Problems in current text simplification research: New data can help. *Transactions of the Association for Computational Linguistics*, 3:283–297.

Wei Xu, Courtney Napoles, Ellie Pavlick, Quanze Chen, and Chris Callison-Burch. 2016. Optimizing statistical machine translation for text simplification. *Transactions of the Association for Computational Linguistics*, 4:401–415.

Shira Yalon-Chamovitz. 2009. Invisible access needs of people with intellectual Disabilities: A conceptual model of practice. *Intellectual and Developmental Disabilities*, 47(5):395–400.

Shira Yalon-Chamovitz and Ornit Avidan-Ziv. 2016. Simultaneous Simplification: Stretching the Boundaries of UDL. In *2016 Universal Design for Learning Implementation and Research Network Summit*, Towson University, Maryland. UDL-IRN.

Shira Yalon-Chamovitz, Ruth Shach, Ornit Avidan-Ziv, and Michal Tenne Rinde. 2016. The call for cognitive ramps. *Work*, 53(2):455–456.

Victoria Yaneva, Irina Temnikova, and Ruslan Mitkov. 2016. A corpus of text data and gaze fixations from autistic and non-autistic adults. In *Proceedings of the Tenth International Conference on Language Resources and Evaluation (LREC'16)*, pages 480–487, Portorož, Slovenia. European Language Resources Association (ELRA).

Xingxing Zhang and Mirella Lapata. 2017. Sentence simplification with deep reinforcement learning. In *Proceedings of the 2017 Conference on Empirical Methods in Natural Language Processing*, pages 584–594, Copenhagen, Denmark. Association for Computational Linguistics.

Sanqiang Zhao, Rui Meng, Daqing He, Andi Saptono, and Bambang Parmanto. 2018. Integrating transformer and paraphrase rules for sentence simplification. In *Proceedings of the 2018 Conference on Empirical Methods in Natural Language Processing*, pages 3164–3173, Brussels, Belgium. Association for Computational Linguistics.

Yang Zhong, Chao Jiang, Wei Xu, and Junyi Jessy Li. 2020. Discourse Level Factors for Sentence Deletion in Text Simplification. *Proceedings of the AAAI Conference on Artificial Intelligence*, 34(05):9709–9716.

A Simplification Operation Definitions

In this section we describe in more detail the different simplification operations, providing full details for each, including sub-operations.

This list is based on cognitive simplification manuals, and includes 2 levels of operations, as many particular operations share similar goals. We describe the similar goals as "Main Operations", and this is the list provided in the main paper. In here, we describe in detail all sub-operations as well.

As explained in the main paper, we focus mainly on the operations that are performed on simplification instances (SIs). We do so both to align with existing research of TS, and to conform with how the simplification manuals describe the process of CS. In addition, we also describe "Document Level" operations. These "Document Level" operations are not distinct to CS, but have an important role in that task.

For each operation, we also describe what type of modification to the source of a SI is this operation aimed at: a modification of its syntactic structure or the modification of its lexical content (i.e., the words used in the SI). We deem the former a structural modification, and the latter a lexical modification. Some operations perform both, but in such cases we chose to assign the type of modification that subsumes the other. For example, Sentence Splitting is a structural modification, since it aims to modify the structure of the original text by splitting a sentence into two or more sentences in the simplification. This structural change might require changing words used in the target (i.e., a lexical modification) but those changes are part of the structural modification.

1. **Proximation**: Proximation is the process of making references in the text closer to the reader, meaning explicit and more relatable. This can be by changing the point of view of the sentence from 3rd to 2nd and/or 1st person, by changing the tenses of verbs to easier to understand tenses[22], or by converting Passive voiced sentences to Active voiced ones[23]. This reduces the potential ambiguity in the source and makes the target more personal, and thus more easily understood to people with cognitive disabilities.

   Proximation, and all of its sub operations, are *structural* modifications, since their goal is to transform the syntax of the sentence (tense, voice, etc.).

2. **Rephrasing**: Modifying the words used in the source such that simpler words and phrases are used in the target instead of complex, ambiguous, and hard to understand ones. Simpler words and simpler phrases makes the text easier to understand for people with lower language comprehension skills, such as those with cognitive disabilities. A rephrasing can be finding a simple synonym to a complex word, but also converting words to phrases and vise-versa. Since Rephrasing changes the words used in a sentence, it is a lexical modification.

3. **Deleting Information**: A main part of simplifying a text is deciding which information is irrelevant or surplus to a reader's comprehension, and removing it from the text. By lowering the information load on the reader, his or her ability to comprehend the text increases. Deleting Information comes in two main types, Removal and Summarization. We chose to assign both into Deleting Information, since in both some of the *information content*[24] of the source is lost in the target, either directly (Removal) or indirectly (Summarization).

   Deleting Information is a *lexical* modification.

4. **Adding Information**: This operation includes adding information to the simplification that never appeared in the source. It includes only one sub-operation, Example Generation, since this is the only type of novel information that can appear in the target of an SI. Any other apparent "new information" is usually implicit information that is part of the source, and requires Explicitation in the target.

   However, finding precise distinctions between new information in the target that is 100% new and new information in the target that is implicit information from the source is a difficult task. As such, we chose to have a general "Adding Information" operation for exactly the type of new information in the target that cannot be precisely associated either as an Explicitation or Example Generation.

   Adding information is a *lexical* modification.

5. **Explicitation**: Many of the texts we read contain implicit information that the writer assumes the reader has prior knowledge of. During simplification, this implicit information will need an explanation or elaboration upon, so that the reader can understand the text.

   This could be achieved by Explanation Generation: explaining the meaning of particular terms and phrases, or explicitly stating the

[22]For example, Present Tenses are generally easier to comprehend than Future Tenses. Another example: in English, Perfect Tenses harder to understand and should usually be converted to other tenses.

[23]Multiple CS manuals state that sentences with an active voice are easier to understand than sentences in passive voice (PLAIN, 2011b; Uziel-Karl et al., 2011). From the Federal Plain Language Guide, Section III.a.1.i, page 20: *"Active voice makes it clear who is supposed to do what. It eliminates ambiguity about responsibilities. Not "It must be done.", but "You must do it.". Passive voice obscures who is responsible for what ...".* Uziel-Karl et al. (2011) even explicitly state that every passive voiced sentence needs to be converted to active voice.

[24]See subsection A.1 for a discussion on this topic

logic and reasoning behind a particular passage in the text. These explanations are crucial for people with cognitive disabilities to understand texts, since they sometimes lack prior common knowledge in many domains.

We consider both Explanation Generation and Example Generation (from the previous main operation) to be forms of *Elaborative Simplification* (Srikanth and Li, 2021). We create a distinction between the two to differentiate between "new information" in the simplification that is from the implicit information of the source and "new information" from the potentially relevant information of the source. See subsection A.1.

In addition, the source might contain pronouns that the writer assumes their co-references can be resolved easily from the text. However, in most cases, people with cognitive disabilities would not necessarily be able to resolve pronoun co-references. As such, most pronouns should be converted in the target to their explicit references. This is Pronoun Explicitation.

Both types of Explicitation are *lexical* modifications.

6. **Intra-Sentence Rearrangement**: At times, the clauses of a sentence can be ordered in such a way that make it harder to comprehend due to its clauses being out of the "correct" logical order. In addition, for many reasons, the ordering of the subject, verb, and object can be out of the "correct" order. When information is presented out of order, it makes the text harder to comprehend, especially for people with cognitive disabilities. Semantic Rearrangement is presenting the information content of a sentence in the source of an SI in a logical and easily followed order, and is a *structural* modification. [25]

7. **Operations on Sentences**: There are often simplification operations that are applied on a whole sentence that is part of a SI, rather than applying to an internal part of a sentence. This includes Scntcncc Splitting, and also Sentence Reordering.

   Splitting long sentences into shorter ones makes texts easier to comprehend by reducing the information load of each sentence. Rearranging the sentences of a paragraph into a correct logical/temporal order also makes a text easier to comprehend, for the same reasons explained above in Intra-Sentence Rearrangement.

   Sentence Operations are *structural* modifications.

8. **Document Level Operations**[26]: In some cases, when simplifying long texts organized as documents and/or documents with subsections, more overarching operations need to be applied. These are almost always modification of *structure*, since information needs to be ordered correctly, as explained in the previous two Main Action types. This can include full chapter/sub-document reordering and full paragraph reordering, but can also cross paragraph reordering of sentences and paragraph splitting.

   In addition, there are *lexical* modifications that we consider a Document Level Operations. These are Adding Paragraphs and Adding Chapters that didn't exist in the original document, and Deleting Paragraphs and Deleting Chapters from the original document. The additions of paragraphs or chapters usually explain particular concepts or ideas crucial to comprehending the document, while deleting paragraphs or chapters in their entirety is usually because the information they provide is not crucial for comprehending the main idea of the document.

A.1 Modifying the Information Content of Simplification Instances

We would like to propose a clear definition of how the information content of a text is modified during the process of simplification. For this, we define the *explicit* information content of a text as being the information that is encoded by the exact words of the text. Each text, in addition to the information explicitly stated by words used in the text, also encodcs *implicit* information about those words and the subjects they describe. This includes assumed

[25] This passage is written on purpose in a convoluted order, to demonstrate to the reader the importance of order to text comprehension.

[26] As stated in the main paper, we focus mainly on the SI operations, and less on the document level operations. We still state them here to present a complete picture.

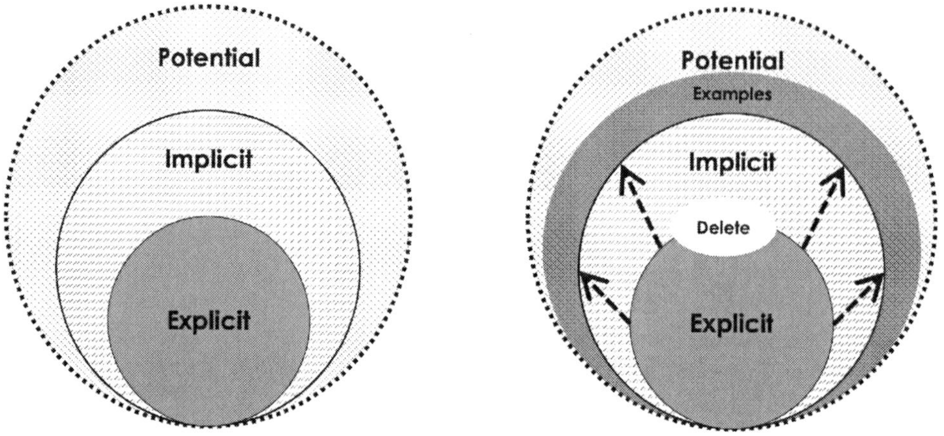

(a) Source (b) Target

Figure 3: Diagrams showing the transformation of *Information Content* between the Source and Target in a simplification instance.

prior knowledge related to the subject of the text or the use of phrases in it, references to other parts of the text, understanding the logic and reasoning behind the information described in the text, and more. The *potentially relevant* information can be defined as all the potential utterances that describe information and knowledge that can be relevant to a particular text. This information is not explicitly stated in the source or needs to be implied to understand it, and if the information appears in the target, the decision to include the particular utterance can't be uniquely predicted given the source. In essence, *potentially relevant* is net new information that can appear in the target. For CS, this happens mainly in the form of Example Generations, and the particular example chosen for a given simplification could easily be switched with other examples.

Using these three types of information content, we can better define the process of CS, and the distinctions between the simplification operations of **Adding Information**, **Explicitation**, and **Deleting Information**.

We can formulate the process of CS as minimizing the distance between the explicit and implicit information content of a text *as much as possible*, while removing redundant or surplus information and adding relevant novel examples, all in the goal of making the text more comprehensible to people with cognitive disabilities. This is juxtaposed with TS, in which the distance between explicit and implicit information content is minimized, but not to the maximal degree.

B Special Token Identification

Each of the operations described in Appendix A can be potentially identified using multiple different methods. In this appendix we describe how we identified each operation and sub-operation in order to prepend the relevant special token as seen in Figure 1.

For the scope of this work, we chose to use deterministic heuristics that can be applied automatically. Although they create noisy classifications, we chose the heuristics such that hey have an emphasis on Precision rather than Recall, and so we find them sufficient for our work.

Most of the operations below are analyzed in the context of simplification instances, and we describe in input as the "source" and simplification as the "target". These will be mathematically noted as S and T respectively when relevant.

The full code that we used to identify these operations is available on GitHub.

1. **Proximation**: All of these operations are tested on a word by word basis using the Universal Dependency parse trees of the source and the target.
   (a) *Change of person point of view*: We check if there was a change in person POV from 3rd to 2nd, 3rd to 1st, or 2nd to 1st.
   (b) *Modify verb tense*: We check if the verbs in the target are in a different tense than the matching verbs in the source.
   (c) *Passive-Active Substitution*: We check if

there exist any passive verbs in the source that share meaning with active verbs in the target.

Any SI that has a Proximation operations was prepended with the token <PROX>.

2. **Rephrasing**: A rephrasing operation will follow the format of replacing one or more words from the source with one or more words with similar meaning in the target. Thus, to identify a rephrasing, we tested every word in the source sentence that did not appear in the target against known paraphrase databases for the relevant language (such as SPPDB (Pavlick and Callison-Burch, 2016) for English) to see if one of their relevant paraphrases appears in the target.

   Phrasing this mathematically, for every word $w \in S \setminus T$, we check if $pp(w) \subset T$, where $pp(w)$ is the result of applying a rule from a paraphrase database on w.

   (a) *Simple synonym*: These operations are defined when one word is paraphrased to another single word.

   (b) *Paraphrasing*

      i. *Word-to-Phrase*: Similar to simple synonym, only a single word is paraphrased into a series of words.

      ii. *Phrase-to-Word*: A phrase is converted to a single word. This is discovered by checking all possible combinations of consecutive words in the source that did not appear in the target for possible paraphrases.

      iii. *Phrase-to-Phrase*: Similar to Phrase-to-Word, when the paraphrase rule is to another phrase instead of a single word.

   Any SI that has a Rephrasing operation was prepended with the token <REPHRASE>.

3. **Deleting Information**: Any words in the source that doesn't appear in the target designate a Deleting Information operation. We discern between Removal and Summarization mainly according to the alignment type. Precisely discerning between the two operations for other alignments types is a more complicated task that cannot be resolved by a simple heuristic, and as such we leave it for future research. For our analysis' purpose, whenever the token length ratio (Martin et al., 2020a) between source and target was greater 1.2 than $(|S|/|T| >= 1.2)$, or that the percentage of deleted words from the source (i.e., that were removed in the target and were not part of another operation such as Rephrasing) was higher than 30% and the token length ratio was > 1, we classified it as a Deleting Information operation.

   (a) *Removal*: If the sentence alignment type of the SI is M-to-0, we count the operation as *Removal*.

   (b) *Summarization*: If the sentence alignment type is M-to-1, we count the operation as *Summarization*.

   Any SI that has a Deleting Information operation was prepended with the token <DEL>.

4. **Adding Information**: To discover if an action was of Adding Information, we check if there are new words in the target, that aren't part of another modification (such as Rephrasing or Passive-Active Substitution) or are function words. Once such words exists, we assume that there is additional explicit information in the target that did not appear in the source. We then test if it is Example Generation or Explanation Generation (see below), and if it is neither, similar to the general classification in Deleting information, if the token length rations between source and target is < 1 (target is longer), we classify as Adding Information.

   (a) *Example Generation*: If the new words are part of a clause that starts with indicative phrases for providing examples (such as "e.g.", "for example", "such as", and more) we classify this operation as *Example Generation*. This is the only case where we would prepend the SI with the token <EXAMPLE>.

   Any SI that satisfied the token length ratio $<$ 1 was prepended with the token <ADD>.

5. **Explicitation**: From a modeling perspective, we grouped Pronoun Explicitation and Explanation Generation together, since their purpose is similar – reducing ambiguity in the source that is related to the implicit information and assumptions. However, from a classi-

Task	Train	Model	SARI	ADD	KEEP	DELETE	BLEU	% Ident.
TS	Manual	T5Large	33.03	2.41	61.78	34.91	0.916	48.75%
		T5Large+Classifier	31.78	2.34	61.27	31.71	0.909	57.66%
		T5Base	30.41	1.77	62.03	27.42	0.920	56.55%
		T5Base+Classifier	30.48	1.87	62.35	27.21	0.920	62.12%
		BART-Large	32.27	2.85	61.27	32.69	0.888	55.43%
		BART-Large+Classifier	**37.66**	**3.87**	59.93	**49.19**	0.842	31.75%
		BART-Base	31.97	1.76	61.83	32.31	0.914	55.15%
		BART-Base+Classifier	32.65	2.45	61.63	33.87	0.876	54.31%
CS	Manual	T5Large	21.10	1.43	41.98	19.91	0.234	69.16%
		T5Large+Classifier	22.43	1.21	42.78	23.30	0.235	72.27%
		T5Base	20.14	1.69	42.35	16.38	0.243	72.90%
		T5Base+Classifier	20.21	0.89	42.26	17.47	0.239	78.82%
		BART-Large	21.42	1.61	42.28	20.39	0.238	75.08%
		BART-Large+Classifier	**26.47**	**2.34**	42.13	**34.94**	0.219	60.12%
		BART-Base	23.48	2.27	42.88	25.29	0.24	72.27%
		BART-Base+Classifier	24.22	2.26	43.52	26.87	0.242	73.52%

Table 3: Results for all models fine-tuned on the Manual dataset (see Appendix C). Metrics include SARI, the percentage of identical generations (% Identical). We also report BLEU for completeness (see text). Highest SARI scores for each fine-tuning setting are **boldfaced**.

fication perspective, each is discovered differently.

(a) *Pronoun Explicitation*: We use a co-reference resolution (CRR) model (Coreferee from Spacy[27]), applied to the concatenated source and target. If the CRR model finds explicit references in the target to pronouns in the source, we classify as Pronoun Explicitation. This is the only case where we would prepend the SI with the token <EXPLICIT>.

(b) *Explanation Generation*: We identify this operation together with Adding Information, since heuristically they can appear very similar. If new words in the target aren't tied to an example, or are tied to a noun phrase in the source that is part of one or more sentences in the target, we assume that this is a form of Explanation. Discerning between the different types of explanation generations is a task for future research, but we list them here for indexing purposes.

    i. For term/phrase
    ii. For logic/reasoning
    iii. For background information

Any SI that was identified containing Explanation Generation <EXPLAIN>.

6. **Intra-Sentence Rearrangement**: This operation is identified when the information order in a text is changed. We use the Universal Dependency parse trees of the source and target to discover rearrangements.

(a) *Clause Reordering*: If the clauses in the target appear in a different order than in the source, then this is a *Clause Reordering* operation.

(b) *SVO* Reordering: For each sentence in the source, we check if the order of subject, verb, and object are maintained in the target. If not, then this is an *SVO Reordering*.

Any SI that has an Intra-Sentence Rearrangement operation was prepended with the token <REORDER>.

7. **Operations on Sentences**: These operations are checked on a sub-document level, as compared to a simplification instance level.

(a) *Sentence Splitting*: This operation is assumed to appear by default in SIs with sentence alignment type of 1-to-N. Any such SI was prepended with the <SPLIT> token.

(b) *Sentence Rearrangement*: Part of the manual alignment process, the original ordering of sentences in the source sub-document and be compared to the order of the original sentences according to their alignment to the target sub-document. So, if the source sub-document consists of sentence $[s_1, s_2, s_3, ..., s_n]$ and their align-

[27]https://spacy.io/universe/project/coreferee

ment to the target sub-document sentences is some permutation of their indexes I, such that the source sentences ordered by the target's order is $[s_{i_1}, s_{i_2}, ..., s_{i_n}]$, we look for the longest increase sub-sequence in this permutation $L \subset I$. Any sentence indexed by $i_j \notin L$ is a Sentence Rearrangement. From an SI perspective, a similar analysis was done for *Clause Reordering*, in order to discover to which SIs to prepend the <REORDER> token.

8. **Document Level Operations**: We list here the Document Level Operations, but for our analysis we only focused on identifying Adding/Deleting Paragraphs and Subdocuments, which were respectively classified as Adding/Deleting Information. In addition, as part of our reordering analysis, we were able to discover Cross-Paragraph Sentence Reordering if they occurred in the same Sub-Document.
   (a) Paragraph Splitting
   (b) Cross-Paragraph Sentence Reordering
   (c) Paragraph Rearrangement
   (d) Sub-Document Rearrangement
   (e) Adding Paragraphs
   (f) Adding Sub-Documents
   (g) Deleting Paragraphs
   (h) Deleting Sub-Documents

C Experiment and Results on the Manually-aligned Dataset

In this section, we describe the experimental setting and results for training TS models on a manually aligned dataset. We do so for completeness, since manually aligned datasets can potentially capture more complex relationships between source and target sentences than automatic alignments can, and the test dataset in CS is manually aligned. We report results for this series of experiments in an appendix, since no prior work used these datasets to train TS models.

The Manual dataset is created by combining WikiManual and Newsela Manual from Jiang et al. (2020). Jiang et al. (2020) used WikiManual and NewselaManual to train their NeuralCRF sentence alignment models for the WikiLarge and Newsela corpora, respectively. In addition, we use these datasets as other comparison points between TS and CS data presented in §8.

With respect to SI counts, for the Manual dataset we use 1522/280 SIs from WikiManual and 11728/1418 SIs from NewselaManual to create combined training and validation sets of 11728/1418 SIs respectively. Although both WikiManual and NewselaManual contain tests sets that Jiang et al. (2020) used to test their CRF models, we use other datasets as the tests sets for our experiments (see §6.2).

We should note, that there are more SIs in the original datasets than the number of SIs we used for fine-tuning. This difference is because the missing SIs are either complete deletions (sentences from the source that are removed in the simplification) or complete additions (sentences in the simplification with no source). See Table 6 in Appendix I for additional details regarding SI counts in each corpus.

Results. When trained in this setting, which uses a considerably smaller albeit cleaner dataset, we notice two phenomena when compared to the results in §7 when tested on TS. First, for all models except T5Large, the +Classifier variant still outperforms the baseline model, though by a smaller margin than in the classic training setting. Second, model size now has a consistent trend, with larger models outperforming their matching smaller counterparts. Further work is required to ascertain this different pattern of performance on this setting. In general, the best TS performance on SARI is achieved by the BART-Large+Classifier variant in this training setting, repeating the performance in §7.

Examining the performance on CS, we find that the +Classifier variants achieved superior results for all model architectures and sizes in this training setting as well. Unlike the results presented in §7, here the difference in SARI scores is more pronounced for larger models, with differences of more than 1.3 SARI points for both large model architectures, while the differences in the base-sized models is under 0.8 SARI points. The model with the highest performance difference in this training setting is BART-Large+Classifier, with a difference of 5.05 SARI points on CS data, while in §7 this was the T5Base+Classifier model.

In both evaluation settings, the best performing model is still BART-Large+Classifier, similar to the results in §7.

Discussion. The results shown here further demonstrates the potential benefit of adding inductive bias towards simplification operations to a TS trained model. Potential future research could also look into performances of different models when trained on datasets of different sizes and quality, since many language lack resources for automatic text simplification, let alone cognitive simplification.

D SARI Calculation

The main metric used for evaluating TS models is SARI (Xu et al., 2016), which is computed based on three token-level operations: ADD, KEEP, and DELETE. Precision and Recall are computed for each with respect to n-grams for $n = 1 \ldots 4$, and averaged together to yield overall Precision and Recall scores per operation. SARI is defined as:

$$SARI = \frac{\text{F1}_{ADD} + \text{F1}_{KEEP} + \text{P}_{DELETE}}{3} \quad (1)$$

E Model Training times

Train Dataset	Model Size	Train Time
WikiAuto	T5-Large	7 days
	T5-Base	4 days
	BART-Large	5 days
	BART-Base	2 days
Manual	T5-Large	1 day
	T5-Base	12 hours
	BART-Large	20 hours
	BART-Base	11 hours

Table 4: Approximate training times on a single GPU for our models trained in §6 and Appendix C.

F Comparing automatic identification of simplification operation to human annotations

We asked a human annotator to manually assign simplification operations to 50 random SI from the WikiAuto training set. Below are the particular Precision, Recall, and F1 scores for each operation on that subset, using the human annotations as ground-truth.

G Simplification Instance Counts

Table 6 contains the details regarding the counts of SIs in each dataset, as used to fine-tune our models

Operation	P.	R.	F1	#
<PROX>	0	0	0	0
<REPHRASE>	80.43	97.37	88.1	38
<DEL>	80	84.21	82.05	19
<ADD>	12.5	50	20	2
<EXAMPLE>	0	0	0	0
<EXPLAIN>	0	0	0	0
<EXPLICIT>	42.86	42.86	42.86	7
<REORDER>	32.43	1	48.98	12
<SPLIT>	1	1	1	13

Table 5: Precision, Recall, and F1 scores for each operation token, when comparing our automatic identification rules to a human annotator. We also describe the number of SI with each operation in the random sample analyzed, and the expected number SI.

in §6, and the full dataset, including deletions of complete sentences from the source and additions complete sentences to the target.

Dataset	Fine-Tuning	Full Corpus
FA	- / - / 321	- / - / 380
NewM	11.7K / 1.4K / 3.6K	17.8K / 2.6K / 5.1K
WikiM	1.5K / 280 / 531	29.9K / 4.4K / 7.9K
ASSET	- / 2K / 359	- / 2K / 359
WikiA	483K / 20K / -	483K / 20K / -

Table 6: Number of SIs used for fine-tuning our models in §7 and Appendix C as compared to the number of SIs in the respective full corpus. The differences are because in the fine-tuning setting we ignored complete deletions of sentences from the source and complete additions of sentences to the target. For each dataset and each setting, the number of SIs are for the train / valid / test sets respectively. We shorten dataset names as follows: FA=FestAbility, NewM=NewselaManual, WikiM/A=WikiManual/Auto.

H Simplification Operations per Dataset

In this appendix, we present the results of 3 key point of information regarding the use of simplification operations in the TS and CS datasets. First, we show the distribution of each simplification operations per dataset (Figure 5). Then, we show the histograms of the number of simplification operations used in each SI (Figure 6). Finally, we present the correlation matrices for each dataset used in our analysis in §8 (Figure 7).

I Full Corpora Analysis

In the main paper §8, we analyzed simplification operations in the datasets as they were used to train our models. However, each dataset also has SIs that are complete deletions (whole sentences in

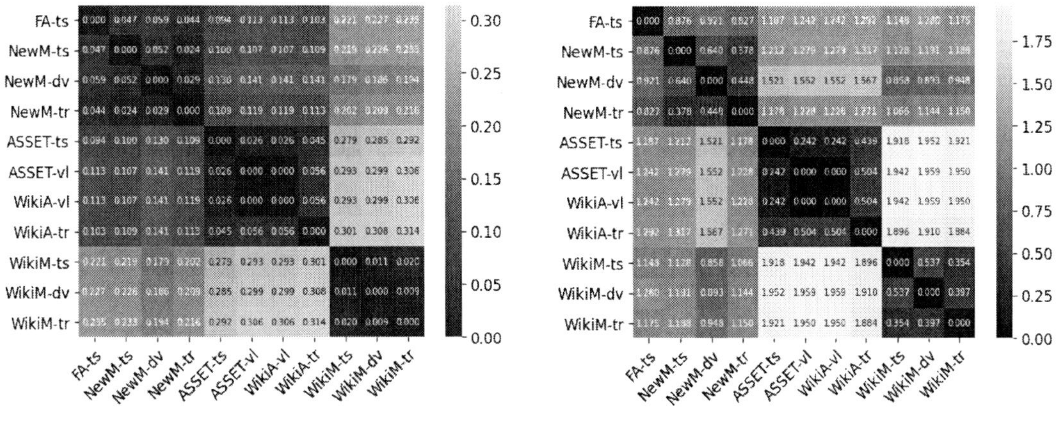

(a) $\overline{JSD}$ distances between distributions

(b) ℓ_2 distances between correlation matrices

Figure 4: Heatmaps of the distances between dataset sub-sets. We abbreviate sub-set names such that FA=FestAbility, NewM=NewselaManual, WikiM/A=WikiManual/Auto. The final two letters signify ts=test, vl=valid, dv=dev, and tr=train sets. For each sub-set pair, we report the numerical distance in the matching cell.

the source that don't have matching sentence(s) in the target) or complete additions (sentences in the target with no matching source sentence(s)). In figure Figure 4 we present the results of the same analysis but for the full dataset.

When analyzing the full datasets, similar patterns to §8 emerge. Sub-sets of the same dataset are still clustered together, although now the in-cluster distance is $\overline{JSD} < 0.06$ and between clusters distance is $\overline{JSD} > 0.09$. Moreover, if considering clusters to have $\overline{JSD} < 0.04$ like in the main paper, then the similar relationships between sub-sets described in the main paper emerge – FestAbility is clustered with itself, ASSET and WikiAuto validation are clustered, and WikiManual is also clustered, and WikiAuto train is separated from the ASSET and WikiAuto validation cluster and the WikiManual cluster. However, there are some differences – NewselaManual development is not clustered with the other NewselaManual sub-sets if considering clusters to have $\overline{JSD} < 0.04$, and WikiAuto train is not closer to the WikiManual cluster than to the ASSET and WikiAuto validation cluster.

These results strengthen our findings from the main paper that the simplification operations are used similarly in CS and TS. They also emphasize the differences between the Newsela corpus and the WikiLarge corpus, as highlighted by Xu et al. (2015). The difference between WikiManual and all the other datasets is the prevalence for "full deletions" in WikiManual, which shows that the relationship between English Wikipedia and Simple English Wikipedia contains many more cases of Information Deletion than other corpora.

In addition, the distances between the operation correlation matrices show that the difference in joint application of simplification operations between CS and TS is similar when considering the full datasets, as the distances between FestAbility and the other sub-sets are maintained (changing by at most ± 0.26, while the other distances outside of clusters increase more).

J Example Simplifications

Shown in Table 7 and Table 8 below.

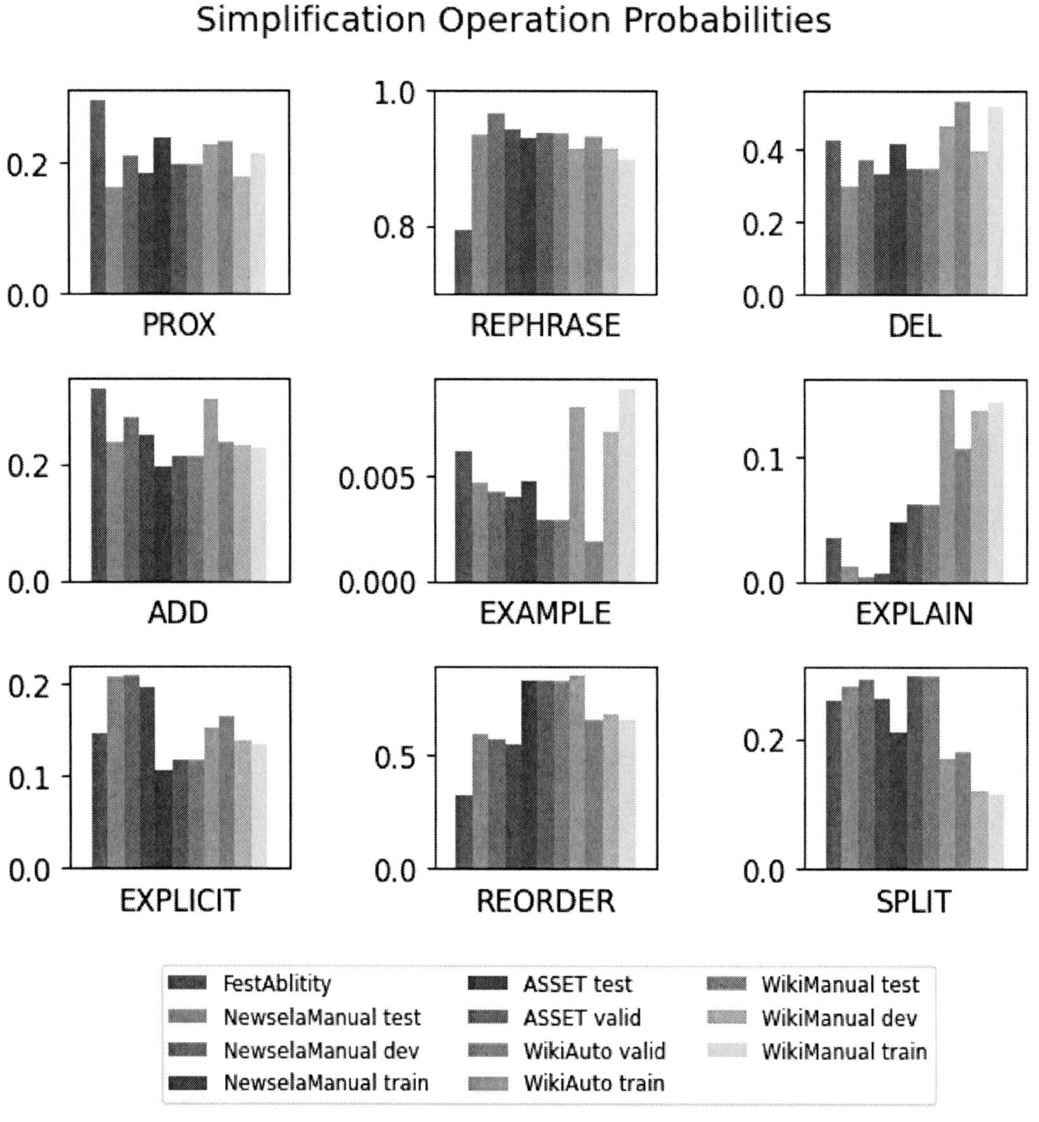

Figure 5: Probabilities each simplification operation is used in every dataset sub-set

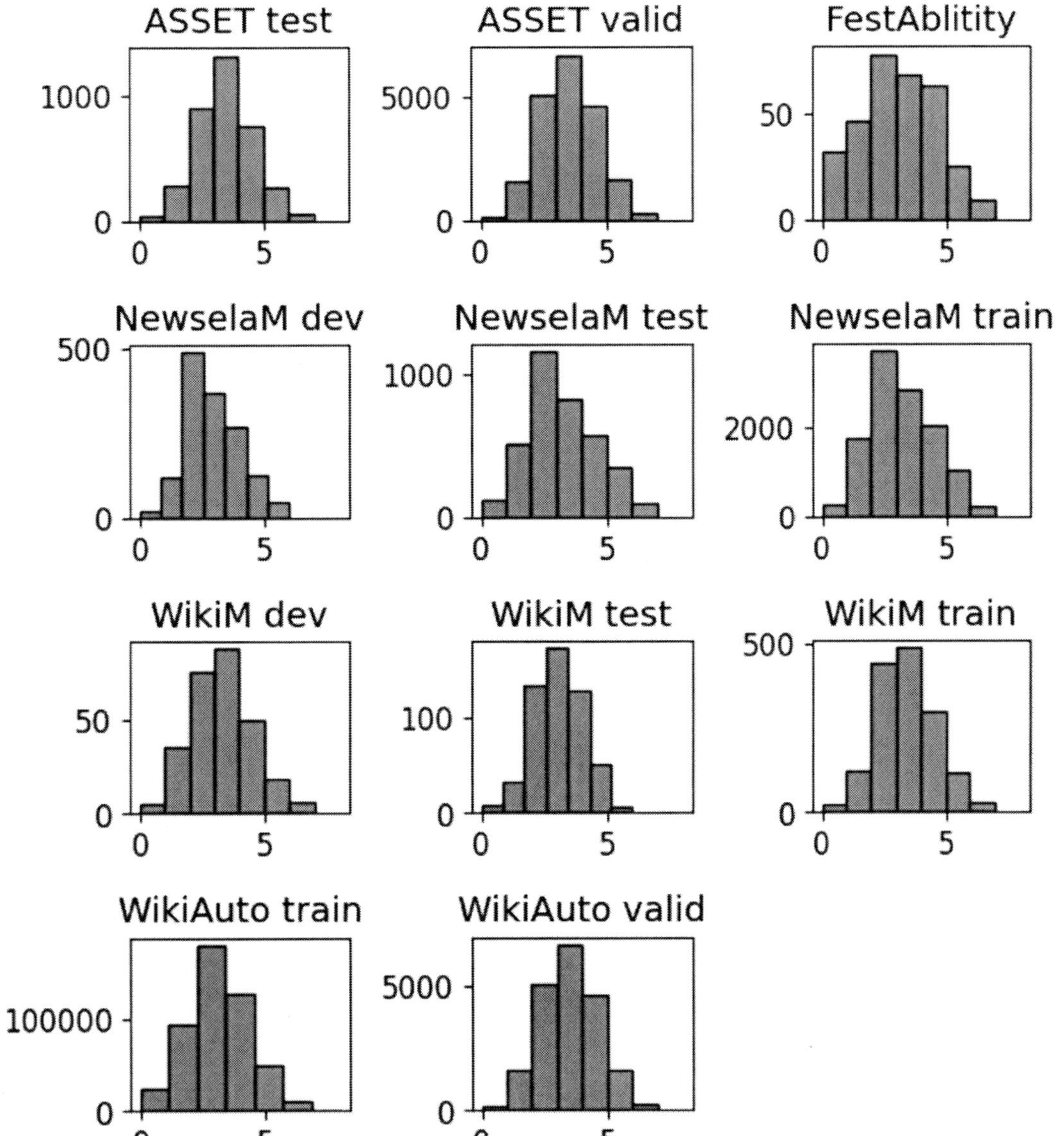

Figure 6: Histograms of the number of simplification operations used in each SI for each dataset sub-set.

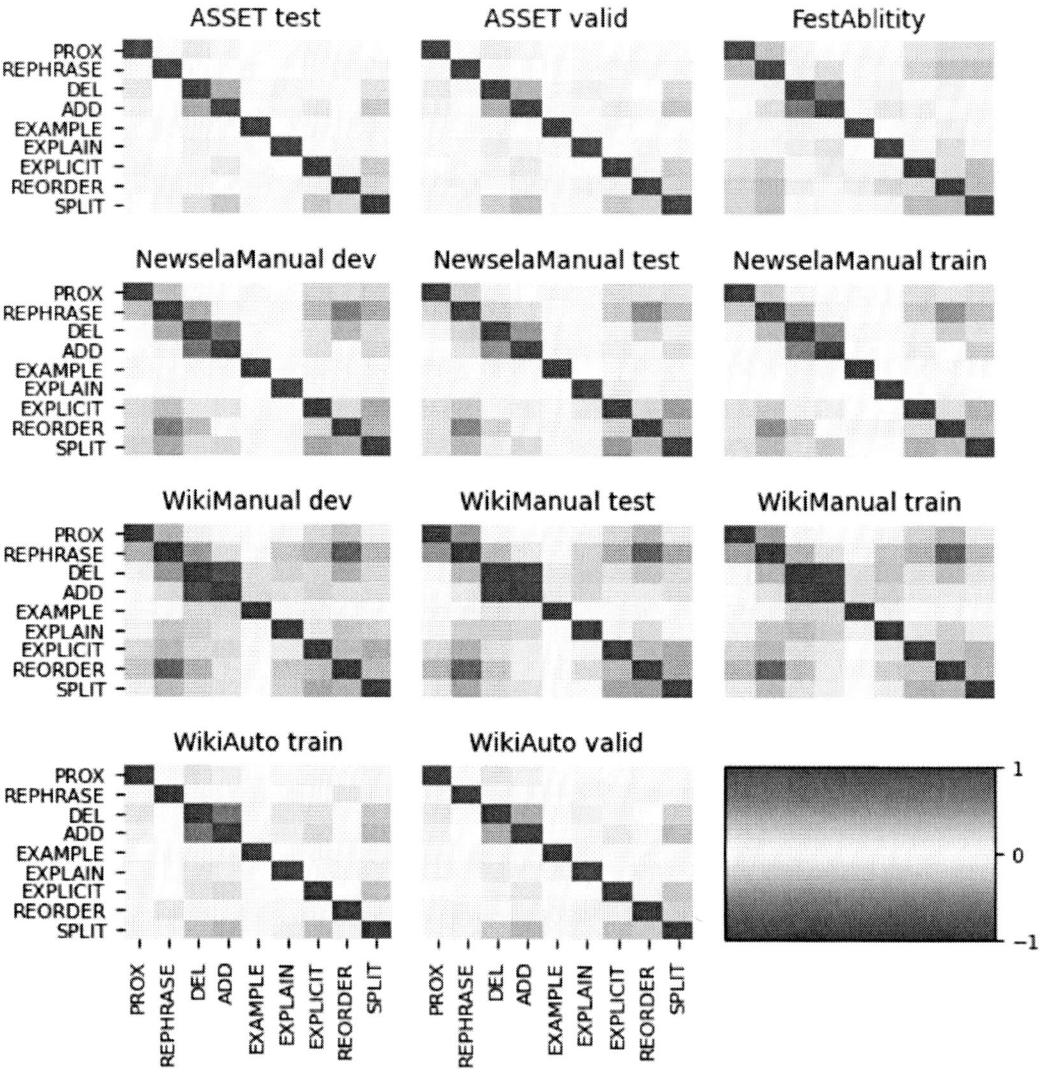

Figure 7: The simplification operations correlations matrices for each dataset subset presented as heatmaps.

Source:	Jeddah is the **principal** gateway to Mecca, Islam's holiest city, *which able-bodied Muslims are required to visit at least once in their lifetime.*
Simplification:	Jeddah is the **main** gateway to Mecca, Islam's holiest city.
Source:	However, the BZ differs a bit *in comparison* to the Freedom Party, as is in favor of a referendum about the Lisbon Treaty but against an EU-Withdrawal.
Simplification:	However, the BZ differs a bit from the Freedom Party**. The BZ** is in favor of a referendum about the Lisbon Treaty but against an EU-Withdrawal.
Source:	Many species had **vanished** by the end of the nineteenth century*, with European settlement.*
Simplification:	Many species had **disappeared** by the end of the nineteenth century.
Source:	**Fearing that Drek will destroy the galaxy, Clank asks Ratchet** to help him find the famous superhero Captain Qwark, *in an effort to stop Drek.*
Simplification:	**Clank fears that Drek will destroy the galaxy. He asks Ratchet** to help him find the famous superhero Captain Qwark.

Table 7: Example Simplifications from ASSET of the T5-Base Classifier model fine-tuned on the WikiAuto dataset. Differences between the source and Simplification are bolded and italicized per example.

Source:	Know that there are absentee ballot options available, *and there may be other options available depending on what situation we find ourselves in.*
Simplification:	There are **many** options for absentee ballots.
Reference:	You should know if you could vote from home. You should check if there are other ways of voting this year because of covid-19.
Source:	Zazel O'Garra**, founder** and artistic director of ZCO Dance Project, *is a force to be reckoned with.*
Simplification:	Zazel O'Garra **is the founder** and artistic director of ZCO Dance Project.
Reference:	Zazel O'Garra is the founder and artistic director of ZCO Dance Project. She is a very strong and important woman.
Source:	*I was diagnosed at the age of five* and completely stopped walking when I was 12 years old.
Simplification:	I stopped walking when I was 12 years old.
Reference:	It started when I was five years old. I stopped walking when I was 12 years old.
Source:	*And in trying to get towards where I really wanted to be in life*, I really thought about giving back and being of service to someone else.
Simplification:	I really thought about giving back and being of service to someone else.
Reference:	I thought about what I really wanted to do. I wanted to help other people.

Table 8: Example simplifications from FestAbility Transcripts of the T5-Base Classifier model fine-tuned on the WikiAuto dataset. Differences between the source and simplification are bold-faced and italicized, per example. We add the CS reference for each example as well to highlight where the model succeeds and fails in the task.

On Language Spaces, Scales and Cross-Lingual Transfer of UD Parsers

Tanja Samardžić[1] Ximena Gutierrez-Vasques[1] Rob van der Goot[2]

Max Müller-Eberstein[2] Olga Pelloni[1] Barbara Plank[2,3]

[1] Text Group, URPP Language and Space, University of Zurich, Switzerland
[2] Department of Computer Science, IT University of Copenhagen, Denmark
[3] Center for Information and Language Processing, LMU Munich, Germany
{tanja.samardzic, ximena.gutierrezvasques, olga.pelloni}@uzh.ch
{robv, mamy}@itu.dk
b.plank@lmu.de

Abstract

Cross-lingual transfer of parsing models has been shown to work well for several closely-related languages, but predicting the success in other cases remains hard. Our study is a comprehensive analysis of the impact of linguistic distance on the transfer of Universal Dependencies (UD) parsers. As an alternative to syntactic typological distances extracted from URIEL, we propose three text-based feature spaces and show that they can be more precise predictors, especially on a more local scale, when only shorter distances are taken into account. Our analysis also reveals that the good coverage in typological databases is not among the factors that explain good transfer.[1]

1 Introduction

The goal of cross-lingual parsing is to process a target language as well as possible by exploiting training data available from (an)other language(s). While we know that parsing models can be transferred well across some well-known closely related languages (de Lhoneux et al., 2018), the success of cross-lingual transfer in all other cases remains hard to predict. Surprising cases of syntactic transfer between unrelated languages such as Irish and Indonesian (Lynn et al., 2014) illustrate well this unpredictability.

A possible explanation for such cases is that genealogically unrelated languages can still be similar enough to allow transfer. But what is the relevant measure of language similarity in such cases? One possible solution is to rely on language features stored in typological databases such as WALS (Dryer and Haspelmath, 2013; Comrie et al., 2013) or Glottolog (Hammarström et al., 2018). Taking these features as vector representations, languages can be embedded and compared regardless of their genealogical relations. A popular library URIEL (Littell et al., 2017) has facilitated the use of typological features to measure similarity between languages at different levels (phonology, syntax, geographical distribution). The problem with this solution is that the information in linguistic databases is often incomplete and unevenly distributed. Some languages are fully described, while only a few feature values are known for others (Ponti et al., 2019). Nevertheless, a study by Lauscher et al. (2020) on transferring models from English to several other languages suggests that the URIEL language similarity score is a good predictor of cross-lingual transfer for parsing Universal Dependencies (UD).

Our study brings a comprehensive analysis of the relationship between language similarity and the cross-lingual transfer in UD parsing. It extends previous work in two directions: first, we cover many more languages than any previous study (which are typically limited to a small set); second, we compare the URIEL representation with three text-based alternatives. These extensions allow us to ask new questions such as: What should we do for languages that do not have close relatives? Do measures of language similarity predict the transfer at any scale (for close and for distant languages)? Are there good alternatives to linguistic databases for measuring language similarity? We perform correlation tests between linguistic distances and parsing scores on various samples of UD treebanks designed to neutralize two kinds of biases. First, we balance the samples at the level of language, genus, and family,[2] reducing gradually the known bias of the UD towards Indo-European languages. Second,

[1] The analysis notebooks are available at https://github.com/MorphDiv/transfer-lang.

[2] Genus and family are two levels of language genealogy commonly used to group languages of the world. A list of families and genera can be found at https://wals.info/languoid/genealogy.

Proceedings of the 26th Conference on Computational Natural Language Learning (CoNLL), pages 266 - 281
December 7-8, 2022

we investigate the impact of the scale by comparing global correlations (considering a whole language space) with local correlations (considering smaller partitions of a language space).

We show that typological distances extracted from URIEL are reasonably good global predictors, while text-based distances are better local predictors. A surprising outcome of our analysis concerns the uneven coverage of languages in typological databases: most of the UD languages with many missing features are Indo-European. On the other hand, good database coverage does not guarantee good predictability of transfer for the languages outside of the Indo-European family.

2 Related Work

Thanks to evident structural alignments between languages the possibility of transferring syntactic parsing models across languages was investigated even before the wide-spread adoption of pre-trained language models in NLP (McDonald et al., 2006; Zeman and Resnik, 2008). However, this task proved non-trivial because such clear alignments tend to be found in similar languages, but are much rarer overall (Seeker and Kuhn, 2013; Goldberg and Elhadad, 2013).

The idea of using data from another language or a set of languages to improve syntactic parsing on any given language is tempting because annotated data is not available for the majority of the world's languages. Early work typically focused on several languages selected according to the availability of training data. In the meantime, the Universal Dependencies (UD) treebanks have become available for many different languages (Zeman et al., 2021)[3] opening the question of what language pairs are most suitable for model transfer. Most of the time, polyglot[4] models are trained on multiple languages, but preserving the identity of the languages (by adding the language ID to the text representation) turns out useful (Ammar et al., 2016). Smith et al. (2018) cluster languages according to similarity before training polyglot models. Cross-lingual parameter sharing is found to improve the performance overall, but especially for closely-related languages, which can share parameters in different layers of neural representation (de Lhoneux et al., 2018; van der Goot and de Lhoneux, 2021).

[3]http://universaldependencies.org

[4]We here used the term *polyglot* model (Mulcaire et al., 2019) most often also referred to as *multilingual* model.

Cross-lingual transfer started being explored in other tasks too after the introduction of large pre-trained models (Pires et al., 2019), making the question of linguistic similarity relevant to a more general scope of NLP research. Lin et al. (2019) propose a range of measures that can be used in order to choose the best transfer language, which they divide into data-dependent (data size, token overlap, TTR) and data independent (various distance measures extracted from the URIEL database). Lauscher et al. (2020) study how well different similarity scores predict the success of the transfer on different tasks (with mBERT and XLM-R as pretrained models) and find that syntactic features extracted from URIEL correlate strongly with the zero-shot cross-lingual UD parsing performance. Interestingly, these features are better predictors than genealogical relatedness, but data-dependent measures, such as the size of the training data, seem to predict better the cross-lingual zero-shot performance on other tasks such as XQuAD (Artetxe et al., 2020; Rajpurkar et al., 2016) or XNLI (Conneau et al., 2018; Bowman et al., 2015; Williams et al., 2018). While English turns out to be a good transfer language for many tasks due to the size of the training data, Turc et al. (2021) show that German is a better transfer language than English for quite a few, even less-related, languages. The fact that English is not the best transfer language on the task of part-of-speech (POS) tagging is confirmed by the most wide-scope study of cross-lingual transfer up to now (de Vries et al., 2022). Similarly to Lauscher et al. (2020), this study too finds that a surface string similarity measure (LDND distance, Wichmann et al. (2010)) is a better predictor of the transfer than genealogical relatedness. Somewhat contrary to this, Kudugunta et al. (2019) find an interesting genealogical clustering in the representations created by machine translation models.

Having counted mentions of successful cross-lingual transfer on many different tasks in the previous works (Ruder et al., 2021; Turc et al., 2021; Vázquez et al., 2021; Hu et al., 2020; Lauscher et al., 2020; Lin et al., 2019; Paul et al., 2013), we notice that English is most frequently mentioned as the best transfer language overall, but these mentions are almost entirely related to European target languages. For targets located outside of Europe, the best transfer languages are different and hard to predict. For instance, Greek is a good transfer language for Thai and Hindi, while Russian works well for these two languages and Arabic.

Our study shares the wide cross-lingual scope with de Vries et al. (2022). In contrast to their work, we focus on syntactic parsing models, rather than POS tagging. We follow some other previous studies in working with both typological and text-based language similarity measures, but our text-based measures can be regarded as generic rather than data-dependent and can be used as an alternative to URIEL in many cases.

3 Language Spaces and Similarity: Genealogy, Typology, Text

The most widely accepted method for comparing languages relies on *genealogical* classification: we consider languages located in the same region of a phylogenetic tree to be similar. This method currently prevails in NLP. Practitioners often discuss language similarity in terms of language family (Ponti et al., 2019; Tan et al., 2019; Shaffer, 2021). However, language families can be too broad for a meaningful comparison as they include typologically very different languages. For instance, English and Armenian belong to the same family (Indo-European), but are very different in terms of phoneme inventories, morphology, and word order. On the other hand, languages can be rather similar even if they are genealogically unrelated. For example, Bulgarian is closely related to other Slavic languages, but its morphology, word order and the use of the definite article makes it more similar to English than to other Slavic languages.

Typological features and geographical placement of languages can be regarded as potentially more objective and fine-grained alternatives to genealogical similarity. In other words, genealogically unrelated languages can turn out to be close in a typological vector space or in the geographical (physical) space. It is less common to have an intuitive perception of languages that are close in such spaces as similar, but typological proximity seems to be more useful as a predictor of cross-lingual transfer than genealogical relatedness (see Section 2).

The URIEL database and its associated Python library `lang2vec` (Littell et al., 2017) are very convenient resources for measuring the distance between languages in all of these spaces. URIEL combines features from several linguistic databases: Ethnologue (Lewis et al., 2015), Glottolog, PHOIBLE (Moran et al., 2014), SSWL[5] and WALS. It describes over 4,000 languages, but the available information strongly depends on the types of features. For example, geographic and genealogical feature values are known for all languages, while syntactic feature values, which are relevant to our study, are often missing.

When assessing linguistic similarity with `lang2vec`, one can use various subsets of features and the `knn` prediction option to fill in the missing features, which is what is typically used in previous research. With this option, all feature slots are filled with some predicted value. If a value is missing for some feature, the corresponding value from the most similar language (nearest neighbor) is returned. We work with the union of syntactic features (WALS + SSWL) completed with the `knn` prediction, but we also analyze the coverage of the UD languages in the URIEL sources by extracting the values before the `knn` prediction.

Text-based features can be regarded as a potential alternative to the features extracted from typological databases. Type-token ratio (TTR), for instance, is higher in morphologically rich than in morphologically poor languages and can be used for language comparison when the data size is controlled (Biber, 1988; Tweedie and Baayen, 1998; Bentz et al., 2017). Other text statistics, such as the *mean word length* (MWL) are also characteristic of languages (words are longer in morphologically rich languages), while being even less dependent on the data. In the work on cross-lingual transfer, it is common to consider all text-based measures to be *data-dependent* as opposed to typological measures, which are *data-independent* (Lin et al., 2019).[6] We assume that text-based features can reach various levels of data-independence, while providing a means for measuring language similarity at a more fine-grained level.

In the remainder of this section, we describe two text-based measures that we propose for comparing languages at two structural levels, morphology and syntax. Our morphological measure is more generic than the syntactic measure, which is more data-dependent.

[5] *Syntactic Structures of the World's Languages* by Chris Collins and Richard Kayne

[6] In NLP, data-dependent measures require access to text samples of the languages to estimate similarity statistics, which are viewed as specific to the samples (not easily generalized). In contrast to this, data-independent measures are often derived from data or linguistic observations yet the text sample is not required at estimation time.

3.1 The Language Space of BPE Subword Productivity

Capturing morphological phenomena, this measure departs from the observation that subword tokenization with BPE compresses the text vocabulary in a way that depends on typological properties of languages. Analyzing subword tokens formed in the first few hundred merges (Gutierrez-Vasques et al., 2021), we can distinguish between languages that have productive morphology (e.g. Hungarian), from languages that form words in a more idiosyncratic fashion (e.g. Chinese).

Following this intuition, we describe each language in terms of three features calculated over the tokens formed in the first 200 BPE merges. The first feature, *subword productivity* is the number of word types in which a subword appears. The second feature, *subword frequency* is the cumulative frequency of all word types in which a given subword appears. The third feature, *subword idiosyncrasy* is the ratio between the subword frequency and the subword productivity. A single vector representation for each language is constructed by averaging the values of all subword tokens. The resulting three-dimensional vectors are centered around zero and scaled with respect to the standard deviation. In this way, we construct a new space for comparing languages distinguishing between morphological types such as analytic, synthetic, and polysynthetic languages.

It is noteworthy that this approach does not depend on access to the information extracted from grammars and stored in typological databases. It also does not require any annotation: the scores are extracted directly from a relatively small sample of raw text (e.g. 50,000 words, fixed for our UD samples) in an unsupervised fashion. It thus provides a good alternative to hand-crafted descriptions which are hard to obtain. The drawback of this method is that it captures morphological features, which, despite the known universal trade-offs between syntax and morphology (Sinnemäki, 2010; Ehret and Szmrecsanyi, 2016; Futrell et al., 2015), might not be the most useful features for predicting the transfer of syntax.

3.2 The Language Space of Dependency Probes

To obtain text-based features capturing more precisely syntactic phenomena, we make use of *syntactic probes*, minimal models that can perform the dependency parsing task at hand. In constructing a language space with dependency probes, we build on the DepProbe approach of Müller-Eberstein et al. (2022) and the intuition that linear subspaces capture syntactic information while being much easier to interpret than the parameters of full parsers. Measuring the similarity of these linear subspaces using subspace angles (Knyazev and Argentati, 2002), we can further compare whether dependency structures and relations are represented similarly or dissimilarly across languages — even across unrelated languages not covered by manual typological annotations — which is crucial for cross-lingual transferability.

Conceptually, each probe contains the information on how pre-trained embeddings map to dependency structures. Therefore, similar mappings are expected to indicate similar languages. Comparing these subspaces for the purpose of transferability estimation has shown to be highly predictive (Müller-Eberstein et al., 2022). We rely on the same intuition, but use the probes for a different purpose: instead of predicting the performance of a full parser, which was the main goal for Müller-Eberstein et al. (2022), we see the probes as a sort of language embeddings for comparing different languages. This leads us to extend this initial study to the full set of languages in UD, and to analyze how these data-driven measures relate to linguistically motivated typological information.

There has been debate regarding what constitutes an appropriately parametrized probe (Hewitt and Liang, 2019; Voita and Titov, 2020). We follow the most common linear probing paradigm for dependency parsing by Hewitt and Manning (2019). It can be seen as learning a linear subspace within the existing, pre-trained latent space in which dependency information is particularly salient. For DepProbe specifically, these are the dependency structural subspace A and the dependency relational subspace L, which are respectively learned using the mean square error and cross-entropy loss to the target dependency tree. This approach is intermediary to training a full parser, which is computationally expensive, and manual features such as those from URIEL, which may lack coverage of the specific language variant used in any particular treebank. However, this measure requires at least some syntactically annotated data.

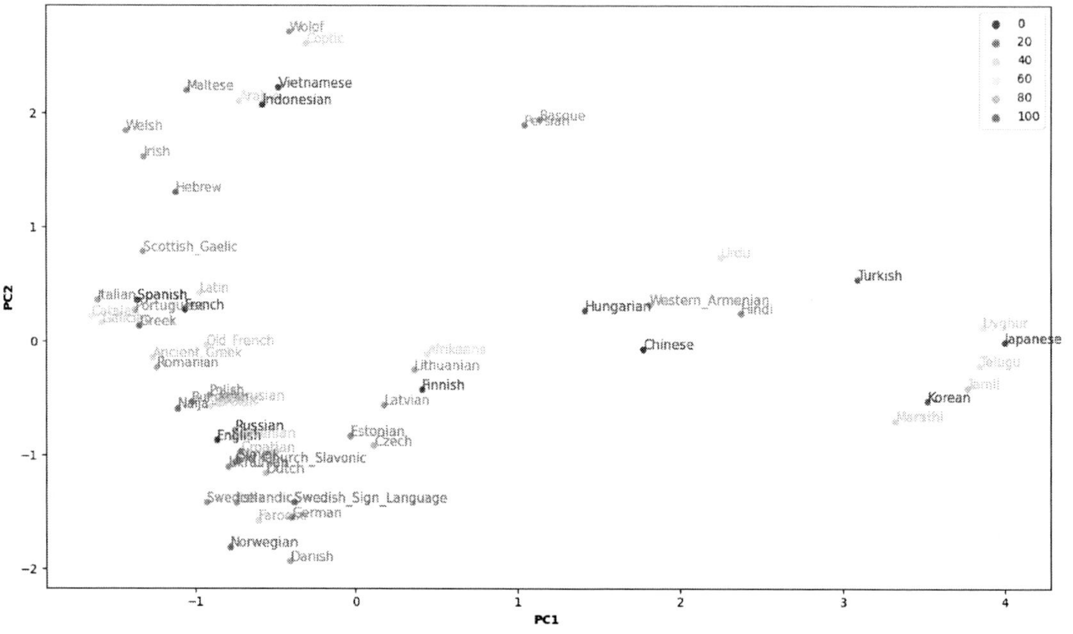

Figure 1: URIEL embeddings (reduced to 2 dimensions using PCA) for 62 UD languages that appear as target languages in our experiments. The color indicates the percentage of missing features in the URIEL sources. Languages with most missing features are located in the densely populated regions.

URIEL	Squared Euclidean distance in the URIEL space using WALS+SSWL syntax features and KNN prediction
probe-A	The distance between dependency probes trained on our UD samples to predict the dependency link (attachment)
probe-L	The distance between dependency probes trained on our UD samples to predict the dependency label
BPE	Squared Euclidean distance in the BPE productivity space constructed from the raw text extracted from our UD samples
MWL	The difference between mean word lengths, estimated on the raw text extracted from our UD samples as the average number of characters per word token in a treebank
MSL	The difference between mean sentence lengths, estimated on the raw text extracted from our UD samples as the average number of word tokens per sentence in a treebank

Table 1: Linguistic distances and baselines as experimental settings. Note: the MWL and MSL differences are, in fact, distances in a monodimensional space.

4 Data and Methods

From the linguistic spaces and measures described in Section 3, we create distance matrices. We then calculate multiple correlation scores between each of the linguistic distance matrices on one side and the scores obtained while testing parsers on a set of languages on the other. For each pair transfer-target language, we have one labeled attachment score (LAS), which we name xLAS in our experiments to underline the fact that these scores are obtained via cross-lingual transfer.[7] We expect higher xLAS scores when linguistic distances are smaller, thus a negative correlation.

In this section, we describe the details of the experimental design and the analyses.

4.1 Data

We carry out all our experiments on the Universal Dependencies V2.9 data (Zeman et al., 2021), and the additional unofficial set of treebanks used in van der Goot et al. (2021). In total our data has 116 languages in 223 treebanks. We removed all multi-word tokens with `ud-conversion-tools`.[8]

[7]We exclude all self-tranfer cases.

[8]Code-switched pairs are considered a new language as specified by the treebank-creators. Arabic-NYUAD and

Since data size has been identified as a factor that has an impact on cross-lingual transfer, controlling for the data size is necessary in order to isolate potential effects of linguistic distances, which are of interest for our study. We fix the training data size to 50,000 tokens for each transfer language. This size is determined as a good balance between the size of the data needed to achieve a reasonable parsing performance and the availability of the data for different languages. We thus use only treebanks with more than 50,000 tokens for training and cap them to the fixed size. This leaves us with 78 treebanks in 47 languages for training. Because we are not attempting to improve the state-of-the-art in this work and we do not tune the parser, we report our scores on the development data. To cover as many language varieties as possible in our analysis, we decided to use the test data set if there is no development set available for a treebank. On the target side, we have 116 treebanks in 62 languages.

4.2 Parser

To investigate how well linguistic distances defined by the three different language spaces (Section 3) predict the cross-lingual transfer of UD models, we perform zero-shot cross-lingual transfer from each of the 78 transfer treebanks to each of the 116 target treebanks (in a one-to-one setting). For this, we use MaChAmp, an NLP toolkit for training and testing models in a transfer-learning framework. This toolkit uses a transformer based language model as encoder, and can employ multiple decoder heads for multiple tasks. In our setup, we use the default UD model, but remove the morphological tagging and lemmatization task, as not all treebanks have annotation for these tasks. We use MaChAmp v0.3 beta (van der Goot et al., 2021) with default settings and mBERT embeddings (Devlin et al., 2019).

We train a single parser for each of the transfer treebanks, and evaluate on all of the target treebanks using the official CoNLL2018 evaluation script (Zeman et al., 2018). We disable early stopping in all experiments, and take the model after the whole training procedure (20 epochs) to avoid overfitting on the development data. Thus, for each target treebank, we test 78 parsers fine-tuned on transfer treebanks, one parser per transfer treebank. This results in a matrix of 78 $\times$ 116 labeled accuracy scores (xLAS). From these scores, we create various samples on which we then calculate correlation scores. For the 78 datasets, we checked the amount of unknown subwords assigned by the tokenizer of mBERT, which were on average only 0.4%. Outliers are Ancient Greek (~6%) and Old East Slavic (~14%). So, the scripts are mostly covered, and altough some languages might be underrepresented (Rust et al., 2021), at least almost all subwords are represented in the vocabulary.

Japanese-BCCWJ are excluded as they are not freely available.

4.3 Stratified sampling: language, genus, family

Recall that the UD data set is biased towards Indo-European languages in two ways. First, it contains many more treebanks in Indo-European languages than in language from any other family (Nivre et al., 2020). Second, for some languages (and those are usually Indo-European), there are multiple treebanks in the data set, while only single treebanks are available for other languages. To deal with the representation biases in the UD data set, we create stratified samples at three levels. Stratified sampling at the level of *language* means that we select one treebank per language; at the level of *genus* one treebank per genus; at the level of *family*, one treebank per family. The representatives of the three categories are selected randomly, but we repeat the tests 30 times to account for the variance in random sampling. We always report mean correlation scores of 30 random selections. The only level that neutralizes the bias towards Indo-European languages is the level of family, but we perform analyses at all the three levels to see how the scores change between them. Also, the analysis of the scales of the linguistic distances (Section 4.4) is performed only at the level of language.

4.4 Scales: global vs. local

When analyzing the effects of linguistic distances on the cross-lingual parsing scores, we distinguish between two scales. In the first case, which we call the *global scale*, we consider the whole spaces, that is all the data points sampled at the level of language regardless of where they are located in a linguistic space. The global scale thus includes both short and long distances. In the second case, called the *local scale*, we partition the linguistic spaces into smaller regions and consider the correlation scores within each region separately. To make the comparison between different spaces more straightforward, we consider only one partition created with the URIEL space and map all the other linguistic measures to this partition. The local scale

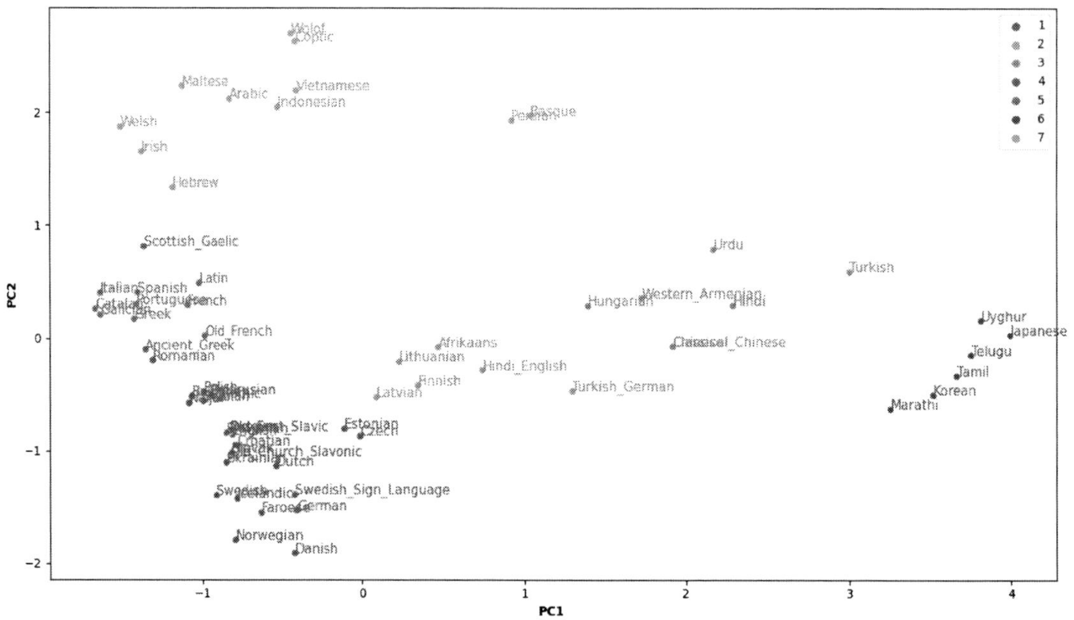

Figure 2: K-means clustering over URIEL embeddings (reduced to 2 dimensions using PCA) for 62 UD languages that appear as target languages in our experiments.

setting thus includes only short distances.

This analysis is motivated by some previous work on the interaction between linguistic variation and geographical phenomena, which has identified potential scale-related limitations. For instance, Jeszenszky et al. (2017) find that traveling times correlate with linguistic distances between Swiss dialects, but the correlation is stronger at shorter distances suggesting a non-linear relationship between the two measures. In other words, traveling times predict linguistic diversity well at short distances, but not so well at longer distances. On the other hand, if a correlation only holds on the global scale, then the observed effect might be driven by (or limited to) a subset of data points, while the rest of the data remains largely unexplained, as pointed out by Moran et al. (2012). Ideally, the correlation scores should not vary depending on the scale and this analysis is expected to show potential limitations of the observed effects.

	Correlation with xLAS		
Linguistic distance	Language level	Genus level	Family level
URIEL	-0.48	-0.39	-0.35
probe-A	**-0.66**	**-0.53**	**-0.50**
probe-L	-0.57	-0.38	-0.32
BPE	-0.39	-0.26	-0.10
MWL	-0.38	-0.36	-0.34
MSL	-0.12	-0.14	-0.16

Table 2: Global Spearman rank correlation between linguistic distance and xLAS scores. The reported values are the means of 30 random selections.

4.5 Correlation settings

In all our correlation tests, the xLAS scores constitute the predicted variable and the linguistic distances are predictors. When calculating global correlations, we distinguish between three xLAS settings, depending on the sampling level: language, genus, family. Local correlations are only calculated in one setting, language, because other levels would give extremely sparse observations. However, we comment on the phenomena related to linguistic diversity in presenting the results.

Table 1 summarizes the settings regarding the linguistic distances. Each of the spaces described in Section 3 is one predictor. In addition to these distances, we perform tests with two kinds of data statistics. We choose MWL as a good representative of text statistics that can be data-independent (see Section 3) and MSL as a representative of data-dependent text statistics.

5 Results

5.1 UD languages in URIEL

Having checked the coverage of the UD languages, we find that more than half of the feature values are missing. We note that missing features are not equally distributed across languages: some languages are well described with over 100 feature values, while for some no syntactic feature values are known. The full list of languages with the counts of missing features is in Appendix A.

To see how the UD languages are distributed in the URIEL space, we create a two-dimensional transformation of the original space with principle component analysis (PCA) and plot in Figure 1 all the languages tested as targets of UD transfer in our experiments (N=62). We color each data point according to the percentage of missing features.

The first thing that can be observed in the plot is a considerable asymmetry in the space density: the most populated area (in the left lower corner) hosts mostly European languages, showing the known bias of the UD data sets. We can also see a considerable covariance between typological, genealogical and geographical factors, which holds only at a very coarse level: Asian languages tend to occupy the right-hand side of the plot, African the upper-left corner. When we zoom in, we see quite a few mismatches between genealogical and syntactic (typological) proximity, especially in the areas outside of the the European corner. For instance, Hungarian and Chinese are rather close in URIEL but they are very far apart in the phylogenetic tree. Interestingly, one such case is the pair Irish-Indonesian mentioned before. Indonesian is an Austronesian language, but it is closer to Irish (which is an Indo-European language) than any other Indo-European language outside of the Celtic group.

Regarding the missing feature values, we notice that all the languages for which more than 50% of feature values are missing are European and their placement with the `knn` prediction is globally correct. At a more fine-grained level, we see some mismatches with what would be expected knowing the properties of languages. For example, Croatian and Serbian are placed rather far apart although they are syntactically identical, genealogically the same language and geographically adjacent. Also, the six languages in the rightmost cluster (Marathi, Korean, Tamil, Telugu, Japanese, Uyghur) come from five different languages families (genealogically distant).

We conclude that the URIEL space represents rather well the knowledge about language similarity globally, but it is rather imprecise at a more fine-grained level.

5.2 Global correlation

Table 2 shows the results of one-to-one correlation tests (one for each predictor). We report the Spearman rank correlation score, which is a non-parametric test best suited for our data. In this setting, we ask how well different linguistic distances predict xLAS scores generally, taking into account the whole spaces. First of all, we can see that the mean sentence (MSL) is the worst predictor despite the fact that its values vary considerably across treebanks. MWL, on the other hand, approaches some of the more elaborated linguistic distances. The values for these two statistics are listed in Appendix B.

The best predictor with solid scores turns out to be `probe-A`, the probe that encodes most of the structural information. This is not very surprising given the fact that the probes are trained to perform lightweight UD parsing. However, it is interesting to see that `probe-A` is a much better predictor than `probe-L` and more consistent across the samples. This means that the representations obtained for a structural task can be regarded as more relevant linguistic features than the representations obtained in a labeling task. The URIEL language space is a reasonably good predictor with moderate scores.[9] The BPE productivity space is close to MWL and sometimes even below it. A reason for this could be the fact that this space captures morphological properties which are not informative enough for predicting xLAS.

All the scores with linguistic distances and MWL decrease with higher sampling levels, which means that the scores at the level of language and genus might still be driven by representation biases in the data. While confirming the expected trends, our results provide a general sense of how big the change is.

5.3 Local correlations

To investigate the impact of the scale on the correlation between linguistic distances and xLAS,

[9]The scores that we observe are considerably lower than what was observed in previous work (Lauscher et al., 2020). This could be due to many reasons since our settings are very different, but it is most likely due to the different sampling approaches.

Linguistic distance	Correlation with xLAS						
	Cluster 1	Cluster 2	Cluster 3	Cluster 4	Cluster 5	Cluster 6	Cluster 7
URIEL	-0.35	-0.14	-0.11	-0.42	-0.54	0.03	0.11
probe-A	**-0.86**	**-0.82**	**-0.63**	**-0.83**	**-0.79**	**-0.11**	-0.34
probe-L	-0.71	-0.51	-0.55	0.80	-0.59	-0.08	-0.35
BPE	-0.55	0.11	-0.30	-0.38	-0.55	-0.01	-0.30
MWL	-0.55	-0.09	-0.45	-0.33	-0.18	**-0.11**	**-0.39**
MSL	-0.80	-0.21	-0.44	0.06	-0.30	0.14	0.31

Table 3: Local Spearman rank correlation between linguistic distance and xLAS scores. Cluster obtained from the URIEL space with k-means.

we measure local correlations within smaller areas. Figure 2 shows the partition of the URIEL space obtained by k-means clustering. The local correlation scores are given in Table 3. Dependency probes are still the best predictors within this scope, but the URIEL space is often below BPE and MWL. An important finding of this analysis is the difference in the correlations between the clusters: the correlations are stronger in clusters 1, 4, and 5, while they are very low in the other clusters (except for MWL in the cluster no. 7). An extreme case is the cluster no. 6, where no measure provides any explanation for the xLAS scores. We note that languages in this cluster come from many different families (6 languages from 5 families). The exceptional linguistic diversity is likely to be the reason for this result, but the exact explanation is still to be found. One possible explanation might be that these languages might be wrongly grouped together due to insufficient or inadequate linguistic descriptions in the linguistic databases. This might lead to overestimating their linguistic proximity, while cross-linguistic parser are struggling with real differences. Overall, predicting xLAS scores seems much more straightforward if the languages in a given sample come from the same language family.

6 Conclusion

In this paper, we have shown that various linguistic features can be good predictors of cross-linguistic transfer of UD parsing models. As an alternative to the typological syntactic features extracted from the URIEL database, we propose several text-based features and show that they are often better predictors. Those that encode syntactic structural information by design (dependency probes) are the strongest predictors, while those that capture morphology (BPE, MWL) are comparable to syntactic features extracted from URIEL, especially on a more local scale. In addition to the distance scales, all the scores are impacted by the genealogical composition of the language samples. Explanations for these findings remain an open question for future work.

Limitations

Focusing on the linguistic distances in this paper, we have not addressed the variation in xLAS scores, that is whether it is easier to predict higher than lower scores. Investigating different cases, we noticed that moderate scores seem to be associated with more noise in the correlation analysis, but this effect would need to be quantified and established in a separate study.

Another limitation of our work concerns potential interaction between the predictors that we studied. It might turn out that a combination of two or more of our predictors in a linear model would provide a better explanation for the xLAS scores than any individual predictor. Since we have introduced two novel measures, our principal goal in this paper was to test them in isolation. We leave the question of potential interactions for future work.

Acknowledgements

This research is supported by the Swiss National Science Foundation (SNSF) grant 176305 and by the Independent Research Fund Denmark (DFF) grant 9063-00077B.

References

Waleed Ammar, George Mulcaire, Miguel Ballesteros, Chris Dyer, and Noah A. Smith. 2016. Many languages, one parser. Transactions of the Association for Computational Linguistics, 4:431–444.

Mikel Artetxe, Sebastian Ruder, and Dani Yogatama. 2020. On the cross-lingual transferability of monolingual representations. In Proceedings of the 58th Annual Meeting of the Association for Computational Linguistics, pages 4623–4637, Online. Association for Computational Linguistics.

Christian Bentz, Dimitrios Alikaniotis, Michael Cysouw, and Ramon Ferrer-i Cancho. 2017. The entropy of words—learnability and expressivity across more than 1000 languages. Entropy, 19(6):275.

Douglas Biber. 1988. Variation across Speech and Writing. Cambridge University Press.

Samuel R. Bowman, Gabor Angeli, Christopher Potts, and Christopher D. Manning. 2015. A large annotated corpus for learning natural language inference. In Proceedings of the 2015 Conference on Empirical Methods in Natural Language Processing, pages 632–642, Lisbon, Portugal. Association for Computational Linguistics.

Bernard Comrie, Matthew S. Dryer, David Gil, and Martin Haspelmath. 2013. Introduction. In Matthew S. Dryer and Martin Haspelmath, editors, The World Atlas of Language Structures Online. Max Planck Institute for Evolutionary Anthropology, Leipzig.

Alexis Conneau, Ruty Rinott, Guillaume Lample, Adina Williams, Samuel Bowman, Holger Schwenk, and Veselin Stoyanov. 2018. XNLI: Evaluating cross-lingual sentence representations. In Proceedings of the 2018 Conference on Empirical Methods in Natural Language Processing, pages 2475–2485, Brussels, Belgium. Association for Computational Linguistics.

Miryam de Lhoneux, Johannes Bjerva, Isabelle Augenstein, and Anders Søgaard. 2018. Parameter sharing between dependency parsers for related languages. In Proceedings of the 2018 Conference on Empirical Methods in Natural Language Processing, pages 4992–4997, Brussels, Belgium. Association for Computational Linguistics.

Wietse de Vries, Martijn Wieling, and Malvina Nissim. 2022. Make the best of cross-lingual transfer: Evidence from POS tagging with over 100 languages. In Proceedings of the 60th Annual Meeting of the Association for Computational Linguistics (Volume 1: Long Papers), pages 7676–7685, Dublin, Ireland. Association for Computational Linguistics.

Jacob Devlin, Ming-Wei Chang, Kenton Lee, and Kristina Toutanova. 2019. BERT: Pre-training of deep bidirectional transformers for language understanding. In Proceedings of the 2019 Conference of the North American Chapter of the Association for Computational Linguistics: Human Language Technologies, Volume 1 (Long and Short Papers), pages 4171–4186, Minneapolis, Minnesota. Association for Computational Linguistics.

Matthew S. Dryer and Martin Haspelmath, editors. 2013. WALS Online. Max Planck Institute for Evolutionary Anthropology, Leipzig.

Katharina Ehret and Benedikt Szmrecsanyi. 2016. An information-theoretic approach to assess linguistic complexity. In Complexity, isolation, and variation, pages 71–94. de Gruyter.

Richard Futrell, Kyle Mahowald, and Edward Gibson. 2015. Quantifying word order freedom in dependency corpora. In Proceedings of the third international conference on dependency linguistics (Depling 2015), pages 91–100.

Yoav Goldberg and Michael Elhadad. 2013. Word segmentation, unknown-word resolution, and morphological agreement in a Hebrew parsing system. Computational Linguistics, 39(1):121–160.

Ximena Gutierrez-Vasques, Christian Bentz, Olga Sozinova, and Tanja Samardzic. 2021. From characters to words: the turning point of BPE merges. In Proceedings of the 16th Conference of the European Chapter of the Association for Computational Linguistics: Main Volume, pages 3454–3468, Online. Association for Computational Linguistics.

Harald Hammarström, Robert Forkel, and Martin Haspelmath. 2018. Glottolog 3.3. Leipzig.

John Hewitt and Percy Liang. 2019. Designing and interpreting probes with control tasks. In Proceedings of the 2019 Conference on Empirical Methods in Natural Language Processing and the 9th International Joint Conference on Natural Language Processing (EMNLP-IJCNLP), pages 2733–2743, Hong Kong, China. Association for Computational Linguistics.

John Hewitt and Christopher D. Manning. 2019. A structural probe for finding syntax in word representations. In Proceedings of the 2019 Conference of the North American Chapter of the Association for Computational Linguistics: Human Language Technologies, Volume 1 (Long and Short Papers), pages 4129–4138, Minneapolis, Minnesota. Association for Computational Linguistics.

Junjie Hu, Sebastian Ruder, Aditya Siddhant, Graham Neubig, Orhan Firat, and Melvin Johnson. 2020. Xtreme: A massively multilingual multi-task benchmark for evaluating cross-lingual generalisation. In International Conference on Machine Learning, pages 4411–4421. PMLR.

Péter Jeszenszky, Philipp Stoeckle, Elvira Glaser, and Robert Weibel. 2017. Exploring global and local patterns in the correlation of geographic distances and morphosyntactic variation in swiss german. Journal of Linguistic Geography, 5(2):86–108.

Andrew V. Knyazev and Merico E. Argentati. 2002. Principal angles between subspaces in an a-based scalar product: Algorithms and perturbation estimates. SIAM Journal on Scientific Computing, 23(6):2008–2040.

Sneha Kudugunta, Ankur Bapna, Isaac Caswell, and Orhan Firat. 2019. Investigating multilingual NMT representations at scale. In Proceedings of the 2019 Conference on Empirical Methods in Natural Language Processing and the 9th International Joint Conference on Natural Language Processing (EMNLP-IJCNLP), pages 1565–1575, Hong Kong, China. Association for Computational Linguistics.

Anne Lauscher, Vinit Ravishankar, Ivan Vulić, and Goran Glavaš. 2020. From zero to hero: On the limitations of zero-shot language transfer with multilingual Transformers. In Proceedings of the 2020 Conference on Empirical Methods in Natural Language Processing (EMNLP), pages 4483–4499, Online. Association for Computational Linguistics.

M. Paul Lewis, Gary F. Simons, and Charles D. Fennig, editors. 2015. Ethnologue: Languages of the World, nineteenth edition. SIL International, Dallas, TX, USA.

Yu-Hsiang Lin, Chian-Yu Chen, Jean Lee, Zirui Li, Yuyan Zhang, Mengzhou Xia, Shruti Rijhwani, Junxian He, Zhisong Zhang, Xuezhe Ma, Antonios Anastasopoulos, Patrick Littell, and Graham Neubig. 2019. Choosing transfer languages for cross-lingual learning. In Proceedings of the 57th Annual Meeting of the Association for Computational Linguistics, pages 3125–3135, Florence, Italy. Association for Computational Linguistics.

Patrick Littell, David R. Mortensen, Ke Lin, Katherine Kairis, Carlisle Turner, and Lori Levin. 2017. URIEL and lang2vec: Representing languages as typological, geographical, and phylogenetic vectors. In Proceedings of the 15th Conference of the European Chapter of the Association for Computational Linguistics: Volume 2, Short Papers, pages 8–14, Valencia, Spain. Association for Computational Linguistics.

Teresa Lynn, Jennifer Foster, Mark Dras, and Lamia Tounsi. 2014. Cross-lingual transfer parsing for low-resourced languages: An Irish case study. In Proceedings of the First Celtic Language Technology Workshop, pages 41–49, Dublin, Ireland. Association for Computational Linguistics and Dublin City University.

Ryan McDonald, Kevin Lerman, and Fernando Pereira. 2006. Multilingual dependency analysis with a two-stage discriminative parser. In Proceedings of the Tenth Conference on Computational Natural Language Learning (CoNLL-X), pages 216–220, New York City. Association for Computational Linguistics.

Steven Moran, Daniel McCloy, and Richard Wright. 2012. Revisiting population size vs. phoneme inventory size. Language, 88(4):877–893.

Steven Moran, Daniel McCloy, and Richard Wright, editors. 2014. PHOIBLE Online. Max Planck Institute for Evolutionary Anthropology, Leipzig.

Phoebe Mulcaire, Jungo Kasai, and Noah A. Smith. 2019. Polyglot contextual representations improve crosslingual transfer. In Proceedings of the 2019 Conference of the North American Chapter of the Association for Computational Linguistics: Human Language Technologies, Volume 1 (Long and Short Papers), pages 3912–3918, Minneapolis, Minnesota. Association for Computational Linguistics.

Max Müller-Eberstein, Rob Goot, and Barbara Plank. 2022. Probing for labeled dependency trees. In Proceedings of the 60th Annual Meeting of the Association for Computational Linguistics (Volume 1: Long Papers), pages 7711–7726, Dublin, Ireland. Association for Computational Linguistics.

Joakim Nivre, Marie-Catherine de Marneffe, Filip Ginter, Jan Hajič, Christopher D. Manning, Sampo Pyysalo, Sebastian Schuster, Francis Tyers, and Daniel Zeman. 2020. Universal Dependencies v2: An evergrowing multilingual treebank collection. In Proceedings of the 12th Language Resources and Evaluation Conference, pages 4034–4043, Marseille, France. European Language Resources Association.

Michael Paul, Andrew Finch, and Eiichrio Sumita. 2013. How to choose the best pivot language for automatic translation of low-resource languages. ACM Transactions on Asian Language Information Processing (TALIP), 12(4):1–17.

Telmo Pires, Eva Schlinger, and Dan Garrette. 2019. How multilingual is multilingual BERT? In Proceedings of the 57th Annual Meeting of the Association for Computational Linguistics, pages 4996–5001, Florence, Italy. Association for Computational Linguistics.

Edoardo Maria Ponti, Helen O'Horan, Yevgeni Berzak, Ivan Vulić, Roi Reichart, Thierry Poibeau, Ekaterina Shutova, and Anna Korhonen. 2019. Modeling language variation and universals: A survey on typological linguistics for natural language processing. Computational Linguistics, 45(3):559–601.

Pranav Rajpurkar, Jian Zhang, Konstantin Lopyrev, and Percy Liang. 2016. SQuAD: 100,000+ questions for machine comprehension of text. In Proceedings of the 2016 Conference on Empirical Methods in Natural Language Processing, pages 2383–2392, Austin, Texas. Association for Computational Linguistics.

Sebastian Ruder, Noah Constant, Jan Botha, Aditya Siddhant, Orhan Firat, Jinlan Fu, Pengfei Liu, Junjie Hu, Dan Garrette, Graham Neubig, and Melvin Johnson. 2021. XTREME-R: Towards more challenging and nuanced multilingual evaluation. In Proceedings of the 2021 Conference on Empirical Methods in Natural Language Processing, pages 10215–10245, Online and Punta Cana, Dominican Republic. Association for Computational Linguistics.

Phillip Rust, Jonas Pfeiffer, Ivan Vulić, Sebastian Ruder, and Iryna Gurevych. 2021. How good is your tokenizer? on the monolingual performance of multilingual language models. In Proceedings of the 59th Annual Meeting of the Association for Computational Linguistics and the 11th International Joint Conference on Natural Language Processing (Volume 1: Long Papers), pages 3118–3135, Online. Association for Computational Linguistics.

Wolfgang Seeker and Jonas Kuhn. 2013. Morphological and syntactic case in statistical dependency parsing. Computational Linguistics, 39(1):23–55.

Kyle Shaffer. 2021. Language clustering for multilingual named entity recognition. In Findings of the Association for Computational Linguistics: EMNLP 2021, pages 40–45, Punta Cana, Dominican Republic. Association for Computational Linguistics.

Kaius Sinnemäki. 2010. Word order in zero-marking languages. Studies in Language. International Journal sponsored by the Foundation "Foundations of Language", 34(4):869–912.

Aaron Smith, Bernd Bohnet, Miryam de Lhoneux, Joakim Nivre, Yan Shao, and Sara Stymne. 2018. 82 treebanks, 34 models: Universal Dependency parsing with multi-treebank models. In Proceedings of the CoNLL 2018 Shared Task: Multilingual Parsing from Raw Text to Universal Dependencies, pages 113–123, Brussels, Belgium. Association for Computational Linguistics.

Xu Tan, Jiale Chen, Di He, Yingce Xia, Tao Qin, and Tie-Yan Liu. 2019. Multilingual neural machine translation with language clustering. In Proceedings of the 2019 Conference on Empirical Methods in Natural Language Processing and the 9th International Joint Conference on Natural Language Processing (EMNLP-IJCNLP), pages 963–973, Hong Kong, China. Association for Computational Linguistics.

Iulia Turc, Kenton Lee, Jacob Eisenstein, Ming-Wei Chang, and Kristina Toutanova. 2021. Revisiting the primacy of English in zero-shot cross-lingual transfer. arXiv preprint arXiv:2106.16171.

Fiona J Tweedie and R Harald Baayen. 1998. How variable may a constant be? measures of lexical richness in perspective. Computers and the Humanities, 32(5):323–352.

Rob van der Goot and Miryam de Lhoneux. 2021. Parsing with pretrained language models, multiple datasets, and dataset embeddings. In Proceedings of the 20th International Workshop on Treebanks and Linguistic Theories (TLT, SyntaxFest 2021), pages 96–104, Sofia, Bulgaria. Association for Computational Linguistics.

Rob van der Goot, Ahmet Üstün, Alan Ramponi, Ibrahim Sharaf, and Barbara Plank. 2021. Massive choice, ample tasks (MaChAmp): A toolkit for multi-task learning in NLP. In Proceedings of the 16th Conference of the European Chapter of the Association for Computational Linguistics: System Demonstrations, pages 176–197, Online. Association for Computational Linguistics.

Raúl Vázquez, Yves Scherrer, Sami Virpioja, and Jörg Tiedemann. 2021. The Helsinki submission to the AmericasNLP shared task. In Proceedings of the First Workshop on Natural Language Processing for Indigenous Languages of the Americas, pages 255–264, Online. Association for Computational Linguistics.

Elena Voita and Ivan Titov. 2020. Information-theoretic probing with minimum description length. In Proceedings of the 2020 Conference on Empirical Methods in Natural Language Processing (EMNLP), pages 183–196, Online. Association for Computational Linguistics.

Søren Wichmann, Eric W. Holman, Dik Bakker, and Cecil H. Brown. 2010. Evaluating linguistic distance measures. Physica A: Statistical Mechanics and its Applications, 389(17):3632–3639.

Adina Williams, Nikita Nangia, and Samuel Bowman. 2018. A broad-coverage challenge corpus for sentence understanding through inference. In Proceedings of the 2018 Conference of the North American Chapter of the Association for Computational Linguistics: Human Language Technologies, Volume 1 (Long Papers), pages 1112–1122, New Orleans, Louisiana. Association for Computational Linguistics.

Daniel Zeman, Jan Hajič, Martin Popel, Martin Potthast, Milan Straka, Filip Ginter, Joakim Nivre, and Slav Petrov. 2018. CoNLL 2018 shared task: Multilingual parsing from raw text to Universal Dependencies. In Proceedings of the CoNLL 2018 Shared Task: Multilingual Parsing from Raw Text to Universal Dependencies, pages 1–21, Brussels, Belgium. Association for Computational Linguistics.

Daniel Zeman, Joakim Nivre, Mitchell Abrams, Elia Ackermann, Noëmi Aepli, Hamid Aghaei, Željko Agić, Amir Ahmadi, Lars Ahrenberg, Chika Kennedy Ajede, Gabrielė Aleksandravičiūtė, Ika Alfina, Lene Antonsen, Katya Aplonova, Angelina Aquino, Carolina Aragon, Maria Jesus Aranzabe, Bilge Nas Arıcan, Hórunn Arnardóttir, Gashaw Arutie, Jessica Naraiswari Arwidarasti, Masayuki Asahara, Deniz Baran Aslan, Luma Ateyah, Furkan Atmaca, Mohammed Attia, Aitziber Atutxa, Liesbeth Augustinus, Elena Badmaeva, Keerthana Balasubramani, Miguel Ballesteros, Esha Banerjee, Sebastian

Bank, Verginica Barbu Mititelu, Starkaður Barkarson, Rodolfo Basile, Victoria Basmov, Colin Batchelor, John Bauer, Seyyit Talha Bedir, Kepa Bengoetxea, Gözde Berk, Yevgeni Berzak, Irshad Ahmad Bhat, Riyaz Ahmad Bhat, Erica Biagetti, Eckhard Bick, Agnė Bielinskienė, Kristín Bjarnadóttir, Rogier Blokland, Victoria Bobicev, Loïc Boizou, Emanuel Borges Völker, Carl Börstell, Cristina Bosco, Gosse Bouma, Sam Bowman, Adriane Boyd, Anouck Braggaar, Kristina Brokaitė, Aljoscha Burchardt, Marie Candito, Bernard Caron, Gauthier Caron, Lauren Cassidy, Tatiana Cavalcanti, Gülşen Cebiroğlu Eryiğit, Flavio Massimiliano Cecchini, Giuseppe G. A. Celano, Slavomír Čéplö, Neslihan Cesur, Savas Cetin, Özlem Çetinoğlu, Fabricio Chalub, Shweta Chauhan, Ethan Chi, Taishi Chika, Yongseok Cho, Jinho Choi, Jayeol Chun, Juyeon Chung, Alessandra T. Cignarella, Silvie Cinková, Aurélie Collomb, Çağrı Çöltekin, Miriam Connor, Marine Courtin, Mihaela Cristescu, Philemon Daniel, Elizabeth Davidson, Marie-Catherine de Marneffe, Valeria de Paiva, Mehmet Oguz Derin, Elvis de Souza, Arantza Diaz de Ilarraza, Carly Dickerson, Arawinda Dinakaramani, Elisa Di Nuovo, Bamba Dione, Peter Dirix, Kaja Dobrovoljc, Timothy Dozat, Kira Droganova, Puneet Dwivedi, Hanne Eckhoff, Sandra Eiche, Marhaba Eli, Ali Elkahky, Binyam Ephrem, Olga Erina, Tomaž Erjavec, Aline Etienne, Wograine Evelyn, Sidney Facundes, Richárd Farkas, Jannatul Ferdaousi, Marília Fernanda, Hector Fernandez Alcalde, Jennifer Foster, Cláudia Freitas, Kazunori Fujita, Katarína Gajdošová, Daniel Galbraith, Marcos Garcia, Moa Gärdenfors, Sebastian Garza, Fabrício Ferraz Gerardi, Kim Gerdes, Filip Ginter, Gustavo Godoy, Iakes Goenaga, Koldo Gojenola, Memduh Gökırmak, Yoav Goldberg, Xavier Gómez Guinovart, Berta González Saavedra, Bernadeta Griciūtė, Matias Grioni, Loïc Grobol, Normunds Grūzītis, Bruno Guillaume, Céline Guillot-Barbance, Tunga Güngör, Nizar Habash, Hinrik Hafsteinsson, Jan Hajič, Jan Hajič jr., Mika Hämäläinen, Linh Hà Mỹ, Na-Rae Han, Muhammad Yudistira Hanifmuti, Sam Hardwick, Kim Harris, Dag Haug, Johannes Heinecke, Oliver Hellwig, Felix Hennig, Barbora Hladká, Jaroslava Hlaváčová, Florinel Hociung, Petter Hohle, Eva Huber, Jena Hwang, Takumi Ikeda, Anton Karl Ingason, Radu Ion, Elena Irimia, Ọlájídé Ishola, Kaoru Ito, Siratun Jannat, Tomáš Jelínek, Apoorva Jha, Anders Johannsen, Hildur Jónsdóttir, Fredrik Jørgensen, Markus Juutinen, Sarveswaran K, Hüner Kaşıkara, Andre Kaasen, Nadezhda Kabaeva, Sylvain Kahane, Hiroshi Kanayama, Jenna Kanerva, Neslihan Kara, Boris Katz, Tolga Kayadelen, Jessica Kenney, Václava Kettnerová, Jesse Kirchner, Elena Klementieva, Elena Klyachko, Arne Köhn, Abdullatif Köksal, Kamil Kopacewicz, Timo Korkiakangas, Mehmet Köse, Natalia Kotsyba, Jolanta Kovalevskaitė, Simon Krek, Parameswari Krishnamurthy, Sandra Kübler, Oğuzhan Kuyrukçu, Aslı Kuzgun, Sookyoung Kwak, Veronika Laippala, Lucia Lam, Lorenzo Lambertino, Tatiana Lando, Septina Dian Larasati, Alexei Lavrentiev, John Lee, Phuong Lê Hồng, Alessandro Lenci, Saran Lertpradit, Herman Leung, Maria Levina, Cheuk Ying Li, Josie Li, Keying Li, Yuan Li, KyungTae Lim, Bruna Lima Padovani, Krister Lindén, Nikola Ljubešić, Olga Loginova, Stefano Lusito, Andry Luthfi, Mikko Luukko, Olga Lyashevskaya, Teresa Lynn, Vivien Macketanz, Menel Mahamdi, Jean Maillard, Aibek Makazhanov, Michael Mandl, Christopher Manning, Ruli Manurung, Büşra Marşan, Cătălina Mărănduc, David Mareček, Katrin Marheinecke, Héctor Martínez Alonso, Lorena Martín-Rodríguez, André Martins, Jan Mašek, Hiroshi Matsuda, Yuji Matsumoto, Alessandro Mazzei, Ryan McDonald, Sarah McGuinness, Gustavo Mendonça, Tatiana Merzhevich, Niko Miekka, Karina Mischenkova, Margarita Misirpashayeva, Anna Missilä, Cătălin Mititelu, Maria Mitrofan, Yusuke Miyao, AmirHossein Mojiri Foroushani, Judit Molnár, Amirsaeid Moloodi, Simonetta Montemagni, Amir More, Laura Moreno Romero, Giovanni Moretti, Keiko Sophie Mori, Shinsuke Mori, Tomohiko Morioka, Shigeki Moro, Bjartur Mortensen, Bohdan Moskalevskyi, Kadri Muischnek, Robert Munro, Yugo Murawaki, Kaili Müürisep, Pinkey Nainwani, Mariam Nakhlé, Juan Ignacio Navarro Horñiacek, Anna Nedoluzhko, Gunta Nešpore-Bērzkalne, Manuela Nevaci, Luong Nguyễn Thị, Huyền Nguyễn Thị Minh, Yoshihiro Nikaido, Vitaly Nikolaev, Rattima Nitisaroj, Alireza Nourian, Hanna Nurmi, Stina Ojala, Atul Kr. Ojha, Adèdayọ̀ Olúòkun, Mai Omura, Emeka Onwuegbuzia, Petya Osenova, Robert Östling, Lilja Øvrelid, Şaziye Betül Özateş, Merve Özçelik, Arzucan Özgür, Balkız Öztürk Başaran, Hyunji Hayley Park, Niko Partanen, Elena Pascual, Marco Passarotti, Agnieszka Patejuk, Guilherme Paulino-Passos, Angelika Peljak-Łapińska, Siyao Peng, Cenel-Augusto Perez, Natalia Perkova, Guy Perrier, Slav Petrov, Daria Petrova, Jason Phelan, Jussi Piitulainen, Tommi A Pirinen, Emily Pitler, Barbara Plank, Thierry Poibeau, Larisa Ponomareva, Martin Popel, Lauma Pretkalniņa, Sophie Prévost, Prokopis Prokopidis, Adam Przepiórkowski, Tiina Puolakainen, Sampo Pyysalo, Peng Qi, Andriela Rääbis, Alexandre Rademaker, Mizanur Rahoman, Taraka Rama, Loganathan Ramasamy, Carlos Ramisch, Fam Rashel, Mohammad Sadegh Rasooli, Vinit Ravishankar, Livy Real, Petru Rebeja, Siva Reddy, Mathilde Regnault, Georg Rehm, Ivan Riabov, Michael Rießler, Erika Rimkutė, Larissa Rinaldi, Laura Rituma, Putri Rizqiyah, Luisa Rocha, Eiríkur Rögnvaldsson, Mykhailo Romanenko, Rudolf Rosa, Valentin Roșca, Davide Rovati, Olga Rudina, Jack Rueter, Kristján Rúnarsson, Shoval Sadde, Pegah Safari, Benoît Sagot, Aleksi Sahala, Shadi Saleh, Alessio Salomoni, Tanja Samardžić, Stephanie Samson, Manuela Sanguinetti, Ezgi Sanıyar, Dage Särg, Baiba Saulīte, Yanin Sawanakunanon, Shefali Saxena, Kevin Scannell, Salvatore Scarlata, Nathan Schneider, Sebastian Schuster, Lane Schwartz, Djamé Seddah, Wolfgang Seeker, Mojgan Seraji, Syeda Shahzadi, Mo Shen, Atsuko Shimada, Hiroyuki Shirasu, Yana Shishkina, Muh Shohibussirri, Dmitry Sichinava, Janine Siewert, Einar Freyr Sigurðsson, Aline Silveira, Natalia Silveira, Maria Simi, Radu Simionescu, Katalin Simkó, Mária Šimková, Kiril Simov, Maria Skachedubova, Aaron Smith, Isabela Soares-Bastos, Shafi Sourov, Carolyn Spadine, Rachele Sprugnoli, Steinhór Steingrímsson, Antonio Stella, Milan Straka, Emmett Strickland, Jana Strnadová, Alane Suhr, Yogi Lesmana Sulestio, Umut Sulubacak, Shingo Suzuki, Zsolt Szántó, Chihiro Taguchi, Dima Taji, Yuta Takahashi, Fabio Tamburini, Mary Ann C. Tan, Takaaki Tanaka, Dipta Tanaya, Samson Tella, Isabelle Tellier, Marinella Testori, Guillaume Thomas, Liisi Torga, Marsida Toska, Trond Trosterud, Anna Trukhina, Reut Tsarfaty, Utku Türk, Francis Tyers, Sumire Uematsu, Roman Untilov, Zdeňka Urešová, Larraitz Uria, Hans Uszkoreit, Andrius Utka, Sowmya Vajjala, Rob van der Goot, Martine Vanhove, Daniel van Niekerk, Gertjan van Noord, Viktor Varga, Eric Villemonte de la Clergerie, Veronika Vincze, Natalia Vlasova, Aya Wakasa, Joel C. Wallenberg, Lars Wallin, Abigail Walsh, Jing Xian Wang, Jonathan North Washington, Maximilan Wendt, Paul Widmer, Sri Hartati Wijono, Seyi Williams, Mats Wirén, Christian Wittern, Tsegay Woldemariam, Tak-sum Wong, Alina Wróblewska, Mary Yako, Kayo Yamashita, Naoki Yamazaki, Chunxiao Yan, Koichi Yasuoka, Marat M. Yavrumyan, Arife Betül Yenice, Olcay Taner Yıldız, Zhuoran Yu, Arlisa Yuliawati, Zdeněk Žabokrtský, Shorouq Zahra, Amir Zeldes, He Zhou, Hanzhi Zhu, Anna Zhuravleva, and Rayan Ziane. 2021. Universal dependencies 2.9. LINDAT/CLARIAH-CZ digital library at the Institute of Formal and Applied Linguistics (ÚFAL), Faculty of Mathematics and Physics, Charles University.

Daniel Zeman and Philip Resnik. 2008. Cross-language parser adaptation between related languages. In Proceedings of the IJCNLP-08 Workshop on NLP for Less Privileged Languages.

A Missing Syntax Features in URIEL

ISO-3 Lang code	Count feats no value	ISO-3 Lang code	Count feats no value
afr	66	lat	70
grc	70	lav	24
arb	37	lit	29
eus	18	mlt	97
bel	70	mar	37
bul	17	pcm	103
cat	47	nno	103
zho	1	chu	103
cop	36	fro	70
hrv	91	pes	18
ces	30	pol	29
dan	29	por	26
nld	32	ron	29
eng	0	rus	13
est	23	gla	28
fao	70	srp	68
fin	5	slk	103
fra	6	slv	43
glg	70	spa	2
deu	16	swe	23
got	71	swl	103
ell	17	tam	33
heb	16	tel	42
hin	21	tur	14
hun	12	ukr	26
isl	28	urd	40
ind	3	uig	45
gle	27	vie	10
ita	26	cym	22
jpn	13	hye	26
kor	15	wol	22

Table 4: The counts of missing syntactic features in URIEL for languages included in UD. The table contains some languages that were not included in our experiments (due to sampling), but are listed as available in UD.

B Data Statistics

Treebank	MSL	MWL
UD_Afrikaans-AfriBooms	25.76	4.98
UD_Ancient_Greek-PROIEL	12.46	5.06
UD_Ancient_Greek-Perseus	13.93	4.59
UD_Arabic-PADT	31.58	4.52
UD_Armenian-ArmTDP	21.18	5.0
UD_Basque-BDT	13.52	5.6
UD_Belarusian-HSE	11.95	5.31
UD_Bulgarian-BTB	13.96	4.63
UD_Catalan-AnCora	31.75	4.29
UD_Chinese-GSD	24.67	1.58
UD_Chinese-GSDSimp	24.67	1.58
UD_Classical_Chinese-Kyoto	4.84	1.04
UD_Coptic-Scriptorium	11.89	5.4
UD_Croatian-SET	22.11	5.0
UD_Czech-CAC	20.09	5.06
UD_Czech-CLTT	32.27	5.45
UD_Czech-FicTree	13.1	4.01
UD_Czech-PDT	17.1	4.84
UD_Danish-DDT	18.34	4.41
UD_Dutch-Alpino	15.14	4.7
UD_Dutch-LassySmall	12.98	4.83
UD_English-Atis	11.38	4.71
UD_English-ESL	19.04	3.87
UD_English-EWT	16.1	4.11
UD_English-GUM	18.05	4.18
UD_English-GUMReddit	18.45	3.94
UD_English-LinES	18.06	3.98
UD_English-ParTUT	24.41	4.53
UD_English-Tweebank2	15.1	4.08
UD_Estonian-EDT	13.99	5.55
UD_Estonian-EWT	12.05	4.7
UD_Faroese-FarPaHC	22.64	3.58
UD_Finnish-FTB	8.5	5.95
UD_Finnish-TDT	13.31	6.49
UD_French-FTB	29.96	4.33
UD_French-GSD	23.86	4.41
UD_French-ParTUT	29.04	4.64
UD_French-Rhapsodie	14.67	3.5
UD_French-Sequoia	22.03	4.57
UD_Galician-CTG	31.66	4.86
UD_German-GSD	18.76	5.27
UD_German-HDT	17.99	5.67
UD_German-tweeDE	9.25	4.74
UD_Gothic-PROIEL	10.34	5.21
UD_Greek-GDT	24.8	5.11
UD_Hebrew-HTB	18.76	4.03
UD_Hindi-HDTB	21.13	3.83
UD_Hindi_English-HIENCS	13.95	3.75
UD_Hungarian-Szeged	22.16	5.46
UD_Icelandic-IcePaHC	20.72	4.04
UD_Icelandic-Modern	23.04	4.43
UD_Indonesian-GSD	21.39	5.25
UD_Irish-IDT	23.94	4.52
UD_Italian-ISDT	19.63	4.65
UD_Italian-ParTUT	25.53	4.93
UD_Italian-PoSTWITA	17.77	4.72
UD_Italian-TWITTIRO	19.91	4.56
UD_Italian-VIT	25.22	4.75
UD_Japanese-GSD	23.88	1.65
UD_Japanese-GSDLUW	18.48	2.13
UD_Korean-GSD	12.88	2.84
UD_Korean-Kaist	12.88	2.84
UD_Latin-ITTB	17.16	5.06
UD_Latin-LLCT	26.64	4.91
UD_Latin-PROIEL	10.81	5.38
UD_Latin-UDante	32.76	4.9
UD_Latvian-LVTB	16.92	5.1
UD_Lithuanian-ALKSNIS	20.35	5.58
UD_Lithuanian-HSE	20.98	5.1
UD_Maltese-MUDT	20.37	4.56
UD_Marathi-UFAL	7.32	4.03
UD_Naija-NSC	15.37	2.97
UD_Norwegian-Bokmaal	15.54	4.47
UD_Norwegian-Nynorsk	17.31	4.51
UD_Norwegian-NynorskLIA	10.32	3.15
UD_Old_Church_Slavonic-PROIEL	9.08	4.5
UD_Old_East_Slavic-TOROT	8.9	4.5
UD_Old_French-SRCMF	11.21	3.5
UD_Persian-PerDT	17.01	3.82
UD_Persian-Seraji	25.0	3.78
UD_Polish-LFG	7.6	4.64
UD_Polish-PDB	15.78	5.07
UD_Portuguese-Bosque	22.65	4.42
UD_Portuguese-GSD	24.75	4.34
UD_Romanian-Nonstandard	22.09	3.77
UD_Romanian-RRT	23.02	4.69
UD_Romanian-SiMoNERo	31.19	5.19
UD_Russian-GSD	19.46	5.28
UD_Russian-SynTagRus	17.3	5.04
UD_Russian-Taiga	11.01	4.58
UD_Scottish_Gaelic-ARCOSG	19.02	4.2
UD_Serbian-SET	22.31	4.93
UD_Slovak-SNK	9.5	4.41
UD_Slovenian-SSJ	17.37	4.63
UD_Spanish-AnCora	30.98	4.43
UD_Spanish-GSD	26.44	4.41
UD_Swedish-LinES	17.46	4.46
UD_Swedish-Talbanken	15.49	4.98
UD_Swedish_Sign_Language-SSLC	7.4	8.91
UD_Tamil-TTB	14.34	7.21
UD_Telugu-MTG	4.84	4.66
UD_Turkish-Atis	8.47	6.65
UD_Turkish-BOUN	12.46	5.51
UD_Turkish-FrameNet	7.14	5.36
UD_Turkish-IMST	10.05	5.41
UD_Turkish-Kenet	9.31	5.41
UD_Turkish-Penn	11.21	5.61
UD_Turkish-Tourism	4.64	5.03
UD_Turkish_German-SAGT	17.31	4.53
UD_Ukrainian-IU	16.8	4.64
UD_Urdu-UDTB	26.88	3.57
UD_Uyghur-UDT	11.63	5.48
UD_Vietnamese-VTB	14.49	3.99
UD_Welsh-CCG	19.73	4.06
UD_Western_Armenian-ArmTDP	18.13	5.06
UD_Wolof-WTB	19.21	3.46

Table 5: Mean Sentence Length (MSL) and Mean Word Length (MWL) values per treebank.

Visual Semantic Parsing: From Images to Abstract Meaning Representation

Mohamed A. Abdelsalam[1], Zhan Shi[1,2*], Federico Fancellu[3†], Kalliopi Basioti[1,4*], Dhaivat J. Bhatt[1], Vladimir Pavlovic[1,4], Afsaneh Fazly[1]
[1]Samsung AI Centre - Toronto , [2]Queen's University , [3]3M , [4]Rutgers University
{m.abdelsalam, d.bhatt, a.fazly}@samsung.com, z.shi@queensu.ca
f.fancellu0@gmail.com, {kalliopi.basioti, vladimir}@rutgers.edu

Abstract

The success of scene graphs for visual scene understanding has brought attention to the benefits of abstracting a visual input (e.g., image) into a structured representation, where entities (people and objects) are nodes connected by edges specifying their relations. Building these representations, however, requires expensive manual annotation in the form of images paired with their scene graphs or frames. These formalisms remain limited in the nature of entities and relations they can capture. In this paper, we propose to leverage a widely-used meaning representation in the field of natural language processing, the Abstract Meaning Representation (AMR), to address these shortcomings. Compared to scene graphs, which largely emphasize spatial relationships , our visual AMR graphs are more linguistically informed, with a focus on higher-level semantic concepts extrapolated from visual input. Moreover, they allow us to generate meta-AMR graphs to unify information contained in multiple image descriptions under one representation. Through extensive experimentation and analysis, we demonstrate that we can re-purpose an existing text-to-AMR parser to parse images into AMRs. Our findings point to important future research directions for improved scene understanding.

1 Introduction

The ability to understand and describe a scene is fundamental for the development of truly intelligent systems, including autonomous vehicles, robots navigating an environment, or even simpler applications such as language-based image retrieval. Much work in computer vision has focused on two key aspects of scene understanding, namely, recognizing entities, including object detection (Liu et al., 2016; Ren et al., 2015; Carion et al., 2020; Liu et al., 2020a) and activity recognition (Herath et al., 2017; Kong and Fu, 2022; Li et al., 2018; Gao et al., 2018), as well as understanding how entities are related to each other, e.g., human–object interaction (Hou et al., 2020; Zou et al., 2021) and relation detection (Lu et al., 2016; Zhang et al., 2017; Zellers et al., 2018).

A natural way of representing scene entities and their relations is in graph form, so it is perhaps unsurprising that a lot of work has focused on graph-based scene representations and especially on scene graphs (Johnson et al., 2015a). Scene graphs encode the salient regions in an image (mainly, objects) as nodes, and the relations among these (mostly spatial in nature) as edges, both labelled via natural language tags; see Fig. 1(b) for an example scene graph. Along the same lines, Yatskar et al. (2016) propose to represent a scene as a semantic role labelled frame, drawn from FrameNet (Ruppenhofer et al., 2016) — a linguistically-motivated approach that draws on semantic role labelling literature.

Scene graphs and situation frames can capture important aspects of an image, yet they are limited in important ways. They both require expensive manual annotation in the form of images paired with their corresponding scene graphs or frames. Scene graphs in particular also suffer from being limited in the nature of entities and relations that they capture (see Section 2 for a detailed analysis). Ideally, we would like to capture event-level semantics (same as in situation recognition) but as a structured graph that captures a diverse set of relations and goes beyond low-level visual semantics.

Inspired by the linguistically-motivated image understanding research, we propose to represent images using a well-known graph formalism for language understanding, i.e., Abstract Meaning Representations (AMRs Banarescu et al., 2013). Similarly to (visual) semantic role labeling, AMRs also represent "who did what to whom, where,

*Work done during an internship at Samsung AI Centre - Toronto

†Work done while at Samsung AI Centre - Toronto

Proceedings of the 26th Conference on Computational Natural Language Learning (CoNLL), pages 282 - 300
December 7-8, 2022 ©2022 Association for Computational Linguistics

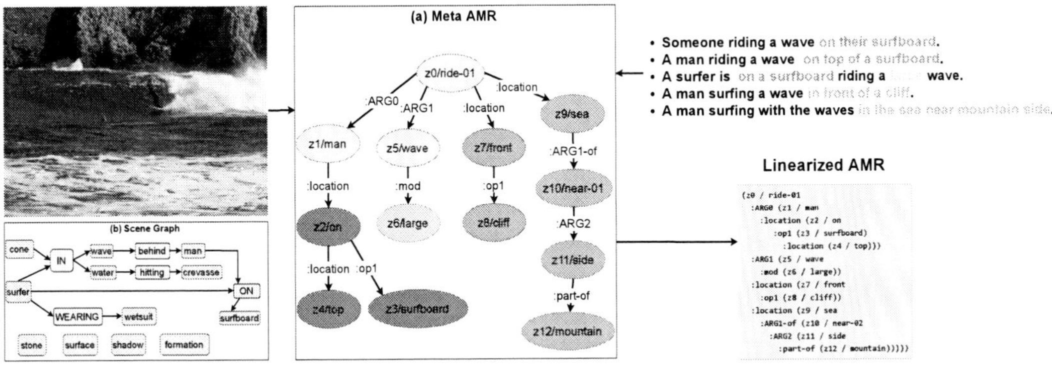

Figure 1: An image from MSCOCO and Visual Genome dataset, along with its five human-generated captions, and: (a) an image-level meta-AMR graph capturing its overall semantics, (b) its human-generated scene graph.

when, and how?" (Màrquez et al., 2008), but in a more structured way via transforming an image into a graph representation. AMRs not only encode the main events, their participants and arguments, as well as their relations (as in semantic role labelling/situation recognition), but also relations among various other participants and arguments; see Fig. 1(a). Importantly, AMR is a broadly-adopted and dynamically evolving formalism (e.g., Bonial et al., 2020; Bonn et al., 2020; Naseem et al., 2021), and AMR parsing is an active and successful area of research (e.g., Zhang et al., 2019b; Bevilacqua et al., 2021; Xia et al., 2021; Drozdov et al., 2022). Finally, given the high quality of existing AMR parsers (for language), we do not need manual AMR annotations for images, and can rely on existing image–caption datasets to create high quality silver data for image-to-AMR parsing. In summary, we make the following contributions:

- We introduce the novel problem of parsing images into Abstract Meaning Representations, a widely-adopted linguistically-motivated graph formalism; and propose the first image-to-AMR parser model for the task.
- We present a detailed analysis and comparison between scene graphs and AMRs with respect to the nature of entities and relations they capture, results of which further motivates research in the use of AMRs for better image understanding.
- Inspired by work on multi-sentence AMR, we propose a graph-to-graph transformation algorithm that combines the meanings of several image caption descriptions into image-level meta-AMR graphs. The motivation behind generating the meta-AMRs is to build a graph that covers most of entities, predicates, and semantic relations contained in the individual caption AMRs.

Our analyses suggest that AMRs encode aspects of an image content that are not captured by the commonly-used scene graphs. Our initial results on re-purposing a text-to-AMR parser for image-to-AMR parsing, as well as on creating image-level meta-AMRs, point to exciting future research directions for improved scene understanding.

2 Motivation: AMRs vs. Scene Graphs

Scene graphs (SGs) are a widely-adopted graph formalism for representing the semantic content of an image. Scene graphs have been shown useful for various downstream tasks, such as image captioning (Yang et al., 2019; Li and Jiang, 2019; Zhong et al., 2020), visual question answering (Zhang et al., 2019a; Hildebrandt et al., 2020; Damodaran et al., 2021), and image retrieval (Johnson et al., 2015b; Schuster et al., 2015; Wang et al., 2020; Schroeder and Tripathi, 2020). However, learning to automatically generate SGs requires expensive manual annotations (object bounding boxes and their relations). SGs were also shown to be highly biased in the entity and relation types that they capture. For example, an analysis by Zellers et al. (2018) reveals that clothing (e.g., *dress*) and object/body parts (e.g., *eyes*, *wheel*) make up over one-third of entity instances in the SGs corresponding to the Visual Genome images (Krishna et al., 2016), and that more than 90% of all relation instances belong to the two categories of geometric (e.g., *behind*) and possessive (e.g., *have*).

One advantage of AMR graphs is that we can draw on supervision through captions associated with images. Nonetheless, the question remains as to what types of entities and relations are encoded by AMR graphs, and how these differ from SGs. To answer this question, we follow an approach similar to Zellers et al. (2018), and categorize entities and relations in SG and AMR graphs corresponding to a sample of 50K images. We use the same categories as Zellers et al., but add a few new ones to capture relation types specific to AMRs, namely, Attribute (*small*), Quantifier (*few*), Event (*soccer*), and AMR specific (*date-entity*). Details of our categorization process are provided in Appendix A.

Figure 2 shows the distribution of instances for each Entity and Relation category, compared across SG and AMR graphs. AMRs tend to encode a more diverse set of relations, and in particular capture more of the abstract semantic relations that are missing from SGs. This is expected because our caption-generated AMRs by design capture the essential meaning of the image descriptions and, as such, encode how people perceive and describe scenes. In contrast, SGs are designed to capture the content of an image, including regions representing objects and (mainly spatial/geometric) visually-observable relations; see Fig. 1 for SG and AMR graphs corresponding to an image. In the context of Entities, and a major departure from SGs, (object/body) parts are less frequently encoded in AMRs, pointing to the well-known whole-object bias in how people perceive and describe scenes (Markman, 1990; Fei-Fei et al., 2007). In contrast, location is more frequent in AMRs.

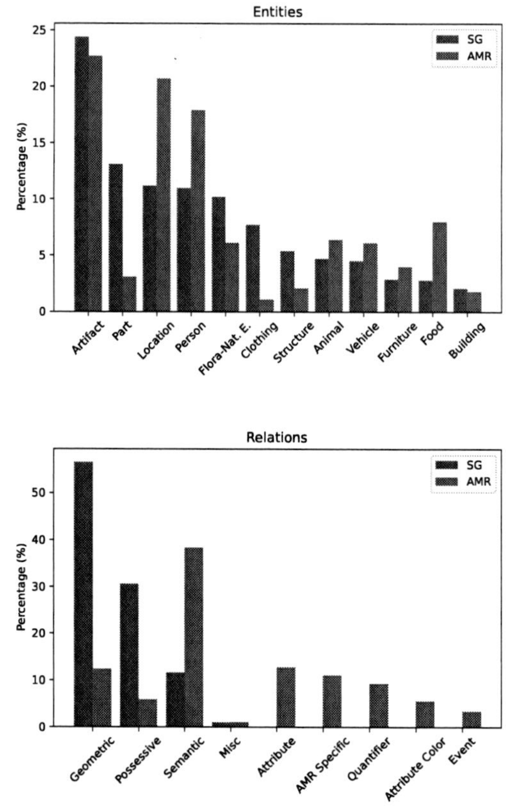

Figure 2: Statistics on a selected set of top-frequency Entity and Relation categories, extracted from the AMR and SG graphs corresponding to around 50K images that appear in both Visual Genome and MSCOCO.

The focus of AMRs on abstract content suggests that they have the potential for improving downstream tasks, especially when the task requires an understanding of the higher level semantics of an image. Interestingly, a recent study showed that using AMRs as an intermediate representation for textual SG parsing helps improve the quality of the parsed SGs (Choi et al., 2022), even though AMRs and SGs encode qualitatively different information. Since AMRs tend to capture higher level semantics, we propose to use them as the final image representation. The question remains as to how difficult it is to directly learn such representations from images. The rest of the paper focuses on answering this question.

3 Method

3.1 Parsing Images into AMR Graphs

We develop image-to-AMR parsers based on a state-of-the-art seq2seq text-to-AMR parser, SPRING (Bevilacqua et al., 2021), and a multimodal VL-BART (Cho et al., 2021). Both are transformer-based architectures with a bidirectional encoder and an auto-regressive decoder. SPRING extends a pre-trained seq2seq model, BART (Lewis et al., 2020), by fine-tuning it on AMR parsing and generation. Next, we describe our models, input representation, and training.

Models. We build two variants of our image-to-AMR parser, as depicted in Fig. 3(a) and (b).

- Our first model, which we refer to as IMG2AMR$_{\text{direct}}$, modifies SPRING by replacing BART with its vision-and-language counterpart, VL-BART (Cho et al., 2021). VL-BART extends BART with visual understanding ability through fine-tuning on multiple vision-and-language tasks. With this modification, our model can receive visual features (plus text) as input, and generate linearized AMR graphs.

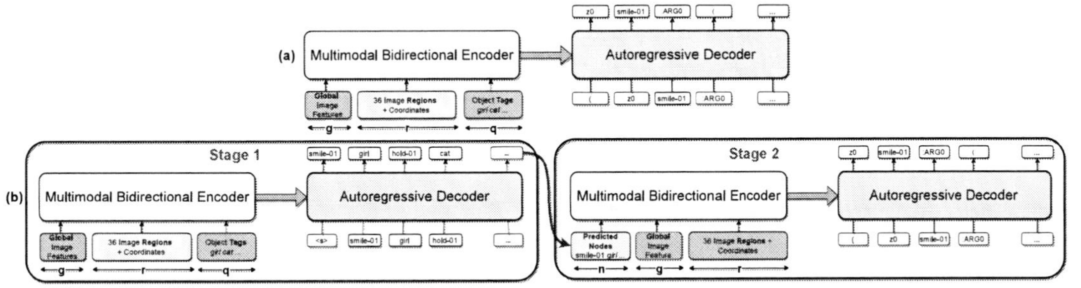

Figure 3: Model architecture for our two image-to-AMR models: (a) IMG2AMR$_{\text{direct}}$: A direct model that uses a single seq2seq encoder–decoder to generate linearlized AMRs from input images; and (b) IMG2AMR$_{\text{2stage}}$: A two-stage model containing two independent seq2seq components. $\mathbf{g}$ and $\mathbf{r}$ stand for global and region features, $\mathbf{q}$ for tag embeddings, and $\mathbf{n}$ for the embeddings of the predicted nodes. The input and output space of the decoders come from the AMR vocabulary.

- Our second model, inspired by text-to-graph AMR parsers (e.g., Zhang et al., 2019b; Xia et al., 2021), generates linearized AMRs in two stages by first predicting the nodes, and then the relations. Specifically, we first predict the nodes of the linearized AMR for a given image. These predicted nodes are then fed (along with the image) as input into a second seq2seq model that generates a linearized AMR (effectively adding the relations). We refer to this model as IMG2AMR$_{\text{2stage}}$.

Input Representation. To represent images, we follow VL-BART, which takes the output of Faster R-CNN (Ren et al., 2015) (i.e., region features and coordinates for 36 regions) and projects them onto $d = 768$ dimensional vectors via two separate fully-connected layers. Faster R-CNN region features are obtained via training for visual object and attribute classification (Anderson et al., 2018) on Visual Genome. The visual input to our model is composed of position-aware embeddings for the 36 regions, plus a global image-level feature ($\mathbf{r}$ and $\mathbf{g}$ in Fig. 3). To get the position-aware embeddings for the regions, we add together the projected region and coordinate embeddings. To get the global image feature, we use the output of the final hidden layer in ResNet-101 (He et al., 2016), which is passed through the same fully connected layer as the regions to obtain a 768-dimensional vector.

Training. To benefit from transfer learning, we initialize the encoder and decoder weights of both our models from the pre-trained VL-BART. This is a reasonable initialization strategy, given that VL-BART has been pre-trained on input similar to ours. Moreover, a large number of AMR labels are drawn from the English vocabulary, and thus the pre-training of VL-BART should also be appropriate for AMR generation. We fine-tune our models on the task of image-to-AMR generation, using images paired with their automatically-generated AMR graphs. We consider two alternative AMR representations: (a) *caption AMRs*, created directly from captions associated with images (see Section 4 for details); and (b) image-level *meta-AMRs*, constructed through an algorithm we describe below in Section 3.2. We perform experiments with either caption or meta-AMRs, where we train and test on the same type of AMRs. For the various stages of training, we use the cross-entropy loss between the model predictions and the ground-truth labels for each token, where the model predictions are obtained greedily, i.e., choosing the token with the maximum score at each step of the sequence generation.

3.2 Learning per-Image meta-AMR Graphs

Recall that, in order to collect a data set of images paired with their AMR graphs, we rely on image–caption datasets such as MSCOCO. Specifically, we use a pre-trained AMR parser to generate AMR graphs from each caption of an image. Images can be described in many different ways, e.g., each image in MSCOCO comes with five different human-generated captions. We hypothesize that these captions collectively represent the content of the image they are describing, and as such propose to also combine the caption AMRs into image-level meta-AMR graphs through a merge and refine process that we explain next.

Prior work has used graph-to-graph transformations for merging sentence-level AMRs into document-level AMRs for abstractive and multi-

Algorithm 1 META-AMR Graph Construction

Input: k human-generated image descriptions $\{c_i\}_{i=1}^{k}$ for a given image i; a set of pre-defined AMR relation types $\mathcal{R}$;
Output: A meta-AMR graph g_{meta};
Initialize: Generate AMR graphs $\{g_i\}$ for the k descriptions using a pre-trained AMR semantic parser; Initialize $g_m = (\mathcal{N}, \mathcal{E})$ to be the null graph.
$\mathcal{N} = \cup_{i=1}^{k} \mathcal{N}_i$
for $i = 1 \sim k$ **do**
  $\mathcal{E}_i$ = getEdges(g_i)
  for $(n_s, n_t) : r \in \mathcal{E}_i$ **do** ▷ (n_s, n_t) is a pair of nodes connected via an edge labeled as r
    if $(n_s, n_t) \notin \mathcal{E}$.keys() $\hookrightarrow \wedge (n_t, n_s) \notin \mathcal{E}$.keys() $\hookrightarrow \wedge r \in \mathcal{R}$ **then**
      $\mathcal{E}$.add($\{(n_s, n_t) : r\}$) ▷ Add a new edge when neither (n_s, n_t) nor (n_t, n_s) previously included, and r belongs to a pre-selected set of AMR relation types $\mathcal{R}$
$\mathcal{G}_m$ = weaklyConnectedComponents(g_m) ▷ Get all connected components as g_{meta} candidates since it should be a connected graph according to the definition of AMR
g_{meta} = getLargestComponent($\mathcal{G}_m$) ▷ Get the candidate with the largest number of nodes as it can cover most entities and predicates in the image
g_{meta} = refineNodes(g_{meta}) ▷ Replace node types by their frequent hypernym if available
return g_{meta}

document summarization (e.g., Liu et al., 2015; Liao et al., 2018; Naseem et al., 2021). Unlike in a summarization task, captions do not form a coherent document, but instead collectively describe an image. Inspired by prior work, we propose our graph-to-graph transformation algorithm that learns a unified meta-AMR graph from caption graphs; see Algorithm 1. Specifically, we first merge the nodes and edges from the original set of k caption-level AMRs, only including a pre-defined set of relation/edge labels. We then select the largest connected component of this merged graph, which we further refine by replacing non-predicate nodes by their more frequent hypernyms, when available. The motivation behind this refinement process is to reduce the complexity of the meta-AMR graphs (in terms of their size), which would potentially improve parsing performance. An example of a meta-AMR graph generated from caption AMRs is given in Appendix C.

AMR graphs of the MSCOCO training captions contain more than 90 types of semantic relations and more than 21K node types, with long-tailed distributions; see Fig. 6 in Appendix B. To refine meta-AMR graphs, we only maintain the top-20 most frequent relation types that include core roles, such as ARG0, ARG1, etc., as well as high-frequency non-core roles, such as mod and location. To further refine the graphs, we replace each non-predicate node (e.g., *salmon*) with its most frequent hypernym (e.g., *fish*) according to WordNet (Fellbaum, 1998). This results in just about 30% reduction in the number of node types (to 15K). The average complexity of graphs is also reduced from 19 nodes and 23 relations to 16 and 18, respectively.

4 Experimental Setup

Data. For our task of AMR generation from images, we use an augmented version of the standard MSCOCO image–caption dataset, which is composed of images paired with their captions, automatically generated caption-level linearized AMR graphs, and an image-level linearized meta-AMR graph. We use the splits established in previous work (Karpathy and Fei-Fei, 2015), containing 113,287 training, 5000 VALidation, and 5000 TEST images, where each image is associated with five manually-annotated captions. Following the cross-modal retrieval work involving MSCOCO (e.g., Lee et al., 2018), we use a subset of the VAL and TEST sets, containing 1000 images each. AMR graphs of the captions are obtained by running the SPRING text-to-AMR parser (Bevilacqua et al., 2021) that is trained on AMR2.0 dataset.[1] The meta-AMR graph is created from the individual AMRs through our merge and refine process described in Algorithm 1 of Section 3.

Parser implementation details. We initialize our IMG2AMR models from VL-BART, which is based on BART$_{\text{Base}}$. BART uses a sub-word tokenizer with a vocabulary size of 50,265. Following SPRING, we expand the vocabulary to include frequent AMR-specific tokens and symbols (e.g., :OP, ARG1, temporal-entity), resulting in a vocabulary size of 53,587. The addition of AMR-specific symbols in vocabulary improves efficiency by avoiding extensive sub-token splitting. The embeddings of these additional tokens are initialized by taking the average of the embeddings of their sub-word constituents. The IMG2AMR$_{\text{direct}}$ models are trained for 60 epochs, while the IMG2AMR$_{\text{2stage}}$ models are trained for 30 epochs per stage. We use a batch size of 10 with gradients being accumulated for 10 batches (hence an effective batch size of 100), the batch size was limited due to the length of the linearized meta-AMRs. The optimizer used is RAdam (Liu et al., 2020b), with a learning rate

[1] https://catalog.ldc.upenn.edu/LDC2017T10

Model	Train/Test AMRs	SMATCH	SEMBLEU-1	SEMBLEU-2
IMG2AMR$_{\text{direct}}$	meta-AMRs	37.7 ± 0.2	32.6 ± 0.8	15.2 ± 0.5
IMG2AMR$_{\text{2stage}}$	meta-AMRs	38.6 ± 0.3	30.9 ± 0.4	15.6 ± 0.3
IMG2AMR$_{\text{direct}}$	caption AMRs	52.3 ± 0.4	68.6 ± 0.4	38.4 ± 0.8

Table 1: TEST results, averaged over 3 runs, for our IMG2AMR models that follow the best setting, when trained and tested on either meta-AMRs or caption AMRs.

of 10^{-5}, and a dropout rate of 0.25. Each experiment is run on one Nvidia V100-32G GPU. Model selection is done based on the best SEMBLEU-1.

5 Results

5.1 Image-to-AMR Parsing Performance

We use the standard measures of SMATCH (Cai and Knight, 2013) and SEMBLEU (Song and Gildea, 2019) to evaluate our various image-to-AMR models. SMATCH compares two AMR graphs by calculating the F1-score between the nodes and edges of these two graphs. This score is calculated after applying a one-to-one mapping of the two AMRs based on their nodes. This mapping is chosen so that it maximizes the F1-score between the two graphs. However, since finding the best exact mapping is NP-complete, a greedy hill-climbing algorithm with multiple random initializations is used to obtain this best mapping. SEMBLEU extends the BLEU (Papineni et al., 2002) metric to AMR graphs, where each AMR node is considered a unigram (used in SEMBLEU-1), and each pair of connected nodes along with their connecting edge is considered a bigram (used in SEMBLEU-2). These metrics are calculated between the model predictions and the noisy AMR ground-truth.

We report results on generating caption AMRs (when the models are trained and tested on these AMRs), as well as meta-AMRs. When evaluating on caption AMR generation, we compare the model output to the five reference AMRs, and report the maximum of these five scores. The intuition is to compare the predicted AMR to the most similar AMR from the five references. Table 1 (top two rows) shows the performance of the models on the task of generating meta-AMRs from TEST images. We perform ablations of the model input combinations on VAL set (see Section D below), and report TEST results for the best setting, which uses all the input features for both models. The 2stage model does slightly better on this task, when looking at the SMATCH and SEMBLEU-2 metrics that take the structure of AMRs into account. Note that SEMBLUE-1 only compares the nodes of the predicted and ground-truth graphs.

Meta-AMR graphs tend to, on average, be longer than individual caption AMRs (~34 vs ~12 nodes and relations). We thus expect the generation of meta-AMRs to be harder than that of caption AMRs. Moreover, although we hypothesize that meta-AMRs capture a holistic meaning for an image, the caption AMRs still capture some (possibly salient) aspect of an image content, and as such are useful to predict, especially if they can be generated with higher accuracy. We thus report the performance of our direct model on generating caption AMRs (when trained on caption AMR graphs); see the final row of Table 1. We can see that, as expected, performance is much higher on generating caption AMRs vs. meta-AMRs.

Given that AMRs and natural language are by design closer in the semantic space, unlike for AMRs and images, it is not unexpected that the results for our image-to-AMR task are not comparable with those of SoTA text-to-AMR parsers, including SPRING. Our results highlight the challenges similar to those of general image-to-graph parsing techniques, including visual scene graph generation (Zhu et al., 2022), where there still exists a large gap in predictive model performance.

5.2 Image-to-AMR for Caption Generation

To better understand the quality of our generated AMRs, we use them to automatically generate sentences from caption AMRs (using an existing AMR-to-text model), and evaluate the quality of these generated sentences against the reference captions of their corresponding images. Specifically, we use the SPRING AMR-to-text model that we train from scratch on a dataset composed of AMR2.0, plus the training MSCOCO captions paired with their (automatically-generated) AMRs.

Model	BLEU-4	CIDEr	METEOR	SPICE
IMG2AMR$_{\text{direct}}$ + AMR2TXT	31.7	111.7	26.8	20.4
VL-BART*	35.1	116.6	28.7	21.5

Table 2: Image captioning results on TEST set, compared with the best reported captioning results for VL-BART.

We evaluate the quality of our AMR-generated captions using standard metrics commonly used in the image captioning community, i.e., CIDEr (Vedantam et al., 2015), METEOR (Denkowski and Lavie, 2014), BLEU-4 (Papineni et al., 2002), and SPICE (Anderson et al., 2016), and compare against VL-BART's best captioning performance as reported in the original paper (Cho et al., 2021). Reported in Table 2, the results clearly show that the quality of the generated AMRs are such that reasonably good captions can be generated from them, suggesting that AMRs can be used as intermediate representations for such downstream tasks. Future work will need to explore the possibility of further adapting the AMR formalism to the visual domain, as well as the possibility of enriching image AMRs via incorporating additional linguistic or commonsense knowledge, that could potentially result in better quality captions.

5.3 Performance per Concept Category

The analysis presented in Section 2 suggests many concepts in AMR graphs tend to be on the more abstract (less perceptual) side. We thus ask the following question: What are some of the categories that are harder to predict? To answer this question, we look into the node prediction performance of our two-stage model for the different entity and relation categories of Section 2. Note that this categorization is available for a subset of nodes only. To get the per-category recall and precision values, we take the node predictions of the first stage of the IMG2AMR$_{\text{2stage}}$ model (trained to predict meta-AMR nodes) on the VAL set. For each VAL image i, we have a set of predicted nodes, which we compare to the set of nodes in the ground-truth meta-AMR associated with the image. When calculating per-category recall/precision values, we only consider nodes that belong to that category. We calculate per-image true positive, true negative, and false positive counts, which are used to obtain the recall and precision using micro-averaging. Fig. 4 presents the per-category (as well as overall) recall and precision values over the VAL set.

Interestingly, events (e.g., *festival*, *baseball*, *tennis*) have the highest precision and recall. These are abstract concepts that are largely absent from SGs, suggesting that relying on a linguistically-motivated formalism is beneficial in capturing such abstract aspects of an image content. The event category contains 14 different types, many referring to sports that have a very distinctive setup, e.g., people wearing specific clothes, holding specific objects, etc. The possibility of encoding such abstract concepts in the training AMRs (generated from human-written descriptions likely to mention the event) helps the model learn to generate them for the relevant images during inference. The next group with high precision and recall are entities (which are likely to be more closely tied to the image regions), and possessives (containing a small number of high-frequency relations, e.g., *have* and *wear*). Semantic relations have a decent performance, but contain a diverse number of types, and need to be further analyzed to disentangle the effect of category vs. frequency.

Quantifiers (many of which are related to counting), geometric relations, and attributes seem to be particularly hard to predict. Counting is known to be hard for deep learning models. Geometric relations are much less frequent in AMRs, compared to SGs. Perhaps, we do need to rely on special features (e.g., relative position of bounding boxes) to improve performance on these relations. Attributes (such as *young*, *old*, *small*) require the model to learn subtle visual cues. In addition to understanding what input features may help improve performance on these categories, we need to further adapt the AMR formalism to the visual domain.

5.4 Qualitative Samples: Generating Descriptive Captions from meta-AMRs

In Section 5.2, we showed that caption AMRs produced by our IMG2AMR model can be used to generate reasonably good quality captions via an AMR-to-text model. Here, we provide samples of how meta-AMRs can be used as rich intermediate representations for generating descriptive captions; see Fig. 5 and Section E. To get these captions, we apply the same AMR-to-text model that we trained

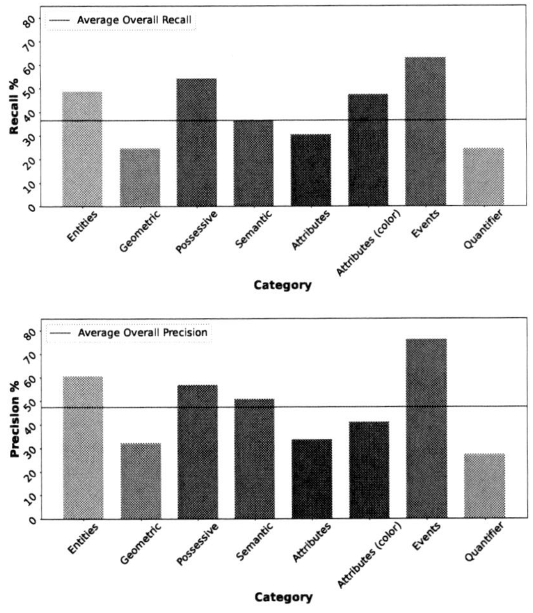

Figure 4: Node prediction performance on VAL, for the two-stage model, broken down by category.

as described in Section 5.2 to the meta-AMRs predicted by our IMG2AMR$_{\text{direct}}$ model. Captions generated from meta-AMRs tend to be longer than the original human-generated captions, and contain much more details about the scene. These captions, however, sometimes contain repetitions of the same underlying concept/relation (though using different wordings), e.g., caption (a) contains both *in grass* and *in a grassy area*. We also see that our hypernym replacement sometimes results in using a more general term in place of a more specific but more appropriate term, e.g., *woman* instead of *girl* in (d). Nonetheless, these results generally point to the usefulness of AMRs and especially meta-AMRs for scene representation and caption generation.

6 Discussion and Outlook

In this paper, we proposed to use a well-known linguistic semantic formalism, i.e., Abstract Meaning Representation (AMR) for scene understanding. We showed through extensive analysis the advantages of AMR vs. the commonly-used visual scene graphs, and proposed to re-purpose existing text-to-AMR parsers for image-to-AMR parsing. Additionally we proposed a graph transformation algorithm that merges several caption-level AMR graphs into a more descriptive meta-AMR graph. Our quantitative (intrinsic and extrinsic) and qualitative evaluations demonstrate the usefulness of (meta-)AMRs as a scene representation formalism.

Our findings point to a few exciting future research directions. Our image-to-AMR parsers can be improved by incorporating richer visual features, a better understanding of the entity and relation categories that are particularly hard to predict for our current models, as well as drawing on methods used for scene graph generation (e.g., Zellers et al., 2018; Zhu et al., 2022). Our meta-AMR generation algorithm can be further tuned to capture visually-salient information (e.g., quantifiers are too hard to learn from images, and perhaps can be dropped from a visual AMR formalism).

Our qualitative samples of captions generated from meta-AMRs show their potential for generating descriptive and/or controlled captions. Controllable image captioning has received a great deal of attention lately (e.g., Cornia et al., 2019; Chen et al., 2020, 2021). It focuses on the use of subjective control, including personalization and style-focused caption generation, as well as objective control on content (controlling what the caption is about, e.g., focused on a set of regions), or on the structure of the output sentence (e.g., controlling sentence length). We believe that by using AMRs as intermediate scene representations, we can bring together the work on these various types of control, as well as draw on the literature on controllable natural language generation (Zhang et al., 2022) for advancing research on rich caption generation.

References

Peter Anderson, Basura Fernando, Mark Johnson, and Stephen Gould. 2016. Spice: Semantic propositional image caption evaluation. In *European Conference on Computer Vision*.

Peter Anderson, Xiaodong He, Chris Buehler, Damien Teney, Mark Johnson, Stephen Gould, and Lei Zhang. 2018. Bottom-up and top-down attention for image captioning and visual question answering. In *IEEE Conference on Computer Vision and Pattern Recognition*.

Laura Banarescu, Claire Bonial, Shu Cai, Madalina Georgescu, Kira Griffitt, Ulf Hermjakob, Kevin Knight, Philipp Koehn, Martha Palmer, and Nathan Schneider. 2013. Abstract meaning representation for sembanking. In *7th Linguistic Annotation Workshop and Interoperability with Discourse*.

Michele Bevilacqua, Rexhina Blloshmi, and Roberto Navigli. 2021. One SPRING to rule them both: Symmetric AMR semantic parsing and generation without a complex pipeline. In *Association for the Advancement of Artificial Intelligence*.

(a) A couple of giraffe standing next to each other in a field near rocks walking in grass in a grassy area.

(b) A yellow and blue fire hydrant on a city street in front at an intersection sitting on the side of the road near a traffic position.

(c) A large long passenger train going across a wooden beach plate, traveling and passing by water.

(d) A woman sitting at a table eating a sandwich and holding a hot dog in a building smiling while eating.

(e) A white area filled with lots of different kinds of donuts with various toppings sitting on them.

(f) A group of people sitting around at a dining table with water posing for a picture.

(g) A person in a red jacket cross country skiing down a snow covered ski slope with a couple of people riding skis and walking on the side of the snowy mountain.

(h) A person in black shirt sitting at a table in a building with a plate of food with and smiling while having meal.

Figure 5: A sample of images, along with descriptive captions automatically generated from the meta-AMRs predicted by our IMG2AMR$_{\mathrm{direct}}$ model. Refer to Section E for the generated meta-AMRs. The url and license information for each of these images is available in Section E. Faces were blurred for privacy.

Claire Bonial, Lucia Donatelli, Mitchell Abrams, Stephanie M. Lukin, Stephen Tratz, Matthew Marge, Ron Artstein, David Traum, and Clare Voss. 2020. Dialogue-AMR: Abstract Meaning Representation for dialogue. In *Proceedings of the 12th Language Resources and Evaluation Conference*.

Julia Bonn, Martha Palmer, Zheng Cai, and Kristin Wright-Bettner. 2020. Spatial AMR: Expanded spatial annotation in the context of a grounded Minecraft corpus. In *Proceedings of the 12th Language Resources and Evaluation Conference (LREC)*.

Shu Cai and Kevin Knight. 2013. Smatch: an evaluation metric for semantic feature structures. In *51st Annual Meeting of the Association for Computational Linguistics*.

Nicolas Carion, Francisco Massa, Gabriel Synnaeve, Nicolas Usunier, Alexander Kirillov, and Sergey Zagoruyko. 2020. End-to-end object detection with transformers. In *European Conference on Computer Vision*.

Long Chen, Zhihong Jiang, Jun Xiao, and Wei Liu. 2021. Human-like controllable image captioning with verb-specific semantic roles. In *Proceedings of the IEEE Conference on Computer Vision and Pattern Recognition*.

Shizhe Chen, Qin Jin, Peng Wang, and Qi Wu. 2020. Say as you wish: Fine-grained control of image caption generation with abstract scene graphs. In *Proceedings of the IEEE Conference on Computer Vision and Pattern Recognition*.

Jaemin Cho, Jie Lei, Hao Tan, and Mohit Bansal. 2021. Unifying vision-and-language tasks via text generation. In *International Conference on Machine Learning*.

Woo Suk Choi, Yu-Jung Heo, Dharani Punithan, and Byoung-Tak Zhang. 2022. Scene graph parsing via Abstract Meaning Representation in pre-trained language models. In *Proceedings of the 2nd Workshop on Deep Learning on Graphs for Natural Language Processing (DLG4NLP 2022)*.

Marcella Cornia, Lorenzo Baraldi, and Rita Cucchiara. 2019. Show, control, and tell: A framework for generating controllable and grounded captioning. In

Proceedings of the IEEE Conference on Computer Vision and Pattern Recognition.

Vinay Damodaran, Sharanya Chakravarthy, Akshay Kumar, Anjana Umapathy, Teruko Mitamura, Yuta Nakashima, Noa Garcia, and Chenhui Chu. 2021. Understanding the role of scene graphs in visual question answering. *arXiv preprint arXiv:2101.05479.*

Michael Denkowski and Alon Lavie. 2014. Meteor universal: Language specific translation evaluation for any target language. In *Workshop on Statistical Machine Translation.*

Andrew Drozdov, Jiawei Zhou, Radu Florian, Andrew McCallum, Tahira Naseem, Yoon Kim, and Ramon Fernandez Astudillo. 2022. Inducing and using alignments for transition-based AMR parsing. In *North American Chapter of the Association for Computational Linguistics.*

Li Fei-Fei, Asha Iyer, Christof Koch, and Pietro Perona. 2007. What do we perceive in a glance of a real-world scene? *Journal of Vision*, 7(1).

Christiane Fellbaum, editor. 1998. *WordNet: An Electronic Lexical Database.* Cambridge, MA: MIT Press.

Ruohan Gao, Bo Xiong, and Kristen Grauman. 2018. Im2flow: Motion hallucination from static images for action recognition. In *Proceedings of the IEEE Conference on Computer Vision and Pattern Recognition.*

Kaiming He, Xiangyu Zhang, Shaoqing Ren, and Jian Sun. 2016. Deep residual learning for image recognition. In *Proceedings of the IEEE Conference on Computer Vision and Pattern Recognition.*

Samitha Herath, Mehrtash Harandi, and Fatih Porikli. 2017. Going deeper into action recognition: A survey. *Image and vision computing*, 60.

Marcel Hildebrandt, Hang Li, Rajat Koner, Volker Tresp, and Stephan Günnemann. 2020. Scene graph reasoning for visual question answering. *arXiv preprint arXiv:2007.01072.*

Zhi Hou, Xiaojiang Peng, Yu Qiao, and Dacheng Tao. 2020. Visual compositional learning for human-object interaction detection. In *European Conference on Computer Vision.*

J. Johnson, R. Krishna, M. Stark, L. J. Li, D. A. Shamma, M. S. Bernstein, and F. F. Li. 2015a. Image retrieval using scene graphs. In *IEEE Conference on Computer Vision and Pattern Recognition.*

Justin Johnson, Ranjay Krishna, Michael Stark, Li-Jia Li, David Shamma, Michael Bernstein, and Li Fei-Fei. 2015b. Image retrieval using scene graphs. In *Proceedings of the IEEE conference on computer vision and pattern recognition.*

A. Karpathy and L. Fei-Fei. 2015. Deep visual-semantic alignments for generating image descriptions. In *IEEE Conference on Computer Vision and Pattern Recognition.*

Yu Kong and Yun Fu. 2022. Human action recognition and prediction: A survey. *International Journal of Computer Vision*, 130(5).

Ranjay Krishna, Yuke Zhu, Oliver Groth, Justin Johnson, Kenji Hata, Joshua Kravitz, Stephanie Chen, Yannis Kalantidis, Li-Jia Li, David A Shamma, Michael Bernstein, and Li Fei-Fei. 2016. Visual genome: Connecting language and vision using crowdsourced dense image annotations.

Kuang-Huei Lee, Xi Chen, Gang Hua, Houdong Hu, and Xiaodong He. 2018. Stacked cross attention for image-text matching. In *European Conference on Computer Vision.*

M. Lewis, Y. Liu, N. Goyal, M. Ghazvininejad, A. Mohamed, O. Levy, V. Stoyanov, and L. Zettlemoyer. 2020. BART: Denoising sequence-to-sequence pre-training for natural language generation, translation, and comprehension. In *Association for Computational Linguistics.*

Xiangyang Li and Shuqiang Jiang. 2019. Know more say less: Image captioning based on scene graphs. *IEEE Transactions on Multimedia*, 21(8):2117–2130.

Yijun Li, Chen Fang, Jimei Yang, Zhaowen Wang, Xin Lu, and Ming-Hsuan Yang. 2018. Flow-grounded spatial-temporal video prediction from still images. In *Proceedings of the European Conference on Computer Vision.*

Kexin Liao, Logan Lebanoff, and Fei Liu. 2018. Abstract Meaning Representation for multi-document summarization. In *the 27th International Conference on Computational Linguistics.*

Tsung-Yi Lin, Michael Maire, Serge Belongie, James Hays, Pietro Perona, Deva Ramanan, Piotr Dollár, and C. Lawrence Zitnick. 2014. Microsoft COCO: Common objects in context. In *European Conference on Computer Vision.*

Fei Liu, Jeffrey Flanigan, Sam Thomson, Norman Sadeh, and Noah A. Smith. 2015. Toward abstractive summarization using semantic representations. In *North American Chapter of the Association for Computational Linguistics.*

Li Liu, Wanli Ouyang, Xiaogang Wang, Paul Fieguth, Jie Chen, Xinwang Liu, and Matti Pietikäinen. 2020a. Deep learning for generic object detection: A survey. *International Journal of Computer Vision*, 128(2).

Liyuan Liu, Haoming Jiang, Pengcheng He, Weizhu Chen, Xiaodong Liu, Jianfeng Gao, and Jiawei Han. 2020b. On the variance of the adaptive learning rate and beyond. In *International Conference on Learning Representations.*

Wei Liu, Dragomir Anguelov, Dumitru Erhan, Christian Szegedy, Scott Reed, Cheng-Yang Fu, and Alexander C Berg. 2016. Ssd: Single shot multibox detector. In *European Conference on Computer Vision*.

Cewu Lu, Ranjay Krishna, Michael Bernstein, and Li Fei-Fei. 2016. Visual relationship detection with language priors. In *European Conference on Computer Vision*.

Ellen M. Markman. 1990. Constraints children place on word meanings. *Cognitive Science*, 14.

Lluís Màrquez, Xavier Carreras, Kenneth C. Litkowski, and Suzanne Stevenson. 2008. Special issue introduction: Semantic role labeling: An introduction to the special issue. *Computational Linguistics*, 34(2).

Tahira Naseem, Austin Blodgett, Sadhana Kumaravel, Tim O'Gorman, Young-Suk Lee, Jeffrey Flanigan, Ramón Fernandez Astudillo, Radu Florian, Salim Roukos, and Nathan Schneider. 2021. DocAMR: Multi-sentence AMR representation and evaluation. In *arXiv*.

Kishore Papineni, Salim Roukos, Todd Ward, and Wei-Jing Zhu. 2002. Bleu: a method for automatic evaluation of machine translation. In *40th Annual Meeting of the Association for Computational Linguistics*.

Shaoqing Ren, Kaiming He, Ross Girshick, and Jian Sun. 2015. Faster R-CNN: Towards real-time object detection with region proposal networks. *Advances in Neural Information Processing Systems*, 28.

Josef Ruppenhofer, Miriam R. L Petruck Michael Ellsworth, Christopher R. Johnson, Collin F. Baker, and Jan Scheffczyk. 2016. *FrameNet II: Extended Theory and Practice*.

Brigit Schroeder and Subarna Tripathi. 2020. Structured query-based image retrieval using scene graphs. In *Proceedings of the IEEE/CVF Conference on Computer Vision and Pattern Recognition Workshops*, pages 178–179.

Sebastian Schuster, Ranjay Krishna, Angel Chang, Li Fei-Fei, and Christopher D Manning. 2015. Generating semantically precise scene graphs from textual descriptions for improved image retrieval. In *Proceedings of the fourth workshop on vision and language*, pages 70–80.

Linfeng Song and Daniel Gildea. 2019. SemBleu: A robust metric for AMR parsing evaluation. In *57th Annual Meeting of the Association for Computational Linguistics*.

Ramakrishna Vedantam, C. Lawrence Zitnick, and Devi Parikh. 2015. Cider: Consensus-based image description evaluation. In *IEEE Conference on Computer Vision and Pattern Recognition*.

Sijin Wang, Ruiping Wang, Ziwei Yao, Shiguang Shan, and Xilin Chen. 2020. Cross-modal scene graph matching for relationship-aware image-text retrieval. In *Proceedings of the IEEE/CVF winter conference on applications of computer vision*, pages 1508–1517.

Qingrong Xia, Zhenghua Li, Rui Wang, and Min Zhang. 2021. Stacked AMR parsing with silver data. In *Findings of the Association for Computational Linguistics: EMNLP*.

Xu Yang, Kaihua Tang, Hanwang Zhang, and Jianfei Cai. 2019. Auto-encoding scene graphs for image captioning. In *Proceedings of the IEEE/CVF Conference on Computer Vision and Pattern Recognition*, pages 10685–10694.

Mark Yatskar, Luke Zettlemoyer, and Ali Farhadi. 2016. Situation recognition: Visual semantic role labeling for image understanding. In *IEEE Conference on Computer Vision and Pattern Recognition*.

Rowan Zellers, Mark Yatskar, Sam Thomson, and Yejin Choi. 2018. Neural motifs: Scene graph parsing with global context. In *IEEE Conference on Computer Vision and Pattern Recognition*.

Cheng Zhang, Wei-Lun Chao, and Dong Xuan. 2019a. An empirical study on leveraging scene graphs for visual question answering. *arXiv preprint arXiv:1907.12133*.

Hanqing Zhang, Haolin Song, Shaoyu Li, Ming Zhou, and Dawei Song. 2022. A survey of controllable text generation using transformer-based pre-trained language models. *arXiv:* `https://arxiv.org/abs/2201.05337`.

Hanwang Zhang, Zawlin Kyaw, Shih-Fu Chang, and Tat-Seng Chua. 2017. Visual translation embedding network for visual relation detection. In *Proceedings of the IEEE Conference on Computer Vision and Pattern Recognition*.

Sheng Zhang, Xutai Ma, Kevin Duh, and Benjamin Van Durme. 2019b. AMR parsing as sequence-to-graph transduction. In *Proceedings of the 57th Annual Meeting of the Association for Computational Linguistics*.

Yiwu Zhong, Liwei Wang, Jianshu Chen, Dong Yu, and Yin Li. 2020. Comprehensive image captioning via scene graph decomposition. In *European Conference on Computer Vision*, pages 211–229. Springer.

Guangming Zhu, Liang Zhang, Youliang Jiang, Yixuan Dang, Haoran Hou, Peiyi Shen, Mingtao Feng, Xia Zhao, Qiguang Miao, Syed Afaq Ali Shah, et al. 2022. Scene graph generation: A comprehensive survey. *arXiv preprint arXiv:2201.00443*.

Cheng Zou, Bohan Wang, Yue Hu, Junqi Liu, Qian Wu, Yu Zhao, Boxun Li, Chenguang Zhang, Chi Zhang, Yichen Wei, et al. 2021. End-to-end human object interaction detection with hoi transformer. In *Proceedings of the IEEE/CVF conference on computer vision and pattern recognition*.

A AMR vs. SG: Entity and Relation Categorization Details

The analysis provided in Section 2 requires us to annotate the entities and relations of a sample of AMRs and SGs into a pre-defined set of categories. We first select all images that appear in both MSCOCO (Lin et al., 2014) and Visual Genome, so we have access to ground-truth scene graphs, as well as captions from which we can generate AMR graphs for the same set of images. We use a single AMR per image, generated from the longest caption, but include all SGs associated with an image in our analysis. For each SG and AMR graph, we consider the entities and relations corresponding to ~900 most frequent types (around 1.3M entity and 1M relation instances for SGs; and around 130K entity and 150K relation instances for AMRs). We annotate these into a pre-defined set of entity and relation categories, including those defined by (Zellers et al., 2018) plus a few we add to cover new AMR relations. Table 5 provides a breakdown of the categories, as well as examples of word types we considered to belong to each category. The table also provides the total number of word types per category and percentages of instances across all types for each category.

Next, we describe our annotation process. SG nodes (entities) come with their most common WordNet sense annotations, which we use to identify their categories. For SG relations, we manually annotate their categories. To annotate AMR entities and relations, we follow a similar procedure, by automatically finding the most common WordNet sense for non-predicate AMR nodes (assuming most of these will be entities) and correcting them if needed. For example, the automatically-identified most common sense of *mouse* is the Animal sense, whereas in our captions, almost all instances of the word point to the computer mouse (Artifact). For any remaining concepts, including predicate nodes (e.g., *eat*, *stand*) and entities for which a category cannot be assigned automatically, we manually identify their categories.

B Distribution of AMR Node Types

Fig. 6 shows the distribution of the 90 AMR role/edge types in our training data. As we can see, keeping the top-20 types is justified given the skewed distribution of the types. Future work will need to examine the nature of the less frequent relations, and the implications of removing them from AMR graphs.

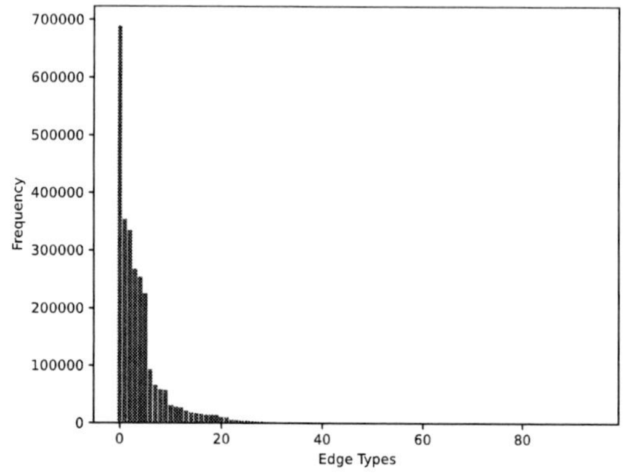

Figure 6: Frequency of the 90 AMR role/edge types prior to the refinement process, which exhibits the characteristics of a long-tail distribution.

C Meta-AMR Construction Example

Fig. 7 shows an example of how a meta-AMR is constructed from five caption-level AMRs. The corresponding captions are provided in red, and the AMR graphs are given in PENMAN notation.

D Ablations

Effect of input on node prediction performance. Table 3 presents performance of meta-AMR node prediction (first stage of IMG2AMR$_{\text{2stage}}$) with different input combinations, in terms of Precision and Recall (when predicted and ground-truth nodes are taken as sets), and BLEU-1 (when the order of nodes in the final linearized AMR is taken into consideration). These results suggest that an overall best performance is achieved by using all input features, namely regions, tags and global image feature.

{r}	{q}	{g}	Recall	Precision	BLEU-1
✓	-	-	34.5	47.1	33.1
-	✓	-	30.4	42.8	29.7
-	-	✓	30.6	39.9	29.1
✓	✓	-	35.8	**49.0**	34.3
✓	-	✓	35.1	47.5	33.9
-	✓	✓	32.9	46.5	32.1
✓	✓	✓	**36.7**	48.4	**35.6**

Table 3: VAL performance of meta-AMR node prediction (first stage of IMG2AMR$_{\text{2stage}}$) with different input combinations.

Effect of input on parsing performance. We train our IMG2AMR models with different inputs to the encoders, and evaluate on VAL set. Specifically, the input to the model may contain the global image feature $\mathbf{g}$, region embeddings $\mathbf{r}$, tag embeddings $\mathbf{q}$ (for the first encoder), and node embeddings $\mathbf{n}$ (for the second encoder of IMG2AMR$_{\text{2stage}}$). Table 4 reports the VAL results of our two models (trained and tested with meta-AMRs) with different input combinations (region embeddings, tag embeddings, global image features) for the direct model, and (node embeddings, global image features, region embeddings) for the second encoder of the 2stage model. For IMG2AMR$_{\text{2stage}}$, we fix the input of the first encoder to the best combination according to Table 3 above, and ablate over the input of the second encoder. Both models are trained and tested with meta-AMRs. As we can see, richer input generally results in better performance. We can also see a big drop in the performance of IMG2AMR$_{\text{direct}}$ when only region features are used as input, suggesting that tags can help associate mappings between regions and AMR concepts.

Model Input	SMATCH	SEMBLEU-1	SEMBLEU-2
IMG2AMR$_{\text{direct}}$			
$\{\mathbf{r}\}$	30.3	18.6	5.4
$\{\mathbf{r}, \mathbf{q}\}$	**39.1**	32.9	16.2
$\{\mathbf{r}, \mathbf{q}, \mathbf{g}\}$	39.0	**33.7**	**16.4**
IMG2AMR$_{\text{2stage}}$			
$\{\mathbf{n}\}$	39.3	31.3	16.1
$\{\mathbf{n}, \mathbf{g}\}$	39.6	31.9	16.3
$\{\mathbf{n}, \mathbf{g}, \mathbf{r}\}$	**40.4**	**32.6**	**16.9**

Table 4: Ablation over model inputs on VAL, for both IMG2AMR models. For IMG2AMR$_{\text{2stage}}$ we use all features $\{\mathbf{r}, \mathbf{q}, \mathbf{g}\}$ as the 1st encoder input.

Cateogry	Example Types per Category	#Types AMR	#Types SG	%Tokens AMR	%Tokens SG
	ENTITIES				
Artifact	clock, umbrella, bottle	128	128	22.7	24.4
Part	eyes, finger, wing	21	44	3.1	13.1
Location	beach, mountain, kitchen	86	52	20.7	11.2
Person	man, women, speaker	30	19	17.9	11
Flora/Nature	ocean, tree, flower	20	34	6.1	10.2
Clothing	dress, scarf, suit	11	31	1.1	7.7
Food	orange, donut, bread	52	23	8	2.8
Animal	horse, bird, cat	16	20	6.4	4.7
Vehicle	car, motorcycle, bicycle	18	17	6.1	4.5
Furniture	table, chair, couch	9	10	4.0	2.9
Structure	window, tower, circle	13	18	2.1	5.4
Building	brick, house, cement	6	6	1.8	2.1
	RELATIONS				
Geometric	down, edge, between	48	122	12.4	56.6
Possessive	have, wear, contain	5	42	5.9	30.6
Semantic	attempt, carry, eat	183	275	38.3	11.6
Attribute Color	color, white, blue	13	8	5.6	0.1
Attribute	young, small, colorful	82	-	12.8	-
AMR specific	and, or, date-entity	8	-	11.1	-
Quantifier	more, both, few	31	1	9.3	0.1
Event	soccer, party, festival	14	-	3.4	-
Misc	they, something, you	6	13	1.1	1.0

Table 5: The list of AMR and SG entity and relation categories, as well as examples of word types, number of types, and percentage of tokens per category.

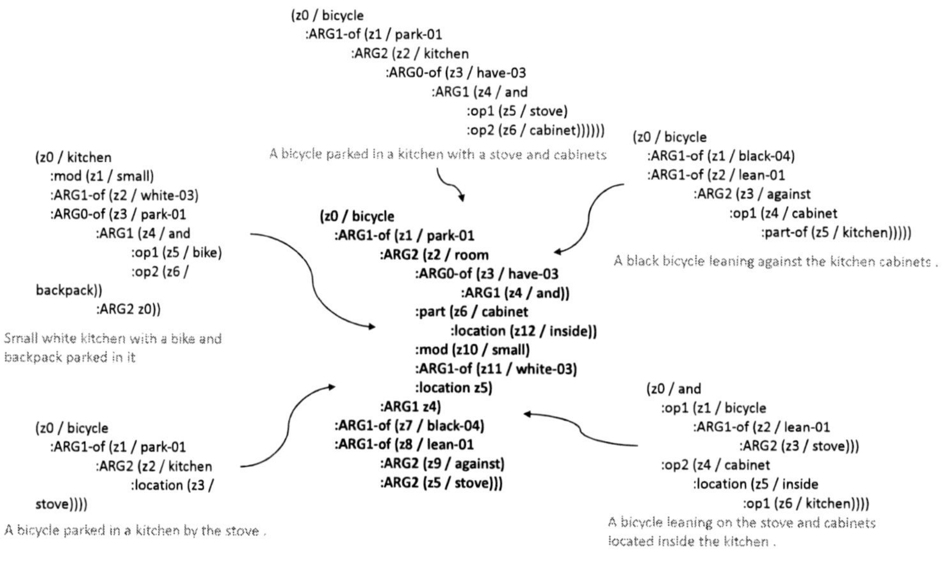

Figure 7: An example of five caption AMRs and their corresponding meta-AMR. Captions are marked as red.

E Generated AMRs for the Qualitative Samples

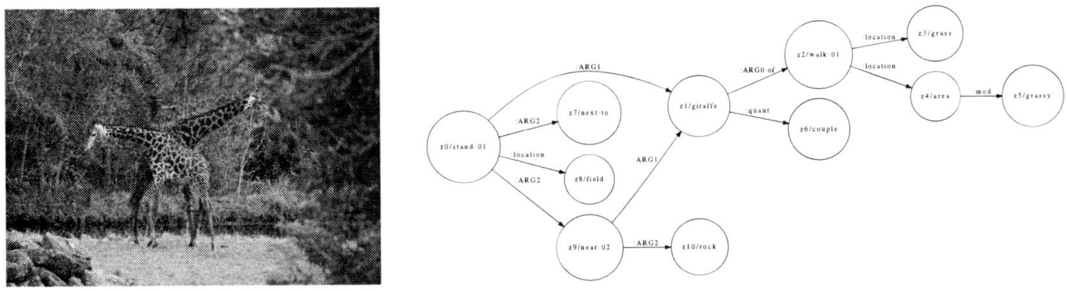

(a) A couple of giraffe standing next to each other in a field near rocks walking in grass in a grassy area.

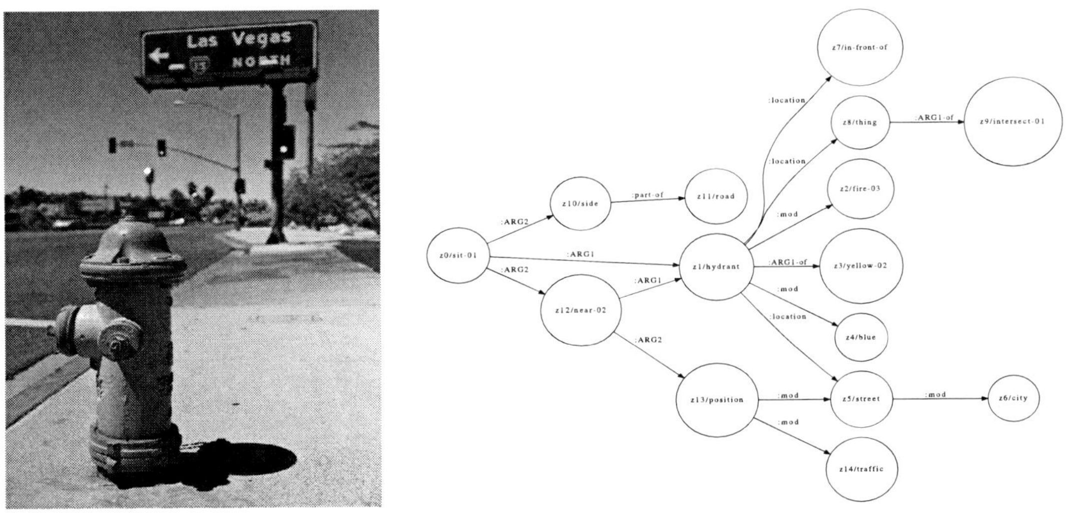

(b) A yellow and blue fire hydrant on a city street in front at an intersection sitting on the side of the road near a traffic position.

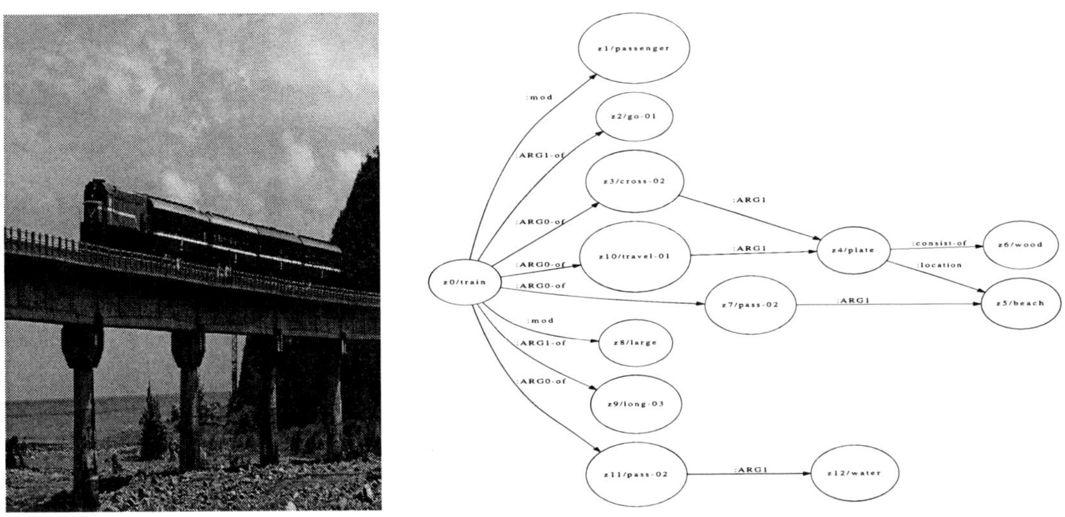

(c) A large long passenger train going across a wooden beach plate, traveling and passing by water.

Figure 8: Images used in Section 5.4, along with their predicted AMRs and generated captions. Refer to Section 5.4 for more details.

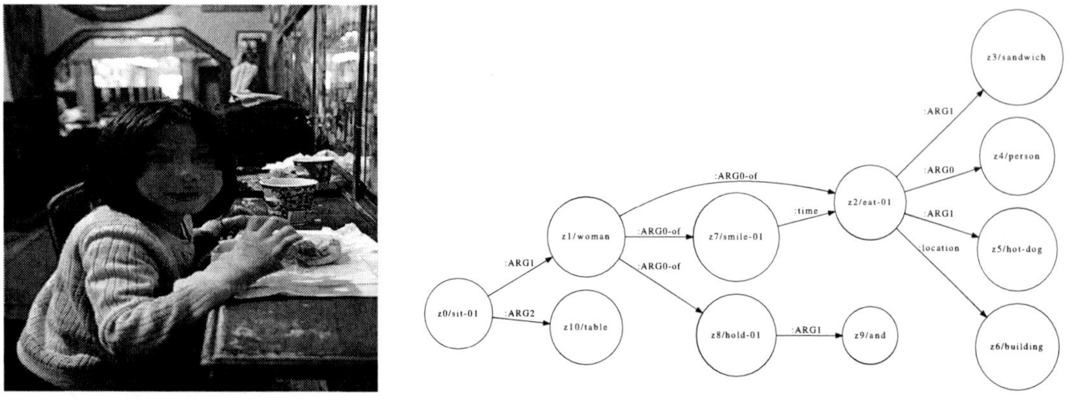

(a) A woman sitting at a table eating a sandwich and holding a hot dog in a building smiling while eating.

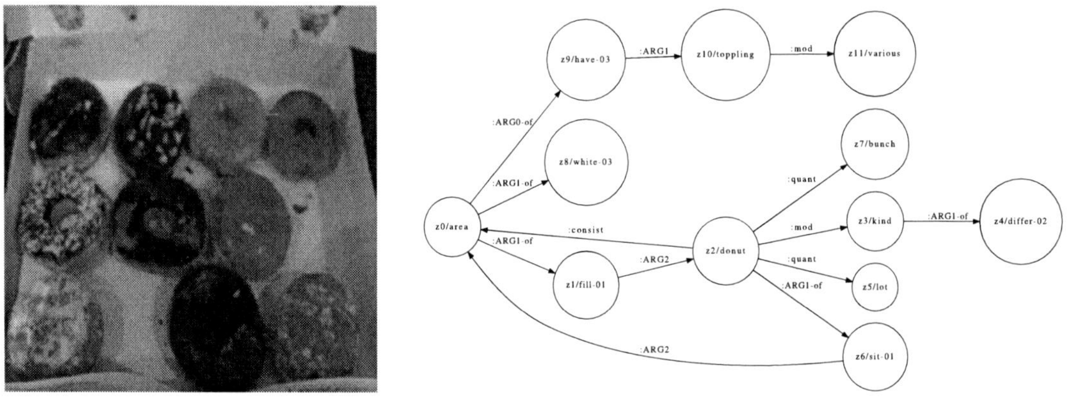

(b) A white area filled with lots of different kinds of donuts with various toppings sitting on them.

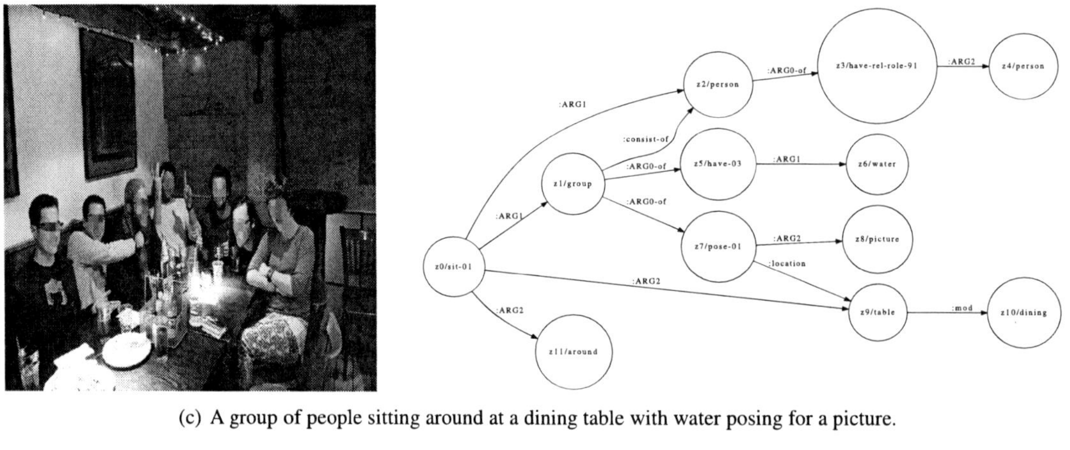

(c) A group of people sitting around at a dining table with water posing for a picture.

Figure 9: (cont) Images used in Section 5.4, along with their predicted AMRs and generated captions. Refer to Section 5.4 for more details.

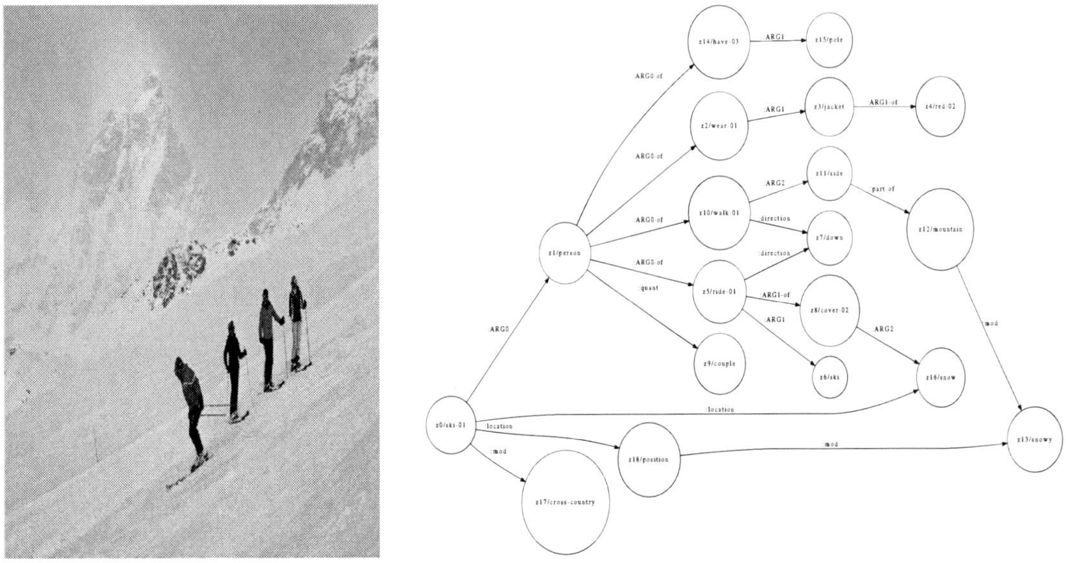

(a) A person in a red jacket cross country skiing down a snow covered ski slope with a couple of people riding skis and walking on the side of the snowy mountain.

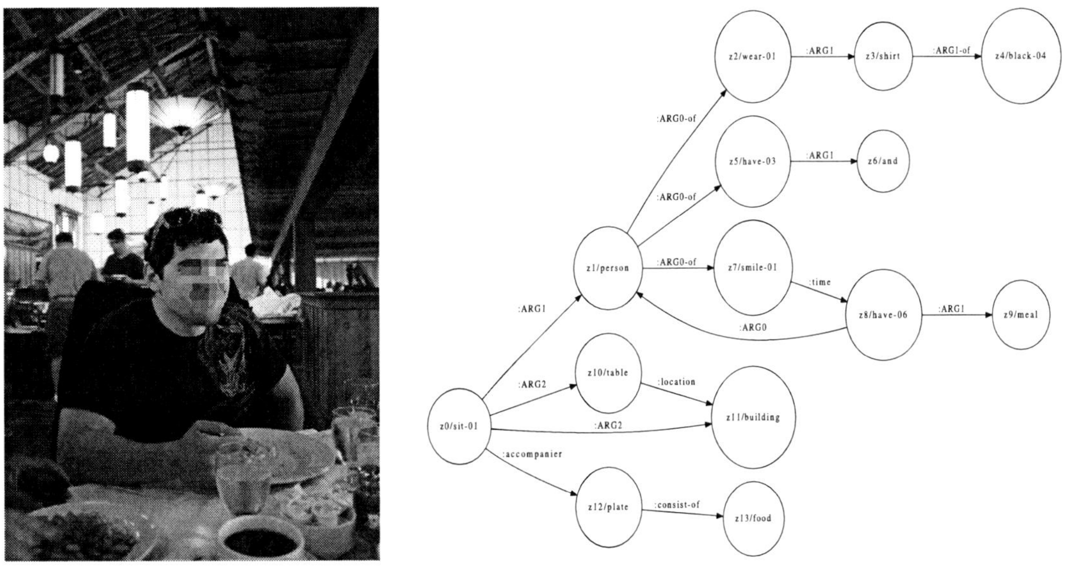

(b) A person in black shirt sitting at a table in a building with a plate of food with and smiling while having meal.

Figure 10: (cont) Images used in Section 5.4, along with their predicted AMRs and generated captions. Refer to Section 5.4 for more details.

Images used in this section (and the rest of the paper) are under a Creative Commons Attribution License 2.0. They are available at (by the order of their appearance in this section):

- http://farm6.staticflickr.com/5299/5465041730_3fe1246cae_z.jpg and http://cocodataset.org/#explore?id=505440
- http://farm6.staticflickr.com/5294/5461489420_1e4141517b_z.jpg and http://cocodataset.org/#explore?id=332654
- http://farm4.staticflickr.com/3719/9115013219_344a42ce47_z.jpg and http://cocodataset.org/#explore?id=329486
- http://farm4.staticflickr.com/3091/3187069218_162b55b720_z.jpg and http://cocodataset.org/#explore?id=569839
- http://farm3.staticflickr.com/2020/1932016761_934411ac16_z.jpg and http://cocodataset.org/#explore?id=5754
- http://farm4.staticflickr.com/3703/10047186866_e6b43fbd32_z.jpg and http://cocodataset.org/#explore?id=298443
- http://farm8.staticflickr.com/7170/6795850593_435a36bcd9_z.jpg and http://cocodataset.org/#explore?id=239235
- http://farm4.staticflickr.com/3786/9676804086_dbb624af5c_z.jpg and http://cocodataset.org/#explore?id=386559

Syntactic Surprisal From Neural Models Predicts, But Underestimates, Human Processing Difficulty From Syntactic Ambiguities

Suhas Arehalli
Johns Hopkins University
suhas@jhu.edu

Brian Dillon
University of Massachusetts, Amherst
brian@linguist.umass.edu

Tal Linzen
New York University
linzen@nyu.edu

Abstract

Humans exhibit garden path effects: When reading sentences that are temporarily structurally ambiguous, they slow down when the structure is disambiguated in favor of the less preferred alternative. Surprisal theory (Hale, 2001; Levy, 2008), a prominent explanation of this finding, proposes that these slowdowns are due to the unpredictability of each of the words that occur in these sentences. Challenging this hypothesis, van Schijndel and Linzen (2021) find that estimates of the cost of word predictability derived from language models severely underestimate the magnitude of human garden path effects. In this work, we consider whether this underestimation is due to the fact that humans weight syntactic factors in their predictions more highly than language models do. We propose a method for estimating syntactic predictability from a language model, allowing us to weigh the cost of lexical and syntactic predictability independently. We find that treating syntactic predictability independently from lexical predictability indeed results in larger estimates of garden path. At the same time, even when syntactic predictability is independently weighted, surprisal still greatly underestimate the magnitude of human garden path effects. Our results support the hypothesis that predictability is not the only factor responsible for the processing cost associated with garden path sentences.

1 Introduction

Readers exhibit *garden path effects*: When reading a temporarily syntactically ambiguous sentence, they tend to slow down when the sentence is disambiguated in favor of the less preferred parse. For example, a participant who reads the sentence fragment

(1) The suspect sent the file ...
a. ... to the lawyer.
b. ... deserved further investigation.

can construct a partial parse in at least two distinct ways: In one reading, the verb *sent* acts as the main verb of the sentence, and the continuation of the sentence as an additional argument to *sent* (as in 1a). In another, less likely, reading, *sent the file* acts as a modifier in a complex subject, which then requires an additional verb phrase to form a complete sentence (as in 1b). Prior work has demonstrated that regions like *deserved further investigation*, which disambiguate these temporarily ambiguous sentences in favor of the modifier parse (1b), are read slower than those same words would be in an unambiguous version of sentence, such as the following:

(2) The suspect *who was* sent the file deserved further investigation.

In (2), the presence of *who was* signals to the reader that *sent the file* acts as a modifier (Frazier and Fodor, 1978).

One account of this phenomenon, surprisal theory (Hale, 2001; Levy, 2008), suggests that readers maintain a probabilistic representation of all possible parses of the input as they process the sentence incrementally. Processing difficulty in garden path sentences is the cost associated with updating this representation; this cost is proportional to the negative log probability, or surprisal, of the newly observed material under the reader's model of upcoming words. This theory predicts that the slowdown associated with garden path sentences can be entirely captured by the differences in surprisal between the disambiguating region in ambiguous garden path sentences and that same region in a matched unambiguous sentence.

Van Schijndel and Linzen (2021) tested this hypothesis. They estimated the surprisals associated with garden path sentences using LSTM language models (LMs) trained over large natural language

Proceedings of the 26th Conference on Computational Natural Language Learning (CoNLL), pages 301 - 313
December 7-8, 2022 ©2022 Association for Computational Linguistics

corpora. Based on the core assumption of surprisal theory—that processing difficulty on a word, when all lexical factors are kept constant, stands in a constant proportion to the word's surprisal, regardless of its syntactic context—they estimated a conversion factor between surprisal and reading times from non-garden path sentences. Applying this conversion factor to the critical words in garden path sentences, van Schijndel and Linzen found that surprisal theory, when paired with the surprisals estimated by their models, severely underestimated the magnitude of the garden path effect for three garden path constructions, consistent with attempts to estimate the magnitude of other syntactically-modulated effects (Wilcox et al., 2021). Moreover, the predicted reading times did not correctly predict differences across the difference garden path constructions, suggesting that no single conversion factor between surprisal and reading times could predict the magnitude of the garden path effect in all three constructions.

The underestimation documented by van Schijndel and Linzen can be interpreted in one of two ways: Either (1) surprisal theory cannot, on its own, account for garden path effects; or (2) predictability estimates derived from LSTM LMs fail to capture some aspect of human prediction that is crucial to explaining the processing of garden path sentences. This work investigates the latter possibility. We ask if the gap between the magnitude of human garden path effects in humans and the magnitude that surprisal theory predicts from LMs is due to a mismatch between how humans and LMs weigh two contributors to word-level surprisal: syntactic and lexical predictability. We hypothesize that the LM next-word prediction objective does not sufficiently emphasize the importance that syntactic structure carries for human readers, who may be more actively concerned with interpreting the sentence. In this scenario, since garden paths are the product of unpredictable syntactic structure—as opposed to an unpredictable lexical item—using a LM predictability estimate for the next word could lead to underestimation of garden path effects.

We test the hypothesis that the gap between model and human effects can be bridged by teasing apart the overall predictability of a word from the surprisal associated with the syntactic structure implied by the word (see Figure 1) and weighting the two factors independently, possibly assigning a higher weight to syntactic surprisal. In this rea-

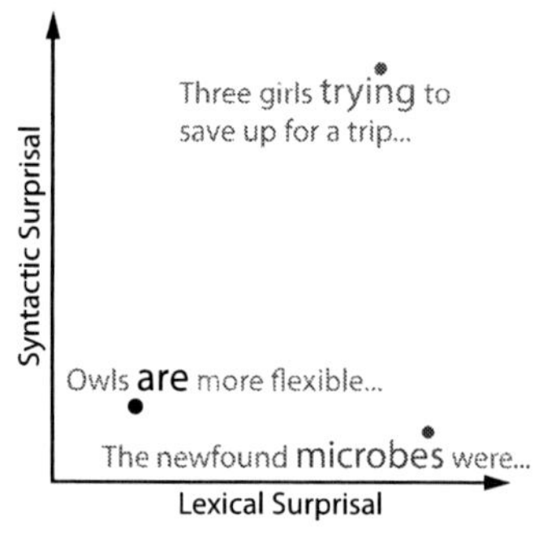

Figure 1: A depiction of the relationship between syntactic and lexical surprisal. Some word tokens, such as *are* in the context of *owls are more flexible*, are highly predictable in all respects. Others are unpredictable due to the syntactic structures they imply (*trying* in *girls trying to save up*), and are expected to be assigned high syntactic and lexical surprisal. Tokens such as *microbes* in the context *the newfound microbes were*, on the other hand, appear in a predictable syntactic environment, but are unpredictable due to their low lexical frequency; such words should be assigned low syntactic surprisal but high lexical surprisal. Since words that appear in unpredictable syntactic environments are themselves unpredictable, we do not expect to find words with high syntactic surprisal but low lexical surprisal.

soning, we follow prior work on syntactic or unlexicalized surprisal carried out in the context of symbolic parsers, where the probability of a structure and particular lexical item can be explicitly disentangled (Demberg and Keller, 2008; Roark et al., 2009). But while past work has demonstrated that that unlexicalized suprisal from symbolic parsers correlates with measures of human processing difficulty (Demberg and Keller, 2008), simple recurrent neural networks trained to predict sequences of part-of-speech tags have been shown to track processing difficulty even more strongly (Frank, 2009), suggesting that even fairly limited syntactic representations like part-of-speech tags can act as a reasonable proxy of syntactic structure when modeling human behavior.

To compute LSTM-based syntactic surprisal, we train the LM with an auxiliary objective—estimating the likelihood of the next word's supertag under the Combinatory Categorial Grammar (CCG) framework (Steedman, 1987)—following Enguehard et al. (2017). Such supertags can be viewed as enriched part-of-speech tags that encode syntactic information about how a particular word can be combined with its local environment. We then define syntactic surprisal in terms of the likelihood of the next word's CCG supertag, and propose a method of estimating that likelihood using our modified LMs. We validate our formulation of syntactic surprisal by demonstrating that it captures syntactic processing difficulty in garden path sentences, while, crucially, not tracking unpredictability that is due to low frequency lexical items. Following van Schijndel and Linzen (2021), we then use the syntactic and lexical surprisal values derived from those models to predict reading times for three types of garden path sentences. We find that adding syntactic surprisal as a separate predictor does lead to larger estimates of garden path effects, but those estimates are still an order of magnitude lower than empirical garden path effects. Finally, we discuss the implications of these findings for surprisal theory and single-stage models of syntactic processing.

2 Computing Syntactic Surprisal

Each incoming word can cause an adjustment in the reader's beliefs about the syntactic structure of the sentence; when a syntactic structure that was assigned a low probability prior to reading the word now has high probability, the word can be said to have high syntactic surprisal. We will operationalize this intuition as the predictability of next word's supertag under the Combinatory Categorial Grammar (CCG) formalism (Steedman, 1987):

$$\text{surp}_{\text{syn}} = -\log(P(c_n \mid w_1, ..., w_{n-1})), \quad (1)$$

where c_n is the CCG supertag of the n-th word. A CCG supertag encodes how a word combines syntactically with adjacent constituents. For example, a token with the tag S\NP combines with an NP to its left to form an S constituent, and a token with the tag (S\NP)/NP combines with an NP to its right to form an S\NP constituent. Since the sequence of supertags associated with all of the words of a sentence often allows only one valid parse, accurately predicting a sentence's supertags has been described as "almost parsing" (Bangalore and Joshi, 1999); consequently, incremental CCG supertagging can be seen as almost *incremental* parsing.

We contrast this syntactic surprisal measure with the standard token surprisal measure, which we refer to as *lexical* surprisal:

$$\text{surp}_{\text{lex}} = -\log(P(w_n \mid w_1, ..., w_{n-1})). \quad (2)$$

Note that what we call lexical surprisal captures *all* factors that contribute to a token's predictability, including syntactic ones.

In order to compute syntactic and lexical surprisal for a given word, we need models that predict, given a left context, not only the next token, as a standard LM does, but also the next token's supertag. To do this, we train models with both a language modeling and CCG supertagging objective, and estimate the distribution over the next word's tag by marginalizing over the distribution over the next word that is defined by the LM. Formally, for a sequence of words $w_1, ..., w_n \in W$ with supertags $c_1, ..., c_n \in C$, our model estimates the probability of the next word given all observed words, $p_{w_{n+1}} = P(w_{n+1} \mid w_1, ..., w_n)$, and the probability of the most recent word's supertag given all currently observed words, $p_{c_n|w_n} = P(c_n \mid w_1, ..., w_n)$. We then infer the distribution over the next word's supertag as

$$P(c_{n+1}|w_1, ..., w_n) = \sum_{w^*_{n+1} \in W} p_{c_{n+1}|w^*_{n+1}} p_{w^*_{n+1}} \quad (3)$$

If we knew the supertag of the next word c_{n+1}, we could simply compute the surprisal of that supertag, $-\log P(c_{n+1} \mid w_1, ..., w_n)$. By contrast with lexical surprisal, however—where there is no uncertainty about the identity of w_{n+1} once that word has been read—a word's supertag is often ambiguous during incremental processing. Consider the verb *gathered* in the following sentences, for example:

(3) The squirrels gathered near the tree.

(4) The squirrels gathered a few acorns.

In (3), *gathered* would eventually be assigned the supertag S\NP, indicating that *gathered* is used in its intransitive frame—a number of squirrels assembled together as a group—and takes no direct object. In (4), on the other hand, the appropriate supertag would be (S\NP)/NP, which indicates that in this sentence *gathered* is used in a transitive frame and takes the noun phrase *a few acorns* as a direct object. When processing this sentence incrementally, a reader must maintain this uncertainty over the appropriate supertag for a word past the point at which they have read that word. A measure of syntactic surprisal that aims to model processing difficulty at a particular word should similarly take into account uncertainty over the supertag of a word even after the word itself has been processed. We take this uncertainty into account by using the distribution $p_{c_n|w_n}$ that our models define over supertags, and computing syntactic surprisal by marginalizing over this distribution:

$$p_{c_{n+1}|w_n} = P(c_{n+1} \mid w_1, ..., w_n) \quad (4)$$

$$surp_{syn} = -\log \sum_{c^*_{n+1} \in C} p_{c^*_{n+1}|w_n} p_{c_{n+1}|w_{n+1}} \quad (5)$$

2.1 Model Architecture and Training

We trained four models, differing only in their random seed, on both a language modeling and CCG supertagging objective. The models consisted of an LSTM shared across the two objectives, which we refer to here as the encoder, and two classifiers, one for language modeling and another for CCG supertagging, which we refer to as the decoders.

Following Gulordava et al. (2018), the encoder was a two-layer LSTM with 650 units per layer. Each decoder consists of a single linear layer followed by the softmax operation. For the supertagging objective, we trained using CCGBank (Hockenmaier and Steedman, 2007), a set of CCG annotations for the Wall Street Journal section of the Penn Treebank (Marcus et al., 1993). The corpus we used for language modeling was a concatenation of the Wall Street Journal portion of the Penn Treebank and the 80 million words from the English Wikipedia used by Gulordava et al. (2018). Language modeling and supertagging losses were weighted equally during training.

Models achieved language modeling perplexities ranging from 74.76 to 75.70 on the test portion of the Gulordava et al. (2018) corpus, while Gulordava et al. (2018)'s best language model achieved a perplexity of 52.0. Models assigned the highest likelihood to the correct CCG supertag in the CCGBank test set between 84.1% and 84.5% of the time, compared to bi-LSTM supertaggers which can achieve an accuracy of 94.1% (Vaswani et al., 2016). Note that these supertagging numbers are not directly comparable, as our models use unidirectional LSTMs and thus have no access to a word's right context when supertagging.

2.2 Experimental data

We evaluated our model on a subset of the Syntactic Ambiguity Processing (SAP) Benchmark (Huang et al., 2022), a dataset containing self-paced reading times from 2000 native English speakers who read a variety of syntactically complex constructions as well as comparatively simple filler sentences. The large size of the dataset allows us to get precise estimates of the magnitude of the garden path effect for each of the three types of garden path sentences it contains. We describe each of these constructions in what follows.

Main Verb/Reduced Relative (MVRR) This ambiguity is illustrated in (5):

(5) The suspect sent the file **deserved** further investigation given the new evidence.

(6) The suspect who was sent the file **deserved** further investigation given the new evidence.

In (5), before reading the word *deserved*, the reader can interpret *sent the file* either as a main verb and direct object (where the subject has sent the file) or as a reduced relative clause (where the subject has had the file sent to them). This is disambiguated in favor of the reduced relative clause reading by the next word, *deserved*, which is the true main verb of the complete sentence. We can measure the processing difficulty incurred by this disambiguation by comparing the reading times at *deserved* in (5) with the reading times at *deserved* in (6), where the relative clause *who was sent the file* is unreduced and thus unambiguous.

Noun Phrase/Sentence (NPS) The NPS ambiguity is illustrated in (7):

(7) The suspect showed the file **deserved** further investigation during the murder trial.

(8) The suspect showed that the file **deserved** further investigation during the murder trial.

Before reading *deserved* in (7), *the file* can be interpreted as either a direct object, where the suspect is presenting a file to someone, or as the beginning of a sentential complement, where the suspect is making a point. The word *deserved* disambiguates the sentence in favor of the less frequent sentential complement reading. As before, the matched control sentence (8) avoids the ambiguity, here by using the explicit complementizer *that* before *the file*; this control makes it possible to measure the slowdown associated with disambiguation.

Noun Phrase/Zero (NPZ): Finally, in (9), before reading *deserved*, *changed* can be interpreted in two ways: as a transitive verb taking *the file* as a noun phrase direct object (where the file was changed by the suspect); or as an intransitive verb, with *the file* as the subject of a separate clause (where the suspect was changed):

(9) Because the suspect changed the file **deserved** further investigation during the jury discussions.

(10) Because the suspect changed, the file **deserved** further investigation during the jury discussions.

The word *deserved* disambiguates the sentence in favor of the less frequent intransitive reading. Introducing a comma between the clauses in the matched sentence (10) removes the ambiguity.

3 Validating Syntactic Surprisal

We first validate that our syntactic surprisal measure successfully isolates syntactic predictability from word predictability. To be satisfied that that is the case, we will require two things be true: first, we expect syntactic surprisal to capture processing difficulty that is the result of syntactic unpredictability; and second, we expect that syntactic surprisal is **not** redundant with lexical predictability. We will evaluate each of these desiderata in turn.

3.1 Syntactic Surprisal Captures Syntactic Processing Difficulty

To verify that syntactic surprisal can capture syntactic unpredictability, we investigate differences in syntactic surprisal between the ambiguous and unambiguous garden path sentences in Huang et al. (2022). Since garden path effects are the result of ambiguity about the syntactic structure of a sentence, a difference in surprisal at the point of disambiguation indicates sensitivity to differences in syntactic predictability.

We found differences in the expected direction for all three types of garden sentences. This was the case both for lexical surprisal—consistent with prior work (Hale, 2001; van Schijndel and Linzen, 2021)—and for syntactic surprisal (Figure 2). We did not find differences in the same direction before the point of disambiguation, indicating that the differences we observe after disambiguation are not a consequence differences in surprisal earlier in the sentence that the LM has not fully recovered from.

3.2 Syntactic Surprisal Captures Only Syntactic Predictability

To verify that syntactic surprisal successfully isolates syntactic factors on predictability, we make two comparisons: first, to lexical surprisal, to verify that syntactic surprisal does not capture all of the variance captured by lexical surprisal; and second, to unigram frequency, to verify that syntactic surprisal is not driven by the frequency of specific lexical items.

Syntactical surprisal does not capture all of the variance captured by lexical surprisal If syntactic surprisal captures a strict subset of the variance captured by lexical surprisal, we expect to see a subset of words with high lexical surprisal and low syntactic surprisal (in addition, perhaps, to words with highly correlated syntactic and lexical surprisals). This subset should represent words that are unpredictable for reasons that are independent of the syntactic structures they imply. By contrast, words that introduce infrequent syntactic structures should have both high syntactic surprisal and high lexical surprisal, as the unpredictability of the syntactic structure means that a word that implies that structure is necessarily unpredictable. This matches what we see in Figure 3a: The relatively frequent verb *trying* introducing a reduced relative clause has high syntactic and lexical surprisal, while infrequent nouns like *microbe* have low syntactic surprisal but high lexical surprisal.

High syntactic surprisal does not reflect low unigram frequency In Figure 3b, we plot the syntactic surprisals of words from the filler items with their log-frequency in the Corpus of Contemporary American English (COCA; Davies 2008–). We find a significant but small positive correlation between the two ($r = 0.064$, $t = 3.18$, $p < 0.005$), indicating that more frequent words have a *higher* syntactic surprisal — the opposite of what we would expect if lexical frequency were driving syntactic surprisal effects. This may be due to the fact that function words, which are generally high-frequency, typically introduce additional syntactic structure

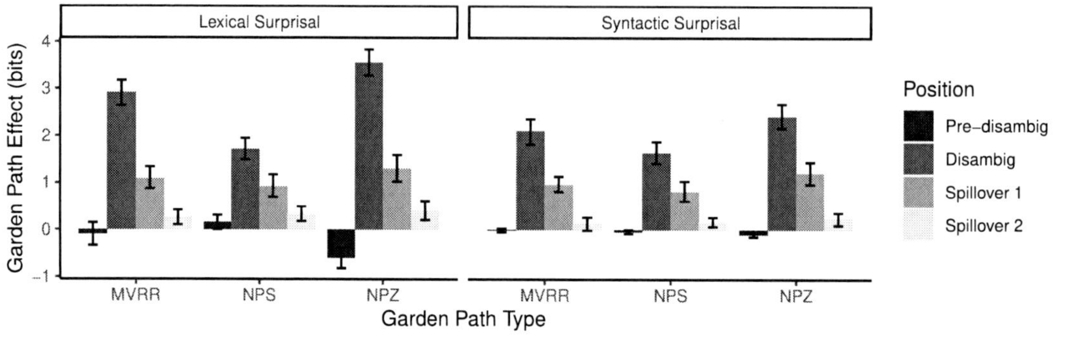

Figure 2: Differences in surprisal estimates between ambiguous and unambiguous garden path sentences at and around the disambiguating verb. Bars indicate 95% confidence intervals.

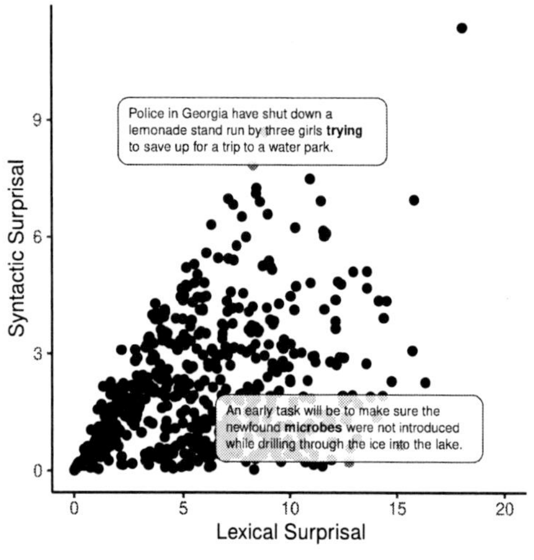

(a) Lexical vs. syntactic surprisal.

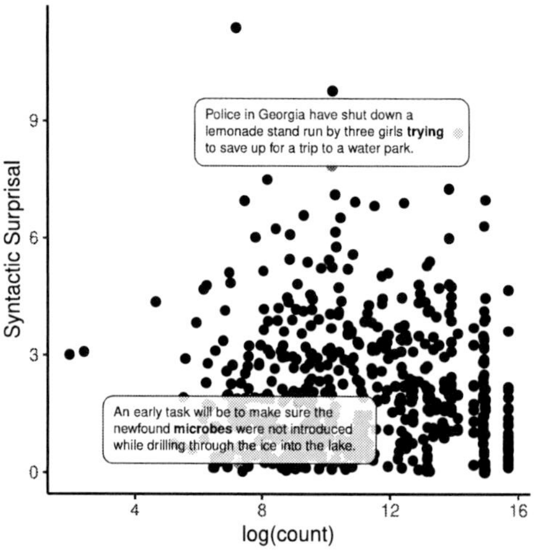

(b) Log unigram frequency vs. syntactic surprisal.

Figure 3: Correlations between syntactic surprisal, lexical surprisal, and unigram frequency for each word in the filler items of Huang et al. (2022). Since these results are fairly consistent across model instances, we present results from a single instance. Two words — one with high syntactic surprisal and high lexical surprisal and one with high lexical surprisal but low syntactic surprisal — are labeled with their context.

and thus have higher-than-average syntactic surprisal.

These three results — that syntactic surprisal captures garden path effects, that we find a subset of words with low syntactic surprisal and high lexical surprisal, and that we find no evidence of low lexical frequency driving syntactic surprisal — suggest that syntactic surprisal captures only the syntactic contributions to a word's unpredictability. We will now use syntactic surprisal in concert with lexical surprisal to directly predict the magnitude of garden path effects.

4 Evaluating Against Human Reading Times

Recall that surprisal theory assumes a linear relationship between surprisal and measures of processing difficulty such as reading times. We follow van Schijndel and Linzen (2021) and estimate a mapping between our surprisal measures and reading times by fitting linear mixed-effects models to the filler (i.e., non-garden path) materials from Huang et al. (2022). In order to compare syntactic and lexical surprisal, we fit four conversion models: one with syntactic surprisal as a predictor, one with lexical surprisal, one with both types of surprisal, and one that does not include either surprisal measure. All four models included baseline predictors other than surprisal — unigram frequency, word position, and word length — which on their own are not expected to capture garden path effects. To account for spillover effects, where processing difficulty from a word spills over to affect reading times at future words, we included all of the aforementioned factors (except word position) not only for the current word but also for the two prior words (a simplification of the technique of van Schijndel and Linzen 2021). This process is repeated with each of the four sets of surprisals extracted from our four language model/supertagger instances. Further details about the surprisal-to-RT conversion process are presented in Appendix A.1. After all four of our models have been fit to the filler items, we use the estimated coefficients to predict reading times for the each of the critical items.

5 Results

Predicted RT differences from our conversion models, as well as the RT differences observed in humans, are presented in Figure 4a. Regardless of the predictors used in the mixed-effects model—lexical surprisal, syntactic surprisal, neither, or both—predicted reading time differences greatly underestimate the reading time differences observed in humans. This is unlikely to be an issue with our surprisal-to-reading-times conversion method more broadly, as at the pre-disambiguation word, RTs and predicted RTs match much more closely than in post-disambiguation regions (particularly in capturing effects in the pre-disambiguation region in NPS sentences), indicating that the difference in magnitudes is due specifically to an underestimation of the garden path effect.

While the inclusion of syntactic surprisal does not close the gap between model predictions and the empirical reading times, it does typically lead to a larger predicted garden path effect. To see this difference more clearly, in Figure 4b we exclude the human reading times and zoom in on the garden path effects predicted by the models. To determine whether adding syntactic surprisal as a predictor affected the magnitude of the garden path effects we predicted, we fit a Linear Mixed Effects Model over all of our conversion models' predicted reading times for each garden path construction at each word in the critical region. We present the results of this analysis for the effect of interest (the interaction between the conversion model and the garden path effect) in Table 1. We find that (1) models containing both surprisals predicted the largest garden path effects at the disambiguating word and first spillover word, (2) models with only syntactic surprisal predicted greater garden path effects than models with only lexical or no surprisal at the disambiguating word, and (3) models with only lexical surprisal predicted larger garden path effects than models with only syntactic or no surprisal in the spillover regions. Note that while models with only lexical surprisal did predict larger effects than other conversion models at the second spillover word, the fact that this only takes place long after the disambiguating word suggests that this difference is due to differing spillover profiles amongst our surprisal measures. Since this work focuses on the estimation of the magnitude of garden path effects, we leave an investigation of this to future work.

6 Discussion

What is the source of the discrepancy between the magnitude of garden path effects in humans and surprisal-based estimates of those magnitudes from neural network language models? In this paper, we have evaluated one possible answer to this question: that word predictability estimates from LMs underweight the importance of syntax to the predictions made by humans. We have proposed a method of estimating syntactic predictability from LSTM LMs augmented with a CCG supertagging auxiliary objective; confirmed that this measure matches our intuitive desiderata from a syntactic surprisal measure; and compared garden path effect magnitude predictions derived from standard, lexical surprisal and syntactic surprisal. Our main finding is that while the syntactic surprisal measure we propose does typically lead to larger predicted garden path effects, model-predicted garden path effects still vastly underestimate the magnitude of garden path effects found in humans.

We defined syntactic surprisal in terms of the predictability of the next word's CCG supertag. This choice is motivated by the relative simplicity of computing this measure—a straightforward auxiliary objective that can be added to any conceivable neural language model—as well as two substantive desiderata: First, we would like the measure to capture processing difficulty due to syntactic unpredictability. Since a word's CCG supertags captures how the word combines with the local syntactic structure, we hypothesize that the surprisal of that

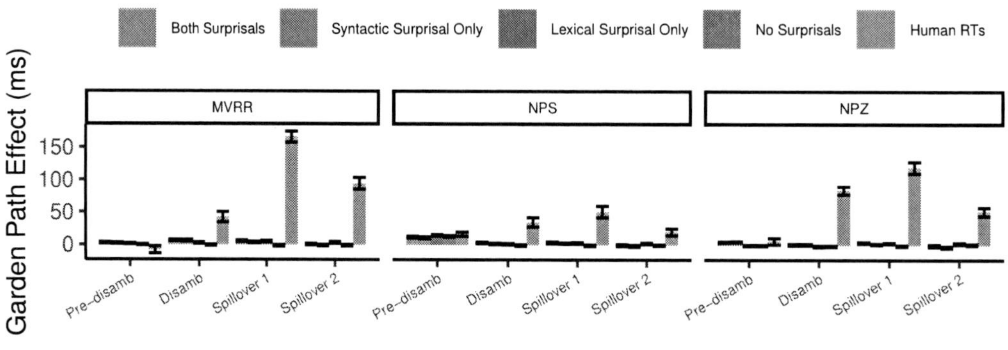

(a) Model predictions and human results.

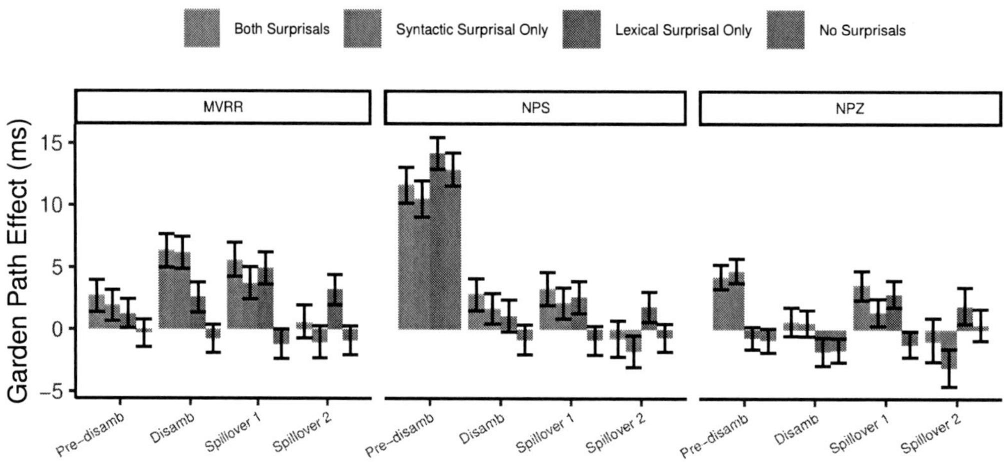

(b) Model predictions only.

Figure 4: Empirical and model-predicted readings times for the three garden path constructions. Bars indicate the difference between the mean readings times for the ambiguous and unambiguous sentences across participants for each condition. Error bars indicate bootstrapped 95% confidence intervals.

supertag—which indicates the extent to which that syntactic combination is unexpected—is a good predictor of syntactic unpredictability. This was borne out in our analysis that showed that syntactic surprisal predicts differences in the correct direction in three garden path constructions.

Second, since syntactic surprisal is designed to isolate *syntactic* predictability from other forms of predictability, it should *not* be perfectly correlated with lexical factors. The comparisons to lexical surprisal and word frequency showed that this desideratum was met: We were able to identify in our materials words that were lexically surprising but had low syntactic surprisal, and we found a *positive* correlation between frequency and syntactic surprisal — the opposite of what would be predicted if high syntactic surprisal was driven by low word frequency.

The increase in model-predicted garden path magnitudes when we use syntactic surprisal, compared to using just standard lexical surprisal, suggests that predictability estimates from LSTM LMs indeed understate the role that syntactic factors play in human prediction. To see why that is, recall that syntactic surprisal captures a subset of the variance that lexical surprisal does. The fact that adding syntactic surprisal produces a better fit to human reading times than lexical surprisal, then, suggests that syntactic factors affect lexical surprisal less than they would need to in order to capture variation in human reading times. One potential explanation for this discrepancy is the difference in

Disambig	MVRR	NPS	NPZ
Both vs. Syntactic Only	$\beta = 0.37, p < 0.001$	$\beta = 1.19, p < 0.001$	$\beta = 0.15, p = 0.056$
Syntactic Only vs. Lexical Only	$\beta = 3.26, p < 0.001$	$\beta = 0.89, p < 0.001$	$\beta = 1.89, p < 0.001$
Syntactic Only vs. Neither	$\beta = 6.77, p < 0.001$	$\beta = 2.85, p < 0.001$	$\beta = 1.77, p < 0.001$
Spillover 1	MVRR	NPS	NPZ
Both vs. Syntactic Only	$\beta = 1.80, p < 0.001$	$\beta = 1.25, p < 0.001$	$\beta = 2.09, p < 0.001$
Syntactic Only vs. Lexical Only	$\beta = -1.02, p < 0.001$	$\beta = -0.53, p < 0.001$	$\beta = -1.62, p < 0.001$
Syntactic Only vs. Neither	$\beta = 5.10, p < 0.001$	$\beta = 3.27, p < 0.001$	$\beta = 2.36, p < 0.001$
Spillover 2	MVRR	NPS	NPZ
Both vs. Syntactic Only	$\beta = 1.68, p < 0.001$	$\beta = 0.92, p < 0.001$	$\beta = 2.10, p < 0.001$
Syntactic Only vs. Lexical Only	$\beta = -4.59, p < 0.001$	$\beta = -3.86, p < 0.001$	$\beta = -5.03, p < 0.001$
Syntactic Only vs. Neither	$\beta = -0.30, p < 0.001$	$\beta = -0.92, p < 0.001$	$\beta = -3.61, p < 0.001$

Table 1: Results of a Linear Mixed Effects analysis over our model-predicted reading times for our effect of interest: the interaction between ambiguity and the conversion model. A significant result with a positive coefficient indicates that the conversion model on the left side of the contrast label predicted a significantly larger garden path effect than the model on the right. See Appendix A.2 for further details.

the tasks humans and LMs perform: While LMs need only predict words in corpora, humans must to comprehend what they read. While both tasks demand some sensitivity to syntactic structure, the need to interpret sentences may place greater importance on predicting structure, leading to a higher sensitivity to syntactic unpredictability.

While models with syntactic surprisal provided a better fit to the human data than those with just lexical surprisal, there remained a very large discrepancy between model-predicted and human garden path effect sizes. It may be possible to further close this gap within the surprisal framework using different approaches to estimating syntactic predictability; one such approach could rely on Recurrent Neural Network Grammars (Dyer et al., 2016), which derive word-level predictability estimates from explicit syntactic parsing mechanisms.

Another possibility is that the discrepancy is not due to flaws in our estimates of human predictability: perhaps surprisal, even based on a perfect simulation of human predictions, is simply not the correct account of the magnitude of the garden path effect observed in humans (van Schijndel and Linzen, 2021). One family of alternative accounts consists of *two-stage, serial* models of processing (Frazier and Fodor, 1978; Fodor and Inoue, 1994; Lewis, 1998; Bader, 1998; Sturt et al., 1999). In such a model, when readers first read through the ambiguous fragment of the sentence, they commit to a small set of preferred parses. When they reach a disambiguating region where all of the parses they have committed to are no longer consistent with the input, a reader would engage a separate, costly reanalysis process in order to construct a new partial parse consistent with the all of the currently available input. The processing cost associated with this reanalysis procedures incurs a slowdown in reading times that does not occur in an unambiguous sentence where the incorrect initial parse is not available, resulting the garden path effects that we observe. Unlike surprisal-based accounts, however, it is often unclear how to derive broad-coverage, quantitative predictions for the size of garden path effects from existing two-stage accounts. As a result, it is difficult to know whether the quantitative mismatches between surprisal-accounts and human reading times that we observed should be taken as evidence for an explicit reanalysis process. This further highlights the need for precise implementations of two-stage serial models that we can quantitatively evaluate against surprisal accounts.

Acknowledgements

This work was supported by the National Science Foundation, grant nos. BCS-2020945 and BCS-2020914, by the United States–Israel Binational Science Foundation (award no. 2018284), and in part through the NYU IT High Performance Computing resources, services, and staff expertise. We would also like to thank members of the NYU Computation and Psycholinguistics lab, as well as members of the Society for Human Sentence Processing community, for insightful discussion around this work.

References

Markus Bader. 1998. Prosodic influences on reading syntactically ambiguous sentences. In Janet Dean Fodor and Fernanda Ferreira, editors, *Reanalysis in Sentence Processing*, pages 1–46. Springer Netherlands, Dordrecht.

Srinivas Bangalore and Aravind K. Joshi. 1999. Supertagging: An approach to almost parsing. *Computational Linguistics*, 25(2):237–265.

Mark Davies. 2008–. The Corpus of Contemporary American English (COCA).

Vera Demberg and Frank Keller. 2008. Data from eyetracking corpora as evidence for theories of syntactic processing complexity. *Cognition*, 109(2):193–210.

Chris Dyer, Adhiguna Kuncoro, Miguel Ballesteros, and Noah A. Smith. 2016. Recurrent neural network grammars. In *Proceedings of the 2016 Conference of the North American Chapter of the Association for Computational Linguistics: Human Language Technologies*, pages 199–209, San Diego, California. Association for Computational Linguistics.

Émile Enguehard, Yoav Goldberg, and Tal Linzen. 2017. Exploring the syntactic abilities of RNNs with multi-task learning. In *Proceedings of the 21st Conference on Computational Natural Language Learning (CoNLL 2017)*, pages 3–14, Vancouver, Canada. Association for Computational Linguistics.

Janet Dean Fodor and Atsu Inoue. 1994. The diagnosis and cure of garden paths. *Journal of Psycholinguistic Research*, 23(5):407–434.

Stefan Frank. 2009. Surprisal-based Comparison between a Symbolic and a Connectionist Model of Sentence Processing. In *Proceedings of the 31st Annual Meeting of the Cognitive Science Society*, pages 1139—1144. Cognitive Science Society.

Lyn Frazier and Janet Dean Fodor. 1978. The sausage machine: A new two-stage parsing model. *Cognition*, 6(4):291–325.

Kristina Gulordava, Piotr Bojanowski, Edouard Grave, Tal Linzen, and Marco Baroni. 2018. Colorless green recurrent networks dream hierarchically. In *Proceedings of the 2018 Conference of the North American Chapter of the Association for Computational Linguistics: Human Language Technologies, Volume 1 (Long Papers)*, pages 1195–1205, New Orleans, Louisiana. Association for Computational Linguistics.

John Hale. 2001. A probabilistic Earley parser as a psycholinguistic model. In *Second Meeting of the North American Chapter of the Association for Computational Linguistics*.

Julia Hockenmaier and Mark Steedman. 2007. CCGbank: A corpus of CCG derivations and dependency structures extracted from the Penn Treebank. *Computational Linguistics*, 33(3):355–396.

Kuan-Jung Huang, Suhas Arehalli, Mari Kugemoto, Grusha Prasad Christian Muxica, Brian Dillon, and Tal Linzen. 2022. SPR mega-benchmark shows surprisal tracks construction- but not item-level difficulty. In *35th Annual Conference on Human Sentence Processing*, Santa Cruz, California. Society for Human Sentence Processing.

Roger Levy. 2008. Expectation-based syntactic comprehension. *Cognition*, 106(3):1126–1177.

Richard L Lewis. 1998. Reanalysis and Limited Repair Parsing: Leaping off the Garden Path. In Janet Dean Fodor and Fernanda Ferreira, editors, *Reanalysis in Sentence Processing*, pages 247–285. Springer Netherlands, Dordrecht.

Mitchell P. Marcus, Beatrice Santorini, and Mary Ann Marcinkiewicz. 1993. Building a large annotated corpus of English: The Penn Treebank. *Computational Linguistics*, 19(2):313–330.

Brian Roark, Asaf Bachrach, Carlos Cardenas, and Christophe Pallier. 2009. Deriving lexical and syntactic expectation-based measures for psycholinguistic modeling via incremental top-down parsing. In *Proceedings of the 2009 Conference on Empirical Methods in Natural Language Processing*, pages 324–333, Singapore. Association for Computational Linguistics.

Mark Steedman. 1987. Combinatory grammars and parasitic gaps. *Natural Language & Linguistic Theory*, 5(3):403–439.

Patrick Sturt, Martin J Pickering, and Matthew W Crocker. 1999. Structural Change and Reanalysis Difficulty in Language Comprehension. *Journal of Memory and Language*, 40(1):136–150.

Marten van Schijndel and Tal Linzen. 2021. Single-stage prediction models do not explain the magnitude of syntactic disambiguation difficulty. *Cognitive Science*, 45(6):e12988.

Ashish Vaswani, Yonatan Bisk, Kenji Sagae, and Ryan Musa. 2016. Supertagging with LSTMs. In *Proceedings of the 2016 Conference of the North American Chapter of the Association for Computational Linguistics: Human Language Technologies*, pages 232–237, San Diego, California. Association for Computational Linguistics.

Ethan Wilcox, Pranali Vani, and Roger Levy. 2021. A targeted assessment of incremental processing in neural language models and humans. In *Proceedings of the 59th Annual Meeting of the Association for Computational Linguistics and the 11th International Joint Conference on Natural Language Processing (Volume 1: Long Papers)*, pages 939–952, Online. Association for Computational Linguistics.

A Appendix

A.1 Converting Surprisals to Reading Times

In order to gauge the impact of syntactic surprisal on the predicted reading time at word n, rt_n, we fit four mixed effects models over the filler data: one containing only lexical surprisal (s_n^{lex}), one containing only syntactic surprisal (s_n^{syn}), one containing both, and one containing neither. As reading times are sensitive to other features of the word being read like unigram frequency (f_n), position in sentence p, and length in characters (c_n), we include those variables as additional factors in the regression. In order to account for spillover effects, where processing difficulty from a word often surfaces in the reading times of subsequent words, we include all of the aforementioned factors for the prior two words. We additionally include random intercepts by item and by participant, as well as random slopes by item for all of the surprisal fixed effects. This gives us the following linear mixed effects model formulas:

$$\begin{aligned} rt_n \sim\ & f_n * c_n + f_{n-1} * c_{n-1} \\ & + f_{n-2} * c_{n-2} + p \\ & + (1 \mid \text{item}) + (1 \mid \text{participant}) \end{aligned} \tag{neither}$$

$$\begin{aligned} rt_n \sim\ & s_n^{lex} + s_{n-1}^{lex} + s_{n-2}^{lex} \\ & + f_n * c_n + f_{n-1} * c_{n-1} \\ & + f_{n-2} * c_{n-2} + p \\ & + (1 + s_n^{lex} + s_{n-1}^{lex} + s_{n-2}^{lex} \mid \text{item}) \\ & + (1 \mid \text{participant}) \end{aligned} \tag{lexical}$$

$$\begin{aligned} rt_n \sim\ & s_n^{syn} + s_{n-1}^{syn} + s_{n-2}^{syn} + \\ & + f_n * c_n + f_{n-1} * c_{n-1} \\ & + f_{n-2} * c_{n-2} + p \\ & + (1 + s_n^{syn} + s_{n-1}^{syn} + s_{n-2}^{syn} \mid \text{item}) \\ & + (1 \mid \text{participant}) \end{aligned} \tag{syntactic}$$

$$\begin{aligned} rt_n \sim\ & s_n^{lex} + s_{n-1}^{lex} + s_{n-2}^{lex} \\ & + s_n^{syn} + s_{n-1}^{syn} + s_{n-2}^{syn} \\ & + f_n * c_n + f_{n-1} * c_{n-1} \\ & + f_{n-2} * c_{n-2} + p \\ & + (1 + s_n^{lex} + s_{n-1}^{lex} + s_{n-2}^{lex} \\ & + s_n^{syn} + s_{n-1}^{syn} + s_{n-2}^{syn} \mid \text{item}) \\ & + (1 \mid \text{participant}) \end{aligned} \tag{both}$$

These models were fit using filler data from Huang et al. (2022), and the coefficients from each model were used to predict reading times for all of the critical, garden path items from the corresponding surprisals, frequencies, lengths, and positions.

A.2 Statistical Analysis of Predicted RTs

To analyze the predicted reading times that come from our four models of surprisal-to-reading time conversion, we fit three separate linear mixed effects models: one over MVRR garden paths, one over NPS garden paths, and one over NPZ garden paths. Each model includes fixed effects of ambiguity and the types of surprisals used in predicting reading times: syntactic surprisal only, lexical surprisal only, both surprisals, or neither. Crucially, we include the interaction between these two factors, representing how our choice of surprisal-to-RT conversion model affects the size of the predicted garden path effect. We additionally include random intercepts by item and by participant. This results in the following mixed effects model formula:

$$\begin{aligned} pred\_rt \sim\ & ambiguity * model \\ & + (1 \mid \text{item}) + (1 \mid \text{participant}). \end{aligned}$$

Since we have four different models converting between surprisals and RTs, we estimate three contrasts for the interaction term: the model with both surprisals vs. the model with only syntactic surprisals, the model with only syntactic surprisals vs. the model with only lexical surprisals, and the model with only lexical surprisals vs. the model with neither surprisal. The estimated magnitude (represented by the β coefficient) as well as significance of the difference for each of these contrasts is reported in the main text in Table 1.

A.3 Variability in Conversion Analysis Results Across Model Instances

In order to assess the robustness of our results with respect to the randomness in the training of our neural network models, we repeated our analysis using surprisals generated from four instances of our LM/supertagging model. These models differed only in the random seed used during the initialization and training procedure. In Figure 4b in the main text, we presented predicted reading times averaged across these analyses. In Figure 5 we present the same results broken out across each model instance.

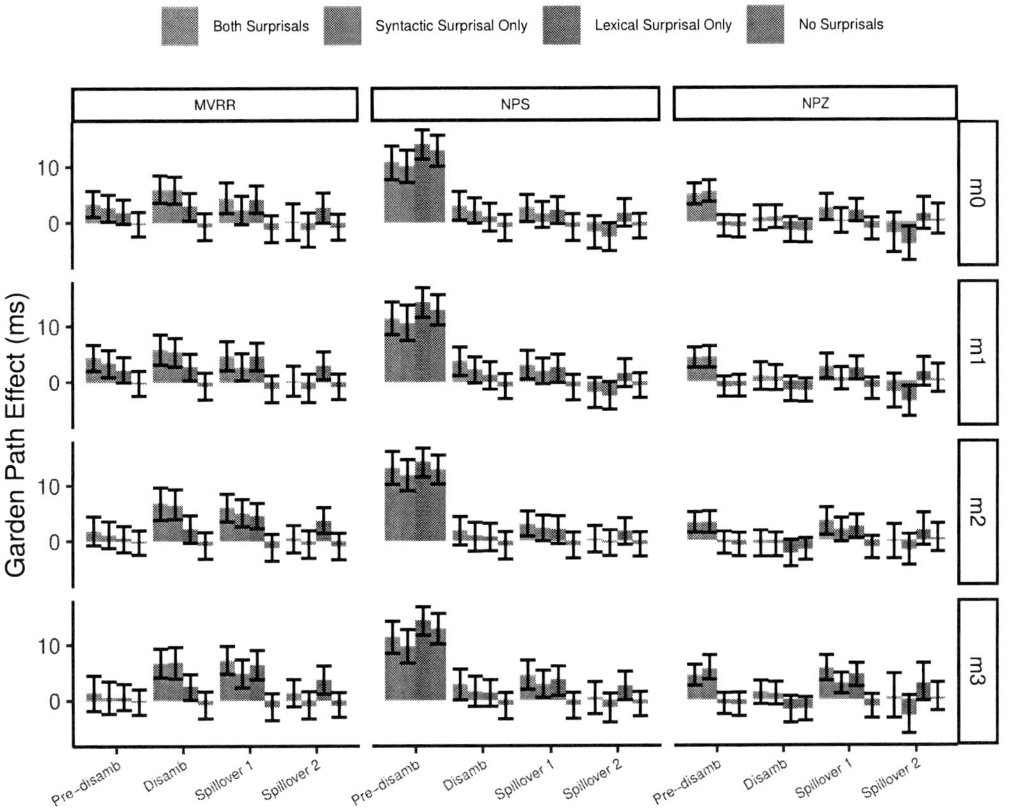

Figure 5: Empirical and model-predicted readings times for the three garden path constructions, broken out by the LM/Supertagger models used to generate the surprisals. Bars indicate the difference between the mean readings times for the ambiguous and unambiguous sentences across participants for each condition. Error bars indicate bootstrapped 95% confidence intervals.

OpenStance: Real-world Zero-shot Stance Detection

Hanzi Xu, Slobodan Vucetic and **Wenpeng Yin**
Temple University
{hanzi.xu; slobodan.vucetic; wenpeng.yin}@temple.edu

Abstract

Prior studies of zero-shot stance detection identify the attitude of texts towards unseen topics occurring in the same document corpus. Such task formulation has three limitations: (i) *Single domain/dataset.* A system is optimized on a particular dataset from a single domain; therefore, the resulting system cannot work well on other datasets; (ii) the model is evaluated on *a limited number of unseen topics*; (iii) it is assumed that *part of the topics has rich annotations*, which might be impossible in real-world applications. These drawbacks will lead to an impractical stance detection system that fails to generalize to open domains and open-form topics.

This work defines OpenStance: open-domain zero-shot stance detection, aiming to handle stance detection in an open world with neither domain constraints nor topic-specific annotations. The key challenge of OpenStance lies in the *open-domain generalization*: learning a system with fully unspecific supervision but capable of generalizing to any dataset. To solve OpenStance, we propose to combine **indirect supervision**, from textual entailment datasets, and **weak supervision**, from data generated automatically by pretrained Language Models. Our single system, without any topic-specific supervision, outperforms the supervised method on three popular datasets. To our knowledge, this is the first work that studies stance detection under the open-domain zero-shot setting. All data and code are publicly released.[1]

1 Introduction

Stance detection differentiates the attitude (e.g., support, oppose, or neutral) of a text towards a topic (Walker et al., 2012a). The topic can be a phrase or a complete sentence. The same text can express the author's positions on many different topics. For example, a tweet on climate warming may also express attitudes about environmental policies as well as the debate between electric or fuel cars. Such compound expression can be seen on all online platforms, including News outlets, Twitter, blogs, etc. Therefore, stance detection can be a complicated task that is essential for developing the inference capability of NLP models as well as other disciplines such as politics, journalism, etc.

Since the textual expressions and the size of topics in the real world are unpredictable, zero-shot stance detection has become the mainstream research direction in this area: topics in the test set are unseen during training. For example, Mohammad et al. (2016) created a dataset SemT6 based on tweets with six noun phrases as topics. One of the topics was reserved for testing and the remaining were used for training. Allaway and McKeown (2020) extended the topic size on the domain of news comments by covering 4,000 topics in training and 600 unseen topics in testing.

However, despite the change in the domain and topic size, there are three major limitations in previous studies *which make the task not a real zero-shot task*: (i) the dataset only contains texts from a single domain, such as news comments in VAST (Allaway and McKeown, 2020) and tweets in SemT6 (Mohammad et al., 2016); (ii) most literature studied only a limited size of topics with a single textual form (either noun phrases or sentential claims), e.g., (Mohammad et al., 2016; Conforti et al., 2020); (iii) rich annotation for at least part of the topics is always required, which is not possible in real-world applications because data collection can be very time-consuming and costly (Enayati et al., 2021). Those limitations lead to an impractical zero-shot stance detection system that cannot generalize well to unseen domains and open-form topics.

In this work, we re-define what a zero-shot stance detection should be. Specifically, we define OpenStance: an open-domain zero-shot stance

[1] https://github.com/xhz0809/OpenStance

Proceedings of the 26th Conference on Computational Natural Language Learning (CoNLL), pages 314 - 324
December 7-8, 2022 ©2022 Association for Computational Linguistics

detection, aiming to build a system that can work in the real world without any specific attention to the text domains or topic forms. More importantly, no task-specific supervision is needed. To achieve this, we propose to combine two types of supervision: *indirect supervision* and *weak supervision*. The indirect supervision comes from textual entailment—we treat the stance detection problem as a textual entailment task since the attitude toward a topic should be inferred from the input text. Therefore, the existing entailment datasets, such as MNLI (Williams et al., 2018), can contribute supervision to the zero-shot setting. To collect supervision that is more specific to the `OpenStance` task, we design two MASK choices (`MASK-topic` and `MASK-text`) to prompt GPT-3 (Brown et al., 2020) to generate weakly supervised data. Given an input text and a stance label (`support`, `oppose`, or `neutral`), `MASK-topic` predicts what topic is appropriate based on the content; given a topic and a label, `MASK-text` seeks the text that most likely holds this stance. The collection of weakly supervised data only needs the unlabeled texts and the set of topics that users want to include. The joint power of indirect supervision and weak supervision will be evaluated on VAST, SemT6 and Perspectrum (Chen et al., 2019), three popular datasets that cover distinct domains, different sizes and diverse textual forms of topics. Experimental results show that although no task-specific supervision is used, our system can get robust performance on all three datasets, even outperforming the task-specific supervised models (72.6 vs. 69.3 by mean F1 over the three datasets).

Our contributions are threefold: (i) we define `OpenStance`, an open-domain zero-shot stance detection task, that fulfills real-world requirements while having never been studied before; (ii) we design a novel masking mechanism to let GPT-3 generate weakly supervised data for `OpenStance`. This mechanism can inspire other NLP tasks that detect relations between two pieces of texts; (iii) our approach, integrating indirect supervision and weak supervision, demonstrates outstanding generalization among three datasets that cover a wide range of text domains, topic sizes and topic forms.

2 Related Work

Stance detection. Stance detection, as a recent member of the NLP family, was mainly driven by newly created datasets. In the past studies, datasets have been constructed from diverse domains like online debate forums (Walker et al., 2012b; Hasan and Ng, 2014; Abbott et al., 2016), news comments (Krejzl et al., 2017; Lozhnikov et al., 2018), Twitter (Mohammad et al., 2016; Küçük, 2017; Tsakalidis et al., 2018)), etc.

Zero-shot stance detection. Recently, researchers started to work on zero-shot stance detection in order to build a system that can handle unseen topics. Most work split the collected topic-aware annotations into *train* and *test* within the same domain. Allaway and McKeown (2020) made use of topic similarity to connect unseen topics with seen topics. Allaway et al. (2021) designed adversarial learning to learn domain-independent information and topic-invariant representations. Similarly, Wang and Wang (2021) applied adversarial learning to extract stance-related but domain-invariant features existed among different domains. Liu et al. (2021) utilized common sense knowledge from ConceptNet (Speer et al., 2017) to introduce extra knowledge of the relations between the texts and topics. Most prior systems worked on a single domain and were tested on a small number of unseen topics. Li et al. (2021) tried to test on various unseen datasets by jointly optimizing on multiple training datasets. However, they still assumed that part of the topics or domains has rich annotations. In contrast, our goal is to design a system that can handle stance detection in an open world without requiring any domain constraints or topic-specific annotations.

Textual entailment as indirect supervision. Textual entailment studies if a hypothesis can be entailed by a premise; this was proposed as a unified inference framework for a wide range of NLP problems (Dagan et al., 2005). Recently, textual entailment is widely utilized to help solve many tasks, such as few-shot intent detection (Xia et al., 2021), ultra-fine entity typing (Li et al., 2022), coreference resolution (Yin et al., 2020), relation extraction (Xia et al., 2021; Sainz et al., 2021), event argument extraction (Sainz et al., 2022), etc. As far as we know, our work is the first one that successfully leverages the indirect supervision from textual entailment for stance detection.

Weak supervision from GPT-3. As the currently most popular and (arguably) well-behaved pre-trained language model, GPT-3 (Brown et al., 2020) has been a great success on few-shot and zero-shot NLP. As an implicit knowledge base fully in the form of parameters, it is not surprising that researchers attempt to extract knowledge from it to construct synthetic data, e.g., (Yoo et al., 2021; Wang et al., 2021). We use GPT-3 to collect distantly supervised data by two novel masking mechanisms designed specifically for the `OpenStance`.

3 Problem definition

`OpenStance` has the following requirements:

- An instance includes three items: text s, topic t and a stance label l ($l \in \{\texttt{support}, \texttt{oppose}, \texttt{neutral}\}$); the task is to learn the function $f(s,t) \to l$;
- The text s can come from any domain; the topic t can be any textual expressions, such as a noun phrase "gun control" or a sentential claim "climate change is a real concern";
- All labeled instances $\{(s, t, l)\}$ only exist in *test*; no *train* or *dev* is provided;
- Previous work used different metrics for the evaluation. For example, VAST (Allaway and McKeown, 2020) used macro-averaged F1 regarding stance labels, while studies on SemT6 (Allaway et al., 2021; Liang et al., 2022) reported the F1 scores per topic. To make systems be comparable, we unify the evaluation and use the label-oriented macro F1 as our main metric.

`OpenStance` vs. prior zero-shot stance detection. Prior studies of zero-shot stance detection worked on a single dataset D^i in which all texts s comes from the same domain. Topics t in the dataset are split into $train$, dev and $test$ disjointly. The main issue is that a model that fits D^i does not work well on a new dataset D^j that may contain s of different domains and unseen t. For example, a model trained on VAST can only get F1 49.0% on Perspectrum, which is around the performance of random guess. `OpenStance` aims at handling multiple datasets of open domains and open-form topics without looking at their $train$ and dev.

`OpenStance` vs. textual entailment. Stance detection is essentially a textual entailment problem if we treat the text s as the premise, and the stance towards the topic t as the hypothesis. This motivates us to use indirect supervision from textual entailment to deal with the stance detection problem. Nevertheless, there are two distinctions between them: (i) even though we can match l of stance detection with the labels of textual entailment: `support` $\to$ `entailment`, `oppose` $\to$ `contradict` and `neutral` $\to$ `neutral`, whether a topic t in stance detection can be treated as a hypothesis depends on the text form of t. If t is noun phrases such as "gun control", t cannot act as a hypothesis alone as there is no stance in it; if t is a sentential claim such as "climate change is a real concern", inferring the truth value of this hypothesis is exactly a textual entailment problem. This observation motivates us to test `OpenStance` on topics of both phrase forms and sentence forms; (ii) Zero-shot textual entailment means the size of the annotated instances for *labels* is zero, while `OpenStance` requires the *topics* have zero labeled examples.

4 Methodology

This section introduces how we collect and combine *indirect supervision* and *weak supervision* to solve `OpenStance`.

Indirect Supervision. As we discussed in Section 3, stance detection is a case of textual entailment since the stance l towards a topic t should be inferred from the text s. To handle the zero-shot challenge in `OpenStance`, textual entailment is a natural choice for indirect supervision.

Specifically, we first cast stance detection instances into the textual entailment format by combining l and t as a sentential hypothesis h, such as "it `supports topic`", and treating the s as the premise p; then a pretrained model on MNLI (Williams et al., 2018), one of the largest entailment dataset, is ready to predict the relationship between the p and h. An entailed (resp. contradicted or neutral) h means the topic t is supported (resp. opposed or neutral) by the text s.

Unfortunately, the indirect supervision from textual entailment may not perform well enough in real-world `OpenStance` considering the widely known brittleness of pretrained entailment models and the open domains and open-form topics in `OpenStance`. Therefore, in addition to the indirect supervision from textual entailment, we will collect weak supervision that is aligned better with the texts $\{x\}$ and the topics $\{t\}$.

Weak Supervision. For the next step, we would like to create some weakly supervised data using easily available resources to obtain a better understanding of the target task. We used GPT-3 (Brown et al., 2020), a pre-trained autoregressive language model that can perform text completion at (arguably) a near-human level, to help us create some weakly labeled instances.

We form incomplete sentences using prompts, and let the GPT-3 complete them. Since a stance label l connects the text s and the topic t and such connection is unavailable in a zero-shot setting, the construction of incomplete sentences is driven by two questions: (i) given an input text s and a stance, e.g., `support`, what topics are supported by s? (ii) given a topic and a stance, for example, `support`, what texts support this topic? As a result, there are two kinds of prompts: `MASK-Topic` and `MASK-Text`. To implement the two masking mechanisms, we need to prepare three sets: the raw texts $\{s\}$, a set of topics $\{t\}$, and the known stance labels {`support`, `oppose`, `neutral`}. It is noteworthy that no topic-specific human annotations are used here.

•**`MASK-Topic`**: In this masking framework, we randomly choose a `text` from $\{s\}$ and a stance label from {`support`, `oppose`, `neutral`}, then build the prompt as:

S/he claims `text`, so s/he `label` the idea of <u>MASK</u>

For example, when the `text` is "Coldest and wettest summer in memory" and the label is `oppose`, the prompt would be "S/he claims coldest and wettest summer in memory, so s/he opposes the idea of". Then, this prompt is fed into GPT-3, and the completion "global warming" would be the predicted topic.

•**`MASK-Text`**: In this case, we randomly choose a `topic` from $\{t\}$ and a stance `label` towards it, then build the prompt as:

His/her attitude towards `topic` is `label` because s/he thinks <u>MASK</u>

For example, when the `topic` is "climate change is a real concern", the `label` is "oppose", the completed sentence filled by GPT-3 could be "His attitude towards climate change is a real concern is opposition because s/he thinks <u>the science behind climate change is not settled</u>".

For any dataset of stance detection, we first collect the three sets (i.e., $\{s\}$, $\{t\}$, and $\{l\}$) *from the label-free training set* without peeking at any gold annotations, then use `MASK-Topic` and `MASK-Text` prompts to generate equal number of weakly supervised examples. We will study which masking scheme is more effective in experiments. In addition, to have a fair comparison with supervised methods that learn on the $train$ of a task, we make sure our generated weakly supervised data has the same size as the $train$ for any target task.

Although noise is common in weakly supervised data, GPT-3 performs badly on `neutral` completions for both `MASK-Topic` and `MASK-Text` tasks. This is not a surprise for the `MASK-Topic` since the GPT-3 is asked to provide a topic that the given text has a neutral attitude for, while most texts, obtained from unlabeled *train* and originally extracted from social networks, usually express a strong attitude. Furthermore, in `MASK-Text`, even though the GPT-3 can output a text given the `neutral` label towards a topic, the response is very general and does not provide any insights. For example, when the template is "His attitude towards high school writing skills is `neutral` because he thinks [MASK]", GPT-3 fills out the MASK with "that they are important but not essential." Obviously, it is much easier to generate text with a clear attitude compared to a neutral stance. On the one hand, GPT-3 may not really understand what a `neutral` stance is. On the other hand, even humans cannot easily write a neutral opinion towards a topic. Since the quality of generated `neutral` instances is not very promising, we take the same approach as how VAST (Allaway and McKeown, 2020) collected its neutral samples: matching texts with random topics in the dataset.

Training strategy. To keep consistent format and make full use of the entailment reasoning framework, we convert all phrase-form `topic` in the weak supervision data into a sentence-form hypothesis with the positive stance, i.e., "he is in favor of `topic`" (note that this does not change the original label). Then, we randomly split the weak supervision data as *train* (80%) and *dev* (20%). Given the entailment dataset MNLI as the indirect supervision data (D_{ind}) and weakly supervised data (D_{weak}) from GPT-3, we first pretrain a RoBERTa-large (Liu et al., 2019) on D_{ind}, then finetune on D_{weak}. In inference, we test the final model on the *test* of each task, checking the system's generalization ability on diverse domains without optimizing on any domain-specific *train*.

	domain	#topic train/test	topic form	#labels
SemT6	tweet	6	phrase	3
VAST	debate	4641/600	phrase	3
Persp.	debate	541/227	sentence	2

Table 1: Dataset statistics.

5 Experiments

5.1 Datasets

We choose datasets that can cover (i) multiple domains, (ii) different sizes of unseen topics, and (iii) various textual forms of topics (phrase-form and sentence-form). Therefore, we evaluate on three mainstream stance detection datasets: SemT6 (Mohammad et al., 2016), VAST (Allaway and McKeown, 2020) and Perspectrum (Chen et al., 2019). We discard their training sets and dev sets to satisfy the definition of `OpenStance`.

SemT6 (Mohammad et al., 2016) contains texts from the tweet domain regarding 6 topics: `Donald Trump`, `Atheism`, `Climate Change is a real Concern`, `Feminist Movement`, `Hillary Clinton`, and `Legalization of Abortion`. It is a three-way stance detection problem with labels {`support`, `oppose`, `neutral`}. Note that the prior applications of SemT6 for zero-shot stance detection always trained on five topics and tested on the remaining one. To match the motivation of `OpenStance`, we treat the whole SemT6 data as *test*, i.e., all six topics are unseen. When we report the data-specific supervised performance, we follow prior work to regard any five topics as seen and test on the sixth topic; each topic will have the chance to be unseen, and the average performance is reported.

VAST (Allaway and McKeown, 2020). In contrast to SemT6, VAST contains text from the New York Times "Room for Debate" section, and many more topics (4,003 in $train$, 383 in dev and 600 in $test$). Those diverse topics, covering various themes, such as education, politics, and public health, are short phrases that are first automatically extracted and then modified by human annotators. Like SemT6, it also has three stance labels, but the `neutral` topics were randomly picked from the whole topic set. For our `OpenStance` task, we only use its $test$ to evaluate our system and do not touch the gold labels of its $train$ and dev.

Perspectrum (Chen et al., 2019) is a binary stance detection benchmark (label is `support` or `oppose`) with two main distinctions with SemT6 and VAST: (i) both its text and topics were collected from several debating websites, and (ii) the topics are sentences rather than noun phrases. Similar to VAST, we do not train our model on its $train$ and dev. The performance on $test$ will be reported. Since there are no neutral samples in this dataset, when the model is pretrained as a 3-way classifier, we set the probability threshold as 1/3 on the `oppose` label: any prediction that has the `oppose` probabilities *lower than 1/3* will be considered as `support`. Otherwise, the label would be `oppose`.

The detailed statistics of the three datasets are listed in Table 1.

5.2 Baselines

There are no prior systems that work on this new `OpenStance` problem since no training data is available. Here, we consider three baselines that can work on an unsupervised scheme.

BERT (Devlin et al., 2019). Given the (`text`, `topic`) as input, "BERT-large-uncased" is used as a masked language model to predict the masked token in "`text`, it [MASK] `topic`". BERT will output the probabilities of the three label tokens {`support`, `oppose`, `neutral`} and the label that receives the highest probability would be the predicted stance.

GPT-3 (Brown et al., 2020). Given the `text` and the `topic` with the instruction telling the model what task we are trying to accomplish, GPT-3 is able to complete the prompt by choosing one of the given labels {`support`, `oppose`, `neutral`}. GPT-3 also has functions designed for classification, but the text completion scheme does a better job on this stance detection task. Our prompt:

> Given a topic and a text, determine whether the stance of the text is support, against, or neutral to the topic.
> `Topic`: Atheism
> `Text`: Everyone is able to believe in whatever they want.
> `Stance`: ________

Cosine similarity. We compare the similarities between the `text` and a hypothesis sentence that combines `label` and `topic`, such as "it `supports` the `topic`", "it `opposes` the

			F1 Score SemT6	VAST	Persp.	mean
random guess			32.0	33.3	49.8	38.3
data-specific supervised learning (prior SOTA)			38.9	78.0	91.0	69.3
cross-domain transfer		SemT6 as *train*	38.9	28.9	47.7	38.5
		VAST as *train*	55.4	78.0	49.0	60.8
		Pers as *train*	26.7	27.0	91.0	48.2
open-domain transfer	baseline	BERT	22.7	36.8	36.5	32.0
		GPT-3	30.5	34.2	39.9	34.9
		Cosine	31.5	35.9	62.7	43.4
	ours	D_{ind} and SemT6-based D_{weak}	63.7	69.8	82.8	72.1
		D_{ind} and VAST-based D_{weak}	64.3	72.0	80.4	72.2
		D_{ind} and Persp-based D_{weak}	64.5	68.7	79.5	70.9
		D_{ind} and joint D_{weak}	63.2	73.5	81.0	**72.6**
		w/o indirect	49.6	64.6	38.2	50.8
		w/o weak	45.3	53.7	79.1	59.4
		w/o `MASK-Topic`	45.5	65.2	74.2	61.6
		w/o `MASK-Text`	63.4	70.8	78.2	70.8

Table 2: Open-domain experiment results on SemT6, VAST and Perspectrum. Our final number is in bold.

`topic`", or "it is `unrelated` to the `topic`". We first get the sentential representations by sentence-BERT (Reimers and Gurevych, 2019), then choose the label whose resulting hypothesis obtains the highest cosine similarity score.

In addition to the unsupervised baselines, we further consider the data-specific supervised training as the upperbound, and the following variants of our system: i) only `MASK-Text` or `MASK-Topic`; ii) only indirect supervision or weak supervision.

5.3 Setting

GPT-3 for D_{weak} collection. The engine we chose for GPT-3 is "curie", which gives good quality at a reasonable price. There are several parameters that we played with. We set the temperature, which goes from 0 to 1 and controls the randomness of the completion generated, as 0.8 for `MASK-Topic` and 0.9 for `MASK-Text` for more diverse results. The randomness for `MASK-Text`is slightly higher because for some datasets the number of topics is extremely limited, such as SemT6, which only has 6 topics in total; therefore, we want to force diverse responses from GPT-3. The max number of tokens GPT-3 can generate is 6 for `MASK-Topic` and 150 for `MASK-Text`. It is worth mentioning that GPT-3 will not necessarily generate as much as the upper bound, sometimes not even close. We let the stop word be "\n", so that it stops generating when it reaches a new paragraph. "top_p" is set as 1, letting all tokens in the vocabulary been used. "frequency_penalty" is 0.3 for `MASK-Text` to avoid the model producing the same line again and again.

Training details. All models are optimized using AdamW (Loshchilov and Hutter, 2019). Learning rate 1e-6, batch size 16, maximal (premise, hypothesis) length is 200. The system is trained for 20 epochs on *train* and the best model on *dev* is kept.

5.4 Result

Table 2 lists the main results. We first include "data-specific supervised learning" as the upperbound performance and the "cross-domain transfer" that takes each dataset as the source domain and tests on others respectively. Both settings try to explore the upper limit when we apply human-annotated supervision. Our core task, `OpenStance`, is evaluated in the last three blocks.

From the baseline block, we can observe that for all domains, baseline methods mostly perform like random guess, except for the slight improvement of the "cosine" approach over Perspectrum. This result indicates the difficulty of the real-world OpenStance task we proposed. Although BERT and GPT-3 are the top-tier pre-trained language models, they still cannot handle OpenStance well.

Then look at our approach that combines indirect supervision data (D_{ind}) and weak supervision data (D_{weak}). Note that D_{weak} can be collected based on the *label-free train* of VAST, SemT6 or Perspectrum. We try D_{weak} for each of the task domains and also put them jointly (i.e., "joint D_{weak}"). We note that all four versions of D_{weak} result in very consistent performance—mostly around 72% by the "mean". This clearly supports the *robustness of our method*: it is less affected by the original domain where text and topic come from, and a single system based on each of the domain or their combination can perform well on all domains.

The last block of Table 2 reports the ablation study, where we discard individual source of supervision (indirect or weak) or individual masking scheme (MASK-Text or MASK-Topic). We observe that i) indirect supervision and weak supervision play complementary roles for the task OpenStance; and they both outperform baselines by large margins, and ii) both masking schemes help, and the MASK-Topic contributes more. This is maybe because MASK-Topic requires the GPT-3 to generate shorter texts than MASK-Text so that MASK-Topic can yield higher-quality data. Additionally, deriving supporting sentences for a given topic sometimes requires substantial background knowledge and solid reasoning, which is still a difficult task for GPT-3.

5.5 Analysis

Next, we conduct a deep analysis for the system robustness towards prompts ($\mathcal{Q}_1$), the required size of D_{weak} ($\mathcal{Q}_2$), the noise in generated D_{weak} ($\mathcal{Q}_3$), and the error patterns made by our system ($\mathcal{Q}_4$).

$\mathcal{Q}_1$: Robustness of dealing with prompts. Prompt design takes place in both GPT-3 completion and the conversion from stance detection to textual entailment. When generating the prompt for GPT-3, how we construct the prompt in MASK-Topic and MASK-Text can make a huge impact on the completion received. In MASK-Topic, we use the prompt "He said text, so he label the idea of [MASK]". The reason why we add "*the idea of*" at the end of the prompt is because it helps the model understand that we want a noun phrase. Otherwise, we will see completions

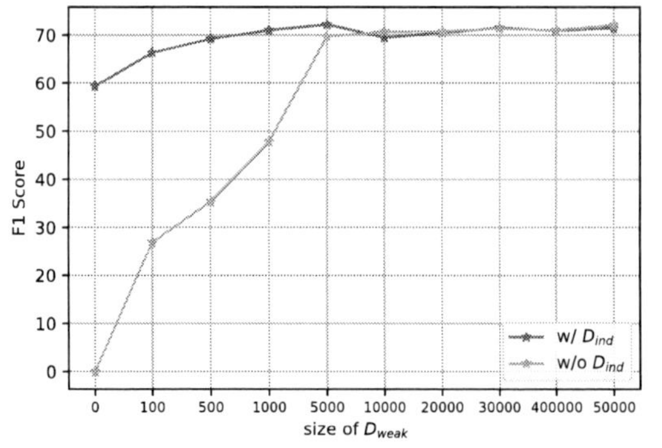

Figure 1: Mean F1 vs. size of D_{weak}.

like "that", "it", etc. Similarly, in MASK-Text, the final prompt we use is "His attitude towards topic is label because he thinks [MASK]". Considering the freedom of GPT-3 completion, we add "s/he thinks" at the end of the prompt, forcing GPT-3 to generate a reasoning for the given topic/label pair. If we don't add "*he thinks*" at the end, it would be common to see GPT-3 repeating the given sentence in the generated completion. In addition, when the label is neutral, such as the prompt "His attitude towards high school writing skills is neutral because he thinks [MASK]", GPT-3 would output sentences like "he does not have a strong opinion either way" if we don't have "*he thinks*" at the end. After the modification, responses would make more sense, such as "that they are important but not essential." These tricks in prompt design suggest that it is essential to make the sentence structure as clear as possible and provide content that helps to instruct the model on what we want.

When we convert the topic phrase into a sentential hypothesis, we again get involved in the prompt design. During training, we stick with "he is in favor of topic" template to limit the training size, but in the testing, we found the majority voting of four templates ("he/she is in favor of topic" and "he/she opposes topic") lead to comparable performance with "he is in favor of topic". This indicates the pre-trained entailment system is considerably robust in dealing with hypotheses derived from different templates.

$\mathcal{Q}_2$: How much weakly supervised data is needed? We answer this question by applying D_{weak} alone or together with D_{ind}. For each case, we test on sizes varying from 100 to 50,000 and report the average results over 3 random seeds. From the Figure 1, we can see that both settings can reach similar performance when we collect over 10k data of D_{weak}, but the pretraining on D_{ind} can dramatically reduce the required size of D_{weak}: from 10k to around 500.

Q_3: Error patterns of weakly supervised data. We collect typical error patterns in D_{weak} derived by `MASK-Topic` and `MASK-Text` separately.

`MASK-Topic`. Three typical error types.

•*Incomplete generation.* Sometimes GPT-3 fails to give a complete topic phrase and cuts in the middle even though it hasn't reached the maximum token limit. For example:

He claims `16 year olds are informed enough to cast a vote,` so he `supports` the idea of <u>GIVING 16-YEAR-OLDS</u>

In this example, the topic given by GPT-3 is "giving 16-year-olds", which is not a complete phrase as we expected. This kind of errors indicate that GPT-3 sometimes stops generating before providing a complete idea even when the word limit is not exceeded.

•*Failure in understanding the stance.* Since we are providing opposite labels (i.e., `support` and `oppose`), we hope that GPT-3 would produce distinct topics that hold opposite stances. However, sometimes GPT-3 fails to understand the stances when generating topics. For example:

He claims `A higher minimum wage means less crime,` so he `supports` the idea of <u>A MINIMUM WAGE</u>
He claims `A higher minimum wage means less crime,` so he `opposes` the idea of <u>A MINIMUM WAGE</u>

This error type is the most common one in the weakly supervised data (approximately 85% error instances), indicating that GPT-3 is still less effective to interpret negated information.

•*Misunderstanding the text.* The GPT-3 does not always understand the meaning of the sentence correctly. For example:

He claims `women who are housewives should be paid,` so he `supports` the idea of <u>WOMEN BEING PAID LESS THAN MEN</u>

Here, the predicted topic is related but not the main subject of the sentence. Such a mistake is rare but still exists weak supervision.

`MASK-Text`. Even though GPT-3 can mostly provide a sentence that is related to the topic and align with the correct stance, more than 50% of the time the content is very short and less informative compared to the texts from the datasets. For example:

His attitude towards `middle east oil` is `opposition` because he thinks <u>IT IS A WASTE</u>

His attitude towards `miss america` is `support` because he thinks <u>SHE IS TALENTED</u>

This is not that surprising since GPT-3 was trained to mainly satisfy the language modeling criterion; thus, it would be "lazy" to return with a solid and long response. These `MASK-Text` instances are never wrong in the judgment of attitudes, so they can still give the model some help, although limited, in determining the attitudes.

Q_4: Error analysis of our system. Due to space limitation, we summarize two common error patterns made by our system.

•*Failed to connect the topic and text.* The text often mentions the topic with distinct expressions and contains its stance implicitly. Therefore, it brings more difficulty to the model to successfully locate the topic and identify the stance. For example:

`Topic:` musician `Text:` Spotify and Pandora pay usage rates that are much lower than the radio, records and legal downloads that they are replacing. Low enough to where many potential new artists won't be able to even earn a living. There must be some alternative other than artists simply being forced to accept the new streaming model that destroys royalties. For example, who set streaming royalty rates? Can artists unionize and negotiate collectively with the streaming services? If we don't sort this out, we will lose a new generation of artists – which is bad for everyone. Gold `label:` support Predicted `label:` neutral

•*Incorrect ground-truth labels.* The gold labels are not always correct. Sometimes the model makes a more appropriate judgement than the data provides. For example:

`Topic:` keep weight `Text:` "All the medical evidence points to the fact that it's nearly impossible to keep off weight once lost. The body just won't let you." This is incorrect, and could lead to fatalism that could harm people who are overweight. For example, I lost 70 pounds. That was at least a year ago. It has not come back. It is easy to keep off......" Gold `label:` neutral Predicted `label:` support

6 Conclusion

In this work, we define `OpenStance`, a more realistic and challenging zero-shot stance detection problem in an open world. Under such a setting, multiple domains and numerous topics can be involved, while no topic-specific annotations are required. To solve this problem, we proposed to combine indirect supervision from textual entailment and weak supervision collected from GPT-3. Our system, without the help of any task-specific supervision, outperforms the supervised method on three benchmark datasets that cover various domains and free-form topics.

Acknowledgment

The authors appreciate the reviewers for their insightful comments and suggestions.

References

Rob Abbott, Brian Ecker, Pranav Anand, and Marilyn A. Walker. 2016. Internet argument corpus 2.0: An SQL schema for dialogic social media and the corpora to go with it. In *Proceedings of the Tenth International Conference on Language Resources and Evaluation LREC 2016, Portorož, Slovenia, May 23-28, 2016*. European Language Resources Association (ELRA).

Emily Allaway and Kathleen R. McKeown. 2020. Zero-shot stance detection: A dataset and model using generalized topic representations. In *Proceedings of the 2020 Conference on Empirical Methods in Natural Language Processing, EMNLP 2020, Online, November 16-20, 2020*, pages 8913–8931. Association for Computational Linguistics.

Emily Allaway, Malavika Srikanth, and Kathleen R. McKeown. 2021. Adversarial learning for zero-shot stance detection on social media. In *Proceedings of the 2021 Conference of the North American Chapter of the Association for Computational Linguistics: Human Language Technologies, NAACL-HLT 2021, Online, June 6-11, 2021*, pages 4756–4767. Association for Computational Linguistics.

Tom B. Brown, Benjamin Mann, Nick Ryder, Melanie Subbiah, Jared Kaplan, Prafulla Dhariwal, Arvind Neelakantan, Pranav Shyam, Girish Sastry, Amanda Askell, Sandhini Agarwal, Ariel Herbert-Voss, Gretchen Krueger, Tom Henighan, Rewon Child, Aditya Ramesh, Daniel M. Ziegler, Jeffrey Wu, Clemens Winter, Christopher Hesse, Mark Chen, Eric Sigler, Mateusz Litwin, Scott Gray, Benjamin Chess, Jack Clark, Christopher Berner, Sam McCandlish, Alec Radford, Ilya Sutskever, and Dario Amodei. 2020. Language models are few-shot learners. In *Advances in Neural Information Processing Systems 33: Annual Conference on Neural Information Processing Systems 2020, NeurIPS 2020, December 6-12, 2020, virtual*.

Sihao Chen, Daniel Khashabi, Wenpeng Yin, Chris Callison-Burch, and Dan Roth. 2019. Seeing things from a different angle: Discovering diverse perspectives about claims. In *Proceedings of the 2019 Conference of the North American Chapter of the Association for Computational Linguistics: Human Language Technologies, NAACL-HLT 2019, Minneapolis, MN, USA, June 2-7, 2019, Volume 1 (Long and Short Papers)*, pages 542–557. Association for Computational Linguistics.

Costanza Conforti, Jakob Berndt, Mohammad Taher Pilehvar, Chryssi Giannitsarou, Flavio Toxvaerd, and Nigel Collier. 2020. Will-they-won't-they: A very large dataset for stance detection on twitter. In *Proceedings of the 58th Annual Meeting of the Association for Computational Linguistics, ACL 2020, Online, July 5-10, 2020*, pages 1715–1724. Association for Computational Linguistics.

Ido Dagan, Oren Glickman, and Bernardo Magnini. 2005. The PASCAL recognising textual entailment challenge. In *Machine Learning Challenges, Evaluating Predictive Uncertainty, Visual Object Classification and Recognizing Textual Entailment, First PASCAL Machine Learning Challenges Workshop, MLCW 2005, Southampton, UK, April 11-13, 2005, Revised Selected Papers*, volume 3944 of *Lecture Notes in Computer Science*, pages 177–190. Springer.

Jacob Devlin, Ming-Wei Chang, Kenton Lee, and Kristina Toutanova. 2019. BERT: pre-training of deep bidirectional transformers for language understanding. In *Proceedings of the 2019 Conference of the North American Chapter of the Association for Computational Linguistics: Human Language Technologies, NAACL-HLT 2019, Minneapolis, MN, USA, June 2-7, 2019, Volume 1 (Long and Short Papers)*, pages 4171–4186. Association for Computational Linguistics.

Saman Enayati, Ziyu Yang, Benjamin Lu, and Slobodan Vucetic. 2021. A visualization approach for rapid labeling of clinical notes for smoking status extraction. In *Proceedings of the Second Workshop on Data Science with Human in the Loop: Language Advances*, pages 24–30, Online. Association for Computational Linguistics.

Kazi Saidul Hasan and Vincent Ng. 2014. Why are you taking this stance? identifying and classifying reasons in ideological debates. In *Proceedings of the 2014 Conference on Empirical Methods in Natural Language Processing, EMNLP 2014, October 25-29, 2014, Doha, Qatar, A meeting of SIGDAT, a Special Interest Group of the ACL*, pages 751–762. ACL.

Peter Krejzl, Barbora Hourová, and Josef Steinberger. 2017. Stance detection in online discussions. *CoRR*, abs/1701.00504.

Dilek Küçük. 2017. Stance detection in turkish tweets. In *Workshops Proceedings and Tutorials of the 28th ACM Conference on Hypertext and Social Media (HT 2017), Prague, Czech Republic, July 4-7, 2017*, volume 1914 of *CEUR Workshop Proceedings*. CEUR-WS.org.

Bangzheng Li, Wenpeng Yin, and Muhao Chen. 2022. Ultra-fine entity typing with indirect supervision from natural language inference. *Trans. Assoc. Comput. Linguistics*, 10:607–622.

Yingjie Li, Chenye Zhao, and Cornelia Caragea. 2021. Improving stance detection with multi-dataset learning and knowledge distillation. In *Proceedings of the 2021 Conference on Empirical Methods in Natural Language Processing, EMNLP 2021, Virtual Event / Punta Cana, Dominican Republic, 7-11 November,*

2021, pages 6332–6345. Association for Computational Linguistics.

Bin Liang, Zixiao Chen, Lin Gui, Yulan He, Min Yang, and Ruifeng Xu. 2022. Zero-shot stance detection via contrastive learning. In *WWW '22: The ACM Web Conference 2022, Virtual Event, Lyon, France, April 25 - 29, 2022*, pages 2738–2747. ACM.

Rui Liu, Zheng Lin, Yutong Tan, and Weiping Wang. 2021. Enhancing zero-shot and few-shot stance detection with commonsense knowledge graph. In *Findings of the Association for Computational Linguistics: ACL/IJCNLP 2021, Online Event, August 1-6, 2021*, volume ACL/IJCNLP 2021 of *Findings of ACL*, pages 3152–3157. Association for Computational Linguistics.

Yinhan Liu, Myle Ott, Naman Goyal, Jingfei Du, Mandar Joshi, Danqi Chen, Omer Levy, Mike Lewis, Luke Zettlemoyer, and Veselin Stoyanov. 2019. Roberta: A robustly optimized BERT pretraining approach. *CoRR*, abs/1907.11692.

Ilya Loshchilov and Frank Hutter. 2019. Decoupled weight decay regularization. In *7th International Conference on Learning Representations, ICLR 2019, New Orleans, LA, USA, May 6-9, 2019*. OpenReview.net.

Nikita Lozhnikov, Leon Derczynski, and Manuel Mazzara. 2018. Stance prediction for russian: Data and analysis. In *Proceedings of 6th International Conference in Software Engineering for Defence Applications, SEDA 2018, Rome, Italy, June 7-8, 2018*, volume 925 of *Advances in Intelligent Systems and Computing*, pages 176–186. Springer.

Saif M. Mohammad, Svetlana Kiritchenko, Parinaz Sobhani, Xiao-Dan Zhu, and Colin Cherry. 2016. Semeval-2016 task 6: Detecting stance in tweets. In *Proceedings of the 10th International Workshop on Semantic Evaluation, SemEval@NAACL-HLT 2016, San Diego, CA, USA, June 16-17, 2016*, pages 31–41. The Association for Computer Linguistics.

Nils Reimers and Iryna Gurevych. 2019. Sentence-bert: Sentence embeddings using siamese bert-networks. In *Proceedings of the 2019 Conference on Empirical Methods in Natural Language Processing and the 9th International Joint Conference on Natural Language Processing, EMNLP-IJCNLP 2019, Hong Kong, China, November 3-7, 2019*, pages 3980–3990. Association for Computational Linguistics.

Oscar Sainz, Oier Lopez de Lacalle, Gorka Labaka, Ander Barrena, and Eneko Agirre. 2021. Label verbalization and entailment for effective zero and few shot relation extraction. In *Proceedings of the 2021 Conference on Empirical Methods in Natural Language Processing, EMNLP 2021, Virtual Event / Punta Cana, Dominican Republic, 7-11 November, 2021*, pages 1199–1212. Association for Computational Linguistics.

Oscar Sainz, Itziar Gonzalez-Dios, Oier Lopez de Lacalle, Bonan Min, and Eneko Agirre. 2022. Textual entailment for event argument extraction: Zero- and few-shot with multi-source learning. In *Findings of the Association for Computational Linguistics: NAACL 2022, Seattle, WA, United States, July 10-15, 2022*, pages 2439–2455. Association for Computational Linguistics.

Robyn Speer, Joshua Chin, and Catherine Havasi. 2017. Conceptnet 5.5: An open multilingual graph of general knowledge. In *Proceedings of the Thirty-First AAAI Conference on Artificial Intelligence, February 4-9, 2017, San Francisco, California, USA*, pages 4444–4451. AAAI Press.

Adam Tsakalidis, Nikolaos Aletras, Alexandra I. Cristea, and Maria Liakata. 2018. Nowcasting the stance of social media users in a sudden vote: The case of the greek referendum. In *Proceedings of the 27th ACM International Conference on Information and Knowledge Management, CIKM 2018, Torino, Italy, October 22-26, 2018*, pages 367–376. ACM.

Marilyn A. Walker, Pranav Anand, Rob Abbott, and Ricky Grant. 2012a. Stance classification using dialogic properties of persuasion. In *Human Language Technologies: Conference of the North American Chapter of the Association of Computational Linguistics, Proceedings, June 3-8, 2012, Montréal, Canada*, pages 592–596. The Association for Computational Linguistics.

Marilyn A. Walker, Jean E. Fox Tree, Pranav Anand, Rob Abbott, and Joseph King. 2012b. A corpus for research on deliberation and debate. In *Proceedings of the Eighth International Conference on Language Resources and Evaluation, LREC 2012, Istanbul, Turkey, May 23-25, 2012*, pages 812–817. European Language Resources Association (ELRA).

Limin Wang and Dexin Wang. 2021. Solving stance detection on tweets as multi-domain and multi-task text classification. *IEEE Access*, 9:157780–157789.

Shuohang Wang, Yang Liu, Yichong Xu, Chenguang Zhu, and Michael Zeng. 2021. Want to reduce labeling cost? GPT-3 can help. In *Findings of the Association for Computational Linguistics: EMNLP 2021, Virtual Event / Punta Cana, Dominican Republic, 16-20 November, 2021*, pages 4195–4205. Association for Computational Linguistics.

Adina Williams, Nikita Nangia, and Samuel R. Bowman. 2018. A broad-coverage challenge corpus for sentence understanding through inference. In *Proceedings of the 2018 Conference of the North American Chapter of the Association for Computational Linguistics: Human Language Technologies, NAACL-HLT 2018, New Orleans, Louisiana, USA, June 1-6, 2018, Volume 1 (Long Papers)*, pages 1112–1122. Association for Computational Linguistics.

Congying Xia, Wenpeng Yin, Yihao Feng, and Philip S. Yu. 2021. Incremental few-shot text classification with multi-round new classes: Formulation, dataset and system. In *Proceedings of the 2021 Conference of the North American Chapter of the Association for Computational Linguistics: Human Language Technologies, NAACL-HLT 2021, Online, June 6-11, 2021*, pages 1351–1360. Association for Computational Linguistics.

Wenpeng Yin, Nazneen Fatema Rajani, Dragomir R. Radev, Richard Socher, and Caiming Xiong. 2020. Universal natural language processing with limited annotations: Try few-shot textual entailment as a start. In *Proceedings of the 2020 Conference on Empirical Methods in Natural Language Processing, EMNLP 2020, Online, November 16-20, 2020*, pages 8229–8239. Association for Computational Linguistics.

Kang Min Yoo, Dongju Park, Jaewook Kang, Sang-Woo Lee, and Woo-Myoung Park. 2021. Gpt3mix: Leveraging large-scale language models for text augmentation. In *Findings of the Association for Computational Linguistics: EMNLP 2021, Virtual Event / Punta Cana, Dominican Republic, 16-20 November, 2021*, pages 2225–2239. Association for Computational Linguistics.

Optimizing text representations to capture (dis)similarity between political parties

Tanise Ceron[△] **Nico Blokker**[□] **Sebastian Padó**[△]
[△] Institute for Natural Language Processing, University of Stuttgart, Germany
[□] Research Center on Inequality and Social Policy, University of Bremen, Germany
{tanise.ceron,pado}@ims.uni-stuttgart.de, blokker@uni-bremen.de

Abstract

Even though fine-tuned neural language models have been pivotal in enabling "deep" automatic text analysis, optimizing text representations for specific applications remains a crucial bottleneck. In this study, we look at this problem in the context of a task from computational social science, namely modeling pairwise similarities between political parties. Our research question is what level of structural information is necessary to create robust text representation, contrasting a strongly informed approach (which uses both claim span and claim category annotations) with approaches that forgo one or both types of annotation with document structure-based heuristics. Evaluating our models on the manifestos of German parties for the 2021 federal election. We find that heuristics that maximize within-party over between-party similarity along with a normalization step lead to reliable party similarity prediction, without the need for manual annotation.

1 Introduction

A party manifesto, also known as electoral program, is a document in which parties express their views, intentions and motives for the next coming years. Since this genre of text is written not just to inform, but to persuade potential voters that the parties compete for (Budge et al., 2001), it provides a strong basis to understand the position taken by parties according to various policies because of its direct access to the parties' opinions. Political scientists study the contents of party manifestos, for instance, to investigate parties' similarity with respect to the several policies (Budge, 2003), to predict party coalitions (Druckman et al., 2005), and to evaluate the extent to which the parties that they vote for actually corresponds to their own world view (McGregor, 2013).

To carry out systematic analyses of party relations while taking into account differences in style and level of detail, these analyses are increasingly grounded in two types of manual annotation about *claims*, statements that contain a position or a view towards an issue, that can be argued or demanded for (Koopmans and Statham, 1999): First, *abstract claim categories* (Burst et al., 2021) are used to group together diverse forms and formulations of demands. Second, annotation often includes the *stance* that parties take towards specific political claims to abstract away from the many ways to express support or rejection in language. In addition, these types of annotation offer a direct way to empirically ground party similarity in claims and link these to concrete textual statements. At the same time, such manual annotation is extremely expensive in terms of time and resources and has to be repeated for every country and every new election.

In this paper, we investigate the extent to which this manual effort can be reduced given appropriate text representations. We build on the advances made in recent years in neural language models for text representations and present a series of fine-tuning designs based on manifesto texts to compute party similarities. Our main hypothesis is that the proximity between groups can be more easily captured when the model receives adequate indication of the differences between groups (and their stances) and this can be done via fine-tuning for instance. This can be achieved by using signal that is freely available in the manifestos' *document structure*, such as groupings by party or topic. Information of this type can serve as an alternative feedback for fine-tuning in order to create robust text representations for analysing party proximity.

We ask three specific questions: (1) How to create robust representations for identifying the similarity between groups such as in the case of party relations? (2) What level of document structure is necessary for this purpose? (3) Can computational methods capture the relation between parties in unstructured text? We empirically investigate these questions on electoral programs from the Ger-

Proceedings of the 26th Conference on Computational Natural Language Learning (CoNLL), pages 325 - 338
December 7-8, 2022 ©2022 Association for Computational Linguistics

man 2021 elections, comparing party similarities against a ground truth built from structured data. We find that our hypothesis is borne out: We can achieve competitive results in modelling the party proximity with textual data provided that the text representations are optimized to capture the differences across parties and normalized to fall in a certain distribution that is appropriate for computing text similarity. More surprisingly, we find that completely unstructured data reach higher correlations than more informed settings that consider exclusively claims and/or their policy domain. We make our code and data available for replicability.[1]

Paper structure. The paper is structured as follows. Section 2 provides an overview of related work. Section 3 describes the data we work with and our ground truth. Section 4 presents our modeling approach. Sections 5 and 6 discuss the experimental setup and our results. Section 7 concludes.

2 Related Work

2.1 Party Characterization

The characterization of parties is an important topic in political science, and has previously been attempted with NLP models. Most studies, however, have focused on methods to place parties along the left to right ideological dimension. For instance, an early example is Laver et al. (2003) who investigate the scaling of political texts associated with parties (such as manifestos or legislative speeches) with a bag of words approach in a supervised fashion, with position scores provided by human domain experts. Others, instead, have implemented unsupervised methods for party positioning in order to avoid picking up on biases of the annotated data and to scale up to large amounts of texts from different political contexts while still implementing word frequency methods (Slapin and Proksch, 2008). More recent studies have sought to overcome the drawbacks of word frequency models such as topic reliance and lack of similarity between synonymous pairs of words, e.g. Glavaš et al. (2017) and Nanni et al. (2022) implement a combination of distributional semantics methods and a graph-based score propagation algorithm for capturing the party positions in the left-right dimension.

Our study differs from previous ones in two main aspects. First, our aim is not to place parties a left-to-right political dimension but to assess party similarity in a latent multidimensional space of policy positions and ideologies. Second, our focus is not on the use of specific vocabulary, but on representations of whole sentences. In other words, our proposed models work well if they manage to learn how political viewpoints are expressed at the sentence level in party manifestos.

2.2 Optimizing Text Representations for Similarity

Fine Tuning. Recent years have seen rapid advances in the area of neural language models, including models such as BERT, RoBERTa or GPT-3 (Devlin et al., 2019; Liu et al., 2020; Brown et al., 2020). The sentence-encoding capabilities of these models make them generally applicable to text classification and similarity tasks (Cer et al., 2018). Both for classification and for similarity, it was found that pre-trained models already show respectable performance, but fine-tuning them on task-related data is crucial to optimize the models' predictions – essentially telling the model which aspects of the input matter for the task at hand.

On the similarity side, a well-known language model is Sentence-BERT Reimers and Gurevych (2019), a siamese and triplet network based on BERT (Devlin et al., 2019) or RoBERTa (Liu et al., 2020) which aims at better encoding the similarities between sequences of text. Sentence-BERT (SBERT) comes with its own fine-tuning schema which is informed by ranked pairs or triplets and tunes the text representations to respect the preferences expressed by the fine-tuning data. Of course, this raises the question of how to obtain such fine-tuning data: The study experiments both with manually annotated datasets (for entailment and paraphrasing tasks) and with the use of heuristic document structure information, assuming that sentences from the same Wikipedia section are semantically closer and sentences from different sections are further away. Parallel results are also found by Gao et al. (2021) in their SimCSE model, which reach even better results when fine-tuning with contrastive learning: They also compare a setting based on manually annotated data from an inference dataset with a heuristic setting based on combining a pair of sentences with its drop-out version as positive examples and different pairs as negative examples.

Both studies find slightly lower performance for

[1] https://github.com/tceron/capture_similarity_between_political_parties.git

Party	Sentence	Domain
AfD	People's insecurities and fears, especially in rural regions, must be taken seriously.	Social Groups
CDU	We want to strengthen our Europe together with the citizens for the challenges of the future.	External Relations
Linke	The policies of federal governments that ensure private corporations and investors can make big money off our insurance premiums, co-pays and exploitation of health care workers are endangering our health!	Political System
FDP	In this way, we want to create incentives for a more balanced division of family work between the parents.	Welfare and Quality of Life
Grüne	After the pandemic, we do not want a return to unlimited growth in air traffic, but rather to align it with the goal of climate neutrality.	Economy
SPD	We advocate EU-wide ratification of the Council of Europe's Istanbul Convention as a binding legal norm against violence against women.	Fabric of Society

Table 1: Examples from the 2021 party manifestos and their annotated domains.

the heuristic versions of their fine-tuning datasets, but still obtain a relevant improvement over the non-fine-tuned versions of their models, pointing to the usefulness of heuristically generated fine-tuning data, for example based on document structure.

Postprocessing to Improve Embeddings A problem of the use of neural language models to create text representations that was recognized recently concerns the distributions of the resulting embeddings: They turn out to be highly anisotropic (Ethayarajh, 2019; Gao et al., 2019), meaning that their semantic space takes a cone rather than a sphere format - in the former two random vectors are highly correlated while in the latter they should be highly uncorrelated. This can cause similarities between tokens or sentences to be very similar even when they should not. To counteract this tendency, Li et al. (2020) impose an isotropic distribution onto the embeddings via a flow-based generative model. Su et al. (2021) propose a lightweight, even slightly more effective approach: The text embeddings undergo a linear so-called whitening transformation, which ensures that the bases of the space are uncorrelated and each have a variance of 1.

3 Data

Before we describe the methods we will use, we describe our textual basis and the ground truth we will aim to approximate.

3.1 The Manifesto Dataset

As stated above, we are interested in deriving party representations from party manifestos. Party manifestos generally contain sections roughly separated by policy topics, however, some party manifestos are organized more strictly by topics than others. For this reason, we utilize the manifesto dataset provided by the Manifesto Project (Burst et al., 2021), which provides manifestos from around the world and offers consistent markup of policy domains and categories [2].

More specifically, every sentence from the manifestos is annotated with domain names and categories. In this paper, consistent with our goal of reducing annotation effort, we consider only the domain. The domain corresponds to a broad policy field such as 'political system' and 'freedom and democracy'. In most cases, an entire sentence is annotated with a single domain, but some sentences have been split when falling into two distinct domains. Nearly every sentence is annotated with a domain label, except the introduction and end sections which usually contain an appeal to the voter and do not belong to any policy category.

For reasons that will become clear in the next subsection, we focus on German data and use the party manifestos written by the six main German parties (CDU/CSU, SPD, Grüne, Linke, FDP, AFD) for the federal elections in 2013, 2017 and 2021. Table 1 shows some examples of sentences with their respective domain names. Due to space constraints, more information about the description of the dataset is found in appendix A.1.

[2]More information on `https://manifesto-project.wzb.eu/information/documents/corpus`

3.2 Ground Truth: Wahl-o-Mat

A problem with the task of predicting party proximity is to find a suitable ground truth against which to evaluate the models. In this study, we make use of a highly structured dataset, Wahl-o-Mat (WoM) from which we can construct a ground truth of party similarities with minimal manual involvement.

Wahl-o-Mat (WoM, Wagner and Ruusuvirta (2012)) is an online application that provides voting advice. The application collects users' stances on a range of policy issues via a questionnaire. There are 38 issues in total and they cover a wide range of topics, e.g. 'Germany should increase its defense spending' or 'The promotion of wind energy is to be terminated'. The users' stances are then matched against those of the German parties in order to suggest the closest choices for users. The database behind WoM consists of the stances that each party takes towards each policy issue, which can be 'agree', 'disagree', or 'neutral'.

WoM provides each user with a "percentage overlap" that they have with the different parties, suggesting that the set of policy issues and the stances are an informative basis for computing positional similarity (Wagner and Ruusuvirta, 2012). In this spirit, we define as our ground truth the *party distance matrix* which we obtain by representing each party by its vector of stances (represented -1, 1, 0) towards the different policy issues and computing the Hamming (L1) distances among them. Such distance calculations are used by political scientists to understand the overall (dis)similarity between party and voters (McGregor, 2013).

Figure 1a shows the distance matrix between parties: the higher the distance, the more they disagree on WoM policy issues. Figure 1b visualizes the ground truth differently, as an agglomerative clustering of the distance matrix. This ground truth arguably stands up to scrutiny: The two most left-oriented parties, Grüne (greens) and Linke (left), are most similar (distance 0.18), due to their similar environmental programs and shared concern about foreign policy. They are then most similar to social democratic SPD. On the other main branch of the clustering tree, which covers the right-oriented parties, AFD (right wing) and CDU/CSU (center conservative) are most similar, although less than the left parties (distance 0.45). Finally, the liberal party FDP groups with the conservative parties, but reluctantly so: it assumes a kind of bridge position between the left and right oriented parties.

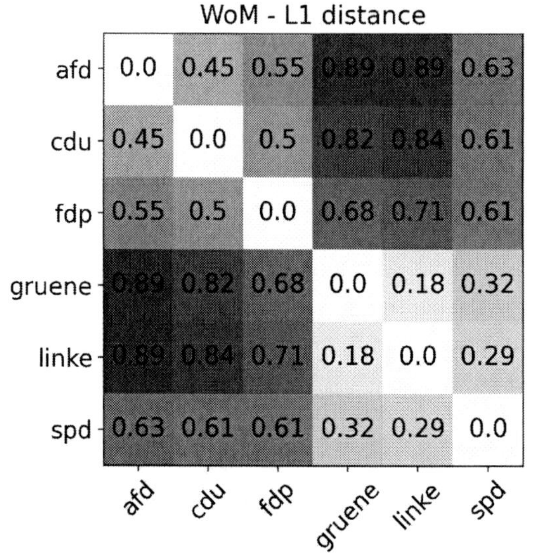

(a) Distances between parties

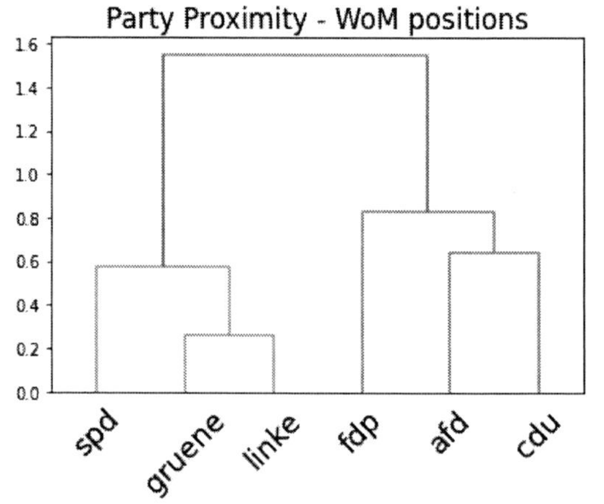

(b) Aggloremative clustering

Figure 1: Based on Wahl-o-Mat policy positions.

4 Methods

We describe our method in three steps: (a) we define a set of informative text representations models; (b) we compute party similarities, parallel to Section 3.2, on the basis of these text representations; (c) we post-process the data.

4.1 Building Informative Text Representations

The first step is to build text representations that are informative for party similarity. As sketched above, we use neural language models (NLMs) as the current state of the art. This involves selecting a base embedding model and defining the different fine-tuning schemes.

Base embedding model: SBERT. We choose SBERT as the basis for our models. With its focus on sentence similarity and its computational efficiency, it is arguably the most appropriate model for our goals. Pre-trained SBERT without any fine-tuning [3] serves directly as our first model.

Fine-tuning SBERT. Fine-tuning of SBERT can take place in different ways, but given our type of data, we use the triplet objective function where the model receives as input an anchor sentence *a*, a positive sentence *p* that is similar to the anchor sentence and a negative sentence *n* unrelated to both previous sentences. The objective of the fine-tuning is to minimize

$$max(\|S_a - S_p\| - \|S_a - S_n\| + \epsilon, 0) \quad (1)$$

which encourages the model to learn that S_p is at least ϵ closer to S_a than to S_n. $\|\cdot\|$ is the distance metric, which is kept as the default Euclidean [4]. We experiment with two ways of constructing triplets for fine-tuning, first by *domain* and then by *party*.

SBERT$_{domain}$ follows the same logic as in Dor et al. (2018) with the Wikipedia sections (and replicated in Reimers and Gurevych (2019)). We use the domain information from the manifestos (cf. Section 3) to construct triplets: The anchor and the positive sentences are part of the same domain and the negative sentence is from a different domain across party manifestos. The hypothesis is that aligning sentences by topic should help the model focus on relevant policy distinctions across parties.

SBERT$_{party}$, in contrast, intends to learn the distinction between the way parties express their claims or their ideologies and opinion. Here, we construct triplets by combining anchor sentences with positive sentences from the same party – irrespective of the domain – and negative sentences from the other parties' manifestos. The hypothesis of this setup is that the embeddings incorporate the parties' stances along with the way that particular sentences are presented, or styles used. We assume that many aspects of the text contribute to capturing the stance such as sentiment, text style and word usage.

[3]Pre-trained model: `https://huggingface.co/sentence-transformers/paraphrase-multilingual-mpnet-base-v2`

[4]Loss function and more details on: `https://www.sbert.net/docs/package_reference/losses.html#sentence_transformers.losses.BatchAllTripletLoss`

ID	Grouping	Filtering	Infor.
CLAIMDOM	Domain	Claims only	++++
CLAIM	-	Claims only	+++
DOM	Domain	All sentences	++
NONE	-	All sentences	+

Table 2: Models for the computational of party similarity, varying in the amount of information used

4.2 Four Models for Party Similarities

With the methods described in the previous subsection, we can obtain representations for individual sentences. We now need to define how to *aggregate* these sentences into global party representations – or rather, their similarities.

Table 2 shows four aggregating strategies that differ in the amount of information that they take into account. They differ in two main dimensions: (a), the *grouping*: is the similarity computed globally, over the complete manifestos, or domain by domain (b), the *filtering*: is the similarity based on all sentences in the manifestos, or only on sentences that contain concrete claims (cf. Section 1).

Regarding grouping, we hypothesize that it is easier for language models to assess the proximity between parties if sentences from matching topics are compared. Similarly, we expect that filtering by claims serves to focus the models on the 'core' of the parties' policies.

CLAIMDOM: using claims and domains. In this, the most informed, model, we represent parties by the claims that they make, compare these claims by domain, and then average the by-domain similarities. Formally, let $\vec{s}$ be the embedding produced for a sentence by an (implicit) encoder model, $cl(T)$ the set of claim sentences contained a text T, and $dom(P, i)$ the set of sentences for domain i in the manifesto of a party P. Then we can define the representation of a domain (Equation 1), the similarity for domain i (Equation 2), and a global similarity (Equation 3):

$$\vec{dom}(P, i) = \sum_{s \in cl(dom(P,i))} \vec{s} \quad (2)$$

$$\text{sim}(P_1, P_2, i) = \cos(\vec{dom}(P_1, i), \vec{dom}(P_2, i)) \quad (3)$$

$$\text{sim}(P_1, P_2) = \frac{1}{|Dom|} \sum_i \text{sim}(P_1, P_2, i) \quad (4)$$

CLAIM: using claims, but no domains. To compute similarities without domain information, we

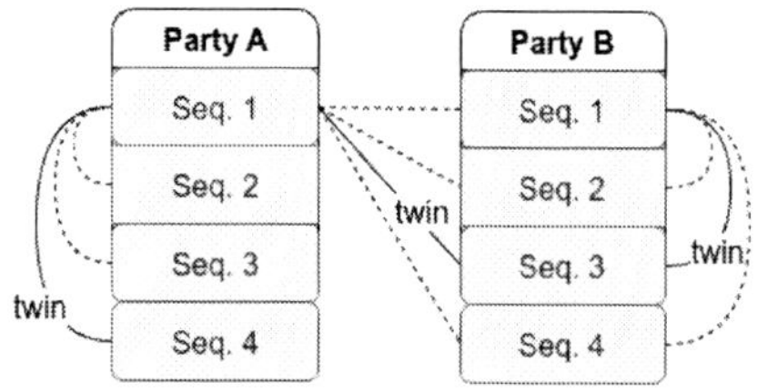

Figure 2: Twin matching: Solid lines mean pairings of maximal similarity.

could simply average over all sentences of the manifestos. However, pilot experiments showed that this procedure resulted in a severe loss of information. To avoid this, we introduce a method called *twin matching*, visualized in Figure 2. Twin matching maps each sentence in one manifesto to its nearest neighbor in the other manifesto (Equation 5) – in most cases, this will be a sentence of the same domain. Furthermore, we normalize the similarity to the twin by dividing by the maximum inter-claim similarity to both manifestos, and average over all sentences in the manifesto (Equation 7). Our hypothesis is that this procedure provides an approximating to domain-based grouping without the need for explicit domain labeling.

Formally, let $tw(s, T)$ denote the nearest neighbor, or twin, of sentence s in text T:

$$tw(s,T) = \arg\max_{t \in T} \cos(s,t) \tag{5}$$

Then the maximum inter-claim similarity C of a manifesto P, is

$$C(P) = \max_{p,p' \in cl(P) \wedge p \neq p'} cos(p, p') \tag{6}$$

Then the similarity of two texts is:

$$\text{sim}(P_1, P_2) = \sum_{s \in cl(P_1)} \frac{\cos(s, tw(s, P_2))}{|cl(P_1)|(C(P_1) + C(P_2))} \tag{7}$$

DOM: using domains, but no claims. This model is identical to CLAIMDOM, but uses all sentences instead of just claims in Equation (2).

NONE: using neither domains nor claims. This model is identical to CLAIM, but uses all sentences instead of just claims in Equations (6) and (7).

4.3 Post-processing

As mentioned in Section 2, sequence representations should form an isotropic space for good similarity prediction. Therefore, we also experiment with post-processed embeddings of the sentences by applying whitening transformation to our embeddings as suggested in Su et al. (2021). Following their normalization procedure, we start with a matrix $\mathbb{R}^{n \times d}$ representing n sequence vectors from a given encoding model with dimension d.[5] Then, matrix W ($\mathbb{R}^{d \times d}$) is computed through singular value decomposition (SVD) and saved along with the mean vector μ ($\mathbb{R}^{1 \times d}$) retrieved from the initial input embedding matrix. Finally, every vector ($\tilde{x}_i$) of interest for the analysis is converted into our final representation as in $\tilde{x}_i = (x_i - \mu)W$.

Su et al. (2021) compute W and μ either with the data from the task at hand (train, validation and test set) or with data from another NLI task. In this study, we experiment with the same data of the analysis, i.e., the entire MaClaim21 in the CLAIMDOM and CLAIM models and Manifesto21 in the DOM and NONE models. This means that each sequence representation of the dataset is stacked into a matrix for the computation of W and μ.

5 Experimental Setup

5.1 Datasets

Fine tuning. We use the German Manifesto data for 2013 and 2017 to fine-tune SBERT following Section 4.1. There is a deliberate temporal gap between the fine tuning datasets and the year of our ground truth, namely 2021, to ensure that the model picks up generalizable differences between parties rather than overfitting. However, we acknowledge the drawback that fine-tuning does not receive any signal from newly emerged topics (e.g. Covid19) and that party communication has not transformed drastically over the last four years.

Appendix A.3 provides more details and statistics, including evaluation on a 20% held-out validation set, which shows that fine-tuning improves both SBERT$_{party}$ and SBERT$_{domain}$ over plain SBERT, with SBERT$_{domain}$ gaining most.

Party representation. To compute party similarities following Section 4.2, we use the 2021 manifestos, which arguably form the right textual basis to evaluate against our Wahl-o-Mat ground truth for the 2021 German elections (Section 3.2). Recall that the Manifesto data comes with annotated domains, but not with annotated claims. We therefore applied an automatic claim classifier to identify claims (Blokker et al., 2020). We evaluated the

[5] The pre-trained model we use has 768 dimensions.

Model + postproc.	MaClaim21		Manifesto21	
	CLAIMDOM (++++)	CLAIM (+++)	DOM (++)	NONE (+)
fasttext_{avg}	0.17	0.30	0.27	0.28
fasttext_{avg}+whiten	0.54*	0.35	0.44*	0.41
BERT_{german}	0.12	0.28	0.11	0.27
BERT_{german} +whiten	0.37	0.47*	0.36	0.48*
RoBERTa_{xml}	0.03	0.35	0.08	0.33
RoBERTa_{xml}+whiten	0.39	0.51*	0.46*	0.54*
SBERT	0.38	0.47*	0.31	0.47*
SBERT(whiten)	**0.57***	0.50*	**0.53***	0.57*
SBERT_{domain}	0.22	0.23	0.32	0.16
SBERT_{domain}+whiten	0.44*	0.45*	0.41	0.52*
SBERT_{party}	0.45	0.13	0.32	0.16
SBERT_{party}+whiten	0.53*	**0.70***	0.50*	**0.69***

Table 3: Experimental results: Mantel's correlation between categorical and textual distance matrices. *+whiten* means that the models have undergone whitening postprocessing. The + symbol indicates the level of informativeness from Table 2. Highest correlation for each model in boldface. * p-value < 0.05.

results of the classifier by calculating the precision on a subset of 324 manually labeled claims from the 2021 manifestos and obtained a reasonable precision of 75,6%. More information about data and classifier can be found in Appendix C.1.

This procedure results in two datasets for model training: Manifesto21 (with domain annotation) has 17,052 sentences; MaClaim21 (with domain and claim annotation) consists of 9,814 claims. More details and statistics are in Appendix B.

5.2 Models

In our empirical evaluation below, we vary the following three parameters: (1), Embedding model and fine-tuning (SBERT plain vs. SBERT_{domain} vs. SBERT_{party}). (2), Party similarity computation (CLAIMDOM vs. CLAIM vs. DOM vs. NONE). (3), Postprocessing (whitening vs. none). We consider all combinations of these parameters.

Baselines We consider three baselines. The first and simplest one is a pre-trained FastText model for German based on character n-gram embeddings (Bojanowski et al., 2017). We compute sentence representations by tokenizing the sentences based on the FastText tokenizer and averaging all FastText token representations.[6]

The other two baselines use transformer-driven (sub)word embeddings, namely from BERT-German [7] and multilingual RoBERTa-XLM [8]. We choose the former because monolingual models often perform better than multilingual ones and the latter because it is the student model with which SBERT has been trained, which allows us to check how much better SBERT can be in a text similarity task in the political domain. Again, we feed each sentence to these models and compute the final representations by averaging all token representations from the two last layers of the model, a strong baseline for similarity tasks (Li et al., 2020; Su et al., 2021).

5.3 Evaluation

To evaluate the pairwise party similarities computed by the models, we turn them into distances and compare them against our ground truth distance matrix (Section 3.2) with the Mantel test (Mantel, 1967). This test is a variant of standard correlation tests (such as Spearman's rho) which are not applicable to distance matrices because they assume that the observations are independent of one another. In our case, changing the position of one value in the matrix would change the correlation between a pair or parties. Having said that, the Mantel test addresses this problem by calculating correlations on

[6] We evaluated both on the general version of fasttext for German available on `fasttext.cc` and also on a trained version with newspaper articles from TAZ for a more domain specific model. Since both models obtained comparable results, we report only results for the former.

[7] `https://huggingface.co/bert-base-german-cased`

[8] `https://huggingface.co/xlm-roberta-base`

all permutations of the flattened distance matrix. The two-tail hypothesis tests whether the correlation between the ground truth matrix and the target distance matrix is statistically significant or not. We use the nonparametric version of the test since the party distances are not normally distributed.

6 Results and Discussion

Table 3 shows the quantitative results of our experiments. We first discuss the effect of our various experimental parameters.

Effect of postprocessing. By comparing the upper and the lower row in each colored block, we observe that the the whitening transformation is beneficial in nearly all models, and where it is not, the loss is minor. On average, post-processed model embeddings are 22 percentage points higher in the correlations, and consistently obtain significant correlations with the ground truth. This suggests that the benefit of enforcing isotropic distributions extends to the domain and genre of political texts. Given the substantially higher performance of the models with the post-processing step, we focus on their results for the remainder of this discussion.

Effect of embedding models and fine-tuning. Comparing the rows in the table, we observe that our two baseline models, BERT and RoBERTa, show generally worse performance than even the non fine-tuned SBERT. BERT is generally the worst performer among the three, despite its monolinguality, which we interpret as evidence that the architectures more geared towards similarity tasks have an advantage. We take these results as validation of our choice of SBERT as embedding model.

Interestingly, our simplest baseline, fasttext$_{avg}$, performs better than most models in the most informative scenario (Mantel=0.54) and relatively well with domain information (Mantel=0.44), but degrades when less information is available. This suggests that FastText embeddings are informative enough to support generalization from rich annotation, but are not able to align semantically similar sentences well in a less informative scenario such as in the twin matching approach.

Among the fine-tuned variants of SBERT, SBERT$_{domain}$ performs surprisingly badly and is generally outperformed by vanilla RoBERTa. This suggests that optimizing the model to pick up on domain contrasts is distracting the model from capturing the dis(similarity) between parties.

In contrast, SBERT$_{party}$ does very well, and competes with vanilla SBERT for the best results. Indeed, SBERT wins in both setups that are grouped by the domain category (CLAIMDOM and DOM), reaching 0.57 and 0.53, respectively. Conversely, SBERT$_{party}$ wins the two scenarios without the grouping by domains (CLAIM's Mantel=0.70 and NONE's Mantel=0.69), and achieves the overall highest correlations here.

These results suggest that SBERT, without any fine-tuning, is reasonably good at capturing the proximity between parties if more information is provided: if we have both only claim structure and the domain category then SBERT can be enough (Mantel=0.57). If there is unstructured data, but there is still domain information, despite having a drop in performance, it can still achieve a reasonable correlation (Mantel=0.53).

SBERT$_{party}$, in contrast, performs better in the settings without domain information, that is, when the party similarity is based on twin sentence similarity (Section 4.2). We believe that this is the case because the sentence-level fine-tuning of SBERT$_{party}$ is most directly carried forward into the predictions of the model. In effect, therefore, fine-tuning SBERT by contrasting the party difference is the best way to encode fine-grained differences between parties' views and ideologies.

Analysis by agglomerative clustering. To complement the analysis by correlation coefficients in Table 3, we compute agglomerative clusterings with average linkage for the best models from Table 3. The results, shown in Figure 3, show a good correspondence to the quantitative results, thus lending support our use of the Mantel test.

Indeed, the two SBERT models in 3(a) and 3(c), which reach moderate correlation coefficients, disagree substantially with the ground truth clustering: they group, for example, the far right AFD with the liberal FDP in (a), and with the left wing Linke in (c). Also, the conservative CDU is grouped with Grüne (greens) and social democratic SPD. In contrast, the two SBERT$_{party}$ models in 3(b) and 3(d) show a better match with the ground truth, even though both group Grüne with SPD instead of Linke, and (b) has AFD as an outlier altogether.

General outcome. Probably the most striking outcome of our experiment is that the best results – both in terms of the correlation coefficient and in terms of the clustering – results from models

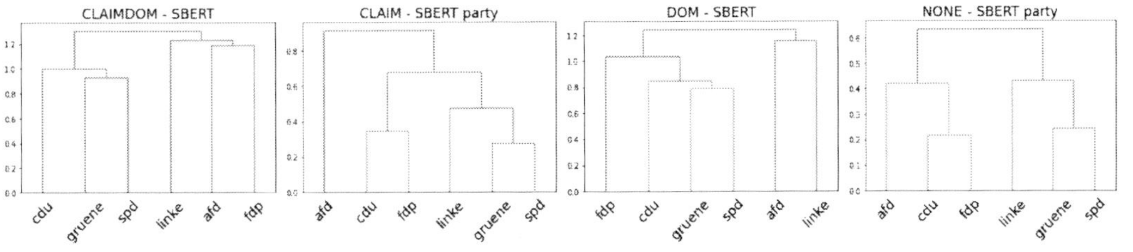

(a) CLAIMDOM model (0.57) (b) CLAIM model (0.70) (c) DOM model (0.53) (d) NONE model (0.69)

Figure 3: Agglomerative clustering for the best model of each setting. Mantel correlation in parenthesis. Ground truth's comparison in Fig. 1b.

that use very little structured information (CLAIM, NONE). The difference among the two is small, and can be seen as a trade-off between using a larger, more noisy dataset (all sentences: Manifesto21) and a more focused dataset (just the claims: MaClaim21) of about half the size. These results confirm the idea that it is possible to use natural language processing methods to identify the dis(similarity) between party according to their policy positions with unstructured data.

We believe that this result is a combination of a good choice of fine-tuning regimen – providing the embeddings with a signal concerning the contrast between parties – with an appropriate way to model similarity, with our twin matching approach which helps to match the most relevant parts of the two manifestos to one another. These two aspects reinforce each other, since a well fine-tuned model is better able to push away dissimilar parties while bringing closer together similar ones.

7 Conclusion

In this paper, we have investigated to what degree text representations can capture the proximity of parties and how to best fine-tune representations for this task. Our results indicate that aspects that have been proposed as important for this type of analysis in political science, namely annotation of domains (Burst et al., 2021) and claims (Koopmans and Statham, 1999), do not appear to matter greatly for this task – or at least, manual annotation can be replaced by NLP tools: we have recognized claims with a classifier (Blokker et al., 2020) and have proposed a weekly supervised method, "twin matching", to approximate domain-level similarity computation. Indeed, one of our models that does not use any manual annotation is among the top contenders. Of rather greater importance for party similarity prediction, according to our findings, is fine-tuning the text representations and postprocessing them.

This is good news for computational political science: the judicious use of document structure appears able to help alleviate the effort of having domain experts annotate large corpora. The two main limitations of our current study relate to this outlook: (a) we only experimented with a single language and ground truth – future work should take into account multiple languages and time periods, with a potential long term goal of text-based models for party development (König et al., 2013); (b) we only scratched the surface of cues available for fine-tuning. Future work could, for example, take into account other aspects of parties such as ideological position (Glavaš et al., 2017), or reach beyond manifestos to include information from other types of party interactions (Strom, 1990). In addition to that, work on interpreting both the fine-tuned and vanilla SBERT models would be interesting to better understand the predominant dimensions of the sentence representations in the political domain.

Acknowledgments

We acknowledge funding by Deutsche Forschungsgemeinschaft (DFG) for project MARDY 2 (375875969) within the priority program RATIO.

Ethics Statement

We believe that this study does not carry major ethical implications in terms of data privacy or handling, given that our datasets are based on publicly available party manifestos from the German elections and from a public and freely accessible voting advice application (Wahl-o-Mat). The annotators that provided us with a subset of labeled claims to estimate the quality of the claim classifier were student assistants from the university remunerated fairly according to their working hours.

References

Nico Blokker, Erenay Dayanik, Gabriella Lapesa, and Sebastian Padó. 2020. Swimming with the tide? positional claim detection across political text types. In *Proceedings of the Fourth Workshop on Natural Language Processing and Computational Social Science*, pages 24–34, Online. Association for Computational Linguistics.

Piotr Bojanowski, Edouard Grave, Armand Joulin, and Tomas Mikolov. 2017. Enriching word vectors with subword information. *Transactions of the Association for Computational Linguistics*, 5:135–146.

Tom Brown, Benjamin Mann, Nick Ryder, Melanie Subbiah, Jared D Kaplan, Prafulla Dhariwal, Arvind Neelakantan, Pranav Shyam, Girish Sastry, Amanda Askell, Sandhini Agarwal, Ariel Herbert-Voss, Gretchen Krueger, Tom Henighan, Rewon Child, Aditya Ramesh, Daniel Ziegler, Jeffrey Wu, Clemens Winter, Chris Hesse, Mark Chen, Eric Sigler, Mateusz Litwin, Scott Gray, Benjamin Chess, Jack Clark, Christopher Berner, Sam McCandlish, Alec Radford, Ilya Sutskever, and Dario Amodei. 2020. Language models are few-shot learners. In *Advances in Neural Information Processing Systems*, volume 33, pages 1877–1901.

Ian Budge. 2003. Validating the manifesto research group approach: theoretical assumptions and empirical confirmations. In *Estimating the policy position of political actors*, pages 70–85. Routledge.

Ian Budge, Hans-Dieter Klingemann, Andrea Volkens, Judith Bara, and Eric Tanenbaum, editors. 2001. *Mapping Policy Preferences: Estimates for Parties, Electors, and Governments 1945-1998*. Oxford University Press, Oxford, New York.

Tobias Burst, Werner Krause, Pola Lehmann, Jirka Lewandowski, Theres Matthieß, Nicolas Merz, Sven Regel, and Lisa Zehnter. 2021. Manifesto corpus. version: 2021.1. *Berlin: WZB Berlin Social Science Center.*

Daniel Cer, Yinfei Yang, Sheng-yi Kong, Nan Hua, Nicole Limtiaco, Rhomni St. John, Noah Constant, Mario Guajardo-Cespedes, Steve Yuan, Chris Tar, Brian Strope, and Ray Kurzweil. 2018. Universal sentence encoder for English. In *Proceedings of the 2018 Conference on Empirical Methods in Natural Language Processing: System Demonstrations*, pages 169–174, Brussels, Belgium. Association for Computational Linguistics.

Jacob Devlin, Ming-Wei Chang, Kenton Lee, and Kristina Toutanova. 2019. BERT: Pre-training of deep bidirectional transformers for language understanding. In *Proceedings of the 2019 Conference of the North American Chapter of the Association for Computational Linguistics: Human Language Technologies, Volume 1 (Long and Short Papers)*, pages 4171–4186, Minneapolis, Minnesota. Association for Computational Linguistics.

Liat Ein Dor, Yosi Mass, Alon Halfon, Elad Venezian, Ilya Shnayderman, Ranit Aharonov, and Noam Slonim. 2018. Learning thematic similarity metric from article sections using triplet networks. In *Proceedings of the 56th Annual Meeting of the Association for Computational Linguistics (Volume 2: Short Papers)*, pages 49–54, Melbourne, Australia. Association for Computational Linguistics.

James N Druckman, Lanny W Martin, and Michael F Thies. 2005. Influence without confidence: Upper chambers and government formation. *Legislative Studies Quarterly*, 30(4):529–548.

Kawin Ethayarajh. 2019. How contextual are contextualized word representations? Comparing the geometry of BERT, ELMo, and GPT-2 embeddings. In *Proceedings of the 2019 Conference on Empirical Methods in Natural Language Processing and the 9th International Joint Conference on Natural Language Processing (EMNLP-IJCNLP)*, pages 55–65, Hong Kong, China. Association for Computational Linguistics.

Jun Gao, Di He, Xu Tan, Tao Qin, Liwei Wang, and Tie-Yan Liu. 2019. Representation degeneration problem in training natural language generation models. In *7th International Conference on Learning Representations, ICLR 2019, New Orleans, LA, USA, May 6-9, 2019*. OpenReview.net.

Tianyu Gao, Xingcheng Yao, and Danqi Chen. 2021. SimCSE: Simple contrastive learning of sentence embeddings. In *Proceedings of the 2021 Conference on Empirical Methods in Natural Language Processing*, pages 6894–6910, Online and Punta Cana, Dominican Republic. Association for Computational Linguistics.

Goran Glavaš, Federico Nanni, and Simone Paolo Ponzetto. 2017. Unsupervised cross-lingual scaling of political texts. In *Proceedings of the 15th Conference of the European Chapter of the Association for Computational Linguistics: Volume 2, Short Papers*, pages 688–693, Valencia, Spain. Association for Computational Linguistics.

Ruud Koopmans and Paul Statham. 1999. Political claims analysis: Integrating protest event and political discourse approaches. *Mobilization: an international quarterly*, 4(2):203–221.

Thomas König, Moritz Marbach, and Moritz Osnabrügge. 2013. Estimating party positions across countries and time—a dynamic latent variable model for manifesto data. *Political Analysis*, 21(4):468–491.

Gabriella Lapesa, André Blessing, Nico Blokker, Erenay Dayanık, Sebastian Haunss, Jonas Kuhn, and

Sebastian Padó. 2020. DEbateNet-mig15: tracing the 2015 immigration debate in germany over time. In *Proceedings of The 12th Language Resources and Evaluation Conference*, pages 919–927.

Michael Laver, Kenneth Benoit, and John Garry. 2003. Extracting policy positions from political texts using words as data. *American political science review*, 97(2):311–331.

Bohan Li, Hao Zhou, Junxian He, Mingxuan Wang, Yiming Yang, and Lei Li. 2020. On the sentence embeddings from pre-trained language models. In *Proceedings of the 2020 Conference on Empirical Methods in Natural Language Processing (EMNLP)*, pages 9119–9130, Online. Association for Computational Linguistics.

Yinhan Liu, Myle Ott, Naman Goyal, Jingfei Du, Mandar Joshi, Danqi Chen, Omer Levy, Mike Lewis, Luke Zettlemoyer, and Veselin Stoyanov. 2020. RoBERTa: A robustly optimized BERT pretraining approach. *ArXiv*, abs/1907.11692.

Nathan Mantel. 1967. The detection of disease clustering and a generalized regression approach. *Cancer research*, 27(2):209–220.

R Michael McGregor. 2013. Measuring "correct voting" using comparative manifestos project data. *Journal of Elections, Public Opinion and Parties*, 23(1):1–26.

Federico Nanni, Goran Glavaš, Ines Rehbein, Simone Paolo Ponzetto, and Heiner Stuckenschmidt. 2022. Political text scaling meets computational semantics. *ACM/IMS Transactions on Data Science (TDS)*, 2(4):1–27.

Nils Reimers and Iryna Gurevych. 2019. Sentence-bert: Sentence embeddings using siamese bert-networks. In *Proceedings of EMNLP/IJCNLP*, pages 3980–3990. Association for Computational Linguistics.

Jonathan B Slapin and Sven-Oliver Proksch. 2008. A scaling model for estimating time-series party positions from texts. *American Journal of Political Science*, 52(3):705–722.

Kaare Strom. 1990. A behavioral theory of competitive political parties. *American Journal of Political Science*, 34(2):565–598.

Jianlin Su, Jiarun Cao, Weijie Liu, and Yangyiwen Ou. 2021. Whitening sentence representations for better semantics and faster retrieval. *ArXiv*, abs/2103.15316.

Markus Wagner and Outi Ruusuvirta. 2012. Matching voters to parties: Voting advice applications and models of party choice. *Acta Politica*, 47(4):400–422.

A Appendix

A.1 Fine-tuning data

Party	Num. inst.
Grüne	5913
Die Linke	4243
Social Democratic Party of Germany (SPD)	3566
Free Democratic Party (FDP)	3149
Christian Democratic Union (CDU)	2569
Alternative for Germany (AfD)	770

Table 1: Number of instances in the train set of the fine-tuning of SBERT$_{party}$. Data from the 2013 and 2017 manifestos.

Domain name	Num. inst
Welfare and Quality of Life	7078
Economy	6330
Fabric of Society	2586
Freedom and Democracy	2395
External Relations	2306
Social Groups	2144
Political System	1682

Table 2: Number of instances in the train set of the fine-tuning of SBERT$_{domain}$. Data from the 2013 and 2017 manifestos. More information about the categories can be found on https://manifesto-project.wzb.eu/coding_schemes/mp_v5

Party	Year	Sentence	Domain
AfD	2017	This oligarchy holds the levers of state power, political education and informational and media influence over the population.	Political System
CDU	2017	We have set ourselves an ambitious goal: We want full employment for all of Germany by 2025 at the latest.	Social Groups
FDP	2013	We want to continue to give people the freedom to pursue their ideas - creating growth, progress and prosperity for all.	Freedom and Democracy
Grüne	2013	We want to make a change today to move towards an economy that benefits everyone, not just a few.	Welfare and Quality of Life
Die Linke	2013	But the populations and workers of these countries have common interests: the fight against wage depression, recession and mass unemployment.	Economy
SPD	2017	This includes ensuring that social cohesion in our country becomes stronger again and that decent dealings with one another are not lost to political radicalization.	Fabric of Society

Table 3: Examples from the training dataset with their corresponding domain names translated from German.

A.2 S-BERT training parameters

- Pre-trained model: paraphrase-multilingual-mpnet-base-v2
- Maximum sequence length: 128
- Train batch size: 16
- Number of training epochs: 5
- Learning rate: 2e-5
- Warm up steps: 100

A.3 Fine-tuning evaluation

Model	f1	SBERT (f1)
SBERT_{domain}	71,39%	66,66%
SBERT_{party}	68,79%	66,66%

Table 4: Comparison of the f1 scores between the non-fine-tuned and fine-tuned SBERT models on the held out validation set.

B Appendix

B.1 Data for the evaluation

Party	Num. claims
Die Linke	2770
Gruene	2380
CDU	1685
FDP	1388
SPD	952
AfD	638

Table 5: Number of claims per party in MaClaim21.

Party	Num. sentences
Die Linke	4850
Gruene	3947
CDU	2775
FDP	2239
SPD	1665
AfD	1574

Table 6: Number of sentences per party in Manifesto21.

C Appendix

C.1 Claim identifier

The claim identifier was trained on annotated data from the DebateNet dataset (Lapesa et al., 2020). The annotations are based on news articles from the German newspaper TAZ regarding the migration in the domestic scenario. Sentences that contain a claim are considered as positive and sentences without any claims are negative. It has been verified that the claim identifier trained on DebateNet can transfer reasonably well to the party manifestos (Blokker et al., 2020) with an averaged f1 score of 82% across the election campaigns of 2013 and 2017. More information regarding the training process:

- Number of training instances: 13,283
- Number of validation instances: 1,477
- Number of testing instances: 1,641
- Maximum sequence length: 128
- Train batch size: 32
- Number of training epochs: 5
- Learning rate: 3e-5

C.2 Evaluation on 2021 party manifestos

Expert annotators from the political science faculty annotated 324 unique political claims from six major German parties competing in the federal election of 2021. Annotations of claims followed a fine-grained hierarchical ontology (*codebook*) yielding 75 unique sub-categories that are divided into eight major categories. While the latter broadly corresponds to relevant policy fields, such as 'health', 'economy and finance', or 'education', the former specifies the concrete policy measure to be taken, for instance, 'mandatory vaccination', 'raise taxes', 'expansion of education and care services'. We do not provide the inter-annotator agreement because annotators worked closely together in this task. However, we verified the quality of the dataset by having a third annotator gold standardizing the dataset.

The classifier detected 245 out of the 324 annotated claims, reaching a reasonable precision of 75,6%. In total, the classifier predicted 9,814 claims out of 17,052 sentences.

Computational cognitive modeling of predictive sentence processing in a second language

Umesh Patil (umesh.patil@gmail.com)
University of Cologne
50923 Cologne, Germany

Sol Lago (sollago@em.uni-frankfurt.de)
Goethe University Frankfurt
60629 Frankfurt, Germany

Abstract

We propose an ACT-R cue-based retrieval model of the real-time gender predictions displayed by second language (L2) learners. The model extends a previous model of native (L1) speakers according to two central accounts in L2 sentence processing: (i) the Interference Hypothesis, which proposes that retrieval interference is higher in L2 than L1 speakers; (ii) the Lexical Bottleneck Hypothesis, which proposes that problems with gender agreement are due to weak gender representations. We tested the predictions of these accounts using data from two visual world experiments, which found that the gender predictions elicited by German possessive pronouns were delayed and smaller in size in L2 than L1 speakers. The experiments also found a "match effect", such that when the antecedent and possessee of the pronoun had the same gender, predictions were earlier than when the two genders differed. This match effect was smaller in L2 than L1 speakers. The model implementing the Lexical Bottleneck Hypothesis captured the effects of smaller predictions, smaller match effect and delayed predictions in one of the two conditions. By contrast, the model implementing the Interference Hypothesis captured the smaller prediction effect but it showed an earlier prediction effect and an increased match effect in L2 than L1 speakers. These results provide evidence for the Lexical Bottleneck Hypothesis, and they demonstrate a method for extending computational models of L1 to L2 processing.

1 Introduction

Although the world population is quickly becoming bilingual, there are very few computational models of bilingual sentence processing. Because most of these models were developed for technological applications—e.g., automatic translation—, this results in a scarcity of models that are cognitively realistic or even evaluable with human data (Frank, 2021; Frank et al., 2016; Hinaut et al., 2015; Hendriks and Vogelzang, 2020). However, such models are crucial to develop computational research that is informed by state-of-the-art psycholinguistic work. With this goal, we propose a computational cognitive model of bilingual processing built in an architecture, ACT-R, which is designed to model human cognition and can be evaluated with human data (Anderson, 2007; Ritter et al., 2019). The ACT-R architecture has also been used to model a number of linguistic phenomena, such as retrieval interference effects in linguistic dependency resolution (Vasishth et al., 2008), the influence of prominence on pronoun resolution (Patil et al., 2016b; Patil and Schumacher, 2022), the effect of memory load on sentence processing (van Rij et al., 2013), sentence processing in patients with aphasia (Crescentini and Stocco, 2005; Patil et al., 2016a), the interaction of sentence processing and eye movements (Engelmann et al., 2013), and incremental formal semantic processing (Brasoveanu and Dotlačil, 2020).

Accounts of bilingual processing can be divided in terms of how they explain differences between native (L1) and non-native (L2) processing. Here we focus on two different explanations of L1–L2 differences. The first, the Interference Hypothesis (IH), makes reference to the cue-based retrieval theory (Cunnings, 2017b,a). The Interference Hypothesis stipulates that memory retrieval is key for different parts of sentence processing, including the processing of non-local pronoun-antecedent dependencies like "<u>*John*</u> *noticed that* ***Richard***$_i$ *had cut* ***himself***$_i$ *with a knife*". When "*himself*" is encountered, speakers attempt to retrieve an antecedent matching the pronoun features. Retrieval success requires suppressing interfering elements that match some but not all of the relevant features (e.g., "*John*" has the appropriate gender and number features but not the syntactic ones, because it is outside the clause of the pronoun). The Interference Hypothesis proposes that L1 and L2 speakers

Proceedings of the 26th Conference on Computational Natural Language Learning (CoNLL), pages 339 - 349
December 7-8, 2022

are similar in their likelihood of initiating retrieval operations, but that L2 speakers are more prone to interference, yielding more misretrievals (e.g., wrongly recovering "*John*" as the pronoun's antecedent).

By contrast, the Lexical Bottleneck Hypothesis (LBH) is framed within so-called capacity-based accounts, which propose that L1–L2 differences arise because speakers process an L2 in a noisier cognitive architecture, resulting in slower and more error-prone parsing (Just and Carpenter, 1992; McDonald, 2006; Hopp, 2022). The Lexical Bottleneck Hypothesis proposes that L1–L2 parsing differences are due to variability in the bilingual lexicon. Specifically, because lexical processing "precedes and feeds into syntactic processing, key characteristics of bilingual lexical processing may cause aspects of non-target parsing" (Hopp, 2018, pp. 6). With regard to grammatical features like gender—the focus of this paper—the claim is that L2 speakers fail to use this information for syntactic processing because L2 words have weaker or more unstable gender representations, making the retrieval of gender information less robust in L2 than in L1. An additional factor—not modeled here—is L1 transfer, such that L2 gender processing may be harder in syntactic contexts that differ between the L1 and the L2.

We evaluate the Interference Hypothesis and the Lexical Bottleneck Hypothesis by using their claims to modify an ACT-R model that was previously shown to capture L1 predictive processing (Patil and Lago, 2021). The predictions of the modified ACT-R models are evaluated against the results of two eye-tracking experiments that examined how L1 and L2 speakers use gender features to do memory retrieval and to predict upcoming referents (Stone et al., 2021b; Lago et al., under review). We show that the ACT-R version that implements the Lexical Bottleneck Hypothesis does a better job at capturing L2 gender predictions. Our results—although currently limited to gender—suggest that the Lexical Bottleneck Hypothesis provides a suitable framework to model the predictive use of morphosyntactic information in L2, and could be extended to other features such as number, case and animacy.

2 Modeling L2 processing

2.1 Starting point: The L1 model

We consider Patil and Lago's (2021) model of processing possessive pronouns as our starting point. They modeled visual-world eye-tracking data from Stone et al. (2021b) in ACT-R and the cue-based retrieval framework (CBR, henceforth) (Lewis and Vasishth, 2005; Lewis et al., 2006). Our goal is to model the L2 visual-world eye-tracking data from Lago et al. (under review) by modifying the model to reflect the processing assumptions of the IH and the LBH. The model has the following structure most of which is inherited from ACT-R and CBR.

Sentence processing takes place as an incremental word-by-word left-corner parsing. Parsing rules are part of ACT-R's procedural memory, whereas the lexical entries, syntactic phrases and the incremental parse tree (NP, DP, VP, IP, etc.) are part of ACT-R's declarative memory. Each declarative memory element, called a *chunk*, has an activation associated with it which is determined by the equation 1.[1] At each input word, parsing rules are applied on chunks that are available in short-term memory to process the word. If a required chunk is not available in short-term memory, it is retrieved from declarative memory by specifying a set of cues as feature-value pairs, a cue-based retrieval mechanism.

The speed, accuracy and success of retrieving a chunk depends on its current activation level. The activation of $chunk_i$ is influenced by its usefulness in the past (the *base level activation* B_i), relevance in the current context (the *spreading activation* received through retrieval cues which is determined by the first summation component in eq. 1), degree of match with the retrieval request (the *partial matching* determined by the second summation component in eq. 1) and stochastic noise (ϵ_i). The *strength of association* S_{ji} is calculated by eq. 2 which is influenced by fan_j, the number of chunks matching cue_j. The value for Mji is calculated by the degree of match between a retrieval cue (cue_j) and $chunk_i$. The values for W (the maximum spreading activation), P (the partial match scale) and S (the maximum associative strength) in the calculation of A_i are constants across all simula-

[1]This is a simplified version of ACT-R's activation equation and it represents how activation is calculated in CBR. The equation can be simplified further to have only one summation term but for comparability with the original ACT-R equation we have kept the two summations separate.

tions and are set as ACT-R's parameter values.

$$A_i = B_i + \sum_{cue_j} WS_{ji} + \sum_{cue_j} PM_{ji} + \epsilon_i \quad (1)$$

$$S_{ji} = S - ln(fan_j) \quad (2)$$

For modeling the visual-world eye-tracking task from Stone et al. (2021b), Patil and Lago (2021) extended the existing architecture with the following new assumptions: (i) the model predicts the target picture at each input word, (ii) prediction of the target picture is implemented as a cue-based memory retrieval, and (iii) the probability of fixating an object is determined by the activation of the chunk representing that object. To incorporate the variable influence of different retrieval cues, Patil and Lago (2021) also proposed a cue-weighting mechanism as a modification to the *strength of association* equation (as in eq. 3) such that the amount of activation spreading from cue_j to $chunk_i$ is influenced by the importance of that cue.

$$S_{ji} = weight_j S - ln(fan_j) \quad (3)$$

The next two sections describe two possible modifications of the L1 model to implement two theories of L2 processing: (i) the Interference Hypothesis, and (ii) the Lexical Bottleneck Hypothesis.

2.2 The IH model

IH proposes that L2 speakers are prone to higher interference compared to L1 speakers and that leads L2 speakers to misretrieve non-target elements more often during sentence processing. Although IH is not a computationally implemented theory, it is described in terms of the CBR framework of sentence processing, and, hence, an L1 model implemented in CBR can be straightforwardly extended to L2 processing. In ACT-R and CBR, misretrievals due to interference take place through the mechanism of partial matching (the second summation term in eq. 1). Partial matching enables non-target chunks (chunks that match some of the cues from the retrieval request but not all) to be considered in the retrieval process. Due to random fluctuation in the activation of chunks (the random noise ϵ_i eq. 1), partially matching chunks can get retrieved instead of the target chunk in some of the retrieval requests (a misretrieval). Misretrievals happen in L1 speakers as well. In fact, in psycholinguistics misretrievals due to partial matching have been suggested to explain some of the grammatical illusions such as agreement attraction and spurious NPI licensing (Wagers et al., 2009; Vasishth et al., 2008). But as per IH, misretrievals happen more often in L2 speakers.

In ACT-R the frequency of misretrievals is controlled by defining the penalty to the activation of a chunk when its feature doesn't match the retrieval cue. The penalty is specified through a parameter called *maximum difference*, the highest penalty for a perfect mismatch. By default the value of *maximum difference* is -1.[2] This means that the activation penalty increases as a function of the number of cues mismatched by a chunk, making its retrieval less likely. The value of *maximum difference* can be changed to calibrate the penalty of a mismatch. Reducing this penalty leads the non-target chunks to get retrieved more often, i.e. higher misretrievals. We propose that reducing the value of *maximum difference* would be the way of extending the L1 model to L2 processing in terms of IH.

2.3 The LBH model

LBH proposes that L2 speakers fail to use grammatical features such as gender in syntactic processing because the gender representations of L2 words are weaker or more unstable, and speakers process an L2 in a noisier cognitive architecture. Although LBH is not specified in connection with a specific cognitive or sentence processing architecture, it can be realized in CBR. A possible implementation of LBH in the ACT-R and CBR frameworks could be done by: (i) having weaker representation of the gender feature in chunks representing various referents present in the input, and (ii) making the representations of the referents noisier compared to their representations in the L1 model.

In a typical CBR model the gender features have discrete values (e.g. *feminine*, *masculine* and *neuter*), and chunks denoting various referents have a certain, relatively low, activation noise associated with them (ϵ_i eq. 1). We propose the following two modifications to the L1 model for implementing LBH.

First, the gender features have values that are encoded as weaker than corresponding L1 values – *feminine-weak*, *masculine-weak* and *neuter-weak*. This leads the corresponding chunk to only *weakly* match a retrieval cue for a specific gender. For

[2] Conversely, ACT-R also provides a parameter called *maximum similarity* that specifies the least penalty for a perfect match which is set to 0 by default.

example, a chunk for a feminine referent encoding gender as *feminine-weak* will weakly match a retrieval request of type 'gender = feminine'. As a consequence, the chunk receives less spreading activation from the retrieval cue than a chunk that encodes gender clearly as *feminine*. This is equivalent to saying that the referent does not have exactly the same value of the feature as the parser expects but is similar enough to be considered in the retrieval request.

We implement this behavior partly by using ACT-R's built-in functionality of setting similarities between a retrieval cue and a feature value (the M_{ji} values in the *partial matching* component of eq. 1), and partly by modifying the *spreading activation* component in eq. 1. The *partial matching* component in the activation equation sums to a negative value since M_{ji} values vary between 0 (for a perfect match between a retrieval cue and a feature) and -1 (for a mismatch); effectively a penalty to a chunk for not fully matching a retrieval request. In ACT-R by default M_{ji}'s are either equal to the value of the parameter *maximum similarity* (0 by default) or to the value of the parameter *maximum difference* (-1 by default), but they can be set to any value between 0 and -1 to reflect the degree of similarity between a pair of values (e.g. feminine and feminine-weak or red and maroon). We propose that for the LBH model the similarity between an expected gender and the weaker value lies between the two extremes 0 and -1 but closer to 0 since a weak gender is more similar than dissimilar to the corresponding strong gender. Reciprocally, the similarity between an expected gender and any other weak gender (e.g. feminine and masculine-weak) also lies between the two extremes and, in this case, closer to -1 since it is more dissimilar than the same weaker gender but less dissimilar than a different strong gender (e.g. feminine and masculine).

We also propose that this graded similarity between a cue and a feature value also influences the *spreading activation* component. This is not part of the original ACT-R framework, so we consider a further modification to the computation of the *strength of association*, S_{ji}, as in 4–6. The *strength of association* now reflects how well the feature value matches the retrieval cue. This modification has influence on the calculations of activation only when a cue and a value don't perfectly match or mismatch, when they do, the value of activation is the same as in the original ACT-R framework. When a value perfectly matches a requested cue (i.e. M_{ji} = 0) eq. 4 reduces to eq. 3, and when a value perfectly mismatches (i.e. M_{ji} = -1) it leads to no activation spreading.

$$S_{ji} = weight_j sim_{ji} S - ln(fan_j) \tag{4}$$

$$fan_j = \sum_{chunk_k} sim_{jk} \tag{5}$$

$$sim_{jk} = (1 + M_{jk}) \tag{6}$$

To implement the LBH proposal that speakers process an L2 in a noisier cognitive architecture, we propose a second change to the L1 model in terms of its activation noise. This change is more intrinsic to ACT-R because the activation equation includes a noise term that controls the random fluctuations in the activation of chunks (ϵ_i in eq. 1). Higher noise value makes the representation of chunks noisier. We suggest that a noisier L1 model, along with weaker gender representation, should be the L2 model representing LBH.

Note that an alternative implementation of the LBH could test if both weak gender and noisier representations are necessary to capture the L2 data. Moreover, ACT-R also assumes another type of noise, the noise in procedural memory. It is conceivable that the noisier representation proposed by the LBH is realized as noisier procedural memory (e.g. Patil et al. 2016a used the noise in procedural memory to model data from patients with aphasia). However, we consider that weak gender and activation noise are the closest realization of the LBH in ACT-R, and a good starting point for modeling LBH. We leave other possible implementations for future research.

3 Human data

The human data was taken from two visual world eye-tracking experiments with the same materials and design but two different groups of participants: 74 L1 German speakers (Stone et al., 2021b, Experiment 2) and 132 L2 German learners (Lago et al., under review, Experiment 2). The L2 group comprised native speakers of Spanish and English. Because they did not differ behaviorally, the comparisons below consider a unified group of L2 participants. We reanalyzed the two experiments to directly compare L1 and L2 processing.

In the experiments, L1 and L2 participants were asked to help find the belongings of two fictional characters, Martin and Sarah. They were told that they would see images and hear instructions, and that their task was to select the object mentioned by the instruction. The instructions always contained a possessive pronoun doubly-marked for gender: the gender of the pronoun stem (*sein-/ihr-*) agreed in gender with the antecedent (*Martin* or *Sarah*). The gender of the pronoun suffix agreed in gender with the upcoming noun, which allowed participants to predict the identity of the target object prior to hearing it in the instruction, e.g.: 'Click on **his.**$_{\text{MASC}}$ blue.$_{\text{MASC}}$ button.$_{\text{MASC}}$'.

The experimental trials showed 2 colored objects: a target object (e.g. a blue button.$_{\text{MASC}}$) and a competitor of a different gender (e.g. a blue bottle.$_{\text{FEM}}$). The 96 items were distributed in two conditions (1). In the MATCH condition, the possessor and target noun had the same gender, i.e., both masculine or both feminine. In the MISMATCH condition, the possessor mismatched the gender of the target object but matched the competitor's. The results of the experiments showed that the gender of the pronoun was used predictively, such that participants showed a target-over-competitor looking preference prior to hearing the noun. In addition, there was a "match effect", with predictions starting earlier in the match than in the mismatch condition (Figure 1). We examined whether the size and onset of predictions and/or the onset of match effects differed between L1 and L2.

(1) a. **MATCH condition**
Klicke auf <u>seinen</u> blauen Knopf!
Click on his.MASC blue.MASC button.MASC

b. **MISMATCH condition**
Klicke auf <u>ihren</u> blauen Knopf!
Click on her.MASC blue.MASC button.MASC

The size of predictions was quantified as the target-over-competitor looking preference in the entire time-window before the target noun was heard (i.e., from pronoun onset to noun onset plus 200ms to account for saccade planning). The onset of prediction was quantified as the earliest point in time at which fixations to the target object significantly differed from fixations to the competitor. This time-point, together with a 95% confidence interval, was taken as the prediction onset (Stone et al., 2021a). Our L1–L2 comparisons revealed the following differences: (i) The size of predictions was approximately 9 percentage points smaller in L2 than in L1 (henceforth **SMALLER-PREDICTION**). The target-over-competitor advantage was 58 [56, 60] % in the L2 group vs. 67 [65, 69] % in the L1 group. (ii) The onset of predictions was always later in L2 than L1 (**LATER-PREDICTION**). In the match condition, the difference in L1–L2 onsets was 211 [60, 320] ms. In the mismatch condition, the difference in L1–L2 onsets was 108 [60, 160] ms. (iii) The match effect—the difference between mismatch vs. match onsets—occurred in both groups: L1 match effect 303 [160, 400] ms and L2 match effect 200 [120, 280] ms. The match effect in onset times was numerically smaller in the L2 group (**SMALLER-MATCH**), but the between-group difference was not statistically reliable (as evidenced by the 95% CI crossing 0): 103 [-40, 220] ms.

4 Computational models

4.1 Modeling details

We generate predictions of IH model and LBH model based on the L2 modeling hypotheses and extensions proposed in sections 2.2 and 2.3. We use the L1 model reported in Patil and Lago (2021) and extend the model to capture the effects of L2 processing from Lago et al. (under review). The goal is to capture the three L2 vs. L1 effects observed in the data presented in section 3: (***SMALLER-PREDICTION***) smaller size of predictions in L2, (***LATER-PREDICTION***) later prediction onsets in L2 for both MATCH and MISMATCH conditions, and (***SMALLER-MATCH***) smaller match effect in L2.

The IH and LBH models were used to generate predicted fixation patterns from the onset of the (possessive) pronoun to the onset of noun. From these predicted fixation profiles, the three effects concerning L1-L2 differences were calculated as follows. The SMALLER-PREDICTION effect was calculated by averaging the size of predictions (i.e. mean fixation probability) in the temporal window between the onsets of the possessive pronoun and the noun across match and mismatch conditions. The effect of LATER-PREDICTION was calculated by subtracting the onset predicted by the L1 model from the onset predicted by each of the two L2 models for each condition separately. Finally, the SMALLER-MATCH effect was calculated by subtracting the prediction onsets of the match vs. mismatch conditions. All model predic-

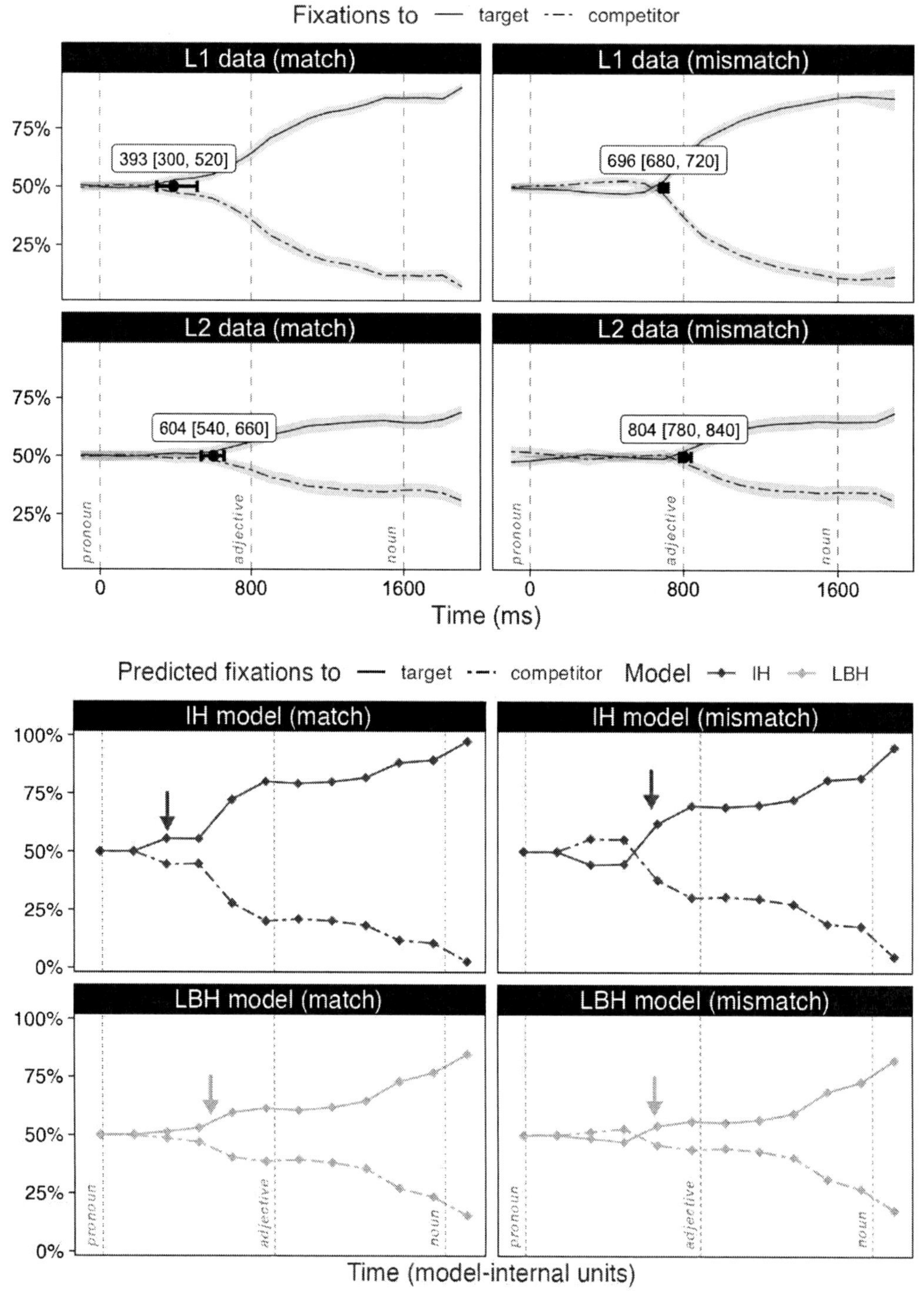

Figure 1: **Human data (top two rows)**: Fixation curves to the target and competitor object averaged across items and participants. The predictive time-window extended from the onset of the pronoun to the onset of the noun, shifted 200 ms to the right. The x-axis is time-locked to the pronoun. Estimated predictive onsets and their 95% confidence intervals (in ms) are overlaid on the fixation curves in each condition. **Model data (bottom two rows)**: Predictions of the model for fixation probabilities to the target and competitor object in the L2 groups. The x-axis reflects processing time in model-internal units. Vertical arrows show the model-predicted onsets.

tions are generated by running 100,000 simulations of each model including the L1 model. Due to ACT-R's stochastic noise component, some of the predicted the values deviate from the ones reported in Patil and Lago (2021), but the qualitative effects remain the same as reported by them. We consider our calculations of L1 predictions as reliable as theirs because we calculated the values by running a higher number of simulations (10,000 vs. 100,000). The ACT-R parameter values that were changed to implement the assumptions of the IH and LBH models are listed in Table 1. We also tested how the predictions of the two models varied as a function of variation in the values of these parameters (see section 4.3).

4.2 Model predictions

The predictions of the two L2 models for prediction onsets and fixation probabilities are shown in Figure 1 (lower panels). The three effects observed in the data and the corresponding predictions of the two L2 models are summarized in Table 2. Both L2 models capture the SMALLER-PREDICTION effect — they show a smaller prediction size compared to the L1 model; however, numerically, the LBH model's prediction is closer to the human data. With regard to the LATER-PREDICTION effect, it is only captured by the LBH model and only in the match condition. While LBH also predicts a delayed L2 prediction onset in the mismatch condition (18 ms), visual inspection of the data revealed that the effect was driven by a few outlier simulations (around 10% of the simulations). On the other hand the IH model doesn't capture the LATER-PREDICTION effect in either the match or mismatch conditions. The SMALLER-MATCH effect is captured only by the LBH model but not by the IH model, which predicts the effect to be in the opposite direction. In both conditions the IH model in fact predicts earlier prediction onsets for L2 than L1 speakers (a negative effect).

4.3 Model predictions across parameter variation

To test if the predictions of the two models were restricted to the specific values selected for the parameters, we generated predictions of the models by varying the parameter values around the values we selected. We only varied the parameters that were modified for implementing the IH and LBH, and only within a range that was still meaningful to represent the hypotheses that were implemented. For parameter variation we randomly sampled 200 values from a uniform distribution with bounds defining a range of values around a selected parameter value. For each random value of a parameter we generated predictions by running 1000 simulations of the model.

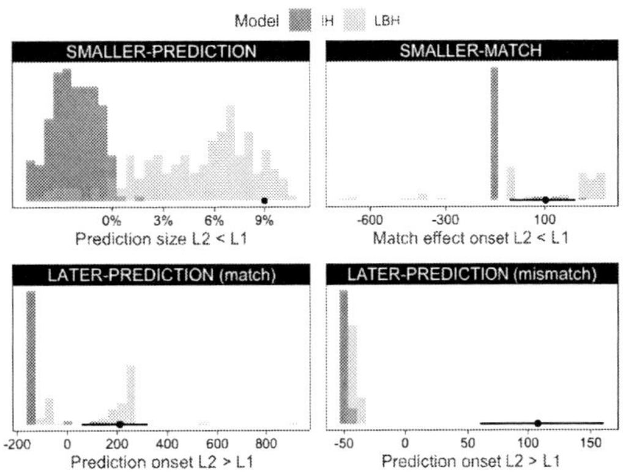

Figure 2: Distributions in terms of histograms of the effects predicted by the IH and the LBH models. The y-axis depicts the frequency of the predicted effects and it has different heights for different panels. Black dots represent the mean effects observed in the L2 data. Prediction distributions for the IH model are generated by varying ACT-R's *maximum difference* parameter, whereas those for the LBH model are generated by varying the *activation noise* parameter and the similarity values between strong and weak genders. These are the same parameters that were used to implement the respective L2 hypothesis through those models (c.f. Table 1).

For the IH model we varied ACT-R's *maximum difference* (penalty) parameter between the values of -0.7 to -0.3 ($U(-0.7, -0.3)$) because a value higher than -0.3 would be too close to the value of no penalty (i.e. 0) for a retrieval cue mismatch and a value lower than -0.7 would be too close to the default penalty (i.e. -1) in the L1's model. For the LBH model we varied ACT-R's *activation noise* parameter and the similarity values between strong and weak genders. We varied the *activation noise* in the range 0.3 to 0.7 ($U(0.3, 0.7)$), and the similarity between the strong and weak gender values of the same gender in the range -0.4 to -0.1 ($U(-0.4, -0.1)$) and between the strong and weak values of different genders in the range -0.9 to -0.6 ($U(-0.9, -0.6)$). Since the *activation noise* value for the L1 model was 0.25 we chose values higher than that, but at the same time if the *activation noise* is too high, the activation has too high impact of the random noise compared to other crucial com-

Table 1: ACT-R parameters values that were modified to model the proposals of the IH and LBH of L2 processing. The column "L1" show the original parameter values used in Patil and Lago (2021), while the columns "IH" AND "LBH" show the values modified to model the L2 data. The values that were modified are in bold face. All other ACT-R parameters had the same value as used in the L1 model.

ACT-R parameter	L1	IH	LBH
Activation noise (ANS)	0.25	0.25	**0.5**
Maximum difference (MD)	-1	**-0.5**	-1
Similarity between weak & strong gender values of the same gender	—	—	**-0.25**
Similarity between weak & strong gender values of different genders	—	—	**-0.75**

Table 2: Comparison of effects of interest in the L2 human data and in the predictions of the IH and LBH models.

Effect	Condition	Human data	IH model	LBH model
SMALLER-PREDICTION		9%	3.2%	11.1%
LATER-PREDICTION	match	211 [60, 320] ms	-58 ms	207 ms
	mismatch	108 [60, 160] ms	-1 ms	18 ms
SMALLER-MATCH		103 [-40, 220] ms	-57 ms	189 ms

ponents influencing the activation and hence the retrievals (see eq. 1). For similarity, values below -0.4 would mean that the strong and weak genders are 40% or more dissimilar, and values above -0.1 would mean they are almost similar (less than 10% dissimilar). The range for similarity between the strong and weak values of different genders was just a mirror image of the range for similarity between the strong and weak values of the same gender in the interval $[0, -1]$.[3]

The distribution of the three effects of interest for above-mentioned range of parameter values for the two L2 models are shown in Figure 2, along with the mean effects observed in the data. A visual inspection supports the generalizations drawn in section 4.2 — the LBH captures the effects SMALLER-PREDICTION, LATER-PREDICTION in the match condition (but not in the mismatch condition) and SMALLER-MATCH for most of the parameter combinations, whereas the IH qualitatively (but not quantitatively) captures the SMALLER-PREDICTION effect (since it predicts positive values for the effect) but barely captures any of the other effects.

[3]As another approach one could also vary the values of these three parameters for a broader range of the intervals. Although these values might not represent either of the theories, they are informative to find the broadest range of values for which the current implementation does not break. Moreover, it is also possible to test other parameters in ACT-R that do not represent either of the L2 hypotheses, the "hyperparameters", to see if they influence predictions. Due to time constraints, we restricted our simulations to narrower intervals around the chosen values.

5 Discussion

We proposed computational cognitive models of two main theories of L2 processing — the Interference Hypothesis and the Lexical Bottleneck Hypothesis. Both are verbally stated theories of processing differences between L2 and L1 speakers, and ours is, to our knowledge, the first computational cognitive realization of those theories. The theories were implemented by extending an existing L1 processing model (Patil and Lago, 2021). We used visual-world eye-tracking data from a predictive sentence processing task to test the models. The results showed that the LBH performed better than IH in capturing the three key effects observed in the data. With the exception of one effect, the IH predicted effects that were opposite to the ones observed in human speakers. Overall the LBH appears to be a more likely explanation of L2 sentence processing as far as the predictive use of gender in processing is concerned. Therefore, we propose that the well-attested difficulty shown by L2 speakers in using gender predictively (as compared to L1 speakers) is more likely attributable to problems in how L2 speakers represent gender information in a non-native language (Gollan et al., 2008; Kroll and Gollan, 2014; Hopp, 2018) and/or to difficulties in using this information as quickly as L1 speakers (Grüter et al., 2017; Kaan, 2014).

An important qualification is that the two implementations evaluated here did not model the potential effect of L1 transfer. Recall that the L2 group consisted of both Spanish and English learners of

German. Because the majority of nouns used in the human experiments had the same gender across Spanish and German, and because there was no evidence of between-group differences, we think that the current dataset is not suitable for modeling L1 transfer effects. Research using other datasets will be relevant to address the role of L1 transfer, which is hypothesized to play a role in the Lexical Bottleneck Hypothesis (Hopp, 2018, 2022). The role of L1 transfer in the IH is less clear, but it may affect the current implementation if, for example, both L1- and L2-based gender features are available for retrieval in the memory chunks corresponding to the objects on-screen.

The effects reported in the L1 and L2 data were possibly born out of retrieval interference during predictive processing (Patil and Lago, 2021). Hence we expected the IH account to capture the effects better as the IH is rooted in the cue-based retrieval framework of sentence processing, and cue-based retrieval theory has rendered explanation to various psycholinguistic phenomenon through retrieval interference. A possible reason for the IH predicting opposite patterns to the ones observed in the data could because retrieval interference as per the cue-based retrieval theory can lead to two opposite processing phenomena — inhibitory vs. facilitory processing — depending on the context (Dillon et al., 2013; Patil et al., 2016b; Parker et al., 2017). The precise nature of the interference effect in a given context can only be predicted through an actual implementation of the model. Our results emphasize the importance of computationally formalizing the predictions of the cue-based retrieval theory in particular (Vasishth et al., 2019), and of verbal theories in cognition in general (Guest and Martin, 2021).

Although the LBH model captured crucial patterns in the differences between L2 and L1 processing, one serious limitation of the model (and also of the IH model) was in terms of capturing the effect of delayed prediction onsets (LATER-PREDICTION) in the mismatch condition for L2 speakers. Since both the L2 models failed at capturing this effect, we think it is also unlikely that a combination of the two models would be able to capture this effect. This also implies that the gender prediction in L2 speakers possibly also involves a process that cannot be explained by either of the hypotheses. We think a computational implementation of another L2 processing hypothesis, in combination with the LBH model, might help capture this effect.

Acknowledgements

The research for this project has been funded by the Deutsche Forschungsgemeinschaft (DFG, German Research Foundation): Project-ID 281511265 – SFB 1252 "Prominence in Language" in the project C07 "Forward and backward functions of discourse anaphora" at the University of Cologne, Department of German Language and Literature I, Linguistics, and Project-ID 317308350 – "AGREE: Agreement in native and second language processing". We furthermore thank the Regional Computing Center of the University of Cologne (RRZK) for providing computing time on the DFG-funded (Funding number: INST 216/512/1FUGG) High Performance Computing (HPC) system CHEOPS as well as support.

Supplementary files

The model code and supplementary files are available at: `https://osf.io/p28k6/`

References

John R. Anderson. 2007. *How can the human mind occur in the physical universe?* Oxford series on cognitive models and architectures. Oxford University Press, New York, NY, US.

Adrian Brasoveanu and Jakub Dotlačil. 2020. *Computational Cognitive Modeling and Linguistic Theory*. Language, Cognition, and Mind. Springer International Publishing, Cham.

Cristiano Crescentini and Andrea Stocco. 2005. Agrammatism as a failure in the lexical activation process. In *Proceedings of the 27th Annual Conference of the Cognitive Science Society*, Mahwah, NJ. Lawrence Erlbaum Associates.

Ian Cunnings. 2017a. Interference in native and non-native sentence processing. *Bilingualism: Language and Cognition*, 20(4):712–721.

Ian Cunnings. 2017b. Parsing and working memory in bilingual sentence processing. *Bilingualism: Language and Cognition*, 20(4):659–678.

Brian Dillon, Alan Mishler, Shayne Sloggett, and Colin Phillips. 2013. Contrasting intrusion profiles for agreement and anaphora: Experimental and modeling evidence. *Journal of Memory and Language*, 69(2):85–103.

Felix Engelmann, Shravan Vasishth, Ralf Engbert, and Reinhold Kliegl. 2013. A framework for modeling the interaction of syntactic processing and eye movement control. *Topics in Cognitive Science*, 5(3):452–474.

Stefan L. Frank. 2021. Toward computational models of multilingual sentence processing. *Language Learning*, 71(S1):193–218.

Stefan L. Frank, Thijs Trompenaars, and Shravan Vasishth. 2016. Cross-linguistic differences in processing double-embedded relative clauses: Working-memory constraints or language statistics? *Cognitive Science*, 40(3):554–578.

Tamar H. Gollan, Rosa I. Montoya, Cynthia Cera, and Tiffany C. Sandoval. 2008. More use almost always means a smaller frequency effect: Aging, bilingualism, and the weaker links hypothesis. *Journal of Memory and Language*, 58(3):787–814.

Theres Grüter, Hannah Rohde, and Amy J. Schafer. 2017. Coreference and discourse coherence in l2: The roles of grammatical aspect and referential form. *Linguistic Approaches to Bilingualism*, 7(2).

Olivia Guest and Andrea E. Martin. 2021. How computational modeling can force theory building in psychological science. *Perspectives on Psychological Science*, 16(4):789–802. PMID: 33482070.

Petra Hendriks and Margreet Vogelzang. 2020. Pronoun processing and interpretation by l2 learners of italian: Perspectives from cognitive modelling. *Discours : A journal of linguistics, psycholinguistics and computational linguistics*, 26.

Xavier Hinaut, Johannes Twiefel, Maxime Petit, Peter Dominey, and Stefan Wermter. 2015. A recurrent neural network for multiple language acquisition: Starting with english and french. In *Proceedings of the 2015 International Conference on Neural Information Processing Systems (NIPS 2015), Workshop on Cognitive Computation: Integrating Neural and Symbolic Approaches*, volume 1583, Montreal, CA.

Holger Hopp. 2018. The bilingual mental lexicon in l2 sentence processing. *Second Language*, 17:5–27.

Holger Hopp. 2022. Second language sentence processing. *Annual Review of Linguistics*, 8(1):235–256.

Marcel A. Just and Patricia A. Carpenter. 1992. A capacity theory of comprehension: Individual differences in working memory. *Psychological Review*, 99(1):122–149.

Edith Kaan. 2014. Predictive sentence processing in l2 and l1: What is different? *Linguistic Approaches to Bilingualism*, 4:257–282.

Judith F. Kroll and Tamar H. Gollan. 2014. *Speech planning in two languages: What bilinguals tell us about language production.*, Oxford library of psychology., pages 165–181. Oxford University Press, New York, NY, US.

Sol Lago, Kate Stone, Elise Oltrogge, and João Veríssimo. under review. Possessive processing in bilingual comprehension. Submitted to Language Learning.

Richard L. Lewis and Shravan Vasishth. 2005. An activation-based model of sentence processing as skilled memory retrieval. *Cognitive Science*, 29:1–45.

Richard L. Lewis, Shravan Vasishth, and Julie A. Van Dyke. 2006. Computational principles of working memory in sentence comprehension. *Trends in Cognitive Sciences*, 10(10):447–454.

Janet L. McDonald. 2006. Beyond the critical period: Processing-based explanations for poor grammaticality judgment performance by late second language learners. *Journal of Memory and Language*, 55(3):381–401.

Dan Parker, Michael Shvartsman, and Julie A. Van Dyke. 2017. The cue-based retrieval theory of sentence comprehension: New findings and new challenges.

Umesh Patil, Sandra Hanne, Frank Burchert, Ria De Bleser, and Shravan Vasishth. 2016a. A computational evaluation of sentence processing deficits in aphasia. *Cognitive Science*, 40(1):5–50.

Umesh Patil and Sol Lago. 2021. Prediction advantage as retrieval interference: an ACT-R model of processing possessive pronouns. In *Proceedings of the 19th International Conference on Cognitive Modeling*, pages 213–219. University Park, PA: Applied Cognitive Science Lab, Penn State.

Umesh Patil and Petra B. Schumacher. 2022. Modeling prominence constraints for German pronouns as weighted retrieval cues. In *Proceedings of the 20th International Conference on Cognitive Modeling*.

Umesh Patil, Shravan Vasishth, and Richard L. Lewis. 2016b. Retrieval interference in syntactic processing: The case of reflexive binding in english. *Frontiers in Psychology*, 7:329.

Frank E. Ritter, Farnaz Tehranchi, and Jacob D. Oury. 2019. Act-r: A cognitive architecture for modeling cognition. *WIREs Cognitive Science*, 10(3):e1488.

Kate Stone, Sol Lago, and Daniel J. Schad. 2021a. Divergence point analyses of visual world data: applications to bilingual research. *Bilingualism: Language and Cognition*, 24(5):833–841.

Kate Stone, João Veríssimo, Daniel J. Schad, Elise Oltrogge, Shravan Vasishth, and Sol Lago. 2021b. The interaction of grammatically distinct agreement dependencies in predictive processing. *Language, Cognition and Neuroscience*, 36(9):1159–1179.

Jacolien van Rij, Hedderik van Rijn, and Petra Hendriks. 2013. How wm load influences linguistic processing in adults: A computational model of pronoun interpretation in discourse. *Topics in Cognitive Science*, 5(3):564–580.

Shravan Vasishth, Sven Brüssow, Richard L. Lewis, and Heiner Drenhaus. 2008. Processing polarity: How the ungrammatical intrudes on the grammatical. *Cognitive Science*, 32(4):685–712.

Shravan Vasishth, Bruno Nicenboim, Felix Engelmann, and Frank Burchert. 2019. Computational models of retrieval processes in sentence processing. *Trends in Cognitive Sciences*, 23(11):968–982.

Matthew W. Wagers, Ellen F. Lau, and Colin Phillips. 2009. Agreement attraction in comprehension: Representations and processes. *Journal of Memory and Language*, 61(2):206–237.

PIE-QG: Paraphrased Information Extraction for Unsupervised Question Generation from Small Corpora

Dinesh Nagumothu, Bahadorreza Ofoghi, Guangyan Huang, Peter W. Eklund
School of Information Technology, Deakin University, 221 Burwood Hwy, Burwood 3125
Victoria, Australia
{dnagumot,b.ofoghi,guangyan.huang,peter.eklund}@deakin.edu.au

Abstract

Supervised Question Answering systems (QA systems) rely on domain-specific human-labeled data for training. Unsupervised QA systems generate their own question-answer training pairs, typically using secondary knowledge sources to achieve this outcome. Our approach (called PIE-QG) uses Open Information Extraction (OpenIE) to generate synthetic training questions from paraphrased passages and uses the question-answer pairs as training data for a language model for a state-of-the-art QA system based on BERT. Triples in the form of <subject, predicate, object> are extracted from each passage, and questions are formed with subjects (or objects) and predicates while objects (or subjects) are considered as answers. Experimenting on five extractive QA datasets demonstrates that our technique achieves on-par performance with existing state-of-the-art QA systems with the benefit of being trained on an order of magnitude fewer documents and without any recourse to external reference data sources.

1 Introduction

Question Answering systems (QA systems) provide answers to input questions posed in natural language. Answering questions from unstructured text can be performed using Machine Reading Comprehension (MRC). Given a passage, several sentences or a paragraph, and a question posed, the QA system produces the best suitable answer. Extractive Question Answering systems (EQA systems) are a subset of QA systems and involve an MRC task where the predicted answer is a span of words from the passage. With pre-trained language models (Radford et al., 2018), EQA systems achieve excellent results, surpassing even human performance. Pre-trained language models, such as BERT (Devlin et al., 2019) and GPT (Radford et al.), can be fine-tuned to perform downstream tasks such as QA. However, huge amounts of data are required to train these models for specific domains, making the task labor-intensive, in terms of the effort required to assemble suitable domain-specific training data.

A single training instance for an EQA system dataset requires a question, a passage, and an answer. Domain-relevant documents can be collected with advanced information retrieval tools, and passages are formed by splitting documents into several related sentences or a paragraph. However, generating the question and answer pairs, that provide the training set for the QA system from a given passage, is considered the most difficult challenge, an approach known as unsupervised QA (Cui et al., 2004).

Existing unsupervised QA system techniques such as (Lewis et al., 2019) and (Lyu et al., 2021) use an out-of-domain dataset for question generation, namely, they require additional training sources beyond what can be provided by the target corpus and a pre-trained generic model. On the other hand, rule-based QA system methods, those constrained to generate question-answer pairs from only the corpus itself, run the risk of generating questions with high lexical overlap with the passage, at risk of forcing the model to learn word matching patterns. The work of (Fabbri et al., 2020) and (Li et al., 2020) use information retrieval-based methods, such as elastic search and citation navigation, to create questions from passages other than those presented within the target dataset. However, these methods may not generate sufficient training questions, especially when the corpus is small and has no citation or inter-document linking structure.

In this paper, we focus on addressing the limitations of EQA systems using a novel unsupervised Paraphrased Information Extraction for Question Generation (PIE-QG) method that generates synthetic training data through the extraction of <subject, relation, object> triples from a given corpus. We use the original passage to produce question-

Proceedings of the 26th Conference on Computational Natural Language Learning (CoNLL), pages 350 - 359
December 7-8, 2022 ©2022 Association for Computational Linguistics

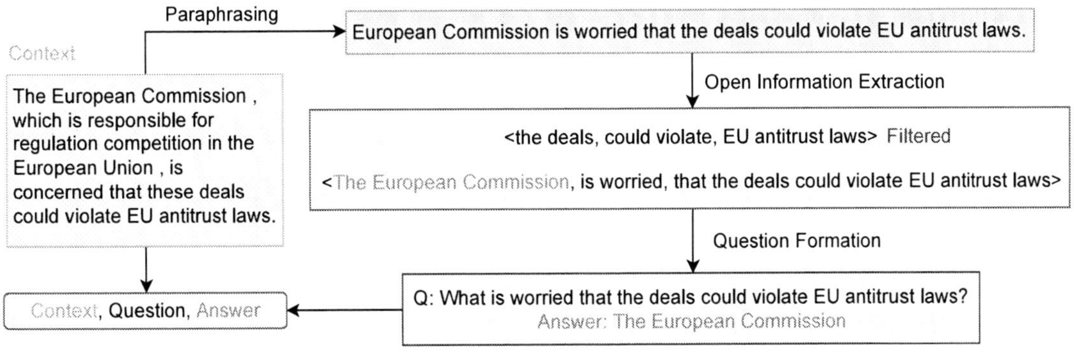

Figure 1: Question Generation from a context (left) by paraphrasing followed by information extraction using OpenIE. Note: The text in green indicates the selected answer.

answer training pairs by generating a paraphrased version of the original passage to avoid lexical overlap between the passage and the question-answers. We adopt Open Information Extraction (Kolluru et al., 2020) to extract <subject, relation, object> triples from every sentence of the paraphrased passage. These triples are rich in semantics and represent raw facts; therefore, generating question-answer pairs from triples results in well-formed and effective training data. Furthermore, many sentences in the passage contribute to generating meaningful extractions, thus helping to pose questions in different ways from a single passage. An example of the question generation process we propose (called PIE-QG for Paraphrasing, Information Extraction Question Generation) is shown in Figure 1. The contributions of this paper are as follows:

1. We describe the PIE-QG method in which paraphrased passages from the original corpus are used to generate question-answer pairs without reliance on external reference data sources, such as retrieval-based or inter-document link navigation methods. Paraphrasing passages reduces the effect of lexical overlap between the passage and the question.

2. We generate multiple questions from a single paraphrased passage by adopting Open Information Extraction to extract facts, thus increasing the number of question-answer pairs extracted from the corpus.

We have conducted experiments on four Extractive QA datasets and demonstrate that the proposed PIE-QG method achieves comparable performance in terms of Exact Match (EM) and F1 score while requiring significantly fewer passages.

The remainder of this paper is organized as follows. We present related work in Section 2. In Section 3, we describe the proposed PIE-QG method. Section 4 discusses the experimental setup. In Section 5, we evaluate the performance of our method. Section 6 presents the limitations of the proposed method and Section 7 offers some concluding remarks.

2 Related Work

Pre-trained language models, such as BERT (Devlin et al., 2019), can be fine-tuned for downstream tasks like Extractive QA systems (EQA systems). A comprehensive natural language (NL) passage, which might be several sentences or a paragraph of NL-text, is considered as the context where the model finds the answer span. The input question and the context are represented as a single sequence, passed to a pre-trained model and the answer is predicted by calculating the probabilities of the first and last tokens of the answer span. Pre-trained language models such as BERT (Devlin et al., 2019), T5 transformer (Raffel et al., 2020) and XLNet (Yang et al., 2019), achieve exceptional performance in EQA systems, however at the cost of reliance on large human-annotated supervised datasets. The Stanford Question Answering Dataset (SQuAD) (Rajpurkar et al., 2016) is a widely used dataset for EQA systems.

Lewis et al. (2019), Fabbri et al. (2020), Li et al. (2020), and Lyu et al. (2021) used randomly sampled passages from Wikipedia, where named entities, or noun chunks, are identified as answers as these tend to be useful for question answering. The questions are then formed in natural language according to the passage and a selected answer phrase.

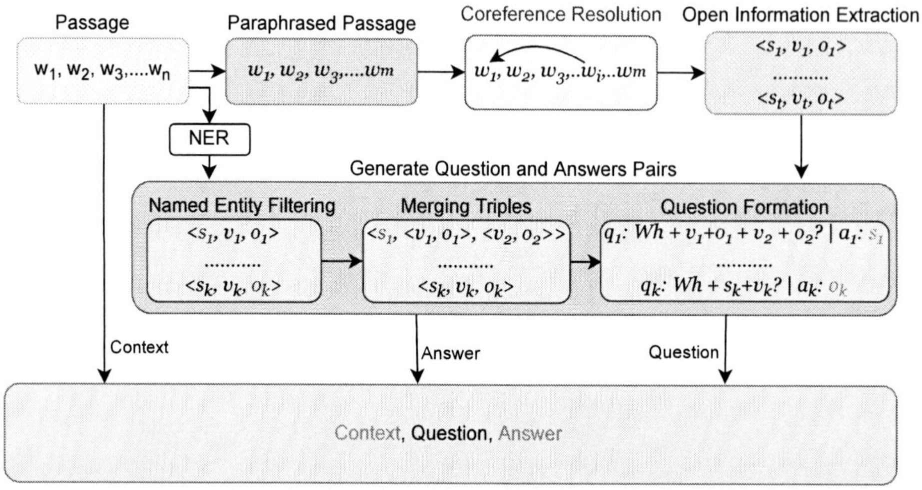

Figure 2: The general pipeline of PIE-QG for question generation using paraphrasing and OpenIE. Note: Blue indicates named entities, red merged triples with a common subject and green the selected answers.

Unsupervised EQA is achieved using the cloze-translation method (Lewis et al., 2019) by forming passage, question-answer triples from a given target corpus. The answers present in the passages are masked to form "fill in the blanks" styled questions, so-called cloze questions. The authors translate natural language questions using a neural machine translation (NMT) model trained with different corpora that contain cloze questions and natural question pairs.

Questions generated directly from the passage can only answer simple cloze questions by matching text within the passage, an approach that can not give correct answers for differently phrased questions. In an effort to broaden the questions used to train an EQA system, Fabbri et al. (2020) generated questions using a similar sentence taken from a different passage. The actual passage is considered a query and sentences are retrieved using elastic search. The most similar sentence, which contains the answer but excludes the original query passage, and with less than 95% similarity, to avoid plagiarised sentences, is used to form the question-answer pairs. The answer from these sentences is masked and a question in the form of a "Wh+B+A?" rule, where "wh" (one of what, when, or who) is selected based on the answer-entity type ("B" is a fragment of the sentence that comes after the answer mask, and "A" is the fragment that is present before the answer mask).

Li et al. (2020) uses citations to form a summary of the passage. The cited passage is considered the context, and the sentence where the citation appeared is used for question generation, to avoid lexical overlap. The question generation process involves masking the answer with a cloze mask, where the mask mentions only the type of the answer entity. The dependency tree for the sentence is altered in such a way that the cloze mask is brought to the beginning. The question is then created by replacing the cloze mask with the suitable "wh" word, again determined by the type of the answer entities.

Lyu et al. (2021) perform unsupervised QA by creating a question generation model from text summaries. The model uses dependency trees and semantic role labels extracted from the summary to generate a question. A neural encoder-decoder model is then trained to translate articles to summary-informed questions. The trained model is applied to the actual passages to create questions. However, we consider this method as a transfer learning task rather than unsupervised question generation due to its dependency on a text-summary dataset. Our method compares to Fabbri et al. (2020) and Li et al. (2020), avoids the sentence and citation-based retrieval, and minimizes the requirement of having a large corpus to generate question-answer pairs.

3 Paraphrased Information Extraction for Question Generation

To overcome the reliance on external reference data sources with a large number of passages, we made use of OpenIE and paraphrased passages for unsupervised synthetic question generation. The actual passages are first altered to a paraphrased form and <subject, predicate, object> triples are then extracted from the paraphrased passages. These triples, combined with certain heuristics, form question-answer pairs which are then used alongside the original passage as context to fine-tune the QA model.

The pipeline of our proposed EQA question generation process is illustrated in Figure 2. The steps in this pipeline are detailed as follows.

(i) Paraphrasing: Question-answer pairs generated directly from the passage result in inferior QA system performance, as they produce models that have little ability to generalize (Fabbri et al., 2020). Paraphrasing is therefore adopted to alter the passage without changing its actual meaning. The intuition behind this is to create questions from passages that are semantically similar but lexicographically different from the original passage. Paraphrasing question-answer pairs themselves has been shown to cause semantic drift (Pan et al., 2021). By contrast, in our approach, the passage is paraphrased, rather than question-answer pair. This improves the model's performance. The effect of paraphrasing is discussed in Section 5.

(ii) Co-reference resolution: As we aim to make use of every sentence in the passage to generate questions, some sentences are ineffective due to the presence of pronouns (Ma et al., 2021). This problem is solved by implementing co-reference resolution, replacing pronouns in the paraphrased passages with the proper name of the referring noun.

(iii) Information Extraction: OpenIE is applied on paraphrased passages to generate extractions in the form of arguments and relations from natural language text (Mausam, 2016). Given a sentence w_i in the passage, $\{w_1, w_2, w_3, ..w_N\}$, OpenIE generates extractions $\{T_1, T_2, T_3, ...T_M\}$, where each extraction is in the form <subject, predicate, object>, namely triples. OpenIE is proven to be an efficient solution for downstream tasks such as complex question answering (Khot et al., 2017).

(v) Question formation: OpenIE extractions produced from a passage are used to form questions as a synthetic training set for QA system fine-tuning.

(vi) Named entity filtering: Since triples extracted from a passage have different types of extractions, we select the triples that contain named entities in the answer. In other words, the subject (or object) is selected as an answer only if it is a named entity.

Algorithm 1: PIE-QG: Question generation from passages.

Input : Given a passage P from the corpus
Output : A list of Question-Answer Pairs

P' = Paraphrase(P)
CP = Coreference_Resolution(P')
T = Open_IE(CP)
named_entities = NER(CP)
T_{ne} = NE_filter(T, *named_entities*)
T_{IF} = IdenticalTriple_filter(T_{ne})
T_M = Merge_Triples(T_{IF})
T_{IF} = Remove_Merged_Triples(T_{IF}, T_M)
$QA\_Pairs \leftarrow newlist$
for t_n *in* T_M **do**
    A = *Select_Answer*(t_n)
    Q = *Wh*
    for *<subject, relation, object> in* t_n **do**
        Q = Q + *relation* + *object/subject*
        $QA\_Pairs \leftarrow$ *append*($\langle Q, A, P\rangle$)
    end
end
for *<subject, relation, object> in* T_{IF} **do**
    Q = *Wh* + *relation* + *object?*
    A = *subject*
    QA_Pairs $\leftarrow$ *append*($\langle Q, A, P\rangle$)
    Q = *Wh* + *relation* + *object?*
    A = *object*
    QA_Pairs $\leftarrow$ *append*($\langle Q, A, P\rangle$)
end
return QA_Pairs

(vii) Eliminating duplicate triples: One downside of open information extraction is the presence of duplicate or semantically redundant triples. Generating separate questions from similar or duplicate triples causes inferior performance in the EQA system model, hence redundant triples are sorted and the longest triple from the sort is selected as the single source for final question generation.

(viii) Merging triples: Questions generated from the triples using the above methods result in simple and easy-to-answer questions. For robust model training, we generate more complex questions from multiple triples by grouping triples with the same subject or object. For instance, if there are two triples of the form $\{\langle s_1, r_1, o_1\rangle, \langle s_2, r_2, o_2\rangle\}$ and $s_1 = s_2$, we form a question-answer pair with "Wh

+ r_1 + o_1, r_2 + o_2?" as the question and s_1 (or s_2) as the answer.

Each triple extracted from a paraphrased passage can form two questions with either subject or object as an answer. When a subject is selected as an answer, the question is formulated as "Wh + relation + object?". Conversely, when an object is selected as the answer, the question generated is of the form "Wh + subject + relation?". "Wh" is the question word in these formulations and the appropriate form is selected from a list, based on the answer entity type as earlier described.

4 Experimental Platform

Datasets The performance of our question generation method is evaluated in terms of Exact-Match (EM) and F-1 score using existing EQA datasets, namely SQuAD v1.1 (Rajpurkar et al., 2016) development set, and NewsQA (Trischler et al., 2016), BioASQ (Tsatsaronis et al., 2015) and DuoRC (Saha et al., 2018) test sets. SQuAD version 1.1 is acquired from the official version[1] while the Fisch et al. (2019) published versions of test sets are considered for NewsQA, BioASQ, and DuoRC. A more recent SQuAD v2.0 (Rajpurkar et al., 2018) is considered unsuitable for our experiments as the synthetic training set does not contain unanswerable questions.

Question Generation We take a relatively small subset of 30,000 passages from the (Li et al., 2020) sampled Wikipedia dataset for question generation and for training the model. The pseudo-code for the proposed question generation technique is presented in Algorithm 1.

Some of the questions resulting from this process can be grammatically incorrect. We rely on questions posed to the model during inference to be in natural language with correct grammar, we experiment by introducing a grammar correction module in the pipeline to synthesize syntactically accurate questions but later removed this due to its effect discussed in Section 5.

Sourced Wikipedia passages are transformed into paraphrased passages with a pre-trained model[2] based on the PEGASUS transformer (Zhang et al., 2020). Pronouns in the paraphrased passage are replaced with the nouns they refer to. We used neuralcoref[3] for this purpose, the spaCy implementation of pre-trained co-referent resolution based on reinforcement learning (Clark and Manning, 2016). OpenIE6 is used to extract <subject, predicate, object> triples from the pronoun-replaced paraphrased passages. OpenIE6 uses Iterative Grid Labeling and is based on BERT. A spaCy-based named-entity recognition (NER) module (Honnibal et al., 2020) is used to generate a list of named-entities from the passage. Named-entity recognition (NER) is particularly helpful for filtering triples and determining the answer-entity type for appropriate "wh" word selection. The simplest version of "Wh" word is selected for a particular named entity based on Fabbri et al. (2020). Questions generated from this process are grammatically corrected using a RoBERTa-based (Liu et al., 2019) grammar correction module named "GECToR" (Omelianchuk et al., 2020). All models are applied from the above-mentioned sources out-of-the-box, namely with no domain specific fine-tuning.

QA fine-tuning We use pre-trained BERT models from Devlin et al. (2019) as the baseline and fine-tune the models for downstream QA system tasks with the generated training data. The generated question, and its context (the actual NL-passage that contains both the question and its answer), are represented as a single sequence, separated by different segment masks and the "[SEP]" token. The final linear layer of the model is trained, to identify the start and end spans of the answer, by computing log-likelihood for each token. All experiments are performed on the uncased version of the BERT-base model with a learning rate of 3e-5, a maximum sequence length of 384, a batch size of 12, a document stride of 128 for 2 epochs, and a check-point at every 500 steps. The best checkpoint was selected by validating each against 5000 QA pairs randomly sampled from the synthetic training data. We use the Huggingface[4] implementation for input tokenization, model initialization, and training. For comparison with the state-of-the-art EQA models, we also experimented on the BERT-large whole-word masking version with the same training data. All models are trained and validated on a single NVIDIA Tesla A100 GPU.

[1] https://rajpurkar.github.io/SQuAD-explorer/

[2] https://huggingface.co/tuner007/pegasus_paraphrase

[3] https://spacy.io/universe/project/neuralcoref

[4] https://huggingface.co

	SQuAD1.1		NewsQA		BioASQ		DuoRC	
PIE-QG Heurisitcs	**EM**	**F-1**	**EM**	**F-1**	**EM**	**F-1**	**EM**	**F-1**
Open IE	22.8	36.5	13.0	23.9	16.6	24.3	22.0	28.5
+ Paraphrasing	37.7	53.6	19.9	32.3	20.3	31.6	32.6	40.7
+ Co-reference Resolution	44.2	53.4	21.1	31.8	26.5	34.7	34.8	40.4
+ Named-Entity filter	46.6	56.5	21.7	32.5	**30.3**	36.9	**36.9**	**42.4**
+ Filtering Identical Triples	47.5	57.8	21.8	32.2	30.1	37.1	35.1	41.1
+ Merging Triples	**48.6**	**58.7**	21.8	**32.8**	29.6	**37.5**	34.3	40.1
+ Grammar Correction	47.1	56.8	**21.9**	32.3	29.1	36.5	35.2	40.7

Table 1: Ablation study of the different techniques used in PIE-QG and their subsequent impacts on the EM and F-1 after fine-tuning the BERT-base model. Note: Each step represents an incremental upgrade to the previous step in question generation.

5 Results and Discussion

The effectiveness of the question-answer data generated using the PIE-QG method is measured by training the BERT-base model and evaluating it against existing EQA development and test sets. The Exact Match (EM) and F-1 scores are selected as the metrics to evaluate the effectiveness of each component in the QA models. The initial set of questions is created using OpenIE, where the passage is directly used to form triples and generate questions as described in Section 3. The intuition behind using OpenIE is to generate multiple questions from a single passage. However, as previously described, such a simple-minded approach suffers from having pronouns as answers, ungrammatical questions, and high degrees lexical similarity between passage and question, making most extracted triples suitable for word matching only.

Effect of Paraphrasing Using paraphrased passages for question generation avoids lexical overlaps with the passage and improves model performance. Ten different paraphrases are generated for each sentence in the passage using the PEGASUS (Zhang et al., 2020) paraphrasing generation model. Jensen-Shannon Divergence (JSD) is calculated for each paraphrase against the original sentence. JSD calculates a divergence score based on the word distributions between two sentences, a higher value for JSD accounts for a more different sentence, while a lower value JSD score represents higher lexical overlap. In our PIE-QG pipeline, sentences with the highest JSD values are selected for question generation to make the question syntactically different. Paraphrasing has a strong positive effect on the model, improving the EM F-1 score by at least 4% and 7% respectively on all evaluation sets.

Effect of Co-reference Resolution The presence of pronouns in passages results in meaningless question-answer pairs. For instance, *"Vaso Sepashvili (; born 17 December 1969) is a retired Georgian professional footballer. He made his professional debut in the Soviet Second League B in 1990 for FC Aktyubinets Aktyubinsk"* is the passage. This produces a triple *"<He, made, his professional debut in the Soviet Second League B in 1990 for FC Aktyubinets Aktyubinsk>"*. While the relation and object form a question "Who made his professional debut in the Soviet Second League B in 1990 for FC Aktyubinets Aktyubinsk?" with the subject "He" selected as the answer. The best answer for this question is found co-referenced in the previous sentence where the pronoun "He" refers to "Vaso Sepashvili". To address this we alter the passage with co-reference resolution to replace all pronouns with the referring proper noun. The above sentence is changed in such a way that the extracted triple becomes *"<Vaso Sepashvili, made, his professional debut in the Soviet Second League B in 1990 for FC Aktyubinets Aktyubinsk>"* and the ideal answer is selected. Pronouns were replaced with their referring nouns using this method to generate meaningful questions while the original passage is retained for training the QA model. In this way, co-referent resolution has a positive impact on the model performance increasing the EM by 2%-6% across all the sets.

Named-Entity Filtering As triples are the direct source of training questions, the quality of triples leads to better training questions for the PIE-QG model. In general, OpenIE6 returns all possible triples from a sentence, but selecting suitable triples, to generate better question-answer pairs, becomes important. To assist in identifying the best set of triples, we filter triples that do not contain named entities. We use Named Entity Recogni-

Fine-tuning Models	SQuAD1.1 EM	SQuAD1.1 F-1	NewsQA EM	NewsQA F-1	BioASQ EM	BioASQ F-1	DuoRC EM	DuoRC F-1	#Training Contexts
BERT-base									
Sentence Retrieval (Fabbri et al., 2020)	46.1†	56.8†	20.1	31.1	29.4	**38.1**	28.8	35.0	45K
PIE-QG (Ours)	**48.6**	**58.7**	**21.8**	**32.5**	**29.6**	37.5	**34.3**	**40.1**	**20-28K**
BERT-large									
Cloze Translation (Lewis et al., 2019) †	45.4	55.6	19.6	28.5	18.9	27.0	26.0	32.6	782K
RefQA (Li et al., 2020)	57.1 †	66.8 †	27.6	41.0	42.0	54.9	41.6	49.7	178K
+ Iterative Data Refinement	**62.5** †	**72.6** †	**32.1**	**45.1**	**44.1**	**57.4**	**45.7**	**54.2**	240K
PIE-QG (Ours)	61.2	**72.6**	29.7	44.1	43.6	55.1	44.6	52.9	**20-28K**

Table 2: Comparison of PIE-QG with state-of-the-art unsupervised QA models. Note: Iterative refinement achieves the best performance through structural analysis of the corpus via citation and intra-document links, a model that requires $\times 8$ as many contexts as the PIE-QG model we propose.'†' indicates results taken from the existing literature, and all other figures are evaluated with published synthetic training data (or) pre-trained models. "#Training Contexts" are measured based on respective published synthetic datasets. Each model uses the same synthetic training data sourced from Wikipedia for fine-tuning and is evaluated against the standard EQA datasets.

tion (NER) to extract all named entities from the passage. To become a candidate to be selected for the question generation process, either the subject or object from the triple must contain at least one named entity. This NER filtering method is beneficial to the model, it eliminates many impractical question-answer pairs from the training set and improves the overall Exact Match (EM) and F-1 score by 2% except for NewsQA.

Effect of Filtering Identical Triples Semantically similar triples are formed using OpenIE6 with a high degree of lexical overlap. Constructing questions from these triples causes question duplication and has the potential to deteriorate model performance and even result in over-fitting. To filter similar or duplicate triples, each triple is verified with other triples extracted from the passage to discover lexical overlaps between them. If a triple formed as a sentence is a sub-string of another, the shorter is removed from the training set to avoid the production of redundant questions. From Figure 1, triples such as <*the deals, could violate, EU antitrust laws*> and <*The European Commission, is worried, that the deals could violate EU antitrust laws*> convey the same meaning with a high degree of lexical overlap, hence the former is removed. *Filtering identical triples* in this way has a small but favorable impact on the model as shown in the ablation summary in Table 1.

Effect of Merging Triples A subject (or object) in a passage can exhibit relations to multiple objects (or subjects). Triples with common subjects are merged to form complex questions such that QA model can understand complex relationships. Merging triples has a small but positive effect on the model performance improving EM by 1.2% and F-1 by 0.9% as shown in Table 1.

Effect of Grammar Correction Questions generated from the above process often contain grammatical errors which can negatively impact model performances. We experimented with "GECToR" [5], a grammar correction module that tags and corrects input questions with grammar errors. For instance, the question "What is is worried that the deals could violate EU antitrust laws?" is formulated. The repeat occurrence of the verb "is" is an obvious error. The grammar correction module alters the question where the final question is formulated correctly as "What is worried that the deals could violate EU antitrust laws?". Based on heuristics presented in Table 1, all incremental upgrades until "Merging Triples" improve the model performance, but Grammar correction does not and is hence removed from the pipeline.

Effect of Training Data Size Experiments were conducted to measure the EM and F-score at different synthetic data sizes to identify the optimal number of training questions. Figure 3 presents the results of these experiments and reveals that PIE-QG achieves peak performance between 30K-50K training questions using BERT-large model and begin to over-fit beyond that number. The same effect is also observed in (Fabbri et al., 2020). The method to determine the optimal number of training questions is to split the generated question-answer pairs into blocks each of 10K. These are then split into training and validation sets. At fixed points of 500 training steps, the validation set is

[5]https://github.com/grammarly/gector

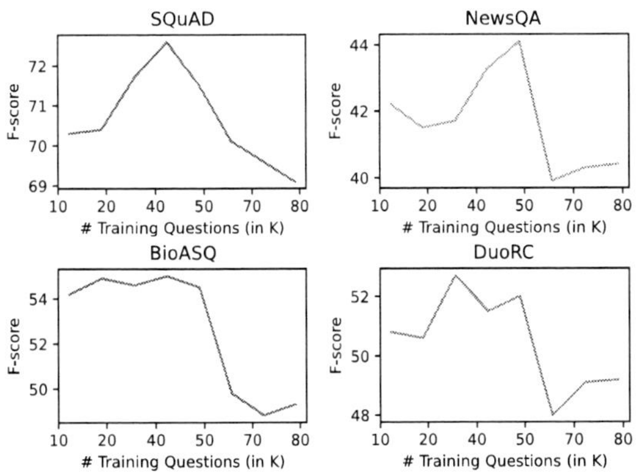

Figure 3: Evaluation of the PIE-QG model F-score for different datasets against the number of questions in the training set using the BERT-large model, the optimal number for each dataset is in the range 30-50K.

measured against the QA model. This incrementally informs the process of when the model optimizes against the number of question-answer pairs used to train it. It is observed, shown in Figure 3, that this occurs for each of the datasets in the range 30-50K. Increasing the number of template-styled training questions negatively affects the evaluation performance after a certain point because of memorisation of synthetic data patterns.

Comparison with the State-of-the-Art Fabbri et al. (2020) use a BERT-base model as the backbone for their experiments while Lewis et al. (2019) and Li et al. (2020) employed the BERT-large whole word masking pre-trained model. Questions generated from the PIE-QG model performed better than the information retrieval-based method presented by Fabbri et al. (2020) and produced an absolute improvement of 2.5% on EM and 1.9% on F-1 on the SQuAD 1.1 development set. Comparing BERT-large models, the PIE-QG model outperforms citation retrieval-based RefQA, a method that involves dependency tree reconstruction. However, RefQA, which includes a refinement technique, achieves the best performance, achieving 1-2.5% higher F-1 score than that of PIE-QG, but at the cost of using 8× more passages and 10× more training questions. Also, refinements in RefQA are performed on the training data through iterative cross-validations on the SQuAD 1.1 development set, whereas the PIE-QG model does not involve such a process. The number of passages and questions used by each method are presented in detail in Table 3. PIE-QG outperforms retrieval-

System	#Contexts	#Questions
Fabbri et al. (2020)	45K	50K
RefQA Li et al. (2020)	178K	300K
+ IDR	240K	480K
PIE-QG	20-28K	30-50K

Table 3: Comparison of statistics of the synthetic training data generated by existing unsupervised question generation methods with PIE-QG.

based question generation on every dataset and produces comparable performance with RefQA with 8× fewer passages.

To summarise, the experimental results demonstrate the advantages of the PIE-QG method;

1. Paraphrasing the original passage eliminates the need of using external knowledge sources to avoid lexical overlap;

2. Multiple questions generated using OpenIE with our proposed method minimizes the requirement of a large corpus without having to sacrifice the performance.

6 Limitations

The downside of the PIE-QG unsupervised question generation pipeline is the use of external modules like paraphrasing, OpenIE, and NER, which may not exist in languages other than English. The quality of question-answer pairs generated to train the QA model is therefore dependent on the performance of these modules on the selected corpus. It is however anticipated that PIE-QG will perform similarly well on any English language corpus. It is future work to apply these modules within the PIE-QG pipeline to other languages where comparable language-specific models can be sourced and performance outcomes analyzed.

7 Conclusion

With no reliance on any external reference corpora, the PIE-QG model uses paraphrasing and Open Information Extraction (OpenIE) to generate synthetic training questions for fine-tuning the language model in a QA system based on BERT. Triples in the form of <subject, predicate, object> are extracted from paraphrased passages, and questions are formed with subjects (or objects) as answers. Pronoun co-referents are resolved and where possible, triples are merged, and duplicate and highly similar triples are removed. Furthermore, triples that do not contain named entities

P	Georgia Tech undergraduate programs continue to excel, and I'm pleased that we've been able to maintain this measure of excellence for so long, " said Interim President and Provost Gary Schuster.
Q	Who was said that he was pleased that Georgia Tech undergraduate programs continued to excel?
A	**Gary Schuster**
P	"We're very upset, very angry," said Raphael Felli, 35, a U.S.- based attorney and son of executed Colonel Roger Felli, who was foreign minister in the Acheampong administration.
Q	Who was is an attorney based in the U.S., is the son of executed Colonel Roger Felli?
A	**Raphael Felli**
P	Liberty and Tyranny Sells a Million. Politics Radio host Mark R. Levin's bestselling Liberty and Tyranny : A Conservative Manifesto has sold one million copies, according to publisher Threshold Editions.....Published on March 24, 2009, Liberty debuted at # 1 on the New York Times bestseller list.
Q	What sell a million, made it to the New York Times bestsellers list?
A	**Liberty**

Table 4: Example synthetic question-answer pairs generated using PIE-QG. Note: **P** represents the passage extracted from a document. **Q** and **A** are the generated question and the selected answer from the passage, respectively.

are eliminated. The PIE-QG pipeline results in a high-quality question-answer training set that informs the QA model. Using the PIE-QG pipeline results in a QA model that achieves performance comparable to the state-of-the-art performance using significantly fewer passages. It is only narrowly outperformed by RefQA, an approach that uses iterative data refinement, and therefore relies on the citation structure of corpora and $\times 10$ more training questions.

References

Kevin Clark and Christopher D. Manning. 2016. Deep reinforcement learning for mention-ranking coreference models. In *Proceedings of the 2016 Conference on Empirical Methods in Natural Language Processing*, pages 2256–2262, Austin, Texas. Association for Computational Linguistics.

Hang Cui, Min-Yen Kan, and Tat-Seng Chua. 2004. Unsupervised learning of soft patterns for definitional question answering. In *Proceedings of the Thirteenth World Wide Web conference (WWW 2004)*, pages 90–99.

Jacob Devlin, Ming-Wei Chang, Kenton Lee, and Kristina Toutanova. 2019. BERT: Pre-training of deep bidirectional transformers for language understanding. In *Proceedings of the 2019 Conference of the North American Chapter of the Association for Computational Linguistics: Human Language Technologies, Volume 1 (Long and Short Papers)*, pages 4171–4186, Minneapolis, Minnesota. Association for Computational Linguistics.

Alexander Fabbri, Patrick Ng, Zhiguo Wang, Ramesh Nallapati, and Bing Xiang. 2020. Template-based question generation from retrieved sentences for improved unsupervised question answering. In *Proceedings of the 58th Annual Meeting of the Association for Computational Linguistics*, pages 4508–4513, Online. Association for Computational Linguistics.

Adam Fisch, Alon Talmor, Robin Jia, Minjoon Seo, Eunsol Choi, and Danqi Chen. 2019. MRQA 2019 shared task: Evaluating generalization in reading comprehension. In *Proceedings of 2nd Machine Reading for Reading Comprehension (MRQA) Workshop at EMNLP*.

Matthew Honnibal, Ines Montani, Sofie Van Landeghem, and Adriane Boyd. 2020. spaCy: Industrial-strength Natural Language Processing in Python.

Tushar Khot, Ashish Sabharwal, and Peter Clark. 2017. Answering complex questions using open information extraction. In *Proceedings of the 55th Annual Meeting of the Association for Computational Linguistics (Volume 2: Short Papers)*, pages 311–316, Vancouver, Canada. Association for Computational Linguistics.

Keshav Kolluru, Vaibhav Adlakha, Samarth Aggarwal, Mausam, and Soumen Chakrabarti. 2020. OpenIE6: Iterative Grid Labeling and Coordination Analysis for Open Information Extraction. In *Proceedings of the 2020 Conference on Empirical Methods in Natural Language Processing (EMNLP)*, pages 3748–3761, Online. Association for Computational Linguistics.

Patrick Lewis, Ludovic Denoyer, and Sebastian Riedel. 2019. Unsupervised question answering by cloze translation. In *Proceedings of the 57th Annual Meeting of the Association for Computational Linguistics*, pages 4896–4910, Florence, Italy. Association for Computational Linguistics.

Zhongli Li, Wenhui Wang, Li Dong, Furu Wei, and Ke Xu. 2020. Harvesting and refining question-answer pairs for unsupervised QA. In *Proceedings of the 58th Annual Meeting of the Association for Computational Linguistics*, pages 6719–6728, Online. Association for Computational Linguistics.

Yinhan Liu, Myle Ott, Naman Goyal, Jingfei Du, Mandar Joshi, Danqi Chen, Omer Levy, Mike Lewis, Luke Zettlemoyer, and Veselin Stoyanov. 2019. Roberta: A robustly optimized bert pretraining approach. *arXiv preprint arXiv:1907.11692*.

Chenyang Lyu, Lifeng Shang, Yvette Graham, Jennifer Foster, Xin Jiang, and Qun Liu. 2021. Improving unsupervised question answering via summarization-informed question generation. In *Proceedings of the 2021 Conference on Empirical Methods in Natural Language Processing*, pages 4134–4148, Online and Punta Cana, Dominican Republic. Association for Computational Linguistics.

Kaixin Ma, Filip Ilievski, Jonathan Francis, Yonatan Bisk, Eric Nyberg, and Alessandro Oltramari. 2021. Knowledge-driven data construction for zero-shot evaluation in commonsense question answering. In *Proceedings of the AAAI Conference on Artificial Intelligence*, volume 35, pages 13507–13515.

Mausam Mausam. 2016. Open information extraction systems and downstream applications. In *Proceedings of the twenty-fifth international joint conference on artificial intelligence*, pages 4074–4077.

Kostiantyn Omelianchuk, Vitaliy Atrasevych, Artem Chernodub, and Oleksandr Skurzhanskyi. 2020. GECToR – grammatical error correction: Tag, not rewrite. In *Proceedings of the Fifteenth Workshop on Innovative Use of NLP for Building Educational Applications*, pages 163–170, Seattle, WA, USA → Online. Association for Computational Linguistics.

Liangming Pan, Wenhu Chen, Wenhan Xiong, Min-Yen Kan, and William Yang Wang. 2021. Unsupervised multi-hop question answering by question generation. In *Proceedings of the 2021 Conference of the North American Chapter of the Association for Computational Linguistics: Human Language Technologies*, pages 5866–5880, Online. Association for Computational Linguistics.

Alec Radford, Karthik Narasimhan, Tim Salimans, and Ilya Sutskever. 2018. Improving language understanding by generative pre-training.

Alec Radford, Jeffrey Wu, Rewon Child, David Luan, Dario Amodei, and Ilya Sutskever. Language models are unsupervised multitask learners.

Colin Raffel, Noam Shazeer, Adam Roberts, Katherine Lee, Sharan Narang, Michael Matena, Yanqi Zhou, Wei Li, Peter J Liu, et al. 2020. Exploring the limits of transfer learning with a unified text-to-text transformer. *J. Mach. Learn. Res.*, 21(140):1–67.

Pranav Rajpurkar, Robin Jia, and Percy Liang. 2018. Know what you don't know: Unanswerable questions for SQuAD. In *Proceedings of the 56th Annual Meeting of the Association for Computational Linguistics (Volume 2: Short Papers)*, pages 784–789, Melbourne, Australia. Association for Computational Linguistics.

Pranav Rajpurkar, Jian Zhang, Konstantin Lopyrev, and Percy Liang. 2016. SQuAD: 100,000+ questions for machine comprehension of text. In *Proceedings of the 2016 Conference on Empirical Methods in Natural Language Processing*, pages 2383–2392, Austin, Texas. Association for Computational Linguistics.

Amrita Saha, Rahul Aralikatte, Mitesh M. Khapra, and Karthik Sankaranarayanan. 2018. DuoRC: Towards complex language understanding with paraphrased reading comprehension. In *Proceedings of the 56th Annual Meeting of the Association for Computational Linguistics (Volume 1: Long Papers)*, pages 1683–1693, Melbourne, Australia. Association for Computational Linguistics.

Adam Trischler, Tong Wang, Xingdi (Eric) Yuan, Justin D. Harris, Alessandro Sordoni, Philip Bachman, and Kaheer Suleman. 2016. Newsqa: A machine comprehension dataset.

George Tsatsaronis, Georgios Balikas, Prodromos Malakasiotis, Ioannis Partalas, Matthias Zschunke, Michael R Alvers, Dirk Weissenborn, Anastasia Krithara, Sergios Petridis, Dimitris Polychronopoulos, et al. 2015. An overview of the bioasq large-scale biomedical semantic indexing and question answering competition. *BMC bioinformatics*, 16(1):1–28.

Zhilin Yang, Zihang Dai, Yiming Yang, Jaime Carbonell, Russ R Salakhutdinov, and Quoc V Le. 2019. Xlnet: Generalized autoregressive pretraining for language understanding. *Advances in neural information processing systems*, 32.

Jingqing Zhang, Yao Zhao, Mohammad Saleh, and Peter Liu. 2020. Pegasus: Pre-training with extracted gap-sentences for abstractive summarization. In *International Conference on Machine Learning*, pages 11328–11339. PMLR.

Probing for targeted syntactic knowledge through grammatical error detection

Christopher Davis[†] **Christopher Bryant**[†] **Andrew Caines**[†]
Marek Rei[‡†] **Paula Buttery**[†]
[†]ALTA Institute, Department of Computer Science & Technology,
University of Cambridge, U.K.
[‡]Imperial College London, U.K.
[†]{ccd38,cjb255,apc38,pjb48}@cam.ac.uk
[‡]marek.rei@imperial.ac.uk

Abstract

Targeted studies testing knowledge of subject-verb agreement (SVA) indicate that pre-trained language models encode syntactic information. We assert that if models robustly encode subject-verb agreement, they should be able to identify when agreement is correct and when it is incorrect. To that end, we propose grammatical error detection as a diagnostic probe to evaluate token-level contextual representations for their knowledge of SVA. We evaluate contextual representations at each layer from five pre-trained English language models: BERT, XLNET, GPT-2, ROBERTA, and ELECTRA. We leverage public annotated training data from both English second language learners and Wikipedia edits, and report results on manually crafted stimuli for subject-verb agreement. We find that masked language models linearly encode information relevant to the detection of SVA errors, while the autoregressive models perform on par with our baseline. However, we also observe a divergence in performance when probes are trained on different training sets, and when they are evaluated on different syntactic constructions, suggesting the information pertaining to SVA error detection is not robustly encoded.

1 Introduction

Recent work investigates whether linguistic information is encoded in pre-trained transformer-based language models (Peters et al., 2018; Devlin et al., 2019). Research using diagnostic methods (Shi et al., 2016; Alain and Bengio, 2017; Adi et al., 2017; Conneau et al., 2018; Hupkes et al., 2018) indicates models encode syntax via experiments targeting, for example, part-of-speech and dependency labelling (Tenney et al., 2019; Jawahar et al., 2019; Hewitt and Manning, 2019), while targeted syntactic evaluation studies show models encode a large amount of hierarchical syntactic information in tests for subject-verb agreement (Linzen et al., 2016; Marvin and Linzen, 2018; Goldberg, 2019). Although previous research has covered a large number of probing tasks (Tenney et al., 2019; Liu et al., 2019a), no one has yet fully explored grammatical error detection (GED) as a probe. We assert that the ability to detect ungrammatical tokens serves as a complementary evaluation to assess linguistic competence.

GED is a natural and complex NLP task that assesses a model's ability to detect which tokens in a sentence are grammatically incorrect. Ungrammatical tokens may be categorised within a taxonomy[1] comprising three operational categories (replacement, unnecessary, and missing) and twenty-five categories based on parts-of-speech. For example:

(1) [Replacement subject-verb agreement] *The train are a good option for long trips.*

(2) [Replacement pronoun] *Everybody must have free time for yourself.*

(3) [Missing determiner] *The birth of [a] new star.*

(4) [Unnecessary preposition] *Public transport means travelling around [...] by using trains, buses, and planes.*

To do well in the task, a model must encode and make use of a wide array of linguistic information. For example, detecting subject-verb agreement errors in English tests a model's capacity to identify i) verbs, ii) the subjects of the verbs, iii) the grammatical number (singular/plural) of both, and iv) whether their number agrees.

The above makes the task a very interesting testbed for evaluating a model's syntactic knowledge. We operationalise the GED task and train probes to detect replacement subject-verb agreement errors (as in Example 1) using contextual representations from different hidden layers from five pre-trained English language models – BERT (Devlin et al.,

[1]Much recent research in GED uses error-type labels based on ERRANT (Bryant et al., 2017).

Proceedings of the 26th Conference on Computational Natural Language Learning (CoNLL), pages 360 - 373
December 7-8, 2022 ©2022 Association for Computational Linguistics

2019), XLNET (Yang et al., 2019), GPT-2 (Radford et al., 2019), ROBERTA (Liu et al., 2019b), and ELECTRA (Clark et al., 2020).

To ensure a robust and thorough evaluation, we leverage existing publicly annotated data from two domains for training: essays by learners of English as a second language from both the Cambridge English Write & Improve + LOCNESS (W&I) corpus (Bryant et al., 2019) and the First Certificate in English corpus (FCE) (Yannakoudakis et al., 2011), along with a corpus of automatically extracted edited sentences from native English Wikipedia edit histories (Grundkiewicz and Junczys-Dowmunt, 2014). For evaluation, we reframe the minimal-pair dataset from Marvin and Linzen (2018) to create targeted evaluation sets annotated for GED. In doing so, we demonstrate how existing minimal-pair datasets can be leveraged to create challenging and interpretable test sets for GED models[2] (Hu et al., 2020).

We find that ELECTRA, BERT, and ROBERTA linearly encode information for the detection of SVA errors in the contextual representations of verbs, however, we observe a gap in performance when probes are trained on data from different domains, implying the information is not encoded consistently or robustly. The results show consistent patterns across layers: both BERT and ELECTRA encode information related to SVA errors in the middle-to-late layers, while ROBERTA seems to encode information earlier in the model. Probes trained on representations from GPT-2 and XLNET (with uni- and bi-directional decoding) perform poorly on the evaluation set, indicating a fundamental difference from either the training objective or pre-training data. Finally, we show that GED probes can complement existing tools for syntactic evaluation: our results suggest that although neural language models perform well on targeted syntactic evaluation tasks, their encoding of SVA does not robustly extend to the detection of SVA errors.[3]

2 Token-level grammaticality

We motivate the use of GED-probes by first reviewing previous literature involving grammaticality judgements and tests for subject-verb agreement, then discuss the advantages in tests for GED.

Boolean acceptability judgements have long been used as a primary behavioural measure to observe humans' grammatical knowledge (Chomsky, 1957; Pater, 2019), and have recently been employed in computational linguistics to evaluate grammatical knowledge in neural models. For example, Warstadt et al. (2019) train classifiers to predict sentence-level Boolean acceptability judgements on example sentences from the linguistics literature. As each sentence is designed to demonstrate a particular grammatical construction, performance on the task is interpreted as a reflection of the implicit knowledge of the classifier.

An alternative approach frames acceptability as a choice between minimal pairs of sentences – one grammatical and another ungrammatical, where the difference between the two is typically one or two tokens. Marvin and Linzen (2018) evaluate linguistic knowledge by testing whether a language model assigns higher probability to a grammatical sentence relative to its minimally different ungrammatical counterpart. Similar to Warstadt et al. (2019), fine-grained grammatical knowledge is evaluated by controlling the evaluation stimuli, with the hypothesis that models must have implicit knowledge of the underlying grammatical concept to succeed.

Rather than evaluating sentence-level scores, Linzen et al. (2016) compare predicted probabilities assigned to target verbs in minimal pair sentences, where each sentence in a pair uses a different form of the verb. Goldberg (2019) extends this to masked language models where he replaces a target verb with the [MASK] token and feeds the entire sentence to a BERT model. A model is considered successful, and thereby has knowledge related to SVA, if it assigns higher probability to the correct form of the verb.

Our work differs from the above in three important ways. First, we don't assume to know where the incorrect token is – the probe is trained to detect errors for all tokens in a sentence, given each token's contextual representation. This is a more fine-grained evaluation compared to sentence-level judgements and tests whether probes know where the error is located. Second, instead of targeting information in the masked token, we investigate whether the model implicitly encodes SVA information in a token's contextual representation. Third, we test for knowledge of SVA without comparing to the counterpart token or sentence. We argue that if a model has knowledge of SVA, it should

[2]In principle these minimal-pair datasets can also be used to evaluate grammatical error correction systems.

[3]We release our code at `https://github.com/chrisdavis90/ged-syntax-probing`

Syntactic Construction	Example
Simple agreement	The **author** laughs/laugh*
Agreement in a sentential complement	The bankers knew the **officer** smiles/smile*
Agreement across a prepositional phrase	The **farmer** near the parents smiles/smile*
Agreement across a subject relative clause	The **officers** that love the skater smile/smiles*
Short verb-phrase coordination	The **senator** smiles and laughs/laugh*
Long verb-phrase coordination	The **manager** writes in a journal every day and likes/like* to watch television shows
Agreement across an objective relative clause	The **farmer** that the parents love swims/swim*
Agreement within an objective relative clause	The farmer that the **parents** love/loves* swims

Table 1: Examples for the main syntactic constructions from the subject-verb-agreement stimuli from Marvin and Linzen (2018). **Bold** indicates the subject-noun, and underlined tokens indicate the grammatical/ungrammatical* verb.

be able to detect SVA-errors without requiring a comparison.

3 Data

3.1 Second language learner corpora

Following previous work in grammatical error correction and detection, we use the Cambridge English Write & Improve + LOCNESS corpus (Bryant et al., 2019) and the First Certificate in English (Yannakoudakis et al., 2011), hereinafter W&I-FCE.[4]

The edit annotations in these corpora were preprocessed and standardised using the ERRANT annotation framework (Bryant et al., 2017). One advantage of this framework is that error types are modular, and consist of "operation" + "main" type tags. This provides us flexibility to target grammatical errors at different levels of granularity. E.g. all `NOUN` errors or only `R:NOUN` for replacement nouns. In addition, we can take advantage of the corrections provided with each edit annotation to control the number and variation of grammatical errors. Since we focus only on replacement subject-verb-agreement errors, `R:VERB:SVA`, we correct all other error types and keep only those sentences containing at least one grammatical error. This leaves 1936 sentences for training and 142 sentences for validation.

3.2 Dataset of Wikipedia edits

As an alternative to the learner corpora, we additionally experiment with a corpus of automatically extracted edited sentences from native English Wikipedia edit histories (WIKED) (Grundkiewicz and Junczys-Dowmunt, 2014). We use the clean and preprocessed version of English Wikipedia edits, consisting of ~29 million sentences.[5] We follow the same procedure as above and retain only sentences with `R:VERB:SVA` errors by correcting all other error types, and keep only the sentences containing at least one error. This leaves ~233K sentences, from which we sample five training sets each with 1936 sentences each to match the amount of sentences in the learner corpora after processing, and 5839 sentences for the validation set. Statistics for both corpora are given in Appendix A. We refer to the sampled training sets as WIKED-S.

3.3 Minimal-pair datasets

We use the manually constructed subject-verb agreement stimuli from Marvin and Linzen (2018) (M&L) to evaluate the GED-probes – this enables a more controlled evaluation compared to the naturally occurring sentences in W&I-FCE and WIKED. The dataset consists of seven main syntactic constructions, shown in Table 1. In addition to those shown in the table, sentences with multiple nouns (except for those testing VP coordination) include instances with two nouns and one acts as a distractor, potentially agreeing with the verb even though it is not the subject:

(5) a. The farmer near the parent smiles/smile*.
b. The farmer near the parents smiles/smile*.
c. The farmers near the parent smiles*/smile.
d. The farmers near the parents smiles*/smile.

In the above sentences, the verbs marked with an asterisk are ungrammatical. The dataset also expands on sentences testing agreement with object relative clauses: agreement is tested across

[4]Public data for W&I and the FCE are available at: `https://www.cl.cam.ac.uk/research/nl/bea2019st#data`

[5]`https://github.com/snukky/wikiedits`

and within the clause, using animate and inanimate main subjects, and with and without the *that*-complementizer.

We process the M&L minimal pairs to create token-level GED annotations, where the ungrammatical verbs are tagged as R:VERB:SVA.[6] We include all of the ungrammatical and grammatical sentences for evaluation – to be successful, the GED-probe should recognise when the agreement is correct and label all tokens as grammatical.[7] Finally, we capitalise the first word in each sentence and add a full stop if one doesn't already exist. Appendix B contains details about the processed dataset.

4 Experiment 1: Per Layer Probes

We first investigate whether models encode SVA-errors by examining probing performance at each layer; we want to test whether models encode this information in the final layer, the token representation, but also how this information develops across the layers. We then break-down performance by syntactic construction to better understand how the SVA-error encoding generalizes. Finally, we carry out a follow-up experiment to investigate the impact of training data size and verb frequency.

4.1 Experimental setup

For each model, we extract contextual representations for every token in a sentence for every one of the twelve layers in the model. We then train a linear probe (Tenney et al., 2019; Hupkes et al., 2018; Liu et al., 2019a) per layer to predict whether each token-level contextual representation is ungrammatical. We train two versions of each probe: one trained using W&I-FCE, and the other using WIKED-S. Every probe is evaluated on the M&L stimuli

Since the probe is trained to detect R:VERB:SVA errors, high probing performance would indicate the probe has learned to extract features to identify subject-verb agreement errors from the contextual representations of the verbs. This implicitly includes sub-tasks to identify the verb, the subject noun, the number of both the verb and noun, and that their number disagrees. Furthermore, as this is a token labelling probe, high probing performance would indicate the pre-trained model has encoded the relevant features in the contextual representations of the verbs.

We evaluate probes using F_1 on the evaluation stimuli from M&L containing an equal number of grammatical and ungrammatical sentences.[8] We compare probes to a VERB-ONLY baseline which incorrectly tags all verbs as ungrammatical. The number of verbs per sentence varies across syntactic constructions; constructions with one verb have an equal number of grammatical and ungrammatical verbs, and therefore have a baseline score of 0.67. Constructions with two and three verbs have scores of 0.40 and 0.30, respectively. Evaluating the baseline over all constructions yields a score of 0.43.

We evaluate five pre-trained models: BERT-BASE-CASED, GPT-2 (small), ROBERTA-BASE, XLNET with both uni-directional (XLNET-UNI) and bi-directional XLNET-BI decoding, and ELECTRA-BASE (discriminator). As all five models use sub-word tokenisation, we follow Liu et al. (2019a) and use the last sub-word unit for token classification. We train the probes for 50 epochs with a patience of 10 epochs for early stopping based on in-domain validation sets.

Four of the five models were pre-trained with a language modelling objective: either masked language modelling (MLM) or autoregressive language modelling (ALM). Whereas ELECTRA is the exception – the *replaced token detection* training objective is somewhat aligned with GED and therefore we may expect representations to encode grammatically discriminative information.[9] Indeed, Yuan et al. (2021) find ELECTRA outperforms BERT when fine-tuned for binary GED targeting a wide range of error-types. BERT and ROBERTA also detect replaced tokens during training, but only on 1.5% of tokens.

[6]In principle, any minimal-pair dataset can be converted to token-level annotations using ERRANT, but not all grammatical errors map cleanly to ERRANT categories. For example, replacement pronouns (R:PRON) includes reflexive anaphor gender- and number- agreement errors.

[7]While the evaluation stimuli consists of minimal pairs, the training data does not.

[8]This departs from $F_{0.5}$ used in the GED literature, which was motivated from educational applications where high precision is preferred over recall because false-positives can be more harmful for language learners compared to false-negatives.

[9]The ELECTRA discriminator model is trained to detect substituted tokens in a grammatical sentence, where an original token is substituted with a plausible alternative from a masked language model.

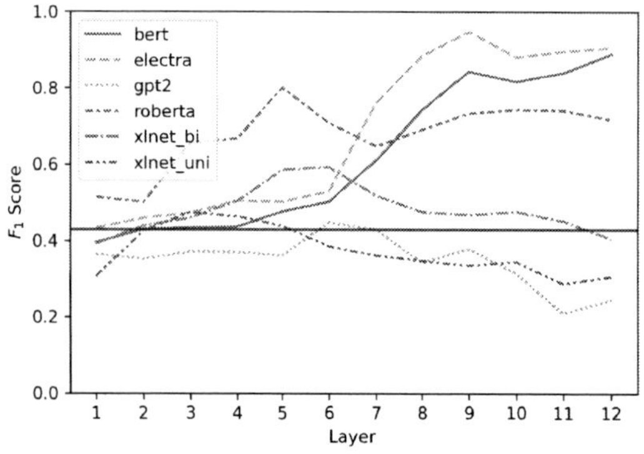

(a) W&I-FCE

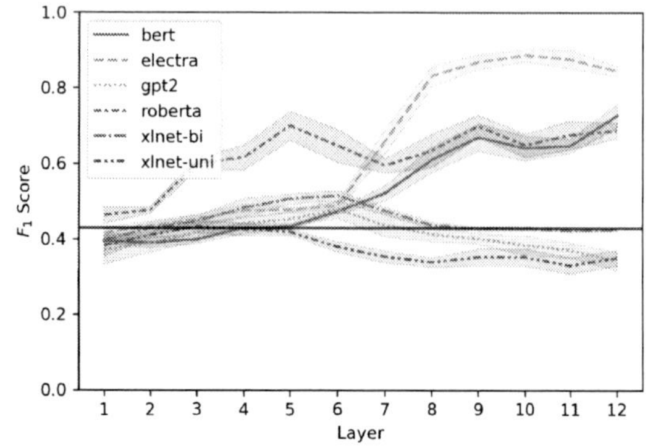

(b) WIKED-S

Figure 1: F_1 scores for probes trained on contextual representations at different layers from BERT, ELECTRA, ROBERTA, XLNET with bidirectional decoding (XLNET-BI), XLNET with unidirectional decoding (XLNET-UNI), and GPT-2. 1a and 1b show results for probes trained on W&I-FCE and the WIKED-S training sets respectively. The VERB-ONLY baseline scores are illustrated using grey horizontal lines. 1b shows the mean and standard deviation across the five training sets (§3.2). All probes are evaluated on the M&L stimuli (§3.3).

	W&I-FCE		WIKED-S	
Model	Layer	F_1	Layer	F_1
ELECTRA	9	0.95	10	$0.89_{\pm 0.02}$
BERT	12	0.89	12	$0.73_{\pm 0.03}$
ROBERTA	5	0.80	5	$0.70_{\pm 0.04}$
XLNET-BI	6	0.59	6	$0.51_{\pm 0.01}$
XLNET-UNI	3	0.48	3	$0.43_{\pm 0.02}$
GPT-2	6	0.45	6	$0.48_{\pm 0.02}$
VERB-ONLY	-	0.43	-	0.43

Table 2: Top F_1 scores on the M&L evaluation set, for probes trained on either W&I-FCE or WIKED-S. Scores for probes trained on WIKED-S are reported as the *mean* ± 1 standard deviation over the five sampled training sets.

4.2 Results

Figure 1 shows F_1 scores for probes trained on W&I-FCE and WIKED-S, and evaluated on the M&L stimuli.[10] For the latter, we plot the mean and standard deviation evaluated over the five sampled training sets. We illustrate the VERB-ONLY baseline score with a grey horizontal line. Table 2 shows layers which obtained the top F_1 score per model.

The figure and table shows ELECTRA encodes the most salient information for SVA error detection, with probes obtaining maximum scores of 0.95 and 0.89 (σ=0.02) when trained on W&I-FCE and WIKED-S, respectively. Though this may not be surprising given the *replaced token detection* pre-training objective, it illustrates that probes trained on representations from a model capable of SVA error detection can obtain high performance using both training sets.

We observe a divergence in performance between MLM-probes and ALM-probes; the MLM-probes tend to perform better, obtaining maximum scores between 0.70 and 0.89 F_1, while the ALM-probes don't score above 0.59 on either training set. In fact, probes trained on representations from GPT-2 and XLNET-UNI often perform worse than the VERB-ONLY baseline at 0.43 and don't score above 0.50 F_1. These results imply that GPT-2 and XLNET-UNI representations do not linearly encode enough information to differentiate between grammatical and ungrammatical verbs in SVA.

The MLM-ALM performance gap could be due to the language model directionality: the two unidirectional models (GPT-2 and XLNET-UNI) do perform the worst, but this fails to account for the performance of XLNET-BI – a bi-directional language model which does not perform much better. It may be that the MLM training objective helps to imbue contextual representations with information useful for detecting SVA errors, but we cannot discount the inclusion of the *replaced token detection* objective, even though it is rarely included. Finally, we note key differences in the pre-training data used by the models: BERT and ELECTRA use the BooksCorpus and English Wikipedia, GPT-2 uses

[10]We additionally evaluate probes against the other error types in the W&I dataset and verify that probes only detect SVA errors. Probes trained on either BERT or ELECTRA obtain mean scores of 0.04 (σ=0.04), verifying that information extracted by the probe is isolated to subject-verb agreement errors.

web-scraped data, and XLNET and ROBERTA use a combination of BooksCorpus, Wikipedia, and web-scraped data.

When we examine performance across layers we see that ELECTRA- and BERT-probes follow a similar trajectory, with performance on par with the baseline from layers 1-5 and higher performance only in layers 8-12. SVA-error information is highest in the final layer for BERT (the token representation) while layers 9 and 10 seem to encode the most useful information for ELECTRA. In contrast, probes trained with representations from ROBERTA peak at layer 5 but have mostly consistent performance until 12, apart from a drop in layer 7.

The results for BERT support those from Jawahar et al. (2019), where they find probes encode elements of syntax in the middle to late layers. Liu et al. (2019a) also find that later layers obtain the best performance for a general GED probe, though they experiment on a single dataset (FCE (Yannakoudakis et al., 2011)) and include all grammatical error types. Recent results from Lasri et al. (2022b) show that removing *number* information from nouns at different layers has a detrimental effect on the number-agreement task up until layer 8. They hypothesise that some transfer of noun-*number* takes place in the previous layers. Our results seem to support this: low probing performance in layers 1-5 (when the noun-*number* has yet to be transferred to the verb), and high probing performance in layers 8-12 after transfer has taken place. Interestingly, performance for ELECTRA takes the same shape, suggesting that the pre-training objective (*replace token detection* versus MLM) may not have an important role in how models encode SVA information, especially given that ROBERTA, trained using masked-language modelling, displays a different pattern across layers. Finally, if GED-probe-performance can be taken as a proxy for noun-*number* transfer, then results for ROBERTA-probes suggest that noun-*number* information is transferred to the target verb earlier, possibly due to the more robust optimization.

Turning to probe performance across training sets, we find that probes trained on W&I-FCE consistently perform better than those trained on WIKED-S, for all models tested apart from GPT-2. This could be due to a domain mismatch, where learner writing may be more similar to the M&L stimuli than data from WIKED-S. Though, at the very least this indicates that information pertaining to SVA errors is not consistently encoded.

Previous work finds some evidence that BERT's representations encode knowledge of SVA (Goldberg, 2019; Jawahar et al., 2019; Newman et al., 2021; Lasri et al., 2022a) but that this knowledge is based on heuristics rather than robust SVA rule learning (Chaves and Richter, 2021; McCoy et al., 2019). Our results indicate that information encoded in contextual representations extends to the detection of SVA errors in ELECTRA, BERT, and to a lesser extent, ROBERTA. However, we find the encoding is not robust across domains, supporting the heuristic-learning claim. These results illustrate the importance of utilising training and evaluation datasets from disparate domains to evaluate probes.

4.3 Results per syntactic construction

We break down the performance of probes for each syntactic construction in the M&L dataset. Figure 2 illustrates F_1 scores for probes trained on W&I-FCE and WIKED-S using representations from each layer of BERT and ROBERTA.[11] The VERB-ONLY baseline is shown as grey horizontal lines. For brevity, we present results on sentences with simple agreement, sentential complements, prepositional phrases, subject relative clauses, and object relative clauses (agreement within and across the clause). Results for the other models and syntactic constructions are included in Appendix E.

The trends across layers observed in Figure 1 are generally consistent within syntactic constructions: probes trained on BERT representations improve in the later layers, while layers 5 and 8-12 seem to be the most salient for probes trained on ROBERTA.

Probes for both models detect SVA errors in the simple agreement constructions – with only the BERT-probe trained on WIKED-S scoring less that 0.90 F_1. We find BERT-probes perform well for most constructions, especially in layer 12, but performance for ROBERTA-probes drops for sentences with subject-relative clauses, prepositional phrases, and object-relative clasues (agreement within the clause), particularly when trained on WIKED-S data. This suggests that the token representation from BERT models, potentially used in downstream tasks, already encodes a lot of information related to SVA before any fine-tuning.

When comparing performance between probes across training sets, we observe a noticeable differ-

[11]We select BERT and ROBERTA because they are both MLMs, whereas the ELECTRA-discriminator is trained using a *replaced token detection* objective.

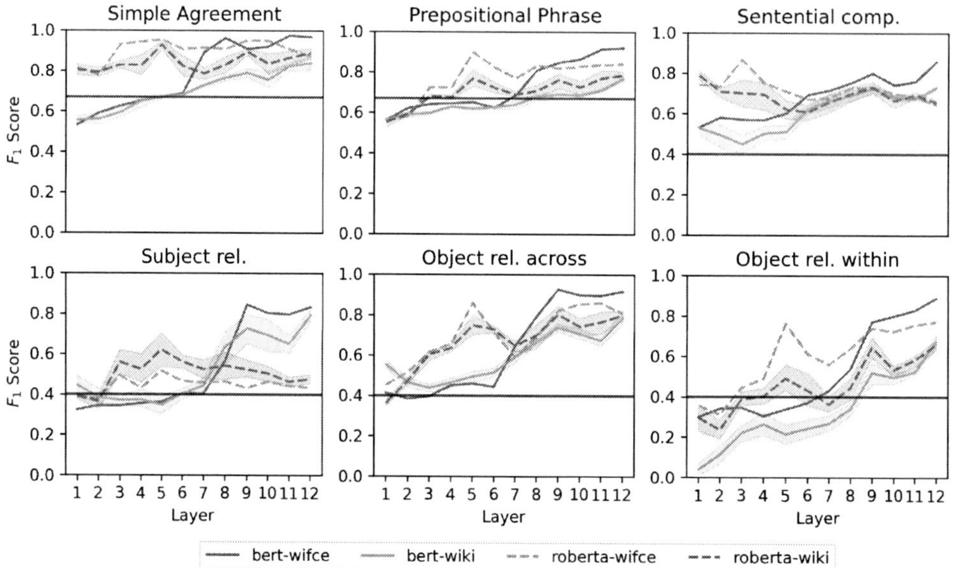

Figure 2: F_1 scores for probes trained on contextual representations from BERT and ROBERTA, using both the W&I-FCE and WIKED-S training sets. The probes are evaluated on M&L stimuli. The VERB-ONLY baseline is illustrated using grey horizontal lines.

ence in performance between BERT-probes trained on W&I-FCE versus those trained on WIKED-S, most evidently in five out of the six syntactic constructions shown. On the other hand, probes trained on ROBERTA don't always display a performance gap – performance is more comparable between probes on sentences testing simple agreement, sentential complements, and agreement across object relative clauses. For sentences with subject relative clauses we find the probes trained on WIKED-S outperform those trained on W&I-FCE. These results may indicate that information pertaining to the detection of SVA errors is more robustly encoded in ROBERTA than BERT – that is, the information is more invariant to the choice of probe training set.

5 Experiment 2: Generalisation to unseen verbs

In our first experiment, we observe that although the MLMs encode more information for SVA error detection compared to the ALMs, the information does not always generalize across domains or syntactic constructions. We carry out a follow-up experiment to investigate whether the information generalizes across verbs using probes trained on BERT representations and WIKED data. We focus on layers 6 to 12 as these were the layers where performance was above the baseline. There are 13 target verbs in the M&L stimuli, of which "to be" is the most frequent with 946 occurrences in WIKED-S. The remaining verbs appear very infrequently – for example, eight verbs have frequencies less than 30. To test generalization across verbs we remove all sentences from the training and development sets which contain a verb from the M&L stimuli except for "to be". We then re-sample sentences from the full WIKED data to maintain 1936 sentences as in the first experiment. Due to the infrequency of many verbs and to ensure a more thorough evaluation, we also increase the training set size by 4- and 8-times to yield training sets with 7744 and 15488 sentences, respectively. We refer to the three sizes as small, medium, and large. This results in paired training sets: for each training set size, there is one set "with M&L verbs" and a set "without M&L verbs". We sample each training set five times and report the mean and standard deviation over the samples. For example, we sample five training sets with 7744 sentences "with M&L verbs", and another five "without M&L verbs". Since we are only interested in the performance of 12 verbs, we modify the evaluation stimuli to remove a) sentences containing only "to be" verbs, and for sentences with multiple verbs we remove the "to be" token from evaluation. For example, in the sentence "The movie the security guards like is good", we remove "is" from evaluation.

Figure 3 illustrates the F_1 scores: the left and

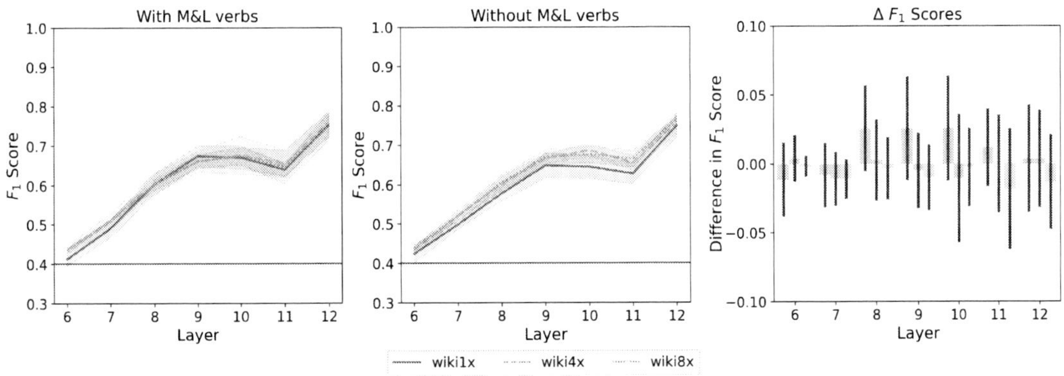

Figure 3: F_1 scores for probes trained on BERT representations, with varying amounts of data (left and centre); 1x=1936, 4x=7744, 8x=15488 sentences. The plots show the mean and standard deviation across five training sets (§5). On the left, probes are trained on data including M&L verbs, while the centre shows scores for probes trained on data without M&L verbs (apart from "is" and "are", as described in §5). The right-hand plot shows the mean and standard deviation of differences in F_1 scores between probes trained on the two types of dataset: with and without M&L verbs. The VERB-ONLY baseline is shown as a grey horizontal line.

centre plots show results for probes trained on data with and without M&L verbs, respectively. The plot on the right presents the mean and standard deviation for the pairwise differences between probes trained on datasets of the same size. The right-hand plot shows that for the smallest training set size we observe a slight benefit when including the M&L verbs, but this is limited to ~0.05 F_1 and restricted to layers 8-10. We generally observe no difference in performance for the medium and large training sets, indicating that SVA-error information does generalize across verbs. Furthermore, we observe no difference when comparing results across training set sizes in the left and central plots, except for probes trained on the small training set without M&L verbs. These results indicate that SVA-error information is linearly accessible and generalizable across across the verbs we test, even when probes are trained with limited data. Future work may expand the investigation to cover more verbs, though we expect performance to deteriorate as verbs become infrequent in the pre-training data (Wei et al., 2021).

6 Discussion

Our experiments test whether information for SVA errors is implicitly encoded in the contextual representations of verbs, but they don't provide any indication as to *how* the information is encoded: is grammaticality encoded atomically or compositionally? Furthermore, we note that selecting the "erroneous token" can be an ambiguous choice between the noun and the verb, for example in "The authors laughs". Yet, the probes we evaluate never tag the nouns. This could indicate that a) the probes learn to only tag verbs, and/or b) that SVA-grammaticality is disparately encoded between nouns and verbs. A compositional account of grammatical encoding is a plausible explanation given the results provided in Lasri et al. (2022b) – that nouns and verbs have different encodings for *number*. We plan to investigate how grammaticality is encoded in future work, both in pre-trained language models as well as models trained specifically for GED.

7 Conclusion

We analyse whether pre-trained transformer-based language models implicitly encode knowledge of SVA errors using GED probes. We carry out a thorough evaluation on five models, using two public training sets from different domains, and evaluate on a manually constructed evaluation set. This enables us to get a more complete and reliable picture of a models' performance.

Grammatical error detection is a challenging and linguistically aligned task to assess the knowledge of neural language models; we show that GED-probes can be used as a complementary analysis tool to evaluate a models' linguistic capabilities.

Our results show that ELECTRA, BERT, and ROBERTA encode information for SVA-error detection, but GPT-2 and XLNET do not. For BERT and ROBERTA, we find that the SVA-error encoding is not robust across all syntactic constructions or training set domains, though we do find some evidence that the encoding generalizes across verbs for BERT. Furthermore, a layer-wise analysis reveals the final layers in ELECTRA and BERT are the most salient for SVA-error detection.

Acknowledgements

We thank Guy Aglionby, Rami Aly, Paula Czarnowska, and Tiago Pimentel for helpful discussions and feedback on early drafts of this work. We also thank the anonymous reviewers for their helpful feedback. This paper reports on research supported by Cambridge University Press & Assessment. We thank the NVIDIA Corporation for the donation of the Titan X Pascal GPU used in this research.

References

Yossi Adi, Einat Kermany, Yonatan Belinkov, Ofer Lavi, and Yoav Goldberg. 2017. Fine-grained analysis of sentence embeddings using auxiliary prediction tasks. In *5th International Conference on Learning Representations, ICLR 2017, Toulon, France, April 24-26, 2017, Conference Track Proceedings*. OpenReview.net.

Guillaume Alain and Yoshua Bengio. 2017. Understanding intermediate layers using linear classifier probes. In *5th International Conference on Learning Representations, ICLR 2017, Toulon, France, April 24-26, 2017, Workshop Track Proceedings*. OpenReview.net.

Christopher Bryant, Mariano Felice, Øistein E Andersen, and Ted Briscoe. 2019. The BEA-2019 shared task on grammatical error correction. In *Proceedings of the Fourteenth Workshop on Innovative Use of NLP for Building Educational Applications*, pages 52–75.

Christopher Bryant, Mariano Felice, and Edward Briscoe. 2017. Automatic annotation and evaluation of error types for grammatical error correction. Association for Computational Linguistics.

Rui P Chaves and Stephanie N Richter. 2021. Look at that! BERT can be easily distracted from paying attention to morphosyntax. *Proceedings of the Society for Computation in Linguistics*, 4(1):28–38.

Noam Chomsky. 1957. *Syntactic structures's*. Mouton: The Hague, The Netherlands.

Kevin Clark, Minh-Thang Luong, Quoc V. Le, and Christopher D. Manning. 2020. ELECTRA: Pre-training Text Encoders as Discriminators Rather Than Generators. In *International Conference on Learning Representations*.

Alexis Conneau, German Kruszewski, Guillaume Lample, Loïc Barrault, and Marco Baroni. 2018. What you can cram into a single $&!#* vector: Probing sentence embeddings for linguistic properties. In *Proceedings of the 56th Annual Meeting of the Association for Computational Linguistics (Volume 1: Long Papers)*, pages 2126–2136, Melbourne, Australia. Association for Computational Linguistics.

Jacob Devlin, Ming-Wei Chang, Kenton Lee, and Kristina Toutanova. 2019. BERT: pre-training of deep bidirectional transformers for language understanding. In *Proceedings of the 2019 Conference of the North American Chapter of the Association for Computational Linguistics: Human Language Technologies, NAACL-HLT 2019, Minneapolis, MN, USA, June 2-7, 2019, Volume 1 (Long and Short Papers)*, pages 4171–4186. Association for Computational Linguistics.

Yoav Goldberg. 2019. Assessing BERT's syntactic abilities. *arXiv preprint arXiv:1901.05287*.

Roman Grundkiewicz and Marcin Junczys-Dowmunt. 2014. The WikEd Error Corpus: A corpus of corrective Wikipedia edits and its application to grammatical error correction. In *Advances in Natural Language Processing – Lecture Notes in Computer Science*, volume 8686, pages 478–490. Springer.

John Hewitt and Christopher D. Manning. 2019. A structural probe for finding syntax in word representations. In *Proceedings of the 2019 Conference of the North American Chapter of the Association for Computational Linguistics: Human Language Technologies, Volume 1 (Long and Short Papers)*, pages 4129–4138, Minneapolis, Minnesota. Association for Computational Linguistics.

Jennifer Hu, Jon Gauthier, Peng Qian, Ethan Wilcox, and Roger Levy. 2020. A systematic assessment of syntactic generalization in neural language models. In *Proceedings of the 58th Annual Meeting of the Association for Computational Linguistics*, pages 1725–1744, Online. Association for Computational Linguistics.

Dieuwke Hupkes, Sara Veldhoen, and Willem Zuidema. 2018. Visualisation and 'diagnostic classifiers' reveal how recurrent and recursive neural networks process hierarchical structure. *Journal of Artificial Intelligence Research*, 61:907–926.

Ganesh Jawahar, Benoît Sagot, and Djamé Seddah. 2019. What does BERT learn about the structure of language? In *ACL 2019 - 57th Annual Meeting of the Association for Computational Linguistics*, Florence, Italy.

Karim Lasri, Alessandro Lenci, and Thierry Poibeau. 2022a. Does BERT really agree? fine-grained analysis of lexical dependence on a syntactic task. In *Findings of the Association for Computational Linguistics: ACL 2022*, pages 2309–2315.

Karim Lasri, Tiago Pimentel, Alessandro Lenci, Thierry Poibeau, and Ryan Cotterell. 2022b. Probing for the usage of grammatical number. In *Proceedings of the 60th Annual Meeting of the Association for Computational Linguistics (Volume 1: Long Papers)*, pages 8818–8831.

Tal Linzen, Emmanuel Dupoux, and Yoav Goldberg. 2016. Assessing the ability of LSTMs to learn syntax-sensitive dependencies. *Transactions of the Association for Computational Linguistics*, 4:521–535.

Nelson F Liu, Matt Gardner, Yonatan Belinkov, Matthew E Peters, and Noah A Smith. 2019a. Linguistic knowledge and transferability of contextual representations.

Yinhan Liu, Myle Ott, Naman Goyal, Jingfei Du, Mandar Joshi, Danqi Chen, Omer Levy, Mike Lewis, Luke Zettlemoyer, and Veselin Stoyanov. 2019b. RoBERTa: A robustly optimized BERT pretraining approach. *arXiv preprint arXiv:1907.11692*.

Rebecca Marvin and Tal Linzen. 2018. Targeted syntactic evaluation of language models. In *Proceedings of the 2018 Conference on Empirical Methods in Natural Language Processing*, pages 1192–1202, Brussels, Belgium. Association for Computational Linguistics.

Tom McCoy, Ellie Pavlick, and Tal Linzen. 2019. Right for the wrong reasons: Diagnosing syntactic heuristics in natural language inference. In *Proceedings of the 57th Annual Meeting of the Association for Computational Linguistics*, pages 3428–3448.

Benjamin Newman, Kai-Siang Ang, Julia Gong, and John Hewitt. 2021. Refining targeted syntactic evaluation of language models. In *Proceedings of the 2021 Conference of the North American Chapter of the Association for Computational Linguistics: Human Language Technologies*, pages 3710–3723.

Joe Pater. 2019. Generative linguistics and neural networks at 60: Foundation, friction, and fusion. *Language*, 95(1):e41–e74.

Matthew E. Peters, Mark Neumann, Mohit Iyyer, Matt Gardner, Christopher Clark, Kenton Lee, and Luke Zettlemoyer. 2018. Deep contextualized word representations. In *Proceedings of the 2018 Conference of the North American Chapter of the Association for Computational Linguistics: Human Language Technologies, Volume 1 (Long Papers)*, pages 2227–2237, New Orleans, Louisiana. Association for Computational Linguistics.

Alec Radford, Jeffrey Wu, Rewon Child, David Luan, Dario Amodei, Ilya Sutskever, et al. 2019. Language models are unsupervised multitask learners. *OpenAI blog*, 1(8):9.

Xing Shi, Inkit Padhi, and Kevin Knight. 2016. Does string-based neural MT learn source syntax? In *Proceedings of the 2016 conference on empirical methods in natural language processing*, pages 1526–1534.

Ian Tenney, Patrick Xia, Berlin Chen, Alex Wang, Adam Poliak, R Thomas McCoy, Najoung Kim, Benjamin Van Durme, Samuel R Bowman, Dipanjan Das, et al. 2019. What do you learn from context? probing for sentence structure in contextualized word representations. *arXiv preprint arXiv:1905.06316*.

Alex Warstadt, Amanpreet Singh, and Samuel R Bowman. 2019. Neural network acceptability judgments. *Transactions of the Association for Computational Linguistics*, 7:625–641.

Jason Wei, Dan Garrette, Tal Linzen, and Ellie Pavlick. 2021. Frequency effects on syntactic rule learning in transformers. In *Proceedings of the 2021 Conference on Empirical Methods in Natural Language Processing*, pages 932–948.

Zhilin Yang, Zihang Dai, Yiming Yang, Jaime Carbonell, Russ R Salakhutdinov, and Quoc V Le. 2019. XLNet: Generalized autoregressive pretraining for language understanding. *Advances in neural information processing systems*, 32.

Helen Yannakoudakis, Ted Briscoe, and Ben Medlock. 2011. A new dataset and method for automatically grading ESOL texts. In *Proceedings of the 49th Annual Meeting of the Association for Computational Linguistics: Human Language Technologies*, pages 180–189, Portland, Oregon, USA. Association for Computational Linguistics.

Zheng Yuan, Shiva Taslimipoor, Christopher Davis, and Christopher Byrant. 2021. Multi-Class Grammatical Error Detection for Correction:A Tale of Two Systems. In *Proceedings of the 2021 Conference on Empirical Methods in Natural Language Processing (EMNLP-2021)*.

A Corpus statistics

	Corpus	**# sentences**	**μ sent. length (σ)**	**μ errors per sentence (σ)**
	FCE-train	28K	16 (11)	1.9 (2.5)
Original	W&I-train	34K	18 (12)	2.0 (2.8)
	BEA-dev	4K	20 (12)	1.9 (2.8)
	WikEd (total)	28M	22 (12)	1.6 (1.6)
	FCE-train	626	25 (14)	1.1 (0.3)
Processed	W&I-train	1310	27 (21)	1.1 (0.3)
	BEA-dev	142	26 (19)	1.1 (0.3)
	WikEd-train	1936	24 (12)	1.0 (0.2)
	WikEd-dev	5839	23 (11)	1.0 (0.2)

Table 3: Corpus statistics.

B Marvin & Linzen statistics

Statistics per construction.

Construction	**# sentences**	**μ sent. length (σ)**
Simple agr.	280	4.57 (0.49)
In sent. comp.	3360	7.57 (0.49)
Across prep.	44800	8.85 (1.17)
Across subj. rel.	22400	8.77 (0.64)
Short VP coord	1680	7.14 (0.64)
Long VP coord	800	14.40 (0.49)
Across obj. rel.	44800	9.18 (0.86)
Across obj. rel. (no comp)	44800	8.18 (0.86)
Within obj. rel.	44800	9.18 (0.86)
Within obj. rel. (no comp)	44800	8.18 (0.86)

Table 4: Details for the evaluation stimuli from (Marvin and Linzen, 2018).

C Results for probes trained on W&I-FCE

Model	1	2	3	4	5	6	7	8	9	10	11	12
BERT	0.40	0.43	0.43	0.44	0.48	0.50	0.61	0.74	0.84	0.82	0.84	0.89
ELECTRA	0.43	0.46	0.47	0.50	0.50	0.53	0.76	0.88	0.95	0.88	0.90	0.91
ROBERTA	0.51	0.50	0.66	0.67	0.80	0.71	0.65	0.69	0.73	0.74	0.74	0.72
GPT-2	0.37	0.35	0.37	0.37	0.36	0.45	0.43	0.34	0.38	0.31	0.21	0.25
XLNET-BI	0.39	0.44	0.46	0.50	0.59	0.59	0.52	0.48	0.47	0.48	0.45	0.41
XLNET-UNI	0.31	0.43	0.48	0.46	0.44	0.39	0.36	0.35	0.33	0.34	0.29	0.31

Table 5: F_1 scores for probes trained on contextual representations at different layers from BERT, ELECTRA, ROBERTA, XLNET with bidirectional decoding, XLNET with unidirectional decoding, and GPT-2. Probes were trained on learner data described in §3.1, and evaluated on the Marvin and Linzen (2018) stimuli (§3.3).

D Results for probes trained on WIKED-S

Model	1	2	3	4	5	6	7	8	9	10	11	12
BERT	0.39	0.39	0.40	0.43	0.43	0.47	0.53	0.62	0.68	0.65	0.65	0.73
ELECTRA	0.42	0.43	0.45	0.48	0.48	0.49	0.66	0.83	0.87	0.89	0.88	0.84
ROBERTA	0.46	0.48	0.60	0.62	0.70	0.65	0.59	0.63	0.70	0.65	0.68	0.69
GPT-2	0.37	0.39	0.42	0.44	0.45	0.48	0.44	0.41	0.40	0.38	0.37	0.34
XLNET-UNI	0.38	0.41	0.43	0.43	0.42	0.38	0.35	0.34	0.35	0.35	0.33	0.35
XLNET-BI	0.40	0.43	0.45	0.48	0.51	0.51	0.48	0.44	0.43	0.43	0.42	0.43

Table 6: F_1 scores for probes trained on contextual representations at different layers from BERT, ELECTRA, ROBERTA, XLNET with bidirectional decoding, XLNET with unidirectional decoding, and GPT-2. Probes were trained on wikipedia data described in §3.2, and evaluated on the Marvin and Linzen (2018) stimuli (§3.3).

E Results across syntactic constructions

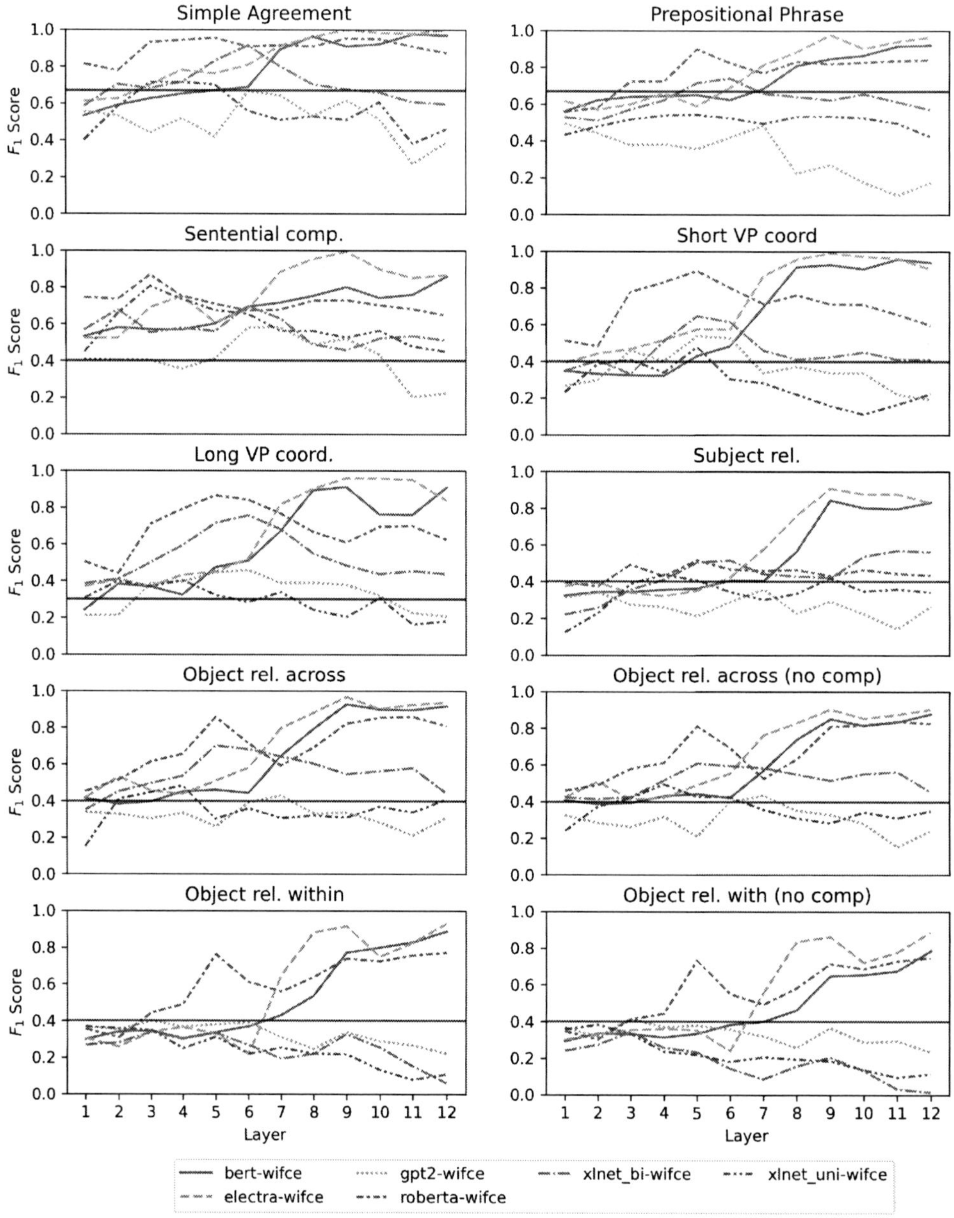

Figure 4: F_1 scores for probes trained the W&I-FCE and training set. The probes are evaluated on M&L stimuli. The VERB-ONLY baseline is illustrated using grey horizontal lines.

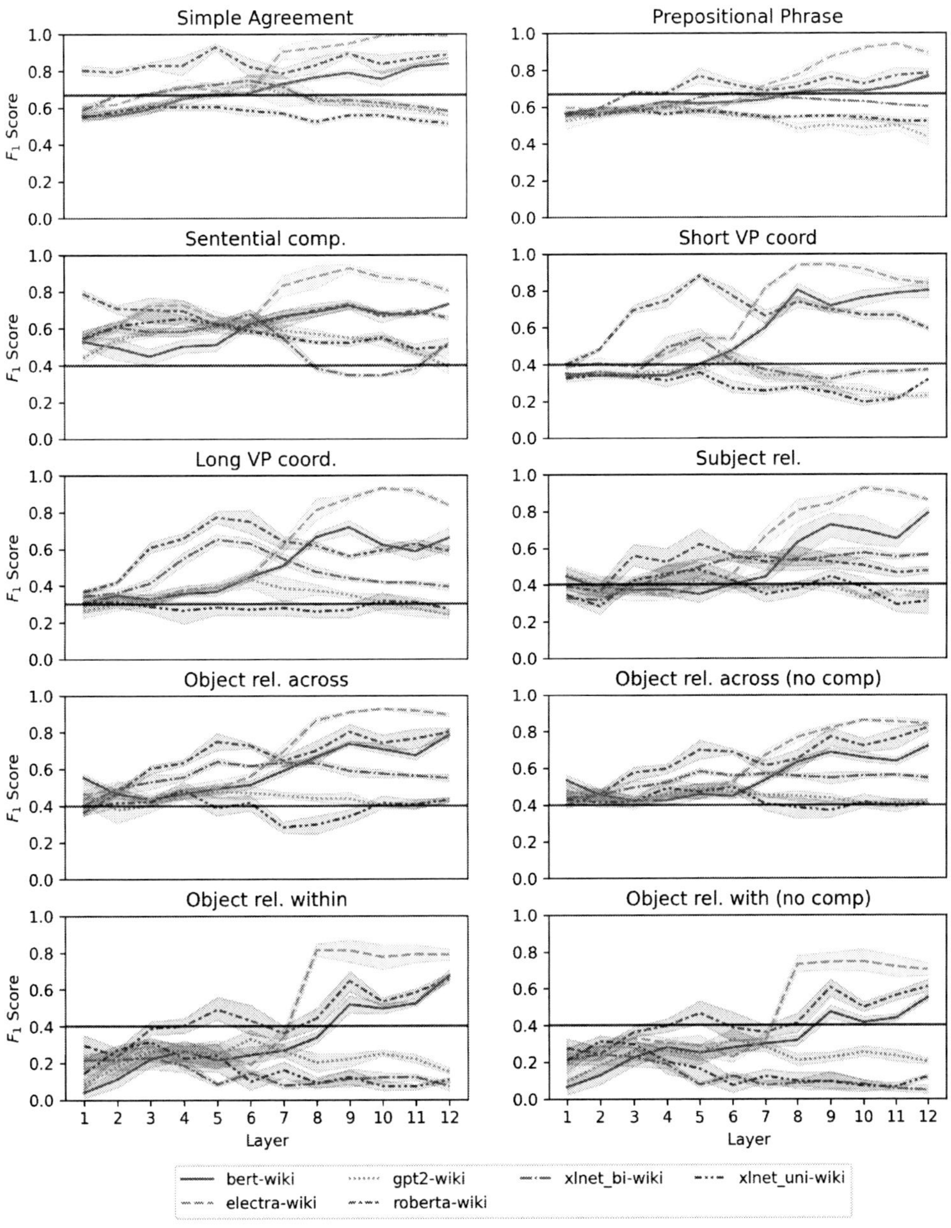

Figure 5: F_1 scores for probes trained the WIKED and training set. The probes are evaluated on M&L stimuli. The VERB-ONLY baseline is illustrated using grey horizontal lines.

An Alignment-based Approach to Text Segmentation Similarity Scoring

Gerardo Ocampo Diaz and Jessica Ouyang
Department of Computer Science
University of Texas at Dallas
Richardson, TX 75083
{godiaz,jessica.ouyang}@utdallas.edu

Abstract

Text segmentation is a natural language processing task with popular applications, such as topic segmentation, element discourse extraction, and sentence tokenization. Much work has been done to develop accurate segmentation similarity metrics, but even the most advanced metrics used today, B, and WindowDiff, exhibit incorrect behavior due to their evaluation of boundaries in isolation. In this paper, we present a new segment-alignment based approach to segmentation similarity scoring and a new similarity metric A. We show that A does not exhibit the erratic behavior of B and WindowDiff, quantify the likelihood of B and WindowDiff misbehaving through simulation, and discuss the versatility of alignment-based approaches for segmentation similarity scoring. We make our implementation of A publicly available and encourage the community to explore more sophisticated approaches to text segmentation similarity scoring.

1 Introduction

Text segmentation is a natural language processing (NLP) task that consists of dividing a sequence of text elements into segments.

Let $T = e_1, e_2, e_3 ... e_n$ be a sequence of text elements (e.g. words, sentences, paragraphs, etc...). A segmentation S of T is given by a binary string $Q = [0|1]^{n-1}$ that encodes boundaries between the elements of T. The ith character of Q codifies the presence of a boundary (1) or lack thereof (0) between e_i and e_{i+1} in S. S contains $m - 1$ boundaries and partitions T into m segments[1].

Measuring similarity between segmentations is not simple. The most straightforward approach is to frame a segmentation as a series of decisions made at every *potential boundary position* (PBP),

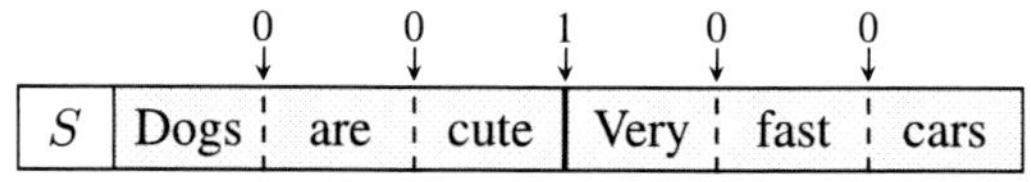

Figure 1: Example segmentation with $Q = 00100$.

which exist between every pair of elements in T, and to calculate the average PBP agreement, but this does not match human intuition well.

Consider how S in Figure 1 compares with $h1$ and $h2$ in Figure 2: h_1 agrees with S in 4 out of 5 positions (one missing boundary), while h_2 agrees with S in only 3 out of 5 positions (one missing and one "extra" boundary). Yet it is easy to agree that h_2 is actually closer to S, as it has simply "shifted" the boundary in S one unit to the right.

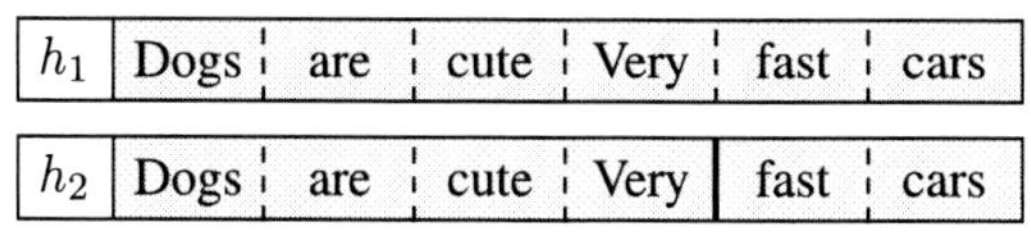

Figure 2: Alternate segmentations to S from Figure 1.

To address this, researchers have proposed a variety of similarity metrics that distinguish "soft" and "hard" errors (shifted versus missing/extra boundaries). However, existing metrics look at boundary errors in isolation; they do not consider the impact that errors have on segments around them.

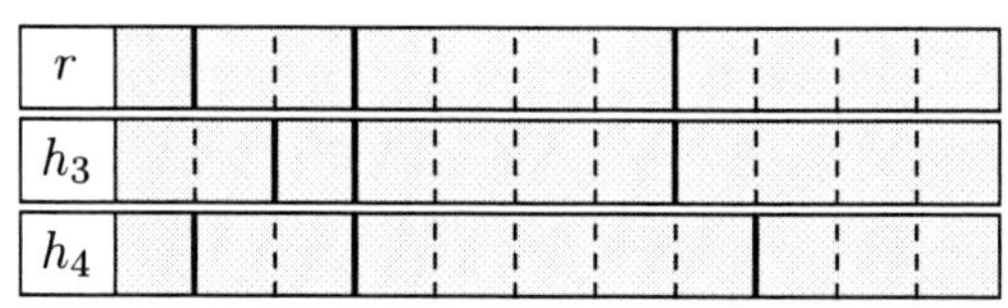

Figure 3: Three similar segmentations.

Consider how hypothesis segmentations h_3 and h_4 compare to a reference segmentation r in Figure 3. Both have a boundary that is shifted one PBP to the right, which results in an"extra" element in the segment to the left of the PBP and a missing element in the segment to the right. However, the

[1] This definition corresponds to *single-type* segmentation. A *multi-type* version also exists where different boundary types are considered, enabling the encoding of different types of segments and even hierarchical relations between them.

Proceedings of the 26th Conference on Computational Natural Language Learning (CoNLL), pages 374 - 383
December 7-8, 2022 ©2022 Association for Computational Linguistics

resulting segment distortion is not the same. In h_3, only $1/2$ of the elements in the the first segment are correct, while $1/2$ of the reference elements are missing from the second segment; in h_4, the third segment has $4/5$ correct elements, and the fourth segment has $1/4$ missing elements. It is easy to argue then that h_4 is closer to r than h_3, but current metrics are unable to distinguish between them.

We propose a new similarity metric based on segment alignment, which scores segmentations based on how well their *segments* match, rather than their boundaries (Section 3). We show that our metric aligns more closely with human intuition than existing metrics (Section 4) and quantify the errors encountered by those metrics (Section 5). Code for our new metric and relevant materials are made publicly available at https://github.com/sierra98x/resources.

2 Existing Metrics

Current segmentation similarity metrics fall into two categories: **window-based** metrics try to capture errors by sliding a window across the element sequence T and comparing the boundaries in both segmentations; in contrast, **edit-based** metrics try to find a sequence of boundary edit operations that would make both segmentations equal.

2.1 Window-Based Metrics

WindowDiff (Pevzner and Hearst, 2002) and P_k (Beeferman et al., 1999) are the most popular similarity metrics currently used.

$\mathbf{P_k}$ is defined as "the probability that a random pair of elements, k elements apart, will be classified inconsistently by two segmentations as belonging/not belonging in the same segment." Given an element sequence T of length n, a reference segmentation r, and an alternate segmentation h, a window of size $k+1$ is slid across the elements (k is recommended by the authors to be half the average segment size in r); at every window position, the segmentations are compared based on the elements at the edges of the window, e_i and e_{i+k}; if the segmentations disagree on whether the elements belong in the same segment, a penalty of 1 is added; finally, the penalty sum is divided by the number of windows:

$$P_k(r,h) = \frac{1}{n-k} \sum_{i=1,j=i+k}^{i=n-k} \delta(r_{i,j}) \neq \delta(h_{i,j})$$

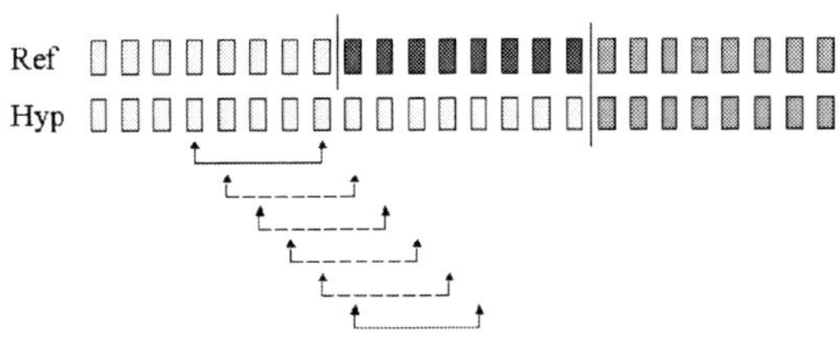

Figure 4: Illustration of P_k and WindowDiff with $k=4$ (Pevzner and Hearst, 2002). Penalized windows indicated by dashed lines.

where $\delta(x_{i,j})$ is true iff e_i, e_j are in the same segment in segmentation x.

There are a variety of situations where P_k penalizes errors inconsistently (Pevzner and Hearst, 2002): it penalizes missing boundaries more than extra boundaries, fails to penalize extra boundaries that are in close proximity to correct boundaries, and is also quite sensitive to the window size k.

WindowDiff improves on P_k by using a different penalty criteria. Instead of comparing the elements at the window edges, WindowDiff counts the number of boundaries between the edge elements and assigns a penalty of 1 if the number is inconsistent between segmentations:

$$\text{WD}(r,h) = \frac{1}{n-k} \sum_{i=1,j=i+k}^{i=n-k} b(r_{i,j}) \neq b(h_{i,j})$$

where $b(x_{i,j})$ is the boundary count between e_i and e_j in segmentation x.

WindowDiff solves some of P_k's inconsistency problems, but still produces unintuitive scores and penalizes errors at the edges of the element sequence less than those towards the middle (a weakness shared with P_k). WindowDiff is usually reported along with P_k rather than instead of it.

Lamprier et al. (2007) present a simple correction to WindowDiff: adding $k-1$ extra elements at the beginning and end of the sequence T ensures that errors at every PBP are penalized an equal number of times. Further, they argue that WindowDiff is unfair because the expected score of a random segmenter depends on the number of boundaries in the reference r. To address this, they present two normalized versions of WindowDiff, **NWin** and **TNWin**, which take into account the expected WindowDiff scores of two random segmentations with the same cardinality as the reference and hypothesis segmentations being evaluated.

Finally, Scaiano and Inkpen (2012) propose **WinPR**, which uses the element padding correction from (Lamprier et al., 2007) and categorizes the errors at each window into true positives (correct boundaries), false positives (extra boundaries), true negatives (correct empty PBPs), and false negatives (missing boundaries), allowing for finer-grained error analysis and the calculation of F1 scores.

Although WinPR is an improvement on WindowDiff, it has not been widely adopted by the community and, like NWin, depends on the correctness of WindowDiff; the improvements presented in WinPR and NWin do not offset the core theoretical issues with WindowDiff. The th Thus, throughout the rest of this paper, we will limit our discussion of window-based metrics to WindowDiff and P_k.

2.2 Edit-Based Metrics

Edit-based segmentation similarity metrics are based on ideas introduced by Damerau-Levenshtein string edit distance (Damerau, 1964; Levenshtein, 1966) and partially replicated by Generalized Hamming Distance (Bookstein et al., 2002). The general idea is that every segmentation can be framed as a sequence of boundaries, each placed at a specific position. If we define a set of edit operations (with costs) that can modify any sequence of boundaries, the distance between two segmentations can be measured as the cost of the optimal sequence of edit operations required to make the two segmentations equal. The optimal sequence of edit operations is equivalent to a boundary alignment between the segmentations.

Segmentation Similarity (Fournier and Inkpen, 2012) and Boundary Similarity (Fournier and Inkpen, 2012) are both based on the same set of boundary edit operations:

- Match: Mark a boundary as correct (no cost).
- Addition/Deletion: Insert or delete a boundary.
- K-Transposition: Shift a boundary to the left or right by a max of k units[2]. Default $k = 1$[3].
- Substitution: Replace a boundary with one of a different type[4].

Segmentation Similarity (S) (Fournier and Inkpen, 2012) assigns a constant cost to all edit operations and normalizes the resulting distance based on the total number of possible boundaries for the given element sequence. The idea behind this normalization is to scale the cost based on the potential complexity of the segmentation in question; the intuition is that a constant cost is less impactful on a longer/more complex sequence than it is on a shorter/simpler one.

[2]If a boundary can not be transposed, it must be deleted and a boundary must be inserted at the corresponding location.

[3]When $k > 1$, Segmentation Similarity and Boundary Similarity allow transpositions across existing boundaries.

[4]Only required for multi-type segmentation.

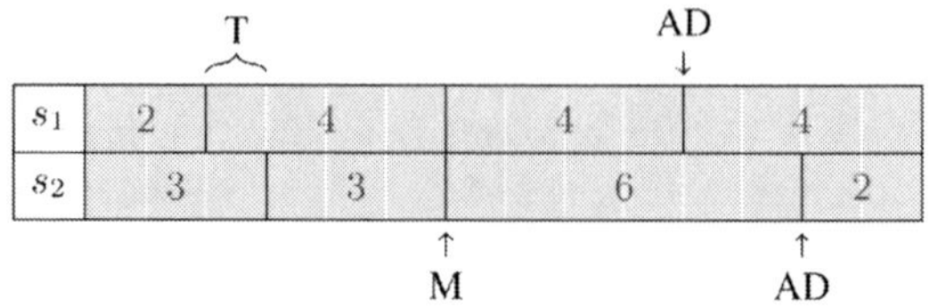

Figure 5: Example segmentation alignment with boundary edit operations (Fournier, 2013).

Let A_e, T_e S_e be the sets of the optimal boundary addition/deletion, transposition, and substitution operations required to align a pair of segmentations, h_1 and h_2, over a sequence of elements T. Further, let b be the number of boundary types (in the case of multi-type segmentation) available.

$$S(h_1, h_2, T) = 1 - \frac{|A_e| + |T_e| + |S_e|}{b(|T| - 1)}$$

Fournier and Inkpen argue that S a) produces scores that align favorably with human intuition compared to WindowDiff in three key examples, b) has reduced sensitivity to variations in segment sizes compared to WindowDiff, and c) produces more accurate inter-annotator agreement scores than WindowDiff in one dataset. It is also noted that S can be used for multi-type segmentation, where traditional window-based methods can not.

Boundary Similarity (B) (Fournier, 2013) improves S by introducing weighted-costs transpositions/substitutions, improving the edit distance normalization factor, and producing a confusion matrix from the edit operations to calculate F1 scores.

$$B(h_1, h_2, T) = 1 - \frac{|A_e| + t(T_e, k) + s(S_e, B_t)}{|A_e| + |T_e| + |S_e| + |M|}$$

where k is the maximum transposition distance, $|M|$ is the number of matching boundary pairs between the two segmentations, B_t is the set of boundary types, and t and s are functions that return the weighted sums of T_e (transpositions) and S_e (substitutions). The normalization factor in B produces behavior that aligns more closely with human judgement than in S.

When comparing scores generated by WindowDiff, P_k, S, and B on a handful of key examples, Fournier argues that B produces behavior that falls more in line with human intuition. B is further shown on one dataset to produce more reliable inter-annotator agreement scores when compared to S, as S-based inter-annotator agreement scores are shown to be inflated, and also to overcome WindowDiff's bias towards segmentations with few or tightly-clustered boundaries when evaluating three segmenters.

As we will demonstrate Section 4, however, B (and WindowDiff) disregards the impact of individual mistakes on the surrounding segments, which leads to scores that do not align well with human judgement in key scenarios.

3 An Alignment-Based Approach to Segmentation Similarity Scoring

In Section 1, Figure 2, we presented an example that showcased the importance of weighing boundary differences in terms of the impact they have on their corresponding segments. None of the current metrics attempt to do this, and they can not be easily modified to do so.

We propose to measure similarity between a pair of segmentations by comparing the segments defined in them. The intuition is straightforward: two segmentations are similar iff the segments defined by them are similar. Inspired by alignments from machine translation and string comparison, our approach measures segmentation similarity by *finding the maximum likelihood segment alignment and scoring its correctness.*

The concept of the most likely alignment is based on two key observations. First, it only makes sense to align overlapping segments. Second, the overlap between two segments is a good indicator for their "closeness", which tells us if they should be aligned. Thus, the maximum likelihood alignment (MLA) is one where every segment is aligned to its closest other segment.

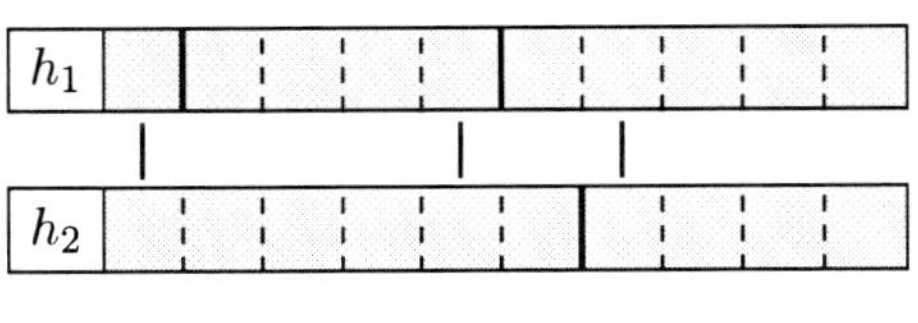

Figure 6: Sample maximum likelihood alignment.

Consider the example alignment in Figure 6: h_2 has fuzzily merged the first two segments in h_1 into a single segment, which results in the third segment from h_1 having a slightly shifted boundary in h_2. Here, it does not make sense to align the third segment in h_1 with the first segment in h_2; even if they overlap, the third segment in h_1 overlaps mainly with the second segment in h_2.

The MLA can be found greedily in $O(m_1 + m_2)$ time, where m_1 and m_2 are the number of segments in h_1 and h_2, respectively. We only need to find the closest segment for any given segment[5]. Figure 7 shows pseudocode for generating the MLA[6].

```
MLA(h1,h2,fn: c):

for each segment p in h1
| for each p-overlapping segment q in h2
| |  closeness = c(p,q)
| r = max c(p,x) segment in h2
| align p (source) to r (target)

repeat for h2
return list of alignment edges
```

Figure 7: Maximum likelihood alignment algorithm.

The MLA depends on the closeness function c. For a generic alignment, where all elements in the element sequence are considered equal, we recommend a simple intersect ratio function i between two segments, x and y:

$$i(x, y) = \frac{\text{intersect}(x, y)}{|x|}$$

The MLA explains the differences between a pair of segmentations in terms of boundaries: in Figure 8, missing/extra boundaries are indicated by the existence of segments with more than one aligned segment. The first segment in h_3 is aligned to two segments in h_4 because h_4 contains an extra boundary; similarly, the third segment in h_4 is aligned to two segments in h_3 because the third segment in h_4 is missing a boundary present in h_3. Furthermore, the existence of pairs of aligned segments with no alignments to any other segments are indicators of matches or transpositions, such as the last segments in h_3 and h_4.

[5]We resolve max closeness ties with Jaccard index scores (see next page); if the tie can not be broken, the left-most segment is chosen to align. Other tie-breaking strategies may be used.

[6]Pseudocode is not $O(m_1 + m_2)$; presented for brevity.

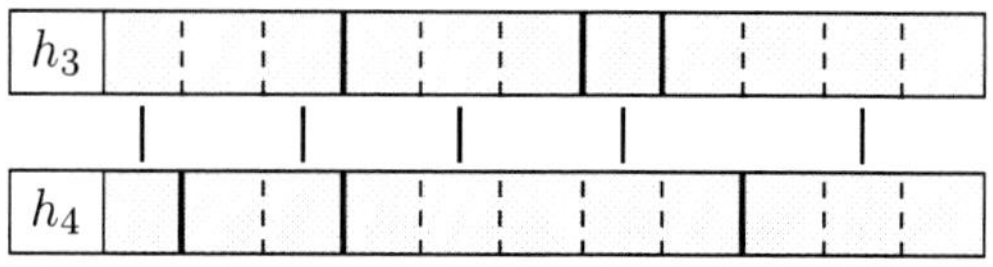

Figure 8: Maximum likelihood alignment.

Once the MLA has been generated, a function should be chosen to map the MLA to a similarity score. A simple approach is to assign a weight to every alignment edge, using a function g, and normalize by the number of edges in the MLA. This generic similarity score A is defined as:

$$A(h_1, h_2, c, g) = \frac{\sum_{\text{edge} \in \text{MLA}(h_1, h_2, c)} g(\text{edge})}{\text{\# edges in MLA}(h_1, h_2, c)}$$

A variety of edge weighting functions can be used: clustering similarity functions such as the rand index, or set similarity metrics such as the overlap coefficient, the Sørensen–Dice coefficient, or the Jaccard index. Both symmetric and asymmetric weighting functions can be used, as the edges generated by the MLA function are directed; we recommend the Jaccard index, since it guarantees a symmetrical segmentation similarity score. Further, the Jaccard version of A can be easily modified to distinguish between "soft" and "hard" mistakes by penalizing edges with weights under some threshold t. The Jaccard index, $J \in [0, 1]$, between two sets S and T is defined as:

$$J(S, T) = \frac{|\text{intersect}(S, T)|}{|\text{union}(S, T)|}$$

The MLA approach with similarity score function A compares favorably to WindowDiff, B, and similar metrics in terms of error analysis, as the MLA structure and edge weights provide information about segmentation differences in terms of both boundaries and segments.

Further, the separation between the MLA algorithm and the similarity score function A makes our approach quite versatile, as the MLA may instead be scored with a different, task-specific similarity scoring function. Consider the reference segmentation r and candidate segmentations h_1 and h_2 in Figure 9: h_1 and h_2 are equidistant to r under A with Jaccard (0.58), B, and WindowDiff. However, for a task like topic segmentation, h_2 may be preferred, as it contains "meta" topics that consistently match two topics each in r, whereas h_1 contains two correct topics, but one really bad third topic, which is a mixture of four topics in r. Conversely, for a task like sentence segmentation, h_1 may be preferred, as it correctly identifies two sentences, where h_2 contains only incorrect sentences. The MLA could be used in conjunction with a similarity scoring function that imposes exponentially increasing penalties on segments with many alignments to favor h_2, while a scoring function that considers only the highest weighted edge for any given segment would favor h_1.

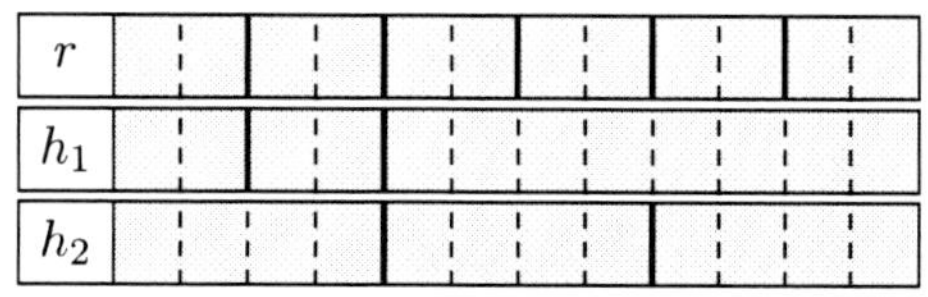

Figure 9: Reference segmentation and two candidates.

Finally, as we will show in the following section, a straightforward implementation of A, using the intersect ratio i as the closeness function and the Jaccard index J as the edge weight function, behaves favorably compared to current metrics in a key set of examples.

4 Similarity Metric Behavior

In this section, we outline three erratic behaviors from B and WindowDiff, and compare these metrics against A in a series of example segmentations.

4.1 Cross-Boundary Transpositions

Since B and WindowDiff look at each boundary in isolation, they consider all boundary shifts with the same distance to be equally bad, resulting in *pseudo-transpositions*, where one boundary crosses over another, being penalized the same as standard transpositions. It is easy to argue against this, as a boundary shift that crosses another boundary is not a true transposition, but rather a pair of over- and under-segmentations. This is illustrated in Figure 10, where h_1 is clearly closer to the reference segmentation r than is h_2. h_1 transposes the leftmost boundary of r two units to the right, while h_2 pseudo-transposes the rightmost boundary two units to the left, crossing over the middle boundary. h_2 results in an oversegmentation of the second segment and undersegmentation of the third and fourth segments of r. A correctly identifies this behavior because it works on segment alignments; B and WindowDiff, however, incorrectly score h_1 and h_2 as being equally close to r.

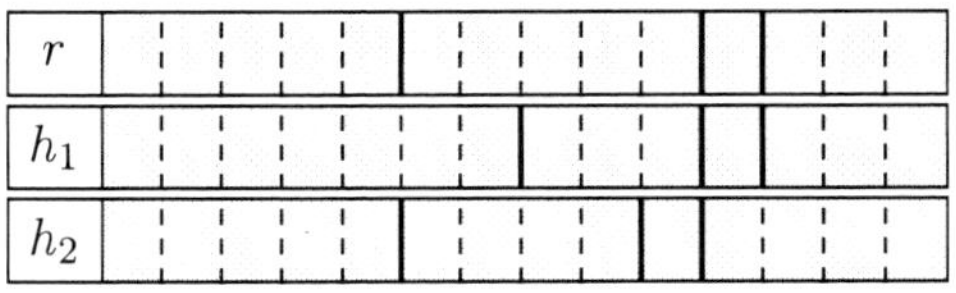

Pair	A	B (k=1)	$1 - \text{WD}$ (k=2)
(r, h_1)	0.83	0.50	0.67
(r, h_2)	0.60	0.50	0.67

Figure 10: Cross-boundary pseudo-transposition.

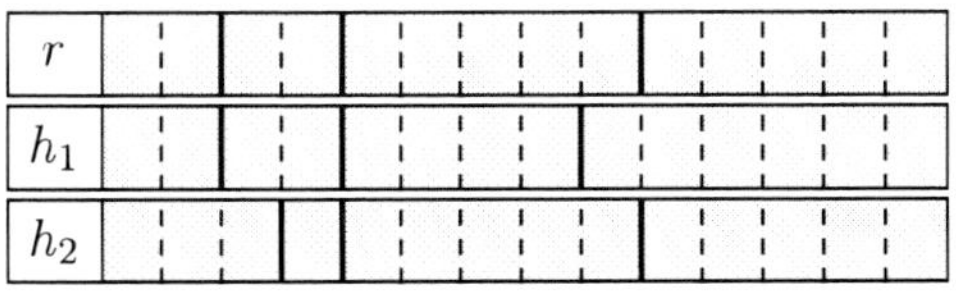

Pair	A	B (k=1)	$1 - \text{WD}$ (k=2)
(r, h_1)	0.91	0.83	0.83
(r, h_2)	0.79	0.83	0.83

Figure 11: Constant cost transpositions.

4.2 Constant Cost Transpositions

B and WindowDiff measure the cost of a transposition based on its absolute distance, without considering the impact it has on the surrounding segments. This quickly leads to problematic behavior, as any given pair of segmentations that contain transpositions with the same distance will get the same score (assuming all other boundary operations are the same). Figure 11 illustrates this problem: B and WindowDiff score both segmentations equally, even though the impact of the transposed boundaries is not the same. Both h_1 and h_2 transpose a boundary by one unit, but in h_1 this results in a single extra/missing token in segments originally of size five, while in h_2, the extra/missing token affects segments originally of size two, impacting them more significantly. A produces proper behavior here, weighing the distance of the transposition in relation to the corresponding segment sizes.

4.3 Vanishing Transpositions

Unlike A, the sensitivity of B and WindowDiff to "near-misses" (transpositions) is regulated by constants. B defines a maximum transposition distance, while WindowDiff utilizes a fixed window size. This causes problematic behavior, as boundary shifts beyond the maximum transposition distance for each metric look the same, which is compounded with the disregard for segment sizes mentioned in the previous subsection.

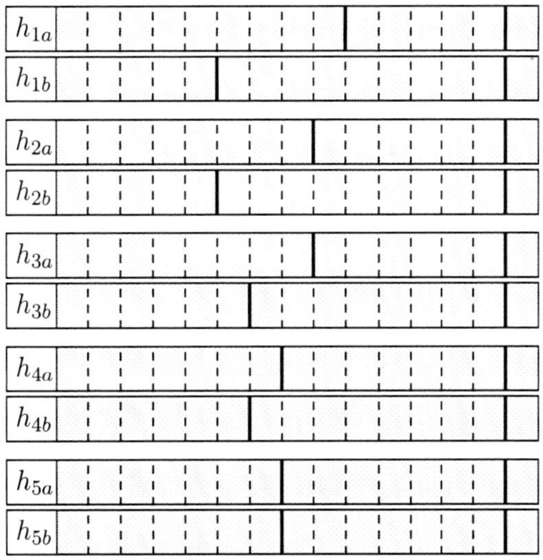

Pair	A	B (k=1)	$1 - \text{WD}$ (k=2)
(h_{1a}, h_{1b})	0.70	0.33	0.69
(h_{2a}, h_{2b})	0.76	0.33	0.69
(h_{3a}, h_{3b})	0.83	0.33	0.69
(h_{4a}, h_{4b})	0.91	0.75	0.85
(h_{5a}, h_{5b})	1	1	1

Figure 12: Vanishing Transpositions

The five segmentation pairs in Figure 12 illustrate this behavior. Although the pairs are ordered by increasing similarity, B and WindowDiff score three out of five pairs equally using their default maximum transposition distance values of 1. The behavior of B is particularly concerning, as it jumps from a relatively high score of 0.75 for the fourth pair, to a very low score of 0.33 for the third pair. In contrast, A correctly matches the first segments and second segments in each pair and considers the relative impact of the transposition given the size of the segments involved.

4.4 Alignment with Human Intuition

We perform a simple experiment to verify whether human judgement of segmentation similarity is sensitive to the kind of errors previously described. We hand-craft 3 reference segmentations r, each with a pair of alternate segmentations, h_1 and h_2, that exemplify each of the problems described in this section (cross-boundary transpositions, constant cost transpositions, and vanishing transpositions). We present each of these 3 instances to 6 NLP graduate students and ask them to indicate whether the alternate segmentations, h_1 and h_2 are equally similar to their reference segmentation r, or whether one is more similar than the other. For all 3 reference segmentations, all 6 students agree that h_1 and h_2 are *not* equally similar to r; in fact, they prefer the candidate segmentation that has the smallest relative impact on the segments being transposed. The document presented to students and the tally of their responses is available in Appendix A.

5 Error Quantification

We quantify the likelihood of WindowDiff and B behaving erroneously through simulation[7]. For the three main error types described in Section 4, we first instantiate every possible reference segmentation r for sequences of length $n \in [5, 20]$. We then try to find two alternate segmentations h_1 and h_2 that B or WindowDiff score as equally similar to r, but in fact are not. Finally, for both B and WindowDiff, we present the ratio of reference segmentations r of length n for which such error-producing pairs h_1 and h_2 exist. We also include A in our simulations and verify that it does not behave erroneously in any of the tested scenarios, so it is not included in our discussion.

To simplify our analysis, we use the Lamprier-corrected version of WindowDiff (Lamprier et al., 2007), which pads the beginning and end of the sequence with $k - 1$ elements. The number of errors produced by this version is a lower bound on the number of errors produced by the original WindowDiff, which penalizes boundary mismatches at the edges less than those at the center.

5.1 Cross-Boundary Transpositions

We consider *B* and WindowDiff (*WD*) to behave erroneously if a pair of segmentations h_1 and h_2 are judged equally similar to r, where h_2 pseudo-transposes a boundary by x units, crossing an existing boundary from r, and h_1 performs a standard transposition on any boundary, i.e., does not transpose across boundaries, also by x units. We only consider h_1 where the two segments on either side of the transposed boundary have Jaccard > 0.5 with their corresponding original segments in r, i.e. the transposition can reasonably be considered a "soft" mistake where the affected segments are still more similar to the originals than not, in contrast to the pseudo-transposition in h_2, where, by crossing a boundary, h_2 effectively oversegments one reference segment and undersegments another (Figure 10).

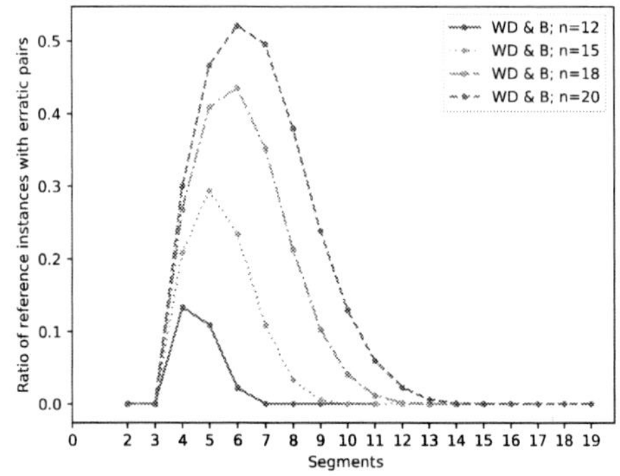

Figure 13: Ratio of potential cross-transposition errors for B and WindowDiff.

Figure 13 shows the percentage of the reference segmentation space for which such erroneous pairs h_1, h_2 exist, for both *B* and *WD* with various sequence lengths n. First, note that *B* and *WD* behave similarly; both *B* and *WD* penalize transpositions based solely on distance, so it is expected that they would judge any erroneous pair h_1, h_2 to be equidistant to r if both h_1, h_2 transpose one boundary by the same distance. Second, the relationship between the number of segments m and the total number of elements in the sequence n reveals an interesting trend: when the number of segments is too low or too high, it is impossible to construct erroneous pairs. For example, erroneous pairs cannot be constructed for $m = 2$ because there is no "second" boundary to transpose across; similarly, when m approaches n, the segments become unit-sized and can no longer be involved in either normal or cross-boundary transpositions. Thirdly, the increasing-decreasing behavior of the curves stems from the "soft" transposition constraint that we impose on h_1. It can be shown that the smallest possible sizes for two adjacent segments containing a "soft" transposition are 5 and 3; this is because the minimum (pseudo-)transposition distance required to cross a boundary is 2 units. Once m is large enough that the average segment size is less than 3, it becomes increasingly hard to find such adjacent segments of sizes 5 and 3, so the number of erroneous h_1, h_2 pairs decreases steadily.

[7]We use the implementation of B from the segeval Python 3 package (Fournier, 2013) and WindowDiff from the Python 3 NLTK package (Bird et al., 2009). Simulation code is available at https://github.com/sierra98x/resources.

5.2 Constant Cost Transpositions

Here, *B* and *WD* behave erroneously if a pair of segmentations h_1 and h_2 are judged equally similar to r, where h_1 "soft" transposes a boundary by x units, and h_2 "hard" transposes any boundary by x units, i.e., the segments on either side of the transposition in h_2 have Jaccard < 0.5 with their corresponding original segments in r.

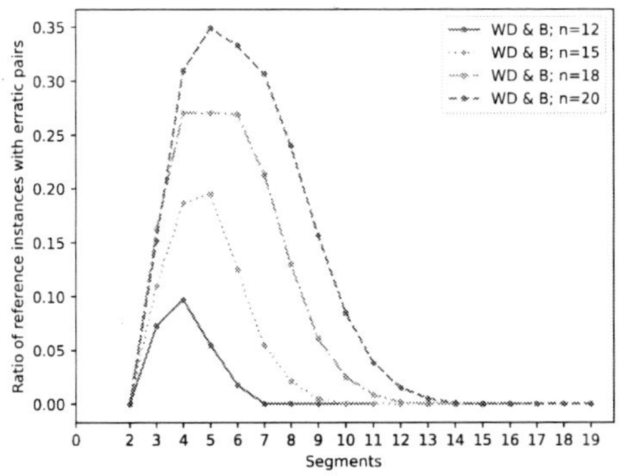

Figure 14: Ratio of potential constant cost transposition errors for B and WindowDiff.

The trend in Figure 14 can be explained as follows: if the ratio between the number of segments m and the sequence length n is too low, the segments are so large that it is rare to find a pair of segments such that transposing their boundary results in a "hard" error; conversely, when the ratio is too high, all segments are small, so it becomes increasingly hard to find "soft" transpositions. Like in Figure 10, *B* and *WD* follow the same trend because h_1, h_2 transpose by the same number of units; in addition, we see once again that the number of erroneous pairs starts decreasing once the average segment size (*m/n* ratio) drops below 3.

5.3 Vanishing Transpositions

Here, *B* and *WD* behave erroneously if a pair of segmentations h_1 and h_2 are judged equally similar to r, where h_1 transposes a boundary by x units and h_2 transposes the same boundary by $y > x$ units. Again, we only consider h_1 with "soft" transpositions, where the two segments on either side of the transposed boundary have Jaccard > 0.5 with the corresponding original segments from r; h_2 may have a "soft" or "hard" transposition.

Figure 15 differs from Figures 13 and 14 in that *B* and *WD* behave differently for this error type, which makes sense, given that this is the only ex-

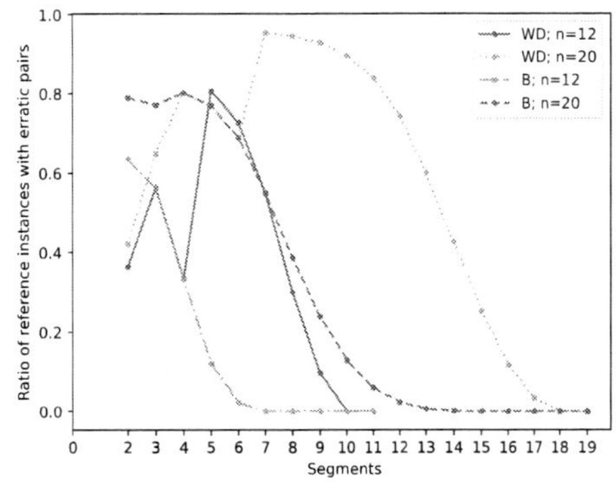

Figure 15: Ratio of potential vanishing transposition errors for B and WindowDiff.

periment where h_1, h_2 do not transpose by the same number of units: recall that *B* has a fixed maximum transposition size (default value of 1) beyond which transpositions can not be distinguished, while *WD*'s maximum transposition size depends on the window size k, which is equal to half the average segment size, and thus a function of m and n. The global peak in error rate for *WD* occurs when k is so small that no transpositions are allowed; *B* makes fewer mistakes than *WD* because *B* always allows transpositions of size 1. The local minimum between the first and second maxima for *WD* is caused by the step-wise nature of the k function, since the window size must be a whole number.

6 Limitations

While we have seen that A performs favorably when compared to B and WindowDiff, further investigation may be warranted on the general MLA approach. First, the space of potential alignments for a given pair of segmentations can be quite large, and while a simple greedy intersection ratio approach generates sensible alignments, edge cases may exhibit undesirable behavior.

Consider Figure 16: h_0 deletes a boundary from r, while h_1 and h_2 transpose it different distances. However, A gives h_2 a worse score than h_0; this behavior is explained by the MLA between r and h_2 containing a diagonal alignment between the first segment in h_2 and the second segment in r, due to the first segment in r being very small — so small that transposing its boundary by two units is considered worse than deleting it. The intersect ratio closeness function in A uses segment size to distinguish "soft" and "hard" transpositions; as we

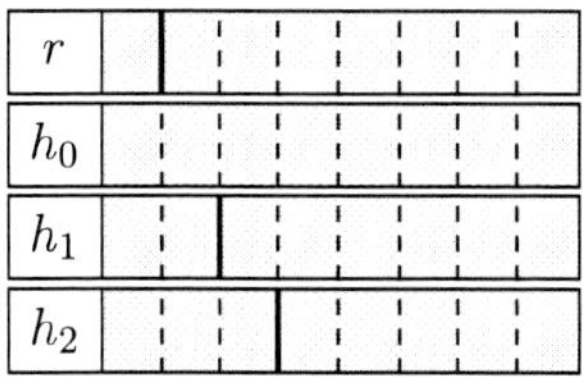

Pair	A	B (k=1)	$1 - \text{WD}$ (k=2)
(r, h_0)	0.67	0.50	0.88
(r, h_1)	0.79	0.75	0.88
(r, h_2)	0.58	0.33	0.62

Figure 16: Intricate behavior of A.

saw in Figure 12, when the segments are longer, A will match the left and right segments of a two-unit transposition with the original segments in r, resulting in a similarity score greater than h_0.

However, specific applications may lean towards favoring "soft" transpositions over deletions regardless of segment size, which would require a) a different segment-to-segment closeness function c, or b) maximizing some global MLA function, such as Maximum Spanning Tree.

Second, in Figure 9, we presented a reference segmentation r and two different candidate segmentations h_1 and h_2 that are scored equally by A, B, and *WD*. Here, the fact that A can not distinguish between them is not due to the MLA, as there is only one possible alignment between each candidate and r. Thus, it may be of interest to develop more sophisticated MLA scoring functions, in order to distinguish between h_1 and h_2.

7 Conclusion

In this paper, we present a new alignment-based approach to text segmentation similarity scoring and present a new similarity metric A. We show that, unlike A, the most advanced segmentation similarity metrics, B and WindowDiff, behave erratically in three key scenarios. We discuss the versatility of alignment-based approaches when paired with different alignment and scoring functions, and show that A, B, and WindowDiff exhibit intricate behaviors that should be explored in the future. We make our implementation of A publicly available[8] in hope that it encourages the NLP community to explore more sophisticated approaches to text segmentation similarity scoring.

[8]Our implementation of A, along with relevant materials, can be found at https://github.com/sierra98x/resources.

References

Doug Beeferman, Adam Berger, and John Lafferty. 1999. Statistical models for text segmentation. *Machine learning*, 34(1):177–210.

Steven Bird, Ewan Klein, and Edward Loper. 2009. *Natural language processing with Python: analyzing text with the natural language toolkit.* " O'Reilly Media, Inc.".

Abraham Bookstein, Vladimir A. Kulyukin, and Timo Raita. 2002. Generalized hamming distance. *Inf. Retr.*, 5(4):353–375.

Fred J. Damerau. 1964. A technique for computer detection and correction of spelling errors. *Commun. ACM*, 7(3):171–176.

Chris Fournier. 2013. Evaluating text segmentation using boundary edit distance. In *Proceedings of the 51st Annual Meeting of the Association for Computational Linguistics (Volume 1: Long Papers)*, pages 1702–1712, Sofia, Bulgaria. Association for Computational Linguistics.

Chris Fournier and Diana Inkpen. 2012. Segmentation similarity and agreement. In *Proceedings of the 2012 Conference of the North American Chapter of the Association for Computational Linguistics: Human Language Technologies*, pages 152–161, Montréal, Canada. Association for Computational Linguistics.

Sylvain Lamprier, Tassadit Amghar, Bernard Levrat, and Frederic Saubion. 2007. On evaluation methodologies for text segmentation algorithms. In *19th IEEE International Conference on Tools with Artificial Intelligence(ICTAI 2007)*, volume 2, pages 19–26.

Vladimir I. Levenshtein. 1966. Binary codes capable of correcting deletions, insertions and reversals. In *Soviet Physics Doklady*, volume 10, page 707.

Lev Pevzner and Marti A. Hearst. 2002. A critique and improvement of an evaluation metric for text segmentation. *Computational Linguistics*, 28(1):19–36.

Martin Scaiano and Diana Inkpen. 2012. Getting more from segmentation evaluation. In *Proceedings of the 2012 Conference of the North American Chapter of the Association for Computational Linguistics: Human Language Technologies*, pages 362–366, Montréal, Canada. Association for Computational Linguistics.

A Human Judgement Test

The following text was presented to 6 graduate NLP students to verify their sensibility to cross-boundary transposition, constant cost transposition, and vanishing transposition errors. For clarity, we have added error type labels to the questions, but the students were not shown these labels during the evaluation.

```
Intro====

A segmentation splits a sequence of elements
into meaningful, non-overlapping segments.

Ex. Split a transcript into utterances:

I did not go to work yesterday, did you? |
No, Johnathan filled in for me.

Note: For simplicity, the elements in every
segmentation example are masked.

The previous example would look like this:
A.A.A.A.A.A.A.A.A|B.B.B.B.B.B

Questions===

For each of the following instances, 3 segmentations
are presented: Gold, H1, and H2.

Determine whether H1 or H2 is closer to gold, or if
they are the same, according to your interpretation.

-AT [Cross-Boundary Transposition (LABEL NOT SHOWN)]

A|B|C.C.C.C.C.C.C.C.C.C|D.D.D.D.D.D.D.D.D.D - Gold
A.B|C|C.C.C.C.C.C.C.C.C|D.D.D.D.D.D.D.D.D.D - H1

A|B|C.C.C.C.C.C.C.C.C.C|D.D.D.D.D.D.D.D.D.D - Gold
A|B|C.C.C.C.C.C.C.C.C.C.D.D|D.D.D.D.D.D.D.D - H2

-RTC [Constant Cost Transposition (LABEL NOT SHOWN)]

A|B.B|C.C.C.C.C.C.C.C|D.D.D.D.D.D.D.D - Gold
A|B.B|C.C.C.C.C.C.C.D|D.D.D.D.D.D.D - H1


A|B.B|C.C.C.C.C.C.C.C|D.D.D.D.D.D.D.D - Gold
A.B|B|C.C.C.C.C.C.C.C|D.D.D.D.D.D.D.D - H2


-VT [Vanishing Transposition (LABEL NOT SHOWN)]

A.A.A.A.A.A.A.A|B.B.B.B.B.B.B.B - Gold
A.A.A.A.A.A.A.A.B.B|B.B.B.B.B.B - H1

A.A.A.A.A.A.A.A|B.B.B.B.B.B.B.B - Gold
A.A.A.A.A.A.A.A.B.B.B|B.B.B.B.B - H2
```

The students achieved perfect agreement on the evaluation and judged as more similar the candidate segmentation with the smallest impact on the gold segments.

Instance	H1 Votes	H2 Votes	Same Votes
AT	0	6	0
RTC	6	0	0
VT	6	0	0

Table 1: Human evaluation results

Enhancing the Transformer Decoder with Transition-based Syntax

Leshem Choshen
Department of Computer Science
Hebrew University of Jerusalem
leshem.choshen@mail.huji.ac.il

Omri Abend
Department of Computer Science
Hebrew University of Jerusalem
omri.abend@mail.huji.ac.il

Abstract

Notwithstanding recent advances, syntactic generalization remains a challenge for text decoders. While some studies showed gains from incorporating source-side symbolic syntactic and semantic structure into text generation Transformers, very little work addressed the decoding of such structure. We propose a general approach for tree decoding using a transition-based approach. Examining the challenging test case of incorporating Universal Dependencies syntax into machine translation, we present substantial improvements on test sets that focus on syntactic generalization, while presenting improved or comparable performance on standard MT benchmarks. Further qualitative analysis addresses cases where syntactic generalization in the vanilla Transformer decoder is inadequate and demonstrates the advantages afforded by integrating syntactic information.[1]

1 Introduction

In parallel to the impressive achievements of large neural networks in a variety of NLP fields, more and more work emphasizes the importance of the inductive biases models possess and the types of generalizations they make (Welleck et al., 2021; Csordás et al., 2021; Ontanón et al., 2021). Syntactic generalization has been repeatedly identified as a problem in text generation (Linzen and Baroni, 2020; Hu et al., 2020), an issue that we address here. Importantly, language models may fail, sometimes unexpectedly, on constructions that can be reliably parsed using standard syntactic parsers. In this work, we propose a method for incorporating syntax into the decoder to assist in mitigating these challenges, focusing on NMT as a test case.

The use of (mostly syntactic) structure in machine translation dates back to the early days of the field (Lopez, 2008). While focus has shifted to string-to-string methods since the introduction of neural methods, considerable work has shown gains from integrating linguistic structure into NMT and text generation technologies. We briefly survey such methods in §7.

Incorporating target-side syntax has been less frequently addressed than source-side syntax, possibly due to the additional conceptual and technical complexity it entails, as it requires to jointly generate the translation and its syntactic structure. In addition to linearizing the structure into a string, that allows to easily incorporate source and target structure (Aharoni and Goldberg, 2017b; Nadejde et al., 2017), several works generated the nodes of the syntactic tree using RNNs (Gū et al., 2018; Wang et al., 2018; Wu et al., 2017). Others have shown gains from multi-task training of a decoder with a syntactic parser (Eriguchi et al., 2016). However, we are not aware of any Transformer-based architecture to support the integration of target-side structure in the form of a tree or a graph. Addressing this gap, we propose a flexible architecture for integrating graphs into a Transformer decoder.

Our approach is based on predicting the output tree as a sequence of transitions (§3), following the transition-based tradition in parsing (Nivre, 2003, and much subsequent work). The method (presented in §4) is based on generating the structure incrementally, as a sequence of transitions, as is customary in transition-based parsers. However, unlike standard linearization approaches, our proposed decoder re-encodes the intermediate graph (and not only the generated tokens), thus allowing the decoder to take advantage of the hitherto produced structure in its further predictions.

In §2, we discuss the possibilities offered by such decoders, that do not only auto-regress on their previous outputs, but also on (symbolic) structures defined by those outputs. Indeed, a decoder thus built can condition both on information it did not predict (e.g., external knowledge bases) and

[1]Code supplied in github.com/borgr/nematus

Proceedings of the 26th Conference on Computational Natural Language Learning (CoNLL), pages 384 - 404
December 7-8, 2022 ©2022 Association for Computational Linguistics

information predicted later on. We introduce *bidirectional attention* into the decoder, that allows token representations to encode the following tokens that were predicted. This is similar to the bidirectional attention in the encoder, where any token can attend to any token, and not only to preceding ones.

Our architecture is flexible, supporting decoding not only into trees, but into any graph structure for which a transition system exists. We test two architectures for incorporating the syntactic graph. One inputs the graph into a Graph Convolutional Network (GCN; Kipf and Welling, 2016), and another dedicates an attention head to point at the syntactic parent of each token, which does not yield any increase in the number of parameters.

We assess in §6 the impact of the proposed architecture on syntactically challenging translation cases (Choshen and Abend, 2019) and in general. We experiment with a 4 layered model in three target languages, and a 6 layered on En-De. Due to the high computational cost, we experiment with the model on a single language pair only. We find that on the syntactic challenge sets proposed by Choshen and Abend (2019), the proposed decoder achieves substantial improvements over the vanilla decoder, which do not diminish (and even slightly improve) when increasing the size of the model. In addition, evaluating on the standard MT benchmarks, we find that the syntactic decoders outperform the vanilla Transformer for the smaller model size on all examined language pairs: on the English-German (En-De) and German-English (De-En) challenge sets and on En-De, De-En and English-Russian (En-Ru) test sets, and obtain comparable results to the vanilla when experimenting with a larger model on En-De. Finally, we analyse the different modifications in isolation, finding that the ablated versions' performance resides between the full model and the vanilla decoder.

2 Decoding Approach

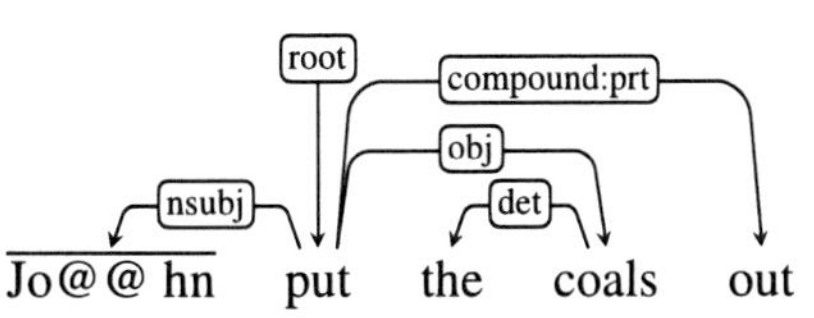

Example 1: Target-side structure reduces the ambiguity of "put". De source: "John löschte die Kohlen" (lit. John put-out the coals).

Disambiguating and connecting distant words is a known challenge in NMT (Avramidis et al., 2020). In Example 1 to disambiguate "put" as not having the sense "lay" but "extinguish", "out" must be considered. To achieve this from the autoregressed output, the decoder's representation may need to be re-computed after predicting "out". We note that while source-side information can potentially be used to disambiguate "put", it may still be beneficial to enhance the auto-regressive decoder with disambiguating information.

Current implementations impose an architectural bias, namely, a decoded token's representation may not attend to future tokens. Transformer models mask attention in the following manner (we did not find any alternative methods): Token embeddings attend only to previously generated tokens, even when the following tokens are already known. This practice "ensures that the predictions for position i can depend only on the known outputs at positions less than i" (Vaswani et al., 2017).

We propose to allow attending to any known token (Fig. 1), as done on the encoder side. Due to its conceptual resemblance to Bidirectional RNN, we name this *Bidirectional Transformer* or biTran.

Formally, let $o_1 \dots o_n$ be a hitherto predicted sequence and d max sentence length. Attention is $softmax\,(L + M)$ where $L \in \mathbb{R}^{d \times d}$ are the logits and $M \in \mathbb{R}^{d \times d}$ is a mask. Hence, $M(i, j) = -\infty$ masks a token j from representation i.

$$M_v(i,j) = \begin{cases} 0 & j < i \\ -\infty & o.s. \end{cases}$$

while Bidirectional attention mask is

$$M_{bi}(i,j) = \begin{cases} 0 & n < j \\ -\infty & o.s. \end{cases}$$

This change does not introduce any new parameters or hyperparameters, but still increases the expressivity of the model. We note, however, that this modification does prevent some commonly implemented speed-ups relying on unidirectionality (e.g., in NEMATUS; Sennrich et al., 2017).

Apart from the technical contribution, we emphasize that this and the following approaches take advantage of attention-based models being stateless. Transformers can, therefore, be viewed as conditional language models, namely as models for producing a distribution for the next word, given the generated prefix and source sentence. Viewing them as such opens possibilities that were not native to RNNs, such as predicting only partial outputs and conditioning on per-token or non-autoregressed context (see App. A).

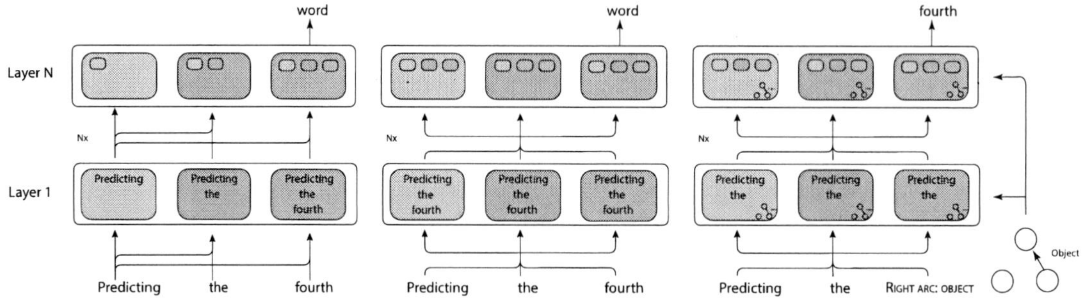

Figure 1: Illustration of the information fed into the decoder with each method. Left: Vanilla. Center: Bidirectional Decoder Right: Structural Decoder. At a given step Bidirectional Decoder attends to all predicted words and Syntactic Transformer predicts edges and receives both edges and words as input.

3 Transition-based Structure Generation

We turn to describe how we represent structure within the proposed decoder.

We generate the target-side structure with a transition-based approach, motivated by the practical strength of such methods, as well as their sequential nature, which fits neural decoders well. We therefore augment the vocabulary with transitions. Our work is inspired by RNNG (Dyer et al., 2016), a conceptually similar architecture that was developed for RNNs. At each step, the input to the decoder includes the tokens and the parse graph that was generated thus far. As edges and their tokens are not generated simultaneously (but rather by different transitions; see below), we rely on bidirectional attention to update the past embeddings when a new edge connects previously generated tokens. In this section, we present the syntactic transitions and in the next (§4), the ways we incorporate it back into the model.

In this work, we represent syntax through Universal Dependencies (UD; Nivre et al., 2016), but note that other syntactic and semantic formalisms that have transition-based parsers (Hershcovich et al., 2018; Stanojević and Steedman, 2020; Oepen et al., 2020) fit the framework as well. We select UD due to its support for over 100 languages and its status as the de facto standard for syntactic representation.

We base our transition system on arc-standard (Nivre, 2003), which can produce any projective tree. Both contain a transition connecting two words by a labeled edge. However, we replace SHIFT that reads the next word by SUBWORD$_t$ generating a new sub-word t. Sub-words are generated successively until a full word is formed. To avoid suboptimal representation of transition tokens, we add the edges going through them to the graph (e.g., the edge LEFT-ARC:*det* $\xrightarrow{\text{det}}$ *the*).

We denote with f the transition functions updating a word stack Σ and the labeled graph G. If a, b are the top and second words in Σ respectively, and x a transition, then $f(x; \Sigma)$ is defined as:

x (token)	Σ	Edges Added
$Subword_t$	t,a,b	$\emptyset$
LEFT-ARC:*l*	a	$a \xrightarrow{l} b, x \xrightarrow{l} b, a \xrightarrow{l} x$
RIGHT-ARC:*l*	b	$b \xrightarrow{l} a, x \xrightarrow{l} a, b \xrightarrow{l} x$

For brevity, we denote an edge from/to every subword of a as an edge from/to a. Overall, the translation sequence to create the graph in Example 1 is: Jo@@ hn put LEFT-ARC:*nsubj* the coals LEFT-ARC:*det* RIGHT-ARC:*obj* out RIGHT-ARC:*compound:prt* (more details in App. B)

4 Regressing on Generated Structure

As discussed in §2, the state-less nature of the Transformer allows re-encoding not only the previous predictions, but any information that can be computed based on them. So far, we proposed to autoregress on the syntactic structure, token by token. However, as f is deterministic, learning to emulate it, is pointless. Instead, we can autoregress on the generated graph itself, $G = f(o_1 \ldots o_n)$, as well as the encoder output, $o_1 \ldots o_n$.

Our approach is modular and works with any graph encoding method. We experiment with two prominent methods for source-side graph encoding.

GCN Encoder. Graph Convolutional Networks (GCN; Kipf and Welling, 2016) are a type of graph neural network. GCNs were used successfully by previous work to encode source-side syntactic and semantic structure for NMT (Bastings et al., 2017; Marcheggiani et al., 2018). The GCN layers are stacked immediately above the embedding layer.

The GCN contains weights per edge type and label as well as gates, that allow placing less emphasis on the syntactic cue if the network so chooses. Gating is assumed to help against noisy structure, which machine output is expected to be. See ablation experiments to assess the impact of gating in §6.3.

Following Kipf and Welling (2016), we introduce 3 edge types. *Self* from a token to itself, *Left* to the parent tokens and *Right* from the parents.

A GCN layer over input layer h, a node v and a graph G containing nodes of size d, with activation ρ, edge directions dir, labels lab, and a function N from a node in G to its neighbors is

$$\mathbf{gcn}(h, v, G) = \rho\Big(\sum_{u \in \mathcal{N}(v)} g_{u,v} \cdot f_{u,v}\Big)$$

where $f_{u,v}$ are graph weighted embedding:

$$f_{u,v} = \big(W_{\text{dir}(u,v)}\,\mathbf{h}_u + \mathbf{b}_{\text{lab}(u,v)}\big)$$

and $g_{u,v}$ is the applied gate:

$$g_{u,v} = \sigma\Big(\mathbf{h}_u \cdot \hat{\mathbf{w}}_{\text{dir}(u,v)} + \hat{b}_{\text{lab}(u,v)}\Big)$$

where σ is the logistic sigmoid function and $\hat{\mathbf{w}}_{\text{dir}(u,v)} \in \mathbb{R}^d$, $W \in \mathbb{R}^{d \times d}$, $\hat{b}_{\text{lab}(u,v)} \in \mathbb{R}$, $\mathbf{b} \in \mathbb{R}^d$ are the learned parameters for the GCN.

Attending to Parent Token. The second re-encoding method we test, PARENT, dedicates an attention head only to the parent(s) of the given token. Commonly, the parent is given by an external parser (Hao et al., 2019) or learned locally in each layer, to focus the attention (Strubell et al., 2018). Unlike such approaches, we define the parents by the self-generated graph. To allow ignoring it when preferable or when no parent was generated, we also allow attending to the current token. To recap, for a token o_i, we mask all but o_i and its parents.

PARENT differs from GCN considerably. On the one hand, PARENT requires minimal architectural changes and no additional hyperparameters. It also affects different network parts, some attention heads, rather than an additional embedding. On the other hand, only GCN represents the labels and the whole graph, specifically children. By considering both architectures, we show that graph methods for the encoder (Bastings et al., 2017) may be easily adapted to the decoder, demonstrating the flexibility of the proposed framework.

5 Experimental Setup

Metrics. We report BLEU (Papineni et al., 2002) and chrF+ (Popovic, 2017) and note that chrF+ has been deemed more reliable (Ma et al., 2019).

Model. Medium (large) models are trained with batch size 128, embedding size 256 (512), 4 (6) decoder and encoder blocks, 8 attention heads (PARENT replaces one). We train for 90K (150K) steps, where empirically some saturation is reached, allowing a fair system comparison (Popel and Bojar, 2018). The GCN architecture includes 2 layers with residual connections. Parses are extracted by UDPipe (Straka, 2018), UD2.0 for English and German and UD2.5 syntagrus for Russian.

Unable to identify a preexisting implementation, we implemented labeled sparse GCNs with gating in Tensorflow. Implementation mostly focused on memory considerations, and was optimized for runtime when possible. More on implementation details, filtering and preprocessing in App. B.

Language Pairs. We experiment on 3 language pairs with 3 target languages: English (De-En), German (En-De) and Russian (En-Ru). We use the WMT16 data (Bojar et al., 2016) for En-De, and either the clean News commentary or the full noisy WMT20 data (Barrault et al., 2020) for En-Ru.

Test sets. Newstest 2012 served as a development set. To measure the overall system performance we used newstest 2013-15.

To test syntactic generalization, we used the challenge sets by Choshen and Abend (2019). Those are sub-sets of the books and newstest corpora in En↔De, automatically filtered by a syntactic parser to contain *lexical long-distance dependencies*. i.e., sentences where two or more non-consecutive words correspond to a single word. E.g., "put ... out" in Example 1 corresponds to the German "löschte" (see also Example 2). Previous work has shown such phenomena to be challenging for present-day NMT systems.

Improving the automatic measures on one such challenge set indicates better performance on a specific phenomenon, while better overall challenge set performance implies better handling of lexical long-distance dependencies. The various challenge set settings are represented as a triplets (dir, p, dom), corresponding to the direction, inspected phenomenon and domain. *Direction* can be either "source" or "target", indicating whether the long distance dependency is in the source or the target reference. Representing the target-side syntax more effectively should improve target challenges and potentially also the source side's, by increasing the model's "awareness" to syntactic structure. By

Source	der gruppe, an die sich der Plan richtet
Gloss	the group to which himself the plan aims
Ref.	the group to whom the plan is aimed
PARENT	the group to which the plan is aimed
Vanilla	the group aimed at the plan

Example 2: A part of a sentence with a long-distance German reflexive verb from the challenge set.

phenomenon, we refer to the syntactic phenomenon in question. There are three test cases for English phenomena and two for German. By *domain* we refer to the origin of the examples, which can be either the sizable *books* corpus (Tiedemann, 2012), or a smaller news corpus (Barrault et al., 2020).

6 Results

We compare the syntactic generalization abilities of the different decoders in §6.1, and continue by examining their overall performance (§6.2). We then assess the contribution of the components of the system through ablation experiments (§6.3) and evaluate the effects of noisy training data (§6.4).

6.1 Syntactic Generalization

We evaluate the syntactic generalization abilities of the models using the syntactic challenge sets. Results (Table 1) show that the medium PARENT (GCN) improves over the Vanilla in 18 (20) of 20 target challenge settings and 19 (19) of 20 in the source challenges. The large model improves in 18/20 of the challenges and gains seem similar or even larger. The latter results suggest that simply using larger models is unlikely to address these gaps in syntactic generalization. See also E.

6.2 Overall Performance

Table 2 presents the test performance for all models. For medium-sized models, the UD-based decoders (GCN and PARENT rows) outperform the vanilla decoder in all settings, with 0.7-1.1 average BLEU improvements and 1-2.4 chrF+. We see a slight advantage to the GCN decoder on De-En, and an advantage to PARENT on En-De and En-Ru. We apply a sign test on all medium size test sets and separately on challenge sets. GCN and PARENT are significantly ($p < 0.01$) better than BiTran, which is significantly better than Vanilla Transformer.

With the large models, PARENT performs comparably to the vanilla (Table 2b), despite the superior results it obtains on syntactic generalization.

6.3 Ablation Experiments

To better understand the contribution of different parts of the architecture, we consider ablated versions (See Table 2 and App. E). Differences are small but consistent. In one, *Linearized*, we train the vanilla Transformer over the transitions, linearized to a string, without encoding the graph through GCN or attention. This is reminiscent of the approaches taken by Aharoni and Goldberg (2017b); Nadejde et al. (2017), albeit with a different form of linearization. Results place Linearized in a clear place: consistently better than the structure-unaware models but not as good as the structure-aware ones.

We turn to experiment with ablated versions of the GCN decoder. *Unlabeled* ignores the labels and relies only on the graph structure, while *Ungated*, also removes the gate g. Gating was hypothesized to be important to avoid over-reliance on the erroneous edges (Bastings et al., 2017; Hao et al., 2019). As our graphs are generated by the network, rather than fed into it by an external parser, this is a good place to test this hypothesis.

Comparing GCN with and without labels, we find their contribution to be limited. Despite some improvement in overall BLEU, as often as not, *Unlabeled* is better on the challenges. We advise caution, however, in interpreting these results, as they may not necessarily indicate that syntactic labels are redundant. There are two technical points to consider. First, the labels' role in GCNs is small, they contribute many hyperparameters, while only affecting a bias term. Presumably, this is an inefficient use that should be addressed in future work. Second, the labels are incorporated also through the transitions, and hence have token embeddings. These could compensate for the disregard of labels.

Unlike labels, gating appears to be crucial. The Ungated scores are lower than the Unlabeled variant in 34/40 challenges. This might indirectly support the hypothesis that gating aids with erroneous parses. It also hints introducing similar mechanisms to PARENT may also be beneficial.

Even BiTran provides a small (up to .28 BLEU,.42 chrF+) but consistent improvement. Indeed, it outperforms the vanilla on average and in 10/12 scores in each pair. We observe a similar trend in the challenge sets (Table 1): BiTran improves scores in 26/40 syntactic challenge sets. In conclusion, bidirectionality in itself is somewhat beneficial, both in general and specifically for ag-

	Preposition Stranding				Particle				Reflexive			
	Books		News		Books		News		Books		News	
	BLEU	chrF+	BLEU	chrF+	BLEU	chrF+	BLEU	chrF+	BLEU	chrF+	BLEU	chrF+
Vanilla	–	–	–	–	4.14	20.72	20.31	49.04	8.08	32.38	20.65	49.09
PARENT	–	–	–	–	**8.37**	**33.78**	**20.54**	**49.99**	**8.60**	**33.49**	**21.39**	**50.01**
(a) Target challenge sets for En-De, large models (Preposition Stranding is omitted as it is not present in German)												
Vanilla	8.70	33.58	**13.82**	43.41	8.59	32.66	**15.28**	44.28	8.54	32.85	18.90	45.82
PARENT	**9.03**	**34.83**	11.53	**45.12**	**8.59**	**33.71**	14.99	**45.90**	**9.05**	**34.11**	**20.79**	**46.73**
(b) Source challenge sets for En-De, large models												
Vanilla	5.95	25.88	9.96	36.96	5.37	24.69	9.39	39.19	5.32	24.71	**16.48**	42.04
PARENT	**6.21**	**28.12**	11.17	**41.13**	5.47	**25.74**	**11.93**	**41.24**	**5.71**	**26.22**	15.56	42.76
GCN	**6.21**	27.27	**11.31**	40.48	**5.51**	25.53	10.35	39.83	5.46	25.70	16.45	**43.03**
(c) Source challenge sets for En-De, medium models												
Vanilla	6.38	27.30	9.18	38.22	6.53	25.70	10.54	38.28	6.15	25.94	17.20	43.12
PARENT	**7.59**	**27.87**	**10.81**	39.22	**7.07**	**26.50**	9.72	39.57	**6.82**	**26.58**	17.56	44.00
GCN	6.33	26.60	10.14	**41.00**	6.69	26.16	**10.60**	**39.81**	6.33	25.83	**20.16**	**44.19**

(d) Target challenge sets for De-En, medium models

Table 1: Results on the syntactic challenge sets, both on the larger sets from books and the smaller ones from news. Models include Vanilla and the GCN and PARENT UD-based decoders. Models can be large or medium in size and trained on En-De or De-En. Challenges are either in the source or target translation. See also App. E.

	2013		2014		2015	
	BLEU	chrF+	BLEU	chrF+	BLEU	chrF+
Vanilla	17.61	45.54	18.23	47.29	19.57	47.50
PARENT	**18.11**	**46.75**	18.6	**48.46**	**20.55**	**49.20**
GCN	18.03	46.43	**18.86**	**48.46**	20.32	48.90
BiTran	17.64	45.66	18.34	47.53	19.33	47.61
Linearized	17.71	46.07	18.39	47.69	19.81	48.36
- Gates	17.81	46.12	18.43	48.08	20.06	48.62
- Labels	17.98	46.40	18.77	48.29	19.96	48.73
(a) Overall performance for En-De, medium models						
Vanilla	**23.64**	53.44	21.94	53.13	**21.60**	**50.84**
PARENT	23.56	**54.08**	**22.11**	**53.77**	20.69	49.16
(b) Overall performance for En-De translation, large models						
Vanilla	21.51	48.20	21.4	48.46	21.44	48.13
PARENT	**22.46**	49.24	21.75	49.41	22.14	49.31
GCN	22.33	49.27	21.76	49.71	**22.43**	**49.73**
BiTran	21.63	48.48	21.42	48.86	21.38	48.54
Linearized	21.95	49.27	21.83	**49.79**	22.2	49.70
- Gates	22.28	49.33	**21.89**	49.68	22.04	49.39
- Labels	22.21	**49.46**	21.75	49.73	22.26	49.57
(c) Overall performance for De-En translation, medium models						
Vanilla	13.2	38.72	17.17	43.69	14.19	40.87
PARENT	**13.61**	**40.67**	**18.53**	**46.44**	**15.75**	**43.57**
GCN	13.25	40.31	17.86	46.09	15.38	43.09

(d) Overall performance for En-Ru

Table 2: Overall performance in different settings. Ablated models (where applicable), appear in the bottom part of the table and include the Bidirectional Transformer (BiTran), with linearized syntax (Linearized), GCN without labels or gating (-Gates) and GCN without labels (-Labels). The syntactic variants consistently outperform the vanilla and ablated variants in the medium size setting and are comparable to it in the large one. The Bidirectional Transformer (BiTran) slightly outperforms Vanilla Transformer.

gregating the syntactically correct context tokens.

As a next step, we compare GCN ablations to PARENT. Like unlabeled GCNs, PARENT does not rely on the labels and successfully provides a different way to incorporate the graph structure. We note that while labels are not incorporated, they appear as transition inputs and can be attended to. Comparing the two architectures, PARENT shows significant gains over Unlabeled GCN. Despite being easier to implement and being much lighter in terms of memory, time and hyperparameters, PARENT generally outperforms Unlabeled GCN in both performance and specific challenges. PARENT is slightly better than unablated? GCN on En-De and slightly worse on De-En. It is better on 3 of 5 De-En phenomena and one of the En-De, when compared to the GCN variant.

6.4 Noise Robustness

Preliminary experiments indicate that syntactic architectures may be more sensitive to noisy training data than the vanilla Transformer, possibly amplifying parser errors. To test this, we trained on the full WMT data for En-Ru, which is mostly crawled data. Results show that the improvement in chrF+ is smaller, 1 point instead of 1.5-2.5 in other settings, and BLEU scores are somewhat worse (see App. §E.1). It seems then that overall, the inclusion of noisy data diminishes the relative improvement.

An alternative explanation to these results may be that our methods contribute less in the presence of more training data. Our positive results on En-De and De-En, that use relatively large amounts of data (4.5M sentence pairs), show that if this is indeed the case, saturation is slow.

6.5 Qualitative Analysis

To complement the automatic challenges, we compile a set of 99 simple subject-verb-object sentences where the German object and subject can swap locations without affecting the meaning. We created three sets of sentences, where the case marking for the subject and object may or may not be ambiguous. For example, *Das Pferd bringt der Vater* and *Der Vater bringt das Pferd* both translate to *the father brings the horse*. Such examples are of particular interest to us here, as the case of the first noun phrase is ambiguous ("Das Pferd" could be either a subject or an object) and is only disambiguated by the case marking of the second one. These cases require some understanding of the syntax to translate correctly. See App. §C.

A native-speaking German annotator, fluent in English, evaluated the medium-size PARENT and Vanilla outputs on these sentences. The ambiguous examples were challenging for both systems, especially the ambiguous case markings. However, overall, PARENT is more robust to the changes in order. Interestingly, both models (PARENT more consistently) translate some sentences to passive voice, keeping both (changed) order and meaning.

7 Related Work

While there are indications that Transformers implicitly learn some syntactic structure when trained as language models or as NMT (e.g., Jawahar et al., 2019; Manning et al., 2020; Don-Yehiya et al., 2022), it is not at all clear whether such information replaces the utility of incorporating syntactic structure. Indeed, a considerable body of work suggests the contrary. Much previous work tested RNN-based and attention-based systems for their ability to make structural generalizations (Welleck et al., 2021; Csordás et al., 2021; Ontañón et al., 2021). Syntactic generalizations seem to pose a particularly difficult challenge (Ravfogel et al., 2019; McCoy et al., 2019). Moreover, while NMT often succeeds in translating inter-dependent linearly distant words, their performance is unstable: the same systems may well fail on other "obvious" cases of the same phenomena (Belinkov and Bisk, 2017; Choshen and Abend, 2019). This evidence provides motivation for efforts such as ours, to incorporate linguistic knowledge into the architecture.

Syntactic structure was used to improve various tasks, including code generation (Chakraborty et al., 2018), question answering (Bogin et al., 2020), automatic proof generation (Gontier et al., 2020) language modelling (Wilcox et al., 2020) and grammatical error correction (Harer et al., 2019). Such approaches, however, are task specific. E.g., the latter makes strong conditional independence assumptions, and is less suitable for MT where the source and target syntax may diverge considerably.

In NMT, some works used structural cues by reinforcement learning (Wieting et al., 2019; Yehudai et al., 2022), but the gain from such methods seems to be limited (Choshen et al., 2020). Aharoni and Goldberg (2017a) and Nadejde et al. (2017) proposed to replace the source and target tokens with a linearized constituency graph or CCG parses. Eriguchi et al. (2016) proposed an RNN to encode the source syntax. Some works suggested modifying RNNs to encode source-side syntax (Chen et al., 2017, 2018; Li et al., 2017). Song et al. (2019) used a graph RNN to encode source-side AMR structures. Few works suggested changes in the Transformer to incorporate source-side syntax: Nguyen et al. (2020) and Bugliarello and Okazaki (2020) proposed a tree-based attention mechanism to encode syntax; Zhang et al. (2019) incorporated the first layers of a parser in addition to the token embeddings. Relatedly, previous work showed gains from using syntactic information for preprocessing (Ponti et al., 2018; Zhou et al., 2019a).

Much fewer works focused on structure-based decoding. Eriguchi et al. (2017), building on Dyer et al. (2016), train a decoder in a multi-task setting of translation and parsing. Notably, unlike in the method we propose, their generated translation is not constrained by the parse during the decoding. Few works proposed alternating between two connected RNNs one translating and one creating a linearized graph using a tree-based RNN (Wang et al., 2018) or transition-based parsing (Wu et al., 2017). Gū et al. (2018) both parse and generate, using a recursive RNN representation.

Other work changed RNNs (Tai et al., 2015) or Transformers to include structural inductive biases, but without explicit syntactic information. Wang et al. (2019) suggested an unsupervised way to train Transformers that learn tree-like structures following the intuition that such representations are more similar to syntax. Shiv and Quirk (2019) encoded tree-structured data in the positional embeddings.

8 Discussion

The work we presented is motivated from several angles. First, we note that Transformers are trained in the same way that former sequence to sequence models are trained (e.g., RNNs) and to many, they are just a better architecture for the same task. Instead, our work emphasizes the possibility of conditional training using Transformers; namely, Transformers should be able to predict the third token given the first two, even without previously predicting them. Although generally not implemented this way, Transformers are already conditional networks, and allow for flexibility not found in RNNs.

The finding that MT quality changes between beginnings and ends of predicted sentences both in RNNs and in Transformers (Liu et al., 2016; Zhou et al., 2019b), further motivates conditional translation. This is often explained by lack of context and disregard for the future tokens. Such future context is used by humans (Xia et al., 2017) and can potentially improve NMT (Tu et al., 2016; Mi et al., 2016). Moreover, as the encoded input is constant throughout the prediction, the varying performance is likely due to the decoder. Attending to all predictions from lower layers, as we propose here, aims to provide more of this required information.[2]

[2]Admittedly, for the very first generated tokens, bidirectionality will not help, as there is nothing to attend to.

Finally, previous work investigated the reasons why incorporating source syntax helps RNNs (Shi et al., 2018) and Transformers (Pham et al., 2019; Sachan et al., 2020). These works show evidence that similar gains can be obtained when incorporating either syntactic trees or non-syntactic, syntactically uninformative, ones. A hypothesis followed, that graph-like architectures are helpful, but that syntactic information is redundant. While GCN creates such an architecture, linearized syntax, arguably PARENT and to some extent the labels GCN component, do not. Still, they allow gains over the vanilla decoder, which challenges this hypothesis.

9 Conclusion

We presented a flexible method for constructing decoders capable of outputting trees and graphs. We show that the improved decoder achieves notable gains in syntactic generalization, and in some settings improves overall performance as well. Our proposal is based on two main modifications to the standard Transformer decoder: (1) autoregression on structure; (2) bidirectional attention in the decoder, which allows recomputing token embeddings in light of newly decoded tokens. Testing on two variants for the decoder, we find that they both show superior syntactic generalization abilities over the vanilla Transformer, and that the gap does not diminish with model size. The method is flexible enough to allow decoding into a wide variety of graph and tree structures.

Our work opens many avenues for future work. One direction would be to focus on conditional networks, training with (intentionally) noisy prefixes, randomly masking "predicted" spans during training (as done in masked language models, Devlin et al., 2019), and data augmentation through hard words or phrases rather than full sentences. Another direction might enhance bidirectionality by allowing "regretting" and changing past predictions. Finally, the work opens possibilities for better incorporating structure into language generators, of incorporating semantic structure and of enforcing meaning preservation (thus targeting hallucinations, Wang and Sennrich, 2020), by incorporating source and target structure together.

10 Acknowledgements

We thank Daniel Lehmann for help the analysis. The work was supported by the Israel Science Foundation (grant no. 929/17) and the Kamin project.

References

Roee Aharoni and Yoav Goldberg. 2017a. Morphological inflection generation with hard monotonic attention. In *Proc. of ACL*, pages 2004–2015.

Roee Aharoni and Yoav Goldberg. 2017b. Towards string-to-tree neural machine translation. In *ACL*.

Eleftherios Avramidis, Vivien Macketanz, Ursula Strohriegel, Aljoscha Burchardt, and Sebastian Möller. 2020. Fine-grained linguistic evaluation for state-of-the-art machine translation. In *Proceedings of the Fifth Conference on Machine Translation*, pages 346–356.

Loïc Barrault, Magdalena Biesialska, Ondrej Bojar, Marta R. Costa-jussà, C. Federmann, Yvette Graham, Roman Grundkiewicz, B. Haddow, Matthias Huck, E. Joanis, Tom Kocmi, Philipp Koehn, Chi kiu Lo, Nikola Ljubesic, Christof Monz, Makoto Morishita, M. Nagata, T. Nakazawa, Santanu Pal, Matt Post, and Marcos Zampieri. 2020. Findings of the 2020 conference on machine translation (wmt20). In *WMT*.

Jasmijn Bastings, Ivan Titov, Wilker Aziz, Diego Marcheggiani, and Khalil Simaán. 2017. Graph convolutional encoders for syntax-aware neural machine translation. In *Proc. of EMNLP*.

Yonatan Belinkov and Yonatan Bisk. 2017. Synthetic and natural noise both break neural machine translation. *ICLR*, abs/1711.02173.

Arianna Bisazza, A. Ustun, and Stephan Sportel. 2021. On the difficulty of translating free-order case-marking languages. *ArXiv*, abs/2107.06055.

Ben Bogin, Sanjay Subramanian, Matt Gardner, and Jonathan Berant. 2020. Latent compositional representations improve systematic generalization in grounded question answering. *arXiv preprint arXiv:2007.00266*.

Ondřej Bojar, Rajen Chatterjee, Christian Federmann, Yvette Graham, Barry Haddow, Matthias Huck, Antonio Jimeno Yepes, Philipp Koehn, Varvara Logacheva, Christof Monz, et al. 2016. Findings of the 2016 conference on machine translation. In *Proceedings of the First Conference on Machine Translation: Volume 2, Shared Task Papers*, pages 131–198.

Emanuele Bugliarello and N. Okazaki. 2020. Enhancing machine translation with dependency-aware self-attention. In *ACL*.

Saikat Chakraborty, Miltiadis Allamanis, and Baishakhi Ray. 2018. Tree2tree neural translation model for learning source code changes. *ArXiv*, abs/1810.00314.

Kehai Chen, Rui Wang, Masao Utiyama, Lemao Liu, Akihiro Tamura, Eiichiro Sumita, and Tiejun Zhao. 2017. Neural machine translation with source dependency representation. In *Proc. of EMNLP*.

Kehai Chen, Rui Wang, Masao Utiyama, Eiichiro Sumita, and Tiejun Zhao. 2018. Syntax-directed attention for neural machine translation. In *Proc. of AAAI*.

Leshem Choshen and Omri Abend. 2019. Automatically extracting challenge sets for non-local phenomena in neural machine translation. In *Proceedings of the 23rd Conference on Computational Natural Language Learning (CoNLL)*, pages 291–303, Hong Kong, China. Association for Computational Linguistics.

Leshem Choshen, Lior Fox, Zohar Aizenbud, and Omri Abend. 2020. On the weaknesses of reinforcement learning for neural machine translation. *ArXiv*, abs/1907.01752.

Róbert Csordás, Kazuki Irie, and Jürgen Schmidhuber. 2021. The devil is in the detail: Simple tricks improve systematic generalization of transformers. *ArXiv*, abs/2108.12284.

Jacob Devlin, Ming-Wei Chang, Kenton Lee, and Kristina Toutanova. 2019. BERT: Pre-training of deep bidirectional transformers for language understanding. In *Proceedings of the 2019 Conference of the North American Chapter of the Association for Computational Linguistics: Human Language Technologies, Volume 1 (Long and Short Papers)*, pages 4171–4186, Minneapolis, Minnesota. Association for Computational Linguistics.

Shuoyang Ding, Adithya Renduchintala, and Kevin Duh. 2019. A call for prudent choice of subword merge operations in neural machine translation. In *Proceedings of Machine Translation Summit XVII Volume 1: Research Track*, pages 204–213, Dublin, Ireland. European Association for Machine Translation.

Shachar Don-Yehiya, Leshem Choshen, and Omri Abend. 2022. Prequel: Quality estimation of machine translation outputs in advance. *arXiv preprint arXiv:2205.09178*.

Chris Dyer, Victor Chahuneau, and Noah A. Smith. 2013. A simple, fast, and effective reparameterization of ibm model 2. In *HLT-NAACL*.

Chris Dyer, Adhiguna Kuncoro, Miguel Ballesteros, and Noah A. Smith. 2016. Recurrent neural network grammars. In *HLT-NAACL*.

Akiko Eriguchi, Kazuma Hashimoto, and Yoshimasa Tsuruoka. 2016. Tree-to-sequence attentional neural machine translation. In *Proceedings of the 54th Annual Meeting of the Association for Computational Linguistics (Volume 1: Long Papers)*, pages 823–833, Berlin, Germany. Association for Computational Linguistics.

Akiko Eriguchi, Yoshimasa Tsuruoka, and Kyunghyun Cho. 2017. Learning to parse and translate improves neural machine translation. *ArXiv*, abs/1702.03525.

Daniel Fernández-González and Carlos Gómez-Rodríguez. 2018. Non-projective dependency parsing with non-local transitions. In *Proceedings of the 2018 Conference of the North American Chapter of the Association for Computational Linguistics: Human Language Technologies, Volume 2 (Short Papers)*, pages 693–700, New Orleans, Louisiana. Association for Computational Linguistics.

Nicolas Gontier, Koustuv Sinha, Siva Reddy, and Christopher Pal. 2020. Measuring systematic generalization in neural proof generation with transformers. *arXiv preprint arXiv:2009.14786*.

Jetic Gū, Hassan S. Shavarani, and Anoop Sarkar. 2018. Top-down tree structured decoding with syntactic connections for neural machine translation and parsing. In *Proceedings of the 2018 Conference on Empirical Methods in Natural Language Processing*, pages 401–413, Brussels, Belgium. Association for Computational Linguistics.

Jie Hao, Xing Wang, Shuming Shi, Jinfeng Zhang, and Zhaopeng Tu. 2019. Multi-granularity self-attention for neural machine translation. In *Proceedings of the 2019 Conference on Empirical Methods in Natural Language Processing and the 9th International Joint Conference on Natural Language Processing (EMNLP-IJCNLP)*, pages 887–897, Hong Kong, China. Association for Computational Linguistics.

Jacob Harer, C. Reale, and P. Chin. 2019. Tree-transformer: A transformer-based method for correction of tree-structured data. *ArXiv*, abs/1908.00449.

Daniel Hershcovich, Omri Abend, and Ari Rappoport. 2018. Multitask parsing across semantic representations. In *Proc. of ACL*, pages 373–385.

Jennifer Hu, Jon Gauthier, Peng Qian, Ethan Wilcox, and Roger Levy. 2020. A systematic assessment of syntactic generalization in neural language models. In *Proceedings of the 58th Annual Meeting of the Association for Computational Linguistics*, pages 1725–1744.

Ganesh Jawahar, Benoît Sagot, and Djamé Seddah. 2019. What does BERT learn about the structure of language? In *Proceedings of the 57th Annual Meeting of the Association for Computational Linguistics*, pages 3651–3657, Florence, Italy. Association for Computational Linguistics.

Diederik P. Kingma and Jimmy Ba. 2015. Adam: A method for stochastic optimization. *CoRR*, abs/1412.6980.

Thomas N. Kipf and Max Welling. 2016. Semi-supervised classification with graph convolutional networks. *CoRR*, abs/1609.02907.

Philipp Koehn, Hieu Hoang, Alexandra Birch, Chris Callison-Burch, M. Federico, N. Bertoldi, B. Cowan, Wade Shen, C. Moran, R. Zens, Chris Dyer, Ondrej Bojar, A. Constantin, and E. Herbst. 2007. Moses: Open source toolkit for statistical machine translation. In *ACL*.

Junhui Li, Deyi Xiong, Zhaopeng Tu, Muhua Zhu, Min Zhang, and Guodong Zhou. 2017. Modeling source syntax for neural machine translation. In *Proc. of ACL*.

Tal Linzen and Marco Baroni. 2020. Syntactic structure from deep learning. *Annual Review of Linguistics*, 7.

L. Liu, M. Utiyama, A. Finch, and Eiichiro Sumita. 2016. Agreement on target-bidirectional neural machine translation. In *HLT-NAACL*.

Adam Lopez. 2008. Statistical machine translation. *ACM Computing Surveys (CSUR)*, 40:8.

Marco Lui and Timothy Baldwin. 2012. langid. py: An off-the-shelf language identification tool. In *Proceedings of the ACL 2012 system demonstrations*, pages 25–30.

Qingsong Ma, Johnny Wei, Ondřej Bojar, and Yvette Graham. 2019. Results of the WMT19 metrics shared task: Segment-level and strong MT systems pose big challenges. In *Proceedings of the Fourth Conference on Machine Translation (Volume 2: Shared Task Papers, Day 1)*, pages 62–90, Florence, Italy. Association for Computational Linguistics.

Christopher D. Manning, Kevin Clark, John Hewitt, Urvashi Khandelwal, and Omer Levy. 2020. Emergent linguistic structure in artificial neural networks trained by self-supervision. *PNAS*.

Diego Marcheggiani, Jasmijn Bastings, and Ivan Titov. 2018. Exploiting semantics in neural machine translation with graph convolutional networks. In *Proc. of NAACL*.

Tom McCoy, Ellie Pavlick, and Tal Linzen. 2019. Right for the wrong reasons: Diagnosing syntactic heuristics in natural language inference. In *Proceedings of the 57th Annual Meeting of the Association for Computational Linguistics*, pages 3428–3448.

Haitao Mi, B. Sankaran, Z. Wang, and Abe Ittycheriah. 2016. Coverage embedding models for neural machine translation. In *EMNLP*.

Maria Nadejde, Siva Reddy, Rico Sennrich, Tomasz Dwojak, Marcin Junczys-Dowmunt, P. Koehn, and Alexandra Birch. 2017. Predicting target language ccg supertags improves neural machine translation. In *WMT*.

Xuan-Phi Nguyen, Shafiq R. Joty, S. Hoi, and R. Socher. 2020. Tree-structured attention with hierarchical accumulation. *ArXiv*, abs/2002.08046.

Joakim Nivre. 2003. An efficient algorithm for projective dependency parsing. In *IWPT*.

Joakim Nivre, Marie-Catherine de Marneffe, Filip Ginter, Yoav Goldberg, Jan Hajic, Christopher D. Manning, Ryan McDonald, Slav Petrov, Sampo Pyysalo, Natalia Silveira, Reut Tsarfaty, and Daniel Zeman. 2016. Universal dependencies v1: A multilingual treebank collection. In *Proc. of LREC*, pages 1659–1666.

Stephan Oepen, Omri Abend, Lasha Abzianidze, Johan Bos, Jan Hajic, Daniel Hershcovich, Bin Li, Tim O'Gorman, Nianwen Xue, and Daniel Zeman. 2020. MRP 2020: The second shared task on cross-framework and cross-lingual meaning representation parsing. In *Proceedings of the CoNLL 2020 Shared Task: Cross-Framework Meaning Representation Parsing*, pages 1–22, Online. Association for Computational Linguistics.

Santiago Ontanón, Joshua Ainslie, V. Cvicek, and Zachary Kenneth Fisher. 2021. Making transformers solve compositional tasks. *ArXiv*, abs/2108.04378.

Kishore Papineni, S. Roukos, T. Ward, and Wei-Jing Zhu. 2002. Bleu: a method for automatic evaluation of machine translation. In *ACL*.

Thuong-Hai Pham, Dominik Machácek, and Ondrej Bojar. 2019. Promoting the knowledge of source syntax in transformer nmt is not needed. *Computación y Sistemas*, 23.

Edoardo Maria Ponti, Roi Reichart, Anna Korhonen, and Ivan Vulić. 2018. Isomorphic transfer of syntactic structures in cross-lingual nlp. In *Proc. of ACL*, volume 1.

Martin Popel and Ondřej Bojar. 2018. Training tips for the transformer model. *The Prague Bulletin of Mathematical Linguistics*, 110(1):43–70.

Maja Popovic. 2017. chrf++: words helping character n-grams. In *WMT*.

Shauli Ravfogel, Y. Goldberg, and Tal Linzen. 2019. Studying the inductive biases of rnns with synthetic variations of natural languages. *ArXiv*, abs/1903.06400.

D. Sachan, Yuhao Zhang, Peng Qi, and W. Hamilton. 2020. Do syntax trees help pre-trained transformers extract information? *ArXiv*, abs/2008.09084.

Rico Sennrich, Orhan Firat, K. Cho, Alexandra Birch, B. Haddow, Julian Hitschler, Marcin Junczys-Dowmunt, Samuel Läubli, A. Barone, Jozef Mokry, and Maria Nadejde. 2017. Nematus: a toolkit for neural machine translation. In *EACL*.

Rico Sennrich, Barry Haddow, and Alexandra Birch. 2016. Neural machine translation of rare words with subword units. In *Proceedings of the 54th Annual Meeting of the Association for Computational Linguistics (Volume 1: Long Papers)*, pages 1715–1725, Berlin, Germany. Association for Computational Linguistics.

Haoyue Shi, Hao Zhou, J. Chen, and Lei Li. 2018. On tree-based neural sentence modeling. In *EMNLP*.

Vighnesh Leonardo Shiv and Chris Quirk. 2019. Novel positional encodings to enable tree-based transformers. In *NeurIPS*.

Linfeng Song, Daniel Gildea, Yue Zhang, Zhiguo Wang, and Jinsong Su. 2019. Semantic neural machine translation using AMR. *TACL*, 7.

Miloš Stanojević and Mark Steedman. 2020. Max-margin incremental CCG parsing. In *Proceedings of the 58th Annual Meeting of the Association for Computational Linguistics*, pages 4111–4122, Online. Association for Computational Linguistics.

Milan Straka. 2018. Udpipe 2.0 prototype at conll 2018 ud shared task. In *Proceedings of the CoNLL 2018 Shared Task: Multilingual Parsing from Raw Text to Universal Dependencies*, pages 197–207.

Emma Strubell, Patrick Verga, Daniel Andor, David Weiss, and Andrew McCallum. 2018. Linguistically-informed self-attention for semantic role labeling. In *Proceedings of the 2018 Conference on Empirical Methods in Natural Language Processing*, pages 5027–5038, Brussels, Belgium. Association for Computational Linguistics.

Kai Sheng Tai, R. Socher, and Christopher D. Manning. 2015. Improved semantic representations from tree-structured long short-term memory networks. In *ACL*.

J. Tiedemann. 2012. Parallel data, tools and interfaces in opus. In *LREC*.

Zhaopeng Tu, Z. Lu, Y. Liu, X. Liu, and Hang Li. 2016. Modeling coverage for neural machine translation. *arXiv: Computation and Language*.

Ashish Vaswani, Noam Shazeer, Niki Parmar, Jakob Uszkoreit, Llion Jones, Aidan N Gomez, Łukasz Kaiser, and Illia Polosukhin. 2017. Attention is all you need. In *Advances in Neural Information Processing Systems*, pages 5998–6008.

Chaojun Wang and Rico Sennrich. 2020. On exposure bias, hallucination and domain shift in neural machine translation. In *Proceedings of the 58th Annual Meeting of the Association for Computational Linguistics*, pages 3544–3552, Online. Association for Computational Linguistics.

Xinyi Wang, Hieu Pham, Pengcheng Yin, and Graham Neubig. 2018. A tree-based decoder for neural machine translation. *arXiv preprint arXiv:1808.09374*.

Yau-Shian Wang, Hung yi Lee, and Yun-Nung Chen. 2019. Tree transformer: Integrating tree structures into self-attention. In *EMNLP/IJCNLP*.

Sean Welleck, Peter West, Jize Cao, and Yejin Choi. 2021. Symbolic brittleness in sequence models: on systematic generalization in symbolic mathematics. *arXiv preprint arXiv:2109.13986*.

J. Wieting, Taylor Berg-Kirkpatrick, Kevin Gimpel, and Graham Neubig. 2019. Beyond bleu: Training neural machine translation with semantic similarity. In *ACL*.

Ethan Wilcox, Peng Qian, Richard Futrell, Ryosuke Kohita, Roger Levy, and Miguel Ballesteros. 2020. Structural supervision improves few-shot learning and syntactic generalization in neural language models. *arXiv preprint arXiv:2010.05725*.

Shuangzhi Wu, Dongdong Zhang, Nan Yang, Mu Li, and Ming Zhou. 2017. Sequence-to-dependency neural machine translation. In *Proc. of ACL*.

Yingce Xia, Fei Tian, Lijun Wu, Jianxin Lin, T. Qin, N. Yu, and T. Liu. 2017. Deliberation networks: Sequence generation beyond one-pass decoding. In *NIPS*.

Asaf Yehudai, Leshem Choshen, Lior Fox, and Omri Abend. 2022. Reinforcement learning with large action spaces for neural machine translation. In *COLING*.

Meishan Zhang, Zhenghua Li, Guohong Fu, and Min Zhang. 2019. Syntax-enhanced neural machine translation with syntax-aware word representations. In *Proceedings of the 2019 Conference of the North American Chapter of the Association for Computational Linguistics: Human Language Technologies, Volume 1 (Long and Short Papers)*, pages 1151–1161, Minneapolis, Minnesota. Association for Computational Linguistics.

Xiangwen Zhang, Jinsong Su, Yue Qin, Y. Liu, R. Ji, and Hongji Wang. 2018. Asynchronous bidirectional decoding for neural machine translation. *ArXiv*, abs/1801.05122.

Chunting Zhou, Xuezhe Ma, Junjie Hu, and Graham Neubig. 2019a. Handling syntactic divergence in low-resource machine translation. In *Proc. of EMNLP-IJCNLP*, pages 1388–1394.

Long Zhou, Jiajun Zhang, and Chengqing Zong. 2019b. Synchronous bidirectional neural machine translation. *Transactions of the Association for Computational Linguistics*, 7:91–105.

A From sequence-to-sequence to conditional

Attention-based models are characterized by being state-less. They can, therefore, be viewed as conditional language models, namely as models for producing a distribution for the next word, given the generated prefix and source sentence It is possible to re-encode other information (not only the decoded output) into the decoder at each step, or predict only tokens of interest, rather than the complete sequence. It is also possible to change the source sentence partially or completely (e.g., adding noise to increase robustness), condition on additional information (§4) and adjust this information during prediction (e.g. force predicted word characteristics). Nevertheless, the standard practice is to only re-encode past predictions.[3]

Unlike RNNs, attention-based models do not inherently rely on past predictions in terms of inputs, weights and gradients. The only connection to past predictions is mediated through their re-encoding back into the decoder.

RNNs receive past states as inputs. Backpropagation through time sees the current network as connected to the previous networks supplying the state input. Thus, the gradients take into account past predictions as well.

In contrast, Transformers have gradients over representation of past words only if they are fed into the network. Unlike backpropagation through time, the preceding tokens can be changed, or even omitted (e.g., in a limited window size scenario). Specifically, in our case, preceding tokens may have different representations at each generation step.

To sum, the representation is updated to provide good representation for the current step, but it is not calculated over the actual network of the previous step. It is often the case, though, that the previous decoded words are auto-regressed and hence updated.

This architecture, therefore, allows more flexibility than RNNs. Still, Transformers are often thought about as an extension to RNNs, i.e., sequnce-to-sequence models. For that reason it is rare to find changes to the training schedule that incorporate more knowledge, change "past" information or translate only parts of a sentence with a network. With such methods, for example, one can dynamically force features of the next prediction (by a changing input) or augment learning by teaching the network only over hard cases. Such an approach may choose augmented data in a regular way, but stop the prediction at the part in the sentence one wishes the network to learn, or even teach it several alternatives with the same prefix.

[3]This is true even in cases of bidirectional generation (e.g., Zhang et al., 2018).

B Experimental Setup

The code is adapted from the NEMATUS code repository (Sennrich et al., 2017) and will be released upon publication. All hyperparameters are either taken from the original suggestions or optimized for the vanilla Transformer and used as is for our suggested models.

Networks are all trained with batch size 128, embedding size 256, 4 decoder and encoder blocks, 8 attention heads (one of which might be a parent head §4), 90K steps (where empirically some saturation is reached. This is a relatively fair comparison (Popel and Bojar, 2018)), learning rate $1e^{-4}$, 4K warm-up steps, Adam (Kingma and Ba, 2015) optimizer with beta 0.9 and 0.999 for the first and second moment and epsilon of $1e^{-8}$. We use the standard (structure-unaware) Transformer encoder in all our experiments. Each model was trained on 4 NVIDIA Tesla M60 or RTX 2080Ti GPUs for approximately a week (2 for GCN architecture), large models on RTX6000.

Preprocessing includes truecasing, tokenization as implemented by Moses (Koehn et al., 2007) and byte pair encoding (Sennrich et al., 2016) without tying. Empty source or target sentences were dropped. In training, the maximum target sentence length is 40 non-transition tokens (BPE).

We used UDPipe English and German over UD 2.0 and Russian with 2.5 with syntagrus version.

In unreported trials, we found that whenever noisy and crawled data is used, filtering is crucial for even the baselines to show reasonable results. On full En-Ru (See §6.2), we filter unexpected languages by langID (Lui and Baldwin, 2012) and improbable alignment ($p < -180$) with FastAlign (Dyer et al., 2013). Overall, about half the sentences were filtered by those measures or length.

There were 4,066,323 training sentences after filtering En-De and 4,468,840 before. In En-Ru, there were 19,557,568 after and 37,948,456 before. The English challenge sets on books and news sizes are respectively, 1,188 and 11 reflexive, 3,953 and 17 particle, 191 and 8 prepositions stranding, and the German 2,628 and 261 reflexive and 7,584 and 232 particle. WMT dev and test sets are always of about 3K sentences in size.

We use *chrF++.py* with 1 word and beta of 3 to obtain chrF+ (Popovic, 2017) score as in WMT19 (Ma et al., 2019) and detokenized BLEU (Papineni et al., 2002) as implemented in Moses. We use two automatic metrics: BLEU as the standard measure and chrF+ as it was shown to better correlate with human judgments, while still being simple and understandable (Ma et al., 2019). Both metrics rely on n-gram overlap between the source and reference, where BLEU focuses on word precision, and chrF+ balances precision and recall and includes characters, as well as word n-grams.

Transitions. We made two practical choices when creating the transition graph. First, we deleted the root edge, as the root is not a word in the translation. Second, we train only on projective parses. This choice reduces noise due to the low reliability of current non-projective parsers (Fernández-González and Gómez-Rodríguez, 2018), while not losing many training sentences. We do note, however, that this choice is not without its risks: it might be less fitting for some languages in which non-projective sentences are common.

The transitions serve as the NMT vocabulary. There are 45 labels and two directions of connections, summing up to 90 new tokens. This hardly affects the standard vocabulary size, which usually consists of tens of thousands of tokens(Ding et al., 2019). We treat both token and transition predictions in the same way, and do not rescale their score as done in Stanojević and Steedman (2020). If anything, the need to memorize more should hurt performance, and so increased performance should come despite enlarging the vocabulary and not because of it. It is possible to split the tokens into directions and labels (summing to 47). This comes at the cost of lengthy sentences which increase training time and memory consumption. We did not experiment with other methods for encoding the transitions (e.g., embedding labels and edges separately).

C Mixup challenge

We follow the results of (Bisazza et al., 2021) that Transformers are able to learn languages with free order, given case markings. Given those findings, we wonder whether indeed Transformers are robust to mixing the order where case marking exists.

	Vanilla	PARENT
Object	6	6
Subject	5	8
Both	10	13

Table 3: Amount of sentences where the rare order (OVS) in German was still well corrected. In rows, what had unambiguous casing.

To do that, we take lists of nouns and verbs to create simple sentences from. Then, we create three types of sentences, validated to be correct and convey the same meaning in both orders by an in-house annotator who is a native German speaker. Ones with both marked such as: *den Ball bringt der Hund* (lit. the dog brings the ball), ones with only the subject marked: *das Pfred drängt der Hund* (the dog urges the horse), and ones with only the object.

The three lists of sentences are:

- Den {Ball, Stein, Tisch, Hamster} {bringt, wirft, drückt} {das Kind, die Mutter, das Mädchen}
- Das {Pferd, Kind, Mädchen} {drängt, drückt, zieht} der {Vater, Hund, Student}
- Den {Ball, Stein, Tisch, Hamster} {bringt, wirft, drückt} der {Vater, Hund, Student}

Then, we switch the object and subject and calculate how often is the translation correct in terms of places. We disregard other errors such as choice of verb in English.

Interestingly, as seen in the results section §E, both networks are quite bad at it (although the syntactic variant is better).

D Results with the Large

We include the full results over the two larger models PARENT and the Vanilla. While overall results are comparable, PARENT consistently performs better on the challenge sets, often with large margins.

	Preposition Stranding				Particle				Reflexive			
	Books		News		Books		News		Books		News	
	BLEU	chrF+	BLEU	chrF+	BLEU	chrF+	BLEU	chrF+	BLEU	chrF+	BLEU	chrF+
Vanilla	8.70	33.58	**13.82**	43.41	8.59	32.66	**15.28**	44.28	8.54	32.85	18.90	45.82
PARENT	**9.03**	**34.83**	11.53	**45.12**	**8.59**	**33.71**	14.99	**45.90**	**9.05**	**34.11**	**20.79**	**46.73**

Table 4: Source challenge sets for En-De translation of large models. PARENT outperforms the Vanilla.

	2013		2014		2015		Average	
	BLEU	chrF+	BLEU	chrF+	BLEU	chrF+	BLEU	chrF+
Vanilla	**23.64**	53.44	21.94	53.13	**21.60**	**50.84**	22.39	52.47
PARENT	23.56	**54.08**	**22.11**	**53.77**	20.69	49.16	22.12	52.34

Table 5: Test sets for En-De translation of large models.

	Particle				Reflexive			
	Books		News		Books		News	
	BLEU	chrF+	BLEU	chrF+	BLEU	chrF+	BLEU	chrF+
Vanilla	4.14	20.72	20.31	49.04	8.08	32.38	20.65	49.09
PARENT	**8.37**	**33.78**	**20.54**	**49.99**	**8.60**	**33.49**	**21.39**	**50.01**

Table 6: Target challenge sets for En-De translation of large models. PARENT outperforms the Vanilla.

E Additional Results

We include here the full results including ablations that were omitted in the paper due to space considerations. For ease of comparison we also split them by challenge direction (source Table 7 and target Table 8). Note that improvements in the syntactic aspect could also be seen in the ablations (not reported in the main paper). Moreover, BiTran improves over the Vanilla even as a standalone architecture.

	Particle				Reflexive			
	Books		News		Books		News	
	BLEU	chrF+	BLEU	chrF+	BLEU	chrF+	BLEU	chrF+
Vanilla	7.15	27.66	17.79	44.91	6.83	26.84	19.68	45.06
PARENT	**7.82**	28.43	19.66	46.32	**7.49**	27.70	**20.97**	47.07
GCN	7.32	27.67	**20.13**	**46.77**	7.11	27.16	20.68	47.15
BiTrans	7.02	27.60	18.58	45.09	6.8	26.90	19.87	45.89
Linearized	7.44	28.05	19.2	46.21	7.27	27.43	20.25	46.92
- Gates	7.62	28.23	19.71	46.36	7.38	27.65	20.74	47.19
- Labels	7.75	**28.60**	19.01	46.51	7.44	**27.90**	20.81	**47.32**

(a) Syntactic source challenge sets for De-En

	Preposition Stranding				Particle				Reflexive			
	Books		News		Books		News		Books		News	
	BLEU	chrF+	BLEU	chrF+	BLEU	chrF+	BLEU	chrF+	BLEU	chrF+	BLEU	chrF+
Vanilla	5.95	25.88	9.96	36.96	5.37	24.69	9.39	39.19	5.32	24.71	16.48	42.04
PARENT	**6.21**	**28.12**	11.17	**41.13**	5.47	25.74	11.93	41.24	5.71	**26.22**	15.56	42.76
GCN	**6.21**	27.27	11.31	40.48	5.51	25.53	10.35	39.83	5.46	25.70	16.45	**43.03**
BiTrans	5.3	26.38	10.56	38.05	**6.07**	**26.08**	10.21	39.48	**5.77**	26.01	13.91	37.74
Linearized	5.99	26.90	8.86	39.12	5.24	25.42	10.45	39.56	5.48	25.47	14.94	42.15
- Gates	5.29	25.86	**11.64**	40.51	5.3	25.03	10.01	38.64	5.31	25.41	12.08	37.00
- Labels	5.83	27.05	8.62	38.33	5.41	25.62	**11.98**	**41.79**	5.42	25.67	**16.55**	41.65

(b) Syntactic source challenge sets for En-De

Table 7: Results on the syntactic challenge sets, both on the large challenges from book domain and the smaller ones from news. Models include Vanilla and Bidirectional Transformer baselines (top) and the GCN and PARENT syntactic variants (middle). Ablated models (bottom) include Vanilla with linearized syntax (Linearized), GCN without labels or gating (-Gates) and GCN without labels (-Labels). Among the baselines, BiTrans is better. It is inconclusive which syntactic method is best, but they are significantly superior to both baselines.

	Preposition Stranding				Particle				Reflexive			
	Books		News		Books		News		Books		News	
	BLEU	chrF+	BLEU	chrF+	BLEU	chrF+	BLEU	chrF+	BLEU	chrF+	BLEU	chrF+
Vanilla	6.38	27.30	9.18	38.22	6.53	25.70	10.54	38.28	6.15	25.94	17.2	43.12
PARENT	**7.59**	**27.87**	**10.81**	39.22	**7.07**	**26.50**	9.72	39.57	**6.82**	26.58	17.56	44.00
GCN	6.33	26.60	10.14	**41.00**	6.69	26.16	10.6	39.81	6.33	25.83	**20.16**	44.19
BiTrans	6.75	27.44	8.92	37.76	6.29	25.69	10.77	39.15	6.24	25.93	17.22	43.96
Linearized	6.79	27.46	7.79	39.62	6.55	25.96	**12.95**	**40.78**	6.56	26.28	16.38	43.76
- Gates	6.89	27.31	10.46	40.80	6.53	26.26	12.45	40.70	6.62	26.50	15.97	43.10
- Labels	7.05	27.51	9.89	38.24	6.98	26.42	12.83	40.18	6.62	**26.65**	18.9	**46.59**

(a) Syntactic target challenge sets for De-En

	Particle				Reflexive			
	Books		News		Books		News	
	BLEU	chrF+	BLEU	chrF+	BLEU	chrF+	BLEU	chrF+
Vanilla	5.4	25.84	**16.24**	43.22	5.12	24.94	16.47	42.71
PARENT	5.52	**26.96**	16.19	**44.83**	5.37	**26.31**	**16.86**	**44.30**
GCN	5.6	26.74	15.57	43.23	5.34	25.91	16.44	43.52
BiTrans	**5.81**	26.79	15.84	43.25	**5.43**	25.88	16.33	42.44
+ Linearized	5.32	26.30	15.69	43.77	5.07	25.57	16.19	43.07
- Gates	5.31	26.21	15.49	43.45	5.01	25.30	15.67	43.13
- Labels	5.56	26.55	15.78	43.96	5.24	25.67	16.8	43.65

(b) Syntactic target challenge sets for En-De

Table 8: Results on the syntactic challenge sets, both on the large challenges from book domain and the smaller ones from news. Models include Vanilla and Bidirectional Transformer baselines (top) and the GCN and PARENT syntactic variants (middle). Ablated models (bottom) include the Vanilla with linearized syntax (Linearized), GCN without labels or gating (-Gates) and GCN without labels (-Labels). Among the baselines, BiTrans is better. It is inconclusive which syntactic method is best, but they are significantly superior to both baselines.

	2013		2014		2015		Average	
	BLEU	chrF+	BLEU	chrF+	BLEU	chrF+	BLEU	chrF+
Vanilla	17.61	45.54	18.23	47.29	19.57	47.50	18.47	46.78
BiTrans	17.64	45.66	18.34	47.53	19.33	47.61	18.44	46.93
PARENT	**18.11**	**46.75**	18.6	**48.46**	**20.55**	**49.20**	**19.09**	**48.14**
GCN	18.03	46.43	**18.86**	**48.46**	20.32	48.90	19.07	47.93
Linearized	17.71	46.07	18.39	47.69	19.81	48.36	18.64	47.37
- Gates	17.81	46.12	18.43	48.08	20.06	48.62	18.77	47.61
- Labels	17.98	46.40	18.77	48.29	19.96	48.73	18.90	47.80

(a) Test sets for En-De translation

	2013		2014		2015		Average	
	BLEU	chrF+	BLEU	chrF+	BLEU	chrF+	BLEU	chrF+
Vanilla	21.51	48.20	21.40	48.46	21.44	48.13	21.45	48.26
BiTrans	21.63	48.48	21.42	48.86	21.38	48.54	21.48	48.63
PARENT	**22.46**	49.24	21.75	49.41	22.14	49.31	22.12	49.32
GCN	22.33	49.27	21.76	49.71	**22.43**	**49.73**	**22.17**	49.57
Linearized	21.95	49.27	21.83	**49.79**	22.20	49.70	21.99	**49.59**
- Gates	22.28	49.33	**21.89**	49.68	22.04	49.39	22.07	49.46
- Labels	22.21	**49.46**	21.75	49.73	22.26	49.57	22.07	**49.59**

(b) Test sets for De-En translation

Table 9: En-De and De-En results on newstest 2013-15. Ablated models include the Transformer decoder with linearized syntax (Linearized), GCN without labels or gating (-Gates) and GCN without labels (-Labels). The syntactic variants consistently outperfom the vanilla and ablated variants, and the Bidirectional Transformer (BiTrans) slightly outperforms Vanilla Transformer.

E.1 Noisy data

Table 10a presents the two tables side by side for ease of comparison. The one on larger noisy Russian train set and the cleaner one.

	2013		2014		2015		Average	
	BLEU	chrF+	BLEU	chrF+	BLEU	chrF+	BLEU	chrF+
Vanilla	13.20	38.72	17.17	43.69	14.19	40.87	14.85	41.09
BiTran	13.13	39.10	17.63	44.63	14.59	41.52	15.12	41.75
GCN	13.25	40.31	17.86	46.09	15.38	43.09	15.50	43.16
PARENT	**13.61**	**40.67**	**18.53**	**46.44**	**15.75**	**43.57**	**15.96**	**43.56**

(a) Test sets for En-Ru translation trained on news data

	2013		2014		2015		Average	
	BLEU	chrF+	BLEU	chrF+	BLEU	chrF+	BLEU	chrF+
Vanilla	16.84	44.28	20.12	47.7	14.74	40.92	17.23	44.30
BiTran	16.84	44.46	**20.61**	48.17	**14.79**	41.05	**17.41**	44.56
GCN	**17.11**	**45.55**	20.29	48.67	14.6	41.63	17.33	45.28
PARENT	16.8	45.42	20.2	**48.95**	14.59	**41.73**	17.20	**45.37**

(b) Test sets for En-Ru translation trained on noisy data

Table 10: En-Ru results on newstest 2013-15 trained on clean (top) or noisy (bottom) data. Models include Vanilla, Bidirectional Transformer and syntactic variants. The syntactic ones improve over all datasets and on average.

Characterizing Verbatim Short-Term Memory in Neural Language Models

Kristijan Armeni
Johns Hopkins University
karmeni1@jhu.edu

Christopher Honey
Johns Hopkins University
chris.honey@jhu.edu

Tal Linzen
New York University
linzen@nyu.edu

Abstract

When a language model is trained to predict natural language sequences, its prediction at each moment depends on a representation of prior context. What kind of information about the prior context can language models retrieve? We tested whether language models could retrieve the exact words that occurred previously in a text. In our paradigm, language models (transformers and an LSTM) processed English text in which a list of nouns occurred twice. We operationalized retrieval as the reduction in surprisal from the first to the second list. We found that the transformers retrieved both the identity and ordering of nouns from the first list. Further, the transformers' retrieval was markedly enhanced when they were trained on a larger corpus and with greater model depth. Lastly, their ability to index prior tokens was dependent on learned attention patterns. In contrast, the LSTM exhibited less precise retrieval, which was limited to list-initial tokens and to short intervening texts. The LSTM's retrieval was not sensitive to the order of nouns and it improved when the list was semantically coherent. We conclude that transformers implemented something akin to a working memory system that could flexibly retrieve individual token representations across arbitrary delays; conversely, the LSTM maintained a coarser and more rapidly-decaying semantic gist of prior tokens, weighted toward the earliest items.

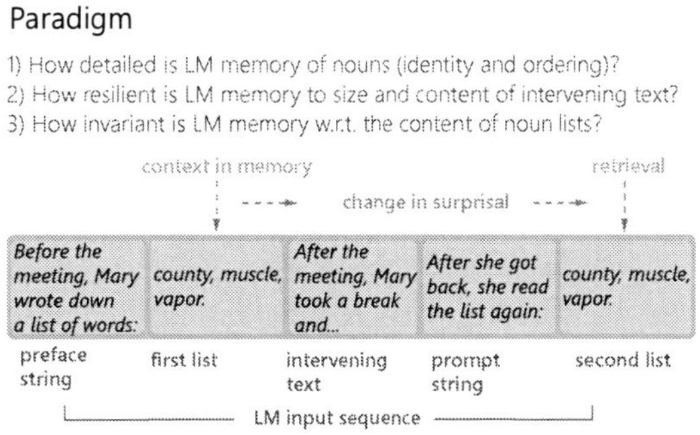

Figure 1: Characterizing verbatim memory retrieval in neural language models. In our paradigm, language models processed English text in which a list of nouns occurred twice. We operationalized retrieval as the reduction in surprisal from the first to the second list presentation. We measured retrieval while varying: a) set size, b) the structure of the second list, c) the length of the intervening text, and d) the content and structure of the intervening text.

1 Introduction

Language models (LMs) are computational systems trained to predict upcoming tokens based on past context. To perform this task well, they must construct a coherent representation of the text, which requires establishing relationships between words that occur at non-adjacent time points.

Despite their simple learning objective, LMs based on contemporary artificial neural network architectures perform well in contexts that require maintenance and retrieval of dependencies spanning multiple words. For example, LMs learn to correctly match the grammatical number of the subject and a corresponding verb across intervening words; for example, they prefer the correct *The **girls** standing at the desk **are** tall*, to the incorrect *The **girls** standing at the desk **is** tall* (Linzen et al., 2016; Marvin and Linzen, 2018; Gulordava et al., 2018; Futrell et al., 2018). The ability to maintain context across multiple words is likely to be a central factor explaining the success of these models, potentially following fine-tuning, in natural language processing tasks (Devlin et al., 2019; Brown et al., 2020).

The work discussed above has shown that LMs extract linguistically meaningful signals and that, over the course of learning, they develop a short-term memory capacity: the ability to store and access recent past context for processing, possibly akin to the working memory systems thought to enable flexible human cognitive capacities (Baddeley, 2003). What is the nature of the memory processes

Proceedings of the 26th Conference on Computational Natural Language Learning (CoNLL), pages 405 - 424
December 7-8, 2022

that LMs learn? Are these memory processes able to access individual tokens from the recent past *verbatim*, or is the memory system more implicit, so that only an aggregate *gist* of the prior context is available to subsequent processing?

Here, we introduce a paradigm (Fig. 1), inspired by benchmark tasks for models of human short-term memory (Oberauer et al., 2018), for characterizing short-term memory abilities of LMs. We apply it to two particular neural LM architectures that possess the architectural ingredients to hold past items in memory: attention-based transformers (Vaswani et al., 2017) and long short-term memory networks (Hochreiter and Schmidhuber, 1997, LSTM). Whereas LSTMs incorporate the past by reusing the results of processing from previous time steps through dedicated memory cells, transformers use the internal representations of each of the previous tokens as input. These architectural ingredients alone, however, are not sufficient for a model to have memory. We hypothesize that whether or not the model puts this memory capacity to *use* depends on whether the training task (next word prediction) requires it — the parameters controlling the activation of context representations and subsequent retrieval computations are in both cases *learned*.

Our goal is to determine whether and when the LMs we study maintain and retrieve verbatim representations of individual prior tokens. First, we measure the *detail* of the context representation: does the LM maintain a verbatim representation of all prior tokens and their order, or does it instead combine multiple prior tokens into a summary representation, like a semantic gist? Second, we consider the *resilience* of the memory to interference: after how many intervening tokens do the representation of prior context become inaccessible? Third, we consider the *content-invariance* of the context representations: does the resilience of prior context depend on semantic coherence of the prior information, or can arbitrary and unrelated information sequences be retrieved?

2 Related Work

Previous studies examined how properties of linguistic context influenced next-word prediction accuracy in transformer and LSTM LMs trained on text in English. Khandelwal et al. (2018) showed that LSTM LMs use a window of approximately 200 tokens of past context and word order information of the past 50 words, in the service of predicting the next token in natural language sequences. Subramanian et al. (2020) applied a similar analysis to a transformer LM and showed that LM loss on test-set sequences was not sensitive to context perturbations beyond 50 tokens. O'Connor and Andreas (2021) investigated whether fine-grained lexical and sentential features of context are used for next-word prediction in transformer LMs. They showed that transformers rely predominantly on local word co-occurrence statistics (e.g. trigram ordering) and the presence of open class parts of speech (e.g. nouns), and less on the global structure of context (e.g. sentence ordering) and the presence of closed class parts of speech (e.g. function words). In contrast with these studies, which focused on how specific features of past context affect LM performance on novel input at test time, our paradigm tests for the ability of LMs to retrieve nouns that are exactly repeated from prior context.

In a separate line of work bearing on memory maintenance in LSTMs, Lakretz et al. (2019, 2021) studied an LSTM's capacity to track subject-verb agreement dependencies. They showed that LSTM LMs relied on a small number of hidden units and the gating mechanisms that control memory contents. Here, we are similarly concerned with memory characteristics that support LM performance, but — akin to behavioral tests in cognitive science — we infer the *functional properties* of LM memory by manipulating properties of repeated noun lists and observing the effects these manipulations have on the behavior (surprisal) of the LM rather than on its internal representation.

A third related area of research proposes *architectural* innovations that augment RNNs and LSTMs with dedicated memory components (e.g. Weston et al., 2015; Yogatama et al., 2018) or improve the handling of context and memory in transformers (see Tay et al., 2020, for review). Here, we are not concerned with improving architectures, but with developing a paradigm that allows us to study how LMs put to use their memory systems, whether those are implicit or explicit.

3 Methods

3.1 Paradigm: Lists of Nouns in Context

Noun lists were embedded in brief vignettes (Figure 1, A and B). Each vignette opened with a *preface string* (e.g. "Before the meeting, Mary wrote down the following list of words:"). This string was followed by a list of nouns (the *first list*), which were separated by commas; the list-final noun was followed by a full stop (e.g. "county, muscle, vapor."). The first list was followed by an *intervening text*, which continued the narrative established by the preface string ("After the meeting, she took a break and had a cup of coffee."). The intervening text was followed by a short *prompt* string (e.g. "After she got back, she read the list again:") after which another list of nouns, either identical to the first list or different from it, was presented (we refer to this list as the *second list*). The full vignettes are provided in Section A.1 of the Appendix.

3.2 Semantic Coherence of Noun Lists

We used two types of word lists: arbitrary and semantically coherent. Arbitrary word lists (e.g. "device, singer, picture") were composed of randomly sampled nouns from the Toronto word pool.[1] Semantically coherent word lists were sampled from the categorized noun word pool,[2] which contains 32 lists, each of which contains 32 semantically related nouns (e.g. "robin, sparrow, heron, ..."). All noun lists used in experiments are reported in Tables 1 and 2 of the Appendix.

After ensuring there were at least 10 valid, in-vocabulary nouns per semantic set (as this was the maximal list length we considered), we were able to construct 23 nouns lists. Finally, to reduce the variance attributable to tokens occurring in specific positions, we generated 10 "folds" of each list by circularly shifting the tokens in the first list 10 times. In this way, each noun in each list was tested in all possible ordinal positions. This procedure resulted in a total of $23 \times 10 = 230$ noun lists.

3.3 Language Models

LSTM We used an adaptive weight-dropped (AWD) LSTM released by Merity et al. (2018)[3], which had 3 hidden layers with 400-dimensional input embeddings, 1840-dimensional hidden states, and a vocabulary size of 267,735. The model contained 182.3 million trainable parameters. It was trained on the Wikitext-103 corpus (Merity et al., 2016) and achieved a test-set perplexity of 41.8. Full training hyperparameters are reported in Section A.4 of the Appendix.

Transformer We trained a transformer LM on approximately 40 million subset of the Wikitext-103 benchmark.[4] We retrained the BPE tokenizer on the concatenated Wikitext-103 training, evaluation, and test sets and set. The vocabulary had 28,439 entries. We trained both the 12-layer GPT-2 architecture (known as "GPT-2 small", 107.7 million trainable parameters) and, as a point of comparison, smaller, 1-, 3-, and 6-layer transformers (29.7, 43.9, and 65.2 million trainable parameters, respectively). The context window was set to 1024 tokens and embedding dimension was kept at 768 across the architectures. The perplexities for the 12-, 6-, 3- and 1-layer models on the Wikitext-103 test set were 40.3, 46.7, 60.1, and 93.2, respectively. The full transformer training details are reported in Section A.5 of the Appendix.

We also evaluated the transformer LM pretrained by Radford et al. (2019), accessed through the Hugging Face Transformers library (Wolf et al., 2020). We refer to this model simply as GPT-2. It was trained on the WebText corpus, which consists of approximately 8 million online documents. We used the GPT-2-small checkpoint which has 12 attention layers and 768-dimensional embedding layer. The model contains 124 million parameters and has a vocabulary of 50,257 entries. We used the maximum context size of 1024 tokens.

3.4 Surprisal

For each token w_t in our sequence, we computed the negative log likelihood (surprisal): $\texttt{surprisal}(w_t) = -\log_2 P(w_t|w_1, \ldots, w_{t-1})$. In cases when the transformer byte-pair encoding tokenizer split a noun into multiple tokens—e.g. "sparrow" might be split into "sp" and "arrow"—we summed the surprisals of the resulting tokens.

Quantifying retrieval: repeat surprisal To quantify how the memory trace of the first list affected the model's expectations on the second list, we measured the ratio between the surprisal on the second list and the surprisal on the first list: $\texttt{repeat surprisal} = \frac{\bar{s}(L_2)}{\bar{s}(L_1)} \times 100$, where $\bar{s}(L_1)$ refers to mean surprisal across non-initial nouns in the first list and $\bar{s}(L_2)$ to mean surprisal across all non-initial nouns in the second list. We

[1] `http://memory.psych.upenn.edu/files/wordpools/nouns.txt`

[2] `http://memory.psych.upenn.edu/files/wordpools/catwpool.txt`

[3] Our code is available at: `https://github.com/KristijanArmeni/verbatim-memory-in-NLMs`. Our experiment data are available at: `https://doi.org/10.17605/OSF.IO/5GY7X`

[4] After retokenization with the BPE tokenizer, the training corpus contained 44,824,396 subword tokens.

take a *reduction* in surprisal on second lists to indicate the extent to which an LM has retrieved tokens from the first list.

4 Transformer Results

We first describe the results of our experiments with the two largest transformer models, the off-the-shelf GPT-2 and the 12-layer transformer we trained; LSTM results are discussed in Section 5, and results with smaller transformers are discussed towards the end of this section.

The transformers retrieved prior nouns and their order; this capacity improved when the model was trained on a larger corpus. We tested whether the transformers could retrieve the identity and order of 10-token noun lists (arbitrary or semantically coherent). To this end, we constructed vignettes in which the second list was either (a) identical to the first list, (b) a permutation of the first list, or (c) a list of novel nouns not present in the first list.[5] We then measured retrieval as reduction in surprisal from first to second list.

When the two transformers were presented with second lists that were repeated version of the first ones (blue in Fig. 2, B and C), token-by-token surprisal decreased compared to novel tokens, suggesting that the transformers were able to access verbatim representations of past nouns from context. When the second list was a permutation of the first one, surprisal was higher compared to when it was repeated, indicating that the transformers expected the nouns to be ordered as in the first list. Training set size played an important role in supporting verbatim recall: surprisal differences were considerably smaller for the transformer trained on the 44 million Wikitext-103 corpus (Fig. 2, B) compared to GPT-2 (Fig. 2, C).

In order to contextualize the magnitude of these retrieval effects, we computed the relative surprisal across all tokens in lists except the first one (Fig. 3). When the first and second lists were identical (e.g. with $N = 10$ arbitrary nouns), the Wikitext-103 transformer's median relative surprisal was at 81% of the first list, compared to 87% for the permuted lists, and 101% for the novel lists. In GPT-2, repeat surprisal was only 2% of the first list, much lower than the 58% for the permuted lists, and 96% of the novel list.

Retrieval in GPT-2 was robust to the exact phrasing of the text that introduced the lists. Replacing the subject 'Mary' with 'John' in the vignette, replacing the colon with a comma or randomly permuting the preface or the prompt strings did not affect the results (Fig. 7, bottom, Appendix A). By contrast, the same perturbations reduced retrieval effects for Wikitext-103 (Fig. 7, top, Appendix A), supporting the conclusion that larger training corpus size contributes to robustness of transformer retrieval.

Transformer retrieval was robust to the number of items being retrieved. In studies of human short-term memory, performance degrades as the number of items that need to be retained increases ("set-size effects", Oberauer et al. 2018). Is our LMs' short-term memory similarly taxed by increasing the set size? We varied the number of tokens to be held in memory with $N^{tokens} \in \{3, 5, 7, 10\}$. For this comparison, the length of the intervening text was kept at 26 tokens. Results reported in Fig. 3 show that for both the smaller Wikitext-103 transformer and the larger GPT-2, verbatim recall was, for the most part, consistent across the different set sizes. For GPT-2, repeat surprisal increased monotonically with set size only when the order of nouns in second list, either semantically coherent or arbitrary, was permuted.[6]

Transformer retrieval was robust to the length and content of intervening text, but scrambling the intervening text reduced retrieval of order information. For how long are individual items retained in the memory of the LM? We tested this by varying the length of the intervening text for $N^{tokens} \in \{26, 99, 194, 435\}$ (see Fig. 1, panel B). To generate longer intervening text samples, we continued the narrative established by the initial preface string ("Before the meeting, Mary wrote down the following list of words:"). All intervening text strings ended with the same prompt string ("When she got back, she read the list again:") which introduced the second list.

[5]Novel nouns in the string were introduced by randomly selecting a list of nouns from one the 22 remaining lists in the noun pool. In semantically coherent lists, novel nouns were drawn from a different semantic category than the nouns in the first list.

[6]This increase in surprisal with set size for permuted sequences is to be expected, of course, because, if the model has perfect memory of the list of tokens, but cannot predict the order in which they will reoccur, then its probability of guessing the next item in a permuted list where k items have yet to be observed will be $1/k$, and the mean value of k is larger for larger set sizes.

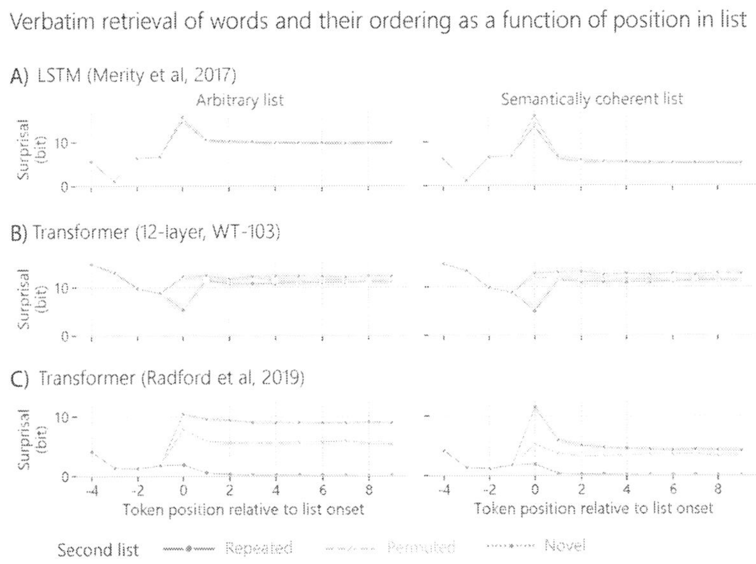

Figure 2: Median surprisal (over $N^{list} = 230$) broken down per token position in second lists of arbitrary nouns and semantically coherent nouns. Negative values on x-axis represent 4 tokens of prompt string that introduced the second list: "(she) read the list again". The 0-index marks the first noun in the list. Line style and hue denote manipulation of the second list relative to the first list. Error bands denote 95% confidence interval around the median (bootstrap estimate).

Memory retrieval in the transformer models, whether trained on Wikitext-103 or a much larger corpus size, was largely invariant to the size of the intervening text between the first and second lists (Fig. 3, B and C, respectively). The results suggest that the two transformers were retrieving prior nouns using a form of direct indexing of the relevant words from the input buffer, rather than implementing a generic memory heuristic, such as predicting that the nouns that have occurred in the most recent 20 tokens will recur.

Increasing the length of *well-formed, semantically coherent* intervening text does not, then, interfere with memory retrieval in the transformer. In models of human memory, current context, such as immediately preceding text, can indeed be used as a cue for recalling the encoded items (Kahana, 2020). Does the transformers' capacity to retrieve copies of past nouns rely on the content and structure of the intervening text? We tested this by creating incongruent and scrambled versions of the longest intervening text (435 tokens). An incongruent condition was created by using intervening text that was syntactically well-formed but semantically incongruent with respect to the preface. The scrambled version was created by randomly permuting the tokens of the intervening text.

The transformers' retrieval of past tokens was largely unaffected by the specific content of the intervening text, as long as the intervening text was coherent/well-formed (Fig. 4). However, in GPT-2, median surprisal across permuted arbitrary lists of nouns increased by 8% when the intervening text was scrambled (Fig. 4, bottom) compared to well-formed text. This suggests that GPT-2 relied on narrative coherence of the intervening text, rather than its aggregate semantic content alone, as a cue for retrieving the ordering information of arbitrary word lists.

Transformer verbatim recall is learned, guided by attention, and requires increase in size. Having shown that the transformer LMs could flexibly and robustly retrieve words and their ordering verbatim from short-term memory (Figs. 3 and 4), we next asked: is this ability learned, or does it derive directly from the architecture? To address this question, we re-ran the experiment with varying number of tokens in lists with a randomly initialized transformer model (architecture as in Section 3.3). This random-weights model was unable to retrieve words or their order: for example, repeat surprisal remained at 100% relative to first lists regardless of whether or not the nouns in the second list have appeared before (Fig. 8, top, Appendix A).

Next we tested whether the transformers' abil-

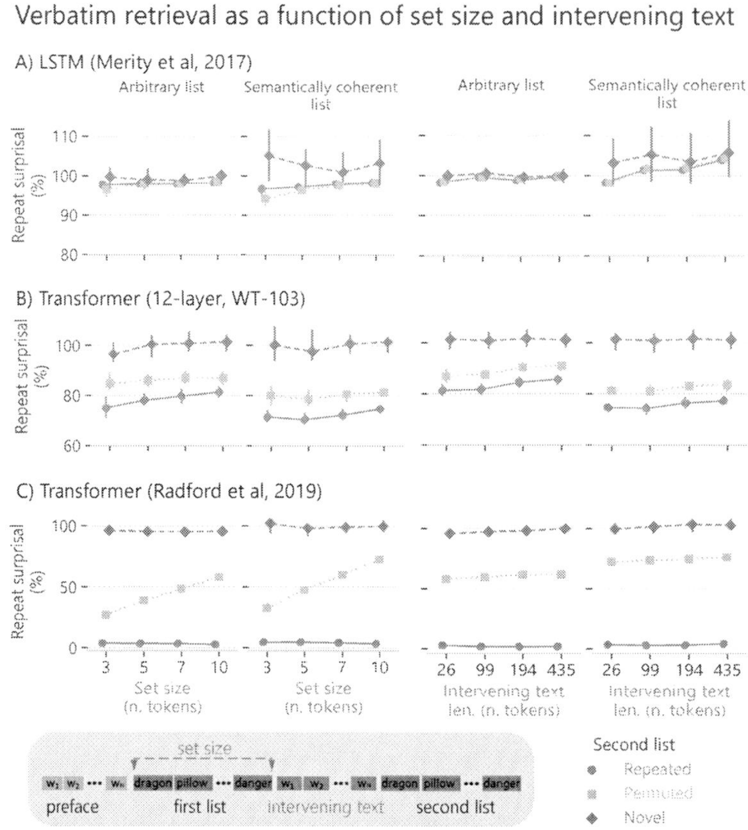

Figure 3: Verbatim token retrieval for varying number of tokens being retrieved (left) and the length of the intervening text (right). Reported is proportion of list-averaged surprisal on second relative to first list of nouns. Points show group median (over $N^{list} = 230$). Error bars denote 95% confidence interval around the median (bootstrap estimate). For set size manipulation, intervening text is fixed at 26 tokens. For intervening text manipulation, set size is fixed at 10 tokens.

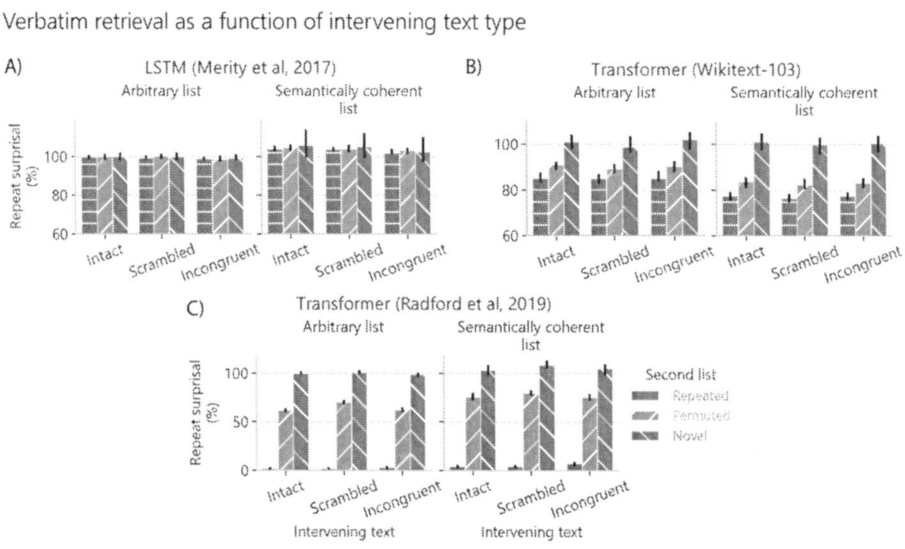

Figure 4: LM memory retrieval for different intervening texts. We plot relative list-averaged surprisal over all non-initial tokens in lists. Points show group median (over $N^{list} = 230$). Error bars denote 95% confidence interval around the median (bootstrap estimate). Note that in the top-row plots y-axis starts at 60%.

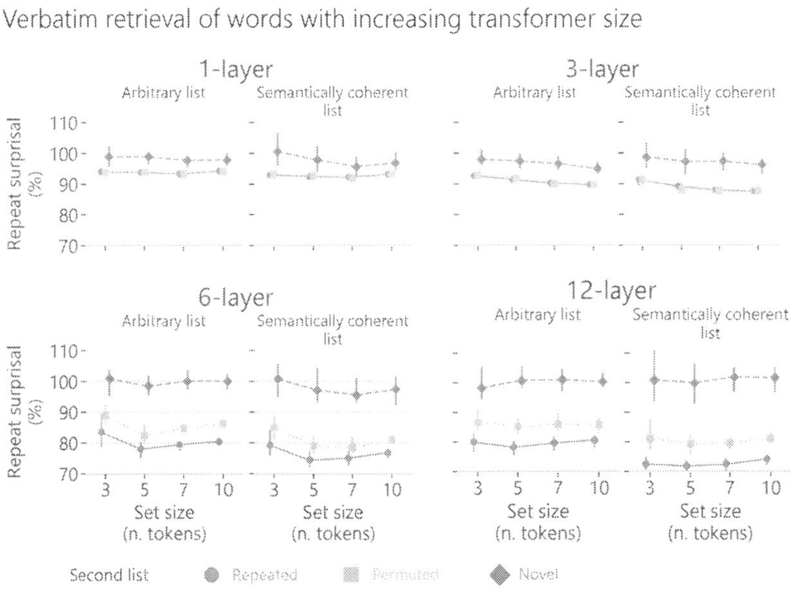

Figure 5: LM memory retrieval for models of different sizes. Reported is relative list-averaged surprisal over all non-initial tokens in lists. Points show group median (over N^{list} = 230). Error bars denote 95% confidence interval around the median (bootstrap estimate). Note that in these plots y-axis starts at 70%.

ity to recall past tokens depended on the attention mechanism (Bahdanau et al., 2014; Vaswani et al., 2017) which allows it, in principle, to use all past words, weighted according to their relevance, for next word prediction. To test for the role of attention in verbatim retrieval, we randomly permuted the rows of key and query matrices in each of the 12 attention layers of GPT-2 and reran the experiment with varying number of tokens in lists. The shuffled-attention model retained some capacity to retrieve past nouns (Fig. 8, bottom, Appendix A), but the effect was greatly reduced. For example, repeat surprisal for lists of $N = 10$ semantically coherent nouns was at 90% relative to first lists for shuffled-attention, compared with 3% for the intact model. Intriguingly, this shuffled-attention model showed the same surprisal for repeated and permuted lists, indicating that it was no longer accessing word order information from the original list. Thus, the attention mechanism is necessary for transformers to index past nouns and their order from memory.

Finally, a deep layered architecture is a key characteristic of transformers and performance typically scales with model size (Radford et al., 2019; Kaplan et al., 2020). Does the capacity to perform verbatim recall depend on model size? To address this question, we trained transformers with 1, 3, 6 and 12 layers on our 40-million subset of Wikitext-103. Consistent with the hypothesis that size – in addition to architecture – is crucial, the smaller 1- and 3-layer models showed a modest verbatim recall capacity, but were not sensitive to order (e.g. the 3-layer model shows 90% repeat surprisal for repeated and permuted lists of $N = 10$ tokens, Fig. 5). Sensitivity to order progressively emerged in 6- and 12-layer models, where in the 12-layer model repeat surprisal levels were 5% and 7% lower for repeated relative to permuted 10-token lists (Fig. 5). While this result confirms that even transformers trained on smaller amounts of text can exhibit short-term memory with sufficient increase in complexity, it remains unclear whether it is the increased depth or the parameter count alone that contribute to this increase in performance.

5 LSTM Results

The LSTM retrieves gist-like memories over short intervening distances, facilitated by semantic coherence. The LSTM language model expected nouns in the second list to belong to the same semantic category as the first list, and especially to the category of the earliest nouns in the first list. If the intervening text was no longer than 26 tokens, LSTM repeat surprisal across non-initial token positions (Fig. 3, A) showed a modest decrease (5%) relative to first list, but only when the nouns in the first and second lists came from

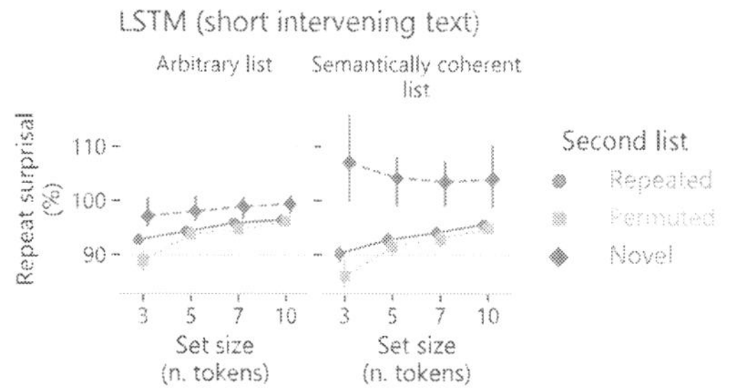

Figure 6: LSTM verbatim token retrieval for varying number of tokens being retrieved at short (4-token) intervening text. Reported is proportion of list-averaged surprisal on second relative to first list of nouns (repeat surprisal). Points show group median (over N^{list} = 230). Error bars denote 95% confidence interval around the median (bootstrap estimate).

the same semantic category. Examining surprisal values broken down by token position in the list (Fig. 2, top) shows that in semantically coherent lists of nouns, surprisal was higher for novel lists than for repeated or permuted lists, but this memory effect was only present for tokens near the beginning of the list.

In light of this limited evidence for retrieval in the LSTM across 26 intervening tokens, we examined whether the LSTM retrieves more successfully over shorter intervals. We reduced the intervening text to 4 tokens of coherent text ("Before the meeting, Mary wrote down the following lists of words. One was: <first list> **And the other:** <second list>"). In this short-range retrieval setting, we now observed a small reduction of relative repeat surprisal of 5% and 4% for arbitrary lists of 3 or 5 nouns, respectively, as well as a stronger reductions ranging from 12% (3-token list) to 5% (10-token list) for semantically coherent lists (Fig. 6).

Overall, the reduction in surprisal was comparable for repeated and permuted lists, indicating that the LSTM did not predict that words would occur in their original order. Taken together, the experiments described in the section suggest that the LSTM retrieves a semantic gist of the prior list, rather than individual tokens in order. Consistent with this notion of an aggregate semantic memory, we found that retrieval was stronger for semantically coherent lists, for which an aggregated semantic representation would be closer to each of the individual words in the list.

6 Discussion

Short-term memory—the capacity to temporarily store and access recent context for current processing—is a crucial component of language prediction. In this paper, we introduced a paradigm for characterizing a language model's short-term memory capabilities, based on retrieval of verbatim content (sequences of nouns) from prior context, and used this paradigm to analyze LMs with transformer and LSTM architectures.

The transformers we tested were able to access verbatim information – individual tokens and their order – from past context. Furthermore, this verbatim retrieval was learned and largely *resilient* to interference from intervening context. This indicates that the models (especially those trained on the largest corpora) implemented, via learning, a high-resolution memory system. The ability to access individual tokens may in turn support functions that rely on token indexing, akin to the functionality of the general-purpose working memory (WM) buffer proposed in cognitive science (Baddeley, 2003).

Such flexible WM could subserve the reported ability of transformers to rapidly generalize to new tasks at runtime (Brown et al., 2020), also known as "in-context learning". Indeed, in concurrent work to ours, Olsson et al. (2022) observed that small (2 or 3-layer) attention-only transformers developed attention heads that functioned as so-called "induction heads". These effectively performed pattern matching by looking over the past context for any occurrences of the current token and predicting the same (or similar) sequence completions. Attention heads that learned this basic inductive computation were also shown to perform more general in-context learning for complex tasks such as language translation. Similarly, it has been suggested that in standard RNNs such meta-learning requires a short-term memory mechanism known as fast weights (Schmidhuber, 1992; Ba et al., 2016) which can be thought of as analogous to self-attention in transformers (Schlag et al., 2021).

However, a highly resilient verbatim memory system could also be disadvantageous if it causes the LM to place too much confidence on verbatim features of prior context for next-word prediction. Indeed, text generated from a transformer LM's predictions can be highly repetitive (Holtzman et al., 2020) – it is possible that an over-reliance on accessing short-term memory may underlie this tendency.

In contrast to the transformers, the LSTM model only retrieved a coarse semantic category of previous lists, without fine-grained information about word order, and was only able to do so when the intervening text was short. This is in spite of the fact that the LSTM had a larger parameter count than the transformer models and obtained comparable perplexity on WikiText103 (Table 3). The tendency of LSTMs to rely on the fuzzy representation of past context for next-word prediction has been reported previously (Khandelwal et al., 2018). Whereas in sequence-to-sequence tasks requiring recall of short lists of pseudowords, recurrent neural networks are a good model of human short-term memory (Botvinick and Plaut, 2006), later research has shown that the copying capacity of LSTMs does not generalize to longer sequences of symbols (Grefenstette et al., 2015).

Is tracking a shallow representation of context always a limitation? Not necessarily. Humans frequently maintain a "good-enough" (i.e. gist-like) representation of context (Ferreira and Patson, 2007). When the potential for memory capacity is limited (e.g. when context must be compressed to a single hidden state as in an RNN) maintaining a broad, gist-like – as opposed to token-specific – memory of context may be more *efficient* overall.

The memory paradigm and the measure of repeat surprisal introduced here allowed us to pinpoint computational differences in how neural LMs put their architectural capacities to use for storing and accessing context in short-term memory when processing English text. While our decision to use autoregressive (left-to-right) LMs was ultimately based on our initial cognitive psycholinguistic motivation, it may be fruitful to apply our paradigm to other classes of transformer models, for example, bidirectional encoder-only transformers such as BERT (Devlin et al., 2019) and encoder-decoder models such as T5 (Raffel et al., 2020). These architectures have gained traction in applied NLP settings and it would be informative to test whether this paradigm can provide diagnostic value for LM performance on other benchmarks. Similarly, if the compressed context representation in LSTMs serves as a short-term memory bottleneck, it would be instructive to test LSTM LM architectures when explicitly augmented with attention (Bahdanau et al., 2014) or a copy-mechanism (Gu et al., 2016). Finally, our attention-ablation experiment in the transformer was performed uniformly across layers; future studies could focus on targeted ablations of specific attention heads to pinpoint the mechanistic locus of short-term memory (Olsson et al., 2022).

7 Conclusions

Pretrained language models, and self-supervised predictive learning broadly, have received increased attention in terms of their (in)sufficiency as a framework for achieving feats of human-like language processing (Kaplan et al., 2020; Linzen and Baroni, 2021). Here, akin to the line of work evaluating cognitive linguistic capacities of neural LMs (Futrell et al., 2019; Ritter et al., 2017), we tested the ability of language models to perform an important aspect of human intelligence for natural language — flexibly accessing items from short-term memory — and showed that the transformer model, even though not trained with a short-term memory objective, retrieved remarkably detailed representations of past context. This capacity emerged from training: a transformer trained on a small amount of data showed more modest retrieval abilities. The retrieval abilities of LSTM LMs, by contrast, were different; the LSTM maintained a summary representation of the list, which was not sensitive to word order. We conclude that our paradigm can illuminate the memory systems that arise in neural language models.

8 Broader Impact

The research reported here addresses a specific, basic research question about the functional organization of short-term memory in contemporary language processing algorithms. Although from a broader perspective, the nature of (working) memory is likely an important question in developing human-like artificial intelligence systems deployed in real-life scenarios, it is, in our opinion, unlikely that the results reported here could pose or lead to novel societal risks as we are primarily trying to better the understanding of the already developed systems.

Acknowledgements

The authors gratefully acknowledge the support of the National Institutes of Mental Health (grant R01MH119099). The research presented here also benefited from the discussions and feedback during the research visit (by KA) in the context of the collaborative grant "Working Memory Based Assessment of Large Language Models" at the Department of Language Technologies, Institute Jozef Stefan. The visit was in part financially supported by the Slovenian Research Agency (grant BI-US/22-24-170). Finally, this work was supported in part through the NYU IT High Performance Computing resources, services, and staff expertise.

References

Jimmy Ba, Geoffrey Hinton, Volodymyr Mnih, Joel Z. Leibo, and Catalin Ionescu. 2016. Using fast weights to attend to the recent past. In *Proceedings of the 30th International Conference on Neural Information Processing Systems*, NIPS'16, pages 4338–4346, Red Hook, NY, USA. Curran Associates Inc.

Alan Baddeley. 2003. Working memory: looking back and looking forward. *Nature Reviews Neuroscience*, 4(10):829–839.

Dzmitry Bahdanau, Kyunghyun Cho, and Yoshua Bengio. 2014. Neural machine translation by jointly learning to align and translate. *CoRR*, abs/1409.0473.

Matthew M. Botvinick and David C. Plaut. 2006. Short-term memory for serial order: A recurrent neural network model. *Psychological Review*, 113(2):201–233.

Tom Brown, Benjamin Mann, Nick Ryder, Melanie Subbiah, Jared D Kaplan, Prafulla Dhariwal, Arvind Neelakantan, Pranav Shyam, Girish Sastry, Amanda Askell, Sandhini Agarwal, Ariel Herbert-Voss, Gretchen Krueger, Tom Henighan, Rewon Child, Aditya Ramesh, Daniel Ziegler, Jeffrey Wu, Clemens Winter, Chris Hesse, Mark Chen, Eric Sigler, Mateusz Litwin, Scott Gray, Benjamin Chess, Jack Clark, Christopher Berner, Sam McCandlish, Alec Radford, Ilya Sutskever, and Dario Amodei. 2020. Language models are few-shot learners. In *Advances in Neural Information Processing Systems*, volume 33, pages 1877–1901. Curran Associates, Inc.

Jacob Devlin, Ming-Wei Chang, Kenton Lee, and Kristina Toutanova. 2019. BERT: Pre-training of deep bidirectional transformers for language understanding. In *Proceedings of the 2019 Conference of the North American Chapter of the Association for Computational Linguistics: Human Language Technologies, Volume 1 (Long and Short Papers)*, pages 4171–4186, Minneapolis, Minnesota. Association for Computational Linguistics.

Fernanda Ferreira and Nikole D. Patson. 2007. The 'Good Enough' approach to language comprehension. *Language and Linguistics Compass*, 1(1-2):71–83.

Richard Futrell, Ethan Wilcox, Takashi Morita, and Roger Levy. 2018. RNNs as psycholinguistic subjects: Syntactic state and grammatical dependency. *arXiv:1809.01329 [cs]*. ArXiv: 1809.01329.

Richard Futrell, Ethan Wilcox, Takashi Morita, Peng Qian, Miguel Ballesteros, and Roger Levy. 2019. Neural language models as psycholinguistic subjects: Representations of syntactic state. In *Proceedings of the 2019 Conference of the North American Chapter of the Association for Computational Linguistics: Human Language Technologies, Volume 1 (Long and Short Papers)*, pages 32–42, Minneapolis, Minnesota. Association for Computational Linguistics.

Edward Grefenstette, Karl Moritz Hermann, Mustafa Suleyman, and Phil Blunsom. 2015. Learning to transduce with unbounded memory. In *Proceedings of the 28th International Conference on Neural Information Processing Systems - Volume 2*, NIPS'15, pages 1828–1836, Cambridge, MA, USA. MIT Press.

Jiatao Gu, Zhengdong Lu, Hang Li, and Victor O.K. Li. 2016. Incorporating copying mechanism in sequence-to-sequence learning. In *Proceedings of the 54th Annual Meeting of the Association for Computational Linguistics (Volume 1: Long Papers)*, pages 1631–1640, Berlin, Germany. Association for Computational Linguistics.

Kristina Gulordava, Piotr Bojanowski, Edouard Grave, Tal Linzen, and Marco Baroni. 2018. Colorless green recurrent networks dream hierarchically. In *Proceedings of the 2018 Conference of the North American Chapter of the Association for Computational Linguistics: Human Language Technologies, Volume 1 (Long Papers)*, pages 1195–1205, New Orleans, Louisiana. Association for Computational Linguistics.

Sepp Hochreiter and Jürgen Schmidhuber. 1997. Long short-term memory. *Neural Computation*, 9(8):1735–1780.

Ari Holtzman, Jan Buys, Li Du, Maxwell Forbes, and Yejin Choi. 2020. The curious case of neural text degeneration.

Michael J. Kahana. 2020. Computational models of memory search. *Annual Review of Psychology*, 71(1):107–138.

Jared Kaplan, Sam McCandlish, Tom Henighan, Tom B. Brown, Benjamin Chess, Rewon Child, Scott Gray, Alec Radford, Jeffrey Wu, and Dario Amodei. 2020. Scaling laws for neural language models. *arXiv:2001.08361 [cs, stat]*. ArXiv: 2001.08361.

Urvashi Khandelwal, He He, Peng Qi, and Dan Jurafsky. 2018. Sharp nearby, fuzzy far away: How neural language models use context. In *Proceedings of the 56th Annual Meeting of the Association for Computational Linguistics (Volume 1: Long Papers)*, pages 284–294, Melbourne, Australia. Association for Computational Linguistics.

Yair Lakretz, Dieuwke Hupkes, Alessandra Vergallito, Marco Marelli, Marco Baroni, and Stanislas Dehaene. 2021. Mechanisms for handling nested dependencies in neural-network language models and humans. *Cognition*, 213:104699.

Yair Lakretz, German Kruszewski, Theo Desbordes, Dieuwke Hupkes, Stanislas Dehaene, and Marco Baroni. 2019. The emergence of number and syntax units in LSTM language models. In *Proceedings of the 2019 Conference of the North American Chapter of the Association for Computational Linguistics: Human Language Technologies, Volume 1 (Long and Short Papers)*, pages 11–20, Minneapolis, Minnesota. Association for Computational Linguistics.

Tal Linzen and Marco Baroni. 2021. Syntactic structure from deep learning. *Annual Review of Linguistics*, 7(1):195–212. _eprint: https://doi.org/10.1146/annurev-linguistics-032020-051035.

Tal Linzen, Emmanuel Dupoux, and Yoav Goldberg. 2016. Assessing the ability of LSTMs to learn Syntax-sensitive dependencies. *Transactions of the Association for Computational Linguistics*, 4:521–535.

Rebecca Marvin and Tal Linzen. 2018. Targeted syntactic evaluation of language models. In *Proceedings of the 2018 Conference on Empirical Methods in Natural Language Processing*, pages 1192–1202, Brussels, Belgium. Association for Computational Linguistics.

Stephen Merity, Nitish Shirish Keskar, and Richard Socher. 2018. Regularizing and optimizing LSTM language models.

Stephen Merity, Caiming Xiong, James Bradbury, and Richard Socher. 2016. Pointer sentinel mixture models.

Klaus Oberauer, Stephan Lewandowsky, Edward Awh, Gordon D. A. Brown, Andrew Conway, Nelson Cowan, Christopher Donkin, Simon Farrell, Graham J. Hitch, Mark J. Hurlstone, Wei Ji Ma, Candice C. Morey, Derek Evan Nee, Judith Schweppe, Evie Vergauwe, and Geoff Ward. 2018. Benchmarks for models of short-term and working memory. *Psychological Bulletin*, 144(9):885–958.

Joe O'Connor and Jacob Andreas. 2021. What context features can transformer language models use? In *Proceedings of the 59th Annual Meeting of the Association for Computational Linguistics and the 11th International Joint Conference on Natural Language Processing (Volume 1: Long Papers)*, pages 851–864, Online. Association for Computational Linguistics.

Catherine Olsson, Nelson Elhage, Neel Nanda, Nicholas Joseph, Nova DasSarma, Tom Henighan, Ben Mann, Amanda Askell, Yuntao Bai, Anna Chen, Tom Conerly, Dawn Drain, Deep Ganguli, Zac Hatfield-Dodds, Danny Hernandez, Scott Johnston, Andy Jones, Jackson Kernion, Liane Lovitt, Kamal Ndousse, Dario Amodei, Tom Brown, Jack Clark, Jared Kaplan, Sam McCandlish, and Chris Olah. 2022. In-context learning and induction heads. *Transformer Circuits Thread*.

Alec Radford, Jeff Wu, Rewon Child, David Luan, Dario Amodei, and Ilya Sutskever. 2019. Language models are unsupervised multitask learners.

Colin Raffel, Noam Shazeer, Adam Roberts, Katherine Lee, Sharan Narang, Michael Matena, Yanqi Zhou, Wei Li, and Peter J. Liu. 2020. Exploring the limits of transfer learning with a unified text-to-text transformer. *J. Mach. Learn. Res.*, 21(1). Publisher: JMLR.org.

Samuel Ritter, David G. T. Barrett, Adam Santoro, and Matt M. Botvinick. 2017. Cognitive psychology for deep neural networks: A shape bias case study. In *Proceedings of the 34th International Conference on Machine Learning*, pages 2940–2949. PMLR. ISSN: 2640-3498.

Imanol Schlag, Kazuki Irie, and Jürgen Schmidhuber. 2021. Linear transformers are secretly fast weight programmers. In *Proceedings of the 38th International Conference on Machine Learning*, volume 139 of *Proceedings of Machine Learning Research*, pages 9355–9366. PMLR.

Jürgen Schmidhuber. 1992. Learning to control fast-weight memories: An alternative to dynamic recurrent networks. *Neural Computation*, 4(1):131–139.

Sandeep Subramanian, Ronan Collobert, Marc'Aurelio Ranzato, and Y.-Lan Boureau. 2020. Multi-scale transformer language models. *arXiv:2005.00581 [cs]*. ArXiv: 2005.00581.

Yi Tay, Mostafa Dehghani, Dara Bahri, and Donald Metzler. 2020. Efficient transformers: A survey. *arXiv:2009.06732 [cs]*. ArXiv: 2009.06732 version: 2.

Ashish Vaswani, Noam Shazeer, Niki Parmar, Jakob Uszkoreit, Llion Jones, Aidan N. Gomez, Łukasz Kaiser, and Illia Polosukhin. 2017. Attention is all you need. In *Proceedings of the 31st International Conference on Neural Information Processing Systems*, NIPS'17, pages 6000–6010, Red Hook, NY, USA. Curran Associates Inc.

Jason Weston, Sumit Chopra, and Antoine Bordes. 2015. Memory networks. In *3rd International Conference on Learning Representations, ICLR 2015*, San Diego. 3rd International Conference on Learning Representations.

Thomas Wolf, Lysandre Debut, Victor Sanh, Julien Chaumond, Clement Delangue, Anthony Moi, Pierric Cistac, Tim Rault, Remi Louf, Morgan Funtowicz, Joe Davison, Sam Shleifer, Patrick von Platen, Clara Ma, Yacine Jernite, Julien Plu, Canwen Xu, Teven Le Scao, Sylvain Gugger, Mariama Drame, Quentin Lhoest, and Alexander Rush. 2020. Transformers: State-of-the-Art natural language processing. In *Proceedings of the 2020 Conference on Empirical Methods in Natural Language Processing: System Demonstrations*, pages 38–45, Online. Association for Computational Linguistics.

Dani Yogatama, Yishu Miao, Gabor Melis, Wang Ling, Adhiguna Kuncoro, Chris Dyer, and Phil Blunsom. 2018. Memory architectures in recurrent neural network language models.

A Appendix

A.1 Vignettes

Intact intervening text:

Before the meeting, Mary wrote down the following list of words:

$W_1, W_2, ..., W_N$

$intervening\_text_1$: After the meeting, she took a break and had a cup of coffee. When she got back, she read the list again: $W_1, W_2, ..., W_N$

$intervening\_text_2$: After the meeting, Mary went for a walk. It was a busy day and she needed a break. Outside was really beautiful and warm and the flowers in the park were blooming. When she got back, she read the list again: $W_1, W_2, ..., W_N$

$intervening\_text_3$: After the meeting, Mary went for a walk. It was a busy day and she needed a break. Outside was really beautiful and warm and the flowers in the park were blooming. While she was walking, she listened to the wonderful bird songs. During the walk, Mary could not stop thinking about the meeting. She was thinking about the discussions she had with her coworkers. Luckily, she met her neighbors Sarah and Ryan and they talked briefly. When she got back, she read the list again: $W_1, W_2, ..., W_N$

$intervening\_text_4$: After the meeting, Mary went for a walk. It was a busy day and she needed a break. Outside was really beautiful and warm and the flowers in the park were blooming. While she was walking, she listened to the wonderful bird songs. During the walk, Mary could not stop thinking about the meeting. She was thinking about the discussions she had with her coworkers. Luckily, she met her neighbors Sarah and Ryan and they talked briefly. The couple has just moved to the area from a different city. Mary thought they were very a lovely couple and made good company. They were just getting to know the neighborhood and this was their first time in the park. Mary was curious what were their first impressions of the town. The neighborhood felt very safe to them and they absolutely loved the park. This was only their second time visiting the park. There was so much to discover, so many winding paths and hidden gardens. When she got back, she read the list again: $W_1, W_2, ..., W_N$

$intervening\_text_5$: After the meeting, Mary went for a walk. It was a busy day and she needed a break. Outside was really beautiful and warm and the flowers in the park were blooming. While she was walking, she listened to the wonderful bird songs. During the walk, Mary could not stop thinking about the meeting. She was thinking about the discussions she had with her coworkers. Luckily, she met her neighbors Sarah and Ryan and they talked briefly. The couple has just moved to the area from a different city. Mary thought they were very a lovely couple and made good company. They were just getting to know the neighborhood and this was their first time in the park. Mary was curious what were their first impressions of the town. The neighborhood felt very safe to them and they absolutely loved the park. This was only their second time visiting the park. There was so much to discover, so many winding paths and hidden gardens. It was not a big park by any means, but it offered a quiet refuge where one can escape the worries of everyday life. It also offered opportunities to do sports of all kinds. Young people from around the area played basketball, football, or volleyball. Others took part in outdoor workout sessions. Young families were going on a stroll with their children. Finally, there were so many people who brought their dogs for a walk. It was incredibly satisfying to see the joy our animal friends get when you throw them a ball. All this diversity of people and activities made a walk in this park a truly rewarding and relaxing daily routine. In fact, Sarah and Ryan were thinking of getting a dog. They have not fully decided yet but they really wanted to spend more time outdoors. Mary liked dogs as well, but she was more of a cat person herself. She and her husband had two cats. One was two and the other four years old. They were very independent and spent most of their time outdoors. Mary thought having an animal was a great idea. They talked for a little bit and then Sarah and Ryan invited her to come over for a cup of coffee. Mary said she had time over the weekend. When she got back, she read the list again: $W_1, W_2, ..., W_N$

Scrambled intervening text:

Before the meeting, Mary wrote down the following list of words:

$W_1, W_2, ..., W_N$

$intervening\_text_1$: After a break, a cup and coffee of had she the took meeting. When she got back, she read the list again: $W_1, W_2, ..., W_N$

$intervening\_text_2$: Outside the the beautiful and park flowers blooming were in and was warm really. After, walk for Mary the a went meeting. It needed busy break she day was a and a. When she got back, she read the list again: $W_1, W_2, ..., W_N$

$intervening\_text_3$: Luckily and and met Sarah they Ryan briefly talked her, neighbors she. Thinking during, stop meeting the not about Mary the could walk. The while walking to songs bird listened wonderful, she she was. After, walk for Mary the a went meeting. Had she about she coworkers her with the was discussions thinking. Outside the the beautiful and park flowers blooming were in and was warm really. It needed busy break she day was a and a. When she got back, she read the list again: $W_1, W_2, ..., W_N$

$intervening\_text_4$: First they their was neighborhood getting and the in park the this to were time know just. There paths so much, and many gardens hidden winding to was discover so. The while walking to songs bird listened wonderful, she she was. Had she about she coworkers her with the was discussions thinking. From the just area city different the a moved couple to has. The absolutely and very them loved they park the safe neighborhood to felt. Outside the the beautiful and park flowers blooming were in and was warm really. And Mary were couple company good lovely made very thought a they. Luckily and and met Sarah they Ryan briefly talked her, neighbors she. Thinking during, stop meeting the not about Mary the could walk. After, walk for Mary the a went meeting. Their this park visiting second was the time only. Impressions Mary what first town the of were was their curious. It needed busy break she day was a and a. When she got back, she read the list again: $W_1, W_2, ..., W_N$

$intervening\_text_5$: It needed busy break she day was a and a. First they their was neighborhood getting and the in park the this to were time know just. Had she about she coworkers her with the was discussions thinking. Of they independent most outdoors time their and were spent very. Get it friends them our joy satisfying when the throw ball a animal to was you see incredibly. The while walking to songs bird listened wonderful, she she was. Weekend had time Mary said the over she. An Mary idea a animal thought great was having. Mary a she was as but cat of herself person more well liked, dogs. It of opportunities kinds sports to also all do offered. Cats husband had she and two her. They spend they really fully but more to outdoors time wanted decided have yet not. A a and of rewarding park all in made this activities relaxing routine daily truly walk people this and diversity. There paths so much, and many gardens hidden winding to was discover so. Finally dogs who were people for brought walk a their so, many there. Luckily and and met Sarah they Ryan briefly talked her, neighbors she. The absolutely and very them loved they park the safe neighborhood to felt. Outside the the beautiful and park flowers blooming were in and was warm really. Young football basketball around played,, volleyball or the people area from. Their this park visiting second was the time only. To Sarah a a for her they Ryan then invited and cup coffee of over come and little talked bit for. From the just area city different the a moved couple to has. And Mary were couple company good lovely made very thought a they. Young with going children stroll on families their a were. Worries a means escape where a offered but one refuge can it by any it the quiet of life everyday, big was park not. Of in Sarah thinking dog a were getting and fact Ryan,. Thinking during, stop meeting the not about Mary the could walk. After, walk for Mary the a went meeting. And one old four the was years other two. Impressions Mary what first town the of were was their curious. Sessions in outdoor others took workout part. When she got back, she read the list again: $W_1, W_2, ..., W_N$

Incongruent intervening text:

Before the meeting, Mary wrote down the following list of words:

$W_1, W_2, ..., W_N$

$intervening\_text_1$: There is a voice in the waters of the great sea. It calls to man continually. When she got back, she read the list again: $W_1, W_2, ..., W_N$

$intervening\_text_2$: Sometimes it thunders in the tempest, when the waves leap high and strong and the wild winds shriek and roar. Sometimes it whispers in the calm, small voice, as if to solicit our regard. When she got back, she read the list again: $W_1, W_2, ..., W_N$

$intervening\_text_3$: After the meeting, Mary went for a walk. It was a busy day and she needed a break. Outside was really beautiful and warm and the flowers in the park were blooming. The sea has much to say; far more than could possibly be comprehended in one volume, however large. It tells us of the doings of man on its broad bosom, from the day in which he first ventured to paddle along shore to the day when he launched his great iron ship, and rushed out to sea. When she got back, she read the list again: $W_1, W_2, ..., W_N$

$intervening\_text_4$: After the meeting, Mary went for a walk. It was a busy day and she needed a break. Outside was really beautiful and warm and the flowers in the park were blooming. The sea has much to say; far more than could possibly be comprehended in one volume, however large. It tells us of the doings of man on its broad bosom, from the day in which he first ventured to paddle along shore to the day when he launched his great iron ship, and rushed out to sea. Before proceeding to the consideration of the wonders connected with and contained in the sea, we shall treat of the composition of the sea itself and of its extent, depth, and bottom. What is the sea made of? Salt water, is the ready reply that rises naturally to every lip. But to this we add the question, what is salt water? To these queries we give the following reply, which, we doubt not, will rather surprise some of our readers. The salt of the ocean varies considerably in different parts. When she got back, she read the list again: $W_1, W_2, ..., W_N$

$intervening\_text_5$: After the meeting, Mary went for a walk. It was a busy day and she needed a break. Outside was really beautiful and warm and the flowers in the park were blooming. The sea has much to say; far more than could possibly be comprehended in one volume, however large. It tells us of the doings of man on its broad bosom, from the day in which he first ventured to paddle along shore to the day when he launched his great iron ship, and rushed out to sea. Before proceeding to the consideration of the wonders connected with and contained in the sea, we shall treat of the composition of the sea itself and of its extent, depth, and bottom. What is the sea made of? Salt water, is the ready reply that rises naturally to every lip. But to this we add the question, what is salt water? To these queries we give the following reply, which, we doubt not, will rather surprise some of our readers. The salt of the ocean varies considerably in different parts. Near the equator, the great heat carries up a larger proportion of water by evaporation than in the more temperate regions. Thus, as salt is not removed by evaporation, the ocean in the torrid zone is salter than in the temperate or frigid zones. The salts of the sea, and other substances contained in it, are conveyed there by the fresh water streams that pour into it from all the continent of the world Here, as these substances cannot be evaporated, they would accumulate to such a degree as to render the ocean uninhabitable by living creatures.The operations of the ocean are manifold. But we cannot speak of these things without making passing reference to the operations of water, as that wonder-working agent of which the ocean constitutes but a part. Nothing in this world is ever lost or annihilated. As the ocean receives all the water that flows from the land, so it returns that water, fresh and pure, in the shape of vapour, to the skies. where, in the form of clouds, it is conveyed to those parts of the earth where its presence is most needed. After having gladdened the heart of man by driving his mills and causing his food to grow, it finds its way again into the sea: and thus the good work goes on with ceaseless regularity. When she got back, she read the list again: $W_1, W_2, ..., W_N$ [7]

[7]The incongruent intervening text was sampled from: "The ocean and its wonder" by R. M. Ballantyne (obtained from: `https://www.gutenberg.org/ebooks/21754`).

Short intervening text:
Before the meeting, Mary wrote down the following lists of words. One was:
$W_1, W_2, ..., W_N$
$intervening\_text_1$: And the other: $W_1, W_2, ..., W_N$

A.2 Noun Lists

A.3 Model Parameter Comparison

Comparison of model parameters across the three main models used in the present study is reported in Table 3.

A.4 LSTM Training Details

The AWD LSTM model was trained using our own version of the original repository. The hyperparameters used for training are reported in Table 4 (essentially input arguments to the original training script which we used: `https://github.com/salesforce/awd-lstm-lm/blob/master/main.py`).

To deploy the training job on an HPC cluster, we used a single GPU (NVIDIA RTX8000), requested 14GB of RAM and a job time of 48 hours. This was sufficient for the model to converge to the perplexity reported in Table 3.

A.5 Transformer Training Details

Transformer training hyperparameters are reported in Table 5. These are effectively input arguments to the HuggingFace `Trainer()` (`https://huggingface.co/transformers/v4.6.0/main_classes/trainer.html`) and `GPT2Config()` (`https://huggingface.co/transformers/v4.6.0/model_doc/gpt2.html#gpt2config`) classes. The model was trained until convergence and training was stopped (early stopping) when the loss did not decrease for at least 0.01 bits in 5 consecutive evaluations.

To train the transformer model on a HPC cluster, we requested a single GPU (NVIDIA RTX8000) with 44GB RAM and 12 hours of job time.

A.6 Compute Resources for Short-term Memory Evaluation Tasks

For a single job (single experimental condition, e.g., evaluating GPT-2 on vignettes with $N = 230$ input sequences containing exactly repeated, abstract noun lists of length 10 and intervening text set to 26 tokens), a single GPU device was used and we typically requested $\sim$12 hours of core-walltime and $\sim$ 4 GB of RAM. To evaluate the RNN models, requesting 06:00 (hh:mm) of walltime and 4GB was typically more than sufficient to avoid any memory overflows.

Table 1: Arbitrary lists of nouns used in present experiments.

	list
1	patience, notion, movie, women, canoe, novel, folly, silver, eagle, center.
2	pleasure, pattern, leader, culture, worker, master, meadow, writer, apple, costume.
3	paper, belief, factor, total, comrade, angle, battle, pistol, nothing, riches.
4	cabin, doorway, candle, parent, monarch, kindness, lover, copy, soldier, kingdom.
5	future, legend, problem, flavor, prairie, forehead, illness, planet, canvas, chamber.
6	oven, patient, daughter, bubble, colour, product, echo, pepper, fountain, music.
7	village, shipping, beauty, football, merit, autumn, lumber, research, resort, rival.
8	county, muscle, vapor, shepherd, sickness, herald, value, mission, finger, building.
9	iron, onion, opera, attack, prison, butter, interest, colonel, commerce, beggar.
10	blanket, marriage, ticket, baby, treasure, event, weakness, cottage, cotton, judgment.
11	summer, bottom, meaning, campaign, voyage, cannon, helmet, thunder, hatred, stanza.
12	effort, province, parcel, temple, river, major, meeting, career, bargain, chimney.
13	acre, fortune, motive, question, service, minute, tiger, author, sorrow, parlor.
14	motor, lawyer, powder, habit, mountain, district, learning, leather, hero, water.
15	orange, letter, acid, stocking, olive, garden, feeling, motion, compass, model.
16	island, theory, person, season, supper, reason, patent, picture, custom, twilight.
17	dragon, pillow, aspect, chairman, marble, horror, justice, danger, bedroom, canal.
18	writing, pocket, training, circuit, cousin, chapter, quarter, button, turkey, surface.
19	sailor, matter, darkness, scatter, captain, tunnel, method, wagon, effect, arrow.
20	image, butcher, anchor, scholar, compound, tribute, victim, lily, witness, widow.
21	candy, window, detail, ocean, program, traffic, feather, array, pilot, silence.
22	vessel, robber, banner, kitten, lemon, failure, princess, painter, bullet, rifle.
23	engine, timber, harbour, party, level, money, single, system, unit, traitor.

Table 2: Semantically coherent lists of nouns used in present experiments.

	list
1	window, door, roof, wall, floor, ceiling, room, basement, hearth, hall.
2	leg, arms, head, eye, foot, nose, finger, ear, hand, toe.
3	sailboat, destroyer, battleship, cruiser, submarine, yacht, canoe, freighter, tugboat, steamship.
4	robin, sparrow, heron, eagle, crow, hawk, parrot, pigeon, woodpecker, vulture.
5	apple, pear, banana, peach, grape, cherry, plum, grapefruit, lemon, apricot.
6	hammer, saw, nails, level, plane, chisel, ruler, wrench, drill, screws.
7	hurricane, tornado, rain, snow, hail, storm, wind, cyclone, clouds, sunshine.
8	oxygen, hydrogen, nitrogen, carbon, sodium, sulphur, helium, chlorine, calcium, potassium.
9	chemistry, physics, psychology, biology, zoology, botany, astronomy, mathematics, geology, microbiology.
10	piano, drum, trumpet, violin, clarinet, flute, guitar, saxophone, trombone, oboe.
11	knife, spoon, fork, pan, pot, stove, bowl, mixer, cup, dish.
12	trout, shark, herring, perch, salmon, tuna, goldfish, cod, carp, pike.
13	football, baseball, basketball, tennis, swimming, soccer, golf, hockey, lacrosse, badminton.
14	doctor, lawyer, teacher, dentist, engineer, professor, carpenter, salesman, nurse, psychologist.
15	oak, maple, pine, elm, birch, spruce, redwood, walnut, fir, hickory.
16	shirt, socks, pants, shoes, blouse, skirt, coat, dress, hat, sweater.
17	cancer, measles, tuberculosis, polio, malaria, leukemia, pneumonia, smallpox, influenza, encephalitis.
18	mountain, hill, valley, river, rock, lake, canyon, tundra, ocean, cave.
19	murder, rape, robbery, theft, assault, arson, kidnapping, larceny, adultery, battery.
20	log, cat, horse, cow, lion, tiger, elephant, pig, bear, mouse.
21	fly, ant, bee, mosquito, spider, beetle, wasp, moth, flea, butterfly.
22	blue, red, green, yellow, black, purple, white, pink, brown, blonde.
23	cotton, wool, silk, rayon, linen, satin, velvet, denim, canvas, felt.

Table 3: Comparison of main architectural and training parameters between models used in the current study.

Model	GPT-2	transformer (WT-103)	AWD LSTM
Reference	Radford et al (2019)	ours	Merity et al (2017)
Nr. layers	12	12	3
Train set size	40 (GB text data)	40 (M tokens)	102 (M tokens)
Nr. parameters (M)	117	107.7	182
Embedding size	768	768	400
Hidden size	768	768	1,840
Vocabulary size	50,257	28,439	267,735
Context window (n. tokens)	1024	1024	-
WikiText103 perplexity	37.50	40.3	41.9

Table 4: Hyperparameter setup for training AWD LSTM.

	Parameter value
Vocabulary size (nr. tokens)	267,735
Nr. layers	3
Input embedding size	400
Hidden size	1840
Output dropout	0.4
Embedding dropout	0
Hidden dropout	0.01
Input dropout	0.01
Weight drop	0.2
Weight decay	1.2^{-6}
Tie weights	True
Learning rate	1^{-3}
Epochs	44
Lr reduction (epochs)	[25, 35]
Batch size	128
Adam alpha	0
Adam beta	0
BPTT	200

Table 5: Hyperparameters for the transformers trained as part of this work.

	1 layer	3 layer	6 layer	12 layer
Activation function	gelu_new	gelu_new	gelu_new	gelu_new
Nr. layers	1	3	6	12
Nr. heads	3	3	6	12
Context size	1024	1024	1024	1024
Causal mask dimensionality	1024	1024	1024	1024
Vocabulary size	28,439	28,439	28,439	28,439
Per device train batch size	12	12	12	12
Per device eval batch size	12	12	12	12
Learning rate	0.00007	0.00007	0.00007	0.00006
Adam beta1	0.6	0.6	0.6	0.6
Adam beta2	0.05	0.05	0.05	0.1
Nr. parameters (millions)	29.7	43.9	65.2	107.7

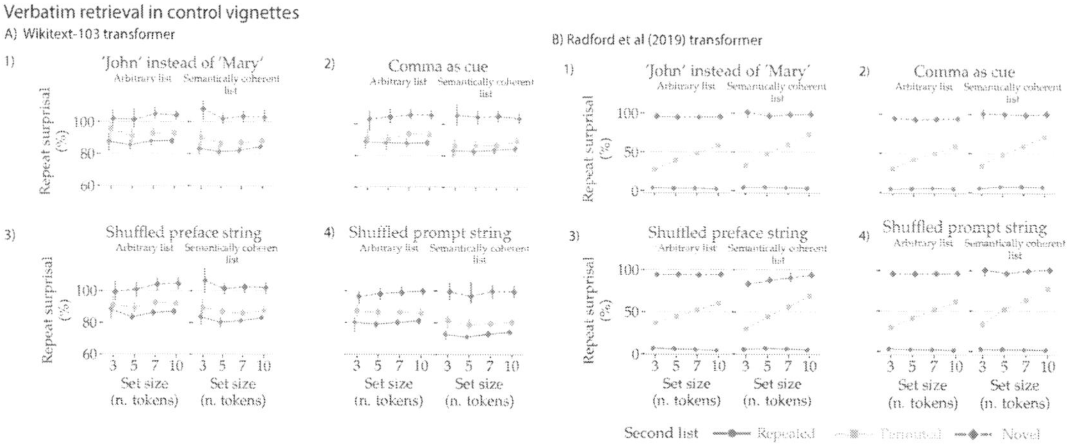

Figure 7: Transformer memory retrieval results for control vignettes. We report relative list-averaged surprisal over all non-initial tokens in lists (group median over N^{list} = 230). Error bars denote 95% confidence interval around the median (bootstrap estimate). Note that in the Wikitext-103 plots the y-axis starts at 70%.

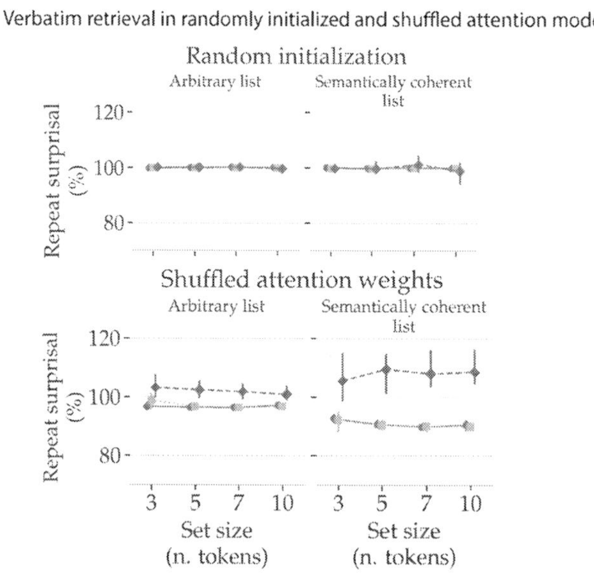

Figure 8: Repeat surprisal for randomly initialized transformer LM and a transformer with permuted attention weights. Reported is relative list-averaged surprisal over all non-initial tokens in lists only. Points show group median (over N^{list} = 230). Error bars denote 95% confidence interval around the median (bootstrap estimate). Note that in these plots y-axis starts at 70%.

Author Index

Abdelsalam, Mohamed Ashraf, 282
Abend, Omri, 194, 241, 384
Agerri, Rodrigo, 228
Arehalli, Suhas, 301
Armeni, Kristijan, 405

Bafna, Niyati, 110
Basioti, Kalliopi, 282
Becerra, Leonor, 213
Bergen, Benjamin, 13
Bhatt, Dhaivat, 282
Bhattacharyya, Pushpak, 132
Blache, Philippe, 213
Blokker, Nico, 325
Brown, David West, 27
Bryant, Christopher, 360
Buttery, Paula, 360

Caines, Andrew, 360
Carley, Kathleen, 27
Ceron, Tanise, 325
Chamovitz, Eytan, 241
Chen, Ying, 70
Choshen, Leshem, 194, 384

Davis, Christopher, 360
Davis, Forrest, 144
Dillon, Brian, 301

Echizen, Isao, 1
Eklund, Peter, 350
España-Bonet, Cristina, 110

Fancellu, Federico, 282
Fazly, Afsaneh, 282

Gupta, Himanshu, 132
Gutierrez-Vasques, Ximena, 266

Halevy, Alon, 50
Honey, Christopher, 405
Hopkins, Mark, 85
Huang, Guangyan, 350

Indurkhya, Sagar, 157

Lago, Sol, 339
Li, Dingcheng, 40
Li, Ping, 40
Linzen, Tal, 95, 176, 301, 405
Liu, Hao, 70

Maës, Eliot, 213
Merrill, William, 176
Michaelov, James, 13
Mueller, Aaron, 95
Müller-Eberstein, Max, 266

Nagumothu, Dinesh, 350
Ng, Lynnette, 27
Nishikawa, Sosuke, 1

Ocampo Diaz, Gerardo, 374
Ofoghi, Bahadorreza, 350
Ouyang, Jessica, 374

Padó, Sebastian, 325
Patel, Gal, 194
Patil, Umesh, 339
Pavlovic, Vladimir, 282
Pelloni, Olga, 266
Peng, Shuyuan, 70
Plank, Barbara, 266

Rei, Marek, 360

Sahoo, Nihar, 132
Samardžić, Tanja, 266
Sanchez-Bayona, Elisa, 228
Shen, Yaozong, 70
Shi, Zhan, 282

Tang, Hongxuan, 70
Tsuruoka, Yoshimasa, 1

van der Goot, Rob, 266
van Genabith, Josef, 110
Vucetic, Slobodan, 314

Wang, Haifeng, 70
Wang, Lijie, 70
Warstadt, Alex, 176
Wu, Hua, 70

Xia, Yu, 95
Xiao, Xinyan, 70

Xu, Hanzi, 314

Yamada, Ikuya, 1
Yang, Peng, 40
Yin, Wenpeng, 314
Yoder, Michael, 27
Yu, Jane, 50

Zhang, Shuai, 70

Žabokrtský, Zdeněk, 110

Association for Computational Linguistics
209 N. Eighth Street
Stroudsburg, Pennsylvania 18360

ISBN 978-1-7138-6762-3

9 781713 867623

CURRAN ASSOCIATES INC.
proceedings
.com